Everyman's

DICTIONARY OF
LITERARY BIOGRAPHY
ENGLISH & AMERICAN

Compiled after

JOHN W. COUSIN

by

D. C. BROWNING
M.A. (Glasgow), B.A., B.Litt.(Oxon.)

LONDON: J. M. DENT & SONS LTD
NEW YORK: E. P. DUTTON & CO. INC.

© J. M. Dent & Sons Ltd, 1958, 1962
All rights reserved
Printed in Great Britain
by
Lowe and Brydone (Printers) Ltd
London N.W.10
for
J. M. DENT & SONS LTD
Aldine House · Bedford Street · London
First published 1958
Revised editions 1960, 1962

INTRODUCTION

SUPERSEDING the *Biographical Dictionary of English Literature* compiled by John W. Cousin (No. 449 in Everyman's Library), this reference volume is for all practical purposes a new work. Cousin's original volume, containing some 1,350 biographies, was compiled fifty years ago, and accordingly many of his articles needed bringing up to date both in the light of modern research and in the altered critical perspective of the present day. Some 350 of his biographies have therefore been replaced by entirely new articles, among the more important of the authors so treated being Jane Austen, both the Brownings, Burns, Byron, Emerson, Keats, Shakespeare, Shelley, and Wordsworth. In addition, all the remaining biographies have been subjected to a complete overhaul which in many cases comes not far short of rewriting.

New Authors

The most important feature of the new volume, however, is the addition of new authors from the last fifty years. About 300 of these had been dealt with in a necessarily makeshift manner in appendices added in recent years to the older volume. For all these authors new biographies have been written on the same scale as the rest of the entries, among the more important being Galsworthy, Hardy, Henry James, Kipling, Bernard Shaw, and H. G. Wells. In addition, there have been added about 650 biographies of authors who were not included either in Cousin's original work or in its appendices; the majority of these authors are of the twentieth century and many are still writing. To sum up, the present volume contains about 2,300 literary biographies, of which 1,300, or considerably more than half, are entirely new articles, while 650, or over a quarter, treat of authors not dealt with at all in the older volume.

American Writers

A significant change from the former work is the increased amount of space claimed by American writers. When the original volume was compiled at the beginning of the century American literature was still regarded merely as an offshoot of English—somewhat as Australian or Canadian literature is looked upon to-day. But it is now manifest that the literature of the United States has developed until in some departments it equals or even surpasses in importance that of the parent country. Accordingly American authors form about a third of the new entries added in the present volume. Many of them are well known in this country. It should be noted, however, that not all are modern. The ever-growing importance of American literature has led to increased interest in its origins and in the earliest writers of the original colony.

Scottish and Irish

Modern Scottish and Irish writers have of course been included as well as English. The Celtic Revival in Ireland is represented by its leader Yeats, and well over a dozen other writers, among whom may be mentioned John Campbell, Padraic Colum, Lord Dunsany, Oliver St John Gogarty, Eva Gore-Booth, Lady Gregory, Seán O'Casey, Seán O'Faoláin, Liam O'Flaherty, Connell O'Riordan, George Russell, James Stephen, John Synge, and Katherine Tynan. Similarly the modern Scottish renaissance is represented not only by such widely known novelists as Cunninghame Graham, Compton Mackenzie, Neil Munro, Neil Gunn, Eric Linklater, and A. J. Cronin, but by a number of Scottish poets from both the traditionalist and the more modern 'Lallans' group, including Marion Angus, C. M. Grieve, Violet Jacob, William Jeffrey, William Soutar, Lewis Spence, and Rachel Annand Taylor. Many well-known writers from oversea countries of the British Commonwealth have also been included.

Literary Range

The literary range of the volume has been purposely kept as catholic as possible, and popular or 'low-brow' authors have been admitted on the same terms as the sophisticated or 'high-brow.' Nat Gould, Ethel M. Dell, and Ella Wheeler Wilcox take their place beside D. H. Lawrence, James Joyce, and Gertrude Stein. There have even been authors put in because of their engaging badness. Robert Montgomery is the classic example from last century and the irrepressible McGonagall from this. On the other hand, scholars and scientists have not been included unless their names are household words or they have written many books of a popular nature. It may be partly a fellow feeling that has led to the inclusion not only of lexicographers like Sir William Craigie and Eric Partridge, but compilers like John Bartlett and Sir Gurney Benham; but all housewives, at least, will approve the insertion of Mrs Beeton.

'Whodunits' and Thrillers

The cult of the 'whodunit' plays such an important part in modern literature that an honoured place has to be given to writers of detective stories and thrillers. The inclusion of such familiar names as Agatha Christie, Dorothy Sayers, John Dickson Carr, and Erle Stanley Gardner on the one hand, and Edgar Wallace, Leslie Charteris, Sydney Horler, and Edgar Rice Burroughs on the other show that this popular department has not been neglected, while 'Westerns' are represented by Zane Grey and Clarence Mulford. Many writers of books for boys and girls are also included, the list on this side of the Atlantic extending from Ballantyne, Henty, and Charlotte Yonge to A. A. Milne and Arthur Ransome, and on the other side from Horatio Alger, Louisa Alcott, and 'Susan Coolidge' to Hugh Lofting and Lucy M. Montgomery.

System of Entry

As this is a biographical work, the usage has been to list each author under his own name, not under a pseudonym, however well known that may be. Thus 'Lewis Carroll' is entered as C. L. Dodgson, and 'John Oxenham' as William Dunkerley, while even 'Mark Twain' is given as Samuel Clemens. When two authors write in collaboration, as in the case of 'Michael Field,' their lives are given separately. There is of course in all these cases a cross-reference from the pen-name to the real one. In some cases an author has actually changed his name, and is therefore listed under the name he adopted; and there are also authors who live a literary Jekyll and Hyde existence, such as Cecil Day Lewis, who under his own name is a learned literary critic, but as Nicholas Blake writes excellent detective stories.

Puzzle of Namesakes

One somewhat unexpected use which the dictionary should have is in distinguishing between different authors who have the same name and are therefore liable to be confused. There are quite a few pairs of writers who may be mis-identified in this fashion. Most readers can distinguish between the two Lawrences, T. E. and D. H., but even well informed readers may find themselves confused between the two Lewises, the two Wyndham Lewises, or the two Pollards, one of whom used to confess that he had actually been an honoured guest at a dinner which was really intended for his namesake. The puzzle is not much simpler when the authors are members of one family, like the three Bensons, the three Powyses, the three Sitwells, and the two Waughs.

Authors' Dates

An innovation which it is hoped will be of use to journalists and others who are interested in authors' anniversaries is the insertion of the exact date (day, month, and year) of each author's birth and death. Sometimes, of course, these are not available. In the case of many writers of the past only the date of baptism and the date of burial are available in parish records, and these have been given for want of better.

A considerable number of modern authors prefer to keep their dates of birth out of reference books, and in such cases the date-bracket has to be left blank.

D. C. B.

1958.

A new edition having been called for, a substantial addition has been made to the number of authors included, more than seventy new entries being added. The most important of these are recent or living writers whose omission has in some cases been pointed out by critics. Among these are the novelists Ivy Compton-Burnett, Nancy Mitford, Anthony Powell, Sir Charles Snow, and Philip Toynbee; the poets Lawrence Durrell, Sidney Keyes, Kathleen Raine, Francis Scarfe, and Henry Treece; and the critics Cyril Connolly and David Daiches. The Scottish renaissance is represented by Maurice Lindsay and Sydney Goodsir Smith; Wales by Rhys Davies; Ireland by Michael O'Donovan, Standish O'Grady, and Maurice Walsh; and American authors newly inserted include Paul Gallico and Betty Mac-Donald. A number of gaps among earlier writers have been filled by the insertion of St Patrick, Eadmer, Juliana, Sir John Cheke, Sir Thomas Bodley, and those literary patronesses the Countess of Pembroke and Lady Mary Wroth. Writers for young people include Angela Brazil and Beatrix Potter; John Jamieson and Joseph Wright represent philology; while other additions are Gertrude Bell the traveller, George Grossmith the humorist, Arthur Mee the compiler, and George Moore the philosopher. A number of slips and misprints have been corrected, and dates have been inserted of those authors who have died since the first edition was published.

D. C. B.

1960.

In the third edition additional material has been added to a few entries to bring them up to date, deaths of authors during the past year have been recorded, and one or two errors corrected.

D. C. B.

1961.

NOTE

A dictionary that includes in its scope the lives and
works of living authors must necessarily be a growing
concern, because fresh items keep demanding admission.
Accordingly, blank pages or spaces have been left throughout the volume at the end of each letter-group of authors
(the A's, the B's, the C's, and so on) to allow for future
expansion of existing articles and the insertion of new ones.

A

Abbott, Eleanor Hallowell (22 Sept. 1872—   ), novelist, grand-daughter of Jacob Abbott (q.v.), was born and educated at Cambridge, Massachusetts, and later wrote about her early life in *Being Little in Cambridge When Everybody Else Was Big*. She became teacher of English composition at Lowell State Normal School, and in 1908 married Dr Fordyce Coburn. Among her novels, which had great popularity, were *Molly Make-Believe* (1912), *White Linen Nurse* (1913), and *Little Eve Edgerton* (1914).

Abbott, Jacob (14 Nov. 1803—31 Oct. 1879), clergyman and author, born at Hallowell, Maine, educated at Bowdoin College and Andover, entered the ministry of the Congregational Church, but was best known as an educationist and writer of religious and other books, mainly for the young. Among them are *Beechnut Tales* and *The Rollo Books*, which ran to 28 volumes.

Abbott, John Stevens Cabot (18 Sept. 1805—17th June 1877), clergyman and historian, brother of the above, born at Brunswick, Maine, and educated at Bowdoin College, studied theology and became a minister of the Congregational Church. Owing to the success of a little work, *The Mother at Home*, he devoted himself, from 1844 onwards, to literature, and especially to historical writing. Among his principal works, which were very popular, are *History of Napoleon Bonaparte* (1852—5), *History of the Civil War in America* (1863—6), and *History of Frederick the Great* (1871).

À Beckett, Gilbert Abbott (9 Jan. 1811—30 Aug. 1856), humorous writer, born in London, the son of a lawyer, belonged to a family claiming descent from Archbishop Thomas à Becket. Destined for the legal profession, he was called to the Bar, and became a metropolitan police magistrate. In addition to contributions to various periodicals including *Punch*, *The Illustrated London News*, *The Times*, and *Morning Herald*, he produced over 50 plays, many of which attained great popularity, and he also helped to dramatize some of Dickens's works. He is perhaps best known as the author of the *Comic History of England*, *Comic History of Rome*, and *Comic Blackstone*.

Abercrombie, John (10 Oct. 1780—14 Nov. 1844), doctor, son of a minister, was born at Aberdeen, and educated at the Grammar School and Marischal College there. He studied medicine at Edinburgh, in which city he practised as a physician. He made valuable contributions to the literature of his profession, and published two

1

works, *Enquiry Concerning the Intellectual Powers* (1830) and *The Philosophy of the Moral Feelings* (1833), which have long been superseded. He was elected Lord Rector of Marischal College in 1836.

Abercrombie, Lascelles (9 Jan. 1881—27 Oct. 1938), poet and scholar, son of a stockbroker, was born at Ashton-upon-Mersey and educated at Malvern and Manchester University, after which he turned to journalism and worked for a time as a reviewer. His first volume of verse, *Interludes and Poems* (1908) was followed by *Mary and the Bramble* (1910). A play, *The Sale of St Thomas*, appeared in 1911. After working as a munitions inspector during the First World War, he became a lecturer at Liverpool in 1919, held the Chairs of English at Leeds from 1922 and in London from 1929, and was appointed Goldsmith's Reader in English at Oxford in 1935. His critical works include *Thomas Hardy, a Critical Study* (1912), *The Idea of Great Poetry* (1925) and *Romanticism* (1926). The style of his poems has been described as difficult, abstract, and intellectual; a collected edition was published in 1930.

Abercrombie, Patrick (1656—1716?), antiquary and historian, born at Forfar, graduated at St Andrews in 1685, and was physician to James II. He was a Jacobite and opposed the Union in various pamphlets. His chief work was *Martial Achievements of the Scots Nation* (1711—16).

Acton, John Emerich Edward Dalberg Acton, 1st Baron (10 Jan. 1834—19 June 1902), historian, born at Naples of an English Roman Catholic family, was educated at Paris, Oscott, and Munich. After visiting America, Russia, and Italy, he settled at Aldenham, the family seat, in 1858, and from 1859 to 1865 was Liberal M.P. for Carlow. In 1869 he was raised to the peerage by Gladstone's influence. For a time he edited the Roman Catholic periodicals *Rambler* and *Home and Foreign Review*, but his views proved too advanced to be acceptable. In 1886 he helped to found the *English Historical Review*. In 1891 he was made a Fellow of All Souls, and from 1895 he was Professor of Modern History at Cambridge. Shortly before his death he planned the great Cambridge Modern History and edited the first outline of it. His chief works, all published posthumously, were *Lectures in Modern History* (1906), *Historical Essays and Studies* (1907), and *Lectures on the French Revolution* (1910).

Adam, Jean (1710—3 April 1765), poetess, was born in Greenock, daughter of a ship's captain. Orphaned at an early age, she became governess in a minister's family, educated herself from his library, and wrote many religious poems, a volume of which was published in 1734. She started a girls' school, but it was a failure, and she was reduced to making a living as a hawker, and died in the poorhouse. She is sometimes credited with the lively 'Song of the Mariner's Wife,' better known as 'There's nae luck aboot the hoose,' often attributed to Meikle (q.v.).

Adamnan, St (625?—23 Sept. 704), historian, born in Donegal, became Abbot of Iona in 679. Like other Irish churchmen he was a statesman as well as an ecclesiastic, and appears to have been sent on various political missions. In the great controversy on the tonsure and the holding of Easter, he sided with Rome against the Irish Church. He left the earliest account we have of the state of Palestine in the early ages of the Church; but of even more value is his Latin life of St Columba, giving a minute account of the condition and discipline of the church of Iona.

Adams, Arthur Henry (6 June 1872—4 March 1936), poet and novelist, was born at Lawrence, New Zealand, and educated at Otago High School and University. In 1898 he became a journalist in Sydney, and during the Boer War was a special correspondent in South Africa. He spent some time in England, but the greater part of his work was done in Australia, where he wrote poems, plays, and novels. His *Collected Verse* was published in 1913. His novels are *Tussock Land* (1904), *Galahad Jones* (1910), *A Touch of Fantasy* (1912), and *Grocer Greatheart* (1915). *A Man's Life* (1929) is autobiographical.

Adams, Charles Follen (21 April 1842—8 March 1918), dialect poet, was born in Dorchester, Massachusetts. In August 1862 he enlisted in the 13th Massachusetts Infantry, and fought at the battle of Bull Run. He became a dealer in dry and fancy goods in Boston, authorship being only a diversion. About 1870 he began writing in the German dialect, in imitation of Leland's Hans Breitmann ballads, though he himself was not of German descent. In 1876 'Leedle Yawcob Strauss,' first printed in the *Detroit Free Press*, made him famous. His entire poems were published as *Yawcob Strauss and Other Poems* (1910).

Adams, Francis William Lauderdale (27 Sept. 1862—4 Sept. 1893), poet, was born at Malta, son of a Scottish scientist, and educated at a private school in Shrewsbury, and in Paris. After two years as a schoolmaster in England he married and went to Australia, where he joined the staff of the *Sydney Bulletin*, in which many of his poems appeared. Incurable lung disease brought about his suicide at an early age. He wrote *Henry and Other Tales* (1884), *Leicester*, an autobiographical novel (1884), *Australian Essays* (1886), *Poetical Works* (1886), and *Songs of the Army of the Night* (1888). A play, *Tiberius*, was published posthumously in 1894.

Adams, Henry Brooks (16 Feb. 1838—27 March 1918), historian, born in Boston, was a great grandson of John Adams (q.v.). Educated at Harvard, he studied law in Germany, and then became secretary to his father, who was United States Minister to Britain. For a number of years he taught history at Harvard and edited the *North American Review*. His works include a *History of the United States During the Administration of Thomas Jefferson and James Madison* (1889—91). His study of medieval culture and its contrast with the disunity of modern life found expression in *Mont-Saint-Michel and Chartres* (1904) and *The Education of Henry Adams* (1907), while *A Letter to American Teachers of History* (1910) deals with social problems. He also wrote some novels.

Adams, James Truslow (18 Oct. 1878—18 May 1949), historian, born at Brooklyn and educated at Brooklyn Polytechnic and Yale, became director of a bank and of a manufacturing company. During the First World War he took part in Col. House's mission to Great Britain, and subsequently turned to writing history, his work *The Founding of New England* (1921) being awarded the Pulitzer Prize; it was the first of a trilogy which was completed by *Revolutionary New England* (1923) and *New England in the Republic* (1926). Others of his works are *The Epic of America* (1931), *The March of Democracy* (1932–3), *Frontiers of American Culture* (1944), and two books on the distinguished Adams family of Massachusetts, to which however he was not related. He was a Fellow of the Royal Society of Literature.

Adams, John (30 Oct. 1735—4 July 1826), 2nd President of the United States, was born at Braintree, now Quincy, Massachusetts, son of a farmer. Educated at Harvard, he studied law and was admitted to the Bar in 1758. In 1768 he settled in Boston, and in 1774 was chosen as a delegate from Massachusetts to the first Continental Congress. A member of over 90 committees, he worked incessantly, was one of the framers of the Declaration of Independence, and on his retiral in 1777 was sent to France as a commissioner; from 1785 to 1788 he was United States Minister to Britain. While in London he published his *Defence of the Constitution of the United States* (1787). In 1796 he was elected President, and had a stormy term of office. His publications include *A History of the Dispute with America* (1774), *Thoughts on Government* (1776), *A Collection of State Papers* (1782), and *The Inadmissible Principles* (1809). His *Works* were edited in 10 volumes in 1856.

Adams, Joseph Quincy (23 March 1881—10 Nov. 1946), scholar, born at Greenville, South Carolina, the son of a minister, was educated at Chicago, Cornell, London, and Berlin Universities. In 1905 he joined the staff of the English Department at Cornell, and from 1919 to 1931 was professor. Thereafter till his death he was Director of the great Folger Shakespeare Library at Washington. He was a member of many Shakespeare societies in America and Europe. His works include *Shakespearian Playhouses* (1917), a *Life of Shakespeare* (with C. S. Northup) (1923), and *Chief Shakespearian Dramas* (1924). He was also general editor of the *New Variorum Shakespeare*.

Addison, Joseph (1 May 1672—17 June 1719), poet, essayist, and statesman, was the son of Lancelot Addison, Dean of Lichfield. Born near Amesbury, Wiltshire, Addison went to the Charterhouse, where he made the acquaintance of Steele (q.v.), and then at the age of 15 to Oxford, where he had a distinguished career, being specially noted for his Latin verse, and became a Fellow of Magdalen. Though he was intended at first for the Church, various circumstances combined to lead him towards literature and politics. His first attempts in English verse took the form of complimentary addresses, and were so successful as to obtain for him the friendship and interest of Dryden, and of Lord Halifax, by whose means he received, in 1699, a pension of £300 to enable him to travel on the continent with a view to diplomatic employment. He visited Italy, whence he addressed his *Epistle* to his friend Halifax. Hearing of the death of William III, an event which lost him his pension, he returned to England in the end of 1703. For a short time his circumstances were somewhat straitened, but the battle of Blenheim in 1704 gave him a fresh opportunity of distinguishing himself. The government wished the event commemorated by a poem; Addison was commissioned to write this, and produced *The Campaign*, which gave such satisfaction that he was forthwith appointed a Commissioner of Appeals. His next literary venture was an account of his travels in Italy, which was followed by the opera of *Rosamund* (1707).

In 1705, the Whigs having obtained the ascendency, Addison was made Under-Secretary of State and accompanied Halifax on a mission to Hanover, and in 1708 was appointed Chief Secretary for Ireland and Keeper of the Records of that country. It was at this period that Addison found his true vocation, and laid the foundations of his real fame. In 1709 Steele began to bring out the *Tatler*, to which Addison became almost immediately a contributor: thereafter he (with Steele) started the *Spectator*, the first number of which appeared on 1 March 1711. This paper, which at first appeared daily, was kept up (with a break of about a year and a half when the *Guardian* took its place) until 20 Dec. 1714, Addison contributing nearly 300 essays, of which the most famous are those dealing with the imaginary character, Sir Roger de Coverley. In 1713 the drama of *Cato* appeared, and was received with acclamation by both Whigs and Tories, though it is little read now. A comedy, *The Drummer* (1715) met with no success. His last undertaking was *The Freeholder*, a party paper (1715—16). The later events in the life of Addison, namely his marriage in 1716 to the Dowager Countess of Warwick, to whose son he had been tutor, and his promotion to be Secretary of State, did not contribute to his happiness. His wife appears to have been arrogant and imperious; his stepson the Earl was a rake and unfriendly to him; while in his public capacity his inveterate shyness made him of little use in Parliament. He resigned his office in 1718, receiving a pension of £1,500 a year, and, after a period of ill-health, died at Holland House in his forty-eighth year. Besides the works above mentioned, he wrote a *Dialogue on Medals*, and left unfinished a work on the Evidences of Christianity.

The character of Addison, in spite of Pope's famous satirical lines on him under the name of Atticus, was magnanimous and kind. The charm of his manners and conversation made him one of the most popular and admired men of his day; and while he laid his friends under obligations for substantial favours, he showed the greatest forbearance towards his few enemies. His style in his essays is remarkable for its ease, clearness, and grace, and for an inimitable and sunny humour. The famous tribute by Dr Johnson is as true now as when his life of Addison was published, 'Whoever wishes to attain an English style, familiar but not coarse, and elegant but not ostentatious, must give his days and nights to the volumes of Addison.'

Ade, George (9 Feb. 1866—16 May 1944), humorist and playwright, was born in Kentland, Indiana, and educated at Purdue University, where he studied science. From 1887 to 1900 he worked as a journalist, then launched out in a line of his own with *Fables in Slang*. These fables of modern life, written in a vernacular of his own devising, were so successful that he published half a dozen volumes of them, under various titles, between 1900 and 1933. He also wrote novels and short stories and a number of successful plays, including *The County Chairman* (1903), *The College Widow* (1904), *The Bad Samaritan* (1905), and *The Fair Co-ed* (1908).

Adeler, Max, *see* **Clark, Charles Heber.**

Adolphus, John (7 Aug. 1768—16 July 1845), historian, of German extraction, studied law and was called to the Bar in 1807. He wrote *Biographical Memoirs of the French Revolution* (1799) a *History of England from 1760 to 1783* (1802), and other historical and biographical works.

Æ, *see* **Russell, George William.**

Ælfric (955?—1022?), called Grammaticus, a pupil of Ethelwold, was a monk at Winchester, and afterwards Abbot of Cerne and Eynsham successively. He has left works which shed an important light on the doctrine and practice of the early Church in England, including two books of homilies (990—4), a *Grammar*, *Glossary*, *Passiones Sanctorum* (Sufferings of the Saints), translations of parts of the Bible with omissions and interpolations, *Canones Ælfrici*, and other theological treatises. His writings had a great influence on the formation of English prose.

Agate, James Evershed (9 Sept. 1877—6 June 1947), journalist, born at Manchester, was educated at Giggleswick and Manchester Grammar School and also studied music. After a period of freelancing he became dramatic critic successively of the *Daily Dispatch* (1905), the *Manchester Guardian* (1906), the *Saturday Review* and finally the *Sunday Times* (1923). A prolific writer, he published novels, books of essays, and anthologies, and achieved notice with his diary, *Ego*, of which eight volumes appeared in his lifetime and one posthumously.

Aguilar, Grace (2 June 1816—16 Sept. 1847), novelist and historian, born at Hackney, had Jewish parents of Spanish descent. She was delicate from childhood, and early showed great interest in history, especially Jewish. After a few dramas and poems she published in America in 1842 *Spirit of Judaism*, and in 1845 *The Jewish Faith* and *The Women of Israel*. She is, however, best known by her novels, of which the chief are *Home Influence* (1847) and *A Mother's Recompense* (1850).

Aiken, Conrad Potter (5 Aug. 1889—), poet and novelist, was born at Savannah, Georgia, the son of a doctor, and was at Harvard with the famous class of 1911, which included T. S. Eliot and Alan Seeger. After his first marriage in 1912 he settled in Massachusetts and devoted himself to literature. In the First World War he secured exemption from military service on the grounds that as a poet he was engaged in essential industry. His first noteworthy volumes of verse were *Turns and Movies* and *The Jig of Forslin*, both published in 1916. In 1929 his *Selected Poems* won the Pulitzer Prize and the Shelley Memorial Award. Volumes published since the Second World War include *The Soldier* (1944), *The Kid* (1947), and *Skylight One* (1949); his *Collected Poems* appeared in 1953. His novels and short stories show subtle character-drawing, *Blue Voyage* (1927) and *Great Circle* (1933) having echoes of Joyce.

Aikin, John (15 Jan. 1747—7 Dec. 1822), author, was born at Kibworth, studied medicine at Edinburgh and London, and received the degree of M.D. at Leyden. He began practice at Yarmouth but, one of his pamphlets having given offence, he removed to London, where he obtained some success in his profession, devoting all his leisure to literature, to which his contributions were incessant. These consisted of pamphlets, translations, and miscellaneous works, some in conjunction with his sister, Anna Letitia Barbauld (q.v.). Among his chief works are *England Delineated*, *General Biography* in 10 volumes, and lives of Selden and Ussher.

Aikin, Lucy (6 Nov. 1781—29 Jan. 1864), authoress, daughter of above and niece of Mrs Barbauld (q.v.), was born at Warrington. After producing a poem, *Epistles on Women*, and a novel, *Lorimer*, she began the historical works on which her reputation chiefly rests, namely, *Memoirs of the Courts of Elizabeth, James I, and Charles I* (1818—33) and a *Life of Addison* (1843). She also wrote lives of her father and aunt. She was remarkable for her conversational powers, and was also an admirable letter-writer. Like the rest of her family she was a Unitarian.

Ainger, Alfred (9 April 1837—8 Feb. 1904), clergyman and author, was born in London and educated at King's College there and at Cambridge. Ordained in 1860, he became a canon of Bristol in 1887 and Master of the Temple in 1894, and was chaplain to Queen Victoria and King Edward VII. The friend of Charles Dickens (whose sons were among his schoolmates) and of Leslie Stephen and Tennyson, he is chiefly remembered as the biographer and editor of Charles Lamb. Two volumes of his *Lectures and Essays* appeared posthumously in 1905.

Ainsworth, William Harrison (4 Feb. 1805—3 Jan. 1882), novelist, son of a solicitor, was born in Manchester. He was intended for the legal profession, which, however, had no attraction for him; and going to London to complete his studies made the acquaintance of John Ebers, publisher, and at that time manager of the Opera House, by whom he was introduced to literary and dramatic circles, and whose daughter he afterwards married. For a short time he tried the publishing business, but soon gave it up and devoted himself to journalism and literature. His first successful novel was *Rookwood*, published in 1834, of which Dick Turpin is the leading character, and thenceforward he continued to pour forth till 1881 a stream of some 40 novels, of which the best known are *The Tower of London* (1840), *Old St Paul's* (1841), *Lancashire Witches* (1848), and *The Constable* *of the Tower.* The titles of some of his other novels are *Crichton* (1837), *Jack Sheppard* (1839), *Guy Fawkes* (1841), *The Miser's Daughter* (1842), and *Windsor Castle* (1843). Ainsworth depends for his effects on striking situations and powerful descriptions: he has little humour or power of delineating character.

Aird, Thomas (28 Aug. 1802—25 April 1876), poet, born at Bowden, Roxburghshire, studied at Edinburgh, where he became the friend of Professor Wilson, Carlyle, and other men of letters. He contributed to *Blackwood's Magazine*, and was editor of the *Dumfries Herald* (1835—63). His chief poem is *The Captive of Fez* (1830), and in prose he wrote *Religious Characteristics*, and *The Old Bachelor in the Old Scottish Village* (1848), all of which were received with favour. Carlyle said that in his poetry he found everywhere a 'healthy breath as of mountain breezes.'

Akenside, Mark (9 Nov. 1721—23 June 1770), poet, son of a butcher, born at Newcastle upon Tyne, gave early indications of talent, and was sent to the University of Edinburgh with the view of becoming a dissenting minister. While there, however, he changed his mind and studied for the medical profession, going on to Leyden, where he took his degree of M.D. in 1744. In that year appeared his principal poem, *The Pleasures of Imagination,* which was well received, and was subsequently translated into more than one foreign language. After trying Northampton, he settled as a doctor in London, but was for long largely dependent for his livelihood on Jeremiah Dyson, a rich friend. His talents brought him a good deal of consideration in society, but the solemn and pompous manner which he affected laid him open to some ridicule, and he is said to have been satirized by Smollett in his *Peregrine Pickle.* In 1761 he was appointed one of the physicians to the Queen. His collected poems were published in 1772. Gosse has described him as 'a sort of frozen Keats.'

Akers, Elizabeth Chase (9 Oct. 1832—7 Aug. 1911), poetess, was born in Strong, Franklin County, Maine, the daughter of a lawyer. She was three times married, her second husband, whom she married in 1860, being Benjamin Paul Akers, a sculptor. In 1855 she became assistant editor of the Portland *Transcript,* and in 1874 literary editor of the Portland *Daily Advertiser.* Her first volume of poems, *Forest Buds from the Woods of Maine* (1856), was so successful that she was able to go travelling on the Continent. Other volumes were *Poems* (1866), *The Silver Bridge* (1886), and *The Sunset Song* (1902). Her poems have fertility of fancy but little originality, the only one now well known being 'Rock Me to Sleep.'

Albinus, *see* **Alcuin.**

Alcott, Amos Bronson (29 Nov. 1799—4 March 1888), philosopher and educationist, was born near Wolcott, Connecticut, had little education, and was a farm hand at the age of 10. In 1828 he became a schoolmaster, and in 1834 started the Temple School in Boston, but it was a failure, as was also the co-operative community Fruitlands which he founded at Harvard after a visit to England. From 1844 onwards he made his home at Concord, where Emerson was his neighbour. The intuitionist philosophy which he developed profoundly influenced the Transcendentalist movement. His works include *Observations on the Principles and Methods of Infant Instruction* (1830), *The Doctrine and Discipline of Human Culture* (1836), *Tablets* (1868), *Concord Days* (1872), and *Table Talk* (1877). He also published two volumes of indifferent verse, *Sonnets and Canzonets* (1882) and *New Connecticut* (1887). His *Journals* were published in 1938.

Alcott, Louisa May (29 Nov. 1832—6 March 1888), authoress, daughter of the above, was born at Germantown, Pennsylvania, but spent most of her childhood at Boston and Concord, Massachusetts, where she received guidance in her education from Thoreau and Emerson. After some years as a school-teacher, she had work published in the *Atlantic Monthly* in 1860. During the Civil War she was an army nurse, and her *Hospital Sketches* (1863) were popular. Her first novel, *Moods*, appeared in 1864, but she first attained real fame with her story for children, *Little Women* (1868—9), which was followed by *Good Wives* (1871), *Little Men* (1871), *Jo's Boys* (1886), and many others. The charm and naturalness of her writing made her children's books classics which have never lost their popularity.

Alcuin *or* **Ealhwine** *or* **Albinus** (735—19 May 804), theologian and scholar, was born and educated at York, then the main centre of western European learning. While returning from a visit to Rome in 781 he had a meeting with Charlemagne at Parma, and was induced to become the equivalent of his Minister of Education. As a result, Northumbrian scholarship was passed on to the Frankish Empire just before it was obliterated in England by the Danish invasions; Alcuin's work was therefore of enormous importance in the development of European civilization. In 796 he retired as Abbot of Tours. His works include educational and theological treatises and metrical annals.

Aldington, Richard (1892—   ), poet and novelist, was born in Hampshire and educated at Dover College and London University. Having started writing at a very early age, he became in 1913 literary editor of the *Egoist*, the periodical of the Imagists, and in the same year married Hilda Doolittle (q.v.), one of the leading Imagist poets; they were divorced in 1937. After serving in the First World War he worked as reviewer and translator, and published several volumes of poetry, including *War and Love* (1919), *A Fool i' the Forest* (1925), and *A Dream in the Luxemburg* (1930). He then turned to prose, *Death of a Hero* (1929), one of the most noteworthy novels produced by the war, being followed by *The Colonel's Daughter* (1931) and *All Men Are Enemies* (1932). During the Second World War he moved to America, where his *Poetry of the English-Speaking World* (1941) was first published. His biography, *Wellington* (1946) was awarded the Tait Black Memorial Prize. His *Collected Poems* appeared in 1949.

Aldrich, Thomas Bailey (11 Nov. 1836—19 March 1906), poet and author, was born at Portsmouth, New Hampshire, and at 16 became a clerk in New York. A facile writer, he produced 'a lyric or two every day' and in 1855 published a book of poems, *The Bells*. After working as a war correspondent in the Civil War he moved to Boston, where he became friendly with Hawthorne, Longfellow, Whittier, and Lowell. The semi-autobiographical *Story of a Bad Boy* (1870), his best prose work, was followed by the novels *Prudence Palfrey* (1874), *The Queen of Sheba* (1877), and *The Stillwater Tragedy* (1880). *Cloth of Gold* (1874) was a collection of poems. As editor of the *Atlantic Monthly* (1881—90) he exercised a commanding influence on American letters. After 1890 he made two voyages round the world. His collected writings were published in nine volumes in 1907.

Alesius, Alexander (23 April 1500—17 March 1565), reformer, was born in Edinburgh and studied at St Andrews, where he became a canon. His paternal name was Alane, but he took that of Alesius, meaning 'wanderer,' which was only too appropriate, for a great part of his life was spent in exile. He had to flee the country in 1532 after preaching against the corruption of the clergy, and settled at Wittenberg, where he became associated with Melanchthon and Luther and was won over to the Reformation. In 1535 he returned to England and lectured at Cambridge on theology, but as a result of the 'Six Articles' had to go abroad again, this time to Frankfort, where he held the Chair of Theology. In 1543 he moved to Leipzig, where he became Rector of the University. His writings include both commentaries and controversial works.

Alexander, Cecil Frances (1818—12 Oct. 1895), hymn-writer, was born in County Wicklow, the daughter of Major Humphreys, an officer in the Marines. In 1846 she published a volume of devotional poetry, *Verses for Holy Seasons*, and in 1850 *Hymns for Little Children*, for which Keble wrote a preface. In that year also she married the Rev. W. Alexander, who became Bishop of Derry and subsequently Archbishop of Armagh. Her *Collected Poems* were edited by her husband after her death, but she is best remembered for her hymns, such as 'All things bright and beautiful,' 'Once in royal David's city,' and 'There is a green hill far away.'

Alford, Henry (10 Oct. 1810—7 Jan. 1871), theologian, scholar, poet, and miscellaneous writer, son of a clergyman, was born in London. After passing through various private schools, he proceeded to Cambridge, where he had a distinguished career, and after entering the Church and filling various preferments in the country, became minister of Quebec Chapel, London, whence he was promoted to be Dean of Canterbury. His great work was his *Greek Testament* in 4 volumes (1849—61), which was for long the standard work on the subject in this country. Alford was one of the most versatile men, and prolific authors, of his day, his works consisting of nearly 50 volumes, including poetry (*School of the Heart* and *Abbot of Munchelnaye*, and a translation of the *Odyssey*), criticism, and sermons. He also wrote *Chapters on the Greek Poets* (1841), the *Queen's*

English (1863), and many well-known hymns, and was the first editor of the *Contemporary Review*. He was an accomplished artist and musician.

Alfred (849—28 Oct. 901), King of the West Saxons, was born at Wantage, Berkshire, succeeded to his throne in 871, and after defeating the Danes became overlord of all England, so that he is often reckoned the first English king. His work for education was of supreme importance. Though he did not, as tradition asserts, found the University of Oxford, he founded many schools and brought teachers from all parts of the world. By his policy he made Winchester the cradle of English prose, as Whitby under Bede had been of its poetry. His own writings included the translation into English of Boethius's *De Consolatione Philosophiae* (On the Consolation of Philosophy), Bede's *Ecclesiastical History of England*, the *Universal History* of Orosius, and a religious handbook, the *Cura Pastoralis* (Pastoral Care) of Gregory the Great. The earlier part of the *Anglo-Saxon Chronicle* may be his own work.

Alger, Horatio (13 Jan. 1834—18 July 1899), writer of books for boys, was born at Revere, Massachusetts, son of a clergyman, and had a rigidly religious upbringing. Educated at Harvard, he spent some time living a Bohemian life in Paris, but in 1864 returned to America and became a Unitarian minister like his father. In 1866 he turned to social work in New York, befriended many street arabs, and got the idea of writing boys' books. In 1867 his 'Ragged Dick' series began, in 1869 his 'Luck and Pluck' series, and in 1871 his 'Tattered Tom' series. All preached the gospel of success and inculcated the comfortable belief that virtue brings affluence. Success stories about eminent American statesmen include *From Canal Boy to President* (1881), *From Farm Boy to Senator* (1882), and *Abraham Lincoln, the Backwoods Boy* (1883). *Grand'ther Baldwin's Thanksgiving* (1879) is a book of poems. He wrote over 100 books in all, and had an influence on the youth of his generation far exceeding that of more serious writers.

Alison, Archibald (1757—17 May 1839), clergyman, was born in Edinburgh and educated at Glasgow University and Oxford. After being presented to various livings in England, he came to Edinburgh as incumbent of St Paul's Episcopal Chapel, where he attained popularity as a preacher of sermons characterized by quiet beauty of thought and grace of composition. His chief contribution to literature is his *Essay on the Nature and Principles of Taste* (1790).

Alison, Sir Archibald (29 Dec. 1792—23 May 1867), historian, son of the above, was born at Kenley, Shropshire, and after studying under a private tutor, and at Edinburgh University, was, in 1814, called to the Bar, at which he ultimately attained some distinction, becoming in 1834 Sheriff of Lanarkshire. He wrote a *History of Europe*, which deals with the period from the outbreak of the French Revolution to the restoration of the Bourbons, and extends, in its original form (1833—42), to 10 volumes. Disraeli satirized the author in *Coningsby* as Mr Wordy, who wrote a history to prove that Providence was on the side of the Tories. A continuation (1852—

1859) brought the story down to the accession of Louis Napoleon. Alison was also the author of a life of Marlborough, and of two standard works on the criminal law of Scotland. He was elected Lord Rector successively of Marischal College, Aberdeen, and of Glasgow University and was created a baronet by Lord Derby in 1852.

Allen, Charles Grant Blairfindie (24 Feb. 1848—28 Oct. 1899), scientific writer and novelist, born in Canada, to which his father, a clergyman, had emigrated, was educated at Birmingham and Oxford. For a time he was principal of a college for Negroes in Jamaica, but returning to England in 1876 devoted himself to literature. His first books were on scientific subjects, and include *Physiological Aesthetics* (1877) and *Flowers and Their Pedigrees*. After assisting Sir W. W. Hunter in his *Gazetteer of India*, he turned his attention to fiction, and between 1884 and 1899 produced about 30 novels, among which *The Woman Who Did* (1895), promulgating certain startling views on marriage and kindred questions, created some sensation. Another work, *The Evolution of the Idea of God*, propounds a theory of religion on heterodox lines. His scientific works also included *Colour Sense*, *Evolutionist at Large*, *Colin Clout's Calendar*, and the *Story of the Plants*, and among his novels may be added *Philistia*, *Babylon*, *In all Shades*, *The Devil's Die*, and *The British Barbarians*.

Allen, William Hervey (8 Dec. 1889—28 Dec. 1949), novelist, was born at Pittsburgh and educated at the Naval Academy of Annapolis and Pittsburgh University. After serving in the First World War as a 1st lieutenant, he settled in Charleston, where he founded the Poetry Society of South Carolina. For a time he was a teacher of English in Charleston High School and at Vassar. *Anthony Adverse* (1933), the most discussed novel of its time, was written during five years' stay in Bermuda, and may be said to have started the modern revival of 'mammoth' novels several hundred thousand words long. Other novels were *Action at Aquila* (1938), and *The Disinherited* (1943—8), a trilogy; he also wrote several volumes of verse, including *Wampum and Old Gold* (1921), and a life of Poe (1926).

Allingham, Margery (1904—), writer of detective stories, was born in London, educated at Perse Girls' School at Cambridge, and trained to write by her father, who was also an author. Her first novel was written at the age of 16. In 1927 she married P. Youngman Carter, artist and editor. Her detective, mild Albert Campion, was very popular, and her books show effective character-drawing, among the best-known being *The Crime at Black Dudley* (1929), *Flowers for the Judge* (1936), *More Work for the Undertaker* (1949), *The Tiger in the Smoke* (1952), *No Love Lost* (1954), and a volume of short stories, *Mr Campion and Others* (1939). During the Second World War she turned to social history and wrote *The Oaken Heart* and *Dance of the Years*.

Allingham, William (19 March 1824—18 Nov. 1889), poet, son of a banker of English descent, was born at Ballyshannon, Donegal, entered the customs service, and ultimately settled in London, where he contributed to *Leigh Hunt's Journal.* Hunt introduced him to Carlyle and other men of letters, and in 1850 he published a book of poems, which was followed by *Day and Night Songs* (1854), *Laurence Bloomfield in Ireland* (1864), his most ambitious, though not his most successful work, and *Collected Poems* in 6 volumes (1888—93). He also edited *The Ballad Book* for the *Golden Treasury* series in 1864. In 1870 he retired from the civil service and became sub-editor of *Fraser's Magazine* under Froude, whom he succeeded as editor (1874—9). His verse is clear, fresh, and graceful. He married Helen Paterson, the water-colourist. Other works are *Fifty Modern Poems* (1865), *Songs, Poems, and Ballads* (1877), *Evil May Day* (1883), *Blackberries* (1884), *Irish Songs and Poems* (1887), and *Varieties in Prose* (1893). A selection from his diaries and autobiography was published in 1906.

Allston, Washington (5 Nov. 1779—9 July 1843), artist and poet, born in South Carolina, became a distinguished painter, and was known as 'the American Titian.' While in Rome in 1805 he formed a friendship with Coleridge and Washington Irving. Later he wrote a good deal of verse, including *The Sylphs of the Seasons* (1813), and *The Two Painters*, a satire. He also produced a novel, *Monaldi* (1841).

Amory, Thomas (1691?—25 Nov. 1788), author, was born in Ireland but settled in Westminster about 1757. In 1755 he published *Memoirs containing the lives of several ladies of Great Britain, a History of Antiquities and Observations on the Christian Religion*, which was followed by the *Life of John Buncle* (1756), practically a continuation. The contents of these works are of the most miscellaneous description —philology, natural science, theology, and, in fact, whatever occurred to the writer, treated without any system, but with occasional originality and felicity of diction. The author, who was probably more or less insane, is described as having a very peculiar aspect, with the manner of a gentleman, scarcely ever stirring abroad except at dusk. He reached the age of 97.

Anderson, Alexander (30 April 1845—11 July 1909), poet, son of a quarrier at Kirkconnel, Dumfriesshire, became a surfaceman on the railway. Spending all his leisure in self-culture, he mastered German, French, and Spanish sufficiently to read the chief masterpieces in these languages. His poetic vein, which was true if somewhat limited in range, soon manifested itself; his first book, *Songs of Labour*, appeared in 1873, and there followed *Two Angels* (1875), *Songs of the Rail* (1878), and *Ballads and Sonnets* (1879). In the following year he was made assistant librarian in the University of Edinburgh, and after an interval as secretary to the Philosophical Institution there, he returned as chief librarian to the university. Thereafter he wrote little. Of a simple and gentle character, he made many friends, including the Duke of Argyll, Carlyle, and Lord Houghton. He generally wrote under the name of 'Surfaceman.'

Anderson, Maxwell (15 Dec. 1888—28 Feb. 1959), dramatist, was born at Atlantic, Pennsylvania, son of a clergyman, and was educated at the University of North Dakota and Stanford University. After some time as an English teacher he became a journalist in San Francisco and then in New York. In 1920, along with Padraic Colum, he founded *Measure*, a poetry magazine. Writer of some 30 plays, he ranks with O'Neill as a leading dramatist of his generation. His first success was *What Price Glory* (1924), a war play in which he collaborated with Laurence Stallings. With *Elizabeth the Queen* (1930), an historical drama, he started on the type of play with which he was most successful, later examples being *Mary of Scotland* (1933), *Joan of Lorraine* (1946), and *Anne of the Thousand Days* (1948). His political satire *Both Your Houses* (1933) was awarded the Pulitzer Prize, while both *Winterset* (1936) and *High Tor* (1937) received the Drama Critics' Award. Others of his plays are *Saturday's Children* (1927), *Key Largo* (1939), *Journey to Jerusalem* (1940), *Candle in the Wind* (1941), *Truckline Cafe* (1946), *Barefoot in Athens* (1952), and *The Bad Seed* (1955). *The Essence of Tragedy* (1935) embodies his views on dramatic theory.

Anderson, Robert (1 Feb. 1770—26 Sept. 1833), poet, was born at Carlisle and educated at the Quaker school there. At the age of 10 he became assistant to a calico printer and was later apprenticed to a pattern drawer. In the course of his work he spent five years in London. His 'Lucy Gray,' which probably suggested Wordsworth's well-known poem of that name, appeared in his first volume of verses in 1798. In 1805 he published *Cumbrian Ballads*, containing rustic poems in the local dialect; they contain vivid pictures of the country life of the time, and have touches of humour which made them popular. His *Poetical Works*, with an autobiography, were published in 1820.

Anderson, Sherwood (13 Sept. 1876—8 March 1941), novelist, was born at Camden, Ohio, and educated at Wittenberg College. During the Spanish-American War he served in Cuba, and after that became successively manager of a paint works and an advertising copy writer before he turned to literature. His earliest novel, *Windy McPherson's Son*, appeared in 1916, but his first real success was with a collection of stories or sketches, *Winesburg, Ohio* (1919). Other such collections, which are often ranked higher than his novels, were *The Triumph of the Egg* (1921) and *Horses and Men* (1923). His novels include *Poor White* (1920), *Many Marriages* (1923), and *Dark Laughter* (1925). *A Story Teller's Story* (1924) and *Tar, a Midwest Childhood* (1926) are autobiographical. After visiting Europe in 1921 he settled in 1924 in Marion, Virginia, and became editor of the town's two newspapers, one Republican and one Democratic. He was married four times.

Andrewes, Lancelot (1555—27 Sept. 1626), prelate and scholar, was born in London, and educated at Merchant Taylors' School and Cambridge, where he became Master of Pembroke Hall (1589—1603). After receiving various other preferments he became Dean of Westminster, and a chaplain-in-ordinary to Queen Elizabeth. On the accession of James I, to whom his somewhat pedantic learning and style of preaching recommended him, he rose into great favour, and was made successively Bishop of Chichester, of Ely, and, in 1618, of Winchester. He attended the Hampton Court Conference, and took part in the preparation of the Authorized Version of the Bible, his special work being given to the earlier parts of the Old Testament; he acted, however, as a sort of general editor. He was considered as, next to Ussher, the most learned churchman of his day, a master of Patristic learning, and enjoyed a great reputation as an eloquent and impassioned preacher, but the stiffness and artificiality of his style render his sermons unsuited to modern taste. A collection of 96 of them was published in 1629, *Private Devotions* in 1647, and his *Works* in 11 volumes in 1854.

Andrews, Roy Chapman (26 Jan. 1884—11 March 1960), naturalist and explorer, was born at Beloit, Wisconsin, and educated at Beloit College and Columbia University. He became vice-director of the American Museum of Natural History, New York, and from 1908 onwards took part in many exploring expeditions, particularly in Central Asia, where between 1921 and 1930 he mapped much new area in the Gobi Desert, discovered the first dinosaur eggs known to science, and secured part of the skeleton of a baluchitherium, the largest known mammal. He also specialized in the study of whales. Among his books are *Whale Hunting with Gun and Camera* (1916), *Across Mongolian Plains* (1921), *On the Trail of Ancient Man* (1926), *The New Conquest of Central Asia* (1932), *Meet Your Ancestors* (1945), *Heart of Asia* (1951), and *Beyond Adventure* (1954).

Angell, Sir Norman (26 Dec. 1874—), author and journalist, was christened Ralph Norman Angell Lane, but later changed his name. He was educated at St Omer Lycée and Geneva University, and subsequently worked in western America, first at ranching and later at journalism. From 1905 to 1914 he was manager, under Northcliffe, of the Paris edition of the *Daily Mail*, and in 1910 he became world-famous by writing *The Great Illusion*, which demonstrated the disastrous effect of war on victor and vanquished alike, and was published in eleven countries and fifteen languages. In 1931 he was knighted and in 1933 received the Nobel Peace Prize. From 1929 to 1931 he was Labour M.P. for North Bradford. His other books include *The Economic Chaos and the Peace Treaty* (1919), *The Fruits of Victory* (1921), *Chaos and Control* (1933), *The Money Mystery* (1936), *Let the People Know* (1943), and *The Steep Places* (1947). *After All* (1951) is an autobiography.

Angus, Marion (1866—18 Aug. 1946), poetess, was born in Aberdeen, but spent her childhood and youth at Arbroath, where her father was a minister. After his death she settled in an old-fashioned cottage at Hazelhead. She did not begin to write poetry seriously till after the First World War, when she was over 50, but kept on writing till she was 75. Her first volume, *The Lilt and Other Verses* (1922) was followed by *The Tinker's Road* (1924), *Sun and Candlelight* (1927), *The Singin' Lass* (1929), *The Turn of the Day* (1931), and *Lost Country* (1937). *Selected Poems* with a memoir appeared after her death, in 1950. Her themes are nearly always sad, her work having affinities with the Border ballads.

Anstey, Christopher (31 Oct. 1724—3 Aug. 1805), poet, son of the rector of Brinkley, Cambridgeshire, was educated at Eton and

Cambridge. He published in 1766 a poem satirizing contemporary fashions, *The New Bath Guide*, which had great popularity, and from which Smollett is said to have drawn largely in his *Humphrey Clinker*. He made many other excursions into literature which are hardly remembered, and ended his days as a country squire at the age of 80.

Anstey, F., *see* Guthrie, Thomas Anstey.

Arbuthnot, John (29 April 1667—27 Feb. 1735), doctor and satirist, was born in Kincardineshire, and after studying at Aberdeen and Oxford, took his degree of M.D. at St Andrews. Settling in London, he taught mathematics. Being by a fortunate accident at Epsom, he was called in to prescribe for Prince George, who was suddenly taken ill there, and was so successful in his treatment that he was appointed his regular physician. This made his professional fortune, and in 1705 he became physician to the Queen. He became the cherished friend of Swift and Pope, and himself gained a high reputation as a wit and man of letters. His principal works are the *History of John Bull* (1712), mainly against the Duke of Marlborough, *A Treatise concerning the Altercation or Scolding of the Ancients*, and the *Art of Political Lying*. He was the principal author of the satirical *Memoirs of Martinus Scriblerus*, to which Pope was a contributor. He also wrote various medical treatises, and dissertations on ancient coins, weights, and measures. He was one of the very few who retained the sincere regard of Swift, whose style he made the model of his own, with such success that writings by the one were sometimes attributed to the other.

Archer, William (23 Sept. 1856—27 Dec. 1924), journalist, was born at Perth of an Australian father and educated at Perth Academy, George Watson's, and Edinburgh University. In 1883 he was called to the bar at the Middle Temple, but never practised. In 1875 he began journalism as a leader-writer for the Edinburgh *Evening News*, and after a tour of the world he settled in London and became dramatic critic for the *Figaro*, and later for the *World* and the *Star*, his work coinciding with the revival of the London stage under Pinero, Wilde, and Barrie. He was instrumental in introducing Ibsen to the English public, his translation of *Pillars of Society* being the first of that dramatist's plays to be produced in London (1880). Besides editing Ibsen's works he wrote several books about the theatre, including *Masks or Faces* (1888) and *Playmaking* (1912). His own successful play, *The Green Goddess*, was produced in 1923.

Argyll, George John Douglas Campbell, 8th Duke of (30 April 1823— 24 April 1900), statesman and author, was born at Ardencaple Castle, near Helensburgh, and succeeded his father, the 7th duke, in 1847. His talents and eloquence soon raised him to distinction in public life. He acted with the Liberal party until its break-up under the Irish policy of Gladstone, after which he was one of the Unionist leaders. He held the offices of Lord Privy Seal, Postmaster-General, and Indian Secretary. His writings include *The Reign of Law* (1866),

Primeval Man (1869), *The Eastern Question* (1879), *The Unseen Foundations of Society* (1893), *Philosophy of Belief* (1896), and *Organic Evolution Cross-examined* (1898). His *Autobiography* appeared posthumously in 1906.

Arlen, Michael (16 Nov. 1895—23 June 1956), novelist, was born at Rustchuk, Bulgaria, of Armenian parents. His original name was Dikrān Kouyoumdjian, but he changed it by deed poll, becoming a naturalized British subject in 1922. He was educated at Malvern College and studied medicine at Edinburgh University. In 1928 he married the Countess Atalanta Mercati. His first book was published when he was 18, but celebrity came to him with the appearance of *The Green Hat* (1924), which was for a time the most talked-of novel in England, and brought its writer a fortune. His work, which has been described as 'a combination of sexual farce and melodrama' belongs to a Mayfair now long out of date. Other books of his are *These Charming People* (1920), *Young Men in Love* (1927), *Hell! Said the Duchess* (1934), and *Flying Dutchman* (1939).

Armstrong, Anthony, *see* **Willis, George A. A.**

Armstrong, John (1709?—7 Sept. 1779), doctor and poet, son of the minister of Castleton, Roxburghshire, studied medicine at Edinburgh, and practised in London. He is remembered as the friend of Thomson, Mallet, and other literary celebrities of the time, and as the author of a poem on *The Art of Preserving Health* (1744), in which a somewhat unpromising subject for poetic treatment is gracefully and ingeniously handled. His other works, consisting of some poems and prose essays, and a drama, *The Forced Marriage*, are forgotten, with the exception of four stanzas which he contributed to the end of the first part of Thomson's *Castle of Indolence*, describing the diseases incident to sloth.

Armstrong, Terence Ian Fytton (29 June 1912—   ), poet and critic who wrote under the name John Gawsworth, was born in Kensington and educated at Merchant Taylors'. During the Second World War he served with the Royal Air Force in Italy and the Middle East. Founder of the *English Digest*, which he edited from 1939 to 1941, he was later editor of the *Literary Digest* from 1946 and of the *Poetry Review* from 1948. His volumes of verse include *Poems 1930—1932* (1933), *New Poems* (1939), *The Mind of Man* (1940), *Marlow Hill* (1941), *Legacy to Love* (1943), *Snow and Sand* (1945), and *Blow No Bugles* (1945); his *Collected Poems* appeared in 1948. *Above the River* (1931) and *Backwaters* (1932) are prose, and he also wrote critical works on P. Wyndham Lewis (1932) and *Ten Contemporaries* (two series, 1932, 1933), besides editing many anthologies.

Arnim, Countess von, *see* **Russell, Elizabeth, Countess.**

Arnold, Sir Edwin (10 June 1832—24 March 1904), poet, son of a Sussex magistrate, was born at Gravesend, and educated at King's School, Rochester, London, and Oxford, where in 1852 he won the Newdigate with a poem on *Belshazzar's Feast*. Thereafter he was an assistant master at King Edward's School, Birmingham, and was in 1856 appointed Principal of the Government Deccan College, Poona. Here he received the bias towards, and gathered material for, his future works. In 1861 he returned to England and became connected with the *Daily Telegraph*, of which he was ultimately editor. The literary task which he set before him was the interpretation in English verse of the life and philosophy of the East. His chief work with this object is *The Light of Asia* (1879), a poem on the life and teaching of Buddha, which had great popularity. In *The Light of the World* (1891), he attempted, less successfully, a similar treatment of the life and teaching of Jesus. Other works are *The Song of Songs of India* (1875), *With Saadi in the Garden*, and *The Tenth Muse*. He travelled widely in the East, and wrote books on his travels. He was made a Knight Commander of the Indian Empire in 1888, and his collected poetical works appeared in the same year.

Arnold, Matthew (24 Dec. 1822—15 April 1888), poet and critic, son of Dr Thomas Arnold (q.v.), was born at Laleham, a Middlesex village on the Thames, and educated at Rugby, Winchester, and Balliol College, Oxford. He won the Newdigate Prize with a poem on *Cromwell*, and in 1854 became a Fellow of Oriel. Thereafter he was private secretary to Lord Lansdowne, Lord President of the Council, through whose influence he was in 1851 appointed an inspector of schools. Two years before this he had published his first book of poems, *The Strayed Reveller*, and it was followed in 1852 by *Empedocles on Etna*. Both of these volumes were published anonymously and afterwards withdrawn by the author, but the best of their contents, including pieces now famous like 'The Forsaken Merman' and 'Tristram and Iseult' were republished in *Poems* (1853), which also contained the short epic 'Sohrab and Rustum,' and 'The Scholar Gipsy,' and bore the author's name. In 1855 appeared *Poems, second series*, containing ' Balder Dead,' and in 1858 the tragedy, *Merope*. Finally *New Poems* (1867) contained ' Thyrsis,' an elegy on A. H. Clough (q.v.), and ' Rugby Chapel.'

In 1857 Arnold had been appointed to the Chair of Poetry at Oxford, which he held for ten years. After this he produced little poetry and devoted himself to criticism and theology. The most important of his prose works were the *Essays in Criticism* (1865), in which he argued against 'provinciality' in thought and style, and assailed what he called the philistinism of the times. He had previously published a series of lectures *On Translating Homer* (1861), and his discourses *On the Study of Celtic Literature* (1866) were stimulating though not authoritative. *Culture and Anarchy* (1869) dealt with manners and morals rather than literature, and championed the cause of 'sweetness and light,' a phrase which he borrowed from Swift. This was followed by a number of works of religious criticism, including *St Paul and Protestantism* (1870), *Literature and Dogma* (1873), *God and the Bible* (1875), and *Last Essays on Church and Religion* (1877). *Mixed Essays* (1879) is partly political, and *Irish Essays* (1882) sought to deal with the Irish question. In 1883 Arnold visited the United States on a lecture tour, and his *Discourses in America* appeared in 1885. In 1886 he resigned his post as inspector of schools, receiving a pension of £250. A second series of *Essays in Criticism* (1888), put together after his death, collected various articles he had written on poets and poetry, and two volumes of his *Letters* were published in 1895.

The rationalistic tendency in some of Arnold's writings gave offence to many of his generation, and the adequacy of his equipment in scholarship for dealing with some of the subjects he handled was called in question; but he undoubtedly exercised a wholesome influence on his time. His writings are characterized by the finest culture, high purpose, and a style of great distinction. Much of his poetry has an exquisite and subtle beauty, though here also it has been doubted whether high culture and wide knowledge of poetry did not sometimes take the place of the true poetic fire.

Arnold, Thomas (13 June 1795—12 June 1842), schoolmaster, son of an inland revenue officer in the Isle of Wight, was educated at Winchester and Oxford, where he had a distinguished record and became a Fellow of Oriel. In 1818 he took orders, and in 1828 became D.D. From that year till 1842 he was headmaster of Rugby. His learning, earnestness, and force of character enabled him not only to raise his own school to the front rank of public schools, but to exercise an unprecedented reforming influence on the whole educational system of the country. A liberal in politics, and a zealous church reformer, he was involved in many controversies, educational and religious. As a churchman he was a decided Erastian, and strongly opposed to the High Church party. In 1841 he was appointed Professor of Modern History at Oxford. His chief literary works are his unfinished *History of Rome* (3 volumes 1838—1842), and his *Lectures on Modern History*. His life, by Dean Stanley (q.v.), is one of the best works of its class in the language.

Ascham, Roger (1515—30 Dec. 1568), educationist and scholar, son of John Arnold, house-steward in the family of Lord Scrope, was born at Kirby Wiske, Yorkshire, and educated first by Sir Humphrey Wingfield, and then at St John's College, Cambridge, where he devoted himself specially to the study of Greek, then newly revived. In 1534 he became a Fellow, and in 1538 Greek Reader at St John's. He was likewise noted for his skill in penmanship, music, and archery, the last of which is the subject of his first work, *Toxophilus* (1545); dedicated to Henry VIII, it gained him the favour of the king, who bestowed a pension upon him. The objects of the book are twofold, to commend the practice of shooting with the long bow as a manly sport and an aid to national defence, and to set the example of a higher style of composition than had yet been attempted in English. Soon afterwards he was made university orator, and master of languages to the Lady (afterwards Queen) Elizabeth. He then went abroad in various positions of trust, returning on being appointed Latin Secretary to Edward VI. This office he likewise discharged to Mary and then to Elizabeth—a testimony to his tact and caution in these changeful times. His principal work, *The Schoolmaster*, a

treatise on education, was printed by his widow in 1570. His life
was written by Dr Johnson.

Asgill, John (25 March 1659—Nov. 1738), pamphleteer, studied at
the Middle Temple and was called to the Bar in 1692.   In 1699 he
published in an unlucky hour a pamphlet to prove that death was not
obligatory upon Christians, which, much to his surprise, aroused
the public wrath and led to his expulsion from the Irish and English
House of Commons successively.   He thereafter fell on evil days, and
passed the rest of his life between the Fleet and the King's Bench,
where, strange to say, his zeal as a pamphleteer continued unabated.

Ashford, Daisy (   ), authoress, was
born at Petersham, Surrey, and educated at The Priory, Haywards
Heath.   She is remembered only for *The Young Visiters* (1919), a
novel which she wrote at the age of 9, and which was published many
years later with an introduction by J. M. Barrie.   The artless charm
of the book made it very popular and it has become a sort of juvenile
classic.   Miss Ashford subsequently married James Patrick Devlin
and lived in Norwich.

Ashmole, Elias (23 May 1617—18 May 1692), antiquary and
astrologer, was born and educated at Lichfield, and became a
solicitor in 1638.   On the breaking out of the Civil War he sided with
the royalists, and at Brasenose College, Oxford, he studied science,
including astrology.   The result of his studies in this region of
mystery was his *Theatrum Chymicum Britannicum*, which gained him
great repute and the friendship of John Selden.   His last astrological
treatise was *The Way to Bliss*, which dealt with the subject of 'the
philosopher's stone.'   He also wrote various works on antiquarian
subjects, and a *History of the Order of the Garter*.   Ashmole held
various posts under government, and presented to the University of
Oxford a valuable collection of curiosities now known as the Ashmolean Museum.   He also bequeathed his library to the University.
His diary was edited in 1927.

Ashton, Winifred (   ), novelist
who wrote under the name Clemence Dane, was born in London
but brought up in the country and educated at rural schools.   At
the age of 16 she taught French in Geneva for a year.   She then
studied art for three years at the Slade School and in Dresden, and
after a further period as a school-teacher in Ireland went on the
stage in 1913, for some five years under the name Diana Cortis.
When she started to write she took her pseudonym from the famous
London church of St Clement Danes.   Her first novel; *Regiment of
Women* (1917) tells of teachers in a girls' school.   *Legend* (1919) was
made into a very successful play, *A Bill of Divorcement* (1921).
Others of her plays are *Will Shakespeare* (1921), *Wild Decembers*
(1933), which tells of the Brontës, and *Come of Age* (1934), which is
about Chatterton.   Later novels are *Wandering Stars* (1928),
Broome Stages (1931), *The Moon Is Feminine* (1938), *He Brings
Great News* (1944), and *The Flower Girls* (1954).   In 1953 she was
made a C.B.E.

Asquith, Emma Alice Margaret, Countess of Oxford and Asquith (2 Feb. 1864—28 July 1945), was a daughter of Sir Charles Tennant, head of a Glasgow chemical firm. In 1894 she married Herbert Henry Asquith, the Liberal statesman who became Prime Minister and was made an Earl in 1925. She was regarded as one of the wittiest hostesses of her day, and her racy *Autobiography of Margot Asquith* (1922), with its lively pen-sketches of notabilities, was widely read. Later works were *Places and Persons* (1925), *More Memories* (1933), and *Off the Record* (1944).

Asser (died 909?), chronicler, a monk of St David's, afterwards Bishop of Sherborne, was the friend, helper, and biographer of King Alfred. He also wrote a chronicle of England from 849 to 887.

Atherstone, Edwin (17 April 1788—29 Jan. 1872), poet and novelist, was born in Nottingham. His works, which were planned on an imposing scale, attracted some temporary attention and applause, but are now forgotten. His chief poem, *The Fall of Nineveh*, consisting of 30 books, appeared at intervals from 1828 to 1868. He also produced two novels, *The Sea Kings in England* and *The Handwriting on the Wall*.

Atherton, Gertrude (30 Oct. 1857—14 June 1948), novelist, was born Gertrude Franklin Horn in San Francisco and was a great-grand-niece of Benjamin Franklin (q.v.). She started writing while still at school. In 1876 she married George H. B. Atherton, and when he died four years later she went to New York and began a writing career in which she produced some 40 books. She lived for seven years in England and for six in Munich, and was made a Chevalier of the Legion of Honour and an LL.D of the University of California. Her most popular books were *The Conqueror* (1902), *Rezánov* (1906), *Black Oxen* (1923), *The Immortal Marriage* (1927), and *Dido, Queen of Hearts* (1929). *Adventures of a Novelist* (1932) is an autobiography of her earlier years.

Atterbury, Francis (6 March 1663—15 Feb. 1732), prelate, was born near Newport Pagnell, Buckinghamshire, and educated at Westminster School and Oxford. He became the leading protagonist on the High Church side in the ecclesiastical controversies of his time, and is believed to have been the chief author of the famous defence of Dr Sacheverell in 1712. He also wrote most of Boyle's *Examination of Dr Bentley's Dissertations on the Epistles of Phalaris*, and published sermons, which, with his letters to Swift, Pope, and other friends, constitute the foundation of his literary reputation. During the reign of the Tories he enjoyed much preferment, becoming successively Canon of Exeter, Dean of Christ Church, Dean of Westminster, and Bishop of Rochester. His Jacobite principles, however, and his participation in various plots got him into trouble, and in 1722 he was confined in the Tower, deprived of all his offices, and ultimately banished. He died at Paris and was buried privately in Westminster Abbey.

Aubrey, John (12 March 1626—June 1697), antiquary, born at Easton Piercy, Wiltshire, was educated at Malmesbury Grammar

School under Robert Latimer, and at Oxford. In 1646 he was entered at Middle Temple, but was never called to the Bar. An accurate but unsystematic investigator, he described the megalithic remains at Avebury in 1649. In 1652 he inherited large estates, but lost both those and his library through litigation. His folklore *Miscellanies* (1696) was the only work published in his lifetime, but he left much antiquarian and historical material in manuscript. His *Topographical Collections* were edited in 1862, and his *Brief Lives of Contemporaries*, which contains a short biography of Shakespeare, in 1898.

Auden, Wystan Hugh (21 Feb. 1907—   ), poet, son of a doctor, was born at York and educated at Gresham's School, Holt, and Christ Church, Oxford. After visiting Germany, he was a schoolmaster in this country for a short time. His first published work, *Poems* (1930), was followed by *The Orators* (1932), *The Dance of Death* (1933), and *Look, Stranger* (1936). Though not a Communist, he became the leader of a new school of Leftist poets who were prominent in the decade before the Second World War, and whose work showed the influence of T. S. Eliot. In 1937 he served as a stretcher-bearer in the Spanish Civil War, wrote a poem, *Spain*, and was awarded the King's Medal for Poetry. He was co-editor of an anthology, *The Poet's Tongue* (1935), based on the principle that poetry is 'memorable speech,' and editor of the *Oxford Book of Light Verse* (1938). He married Erika Mann, daughter of the German novelist, and in 1938 moved permanently to the United States, adopted American citizenship, and taught in a number of American colleges and universities. Volumes of verse he published subsequently included *Another Time* (1940), *New Year Letter* (1941), *For the Time Being* (1945), and *The Age of Anxiety* (1948); *Collected Shorter Poems* appeared in 1950. In collaboration with Christopher Isherwood he wrote three verse plays, *The Dog Beneath the Skin* (1935), *The Ascent of F6* (1936), and *On the Frontier* (1938). Though often very close to conversational speech, Auden's poetry does not always escape the obscurity common among poets of the period. His work is difficult to assess because he has no definite style, but his influence is undoubted. In 1956 he was elected Professor of Poetry at Oxford.

Aumonier, Stacy (1887—21 Dec. 1928), novelist, son of a sculptor, was educated at Cranleigh, and began his career as a designer and a landscape painter, frequently exhibiting at the Royal Academy and various London galleries. He served as a private in the First World War, and died in Switzerland at the age of 41. *The Querrils*, a study of a war-time family, is his best-known novel, but he was more popular as a short-story writer. Others of his books are *Heartbeat* (1922), *Overheard: Fifteen Tales* (1924), *The Baby Grand* (1926), and *Little Windows* (1931).

Austen, Jane (16 Dec. 1775—18 July 1817), novelist, was born at Steventon in Hampshire, the daughter of a clergyman who had been a Fellow of St John's College, Oxford. In 1784 she was sent to a school at Reading, with her elder sister Cassandra, who was her lifelong friend and confidant, but for the most part she was taught by her father, and thus had a far better education than fell to the lot of the average English girl of her class. She began writing at a very early age, *Love and Freindship* (*sic*) dating from her teens. In 1801 the family moved to Bath, the scene of so many episodes in her books, and after the death of her father in 1805 to Southampton and then to Chawton, a village in Hampshire where the house in which most of her novels were written is still standing. Apart from occasional journeys to London and holidays at Dawlish, Teignmouth, or Lyme Regis, her life was placid and uneventful. In May 1817 the family moved to Winchester so that she might have skilled medical attention for the consumption with which she was threatened, but in spite of every care she died two months later and lies buried in Winchester Cathedral.

The chronology of her six novels is complicated by the fact that the order of publication has little relation to the order of composition. *Pride and Prejudice*, considered by many critics the best, was begun in 1796, the original title being *First Impressions*; offered to a publisher in the following year, it was rejected, and only appeared at last, after revision, in 1813. *Sense and Sensibility* was published two years earlier, though it had not been begun till 1797, having been originally planned with the title *Elinor and Marianne*. *Northanger Abbey*, that satire on the 'horror tales' of the time, also begun in 1797, was sold in 1803 to a publisher who made no use of it; in 1816 the manuscript was recovered, but it was not published till after the writer's death. The remaining three novels are more straightforward in their history. *Mansfield Park*, begun in 1811, was published in 1814; *Emma*, written in 1814, appeared in 1816, the year after *Persuasion*, the last of the novels, was written, to be published posthumously. *Sanditon*, a fragment written in the year of her death, was first published in 1925.

Jane Austen's novels, like her life, are uneventful. Though published in the nineteenth century, they really belong to the eighteenth, for there is little passion or romantic atmosphere in any of them. She lived right through the Napoleonic wars, yet no reference is made to the events of the time, even though naval officers (two of her brothers rose to be admirals) figure so frequently in her pages. But in her own limited sphere, depicting the actions and describing the society of English country families, she is unsurpassed. She herself spoke of 'the little bit (two inches wide) of ivory on which I work with so fine a brush as produces little effect after much labour.' Her genius was at once recognized by such critics as Coleridge, Southey, and Macaulay; and Walter Scott declared 'she had a talent for describing the involvements and feelings and characters of ordinary life which is to me the most wonderful I ever met with.' The standard edition of her works is that of R. W. Chapman (1923), who later edited three additional volumes of the juvenilia and unfinished pieces, and also two volumes of her *Letters* (1932).

Austin, Alfred (30 May 1835—2 June 1913), Poet Laureate, was born at Leeds, son of a wool-stapler, educated at Stonyhurst and Oscott College, and became a B.A. of London in 1853. He was called to the Bar at the Inner Temple in 1857, but forsook law for literature, though his earliest efforts were not very successful. From 1866 to 1896 he was a leader-writer and sometimes foreign correspondent for the *Standard*, and later he edited the *National Review*. After settling at Swineford Old Manor in Kent he produced some 20 volumes of verse between 1871 and 1908, his best work being his poetry of the countryside. In 1896 he was appointed Poet Laureate, a post for which his reverence for authority made him in some ways suitable. He wrote several novels, which are dull and full of moralizing, and a somewhat pompous *Autobiography* (1911).

Austin, John (3 March, 1790—Dec. 1859), jurist, born near Ipswich, served in the army in Sicily and Malta, but, selling his commission, studied law, and was called to the Bar in 1818. He did not long continue to practise, but devoted himself to the study of law as a science, and became Professor of Jurisprudence in London University 1826—32. Thereafter he served on various Royal Commissions. By his works he exercised a profound influence on the views of jurisprudence held in England. These include *The Province of Jurisprudence Determined* (1832), and his *Lectures* (1863).

Avebury, Sir John Lubbock, 1st Baron (30 April 1834—28 May 1913), banker and natural historian, was born in London, son of the banker and astronomer Sir J. W. Lubbock, but from the age of 6 lived in the country at Down, Kent, where he was encouraged in his enthusiasm for natural history by Charles Darwin, who was a friend of his father. Educated at Eton, he entered the banking business at 15, and rose to be the first President of the Institute of Bankers. As M.P. for London University he was instrumental in establishing the August bank holiday and getting the Shop Hours Act passed. He was at different times Vice-Chancellor of London University and President of the British Association and of the London County Council; he was created baron in 1900. As a writer he is best remembered for his excellent books on nature, such as *The Origin and Metamorphoses of Insects* (1874), *Ants, Bees, and Wasps* (1882), and *The Beauties of Nature* (1892). His famous list of the hundred best books was a stimulus to many.

à Wood, Anthony, *see* **Wood.**

Ayton *or* **Aytoun, Sir Robert** (1570—Feb. 1638), poet, was born at Kinaldie in Fife. After graduating at St Andrews, he studied law at Paris, became ambassador to the Emperor, and held other court offices. He appears to have been well-known to his literary contemporaries in England. He wrote poems in Latin, Greek, and French, and was one of the first Scotsmen to write in English. His chief poem is *Diophantus and Charidora*; 'Inconstancy Upbraided' is perhaps the best of his short poems. He is credited with a little poem, 'Old Long Syne,' which possibly suggested Burns's famous 'Auld Lang Syne.'

Aytoun, William Edmonstoune (21 June 1813—4 Aug. 1865), poet and humorist, a Writer to the Signet, was born and educated in Edinburgh and was brought up to the law, which, however, as he said, he 'followed but could never overtake.' He became a contributor to *Blackwood's Magazine* in 1836, and continued his connection with it until his death. In it appeared most of his humorous prose pieces, such as 'The Glenmutchkin Railway,' 'How I Became a Yeoman,' and 'How I Stood for the Dreepdaily Burghs,' all full of vigorous fun. In the same pages began to appear his chief poetical work, the *Lays of the Scottish Cavaliers* (1848), and a novel, partly autobiographical, *Norman Sinclair* (1861). Other works were *The Bon Gaultier Ballads* (1855), which he composed jointly with Theodore Martin, and *Firmilian, a Spasmodic Tragedy* (1854), under the *nom de plume* of T. Percy Jones, intended to satirize a group of poets and critics, including Gilfillan, Dobell, Bailey, and Alexander Smith. In 1845 he obtained the Chair of Rhetoric and Belles Lettres in Edinburgh University, which he filled with great success, raising the attendance from 30 to 150, and in 1852 he was appointed sheriff of Orkney and Shetland. He was married to a daughter of Professor John Wilson (q.v.).

B

Bacon, Francis, Lord Verulam and Viscount St Albans (22 Jan.
1561—9 April 1626), statesman, philosopher, and essayist, was the
youngest son of Sir Nicholas Bacon, Lord Keeper, by his second wife,
a daughter of Sir Anthony Cooke, whose sister married William Cecil,
Lord Burghley, the great minister of Queen Elizabeth. He was born
at York House in the Strand, and in his 13th year was sent with
his elder brother Anthony to Trinity College, Cambridge. Here he
first met the Queen, who was impressed by his precocious intellect,
and was accustomed to call him 'the young Lord Keeper.' Here
also he became dissatisfied with the Aristotelian philosophy then in
vogue, regarding it as being unfruitful and leading only to resultless
disputation. In 1576 he entered Gray's Inn, and in the same year
joined the embassy of Sir Amyas Paulet to France, where he remained
until 1579. The death of his father in that year gave an adverse
turn to his fortunes, and rendered it necessary that he should decide
upon a profession. He accordingly returned to Gray's Inn, and was
called to the Bar in 1582. He did not, however, desert philosophy,
and published a Latin tract, *Temporis Partus Maximus* (the Greatest
Birth of Time), the first rough draft of his own system. Two years
later, in 1584, he entered the House of Commons as member for
Melcombe, sitting subsequently for Taunton (1586), Liverpool (1589),
Middlesex (1593), and Southampton (1597). In the Parliament of
1586 he took a prominent part in urging the execution of Mary Queen
of Scots. About 1591 he formed a friendship with the Earl of
Essex, from whom he received many tokens of kindness, being
presented with a property at Twickenham, which he subsequently
sold for £1,800, equivalent to a far greater sum now. In 1596 he
was made a Queen's Counsel, but missed the appointment of Master
of the Rolls, and in the next year (1597), he published the first edition
of his *Essays*, ten in number. By 1601 Essex had lost the Queen's
favour, and had raised his rebellion, and Bacon was one of those
appointed to investigate the charges against him, and examine
witnesses, in connection with which he showed an ungrateful and
indecent eagerness in pressing the case against his former friend and
benefactor, who was executed on 25 Feb. 1601. This act Bacon
endeavoured to justify in *A Declaration of the Practices and Treasons
of the Earl of Essex*.

The accession of James VI in 1603 gave a favourable turn to his
fortunes: he was knighted, and endeavoured to set himself right with
the new powers by writing his *Apologie* (defence) of his proceedings in
the case of Essex, who had favoured the succession of James. In the
first Parliament of the new king he sat for St Albans, and was
appointed a Commissioner for Union with Scotland. In 1605 he
published *The Advancement of Learning*, dedicated, with fulsome
flattery, to the king. The following year he married Alice Barnham,
the daughter of a London merchant, and in 1607 he was made

Solicitor-General, and wrote *Cogita et Visa*, a first sketch of the *Novum Organum*, followed in 1609 by *The Wisdom of the Ancients*. Meanwhile (in 1608), he had entered upon the Clerkship of the Star Chamber, and was in the enjoyment of a large income; but old debts and present extravagance kept him embarrassed. In 1613 he became Attorney-General, and in this capacity prosecuted Somerset in 1616. The year 1618 saw him Lord Keeper, and the next Lord Chancellor and Baron Verulam, a title which, in 1621, he exchanged for that of Viscount St Albans. Meanwhile he had written the *New Atlantis*, a political romance, and in 1620 he presented to the king the *Novum Organum*, on which he had been engaged for thirty years, and which ultimately formed the main part of the *Instauratio Magna*, his great work for the restoration of knowledge, of which only sections were completed. In his office of Lord Chancellor Bacon showed a failure of character in striking contrast with the majesty of his intellect. He was corrupt alike politically and judicially, and now the hour of retribution arrived. In 1621 a Parliamentary Committee on the administration of the law charged him with corruption under 23 counts; and so clear was the evidence that he made no attempt at defence. He was sentenced to a fine of £40,000, remitted by the king; to be committed to the Tower during the king's pleasure (which was that he should be released in a few days); and to be incapable of holding office or sitting in parliament. He narrowly escaped being deprived of his titles.

Thenceforth he devoted himself to study and writing. In 1622 appeared his *History of Henry VII*, and the 3rd part of the *Instauratio*; in 1623, *History of Life and Death*, the *De Augmentis Scientarum*, a Latin translation of the *Advancement*, and in 1625 the 3rd edition of the *Essays*, now 58 in number. He also published *Apophthegms*, and a translation of some of the *Psalms*. In March 1626, he came to London, and shortly after, when driving on a snowy day, the idea struck him of making an experiment as to the antiseptic properties of snow, in consequence of which he caught a chill, which ended in his death. He left debts to the amount of £22,000. At the time of his death he was engaged upon *Sylva Sylvarum*. The intellect of Bacon was one of the most powerful and searching ever possessed by man, and he is claimed by scientists as the originator of the modern school of experimental research. The most popular of his works is the *Essays*, which convey profound and condensed thought in a style that is at once clear and rich. His moral character was extremely mixed and complex, and bears no comparison with his intellect. Futile attempts, supported sometimes with much ingenuity, have been made to claim for Bacon the authorship of Shakespeare's plays.

Bacon, Roger (1214?—1294), scientist, born at Ilchester in Somerset, studied at Oxford and Paris. His scientific acquirements, regarded in that age as savouring of witchcraft, aroused the suspicion and jealousy of the Franciscan order, to which he belonged, and he was in consequence imprisoned at Paris for ten years. Pope Clement IV, who had been a sympathizer, desired on his accession to see

Bacon's works, and in response Bacon sent him *Opus Majus*, a treatise on the sciences (grammar, logic, mathematics, physics, and philosophy), followed by *Opus Minus* and *Opus Tertium*. Clement, however, was near death when they arrived. Bacon was comparatively free from persecution for the next ten years, but after the appearance in 1272 of his *Compendium Studii Philosophiae*, in which he attacked the ignorance of the clergy, he was again put in confinement for some fourteen years. At the intercession of some English noblemen he was at last released, and spent the rest of his life at Oxford. He possessed one of the most commanding intellects of his own, or perhaps of any, age, and, notwithstanding all the disadvantages and discouragements to which he was subjected, made many discoveries, and came near to many more. He received the sobriquet of 'Doctor Mirabilis.'

Bæda, *see* **Bede.**

Bage, Robert (29 Feb. 1728—1 Sept. 1801), novelist, born at Darley in Derbyshire, carried on his father's business of paper manufacture. It was not until he was 53 that he took to literature; but in the fifteen years following he produced six novels, of which Sir Walter Scott says that 'strong mind, playful fancy, and extensive knowledge are everywhere apparent.' Bage, though brought up as a Quaker, imbibed the principles of the French Revolution. *Hermsprong; or, Man as He is Not* (1796) is considered the best of his novels, of which it was the last. The names of the others are *Mount Kenneth* (1781), *Barham Downs* (1784), *The Fair Syrian* (1787), *James Wallace* (1788), and *Man as He is* (1792).

Bagehot, Walter (3 Feb. 1826—24 March 1877), economist, son of a banker, was born at Langport, Somerset, educated at University College, London, and called to the Bar, but did not practise, and joined his father in business. He wrote for various periodicals, and from 1860 was editor of *The Economist*. He was the author of *The English Constitution* (1867), a standard work which was translated into several languages; also *Physics and Politics* (1872), and *Lombard Street* (1873), a valuable financial work. His *Literary Studies* (1879) contain some excellent criticism of English writers.

Bagnold, Enid (   ), novelist, was educated at Godalming and in Paris and took lessons in painting. In the First World War she served as a V.A.D. and afterwards wrote *A Diary Without Dates* (1917) about her experiences. Later she joined the First Aid Nursing Yeomanry, was attached to the French army, and made that period the subject of *The Happy Foreigner* (1920). In the same year she married Sir Roderick Jones, the chairman of Reuters. In 1925 she published the novel *Serena Blandish*, in 1930 a children's book, *Alice and Thomas and Jane*, and in 1935 her best-known work, *National Velvet*, a story of a racehorse. Later books are *The Loved and Envied* (1951) and *The Girl's Journey* (1954). *Lottie Dundass* (1941) and *Poor Judas* (1946) are plays.

Bailey, Henry Christopher (1 Feb. 1878—24 March 1961), novelist, born in London, was educated at the City of London School and

Oxford, where he coxed his college boat. While an undergraduate he wrote *My Lady of Orange*, which was later followed by several other historical novels, including *The Lonely Queen* and *Knight At Arms*. On leaving Oxford in 1901 he joined the staff of the *Daily Telegraph*, on which he remained for forty-five years. During the First World War he started writing detective stories and created the popular Reggie Fortune, who is known in half a dozen languages, as well as a minor sleuth called Joshua Clunk. Among the best-known of the Fortune books are *Call Mr Fortune* (1920) and *Mr Fortune's Practice* (1922); an omnibus volume, *Meet Mr Fortune*, appeared in 1942.

Bailey, Philip James (22 April 1816—6 Sept. 1902), poet, son of a journalist, was born at Nottingham, and educated there and at Glasgow University, of which he was made an LL.D. in 1891. His life was a singularly uneventful one. He lived at Nottingham, Jersey, Ilfracombe, London, and again at Nottingham, and travelled a good deal on the Continent. He was by profession a barrister, but never practised, and devoted his whole energies to poetry. His poetical drama *Festus* (1839), an imitation of Goethe's *Faust*, had tremendous popularity for a time, Tennyson being among its greatest admirers. Revisions, additions, and the embodiment in it of later unsuccessful compositions made its jubilee edition (1889) a monstrous compilation and overlaid what little merit it ever possessed. The subsequent poems of Bailey, *The Angel World* (1850), *The Mystic* (1855), *The Age* (1858), and *The Universal Hymn* (1867), were failures. In 1856 he was awarded a Civil List pension of £100. Bailey is sometimes regarded as the father of the so-called Spasmodic School of poetry.

Baillie, Lady Grisell *or* **Grizel** (25 Dec. 1665—6 Dec. 1746), poetess, daughter of Sir Patrick Home or Hume, afterwards Earl of Marchmont, was married to George Baillie of Jerviswoode. In her childhood she showed remarkable courage and address in the services she rendered to her father and his friend, Robert Baillie of Jerviswood the eminent Scottish patriot, when under persecution. She shared her father's exile in Utrecht and returned to Scotland at the Restoration. She left many pieces both prose and verse in manuscript, the best known being the beautiful song, 'Werena my heart licht I wad dee.'

Baillie, Joanna (11 Sept. 1762—23 Feb. 1851), dramatist and poetess, was the daughter of the minister of Bothwell, afterwards Professor of Divinity at Glasgow. Her mother was a sister of the great anatomists, William and John Hunter, and her brother was the celebrated physician, Matthew Baillie, of London. She received a thorough education at Glasgow, and at an early age went to London, where the remainder of her long, happy, and honoured, though uneventful, life was passed. In 1798, when she was 36, the first volume of her *Plays on the Passions* appeared, and was received with much favour, being admired by Walter Scott. Other two volumes followed in 1802 and 1812, and she also produced *Miscellaneous Plays* in 1804, and three volumes of *Dramatic Poetry* in 1836.

Baillie, Robert (1599—July 1662), clergyman, son of Baillie of Jerviston, educated at Glasgow University, entered the Church of

Scotland and became minister of Kilwinning in Ayrshire. His abilities soon made him a leading man. He was a member of the historic Assembly of 1638, when Presbyterianism was re-established in Scotland, and also of the Westminster Assembly, 1643, having served as chaplain in the Covenanting army at Duns Law. In 1651 he was made Professor of Divinity in Glasgow, and ten years later Principal. His *Letters and Journals*, edited for the Bannatyne Club by D. Laing (q.v.), are of the greatest value for the light they throw on a period of great importance in Scottish history.

Bain, Alexander (11 June 1818—18 Sept. 1903), philosopher, born in Aberdeen, son of a weaver, left school at 11, but subsequently went to Marischal College, became assistant to the Professor of Moral Philosophy, and in 1860 was appointed Professor of Logic and English. His principal works were *Mental and Moral Science* (1868), *Logic* (1870), and *Mind and Body* (1872), and he also published several books on English grammar. In 1876 he founded the philosophical journal, *Mind*, and in 1881 was elected Lord Rector of Aberdeen University. His *Autobiography* appeared in 1904.

Baker, Ray Stannard (17 April 1870—12 July 1946), biographer and essayist, was born in Lansing, Michigan, and studied law and literature at Michigan University. Taking up journalism, he worked for the Chicago *Record* from 1892 to 1897, then moved to New York where he was associate editor of *McClure's Magazine* (1899—1905), and afterwards on the *American Magazine* (1906—15). He was appointed editor of President Wilson's papers, and in 1940 when just over 70 received the Pulitzer Prize for the 8 volumes of *Woodrow Wilson: Life and Letters*. Under the pseudonym David Grayson he had a separate writing career, producing a series of studies of country life which included *Adventures in Contentment* (1907), *Adventures in Friendship* (1910), *Adventures in Understanding* (1925), *Adventures in Solitude* (1931), and *The Countryman's Year* (1936). 'David Grayson's' identity was revealed in 1916.

Baker, Sir Richard (1568?—18 Feb. 1645), historian and religious writer, educated at Oxford, studied law in London, was knighted in 1603, and was High Sheriff of Oxfordshire in 1620. He was the author of *The Chronicle of the Kings of England* (1643), which was for long held as a great authority among the country gentlemen. It has, however, many errors. Baker fell on evil days, was thrown into the Fleet for debt incurred by others, for which he had made himself responsible, and died there. It was during his durance that the *Chronicle* and some religious treatises were composed.

Baker, Sir Samuel White (8 June 1821—30 Dec. 1893), explorer, was born in London, son of a West-India merchant, and educated at the College School, Gloucester, and at Frankfurt. After being a planter in Ceylon, and superintending the construction of a railway between the Danube and the Black Sea, he went with his second wife, a Hungarian, in search of the sources of the Nile, and discovered the great lake, Albert Nyanza. Baker was knighted in 1866, and was for four years Governor-General of the Equatorial Nile Basin. His books, which are all on travel and sport, include *Albert Nyanza* (1866),

Nile Tributaries of Abyssinia (1867), *Ismailia* (1874), and *Wild Beasts and their Ways* (1890).

Balchin, Nigel Marlin (3 Dec. 1908—   ), novelist, was born at Potterne in Wiltshire. Educated at Dauntsey's School and Peterhouse, Cambridge, he studied science and became an industrialist and fruit farmer. Under the name Mark Spade he published the humorous satires *How to Run a Bassoon Factory* (1934) and *Business for Pleasure* (1935). During the Second World War he was Deputy Scientific Adviser to the Army Council. Books published under his own name are *No Sky* (1933), *Simple Life* (1934), *Lightbody on Liberty* (1936), *Income and Outcome* (1937), *Darkness Falls from the Air* (1942), *The Small Back Room* (1943), *Mine Own Executioner* (1945), *Lord, I was Afraid* (1947), *A Sort of Traitors* (1949), *The Anatomy of Villainy* (1950), *A Way through the Wood* (1951), *Sundry Creditors* (1953), and *The Fall of the Sparrow* (1955).

Bale, John (21 Nov. 1495—1563), historian and dramatist, was born at Cove, Suffolk, and educated as a Carmelite friar, but becoming a Protestant, engaged in violent controversy with the Roman Catholics. After undergoing persecution and flying to Flanders, he was brought back by Edward VI and made Bishop of Ossory. On the death of Edward he was again persecuted, and had to escape from Ireland to Holland, but returned on the accession of Elizabeth, who made him a Prebendary of Canterbury. His chief work is a Latin *Account of the Lives of Eminent Writers of Great Britain*. Besides this he wrote some dramas on scriptural subjects, and is noteworthy as the author of *King John* (1548), the first English historical play. His others, such as *Moses and Christ*, are of the nature of moralities.

Balfour, Arthur James Balfour, 1st Earl of, O.M. (25 July 1848—19 March 1930), philosopher and statesman, was born at Whittinghame, East Lothian, and educated at Eton and Cambridge. In 1874 he became M.P. for Hertford and in spite of apparent indolence rose to be leader of the Conservative party, holding office at different times as First Lord of the Treasury, First Lord of the Admiralty, Foreign Secretary, Lord President of the Council, and (1902—5) Prime Minister. After his work at the Washington Conference in 1922 he was made an Earl. His earliest book, *A Defence of Philosophic Doubt* (1879), was followed by *The Religion of Humanity* (1888) and *The Foundations of Belief* (1895). In 1915 he delivered the Gifford Lectures, taking as his subject *Theism and Humanism*, and in 1923 he wrote *Theism and Thought*. Among his many other distinctions he was President of the British Association in 1904, Chancellor of Cambridge University in 1919, and President of the British Academy from 1921 onwards. He was awarded the Order of Merit in 1916.

Ball, Sir Robert (1 July 1840—25 Nov. 1913), astronomer, was born in Dublin, son of a well-known naturalist, and educated at Trinity College. A brilliant mathematician, in 1867 he became Professor of Applied Mathematics in the Royal College of Science,

Dublin. In 1873 he was elected a Fellow of the Royal Society, in the following year he succeeded to the Chair of Astronomy at Dublin University, and in 1893 to that at Cambridge. He was best known for his popular works on astronomy, numbering over a dozen, of which *The Story of the Heavens* (1886) was the most successful. In the concluding years of the century he was president successively of the Royal Astronomical Society and of the Mathematical Association.

Ballantine, James (1808—Dec. 1877), artist and author, born in Edinburgh, began life as a house painter. He studied art, and became one of the first to revive the art of glass-painting, on which subject he wrote a treatise. He was the author of *The Gaberlunzie's Wallet* (1843), *Miller of Deanhaugh* (1845), *Poems* (1856), *100 Songs with Music* (1865), and a *Life of David Roberts, R.A.* (1866).

Ballantyne, Robert Michael (24 April 1825—8 Feb. 1894), writer of tales for boys, born in Edinburgh, was a nephew of the printer of Walter Scott's works. As a youth he spent some years in the service of the Hudson's Bay Co., and was then a member of Constable's printing firm. In 1856 he took to literature as a profession, and wrote about 80 tales, which, abounding in interesting adventure and information, and characterized by a manly tone, had great popularity. Among them are *The Young Fur Traders*, *The Coral Island*, *Fighting the Flames*, *Martin Rattler*, *The World of Ice*, *The Dog Crusoe*, *Erling the Bold*, and *Black Ivory*. His autobiographical *Personal Reminiscences in Book-making* appeared in 1893. Ballantyne was also an accomplished water-colour artist, and exhibited at the Royal Scottish Academy. He died at Rome.

Bancroft, George (3 Oct. 1800—17 Jan. 1891), historian, was born at Worcester, Massachusetts, son of a minister, and after graduating at Harvard, studied in Germany, where he became acquainted and corresponded with Goethe, Hegel, and other leaders of German thought. Returning to America he began his *History of the United States* (1834—74); this work covers the period from the discovery of the Continent to the conclusion of the Revolutionary War in 1782. His other great work is *The History of the Formation of the Constitution of the United States* (1882). Bancroft filled various political offices, and was in 1846 United States Minister to Great Britain.

Banim, John (3 April 1798—13 Aug. 1842), novelist, was born at Kilkenny, the son of a farmer. He began life as a miniature painter, but was led by the success of his first book, *Tales of the O'Hara Family*, in which his brother Michael collaborated, to devote himself to literature. The object which he set before himself was to become to Ireland what Scott has been to Scotland, and the influence of his model is distinctly traceable in his writings. His strength lies in the delineation of the characters of the Irish lower classes. The first series of the *O'Hara Tales* appeared in 1825, the second in 1826. Other works are *The Denounced* (1830), *The Smuggler* (1831), and *The Mayor of Windgap*. Most of these deal with the darker and more painful phases of life. Banim latterly suffered from illness and consequent poverty, which was alleviated by a Civil List pension of £190. He also wrote some poems, including *The Celt's Paradise*, and one or two plays, his tragedy, *Damon and Pythias*, being produced at Covent Garden in 1821.

Banim, Michael (5 Aug. 1796—30 Aug. 1874), novelist, was born at Kilkenny, of which he became postmaster. He studied law, but gave it up to collaborate with his brother John Banim (q.v.) in the *O'Hara Tales*, of which he wrote more than half, including *Crohoore of the Billhook*, one of the most successful. He also wrote *The Croppy* (1828) and *Father Connell* (1842).

Bannatyne, George (1545—1608?), compiler, the seventh of a family of twenty-three, became a burgess of Edinburgh in 1587. During the plague of 1568 he made the collection of Scots poetry known as the *Bannatyne Manuscript*, which is one of the main sources for the poems of Dunbar, Henryson, Lyndsay, and Alexander Scott. In 1823 the Bannatyne Club was founded in his memory.

Bannatyne, Richard (died 4 Sept. 1605), secretary to John Knox, compiled *Memorials of Transactions in Scotland from 1569 to 1573*, which are important for historians. After Knox's death he was for thirty years an advocate's clerk.

Barbauld, Anna Letitia (1743—9 March 1825), poetess, sister of John Aikin (q.v.), was born at Kibworth-Harcourt, Leicestershire. Her father kept an academy for boys, whose education she shared, and thus became acquainted with the classics. In 1773 she published a collection of miscellaneous poems, which was well received, and in the following year she married Rochemont Barbauld, a French Protestant and dissenting minister, who also conducted a school near Palgrave in Suffolk. Mainly owing to her talents and reputation, it proved a success and was afterwards carried on at Hampstead and Newington Green. Meantime, she brought out various devotional works, including her *Hymns in Prose for Children* (1781). These were followed by *Evenings at Home* (1796), *Selections from the English Essayists, The Letters of Samuel Richardson*, with a life prefixed, and a 50-volume collection of the British novelists with introductory essay (1810). In her poem *Eighteen Hundred and Eleven* she anticipated Macaulay's New Zealander with a youth who views the ruins of London.

Barbellion, W. N. P., *see* Cummings, Bruce.

Barber, Margaret Fairless (7 May 1869—24 Aug. 1901), essayist who wrote under the name Michael Fairless, was born at Castle Hill, Rastrick, Yorkshire. For a time she worked as a nurse, but owing to an affection of the spine she became a semi-invalid living in a country cottage and latterly in Chelsea. *The Roadmender*, a book of reflective essays written in the last two years before her early death, the final chapter being dictated on her deathbed, went through over thirty impressions in its first ten years. All her books were posthumously published, the best-known of the others being *The Gathering of Brother Hilarius* (1901), and *The Grey Brethren* (1905).

Barbour, John (1316—13 March 1395), poet, is thought to have been born near Aberdeen, of which he was archdeacon from 1357 till his death. There is evidence that he studied at Oxford and Paris, and later he held office in the household of King Robert II. His chief work was *The Brus* (1375), a national epic celebrating in over 13,000 octosyllabic lines the exploits of Robert the Bruce and Sir James Douglas, the heroes of Scottish chivalry. It has some fine descriptive passages, though its style is plain and severe, and it follows historical fact very closely. Other poems doubtfully ascribed to Barbour are *The Legend of Troy* and *Legends of the Saints*. An annuity of 20 shillings, bestowed on him by the king, was devoted to providing Masses for himself and his parents at the church of St Machar, and this was only discontinued at the Reformation.

Barclay, Alexander (born 1475? buried 10 June 1552), poet, probably of Scottish birth, was successively a priest in the college of Ottery St Mary, Devonshire, a monk of Ely, a Canterbury Franciscan, and rector of All Hallows, London. He is remembered for his satirical poem, *The Ship of Fools* (1509), partly a translation, which is of interest as throwing light on contemporary manners and customs. He also translated Sallust's *Bellum Jugurthinum*, and the *Mirrour of Good Manners*, from the Italian of Mancini, and wrote five *Eclogues*, which are the earliest English pastorals. His style is stiff and his verse uninspired.

Barclay, Florence Louisa (2 Dec. 1862—10 March 1921), novelist, was born at Limpsfield, Surrey, where her father, the Rev. S. Charlesworth, was rector, and in 1881 married the Rev. C. W. Barclay, vicar of Little Amwell, Hertford. Her first book, *Wheels of Time* (1908) was followed by the sensationally successful romance *The Rosary* (1909), which sold over a million copies before her death. In 1909 she toured the United States, lecturing on 'Palestine and the Bible.' Others of her novels are *The Mistress of Shenstone* (1910), *The Following of the Star* (1911), *The Broken Halo* (1913), and *My Heart's Right There* (1914). Her biography was written by one of her daughters.

Barclay, John (28 Jan. 1582—15 Aug. 1621), satirist, son of a Scotsman who was Professor of Law at Pont-à-Mousson, Lorraine, came with his father to England about 1603. His best-known works are the *Euphormionis Satyricon* (1603—7), a Latin satire in the manner of Petronius, directed against the Jesuits, and *Argenis*, a political romance, resembling in certain respects the *Arcadia* of Sidney and the *Utopia* of More. *Sylvae* (1606) is a collection of Latin poems.

Barclay, Robert (23 Dec. 1648—3 Oct. 1690), Quaker apologist, born at Gordonstown, near Elgin, was educated at the Scots College in Paris, of which his uncle, a Roman Catholic, was rector, but in spite of the latter's persuasions went back to Scotland and in 1667 became a Quaker like his father. In defence of this sect he published *Truth Cleared of Calumnies* (1670), and *A Catechism and Confession of Faith* (1673), but his great work was his *Apology for the True Christian Divinity Held by the Quakers*, published in Latin (1676) and then in English (1678), which forms the accepted exposition of Quaker principles. He was several times imprisoned, but at last found a protector in the Duke of York, afterwards James II, and in 1683 received, with Penn and other Quakers, the proprietorship of East New Jersey, of which he was appointed nominal governor.

Barham, Richard Harris (6 Dec. 1788—17 June 1845), humorous poet, son of a country gentleman, was born at Canterbury, educated at St Paul's School and Brasenose College, Oxford, entered the church, held various incumbencies, and was Divinity Lecturer, and minor canon of St Paul's. It is not, however, as a churchman that he is remembered, but as the author of the *Ingoldsby Legends*, a series of comic and serio-comic pieces in verse, sparkling with wit, and full of striking and often grotesque turns of expression, which appeared first in *Bentley's Miscellany*, and were published collectively in three series (1840—7). He also wrote, in *Blackwood's Magazine*, a novel, *My Cousin Nicholas*.

Baring, Maurice (27 April 1874—15 Dec. 1945), poet and novelist, son of Lord Revelstoke, was born in London, educated at Eton and Cambridge, and entered the Diplomatic Service, holding posts successively at Paris, Copenhagen, and Rome. Meanwhile he had published several books of verse, including *Pastels and Other Rhymes* (1891) and *The Black Prince* (1902). In 1904 he abandoned diplomacy for journalism and worked as a special correspondent of the *Morning Post* in Russia and the Far East. His *Diminutive Dramas* appeared in 1910 and a play, *The Grey Stocking*, in 1912. During the First World War he served in the Royal Flying Corps and became a Wing Commander. After that he turned to novel writing and produced *C* (1924), *Cat's Cradle* (1925), *Tinker's Leave* (1927), *Comfortless Memory* (1928), and *Friday's Business* (1932). His *Collected Poems* appeared in 1925. He also wrote many short stories, essays, and sketches, *An Outline of Russian Literature* (1914), and a volume of reminiscences, *Puppet Show of Memory* (1922). He was a Fellow of the Royal Society of Literature and a Chevalier of the Legion of Honour.

Baring-Gould, Sabine (28 Jan. 1834—2 Jan. 1924), clergyman and author, born at Exeter, educated privately and at Cambridge, was an assistant master at Hurstpierpoint College from 1857 to 1864. Ordained in 1865, he held various appointments before he succeeded in 1872 to the family estates at Lew Trenchard in Devon, and in 1881 became rector of the parish. He wrote voluminously. Of some 150 published works the most important are *Curious Myths of the Middle Ages* (1866—8), *The Origin and Development of Religious Belief* (1870), and *The Lives of the Saints* in 15 volumes (1872—7). He also published a number of novels, including *John Herring* (1883), *Richard Cable* (1888), *The Pennycomequicks* (1889), and *The Crock of Gold* (1899). He was greatly interested in folklore, wrote of the West Country in *A Book of the West* (1899), and *A Book of Dartmoor* (1900), and was President of the Devonshire Association. His *Early Reminiscences* (1923) were followed by *Further Reminiscences*, published just after his death. Among a number of hymns he wrote is the famous 'Onward, Christian Soldiers.'

Barker, Sir Ernest (23 Sept. 1874—17 Feb. 1960), historian, was educated at Manchester Grammar School and Oxford, where he became a Fellow of Merton in 1898 and subsequently held fellowships of various colleges before becoming Principal of King's College, London, in 1920. In 1927 he was appointed Professor of Political Science at Cambridge and elected a Fellow of Peterhouse. He was knighted in 1944 and also received several foreign Orders, as well as honorary degrees of many universities. His most important works are *The Political Thought of Plato and Aristotle* (1906), *National Character* (1927), *Reflections on Government* (1942), *Aristotle's Politics* (1946), *Traditions of Civility* (1948), and *Principles of Social and Political Theory* (1951). He also contributed to the Cambridge Ancient and Modern Histories, and edited Dent's Library of Greek Thought. *Father of the Man* (1948) is autobiographical.

Barlow, Joel (24 March 1754—24 Dec. 1812), poet, born at Reading, Connecticut, and educated at Yale, served for a time as an army chaplain, thereafter betook himself to law, and finally to commerce and diplomacy, in the former of which he made a fortune. He was much less successful as a poet than as a man of affairs. His writings include *Vision of Columbus* (1787), afterwards expanded into the *Columbiad* (1807), *The Conspiracy of Kings* (1792), and *The Hasty Pudding* (1796), a mock-heroic poem, his best work. In 1811 he was appointed ambassador to France, and met his death in Poland while on a mission to Napoleon.

Barnard, Lady Anne (8 Dec. 1750—6 May 1825), poetess, daughter of James Lindsay, 5th Earl of Balcarres, married Andrew Barnard, afterwards Colonial Secretary at Cape Town. On the death of her husband in 1807, she settled in London. Her exquisite ballad of *Auld Robin Gray* was written in 1771, and published anonymously. She confessed the authorship to Sir Walter Scott in 1823. *South Africa a Century Ago* (1901) is a collection of her letters from the Cape.

Barnes, Barnabe (1569?—1609), poet, son of Dr Richard Barnes, Bishop of Durham, was born in Yorkshire, and studied at Oxford. He wrote *Parthenophil and Parthenophe* (1593), a collection of sonnets, madrigals, elegies, and odes, *A Divine Centurie of Spirituall Sonnets* (1595), and *The Devil's Charter*, a tragedy. When at his best he showed a true poetic vein.

Barnes, Juliana, *see* **Berners.**

Barnes, William (20 March 1801—7 Oct. 1886), dialect poet and philologist, son of a farmer, born at Rushay, Dorset, has been called 'the Dorsetshire Burns.' After being a solicitor's clerk and a schoolmaster, he studied theology at St John's College, Cambridge, and took orders, became pastor of Whitcombe in 1847, and was rector of Came for the last twenty-four years of his life. He first contributed to a newspaper *Poems in Dorset Dialect*, separately published in 1844. *Hwomely Rhymes* followed in 1858, and a collected edition of his poems appeared in 1879. His philological works include *Philological Grammar* (1854), *Se Gefylsta, an Anglo-Saxon Delectus*

C

(1849), *Tiw, or a View of Roots* (1862), and a *Glossary of Dorset Dialect* (1863). Barnes's poems are characterized by a singular sweetness and tenderness of feeling, deep insight into humble country life and character, and fine word-pictures of local scenery.

Barnfield, Richard (baptized 13 June 1574, buried 6 March 1627), poet, eldest son of Richard Barnfield, gentleman, was born at Norbury, Shropshire, and educated at Oxford. In 1594 he published *The Affectionate Shepherd*, a collection of variations in graceful verse of the 2nd Eclogue of Virgil. His next work was *Cynthia, with certain Sonnets and the Legend of Cassandra* in 1595; and in 1598 there appeared *The Encomion of Lady Pecunia*, two songs in which, 'If music and sweet poetrie agree,' and 'As it fell upon a day,' were included in *The Passionate Pilgrim*, and for long attributed to Shakespeare. From this time, 1599, Barnfield produced nothing else, and seems to have retired to the life of a country gentleman at Stone in Staffordshire. He was for long neglected, but his poetry is clear, sweet, and musical.

Barr, Robert (16 Sept. 1850—21 Oct. 1912), novelist, was born in Glasgow but went to Canada at the age of 4, attended the Normal School, Toronto, and became a reporter on the Detroit *Free Press*, where he wrote under the pseudonym of Luke Sharp. In 1881 he returned to Britain and collaborated with Jerome K. Jerome in founding *The Idler*. A facile writer of magazine stories, he is remembered by *The Triumphs of Eugène Valmont* (1906), which introduced a comic French detective who in some ways anticipates Agatha Christie's Hercule Poirot.

Barrett, Eaton Stannard (1786—20 March 1820), poet, born in Cork, was entered at the Middle Temple but never called to the Bar. In addition to *Woman and Other Poems* (1810), which quickly went through five editions, he wrote a number of political satires.

Barrie, Sir James Matthew, Bart., O.M. (9 May 1860—19 June 1937), novelist and playwright, was born at Kirriemuir in Angus (the 'Thrums' of his novels), the son of a weaver, and was educated at Glasgow Academy, Dumfries Academy, and Edinburgh University. From his boyhood he planned to be a writer. In 1883 he joined the staff of the *Nottingham Journal*, and two years later, having established a connection with some London papers, he moved there and for five or six years supported himself with growing confidence and reputation by articles in various periodicals. During this period *When a Man's Single* appeared in the *British Weekly* with the pseudonym Gavin Ogilvy, and two series of sketches, *Auld Licht Idylls* (1888) and *A Window in Thrums* (1889) were published. His first real novel, *The Little Minister* (1891), was an immediate success. In 1894 he married Mary Ansell, an actress, and settled in Kensington, where he wrote three more novels of Scottish life, *Margaret Ogilvy* (1896), a tribute to his mother's memory, *Sentimental Tommy* (1896), and its sequel *Tommy and Grizel* (1900).

His first full-length play, *Walker, London*, had appeared in 1892, and in 1898 *The Little Minister* was dramatized and eventually brought him £80,000. Thenceforward he turned from novels to playwriting, the sentimental comedy of *Quality Street* (1901) and the social satire of *The Admirable Crichton* (1902) being followed by what is usually reckoned his greatest work, *Peter Pan*, in 1904. The success of this epic of boyhood, which is a fairy-tale mixed with the essence of all the best adventure stories, with pirates and redskins playing leading parts, was tremendous, and fifty years later it was still one of the most popular plays for children when it was put on every winter. Its immortality is reflected in the statue of Peter Pan which Barrie had set up in Kensington Gardens, the original home of 'the boy who wouldn't grow up.' No other play of Barrie's followed similar lines, the nearest to it being the fantasy *A Kiss for Cinderella* (1916). His later productions, in the vein of whimsical satire which he made peculiarly his own, include *What Every Woman Knows* (1908) and *The Twelve-Pound Look* (1910), both excellent satirical comedies; *Dear Brutus* (1917), the theme of which is that each man carries his destiny within himself; *Mary Rose* (1920), an eerie fantasy; and *Shall We Join the Ladies?* (1921), an unconcluded murder story. His last play, *The Boy David* (1936), which had a biblical subject, was less successful.

In 1909 Barrie obtained a divorce from his wife and moved to the Adelphi, where he had Bernard Shaw for a neighbour. In 1913 he was made a baronet, and in 1922 he received the Order of Merit, and as Lord Rector of St Andrews University delivered a noteworthy address on *Courage*. The definitive edition of his plays appeared in 1942; the standard life is *The Story of J.M.B.* by Denis Mackail (q.v.).

Barrington, Maurice, *see* **Brogan, D. W.**

Barrow, Isaac (1630—4 May 1677), clergyman and mathematician, the son of a London merchant, was educated at Charterhouse, Felsted, and Trinity College, Cambridge, of which he was made a Fellow in 1649; he also studied abroad. Ordained in 1659, he was in the following year appointed Professor of Greek at Cambridge, and in 1662 Professor of Geometry at Gresham College, London. He was one of the first Fellows of the Royal Society, and in 1663 became the first holder of the Lucasian Chair of Mathematics at Cambridge, in which he was succeeded by his pupil, Isaac Newton, in 1669. For some four years he was chaplain to Charles II and prebendary of Salisbury, being made D.D. by royal mandate in 1670, and from 1672 till his death he was Master of Trinity, Cambridge. He was reckoned one of the greatest preachers of his time, and as a mathematician ranked second only to Newton. His greatest controversial work was his *Treatise on the Pope's Supremacy* (1680).

Barry, Philip (18 June 1896—3 Dec. 1949), playwright, was born at Rochester, New York, of Irish parentage, and educated at Yale and Harvard. For some months in 1918 he was an attaché at the United States embassy in London. From 1923 onwards he wrote about a play a year, beginning with *You and I*, a social comedy; of the same type were *In a Garden* (1925), *Paris Bound* (1927), which was his first box-office success, *Holiday* (1928), *The Philadelphia Story* (1939), *Without Love* (1942), and *Foolish Notion* (1945). Dramas of a more serious philosophical or religious kind were *John* (1927), based on the life of John the Baptist, *Hotel Universe* (1930), which introduces a hypnotherapy motif, *The Joyous Season* (1934), *Bright Star* (1935), and *Here Come the Clowns* (1938). *White Wings* (1926) is a fantasy.

Bartlett, John (14 June 1820—3 Dec. 1905), compiler, was born at Plymouth, Massachusetts, son of a sea captain, and educated at the local schools. At the age of 16 he joined the staff of the university book store at Cambridge, and in 1849 became owner of the store. His knowledge of books was then so wide and he was so often asked for quotation references that he began a collection which developed into his well-known *Familiar Quotations* (1855), which went through nine editions in his lifetime and is still a standard work. In 1882 he published *The Shakespeare Phrase Book*, and in 1894 his complete and authoritative *Concordance to Shakespeare's Dramatic Works and Poems*. A very keen fisherman, he also made a *Catalogue of Books on Angling* (1882). He was an honorary A.M. of Harvard and a member of the American Academy of Arts and Sciences.

Barton, Bernard (31 Jan. 1784—19 Feb. 1849), poet, born at Carlisle, of Quaker parentage, passed nearly all his life at Woodbridge, for the most part as a clerk in a bank. He became the friend of Southey, Lamb, and other men of letters. His chief works are *The Convict's Appeal* (1818), a protest against the severity of the criminal code of the time, and *Household Verses* (1845), which came under the notice of Sir R. Peel, through whom he obtained a pension of £100. His daughter Lucy, who married Edward FitzGerald, the translator of *Omar Khayyám*, published a selection of his poems and letters, to which her husband prefixed a biographical introduction.

Basse *or* **Bas, William** (1583?—1653?), poet, studied at Oxford and lived at Moreton, near Thame. His first production, *Sword and Buckler, or Serving Man's Defence* (1602), was followed in the same year by *Three Pastoral Elegies of Anander, Anetor, and Muridella*. He also wrote an elegy on Henry, Prince of Wales, in 1613, but is best remembered for his poem on Shakespeare, in which he couples his name with Chaucer and Spenser.

Bates, Herbert Ernest (16 May 1905—   ), novelist, born at Rushden, Northamptonshire, was educated at Kettering Grammar School and worked first on a local newspaper, then as a clerk in a warehouse. His first novel, *The Two Sisters*, was published when he was 20; others were *Catherine Foster* (1929), *Charlotte's Row* (1931), *The Fallow Land* (1932), *The Poacher* (1935), *The Purple Plain* (1947), *The Jacaranda Tree* (1949), and *The Sleepless Moon* (1956). He was, however, most successful as a writer of short stories, collections of which include *Day's End* (1928), *Seven Tales and Alexander* (1929), *The Woman Who Had Imagination* (1934), *Cut and Come Again* (1935), *The Flying Goat* (1939), *My Uncle Silas* (1940), and *The Bride Comes to Evensford* (1949). He also wrote *The Day of Glory*, a play, and a text-book, *The Modern Short Story* (1945). During the Second World War he became a squadron-leader in the R.A.F., and many of his stories of service life were originally published under the pseudonym 'Flying-Officer X.'

Bates, Katherine Lee (12 Aug. 1859—28 March 1929), scholar and poetess, was born at Falmouth, Massachusetts, daughter of a Congregational minister, and educated at Wellesley College, where she was appointed instructor and, after a period of study at Oxford, Professor of English Literature from 1891 to 1925. She is best known for her poem 'America the Beautiful,' which is said to have been inspired by the view from the top of Pike's Peak in Colorado and has been suggested for adoption as the national anthem of the United States. She wrote a number of books of verse, her *Selected Poems* appearing in 1930. *From Gretna Green to Land's End* (1907), tells of her travels in England.

Baxter, Richard (12 Nov. 1615—8 Dec. 1691), clergyman, born at Rowton, Shropshire, was educated at Wroxeter School, but went to no university. Ordained in 1638, he was an assistant at Bridgnorth and then went as precentor to Kidderminster in 1641, but adopted Nonconformist views and acted as adviser to Cromwell. Despite this, in 1660 he was chaplain to Charles II, but the Act of Uniformity (1662) put an end to his preaching in the Church of England. In 1685 he was sentenced by Judge Jeffreys to eighteen months' imprisonment, but with the passing of the Toleration Act in 1689 he was free again to continue preaching. His best-known works are *The Saint's Everlasting Rest* (1650), and *The Holy Commonwealth* (1659). *Reliquiae Baxterianae* (1696) is his autobiography.

Bayly, Ada Ellen (25 March 1857—8 Feb. 1903), novelist, daughter of a barrister, was born at Brighton and educated at private schools there. When she started to write she chose as a pseudonym Edna Lyall, an anagram of nine letters from her names. Her first book, *Won by Waiting* (1879), is the story of a girl's life. A 3-volume novel *Donovan* (1882) was admired by Gladstone, but it was the sequel to it, *We Two* (1884), which established her reputation. *In the Golden Days* (1885), an historical novel of the seventeenth century, was one of her best, and *The Autobiography of a Slander* (1887) was also very popular. A supporter of all liberal movements, in *Doreen* (1889) she championed the cause of Irish Home Rule, while her last novel, *The Hinderers* (1902), opposed the Boer War.

Bayly, Thomas Haynes (13 Oct. 1797—22 April 1839), author, was born at Bath, son of a lawyer, and educated at Winchester and Oxford. Originally intended for the law, he changed his mind and thought of entering the Church, but abandoned this idea also, and gave himself to writing for the stage and the periodical press. He is chiefly known for his songs, of which he wrote hundreds, some being set to his own music. Among the best known are 'I'd be a Butterfly,' 'Oh, no, we never mention her,' and 'She wore a Wreath of Roses.' He also wrote five novels and 36 dramatic pieces, of which the best known is *Perfection*.

Baynes, Thomas Spencer (24 March 1823—31 May 1887), philosopher, son of a Baptist minister, born at Wellington, Somerset, intended to study for Baptist ministry, and was at a theological seminary at Bristol with that view, but being strongly attracted to philosophical studies, left it and went to Edinburgh, when he became the favourite pupil of Sir W. Hamilton (q.v.), and acted as his assistant. After working as editor of a newspaper in Edinburgh, in 1858 he became assistant editor of the *Daily News*. In 1864 he was appointed Professor of Logic and English Literature at St Andrews, in which capacity his mind was drawn to the study of Shakespeare, and he contributed to the *Edinburgh Review* and *Fraser's Magazine* valuable papers (chiefly relating to Shakespeare's vocabulary and the extent of his learning) afterwards collected as *Shakespeare Studies*. In 1873 he was appointed to superintend the 9th edition of the *Encyclopaedia Britannica*, in which, after 1880, he was assisted by W. Robertson Smith (q.v.).

Beach, Rex Ellingwood (1 Sept. 1877—7 Dec. 1949), novelist, was born at Atwood, Michigan, where his father had a fruit farm. The family moved to Florida, and Beach was educated at Rollins College. Later he studied law at Chicago and elsewhere, but interrupted this by joining in the gold rush to the Klondike, which, however, he never reached. He also tried zinc mining in Missouri before turning to writing. *Pardners* (1905), his first novel, was followed by *The Spoilers* (1906), which with *The Barrier* (1907) and *The Silver Horde* made up the omnibus *Alaskan Adventures* (1935). Other novels, all of the adventurous he-man type, were *The Iron Trail* (1913), *The Mating Call* (1927), and *Money Mad* (1931). *Personal Experiences* (1941) is an autobiography. Suffering from cancer, he shot himself at the age of 72.

Beaconsfield, Earl of, *see* Disraeli, Benjamin.

Beard, Charles Austin (27 Nov. 1874—1 Sept. 1948), historian, born at Knightstown, Indiana, was educated at De Pauw University and Oxford, where he founded Ruskin Hall, the working-men's college. After some time at Cornell he joined the staff of Columbia University in 1904 and in 1915 became Professor of Politics, but resigned in 1917 as a protest against the dismissal of pacifist professors. Among his more important works are *An Economic Interpretation of the Constitution of the United States* (1913), *American Foreign Policy in the Making, 1932—1940* (1946), and *President Roosevelt and the Coming of the War* (1948), after publication of which he was awarded the gold medal of the American Academy of Arts and Letters. In collaboration with his wife, Mary Ritter Beard, an enthusiastic champion of women's rights, he wrote a number of books including *A History of the United States* (1921), and *The Rise of American Civilization* (1927), an important study of the American background.

Beattie, James (25 Oct. 1735—18 Aug. 1803), poet and philosophical writer, son of a shopkeeper and small farmer at Laurencekirk, Kincardineshire, was educated at Aberdeen University, became a master at Aberdeen Grammar School, and in 1760 was appointed Professor of Moral Philosophy and Logic at Marischal College. In the following year he published a volume of poems, which attracted attention. The two works, however, which brought him most fame were his *Essay on Truth* (1770), intended as an answer to Hume, which had great immediate success, and led to an introduction to the King, a pension of £200, and the degree of LL.D. from Oxford; and his poem of *The Minstrel*, of which the first book was published in 1771 and the second in 1774, and which constitutes his true title to remembrance. It contains much beautiful descriptive writing. Beattie frequently visited London, and became the friend of Johnson, Reynolds, and the poet Gray.

Beauchamp, Kathleen Mansfield (14 Oct. 1888—9 Jan. 1923), who wrote short stories under the name Katherine Mansfield, was born at Wellington, New Zealand, daughter of a banker, who was later knighted. Her first story was published when she was 9, and later when at Queen's College, London, she edited the college magazine, but her plans then were for a musical career. In 1909 she married George Bowden, but left him after a few days. In 1911 she met John Middleton Murry (q.v.), whom she married in 1918 when she obtained a divorce from her first husband. Ill-health due to lung trouble made her move about seeking a congenial climate, and she lived at different times in France and in Germany. In 1920 *Bliss and Other Stories* made her famous. Other collections were *The Garden Party* (1922), *The Doves' Nest* (1923), *Something Childish* (1924), and *The Aloe* (1930). In 1922 she went to Paris for special treatment and died at Fontainebleau. In her mastery of the short story, depending on atmosphere rather than on incident, she has been compared with Chekhov. Her *Poems* were published in 1923 and her autobiographical *Journal* (1927), *Letters* (1928), and *Scrapbook* (1940) were all edited by her husband.

Beaumont, Francis (1584—6 March 1616), dramatist, was born at Grace-Dieu, Leicestershire, son of a judge, matriculated at Broadgates Hall, Oxford, in 1597, and was entered in 1600 at the Inner Temple, for which he wrote a masque in 1613. In 1602 he published *Salmacis and Hermaphroditus*, a poem based on a tale of Ovid's. He became a great friend of Drayton and Ben Jonson, for whose plays he wrote commendatory verses, and from an early age was closely associated with John Fletcher (q.v.). They shared lodgings and servant, and collaborated in writing plays between 1606 and 1616, Beaumont excelling in the construction of plots. He was married about 1613, died not long after, and is buried in Westminster Abbey. The list of over 50 plays attributed to Beaumont and Fletcher is obviously far too long for their period of collaboration, and was a publicity device of the publishers. Much time has been spent in unravelling the puzzle, and it is now thought that Beaumont was solely responsible for *The Woman Hater* (1607), and *The Knight of the Burning Pestle* (1609), and that he and Fletcher together wrote some dozen plays, of which the best are *The Scornful Lady* (1610), *Philaster* (1611), *The Maid's Tragedy* (1611), *A King and No King* (1611), *Bonduca* (1614), and *Thierry and Theodoret* (1616).

Beaumont, Sir John (born 1582, buried 19 April 1627), poet, brother of Francis Beaumont (q.v.), matriculated at Oxford at the age of 14, and was later entered at the Inner Temple. In 1602 he published anonymously his *Metamorphosis of Tobacco*, a mock-heroic poem. He succeeded to his father's estates when his brother Henry died in 1605, and was made a baronet on his introduction to the king by Buckingham in 1626. His poems were published by his son in 1629.

Beaumont, Joseph (13 March 1616—25 Sept. 1699), clergyman and poet, was born at Hadleigh, Suffolk, son of a clothier, and educated at Hadleigh Grammar School and Peterhouse, Cambridge, of which he became a Fellow. In 1644 he was ejected as a Royalist, and returned to Hadleigh, where he wrote *Psyche* (1648), an epic of 30,000 lines. Made a D.D. at the Restoration, he was appointed Master of Jesus College in 1662 and of Peterhouse in 1663. In 1674 he became Professor of Divinity. Of artistic bent, he adorned Peterhouse chapel with scriptural scenes.

Becke, George Lewis (18 June 1855—18 Feb. 1913), novelist, was born at Port Macquarie, New South Wales, where his father was clerk of petty sessions. Educated in Sydney, he went to sea at an early age in Pacific trading vessels, and also worked at different times as gold prospector and bank clerk. In 1892 he turned to writing and published over 30 books, including *By Reef and Palm* (1894), *The Ebbing of the Tide* (1896), *His Native Wife* (1896), *Wild Life in the Southern Seas* (1897), *Rodman the Boatsteerer* (1899), *Tom Wallis* (1900), *Helen Adair* (1903), and *Notes from my South Seas Log* (1905).

Beckford, William (29 Sept. 1760—2 May 1844), novelist, only son of a Lord Mayor of London, was born at Fonthill in Wiltshire, and inherited at the age of 9 an enormous fortune. In these circumstances he grew up wayward and extravagant, showing, however, a strong bent towards literature. His education was entrusted to a private tutor, with whom he travelled extensively on the Continent. At the age of 22 he produced his oriental romance, *Vathek*, written originally in French and, as he was accustomed to boast, at a single sitting of three days and two nights. There is reason, however, to believe that this was a flight of imagination. A pirated English translation was published in 1786, perhaps by the Rev. S. Henley, and in the next year Beckford published the original French. His other principal writings are *Memoirs of Extraordinary Painters* (1780), a satirical work, and *Letters from Italy with Sketches of Spain and Portugal* (1835), full of brilliant descriptions of scenes and manners. Beckford's fame, however, rests nearly as much upon his eccentric extravagances as a builder and collector as upon his literary efforts. In carrying out these he managed to dissipate his fortune of £100,000 a year, only £80,000 of his capital remaining at his death. He sat in parliament for various constituencies, and one of his two daughters became Duchess of Hamilton.

Beddoes, Thomas Lovell (20 July 1803—26 Jan. 1849), poet and physiologist, son of an eminent physician and nephew of Maria

Edgeworth, was born at Clifton and educated at Charterhouse and Oxford. In 1821 he published *The Improvisatore*, which he afterwards endeavoured to suppress. His next venture was *The Bride's Tragedy* (1822), which had considerable success and won for him the friendship of Bryan Waller Procter. Thereafter he went to Göttingen and studied medicine. He then led a wandering life on the Continent as doctor and democrat, and finally poisoned himself with curare. For some time before his death he had been engaged upon a drama, *Death's Jest Book*, which was published in 1850 with a memoir by his friend T. F. Kelsall; his poems were published in the following year.

Bede *or* **Bæda** (673—735), historian and scholar, sometimes referred to as 'the father of English history,' was in his youth placed under the care of Benedict Biscop, Abbot of Wearmouth, and of Ceolfrith, afterwards Abbot of Jarrow. Ordained deacon in 692 and priest in 703, he spent most of his days at Jarrow, where his fame as a scholar and teacher of Latin, Greek, and Hebrew brought him many disciples. Here likewise he died and was buried, but his bones were, towards the beginning of the eleventh century, removed to Durham. The well-deserved title of 'Venerable' usually prefixed to his name first appears in 836. He was the most learned Englishman of his age. His industry was marvellous, and its results remain embodied in about 40 books, of which about 25 are commentaries on books of Scripture. The others are lives of saints and martyrs, and his two great works, *The Ecclesiastical History of England* and the scientific treatise, *De Natura Rerum*. The former of these gives the fullest and most reliable information we have as to the history of England down to the year 731, and the latter is an encyclopaedia of the sciences as then known.

Bede, Cuthbert, *see* **Bradley, Edward.**

Beebe, William (29 July 1877—   ), naturalist, born at Brooklyn, New York, and educated at Columbia University, became curator of ornithology at the Bronx Zoo. His first book, *Two Bird-Lovers in Mexico* (1925), telling of an expedition he made along with his wife, was followed by *Our Search for a Wilderness* (1910). *Tropical Wild Life* (1917), *Jungle Peace* (1918), and *Edge of the Jungle* (1921) relate experiences in British Guiana. Beebe was also the first man to descend more than 3,000 feet into the depths of the ocean, and *Half Mile Down* (1934) tells of descents in his bathysphere off Bermuda.

Beecher, Henry Ward (24 June 1813—8 March 1887), clergyman and reformer, was born at Litchfield, Connecticut, son of a Congregationalist minister, and was a brother of Harriet Beecher Stowe (q.v.). Educated at Amherst College and Lane Theological Seminary, he became a Presbyterian minister in 1837, and ten years later was called to Plymouth Congregational Church, Brooklyn, where he became one of the most famous of American preachers and a great anti-slavery leader. His writings include *Summer in the Soul* (1858), *Freedom and War* (1863), *Yale Lectures on Preaching* (1874), and *Evolution and Religion* (1885).

C*

Beeding, Francis, *see* **Palmer, John Leslie**, and **Saunders, Hilary**.

Beer, Thomas (22 Nov. 1889—18 April 1940), novelist and critic, was born at Council Bluffs, Iowa, and brought up at first in Ohio and later in Yonkers. After graduating at Yale he studied law at Columbia and practised from 1913 to 1917, being the sixth generation of his family to do so. In the First World War he served as lieutenant of artillery. Shy and fastidious, he wrote few books but had a high reputation and has been called 'an aristocrat of letters.' His novels include *The Fair Rewards* (1922), *Sandoval* (1924), and *The Road to Heaven* (1928); *Mrs Egg and Other Barbarians* (1933) is a collection of short stories. He also wrote a biography of *Stephen Crane* (1923), and *The Mauve Decade* (1926), a brilliant study of the eighteen-nineties.

Beerbohm, Sir Max (24 Aug. 1872—20 May 1956), essayist and caricaturist, was born in London, his half-brother being the actor-manager Sir Herbert Beerbohm-Tree, and educated at Charterhouse and Merton College, Oxford. One of the leading lights of the gay nineties, he wrote for the *Yellow Book* and succeeded Bernard Shaw as dramatic critic of the *Saturday Review*. In 1910 he married Florence Kahn, of Memphis, Tennessee, and they made their home at Rapallo in the Italian Riviera. His most famous books are *Zuleika Dobson* (1911), a fantastic novel of Oxford life, and a series of brilliant essays, beginning with *The Works of Max Beerbohm*, published when he was 24, and continuing with *More* (1899), *Yet Again* (1909), *And Even Now* (1920), and *A Variety of Things* (1928). *A Christmas Garland* (1895) showed him one of the cleverest of modern parodists, and he also published a number of books of caricatures. He was knighted in 1939.

Beers, Ethel Lynn (13 Jan. 1827—11 Oct. 1879), poetess, was born Ethelinda Eliot at Goshen, New York, where her father was a druggist and J.P. In 1846 she married W. H. Beers, and in 1861 her famous poem 'The Picket Guard' appeared in *Harper's Magazine*, with its opening line, 'All quiet along the Potomac' taken from a newspaper headline. Her *Collected Poems* were published the day before her death.

Beeton, Isabella Mary (14 March 1836—6 Feb. 1865), authoress, had the maiden name of Mayson, and was educated at Heidelberg, becoming an accomplished pianist. In 1856 she married Samuel Orchard Beeton, an eminent publisher, and contributed articles to *The Englishwoman's Domestic Magazine*, which he had founded. She is remembered by her *Book of Household Management*, a standard manual covering in over a thousand pages not merely cookery in all its branches but the whole field of domestic science; it first came out as a single volume in 1861, having taken four years to compile. Mrs Beeton was under 30 when she died of puerperal fever.

Behn, Aphra (baptized 10 July 1640, died 16 April 1689), novelist and dramatist, daughter of a barber named Johnson, was born at Wye in Kent, but spent her childhood and youth at Surinam (Dutch Guiana), where she became acquainted with the celebrated slave

Oroonoko, afterwards the hero of one of her novels. Returning to England in 1658 she married Behn, a Dutch merchant, but was a widow at the age of 26. She then became attached to the Court, and was employed as a political spy at Antwerp. Leaving that city she cultivated the friendship of various playwrights, and produced a number of very coarse plays, as well as poems and pamphlets. She was the first English professional authoress. The best-known of her plays are *The Forced Marriage* (1671), *The Amorous Prince* (1671), and *The Town Fop* (1677); her novels include *Oroonoko* (1688) and *The Nun* (1689). The former anticipates Rousseau's doctrine of the Noble Savage. She was buried in Westminster Abbey.

Beith, John Hay (17 April 1876—22 Sept. 1952), novelist who wrote under the pen-name Ian Hay, was educated at Fettes and Cambridge. In the First World War he served as a captain in the Argyll and Sutherland Highlanders, was awarded the Military Cross and made a Commander of the Order of the British Empire. He wrote some fine war books, *The First Hundred Thousand* (1915) being followed by *Carrying On* (1917). His light and humorous novels, which were very popular, include *Pip* (1907), *The Right Stuff* (1908), *A Man's Man* (1909), *A Safety Match* (1911), *A Knight on Wheels* (1914), and *The Willing Horse* (1921). His plays *Tilly of Bloomsbury* (1919) and *Housemaster* (1936) were light comedies, and he collaborated in many others, such as *The Middle Watch* (1929) and *Admirals All* (1934), which he wrote with Commander Stephen King-Hall. *The Lighter Side of School Life* (1914) is a series of amusing pen-pictures. In the Second World War Beith was Director of Public Relations at the War Office. A member of the Royal Company of Archers, the Queen's bodyguard in Scotland, he was one of the finest bow-shots in Britain.

Belasco, David (25 July 1859—14 May 1931), dramatist and producer, was born at San Francisco. His father had been a clown, his uncle a well-known actor, and he himself ran away from a monastery to join a travelling circus. At the age of 11 he took the part of the young Duke of York in Charles Keane's production of Shakespeare's *Richard III*. He produced his first play in 1882 and opened his own house, the Belasco, in 1887. In the course of his career he produced well over 300 plays, as well as writing 75 either alone or with various collaborators, the most famous being *Madame Butterfly* (1900), and *The Girl of the Golden West* (1905).

Bell, Adrian Hanbury (4 Oct. 1901—   ), novelist and nature writer, was educated at Uppingham, then went as a pupil on a farm in Suffolk, and became a gentleman-farmer there. As a spare-time occupation he started writing of his experiences on the land and depicting the different types of countryman. His novels *Corduroy* (1930), *Silver Ley* (1931), and *The Cherry Tree* (1932) form a trilogy. Others are *Folly Field* (1933), *The Balcony* (1934), *By-Road* (1937), *Shepherd's Farm* (1939), *Apple Acre* (1942), *Sunrise to Sunset* (1944), *The Budding Morrow* (1946), *The Flower and the Wheel* (1949), *The Black Donkey* (1949), *Music in the Morning* (1954), and *A Young Man's Fancy* (1955). *Men and the Fields* (1939) is a study of agricultural conditions, and in 1935 a collection of his *Poems* was published. He also edited *The Open Air* (1936), an anthology of English country life.

Bell, Gertrude Margaret Lowthian (14 July 1868—12 July 1926), travel writer and archaeologist, was born at Washington Hall, Durham, daughter of an ironmaster, and educated at Queen's College, London, and Lady Margaret Hall, Oxford, where in 1888 she was the first woman to get first-class honours in history. During the next few years she made a voyage round the world and learned Persian, publishing a translation, *Poems from the Divan of Hafiz*. In 1899 she spent the winter in Jerusalem, learning Arabic. She also became an accomplished Alpine climber, scaling some difficult peaks. In 1905 she travelled through Syria and Cilicia and wrote about it in *The Desert and the Sown* (1907). By now a competent archaeologist, she told of further explorations in the Middle East in *The Thousand and One Churches* (1909), *Amurath to Amurath* (1911), and *The Palace and Mosque of Ukhaidir* (1914). She then turned to Arabia, and became so well informed in its politics that during the First World War her special knowledge was invaluable to the British Intelligence Department. Her influence was seen in the post-war settlement which resulted in the setting up of the new state of Iraq. Her last work, on which she was occupied at her death, was the setting up of a national museum at Bagdad. Her *Letters* were published in 1929.

Bell, Henry Glassford (8 Nov. 1803—7 Jan. 1874), poet and historian, born in Glasgow, was a member of the Scottish Bar, and became Sheriff of Lanarkshire. He wrote a *Life of Mary Queen of Scots* (1830), and a well-known poem on her; collections of his verse are *Summer and Winter Hours* (1831), and *My Old Portfolio*, the latter also containing pieces in prose.

Bell, John Joy (7 May 1871—14 Nov. 1934), novelist, was born in Glasgow, son of a tobacco manufacturer, and educated at Kelvinside Academy, Morrison's Academy, Crieff, and Glasgow University, where he studied chemistry. Sketches that he wrote in Glasgow dialect for the Glasgow *Evening Times* were collected for his novel *Wee MacGreegor* (1902), published at his own expense, which sold a quarter of a million copies in this country and was extensively pirated in America. He followed this up with *Wee MacGreegor Again* (1904), and in the First World War *Wee MacGreegor Enlists* (1915). Others of his novels are *Mistress McLeerie* (1903), *Oh Christina* (1909), and *Courtin' Christina* (1913). *Clyde Songs* (1906) is a collection of his verses, *The Glory of Scotland* (1932) and *Scotland's Rainbow West* (1933) are descriptive books, and *I Remember* (1932) is a volume of reminiscences.

Bellamy, Edward (26 March 1850—22 May 1898), novelist, was born and spent most of his life at Chicopee Falls, Massachusetts, where his father was Baptist minister for thirty-five years. Educated locally and at Union College, he studied law and was admitted to the Bar. Taking up journalism he joined in founding the Springfield *Daily News*, and also wrote short stories which were collected after his death in *The Blind Man's World and Other Stories* (1898). Two of his early novels, *Dr Heidenhoff's Process* (1880) and *Mrs Ludington's Sister* (1884), brought in the theme of psychic phenomena.   But his greatest achievement was his utopian romance *Looking Backward, or: 2000—1887* (1888), which pictured a socialist community of the future; it sold a million copies and became a sort of Bible to many of his way of thinking.   In 1897 he published a sequel, *Equality*.

Bellenden, John (1492?—1587?), translator, was educated at St Andrews and Paris.   At the request of James V he translated the *Historia Gentis Scotorum* of Boece.   This translation, *Chroniklis of Scotland*, is a very free one, with a good deal of matter not in the original, so that it may be almost considered as a new work.   It was published in 1536, and is the earliest existing specimen of Scottish literary prose.   He also translated the first five books of Livy.   He enjoyed the royal favour, and was Archdeacon of Moray.

Belloc, Joseph Hilaire Peter (27 July 1870—16 July 1953), historian, poet, essayist, was born at St Cloud, Paris, son of a French barrister by his English wife.   Four of his great-uncles were generals under Napoleon, and he himself did his period of military service as a driver in the French artillery.   From the Oratory School, Birmingham, he went in 1893 to Oxford, where he studied history and became President of the Union.   His first book, *Verses and Sonnets*, appeared in 1895, and in the following year he published *The Bad Child's Book of Beasts*, a delightful nonsensical volume, which had successors in *More Beasts for Worse Children* (1897) and *Cautionary Tales* (1907).   His historical works include lives of *Danton* (1899), *Robespierre* (1901), *Napoleon* (1932), and *Cromwell* (1934).   From 1906 to 1910 he sat as Liberal M.P. for South Salford, and from 1911 to 1913 was head of the English Department of East London College.   Among his novels, most of which were illustrated by his friend G. K. Chesterton (q.v.) were *Emmanuel Burden* (1904), and *Pongo and the Bull* (1910).   He also wrote several travel books, of which *The Path to Rome* (1902), *The Four Men* (1912), and *The Cruise of the 'Nona'* (1925) are the best-known, and a number of books of miscellaneous essays, including *On Nothing* (1908), *On Everything* (1909), and *On Anything* (1910).   In 1934 the Pope conferred on him the rank of Knight Commander of the Order of St Gregory the Great; he also received honorary degrees from Glasgow and Dublin.

Benchley, Robert Charles (15 Sept. 1889—21 Nov. 1945), humorist and actor, was born at Worcester, Massachusetts, and educated at Harvard.   Taking up journalism, he became dramatic critic of *Life* in 1920 and its editor in 1924, and in 1929 dramatic critic of the *New Yorker*, for which he wrote many humorous articles.   One of his first appearances on the stage was in his own skit *The Treasurer's Report* (1930), which was later made into the first all-talking motion picture and formed the first of a series of one-reel comedies which he wrote.   Among his books are *20,000 Leagues under the Sea, or, David Copperfield* (1928), *From Bed to Worse* (1934), *My Ten Years in a Quandary* (1936), *Inside Benchley* (1942), *Benchley Beside Himself* (1943), and *One Minute Please* (1945).

Benét, Stephen Vincent (22 July 1898—13 March 1943), poet, was born at Bethlehem, Pennsylvania, of a writing family, and was educated at Yale and the Sorbonne. His first book, six monologues in verse, was published when he was 17. In 1921 he shared with Carl Sandburg the prize of the Poetry Society of America, and in 1929 he was awarded the Pulitzer Prize for his long poem on the Civil War, *John Brown's Body*. Others of his poems are *King David* (1923), *Burning City* (1936), and *Western Star* (1943). He wrote five novels, including *John Huguenot* (1923), and *Spanish Bayonet* (1926), but was at his best in short stories; his tale 'The Devil and Daniel Webster,' published in *Thirteen O'Clock* (1937) became a classic and was made into a play. His *Selected Works* were published in 1942.

Benham, Sir William Gurney (16 Feb. 1859—13 May 1944), compiler, was educated at Merchant Taylors', became a journalist, and from 1884 was editor and proprietor of the *Essex County Standard*. He published a book of verse and a number of volumes on Essex archaeology, but his best-known work is his excellent *Book of Quotations, Proverbs, and Household Words* (1907). Mayor of Colchester on three occasions, he was knighted in 1935.

Bennett, Enoch Arnold (27 May 1867—27 March 1931), novelist, born at Hanley in Staffordshire, son of a solicitor, was educated at Burslem and Middle School, Newcastle. He studied law, but abandoned it for journalism, and four years on the staff of *Woman* gave him an insight into feminine psychology. His first novel, *A Man from the North* (1898), was followed by *Anna of the Five Towns* (1901), dealing with the provincial world of the Potteries which he was to make peculiarly his own. In 1902 *The Grand Babylon Hotel* was published, and for the next ten years he lived at Fontainebleau, marrying a Frenchwoman. His best novel, *The Old Wives' Tale* (1908), caused him to be ranked as one of the leading writers of the day. Other highly successful novels were *Buried Alive* (1908), *Clayhanger* (1910) with its sequels *Hilda Lessways* (1911) and *These Twain* (1915), and *The Card* (1911). Returning to England, he collaborated with Edward Knoblock in a play, *Milestones*, which had great popularity. Later novels were *The Pretty Lady* (1918), *Riceyman Steps* (1923), which won the Tait Black Prize, *Lord Raingo* (1926), and *Imperial Palace* (1930). Of the realist school of Zola, Bennett was an adept at portraying lower middle-class life; as one critic observed, 'Nobody has ever succeeded better in making dull people interesting.' *The Journals of Arnold Bennett, 1896—1928* were edited by Newman Flower (1932—3).

Benson, Arthur Christopher (24 April 1862—17 June 1925), scholar and author, was born at Wellington College, where his father, who later became Archbishop of Canterbury, was headmaster; E. F. Benson and R. H. Benson (qq.v.) were his younger brothers. Educated at Eton and King's College, Cambridge, he became a housemaster at Eton, where he wielded great influence. In 1903 he gave up his school post and a year later became a Fellow of Magdalene College, Cambridge, of which from 1915 he was Master.

He collaborated with Viscount Esher in editing *Selections from the Correspondence of Queen Victoria* (1907). In addition to some books of verse, he wrote biographies of *Rossetti* (1904), *Edward FitzGerald* (1905), and *Pater* (1906), but his most popular works were his volumes of essays, *The Upton Letters* (1905), *From a College Window* (1906), and *Beside Still Waters* (1907). He also wrote the words of the song 'Land of Hope and Glory.'

Benson, Edward Frederic (24 July 1867—29 Feb. 1940), novelist, younger brother of A. C. Benson (q.v.) was born at Wellington College and educated at Marlborough and Cambridge. From 1892 to 1895 he worked with the British School of Archaeology at Athens. His novel *Dodo* (1893), which created a sensation, was generally supposed to be based on the character of Margot Tennant, afterwards Lady Oxford; it was followed later by *Dodo the Second* (1914), and *Dodo Wonders* (1921). In the meantime Benson produced a number of light novels including *The Babe B.A.* (1897), *Mammon and Co.* (1900), and *David Blaize* (1915). He also wrote lives of *Alcibiades* (1929), *Charlotte Brontë* (1932), and *King Edward VII* (1933), as well as two volumes of reminiscences, *As We Were* (1930), and *As We Are* (1932). From 1934 to 1937 he was Mayor of Rye.

Benson, Robert Hugh (18 Nov. 1871—19 Oct. 1914), novelist, was born at Wellington College, like his brothers A. C. and E. F. Benson (qq.v.) and educated at Eton and Cambridge. Ordained in the English Church in 1897, he became curate of Kensing, but in 1903 was converted to Roman Catholicism and in 1911 was appointed private chamberlain to Pope Pius X. His early works were historical romances, *The King's Achievement* (1905), telling of Henry VIII, and *The Queen's Tragedy* (1906), of Mary I. Later he wrote novels of modern life with a strongly religious tone, among them being *The Sentimentalists* (1906), *The Conventionalists* (1908), *The Coward* (1912), *Come Rack, Come Rope* (1912), and *Loneliness* (1915).

Benson, Stella (6 Jan. 1892—6 Dec. 1933), novelist, was born at Much Wenlock, Shropshire, and educated at home. In 1912 she made a voyage to the West Indies, of which she wrote in *I Pose* (1915). After her return she took up social work in Hoxton, and during the First World War worked on the land. In 1918 she went to California, returning through China, where she taught in a mission school for a time, and in 1921 she married J. C. O'G. Anderson of the Chinese customs service; *The Little World* (1925) tells of their honeymoon motoring across America. Thereafter she spent most of her life in China. Not long before her death her novel *Tobit Transplanted* (1931) won the Femina Vie Heureuse Prize and the A. C. Benson Silver Medal of the Royal Society of Literature. Others of her novels were *Living Alone* (1919), *The Poor Man* (1922), and *Goodbye, Stranger* (1926). Her *Poems* were published in 1935 and her *Collected Short Stories* in 1936.

Bentham, Jeremy (15 Feb. 1748—6 June 1832), writer on law, born in London, son of a prosperous attorney, educated at Westminster and Oxford, was called to the Bar at Lincoln's Inn, and

devoted himself to the theory of jurisprudence. In 1776 he published anonymously his *Fragment on Government*, an able criticism
of Blackstone's *Commentaries*, which brought him under the notice
of Lord Shelburne, and in 1780 his *Introduction to Principles of
Morals and Legislation*. Other works were *Panopticon*, in which he
suggested improvements on prison discipline, *Discourse on Civil
and Penal Legislation* (1802), *Punishments and Rewards* (1811),
Parliamentary Reform Catechism (1817), and *A Treatise on Judicial
Evidence*. By the death of his father he inherited a competency on
which he was able to live in frugal elegance, not unmixed with
eccentricity. Bentham is the first and perhaps the greatest of the
'philosophical radicals,' and his fundamental principle is utilitarianism or 'the greatest happiness of the greatest number,' a phrase
of which he is often erroneously regarded as the author. The effect
of his writings on legislation and the administration of the law has
been almost incalculable. He left his body to be dissected; and
his skeleton, clothed in his usual attire, is preserved in University
College, London.

Bentley, Edmund Clerihew (10 July 1875—30 March 1956), journalist and novelist, born at Shepherd's Bush, son of a government
official, was at St Paul's School with G. K. Chesterton, his lifelong friend, and went to Oxford, where he was President of the
Union and Captain of the University Boat Club. He studied law in
London, was called to the Bar in 1902 but became a journalist, first
on the *Daily News* and then on the *Daily Telegraph*. His volumes
of ingenious nonsense verse, *Biography for Beginners* (1905), *More
Biography* (1929), and *Baseless Biography* (1939) consisted of 'cleri-
hews,' four-line poems with halting metre, a medium of his own
invention which became nearly as popular as the limerick. In 1913
he became celebrated by publishing *Trent's Last Case*, the first really
light-hearted detective story, which was followed by *Trent Intervenes*
(1938). *Those Days: An Autobiography* appeared in 1940.

Bentley, Phyllis Eleanor (19 Nov. 1894—   ), novelist, born at Halifax, daughter of a cloth manufacturer, was educated
at Cheltenham Ladies' College and London University, and for a time
worked as a teacher. Her first novel, *Environment* (1922), was
followed next year by a sequel, *Cat-in-the-Manger*. After the First
World War she took the job of cataloguing a number of local libraries.
All her early novels have Yorkshire backgrounds, *A Modern Tragedy*
(1934) telling of the effects of the slump, while *Sleep in Peace* (1938)
and *Take Courage* (1940) dealt with local history. Her theory of
novel-writing is set out in *Some Observations on the Art of Narrative*
(1946). She also wrote a study, *The Brontës* (1947).

Bentley, Richard (27 Jan. 1662—14 July 1742), classical scholar,
was born at Oulton, near Wakefield, son of a farmer, and educated
at Wakefield Grammar School and St John's College, Cambridge.
After teaching for a short time as headmaster of a school at Spalding,
in Lincolnshire, in 1683 he became tutor to the son of Dr Stillingfleet,
Dean of St Paul's, afterwards Bishop of Worcester (q.v.), and in

1689 accompanied his pupil to Oxford. There he laid the foundation of his reputation as one of the greatest scholars England has produced by his 'Letter to Mill' which was appended to Dr Mill's edition of the *Chronicle of John Malelas*, and by his *Dissertation on the Letters of Phalaris* (1699), which spread his fame through Europe. After receiving various preferments, including the Boyle lectureship and the Keepership of the Royal Library at St James's, he was, in 1700, appointed Master of Trinity College, Cambridge, and afterwards was, largely owing to his own pugnacity and rapacity, which were almost equal to his learning, involved in a succession of litigations and controversies. These lasted for twenty years, and led to the temporary loss of his academic preferments and honours. In 1717, however, he was appointed Regius Professor of Divinity at Cambridge. During the contentions referred to he continued his literary activity without abatement, and published various editions of the classics, including Horace and Terence. He was much less successful in certain emendations of Milton which he attempted. Having incurred the resentment of Pope he was rewarded by being assigned a niche in *The Dunciad*, while his classical controversies called forth Swift's *Battle of the Books*.

Beresford, James (28 May 1764—29 Sept. 1840), satirist and clergyman, was born at Upham, Hampshire, and educated at Charterhouse and Oxford. He made translations and wrote religious books, but was chiefly known as the author of a satirical work, *The Miseries of Human Life* (1806—7), which was praised by Walter Scott.

Beresford, John Davys (7 March 1873—2 Feb. 1947), novelist, born at Castor in Northamptonshire, where his father was rector, was lame as a result of an accident in infancy. Educated at Oundle and Peterborough, he worked for eight years in an architect's office, then tried advertising, and in 1907 began writing for the *Westminster Gazette*. From 1918 to 1923 he worked for a firm of publishers, and for some years after that lived in France. His novels, quiet and slow-moving, are somewhat reminiscent of those of 'Erewhon' Butler. Among the best are three composing a trilogy, *Jacob Stahl* (1911), *A Candidate for Truth* (1912), and *The Invisible Event* (1915). A later trilogy consisted of *The Old People* (1931), *The Middle Generation* (1932), and *The Young People* (1933). Other books are *What Dreams May Come* (1941), *Long View* (1943), *If This Were True* (1944), and *Hampdenshire Wonder* (1948). In *Writing Aloud* (1928) he gave a description of his methods.

Berkeley, George (12 March 1685—14 Jan. 1753), philosopher, born at Kilcrin near Kilkenny, was educated at Trinity College, Dublin, where he obtained a Fellowship in 1707. His earliest publication was a mathematical one; but the first which brought him into notice was his *Essay towards a New Theory of Vision*, published in 1709. Though giving rise to much controversy at the time, its conclusions are now accepted as an established part of the theory of optics. There next appeared in 1710 the *Treatise concerning the Principles of Human Knowledge*, which was followed in 1713 by

Dialogues between Hylas and *Philonous*, in which he propounded his system of philosophy, the leading principle of which is that the world as represented to our senses depends for its existence on being perceived. Of this theory the *Principles* gives the exposition and the *Dialogues* the defence. One of his main objects was to combat the prevailing materialism of the time. Shortly afterwards Berkeley visited England, and was received into the circle of Addison, Pope, and Steele. He then went to the Continent in various capacities, and on his return was made Lecturer in Divinity and Greek in his university, D.D. in 1721, and Dean of Derry in 1724. In 1725 he formed the project of founding a college in Bermuda for training ministers for the colonies and missionaries to the Indians, in pursuit of which he gave up his deanery with its income of £1,100, and went to America on a salary of £100. Disappointed of promised aid from Government he returned, and was in 1734 appointed Bishop of Cloyne. Soon afterwards he published *Alciphron, or The Minute Philosopher*, directed against Shaftesbury, and in 1734—7 *The Querist*. His last publications were treatises on the medicinal virtues of tar-water. As a thinker his is the greatest name in English philosophy between Locke and Hume.

Berners, Gerald Hugh Tyrwhitt-Wilson, 14th Baron (18 Sept. 1883—19 April 1950), novelist and composer, educated at Eton, was in the Diplomatic Service from 1909 to 1924. He composed a number of operas and ballets and wrote a series of fanciful novels, including *The Camel* (1936), *Far From the Madding War* (1941), and *The Romance of a Nose* (1942). His best-known books are his autobiographical works, *First Childhood* (1934), and *A Distant Prospect* (1945).

Berners, John Bourchier, 2nd Baron (1467—16 March 1553), diplomat and translator, educated at Oxford, held various offices of state, including that of Chancellor of the Exchequer to Henry VIII, and Lieutenant of Calais, where he died. He translated at the King's desire, *Froissart's Chronicles* (1523—5), in such a manner as to make a distinct advance in English historical writing, and the *Golden Book of Marcus Aurelius* (1534); also *The History of Arthur of Lytell Brytaine* (Brittany), and the romance of *Huon of Bordeaux*.

Berners *or* **Bernes** *or* **Barnes, Juliana** (born 1388?), writer on sport, was said to be the daughter of Sir James Berners and to have been Prioress of Sopwell Nunnery near St Albans. The *Boke of St Albans* (1486) has been attributed to her, but she was probably author only of the versified treatise on hunting contained in it.

Besant, Annie (1 Oct. 1847—20 Sept. 1933), theosophist, born in London, the daughter of William P. Wood, and educated privately, married in 1867 the Rev. Frank Besant, brother of Sir Walter Besant (q.v.), but separated from him six years later. Associating with Charles Bradlaugh in Free Thought propaganda, she wrote *The Gospel of Atheism* (1877). Taking up Socialism next, she established the Law and Liberty League and joined the Fabian Society. After being introduced to the writings of Helena Blavatsky, she became an ardent theosophist, succeeded Mme Blavatsky as head of the Esoteric School, and in 1907 became President of the Theosophical Society. In 1894 she went to India, where she discovered a 'new Messiah' in Krishnamurti, a young Hindu, and had considerable influence on the Nationalist movement, founding the Indian Home Rule League. In 1917 she was interned by the Governor of Madras, but was soon released and in 1918 was elected President of the National Congress. Her autobiography, *Through Storm to Peace*, appeared in 1893, and her works include *Reincarnation* (1892), *Death and After* (1893), *Four Great Religions* (1897), *Theosophy and the New Psychology* (1904), and *The Wisdom of the Upanishads* (1906).

Besant, Sir Walter (14 Aug. 1836—9 June 1901), novelist, born at Portsea, was educated at King's College, London, and Cambridge, where his friends included C. S. Calverley (q.v.) and W. W. Skeat (q.v.); Annie Besant was his sister-in-law. After some years as a professor at the Royal College, Mauritius, he returned to London and wrote for various papers. In 1869 he became acquainted with James Rice (q.v.) with whom he collaborated in a number of highly successful novels, including *Ready Money Mortiboy* (1872), *The Golden Butterfly* (1876), and *The Chaplain of the Fleet* (1881). After Rice's death in 1882 Besant carried on alone, making a plea for the East End poor in *All Sorts and Conditions of Men* (1882), which inspired the establishment of the People's Palace in Mile End Road in 1887 for cheap concerts and lectures. He also initiated technical evening schools and founded the Society of Authors, through which the law of copyright was reformed, and in 1892 established the Authors' Club. In 1894 he started a great topographical *Survey of London*, which unfortunately he did not live to complete. In the same year he was elected a Fellow of the Society of Antiquaries, and in the following year he was knighted. His *Autobiography* appeared in 1902.

Besier, Rudolf (July 1878—15 June 1942), dramatist, born in Java of Anglo-Dutch extraction, was educated at Elizabeth College, Guernsey, and Heidelberg, and worked as a journalist in London. His first play, *The Virgin Goddess* (1908), was written during a visit to America. Others were *Don* (1910), *Lady Patricia* (1912), and *Secrets*, which he wrote in collaboration with May Edginton. His best-known work, *The Barretts of Wimpole Street*, was produced at the Malvern Festival in 1930, and later ran for 700 performances in New York, but its depiction of Mrs Browning's father was resented by the Barrett family.

Betjeman, John (1906—   ), poet, was educated at Marlborough and Oxford, where he was contemporary with Auden and MacNeice. In 1933 he married a daughter of Lord Chedwode. During the Second World War he had a post at the Admiralty, and after that worked for a time on the British Council. As a poet he may be styled a lyrical satirist, and frequently makes use of material normally considered prosaic; he himself says 'I love suburbs and gas-lights and Gothic revival churches and mineral railways, provincial towns and garden cities.' But he is also a serious nature poet, and in addition an authority on architecture. Among his ·

books of verse are *Mount Zion* (1933), *Continual Dew* (1937), *New Bats in Old Belfries* (1940), *Old Lights for New Chancels* (1945), and *A Few Late Chrysanthemums* (1954); in 1948 his *Selected Poems* received the Heinemann Award, and in 1958 his *Collected Poems* appeared. Prose works include *Ghastly Good Taste* (1933) and *First and Last Loves* (1952), as well as guides to various English counties.In 1960 he was made a C.B.E.

Bickerstaffe, Isaac (1735?—1812?), playwright, in early life a page to Lord Chesterfield when he was Lord Lieutenant of Ireland, produced between 1756 and 1771 many dramatic pieces, which had considerable popularity, the best known of which are *Love in a Village* (1762), and *The Maid of the Mill* (1797), which was based on Richardson's *Pamela*. Owing to misconduct he was dismissed from being an officer in the Marines, and had ultimately, in 1772, to fly the country. The remainder of his life seems to have been passed in penury and misery.

Bierce, Ambrose Gwinnet (24 June 1842—1914?), journalist, was born in Meigs County, Ohio, son of a farmer, and served through the Civil War. His only education was from reading his father's books. While working in the Mint at San Francisco he wrote for the local weeklies, and in 1871 had his first short story, 'The Haunted Valley' published. On Christmas day of that year he got married and sailed for England, where he joined the staff of *Fun*, made friends with Sala, W. S. Gilbert, and Tom Hood the Younger, and published two collections of humorous sketches, *The Fiend's Delight* and *Cobwebs from an Empty Skull*. Back in San Francisco in 1876 he wrote for the *Sunday Examiner*, and became a sort of literary dictator of the Pacific Coast. *Tales of Soldiers and Civilians* (1891) was a collection of grim short stories, and *Can Such Things Be?* (1893) consisted of weird tales of the supernatural. Embittered by bereavements, he vanished in the Mexican War. His *Collected Works* in 12 volumes appeared between 1909 and 1912, and his *Letters*, with a memoir, in 1922.

Biggers, Earl Derr (26 Aug. 1884—5 April 1933), novelist, born at Warren, Ohio, and educated at Harvard, worked as a journalist in Boston. His mystery novel *Seven Keys to Baldpate* (1913) was a sensational success both in its original form and when dramatized. More than ten years later his popular Chinese detective Charlie Chan made his first appearance in *The House Without a Key* (1925). This original type of sleuth figured in five novels which were collected in an omnibus volume, and made his final appearance, continuing the author's favourite 'key' motif, in *The Keeper of the Keys* (1932).

Billings, Josh, *see* Shaw, Henry Wheeler.

Binyon, Robert Laurence (10 Aug. 1869—10 March 1943), poet, born at Lancaster, son of a clergyman, was a cousin of Stephen Phillips (q.v.). Educated at St Paul's School and Oxford, he entered the service of the British Museum, and from 1913 to 1933 was Keeper of the Oriental Paintings and Prints; his *Painting in the Far East* appeared in 1908. His first book of verse was *Lyric Poems*

(1894), and just after the First World War he published *The Four Years*, containing the well-known poem 'For the Fallen,' which has been quoted innumerable times at war memorial services. His *Collected Poems* appeared in 1931. His plays include *Attila* (1907), *Arthur* (1923), and *Boadicea* (1925). In addition to many other distinctions he was created a Companion of Honour in 1932, and in 1933 succeeded T. S. Eliot as Professor of Poetry for a year at Harvard.

Bird, Robert Montgomery (5 Feb. 1806—23 Jan. 1854), novelist, born in Newcastle, Delaware, became a Professor of Medicine. He wrote three tragedies, *The Gladiator, Oralloossa*, and *The Broker of Bogota*, and several novels, including *Calavar* (1834), *The Infidel* (1835), *The Hawks of Hawk Hollow* (1835), and *Nick of the Woods* (1837), in the first two of which he gives graphic and accurate details and descriptions of Mexican history.

Birmingham, George A., *see* Hannay, James Owen.

Birrell, Augustine (19 Jan. 1850—20 Nov. 1933), statesman and essayist, was born at Wavertree, near Liverpool, son of a Baptist minister. He studied law at Cambridge, was called to the Bar by the Inner Temple, took silk in 1885, and from 1896 to 1899 was Quain Professor of Law in London. Entering Parliament he rose to be President of the Board of Education (1905—7) and Secretary for Ireland (1907—16). He wrote three volumes of *Obiter Dicta* (1884, 1887, 1924), miscellaneous collections of acute literary criticisms, the subjects ranging from Falstaff to Carlyle. He also published books on *William Hazlitt* (1902) and *Andrew Marvell* (1905).

Bishop, Samuel (21 Sept. 1731—17 Nov. 1795), poet, born in London, and educated at Merchant Taylors' School and Oxford, took orders, became curate of Headley in Surrey and then a master at his old school, of which he became head in 1783. His poems on miscellaneous subjects fill two quarto volumes, the best of them being those to his wife and daughter. He also published essays.

Black, William (9 Nov. 1841—10 Dec. 1898), novelist, was born in Glasgow, where he studied at the School of Art, afterwards turning to journalism. In 1864 he went to London, and soon after published his first novel, *James Merle*, which made no impression. In the Austro-Prussian War he acted as a war correspondent. Thereafter he began afresh to write fiction, and was more successful; the publication of *A Daughter of Heth* (1871) at once established his popularity, which reached its highest mark in *A Princess of Thule* (1873). Many other books were added before his death in 1898, among which may be mentioned *In Silk Attire* (1869), *The Strange Adventures of a Phaeton* (1872), and *White Heather* (1886). A collected edition of his works in 26 volumes appeared in 1894.

Blackie, John Stuart (28 July 1809—2 March 1895), scholar, was born in Glasgow, but on his father, a bank manager, removing to Aberdeen, was educated at the Grammar School there, at Marischal College, and at Edinburgh University. Later he took a theological course at Aberdeen and studied in Germany and Italy. Returning to Scotland he was, in 1834, admitted to the Scottish Bar, but did not practise. His first work was his translation of *Faust* (1834), which won the approbation of Carlyle. From 1841 to 1852 he was Professor of Humanity (Latin) in Aberdeen University, and from 1852 till 1882, when he retired, Professor of Greek at Edinburgh. His literary activity was incessant, his works consisting of translations of *Aeschylus* and of the *Iliad*, various books of poetry, including *Lays and Legends of Ancient Greece*, and treatises on religious, philosophical, and political subjects, among which may be mentioned *Self-Culture* (1873), *Horae Hellenicae* (1874), and a life of Burns. He was an enthusiastic champion of Scottish nationality. It was owing to his efforts that a Chair of Celtic Languages and Literature was established in Edinburgh University.

Blacklock, Thomas (1721—7 July 1791), poet, born at Annan in Dumfriesshire, son of a bricklayer, lost his sight by smallpox when 6 months old. He began to write poetry at the age of 12, and studied at Edinburgh for the Church. He was appointed Minister of Kirkcudbright, but was objected to by the parishioners on account of his blindness, and gave up the presentation on receiving an annuity. He then retired to Edinburgh, where he took pupils. In 1745 he published a volume of poems, but is remembered better for his generous encouragement of Burns at the outset of the latter's career. He was made D.D. in 1767.

Blackmore, Sir Richard (1653—9 Oct. 1729), poet, born at Corsham in Wiltshire, was educated at Westminster and Oxford, and became one of the Court Physicians to William III and Anne. He wrote several very long and well-intentioned but dull and tedious epics, which, though praised by Addison and Johnson, are now utterly forgotten. They include *Prince Arthur* (1696) and *Creation* (1712). He was knighted in 1697.

Blackmore, Richard Doddridge (7 June 1825—20 Jan. 1900), novelist, born at Longworth, Berkshire, where his father was vicar, was educated at Tiverton School and Oxford. He practised for a short time as a lawyer but, owing to ill health, gave this up, and took to market-gardening and literature at Teddington. His first publication was *Poems by Melanter* (1853), followed by *Epullia* (1855), and other volumes; but he soon found that fiction, not poetry, was his true vocation. Beginning with *Clara Vaughan* in 1864, he produced 15 novels, all of more than average, and two or three of outstanding merit. Of these much the best in the opinion of the public, though not of the author, is *Lorna Doone* (1869), the two which rank next to it being *The Maid of Sker* (1872), which was the author's favourite, and *Springhaven* (1887). Others are *Cradock Nowell* (1866), *Alice Lorraine* (1875), *Cripps the Carrier* (1876), *Mary Anerley* (1880), and *Christowell* (1882). One of the most striking features of Blackmore's writings is his marvellous eye for, and sympathy with, Nature. He may be said to have done for Devonshire what Scott did for the Highlands.

Blackmur, Richard Palmer (21 Jan. 1904—   ), poet and critic, was born at Springfield, Massachusetts, of Scottish parentage, and worked as a clerk in a bookshop at Cambridge there. From 1936 to 1938 he held a Guggenheim Fellowship, and in 1940 he joined the staff of Princeton, where he became Professor of English in 1951. He published criticisms of a number of modern writers, including both the Lawrences, T. E. and D. H. A collection of critical essays, *The Expense of Greatness* (1940), was followed by a study of *Henry James* (1941), *Language as Gesture* (1952), and *The Lion and the Honeycomb* (1955). His volumes of poetry include *From Jordan's Delight* (1937), *Second World* (1942), and *The Good European* (1947).

Blackstone, Sir William (10 July 1723—14 Feb. 1780), legal writer, posthumous son of a silk mercer in London, was educated at Charterhouse School and Oxford, and entered the Middle Temple in 1741. He was the first Vinerian Professor of English Law (1758—66), sat for a time in the House of Commons, and was latterly a Justice of Common Pleas. His great work is his *Commentaries on the Laws of England*, in four volumes (1765—9), which still remains the best general history of the subject. It had an extraordinary success, and is said to have brought Blackstone £14,000. He had also a turn for neat and polished verse, of which he gave proof in *The Lawyer's Farewell to his Muse*.

Blackwood, Algernon Henry (1869—10 Dec. 1951), novelist, born in Kent, son of Sir Arthur Blackwood and Sidney, Duchess of Manchester, was educated at Wellington and Edinburgh University. At the age of 20 he went to Canada, where he was successively journalist, dairy-farmer, hotel-keeper, prospector, artist's model, actor, and private secretary. He had a great interest in the occult and has been called 'the ghost man' because of his subjects. After two volumes of short stories, *The Empty House* (1906), and *The Listener* (1907), he made his reputation with the weird *John Silence* (1908). Other novels were *The Human Chord* (1910), *The Wave* (1916), and *Dudley and Gilderoy* (1929). *Incredible Adventures* (1914), *Tongues of Fire* (1924), and *Tales of the Uncanny and Supernatural* (1949) are collections of short stories. *Sambo and Snitch* (1927) and *Mr Cupboard* (1928) are children's books, and *Episodes Before Thirty* (1923) tells of his early roving life. He was made a C.B.E. in 1949.

Blair, Eric (25 June 1903—23 Jan. 1950), novelist who wrote under the name of George Orwell, was born at Motihari in Bengal and educated at Eton. From 1922 to 1927 he served with the Indian Imperial Police in Burma, and later he used this experience in *Burmese Days* (1934). A period of poverty during which he was successively tutor, teacher, and bookshop assistant is described in *Down and Out in Paris and London* (1933). In 1936 he fought in the Spanish Civil War, was wounded, and wrote of this in *Homage to Catalonia* (1938). During the Second World War he worked for the B.B.C., and immediately after it published his finest book, *Animal Farm* (1945), a satire on dictatorship. His pessimistic *Nineteen Eighty Four* appeared shortly before his death. Earlier novels were *Keep the Aspidistra Flying* (1936), *The Road to Wigan Pier* (1937), and *Coming Up for Air* (1939). He also published some volumes of essays, including *Inside the Whale* (1940) and *Shooting an Elephant* (1950).

Blair, Hugh (7 April 1718—27 Dec. 1800), minister, was born in Edinburgh and educated at Edinburgh University. After being minister at Collessie in Fife, he was translated to Edinburgh, where he filled various pulpits, latterly that of the High Church. In 1759 he commenced a series of lectures on composition, and soon after the Chair of Rhetoric and Belles Lettres was founded, to which he was appointed. His *Lectures* were published on his resignation of the chair in 1783. His chief fame, however, rests upon his *Sermons*, in four volumes, which had an extraordinary popularity, and obtained for him a pension of £200.

Blair, Robert (1699—4 Feb. 1746), poet, born in Edinburgh, where his father was a clergyman, became minister of Athelstaneford, Haddingtonshire. His sole work was *The Grave* (1743), a poem in blank verse extending to 767 lines of very various merit, in some passages rising to great sublimity, and in others sinking to commonplace. It enjoyed instant success, and was later illustrated by William Blake (q.v.). Blair's son, Robert, was a very distinguished Scottish judge and Lord President of the Court of Session; and his successor in his ministerial charge was Home, the author of *Douglas*.

Blake, George (28 Oct. 1893—29 Aug. 1961), novelist, was born at Greenock and educated at Greenock Academy, afterwards studying law. In the First World War he was wounded at Gallipoli and subsequently turned to journalism, succeeding Neil Munro as literary editor of the *Glasgow Evening News*. In 1924 he became acting editor of *John o' London's Weekly* and in 1928 editor of the *Strand Magazine*. His novel *Mince Collop Close* (1923), portraying the seamy side of Glasgow's slum life, was followed by *The Wild Men* (1925) and a war story, *The Path of Glory* (1929). In 1932 he settled at Helensburgh on the Clyde, which is the background of several of his books, including *Down to the Sea* (1937), which tells of the ship workers, and *The Firth of Clyde* (1952), a tribute to the Firth and its famous fleet of steamers. Among his later novels were *The Valiant Heart* (1940), *The Westering Sun* (1946), *The Five Arches* (1947), and *The Voyage Home* (1952).

Blake, Nicholas, *see* **Lewis, Cecil Day.**

Blake, William (28 Nov. 1757—12 Aug. 1827), poet and painter, born in London, son of a hosier, was from earliest youth a seer of visions and a dreamer of dreams. His teeming imagination sought expression both in verse and in drawing, and in his fourteenth year he was apprenticed to James Basire, an eminent engraver, and thereafter studied at the Royal Academy. Among his chief artistic works were illustrations for Young's *Night Thoughts*, Blair's *Grave*, 'Spiritual Portraits,' and his finest work, 'Inventions to the Book of Job,' all distinguished by originality and imagination. In literature his *Songs of Innocence* appeared in 1789, *Songs of Experience* in 1794. These books were literally made as well as written, poems and designs alike being engraved on copper by Blake and bound by Mrs Blake. In like fashion were produced his mystical books, *The Book of Thel* (1789), *The Marriage of Heaven and Hell* (1790), *The Gates of Paradise, Visions of the Daughters of Albion* (1793), *The Book of Urizen* (1794), *The Book of Los* and *The Book of Ahania* (1795). His last books were *Jerusalem* and *Milton*. His earlier and shorter pieces, e.g. 'The Chimney-Sweeper,' 'Holy Thursday,' 'The Lamb,' 'The Sunflower,' and 'The Tiger,' have an exquisite simplicity arising from directness and intensity of feeling, sometimes tender, sometimes sublime.

Blamire, Susanna (1747—5 April 1794), poetess, daughter of a Cumberland farmer, received the sobriquet of 'The Muse of Cumberland.' Her poems, which were not collected until 1842, depict Cumbrian life and manners with truth and vivacity. She also wrote some fine songs in the Scottish dialect, including 'Ye shall walk in Silk Attire,' and 'What ails this Heart o' Mine.'

Bland, Edith, *see* **Nesbit.**

Blayds, Charles Stuart, *see* **Calverley.**

Blessington, Marguerite, Countess of (1 Sept. 1789—4 June 1849), diarist, daughter of Edmund Power, was born near Clonmel, Tipperary. In 1818 she married as her second husband the 1st Earl of Blessington, with whom she travelled much on the Continent, where she met Lord Byron, her *Conversations* with whom she published in 1834. Author also of some travel books and novels, she held a literary salon at her home in Kensington. Latterly she became bankrupt and went to Paris, where she lived under the protection of the Count d'Orsay.

Blind Harry, *see* **Henry the Minstrel.**

Blind, Mathilde (21 March 1841—26 Nov. 1896), poetess, was born at Mannheim, daughter of a banker named Cohen, but took the name of her stepfather, Karl Blind, who was exiled from Germany for his connection with the Baden insurrection of 1849 and found asylum in London. There Mathilde received an English education and was influenced by other foreign refugees, especially Mazzini. In 1867 she published a book of verse under the pseudonym Claude Lake. Visits to Scotland inspired two poems, *The Prophecy of St Oran* (1881), and *The Heather on Fire* (1886). *The Ascent of Man* (1888) is an epic of Darwinian evolution. She also wrote lives of *George Eliot* and *Madame Roland*, and translated the *Journal of Marie Bashkirtseff* (1890).

Bloomfield, Robert (3 Dec. 1766—19 Aug. 1823), poet, born at Honington in Suffolk, lost his father when he was a year old, and received the rudiments of education from his mother, who kept the village school. While still a boy he went to London, and worked as a shoemaker under an elder brother, enduring extreme poverty. His first and chief poem, *The Farmer's Boy*, was composed in a room where half a dozen other men were at work, and the finished lines he carried in his head until there was time to write them down. The

manuscript, after passing through various hands, fell into those of
Capel Lofft, a Suffolk squire of literary tastes, by whose exertions it
was published in 1800. It had a signal success, twenty-six thousand
copies having been sold in three years. The Duke of Grafton obtained
for him an appointment in the Seal Office, and when, through ill-
health, he was obliged to resign this, allowed him a pension of 1s.
a day. Other works were *Rural Tales* (1802), *Wild Flowers* (1806),
The Banks of Wye (1811), and *May Day with the Muses* (1822). An
attempt to carry on business as a bookseller failed, his health gave
way, his reason was threatened, and he died in great poverty at
Shefford, Bedfordshire.

Blunden, Edmund Charles (1 Nov. 1896—   ), poet
and critic, born at Yalding, Kent, was educated at Christ's Hospital,
of which he wrote later in *Christ's Hospital: a Retrospect*, and Queen's
College, Oxford. In the First World War he served as a lieutenant
and was awarded the Military Cross. His *Undertones of War* (1929)
is one of the best war books. Taking up journalism, he joined the
staff of the *Athenaeum*. In 1921 he paid a visit to America, writing
of it in *The Bonadventure*, and in 1922 his volume of poetry *The
Shepherd* was awarded the Hawthornden Prize. From 1924 to 1927
he was Professor of English at Tokio and published the small volume
Japanese Garland. In 1931 he became Fellow and Tutor of Merton
College, Oxford, and in 1943 he joined the staff of the *Times Literary
Supplement*. Later he returned to the Far East, and from 1953 was
head of the English department at the University of Hong Kong.
Blunden's love of the English countryside is revealed throughout
his *English Poems* (1925), his prose *Face of England* (1932), and his
Poems, 1932—1940; he was pre-eminently a nature poet. He was
also a brilliant critic and an authority in particular on Charles
Lamb, on whom he wrote in *Charles Lamb and his Contemporaries*
(1932). Later works include *Keats's Publisher* (1936), *Thomas Hardy*
(1942), *Cricket Country* (1944), and *Shelley, a Life Story* (1946).
Shells by the Stream (1944), is a book of verse. In 1951 he was made
a C.B.E.

Blunt, Wilfrid Scawen (17 Aug. 1840—10 Sept. 1922), poet, born
in Sussex and educated at Stonyhurst and Oscott, entered the
Diplomatic Service at 18 and served in legations at Athens, Frankfort, Madrid, Paris, Lisbon, Buenos Aires, and Berne. In 1869 he
left the service and married Lady Anne Noel, a descendant of Lord
Byron, who was a brilliant Arabic scholar and more famous among
the Bedouin than even Lord Cromer. Together they travelled over
the Middle East and India, and Blunt wrote *The Future of Islam*
(1882) and other books. An opponent of British imperialism, he
championed the cause of Ireland and was imprisoned in 1888. He
is best known for his poems, which included *Sonnets and Songs of
Proteus* (1875), and *Esther* (1892). His *Collected Poems* were published in 1914, and *My Diaries* in 1920.

Bodenham, John (fl. 1600), anthologist, is said to have edited the
Elizabethan anthologies *Politeuphuia: Wits' Commonwealth* (1597),
Wits' Theater (1598), *Belvedere, or the Garden of the Muses* (1600), and

England's Helicon (1600). Probably he only planned these collections and left the editing to others.

Bodley, Sir Thomas (2 March 1545—28 Jan. 1613), diplomat and scholar, was born at Exeter. His father, a Protestant, fled with him to Geneva in Mary I's reign, but returned to London on the accession of Elizabeth. Thomas went to Magdalen College, Oxford, was elected a Fellow of Merton in 1564, and lectured on Greek. A good linguist from his travels in France, Germany, and Italy, he carried out a number of diplomatic missions. He is chiefly famous for his refounding in 1598 of the Bodleian Library at Oxford, first begun in 1444 by Duke Humphrey of Gloucester. The first catalogue, of 655 pages, appeared in 1605, and in 1610 Bodley arranged with the Stationers' Company that the library should get a copy of every book they published.

Boece, *or* **Boethius, Hector** (1456?—1536), historian, was probably born at Dundee, and educated there and at Paris, where he became a regent or professor from 1492 to 1498, and made the acquaintance of Erasmus. Returning to Scotland he co-operated with Elphinstone, Bishop of Aberdeen, in founding the university there, of which he was the first Principal. His literary fame rests on two works, his *Lives of the Bishops of Mortlach and Aberdeen,* in which his friend Elphinstone figures prominently, and his *History of Scotland* to the accession of James III. These works were, of course, composed in Latin, but the *History* was translated into Scottish prose by John Bellenden in 1533, and into English for Holinshed's *Chronicle.* The work became very popular, and led to ecclesiastical preferment and royal favour.

Boileau, Ethel Mary, Lady (1882—16 Jan. 1942), novelist, born in London, daughter of the Rev. J. F. Young, was educated privately and in Germany, and in 1905 married Sir Raymond Boileau, Bart., Deputy-Lieutenant of Norfolk. Her first book, *Fire of Spring* (1914), was followed by *Hippy Buchan* (1925), a tale of a returned soldier, *The Arches of the Years* (1930) and *Clansmen* (1936), a romance of the Scottish Highlands.

Boker, George Henry (6 Oct. 1823—2 Jan. 1890), playwright, poet, and diplomat, was born at Philadelphia and educated at Princeton. He studied law, but after a foreign tour decided to turn to writing. *Calaynos* (1848) and *Leonor de Guzman* (1853), blank verse tragedies of medieval Spain, were followed by one with a medieval Italian setting, *Francesca da Rimini* (1855), often reckoned the best American play of the century. *Plays and Poems* (1856) is a collection of his early works, and in 1869 he published *Königsmark, The Legend of the Hounds, and Other Poems.* He was outstanding as a writer of sonnets, of which he published over 300. As United States Minister to Turkey in 1871 and to Russia in 1875 he carried through important negotiations.

Boldrewood, Rolf, *see* **Browne, Thomas Alexander.**

Bolingbroke, Henry Saint-John, 1st Viscount (1 Oct. 1678—12 Dec. 1751), statesman and philosopher, was born at Battersea and educated at Eton. After travel on the Continent he became Tory M.P. for Wootton Bassett and rose to be Secretary for War (1704) and Secretary of State (1710). In 1712 he was raised to the peerage for negotiating the Peace of Utrecht. On the accession of George I he was dismissed and attainted for Jacobite sympathies and fled to France, where he joined the Old Pretender. Pardoned in 1723, he returned to England, settled near Uxbridge, and became the associate of Pope and Swift. In France again from 1735 to 1743, he wrote *A Letter on the True Uses of Retirement and Study*, and *Letters on the Study of History*, both of which were published just after his death. His last years were spent at Battersea, where he produced various political works, including *Letters on the Spirit of Patriotism* (1749), and *The Idea of a Patriot King* (1749).

Bolitho, Henry Hector (1898—   ), biographer, born at Auckland, was a newspaper reporter at 17 and at 21 accompanied the Prince of Wales and his party in their tour of the Antipodes and wrote *With the Prince in New Zealand* (1920). In 1921 he was editor of the Sydney *Sunday News*, and in the following year he came to England and wrote two novels, *Solemn Boy* (1927), and *Judith Silver* (1929). Thereafter he became known as a sort of unofficial court biographer with his books *Albert the Good* (1932), *Victoria the Widow and her Son* (1934), and *Victoria and Albert* (1938). The most successful of all, *Edward VIII: His Life and Reign* (1937) was followed in the same year by *King George VI: A Character Study*. Later works are *The Romance of Windsor Castle* (1946), *A Century of British Monarchy* (1951), and *A Penguin in the Eyrie* (1955), reminiscences of the Second World War.

Bonar, Horatius (19 Dec. 1808—31 July 1889), minister and poet, son of James Bonar, Solicitor of Excise for Scotland, born and educated in Edinburgh, entered the Ministry of the Church of Scotland, and was settled at Kelso. He joined the Free Church at the Disruption in 1843, and in 1866 was translated to Edinburgh. In 1853 he was made D.D. of Aberdeen, and in 1883 was Moderator of the General Assembly of the Free Church. He was a voluminous and highly popular author, and in addition to many books and tracts wrote a number of hymns, many of which, e.g., 'I heard the voice of Jesus say,' are known all over the English-speaking world. A selection of these was published as *Hymns of Faith and Hope*.

Bone, Sir David William (1874—17 May 1959), novelist, was born in Glasgow, son of a journalist. His brother Muirhead Bone, the well-known artist, illustrated his *Merchantmen at Arms* (1919), which told of the work of the merchant service in the First World War. David Bone went to sea at 15 as an apprentice in the square-rigged *City of Florence*, and served seven years in sail. In 1899 he joined the Anchor Line, where he rose to be Commodore. His books, which are all about the sea, include *The Brassbounder* (1910), *Broken Stowage* (1915), *The Lookoutman* (1923), *Capstan Bars* (1931), and

Merchantmen Rearmed (1949). *Landfall at Sunset* (1955) is an auto-biography. He was made a C.B.E. in 1943 and knighted in 1946.

Boorde, *or* **Borde, Andrew** (1490?—April 1549), doctor and traveller, born near Cuckfield, Sussex, was brought up as a Carthusian, and held ecclesiastical appointments, then practised medicine at various places, including Glasgow, and was employed on a special mission by Thomas Cromwell. He travelled widely, going as far as Jerusalem, and wrote descriptions of the countries he had visited. His *Dyetary* is the first English book of domestic medicine. The *Fyrst Boke of the Introduction of Knowledge* (1547) describes his journeys on the Continent. Other works are *The Boke of Berdes*, which dissuades from beard-growing, *Handbook of Europe*, and *Itinerary of England*. He died in the Fleet Prison.

Boothby, Guy Newell (13 Oct. 1867—26 Feb. 1905), novelist, born at Adelaide, South Australia, where his father was a member of the State House of Assembly, was educated in England, then lived in Australia from 1883 to 1894 and was secretary to the Mayor of Adelaide. In 1891 he made a journey across Australia from north to south and wrote about it in *On the Wallaby* (1894). After that he settled in England and wrote some 50 adventure stories, hasty and crude but exciting, of which one of the earliest, *A Bid for Fortune: or Dr Nikola's Vendetta* (1895), was so successful that he followed it up with three more Nikola books, including *Dr Nikola's Experiment* (1899). *A Lost Endeavour* (1895) and *Bushigrams* (1897) are novels of Australian life.

Borden, Mary (1887—), novelist, was born in Chicago and educated at Vassar. After an early marriage and divorce and a tour round the world she worked with a mobile hospital in France during the First World War, and was awarded the Croix de Guerre and made a Member of the Legion of Honour. In 1918 she married Major-General Sir Edward Spears, subsequently British Minister to the Republics of Syria and the Lebanon, and settled in London, now a British subject. Her novels include *Jane, Our Stranger* (1922), *Four o'Clock* (1926), *Flamingo* (1927), *Sarah Gay* (1931), *The Black Virgin* (1937), *No. 2, Shovel Street* (1949), *For the Record* (1950), and *Martin Merriedew* (1952).

Borrow, George (5 July 1803—26 July 1881), author and traveller, born at East Dereham, Norfolk, son of a recruiting officer, had a somewhat wandering childhood. He received most of his education in Edinburgh, and showed a peculiar talent for acquiring languages. After being for a short time in the office of a solicitor in Norwich, he travelled widely on the Continent and in the East, acquainting himself with the people and languages of the various countries he visited. He specially attached himself to the Gipsies, with whose language he became so familiar as to publish a dictionary of it. His learning was shown by his publishing at St Petersburg *Targum*, a work containing translations from 30 languages. He became a travelling agent of the Bible Society, and his book, *The Bible in Spain* (1843), giving an account of his remarkable adventures in that country, made his literary reputation. It was followed by *Lavengro* (1851), its sequel,

Romany Rye (1857), and *Wild Wales* (1862), which, though now perhaps his most popular books, were received with less public favour. The two first give a highly coloured account of his own life. In 1840 he married and settled at Oulton Broad, Norfolk, where he died. Borrow was a man of striking appearance and great vigour and originality of character and mind.

Boston, Thomas (17 March 1677—20 May 1732), born at Duns in Berwickshire and educated at Edinburgh University, was successively schoolmaster at Glencairn, and minister of Simprin in Berwickshire, and Ettrick in Selkirkshire. In addition to his best-known work, *The Fourfold State*, one of the religious classics of Scotland, he wrote an original little book, *The Crook in the Lot*, and a learned treatise on the Hebrew accents. His *Autobiography* (1776) is an interesting record of contemporary Scottish life.

Boswell, Sir Alexander (9 Oct. 1775—27 March 1822), antiquary and poet, son of James Boswell (q.v.), born at Auchinleck and educated at Westminster and Oxford, was interested in old Scottish authors, some of whose works he reprinted at his private press. He wrote some popular Scotch songs, of which ' Jenny's Bawbee ' and ' Jenny dang the Weaver ' are the best known. Created a baronet in 1821 he died as the result of a duel over some political lampoons.

Boswell, James (29 Oct. 1740—19 May 1795), biographer, was born in Edinburgh, son of Lord Auchinleck, a prominent advocate. He was educated at Edinburgh High School and the Universities of Edinburgh, Glasgow, and Utrecht, where he studied law, being admitted to the Scottish Bar in 1766. At the age of 21 he published anonymously an *Ode to Tragedy*. A great lion-hunter, he attained the height of his ambition when he was introduced to Dr Johnson in a London bookshop on 16 May 1763 and succeeded in winning his friendship. Later in this year he undertook a continental tour in the course of which he met Rousseau and Voltaire and secured an introduction to Paoli in Corsica; *An Account of Corsica* (1768), his first book, was a great success. In the following year he married his cousin, Margaret Montgomerie, by whom he had seven children, and shortly afterwards began the period of greatest intimacy with Johnson, whose conversation he recorded with such effectiveness until his death in 1784. In 1773 he was elected a member of the famous Club, to which Johnson, Reynolds, Burke, and Goldsmith belonged, and in the same year he induced Johnson to accompany him on the Scottish tour of which he wrote in *A Journal of a Tour to the Hebrides* (1785). In 1782 Boswell succeeded, on his father's death, to a wealthy estate, and made some attempts at a political career, but obtained only the Recordship of Carlisle, which he relinquished after a year. In 1789 his wife died, and he accelerated his own end by the drink and dissipation which had always been his weakness.

Boswell's *Life of Samuel Johnson*, published in 1791, was so successful that a second edition was called for two years later. Unquestionably the greatest biography written in English, it shows a marvellous power of observation and vivid narration. Although an admirer of the great doctor, Boswell was no mere sycophant, and his account is all the more valuable and entertaining because it reveals the weaknesses as well as the greatness of his subject. The standard edition is that by G. B. Hill, revised by L. F. Powell (1934—1950). Boswell's *Letters* were edited in 1924, and his *Notebook, 1776—1777* in 1925. About the same time a vast mass of unpublished diaries and papers was discovered at Malahide Castle in Ireland, the seat of his great-grandson. Sections of it were published as *Boswell's London Journal* (1950), *Boswell in Holland, 1763—4* (1952), and *Boswell on the Grand Tour, 1765—1766* (1955).

Bottome, Phyllis (31 May 1884—   ), novelist, was born at Rochester, Kent, the daughter of an American clergyman, and passed several years of her girlhood in the United States. After studying at a dramatic school she turned to writing, her first novel being accepted by Andrew Lang when she was 17. In 1917 she married A. E. Forbes-Dennis, who took a post in Vienna; later they lived in the Tyrol and after that in England. She was particularly successful as a short story writer, her books including *Raw Material* (1905), *The Dark Tower* (1909), *Windlestraws* (1929), *The Mortal Storm* (1937), *Masks and Faces* (1940), *London Pride* (1941), *From the Life* (1944), *Fortune's Finger* (1950), *The Challenge* (1953), and *Man and Beast* (1954). *Search for a Soul* (1947) is autobiographical.

Bottomley, Gordon (20 Feb. 1874—25 Aug. 1948), poet and playwright, born at Keighley in Yorkshire and educated at the grammar school there, settled in the Lake District and had an uneventful life. His first book, *The Mickle Drede and Other Verses* (1896), was followed by several volumes of verse, including two series of *Chambers of Imagery* (1907 and 1912). He instituted a revival of English verse drama with *The Crier by Night* (1902), *The Riding to Lithend* (1909), and other plays. He also wrote preludes to two of Shakespeare's plays, *King Lear's Wife* (1915), and *Gruach*, a play of Lady Macbeth's early life, which won the Femina Vie Heureuse Prize in 1923. In 1925 he was awarded the Arthur Benson Medal of the Royal Society of Literature. His last plays were *Deirdre* (1944) and *Kate Kennedy* (1945).

Boucicault, Dion (26 Dec. 1822—18 Sept. 1890), actor and dramatist, born in Dublin and educated in London, joined Macready while still young, and made his first appearance upon the stage with Benjamin Webster at Bristol. Soon afterwards he began to write plays, of which the first, *London Assurance* (1841) had an immediate success. He was an excellent actor, especially in pathetic parts, and his plays, though practically all adaptations, are often very ingenious in construction, and have had great popularity. Among the best known are *Faust and Marguerite* (1852), *The Colleen Bawn* (1860), *Arrahna-Pogue* (1865), and *The Shaughraun* (1875). Boucicault died in New York.

Bowdler, Thomas (11 July 1754—24 Feb. 1825), expurgator, born at Ashley, near Bath, son of a gentleman of independent fortune, studied medicine at St Andrews and at Edinburgh, where he took his degree in 1776, but did not practise, devoting himself instead to the cause of prison reform. In 1818 he published his *Family Shakespeare* in 10 volumes, 'in which nothing is added to the original text, but those words and expressions are omitted which cannot with propriety be read aloud in a family.' The work had considerable success, four editions having been published before 1824, and others in 1831, 1853, and 1861. It was, however, subjected to some criticism and ridicule, and gave rise to the expression 'bowdlerize.' Bowdler subsequently essayed a similar enterprise in regard to Gibbon, which, however, was not so successful.

Bowen, Edward Ernest (30 March 1836—8 April 1901), poet and schoolmaster, was born at Woolaston, near Chepstow, where his father was curate, and educated at King's College, London, and Cambridge, where he was first a scholar and then a Fellow of Trinity. In 1859 he became a master at Harrow under Dr Vaughan, and remained there all his life, becoming head of the modern side in 1869. In 1872 he wrote the Harrow school song, 'Forty Years On,' and a volume *Harrow Songs and Other Verses* was published in 1886.

Bowen, Elizabeth Dorothea Cole (7 June 1899—   ), novelist, daughter of an Irish barrister, was born in Dublin; *Seven Winters* (1942) tells of her childhood there. At an early age she was taken to the south of England, and was educated at Downe House in Kent. Leaving home at the age of 19 she lived alone in London and the Continent, and in 1923 married Alan Charles Cameron; later they settled at Oxford. Her first short stories were written when she was 20 and published as *Encounters* (1923); other collections are *Ann Lee's* (1928), *Joining Charles* (1929), *The Cat Jumps* (1934), and *Demon Lover* (1946). Her first novel, *The Hotel* (1927) was written at Bordighera; others are *Friends and Relations* (1931), *To the North* (1932), *The House in Paris* (1935), *The Heat of the Day* (1949), and *A World of Love* (1955). She also wrote *Bowen's Court* (1942), an account of the Bowen family, named from their ancestral seat in County Cork, and a book of essays, *Collected Impressions* (1950). In 1948 she was made a C.B.E., and in 1949 received an honorary doctorate of Trinity College, Dublin.

Bowen, Marjorie, *see* **Long, Margaret.**

Bower, Archibald (17 Jan. 1686—3 Sept. 1766), historian, born at Dundee, and educated at the Scots College, Douay, became a Jesuit, afterwards joined the Church of England, again became a Jesuit, and finally died a Protestant. He wrote a *History of Rome* (1735—44) and a *History of the Popes* (1748—66), which are ill-proportioned and inaccurate.

Bower, *or* **Bowmaker, Walter** (1385—1449), historian, born at Haddington, became Abbot of Inchcolm in the Firth of Forth. He continued the *Scotichronicon* of Fordun (q.v.) from 1153 down to 1437, and wrote an abridgment of it called *The Book of Cupar*.

Bowles, William Lisle (24 Sept. 1762—7 April 1850), clergyman, poet, and antiquary, born at King's Sutton, Northamptonshire, of which his father was vicar, and educated at Winchester and Oxford, was for the most of his life Vicar of Bremhill, Wiltshire, and became Prebendary and Canon Residentiary of Salisbury. His first work, published in 1789, was a little volume containing 14 sonnets composed during a tour through the north of England and Scotland, which was received with extraordinary favour, not only by the general public, but by such men as Coleridge and Wordsworth. It may be regarded as the harbinger of the reaction against the school of Pope, in which these poets were soon to bear so great a part. Bowles published several other poems of much greater length, of which the best are *The Spirit of Discovery* (1805) and *The Missionary of the Andes* (1815), and he also enjoyed considerable reputation as an antiquary, his principal work in that department being *Hermes Britannicus* (1828). In 1806 he published a *Life of Pope*, in which he expressed some views on poetry which resulted in a fierce controversy with Byron, Campbell, and others. He also wrote a *Life of Bishop Ken*. Bowles was an amiable, absent-minded, and rather eccentric man. His poems are characterized by refinement of feeling, tenderness, and pensive thought, but are deficient in power and passion.

Bowmaker, Walter, *see* **Bower.**

Bowra, Sir Cecil Maurice (8 April 1898—), scholar, was the son of a Customs official and was educated at Cheltenham and New College, Oxford. During the First World War he served in France with the artillery. After it he became a Fellow of Wadham College, and in 1938 was elected Warden. In 1946 he was appointed Professor of Poetry and in 1951 became Vice-Chancellor of Oxford and was knighted. An accomplished classical scholar, he had also a wide knowledge of modern works in many literatures. His principal works are *Tradition and Design in the Iliad* (1935), *Ancient Greek Literature* (1935), *Greek Lyric Poetry* (1936), *Early Greek Elegists* (1938), *The Heritage of Symbolism* (1943), *A Book of Russian Verse* (1943), *Sophoclean Tragedy* (1943), *From Vergil to Milton* (1945), *Edith Sitwell* (1947), *A Second Book of Russian Verse* (1948), *The Creative Experiment* (1949), *The Romantic Imagination* (1950), *Heroic Poetry* (1952), *Problems in Greek Poetry* (1953), and *Inspiration and Poetry* (1955).

Bowring, Sir John (17 Oct. 1792—23 Nov. 1872), linguist, writer, and traveller, was born at Exeter. His talent for acquiring languages enabled him at last to say that he knew 200, and could speak 100. He was appointed editor of the *Westminster Review* in 1824, and travelled in various countries with the view of reporting on their commercial position. He was elected M.P. in 1835, and obtained the issue of the florin as a first step towards a decimal currency. His chief literary work was the translation of the folk songs of European nations, and he also wrote original poems and hymns, and works on political and economic subjects. He was knighted in 1854.

Boyd, Andrew Kennedy Hutchison (3 Nov. 1825—1 March 1899), clergyman and essayist, son of the Rev. Dr Boyd of Glasgow, studied

D

at King's College, London, and Middle Temple, but returned to Glasgow University and qualified for the ministry. In 1865 he became a minister at St Andrews and in 1890 was Moderator of the General Assembly. Over the initials A.K.H.B. he wrote in *Fraser's Magazine* a series of light articles subsequently collected as *The Recreations of a Country Parson*. He also published several books of reminiscences, written in a pleasant chatty style, and some sermons. He was D.D. and LL.D.

Boyd, Zachary (1585?—1653), minister, of the family of Boyd of Pinkhill, Ayrshire, was educated at Glasgow, St Andrews, and Saumur Universities. He was minister of the Barony Parish, Glasgow, in 1623, and was thrice elected Rector of the University, where his voluminous manuscript writings are preserved. He translated many parts of Scripture into uncouth verse. Among his works are *The Garden of Zion* and *Zion's Flowers*.

Boyle, Hon. Robert (25 Jan. 1627—31 Dec. 1691), physicist and chemist, seventh son of the 1st Earl of Cork, was born at Lismore, Co. Waterford, and educated at Eton and by private tutors, after which he pursued his studies on the Continent. On his return to England he devoted himself to the study of science, especially natural philosophy and chemistry. He was one of the founders of the Royal Society, by his experiments and observations added to existing knowledge, especially in regard to pneumatics, and formulated the principle of 'Boyle's Law.' All his life he was devoted to religion, and as a director of the East India Co. he did much for the propagation of Christianity in the East, and for the dissemination of the Bible. He also founded the 'Boyle Lectures' in defence of Christianity. He declined the offer of a peerage. Boyle was a man of great intellectual acuteness, and remarkable for his conversational powers. Among his writings are *Origin of Forms and Qualities*, *Experiments touching Colour*, *Hydrostatical Paradoxes*, and *Observations on Cold*; in theology, *Seraphic Love*. His complete works were published in 5 volumes in 1744.

Boyle, Roger, *see* **Orrery, Earl of.**

Braddon, Mary Elizabeth (4 Oct. 1837—4 Feb. 1915), novelist, born in London and educated privately, started writing at an early age. A lurid story, *Three Times Dead*, which she wrote at 19, failed of publication only because the publisher went bankrupt; later it was rewritten as *The Trail of the Serpent*. In 1862 she produced *Lady Audley's Secret*, which had tremendous success, nearly a million copies being sold, so that the book made both her fortune and her publisher's. From then almost till her death she produced with unflagging energy and enthusiasm some 70 novels of a sensational and melodramatic type. Among the more successful were *Aurora Floyd* (1863), *Henry Dunbar* (1864), *Dead Sea Fruit* (1868), *Ishmael* (1884), and *The Green Curtain* (1911). She also wrote plays and edited several magazines. In 1874 she married John Maxwell, the publisher.

Bradford, William (baptized 19 March 1590, died 9 May 1657), administrator and historian, was born at Austerfield in Yorkshire, son of a farmer. Joining the puritan Separatist or Brownist sect he accompanied them to Holland, and in 1620 sailed on the *Mayflower* to Plymouth, New England. In 1621 he was elected Governor, and was re-elected regularly for the next thirty years, except on five occasions, when he 'by importunity gat off.' In collaboration with Edward Winslow he wrote the journal commonly known as *Mourt's Relation* (1622), giving an account of the beginnings of the colony. His *History of Plimmoth Plantation*, first published in 1856, covers the period from 1602 to 1647 and is the principal source for his life.

Bradley, Andrew Cecil (26 March 1851—2 Sept, 1935), critic and scholar, son of the Rev. Charles Bradley and brother of F. H. Bradley (q.v.), was educated at Cheltenham and Balliol College, Oxford, then under the mastership of Dr Jowett. In 1874 he became a Fellow of Balliol, in 1882 was elected to the Chair of Literature and History at Liverpool, and in 1890 became Professor of English at Glasgow. In 1900 he retired to London to devote himself to literary criticism, but in the following year was elected Professor of Poetry at Oxford. His lectures there were collected to form his most famous book, *Shakespearian Tragedy* (1904). He took a prominent part in the formation in 1906 of the English Association, of which he was later president. His other works include *A Commentary on 'In Memoriam'* (1901), and *Oxford Lectures on Poetry* (1909).

Bradley, Edward (25 March 1827—12 Dec. 1889), clergyman and novelist, son of a surgeon, was educated at Kidderminster Grammar School and Durham, after which he stayed a year at Oxford but never matriculated. In 1850 he was ordained and after holding various livings became rector of Stretton in Rutland. Choosing the pseudonym of Cuthbert Bede, the names of the two patron saints of Durham, he wrote a few novels, of which by far the most successful was *The Adventures of Mr Verdant Green, an Oxford Freshman* (1853), a humorous story of Oxford life which has become a classic. A sequel, *Little Mr Bouncer and his Friend Verdant Green* (1878) failed to reach the same standard. Others of Bradley's novels were *Glencraggan* (1861) and *Fotheringhay* (1885).

Bradley, Francis Herbert, O.M. (30 Jan. 1846—18 Sept. 1924), philosopher, son of the Rev. Charles Bradley and brother of A. C. Bradley (q.v.) was educated at Cheltenham, Marlborough, and Oxford. In 1870 he became a Life Fellow of Merton College, which was his home until his death more than fifty years later. Although chronic illness caused him to live a very retired life, he took an important part in college affairs, as well as being a leading influence on contemporary philosophical thought. He received the Order of Merit in 1914. His main works are *Ethical Studies* (1876), *The Principles of Logic* (1883), *Appearance and Reality* (1893), and *Essays on Truth and Reality* (1914). Though inspired by Hegel, he dissented too much from him to be called a Hegelian.

Bradley, Henry (3 Dec. 1845—23 May 1923), lexicographer, was born at Manchester and educated at Chesterfield Grammar School. While working as a clerk he mastered a number of European languages, and in 1884 he took up literary work in London. Gaining attention by a review which he wrote of the first part of the *Oxford English Dictionary*, he joined its staff, and in 1889 became one of its editors, finally succeeding Sir James Murray as senior editor in 1915. In 1916 he was elected a Fellow of Magdalen; he was also three times president of the Philological Society. In addition to his work on the *Oxford Dictionary* he produced a revised edition of Stratmann's *Middle English Dictionary* (1891), and a very popular philological primer, *The Making of English* (1904). He was also an authority on the origin of English place-names.

Bradley, Katharine Harris (27 Oct. 1848—26 Sept. 1914), poetess who wrote in collaboration with her niece Edith Emma Cooper (q.v.) under the pseudonym Michael Field, was born in Birmingham, daughter of a tobacco manufacturer. She was educated at Newnham College, Cambridge, and the Collège de France, Paris, and afterwards studied at University College, Bristol. Described as imperious and witty, she corresponded with Ruskin, and knew Browning, Meredith, Oscar Wilde, and George Moore. From the age of 16 she lived in the same household with her niece, with whom she worked in such close affinity that their productions can only be regarded as if they were by a single author. Imbued with a keen sense of beauty and a fine writing touch, they composed 27 tragedies and eight volumes of verse. The latter include *Long Ago* (1889), *Sight and Song* (1892), *Underneath the Bough* (1893), *Wild Honey* (1908), *Poems of Adoration* (1912), and *Mystic Trees* (1913). Among their plays are *Fair Rosamund* (1884), *Canute the Great* (1887), *Tragic Mary* (1890), and *Borgia* (1905). *Works and Days* (1933) contains extracts from their journal. In 1907 they both became Roman Catholics.

Bradstreet, Anne (1612?—16 Sept. 1672), America's first poetess, was born probably at Northampton. Her father, Thomas Dudley, became steward to the Earl of Lincoln, and she had a good private education before she married Simon Bradstreet in 1628. Going to New England in 1630 she lived at Ipswich and afterwards at North Andover, both her father and her husband becoming Governors of the Province of Massachusetts Bay. Her volume of poems, *The Tenth Muse Lately Sprung Up in America* (1650), was published in London and follows contemporary English fashions, but some of her later writings were less conventional. In 1867 her *Works in Prose and Verse* were published. Among her descendants were Richard Henry Dana, Wendell Phillips, and Oliver Wendell Holmes.

Bradwardine, Thomas (1290?—26 Aug. 1349), theologian, was at Oxford, where he became Professor of Divinity and Chancellor, and afterwards Chaplain to Edward III, whom he attended in his French wars. He was twice elected Archbishop of Canterbury by the monks, and on the second occasion accepted, but died of the plague within forty days. He wrote on geometry, but his great work was *De Causa Dei contra Pelagium* (On the Cause of God against Pelagius), in which he treated theology mathematically, and which earned for him from the Pope the title of the Profound Doctor.

Brady, Nicholas (28 Oct. 1659—20 May 1726), clergyman and poet, born at Bandon, Cork, son of an army officer, was educated at Westminster School and Oxford and Dublin Universities. He took orders and held various livings in Cork. During the Revolution he supported the Orange side, and became chaplain successively to William III, Mary, and Queen Anne. From 1696 till his death he was vicar of Richmond, where he also kept a school, and in 1699 he was made a D.D. of Dublin. He is best known by the metrical version of the Psalms which he made in collaboration with Nahum Tate (q.v.). In 1696 a royal proclamation stated that it might be used in churches, and though it was criticized as being too political it gradually superseded the older version of Sternhold and Hopkins (q.v.). Brady also wrote a tragedy, *The Rape* (1692) and some poems.

Braithwaite, *or* **Brathwaite, Richard** (1588—4 May 1673), poet, born near Kendal, and educated at Oxford, is believed to have served with the Royalist army in the Civil War. He was the author of many works of very unequal merit, of which the best known is *Drunken Barnaby's Four Journeys*, which records his pilgrimages through England, in rhymed Latin (said by Southey to be the best of modern times), and doggerel English verse. *The English Gentleman* (1631), and *English Gentlewoman* are in a much more decorous strain. Other works are *The Golden Fleece* (poems), *The Poet's Willow*, *A Strappado for the Devil* (a satire), and *Art Asleepe, Husband?*

Bramah, Ernest, *see* **Smith, Ernest Bramah.**

Bramston, James (1694?—16 March 1744), satirist, educated at Westminster School and Oxford, took orders and was latterly vicar of two Sussex parishes. His poems are *The Art of Politics* (1729), an imitation of Horace, and *The Man of Taste* (1733), in imitation of Pope. He also parodied Phillips's *Splendid Shilling* in *The Crooked Sixpence*. His verses have some liveliness.

Brathwaite, Richard, *see* **Braithwaite.**

Bray, Anna Eliza (25 Dec. 1790—21 Jan. 1883), novelist, daughter of John Kempe, bullion porter in the Mint, was born at Newington, Surrey. She was married first to C. A. Stothard, son of the famous R.A., and himself an artist, and secondly to the Rev. E. A. Bray. She wrote about a dozen novels, chiefly historical, and *The Borders of the Tamar and Tavy* (1836), an account of the traditions and superstitions of the neighbourhood of Tavistock in the form of letters to Southey, of whom she was a great friend. Her *Autobiography* was published in 1884.

Brazil, Angela (30 Nov. 1868—13 March 1947), writer of school stories, was born at Preston, Lancashire, daughter of a cotton manufacturer, and educated at Manchester High School and Ellerslie College, of which she was head girl. Later she was a fellow-student of Baroness Orczy (q.v.) at an art school. After her father's death she travelled with her mother in Europe and the Middle East; she never married. Starting serious writing at the age of 36, she published over fifty stories of schoolgirl life, which are pleasant and cheerful but free from sentimentalism and true to reality. Among the best are *The Fortunes of Philippa* (1907), *The Manor House School* (1911), *A Pair of Schoolgirls* (1912), *The School by the Sea* (1914), *The Youngest Girl in the Fifth* (1914), *Captain Peggie* (1924), *At School with Rachel* (1928), *Jean's Golden Term* (1934), *An Exciting Term* (1936), *The New School at Scarsdale* (1940), and *The School on the Loch* (1946). *My Own Schooldays* (1935) is autobiographical. Her name is accented on the first syllable.

Breasted, James Henry (27 Aug. 1865—2 Dec. 1935), historian, born at Rockford, Illinois, was educated at North Central College, Napierville, and afterwards studied for the ministry. Later he obtained a Ph.D. of Berlin, and in the early years of scientific excavation was commissioned to arrange the Egyptian inscriptions in European museums for the Berlin Egyptian Dictionary. He became Professor of Egyptology and Director of the Oriental Institute at Chicago, and led a number of archaeological expeditions to Egypt and the Near East. His writings include *A History of Egypt* (1905), which is a standard work, *A History of the Ancient Egyptians* (1908), and *Ancient Times: A History of the Early World* (1916).

Breton, Nicholas (1545?—1626?), poet and satirist, son of a London merchant, was perhaps at Oxford, and was a rather prolific author of considerable versatility. Among his poetical works are *A Floorish upon Fancie* (1577), *The Soul's Heavenly Exercise* (1601), *The Passionate Shepherd* (1604), and *Pasquil's Mad-cappe* (1626). In prose he wrote *Wit's Trenchamour* (1597), an angling idyll, *The Wil of Wit* (1599), *A Mad World, my Masters* (1603), *Adventures of Two Excellent Princes, Grimello's Fortunes* (1604), and *Strange News out of Divers Countries* (1622). His mother married George Gascoigne, the poet (q.v.). His lyrics, eight of which appear in *England's Helicon*, are pure and fresh, and his romances, though full of conceits, are pleasant reading, remarkably free from grossness.

Brewer, Ebenezer Cobham (2 May 1810—6 March 1897), compiler, was born in London and educated privately and at Cambridge, where he took a degree in civil law. In 1836 he took orders, but turned to literature, and in 1870 published his best-known reference work, the *Dictionary of Phrase and Fable*. Others of his thirty compilations are *The Reader's Handbook of Allusions, References, Plots, and Stories* (1880), an *Etymological Dictionary of Difficult Words* (1882), and a *Dictionary of Miracles* (1884).

Brewster, Sir David (11 Dec. 1781—10 Feb. 1868), scientist, born at Jedburgh, originally intended to enter the Church, of which, after a distinguished course at the University of Edinburgh, he became a licentiate. Afterwards, however, he turned scientist, becoming one of the most brilliant of his day, especially in the study of optics, and received almost every kind of honorary distinction open to a man of science. He was one of the founders of the British Association, and his works include a *Life of Newton* (1831), *The Martyrs of Science*

(1841), *More Worlds than One* (1854), and *Letters on Natural Magic* addressed to Sir W. Scott; he also edited, in addition to various scientific journals, *The Edinburgh Encyclopaedia* (1807—29). He likewise held the offices successively of Principal of the United College of St Salvator and St Leonard, St Andrews (1838), and of the University of Edinburgh (1859). He was knighted in 1831.

Brickhill, Paul Chester Jerome (20 Dec. 1916—), journalist, was born in Melbourne and educated at North Sydney High School and Sydney University. From 1935 to 1940 he worked on newspapers, and throughout the Second World War was a fighter pilot in the Royal Australian Air Force. Shot down in Tunis, he was for a time a prisoner of war in Germany. He was best known by his war books, many of which are about the escapes of prisoners. They include *Escape to Danger* (1946), *The Great Escape* (1951), *The Dam Busters* (1951), and *Escape—or Die* (1952); most famous of all is *Reach for the Sky* (1954), which tells the life story of Douglas Bader, the legless English air ace.

Bridges, Robert Seymour, O.M. (23 Oct. 1844—21 April 1930), Poet Laureate, was born at Walmer and educated at Eton and Corpus Christi College, Oxford, where he stroked the college boat when it was second on the river. After studying medicine at St Bartholomew's Hospital, he practised for a time, then retired and after a period of travel published his first volume of poetry in 1873. Between then and 1894 he produced four volumes of lyrics, as well as the longer *Prometheus the Firegiver* (1884), and *Eros and Psyche* (1885). In 1907 he settled at Boars Hill, near Oxford, where he lived a very secluded life. In 1912 his *Poetical Works* appeared in one volume, and in 1913 he was appointed Poet Laureate in succession to Alfred Austin. In 1916 he published an anthology of prose and verse from various authors entitled *The Spirit of Man*. His *New Verse* appeared in 1925, and his long poem, *The Testament of Beauty*, published the year before his death at 85, went through fourteen impressions in its first year. Bridges was one of the founders of the Society for Pure English, and placed posterity in his debt by rescuing the poems of Gerard Manley Hopkins from oblivion. His own work gives an impression of aloofness and frigidity, and attracts mainly by its skilful craftsmanship. He was at his best in short lyrics.

Bridges, Roy (23 March 1885—), journalist and novelist, was born at Hobart and educated at Queen's College there and the University of Tasmania. Becoming a journalist, he was from 1909 to 1925 on the literary staff of the Melbourne *Age*. In 1944 and 1945 he held an Australian Commonwealth Literary Fellowship. His best novels are those dealing with the early history of Tasmania, and include *And All That Beauty* (1929), *Negrohead* (1930), *Cloud* (1932), and *The House of Fendon* (1936). Others are *The Barb of an Arrow* (1909), *By His Excellency's Command* (1910), *On His Majesty's Service* (1914), *The Bubble Moon* (1915), *Dead Men's Gold* (1916), *The Fenceless Ranges* (1920), *Green Butterflies* (1923), *A Mirror of Silver* (1927), *Sullivan's Bay* (1937), *Old Admiral Death* (1940), *The Owl Is Abroad* (1941), and *The League of the Lord* (1949).

Bridie, James, *see* **Mavor, O. H.**

Bright, Mary Chavelita (14 Dec. 1860—12 Aug. 1945), novelist writing under the name George Egerton, was born in Melbourne, daughter of Captain J. J. Dunne, and was married three times, her second husband being Egerton Clairmonte, who died in 1901, and her third Reginald Golding Bright. Educated privately, in her youth she made a voyage in a sailing ship to Valparaiso, then travelled to Wales and Ireland. She at first planned to be an artist, then turned to writing. Her novel *Keynotes* (1893), which gives an intimate picture of married life, was followed by *Discords* (1894), *Symphonies* (1897), *Fantasies* (1898), and *Flies in Amber* (1905). She also translated Knut Hamsun's novel *Hunger* (1926), and was an original member of the Irish Genealogical Society.

Brittain, Vera Mary (   ), novelist, was born at Newcastle under Lyme, but spent her childhood in Cheshire, where her father was proprietor of some paper mills. She was educated at St Monica's, Kingswood, and Somerville College, Oxford, which she entered as an exhibitioner in 1914. During the First World War she served as a Red Cross nurse, and wrote of her experiences afterwards in *Testament of Youth* (1933). In 1919 she returned to Oxford, and in 1922 settled in London and worked as a freelance journalist. Her first novel, *The Dark Tide* (1923), told of Oxford life, and was followed by *Not Without Honour* (1924). In 1925 she married George E. G. Catlin, an Oxford man who was then Professor of Politics at Cornell, and between 1934 and 1946 she made four lecture tours of the United States. Later works were *Testament of Friendship* (1940), a tribute to her lifelong friend, Winifred Holtby (q.v.), *England's Hour* (1940), and the novels *Account Rendered* (1944) and *Born 1925* (1949). *Lady into Woman* (1954) is a history of women from Victoria to Elizabeth II.

Brogan, Denis William (11 Aug. 1900—   ), historian, born at Rutherglen, near Glasgow, of Irish parentage, was educated at Rutherglen Academy, Glasgow University, Balliol College, Oxford, and Harvard. For a time he lectured on American history at London University, in 1934 was elected a Fellow of Corpus Christi College, Oxford, and in 1939 became Professor of Political Science at Cambridge and a Fellow of Peterhouse. During the Second World War he was an intelligence officer with the British Broadcasting Company and received the Legion of Honour. He was one of the greatest interpreters of American history to the British people and of the British outlook to Americans. His works include *The American Political System* (1933), *Proudhon* (1934), *Lincoln* (1935), *The Development of Modern France* (1940), *U.S.A., an Outline* (1941), *The English People* (1943), *The American Problem* (1944), *French Personalities and Problems* (1946), *American Theories* (1948), *The Era of Franklin D. Roosevelt* (1950), *The Price of Revolution* (1951), and *Politics in America* (1954). In 1941 while convalescing from an illness he wrote a detective story *Stop on the Green Light!* under the name Maurice Barrington.

Broke, *or* **Brooke, Arthur** (died 1563), translator, was the author of *The Tragicall Histoire of Romeus and Juliett*, from which Shakespeare probably took the story of his *Romeo and Juliet*. Though indirectly translated, through a French version, from the Italian of Bandello, it is altered and amplified, notably in the character of the Nurse. The only fact known regarding Broke is his death by shipwreck when crossing to France.

Brome, Richard (died 1652), dramatist, the servant and friend of Ben Jonson, produced upwards of 20 plays, some in conjunction with Dekker and others. Among them are *The Northern Lass* (1632), *Late Lancashire Witches* (1634), *A Jovial Crew* (1652), *The Antipodes* (1646), *City Wit* (1653), and *Court Beggar* (1653). He had no original genius, but knew stage-craft well.

Bromfield, Louis (27 Dec. 1896—18 March 1956), novelist, born at Mansfield, Ohio, son of a farmer, studied at Cornell and Columbia Universities. In the First World War he joined the French army as an ambulance driver, and was awarded the Croix de Guerre. For a time he worked as a dramatic critic, and was on the original staff of *Time*. His first novel, *The Green Bay Tree* (1924), tells of life in a mid-western town. Others are *Possession* (1925), *Early Autumn* (1926), which won the Pulitzer Prize, *The Strange Case of Miss Annie Spragg* (1928), *Mrs Parkington* (1943), *Colorado* (1947), and *Mr Smith* (1951). *It Had to Happen* (1936) and *It Takes All Kinds* (1939) are collections of short stories. After living for some years in France, he returned in 1939 to Ohio and bought a farm near his birth-place. *Pleasant Valley* (1943) is partly autobiographical.

Brontë, Anne (25 March 1820—28 May 1849), novelist, was the youngest and gentlest of the famous Brontë sisters, and like the others was born at Thornton and lived at Haworth on the Yorkshire moors. She had no formal education except a few months at Miss Wooler's school at Roe Head in 1835. She went as governess to the Inghams at Blake Hall in 1839 and in 1841 to the Robinsons in Thorp Green, where she remained for four years (a record for her family) but left when her brother Branwell was asked to leave because of his infatuation for Mrs Robinson. In 1845 she wrote *Agnes Grey*, a story of a governess's life, which was published in 1847 along with Emily's *Wuthering Heights*. She also contributed a few poems to the joint volume of 1846. Her second novel, *The Tenant of Wildfell Hall*, appeared in 1848, and a year later she succumbed to tuberculosis at Scarborough, where she had gone for the sea air.

Brontë, Charlotte (21 April 1816—31 March 1855), novelist, was born at Thornton, now part of Bradford, daughter of an eccentric Irish clergyman who removed with his family to Haworth on the Yorkshire moors when she was five. Her mother died of cancer in 1821 and the family of four girls and one boy were brought up by their Aunt Elizabeth, who was unsympathetic. They ran wild upon the moors, read grown-up literature, and wrote a miniature series of romances to fit a regiment of toy soldiers, Charlotte and her brother Branwell using as background an imaginary country of Angria.

D*

Part of these juvenile writings has been published as *Legends of Angria* (1933).

In 1824 all the girls except Anne, the youngest, were sent to a cheap boarding school for clergymen's daughters at Cowan Bridge. The two eldest, Maria and Elizabeth, died, and Charlotte and Emily were brought home to be educated by their father till 1831, when Charlotte went for a year to Miss Wooler's school at Roe Head. In 1835 she returned there as a teacher, but could not endure the drudgery, and tried two posts as governess with the same lack of success. The three sisters then planned to start a private school of their own, and to increase their qualifications Charlotte and Emily attended a school in Brussels. Summoned home on the death of their aunt, from whom they inherited £100 each, they advertised their projected school but got no applicants. In 1843 Charlotte went back to Brussels for a year as English teacher in the school of M. Heger, for whom she formed an attachment revealed in letters which were published in 1913. Returning to Haworth she found Branwell going downhill with drink and dissipation.

In 1845 Charlotte discovered the manuscript of Emily's poems, and after much difficulty persuaded her to let them be published. All three sisters contributed to a small joint volume, writing under the names of Currer, Ellis, and Acton Bell. They paid £50 to get it published, but in the first year (1846) only two copies were sold. Each then started novel writing. Emily's *Wuthering Heights* and Anne's *Agnes Grey* were published, but Charlotte's *The Professor* was at first rejected, and did not appear till after her death; with the rejection, however, she received encouragement which enabled her to finish *Jane Eyre*, which appeared in 1847 and immediately made her famous. At this time she visited London and made the acquaintance of Thackeray and Mrs Gaskell.

Within a year from then all the others were dead and Charlotte was left alone. She wrote *Shirley* (1849), and *Villette* (1852), which told of her days in Brussels. *Emma*, a fragment, appeared in the *Cornhill Magazine* in 1860. In 1854 she married her father's curate, Arthur Bell Nicholls, and died less than a year later. Charlotte with her restless energy was the organizing genius of the family, and has been claimed not only as one of the greatest of our women novelists but as the first writer of 'feminist' novels which transmute into a human story the drab lives of plain women. Her life was afterwards written by Mrs Gaskell (q.v.).

Brontë, Emily Jane (20 Aug. 1818—19 Dec. 1848), poetess and novelist, was born at Thornton and brought up at Haworth in Yorkshire, like her sisters Charlotte and Anne (qq.v.). She had no formal schooling except for some months at Cowan Bridge when she was 6, and a short time with Charlotte at Roe Head ten years later. All her life she showed a furious resentment of restraint and regimentation, and was the stormiest as well as, in the opinion of many, the greatest genius of the three famous sisters. In 1836 she went as a governess to a family in Halifax for six months, and later accompanied Charlotte to Heger's school in Brussels, but like the others, she disliked the drudgery teaching involved. In 1845 Charlotte discovered the manuscript of her poems, some of which dealt with the imaginary country of Gondal which Emily and Anne created in their childhood to match the Angria of Charlotte and Branwell's fancy, and persuaded her to let them be published. In the small volume of poems by the three sisters under the names of Currer, Ellis, and Acton Bell, Emily's contribution was by far the most important; it includes the well-known 'Old Stoic' and 'Last Lines,' which show the spirit of the writer's indomitable nature. A year later, in 1847, her novel *Wuthering Heights* appeared, a grim but powerful story which reflects the atmosphere of her own desolate moors. In the same year she died of consumption, on her feet to the last, having refused to see a doctor.

Brooke, Arthur, *see* Broke.

Brooke, Charlotte (1740—29 March 1793), anthologist, born at Cavan, was one of the twenty-two children of Henry Brooke (q.v.), and was educated by him, among her studies being the Irish language. Reduced to poverty after caring for her father during his last days, in 1789 she published by subscription *Reliques of Irish Poetry*, the first notable collection of translations from early Irish verse. Her *School for Christians* (1791) consisted of dialogues for the use of children.

Brooke, Fulke Greville, 1st Baron (1554—30 Sept. 1628), poet and statesman, was born at Beauchamp Court, Warwickshire, and entered Shrewsbury School in 1564 on the same day as Philip Sydney (q.v.), his lifelong friend, proceeding afterwards to Jesus College, Cambridge. He became a favourite of Queen Elizabeth, sat for Warwickshire in the House of Commons, and rose to hold various political offices, including that of Chancellor of the Exchequer. In 1621 he was made a baron by James VI and I. Brooke belonged to Gabriel Harvey's Areopagus, a group which sought to introduce classical metres into English verse. The only work published in his lifetime was a tragedy, *Mustapha* (1609). Other works, published after his death, were his *Life of Sidney* (1652) and his *Remains* (1670). His complete works were reprinted in 1870.

Brooke, Henry (1703?—10 Oct. 1783), novelist and dramatist, born in Ireland, son of a clergyman, was educated at Trinity College, Dublin, and studied law, but embraced literature as a career. He wrote poems, dramas, and novels; but the only work which has kept its place is *The Fool of Quality* (5 volumes 1766—70), which was a favourite book with John Wesley. His now forgotten poem, *Universal Beauty* (1735), was admired by Pope, and was said to have suggested Erasmus Darwin's *Botanic Garden*.

Brooke, Rupert Chawner (3 Aug. 1887—23 April 1915), poet, was born at Rugby, his father being a housemaster at the school, and educated there and at King's College, Cambridge. At school he won a prize for verse, and at Cambridge he made a special study of Elizabethan drama. After that he settled at the Old Vicarage.

Grantchester, subject of one of his most famous poems, and numbered among his friends Edward Marsh, Gosse, Drinkwater, de la Mare, W. W. Gibson, W. H. Davies, and the Asquiths. In 1911 he was made a Fellow of King's, published a small volume of *Poems*, and planned the anthology *Georgian Poetry* with Harold Monro (q.v.). In 1913 he had a year of travel, crossing America and going on to Hawaii, Samoa, Fiji, New Zealand, and Tahiti, but his plans were interrupted by the First World War. Obtaining a commission in 1914, he was with the Royal Naval Division at Antwerp, and in 1915 was sent to the Dardanelles, but died of septicaemia in Scyros, the fabled island of Achilles. Brooke's poems won great celebrity, both because the war sonnets in the posthumous volume *1914 and Other Poems* caught the prevailing spirit of splendid and selfless patriotism, and because he himself typified the flower of English youth which was being ruthlessly sacrificed in the so-called 'war to end wars.' His *Complete Poems* (1932) show his kinship with Keats and the Elizabethans. His critical volume, *John Webster and the Elizabethan Drama* was published in 1916 and his *Letters* and *Prose* in 1956.

Brooke, Stopford Augustus (14 Nov. 1832—18 March 1916), clergyman and scholar, was born near Letterkenny, County Donegal, and educated at Trinity College, Dublin. Ordained in 1857, after holding various London curacies he was from 1866 to 1875 minister of the proprietary chapel of St James, and from 1875 to 1893 at Bedford Chapel, Bloomsbury. In 1863 he went to Berlin for a time as chaplain to Prince Frederick of Prussia, and in 1867 he was appointed chaplain to Queen Victoria, but in 1880 he seceded from the English Church and adopted Unitarian views. His most successful book was his excellent little *Primer of English Literature* (1876), which sold half a million copies during his lifetime. Others were a *History of Early English Literature* (1892), studies of *Tennyson* (1894) and *Browning* (1902), *A Treasury of Irish Poetry* (1900), *On Ten Plays of Shakespeare* (1907), and *Ten More Plays from Shakespeare* (1913). He published a volume of *Poems* in 1888, and in his later years took up painting.

Brooks, Charles William Shirley (29 April 1816—23 Feb. 1874), journalist, born in London, was articled as a solicitor, but took to journalism, and contributed to various periodicals. In 1851 he joined the staff of *Punch*, to which he contributed 'Essence of Parliament,' and on the death of Mark Lemon (q.v.), he succeeded him as editor. He published a few novels, including *Aspen Court* (1855), and *The Gordian Knot* (1860).

Brooks, Maria (1794?—11 Nov. 1845), poetess, born at Medford, Massachusetts, her baptismal name being Abigail Gowen, in 1810 married John Brooks, a Boston merchant, who died in 1823, after which she wrote highly romantic and impassioned poetry. Her chief work, *Zophiël or The Bride of Swen* (1829), was finished under the auspices of Southey, who called her 'Maria del Occidente,' and regarded her as 'the most impassioned and imaginative of all poetesses,' but time has not sustained this verdict.

Brooks, Van Wyck (16 Feb. 1886—   ), critic, born at Plainfield, New Jersey, and educated at Harvard, worked for a time in England as a journalist. His first book, *The Wine of the Puritans*, a social study, appeared in 1909. From 1908 to 1911 he did lexicographical work in New York, then went to California, where he met Mark Twain and Henry James, and from 1911 to 1913 was Instructor in English at Leland Stanford University. In 1913 he returned to England and wrote *America's Coming of Age* (1915), but on the outbreak of the First World War, he returned to America and in 1920 settled at Westport, Connecticut. His best-known books are *The Ordeal of Mark Twain* (1920), *The Pilgrimage of Henry James* (1925), *The Life of Emerson* (1932), his five-volume *Makers and Finders: A History of the Writers in America, 1800—1915* (1936—52), and *A Pictorial History of American Literature* (1956), in which he collaborated with Otto L. Bettmann. *Scenes and Portraits* (1954) is a volume of reminiscences.

Broome, William (baptized 3 May 1689, died 16 Nov. 1745), poet and translator, born at Haslington, Cheshire, son of a farmer, was educated at Eton and Cambridge, then took orders, and held various incumbencies. He translated the *Iliad* in prose along with others, and was employed by Pope, whom he excelled as a Greek scholar, in his rendering of the *Odyssey*, of which he translated the 8th, 11th, 12th, 16th, 18th, and 23rd books, catching the style of his master so exactly as almost to defy identification, and thus so annoying him as to earn a niche in *The Dunciad*. He published verses of his own of very moderate poetical merit.

Brophy, John (6 Dec. 1899—   ), novelist, was born of Irish parents at Liverpool, which forms the background of two of his novels, *The Bitter End* (1928), and *Waterfront* (1934). In November 1914, while not yet 15, he enlisted and fought for four years in France and Belgium in the First World War. In collaboration with Eric Partridge (q.v.), he compiled *Songs and Slang of the British Soldier, 1914—18* (1930). After the war he took a degree at Liverpool University and studied psycho-analysis at Durham. He spent two years as a teacher in Egypt, then became chief copywriter to a London advertising agency, and subsequently a reviewer of fiction. During the Second World War he edited *John o' London's Weekly*, and wrote two war stories, *Immortal Sergeant* (1942) and *Spearhead* (1943), a story of the commandos. His other books include a novel about Shakespeare, *Gentleman of Stratford* (1939), *Portrait of an Unknown Lady* (1945), *Sarah* (1948), *Julian's Way* (1949), and *Turn the Key Softly* (1951).

Brougham, Henry Peter, 1st Baron Brougham and Vaux (19 Sept. 1778—7 May 1868), lawyer and author, was born in Edinburgh and educated at the High School and University there. Called to the Scottish Bar in 1800 and to the English Bar in 1810, he became famous through his splendid defence of Queen Caroline when she was accused of adultery. Entering Parliament in 1830, he rose to be Lord Chancellor, and was celebrated for his reforms of the laws of libel and of evidence. He took part in founding London University, the Society for the Diffusion of Useful Knowledge, and the *Edinburgh Review*, to which he contributed extensively. He also wrote a prodigious number of works on history and philosophy, of which the most important are *Historical Sketches of Statesmen who Flourished in the Time of George III* (1843), and his last publication, an autobiography written in his eighty-fourth year.

Broughton, John Cam Hobhouse, 1st Baron (27 June 1786—3 June 1869), eldest son of Sir Benjamin Hobhouse, born at Redland near Bristol, was educated at Westminster School and at Cambridge, where he became intimate with Byron; he accompanied him in his journeys in the Peninsula, Greece, and Turkey, and acted as best man at his wedding. In 1816 he was with Byron after his separation from his wife, and contributed notes to the fourth canto of *Childe Harold*, which was dedicated to him. On his return he threw himself into politics with great energy as an advanced Radical, and wrote various pamphlets, for one of which he was in 1819 imprisoned in Newgate. In the following year he entered Parliament, sitting for Westminster. After the attainment of power by the Whigs he held various offices, including those of Secretary at War, Chief Secretary for Ireland, and President of the Board of Control. He published *Journey through Albania* (1813), *Historical Illustrations of the Fourth Canto of Childe Harold* (1818), and *Recollections of a Long Life* (1865), for private circulation, and he left in manuscript *Diaries, Correspondence, and Memoranda*, not to be opened till 1900, extracts from which were published by his daughter Lady Dorchester in 1909.

Broughton, Rhoda (29 Nov. 1840—5 June 1920), novelist, born near Denbigh in Wales, the daughter of a clergyman, was brought up in Staffordshire, but after her father's death lived in North Wales and later at Oxford. Her first two novels, published when she was 27, were *Not Wisely but Too Well*, and *Cometh Up as a Flower*, both of which were in those days reckoned very daring. Thereafter she wrote at the rate of about one novel every two years, among the best-known being *Red as a Rose is She* (1870), *Dr Cupid* (1886), *A Waif's Progress* (1905), and *The Devil and the Deep Sea* (1910). Her books give an entertaining picture of country life in the latter half of the nineteenth century.

Brown, Alice (5 Dec. 1857—21 June 1948), novelist, born on a farm at Hampton Falls, New Hampshire, and educated at Exeter close by, was a teacher for some time and in 1885 joined the staff of *Youth's Companion*. Her first novel, *Love and I*, by 'Martin Redfield,' was told from a man's standpoint. She wrote many short stories of New England life, some of which are collected in *Meadow-Grass* (1895), and *Tiverton Tales* (1899). Her novels include *The Prisoner* (1916), *The Mysteries of Anne* (1925), and *Dear Old Templeton* (1927). In 1915 she won the Winthrop Ames Prize of 10,000 dollars with her play *Children of Earth*. *By Oak and Thorn* (1896) tells of a walking tour in Wales. She also wrote a biography of her friend *Louise Imogen Guiney* (1921).

Brown, Charles Brockden (17 Jan. 1771—22 Feb. 1810), novelist, born in Philadelphia, belonged to a Quaker family, became a lawyer, but exchanged law for literature, and has the distinction of being the first American to adopt a purely literary career. He wrote several novels, including *Wieland* (1798), *Ormond* (1799), *Arthur Mervyn* (1800—1), and his last, *Jane Talbot* (1801). With a good deal of crudeness and sentimentality he has occasional power, but dwells too much on the horrible and repulsive, the result, perhaps, of the morbidity produced by the ill-health from which he all his life suffered.

Brown, George Douglas (26 Jan. 1869—28 Aug. 1902), novelist, born at Ochiltree, Ayrshire, son of a farmer, was educated at Ayr Academy, Glasgow University, and Oxford, after which he settled in London and supported himself by private tuition and reviewing. In 1899, under the pen-name of Kennedy King, he published a boys' book, *Love and a Sword*, and in 1900 he rented a cottage at Hindhead and under the name George Douglas produced the novel by which he is remembered, *The House with the Green Shutters* (1901), a realist counterblast to the Scottish kailyard school. He died unexpectedly in the hour of his success while on a visit to London.

Brown, Ivor John Carnegie (25 April 1891—   ), journalist, born at Penang, son of a doctor, was educated at Cheltenham and Oxford. He entered the Civil Service in 1913, but abandoned it for journalism. He was dramatic critic successively of the *Manchester Guardian*, the *Saturday Review*, the *Weekend Review*, the *Sketch*, and *Punch*, and from 1942 to 1948 was editor of the *Observer*. In 1915 he published a novel, *Years of Plenty*. Other works were *The Meaning of Democracy* (1920), *Masques and Phases* (1927), *Brown Studies* (1930), and *I Commit to the Flames* (1934). He also wrote studies of *H. G. Wells* (1922), and *Shakespeare* (1949), and a series of half a dozen 'word-anthologies,' beginning with *A Word in Your Ear* (1942). In 1939 he was Professor of Drama of the Royal Society of Literature, and from 1940 to 1942 Director of Drama for the Council for the Encouragement of Music and the Arts.

Brown, John (5 Nov. 1715—23 Sept. 1766), poet and playwright, born in Northumberland and educated at Wigton, where his father was curate, and at Cambridge, took orders and became a minor canon of Carlisle. In addition to the poems *Honour* (1743), *Liberty* (1749), and *An Essay on Satire*, he wrote two tragedies, *Barbarossa* (1754), and *Athelstane* (1756), in which Garrick appeared. His *Estimate of the Manners and Principles of the Times* (1757), an attack on the laxness of the age, was highly praised. He was invited to go to St Petersburg as adviser on Russian education, but committed suicide when his doctor forbade the journey.

Brown, John (22 Sept. 1810—11 May 1882), doctor and essayist, was born at Biggar, where his father, a famous biblical scholar, was minister, and educated at the High School and University of Edinburgh. During an uneventful life as a general practitioner in Edinburgh he wrote a number of delightful essays, among which are

'Rab and his Friends,' 'Pet Marjorie,' 'Our Dogs,' 'Minchmoor,' and 'The Enterkine.' These were collected along with papers on art, and medical history and biography, in *Horae Subsecivae* (Leisure Hours). In the mingling of tenderness and delicate humour he has much in common with Lamb and in his insight into dog-nature he is unsurpassed.

Brown, Thomas (1663—16 June 1704), satirist, was born at Shifnal in Shropshire and studied at Christ Church, Oxford, where he made the famous epigram on the Dean, beginning 'I do not love thee, Dr Fell.' Later he made amends by writing Fell's epitaph. He was for a few years schoolmaster at Kingston-upon-Thames, but owing to his irregularities lost the appointment, and went to London, where he wrote satires, epigrams, and miscellaneous pieces, generally coarse and scurrilous. He was buried in the cloisters of Westminster Abbey.

Brown, Thomas (9 Jan. 1778—2 April 1820), metaphysician, son of a minister, studied medicine at Edinburgh and practised for some time there; but his tastes and talents lying in the direction of literature and philosophy, he devoted himself to the cultivation of these, and succeeded Dugald Stewart as Professor of Moral Philosophy in the University of Edinburgh, in which position he had remarkable popularity as a lecturer. His main contribution to literature is his *Lectures*, which ran to twenty editions, but are now out of date.

Brown, Thomas Edward (5 May 1830—30 Oct. 1897), poet, born at Douglas, Isle of Man, where his father was vicar, and educated at King William's College and Christ Church, Oxford, took a Double First and became a Fellow of Oriel. After being vice-principal of his old school from 1858 to 1861, he became one of the original staff of masters at Clifton, where he remained for nearly thirty years. His narrative poems in the Manx dialect made his literary reputation, his chief works being *Fo'c'sle Yarns* (1881), *The Doctor and Other Poems* (1887), *The Manx Witch* (1889), and *Old John* (1893). His *Collected Poems* were edited by Henley in 1900, and his *Letters* were published in the same year.

Browne, Charles Farrar (26 April 1834—6 March 1867), humorist who adopted the pseudonym of Artemus Ward, was born in Waterford, Maine, the son of a civil engineer. He learned the printing trade, and worked for various country newspapers as compositor and writer, his earliest literary production, 'The Surrender of Cornwallis' appearing in the Boston *Carpet Bag* in 1852. At Cleveland, Ohio, he adopted the name of Artemus Ward from some old records of land surveys carried out by one of his forbears, and from 1858 he started the fiction of being a travelling showman of waxworks and tame animals. In the following year he joined the staff of *Vanity Fair* in New York, and his contributions were collected as *Artemus Ward. His Book* (1862). President Lincoln enjoyed his work, and opened the fateful Cabinet meeting of 22 September 1862, which resulted in proclaiming freedom for slaves, by reading Ward's 'High Handed Outrage in Utica.' Going on a lecture tour, he worked through

California and Nevada to Salt Lake City, then returned to New York and lectured on 'Artemus Ward among the Mormons.' In 1866 he sailed for England, where he made the Savage Club his head-quarters, and contributed to *Punch*, but died in the following year at Southampton of consumption. Like other American humorists, Ward secured his comic effects partly by pretended illiteracy, bad spelling, and outrageous puns; to this he added an irresistible sense of fun which made Charles Reade call him 'Artemus the Delicious.' His *Complete Works* appeared in 1871.

Browne, Isaac Hawkins (21 Jan. 1705—14 Feb. 1760), poet, born at Burton-on-Trent, where his father was vicar, and educated at Westminster and Cambridge, is remembered as the author of some clever imitations of contemporary poets on the theme of *A Pipe of Tobacco*, somewhat analogous to the *Rejected Addresses* of a later day. He also wrote a Latin poem on the immortality of the soul. Browne, who was a barrister and M.P., had great conversational powers. He was a friend of Dr Johnson.

Browne, Sir Thomas (19 Oct. 1605—19 Oct. 1682), doctor and author, son of a London merchant, was educated at Winchester and Oxford, after which he studied medicine at various Continental universities, including Leyden, where he graduated. He ultimately settled and practised at Norwich. His first and perhaps best-known work, *Religio Medici* (the Religion of a Physician) was published in 1642. Other books are *Pseudodoxia Epidemica: Enquiries into Vulgar Errors* (1646), *Hydriotaphia, or Urn-burial* (1658); and *The Garden of Cyrus* in the same year. After his death were published his *Letter to a Friend* and *Christian Morals*. Browne is one of the most original writers in the English language. Though by no means free from credulity, and dealing largely with trivial subjects of inquiry, the freshness and ingenuity of his mind invest everything he touches with interest; while on more important subjects his style, if frequently rugged and pedantic, often rises to the highest pitch of grave and stately eloquence. His influence is seen later in such writers as Lamb, Coleridge, and De Quincey. In the Civil War he sided with the King's party, and was knighted in 1671 on the occasion of a Royal visit to Norwich.

Browne, Thomas Alexander (6 Aug. 1826—11 March 1915), nove-list who wrote under the name of Rolf Boldrewood, was born in London and taken to Australia in infancy by his father, one of the founders of Melbourne. After experience as a squatter in western Victoria and as a sheep-farmer in New South Wales, he became a police magistrate and gold-fields commissioner. His literary reputa-tion rests on his exciting novels telling of the early days of bush-rangers and the gold rush, of which the best are *Robbery Under Arms* (1888) and *The Miner's Right* (1890). His *Old Melbourne Memories* (1895) contains vivid sketches of life on the cattle stations.

Browne, William (1590?—1645?), poet, born at Tavistock, was educated at Oxford, after which he entered the Inner Temple. His poems, which are mainly descriptive, are rich and flowing, and true to the phenomena of nature, but deficient in interest. Influenced by Spenser, he in turn had an influence upon such poets as Milton and Keats. His chief works were *Britannia's Pastorals* (1613), and *The Shepheard's Pipe* (1614).

Browning, Elizabeth Barrett (6 March 1806—30 June 1861), poetess, was born Elizabeth Barrett Moulton, her father later changing his name to Barrett. Her original home was Coxhoe Hall, in the county of Durham, but she spent her girlhood in Herefordshire at a house called Hope End. Very precocious, she read Homer in Greek at the age of 8, and her juvenile epic, *The Battle of Marathon*, was privately printed when she was 14. Shortly afterwards a fall from a pony caused spinal injury which compelled her to lie on her back for years, with the result that she never went to school. After her mother's death in 1826 the family moved to Wimpole Street, London. In the same year was published an *Essay on Mind* which she wrote at 18. Her translation of Aeschylus's *Prometheus Bound* (1833) was followed in 1838 by *The Seraphim and Other Poems*, which included the well-known 'Cowper's Grave.' It was at this period that her friend Mary Russell Mitford (q.v.) describes her as 'a slight, delicate figure, with a shower of dark curls falling on each side of a most expressive face; large, tender eyes, richly fringed by dark eyelashes, and a smile like a sunbeam.'

In that same year she suffered a tragic shock which changed her whole life, her favourite brother being drowned on a boating trip at Torquay within sight of the house. She had already been threatened with lung disease, and from that time onwards lived in a darkened room, with few visitors. But she read omnivorously in many languages, and continued to write, becoming famous through her poems, two more volumes of which appeared in 1844. Through admiration of them, Robert Browning, then a little-known poet and six years her junior, began a correspondence and in 1846 was introduced by a friend. They fell in love and decided to elope, in spite of her supposed helpless condition. The step was not so rash as it might appear, for she had been advised on medical grounds to winter abroad, though her father, who was almost insanely jealous and tyrannical, would not hear of this. On 12 September she managed to slip out of the house and married Browning without her father's knowledge, and a week later the couple went off to Paris. Barrett, the perfect example of the 'Victorian' father, never forgave her and never saw her again. But the runaway match, however dangerous, cured her invalidism. The union was ideally happy, she lived to be over 55, and had a son.

The Brownings settled first at Pisa, then in Florence, where they had a floor in the Palazzo Guidi, became known to all the English celebrities then in Italy, and made occasional trips to Paris, Rome, and London. Mrs Browning continued her writing with *Casa Guidi Windows* (1851), which was inspired by her sympathy with the Italian struggle for freedom. Her *Poems* (1850), contained the famous *Sonnets from the Portuguese*, which are not translations but the intensely personal utterance of a wife's feelings for her husband.

In 1856 appeared *Aurora Leigh*, a romance in blank verse, which tells the story of her life and is not very successful. *Poems Before Congress* (1860) and *Last Poems* (1862), dealing chiefly with political themes, were written when her health was failing. She died in her husband's arms, of consumption, and is buried in the Protestant cemetery in Florence. Her *Letters* were published in 1897.

Throughout her lifetime Mrs Browning was much more famous than her husband, and though her work is now less admired she disputes with Christina Rossetti the title of greatest English poetess. She ranks high through the depth of feeling which makes her one of the greatest interpreters of love as viewed from the woman's standpoint. Much of her work, such as the famous 'Cry of the Children' had a political or social appeal which is now only historical. But her greatest weakness is in the matter of poetical technique. Slipshod rhymes like 'angels'—'candles' and 'mountains'—'dauntings' are common, and her use of words is often inaccurate and arbitrary, with such solecisms as 'oftly' and 'fantasque.' A tendency to over-luxuriance was curbed when she used the rigid sonnet form, hence the success of the *Sonnets from the Portuguese*, her greatest work. As a sonnet writer she ranks little behind Milton and Wordsworth.

Browning, Oscar (17 Jan. 1837—6 Oct. 1923), historian, born in London, was educated at Eton, where his tutor was W. J. Cory (q.v.), and King's College, Cambridge, where he became President of the Union. In 1859 he was made a Fellow of King's, and from 1860 to 1875 was an assistant master at Eton, where he encouraged artistic and musical activities in preference to athletics. Returning to King's, he was a popular history lecturer and took a leading part in the social life of the college. His last years were spent in Rome, where he became President of the British Academy of Arts. During this period he wrote *A History of the Modern World, 1815—1910* (1912), *A General History of the World* (1913), and *A Short History of Italy, 375—1915* (1917).

Browning, Robert (7 May 1812—12 Dec. 1889), poet, was born in Camberwell, then a suburb of London. His father was a clerk in the Bank of England, and his mother, Sarah Anna Wiedemann, was of German-Scottish extraction. Robert was educated mainly at home, with little systematic schooling except for some classes in Greek at London University. A beautiful, impetuous boy, he decided at the age of 17 to be a poet, and all his early works were published at his father's expense. His first poem, *Pauline* (1833) shows the influence of Shelley. Little notice was taken of it, and it was partly this early failure of an intensely personal utterance that turned him to the form of dramatic monologue which he made peculiarly his own. *Paracelsus* (1835), the story of one of those out-of-the-way medieval characters who appear so often in his work, was followed by *Sordello* (1840), a long involved poem which started the reputation for obscurity which its writer only partly deserved. At this time also Browning made his first attempt in drama with *Strafford*, which Macready produced at Covent Garden in 1837.

Like his other plays, *King Victor and King Charles* (1842), *The Return of the Druses* (1843), *A Blot in the Scutcheon* (1843), *Colombe's Birthday* (1844), and *Luria* (1846), it fails through excess of psychological analysis. The essence of drama is character in action, but Browning's depiction of character is static, not dynamic.

Far more successful was the dramatic poem *Pippa Passes*, which was written after a visit to Italy and formed part of *Bells and Pomegranates* (a title taken from Exodus xxviii. 33—4), which was published in several sections between 1841 and 1846. The sections *Dramatic Lyrics* (1842) and *Dramatic Romances* (1845), contain many poems of lasting popularity, such as the 'Cavalier Tunes,' 'How They Brought the Good News From Ghent to Aix,' 'The Lost Leader,' 'Home Thoughts from Abroad,' and 'The Pied Piper of Hamelin.' In 1846 he made his romantic runaway marriage with Elizabeth Barrett (*see* Elizabeth Barrett Browning) and lived happily with her until her death sixteen years later, staying chiefly at Florence, in Italy. It was at Florence that their son, Robert Wiedemann Barrett Browning, was born, and *Christmas Eve and Easter Day* was written, a monument to Browning's mother, who died in 1849. There too he further developed the dramatic monologue in *Men and Women* (1855), which contained fifty of his finest poems, such as 'Love Among the Ruins,' 'Evelyn Hope,' 'Fra Lippo Lippi,' 'The Last Ride Together,' and 'The Grammarian's Funeral.' In the definitive edition of his works a great part of this volume was distributed among the others.

After his wife's death in 1861 Browning left Florence, never to return. He settled in London and became a social figure, his sister Sarianna keeping house for him and his son, nicknamed 'Pen,' who later became a sculptor. *Dramatis Personae* (1864) embodied the poet's views on religious and moral questions, and included 'Rabbi Ben Ezra,' 'Caliban upon Setebos,' and 'Prospice.' Then followed what is recognized as his greatest achievement, *The Ring and the Book* (1868—9), which relates in some 21,000 lines the trial of the medieval Count Guido Franceschini for the murder of his wife, and consists of ten dramatic monologues, giving the same story from ten points of view, yet never flagging in interest and intensity. From this time onwards Browning was recognized as the greatest English poet after Tennyson. He was made an honorary M.A. of Oxford, and an honorary Fellow of Balliol, and in 1881 a Browning Society was formed. In 1869, thinking mainly of 'Pen's' welfare, he proposed marriage to the wealthy Lady Ashburton, but the offer was rejected.

In 1871 appeared *Prince Hohenstiel-Schwangau*, a monologue referring to Napoleon III, and in 1872 *Fifine at the Fair*, one of his more obscure works. It was followed in 1873 by *Red Cotton Nightcap Country*, a tragic poem which takes its title from the garb of the fisher folk of Normandy, where its scene is laid. Next came *The Inn Album* (1875), a purely narrative work, and after it the extraordinary poem *Of Pacchiarotto, and How he Worked in Distemper*, which concludes with a flood of invective against the poet's critics and contains the famous rhyme of 'ranunculus' with 'Tommy-make-

room-for-your-uncle us.' Two works appeared in 1878, *La Saisiaz*, another metaphysical poem, and *The Two Poets of Croisic*, which is introduced by one of his most perfect lyrics. Great as the work of this period is, it has less appeal than that of his youth, and gives some force to the criticism that 'Browning wrote too much.'

His interest in classical as well as medieval themes had been shown by his renderings of the *Alcestis* of Euripides, which forms part of *Balaustion's Adventure* (1871), and of the *Agamemnon* of Aeschylus (1877). In 1879 he published *Dramatic Idylls*, a series of vigorous character sketches including 'Pheidippides' and 'Ivan Ivanovitch,' and in 1883 *Jocoseria*, with the oft-quoted 'Never the time and the place.' *Ferishtah's Fancies* appeared in 1884 and in 1888 the literary world was startled by the furious 'Lines to Edward FitzGerald,' which were provoked by a passage in which that poet and critic (q.v.) had disparaged Mrs Browning. Soon afterwards Browning was on his last visit to Italy. *Asolando*, written at Asolo, scene of *Pippa Passes*, where he had planned to have a house called Pippa's Tower, was published on the day that he died in Venice, the magnificent 'Epilogue' which bids us 'Greet the unseen with a cheer' forming a perfect closing utterance to his work. He was brought back to England and buried in Westminster Abbey. The definitive edition of his works was published in 1896.

Browning's perpetual optimism gives a tonic quality to all his work, which maintains throughout the duty of self-development and self-expression. He has been described as a strange blend of Victorian knowledge, Renaissance curiosity, and medieval pedantry, and it is true that in much of his work a sense of the grotesque seems to replace a sense of the beautiful. His intense interest in individual men and women makes him essentially a poet of character as Tennyson was a poet of form. The charge of obscurity so often levelled at him is due mainly to over-compression; his short lyrics, by which he is best remembered, are in most cases simple and direct.

Bruce, James (14 Dec. 1730—27 April 1794), explorer, born at Kinnaird, Stirlingshire, was educated at Harrow and Edinburgh University, where he studied law but disliked it. Although of delicate constitution, he trained himself by exercise and sport till he was athletic, daring, and 6 feet 4 inches in height. After some years as a wine-merchant in London and then as consul in Algiers, he set out in 1768 from Cairo in disguise to explore Abyssinia. In 1770 he reached the head stream of the Blue Nile, then supposed to be the main river, and returned to Scotland in 1774. His *Travels to Discover the Source of the Nile* (1790) was published in 5 volumes with plates and charts, but contained such curious information that parts of it were at first discredited. Bruce eventually died as the result of a fall.

Bruce, Michael (27 March 1746—5 July 1767), poet, son of a poor weaver at Kinnesswood, Kinross-shire, as a child herded cattle, but received a good education, including four sessions at the University of Edinburgh, and for a short time kept a school. His longest poem, *Loch Leven*, shows the influence of Thomson. His best is his *Elegy*—

Written in Spring. His promising career was cut short by consumption in 1767. The authorship of his beautiful 'Ode to the Cuckoo,' beginning 'Hail, beauteous stranger of the grove' has been contested, some authorities claiming it for the Rev. John Logan (q.v.), who edited Bruce's works.

Brunne, Robert of, *see* **Mannyng.**

Brunton, Mary (1 Nov. 1778—19 Dec. 1818), novelist, daughter of Col. Balfour of Elwick, was born on Burray in the Orkneys, and married the. Rev. Dr Brunton, Professor of Oriental Languages in the University of Edinburgh. Her two novels, *Self-Control* (1811), and *Discipline* (1814), were popular in their day.

Bryant, Sir Arthur Wynne Morgan (18 Feb. 1899—   ), historian, born at Dersingham in Norfolk, son of Sir Francis Bryant, was educated at Harrow and Oxford and was called to the Bar at the Inner Temple. During the First World War he was a pilot in the Royal Flying Corps. His works include three volumes on Samuel Pepys, *The Man in the Making* (1933), *The Years of Peril* (1935), and *The Saviour of the Navy* (1938); lives of *King Charles II* (1934), *George V* (1936), and *Stanley Baldwin* (1937); and a British historical series, *The Years of Endurance, 1793—1802* (1942), *Years of Victory, 1802—1812* (1944), and *The Age of Elegance, 1812—1832* (1950). *English Saga* (1940) is a survey of the last hundred years, and *The Turn of the Tide* (1957), based on the diaries of Field Marshal Lord Alanbrooke, deals with the Second World War. Bryant was made a C.B.E. in 1949 and knighted in 1954.

Bryant, Jacob (1715—14 Nov. 1804), scholar, born at Plymouth, and educated at Eton and King's College, Cambridge, of which he became a Fellow, wrote learnedly but paradoxically on mythological and Homeric subjects. His chief works were *A New System or Analysis of Ancient Mythology* (1774—6), *Observations on the Plain of Troy* (1795), and *Dissertation concerning the Wars of Troy* (1796). In the last two he endeavoured to show that the existence of Troy and the Greek expedition were fabulous.

Bryant, William Cullen (3 Nov. 1794—12 June 1878), poet, son of a doctor, was born at a farmhouse in Cummington, Massachusetts, and educated at Williams College, Williamstown. He studied law and was admitted to the Bar in 1815, but gave it up for writing. His *Poems* (1821) contained the remarkable 'Thanatopsis,' written when he was 17, and the well-known stanzas 'To a Waterfowl.' In 1825 he moved to New York, where he was co-editor of the *New York Review,* and from 1829, as editor of the *Evening Post,* took an important part in guiding popular opinion. His connection with this paper lasted for over half a century and left him little time for verse, but he published another volume of poems in 1832 and followed this with *The Fountain* (1842), and *The White-Footed Doe* (1844). In 1871 he translated Homer into blank verse. His *Complete Works* were published in 4 volumes in 1884. Claimed as the father of American poetry, Bryant has been called 'a stately moralist in verse.' His work shows a strong feeling for nature.

Bryce, James Bryce, Viscount, O.M. (10 May 1838—22 Jan. 1922), historian and statesman, was born at Belfast, son of a Scottish schoolmaster, and educated at Glasgow University and Oxford, where he was President of the Union and became a Fellow of Oriel. In 1863 he won the Arnold Historical Essay Prize with his *Holy Roman Empire,* which was later substantially expanded and became a standard work. Having studied law at Heidelberg, he was called to the Bar in 1867 and in 1870 was appointed Professor of Civil Law at Oxford. In 1880 he was elected as a Liberal M.P., and rose to be successively Chancellor of the Duchy of Lancaster, President of the Board of Trade, and Chief Secretary for Ireland. From 1907 to 1913 he was ambassador to the United States. Among his works are *The American Commonwealth* (1888), *Studies in Contemporary Biography* (1903), and *South America: Observations and Impressions* (1912). A keen mountain climber, he was President of the Alpine Club, Mount Bryce in the Rockies being named after him. He received honorary degrees from over thirty universities, was a Fellow of the Royal Society, and was awarded the Order of Merit in 1907 and created a Viscount in 1914.

Brydges, Sir Samuel Egerton (30 Nov. 1762—8 Sept. 1837), bibliographer and genealogist, educated at King's School, Canterbury, and Cambridge, was called to the Bar in 1787, but never practised. He wrote some novels and poems, now forgotten, but rendered valuable service by his bibliographical publications, *Censura Literaria, Titles and Opinions of Old English Books* (10 volumes, 1805—9), his editions of E. Phillips's *Theatrum Poetarum Anglicanorum* (1800), Collins's *Peerage of England* (1812), and of many rare Elizabethan authors. He was M.P. for Maidstone (1812—18) and was made a Baronet in 1814.

Buchan, Anna (died 24 Nov. 1948), novelist who wrote under the name of Olive Douglas, was born at Kirkcaldy, where her father was a Free Church minister, and was a sister of John Buchan (q.v.). Her father was later called to Glasgow, where she attended Hutcheson's Grammar School and the University. Her novel *The Setons* (1917) gives a delightful picture of Glasgow suburban life, but her first was *Olivia in India* (1913), written after a visit to her brother William, who was in the Indian Civil Service. For more than forty years she was mistress of Bank House, the family home in Peebles (the Priorsford of her books), and there she wrote many novels about Fife or the Border country from which her family originally came. The best known are *Penny Plain* (1920), *Ann and her Mother* (1922), *Pink Sugar* (1924), *Eliza for Common* (1928), *Priorsford* (1932), and *The House that is Our Own* (1940). *Unforgettable, Unforgotten* (1945) is an autobiography.

Buchan, John, 1st Baron Tweedsmuir (26 Aug. 1875—11 Feb. 1940), statesman and novelist, a Borderer by extraction, was born in Perth, son of a minister, and educated at Glasgow University and Oxford, where he had a brilliant career and was President of the Union. In 1901 he was called to the Bar at the Middle Temple. As assistant private secretary to Lord Milner in South Africa from 1901 to 1903 he gained practical experience of statesmanship. Of his long list of adventure stories the best known are *The Watcher by the Threshold* (1902), *Prester John* (1910), *The Thirty-Nine Steps* (1915), *Greenmantle* (1916), *The Power House* (1916), *Mr Standfast* (1919), *Huntingtower* (1922), and *The Three Hostages* (1924). During the First World War he became Director of Information and wrote a history of the war in 24 volumes, which was later abridged. Among his other historical works were biographies of *Montrose* (1928), *Sir Walter Scott* (1932), *Cromwell* (1934), and *Augustus* (1937). His *Poems, Scots and English* appeared in 1917. From 1927 to 1935 he was Conservative M.P. for Scottish Universities, and in 1935, on his appointment as Governor-General of Canada, was given the G.C.M.G. and a peerage. He had already been made a Companion of Honour in 1932, and in 1938 he was Chancellor of Edinburgh University. His autobiography, *Memory Hold-the-Door*, appeared in 1940.

Buchanan, George (Feb. 1506—29 Sept. 1582), scholar, was born at Killearn in Stirlingshire, and educated at the Universities of St Andrews and Paris. For writing two satires against the Franciscans, the *Somnium* and the *Franciscanus*, he was imprisoned by Cardinal Beaton, but escaped to Bordeaux and taught Latin at the College de Guyenne, Montaigne being one of his pupils. In 1548 he was appointed head of a college in Coimbra, Portugal. Confined in a monastery as a suspected heretic, he wrote a poetic Latin version of the Psalms. In 1560 he returned to Scotland, and though a Pro-testant was appointed tutor to Queen Mary, but sided against her after Darnley's murder. In 1566 he became Principal of St Leonard's College at St Andrews, and in 1567 was Moderator of the General Assembly of the Church of Scotland. Subsequently he was tutor to the young James VI, and taught him the learning for which he was afterwards famous. From 1570 to 1578 he was Keeper of the Privy Seal. His chief works were *De Jure Regni* (Concerning the Law of the Kingdom), published in 1579, and *Rerum Scoticarum Historia* (History of Scottish Affairs), which appeared in the year of his death. He also wrote two tragedies, *Baptistes* (1554) and *Jepthes* (1578). His *Vernacular Writings* were edited in 1892 by P. Hume Brown. Buchanan is claimed as Scotland's greatest humanist, and had a European reputation as a Latin poet.

Buchanan, Robert Williams (18 Aug. 1841—10 June 1901), poet and novelist, was born at Caverswall, Staffordshire. In 1850 his father removed to Glasgow, and Robert was educated at Glasgow Academy, High School, and University. In 1860 he went to London and wrote for a living, becoming acquainted with Dickens, Peacock, George Eliot, and Browning. In 1865 he published *Idylls and Legends of Inverburn*, and in 1866 *London Poems*. From that year to 1874 he lived near Oban, writing verse and prose sketches, includ-ing *The Land of Lorne* (1871), which describes a yachting tour. A controversy with the Pre-Raphaelites was provoked by his article 'The Fleshly School of Poetry' in the *Contemporary Review* for October 1871. There was a libel action, as a result of which Buchanan was awarded £150, but afterwards he withdrew his allegations. In 1874 he settled at Rossport, County Mayo, and wrote his first novel, *The Shadow of the Sword* (1876). Finally he returned to London, where he produced his most powerful novel, *God and the Man* (1881). His play, *A Nine Days' Queen* (1880) was followed by many others, some written in collaboration with G. R. Sims. In 1900 Buchanan went bankrupt, and died in poverty.

Buck, Pearl (26 June 1892—), novelist, the daughter of Absalom Sydenstricker, a missionary, was born at Hillsboro, West Virginia, but was taken to China at an early age and educated at a boarding-school in Shanghai. In 1917 she married Dr J. L. Buck, a missionary; they lived first in North China, then in Nanking, where she taught English at the University. Her first book, *East Wind, West Wind*, appeared in 1929. *The Good Earth* (1931), the greatest of her Chinese novels, won the Pulitzer Prize and the Howells Medal of the American Academy of Art and Letters, and led ultimately to her receiving the Nobel Prize for Literature in 1938. Later works were *Sons* (1931), *Dragon Seed* (1942), *Peony* (1948), *The Child who Never Grew* (1951), *The Hidden Flower* (1952), *My Several Worlds* (1954), and a number of books for children.

Buckingham, George Villiers, 2nd Duke of (30 Jan. 1628—16 April 1687), dramatist, son of the 1st Duke, who was in 1628 assassinated by Felton, was educated at Trinity College, Cambridge, where he became a friend of Abraham Cowley (q.v.). His life was full of adventure and change of fortune. The Restoration gave him back his already twice lost estates, which he again squandered by a life of wild extravagance and profligacy at Court. He was a member of the 'Cabal' and intrigued against Clarendon. He wrote pamphlets, lampoons, and plays, but his chief contribution to literature was *The Rehearsal* (1671), a comedy, in which he satirized the heroic drama of Dryden and others. It is believed that Samuel Butler (q.v.) had a hand in it. Dryden had his revenge in his picture of Buckingham as Zimri in *Absalom and Achitophel*.

Buckingham and Normanby, John Sheffield, 1st Duke of (7 April 1648—24 Feb. 1721), son of the 2nd Earl of Mulgrave, served in his youth as a soldier under Prince Rupert and Turenne. He was a Privy Councillor under James II, William and Mary, and Anne, with the last of whom he remained a favourite. His magnificent mansion was purchased and pulled down to make way for Buckingham Palace. He wrote *An Account of the Revolution, An Essay on Satire*, and *An Essay on Poetry* (1682). He also remodelled Shakespeare's *Julius Caesar*, making two plays of it.

Buckingham, James Silk (25 Aug. 1786—30 June 1855), traveller, was born at Flushing, near Falmouth. After a youth spent at sea, he joined the staff of the *Calcutta Journal*. In 1823 he was expelled from India for making attacks on the Government, but later he was given a pension of £200 by the East India Company. Returning to England after travelling in the East, he founded and edited various journals, including the *Athenaeum*, which began in January 1828. From 1832 to 1837 he was M.P. for Sheffield, then set out again on his travels, which he made the subject of some 20 books, including *Travels in Palestine* (1822), *Among the Arab Tribes* (1825), *In Mesopotamia* (1827), *In Assyria, Media, and Persia* (1830), and a number about various parts of America and of Europe. His *Autobiography* appeared in 1855.

Buckland, Francis Trevelyan (17 Dec. 1826—19 Dec. 1880), naturalist, born and educated at Oxford, where his father was a canon of Christ Church, studied medicine in London, and was assistant-surgeon in the Life Guards. An enthusiastic lover of natural history, he wrote largely upon it, among his works being *Curiosities of Natural History* (4 volumes 1857—72), *Log Book of a Fisherman and Zoologist* (1876), and *Natural History of British Fishes* (1881). He also founded and edited *Land and Water*. He was for a time Inspector of Salmon Fisheries, and served on various commissions. Though observant, he was not always strictly scientific in his methods and modes of expression, and he was a strong opponent of Darwin.

Buckle, Henry Thomas (24 Nov. 1821—29 May 1862), historian, son of a London shipowner, was born at Lee in Kent. Though never at a university and little at school, he received a high degree of education privately, and inheriting an ample fortune and a large library, he devoted himself to travel and study, with the view of preparing for a great work, which he had projected, *The History of Civilization in England*. As an introduction to this he entered upon the consideration of the state of civilization in various other countries, but this he had scarcely completed when his death took place at Damascus in 1862. The first volume was published in 1857, and the second in 1861 forming a fragment only of the whole, which was to have extended to 14 volumes. It did, however, embody a new idea of history. Buckle was one of the greatest chess-players in Europe.

Budgell, Eustace (19 Aug. 1686—4 May 1737), essayist, educated at Oxford, was a cousin of Addison, who took him to Ireland and got him appointed to a lucrative office, which, however, he was foolish enough to throw away by lampooning the Viceroy. He contributed to the *Spectator*, of which he wrote 37 numbers signed X. In these he imitates Addison's style with some success. Budgell, who was vain and vindictive, fell on evil days, lost a fortune in the South Sea Bubble, was accused of forging a will, and committed suicide by throwing himself out of a boat at London Bridge.

Bull, George (25 March 1634—17 Feb. 1710), theologian, born at Wells, educated at Tiverton and Oxford, took orders, was ordained by an ejected bishop in 1658, and received the living of Suddington near Bristol. He was a strong Royalist, and was privy to a scheme for bringing back the Royal family. After the Restoration he obtained further preferment, and became in 1704 Bishop of St David's. Among his works are *Harmonia Apostolica* (1669—70) in which he endeavoured to reconcile alleged discrepancies between the teaching of St Paul and St James on the relation between faith and works, *Defensio Fidei Nicaenae* (1685) and *Corruptions of the Church of Rome* (1705—7).

Bullen, Frank Thomas (5 April 1857—26 Feb. 1915), writer of sea stories, was born in Paddington of working-class parents, and at the age of 12 was a cabin boy on his uncle's ship *Arabella*. At 18, when in New Bedford, Massachusetts, he signed on in the *Cachalot*, which became the scene of his best book, *The Cruise of the 'Cachalot'* (1898), which told of the whale-fishing. At the age of 27 he became a clerk in the London Meteorological Office, and after that took to writing, producing 36 books in seventeen years. Among his best are *Idylls of the Sea* (1899), *Our Heritage of the Sea* (1906), and *From Wheel and Outlook* (1913). *The Log of a Sea Waif* (1899) is autobiographical.

Bullett, Gerald William (30 Dec. 1893—3 Jan. 1958), poet and novelist, born at Forest Hill, London, and educated at a day school, became a bank clerk at 16. At 21 he wrote his first novel, *The Progress of Kay* (1916). In the First World War he served in the Royal Flying Corps, and after it took a First in English at Cambridge, subsequently working as a reviewer. His volumes of poetry include *Dreams o' Mine* (1915), and *The Bubble* (1934), and he also edited two anthologies, *The English Galaxy* (1933), and *Silver Poets of the Sixteenth Century* (1947), as well as writing studies of G. K. Chesterton and Walt Whitman. Among his best-known novels are *The History of Egg Pandervil* (1928) with its sequel *Nicky Son of Egg* (1929), *The Jury* (1935), *The Snare of the Fowler* (1936), *The Bending Sickle* (1938), *A Man of Forty* (1939), *When the Cat's Away* (1940), *Judgment in Suspense* (1946), *Cricket in Heaven* (1949), and *The Trouble at Number Seven* (1952).

Bulwer, Edward, *see* Lytton.

Bulwer, W. H. L. E., *see* **Dalling and Bulwer.**

Bunner, Henry Cuyler (3 Aug. 1855—11 May 1896), poet and journalist, was born at Oswego, New York, browsed in his father's ample library, and planned to go to college, but had to forgo this and took up journalism. Joining the staff of *Puck*, the earliest American comic weekly, he remained with it all his life, writing prose and verse, parodies, jokes, stories, and editorials. His first published volume, *Airs from Arcady and Elsewhere* (1884), containing his famous poem 'The Way to Arcady,' was followed by *Rowen* (1892). He also wrote two novels, *The Midge* (1886), and *The Story of a New York House* (1887), and a number of volumes of short stories, including *Short Sixes* (1890), and *More Short Sixes* (1894).

Bunyan, John (baptized 30 Nov. 1628, died 31 Aug. 1688), religious writer, was born at Harrowden in Elstow parish, near Bedford, the son of a tinker, and after an elementary education was apprenticed to his father's trade. In 1644 he was drafted into the Parliamentary forces, his commanding officer in the Civil War being Sir Samuel Luke, the original of Butler's Hudibras. In 1646 he married a poor woman who brought him as her dowry only two religious books, *The Plain Man's Pathway to Heaven* and *The Practice of Piety*. Bunyan then experienced a spiritual upheaval, being oppressed by a deep sense of guilt and imagining that he had committed 'the unpardonable sin,' though profanity seems to have been the worst of his vices. Following a period of despair and heart-searching which is later described in his books, he engaged in preaching, and was recognized as a Baptist minister in 1657, having removed to Bedford two years previously. In spite of prohibitive legislation, he refused to desist at the Restoration, and from 1660 to 1672 was imprisoned, supporting his family precariously by making tagged laces. During this period, with no reference library but the Bible and Foxe's *Book of Martyrs*, he wrote *Grace Abounding to the Chief of Sinners* (1666), which relates his own struggles, and *The Holy City*, inspired by a passage in the Book of Revelations.

In 1672 the restrictions on Dissenting ministers were removed, and Bunyan was released and resumed preaching. But three years later the Declaration of Indulgence was withdrawn, and he was again imprisoned for six months, during which he wrote his great work *The Pilgrim's Progress* (1678, second part 1684), of which 100,000 copies were sold in ten years. His later works were *The Life and Death of Mr Badman* (1680), which gives an interesting picture of life in the time of Charles II; *The Holy War* (1682), telling of the siege of Mansoul by the powers of evil; and *The Heavenly Footman* (1698). He died as the result of a chill caught in the course of a journey to mediate between a father and a prodigal son. *The Pilgrim's Progress*, an allegory describing the journey of Christian from the City of Destruction to the Celestial City, and relating his adventures in the Slough of Despond, the Valley of Humiliation, the Valley of the Shadow of Death, and Vanity Fair, is now accepted as the greatest prose work of the Puritan period. It is written entirely without literary ornament, in a simple style modelled on that of the Bible, but carries conviction by its intense sincerity and its imaginative power. Although it quickly found its way in cheap editions to the cottage and the servants' hall, the humble calling of its writer debarred it from full appreciation until the beginning of the nineteenth century, when Southey and Macaulay testified to its greatness.

Burckhardt, John Lewis (24 Nov. 1784—15 Oct. 1817), explorer, born at Lausanne and educated at Leipzig and Göttingen Universities, came to England in 1806 and wrote his books of travel in English. He travelled widely in Africa and in Syria, and the adjoining countries, became a great oriental scholar, and, disguising himself, made the pilgrimage to Mecca, and obtained access to places not open to Christians. He wrote *Travels in Nubia* (1819), *Travels in Syria and the Holy Land* (1822), and a book on *Arabic Proverbs* (1830). He died of dysentery at Cairo when about to start on a new journey into the interior of Africa.

Burgess, Frank Gelett (30 Jan. 1866—18 Sept. 1951), humorist, born at Boston, Massachusetts, and educated at the Institute of Technology, worked as a draughtsman for the Southern Pacific Railway, and in 1891 became instructor in topographical drawing in the University of California. Between 1894 and 1897 he edited a magazine called *The Wave* and another called *The Lark*, in the first issue of which appeared the famous quatrain on the Purple Cow. *Goops and How to Be Them* (1900), a series of children's poems in the 'ruthless rhymes' tradition, was followed by *More Goops* (1903), *The Goop Encyclopaedia* (1915), and *New Goops* (1940). *Are You a Bromide?* (1897) is a satire on platitudes, and *Burgess Unabridged* (1914) introduced a number of new words, one which has become accepted being *Blurb*, interpreted as 'Self-praise; to make a noise like a publisher.'

Burgon, John William (21 Aug. 1813—4 Aug. 1888), clergyman and author, born at Smyrna, son of a merchant who moved to London in 1814, attended classes at London University, went to Oxford in 1841, won the Newdigate Prize with a poem on *Petra*, and became a Fellow of Oriel. In 1863 he was appointed vicar of St Mary's, Oxford, and in 1867 Gresham Professor of Divinity. In 1876 he became Dean of Chichester. *Lives of Twelve Good Men* (1888) was his most popular work.

Burke, Edmund (12 Jan. 1729—9 July 1797), statesman and philosopher, was born in Dublin. His father was a Protestant, his mother a Roman Catholic, and he went to a school in County Kildare run by a Quaker. On leaving Trinity College, Dublin, in 1747 he was entered at the Middle Temple, but was never called to the Bar. In 1756 appeared his first published work, *A Vindication of Natural Society*, which satirized the views of Bolingbroke (q.v.). In the same year he published his *Philosophical Inquiry into the Sublime and Beautiful*, which laid the foundations of the science of aesthetics in England. Along with Dodsley the publisher he founded in 1759 the *Annual Register*, for which he wrote the yearly survey of events till 1788. He acted as private secretary to 'Single-speech' Hamilton and then to the Whig Prime Minister, the Marquis of Rockingham, and in 1765 was himself returned to Parliament as the member for Wendover. In the following year he made his first speech on the vexed question of the American Colonies, and in 1769 published his *Observations on a Late Publication entitled 'The Present State of the Nation,'* followed in 1770 by *Thoughts on the Cause of the Present Discontents*, both pamphlets showing great rhetorical powers. About this time he became one of the circle which revolved round Dr Johnson.

In 1774 he became M.P. for Bristol, at the invitation of its citizens, and during Lord North's administration he attacked the Government's policy in his famous speeches *On American Taxation* and *On Conciliation with the Colonies*. His championing of the cause of Catholic emancipation and of free trade with Ireland lost him his seat at Bristol, and in 1781 he was returned for Malton in Yorkshire. After the fall of North's Ministry in 1782 he was appointed Paymaster of the Forces under Rockingham and Portland, and was made a Privy Councillor. At the impeachment of Warren Hastings in 1788 he opened the trial with a speech which ranks among the masterpieces of English oratory. With the advent to power of the younger Pitt he was again in opposition, and in 1790 he published his *Reflections on the French Revolution*, which reached an 11th edition in a year, and had great influence all over Europe in encouraging resistance to the Revolution; it also split the Whig Party and brought upon him a storm of obloquy which he answered trenchantly in the *Letter to a Noble Lord* (1796). By that time he had retired from politics, having spent almost his whole life in opposition.

Although one of the greatest political thinkers that the British Isles have produced, Burke was more successful as a writer than as a speaker. The continued splendour of his declamation, his inordinate copiousness and vehemence, joined with an awkward delivery, tended to bore his audience. But in both writings and speeches there is a perfect welding of knowledge, thought, and feeling which captivates the reader; as Goldsmith once said, he 'wound himself into his subject like a serpent.' He is the only orator whose speeches claim a permanent place in English literature comparable to its greatest poetry or drama.

Burke, Kenneth (5 May 1897—   ), critic, was born at Pittsburgh and educated at Ohio State University and Columbia. He was music critic of the *Dial* from 1927 to 1929 and of the *Nation* from 1934 to 1936, and in 1928 won the *Dial* award of 2,000 dollars for distinguished service to American literature. In 1935 he was awarded a Guggenheim Fellowship, and in 1950 was Visiting Professor of English at Chicago. His work on the theory of literary criticism and the psychology of literary form is often advanced and involved, so that he has been called 'the critics' critic.' Among his books are *Counter-Statement* (1931), *Permanence and Change: an Anatomy of Purpose* (1935), *Attitudes towards History* (1937), *The Philosophy of Literary Form* (1941), *A Grammar of Motives* (1945), and *A Rhetoric of Motives* (1950). *The White Oxen* (1942) is a collection of stories.

Burke, Thomas (1886—22 Sept. 1945), descriptive writer and novelist, born in London, was left an orphan at an early age, and at 15 started work in an office. He sold his first story when he was 16, and subsequently worked for a second-hand bookseller and a literary agent. He is best remembered as the supreme interpreter of London's East End. *Nights in Town* (1915), a series of London sketches, was followed by *Out and About* (1919), *The Outer Circle* (1921), *The London Spy* (1922), *The Real East End* (1932), *London in My Times* (1934), and *The Streets of London* (1940). His highly successful short stories deal with London's Chinatown; collections of these are *Limehouse Nights* (1916), *Whispering Windows* (1920), and *The Pleasantries of Old Quong* (1931). He also published some books of verse, and several novels, including *Twinkletoes* (1917), and *Abduction* (1939). *The Wind and the Rain* (1924) is autobiographical.

Burnand, Sir Francis Cowley (29 Nov. 1836—21 April 1917), humorist, born in London, son of a stockbroker, was educated at Eton and Cambridge, where he founded the Amateur Dramatic Club. He attended Cuddesdon Theological College to study for holy orders, but was converted to Roman Catholicism. Taking up law, he was called to the Bar, but found writing burlesques more congenial, and in 1863 sent his first contribution to *Punch*. As editor of *Punch* for twenty-six years, from 1880 to 1906, he raised its tone and reputation. At his best in parody, he was an inveterate punster, his best works being *Happy Thoughts* (1866), *A New History of Sandford and Merton* (1872), and *Records and Reminiscences* (1904). He was knighted in 1902.

Burnet, Gilbert (18 Sept. 1643—7 March 1715), bishop and historian, son of a Royalist and Episcopalian lawyer who became a judge, and of the sister of Johnston of Warristoun, a leader of the Covenanters, was born in Edinburgh, and educated at Aberdeen and at Amsterdam, where he studied Hebrew under a Rabbi. Returning to Scotland, he was successively Episcopal minister at Saltoun and Professor of Divinity in Glasgow (1669), and was then offered, but declined, a Scotch bishopric. His energetic and bustling character led him to take an active part in the controversies of the time, and he endeavoured to bring about a reconciliation between Episcopacy and Presbyterianism. Going to London he won favour with Charles II, from whom he received various preferments. His literary reputation was greatly enhanced by the publication in 1679 of the first volume of his *History of the Reformation of the Church of England*, for which he received the thanks of Parliament, and which was completed by other two volumes, in 1682 and 1714. On account of a letter of reproof which he ventured to write to the King, he lost favour at Court, and the policy pursued by James II being very repugnant to him, he betook himself in 1687 to Holland, where he became one of the advisers of the Prince of Orange. Returning to England at the Revolution, he was made Bishop of Salisbury. The work by which his fame is chiefly sustained, his *History of my Own Times* (1723), gives a sketch of the history of the Civil Wars and Commonwealth, and a detailed account of the immediately succeeding period down to 1713. While not free from egotism and some party feeling, it is written with a sincere desire for accuracy and fairness, and it has largely the authority of an eye-witness. Among his other writings are *Memoirs of the Dukes of Hamilton* (1677), and an *Exposition of the 39 Articles* (1699).

Burnet, Thomas (1635—27 Sept. 1715), theologian and writer on cosmogony, was born at Croft near Darlington, and educated at Cambridge, and became Master of Charterhouse and Clerk of the Closet to William III. His literary fame rests on his *Telluris Theoria Sacra, or Sacred Theory of the Earth* (1681), published first in Latin and afterwards in English, a work which, in absence of all scientific knowledge of the earth's structure, was necessarily a mere speculative cosmogony. It is written, however, with much eloquence. Some of the views expressed in another work, *Archaeologiae Philosophicae* (1692), were, however, so unacceptable to contemporary theologians that he had to resign his post at Court.

Burnett, Frances Eliza Hodgson (24 Nov. 1849—29 Oct. 1924), novelist, was born in Manchester, daughter of Edwin Hodgson, a hardware dealer. In 1865 poverty drove the family to a log-cabin life in Knoxville, Tennessee. Frances, a very imaginative child, started writing stories at the age of 17, and in later years she said that she never had a manuscript rejected. In 1873 she married Dr Swan M. Burnett, and moved with him to Washington in 1877. In 1898 they were divorced, and her later marriage with Stephen Townshend had a very brief duration. Mrs Burnett lived in Kent for a time, but finally moved back to America and settled in Long Island. Nicknamed 'Fluffy,' she inhabited a saccharine dreamworld of her own, her most famous work being *Little Lord Fauntleroy* (1886). She wrote more than 40 novels, one of the best being the first, *That Lass o' Lowrie's* (1877), which tells of the Yorkshire coal mines. *The One I Knew Best of All* (1893) describes her early life.

Burnett, James, *see* **Monboddo.**

Burney, Frances *or* **Fanny** (13 June 1752—6 Jan. 1840), novelist and diarist, was born at King's Lynn, Norfolk. Her father was a well-known musician, and after he removed to London in 1760 the house had many notable callers. Fanny, shy, short-sighted, and plain, used them as material for the stories she scribbled incessantly but secretly from the age of 10 onwards. At the age of 15 she destroyed her early efforts, but continued to write, and in 1778 her novel *Evelina: or, A Young Lady's Entrance into the World* appeared anonymously. It caused a great sensation, being fathered on various celebrities before the real authoress became known. Fanny then became famous and a great favourite of Dr Johnson. *Evelina* is cast in letter form and has a conventional plot, but the character description is lively and entertaining. Her second book, *Cecilia: or Memoirs of an Heiress* (1782), though it was sold out in three months, is inferior to the first, being less spontaneous and more mannered. From 1786 to 1791 she held the post of Second Keeper of the Robes to Queen Charlotte, the wife of George III, but she was not happy in the stiff German etiquette of the Court. Her immediate superior was a stupid overbearing German woman, and Fanny was too delicate to stand up to her bullying. In 1791 she resigned, was granted a pension of £100 a year, and went to live with her father in Chelsea.

In 1793 she married a French *émigré*, General Alexandre D'Arblay, a former adjutant of Lafayette. In 1796 was published her third novel, *Camilla: or, A Picture of Youth*; though inferior to her others, it was a commercial success, and is said to have brought 3,000 guineas, with which she built herself a house, Camilla Cottage, near Dorking. She also wrote a tragedy, *Edwy and Elgiva*, which was acted at Drury Lane in 1795, but in spite of Kemble and Mrs Siddons being in the cast was taken off after one performance. Miss Burney had no success as a dramatist, her other attempts, including two comedies, *The Witlings* and *Love and Fashion*, failing to be produced, though the last-named was rehearsed in 1799. From 1802 to 1812 she lived near Paris with her husband, who had secured a post there, and then returned to England with her son Alexander. In 1814 appeared the last of her novels, *The Wanderer: or, Female Difficulties*. In the same year her father died, and in 1815, having rejoined her husband after Napoleon's downfall, she was living in Brussels during the fateful Hundred Days. From Louis XVIII she was given the title of countess. In 1818 D'Arblay died, and she passed the remainder of her life in England, outliving her son, who became a clergyman but died of a decline. In 1832 appeared her *Memoirs of Dr Burney*, written in a ponderous style, and after her death *The Diary and Letters of Madame D'Arblay* was edited in seven volumes by her niece, Charlotte Barrett; they omitted the parts before 1778, which were published in 1889 by Mrs A. R. Ellis as *The Early Diary of Frances Burney*. The diary gives a delightful if sometimes depressing picture of life at George III's Court and of the notabilities that the writer met there and at her home. A pioneer in the art of the domestic novel, Fanny Burney had considerable influence on Jane Austen, who took the title of her greatest novel, *Pride and Prejudice*, from the pages of *Cecilia*.

Burns, John Horne (7 Oct. 1916—10 Aug. 1953), novelist, was born at Andover, Massachusetts, and educated at Phillips Academy there, and at Harvard. From 1937 to 1942 he was instructor in English at the Loomis School, Connecticut. During the Second World War he served as a second lieutenant in Africa and Italy. His first novel, *The Gallery* (1947), a popular success, was followed by *Lucifer with a Book* (1949) and *A Cry of Children* (1952). He was engaged on a fourth novel when he died of cerebral haemorrhage at Leghorn in Italy.

Burns, Robert (25 Jan. 1759—21 July 1796), poet, was born at Alloway near Ayr, in a cottage built by his father, a farmer who had migrated from Kincardineshire and who originally spelt his name Burnes. The careful instruction that Burns got from him and from John Murdoch, the village schoolmaster, seconded by his study of such books as *A Collection of English Songs*, which he took with him to the fields, disposes of the theory that he was inspired but illiterate. From his mother, Agnes Broun, he gained a wealth of traditional ballads and folk-tales. But he was put early to work. His father, who was constantly trying to better his position but seemed fated to be unfortunate, took a farm in 1766 at Mount Oliphant, and in 1777 moved to Lochlea in the parish of Tarbolton. At 15 Burns was a skilled ploughman earning his £7 a year.

Meanwhile he had some additional though intermittent schooling, and when Murdoch was established in Ayr made shift to learn from him the rudiments of French. His first song, 'Handsome Nell' was written when he was 16, inspired by a young partner at the harvesting. About this time he attended a country dancing school, against his father's wishes, and soon after began the succession of love affairs which have made him notorious. In a brief visit to a school at Kirkoswald he learned surveying and also to take his glass, and in 1781, despairing of farming, he went to Irvine to learn the trade of flax-dressing, but that project fell through when the shop was burned down during a Hogmanay carousal. Finally, in 1784, when his father died of consumption, Robert and his brother Gilbert invested what little capital could be saved in the farm of Mossgiel near Mauchline.

Mossgiel proved no more successful than their other ventures, and

E

meanwhile Robert had formed a union with Jean Armour, daughter of a master-mason, but owing to separation following a quarrel with her family considered himself free again and purposed, as a desperate bid for fortune, to emigrate to Jamaica as book-keeper on a plantation. To this time belongs the romance of 'Highland Mary' mentioned in his poems, whose statue stands at Dunoon; Burns intended that Mary Campbell should accompany him to Jamaica as his wife, but meanwhile she died of fever, and his fortunes took a turn for the better which entirely changed his plans. It was to get money for his passage that he published his *Poems Chiefly in the Scottish Dialect* (1786), the famous 'Kilmarnock Burns,' which was an immediate success. It contained much of his best work, including 'The Twa Dogs,' 'Hallowe'en,' 'The Jolly Beggars,' 'To a Mouse,' 'To a Mountain Daisy,' and that idyll of a Scottish fireside, 'The Cotter's Saturday Night.' On seeing the collection Dr Thomas Blacklock (q.v.) dissuaded Burns from going abroad, and arrangements were made for an Edinburgh edition of the poems, which eventually brought him some £500.

In Edinburgh Burns was received as an equal by Dugald Stewart the philosopher, William Robertson the historian, and Hugh Blair the poet, as well as by aristocrats like the Earl of Glencairn. Always a good conversationalist, he made a favourable impression by his frankness and modesty, forming friendships with, among others, Mrs McLehose, the 'Clarinda' of his letters, and Mrs Dunlop of Dunlop, with whom also he corresponded for a time. Walter Scott, then a boy of 15, saw him and described him later as 'of manners rustic, not clownish' . . . 'the eye alone indicated the poetical character and temperament. It was large, and of a dark cast, and literally glowed when he spoke with feeling or interest.' Back in Ayrshire in 1788 Burns acknowledged Jean Armour as his lawful wife, used his capital to try a new farm, Ellisland on the banks of the Nith near Dumfries, and took up the duties of exciseman as a line to fall back upon if farming should again prove unsuccessful.

At Ellisland he was cultivated by the local gentry, and it was suggested that he should be a candidate for the newly founded Chair of Agriculture at Edinburgh University, but he declined. The farm proving a poor bargain, like the others, in 1791 he removed to Dumfries and became a gauger or exciseman pure and simple. Unfortunately the advantages of a steady income were partly offset by the opportunities afforded for hard drinking, which had long been his weakness. Meanwhile he was engaged in one of his most important literary tasks, the provision of songs for the *Scots Musical Museum* compiled by James Johnson, and also for George Thomson's *Select Collection of Original Scottish Airs*. Burns's contribution of over 200 songs, many of his own composition, many based on older verses which he refurbished and revitalized by his genius, is perhaps his supreme achievement. It was entirely a labour of love, for he received no payment whatever. At this time also he wrote in one day what is reckoned the greatest of his longer poems, the rollicking 'Tam o' Shanter.' His work in the Excise was satisfactory, and he could look forward confidently to a supervisorship. His prospects had never been brighter when in 1796 he paid the final penalty of his intemperate habits, an attack of rheumatism bringing on endocarditis to which he succumbed. His collected works were first published in 1800.

Ever since his death Burns has suffered from well-meaning but illogical critics who think it necessary to deplore or explain away his frailties before pointing out the greatness of his genius; as Gregory Smith observes sarcastically, 'the comment on intrigue and whisky rolls on, involving us all in irrelevance.' The simple facts, from a literary point of view, are that Burns was not only the finest Scottish poet but one of the greatest of all writers of love songs; in this he has been compared, not inaptly, with Sappho, who also wrote in dialect. Whether composing original pieces or, as in the case of 'Auld Lang Syne,' revitalizing a song which had already passed through more than one version, he had the sure touch of lyric genius. To this he added a power of vitriolic satire, shown in such poems as 'Holy Willie's Prayer,' and a command of vivid description that appears at its best in 'Tam o' Shanter' and 'The Jolly Beggars.' His poetry owes much to Allan Ramsay and to ill-starred Robert Fergusson, who stands in much the same relation to Burns as Marlowe does to Shakespeare, but he far surpassed them both, and the example of his work was one of the vital influences in the coming Romantic Movement.

Burroughs, Edgar Rice (1 Sept. 1875—19 March 1950), novelist, born at Chicago, was educated at Michigan Military Academy. He enlisted, but was discharged as under age, and in the next fifteen years was successively cattle drover, gold dredger, and railway detective. In 1912 he wrote *Tarzan of the Apes*, the first of some dozen books telling of Tarzan, the boy who was adopted and reared by apes. Burroughs had never seen Africa, where most of these stories are located, but their popularity was such that over 25 million copies were sold. Others in the series were *The Return of Tarzan* (1915), *The Son of Tarzan* (1917), *Tarzan the Untamed* (1920), and *Tarzan Triumphant* (1932). Burroughs wrote a number of other novels, including a series about Mars, beginning with *A Princess of Mars* (1917), but they never attained the same popularity. During the Second World War he was a special correspondent in the Pacific theatre.

Burroughs, John (3 April 1837—29 March 1921), nature-writer, was born at Roxbury, New York; brought up on his father's farm, he had all his life a great love of his native hills, the Catskills. From 1854 to 1863 he taught in a country school, then for the next ten years was a clerk in the Treasury Department at Washington, where he formed a friendship with Walt Whitman, who is the subject of his first book, *Notes on Walt Whitman as Poet and Person* (1867). After leaving Washington he settled on a fruit farm beside the Hudson and wrote popular nature books. *Wake-Robin* (1871) was followed by, among others, *Birds and Poets* (1877), *Locusts and Wild Honey* (1879), *Leaf and Tendril* (1908), and *Under the Apple Trees* (1916). His collected works were published in 1922 and his *Life and Letters* in 1925. He received honorary degrees from Yale, Colgate, and Georgia.

Burton, John Hill (22 Aug. 1809—10 Aug. 1881), historian, born and educated at Aberdeen, was in 1831 called to the Bar, but had little practice, and in 1854 was appointed Secretary to the Prison Board of Scotland, and in 1877 a Commissioner of Prisons. He became at an early period of his life a contributor to *Blackwood's Magazine* and other periodicals, and in 1846 published a life of Hume, which attracted considerable attention, and was followed by lives of Lord Lovat and Lord President Forbes. He began his career as an historian by the publication in 1853 of *History of Scotland from the Revolution to the Extinction of the last Jacobite Insurrection*, to which he added (1867—70) *History of Scotland from Agricola's Invasion to the Revolution*, in 7 volumes, thus completing a continuous narrative. Subsequently he published a *History of the Reign of Queen Anne* (1880). Other works of a lighter kind were *The Book-Hunter* (1862), and *The Scot Abroad* (1864).

Burton, Sir Richard Francis (19 March 1821—20 Oct. 1890), explorer, son of an army officer, was born at Barham House, Hertfordshire. He had no regular schooling, but accompanied his parents on their travels all over Europe, and later spent five terms at Trinity College, Oxford. In 1842 he served in Sind under Sir Charles Napier, and then embarked on a life of travel and adventure in the course of which he mastered thirty-five languages. Disguised as a pilgrim, under the name of Al-Haj Abdullah, he travelled to Mecca in 1853, and described his experiences in *A Personal Narrative of a Pilgrimage to Mecca* (1855), which was very popular. Later he explored Somaliland, served in the Crimea, searched for the source of the Nile with Speke, and became British consul successively at Fernando Po, Santos, Damascus, and Trieste. He was given the K.C.M.G. in 1885. In his later years he translated the great Portuguese epic of Camoens, and made an elaborate and literal rendering of the *Arabian Nights* (1885—8), of which his wife published an expurgated edition.

Burton, Robert (8 Feb. 1577—25 Jan. 1640), author, born at Lindley in Leicestershire, was educated at Nuneaton Grammar School, Sutton Coldfield School, and Brasenose College, Oxford. In 1599 he was elected a Student of Christ Church, where he spent the rest of his life, though he held the Oxford living of St Thomas and was rector of Segrave, Leicestershire. Anthony à Wood says of him 'He was an exact mathematician, a curious calculator of nativities, a general real scholar, a thro' paced philologist. His company was very merry, facete, and juvenile.' He wrote an anti-Catholic comedy, *Philosophaster*, which was acted at Christ Church in 1617. On his death he bequeathed his books to the Bodleian Library. His famous and unique work, the *Anatomy of Melancholy*, by 'Democritus Junior,' first appeared in 1621, and after various alterations and additions reached its final form in the 6th edition thirty years later. It contains everything that can be imagined—science, philosophy, medicine, history, literature—and is a quarry from which every author from Milton to Byron has hewed according to his wishes. Divided into three parts, the first dealing with causes and symptoms of melancholy, the second with cures, and the third with love-melancholy and religious-melancholy, it is an inspired farrago of quotations from classical and medieval writers.

Bury, Lady Charlotte Susan Maria (28 Jan. 1775—31 March 1861), novelist, daughter of the 5th Duke of Argyll, and married first to Col. J. Campbell, and second to Rev. E. J. Bury, wrote a number of novels—*Flirtation, Separation, The Divorced*, and others, but is chiefly remembered in connection with a *Diary illustrative of the Times of George IV* (1838), a somewhat scandalous anonymous work which she is supposed to have written while lady-in-waiting to Caroline, Princess of Wales. She also wrote some poems and two devotional works.

Bury, John Bagnell (16 Oct. 1861—1 June 1927), historian, born at Monaghan, son of a clergyman, was educated at Foyle College, Londonderry, and Trinity College, Dublin, where he got a double First and was made a Fellow in 1885 and Professor of Modern History in 1893. In 1902 he succeeded Lord Acton in the corresponding Cambridge chair. Bury's classical knowledge was shown in his editions of the *Nemean* (1890), and *Isthmian* (1893) *Odes of Pindar*. Having mastered Sanskrit, Hebrew, Syriac, Russian, and Hungarian, he wrote a series of monumental works on the history of the later Roman Empire, the last of which was published in 1923. His one-volume *History of Greece* (1900) is still a standard text-book. He also edited Gibbon's *Decline and Fall of the Roman Empire*, and was one of the editors of the *Cambridge Ancient History*.

Bury, Richard de (24 Jan. 1287—14 April 1345), bibliophile, son of Sir Richard Aungerville, born at Bury St Edmunds, from which he is named, studied at Oxford, and was a Benedictine monk, became tutor to Edward III when Prince of Wales, and Bishop of Durham, and held many offices of State. A patron of learning and one of the first English collectors of books, he wrote his work, *Philobiblon*, in praise of books, and founded a library at Durham College, Oxford.

Butler, Joseph (18 May 1692—16 June 1752), theologian, born at Wantage, son of a Presbyterian linen-draper, was destined for the ministry of that Church, but in 1714 he decided to enter the Church of England, and went to Oxford. After holding various other preferments he became rector of the rich living of Stanhope, Bishop of Bristol (1738), and Bishop of Durham (1750), and was said to have refused the Primacy. In 1726 he published *Fifteen Sermons*, and in 1736 *The Analogy of Religion*. The latter, which has become a classic of English theology, is a defence of revealed religion against the contemporary deistic attacks on it. These two books depend for their effect entirely upon the force of their reasoning, for they have no graces of style. Butler's works were edited by W. E. Gladstone (2 volumes 1896).

Butler, Samuel (baptized 8 Feb. 1612, died 25 Sept. 1680), satirist, was the son of a Worcestershire farmer. In early youth he was page to the Countess of Kent, and thereafter clerk to various Puritan justices, some of whom are believed to have suggested characters in *Hudibras*. After the Restoration he became secretary to the Lord President of Wales, and about the same time married a Mrs Herbert, a widow with a jointure, which, however, was lost. In 1663 the first part of *Hudibras* was published, and the other two in 1664 and 1678 respectively. This mock-heroic poem ridiculing the Puritans, which is to a certain extent modelled on *Don Quixote*, stands high in the satirical literature of England, and for wit and compressed thought has few rivals. Many of its brilliant couplets have passed into the proverbial commonplaces of the language, and few who use them have any idea of their source. Butler, notwithstanding the popularity of his work, was neglected by the Court, and died in poverty.

Butler, Samuel (4 Dec. 1835—18 June 1902), satirist, was born at Langar Rectory, near Bingham, Nottinghamshire, then occupied by his father, who later became a canon of Lincoln. Educated at Shrewsbury and St John's College, Cambridge, Samuel was intended for the Church, but instead became a sheep-farmer at Rangitata in New Zealand, where he was very successful. His letters home form the basis of *A First Year in Canterbury Settlement* (1863). Returning to London in 1864 he lived at Clifford's Inn for the rest of his life. For a time he studied painting, and his picture 'Mr Heatherley's Holiday' is in the Tate Gallery. In 1872 *Erewhon*, a brilliant satire, appeared anonymously; it tells of a country in which crimes are dealt with by surgical or hospital treatment. Books on evolution and on Italy followed, and in 1896 Butler wrote a life of his grandfather, who had been headmaster of Shrewsbury and Bishop of Lichfield. In his latter years he produced *The Authoress of the Odyssey* (1897), in which he maintained that the epic was written by Nausicaa; and he also made colloquial prose versions of both Homer's poems. In 1899 he published *Shakespeare's Sonnets Reconsidered*, which shows typical originality of thought, and in 1901 *Erewhon Revisited*. A year after his death was published his novel *The Way of All Flesh*, which tells of his own childhood and is a scathing indictment of family tyranny. His *Note Books* were edited in 1912.

Byrd, William (28 March 1674—26 Aug. 1744), statesman and historian, was born in Virginia, son of a merchant, but was educated in England and studied law at the Middle Temple. In 1692 he returned to Virginia, where he was elected to the House of Burgesses and in 1709 became a member of the Council of State. In 1728 he was one of the commissioners entrusted with marking out the boundary between Virginia and North Carolina, of which he told in *The History of the Dividing Line*. This, along with his *Journey to the Land of Eden* and *Progress to the Mines*, made up the volume of *Westover Manuscripts* (1841). Like Pepys, he kept a private journal, which was published as *The Secret Diary of William Byrd of Westover* (1940—3).

Byrne, Donn (20 Nov. 1889—18 June 1928), novelist, whose name was originally Brian Oswald Donn-Byrne, was born in Brooklyn, son of an architect, and educated at Dublin, the Sorbonne, and Leipzig. Going to South America, he became a cow-puncher, and later worked in a garage in New York. His first book was *Stories without Women* (1915), but his great success was *Messer Marco Polo* (1920). Returning to Ireland, he bought Castle Coolmaine in County Cork, but was killed in a motor accident soon after. Others of his novels are *The Wind Bloweth* (1922), *Blind Raftery* (1924), *Hangman's House* (1926), *Brother Saul* (1927), and *Destiny Bay* (1928).

Byrom, John (29 Feb. 1692—26 Sept. 1763), poet and stenographer, born at Broughton, near Manchester, was educated at Merchant Taylors' and Trinity College, Cambridge, of which he became a Fellow. He contributed two papers to Addison's *Spectator*, and also a humorous pastoral called *Colin and Phoebe*. In 1716 he travelled abroad and studied medicine. After his marriage in 1721 he took to teaching shorthand, of which he had a new system, his pupils, who included Horace Walpole and Lord Chesterfield, being bound by an oath of secrecy. His system was elegant, but not fast enough for modern needs. In 1724 he became a Fellow of the Royal Society. His collected *Poems* were published in 1773 and his *Private Journal* in 1857.

Byron, George Gordon Noel Byron, 6th Lord (22 Jan. 1788—19 April 1824), poet, was born in London. His father 'Mad Jack' Byron, an officer in the Guards, died when he was 3; his mother, Catherine Gordon, was a Scottish heiress. He spent his early years with her in Aberdeen, where he attended the Grammar School from 1794 to 1798, and received impressions of the mountainous Deeside scenery which left their mark on his poetry. His childhood was embittered by incessant quarrels with his mother, who even taunted him with the deformed foot which had been his from birth. In 1798, by the death of his great-uncle, he succeeded unexpectedly to the family title and went to live at Newstead, and in 1801 went to Harrow, where he overcame his physical disability so far as to play for the school at cricket against Eton, having someone to run for him. In 1805 he went on to Trinity College, Cambridge, where he rode, shot, boxed, and was a particularly fine swimmer; he also gambled, led a dissipated life, and cultivated members of 'the fancy' such as Gentleman Jackson.

While still at Cambridge he published his first book, *Fugitive Poems*, but his first real appeal to the public was with *Hours of Idleness* (1807), an immature collection which was brutally assailed by Brougham in the *Edinburgh Review*. In 1809 Byron retaliated effectively with his *English Bards and Scotch Reviewers*, a brilliant satire written in the heroic couplet of Pope. In the same year he went on a foreign tour with John Cam Hobhouse, afterwards Lord Broughton, his lifelong friend. They visited Spain, Portugal, Greece, and Turkey, and in 1812 appeared the first two cantos of *Childe Harold's Pilgrimage*, a travel poem in Spenserian stanzas inspired by the tour, Childe Harold being Byron himself in his favourite pose of sated voluptuary. The success of the work was immediate, and to use Byron's oft-quoted words, he 'awoke to find himself famous.' He now ousted Scott as the reigning poet, and became the spoilt darling of society.

In 1813 he followed this up with *The Giaour* and *The Bride of Abydos*, narrative poems in Scott's vein but using the East instead of the Scottish highlands as background, and introducing in every case a sinister and romantic hero. These effusions, which are now little read, caught the public taste for the thrilling and exotic, and when *The Corsair* appeared in 1814, 10,000 copies were sold on the day of publication. *Lara* followed in the same year, and in 1816 *The Siege of Corinth*, with its oriental colouring. Meanwhile Byron, tired of being pursued by the silly adoration of women, one of whom, Lady Caroline Lamb, had created a public scandal, married in 1815 Anne Isabella Milbanke, an heiress, and settled in London. Unfortunately the match proved quite unsuitable, Lady Byron being incapable of understanding her temperamental husband. After a year of unhappiness, during which a daughter, Augusta Ada, was born, she obtained a separation, accusing Byron of cruelty and insanity. There were at the same time dark whispers of his having had criminal relations with his half-sister, Augusta Leigh. The scandal ruined Byron socially, and on 25 April 1816, cast out by the society of which he had been the favourite, he left England, never to return.

Having travelled through Belgium and Germany to Switzerland, he stayed for a while at the Villa Diodati on the Lake of Geneva, where he met Shelley and Mary Godwin, and had a liaison with Jane Clairmont, Mary's stepsister; they had a daughter named Allegra, who died at the age of 6. Meanwhile he had written the third canto of *Childe Harold*, with its magnificent stanzas on Waterloo and descriptions of the Rhine scenery. The fourth and last canto was written in 1817 in Venice, where he secured a new mistress in the Countess Guiccioli, with whom and her complaisant husband he lived for several years. Byron was a greater poet in exile than he had ever been in England, and the later cantos of *Childe Harold* have more genuine poetry than the earlier ones. To this period belong his dramas, *Manfred, Marino Faliero, Sardanapalus, The Two Foscari*, and *Cain*, a tragedy which defends sin and brought fresh attacks on its author. During this time also he completed *Don Juan*, generally admitted to be his finest work and the greatest burlesque since *Hudibras*.

In 1821 he settled in a palazzo in Pisa, where he was joined by Leigh Hunt, and they collaborated in producing *The Liberal*, a short-lived magazine in which appeared Byron's satirical 'Vision of Judgment,' outcome of a feud which he had long kept up with Southey. Next year Shelley was drowned just after a visit to Byron, who felt the shock of the tragedy very deeply. In 1823 he was elected a member of the Greek revolutionary committee for the liberation of Greece from Turkish rule. Arriving at Missolonghi in January of 1824 he made great efforts to settle the differences which had arisen among the Greek leaders, but in April he died of rheumatic fever and ever since has been a hero to the Greek nation. His body was conveyed in a warship to England, where his death caused a general shock. Tennyson, then a boy of 14, carved 'Byron is dead' on a rock at Somersby, and declared 'The whole world seemed darkened to me.' In 1830 Thomas Moore (q.v.) published the *Life, Letters, and Journals of Lord Byron*.

Byron's position in literature is not easy to assess. In his own day he was reckoned far the greatest of English poets, and on the Continent his reputation has always been high, his name being coupled with Goethe's as a leading spirit of the age. But his work has little depth; it was Goethe himself who declared 'Directly he begins to reflect, he is a child.' It is true that he typifies one side of the Romantic Movement. Handsome, gloomy, profligate, and misanthropic, he caught the popular imagination, and his exotic verse tales, with their exciting adventures, filled the place of the modern 'thriller.' But much of the poetry which once seemed gorgeous and fascinating has since been found crude and tawdry. The truth is that Byron's romanticism was largely a pose. His Eastern tales were written to please the public and to amuse himself. He had as much kinship with the school of Pope and Dryden as with that of Shelley and Keats; and it was only when he found in the satirical burlesque of *Don Juan* a medium which possessed features of both schools that he was able fully to express his genius.

Byron, Henry James (Jan. 1834—11 April 1884), dramatist, born at Manchester, was apprenticed to a surgeon, but disliked the calling and joined a provincial company of actors. His earliest publication was a monologue, *A Bottle of Champagne Uncorked by Horace Plastic*. In 1858 he was entered at the Middle Temple, and in the same year had a burlesque, *Fra Diavolo*, produced in the West End. He became manager of various theatres in London and Liverpool, his best plays being *Cyril's Success* (1868), *Our Boys* (1875), and *The Upper Crust* (1880), all comedies. He was the first editor of *Fun*.

Byron, Robert (26 Feb. 1905—Feb. 1941), traveller, a distant connection of the poet's family, was educated at Eton and Oxford, had a passion for Greece, and wrote a number of travel books. *Europe in the Looking Glass* (1927) records a journey in Germany, Italy, and Greece; *The Station* (1928) describes Mount Athos; *First Russia, then Tibet* (1933) goes further afield; and *The Road to Oxiana* (1937) tells of a visit to Persia, India, and Afghanistan. *The Byzantine Achievement* (1929) and *The Birth of Western Painting* (1930) deal with Byzantine art. On the outbreak of the Second World War Byron joined the overseas department of the B.B.C., and in 1941, while he was on his way to Egypt as special correspondent for a group of English newspapers, his ship was torpedoed.

E*

C

Cabell, James Branch (14 April 1879—5 May 1958), novelist,
was born at Richmond, Virginia, and educated at William and Mary
College; while still a student he was an instructor in Greek and
French. He then worked for some time as a journalist in Richmond
and New York before devoting himself entirely to literature. In
1913 he was appointed genealogist of the Virginia chapter of the
Sons of the Revolution, and subsequently held other similar posts.
His first novel, *The Eagle's Shadow* (1904) was followed by *The
Cords of Vanity* (1909), *The Soul of Melicent* (1913), *The Rivet in
Grandfather's Neck* (1915), *The Cream of the Jest* (1917), and his best-
known books, the erotic *Jurgen* (1919) and *Figures of Earth* (1921);
all except the last of these were later subjected to revision. Cabell
displays a kind of pseudo-Rabelaisian preoccupation with sex, which
resulted in an attempt being made to ban *Jurgen*. His fiction deals
either with medieval romance and chivalry, usually written round
an imaginary kingdom called Poictesme, or with modern comedy and
gallantry. His style is precious and sophisticated, showing elaborate
rhythm and a preference for out-of-the-way words and expressions.
Among his later novels are *The High Place* (1923), *The Silver Stallion*
(1926), *Something About Eve* (1927), and *The White Robe* (1928).
He also published several collections of short stories and two volumes
of verse, *From the Hidden Way* (1916) and *Ballades from the Hidden
Way* (1928), as well as a number of miscellaneous pieces and sketches.
His *Works* in 18 volumes appeared in 1930. *These Restless Heads*
(1932), an autobiographical work, is signed Branch Cabell, as are
Smirt (1934), *Smith* (1935), and *Smire* (1937), which form a trilogy.
Let Me Lie (1947) and *Quiet, Please* (1952) are collections of essays.

Cable, George Washington (12 Oct. 1844—31 Jan. 1925), novelist,
was born in New Orleans, though descended from an old Virginian
family. After serving in the Civil War with the 4th Mississippi
Cavalry he started as a newspaper reporter, then became an accountant and educated himself, learning French. Starting to write short
stories, he found material in the old records of the Creoles, the
French-speaking natives of Louisiana. The collection *Old Creole
Days* (1879) was followed by the historical romances *Grandissimes*
(1880), *The Creoles of Louisiana* (1884), and *Dr Sevier* (1885). He
then moved to Northampton, Massachusetts. Later novels include
Bonaventure (1888), *The Cavalier* (1901), *Kincaid's Battery* (1908),
Gideon's Band (1914), and *Lovers of Louisiana* (1918). More serious
works, dealing with the colour problem, were *The Silent South* (1885),
and *The Negro Question* (1888).

Caedmon (died 680?), earliest known English poet, is said to have
been a cowherd at the monastery of Whitby, and was an elderly
man when he started making verse. According to the picturesque
account given by Bede (q.v.) he received the gift of song in a vision,

being bidden to sing 'the beginning of all created things.' His verses were recited to the Abbess Hilda, and he then became a monk and devoted himself to writing sacred songs. At one time the scriptural poems in the Bodleian manuscript Junius 11 were attributed to him, but it is now generally agreed that they are of later date, and that the only authentic piece of his work is his first hymn, which Bede quotes.

Caine, Sir Thomas Henry Hall (14 May 1853—31 Aug. 1931), novelist, was born at Runcorn, Cheshire, son of a Manx blacksmith, and educated in the Isle of Man and at Liverpool. He worked as an architect's clerk and then as a schoolteacher, and did journalism in his spare time. At the age of 25 he became acquainted with D. G. Rossetti (q.v.), to whom he acted as a kind of secretary, living in Cheyne Walk, Chelsea; his *Recollections* of Rossetti appeared in 1882. He then retired to the Isle of Wight and wrote his first novel, *The Shadow of a Crime* (1885). *The Deemster* (1887), which was later dramatized, began a run of phenomenal popularity which enabled him to buy Greeba Castle in the Isle of Man, where for some time he sat in the House of Keys, and amass a quarter of a million. He was knighted in 1918 and made a Companion of Honour in 1922. From 1893 onwards he worked on a life of Christ, which appeared posthumously in 1938. Among his best-known books are *The Bondman* (1890), *The Manxman* (1894), *The Eternal City* (1901), and *The Prodigal Son* (1904). *My Story* (1908) tells of his early life.

Caird, Edward (22 March 1835—1 Nov. 1908), philosopher, brother of John Caird (q.v.), was born at Greenock and educated at Greenock Academy, Glasgow and St Andrews Universities, and Balliol College, Oxford, and was elected a Fellow of Merton. In 1866 he was appointed to the Chair of Moral Philosophy at Glasgow, which he held until 1893, when he became Master of Balliol in succession to Dr Jowett (q.v.). He wrote a *Critical Account of the Philosophy of Kant* (1877), *Hegel* (1883), *Social Philosophy and Religion of Comte* (1885), *Evolution of Religion* (1893), and *Evolution of Theology in the Greek Philosophers* (1904).

Caird, John (15 Dec. 1820—30 July 1898), theologian, was born at Greenock, son of the head of a shipbuilding firm, and educated at Glasgow University. After being a minister at Newton on Ayr and in Edinburgh, he was translated to Glasgow, becoming in 1862 Professor of Divinity in Glasgow University, and in 1873 Principal. A sermon on 'Religion in Common Life,' preached before Queen Victoria, made him known throughout the Protestant world. He wrote an *Introduction to the Philosophy of Religion* (1880), and a volume on *Spinoza* (1888).

Calamy, Edmund (Feb. 1599—29 Oct. 1666), Presbyterian minister, born in London, and educated at Cambridge, was one of the five authors of a famous controversial work bearing the title *Smectymnuus*, made up of the initials of the various writers, and published in 1641 in reply to Bishop Hall's *Divine Right of Episcopacy*. His other chief work is *The Godly Man's Ark*. He was a supporter of monarchy, and favoured the Restoration, after which he was offered,

but declined, the see of Coventry and Lichfield.   He was a member
of the Savoy Conference.   The passing of the Act of Uniformity led
to his retiring from ministerial work.   He is said to have died of
melancholy caused by the Great Fire of London.

Calderwood, David (1575—1650), minister and church historian,
born at Dalkeith and educated at Edinburgh, in 1604 became
minister of Crailing, Roxburghshire.   Opposing the designs of James
VI for setting up Episcopacy, he was imprisoned in 1617, and afterwards banished to Holland, where his controversial work, *Altare
Damascenum*, against Episcopacy, was published.   In 1625 he
returned to Scotland, and began his great work, *The Historie of the
Kirk of Scotland*, which was published in an abridged form in 1646.
The complete work was printed (1841—9) for the Woodrow Society.

Caldwell, Erskine Preston (17 Dec. 1903—   ), novelist, was born at White Oak, Georgia, son of a Presbyterian minister.
His boyhood was spent incessantly travelling about the entire
South, of which he was to write later; he had little regular schooling,
though he attended the University of Virginia for a year.   In the
course of his life he was at different times cotton-picker, lumber-mill
hand, hack-driver, stagehand, cook, waiter, and reporter.   During
five years which he spent in Maine he wrote a story 'Country Full of
Swedes' which won the *Yale Review* 1,000 dollar award for fiction in
1933.   At this time also he wrote the novels *God's Little Acre* and
Tobacco Road, the latter being made into a play which had the longest
run in the history of the American theatre.   Others of his books are
Journeyman (1935), *Jackpot* (1940), *A House in the Uplands* (1946),
This Very Earth (1948), *A Lamp for Nightfall* (1952), and *Love and
Money* (1954).   He was a correspondent in Russia during the Second
World War.

Calverley, Charles Stuart (22 Dec. 1831—17 Feb. 1884), poet and
parodist, was born at Martley in Worcestershire, son of a clergyman
named Blayds, who changed his name to Calverley in 1852.   Famous
all his life for his ready repartees and improvisations and his mis-
chievous pranks, young Calverley was educated at Marlborough,
Harrow, Oxford, and Cambridge.   From Oxford he was sent down
because of his escapades, but at Cambridge he was more staid and
became a Fellow of Christ's.   It was there that he compiled his
famous examination paper on Dickens's *Pickwick Papers*, the prizes
for which were won by his contemporaries Walter Besant and Walter
Skeat.   Having studied law, he was called to the Bar in 1865, but in
the following year contracted concussion of the brain as the result
of a skating accident and was a semi-invalid till his death in middle
age.   He translated the Idylls of Theocritus into English verse, but
is best remembered for the parodies, perhaps the cleverest in English
literature, contained in *Fly Leaves* (1872).

Cambridge, Richard Owen (14 Feb. 1717—17 Sept. 1802), poet,
born in London, son of a merchant, was educated at Eton and Oxford,
and studied law at Lincoln's Inn.   He lived as a country gentleman at
Whitminster in Gloucestershire and afterwards at Twickenham, where
he had many notabilities as his guests.   He wrote the *Scribleriad*

(1751), a mock-heroic poem in six books satirizing false poetical taste, and also published some imitations of Horace, as well as a *History of the War upon the Coast of Coromandel* (1761).

Camden, William (2 May 1551—9 Nov. 1623). antiquary, born in the Old Bailey, London, and educated at Christ's Hospital, St Paul's School, and Oxford, was in 1575 appointed Second Master in Westminster School, and Head Master in 1593, and spent his vacations in travelling over England collecting antiquarian information. His great work, *Britannia*, written in Latin, was published in 1586, and at once brought him fame both at home and abroad. In 1597 Camden was made Clarenceux King-at-Arms which, setting him free from his academic duties, enabled him to devote more time to his antiquarian and historical labours. His other principal works are *Annals of the Reign of Elizabeth* (1615—23), *Monuments and Inscriptions in Westminster Abbey* (1600), and a collection of ancient English historians. He was buried in Westminster Abbey. The Camden Society for historical research, founded in 1838, is named after him.

Campbell, George (25 Dec. 1719—6 April 1796), theologian, born and educated in Aberdeen, became a minister and was later Principal and Professor of Divinity in Marischal College. His *Dissertation on Miracles* (1763), in answer to Hume, was in its day considered a masterly argument. He also wrote *The Philosophy of Rhetoric* (1776).

Campbell, Ignatius Roy Dunnachie (2 Oct. 1901—22 April, 1957), South Africa's greatest poet, was born in Durban, son of a doctor. During the First World War, at the age of 15, he joined the 6th South African Infantry, but was sent back to Durban High School. After the war he went to Oxford, but failed to pass his examinations and spent some time in France living among fishermen. In 1922 he married Mary Margaret Garman, and they lived in a fisherman's cabin in Wales, where he wrote *The Flaming Terrapin* (1924). Back in South Africa he edited the review *Voorslag*, which got into trouble with the authorities. Returning to the Mediterranean, he was a professional bullfighter from 1928 to 1931, and in 1932 and 1933 won the steer-throwing contest of Provence; later he served with Franco's forces in the Spanish Civil War, and from 1942 to 1944 was with the British Army in Africa. About 1935 he was converted to Roman Catholicism. His poetry has a strong satirical and rhetorical strain, and he has been called 'the Byron of our time.' His works include *The Wayzgoose* (1928), *Adamastor* (1930), *Poems* (1930), *The Gum Trees* (1930), *The Georgiad* (1931), *Flowering Reeds* (1933), *Mithraic Emblems* (1936), *Flowering Rifle* (1939), *Talking Bronco* (1940), *Sons of the Mistral* (1941), and *Lorca* (1952); his *Collected Poems* appeared in 1949. *Broken Record* (1934) and *Light on a Dark Horse* (1951) are autobiographical.

Campbell, John Campbell, 1st Baron (15 Sept. 1779—22 June 1861), Lord Chancellor, son of the minister of Cupar, went to St Andrews University when he was 11. He had a highly successful career as a lawyer, and held the offices successively of Solicitor and Attorney-General, Lord Chancellor of Ireland, Lord Chief Justice, and Lord Chancellor. His contributions to literature were *Lives of the Lord Chancellors* (1845—7), and *Lives of the Chief Justices* (1849—57). These works, though deficient in research and accuracy, are interesting and full of information.

Campbell, John Francis (29 Dec. 1822—17 Feb. 1885), Celtic scholar, educated at Eton and Edinburgh, was afterwards Secretary to the Lighthouse Commission. He was an authority on Celtic folklore, and published *Popular Tales of the West Highlands* (4 volumes, 1860—2), and various Gaelic texts.

Campbell, Joseph (1879—13 July 1944), poet and playwright, was born in Belfast and took part in the Ulster Theatre Movement. He went to America and was for a time an instructor at Fordham University, New York. His volumes of verse include *The Garden of the Bees* (1905), *Rushlight* (1906), *The Mountainy Singer* (1909), *Irishry* (1913), and *The Earth of Cualann* (1917). *Judgment* (1912) is a play and *Mearing Stones* (1911) is a prose account of a tramp in Donegal.

Campbell, Lewis (3 Sept. 1830—25 Oct. 1908), scholar, born in Edinburgh, son of a naval officer, was educated at Edinburgh Academy, Glasgow University, and Balliol College, Oxford, where Dr Jowett (q.v.) was his tutor. He took orders, and was Vicar of Milford, Hampshire, until 1863, when he was appointed Professor of Greek at St Andrews. He brought out editions of Sophocles and other works on the Greek classics, and in conjunction with E. Abbott a life of Jowett, with whom he had collaborated in editing the Platonic dialogues. He also edited the poems of Thomas Campbell, to whom he was related.

Campbell, Thomas (27 July 1777—15 June 1844), poet, was born in Glasgow when his father, a business man, was 67, and educated at Glasgow University. After a period as a tutor in Mull, where he learned to love highland scenery, he went to Edinburgh to study law, in which, however, he did not make much progress. He first gained fame by producing in 1799, at the age of 21, his principal poem, *The Pleasures of Hope*, a marvellous performance for so young a man. His other longer poems are *Gertrude of Wyoming* (1809), *O'Connor's Child* (1809), and *Theodoric* (1824), but he is best remembered for his war lyrics, 'Ye Mariners of England,' 'Hohenlinden,' and 'The Battle of the Baltic.' He was also distinguished as a critic, and his *Specimens of the British Poets* (1819) is prefaced by an essay which is an important contribution to criticism. Campbell resided in London from 1803 until the year of his death, which took place at Boulogne, where he had gone in search of health. In addition to the works mentioned he wrote various compilations, including *Annals of Great Britain*, covering part of the reign of George III. In 1805 he received a Government pension, and he was three times elected Lord Rector of Glasgow University, once defeating Sir Walter Scott. He is buried in Westminster Abbey. His *Life and Letters*, by W. Beattie, appeared in 1849.

Campbell, William Wilfred (1 June 1861—1 Jan. 1918), poet, was born at Berlin, Ontario, son of a clergyman, and educated at Upper Canada College and the University of Toronto. In 1865 he took orders and became a rector in New Brunswick, but resigned in 1891 and entered the Canadian Civil Service. His volumes of verse include *Lake Lyrics* (1889), *The Dread Voyage* (1893), *Beyond the Hills of Dream* (1899), *Sagas of Vaster Britain* (1914), and *War Lyrics* (1915). In 1895 he published two verse plays, *Mordred* and *Hildebrand*. *Ian of the Orcades* (1906) and *A Beautiful Rebel* (1909) are novels. He also edited the *Oxford Book of Canadian Verse*. In 1893 he was elected to the Royal Society of Canada and in 1906 was made an honorary LL.D. of Aberdeen.

Campion, Thomas (12 Feb. 1567—1 March 1619), poet and musician, born at Witham, Essex, and educated at Cambridge and on the Continent, studied law at Gray's Inn, but discarding it, practised medicine in London. He wrote masques which were presented at court, and many fine lyrics remarkable for their metrical beauty, of which 'Cherry Ripe' and 'Lesbia' are well known. He also wrote *Epigrams* in Latin, and *Observations on the Arte of Poesie* (1602), which advocated the abolition of rhyme. He composed the music for many of the songs in his four *Books of Ayres* (1610—12), and wrote a musical treatise.

Cannan, Gilbert (25 June 1884—30 June 1955), novelist and dramatist, was born in Manchester and educated at Manchester University and Cambridge. He studied law and was called to the Bar in 1908 but never practised, preferring the stage. From 1909 to 1910 he was dramatic critic of the *Star*, and later with John Drinkwater and others he founded the Manchester Repertory Theatre, himself acting in 1918 in Congreve's *Way of the World*. *Peter Homunculus* (1909) was his first novel, but his first real success was with *Round the Corner* (1913). Others are *Young Ernest* (1915), *Three Pretty Men* (1916) with its sequel *The Stucco House* (1917), *Mummery* (1918), *Pink Roses* (1919), *Sembal* (1922), and *The House of Prophecy* (1924). His work was influenced by Romain Rolland, whose *Jean Christophe* he translated. His plays include *Miles Dixon* (1910), *James and John* (1911), *Mary's Wedding* (1912), *Everybody's Husband* (1917), and *The Release of the Soul* (1920). In 1910 he married Mary Ansell after J. M. Barrie divorced her.

Canning, George (11 April 1770—8 Aug. 1827), statesman, was born in London, the son of a lawyer. He lost his father while still an infant, and was brought up by an uncle, who sent him to Eton and Oxford. In 1793 he entered Parliament as a supporter of Pitt, and soon became one of the most brilliant debaters in the House. After filling various offices, including that of Foreign Secretary, with striking ability, he was in 1827 appointed Prime Minister, but died, deeply mourned by the nation, a few months later. He has a place in literature as the leading spirit in the *Anti-Jacobin*, a paper started during the French Revolution, in support of the English Constitution; it had many of the most eminent men of the day as contributors. The 'Needy Knife-Grinder,' in Sapphic verse, is one of his best efforts. His *Collected Poems* were published in 1823.

Capgrave, John (21 April 1393—12 Aug. 1464), historian, born at Lynn in Norfolk, was ordained priest about 1417, became an Augustinian Friar, and rose to be Provincial of the Order of England. He studied probably at Cambridge, visited Rome, and was a client of Humphrey, Duke of Gloucester, whose life he wrote. He was the author of numerous theological and historical works, some of which are of considerable importance, including in Latin, *Nova Legenda Angliae* and *De Illustribus Henricis*; in English, lives of St Gilbert of Sempringham and St Katharine of Alexandria, and a *Chronicle* reaching to 1417.

Carew, Richard (17 July 1555—6 Nov. 1620), translator and antiquary, was born in Cornwall, of which he became high sheriff in 1586. Educated at Oxford, he made a translation of the first five cantos of Tasso's *Jerusalem Delivered* (1594). Other works were *A Survey of Cornwall* (1602), and an *Epistle concerning the Excellencies of the English Tongue* (1695).

Carew, Thomas (1595—22 March 1640), poet, born at West Wickham, son of a lawyer, was educated at Oxford and entered at Middle Temple. He was one of the first and best of the courtly poets who wrote gracefully on light themes of Court life and gallantry. Carew's poems have often much beauty and even tenderness. His chief work is *Coelum Britannicum* (1633), a masque. His poems, consisting chiefly of short lyrics, were collected and published after his death. One of the best known of his songs is that beginning 'He that loves a rosy cheek.'

Carey, Henry (1687?—4 Oct. 1743), poet and musician, was believed to be an illegitimate son of George Savile, Marquis of Halifax. He wrote innumerable burlesques, farces, and songs, often with his own music, including *Chrononhotonthologos* (1734), a burlesque on the mouthing plays of the day, and *The Dragon of Wantley*. His poem, 'Namby Pamby,' in ridicule of Ambrose Phillips (q.v.), added a word to the language, and his 'Sally in our Alley' is one of our best-known songs. 'God Save the King' was also claimed for him, but apparently without reason.

Carleton, Will (21 Oct. 1845—18 Dec. 1912), poet, was born at Hudson, Michigan, son of a farmer, and educated at Hillsdale College. Entering journalism, he edited the Hillsdale *Standard* and the Detroit *Weekly Tribune*. In 1871 he wrote 'Betsy and I are Out,' followed by other poems, which were published as *Farm Ballads* (1873); other volumes are *Farm Legends* (1875), *Young Folks' Centennial Rhymes* (1876), and *Farm Festivals* (1881). After moving to Boston he published *City Ballads* (1885), *City Legends* (1889), and *City Festivals* (1892), and finally *Rhymes of Our Planet* (1896). He gave readings from his poems, which were simple in language and thought, 'Over the Hill to the Poor-House' being one of the best known.

Carleton, William (1794—30 Jan. 1869), novelist, born in Prillisk, County Tyrone, the youngest of a farmer's fourteen children, and brought up among the Irish peasantry, acquired an insight into their ideas and feelings which has never been equalled. His finest work is in his short stories, collected under the title of *Traits and Stories of the Irish Peasantry* (two series, 1830, 1833). He also wrote several longer novels, of which the best is *Fardorougha the Miser* (1837), a work of great power. Others are *The Misfortunes of Barny Branagan* (1841), *Valentine M'Clutchy* (1845), *Rody the Rover* (1847), *The Squanders of Castle Squander* (1854), and *The Evil Eye* (1860). Carleton received a pension of £200 from the Government.

Carlyle, Alexander (26 Jan. 1722—25 Aug. 1805), autobiographer, son of the Minister of Cummertrees, Dumfriesshire, was educated at Edinburgh, Glasgow, and Leyden Universities, and entering the Church became Minister of Inveresk, near Edinburgh, where he remained till his death. He was a man of great ability, shrewdness, and culture, and the friend of most of the eminent literary men in Scotland of his day. He left an autobiography in manuscript, which was edited by Hill Burton, and published in 1860, and which is one of the most interesting contemporary accounts of his time. His stately appearance gained for him the name of ' Jupiter' Carlyle.

Carlyle, Thomas (4 Dec. 1795—4 Feb. 1881), historian and essayist, was born at Ecclefechan in Dumfriesshire, son of a stone-mason. He went to the grammar school at Annan, and when he was 15 to Edinburgh University where, after completing the Arts course, he started studying for the ministry; but he gave this up and became a mathematics teacher at Kirkcaldy. There he became acquainted with Edward Irving (q.v.), his close friend for many years. In 1819 he returned to Edinburgh and studied law, but tired of this and in 1822 got a private tutorship. Making a special study of German thought, then little known, he began his literary career with a series of articles on Schiller written for the *London Magazine* in 1823. In the following year he wrote biographies of Nelson, Montaigne, Montesquieu and others for an encyclopaedia, and also translated Goethe's *Wilhelm Meister*. About this time he became acquainted with Hazlitt, Coleridge, Campbell, and other leading writers. In 1826 he married Jane Baillie Welsh, a girl of shrewd wit and great beauty who had been a pupil of Irving's, and after some time in Edinburgh they settled at her farmhouse of Craigenputtock on the Galloway moors. There during the next six years Carlyle wrote *Sartor Resartus*, his contribution to moral philosophy, which is in some degree autobiographical, and also his essays on Burns, Johnson, Voltaire, Diderot, and Novalis.

In 1834 the Carlyles moved to Cheyne Row, Chelsea, where he spent the rest of his life; the house has been made a Carlyle museum. He was now engaged on his *History of the French Revolution*, the first volume of which met with disaster when the manuscript was accidentally burned while lent to J. S. Mill for annotation. Carlyle set to work and rewrote it, and when the complete work came out in 1837 it established him as one of the foremost men of letters of his day. Through the help of Harriet Martineau and other friends it was arranged that he should give a series of popular lectures in London between 1837 and 1841. The most important were those on ·

German Literature and on *Heroes and Hero Worship*, the latter being published as a book in 1841. His *Chartism* (1839) dealt with the contemporary agitation on the part of the masses for popular rights. In 1843 appeared *Past and Present*, in which he discussed other political problems and stressed the need for a wise and strong ruling class, a theme to which he returned in *Latter-Day Pamphlets* seven years later.

One of his most successful productions was his edition of *Oliver Cromwell's Letters and Speeches* (1845), which entirely altered the public estimate of Cromwell's character. His *Life of John Sterling* (q.v.) appeared in 1851, and he then embarked on his most formidable work, *Frederick the Great*, which took fourteen years to complete, appearing between 1858 and 1865. In that last year he was elected Lord Rector of Edinburgh University. In 1866 his wife died, and after that he wrote little of importance. In 1874 Disraeli offered him a baronetcy, which he declined, but he accepted the Prussian Order of Merit established by Frederick the Great. His *Reminiscences* were edited after his death by J. A. Froude (q.v.), who also wrote his life with a frankness which provoked a good deal of indignation. Although he gave up his plans for the ministry, Carlyle in his writings is always the preacher and prophet, breathing the spirit of the Old Testament rather than the New. He has a twofold gospel. On the one hand he is the apostle of work, which he described as 'the grand cure of all the maladies and miseries that ever beset mankind'; on the other he spreads the cult of the hero, the belief that the history of the world is but the biography of its great men, and idealises the Great Man especially in the person of the dictator Cromwell. This cult was extremely popular at one time, but lost favour when the experience of two world wars showed what mischief dictators could do. As a historian, Carlyle has immense vitality, his style being strong, vivid, and picturesque; his *French Revolution* has been described as an epic-romance rather than a history.

Carman, William Bliss (15 April 1861—8 June 1929), poet, was born at Fredericton, New Brunswick, and educated at the University of New Brunswick and Edinburgh University. For a time he worked as a teacher, and he also studied engineering. In 1885 he went to Harvard, where he met Richard Hovey and they agreed to devote themselves to poetry; together they wrote 3 volumes of *Songs from Vagabondia* (1894, 1896, 1902). Settling in New York, Carman kept himself by journalism; he had a flair for light romantic verse, but his strongest feeling was for nature poetry. His best-known works are *Low Tide on Grand Pré* (1893), *A Seamark* (1895), *Ballads of Lost Haven* (1897), *A Winter Holiday* (1899), *Ballads and Lyrics* (1902), *Pipes of Pan* (1904), *Later Poems* (1922), *Far Horizons* (1925), and *Sanctuary* (1929). He also edited *The World's Best Poetry* in 10 volumes (1904), and the *Oxford Book of American Verse* (1927).

Carpenter, Edward (29 Aug. 1844—28 June 1929), social reformer, was born at Brighton, one of a family of ten, and went to Trinity Hall, Cambridge, of which he became a Fellow, afterwards taking holy orders, which he relinquished in 1874. In 1883 he became a

Socialist and wrote *Towards Democracy*. Buying a farm at Mill-
thorpe, near Sheffield, he lived there till 1919, when he moved to
Guildford. His life was a reaction against Victorian conventions,
and he was an admirer of Walt Whitman, whom he visited in
America. Among his best-known works are *England's Ideal* (1887),
Civilization: Its Cause and Cure (1889), *Love's Coming of Age* (1896),
and *The Intermediate Sex* (1908). *My Days and Dreams* (1916) is
autobiographical.

Carr, John Dickson (1905—   ), who wrote detective
stories under that name and also as Carter Dickson, was born at
Uniontown, Pennsylvania. His father was a member of Congress,
and it was intended that the son should study law, but he turned
instead to journalism, and then became well known as a writer of
ingenious detective stories. His sleuth Dr Gideon Fell features in
many mysteries, including *The Arabian Nights Murder* (1936), *The
Crooked Hinge* (1938), *The Case of the Constant ʾSuicides* (1941), *The
Emperor's Snuff-Box* (1943), *The Sleeping Sphinx* (1947), *Below
Suspicion* (1950), *Death Watch* (1953), and *Captain Cut-Throat*
(1955). As Carter Dickson, who relies on that able investigator
Sir Henry Merrivale, he wrote *The Plague Court Murders* (1935),
The Ten Teacups (1937), *The Judas Window* (1938), *And So To
Murder* (1940), *The Gilded Man* (1942), and *The Skeleton in the
Clock* (1949). He also published a life of Conan Doyle in 1949, and
with Adrian C. Doyle wrote *The Exploits of Sherlock Holmes*, a not
very successful attempt to resuscitate the great detective. During
the Second World War he was bombed out of his London house, and
in 1948 he returned to the United States.

Carroll, Lewis, *see* **Dodgson, Charles Lutwidge.**

Carruthers, Robert (5 Nov. 1799—26 May 1878), journalist, born
in Dumfries, son of a farmer, was for a time a teacher in Huntingdon,
and wrote a *History of Huntingdon* (1824). In 1828 he became
editor of the *Inverness Courier*, which he conducted with great
ability for fifty years. He edited Pope's works with a memoir
(1853), and along with Robert Chambers (q.v.) edited the first edition
of *Chambers's Cyclopaedia of English Literature* (1842—4). He
received the degree of LL.D. from Edinburgh.

Carryl, Charles Edward (30 Dec. 1841—3 July 1920), writer of
children's books, born in New York, was educated at the Irving
Institute, Tarrytown. He became a railway company director, and
from 1874 was a member of the New York stock exchange. His
book for children, *Davy and the Goblin* (1885), contains some delightful verse in the vein of Lewis Carroll; it was followed by *The Admiral's
Caravan* (1892). *The River Syndicate* (1899) was a collection of short
stories for grown-ups. Carryl's career has sometimes been compared
with that of Kenneth Grahame (q.v.). His son Guy, who was making
a name for himself as poet and humorist, died in 1904.

Carson, Rachel Louise (27 May 1907—   ), writer on
science, was born at Springdale, Pennsylvania, daughter of Robert
Warden, and educated at Pennsylvania College for Women and Johns

Hopkins University. After studying at the Marine Biological Laboratory, she joined the zoological staff of the University of Maryland in 1931. She received numerous awards and medals for her scientific work and held honorary degrees of several universities. Her books include *Under the Sea Wind* (1934), and *The Sea Around Us* (1951).

Carswell, Catherine Roxburgh (27 March 1879—18 Feb. 1946), novelist and critic, was born in Glasgow, daughter of George Gray Macfarlane, an East India merchant, and educated at the Park School; afterwards she studied music in Frankfort. Her first marriage, to H. P. M. Jackson in 1903, was terminated by a decree of nullity. In 1907 she became dramatic critic of the *Glasgow Herald*, but lost her post in 1911 owing to a review which she wrote of D. H. Lawrence's banned novel, *The Rainbow*. In 1915 she married Donald Carswell, who was killed in the black-out during the Second World War. Her novels *Open the Door* (1920) and *The Camomile* (1922) were followed in 1930 by a *Life of Burns* which was received unfavourably in Scotland, and *The Savage Pilgrimage: a Narrative of D. H. Lawrence* (1932), written from personal knowledge, which was suppressed as libellous. Her autobiography, *Lying Awake*, was published in 1950.

Carte, Thomas (baptized 23 April 1686, died 2 April 1754), historian, born at Clifton-upon-Dunamoor, Warwickshire, where his father was vicar, and educated at Oxford and Cambridge, took orders but resigned his benefice at Bath when required to take the oath of allegiance to George I. He was secretary to Francis Atterbury (q.v.), and was involved in the consequences of his conspiracy, but escaped to France, where he remained until 1728. After his return he published a life of the Duke of Ormonde (1736), and a *History of England* to 1654 in 4 volumes (1747—54), the latter a work of value for its original material.

Carter, • Elizabeth (16 Dec. 1717—19 Feb. 1806), scholar and poetess, was born at Deal, daughter of a clergyman. Originally backward, she applied herself to study with such perseverance that she became perhaps the most learned Englishwoman of her time, being mistress of Latin, Greek, Hebrew, Arabic, French, Italian, Spanish, German, and Portuguese. She was also well read in science. She translated Epictetus (1758) and wrote a small volume of poems. Dr Johnson, whose friendship she enjoyed for nearly fifty years, asserted that she 'could make a pudding as well as translate.'

Cartwright, William (Sept. 1611—29 Nov. 1643), clergyman and dramatist, son of a gentleman of Gloucestershire, who had run through his fortune and kept an inn at Cirencester, was educated at Westminster School and Oxford. He took orders in 1635, was a zealous Royalist, and a florid preacher. He also wrote spirited lyrics and four plays of which *The Royal Slave*, performed in 1636 before the court at Oxford, was the most successful; others were *The Siege* and *The Lady Errant*. He was the friend of Ben Jonson, Henry Vaughan, and Izaak Walton. He died at Oxford of camp fever.

Cary, Alice (26 April 1820—12 Feb. 1871), poetess, was born on her father's farm near Cincinnati. She had a poem printed when she was 18, and in 1849 joined with her sister Phoebe (q.v.) in publishing *Poems of Alice and Phoebe Cary*. In the following year the sisters made a journey to New York, where they met Whittier. Settling there, they formed a circle of literary friends, and Alice became president of the first women's club in America, now the Sorosis. Other volumes of her poetry are *Lyra and Other Poems* (1852) and *Ballads, Songs, and Hymns* (1866). Of her prose works *Clovernook Papers* (1852) was the most popular.

Cary, Arthur Joyce Lunel (7 Dec. 1888—29 March 1957), novelist, born at Londonderry, was educated at Clifton and Oxford, and studied art in Edinburgh and Paris. In 1913 he joined the Nigerian political service, and from 1915 to 1916 he served with the Nigeria Regiment in the Cameroons. Resigning in 1920 for health reasons, he settled in Oxford and after a long apprenticeship as a writer became a highly successful novelist. His first book was *Aissa Saved* (1932), and one of his greatest successes was *The House of Children* (1941), which won the Tait Black Memorial Prize. Other novels are *The American Visitor* (1933), *The African Witch* (1936), *Mister Johnson* (1939), *Charley is my Darling* (1940), *Herself Surprised* (1941), *To the Moonlight* (1946), *Prisoner of Grace* (1952), and *Not Honour More* (1955). *Marching Soldier* (1945) and *The Drunken Sailor* (1947) are books of verse. He also wrote some political studies, including *Power in Men* (1939), *The Case for African Freedom* (1941), and *The Process of Real Freedom* (1943).

Cary, Henry Francis (6 Dec. 1772—14 Aug. 1844), translator, was born at Gibraltar, and educated at Oxford. Publishing a book of verse at the age of 16, he became a regular contributor to *The Gentleman's Magazine*. He took orders in 1796. His great work is his translation of the *Divina Commedia* of Dante (1805—14), which is not only faithful to the original, but is rendered into such fine English as to be itself literature. He also translated from the Greek. He received a pension in 1841, and was buried in Westminster Abbey.

Cary, Phoebe (4 Sept. 1824—31 July 1871), poetess, was born near Cincinnati, a sister of Alice Cary (q.v.), and contributed in 1849 to the *Poems of Alice and Phoebe Cary*. She followed her sister to New York, and looked after the domestic side of their household. Her literary output was smaller than Alice's, but she had more feeling and humour. Her books include *Poems and Parodies* (1854) and *Poems of Faith, Hope, and Love* (1868), her religious piece 'One Sweetly Solemn Thought' being widely admired. Devoted all their lives, the sisters died within a few months of each other.

Castle, Egerton (12 March 1858—16 Sept. 1920), novelist, was born in London. His father, who was an intimate friend of Browning, George Sand, Verdi, and Liszt, took the boy with him on walking tours on the Continent. He was educated at the universities of Paris, Glasgow, and Cambridge; was entered at the Inner Temple; went to Sandhurst and served three years with the colours; and represented England as an international at fencing. From 1885 to

1894 he was on the staff of the *Saturday Review*. With his wife Agnes he produced a series of romantic novels which include *The Pride of Jennico* (1898), *The Bath Comedy* (1900), *The Secret Orchard* (1901), *The Star Dreamer* (1903), *The Incomparable Bellairs* (1904), and *If Youth But Knew* (1906). He also wrote a play, *Desperate Remedies*.

Cather, Willa Sibert (7 Dec. 1873—24 April 1947), novelist, was born near Winchester, Virginia, but when she was 8 the family removed to a ranch in Nebraska, and she became a Westerner by environment. She paid her way through the University of Nebraska by working as a newspaper correspondent, and later became dramatic critic of the Pittsburgh *Daily Leader*. In 1903 she published a book of poems, *April Twilight*, and in 1905 *The Troll Garden*, a collection of short stories. From 1906 to 1912 she was managing editor of *McClure's Magazine*. *O Pioneers!* (1913), a novel which tells of the Western immigrants, was her first great success, and was followed by *My Antonia* (1918) and *A Lost Lady* (1923). Later novels show the influence of her conversion to Roman Catholicism. *Death Comes for the Archbishop* (1927) depicts the Spanish South West, and *Shadows on the Rock* (1931) French Quebec. In 1933 she received the Prix Femina Americaine, and at various times she was awarded honorary degrees by five universities. Her work shows classic restraint and balance.

Catlin, George (23 July 1796—23 Dec. 1872), artist and author, born at Wilkesbarre, Pennsylvania, practised for some time as a lawyer, but yielding to his artistic instincts he took to painting. He spent the seven years, 1832—9, among the Indians of North America, of whom he painted about 500 portraits. He became thoroughly acquainted with their life, and published *Letters and Notes on the Manners, Customs, and Condition of the North American Indians* (1841), and *Life Among the Indians* (1867).

Cave, Edward (27 Feb. 1691—10 Jan. 1754), printer, who used the pseudonym Sylvanus Urbanus, born near Rugby, started in 1731 *The Gentleman's Magazine*, for which Dr Johnson was parliamentary reporter from 1740. He published many of Johnson's works.

Cavendish, George (1500—1561), biographer, married a niece of Sir Thomas More, and was Gentleman Usher to Cardinal Wolsey, to whom he was so much attached that he followed him in his disgrace, and continued to serve him until his death. He left in manuscript a life of his patron, which is the first separate biography in English, and is the main original authority of the period.

Cavendish, Margaret, *see* **Newcastle.**

Caxton, William (1422?—1491), printer and translator, born in the Weald of Kent, was apprenticed to a London mercer. On his master's death in 1441 he went to Bruges and lived there and in various other places in the Low Countries for over thirty years, engaged as head of an association of English merchants trading in foreign parts, and in negotiating commercial treaties between

England and the Dukes of Burgundy. His first literary labour was a translation of a French romance, which he entitled *The Recuyell of the Historyes of Troye*, and which he finished in 1471. About this time he learned the art of printing, probably in Cologne, and, after being in the service of Margaret Duchess of Burgundy, an English princess, returned to his native country and set up at Westminster in 1476 his printing press, the first in England. His *Recuyell* and *The Game and Playe of Chesse* had already been printed—the first books in English—on the Continent. Here was produced the first book printed in England, *The Dictes and Sayings of the Philosophers* (1477), and also editions of the works of Chaucer and Gower. Caxton printed nearly 80 separate works, many of them translations of his own, which contributed to the formation of an English prose style.

Cecil, Lord Edward Christian David Gascoyne (9 April 1902—), critic, son of the 4th Marquis of Salisbury, was educated at Wadham College, Oxford, of which he became a Fellow, and in 1948 was appointed Goldsmith's Professor of English Literature at Oxford. In 1932 he married a daughter of Desmond MacCarthy (q.v.). His works include *The Stricken Deer* (1929), a study of Cowper, *Sir Walter Scott* (1933), *Early Victorian Novelists* (1934), *Jane Austen* (1935), *The Young Melbourne* (1939), and *Poets and Story Tellers* (1949). He also edited *An Anthology of Modern Biography* (1936) and the *Oxford Book of Christian Verse* (1940). He was made a Companion of Honour in 1949.

Centlivre, Susanna (1667?—1 Dec. 1723), dramatist and actress, whose maiden name was either Freeman or Rawkins, married at 16, lost her husband in a year, then married an officer, who fell in a duel in 18 months, and finally, in 1706, married Joseph Centlivre, chef to Queen Anne, with whom she lived happily for the rest of her days. She wrote 18 or 19 plays, well constructed and amusing, among which may be mentioned *The Perjured Husband* (1700), *The Busybody* (1709), *The Wonder! A Woman Keeps a Secret* (1714), and *A Bold Stroke for a Wife* (1717). She was a strong Whig, and sometimes made her plays the medium of expressing her political opinions.

Chalkhill, John (fl. 1600), poet, wrote a pastoral poem, *Thealma and Clearchus*, which was edited in 1683 by Izaak Walton. As nothing else is known of him it has been held by some that the name was a pseudonym of Walton himself. It has been shown, however, that a gentleman of the name existed during the reign of Elizabeth. Walton says he was a friend of Spenser, and that his life was 'useful, quiet, and virtuous.'

Chalmers, George (1742—31 May 1825), antiquary, born at Fochabers, Elginshire, and educated at King's College, Aberdeen, emigrated to America and practised law in Baltimore; but on the outbreak of the Revolutionary War returned to Britain, and settled in London as a clerk in the Board of Trade. He published in 1780 a *History of the United Colonies*, and wrote lives of Sir David Lyndsay, Defoe, and Mary Queen of Scots. His great work, however, is his *Caledonia*, of which 3 volumes had been published at his death. It was to have been a complete collection of the topography and antiquities of Scotland; and, as it stands, is a monument of industry and research, though not always trustworthy in disputed points.

Chalmers, Thomas (17 March 1780—30 May 1847), minister and philanthropist, born at Anstruther, Fife, one of a merchant's fourteen children, studied at St Andrews and, entering the ministry of the Church of Scotland, was first settled in the small parish of Kilmeny, Fife, but, his talents and eloquence becoming known, he was, in 1815, translated to Glasgow, where he was soon recognized as the most eloquent preacher in Scotland, and where also he initiated his schemes for helping the poor.   In 1823 he became Professor of Moral Philosophy at St Andrews, and in 1828 of Divinity in Edinburgh. In 1834 he began his great scheme of Church extension, the result of which was that in seven years £300,000 had been raised, and 220 churches built.   In the same year, 1834, began the troubles and controversies in regard to patronage and the relations of Church and State, which in 1843 ended in the disruption of the Church, when 470 ministers with Chalmers at their head, resigned their benefices, and founded the Free Church of Scotland.   Chalmers was chosen its first Moderator and Principal of its Theological College in Edinburgh. The remaining four years of his life were spent in organizing the new Church, and in works of philanthropy.   His chief works, which were collected and published in 34 volumes, relate to natural theology, evidences of Christianity, political economy, and general theology and science.   Those which perhaps attracted most attention were his *Astronomical Discourses* and his *Lectures on Church Establishments.* He was D.D., LL.D., D.C.L.(Oxon.), and a Corresponding Member of the Institute of France.

Chamberlayne, William (1619—Jan. 1689), doctor and poet, practised medicine at Shaftesbury.   On the outbreak of the Civil War he joined the Royalists and fought at the second battle of Newbury.   He wrote a play, *Love's Victory* (1658), and an epic *Pharonnida* (1659).   With occasional beauties he is, in the main, heavy and stiff, and is almost forgotten.   He influenced Keats.

Chambers, Charles Haddon (22 April 1860—28 March 1921), playwright, was born in Stanmore, Sydney, of Irish parentage, his father being a member of the Civil Service, which he himself entered at 15; but after two years he gave it up and became a stockrider.   At the age of 22 he went to London and started writing plays.   His first real success was when his comedy *Captain Swift* was produced by Beerbohm Tree at the Haymarket in 1888.   This was followed by *The Idler* (1890), and his best play, a four-act comedy, *The Tyranny of Tears* (1899).   During the First World War he was employed on propaganda work.   Later plays were *The Saving Grace* (1919) and *Passers-by* (1920).

Chambers, Sir Edmund Kerchever (16 March 1866—21 Jan. 1954), scholar, was born in Berkshire, son of a former Fellow of Worcester College, Oxford.   Educated at Marlborough and Oxford, he entered the Education Department in 1892, eventually becoming Second Secretary to the Board.   He was one of the greatest authorities on Shakespeare and the early English theatre, his principal works being

The Medieval Stage (1903), *The Elizabethan Stage* (1923), *Shakespeare: A Survey* (1925), *Arthur of Britain* (1927), *William Shakespeare* (1930), *Samuel Taylor Coleridge* (1938), and *English Literature at the Close of the Middle Ages* (1945). He also edited Donne's and Vaughan's poems, and compiled the *Oxford Book of Sixteenth-Century Verse* (1932). He was made a C.B. in 1912 and knighted in 1925.

Chambers, Robert (10 July 1802—17 March 1871), author and publisher, was born at Peebles, and started business as a bookseller in Edinburgh at the age of 16, devoting all his spare time to study, to such purpose that in 1824 he published *Traditions of Edinburgh*, a work in which he had the assistance of Walter Scott. He joined his brother William (q.v.) in establishing the publishing firm of W. and R. Chambers, and in starting *Chambers's Journal*, to which he was a constant contributor. Later ventures were *The Cyclopaedia of English Literature* (1842—4, latest edition 1938), and *Chambers's Encyclopaedia* (1859—68, latest edition 1950). Among his own works may be mentioned *Vestiges of Creation*, published anonymously (1844), a precursor of Darwinism, *A Life of Burns* (1851), *Popular Rhymes of Scotland* (1847), *History of the Rebellions in Scotland*, *Domestic Annals of Scotland* (1859—61), *Ancient Sea Margins* (1848), *Dictionary of Eminent Scotsmen* and *The Book of Days* (1863). He was LL.D. of St Andrews.

Chambers, William (16 April 1800—20 May 1883), author and publisher, born at Peebles, started in 1832 with his brother Robert (q.v.) *Chambers's Journal*, and soon after joined him in the firm of W. and R. Chambers. Besides contributions to the *Journal* he wrote several books, including a *History of Peeblesshire* (1864), and an autobiography of himself and his brother. Chambers was a man of great business capacity, and, though of less literary distinction than his brother, did much for the dissemination of cheap and useful literature. He was Lord Provost of Edinburgh from 1865 to 1869, was an LL.D. of the university, and restored the ancient church of St Giles.

Chamier, Frederick (1796—Oct. 1870), novelist, was in the navy, rose to the rank of captain, and served in the Walcheren expedition. Retiring in 1827, he wrote several sea novels somewhat in the style of Marryat, including *Life of a Sailor* (1832), *Ben Brace* (1836), *Jack Adams* (1838), and *Tom Bowline* (1841). He also continued James's *Naval History*, and wrote books of travel.

Chandler, John (16 June 1806—1 July 1876), translator, was born at Witley, Godalming, Surrey. Educated at Oxford, he took orders in 1831 and in 1837 became vicar of Witley. He wrote a *Life of William of Wykeham* (1842) and *Horae Sacrae* (1844), a book of prayers, but is remembered chiefly for his *Hymns from the Primitive Church* (1827), which gives text and translation of Latin hymns; many of his renderings have been incorporated in modern hymnals.

Channing, William Ellery (7 April 1780—2 Oct. 1842), Unitarian minister, born at Newport, Rhode Island, was for a time in the Congregationalist Church, but became the leader of the Unitarians in New England. He had a powerful influence on the thought and literature of his time in America, and published *Remarks on American Literature* (1830). His statue in Boston bears the inscription 'He breathed into theology a humane spirit.'

Chapman, George (1559?—12 May 1634), dramatist and translator, was born near Hitchin, and may have been educated at Oxford and Cambridge. His principal tragedies are *Bussy D'Ambois* (1607), *The Conspiracy and Tragedy of Byron* (1608), *The Revenge of Bussy D'Ambois* (1613), and *Caesar and Pompey* (1631); his comedies include *The Blind Beggar of Alexandria* (1598), *An Humorous Day's Mirth* (1599), *All Fools* (1605), *May-Day* (1611), and *The Gentleman Usher* (1606). He also collaborated with Jonson in *Eastward Ho!* (1605) and shared in the imprisonment meted out to its authors. As a dramatist he has humour, and vigour, and occasional poetic fire, but is very unequal. His great work by which he lives in literature is his translation of Homer. The *Iliad* was published in 1611, the *Odyssey* in 1616, and the *Hymns* in 1624. The work is full of energy and spirit, well maintains its place among the many later translations, and had the distinction of suggesting Keats's immortal sonnet. Chapman also translated from Petrarch, and completed Marlowe's unfinished *Hero and Leander*. He has sometimes been identified with the rival poet of Shakespeare's *Sonnet* LXXXVI.

Chapman, Robert William (5 Oct. 1881—20 April 1960), editor, was born at Eskbank, Dalkeith, son of an English clergyman, and educated at Dundee High School, St Andrews University, and Oxford. In 1906 he joined the staff of the Clarendon Press, of which he became secretary from 1920 to 1942, one of its greatest periods, during which the great *Oxford English Dictionary* was published. During the First World War he served with the artillery and found time to edit Dr Johnson's *Tour to the Hebrides*. From 1931 to 1947 he was a Fellow of Magdalen. His authoritative edition of the works of Jane Austen began with the *Novels* in 1923, was continued with the *Letters* in 1932, and completed when the *Juvenilia* came out in 1951. In 1953 he published an edition of Dr Johnson's *Letters*. He was awarded doctorates by St Andrews and Oxford, was a Fellow of the British Academy, and in 1955 was made a C.B.E.

Chapone, Hester (27 Oct. 1727—25 Dec. 1801), born at Twywell, Northamptonshire, daughter of Thomas Mulso, married Chapone, a solicitor, who died a few months afterwards. She was one of the learned ladies who gathered round Mrs Montague (q.v.), and was the author of *Letters on the Improvement of the Mind* (1772), and *Miscellanies*.

Charleton, Walter (2 Feb. 1619—24 April 1707), doctor and antiquary, son of the rector of Shepton Mallett in Somerset, was educated at Oxford and became titular physician to Charles I. He was a copious writer on theology, natural history, and antiquities, and published *Chorea Gigantum* (1663) to prove that Stonehenge was built by the Danes. He was also one of the 'character' writers, and in this kind of literature wrote *A Brief Discourse concerning the Different Wits of Men* (1675).

Charteris, Leslie (12 May 1907—   ), novelist, born at Singapore, son of a Chinese surgeon and an Englishwoman, was christened Leslie Charles Bowyer Yin.   Before he was 12 he had been three times round the world.   At 10 years of age he was writing and editing his own magazine, he got into print at 11, sold his first story when he was 17, and at 18 went to Cambridge.   After having a crime novel accepted he decided to be a writer, but before achieving success earned his living at a great variety of occupations, and was in turn rubber planter, tin miner, gold prospector, pearl fisher, seaman, travelling showman, and bar-tender.   His picaresque stories, which tell of a gentleman-burglar Simon Templar, nicknamed 'the Saint,' began in 1930 with *Enter the Saint* and became immensely popular, being translated into fifteen languages as well as being used on films, radio, and the comic strip.   Others of the series were *Knight Templar* (1930), *Alias the Saint* (1931), *The Brighter Buccaneer* (1933), *The Ace of Knaves* (1937), *The Happy Highwayman* (1939), *The Saint in Miami* (1940), and *The Saint Goes West* (1942).   In 1932 Charteris went to America and in 1941 he became an American citizen.   He was married four times.

Chatterton, Edward Keble (1878—31 Dec. 1944), writer of books about ships, was born at Sheffield and educated at Oxford.   Going to London, he became art and dramatic critic for several journals, but was best known for his numerous works on ships and the sea. During the First World War he served as a lieutenant-commander R.N.V.R.   Among his books are *Sailing Ships* (1909), *Steamships and their Story* (1910), *The Romance of the Ship* (1910), *Fore and Aft* (1911), *King's Cutters and Smugglers* (1912), *Ships and Ways of Other Days* (1913), *The Old East Indiamen* (1914), *The Romance of Piracy* (1914), *Q-Ships and their Story* (1922), *The Mercantile Marine* (1923), *Seamen All* (1924), *Whalers and Whaling* (1925), *Battles by Sea* (1925), *Windjammers and Shellbacks* (1926), *Ventures and Voyages* (1928), *On the High Seas* (1929), *The Yachtsman's Pilot* (1933), *Valiant Sailormen* (1936), and *The Commerce Raiders* (1943).

Chatterton, Thomas (20 Nov. 1752—25 Aug. 1770), poet, was born in Bristol, the posthumous son of a poor schoolmaster, and brought up beside the church of St Mary Redcliffe, of which his uncle was sexton.   Much of the boy's leisure was spent in its muniment room, poring over ancient documents preserved there, round which he wove a world of his own imagining.   Using antique spelling and vocabulary, he started to write poems by an imaginary medieval monk whom he named Thomas Rowley.   One of these deceived a master at Colston's Bluecoat School, which he attended, and in 1768, on the occasion of the opening of a new bridge, he published in the *Bristol Journal* a supposed contemporary account of a similar cere-mony in the thirteenth century.   Going on to fabricate a more ambitious work, 'The Ryse of Peynctynge in England,' he sent it to Horace Walpole, who was at first taken in by it, but was undeceived when he submitted it to the poet Gray, who pronounced it a forgery.

In Bristol Chatterton had been apprenticed to an attorney, and though a mere office drudge working eleven hours a day had found time to study heraldry, metaphysics, astonomy, medicine, and music, as well as his beloved antiquities. But in April of 1770, with some £5 of capital, he took coach to London and found lodgings in Shoreditch, bent on making a living by his pen. Four months later, having removed to Holborn in the meantime, he poisoned himself with arsenic, after having lived for weeks on the verge of starvation and at the last proudly refusing his landlady's invitation to take a meal with her. His tragic death gripped the imagination of poets of the Romantic Revival, and tributes were paid to his memory by Coleridge, Shelley, Keats, and Wordsworth, who calls him 'the sleepless soul that perished in his pride.' But it should be realized that his was not the tragedy of an unworldly poet vainly seeking recognition for his verses. Chatterton had planned to make his way in London as a freelance writer, and at first he met with fair success. Versatile and energetic, he dashed off essays, political articles, stories, and squibs, as well as poems like his graceful 'Balade of Charitie'; in May and June he had articles in six leading magazines, earned 11 guineas, and even sent home a box of presents for his mother and sister. He had also obtained a hopeful interview with Lord Mayor Beckford. But Beckford died suddenly and Chatterton was left without resources to tide him over the summer holiday season, which was then, as it is now, a slack and difficult time for the freelance.

For years there was a heated controversy over the Rowley Poems, but Skeat's edition of 1871 once for all demonstrated that they were fabrications. Chatterton's importance in English literature lies not in his use of terms from old glossaries, which he frequently misunderstood, but in his command of rhythm and his breaking away from eighteenth-century conventions. For example, the rhythm of Coleridge's 'Christabel,' which is said to have inspired Walter Scott's familiar octosyllabic metre, is anticipated in Chatterton's work. Such pieces as the Minstrel's Song in his dramatic interlude 'Aella' justify Watts-Dunton's description of him as 'the Renascence of Wonder incarnate,' and even so cautious a critic as Edmund Gosse declared him 'the most extraordinary phenomenon of infancy in the literature of the world.'

Chaucer, Geoffrey (1340?—25 Oct. 1400), poet, was born in London, the son of John Chaucer, a vintner of Thames Street, who had also a small estate at Ipswich, and was occasionally employed on service for King Edward III; this doubtless was the means of his son's introduction to the Court. The acquaintance which Chaucer displays with all branches of the learning of his time shows that he must have received an ample education; but there is no evidence that he was at either of the universities. In 1357 he appears as a page to the Lady Elizabeth, wife of Lionel Duke of Clarence, and in 1359 he first saw military service in France, when he was made a prisoner, being ransomed in 1360. About 1366 he married Philippa, probably a sister of the third wife of John of Gaunt, whose patronage he thenceforth enjoyed. In 1367 he was one of the valets of the King's Chamber, a post always held by gentlemen, and received a pension of 20 marks, and he was soon afterwards one of the King's esquires. In 1369 the death of Blanche, wife of John of Gaunt, gave occasion for a poem by Chaucer in honour of her memory, *The Boke of the Duchess*. In the same year he again bore arms in France, and during the next ten years he was frequently employed on diplomatic missions. In 1372 he was sent to Genoa to arrange a commercial treaty, on which occasion he may have met Petrarch and Boccaccio, and was rewarded by a grant in 1374 of a pitcher of wine daily. In the same year he got from the corporation of London a lease for life of a house at Aldgate, on condition of keeping it in repair; and soon after he was appointed Comptroller of the Customs and Subsidy of Wool, Skins, and Leather in the port of London; he also received from the Duke of Lancaster a pension of £10. In 1377 he was sent on a mission to Flanders to treat of peace with the French King.

After the accession of Richard II in that year, he was sent to France to treat for the marriage of the King with the French Princess Mary, and thereafter to Lombardy, on which occasion he appointed John Gower (q.v.) to act for him in his absence in any legal proceedings which might arise. In 1382 he became Comptroller of the Petty Customs of the port of London, and in 1385 was allowed to appoint a deputy, which enabled him to devote more time to writing. He had in 1373 begun his *Canterbury Tales*, on which he was occupied at intervals for the rest of his life. In 1386 Chaucer took his seat in Parliament as Knight of the Shire for Kent. His fortunes now suffered some eclipse. His patron, John of Gaunt, was abroad, and the government was presided over by the Duke of Gloucester, who was at feud with him. Owing probably to this cause Chaucer was in December 1386, dismissed from his employments, and was left with no income beyond his pensions, on which he was obliged to raise money. His wife also died about the same time. In 1389, however, Richard took the government into his own hands; prosperity returned to Chaucer, whose friends were now in power, and he was appointed Clerk of the King's works. This office, however, he held for two years only, and again fell into poverty, from which he was rescued in 1394 by a pension from the King of £20. On the accession of Henry IV in 1399 an additional pension of 40 marks was given him. In the same year he took a lease of a house at Westminster, where he died soon afterwards. He is buried in the Poets' Corner, Westminster Abbey, where a monument to him was erected by Nicholas Brigham, a minor poet of the sixteenth century. The fullest edition of his works is by W. W. Skeat (1894—7).

The exact dates of the composition of his various poems are uncertain, but his work clearly shows three stages in his poetic development. In the first the influence of French literature is predominant, a natural thing since the Court was still bilingual. To this period belong his translation of the *Romance of the Rose*, that great French poem of the previous century, and also the *Boke of the Duchesse* (1369). In the second period he came under Italian influence, particularly that of Dante and Boccaccio, and began to make use of the heroic couplet in place of his earlier octosyllabics. It was then that he wrote *The Hous of Fame, The Parlement of*

Foules, The Legende of Good Women, and, greatest of all, *Troilus and Criseyde,* a translation, with numerous alterations, of Boccaccio's *Filostrato.* Boccaccio also provides sources for several of the *Canterbury Tales,* which belong ·to the final or English period of Chaucer's development, when he had reached his full stature as a writer and become one of the greatest of English poets. Chaucer's importance in English literature can hardly be over-estimated. A great creative genius, an artist in verse with an insight into humanity rivalling Shakespeare's, and an elvish but kindly sense of humour, he was both a finished poet and a supreme story-teller. The first of modern English writers, he may be said to have created not only English poetry but the English language, so that the next of our great poets rightly called him 'Dan Chaucer, well of English undefiled.'

Cheke, Sir John (16 June 1514—13 Sept. 1557), scholar, was born in Cambridge at the corner of Petty Cury, son of an esquire-bedel of the university. Educated at St John's, he earned a great reputation by his knowledge of Greek, was first lecturer, then in 1540 professor, of that subject, and introduced the revised pronunciation of Greek now in use. In 1544 he was appointed Public Orator to the university, and also became tutor to the future Edward VI. In 1548 he was appointed Provost of King's College, and in 1552 he was knighted. Later, under Mary I, he was imprisoned in the Tower and compelled to abjure Protestantism. He edited many Greek texts, and his *Letter on English* was prefaced to the translation by Hoby (q.v.) of Castiglione's *The Courtier.*

Cherry, Andrew (11 Jan. 1762—12 Feb. 1812), dramatist, son of a bookseller at Limerick, was a successful actor, and managed theatres in the provinces. He also wrote some plays, of which *The Soldier's Daughter* (1804) is the best. His chief claim to remembrance rests on his songs, 'The Bay of Biscay' and 'The Green Little Shamrock.'

Chesterfield, Philip Dormer Stanhope, 4th Earl of (22 Sept. 1694—24 March 1773) statesman and letter-writer, was born in London, eldest son of the 3rd Earl. After being at Trinity College, Cambridge, he sat in the House of Commons until his accession to the peerage in 1726. He filled many high offices, including those of Ambassador to Holland, Lord Lieutenant of Ireland, and Secretary of State. He was distinguished for his wit, conversational powers, and grace of manner. His place in literature is fixed by his well-known *Letters* addressed to his natural son, Philip Dormer Stanhope. Though brilliant, and full of shrewdness and knowledge of the world, they reflect the low tone of morals prevalent in the age when they were written. He was the recipient of Johnson's famous letter rebuking him for his failure as a patron.

Chesterton, Gilbert Keith (29 March 1874—14 June 1936), essayist, novelist, poet, was born at Campden Hill, London, son of an estate agent; he took the name Keith from the Aberdeen ancestors of his French-Scottish mother. He went to school at St Paul's, where he started a magazine, *The Debater,* and afterwards attended the Slade

School of Art.   Later he was to illustrate the novels of his friend
Hilaire Belloc (q.v.), but now he began the career of journalism
which produced those delightful weekly essays which were collected
in a series of volumes.   His first books, however, were two collections
of verse, *The Wild Knight* and a book of humorous pieces, *Greybeards
at Play*, both published in 1900.   In the following year he married
Frances Blogg and settled at Battersea.   In 1904 appeared *The
Napoleon of Notting Hill Gate*, which embodies his 'Little Englander'
doctrine.   His works of literary criticism began with *Robert Browning*
(1903) followed by studies of *Dickens* (1906) and *Bernard Shaw* (1909).
In 1908 he published *Orthodoxy*, expressing his idea of Christianity,
and in 1910 *What's Wrong with the World*, outlining his social beliefs.

About this time the Chestertons moved from Battersea to Beaconsfield, where they spent the rest of their lives.   Here he began his
series of detective stories with *The Innocence of Father Brown* (1911).
In the same year he published his *Ballad of the White Horse*, and in
1912 the novel *Manalive*, which expresses his supreme zest in living.
The Victorian Age in Literature (1913), a brilliant piece of criticism,
was followed by *A Short History of England* (1917), inaccurate but
inspired.   At the beginning of the First World War he had an almost
fatal illness, but by 1916, when his brother Cecil enlisted in the army,
he was able to take over from him the editorship of the *New Witness*,
which later as *G. K.'s Weekly* proclaimed his gospel of 'distributism,'
championing the small man against the trusts.   In 1922 he was
received into the Roman Catholic Church by his friend Father
O'Connor, the original of 'Father Brown,' his reverend detective.
The remainder of his life was notable mainly for his religious writings,
St Francis of Assisi (1923), *The Everlasting Man* (1925), and *St
Thomas Aquinas* (1933).   His *Collected Poems* were published in
1927 and a study of *Chaucer* in 1932.   In the course of a busy life
he produced over 100 volumes.   Stout, untidy, absent-minded,
good-natured, with a tremendous sense of fun and a genius for
illuminating paradox, Chesterton was one of the most popular writers
of his time.

Chettle, Henry (1565—1607?), dramatist and pamphleteer, son
of a London dyer, edited Greene's *Groat's-worth of Wit* (1592), and
is believed to have written 13 and collaborated in 35 plays.   He also
wrote two satires, *Kind Harts Dreame* (1593), which contains one of
the earliest tributes to Shakespeare, and *Pierce Plainnes Prentiship*
(1595). He was imprisoned for debt in 1599. The only one of his plays
that has survived is *The Tragedy of Hoffman*, written about 1602.

Cheyney, Peter, *see* Southouse-Cheyney.

Child, Francis James (1 Feb. 1825—11 Sept. 1896), philologist, was
born at Boston, son of a sailmaker, and educated at Harvard,
Göttingen, and Berlin.   In 1851 he became Professor of Rhetoric
at Harvard, and in 1876 changed over to the chair of Early English
Literature.   He edited some early English plays and the poems of
Spenser, but his great achievement was his collection of *English and
Scottish Ballads* in 10 volumes (final edition 1882—97), which is the
standard work on the subject.

F

Child, Lydia Maria (11 Feb. 1802—20 Oct. 1880), novelist, was born at Medford, Massachusetts, daughter of Convers Francis, a baker. After publishing *Hobomok* (1824) and *The Rebels* (1825), both novels, she kept a private school for a time, and in 1828 married David Lee Child, a Boston lawyer. They worked together in the campaign against slavery, and she wrote *An Appeal in Favor of That Class of Americans Called Africans* (1838). Her later novels include *Philothea* (1836), a tale of the age of Pericles, and *A Romance of the Republic* (1867), which deals with the American Civil War. Her *Letters* were edited in 1883.

Childers, Robert Erskine (25 June 1870—24 Nov. 1922), novelist, was born in London, son of an oriental scholar. His mother was Irish, and he was brought up in County Wicklow and educated at Haileybury and Cambridge, where he studied law. After serving in the Boer War he wrote a book about his experiences, *In the Ranks of the C.I.V.* (1900). In the same year appeared his best-known novel, *The Riddle of the Sands*, which describes an imaginary German plot to invade Britain. In 1914 he served with the Royal Naval Air Service and was awarded the D.S.C. After the war he devoted himself to the cause of Irish Home Rule and was secretary of the Irish delegation which negotiated the treaty of 1921. After the establishment of the Irish Free State he joined the Republican Army, was captured by Free State soldiers, and was court-martialled and executed in Dublin.

Chillingworth, William (1602—30 Jan. 1644), theologian, born and educated at Oxford, was godson of Archbishop Laud. Falling into theological doubts he subsequently became a convert to Roman Catholicism, and studied at the Jesuit College at Douay, 1630. In the following year he returned to Oxford, and rejoined the Church of England in 1634. This exposed him to violent attacks on the part of the Romanists, in reply to which he published in 1637 his famous polemic, *The Religion of the Protestants a Safe Way to Salvation*. For a time he refused ecclesiastical preferment but ultimately he became Prebendary and Chancellor of Salisbury. He was regarded as one of the ablest controversialists of the Anglican Church.

Cholmondeley, Mary (8 June 1859—15 July 1925), novelist, was born at Hodnet, Shropshire, where her father was rector. All her life she was handicapped by bad health. Her first book, *The Danvers Jewels* (1887), a detective story published under the pseudonym Pax, was followed by *Sir Charles Danvers* (1889), and *Diana Tempest* (1893). In 1896 her father retired and removed to London, and three years later she became famous through her outspoken novel *Red Pottage*, which attacked the shams of the English middle class. Later novels were *Moth and Rust* (1902), *Prisoners* (1906), *The Lowest Rung* (1908), *Notwithstanding* (1913), and *The Romance of his Life* (1921). *Under One Roof* (1918) is a book of reminiscences

Chorley, Henry Fothergill (15 Dec. 1808—16 Feb. 1872), critic and novelist, son of a lock manufacturer, was born at Blackley Hurst in

Lancashire.   While working in an office he wrote musical criticisms and in 1833 obtained a post on the *Athenaeum*, ultimately becoming one of its chief reviewers.   Among his novels are *Conti* (1835), *The Lion* (1839), *Pomfret* (1845), *Roccabella* (1859), and *The Prodigy* (1866).   *Old Love and New Fortune* was the only successful one of his plays.   He also wrote the hymn 'God the All-Terrible.'

Christie, Agatha Mary Clarissa (1891—   ), writer of detective stories, was born at Torquay, daughter of F. A. Miller, an American.   She was educated by her mother, who encouraged her to read widely, and at a school in Paris.   In 1914 she married Archibald Christie, who became a colonel and was awarded the C.M.G. and D.S.O.; while he was fighting in France she worked as a V.A.D. in a Torquay hospital.   In 1920 she published her first detective story, *The Mysterious Affair at Styles*, which introduces the famous Belgian detective Hercule Poirot, with his belief in psychology and the 'little grey cells.'   After two more Poirot books she produced her most famous mystery, *The Murder of Roger Ackroyd* (1926), which surprised the critics by making the narrator the criminal.   At the same time she was given a great deal of publicity through the mystery of her own disappearance from home, when she was finally located in a Yorkshire health resort, a victim of amnesia.   In 1928 she divorced her husband, and after a period travelling with her daughter Rosalind, in 1930 she married Max Edgar Lucien Mallowan, an archaeologist, whom she accompanied on his later expeditions, even weaving a detective story round them, *Murder in Mesopotamia*.   Possibly the most successful financially of all detective-story writers, in 1954 she had three plays running simultaneously in the West End.   Among the best-known of her many novels are *The Mystery of the Blue Train* (1928), *The Seven Dials Mystery* (1929), *Lord Edgware Dies* (1933), *Death on the Nile* (1937), *Ten Little Niggers* (1940), *The Body in the Library* (1942), and *A Murder Is Announced* (1950).   Under the pseudonym Mary Westmacott she also wrote two 'straight' novels, *Absent in the Spring* (1944) and *The Rose and the Yew Tree* (1948).

Church, Richard (26 March 1893—   ), poet and novelist, was born in London and educated at Dulwich Hamlet School.   At the age of 16 he entered the Civil Service, where he remained till he was 40.   His first book of poems, *The Flood of Life* (1917) was followed by over ten others, of which the best-known and most representative are *The Glance Backward* (1930), *News from the Mountain* (1934) and *The Solitary Man* (1941); his *Collected Poems* appeared in 1948, and subsequent volumes were *The Prodigal* (1953) and *The Inheritors* (1957).   His novels include *Oliver's Daughter* (1930), *High Summer* (1931), *The Prodigal Father* (1933), *Apple of Concord* (1935), *The Porch* (1937), which is the best-known and won the Femina Vie-Heureuse Prize, *The Stronghold* (1939), *The Room Within* (1940), *The Sampler* (1942), *Green Tide* (1944), and *The Dangerous Years* (1956).   Among his critical works are *Mary Shelley* (1928), *Eight for Immortality* (1941), *British Authors* (1943), and *The Growth of the English Novel* (1950).   With M. M. Bozman he edited *Poems of Our Time* (1945), and in 1955 published his prize-winning autobiography *Over the Bridge* to which *The Golden Sovereign* (1957) is a sequel. In 1957 he was made a C.B.E.

Church, Richard William (25 April 1815—9 Dec. 1890), clergyman and historian, was born at Lisbon, and educated at Oxford, where he became a friend of J. H. Newman (q.v.). He took orders, and became Rector of Whatley, Somerset, and in 1871 Dean of St Paul's. He was a leading member of the High Church party. Among his writings are *The Beginning of the Middle Ages* (1877), and a *History of the Oxford Movement* (1891). He also wrote Lives of Anselm, Dante, Spenser, and Bacon.

Churchill, Charles (Feb. 1731—4 Nov. 1764), clergyman and satirist, was born in Westminster, son of the rector of Rainham, Essex. At the age of 17, while still at Westminster School, he made a Fleet marriage with a girl named Scott. He took orders in 1754, and on the death of his father in 1758 succeeded him in the curacy of St John's, Westminster. In 1761 he published the *Rosciad*, in which he severely satirized the players and managers of the day. It at once brought him both fame and money; but he fell into dissipated habits, separated from his wife, and outraged the proprieties of his profession to such an extent that he was compelled to resign his preferments. He also incurred the enmity of those whom he had attacked, which led to the publication of two other satirical pieces, *The Apology* (1761), and *Night*. He also attacked Dr Johnson and his circle in *The Ghost* (1762), and the Scots in *The Prophecy of Famine* (1763). He attached himself to John Wilkes, and wrote a great part of his paper, the *North Briton*, but died of fever while visiting him in France.

Churchill, Winston (10 Nov. 1871—12 March 1947), novelist, was born at St Louis and was educated at the Naval Academy at Annapolis but never served in the navy. Having private means he decided, after a short experience of journalism, to devote himself to literature. His first novel, *The Celebrity*, appeared in 1898, and the next, *Richard Carvel* (1899), the story of an officer serving under Paul Jones, was a remarkable success, selling over a million copies. After the publication of *The Crisis* (1901) he was recognized as one of the foremost American novelists. He then settled in New Hampshire, where he was a member of the legislature from 1903 to 1905. Others of his novels are *The Crossing* (1904), *Coniston* (1906), *Mr Crewe's Career* (1908), *A Modern Chronicle* (1910), *The Inside of the Cup* (1913), *A Far Country* (1915), and *The Dwelling Place of Light* (1917). After 1917 he gave up writing, except for one more book, *The Uncharted Way* (1941).

Churchill, Sir Winston Leonard Spencer, O.M. (30 Nov. 1874—   ), statesman and historian, was born at Blenheim Palace, son of Lord Randolph Churchill and his American wife, the former Jennie Jerome. Educated at Harrow and Sandhurst, in 1895 he became a subaltern in the 4th Hussars. Combining journalism with soldiering, he served, while on leave from his own regiment, in the Spanish campaign in Cuba and on the Northwest Frontier of India, and while under Kitchener took part in one of the last cavalry charges of history at Omdurman. During the Boer War he was a special correspondent for the *Morning Post*, and was taken prisoner but made a sensational escape. At this time he wrote *The Story of the Malakand Field Force* (1898), *The River War* (1899), and *London to Ladysmith via Pretoria* (1900).

In 1900 he was elected M.P. for Oldham, and after a rapid rise to ministerial rank became successively President of the Board of Trade (1908), Home Secretary (1910), and First Lord of the Admiralty (1911). In 1916 he served in Flanders as colonel of the Royal Scots Fusiliers. In the following year he was Minister for Munitions, in 1918 Secretary for War, and in 1921 Secretary for the Colonies. In 1906 he had written a life of his father, and in 1922, having been defeated at the polls and being out of politics he wrote the four volumes of *The World Crisis 1911—1918*, a history of the First World War. In 1924 he was returned again, for Epping, and became Chancellor of the Exchequer. After 1929, when the Labour party was in power, he wrote his four-volume *Life of Marlborough* (1933—1938), his famous ancestor. On the outbreak of the Second World War in 1939 he again became First Lord of the Admiralty and in the following year Prime Minister and carried the country through to victory. His war speeches, containing many of his most famous sayings, were later published in several volumes. In 1945 he was out of office as a result of the election which put the Socialists in power, but in 1951 he was Prime Minister again and worked successfully for the country's economic recovery until he retired in 1955.

Meanwhile he had written his monumental history of the Second World War in the successive volumes *The Gathering Storm* (1948), *Their Finest Hour* (1949), *The Grand Alliance* (1950), *The Hinge of Fate* (1950), *Closing the Ring* (1951), and *Triumph and Tragedy* (1954). His *History of the English-Speaking Peoples* was published in four volumes (1956–8). In 1946 he had been awarded the Order of Merit; in 1953 he was made a Knight of the Garter and in the same year he was given the Nobel Prize for Literature; and in 1961 the Royal Society of Literature made him a Companion of Literature. Successful even in his relaxations, he had several pictures hung in the Royal Academy and was elected Academician Extraordinary. Churchill would have been regarded as one of the leading writers of modern times, even if he had not been already distinguished as the greatest English statesman of his own or perhaps of any century.

Churchyard, Thomas (born 1520?—buried 4 April, 1604), poet and pamphleteer, began life as a page to the Earl of Surrey, and subsequently passed through many vicissitudes as a soldier in Scotland, Ireland, France, and the Low Countries. He was latterly a hanger-on at Court, and had a pension of eighteenpence a day from Queen Elizabeth, which was not, however, regularly paid. He wrote innumerable pamphlets and broadsides, and some poems, of which the best are *Shore's Wife* (1563), *The Worthiness of Wales* (1587), and *Churchyard's Chips* (1575), an autobiographical piece.

Chute, Marchette Gaylord (16 Aug. 1909—),
biographer, was born at Minnehaha Creek, Minneapolis, and educated
at the University of Minnesota. Her earliest work was a book of
verses for children, *Rhymes about Ourselves* (1932), which was followed
in the same vein by *Rhymes about the Country* (1941) and *Rhymes
about the City* (1946). Later she became famous for her vivid
biographies of old writers. Her first book, *Geoffrey Chaucer of
England* (1951) was followed by *Shakespeare of London* (1951). She
then made a trip to England, where she knew her way about so well
from her antiquarian studies that she felt quite at home. A later
book was *Ben Jonson of Westminster* (1953).

Cibber, Colley (6 Nov. 1671—12 Dec. 1757), Poet Laureate, actor,
and playwright, was born in Bloomsbury, son of a Danish sculptor,
and educated at Grantham in Lincolnshire. In 1688 he served as a
soldier. He made his first appearance as an actor at Drury Lane in
1691, and later played Richard III in his own adaptation of Shakespeare's play, which for many years ousted the original from the
boards. The first of his own plays was *Love's Last Shift* (1696) and
he wrote some 30 others, one of the best being *The Careless Husband*
(1705). Though an indifferent poet he was appointed to the Laureateship in 1730, and as a result was savagely attacked by Pope, who
made him a central figure of his satirical *Dunciad*. In 1740 he
wrote his autobiography, *Apology for the Life of Mr Colley Cibber,
Comedian*.

Clare, John (13 July 1793—20 May 1864), poet, son of a poor
labourer, was born at Helpstone near Peterborough. Starting work
as a shepherd-boy at the age of 7, he was subsequently an under-
gardener, enlisted in the militia, and worked at a lime-kiln. With
great difficulty he managed to save £1, with which he was able to have
a prospectus of his first book of poems printed; this led to an
acquaintance with Drury, a bookseller in Stamford, by whose help
the poems were published, and brought him £20. The book, *Poems
descriptive of Rural Life* (1820), immediately attracted attention.
Various noblemen befriended him and stocked a farm for him.
But unfortunately Clare had no turn for practical affairs, and got into
difficulties. He, however, continued to produce poetry, and in
addition to *The Village Minstrel*, which had appeared in 1821,
published *The Shepherd's Calendar* (1827), and *Rural Muse* (1835).
Things, however, went on from bad to worse; his mind gave way,
from 1837 he was an inmate in an asylum. Clare excels in description
of rural scenes and the feelings and ideas of humble country life.

Clarendon, Edward Hyde, Earl of (18 Feb. 1608—9 Dec. 1674),
statesman and historian, was born at Dinton in Wiltshire, educated
at Oxford, and studied law at the Middle Temple. Entering Parliament in 1640 he became one of the King's chief supporters. Sharing
Charles II's exile in France, he was appointed his Chancellor and
chief minister and at the Restoration in 1660 was raised to the
peerage and became Earl of Clarendon. Later he was impeached
and in 1667 fled to France, where he wrote *The True Historical Narrative of the Rebellion and Civil Wars in England* (1704—7), a most

valuable account of contemporary events. It was from the profits of this work that the Oxford University Press built their printing house known as the Clarendon Buildings, whence they took the name of the Clarendon Press. Clarendon also wrote a *History of the Civil War in Ireland* (1721), and an account of his own life. He was buried in Westminster Abbey.

Clark, Charles Heber (11 July 1847—10 Aug. 1915), humorous writer who used the pseudonym Max Adeler, was born at Berlin, Maryland, son of an Episcopalian clergyman, and was educated at Georgetown, District of Columbia. He left school at 15 and became a journalist in Philadelphia, working as editorial writer and book reviewer for various papers. His first book, *Out of the Hurly Burly* (1874) consisted of humorous sketches of small-town life and was very popular; of a similar type were *Elbow Room* (1876) and *Random Shots* (1879). *The Fortunate Island* (1882) and *By the Bend in the River* (1914) were books of short stories, and he also wrote several novels.

Clarke, Arthur Charles (16 Dec. 1917—   ), science fiction writer, was born at Minehead, Somerset, son of a farmer. In 1936 he entered the Civil Service. During the Second World War he became a specialist in radar, and afterwards studied at London University, taking a B.Sc. in physics in 1948. From 1949 to 1951 he was assistant editor of *Science Abstracts*. Among his serious works are *Interplanetary Flight* (1950) and *The Exploration of Space* (1951), but he was best known for his science fiction, which is among the best of its kind, and includes *Prelude to Space* (1950), *The Sands of Mars* (1951), *Islands in the Sky* (1952), *Against the Fall of Night* (1953), *Childhood's End* (1953), *Expedition to Earth* (1953), *Going into Space* (1954), and *Earthlight* (1955). For a number of years he was chairman of the British Interplanetary Society, and he was also a Fellow of the Royal Astronomical Society.

Clarke, Charles Cowden (15 Dec. 1787—13 March 1877), critic, was born at Enfield, Middlesex, and was a friend of Keats, who attended his father's school; later he became acquainted with Leigh Hunt, Shelley, Hazlitt, and the Lambs. In 1820 he started as a bookseller in London. In 1828 he married Mary Victoria, daughter of Vincent Novello, a musician, and in the following year she began compiling her famous *Complete Concordance to Shakespeare's Plays*, which appeared in 1845. For twenty years Cowden Clarke gave lectures on Shakespeare, and with his wife he produced *The Shakespeare Key* (1879), a book of commentary, and *Recollections of Writers* (1878). His life was written by his wife in 1887.

Clarke, Marcus Andrew Hislop (24 April 1846—2 Aug. 1881), novelist, was born in Kensington, son of a barrister. His father died when he was 16, and he went to an uncle in Australia, where after four years he joined the staff of the Melbourne *Argus*, and became one of the literary circle to which A. L. Gordon and Kendall (qq.v.) belonged. His novel *Long Odds* (1868) was followed in 1871 by *Old Tales of a Young Country*, and in the same year he became assistant librarian of Melbourne Public Library. In 1874 appeared his most famous novel, *His Natural Life*, sometimes called *For the Term of his Natural Life*, and dealing with the Australian convict days. It was followed by *'Twixt Shadow and Shine* (1875) and *Holiday Peak*, a collection of short stories.

Clarke, Samuel (11 Oct. 1675—17 May 1729), clergyman and philosopher, born at Norwich, was educated at Cambridge, where he became the friend and disciple of Newton. In 1704—5 he delivered the Boyle lectures, *The Being and Attributes of God*, assuming an intermediate position between orthodoxy and deism, and in 1712 he published his *Scripture Doctrine of the Trinity*, which caused a controversy. He was counted the foremost metaphysician of his time.

Clemens, Samuel Langhorne (30 Nov. 1835—21 April, 1910), novelist and travel writer who wrote under the name of Mark Twain, was born at Florida, Missouri, son of a lawyer; when he was 5 the family moved to Hannibal. His education was cut short when his father died in 1847, and he was apprenticed to a printer and wrote articles for his brother Orion, who ran the *Missouri Courier*. As a journeyman printer he travelled east to New York and Philadelphia. In 1857 he became an apprentice pilot on the Mississippi, where he remained until the river boats stopped running on the outbreak of the Civil War. After two weeks as a second lieutenant in the Confederate volunteers he went back to journalism and as city editor of the Virginia City Nevada *Enterprise* first used the pseudonym Mark Twain, the call of the pilots when taking soundings, meaning two fathoms. A meeting with Artemus Ward (q.v.) gave him greater literary ambitions, and later he collaborated with Bret Harte (q.v.). In 1865 his story ' The Celebrated Jumping Frog of Calaveras County ' was published in a New York paper and made him a famous humorist. He was now commissioned by the Sacramento Union as a writer of travel articles, sent first to Hawaii and then told to go round the world. Instead, he joined a party going to the Mediterranean and wrote *The Innocents Abroad* (1869), a debunking account of the trip, which established him as a writer of note. Returning to America he married Olivia Langdon, who belonged to a wealthy New York family, and they lived at Hartford from 1871 to 1891. This was the happiest time of his life, during which he wrote his most famous books, *The Adventures of Tom Sawyer* (1876), *A Tramp Abroad* (1880), *Life on the Mississippi* (1883), *The Adventures of Huckleberry Finn* (1884), and *A Connecticut Yankee in King Arthur's Court* (1889). But misfortune now entered his life. In 1884 he had invested money in the Charles L. Webster Company, a publishing house, which went bankrupt in 1894 and left him penniless. In 1895 he went on a world lecture tour, of which he wrote in *Following the Equator* (1897), and earned enough to pay his debts. Private tragedy followed; his wife and two daughters died, leaving only his daughter Clara. The work of this period is uneven. *Pudd'nhead Wilson* (1894), and *Personal Recollections of Joan of Arc* (1896), rank with his best, but *Tom Sawyer Abroad* (1894) and *Tom Sawyer Detective* (1895) are feeble sequels to the earlier book.

As his life drew to a close public honours were heaped on him. Yale, which had given him an M.A. degree, made him LL.D. in 1901, the University of Missouri followed suit in 1902 and Oxford in 1907. He built himself a house at Redding, Connecticut, where he died, as he had superstitiously expected, during the appearance of Halley's Comet, which had appeared at his birth seventy-five years before. His *Autobiography* was published in 1924, and material from the papers he left behind was edited in several volumes, including *Mark Twain's Travels with Mr Brown* (1940). During his later years he had become a sort of national legend, much as Bernard Shaw did in England. He was an artist in grotesque and somewhat obvious humour, his style and cadence suggesting a talker rather than a writer. He has been called 'the Lincoln of American literature.'

Cleveland, John (baptized 20 June 1613, died 29 April 1658), poet, son of an usher in a charity school, was born at Loughborough, and educated at Cambridge, where he became tutor and lecturer on rhetoric at St John's. A staunch Royalist, he opposed the election of Oliver Cromwell as member for Cambridge in the Long Parliament, and was in consequence ejected from his college in 1645. Joining the King, by whom he was welcomed, he was appointed judge advocate at Newark. In 1655 he was imprisoned at Yarmouth, but released by Cromwell, to whom he appealed, and went to London, where he enjoyed a high reputation till his death. His best work is satirical, giving a faint adumbration of *Hudibras*; his other poems, with occasional passages of great beauty, being affected and artificial. The *Poems* were published in 1656.

Clifford, Lady, *see* **de la Pasture, Mrs Henry.**

Clinton, Henry Fynes (14 Jan. 1781—24 Oct. 1852), chronologist, born at Gamston, Nottinghamshire, where his father was rector, was educated at Southwell, Westminster, and Oxford, where he devoted himself chiefly to the study of Greek. Brought into Parliament by the Duke of Newcastle in 1806, he took no active part in political life, and retired in 1826. He bought in 1810 the estate of Welwyn, and there he compiled *Fasti Hellenici* (1824—41) and *Fasti Romani* (1850—1), dealing with the chronology of ancient Greece and Rome respectively. He also wrote a tragedy, *Solyman* (1807), which was a failure.

Close, Upton, *see* **Hall, Josef Washington.**

Clough, Arthur Hugh (1 Jan. 1819—13 Nov. 1861), poet, son of a cotton merchant in Liverpool, spent his childhood in America, but was sent back to England for his education, which he received at Rugby and Oxford. While at the University, where he was tutor and Fellow of Oriel, he fell under the influence of Newman, but afterwards became a sceptic and resigned his fellowship in 1848. In the same year he published his poem, *The Bothie of Tober-na-Vuolich*, written in hexameters. After travelling on the Continent for a year, he was in 1849 appointed Warden of University Hall, London. In that year appeared *Amours de Voyage*, a rhymed novelette, and the dramatic dialogue, *Dipsychus*. In 1854 he was appointed an

F*

examiner in the Education Office. His last appointment was as Secretary of a Commission on Military Schools, in connection with which he visited various countries, but was seized with illness, and died at Florence. Clough was a man of singularly sincere character, with a passion for truth. His poems, though full of fine and subtle thought, are, with the exception of some short lyrics, deficient in form, and the hexameters which he employed in *The Bothie* are often rough. He was a close friend of Matthew Arnold (q.v.), who commemorated him in his poem *Thyrsis*.

Clouston, Joseph Storer (23 May 1870—23 June 1944), novelist, son of a doctor, was born in Cumberland, but came of an old Orkney family. Educated at Merchiston Castle and Oxford, he was called to the English Bar but never practised. In 1899 he scored a great success with his first novel, *The Lunatic at Large*, which had a series of sequels published at intervals—*Count Bunker* (1906), *The Lunatic at Large Again* (1922), *The Lunatic Still at Large* (1923), and *The Lunatic in Charge* (1926). Other novels were *The Peer's Progress* (1910), *The Jade's Progress* (1928), and *The Best Story Ever* (1932). *The Spy in Black* (1917), and *The Man from the Clouds* (1918) are war thrillers. He also wrote a *History of Orkney* (1932) and several plays. During the First World War he was sub-commissioner under the National Services Department, for Orkney and Shetland.

Clutton-Brock, Arthur (23 March 1868—8 Jan. 1924), critic and essayist, was born at Weybridge, Surrey, the son of a banker, and went to Eton, where he won a prize for English verse. Going to Oxford, he studied law, was called to the Bar of the Inner Temple in 1895 and practised for some years. In 1904 he became literary editor of the *Speaker* (later the *Nation*) and was a frequent contributor to the *Times Literary Supplement*. His critical works include *Shelley: the Man and the Poet* (1909), and *William Morris: his Work and Influence* (1914). During the First World War he published *Thoughts on the War*. *Essays on Art* (1918) was followed by two series of *Essays on Books* (1920, 1921).

Cobb, Irvin Shrewsbury (23 June 1876—10 March 1944), short story writer, was born at Paducah, Kentucky, and was a descendant of the first Governor of Vermont. At the age of 15 he went to work as a message boy, at 16 was a reporter on a newspaper and at 19 its managing editor, the youngest in the United States. He married in 1900 and four years later moved to New York. His first story was written when he was 37, and he soon became famous for his humorous tales of Kentucky life. Among the best-known of some 60 books are *Roughing It De Luxe* (1914), *Paths of Glory* (1915), *Old Judge Priest* (1915), *Fiddle, D.D.* (1916), *The Life of the Party* (1919), *One Third Off* (1921), *A Laugh a Day* (1923), *Prose and Cons* (1926), *All Aboard* (1928), and *Incredible Truth* (1931). In 1938 he moved to Santa Monica. *Myself to Date* (1923), and *Exit Laughing* (1941) are autobiographical.

Cobbe, Frances Power (4 Dec. 1822—5 April 1904), religious and social writer, was born near Dublin. Coming under the influence of Theodore Parker, she became a Unitarian. Her first work, published anonymously, was on *The Intuitive Theory of Morals* (1855). She travelled in the East, and published *Cities of the Past* (1864). Later she became interested in social questions and philanthropic work, and wrote *Criminals, Idiots, Women and Minors* (1869), *Darwinism in Morals* (1872), and *Scientific Spirit of the Age* (1888). She was a strong opponent of vivisection.

Cobbett, William (9 March 1763—18 June 1835), journalist and politician, was born at Farnham, Surrey, son of a farmer. Going to London, he worked for some months as an attorney's clerk, then enlisted in the 54th Foot, where he rose to be a sergeant-major, serving in Florida from 1784 to 1791. In 1792 he was in France for six months, then returned to America and while teaching English to French refugees at Philadelphia penned fierce attacks on the Democrats, writing under the pseudonym of Peter Porcupine. In 1800 he returned to England, and in 1802 started the *Weekly Political Register*, which he continued till his death, and from which in 1830 was reprinted his most famous book, *Rural Rides*; it described various parts of England with comments on their agriculture and politics. He took up farming, settling first at Botley in Hampshire and later starting a seed-farm in Kensington. In 1832 he was elected M.P. for Oldham. He wrote some 50 works, including an *English Grammar* (1818), a *History of the Reformation* (1827), and the shrewd *Advice to Young Men* (1830).

Cockburn, Alicia *or* **Alison** (8th Oct. 1713—22 Nov. 1794), poetess, born at Fairnilee, Selkirkshire, was a daughter of Robert Rutherford and was distantly related to Walter Scott's mother. A very beautiful girl, she married in 1731 Patrick Cockburn, advocate, and was for sixty years a queen of Edinburgh society. She met Scott in his boyhood, and mutual admiration resulted; she also met Burns. Although she cultivated poetry all her life she is remembered almost solely by her poem 'The Flowers of the Forest,' which begins 'I've seen the smiling of fortune beguiling.' It is commonly assumed to have the same subject as the poem of Jean Elliot (q.v.) with the same title, which is a lament for Flodden; but in fact it was occasioned by a wave of financial ruin which afflicted many in the Ettrick Forest neighbourhood. Her *Letters* were edited in 1900.

Cockburn, Henry Thomas, Lord Cockburn (26 Oct. 1779—26 April 1854), judge and biographer, son of the sheriff of Midlothian, educated in Edinburgh, became a distinguished member of the Scottish Bar, and ultimately a judge. He was also one of the leaders of the Whig party in Scotland in its days of darkness prior to the Reform Act of 1832. The lifelong friend of Francis Jeffrey (q.v.), he wrote his life, published in 1852. His chief literary work, however, is his *Memorials of his Time* (1856), continued in his *Journal* (1874). These constitute an autobiography of the writer interspersed with notices of manners, public events, and sketches of his contemporaries.

Cole, George Douglas Howard (25 Sept. 1889—   ), economist and novelist, born at Ealing, was educated at St Paul's and Oxford, where he became a Fellow of Magdalen. In 1925 he was appointed Reader in Economics at Oxford, and in 1944 Chichele

Professor of Social and Political Theory and a Fellow of All Souls. An active Socialist, he was chairman of the Fabian Society. In 1918 he married Margaret Isabel Postgate, a professor's daughter who was educated at Roedean and Girton and was for a time classical mistress at St Paul's Girls' School; she collaborated in a number of his books. Cole's works, which are very numerous, include *Recent Developments in the British Labour Movement* (1918), *Guild Socialism* (1921), lives of *William Cobbett* (1924), *Robert Owen* (1925), and *Samuel Butler* (1947), *Chartist Portraits* (1941), *Fabian Socialism* (1943), *A Century of Co-operation* (1945), *Local and Regional Government* (1947), *The Meaning of Marxism* (1948), *A History of the Labour Party* (1948), and *Socialist Economics* (1950); and (with Mrs Cole) *The Intelligent Man's Review of Modern Europe* (1933), and *A Guide to Modern Politics* (1934). His detective stories, all written in collaboration with Mrs Cole, began with *The Brooklyn Murders* (1923), and include *The Death of a Millionaire* (1925), *Poison in the Garden Suburb* (1929), *Burglars in Bucks* (1930), *Dead Man's Watch* (1932), *Death in the Quarry* (1934), *Knife in the Dark* (1942), and *Toys of Death* (1948).

Colenso, John William (24 Jan. 1814—20 June 1883), Biblical-critic, born at St Austell, Cornwall, and educated at St John's College, Cambridge, of which he became a Fellow, took orders, and published various mathematical treatises and *Village Sermons*. In 1853 he was appointed the first Bishop of Natal. He mastered the Zulu language, introduced printing, compiled a Zulu grammar and dictionary, and wrote many useful reading-books for the natives. His *Commentary on the Romans* (1861) excited great opposition from the High Church party, and his *Critical Examination of the Pentateuch* (1862—79), by its then extreme views, aroused violent criticism. He was in 1863 deposed and excommunicated by Bishop Gray of Cape Town, but confirmed in his see by the law courts.

Coleridge, Hartley (19 Sept. 1796—6 Jan. 1849), poet, eldest son of Samuel. Taylor Coleridge (q.v.), was born at Clevedon, Somerset. A very imaginative child, he was brought up, after his parents' separation, in Southey's household at Keswick, and educated at Oxford, where he was elected to an Oriel fellowship but lost it through intemperance. Depressed by this and by his failure to win the Newdigate, he went to London and wrote for magazines. From 1823 to 1828 he tried keeping a school at Ambleside, which failed, and he then led the life of a recluse at Grasmere until his death. Here he wrote *Biographia Borealis* (1832), comprising a series of lives of Yorkshire and Lancashire worthies, and a *Life of Massinger* (1839). He is remembered chiefly for his sonnets, which are among the finest in the English language. His *Poems* and the unfinished drama *Prometheus* were published with a memoir by his brother Derwent in 1851, and his *Letters* in 1937.

Coleridge, Mary Elizabeth (23 Sept. 1861—25 Aug. 1907), novelist and poetess, a grand-daughter of the elder brother of Samuel Taylor Coleridge, was born in London and educated at home, partly by W. J. Cory (q.v.). She wrote verse while still a child, her first published volume being *Fancy's Following* (1896). Her first novel, *The Seven Sleepers of Ephesus* (1893) was praised by Stevenson, and her reputation as a writer was established by *The King with Two Faces* (1897), an historical romance. Later novels were *The Fiery Dawn* (1901), *The Shadow on the Wall* (1904), and *The Lady on the Drawing Room Floor* (1906). *Non Sequitur* (1900) is a volume of essays, and *Poems Old and New* appeared in 1907 after her death.

Coleridge, Samuel Taylor (21 Oct. 1772—25 July 1834), poet, philosopher, and critic, son of the vicar and schoolmaster of Ottery St Mary, Devonshire, was born there in 1772, the youngest of thirteen children. He was at Christ's Hospital from 1782 to 1790, and had Charles Lamb for a schoolfellow, and the famous scholar and disciplinarian, James Boyer, for his master. Thence he proceeded as a sizar to Jesus College, Cambridge, in 1791, where he read much, but desultorily, and got into debt. The troubles arising thence and also, apparently, a disappointment in love, led to his going to London and enlisting in the 15th Dragoons under the name of Silas Tomkyn Comberback. He could not, however, be taught to ride, and through some Latin lines written by him on a stable door, his identity was discovered, his friends communicated with, and his release accomplished, his brothers buying him off. After this escapade he returned in 1794 to Cambridge. He had by this time imbibed extreme democratic or, as he termed them, pantisocratic principles, and on leaving Cambridge, in the same year he visited Oxford, where he made the acquaintance of Southey, and discussed with him a project of founding a 'pantisocracy' on the banks of the Susquehanna, a location chosen partly for its romantic name. It was considered essential that the emigrants should be married, and after meeting Southey's fiancée, Edith Fricker, Coleridge became engaged to her sister Sara, whom he married in 1795. In the meantime the pantisocratic project had fallen through, mainly for lack of funds. Coleridge had spent one more term at Cambridge, and there in 1794 his first work, *The Fall of Robespierre*, a drama, to which Southey contributed two acts, the second and third, was published.

After his marriage he settled first at Clevedon, and thereafter at Nether Stowey, Somerset, where he had Wordsworth for a neighbour, with whom he formed an intimate association. In 1796 *Poems on various Subjects* appeared, and a little later *Ode to the Departing Year*. While at Nether Stowey he was practically supported by Thomas Poole, a tanner, with whom he had formed a friendship. Here he wrote 'The Ancient Mariner,' the first part of 'Christabel,' and 'Kubla Khan,' and here he joined with Wordsworth in producing the *Lyrical Ballads*. Some time previously he had become a Unitarian, and for a short time acted as a minister at Shrewsbury. Influenced by Josiah and Thomas Wedgwood, who each in 1798 gave him an annuity of £75 on condition of his devoting himself to literature, he resigned this position, and soon afterwards went to Germany, where he remained for over a year, an experience which profoundly influenced the future development of his intellect. On his return he made excursions with Southey and Wordsworth, and at the end of 1799 went to London, where he wrote and reported for the *Morning Post*. His great translation of Schiller's *Wallenstein* appeared in 1800. In the same year he removed to Greta Hall, near Keswick, where he wrote the second part of 'Christabel.' Soon after this his health gave way, and he suffered much; and, whether as the cause or the consequence of this, he had become a slave to opium. In 1804 he went to Malta in search of health, and there became the friend of the governor, Sir Alexander Ball, who appointed him his secretary. Resigning this occupation, of which he had become tired, he travelled in Italy, and in the beginning of 1806 reached Rome, where he enjoyed the friendship of Tieck, Humboldt, and Bunsen.

He returned to England at the end of 1806, and in 1808 delivered his first course of lectures on Shakespeare at the Royal Institution; the following year, leaving his family at Keswick, he went to live with Wordsworth at Grasmere. Here he started *The Friend*, a philosophical and theological periodical, which lasted for nine months. The part of his annuity contributed by T. Wedgwood had been confirmed to him by will in 1805, and this he allowed to his wife, from whom he was now finally separated, but in 1811 the remaining half was stopped. He delivered a second course of lectures in London, and in 1813 his drama, *Remorse*, was acted at Drury Lane with success. Leaving his family dependent upon Southey, he lived with various friends. In 1817 were published *Biographia Literaria*, *Sybilline Leaves*, and an autobiography. In 1818 he appeared for the last time as a lecturer. He found a final resting-place in the household of James Gillman, a surgeon at Highgate. His life thenceforth was a splendid wreck. His nervous system was shattered, and he was a constant sufferer. Yet these last years were, in some respects, his best. He maintained a struggle against opium which lasted till his death, and though he ceased to write much, he became the revered centre of a group of disciples, and thus indirectly continued and increased his influence in the philosophic and theological thought of his time. In 1824 he was elected an Associate of the Royal Society of Literature, which brought him a pension of 100 guineas. His latest publications were *Aids to Reflection* (1825), and *The Constitution of Church and State* (1830). After his death there were published, among other works, *Table Talk* (1835), *Confessions of an Enquiring Spirit* (1840), *Letters* and *Anima Poetae* (1895).

Endowed with an intellect of the first order, and an imagination at once delicate and splendid, Coleridge, from a weakness of moral constitution, fell far short of the performance which he had planned, and which included various epic poems, and a complete system of philosophy, in which all knowledge was to be co-ordinated. Lamb, with his usual gift of vivid phrase, termed him 'an archangel a little damaged.' But he produced poetry of such excellence as to place him in the first rank of English poets, while his knowledge of philosophy, science, theology, and literature was alike wide and deep, and his powers of conversation, or rather monologue, were outstanding.

Coleridge, Sara (22 Dec. 1802–3 May 1852), only daughter of the above, was born at Greta Hall, Keswick, and spent her girlhood with Southey and Wordsworth. In 1829 she married her cousin, Henry

Nelson Coleridge, and they made their home in Hampstead. She translated Dobrizhöffer's *Account of the Abipones* (1822), and the *Memoirs of the Chevalier Bayard* (1825). Her original works are *Pretty Lessons in Verse for Good Children* (1834), which was very popular, and a fairy tale, *Phantasmion* (1837). She also edited her father's works.

Colet, John (1467—16 Sept. 1519), scholar and theologian, was born in London, the son of a wealthy citizen who was twice Lord Mayor. The only survivor of a family of twenty-two, he went to Oxford and Paris, and thence to Italy, where he learned Greek. He took orders, and held many preferments, including the Deanery of St Paul's. He continued to follow out his studies, devoting himself chiefly to St Paul's epistles. He was outspoken against the corruptions of the Church, and would have been called to account but for the protection of Archbishop Warham. He devoted his great fortune to founding and endowing St Paul's School. Among his works are a treatise on the Sacraments and various devotional writings. A pioneer of the Reformation, he was the leading Christian humanist of his time in England.

Collier, Jeremy (23 Sept. 1650—26 April 1726), clergyman, born at Stow, Cambridgeshire, educated at Ipswich and Cambridge, took orders, and became rector of Ampton, Suffolk, lecturer of Gray's Inn, London, and ultimately a nonjuring bishop. He was engaged in controversies almost until his death. His first important one was with Gilbert Burnet, and led to his being imprisoned in Newgate. His chief writings are his *Ecclesiastical History of Great Britain* (1708—14), and especially his *Short View of the Immorality and Profaneness of the English Stage* (1699), on account of which he was attacked by Congreve and Farquhar, for whom, however, he showed himself more than a match. The work materially helped towards the subsequent purification of the stage.

Collins, Cuthbert Dale (7 April 1897—   ), novelist, was born at Sydney. At the age of 11 he contributed a story 'A Kangeroo Hunt,' to the English comic paper *Puck*. At 14 he was office-boy, proof-reader, leader-writer, and 'Evangeline' of the women's column, for a suburban paper, and later became dramatic critic of the Sydney *Bulletin*. Joining a party which made the first motor-boat cruise round the world, he wrote it up as *Sea-Tracks of the Speejacks* (1923). *Ordeal* (1924) is a sea story, and his other novels include *The Haven* (1925), *The Sentimentalists* (1927), *Idolater* (1929), *Rich and Strange* (1931), *Lost* (1933), *The Mutiny of Madam Yes* (1934), and *Gulls Against the Sky* (1936). During the Second World War he was a press censor. Later works are *Winds of Chance* (1947), *The Happy Emigrants* (1948), and the autobiographical *Bright Vista* (1946).

Collins, John (1742?—2 May 1808), actor and poet, born at Bath, son of a tailor, was a staymaker, but took to the stage, on which he was fairly successful. He also gave humorous entertainments and published *Scripscrapologia* (1804), a book of verses. He is worthy of mention for the little piece, 'To-morrow,' which Palgrave included in his *Golden Treasury*.

Collins, John Churton (26 March 1848—12 Sept. 1908), critic, was born at Bourton-on-the-Water, Gloucestershire, son of a doctor, and educated at King Edward's School, Birmingham, and Oxford. He wrote a number of critical works, and it was largely due to his efforts that the Chair of English Literature was established at Oxford; in 1904 he became Professor of English at Birmingham. He was drowned at Oulton Broad near Lowestoft. His works include *Essays and Studies* (1895), *Studies in Shakespeare* (1904), *Studies in Poetry and Criticism* (1905), and editions of Tourneur and Greene.

Collins, Mortimer (29 June 1827—28 July 1876), poet and novelist, son of a solicitor at Plymouth, was for a time a teacher of mathematics in Guernsey. Settling in Berkshire he adopted a literary life, and was a prolific author, writing largely for periodicals. Volumes of his verse are *Idylls and Rhymes* (1855), and *Inn of Strange Meetings* (1871). He also wrote several novels, including *Sweet Anne Page* (1868), *Two Plunges for a Pearl* (1872), and *A Fight with Fortune* (1876). Unconventional in dress, he was known as 'the king of the Bohemians.'

Collins, Norman Richard (3 Oct. 1907—   ), novelist, was born in London and educated at William Ellis School, Hampstead. From 1929 to 1933 he was on the staff of the *News Chronicle*, and in the latter year published *The Facts of Fiction*, a study of the English novel. Subsequently he was in a publishing business, and later became controller of television. Of his novels, which have been compared with Priestley's, one of the best is *London Belongs to Me* (1945). Others are *Penang Appointment* (1934), *The Three Friends* (1935), *Trinity Town* (1936), *Love in our Time* (1938), *Anna* (1942), *Black Ivory* (1947), *Children of the Archbishop* (1951), *The Bat that Flits* (1952), *The Bond Street Story* (1958), and *The Governor's Lady* (1959).

Collins, Tom, *see* **Furphy, Joseph.**

Collins, William (25 Dec. 1721—12 June 1759), poet, was born at Chichester, son of a hatter who was twice elected mayor of the town. William was educated at Winchester, where he was a schoolfellow of Joseph Warton (q.v.), and at Oxford. His *Persian Eclogues* (1742) were published while he was still an undergraduate. Coming to London to work as a writer he was reduced to great straits, and on one occasion Dr Johnson had to rescue him from the bailiffs. His *Odes* were published in 1747, but attracted little attention. In 1749 a legacy enabled him to settle in Chichester, but from 1751 he was afflicted with acute melancholia, and eventually he became imbecile, dying in his sister's house. Collins's output of verse was small but most of it was of the first rank, his finest productions being the odes, especially that 'To Evening,' and the 'Dirge in Cymbeline.' His work had a considerable influence on the development of English poetry, and his *Ode on the Popular Superstitions of the Highlands*, published posthumously in 1788, has been said to foreshadow the whole Romantic School.

Collins, William Wilkie (8 Jan. 1824—23 Sept. 1889), novelist, was born in London, son of a well-known artist who named him after Sir David Wilkie, the R.A. Educated privately, after some years in Italy he was entered at Lincoln's Inn and called to the Bar in 1851. In 1848 he wrote a life of his father, and in 1850 published his first novel, *Antonina*. In 1851 he formed a friendship with Charles Dickens, with whom he collaborated in a number of works. He is best remembered for *The Woman in White* (1860), a mystery story, and *The Moonstone* (1868), which T. S. Eliot once termed 'the first, the longest, and the best of detective novels.' Others of his books were *Hide and Seek* (1854), *No Name* (1862), and *Armadale* (1866).

Colman, George, the elder (baptized 18 April 1732, died 14 Aug. 1794), dramatist, born at Florence, where his father was British envoy, was educated at Westminster and Oxford, and was called to the Bar at Lincoln's Inn. He was a friend of Garrick, and took to writing for the stage with success. He wrote more than 30 dramatic pieces, of which the best known are *The Jealous Wife* (1761), and *The Clandestine Marriage* (1766). Colman was also manager and part proprietor of various theatres. He was a scholar and translated Terence and the *De Arte Poetica* of Horace, wrote essays, and edited the plays of Beaumont and Fletcher and Ben Jonson.

Colman, George, the younger (21 Oct. 1762—17 Oct. 1836), dramatist, son of the above, was educated at Westminster and Oxford. He wrote or adapted numerous plays, including *The Heir at Law* (1797), and *John Bull* (1805). As Examiner of Plays from 1824 to 1836 he was rigorous and prudish. His wit made him popular in society, and he was a favourite with George IV.

Colton, Charles Caleb (1780?—28 April, 1832), clergyman, educated at Eton and Cambridge, took orders and held various livings. He was an eccentric man of talent, with little or no principle, took to gaming, and had to leave the country. He died by his own hand. His books, mainly collections of epigrammatic aphorisms and short essays, had a phenomenal popularity in their day. Among them are *Lacon, or Many Things in Few Words* (1822), and some poems.

Colum, Padraic (8 Dec. 1881—), poet and playwright, was born at Longford, Ireland, and educated at local schools. Moving to Dublin, where he worked as a clerk in a railway office, he became one of the group of writers, including Yeats, George William Russell, J. M. Synge, and Lady Gregory, who are identified with the Irish literary renascence. His play *The Land* (1905) was the Irish Theatre's first success; others were *The Fiddler's House* (1907), *Thomas Muskerry* (1910), *The Desert* (1912), and *Balloon* (1929). With James Stephens and Thomas MacDonagh he founded the *Irish Review*, of which he was editor for a short time. In 1914 he visited America, and later he settled in Connecticut. In 1923, at the invitation of the Hawaiian government, he made a study of Hawaiian folklore and published two volumes dealing with it, *At the Gateways*

of the Day (1924), and *The Bright Islands* (1925). From 1939 he
made his home in New York. His volumes of verse include *Wild
Earth* (1907), *Dramatic Legends* (1922), *Creatures* (1927), *Old Pastures*
(1930), *The Story of Lowry Maen* (1937), and *Flower Pieces* (1939).
He also wrote a novel, *Castle Conquer* (1923), and many books for
children. He edited *An Anthology of Irish Verse* (1948), and *A
Treasury of Irish Folklore* (1955). In 1952 he received the award of
the American Academy of Poets, and in 1953 the Gregory Medal of
the Irish Academy of Letters.

Colvin, Sir Sidney (18 June 1845—11 May 1927), critic, was born
at Woodbridge, Suffolk, son of a wealthy East India merchant;
Ruskin was a friend of the family. He went to Trinity College,
Cambridge, of which he became a Fellow. After a period in London
as art critic of the *Pall Mall Gazette*, in 1873 he was appointed Slade
Professor of Fine Art at Cambridge and three years later Director of
the Fitzwilliam Museum. He resigned both these posts in 1884,
when he was made Keeper of Prints and Drawings at the British
Museum, an appointment which he held till 1912. He knew many
eminent literary men, Stevenson and Conrad being among his
intimate friends. His works include lives of *Landor* (1881), and
Keats (1887), and an edition of the *Letters of Stevenson*. He was
knighted in 1911.

Combe, George (21 Oct. 1788—14 Aug. 1858), phrenologist, one of
a brewer's seventeen children, was born and educated in Edinburgh,
where for some time he practised as a lawyer. Latterly, however,
he devoted himself to the promotion of phrenology, and of his views
on education, for which he in 1848 founded a school. His chief
work was *The Constitution of Man* (1828).

Combe, William (1741—19 June 1823), poet, was born in Bristol,
and educated at Eton and Oxford, where he gave himself up to
dissipation. Having travelled in France and Italy, where he met
Sterne, he lived for a time in princely style and was known as Count
Combe. But evil days followed, during which he was successively
soldier, waiter, and cook, and spent much time in a debtor's prison.
In 1776 he published a satire, the *Diaboliad*. From 1809 to 1811 he
contributed doggerel verses to accompany a series of Rowlandson's
illustrations in the *Poetical Magazine*. They were collected as *The
Tour of Dr Syntax in Search of the Picturesque*, and were very popular.
Dr Syntax reappeared in *A Second Tour in Search of Consolation*
(1820) and *A Third Tour in Search of a Wife* (1821). Combe also
wrote a series of imaginary letters of the second or 'wicked' Lord
Lyttelton, with whom he was at Eton.

Comfort, Alexander (10 Feb. 1920—   ), poet and
novelist, was educated at Highgate, Cambridge, and London Hospital Medical College, where in 1948 he was appointed Lecturer in
Physiology. His novels include *No Such Liberty* (1941), *The Almond
Tree* (1943), *The Power House* (1944), *On This Side Nothing* (1948),
and *A Giant's Strength* (1952); *Letters from an Outpost* (1947) is a book
of short stories. Volumes of his verse are *A Wreath for the Living*
(1943), *The Signal to Engage* (1947), and *All But He Departed* (1951), ·

and he composed two plays, *Into Egypt* (1942), and *Gengulphus* (1948). He also published several sociological works, including *Art and Social Responsibility* (1946), *The Pattern of the Future* (1949), and *Authority and Delinquency in the Modern State* (1950).

Compton-Burnett, Ivy (1892—   ), novelist, born in London, was educated privately and at London University, where she took a degree in Classics. Her novels, which deal with middle- or upper-class people of the early years of this century, have what is termed an oblique approach, because the characters are not described directly but reveal themselves through their conversations; time, place, and background are indicated only hazily, if at all, while under a veneer of polite convention they display the real ugliness of human cruelty and selfishness. The titles, which have a certain similarity of form, are *Pastors and Masters* (1925), *Brothers and Sisters* (1929), *Men and Wives* (1931), *More Women than Men* (1933), *A House and its Head* (1935), *Daughters and Sons* (1937), *A Family and a Fortune* (1939), *Parents and Children* (1941), *Two Worlds and their Ways* (1949), *Darkness and Day* (1951), *Mother and Son* (1955), which was awarded the Tait Black Memorial Prize, and *A Father and his Fate* (1957). In 1951 she was made a C.B.E.

Congreve, William (baptized 10 Feb. 1670, died 19 Jan. 1729), dramatist, was born at Bardsley, near Leeds, son of an army officer who was sent on garrison duty to Ireland. Young Congreve was educated at Kilkenny and Trinity College, Dublin, where he formed a friendship with Swift. In 1688 he returned to England and entered the Middle Temple, but does not appear to have practised, and after publishing a novel, *Incognita*, he took to writing for the stage. His first comedy, *The Old Bachelor*, was produced with great applause in 1693, and was followed by *The Double Dealer* (1693), *Love for Love* (1695), and *The Way of the World* (1700), and by a tragedy, *The Mourning Bride* (1697). His comedies are all remarkable for wit and sparkling dialogue, but their profanity and licentiousness brought them under the lash of Jeremy Collier (q.v.) in his *Short Review of the English Stage*. Congreve rushed into controversy with his critic, who, however, proved too strong for him. Congreve was a favourite at Court, had various lucrative offices conferred upon him, and was finally buried with great pomp in Westminster Abbey. In his latter years he was blind.

Conington, John (10 Aug. 1825—23 Oct. 1869), classical scholar, was born at Boston, Lincolnshire, son of a clergyman, and educated at Rugby and Oxford, where he had a brilliant career, became a Fellow of University College, and was the first occupant of the Chair of Latin. He translated Horace's *Odes* in lyric metres, his *Satires* and *Epistles* in heroic couplets, Virgil's *Aeneid* in the ballad metre of Scott, and Homer's *Iliad* in Spenserian stanzas, but his greatest achievement was his annotated edition of Virgil's works, which is still the best English commentary on them.

Connell, F. Norreys, *see* O'Riordan, Conal.

Connington, J. J., *see* Stewart, Alfred Walter.

Connolly, Cyril Vernon (10 Sept. 1903—   ), critic, was born in Coventry, son of an army officer. Taken to South Africa in childhood, he was educated in England and spent holidays with his mother's relations in Ireland. At his first school he had George Orwell (q.v.) as a schoolmate, and at Balliol, to which he went from Eton, he was a contemporary of Graham Greene. Entering journalism, he became a regular contributor to the *New Statesman* and other periodicals, and from 1942 to 1943 was literary editor of the *Observer*. In 1939, along with Stephen Spender (q.v.), he founded the literary review *Horizon*, which lasted ten years under his editorship. He published one novel, *The Rock Pool* (1935), and a number of collections of essays, including *The Unquiet Grave* (1944), *The Condemned Playground* (1944), and *Ideas and Places* (1953).

Connor, Ralph, *see* **Gordon, Charles William.**

Conrad, Joseph (3 Dec. 1857—3 Aug. 1924), novelist, was born at Berdiczew in Podolia, one of the Ukrainian provinces of Poland, and was christened Jósef Teodor Konrad Naleçz Korzeniowski. When he was 3 his father was exiled to Northern Russia and Conrad, left an orphan a few years later, was brought up at Cracow by an uncle. Reading Victor Hugo's *Toilers of the Sea* is said to have inspired him with a desire for the sea, surprising in one reared so far inland, and in 1874 he travelled to Marseilles to become a sailor. After gaining some experience he joined with three companions in using the vessel *Tremolino* for smuggling, till she was deliberately wrecked; part of the adventures of this period are recounted in *The Mirror of the Sea* (1906) and *The Arrow of Gold* (1919). His first ship was the *Mavis*, in which he visited England for the first time in 1878. Soon afterwards he sailed to Australia in a 'wool-clipper,' and after passing the necessary examination served as third mate in various ships in the Indian Ocean, which he made the scene of many of his best-known stories, such as *The Nigger of the Narcissus* (1897), *Lord Jim* (1900), *The Shadow-Line* (1917), and *The Rescue* (1920).

In 1886 he obtained his certificate as a master mariner and also became a naturalized British subject. Four years later he fulfilled a childhood ambition by commanding a river steamer in the Belgian Congo, of which he told subsequently in 'Heart of Darkness.' He was now writing his first book, *Almayer's Folly*, which appeared in 1895. His last ship was the *Torrens*, a famous sailing vessel, which he left in 1893. In 1896 he married Jessie George and settled down as a writer, but it was not until the publication in America of *Chance* (1913) that he became widely popular. For a time his reputation was second only to Hardy's among living authors, and he made a name as a stylist in English although he was unable to speak a word of the language before he was 19. Although usually thought of as a writer of sea stories, he also wrote a number of novels with other settings, such as *Nostromo* (1904), *The Secret Agent* (1907), and *Under Western Eyes* (1911); his two last, *The Rover* (1923) and the unfinished *Suspense* (1925), tell of the Napoleonic period. Among his finest short stories are 'Youth' (1902), and 'Typhoon' (1903). *Some Reminiscences* (1912) is autobiographical.

Constable, Henry (1562—9 Oct. 1613), poet, son of Sir Robert Constable, was educated at Cambridge, became a Roman Catholic, and spent most of his life in France. In 1592 he published *Diana*, a collection of sonnets, and contributed to *England's Helicon* four poems, including 'Diaphenia' and 'Venus and Adonis.' His style is characterized by fervour and richness of colour.

Cook, Eliza (24 Dec. 1818—23 Sept. 1889), poetess, was born in Southwark, the youngest of eleven children of a brasier. Self-educated, she began to write verses before she was fifteen. Her first published volume, *Lays of a Wild Harp* (1835), was followed by *Melaia* (1838), and *New Echoes* (1864). Her best-known poem 'The Old Arm Chair' first appeared in the *Weekly Dispatch* in 1836. Between 1849 and 1854 she edited *Eliza Cook's Journal*.

Cooke, John Esten (3 Nov. 1830—27 Sept. 1886), novelist, was born at Winchester, Virginia, son of a lawyer, and went to school at Richmond. His novels *Leather Stocking and Silk* (1854), *The Virginia Comedians* (1854), and *Henry St John* (1859), deal with colonial Virginia. Serving throughout the Civil War on the Confederate side, he wrote lives of Stonewall Jackson (1863) and Robert E. Lee (1871). Later novels include *The Heir of Gaymount* (1870), and *My Lady Pokahontas* (1885).

Coolidge, Susan, *see* **Woolsey, Sarah Chauncey.**

Cooper, Alfred Duff, 1st Viscount Norwich (22 Feb. 1890—1 Jan. 1954), statesman and historian, was born at Norwich, son of a surgeon, and educated at Eton and New College, Oxford. Entering the Civil Service, he became a clerk in the Foreign Office. During the First World War he served with the Grenadier Guards as a subaltern in France and was given the Distinguished Service Order. In 1919 he married the famous beauty Lady Diana Manners, daughter of the Duke of Rutland. From 1924 to 1945 he sat in the House of Commons as M.P. first for Oldham and then for St George's, Westminster. He was successively Secretary of State for War (1935), First Lord of the Admiralty (1937), and Minister of Information (1940), and in 1944 was the first British ambassador to France after the liberation. His works include *Talleyrand* (1932), *Haig* (1935—6), *The Second World War* (1939), *David* (1943), and *Old Men Forget* (1953).

Cooper, Anthony Ashley, *see* **Shaftesbury, Earl of.**

Cooper, Edith Emma (12 Jan. 1862—13 Dec. 1913), poetess who wrote in collaboration with her aunt Katharine Bradley under the name Michael Field, was born at Kenilworth, Warwickshire, daughter of a merchant. Educated by her aunt, with whom she lived from the age of 4, she moved with her to Bristol, Reigate, and finally Richmond; in 1907 she became a Roman Catholic. For their joint productions see under Bradley. They died of cancer within a year of each other.

Cooper, James Fenimore (15 Sept. 1789—14 Sept. 1851), novelist, was born at Burlington, New Jersey; his father later became a judge and a member of New York State Legislature. Soon after James was born the family moved to the wild area near Otsego Lake which developed into Cooperstown; there he grew up with an intimate knowledge of wood craft and Red Indian lore. He was educated at Yale, from which he was expelled for an escapade, then obtained a commission in the Navy and was assigned to the section that patrolled the Great Lakes. In 1811 he married Susan de Lacey, resigned his commission, and settled down to the life of a country gentleman. In 1829 he wrote *Precaution* in the style of contemporary English fiction, and followed it next year with *The Spy*, which had an American plot. *The Pioneers* (1823) was the first of the famous Leatherstocking Tales, so called from their hero's nickname; they comprise *The Last of the Mohicans* (1826), *The Pathfinder* (1840), *The Deerslayer* (1841), and *The Redskins* (1846), and give a vivid if idealized picture of the woodsman and the Red Indian. From 1826 Cooper spent seven years in Europe, officially as United States consul at Lyons; he made friends with Lafayette and met Sir Walter Scott. Back in Cooperstown, he became quarrelsome and litigious, wrote a number of satirical works as well as many more novels and a *History of the Navy* (1839). His *Works* in 33 volumes were published between 1895 and 1900, and his *Correspondence* was edited by his grandson in 1922.

Cooper, Thomas (20 March 1805—15 July 1892), Chartist poet, was born at Leicester, son of a dyer, and apprenticed to a shoemaker. In spite of hardships and difficulties, he educated himself, and at 23 was a schoolmaster. He became a leader and lecturer among the Chartists, and in 1842 was imprisoned for sedition in Stafford jail, where he wrote his *Purgatory of Suicides*, a political epic, and *Wise Saws and Modern Instances*, a series of tales. At the same time he adopted sceptical views, which he continued to hold until 1855, when he became a Christian, joined the Baptists, and was a preacher among them. His friends in 1867 raised an annuity for him, and in the last year of his life he received a government pension. In addition to his poems he wrote several novels and an autobiography.

Coppard, Alfred Edgar (4 Jan. 1878—13 Jan. 1957), poet and short story writer, was born at Folkestone, son of a tailor, and educated at a Brighton board school. At the age of 9 he was a shop-boy in Whitechapel, then became an office-boy in Brighton. He educated himself so effectively both mentally and physically that he was at one time a professional sprinter. Later he became an accountant at Oxford, where he started writing. In 1919 he threw up his job to devote himself to literature, and had two years of extreme poverty, during which he wrote *Adam and Eve and Pinch Me* (1921). His stories are vivid and give the impression that he is speaking rather than writing; collections of them include *Clorinda Walks in Heaven* (1922), *The Black Dog* (1923), *Fishmonger's Fiddle* (1925), *The Field of Mustard* (1926), *Silver Circus* (1928), *The Gollan* (1929), *Dunky Fitlow* (1933), *Ninepenny Flute* (1937), *Tapster's Tapestry* (1939), *Ugly Anna* (1944), *Fearful Pleasures* (1946), and *The Dark-Eyed Lady* (1947). *Pink Furniture* (1930) is a book for children. His volumes of poetry include *Hips and Haws* (1922), *Pelagea* (1926), and *Yokohama Garland* (1926); his *Collected Poems* appeared in 1928, and the first part of an autobiography, *It's Me, Oh Lord*, in 1957.

Corbet, Richard (1582—28 July 1635), bishop and poet, born at Ewell, Surrey, son of a gardener, was educated at Westminster School and Oxford, and took holy orders, was Dean of Christ Church at the age of 37, and rose to be Bishop successively of Oxford and Norwich. He was celebrated for his wit, which not seldom passed into buffoonery. His poems, published in 1647, reflect his jovial nature. They include 'Iter Boreale,' the account of a tour from Oxford to Newark, and the well-known 'Farewell, Rewards and Fairies.'

Corelli, Marie, *see* **Mackay, Mary.**

Cornford, Frances Crofts (1866—19 Aug. 1960), poetess, was born at Cambridge, where her mother was a lecturer at Newnham College, and was a grand-daughter of Charles Darwin (q.v.). In 1908 she married Francis Cornford, Professor of Ancient Philosophy. Her first publication was *Death and the Princess, a Morality* (1912). Her books of verse include *Spring Morning* (1915), *Autumn Midnight* (1923), *Different Days* (1928), *Mountains and Molehills* (1934), and *Travelling Home* (1948); her *Collected Poems* appeared in 1954. In 1959 she was awarded the Queen's Medal for Poetry.

Cornwall, Barry, *see* **Procter, B. W.**

Corvo, Baron, *see* **Rolfe, Frederick.**

Cory, William Johnson (9 Jan. 1823—11 June 1892), schoolmaster and poet, was born at Torrington, son of Charles Johnson, a Devon squire. Educated at Eton and King's College, Cambridge, of which he became a Fellow, he was an assistant master at Eton for over twenty-six years. In 1872 he inherited an estate, assumed the name of Cory, and settled at Hampstead. His collection of lyrics, *Ionica*, was first published anonymously in 1858 and *Extracts from Letters and Journals* was edited in 1897. He was a skilful Latin and Greek versifier, and his best-known poem is 'Heraclitus,' a paraphrase from Callimachus. In 1863 he wrote the famous 'Eton Boating Song,' which was first printed in the school magazine two years later.

Coryate, *or* **Coryatt, Thomas** (1577—Dec. 1617), traveller, born at Odcombe, Somerset, where his father was rector, and educated at Westminster and Oxford, entered the household of Prince Henry. In 1608 he made a walking tour in France, Italy, and Germany, walking nearly 2,000 miles in one pair of shoes, which were, until 1702, hung up in Odcombe Church, and known as 'the thousand mile shoes.' He gave an amusing account of this in his *Coryate's Crudities* (1611), prefixed to which were commendatory verses by many contemporary poets. A sequel, *Coryate's Crambé, or Colewort twice Sodden* followed. Next year (1612) Coryate set out on another journey to Greece, Egypt, and India, from which he never returned. He died at Surat. Though odd and conceited, he was a close observer; for a time his work was the only handbook to continental travel.

Costello, Louisa Stuart (1799—24 Oct. 1877), artist and poetess, was born in County Mayo, daughter of an Irish army officer who died when she was a girl. A proficient artist at the age of 15, she went to Paris and kept her mother and sent her brother to Sandhurst with the proceeds of her miniature paintings. She wrote many poems, including *The Maid of Cyprus Isle* (1815), and *Songs of a Stranger* (1825). *Specimens of the Early Poetry of France* (1835) won her the friendship of Walter Scott. A very voluminous writer, she also published topographical books about France, and some historical novels.

Cotton, Charles (28 March 1630—Feb. 1686), poet and translator, was born at Beresford Hall, Staffordshire, and is said to have been educated at Cambridge. He is chiefly remembered for his excellent translation of Montaigne's *Essays* (1685). His *Poems on Several Occasions* (1689) was admired by the Lake Poets for the natural descriptions contained in it. Others of his works are *Scarronides, or the First Book of Virgil Travestied* (1664), *The Compleat Gamester* (1674), and *Wonders•of the Peak* (1681). He was a friend of Izaak Walton and wrote an addition to his *Compleat Angler*.

Cotton, Nathaniel (1705—2 Aug. 1788), doctor and poet, was born in London, son of a merchant, and studied medicine at Leyden. He practised at St Albans, and kept a private asylum in which for a time Cowper was confined. His best-known volume, *Visions in Verse* (1751), moralises the fables of Gay. His *Collected Works* were published in 1791.

Cotton, Sir Robert Bruce (22 Jan. 1571—6 May 1631), antiquary, born at Denton, Huntingdonshire, and educated at Cambridge, was a great collector of charters and records throwing light upon English history, and co-operated with Camden (q.v.). Among his works is a history, the *Reign of Henry III* (1627). He was the collector of the Cottonian library, now in the British Museum, and was the author of various political tracts.

Cottrell, Ida Dorothy Ottley (16 July 1902—   ), novelist, was born at Picton, New South Wales, daughter of Walter B. Wilkinson. At the age of 6 she contracted infantile paralysis, and thereafter was educated privately. In 1922 she married Walter M. Cottrell and moved to California. Her first two books, *The Singing Gold* (1929), and *Earth Battle* (1933), told of pastoral life in Queensland. Later she wrote two animal stories, *Winks* (1936), the story of a terrier, and *Wilderness Orphan* (1940); about a kangaroo.

Couch, Sir Arthur Quiller-, *see* Quiller-Couch.

Coulton, George Gordon (15 Oct. 1858—4 March 1947), scholar, was born at King's Lynn, son of a solicitor, and educated at Felsted, Cambridge, and Heidelberg. After being a master at various public schools he was appointed lecturer in English at Cambridge in 1911 and some years later became a Fellow of St John's. From 1940 to 1943 he was Professor of Medieval History at Toronto. In 1905 he began publishing his long series of Medieval Studies (1905—31).

Others of his works are *Chaucer and his England* (1908), *A Medieval Garner* (1910), *The Medieval Village* (1925), *Life in the Middle Ages* (1929), and *Medieval Panorama* (1938). He also wrote *Five Centuries of Religion* (1927—47), and a number of other religious works. *Fourscore Years* (1943) is autobiographical.

Courthope, William John (17 July 1842—10 April 1917), critic, was born at South Malling near Lewes, in Sussex, where his father was rector, and was educated at Harrow and Oxford, where he won the Chancellor's Prize with an essay on 'The Genius of Shakespeare,' and also the Newdigate. In 1869 he became an examiner in the Education Office, and in the same year he published *Ludibria Lunae*, a satire on the suffragette movement. From 1887 to 1907 he was a Civil Service Commissioner. He is chiefly remembered for his six-volume *History of English Poetry* (1895—1909), which is sound and conservative and secured him a doctorate of Durham. In 1895 he was elected Professor of Poetry at Oxford. His other works include a life of Addison (1882), and *Life in Poetry : Law in Taste* (1901).

Cousin, Anne Ross (27 April 1824—6 Dec. 1906), hymn writer, daughter of a doctor, David Ross Cundell, was born at Hull, the family soon afterwards removing to Leith. Educated privately, she became an expert pianist. She married William Cousin, for many years minister at Melrose, where she is commemorated by a stained glass window. She is best remembered for her hymn 'The Sands of Time Are Sinking,' which appeared in her volume *Immanuel's Land and Other Pieces* (1876). Her son, John William Cousin, compiled the *Biographical Dictionary of English Literature,* on which the present work is based; it was published in 1910, and he died in December of that year.

Coverdale, Miles (born 1488, buried 19 Feb. 1568), translator, was born in Yorkshire, and educated at Cambridge. Originally an Augustinian monk, he became a supporter of the Reformation. In 1535 his translation of the Bible was published, probably at Zurich. It bore the title, *Biblia, the Bible : that is the Holy Scripture of the Olde and New Testament faithfully and newly translated out of the Doutche and Latyn into English*. Coverdale was made Bishop of Exeter in 1551, but, on the accession of Mary, he was imprisoned for two years, at the end of which he went to Denmark and afterwards to Geneva. On the death of Mary he returned to England, but the views he had imbibed in Geneva were adverse to his preferment. He ultimately, however, received a benefice in London, which he resigned before his death. Besides the Bible he translated many treatises of the Continental Reformers.

Coward, Noel Pierce (16 Dec. 1899—   ), actor, dramatist, composer, born at Teddington on the Thames, came of a musical family, and when at the Chapel Royal School, Clapham, developed a fine singing voice. He received his dramatic training at the Italia Conti Academy. One of his earliest stage appearances was as a page-boy in Charles Hawtrey's company, and in 1913 he played Slightly in Barrie's *Peter Pan*. During the First World War he enlisted in the Artists' Rifles, but was discharged for health reasons. Taking to playwriting he achieved his first success with *The Vortex* in 1923. This was followed by *Fallen Angels* (1925), *Hay Fever* (1925), a sophisticated comedy which he wrote in three days, *Easy Virtue* (1926), *The Queen Was in the Parlour* (1926), *Private Lives* (1930), *Design for Living* (1933), *Blithe Spirit* (1941), *This Happy Breed* (1943), and *Relative Values* (1951); *Calvacade* (1931), a story of thirty years in the life of a family, initiated a new type of drama. Coward also composed the revues *On With the Dance* (1925), and *Sigh No More* (1943), and several tuneful operettas, including *Bitter Sweet* (1929), which was so successful in both London and New York that he was able to go on a world tour afterwards; others were *Conversation Piece* (1934), and *Pacific 1860* (1946). Besides writing the words and music he produced most of his plays, as well as acting in them. *Present Indicative* (1937) and *Future Indefinite* (1954) are autobiographical.

Cowley, Abraham (1618—28 July 1667), poet, was born in London, son of a stationer. In childhood he was greatly influenced by reading Spenser, and composed an epical romance at the age of 10. His first book, *Poetic Blossoms* (1633), was published when he was only 15, and *Love's Riddle*, a pastoral drama, appeared five years later. After being at Westminster School he went to Cambridge, where he was distinguished for his graceful translations. On the outbreak of the Civil War he joined the Royalists, was turned out of his college, and in 1646 followed the Queen to Paris, where he remained for ten or twelve years, during which he rendered unwearied service to the Royal Family. At the Restoration he wrote some loyal odes, but was disappointed by being refused the Mastership of the Savoy, and retired to the country. He received a lease of Crown lands, but his life in the country did not yield him the happiness he expected. He is said by Pope to have died of a fever brought on by lying in the fields after a drinking-bout; the drinking-bout, however, is perhaps an ill-natured addition. Cowley's fame among his contemporaries was much greater than that which posterity has accorded to him. His poems are marred by conceits and a forced and artificial brilliancy. In some of them, however, he sings pleasantly of gardens and country scenes. They comprise *The Mistress, or Love Poems* (1647), *Pindaric Odes* (1656) in which he was a pioneer, and *The Davideis*, an epic on David (unfinished). His is the first name in Johnson's *Lives of the Poets*. His prose, especially in his *Essays*, is simple and graceful. Cowley is buried in Westminster Abbey near Spenser.

Cowley, Hannah (1743—11 March 1809), dramatist and poetess, was born at Tiverton, Devon, daughter of Philip Parkhouse, a bookseller, and married Captain Cowley about 1768. Her play *The Runaway* (1776), written in a fortnight, was a great success. Later plays were *Who's the Dupe?* (1779), *The Belle's Stratagem* (1782), *A Bold Stroke for a Husband* (1783), and *A School for Greybeards* (1786). Her poems include *The Maid of Arragon* (1780), *The Scottish Village* (1787), *Edwina* (1794), and *The Siege of Acre* (1799). Her *Works* were published in 1813.

Cowper, William (15 Nov. 1731—25 April 1800), poet, was born at Berkhampstead, Hertfordshire, son of the rector, who was chaplain to George II. His grandfather was a judge, and he was the grand-nephew of the 1st Earl Cowper, the eminent Lord Chancellor. The death of his mother when he was 6 years old, and the sufferings inflicted upon him by a bullying schoolfellow at his first school, wounded his tender and shrinking spirit irrecoverably. He was sent to Westminster School, where he had for schoolfellows Churchill, the poet (q.v.), and Warren Hastings. The powerful legal influence of his family naturally suggested his being destined for the law, and at 18 he entered the chambers of a solicitor, where he had for a companion Thurlow, the future Chancellor, a truly incongruous conjunction; the pair, however, seem to have got on well together, and employed their time chiefly in 'giggling and making giggle.' He then entered the Middle Temple, and in 1754 was called to the Bar. This was perhaps the happiest period of his life, being enlivened by the society of two cousins, Theodora and Harriet Cowper. With the former he fell in love; but his proposal of marriage was opposed by her father, who had observed symptoms of morbidity in him, and he never met her again. The latter, as Lady Hesketh, was in later days one of his most intimate friends. In 1759 he received a small sinecure appointment as Commissioner of Bankrupts, which he held for five years, and in 1763, through the influence of a relative, he received the offer of the desirable office of Clerk of the Journals to the House of Lords. He accepted the appointment, but the dread of having to make a formal appearance before the House so preyed upon his mind as to induce a temporary loss of reason, and he was sent to an asylum at St Albans, where he remained for about a year.

He had now no income beyond a small sum inherited from his father, and no aims in life; but friends supplemented his means sufficiently to enable him to lead with a quiet mind the life of retire-ment which he had resolved to follow. He went to Huntingdon, and there made the acquaintance of the Unwins, with whom he went to live as a boarder. The acquaintance soon ripened into a close friendship, and on the death, from an accident (1767), of Mr Unwin, Cowper accompanied his widow (the 'Mary' of his poems) to Olney, where the Rev. John Newton (q.v.) was curate. Newton and Cowper became intimate friends, and collaborated in producing the well-known *Olney Hymns*, of which 67 were composed by Cowper. He became engaged to Mary Unwin, but a fresh attack of his mental malady in 1773 prevented their marriage. On his recovery he took to gardening, and amused himself by keeping pets, including the hares Tiny and Puss, and the spaniel Beau, immortalized in his works. At the suggestion of Mrs Unwin, he wrote *The Progress of Error; Truth, Table Talk, Expostulation, Hope, Charity, Conversation,* and *Retirement* were added, and the whole were published in one volume in 1782. Its signal merits of freshness, simplicity, graceful humour, and the pure idiomatic English in which it was written gradually obtained recognition, and the fame of the poet-recluse began to spread. His health had now improved, and he enjoyed an unwonted measure of cheerfulness, which was fostered by the friendship of

Lady Austin, who had become his neighbour. From her he received the story of John Gilpin, which he forthwith turned into his immortal ballad. Hers also was the suggestion that he should write a poem in blank verse, which gave its origin to his most famous poem, *The Task*. Before it was published, however, the intimacy had, apparently owing to some little feminine jealousies, been broken off.

The Task, published in 1785, met with immediate and distinguished success. It was the beginning of an uprising against the classical school of poetry, and the founding of a new school in which nature was the teacher. As Stopford Brooke points out: 'Cowper is the first of the poets who loves Nature entirely for her own sake.' About this time he resumed his friendship with his cousin, Lady Hesketh, and, encouraged by her, he began his translation of *Homer*, which appeared in 1791. Before this he had removed with Mrs Unwin to the village of Weston Underwood. His health had again given way; and in 1791 Mrs Unwin became paralytic, and the object of his assiduous and affectionate care. A settled gloom with occasional brighter intervals was now falling upon him. He strove to fight it by engaging in various translations, and in revising his *Homer*, and undertaking a new edition of Milton, which last was, however, left unfinished. In 1794 a pension of £300 was conferred upon him, and in 1795 he removed with Mrs Unwin, now a helpless invalid, to East Dereham. Mrs Unwin died in the following year, and three years later his own death released him from his heavy burden of trouble and sorrow. His last poem was 'The Castaway,' which, with its darkness almost of despair, shows no loss of intellectual or poetic power. In addition to his reputation as a poet Cowper has that of being among the very best of English letter-writers, and in this he shows, in an even easier and more unstudied manner, the same command of pure idiomatic English, the same acute observation, and the same mingling of gentle humour and melancholy. In literature Cowper is the connecting link between the classical school of Pope and the natural school of Burns, Crabbe, and Wordsworth, having, however, much more in common with the latter. The standard edition of his works is Southey's, with memoir (15 volumes 1834—7).

Coxe, William (7 March 1747—16 June 1828), historian, was born in London, son of the king's physician and educated at Eton and Cambridge. He took orders and died Archdeacon of Wiltshire. As tutor to various young men of family he travelled much on the Continent, and published accounts of his journeys. His chief historical work is his *Memoirs of the House of Austria* (1807), and he also wrote lives of Walpole, Marlborough, and others.

Crabbe, George (24 Dec. 1754—3 Feb. 1832), poet, was born at Aldborough, Suffolk, where his father was collector of salt dues, and was apprenticed to a surgeon, but, having no liking for the work, went to London to try his fortune in literature. Unsuccessful and almost destitute, he as a last resource wrote a letter to Burke enclosing some of his writings, and was immediately befriended by him, and taken into his own house, where he met Fox, Reynolds, and others. His first important work, *The Library*, was published in 1781, and received with favour. He took orders, and was appointed by the Duke of Rutland his domestic chaplain, residing with him at Belvoir Castle. Here in 1783 he published *The Village*, which had been revised by Burke and Johnson. It established his reputation, and about the same time he was presented by Lord Thurlow to two small livings. He was now secured from want, made a happy marriage, and devoted himself to literary and scientific pursuits. The *Newspaper* appeared in 1785, and was followed by a period of silence until 1807, when he came forward again with *The Parish Register*, followed by *The Borough* (1810), *Tales in Verse* (1812), and his last work, *Tales of the Hall* (1817—18). In 1819 Murray the publisher gave him £3,000 for the last-named work and the unexpired copyright of his other poems. In 1822 he visited Sir Walter Scott at Edinburgh. Soon afterwards his health began to give way. Crabbe has been called 'the poet of the poor.' He describes in simple, but strong and vivid, verse their struggles, sorrows, weaknesses, crimes, and pleasures, sometimes with racy humour, oftener in sombre hues. He has a marvellous power of depicting both the beauty and the ugliness of natural scenery, so that Byron styled him 'Though Nature's sternest painter, yet the best.' Grimly realistic in outlook, he eschews all sentimentality and breaks down the 'pretty-pretty' convention of the happy unspoiled rustic. He wrote in heroic couplets modelled on Pope's, and has been nicknamed 'Pope in fustian.'

Craigie, Pearl Mary Teresa (3 Nov. 1867—13 Aug. 1906), novelist and dramatist who wrote under the pen-name John Oliver Hobbes, was born at Chelsea, near Boston, Massachusetts. Her father, John Morgan Richards, a merchant, removed with his family to London when she was less than a year old. Most of her education was received in London and Paris, and from childhood she was a great reader and observer. At 19 she married Reginald Walpole Craigie, but the union was unhappy and she divorced him in 1895. In 1892 she became a Roman Catholic. She wrote a number of novels and dramas, distinguished by originality of subject and treatment, and a command of epigram, among which may be mentioned *Some Emotions and a Moral* (1891), a first novel which was well received, *The Gods, Some Mortals, and Lord Wickenham* (1895), *The School for Saints* (1897), *Robert Orange* (1900), and *The Dream and the Business* (1907). Her dramas include *The Ambassador* and *The Bishop's Move*.

Craigie, Sir William Alexander (13 Aug. 1867—2 Sept. 1957), lexicographer, was born at Dundee and educated at St Andrews University and Oxford. In 1893 he was appointed an assistant in Latin at St Andrews, and at this time he collaborated with Andrew Lang (q.v.) in an edition of Burns. In 1897 he joined the staff of the *Oxford English Dictionary*, of which eventually he became editor-in-chief; on its completion in 1928 he received a knighthood and honorary doctorates from both Oxford and Cambridge. Meanwhile he had occupied the chair of Anglo-Saxon at Oxford from 1915, and in 1925 had accepted a professorship of English at Chicago, where he compiled a four-volume *Historical Dictionary of American English* (1944). About the same time he began work on a *Dictionary of the Older Scottish Tongue*, which covers the language to the end of the seventeenth century. In addition to these three vast undertakings he edited many works for the Scottish Text Society, of which he was president, wrote pamphlets for the Society for Pure English, and did so much in connection with Icelandic literature, on which he was an expert, that he was made a Knight Commander of the Icelandic Falcon. His later years were spent on the crest of the Chilterns, near Watlington.

Craik, Dinah Maria Mulock (20 April 1826—12 Oct. 1887), novelist, was born at Stoke-upon-Trent, where her father, Thomas Mulock, was minister. In 1846 she removed to London, where she rapidly made many friends. Her first novel, *The Ogilvies* (1849), was followed by *Olive* (1850), *The Head of the Family* (1851), and *Agatha's Husband* (1853). Established as a successful author, she settled at Hampstead, and in 1857 published *John Halifax, Gentleman*, by which she is chiefly remembered. Later novels were *A Life for a Life* (1859), and *Christian's Mistake* (1865). *The Little Lame Prince* (1874) is a charming children's story, and in 1881 appeared her *Poems of Thirty Years, New and Old*. In 1865 she married George Lillie Craik, a partner in a publishing firm.

Craik, George Lillie (1798—25 June 1866), literary historian, born at Kennoway, Fife, and educated at St Andrews, went to London in 1824, where he wrote largely for the Society for the Diffusion of Useful Knowledge. In 1849 he was appointed Professor of English Literature and History at Belfast. Among his books are *The Pursuit of Knowledge under Difficulties* (1831), *History of British Commerce* (1844), and *History of English Literature and the English Language* (1861). He also wrote books on Spenser and Bacon. Mrs Craik the novelist (q.v.) was married to his nephew.

Crane, Harold Hart (21 July 1899—27 April 1932), poet, was born at Garrettsville, Ohio; in his childhood the family moved to Cleveland, where his father had a large confectionery business, and soon afterwards his parents were divorced. At the age of 13 he wrote verse. At 17 he spent a year on his father's plantations in Cuba, during the First World War he worked on munitions, and later he was a reporter on the Cleveland *Plain Dealer*. His principal works are *White Buildings* (1926), a collection of poems, and *The Bridge* (1930), a mystical poetic interpretation of American history. In 1931 he won a Guggenheim Fellowship and went to Mexico meaning to write an epic of Latin America. But by this time his personality was warped by drink and other excesses, and he ended his life by jumping overboard while on his way back to New York. His *Collected Poems* were published in 1933 and his *Letters* in 1952. He has been described as 'a myth-maker in the grand manner' and though frequently obscure is regarded as one of the leading American poets of modern times.

Crane, Stephen (1 Nov. 1871—5 June 1900), war correspondent, was the fourteenth child of a Methodist minister of Newark, New Jersey. He was educated at Syracuse University, where he captained the baseball team. Taking up journalism, he wrote *Maggie: A Girl of the Streets* (1892), and followed it next year with *The Red Badge of Courage*, a war novel in which, it has been said 'his genius seemed to spring to life fully armed.' Most of the rest of his life was spent seeing and writing of wars. In 1896 he visited London and formed a friendship with Conrad. Later he wrote of the Spanish-American war in *Wounds in the Rain* (1900). His books of verse include *The Black Riders* (1895), and *War is Kind* (1899). He died in Germany of tuberculosis, and his writings were collected in 12 volumes in 1926.

Cranmer, Thomas (2 July 1489—21 March 1556), Archbishop of Canterbury, was born at Aslacton, Nottinghamshire, educated at Cambridge, and became an eminent classical and biblical scholar. He supported Henry VIII in his divorce proceedings against Queen Catherine, gained the King's favour, and obtained rapid preferment, ending with the Primacy. He was one of the chief promoters of the Reformation in England. On the accession of Mary, he was committed to the Tower, and, after a temporary failure of courage and constancy, suffered martyrdom at the stake. It is largely to Cranmer that we owe the stately forms of the Book of Common Prayer, the production of which he supervised in 1552.

Crashaw, Richard (1613?—21 Aug. 1649), poet, son of a clergyman, was born in London, and educated at Charterhouse and Cambridge, where he became a Fellow of Peterhouse, from which, however, he was, in 1643, ejected for refusing to accept the Solemn League and Covenant. Thereafter he went to France, and became a Roman Catholic. He suffered great straits, being almost reduced to starvation, but was, through the influence of Queen Henrietta Maria, appointed Secretary to Cardinal Palotta. About 1649 he went to Italy, and in the following year became a canon of the Church of Loretto. He died the same year. Crashaw is said to have been an eloquent preacher, and was a scholar as well as a poet of a high order in the ecstatic and transcendental style. His chief work is *Steps to the Temple* (1646), consisting mainly of religious poems somewhat in the style of Herbert; but many of his poems contain most extravagant conceits. His friend Cowley commemorated him in a beautiful ode.

Crawford, Francis Marion (2 Aug. 1854—9 April 1909), novelist, son of an American sculptor and nephew of Julia Ward Howe (q.v.), was born at Bagni di Lucca, Tuscany, and had a cosmopolitan education. He wrote in French as easily as in English; he studied German, Swedish, and Spanish at Cambridge; he also studied Sanskrit at Rome and Harvard and knew many Eastern languages. His first novel, *Mr Isaacs* (1882), was a great success and was followed by over 40 others, mainly historical romances, including *Dr Claudius* (1883), *A Roman Singer* (1884), *Zoroaster* (1885), *Saracinesca* (1887), *Sant' Ilario* (1889), *A Cigarette Maker's Romance* (1890), and *The White Sister* (1909). *The Novel—What Is It?* (1893) embodied his theory of fiction. His last years were spent at Sorrento.

Creasy, Sir Edward Shepherd (12 Sept. 1812—27 Jan. 1878), historian, son of a land agent, was born at Bexley in Kent, educated at Eton and Cambridge, and called to the Bar in 1837. He became in 1840 Professor of History, London University, and in 1860 Chief Justice of Ceylon, when he was knighted. His best known contribution to literature is his *Fifteen Decisive Battles of the World* (1852). Other works are *Historical and Critical Account of the Several Invasions of England* (1852), and *History of the Ottoman Turks* (1878).

Creech, Thomas (1659—June 1700), translator, born at Blandford in Dorset and educated at Oxford, became Headmaster of Sherborne School. He translated Lucretius in verse (1682), for which he received a Fellowship at Oxford, also Horace, Theocritus, and other classics. Owing to a disappointment in love and money difficulties he hanged himself.

Creevey, Thomas (March 1768—Feb. 1838), politician, was born in Liverpool, son of a merchant, and educated at Queens' College, Cambridge. From 1802 onwards he was a Whig M.P., first for Thetford and then for Appleby. He married a widow by whom he had sixteen children, and in 1860 became Treasurer of Greenwich Hospital. His claim to remembrance is the *Creevey Papers*, made up of his journals and letters he received. First published in 1903, they throw light on the inner history of his times. A further selection, *Creevey's Life and Times*, was edited in 1934.

Creighton, Mandell (5 July 1843—14 Jan. 1901), prelate and historian, born at Carlisle, and educated at Durham Grammar School and Merton College, Oxford, took orders, and was presented to the living of Embleton, Northumberland, in 1875. In 1882 the first two volumes of his *History of the Papacy* appeared, followed by two more in 1887, and a fifth in 1894. In 1884 he was appointed first Dixie Professor of Ecclesiastical History at Cambridge, and from 1886 to 1891 he edited the *English Historical Review*. In 1891, after having held canonries at Worcester and Windsor, he became Bishop of Peterborough, from which he was in 1897 translated to London, where his duties made the completion of his great historical work an impossibility. He wrote in addition to it various text-books on history, a life of Queen Elizabeth, and a memoir of Sir George Grey.

Crèvecœur, Michel-Guillaume Jean de (31 Jan. 1735—12 Nov. 1813), essayist who used the name J. Hector St John de Crèvecœur, was born near Caen in Normandy. Emigrating to Canada he served under Montcalm. Between 1759 and 1769 he travelled widely in Pennsylvania and New York, then married and settled down and wrote *Letters from an American Farmer* (1782), and *Sketches of Eighteenth-Century America* (1925), describing American rural life. At the Revolution he had to flee to France as a loyalist, and when he returned in 1783 he found that his home had been destroyed by Red Indians. For a time he acted as French consul in New York, and in 1790 returned to France, where he spent the rest of his life.

Crockett, Samuel Rutherford (24 Sept. 1860—21 April 1914), minister and novelist, was born at Little Duchrae in Kirkcudbright-

shire, and educated at Cowper's School, Castle Douglas, and Edinburgh University. After travelling as a tutor in Germany,
Switzerland, and Italy he studied theology in Edinburgh and in
1886 became minister of Penicuik, Midlothian. In the same year
he published a volume of poems, *Dulce Cor*. In 1893 appeared *The
Stickit Minister*, a series of sketches, which was well received. Two
novels which he published in the following year, *The Raiders*, and
The Lilac Sunbonnet, were so successful that he retired from the
ministry and devoted himself to writing. Among some 40 books
which he produced, the best-known are *The Men of the Moss Hags*
(1895), *The Grey Man* (1896), *Kit Kennedy* (1899), *The Loves of Miss
Anne* (1904), and *The White Plumes of Navarre* (1909). One of the
leaders of the so-called Kailyard School of novelists, Crockett was
much admired by R. L. Stevenson, who dedicated to him one of his
best-known poems.

Crofts, Freeman Wills (June 1879—11 April 1957), writer of
detective stories, was born in Dublin, son of an army doctor.
Educated at Campbell College, Belfast, he became a railway engineer.
In 1919, during a long illness, he started writing a story to pass the
time; published in the following year as *The Cask*, it sold over 100,000
copies in twenty years and was regarded as one of the classics of
detective fiction. In 1929 Crofts gave up railway work to devote
himself to writing. He belongs to the matter-of-fact school, unravelling his mysteries by the method of actual police routine, and it
is typical that his hero, Inspector French, is a member of the regular
force. Among his best-known books are *The Pit Prop Syndicate*
(1922), *Inspector French's Greatest Case* (1925), *The Cheyne Mystery*
(1926), *The Starvel Tragedy* (1927), *The Box Office Murders* (1929),
Sudden Death (1932), *The 12.30 from Croydon* (1934), *The Loss of
the 'Jane Vosper'* (1936), *A Losing Game* (1941), *Death of a Train*
(1946), and *French Strikes Oil* (1951).

Croker, John Wilson (20 Dec. 1780—10 Aug. 1857), M.P. and
essayist, was born in Galway, son of a customs official, and educated
at Trinity College, Dublin. He entered Parliament as a Tory, and
was appointed to various offices, including the Secretaryship of the
Admiralty, which he held for twenty years. He was one of the
founders of the *Quarterly Review*, and wrote some of its most violent
political articles and reviews. He published in 1831 an edition of
Boswell's Life of Johnson. His *Correspondence and Diaries* were
edited in 1884.

Croker, Thomas Crofton (15 Jan. 1798—8 Aug. 1854), antiquary,
born at Cork, became a clerk in the Admiralty. He devoted himself
largely to the collection of ancient Irish poetry and folklore. Among
his publications are *Researches in the South of Ireland* (1824), *Fairy
Legends and Traditions of the South of Ireland* (1825—7), *Popular
Songs of Ireland* (1837), *Daniel O'Rourke* (1829), and *Barney Mahoney*
(1832). He assisted in founding the Camden and Percy Societies.

Croly, George (17 Aug. 1780—24 Nov. 1860), clergyman and
author, born in Dublin and educated at Trinity College there, took

G

orders and in 1810 moved to London, where he became rector of St Stephen's, Walbrook, and had a high reputation as a preacher. He wrote poems, dramas, satires, novels, history, and theological works, and attained some measure of success in all. Perhaps his best known works are his novels, *Salathiel* (1829), founded on the legend of 'the wandering Jew,' and *Mareton* (1846). A romantic writer, he belongs to the school of Byron and Moore.

Cronin, Archibald Joseph (19 July 1896—   ), novelist, was born at Cardross, Dumbartonshire, and educated at Dumbarton Academy and Glasgow University, where he took his degree in medicine. After various hospital appointments he married a lady doctor, Agnes Mary Gibson, in 1921, and started practice in South Wales, later moving to London. In 1930 he had a breakdown in health, and while convalescing on a farm near Inveraray wrote *Hatter's Castle* in three months; it had a phenomenal success, was translated into five languages, and enabled him to give up medicine for a literary career. Others of his books, which never quite repeated the success of his first, are *Three Loves* (1932), *Grand Canary* (1933), *The Stars Look Down* (1935), *The Citadel*, which shed a lurid light on Harley Street (1937), *The Keys of the Kingdom* (1941), *The Green Years* (1944), *Shannon's Way* (1948), *The Spanish Gardener* (1950), *Beyond This Place* (1953), and *Crusader's Tomb* (1956). He also wrote a play, *Jupiter Laughs* (1940).

Cross, Mary Ann, *see* **Evans.**

Crowe, Catherine (1800—1876), novelist, was born at Borough Green, Kent, her maiden name being Stevens, but lived mainly in Edinburgh. She wrote dramas, children's books, and one or two novels, including *Susan Hopley* (1841), and *Lilly Dawson* (1847), but is chiefly remembered for her *Night-side of Nature* (1848), a collection of stories of the supernatural.

Crowe, Eyre Evans (20 March 1799—25 Feb. 1868), historian and novelist, son of an army officer, was born near Southampton, and educated at Trinity College, Dublin. He wrote several novels, including *Vittoria Colonna, To-day in Ireland* (1825), *The English in France* (1828), and *Charles Dalmer* (1853). Among his historical works are a *History of France* written for Lardner's *Cabinet Encyclopaedia*, afterwards enlarged and separately published, and a *History of Louis XVIII and Charles X* (1854).

Crowe, Sir Joseph Archer (20 Oct. 1825—6 Sept. 1896), journalist, son of the above, was born in London but spent most of his childhood in Paris. He was for some years engaged in educational work in India, and filled various important consular posts, for which he was in 1890 made K.C.M.G. In collaboration with G. B. Cavalcasselle, an Italian refugee, he was the author of several authoritative works on art, including *The Early Flemish Painters* (1856), *A New History of Painting in Italy* (1864—8), *A History of Painting in North Italy* (1871), *Titian, His Life and Times* (1877), and *Raphael, His Life and Works* (1883—5).

Crowe, William (baptized 13 Oct. 1745, died 9 Feb. 1829), clergyman and poet, born at Midgham, Berkshire, the son of a carpenter, was educated as a foundationer at Winchester, whence he proceeded to Oxford, where he became Public Orator. He wrote a smooth, but somewhat conventional poem, *Lewesdon Hill* (1789), edited Collins's poems (1828), and lectured on poetry at the Royal Institution. His poems were collected in 1827. Crowe was rector of Alton Barnes, Wiltshire.

Crowne, John (1640?—1703?), dramatist, returned from Nova Scotia, to which his father, a Nonconformist minister, had emigrated, and became gentleman usher to a lady of quality. His first work was a romance, *Pandion and Amphigenia* (1665). His first play, *Juliana*, appeared in 1671. He wrote in all about 17 dramatic pieces, of which the best is *Sir Courtly Nice* (1685), adapted from the Spanish; it is amusing, and enjoyed a long continued vogue. In general, however, Crowne is dull.

Cruden, Alexander (31 May 1701—1 Nov. 1770), compiler, the son of an Aberdeen bailie, was educated at Aberdeen Grammar School and Marischal College. After being confined in an asylum owing to mental illness he went to London in 1722 as a private tutor and in 1732 opened a bookshop in the Royal Exchange. His great *Concordance of the Holy Scriptures*, published in 1737, was dedicated to Queen Caroline, who, however, died before she could grant any substantial recognition of it. Cruden again lapsed into insanity and during the rest of his life had to be confined at intervals. He worked as a press reader, and finally died when at prayers in his Islington lodgings.

Cudworth, Ralph (1617—26 June 1688), clergyman, son of the rector of Aller, Somerset, was educated at Cambridge, where he became Master of Clare Hall in 1645, was Professor of Hebrew (1645—88), and Master of Christ's College from 1654. A leader of the Cambridge Platonists, he was celebrated for his *True Intellectual System of the Universe* (1678). A work of vast learning and acuteness, it is directed against the infidelity of the age. He also left in manuscript a *Treatise concerning Eternal and Immutable Morality*, published in 1731.

Cullum, Ridgwell (13 Aug. 1867—3 Nov. 1943), novelist, was born in London. At the age of 17 he joined the Transvaal gold rush, then worked in the diamond mines at Kimberley. Later he went fur-hunting on the Yukon, then cattle-ranching in Montana, and took part in some of the Indian risings. By writing about Canada he broke almost fresh ground, and his fast-moving adventure tales were very popular. They include *The Devil's Keg* (1903), *The Brooding Wild* (1905), *The Night Riders* (1906), *The Watchers of the Plains* (1909), *The Twins of Suffering Creek* (1912), *The Heart of Unaga* (1920). *The Luck of the Kid* (1923), and *The Child of the North* (1926).

Cumberland, Richard (19 Feb. 1732—7 May 1811), dramatist and novelist, born at Cambridge, was at Westminster with Colman and Churchill (qq.v.). He then went on to Cambridge, entered the diplomatic service, and filled several government appointments.

His best plays are *The Brothers* (1769) and *The West Indian* (1771). His novels do not rise much above mediocrity. His *Memoirs* appeared in 1807. Sheridan caricatured him as Sir Fretful Plagiary in *The Critic*.

Cummings, Bruce Frederick (7 Sept. 1889—22 Oct. 1919), essayist and diarist who wrote under the name W. N. P. Barbellion, the initials standing significantly for Wilhelm Nero Pilate, was born at Barnstaple, Devonshire, son of a journalist. At the age of 16 he was a newspaper reporter, but he had always a strong scientific bent, and in 1911 he obtained through open competition a post in the Natural History Museum at South Kensington. He was even then in the grip of disseminated sclerosis, a painful and ultimately fatal illness. In the book which made him famous, *The Journal of a Disappointed Man* (1919), based on a journal which he kept from the age of 13, he tells of what he had to endure; it is an intensely human document, and he himself called it 'a self-portrait in the nude.' Others of his books are *Enjoying Life* (1919), and *A Last Day* (1920).

Cummings, Edward Estlin (14 Oct. 1894—   ), poet, was born at Cambridge, Massachusetts, and educated at Harvard, where his father had been a lecturer. In the First World War he volunteered as an ambulance driver in the French army and wrote of his experiences in *The Enormous Room* (1922). After the war he studied art in Paris, returning to New York in 1924. His *Tulips and Chimneys* had appeared in 1923, and in 1925 he won the *Dial* award for distinguished service to American literature. After some further years in Paris he settled down in Greenwich Village. His works include *XLI Poems* (1925), *&* (1925), *Is 5* (1926), *Viva* (1931), *Eimi* (1933), *No Thanks* (1935), *Tom* (1935), *V20* (1936), *1 x 1* (1944), and *Seventy-One Poems* (1950). His *Collected Poems* appeared in 1938. He also wrote *him* (1928), a phantasmagoria in 21 scenes, and *Santa Claus: a Morality* (1946); *six nonlectures* (1953) is a critical work. An ultra-modernist, he indulged in typographical oddities, preferring to write his name e. e. cummings, and used jazz rhythm and a slang dialect. He has been described as one of the few successful verse-experimenters of his time.

Cummins, Maria Susanna (9 April 1827—1 Oct. 1866), novelist, was born at Salem, Massachusetts, daughter of a judge, and went to school at Lenox. Her moralistic novel *The Lamplighter* (1854) was a popular success and was followed by *Mabel Vaughan* (1857), and *Haunted Hearts* (1864).

Cunningham, Allan (7 Dec. 1784—30 Oct. 1842), poet and man of letters, born near Dalswinton, Dumfriesshire, in his youth knew Burns, who was a friend of his father's. He was apprenticed to his brother, a stone-mason, but gave his leisure to reading and writing imitations of old Scottish ballads, which he contributed to Cromek's *Remains of Nithsdale and Galloway Song* (1810); these gained for him the friendship of Scott and Hogg. Thereafter he went to London, and became a parliamentary reporter, and subsequently assistant to Chantrey, the sculptor, but continued his literary labours. His works include *Traditional Tales of the English and Scottish*

Peasantry (1822); *The Songs of Scotland, Ancient and Modern* (1825), which contains his famous 'A Wet Sheet and a Flowing Sea'; *Lives of the Most Eminent British Painters, Sculptors, and Architects* (1829—33); and a *Life of Sir David Wilkie* (1843). He also edited Burns's works, and wrote three novels.

Cunninghame-Graham, Robert, *see* **Graham.**

Curtis, George William (24 Feb. 1824—31 Aug. 1892), journalist, was born at Providence, Rhode Island, and was a clerk in New York for a few years. After travelling in Europe and the Near East he wrote *Nile Notes of a Howadji* (1851), and *The Howadji in Syria* (1852). *Potiphar Papers* (1853), and the novel *Trumps* (1861) deal with New York social life. *Prue and I* (1857) is a collection of fanciful sketches. From 1865 Curtis was editor of *Harper's Weekly*.

Cynewulf (eighth century), poet, belonged probably to Northumbria. The only poems which can be identified with certainty as his work are four contained in the Exeter Book, preserved at Exeter Cathedral, and the Vercelli Book at Vercelli in north Italy. They are *Elene*, *Juliana*, *The Ascension*, and *The Fates of the Apostles*, in all of which his runic 'signature' is interwoven in the verse. Of these the best is the *Elene*, which tells the story of the finding of the Cross by the Empress Helena, mother of Constantine the Great.

D

Daiches, David (2 Sept. 1912—   ), scholar, was born
in the north of England, son of a clergyman, but was brought up in
Edinburgh, where he attended George Watson's College and took an
English degree at the university; later he went to Balliol College,
Oxford, where he did research work after graduating and became a
Fellow of the college. His *New Literary Values,* a study of modern
writers, appeared in 1936 and his *Literature and Society* in 1938.   In
1937 he accepted an invitation to teach at the University of Chicago,
where he remained till 1943.   After three years as Second Secretary
to the British Embassy in Washington, he was Professor of English
at Cornell till 1951, when he returned to England as a lecturer at
Cambridge.   His critical works include *The Novel and the Modern
World* (1939), *Poetry and the Modern World* (1940), *A Study of
Literature* (1948), *Critical Approaches to Literature* (1956), *The
Present Age* (1958), and studies of Virginia Woolf (1942), Stevenson
(1947), Burns (1950), and Willa Cather (1951).

Dalling and Bulwer, William Henry Lytton Earle Bulwer, 1st Baron
(13 Feb. 1801—23 May 1872), born in London, was the elder brother
of Lord Lytton (q.v.), and a distinguished diplomatist.   He represented England at Madrid, Washington (where he concluded the
Bulwer-Clayton Treaty), Florence, Bucharest, and Constantinople,
and was raised to the peerage in 1871.   He was the author of a
number of books of travel and biography, including *An Autumn in
Greece* (1826), a *Life of Byron* (1835), *Historical Characters* (1868—
1870), and an unfinished life of Lord Palmerston.

Dalrymple, Sir David, *see* **Hailes.**

Dampier, William (baptized 8 June 1652, died March 1715),
explorer and buccaneer, was born near Yeovil, son of a farmer, and
went to sea at the age of 16.   After various seafaring adventures, and
leading a semi-piratical life, he was in 1688 marooned on Nicobar
Island, but escaped to Atchin, returning to England in 1691.   He
published his *Voyage Round the World* (1697), and *A Discourse of
Winds* (1699).   He was then employed by government on a voyage
of survey and discovery (1699—1700), in the course of which he
explored the north-west coast of Australia and the coasts of New
Guinea and New Britain.   In 1701 he was wrecked upon Ascension
Island, from which he was rescued by an East Indiaman, and was
afterwards court-martialled for cruelty.   During a later voyage he
made to the South Seas Alexander Selkirk was rescued from Juan
Fernandez.   His *Voyage to New Holland* appeared in 1709.

Dana, Richard Henry (15 Nov. 1787—2 Feb. 1879), poet and critic,
was born at Cambridge, Massachusetts, son of a famous diplomat,
and educated at Harvard.   He then studied law, but abandoned it

for literature, and was one of the founders of the *North American Review*. In 1821 he started a periodical, *The Idle Man*, which lasted only six months. His first book of verse, *The Buccaneer* (1827) was followed six years later by *Poems and Prose Writings*, and in 1839 he gave lectures on Shakespeare which were very popular but were not printed.

Dana, Richard Henry (1 Aug. 1815—6 Jan. 1882), son of the above, was educated at Harvard, but on his eyesight giving trouble shipped as a common sailor, and wrote of his experiences in *Two Years before the Mast* (1840). Called to the Bar in 1840, he became an authority on maritime law. Other books by him are a manual, *The Seaman's Friend* (1841), and *Vacation Voyage to Cuba* (1859).

Dane, Clemence, *see* **Ashton, Winifred.**

Daniel, Samuel (1562—Oct. 1619), poet and dramatist, son of a music master, was born probably near Taunton, and educated at Oxford. For a time he was tutor to William Herbert, 3rd Earl of Pembroke. In 1592 he published *Delia*, a fine sonnet series, and *The Complaint of Rosamond*. About the same time there is a reference to him in Spenser's works as a poet who has recently become known, and tradition asserts that he succeeded Spenser as Poet Laureate in 1599, the year in which he published *Musophilus or A General Defence of Learning*. A weighty poem in eight books, *The History of the Civil Wars between York and Lancaster* had appeared in 1595. His *Defence of Rhyme*, published about 1602, championed the native English use of rhyme and was an answer to Campion's *Art of English Poesy*, which advocated classical metre. His plays include *Cleopatra* (1594), a Senecan tragedy, but his chief work for the stage consisted of masques and pastorals designed for court functions, such as *The Vision of the Twelve Goddesses* (1604), *The Queen's Arcadia* (1605), and *Hymen's Triumph* (1614). From 1615 to 1618 he was Inspector of the Children of the Queen's Revels, finally retiring to a farm in Somerset. Daniel is said to have enjoyed the friendship of Marlow and Shakespeare, and his poetry was praised by such acute critics as Drummond of Hawthornden, Coleridge, and Hazlitt.

Dannay, Frederic (20 Oct. 1905—   ), writer of detective stories in collaboration with Manfred B. Lee (q.v.) under the names of Ellery Queen and Barnaby Ross, was born in Brooklyn, and at the age of 24 became art director of a New York advertising agency. He and Lee entered for a detective story prize contest, which they won with *The Roman Hat Mystery* (1929). Elaborate precautions were taken to conceal the identity of the authors, who even wore masks when attending literary parties, but later this was abandoned though the pseudonym Ellery Queen was retained, being used also as the name of the detective, who became one of the most famous of these fictitious characters. Others of the novels are *The French Powder Mystery* (1930), *The Dutch Shoe Mystery* (1931), *The Greek Coffin Mystery* (1932), *The Siamese Twin Mystery* (1933), *Halfway House* (1936), *The Four of Hearts* (1938), *The Tragedy of X* (1940), *Calamity Town* (1942), *Ten Days' Wonder* (1948), *Double,*

Double (1950), and *The Glass Village* (1954). Two volumes of *Adventures of Ellery Queen* (1934, 1940) are collections of short stories, and there was an Ellery Queen monthly magazine containing detective stories by various authors.

D'Arblay, Frances, *see* Burney, Frances.

Darley, George (1795—23 Nov. 1846), poet, novelist, and critic, born in Dublin, and educated at Trinity College there, early decided to follow a literary career, and went to London, where he brought out his first poem, *Errors of Ecstasie* (1822). He also wrote for the *London Magazine*, under the pseudonym of John Lacy. In it appeared his best story, *Lilian of the Vale*. Various other books followed, including *Sylvia, or The May Queen*, a poem (1827). Thereafter he joined the *Athenaeum*, in which he showed himself a severe critic. He was also a dramatist and a profound student of old English plays, editing those of Beaumont and Fletcher in 1840. So deeply was he imbued with the spirit of the seventeenth century that his poem, 'It is not beauty I desire,' was included by F. T. Palgrave in the first edition of his *Golden Treasury* as an anonymous lyric of that age. He was also a mathematician of considerable talent.

Darwin, Charles Robert (12 Feb. 1809—19 April 1882), naturalist, son of a doctor, and grandson of Dr Erasmus Darwin (q.v.), and of Josiah Wedgwood, the famous potter, was born and went to school at Shrewsbury. In 1825 he went to Edinburgh to study medicine, but was more interested in marine zoology. After two years he proceeded to Cambridge, where he graduated in 1831. In the same year came the opportunity of his life, his appointment to sail in the *Beagle* as naturalist on a survey of South America. To this voyage, which extended over nearly five years, he attributed the first real training of his mind, and after his return published *Zoology of the Voyage of the 'Beagle'* (1840). After spending a few years in London arranging his collections and writing his *Journal*, he removed to Downe, a retired village near the Weald of Kent, where, in a house surrounded by a large garden, his whole remaining life was passed in the patient building up, from accurate observations, of his theory of Evolution, which created a new epoch in science and in thought generally. His industry was marvellous, especially when it is remembered that he suffered from chronic bad health. After devoting some time to geology, specially to coral reefs, and exhausting the subject of barnacles, he took up the development of his favourite question, the transformation of species. In these earlier years of residence at Downe he published *The Structure and Distribution of Coral Reefs* (1842), and two works on the geology of volcanic islands, and of South America. The publication in 1859 of *The Origin of Species* gave Darwin an acknowledged place among the greatest men of science, and the controversies which, along with other of his works, it raised, helped to carry his name all over the civilized world. Among his numerous subsequent writings may be mentioned *The Fertilization of Orchids* (1862), *Variation of Plants and Animals under Domestication* (1868), *The Descent of Man, and*

Selection in relation to Sex (1871), *The Expression of the Emotions in Man and Animals* (1872), *Insectivorous Plants* (1875), *Climbing Plants* (1875), *Different Forms of Flowers* (1877), and *The Power of Movement in Plants* (1880). His *Life and Letters* were edited by his son, Sir F. Darwin, in 1887.

Darwin, Erasmus (12 Dec. 1731—18 April 1802), doctor and poet, was born at Elston, Nottinghamshire, and educated at Cambridge and at Edinburgh, where he took his degree of M.D. He ultimately settled in Lichfield as a doctor, and attained so high a reputation that he was offered, but declined, the appointment of physician to George III. In 1778 he formed a botanical garden, and in 1789 published his first poem, *The Loves of the Plants*, followed in 1792 by *The Economy of Vegetation*; the two poems were published together as *The Botanic Garden* in 1795. Another poem, *The Temple of Nature*, appeared posthumously. In prose, his *Zoonomia, or the Laws of Organic Life* (1796) foreshadows his grandson's theory of evolution.

Dasent, Sir George Webbe (22 May 1817—11 June 1896), scholar, was born in the island of St Vincent, of which his father was attorney-general, and educated at Westminster School, King's College, London and Oxford. He entered the diplomatic service, and was for several years Secretary to the British Embassy at Stockholm, where he became interested in Scandinavian literature and mythology. Returning to England he was appointed assistant editor of *The Times* (1845—70). In 1852 he was called to the Bar, and in the following year was appointed Professor of English Literature and Modern History at King's College, London, an office which he held for thirteen years. He was knighted in 1876. His principal writings include an *Icelandic Grammar*, *The Prose or Younger Edda* (1842), *Popular Tales from the Norse* (1859), *The Saga of Burnt Njal* (1861), and *The Story of Gisli the Outlaw* (1866). He also translated the Orkney and Hacon Sagas for the Rolls Series, and wrote four novels.

D'Avenant *or* **Davenant, Sir William** (baptized 3 March 1606, died 7 April 1668), poet and dramatist, was born at Oxford, where his father kept an inn, which Shakespeare was in the habit of visiting. There was a story that he was really Shakespeare's son, and in his twelfth year he wrote an 'Ode in Remembrance of Master Shakespeare.' Educated at Oxford, he was afterwards in the service of Lord Brooke, became involved in the troubles of the Civil War, in which he took the Royalist side, and was imprisoned in the Tower, escaped to France, and after returning was, in 1643, knighted by Charles I. Later he was employed on various missions by the King and Queen, but was again in the Tower from 1650 to 1652, when he published his poem *Gondibert*; he is said to have owed his release to the interposition of Milton. In 1656 he practically founded the English Opera with his *Siege of Rhodes* (1656). In 1659 he was again imprisoned, but after the Restoration he seems to have enjoyed prosperity and royal favour, and established a theatre, where he was the first habitually to introduce female players and movable scenery. D'Avenant wrote 25 dramatic pieces, among which are *Albovine*,

King of the Lombards (1629), *Platonick Lovers* (1636), *The Wits* (1633), *Unfortunate Lovers* (1643), *Love and Honour* (1649). He succeeded Ben Jonson as Poet Laureate, collaborated with Dryden in altering (and debasing) *The Tempest*, and was satirized along with him in *The Rehearsal*. He collected his miscellaneous verse under the title of *Madagascar*. He is said to have had the satisfaction of repaying in kind the good offices of Milton when the latter was in danger in 1660. He joined with Waller and others in founding the classical school of English poetry.

Davidson, John (11 April 1857—23 March 1909), poet, was born at Barrhead, Renfrewshire, son of a minister, and educated at Greenock Academy and Edinburgh University. Between 1877 and 1889 he held various teaching appointments in Glasgow, Paisley, Greenock, and Perth. In 1886 appeared his first work, the chronicle play *Bruce*; others of his plays are *Smith* (1888), *An Unhistorical Pastoral* (1889), *A Romantic Farce* (1889), and the poetical *Scaramouch in Naxos*. A novel, *Perfervid*, appeared in 1890, and a volume of verse *In a Music Hall* in 1891, but it was with his *Fleet Street Eclogues* (1893, 1896) that he showed real power as a poet. *Ballads and Songs* appeared in 1894 and *New Ballads* in 1897. In 1906 he was granted a Civil List pension of £100, but still suffered from poverty and ill health, and shortly afterwards drowned himself near Penzance.

Davies, David (15 Jan. 1893—16 Dec. 1951), playwright, composer, actor, manager, who used the stage name Ivor Novello, was born in Cardiff, son of Dame Clara Novello Davies, a well-known musician, and educated at Magdalen College School, Oxford, where he was a chorister. During the First World War he served in the Royal Naval Air Service. He first appeared on the regular stage in London in 1921. Comedies which he wrote, produced, and acted in include *The Truth Game* (1928), *A Symphony in Two Flats* (1929), *Party* (1932), *Proscenium* (1933), and *Comedienne* (1938), but he was best known for his 'Ruritanian' musical plays *Glamorous Night* (1935), *Careless Rapture* (1936), *The Dancing Years* (1939), *Perchance to Dream* (1945), and *King's Rhapsody* (1949). His last play, *Gay's the Word* (1950) burlesqued these successful plays. He wrote about 60 songs and appeared in a number of films.

Davies, John (born 1565? buried 6 July 1618), poet and writing master, was said to be the best penman of his age. He wrote very copiously and rather tediously on theological and philosophical themes. His works include *Mirum in Modum, Microcosmos* (1602), *The Picture of a Happy Man* (1612), *Wit's Bedlam* (1617), and many epigrams on his contemporaries which have some historical interest.

Davies, Sir John (baptized 16 April 1569, died 8 Dec. 1626), lawyer and poet, was educated at Winchester and Oxford, and became a barrister of the Middle Temple in 1595. He was a member successively of the English and Irish Houses of Commons, and held various legal offices. In literature he is known as the writer of two poems, *Orchestra: a Poem of Dancing* (1594), and *Nosce Teipsum* (Know Thyself), in two elegies (1) Of Humane Knowledge (2) Of the Immortality of the Soul. The poem consists of quatrains, each containing a complete and compactly expressed thought. It was published in 1599. He also composed *Astraea*, a series of acrostics on the name Elizabeth.

Davies, Rhys (9 Nov. 1903—), novelist, born at Porth, Glamorgan, was educated at the county school there. After trying various jobs in London he lived in France for a time and stayed with D. H. Lawrence in Paris. During the Second World War he worked at the War Office. His first novel, *The Withered Root* (1927), has the Rhondda valley as its background. Others are *Count Your Blessings* (1932), *The Red Hills* (1932), *A Time to Laugh* (1937), *Jubilee Blues* (1938), *Under the Rose* (1940), *To-morrow to Fresh Woods* (1941), *The Black Venus* (1944), *The Dark Daughters* (1947), *Marianne* (1951), *The Painted King* (1954), and *The Perishable Quality* (1957). He also published half a dozen collections of short stories, beginning with *A Pig in a Poke* (1931), and a play, *No Escape* (1954).

Davies, William Henry (3 July 1871—26 Sept. 1940), poet, was born at Newport, Monmouth, where his grandfather kept a public-house. Apprenticed to a picture-frame maker, he gave up this trade and became a tramp and pedlar. At the age of 22 he went to New York with 10 dollars in his pocket. In America he worked at fruit-picking and as a cattle-man, and learned the hobo's art of getting about by 'train-jumping.' While trying this at Renfrew, Ontario, he slipped and his right leg was severed at the ankle. Returning to England he started to write, keeping himself alive by peddling laces, pins and needles, and singing in the streets. His first book of verse, *The Soul's Destroyer* (1905) was sent to various literary people, who befriended him. Bernard Shaw helped him to become known and Edward Thomas lent him a cottage at Sevenoaks, where he wrote *The Autobiography of a Super-Tramp* (1907), which made him famous. He lived in the country, first at Oxted, Surrey, then at Nailsworth, Gloucestershire. In 1911 he was awarded a Civil List pension, and in 1926 the University of Wales made him an LL.D. His books of verse number a score, and his *Collected Poems* (1943) contains over 600 pieces. The contrast between his life and his work is remarkable, for his lyrics are like the most delicate of Elizabethan verse. He also wrote another autobiographical work, *Later Days* (1925).

Daviot, Gordon, *see* **Mackintosh, Elizabeth.**

Davis *or* **Davys, John** (1550—29 or 30 Dec. 1605), navigator, was born at Sandridge, near Dartmouth, and followed the sea from boyhood days. He was one of the most enterprising of the Eliza-bethan sailors who devoted themselves to the discovery of the North-west Passage. Davis Strait was discovered by, and named after, him. He made many voyages, in the last of which he met his death at the hands of a Japanese pirate. He wrote *The World's Hydrographical Description* (1595), and a work on practical naviga-tion, *The Seaman's Secrets*.

Davis, Richard Harding (18 April 1864—11 April 1916), journalist and novelist, was born in Philadelphia; his father was a newspaper editor, his mother a novelist. Educated at Lehigh University and Johns Hopkins, he began as a journalist on the Philadelphia *Record*, and in 1890 became editor of *Harper's Weekly*. As a war correspondent he covered the Boer, Spanish-American, Russo-Japanese, and First World Wars. *Gallegher* (1890), and *Van Bibber* (1891), both books of short stories, made him famous. The success of his vivid and romantic tales was helped by the fact that he was often depicted as the escort of the famous Gibson Girls, the popular 'pin-ups' of those days. His first novel, *Soldiers of Fortune* (1897) was followed by *The King's Jackal* (1898), *The Bar Sinister* (1903), *Vera the Medium* (1908), and *The White Mice* (1909). Of his 25 plays the best were *Ranson's Folly* (1902), *The Dictator* (1904), and *Miss Civilization* (1905). He also wrote many travel books, including *The West from a Car Window* (1892), *Our English Cousins* (1894), and *About Paris* (1895).

Davis, Thomas Osborne (14 Oct. 1814—16 Sept. 1845), poet, born at Mallow, son of an army surgeon, was educated at Trinity College, Dublin, and called to the Irish Bar in 1838. He was one of the founders of *The Nation* newspaper, and of the Young Ireland party. He wrote some stirring patriotic ballads, published as *Spirit of the Nation*, also a memoir of Curran the great Irish lawyer and orator, prefixed to an edition of his speeches; and he had formed many literary plans which were brought to naught by his untimely death.

Davy, Sir Humphry (17 Dec. 1778—29 May 1829), chemist, son of a wood-carver, was born at Penzance. Apprenticed in 1795 to a surgeon, he became specially interested in chemistry, and assisted Dr Beddoes in his laboratory at Bristol. His *Researches, Chemical and Philosophical* (1799), led to his appointment as Director of the Chemical Laboratory at the Royal Institution, where he also delivered courses of scientific lectures with extraordinary popularity. Thereafter his life was a succession of scientific triumphs and honours. His great discovery was that of the metallic bases of the earths and alkalis. He also discovered various metals, including sodium, calcium, and magnesium. In 1812 he was knighted, and married a wealthy widow. Thereafter he investigated volcanic action and fire-damp, and invented the miner's safety-lamp. In 1818 he was created a baronet, and in 1820 became President of the Royal Society, to which he communicated his discoveries in electro-magnetism. In addition to his scientific writings, which include *Elements of Agricultural Chemistry* (1813), and *Chemical Agencies of Electricity*, he wrote *Salmonia, or Days of Fly Fishing* (1828), somewhat modelled upon Walton, and *Consolations in Travel* (1830), dialogues on ethical and religious questions.

Davys, John, *see* **Davis.**

Day, Clarence Shephard (1874—28 Dec. 1935), essayist, was born in New York, son of a stockbroker, and educated at St Paul's School and Yale. He became his father's partner, but left to join in the

Spanish-American War, where he contracted arthritis, which left him a cripple, so that from middle age onwards he was bedridden and unable to move. Living in a flat overlooking Central Park, he became a sort of humorous philosopher, writing essays which were very popular. Among his studies of American types are *God and My Father* (1932), *Life with Father* (1935), *Life with Mother* (1937), and *Father and I* (1940). *This Simian World* (1920) depicts the apelike nature of man.

Day, John (1574—1640), dramatist, son of a Norfolk yeoman, was educated at Cambridge. He collaborated with Dekker and others in plays, and was the author of *The Isle of Gulls* (1606), *Law Trickes* (1608), and *Humour out of Breath* (1608), but his best work was an allegorical masque, *The Parliament of Bees* (1641).

Day, Thomas (22 June 1748—28 Sept. 1789), author, was born in London, educated at the Charterhouse and at Oxford, and called to the Bar in 1775, but having inherited in infancy an independence, he did not practise. He became a disciple of Rousseau in his social views, and endeavoured to put them in practice in combination with better morality. He was a benevolent eccentric, and used his income, which was increased by his marriage with an heiress, in schemes of social reform as he understood it. He is chiefly remembered as the author of *The History of Sandford and Merton* (1783—9), a moral tale for children.

Deeping, George Warwick (28 May 1877—20 April 1950), novelist, was born at Southend, Essex, son of a doctor. Educated at Merchant Taylors' and Cambridge, he studied science and medicine and for a year worked as a general practitioner in the country. His earliest books were historical novels, including *Uther and Igraine* (1903), *Bertrand of Brittany* (1908), *The Red Saint* (1909), and *Joan of the Tower* (1911). During the First World War he served with the R.A.M.C., and after it he wrote his most popular novel, *Sorrell and Son* (1925), which was a product of his war experiences. It was followed by *Old Pybus* (1928), *Roper's Row* (1929), *Exiles* (1930), *Seven Men Came Back* (1934), *The Woman at the Door* (1937), *Shabby Summer* (1939), *Corn in Egypt* (1941), and *Laughing House* (1947).

Defoe, Daniel (1660?—26 April 1731), journalist, novelist, and pamphleteer, son of James Foe, a butcher, was born in St Giles, Cripplegate; he changed his name to Defoe about 1703. His father being a Dissenter, he was educated at a Dissenting college at Newington with the view of becoming a Presbyterian minister. He joined the army of Monmouth, and on its defeat was fortunate enough to escape punishment. In 1688 he joined William III and later became his trusted confidant. Before settling down to his career as a political writer, Defoe had been engaged in various enterprises as a hosier, a merchant-adventurer to Spain and Portugal, and a brickmaker, all of which proved so unsuccessful that he had to fly from his creditors. Having become known to the government as an effective writer, and employed by them, he was appointed Accountant in the Glass-Duty Office in 1695. Among his more important political writings are an *Essay on Projects* (1698), and *The True-born*

Englishman (1701), which had a remarkable success. In 1702 appeared *The Shortest Way with the Dissenters*, written in a strain of grave irony which was, unfortunately for the author, misunderstood, and led to his being fined, imprisoned, and put in the pillory, which suggested his *Hymn to the Pillory* (1704). Notwithstanding the disfavour with the government which these disasters implied, Defoe's knowledge of commercial affairs and practical ability were recognized by his being sent in 1706 to Scotland to aid in the Union negotiations. In the same year appeared *Jure Divino*, a satire, followed by a *History of the Union* (1709), and *The Wars of Charles XII* (1715). Further misunderstandings and disappointments in connection with political matters led to his giving up this line of activity, and, fortunately for posterity, taking to fiction.

The first and greatest of his novels, *The Life and Strange Surprising Adventures of Robinson Crusoe of York, Mariner* (1719), was followed in the same year by *Further Adventures of Robinson Crusoe*; the two volumes, generally referred to simply as *Robinson Crusoe*, are written with a sobriety of language and an attention to circumstantial detail which give a convincing impression of reality. A sequel, of much inferior interest, *Serious Reflections during the Life and Surprising Adventures of Robinson Crusoe*, appeared in 1720. These were followed by *Captain Singleton* (1720), *Moll Flanders, Colonel Jacque*, and *Journal of the Plague Year* (1722), *Memoirs of a Cavalier* (1724), *A New Voyage Round the World* (1725), and *Captain Carlton* (1728). Among his miscellaneous works are *Political History of the Devil* (1726), *System of Magic* (1727), *The Complete English Tradesman* (1727), and *The Review*, a paper which he edited from 1704 to 1713. In all he published, including pamphlets, about 250 works. All Defoe's writings are distinguished by a clear, nervous style, and his works of fiction by a minute verisimilitude and naturalness of incident which has never been equalled except perhaps by Swift, whose genius his, in some other respects, resembled. His mind was a peculiar amalgam of imagination and matter-of-fact, seeing strongly and clearly what he did see, but little conscious, apparently, of what lay outside his purview.

De Forest, John William (31 May 1826—17 July 1906), novelist, was born at Humphreysville, now Seymour, Connecticut, son of a cotton manufacturer. Illness and bereavement deprived him of a college education. In 1851 he published a *History of the Indians of Connecticut*. Having visited Syria, where his brother kept a girls' school, he wrote *Oriental Acquaintance* (1856), and *European Acquaintance* (1858). His earliest novels were *Witching Times* (1856), and *Seacliff* (1859). In the Civil War he served under Sheridan and rose to the rank of major; subsequently he produced the first realistic novel of that conflict, *Miss Ravenel's Conversion from Secession to Loyalty* (1867). *Kate Beaumont* (1872), another realistic novel of southern life, was followed by *The Wethered Affair* (1873), *Honest John Vane* (1875), *Playing the Mischief* (1876), *Irene the Missionary* (1879), and *A Lover's Revolt* (1898). He was noted for his vigorous character-drawing.

Dekker, Thomas (1570?—1632?), dramatist and pamphleteer, was born and spent most of his life in London. He is first known of as writing plays for the Admiral's Men in 1598. Four of his best plays are *Old Fortunatus* (1600); *The Shoemaker's Holiday* (1600), a realist comedy; *Satiromastix* (1602), a satire on Ben Jonson; and *The Honest Whore* (1604), a tragedy. Less important pieces which can with some confidence be ascribed to him are *The Whore of Babylon* (1607), *If It Be Not Good the Devil Is In It* (1612), and *Match Me in London* (1631). He also collaborated with Middleton and Webster in some plays, and with Ford and Rowley in *The Witch of Edmonton* (1621), which protests against the persecution of witches. Although Dekker suffered from poverty and was at one time imprisoned for debt his work attracts by its sunny kindliness and simplicity, while the beautiful lyrics contained in his plays caused Lamb to declare that he 'had poetry enough for anything.' He was also the author of a number of prose pamphlets. *The Wonderful Year* (1603) describes the plague in London, and the famous *Gull's Hornbook* (1609) pictures the life of London gallants. Moral satires are *The Seven Deadly Sins of London* (1606), *News from Hell* (1606), and *Lanthorn and Candlelight* (1609).

Delafield, E. M., *see* de la Pasture, Edmée.

de la Mare, Walter John, O.M. (25 April 1873—22 June 1956), poet, born at Charlton in Kent; of Huguenot descent, was related on the mother's side to Robert Browning. Educated at St Paul's Cathedral Choir School, where he founded a school magazine, the *Chorister's Journal*, in 1890 he became a clerk in the offices of the Anglo-American Oil Company, and remained there for eighteen years. His first book, *Songs of Childhood*, was published in 1902 under the anagrammatic pseudonym Walter Ramal. In 1908 he was granted a Civil List pension which enabled him to devote all his time to writing. His first novel, *Henry Brocken* (1904) was followed by *The Three Mulla-mulgars* (1910), *The Return* (1910), which won the Polignac Prize, and *Memoirs of a Midget*, which won the Tait Black Memorial Prize for 1922. *The Listeners and Other Poems* (1912) established his reputation as a writer of delicately imaginative verse on the twin domains of childhood and dreamland. Later volumes were *Peacock Pie* (1913), *Down-adown-Derry* (1922), and *Poems for Children* (1930). *Rhymes and Verses* (1944) gathered together the poems written for children, while *Collected Poems* (1942) collected the rest of his verse. All his work is marked by exquisite craftsmanship, with a faerie atmosphere peculiarly his own. In 1948 he was made a Companion of Honour, and in 1953 he was awarded the Order of Merit; he also held honorary degrees from several universities.

de la Pasture, Edmée Elizabeth Monica (9 June 1890—2 Dec. 1943), novelist who wrote under the name E. M. Delafield, was the daughter of Mrs Henry de la Pasture (q.v.). She began to write at 8, and revelled in stories with unhappy endings. During the First World War she was a V.A.D. in Exeter, and drew later on her experiences there for *The War-Workers* (1918). In 1919 she married Major Arthur Paul Dashwood, O.B.E., and after two years in Singapore they settled in Devon. Her novels include *Consequences* (1919), *The Way Things Are* (1927), and *What is Love?* (1928), while *Messalina of the Suburbs* (1924), and *Women Are Like That* (1929) are collections of short stories. In 1931 she published *The Diary of a Provincial Lady*, which first appeared by instalments in *Time and Tide*, and it was so successful that she followed it with *The Provincial Lady Goes Further* (1932), and two more sequels depicting the provincial lady in America (1934) and in war time (1940). *To See Ourselves* (1930), *The Glass Wall* (1933), and *The Mulberry Bush* (1935) are plays.

de la Pasture, Mrs Henry (1866—30 Oct. 1945), novelist, whose maiden name was Elizabeth Lydia Rosabelle Bonham, was born at Naples, daughter of a British consul. In 1887 she married Henry de la Pasture of Llandogo Priory, Monmouth, and after his death in 1908 she married Sir Hugh Clifford. Her best-known novels were *The Little Squire* (1894), and *Deborah of Tod's* (1897), both of which were dramatized, and the later *Peter's Mother* (1905), *The Man from America* (1906), *The Lonely Lady of Grosvenor Square* (1907), *The Tyrant* (1909), and *Michael Ferrys* (1913). Her plays include *The Lonely Millionaires* (1906), and *Her Grace the Reformer* (1907). In 1918 she was awarded the C.B.E.

de la Roche, Mazo (1885—12 July 1961), novelist, was born in Toronto and spent her childhood on her father's fruit farm in Ontario. Educated at Toronto University, she disliked city life and lived in the country. Her first novel, *Explorers of the Dawn* (1922) attracted little notice, but she achieved fame with *Jalna* (1927), which won the *Atlantic Monthly's* 10,000 dollar prize, and was succeeded by a whole series of sequels forming a family chronicle— *Whiteoaks of Jalna* (1929), *Finch's Fortune* (1931), *The Master of Jalna* (1933), *Young Renny* (1935), *Whiteoak Harvest* (1936), *Whiteoak Heritage* (1940), *Wakefield's Course* (1941), *The Building of Jalna* (1944), *Return to Jalna* (1949), *The Whiteoak Brothers* (1953), and *Variable Winds at Jalna* (1953). She also wrote a comedy, *Low Life* (1925), several other plays, and a *History of the Port of Quebec* (1944). In 1930 she removed to England, and in 1938 she was awarded the Lorne Pierce Medal of the Royal Society of Canada.

Dell, Ethel Mary (2 Aug. 1881—17 Sept. 1939), novelist, daughter of an insurance agent, was born at Streatham and educated at a private school there. Her early life was spent at Knockholt, near Sevenoaks, and later she settled in Guildford. Having started to write as a child, she achieved her first great success with *The Way of an Eagle* in 1912. This was followed by *The Knave of Diamonds* (1913), *The Rocks of Valpré* (1914), *The Keeper of the Door* (1915), *The Hundredth Chance* (1917), *Charles Rex* (1922), *The Black Knight* (1926), *Storm Drift* (1930), and *The Serpent in the Garden* (1938). In all she wrote 34 novels, usually containing strong and unrelenting heroes with a strain of sadism, and villains of the deepest dye. Her books had a great vogue during the First World War, but she herself lived a very retired life in the country. In 1922 she married Colonel G. T. Savage, D.S.O., of the Royal Army Service Corps.

De Lolme, John Louis (1740?—March 1807), Swiss writer, born at

Geneva, has a place in English literature for his well-known work, *The Constitution of England*, written in French, and translated into English in 1775. He also wrote *History of the Flagellants* (1777), and *The British Empire in Europe* (1787). He came to England in 1769, lived in great poverty, and having inherited a small fortune, returned to his native place in 1775.

Deloney, Thomas (1543?—1600), balladist and novelist, worked as a silk-weaver in Norwich, but was in London by 1586, and in the course of the next ten years is known to have written about 50 ballads, some of which involved him in trouble, and caused him to turn to prose fiction. Less under the influence of Lyly and other preceding writers than Greene, he is more natural, simple, and direct, and writes of middle-class citizens and tradesmen with a light and pleasant humour. Of his novels, all written between 1596 and 1600, *Thomas of Reading* is in honour of clothiers, *Jack of Newbury* celebrates weaving, and *The Gentle Craft* is dedicated to the praise of shoemakers. His volumes of verse include *Strange Histories* (1602), and *The Garland of Good Will* (1618).

De Morgan, Augustus (1806—18 March 1871), mathematician, was born at Madura in India, son of a colonel. His parents sailed for England when he was a few months old and he was educated at Cambridge, where he was Fourth Wrangler. In 1828 he was appointed the first Professor of Mathematics at London University, and his influence on the study of it was far-reaching. His most important works were his *Essay on Probabilities* (1838) and his brilliant *Budget of Paradoxes* (1872), which discusses mathematical fallacies in a witty fashion.

De Morgan, William Frend (16 Nov. 1839—15 Jan. 1917), novelist, son of the above, was born in London and educated at London University. Later he studied art at the Royal Academy School, where he formed friendships with Morris, Rossetti, and Burne-Jones. For forty years he devoted himself to the designing of artistic pottery and stained glass, and it was only when he retired from this at the age of 67 that he started writing novels in imitation of his idol, Dickens. *Joseph Vance* (1906) was a great success, and in the eight remaining years of his life he wrote five more novels—*Alice-for-Short* (1907), *Somehow Good* (1908), *It Never Can Happen Again* (1909), *An Affair of Dishonour* (1910), *A Likely Story* (1911), and *When Ghost Meets Ghost* (1914). Two novels which he left unfinished were completed by his wife, one of them, *Old Man's Youth*, being largely autobiographical.

Denham, Sir John (1615—10 March 1669), poet, son of an Irish judge, was born in Dublin, and educated at Oxford, after which he lived at Egham, Surrey. He began his literary career with a tragedy, *The Sophy* (1641), which seldom rises above mediocrity. His poem, *Cooper's Hill* (1642), is the work by which he is remembered. It is the first example in English of a poem devoted to local description, and received extravagant praise from Johnson. In his earlier years Denham suffered for his Royalism, but after the Restoration enjoyed prosperity, being knighted in 1661. He made an unhappy marriage, however, and his last years were clouded by insanity. He was an architect by profession, coming between Inigo Jones and Wren as King's Surveyor.

Dennis, Clarence Michael James (7 Sept. 1876—1 June 1938), poet and journalist, was born at Auburn, South Australia, son of a retired sea captain, and educated at the Christian Brothers College, Adelaide, where he collaborated in a school paper, *The Weary Weekly*. For a time he worked as a clerk, then was successively miner, carpenter, and labourer at Broken Hill. Back in Adelaide he founded a periodical, *The Gadfly*, which lasted only a year and a half, then settled at Toolangi near Melbourne, freelanced for a time, and in 1922 joined the staff of the Melbourne *Herald*. His first publication was *Backblock Ballads* (1913), but it was *The Songs of a Sentimental Bloke* (1915) that made him famous. Later books were *The Moods of Ginger Mick* (1916) with its sequel *Rose of Spadgers* (1924), and *Digger Smith* (1918). *The Glugs of Gosh* (1917) is nonsense verse.

Dennis, John (1657—6 Jan. 1734), critic and playwright, son of a saddler, was born in London, and educated at Harrow and Caius College, Cambridge, from the latter of which he was expelled for stabbing a fellow-student, and transferred himself to Trinity Hall. He attached himself to the Whigs, in whose interest he wrote several bitter and vituperative pamphlets. His attempts at play-writing were failures; and he then devoted himself chiefly to criticizing the works of his contemporaries. Unfortunately for him, some of those whom he attacked, such as Pope and Swift, had the power of conferring upon him an unenviable immortality. Embalmed in *The Dunciad*, his name has attained a fame which no work of his own could have given it. Among his plays are *Rinaldo and Armida* (1699) and *Appius and Virginia* (1709). His critical works include *Letters on Milton and Congreve* (1696), *The Advancement and Reformation of Modern Poetry* (1701), *The Grounds of Criticism in Poetry* (1704), and *The Genius and Writings of Shakespeare* (1712). He died in straitened circumstances.

De Quincey, Thomas (15 Aug. 1785—8 Dec. 1859), essayist, was born in Manchester, son of a merchant. The aristocratic 'De' was assumed by himself, his father, whom he lost while he was still a child, having been known by the name of Quincey, and he claimed descent from a Norman family. His *Autobiographic Sketches* give a vivid picture of his early years at the family residence of Greenheys, and show him as a highly imaginative and over-sensitive child, suffering hard things at the hands of a tyrannical elder brother. He was educated first at home, then at Bath Grammar School, next at a private school at Winkfield, Wiltshire, and in 1801 he was sent to the Manchester Grammar School, from which he ran away, and for some time rambled in Wales on a small allowance made to him by his mother. Tiring of this, he went to London at the end of 1802, where he led the strange Bohemian life related in *The Confessions*. His friends, thinking it high time to interfere, sent him in 1803 to Worcester College, Oxford. This did not, however, preclude occasional brief interludes in London, on one of which he made his first acquaintance with opium, which was to play so prominent and disastrous a part in his future life. In 1807 he became acquainted with Coleridge, Wordsworth, and Southey, and soon afterwards with Charles Lamb. During the years 1807—9 he paid various visits to the Lakes, and in the latter year he settled at Townend, Grasmere, where Wordsworth had previously lived. Here he pursued his studies, becoming gradually more and more enslaved by opium, until in 1813 he was taking from 8,000 to 12,000 drops daily. John Wilson (Christopher North), who was then living at Elleray, had become his friend, and brought him to Edinburgh occasionally. His marriage to Margaret Simpson, daughter of a farmer, took place in 1816.

Up to this time he had written nothing, but had been steeping his mind in German metaphysics, and out-of-the-way learning of various kinds; but in 1819 he sketched out *Prolegomena of all future Systems of Political Economy*, which, however, was never finished. In the same year he acted as editor of the *Westmoreland Gazette*. His true literary career began in 1821 with the publication in the *London Magazine* of *The Confessions of an English Opium-Eater*. Thereafter he produced a long series of articles, some of them almost on the scale of books, in *Blackwood's* and *Tait's* magazines, the *Edinburgh Literary Gazette*, and *Hogg's Instructor*. These included 'Murder Considered as One of the Fine Arts' (1827), and in his later and more important period, 'Suspiria de Profundis' (1845), 'The Spanish Military Nun' (1847), 'The English Mail Coach,' and 'The Vision of Sudden Death' (1849). In 1853 he began a collected edition of his works, which was the main occupation of his later years. He had in 1830 brought his family to Edinburgh, which, except for two years (1841—3) when he lived in Glasgow, was his home till his death in 1859, and in 1837, on his wife's death, he placed them in the neighbouring village of Lasswade, while he lived in solitude, moving from one dingy lodging to another as each in turn became choked up with an accumulation of papers. At the time of his death there were six such sets of lodgings, on all of which he was paying rent.

De Quincey stands among the great masters of style in the language. In his greatest passages, as in the 'Vision of Sudden Death' and the 'Dream Fugue,' the cadence of his elaborately piled-up sentences falls like cathedral music, or gives an abiding expression to the fleeting pictures of his most gorgeous dreams. His character unfortunately bore no correspondence to his intellectual endowments. His moral system had in fact been shattered by indulgence in opium. His appearance and manners have been thus described: 'A short and fragile, but well-proportioned frame; a shapely and compact head; a face beaming with intellectual light, with rare, almost feminine beauty of feature and complexion; a fascinating courtesy of manner, and a fulness, swiftness, and elegance of silvery speech.' His own works give very detailed information regarding himself. The standard edition, in 14 volumes, was published in 1890 by Professor Masson (q.v.) who also wrote his life.

Dermody, Thomas (1775—15 July 1802), poet, was born at

Ennis, County Clare, son of a schoolmaster; his father taking to drink, he ran away to Dublin, where he had a book of poems published in 1792. Later he enlisted in the army and obtained a commission, but an irregular life brought about his early death. A complete collection of his poems, *The Harp of Erin*, was published in 1807.

de Selincourt, Ernest (24 Sept. 1870—22 May 1943), scholar and critic, was born at Streatham and educated at Dulwich College and Oxford, where he was a lecturer in English from 1906 to 1909. From then till 1935 he was Professor of English Language at Birmingham, holding the office of Vice-Principal during his last four years, and in 1929 he was appointed Professor of Poetry at Oxford. He was a recognized authority on Wordsworth, his works including *English Poets and the National Ideal* (1915), *The Study of Poetry* (1918), *Dorothy Wordsworth, a Biography* (1933), and *Oxford Lectures on Poetry* (1934). He also edited Dorothy Wordsworth's letters and journals, and the poems of Keats.

de Tabley, John Byron Leicester Warren, 3rd Baron (26 April 1835—22 Nov. 1895), poet, was born at Tabley House in Cheshire, but spent much of his childhood in Italy and Germany. Educated at Eton and Oxford, he was for a time attached to the British Embassy in Constantinople, but his main interest was literature. He wrote blank verse on the Tennysonian model, his earliest volumes *Praeterita* (1863), *Eclogues and Monodramas* (1864), and *Studies in Verse* (1865) appearing under the pseudonym George F. Preston. A tragedy, *Philoctetes* (1866), the most powerful of his works, was followed by *Orestes* (1868). After the disappointing reception of *The Soldier's Fortune* (1876), which did not sell a single copy, he lived like a hermit in London, but later published collections of his best work in *Poems Dramatic and Lyrical* (first and second series, 1893, 1895), which received wider recognition.

Deutsch, · Babette (22 Sept. 1895—), poetess, was born in New York and educated at Columbia University, where she started writing for periodicals while still an undergraduate. In 1921 she married Avrahm Yarmolinsky, chief of the Slavonic department of New York Public Library, with whom she edited two collections of Russian poetry. Her own work employs both regular rhyme forms and loosely constructed free verse. Her poem 'Thoughts at the Year's End' won the *Nation* Poetry Prize in 1929, and appears in her book *Fire for the Night* (1930). Others of her books of verse are *Banners* (1919), *Honey Out of the Rock* (1925), *Epistle to Prometheus* (1931), *One Part Love* (1939), and *Animal, Vegetable, Mineral* (1954); *Take Them, Stranger* (1954) is a volume of collected poems. She also wrote several novels, including *A Brittle Heaven* (1926), *In Such a Night* (1927), and *Mask of Silenus* (1933). Her critical works include *Walt Whitman—Builder for America* (1941) and *Poetry in Our Time* (1952). Her political views were leftist.

de Vere, Aubrey Thomas (10 Jan. 1814—21 Jan. 1902), poet, son of Sir Aubrey de Vere, himself a poet, was born at Adare, County

Limerick, and educated at Trinity College, Dublin. In early life he became acquainted with Wordsworth, by whom he was greatly influenced. Later he was a friend of Landor, Tennyson, and Browning. On the religious and ecclesiastical side he came under the influence of Newman and Manning, and in 1851 was received into the Church of Rome. He was the author of many volumes of poetry, including *The Waldenses* (1842), *The Search after Proserpine* (1843), and *May Carols* (1857). Later he began a series of poems on Irish subjects, including *Innisfail* (1861), *Irish Odes* (1869), and *The Legends of St Patrick* (1872). His interest in Ireland and its people led him to write prose works, including *English Misrule and Irish Misdeeds* (1848); and to criticism he contributed *Essays chiefly on Poetry* (1887). His last work was his *Recollections* (1897). His poetry is characterized by lofty ethical tone, imaginative power, and grave stateliness of expression.

de Vere, Edward, *see* **Oxford.**

Dewey, John (20 Oct. 1859—1 June 1952), philosopher, was born at Burlington, Vermont, and educated at the University of Vermont and Johns Hopkins, where he obtained a doctorate. Professor of Philosophy successively at Michigan, Chicago (1894), and Columbia University (1904), he was also in 1902 appointed Director of the School of Education at Chicago. The chief follower of William James's system of pragmatism, he formulated a practical philosophy of action adapted to American life, sometimes termed instrumentalism or operationalism, and had an enormous influence on American thought and education, though his writing is often obscure. His belief in a democratic view of life is embodied in *The Ethics of Democracy* (1888), and worked out more fully in *Democracy and Education* (1916). Others of his books are *How We Think* (1910), *Reconstruction in Philosophy* (1920), *Human Nature and Conduct* (1922), *Experience and Nature* (1925), *The Quest for Certainty* (1929), *Art As Experience* (1935), and *Experience and Education* (1938). On his ninetieth birthday he was the guest of honour at a testimonial function in New York; among many other distinctions he held honorary degrees of Paris and Pekin.

Dibdin, Charles (4 March 1745—25 July 1814), dramatist and songwriter, son of a silversmith, was born at Southampton, and began his literary career at 16 with a drama, *The Shepherd's Artifice*. His fame, however, rests on his sea songs, which are unrivalled, and include 'Tom Bowling,' 'Poor Jack,' and 'Blow High, Blow Low.' He is said to have written over 1,200 of these, besides many dramatic pieces, two novels, *Hannah Hewitt* (1792), and *The Younger Brother* (1793), and a *History of the Stage* (1795).

Dibdin, Thomas John (21 March 1771—16 Sept. 1841), songwriter, was born in London, the illegitimate son of Charles Dibdin (q.v.). One of his godfathers was Garrick, and he appeared as Cupid with Mrs Siddons at Drury Lane when he was 4 years old. In 1779 he entered the choir of St Paul's. Apprenticed to an upholsterer, he ran away and got a theatrical engagement at Eastbourne. Later he wrote pieces for Sadler's Wells, of which he became stage manager. In 1797 he wrote *The British Raft*, containing his famous song 'The Snug Little Island,' but *The Cabinet* (1801) is reckoned his best opera. In all he wrote nearly 5,000 songs. His *Reminiscences* appeared in 1827.

Dickens, Charles (7 Feb. 1812—9 June 1870), novelist, was born at Landport, near Portsmouth, where his father was a clerk in the Navy Pay Office. The hardships and mortifications of his early life, his want of regular schooling, and his miserable time in the blacking factory, which form the basis of the early chapters of *David Copperfield*, are largely accounted for by the fact that his father was to a considerable extent the prototype of the immortal Mr Micawber; but partly by his being a delicate and sensitive child, unusually susceptible to suffering both in body and mind. He had, however, much time for reading, and had access to the older novelists, Fielding, Smollett, and others. A kindly relative also took him frequently to the theatre, where he acquired his lifelong interest in, and love of, the stage. After a few years' residence in Chatham, the family removed to London, and soon after that his father was imprisoned in the Marshalsea, where by-and-by the whole family joined him, a passage in his life which furnishes the material for parts of *Little Dorrit*. This period of family obscuration happily lasted but a short time: the elder Dickens managed to satisfy his creditors, and soon after retired from his official duties on a pension. About the same time the son had two years of continuous schooling, and shortly afterwards he entered a law office. His leisure he devoted to reading and learning shorthand, in which he became very expert. He then acted as parliamentary reporter, first for *The True Sun*, and from 1835 for the *Morning Chronicle*. Meanwhile he had been contributing to the *Monthly Magazine* and the *Evening Chronicle* the papers which, in 1836, appeared in a collected form as *Sketches by Boz*, Boz being the nickname of a younger brother, and he had also produced one or two comic burlettas.

In the same year he married Catherine Hogarth; and in the following year occurred the turning-point of his life. He was asked by Chapman and Hall to write the letterpress for a series of sporting plates to be done by Robert Seymour who, however, died shortly after, and was succeeded by Hablot Browne (Phiz), who became the illustrator of most of Dickens's novels. In the hands of Dickens the original plan was entirely altered, and became the *Pickwick Papers* which, appearing in monthly parts during 1837—9, took the country by storm. Simultaneously *Oliver Twist* was coming out in *Bentley's Miscellany*. Thenceforward Dickens's literary career was a continued success, and the almost yearly publication of his works constituted the main events of his life. *Nicholas Nickleby* appeared in serial form 1838—9. Next year he projected *Master Humphrey's Clock*, intended to be a series of miscellaneous stories and sketches. It was, however, soon abandoned, *The Old Curiosity Shop* and *Barnaby Rudge* taking its place. The latter, dealing with the Gordon Riots, is, with the partial exception of the *Tale of Two Cities*, the author's only excursion into the historical novel. In 1841

Dickens went to America, and was received with great enthusiasm, which, however, the publication of *American Notes* considerably damped, and the appearance of *Martin Chuzzlewit* in 1843, with its caustic criticisms of certain features of American life, converted into extreme, though temporary, unpopularity. The first of the Christmas books—the *Christmas Carol*—appeared in 1843, and in the following year Dickens went to Italy, where at Genoa he wrote *The Chimes*, followed by *The Cricket on the Hearth*, *The Battle of Life*, and *The Haunted Man*. In January 1846, he was appointed first editor of the *Daily News*, but resigned in a few weeks. The same year he went to Switzerland, and while there wrote *Dombey and Son*, which was published in 1848, and was immediately followed by *David Copperfield* (1849—50). Shortly before this he had become manager of a theatrical company, which performed in the provinces, and he had in 1849 started his magazine, *Household Words*. *Bleak House* appeared in 1852—3, *Hard Times* in 1854, and *Little Dorrit* 1856—7. In 1856 he bought Gadshill Place, which, in 1860, became his permanent home.

In 1858 he began his public readings from his works, which, while eminently successful from a financial point of view, gradually broke down his constitution, through the nervous strain they entailed, and hastened his death. In the same year he separated from his wife, and consequent upon the controversy which resulted he brought *Household Words* to an end, and started *All the Year Round*, in which appeared *A Tale of Two Cities* (1859), and *Great Expectations* (1860—1). *Our Mutual Friend* came out in numbers (1864—5). Dickens was now in the full tide of his readings, and decided to give a course of them in America, where he went at the end of 1867, returning in the following May. He had a magnificent reception, and his profits amounted to £20,000; but the effect on his health was such that he was obliged, on medical advice, finally to abandon all appearances of the kind. In 1869 he began his last work, *The Mystery of Edwin Drood*, which was interrupted by his death from an apoplectic seizure.

One of Dickens's most marked characteristics is the extrordinary wealth of his invention as exhibited in the number and variety of the characters introduced into his novels; outside of Shakespeare, there is no author who can produce a gallery of figures to compare with the Wellers, Mrs Gamp, the Micawbers, and other Dickens immortals. Another, especially, of course, in his earlier works, is his boundless flow of animal spirits. Others are his marvellous keenness of observation and his descriptive power. The English race may well, with Thackeray, be 'grateful for the innocent laughter, and the sweet and unsullied pages which the author of *David Copperfield* gives to [its] children.' On the other hand, his faults are obvious—a tendency to caricature, a mannerism that often tires, and almost disgusts, fun often forced, and pathos not seldom degenerating into mawkishness. Of his popularity there has never been any question; from the first his work conquered the whole English-speaking world, where he is still one of the most commonly quoted authors.

The standard life of Dickens is by John Foster (1872); his *Letters* were edited by Miss Hogarth (1880—2); one of the best studies of his works is by G. K. Chesterton (q.v.).

Dickens, Monica Enid (10 May 1915—   ), novelist, a great-granddaughter of Charles Dickens, was educated at St Paul's Girls' School, Hammersmith.   She was best known for her auto-biographical series *One Pair of Hands* (1939), *One Pair of Feet* (1942), and *My Turn to Make Tea* (1951), but also wrote a number of novels, including *Mariana* (1940), *The Fancy* (1944), *Thursday Afternoons* (1945), *The Happy Prisoner* (1946), *Joy and Josephine* (1948), *Flowers on the Grass* (1949), *No More Meadows* (1953), and *The Winds of Heaven* (1955).

Dickinson, Emily Elizabeth (10 Dec. 1830—15 May 1886), America's greatest woman poet, was born and spent nearly all her life in Amherst, Massachusetts, where her father was a lawyer.   Educated at Amherst Academy and Mount Holyoke Female Seminary, she was noted for her wit and love of fun, and as a young woman took a normal part in village social activities.   In 1854 while on a visit to Washington, her father being then a member of Congress, she is said to have fallen in love with a young preacher, but on learning that he was married to have broken off all communication with him.   Thereafter she lived a very retired life, seeking companionship in nature and recreation in solitary country walks.   After the death of her father in 1874 she immured herself in the home, though still performing the duties of a housewife.   Though her days were uneventful, her poems, jealously guarded as a secret, showed her rich and sympathetic mind.   Only two were printed in her lifetime, but after her death they were discovered and published by her sister Lavinia in three series (1890, 1891, 1896).   Further volumes were *The Single Hound* (1914), *Further Poems* (1929), and *Bolts of Melody* (1945). In all she wrote over 1,000 poems.   Her *Letters* were published in 1894.   Her short lyrics are remarkable for their mystic quality, which is joined to an integrity and originality which led one critic to declare that 'she wrote as though no one had written poetry before.'   Her delicate command of phrase more than compensates for occasional technical flaws in her work, and the Imagists claimed her as their precursor.

Dickinson, Goldsworthy Lowes (6 Aug. 1862—3 Aug. 1932), philosopher, was born in London, son of an artist, and educated at Charterhouse and King's College, Cambridge, where he lived in seclusion as a Fellow from 1887 till his death.   He studied medicine but never practised.   From 1896 to 1920 he was a lecturer in political science.   A graceful and persuasive writer, imbued with Platonic ideals, he became devoted to the cause of international peace, and is credited with inventing the name 'League of Nations' for that institution when it was founded.   His works include *The Greek View of Life* (1896), *Letters from John Chinaman* (1901), *Justice and Liberty* (1908), *Religion and Immortality* (1911), *East and West* (1914), and *The International Anarchy 1904—14* (1926).

Digby, Sir Kenelm (11 July 1603—11 June 1665), diplomat and writer, born near Newport Pagnell, son of Sir Everard Digby, who was executed for his share in the Gunpowder Plot, was educated at Oxford, travelled much, and was engaged in sea-fighting. Brought up first as a Catholic, then as a Protestant, he finally in 1636 joined the Church of Rome. In 1623 he was knighted and became Gentleman of the Privy Chamber to Prince Charles. During the Civil War he was active on the side of the King, and on the fall of his cause was for a time banished. He was the author of several books on religious and quasi-scientific subjects, writing on the *Choice of a Religion*, and on the *Immortality of the Soul* (1644). He also wrote a *Discourse on Vegetation* (1660), and one *On the Cure of Wounds* by means of a 'sympathetic powder' which he imagined he had discovered. His *Private Memoirs* were printed in 1827.

Dilke, Charles Wentworth (8 Dec. 1789—10 Aug. 1864), critic, educated at Cambridge, served for twenty years in the Navy Pay-Office, on retiring from which he devoted himself to literary pursuits. He had in 1814—16 made a continuation of Dodsley's *Collection of English Plays*, and in 1829 he became part proprietor and editor of the *Athenaeum*, the influence of which he greatly extended. In 1846 he resigned the editorship, and assumed that of the *Daily News*, but contributed to the *Athenaeum* studies on Pope, Burke, Junius, and others, which were published in 1875 by his grandson with the title *Papers of a Critic*.

Dine, S. S. van, *see* **Wright, W. H.**

Disraeli, Benjamin, 1st Earl of Beaconsfield (21 Dec. 1804—19 April 1881), statesman and novelist, son of Isaac D'Israeli (q.v.), was born in London and privately educated. His father destined him for the law, and he was articled to a solicitor. The law was, however, uncongenial, and he had already begun to write. After some journalistic work, he brought himself into general notice by the publication, in 1827, of his first novel, *Vivian Grey*, which created a sensation by its brilliance, audacity, and slightly veiled portraits of living celebrities. After producing a *Vindication of the British Constitution*, and some political pamphlets, he followed up his first success by a series of novels, *The Young Duke* (1831), *Contarini Fleming* (1832), *Alroy* (1833), *Venetia* and *Henrietta Temple* (1837). During the same period he had also written *The Revolutionary Epic* and three burlesques, *Ixion*, *The Infernal Marriage*, and *Popanilla*. Leaving literature for politics, after various unsuccessful attempts to enter Parliament, in which he stood, first as a Radical, and then as a Tory, he was in 1837 returned for Maidstone, gradually rose to a commanding position in parliament and in the country, became leader of the Tory party, and was thrice Chancellor of the Exchequer, 1852, 1858—9, and 1866—8, in which last year he became Prime Minister, an office which he again held from 1874 till 1880. Meanwhile, in 1844 he had published *Coningsby*, followed by *Sybil* (1845), and *Tancred* (1847), and in 1848 he wrote a life of Lord G. Bentinck, his predecessor in the leadership of the Protectionist party. His last novels were *Lothair* (1870), and *Endymion* (1880). He was raised to the peerage as Earl of Beaconsfield in 1876, and made a Knight of the Garter. In his later years he was the intimate friend as well as the trusted minister of Queen Victoria. The career of Disraeli is one of the most remarkable in English history. With no family or political influence, and in spite of the current prejudices in regard to his race, he rose by sheer force of will and intellect to the highest honours attainable in this country. As a writer he is generally interesting, and his books teem with striking thoughts, shrewd maxims, and brilliant phrases which stick in the memory. On the other hand he is often artificial, extravagant, and turgid.

D'Israeli, Isaac (11 May 1766—19 Jan. 1848), miscellaneous writer, born at Enfield, was descended from a Jewish family which had been settled first in Spain, and afterwards at Venice. Educated at Amsterdam and Leyden, he devoted himself to literature, producing a number of interesting works of considerable value, including *Curiosities of Literature*, in three series (1791—1823), *Calamities of Authors* (1812), *Quarrels of Authors* (1814), and *Amenities of Literature* (1841); also works dealing with the lives of James I and Charles I. D'Israeli was latterly blind.

Diver, Maud (died 14 Oct. 1945), novelist, was born at Murree in the Himalayas, daughter of a colonel, her maiden name being Katherine Helen Maud Marshal. The wife of Sir Henry Lawrence was her great-aunt, and Rudyard Kipling's sister was one of her greatest friends. Though educated in England, she had a passion for India and a rare understanding of its people. In 1896 she married Lieutenant-Colonel T. Diver, and returned to England with him. Her first novel, *Captain Desmond, V.C.* (1906) had instantaneous success which she followed up with other Anglo-Indian stories, including *The Great Amulet* (1908), *The Hero of Herat* (1912), *The Strong Hours* (1919), *A Wild Bird* (1929), *Ships of Youth* (1931), and *Kabul to Kandahar* (1935).

Dixon, Richard Watson (5 May 1833—Jan. 1900), clergyman and poet, was born in London, son of a Wesleyan minister. He was educated at King Edward's School, Birmingham, and Oxford, where he associated with Morris, Burne-Jones, and others of the Pre-Raphaelite Group. Taking orders, he was a curate in London, a schoolmaster at Carlisle, and then successively vicar of Hayton in Cumberland and Warkworth in Northumberland. His volumes of verse include *Christ's Company* (1861) and *Historical Odes* (1863), and he helped, along with Bridges, to publicize the works of Gerard Manley Hopkins. But his greatest work was his *History of the Church of England from the Abolition of the Roman Jurisdiction* (1900). His life was written by his son.

Dixon, William Hepworth (30 June 1821—27 Dec. 1879), historian and traveller, born near Manchester, went to London in 1846, and in 1854 was called to the Bar at Inner Temple, but never practised. In 1850 he published *John Howard and the Prison World of Europe*, which had a wide circulation, and in 1851 a life of *William Penn*, in answer to Macaulay's onslaught. His lives of *Admiral Blake* and *Lord Bacon* received somewhat severe criticism at the hands of competent authorities. Dixon was editor of the *Athenaeum* 1853—

1869, and wrote many books of travel, including *The Holy Land* (1865), *New America* (1867), and *Free Russia* (1870). His later historical works include *Her Majesty's Tower* (1871), and *The History of Two Queens* (Catherine of Aragon and Anne Boleyn) (1874).

Dobell, Sydney Thompson (5 April 1824—22 Aug. 1874), poet, was born at Cranbrook, Kent, son of a wine merchant, who removed to Cheltenham, where most of the poet's life was passed. His youth was precocious; he was engaged at 15 and married at 20. In 1850 his first work, *The Roman*, appeared under the pseudonym Sydney Yendys, and had great popularity. *Balder* (1854), *Sonnets on the War* (1855), written jointly with Alexander Smith (q.v.), and *England in Time of War* (1856) followed. His later years were passed in Scotland and abroad in search of health; but he was injured by a fall while exploring some ruins at Pozzuoli. His *Life and Letters* were published in 1878. Dobell's poems exhibit fancy and brilliancy of diction, but lack simplicity, and sometimes run into grandiloquence and other faults of the so-called Spasmodic School to which he belonged.

Dobson, Henry Austin (18 Jan. 1840—2 Sept. 1921), poet and critic, was born at Plymouth, son of a civil engineer. He was educated at Beaumaris Grammar School and the gymnase at Strasbourg, then entered the Board of Trade, where he remained from 1856 to 1901. After his retirement he was awarded a Civil List pension of £250. His first book, *Vignettes in Rhyme* (1873) was followed by *Proverbs in Porcelain* (1877) and *At the Sign of the Lyre* (1885), but he was rather a graceful and ingenious writer of light verse than a serious poet. As a critic he was an authority on the eighteenth century, and published three volumes of essays entitled *Eighteenth Century Vignettes* (1892, 1894, 1896), as well as popular biographies of *Fielding* (1883), *Goldsmith* (1888), *Richardson* (1902), and *Fanny Burney* (1903), and the standard life of Hogarth (1891).

Dodd, William (29 May 1729—27 June 1777), clergyman and anthologist, was born at Bourne in Lincolnshire, where his father was vicar, and educated at Cambridge. He became a popular preacher in London, and a Royal Chaplain, but, acquiring expensive habits, and got involved in hopeless difficulties, from which he endeavoured to escape first by an attempted simoniacal transaction, for which he was disgraced, and then by forging a bond for £4,200, for which, according to the then existing law, he was hanged. Great efforts were made to obtain a commutation of the sentence, and Dr Johnson wrote one of the petitions, but on Dodd's book, *Thoughts in Prison*, appearing posthumously, he remarked that 'a man who has been canting all his days may cant to the last.' Dodd is chiefly remembered for his *Beauties of Shakespeare* (1752), an anthology which was long popular.

Doddridge, Philip (26 June 1702—26 Oct. 1751), nonconformist minister, was born in London, the twentieth child of an oilman. Educated for the ministry at a theological institution at Kibworth, he became minister first at Market Harborough, and afterwards at Northampton, where he also acted as head of a theological academy.

He published many religious books, of which the best known is *The Rise and Progress of Religion in the Soul* (1745). In 1736 he received the degree of D.D. from Aberdeen. He died at Lisbon, where he had gone in search of health. Several of his hymns, e.g., 'O Happy Day', and 'O God of Bethel,' are universally used by English-speaking Christians, and have been translated into various languages.

Dodgson, Charles Lutwidge (27 Jan. 1832—14 Jan. 1898), who wrote children's 'books under the pseudonym Lewis Carroll, was born at Daresbury, near Warrington, son of a clergyman who became Archdeacon of Richmond. Educated at Rugby and Oxford, he took double honours in Classics and Mathematics, and was appointed a Student or Fellow of Christ Church, where he spent the rest of his working life. In 1861 he was ordained, but he preached only occasionally. He was very shy, except with little girls, with whom he formed countless friendships and to whom he wrote most delightful whimsical letters. In 1865 he published *Alice's Adventures in Wonderland*, which he had first made up to amuse Alice Liddell, daughter of the Dean of Christ Church; in its original form the book was entitled 'Alice's Adventures Underground.' Along with its sequel *Through the Looking-Glass and What Alice Found There* (1871) it is probably the most popular children's story ever published apart from the more famous fairy-tales, and it was translated into many languages. It was followed in 1876 by *The Hunting of the Snark*, a clever nonsense poem. *Sylvie and Bruno* (1889) and *Sylvie and Bruno Concluded* (1893) were an attempt to write a children's story embodying Christian philosophy, but they are mawkish and confused, although they contain some good comic verse. Dodgson published a large number of humorous articles and puzzles, as well as some works on mathematics, which was the subject he taught. He died and was buried at Guildford. His *Life and Letters* were edited in 1898 by his nephew, Stuart Dodgson Collingwood.

Dodsley, Robert (13 Feb. 1703—25 Dec. 1764), poet and bookseller, was born near Mansfield, Nottinghamshire, and apprenticed to a stocking-weaver, but not liking this employment, he ran away and became a footman. While thus engaged he produced *The Muse in Livery* (1732). This was followed by *The Toy Shop* (1735), a drama, which brought him under the notice of Pope, who befriended him, and assisted him in starting business as a bookseller. In this he became eminently successful, and acted as publisher for Pope, Johnson, and Akenside. He projected and published the *Annual Register*, and made a collection of *Old English Plays* in 12 volumes (1744), also of *Poems by Several Hands* in 6 volumes (1748—58). In addition to the original works above mentioned he wrote various plays and poems, including *The Blind Beggar of Bethnal Green* (1741) and *Cleone* (1758).

Donne, John (1572—31 March 1631), Dean of St Paul's and poet, was born in London, son of a wealthy ironmonger. His mother was a daughter of John Heywood the dramatist (q.v.). Brought up as a Roman Catholic, he was sent to Oxford, where he formed his lifelong friendship with Sir Henry Wotton, and afterwards entered Lincoln's Inn with a view to the law. Here he studied the points of controversy between Catholics and Protestants, with the result that he joined the Church of England. The next two years were somewhat changeful, including travels on the Continent, service under Essex in his expeditions to Cadiz and the Azores, employment as private secretary to Sir Thomas Egerton, Keeper of the Great Seal, and a clandestine marriage with the niece of his patron, which led to dismissal and imprisonment, followed by reconciliation. On the suggestion of James I, who approved of *Pseudo-Martyr* (1610), a book against Rome which he had written, he took orders, and after executing a mission to Bohemia, he was, in 1621, made Dean of St Paul's. Donne had great popularity as a preacher. His poetical works consist of elegies, satires, epigrams, and religious pieces, in which, with some conceits, there is much noble poetry and imagination of a high order. Among his writings may be noted *An Anatomy of the World* (1611) and *Progress of the Soul* (1612), both elegies; his *Epithalamium* (1613) and *Divine Poems*. Collections of his poems appeared in 1633 and 1649. Greatest of the so-called 'metaphysical' poets, he exercised a strong influence on literature for over half a century after his death, and there was a revival of interest in his work after the First World War. Early folios of his remarkable sermons appeared in 1640, 1649, and 1660, and his *Letters* were published in 1651. His life was written by Izaak Walton.

Dooley, Mr, *see* **Dunne, Finley Peter.**

Doolittle, Hilda (10 Sept. 1886—   ), poetess who wrote under the initials H. D., was born at Bethlehem, Pennsylvania, daughter of a professor of mathematics, and educated at the Friends' Central School, Philadelphia, and Bryn Mawr College. Her first published work consisted of stories for children. In 1911 she went on a visit to Europe and remained there, being drawn into the Imagist group of poets, of which she became one of the leaders. In 1913 she married Richard Aldington (q.v.) and when he was absent during the First World War she took over the editorship of the *Egoist*, the Imagist magazine. After their divorce in 1937 she settled in a town near Lake Geneva. Her books of verse include *Sea Garden* (1916), *Hymen* (1921), *Heliodova* (1924), *Collected Poems* (1940), and a trilogy consisting of *The Walls Do Not Fall* (1944), *Tribute to the Angels* (1945), and *Flowering of the Rod* (1946). She also translated the *Ion of Euripides* and wrote some novels. Her faithfulness to Imagist principles gave her work a classically chiselled, objective form reminiscent of ancient Greek art.

Doran, John (11 March 1807—25 Jan. 1878), historian, born in London of Irish parents, worked as a tutor, and obtained a doctor's degree of Marburg in Prussia. He wrote a number of works dealing with the lighter phases of manners, antiquities, and social history, often bearing punning titles, such as *Table Traits with Something on Them* (1854), and *Knights and their Days*. He also wrote *Lives of the Queens of England of the House of Hanover* (1855), and *A History of Court Fools* (1858), and edited Horace Walpole's *Journal of the*

Reign of George III. His books contain much curious and out-of-the-way information. Doran was for a short time editor of the *Athenaeum*, and later of *Notes and Queries*.

Dorset, Charles Sackville, 6th Earl of (24 Jan. 1638—29 Jan. 1706), poet, was one of the dissolute and witty courtiers of Charles II, and a friend of Sir C. Sedley (q.v.), in whose orgies he participated. He was, however, a patron of literature, and a benefactor of Dryden in his later and less prosperous years. He wrote a few satires and songs, among the latter being the well-known 'To All You Ladies Now on Land.' As might be expected, his writings are characterized by the prevailing indelicacy of the time.

Dorset, Thomas Sackville, 1st Earl of (1536—19 April 1608), poet and statesman, was born at Buckhurst, Sussex, the only son of Sir Richard Sackville, Chancellor of the Exchequer, and educated at Oxford and Cambridge. He studied law at the Inner Temple, and while there wrote, in conjunction with Thomas Norton (q.v.), *Ferrex and Porrex*, later called *Gorboduc* (1561—2), the first regular English tragedy. A little later he planned *The Mirror for Magistrates*, which was to have been a series of narratives of distinguished Englishmen, somewhat on the model of Boccaccio's *Falls of Princes*. Finding the plan too large, he handed it over to others—seven poets in all being engaged upon it—and himself contributed two poems only, one on Buckingham, the confederate, and afterwards the victim, of Richard III, and an Induction or introduction, which has been described as the best poem between Chaucer and Spenser. These two pieces are distinguished by strong invention and imaginative power, and a stately and sombre grandeur of style. Dorset played a prominent part in the history of his time, and held many high offices, including those of Lord Steward and Lord Treasurer.

Dos Passos, John Roderigo (14 Jan. 1896—   ), novelist and playwright, was born in Chicago, son of a lawyer of Portuguese extraction, and educated at Harvard. During the First World War he served in the U.S. Medical Corps, and used his experiences in his first book *One Man's Initiation—1917* (1920), which was followed by *Three Soldiers* (1922), another war novel of the debunking type. Later he was a war correspondent in Spain, Mexico, and the Near East. *A Pushcart at the Curb* (1922) is a volume of verse. Further novels were *Streets of Night* (1923) and *Manhattan Transfer* (1925), which tells of New York, while *The 42nd Parallel* (1930), *1919* (1932), and *The Big Money* (1936) were combined as a trilogy entitled *U.S.A.* Another trilogy, *District of Columbia* (1952), is made up of *Adventures of a Young Man* (1939), *Number One* (1943), and *The Grand Design* (1949). *State of the Nation* (1944) and *Tour of Duty* (1946) are collections of essays, and his plays include *The Garbage Man* (1926), *Airways Inc.* (1929), and *Fortune Heights* (1933). *Orient Express* (1927), *All Countries* (1934), and *Journeys Between Wars* (1938), are unconventional travel books. His *Head and Heart of Thomas Jefferson* appeared in 1954.

Douce, Francis (1757—30 March 1834), antiquary, born in London, a lawyer by profession, was for a time Keeper of the Manuscripts at the British Museum. He published *Illustrations of Shakespeare* (1807), and a dissertation on *The Dance of Death* (1833).

Doughty, Charles Montagu (19 Aug. 1843—30 Jan. 1926), explorer and poet, was born at Theberton Hall, Suffolk, son of a clergyman. He was intended for the Navy, but could not pass the medical examination, and went to Cambridge, where he studied geology and developed a passion for the poetry of Chaucer and Spenser. In 1870 he left England and travelled in Europe, North Africa, Syria, Palestine, and finally Arabia, where he spent a year learning Arabic. In 1876 he set out from Damascus, disguised as an Arab, on the pilgrims' trail to Mecca, and spent two years among the Bedouin. From this journey came his *Travels in Arabia Deserta* (1888), written in an obscure archaic style, which has become accepted as a classic of travel. Later he composed an epic of 30,000 rhymed lines entitled *The Dawn in Britain* (1906), and some other books of poetry. He was made an honorary D.Litt. of both Oxford and Cambridge.

Douglas, Lord Alfred Bruce (22 Oct. 1870—20 March 1945), poet, was born at Ham Hill near Worcester, son of the Marquis of Queensberry. A fine runner, he won the school steeplechase at Winchester, and then went to Magdalen College, Oxford, where he was noted for his exceptional good looks and personal charm. In 1891 he met Oscar Wilde (q.v.), and began that unhappy association which resulted in Wilde's disgrace. From 1907 to 1910 he edited the *Academy*, but gave this up because of quarrels. Later he became involved in various lawsuits, and was imprisoned for six months for publishing a libel on Winston Churchill. As a poet he was an acknowledged master of the sonnet form, his principal books being *The City of the Soul* (1899), *Sonnets* (1909), *In Excelsis* (1924), and *Lyrics* (1935). His *Collected Satires* were published in 1927, and he produced some delightful nonsense verse, including *Tales with a Twist* (1896), *The Placid Pug* (1906), and *The Pongo Papers* (1907). His *Autobiography* appeared in 1929, and he wrote two books on Oscar Wilde. He became a Roman Catholic at the age of 41.

Douglas, Gavin *or* **Gawin** (1474—Sept. 1522), poet, son of the 5th Earl of Angus, nicknamed Archibald Bell-the-Cat, was educated at St Andrews for the Church. Promotion came early, and he was in 1501 made Provost of St Giles, Edinburgh, and in 1514 Abbot of Aberbrothock, and Archbishop of St Andrews. But the times were troublous, and he had hardly received these latter preferments when he was deprived of them. He was, however, named Bishop of Dunkeld in 1514 and, after some difficulty, and undergoing imprisonment, was confirmed in the see. In 1520 he was again driven forth, and two years later died of the plague in London. His principal poems are *The Palace of Honour*, and *King Hart*, both allegorical; but his great achievement was his translation of the *Aeneid* in ten-syllabled metre, the first translation into English of a classical work. Douglas's language is more archaic than that of some of his predecessors, his rhythm is rough and unequal, but he had fire, and a power of vivid description, and his allegories are ingenious and felicitous.

H

Douglas, George, *see* **Brown, George Douglas.**

Douglas, George Norman (8 Dec. 1868—9 Feb. 1952), novelist and essayist, was born at Tilquhillie on Deeside, of distinguished Scottish and German ancestry, and educated at Uppingham and Karlsruhe. Entering the Foreign Office, he served in the diplomatic corps at St Petersburg from 1894 to 1896, then went to Italy and eventually settled in Capri. His early travel books, *Siren Land* (1911), *Fountains in the Sand* (1912), which tells of Tunisia, and *Old Calabria* (1915) attracted little attention, but his novel *South Wind* (1917) was hailed as a masterpiece; other novels were *They Went* (1920), *Alone* (1921), and *Together* (1923). *Good-bye to Western Culture* (1930) was a reply to Katherine Mayo's *Mother India*. He also wrote two autobiographical works, *Looking Back* (1933), and *Late Harvest* (1946). Douglas spoke and wrote in German as readily as in English, and like Conrad, who also was bilingual, was much admired as a stylist.

Douglas, Lloyd Cassel (27 Aug. 1877—13 Feb. 1951), novelist, was born in Columbia City, Indiana, son of a minister, and educated at Wittenberg College, Springfield, Ohio, and Hamma Divinity School. He officiated as a Lutheran minister in Washington, Ann Arbor, Akron, Los Angeles, and Montreal successively, but in 1933 retired to devote himself to literature. He was over 50 when his first novel, *Magnificent Obsession* (1929) was published. Both it and *Forgive Us Our Trespasses* (1932) were great successes, though written with an ethical purpose and described by the author himself as 'old-fashioned novels in which the characters are tiresomely decent.' Later books were *Precious Jeopardy* (1933), *Green Light* (1935), *White Banners* (1936), *Disputed Passage* (1939), *Invitation to Live* (1940), *The Robe* (1942), *Home for Christmas* (1949), and *A Time to Remember* (1951).

Douglas, Olive, *see* **Buchan, Anna.**

Dowden, Edward (3 May 1843—4 April 1913), scholar and critic, was born in Cork and educated at Queen's College there and Trinity College, Dublin, where he had a brilliant record and was appointed Professor of English in 1867, four years after he had graduated; this post he held till the end of his life. He is chiefly remembered as a great Shakespearian scholar. *Shakspere: His Mind and Art* appeared in 1875 and his *Shakspere Primer* in 1877, and he also edited many of the plays. Others of his books are *Studies in Literature* (1878), and *Transcripts and Studies* (1888), and biographies of *Southey* (1880), *Shelley* (1886), *Browning* (1904), and *Montaigne* (1905). He was a close friend of Walt Whitman, and published some volumes of verse.

Dowson, Ernest Christopher (2 Aug. 1867—23 Feb. 1900), poet, was born in Kent, but spent much of his youth and his later life in France. Educated at Oxford, he lived for a time in the East End of London, where his father owned a dry dock. There he met the 'Cynara' of his best-known poem; the daughter of a French café proprietor, she eventually married a waiter. In Paris and Dieppe Dowson, already sickly owing to consumption and poverty, undermined his health with drink. As a poet he ranks with the French Decadents. His works include *Dilemmas* (1893), *Verses* (1896), and *Poems* (1905). *The Pierrot of the Minute* (1897) is a poetic drama.

Doyle, Sir Arthur Conan (22 May 1859—7 July 1930), novelist, was born in Edinburgh of an Irish Roman Catholic family. His father was a clerk in the Board of Works, and his uncle, Richard Doyle, was the artist who drew the well-known cover design of *Punch*. Doyle was educated at Stonyhurst and Edinburgh University, where he qualified as a doctor, practising at Southsea from 1882 to 1890. In 1882 he published *A Study in Scarlet*, an adventure story which introduced the famous character Sherlock Holmes. A later Holmes novel was *The Sign of Four* (1890), but he first became really famous with the publication in the *Strand Magazine* of the *Adventures of Sherlock Holmes* (1892), short stories of which the first was 'A Scandal in Bohemia.' Holmes and his friend and chronicler Dr Watson set the fashion for the detective story, the former being modelled on Dr Joseph Bell, under whom Doyle had worked as a surgeon; the name Holmes was taken from the American writer Oliver Wendell Holmes (q.v.), for whose work Doyle had a great admiration. Later volumes of short stories on the same theme were *The Memoirs of Sherlock Holmes* (1894), *The Return of Sherlock Holmes* (1905), *His Last Bow* (1917), and *The Case-Book of Sherlock Holmes* (1927). Of full-length Holmes novels, the most famous was *The Hound of the Baskervilles* (1902).

Among novels which Doyle wrote on other themes the best are *Micah Clarke* (1889) and *Rodney Stone* (1896), a boxing story. *The White Company* (1890) and *Sir Nigel* (1906) are historical romances with a strong appeal to the young, while *The Exploits of Brigadier Gerard* (1895) recounts with humorous irony the adventures of a young Napoleonic officer. Doyle served as a doctor in the South African War and wrote a history of the conflict, *The Great Boer War* (1900). In 1902 he was knighted. Later he created an amusing new character in the belligerent Professor Challenger, who is the hero of the scientific romances *The Lost World* (1912) and *The Poison Belt* (1913). *Songs of Action* is a book of poems, and *Memories and Adventures* (1924) contains his reminiscences. In his latter years Doyle was deeply interested in psychic phenomena, and wrote a *History of Spiritualism* (1926).

Doyle, Sir Francis Hastings, 2nd Baronet (21 Aug. 1810—8 June 1888), poet, was born at Nunappleton in Yorkshire; his father was a general and many of his relations were army officers. Educated at Eton and Oxford, he studied law, was called to the Bar in 1837, and afterwards held various high fiscal appointments, becoming in 1869 Commissioner of Customs. In 1834, he published *Miscellaneous Verses*, followed by *Two Destinies* (1844), and *Return of the Guards* (1866). He was elected in 1867 Professor of Poetry at Oxford. Doyle's best work is his ballads, which include 'The Private of the Buffs,' and 'The Loss of the *Birkenhead*.'

Drake, Joseph Rodman (7 Aug. 1795—21 Sept. 1820), poet, born in New York, studied medicine, and died of consumption. He collaborated with Fitzgreene Halleck (q.v.) in the humorous *Croaker Papers*, and wrote 'The Culprit Fay,' and 'The American Flag.'

Draper, John William (5 May 1811—4 Jan. 1882), scientist and historian, born at St Helen's, near Liverpool, was educated at London University and (having emigrated in 1833) the University of Pennsylvania. In 1839 he became Professor of Chemistry at New York. He wrote *History of the Intellectual Development of Europe* (1863), *History of the American Civil War* (1867—70), and *History of the Conflict between Science and Religion* (1874), beside treatises on various branches of science.

Drayton, Michael (1563—23 Dec. 1631), poet, born at Hartshill, Warwickshire, was in early life a page. His earliest poem, *The Harmonie of the Church*, was condemned by the authorities to be destroyed. His next was *The Shepherd's Garland* (1593), afterwards reprinted as *Eclogues*. Three historical poems, *Gaveston* (1593), *Matilda* (1594), and *Robert, Duke of Normandie* (1596) followed, and he then appears to have collaborated with Dekker, Webster, and others in dramatic work. His *magnum opus*, however, was *Polyolbion* (1622), a topographical description of England in twelve-syllabled verse, full of antiquarian and historical details, so accurate as to make the work an authority on such matters. The rushing verse is full of vigour and gusto. Other poems of Drayton are *Idea's Mirrour* (1594), a collection of sonnets, Idea being the name of the lady to whom they were addressed, which includes the famous 'Since there's no help, come let us kiss and part'; *England's Heroical Epistles* (1598), imaginary letters between Royal lovers such as Henry II and Rosamund; *Poems, Lyric and Heroic* (1606) which contains the fine ballad of 'Agincourt'; *Nymphidia* (1627), a delightful fairy fantasy; and *Muses Elizium* (1630). He was buried in Westminster Abbey.

Dreiser, Theodore Herman Albert (27 Aug. 1871—28 Dec. 1945), novelist, was born at Terre Haute, Indiana, the twelfth of thirteen children, his brother Thomas being a popular song-writer. In early life he was handicapped by poverty and his father's religious bigotry. He attended schools at Warsaw, Indiana, and between 1886 and 1891 held various posts in Chicago, with one year at Indiana University. From 1892 to 1895 he did newspaper work in Chicago and St Louis, and rose to be editor-in-chief of a series of publications. His first novel, *Sister Carrie* (1900) was withdrawn because of its sordid realism, and he fought a long battle with the censorship, but his second, *Jennie Gerhart* (1911) was well received. It was followed by *The Financier* (1912), *The Titan* (1914), *The Genius* (1915), and, most famous of all, *An American Tragedy* (1925), which was based on actual court records. His last two novels were *The Bulwark* (1946) and *The Stoic* (1947). Though a powerful writer, Dreiser was not an artist in words, and his style is unpolished. Among his other works are two travel books, *A Traveller at Forty* (1913) and *A Hoosier Holiday* (1916); a collection of essays, *Hey, Rub-a-Dub-Dub* (1930) reveals his attitude to humanity, and *A Book About Myself* (1922) is autobiographical. A Communist sympathizer, he paid an official visit to Russia in 1927, and published *Dreiser Looks at Russia* in the following year. He was twice married.

Drinkwater, John (1 June 1882—25 March 1937), poet and playwright, was born at Leytonstone in Essex, son of a schoolmaster who became an actor, and educated at the City of Oxford School. In 1897 he entered an insurance office, where he remained for twelve years, being moved in 1901 to Birmingham. His first book, *Poems*, appeared in 1903, followed by *The Death of Leander* (1906). In 1909 he left insurance for literature, and in 1913 was one of the founders of the Birmingham Repertory Theatre. He was best known for his chronicle plays, which include *Abraham Lincoln* (1918), *Mary Stuart* (1921), *Oliver Cromwell* (1921), *Robert E. Lee* (1923), and *Robert Burns* (1925); *Bird in Hand* (1928) is a comedy. His work had an important influence on the revival of serious drama. Among his numerous books of verse may be mentioned *Olton Pools* (1916), *Collected Poems* (1923), *New Poems* (1925), and *Summer Harvest* (1933). He wrote two books of autobiography, *Inheritance* (1931) and *Discovery* (1932). In 1924 he married Daisy Kennedy, the violinist. He was a keen philatelist, specializing in the stamps of the United States.

Drummond, Henry (17 Aug. 1851—11 March 1897), born at Stirling, and educated at Edinburgh, studied for the ministry, but having a decided scientific bent he became in 1884 Professor of Natural Science at the Free Church College in Glasgow. He made geological surveys in the Rocky Mountains and Central Africa, after which he published *Tropical Africa* (1888). His chief contribution to literature was his *Natural Law in the Spiritual World* (1883), which had extraordinary popularity. *The Ascent of Man* (1894) was less successful.

Drummond, William (13 Dec. 1585—4 Dec. 1649), poet, was descended from a very ancient family, and through Annabella Drummond, queen of Robert III, related to the royal house. Educated at Edinburgh High School and University, he studied law on the Continent, but succeeding in 1610 to his paternal estate of Hawthornden, he devoted himself to poetry. *Tears on the Death of Meliades* (Prince Henry) appeared in 1613, and in 1616 *Poems, Amorous, Funerall, Divine, Pastorall*. His finest poem, *Forth Feasting* (1617), is addressed to James VI on his revisiting Scotland. Drummond was also a prose-writer, and composed a *History of the Five Jameses, Kings of Scotland from 1423 to 1524*, and *The Cypress Grove*, a meditation on death. He had a library of over 500 volumes, was also a mechanical genius, and patented 16 inventions. Drummond, though a Scotsman, wrote in the classical English of the day, and was the friend of his principal literary contemporaries, notably Ben Jonson, who visited him at Hawthornden, on which occasion Drummond preserved notes printed first in 1832 as his *Conversations*, which form a pleasant chapter of literary history. As a poet he belonged to the school of Spenser, his verse being sweet, flowing, and harmonious, while his sonnets, on the Italian model, won him the name of the Scottish Petrarch. The Hawthornden Prize for imaginative writing was founded in 1919 to honour his memory.

Drummond, William Henry (13 April 1854—6 April 1907), poet, was born in County Antrim, his father being in the Royal Irish Constabulary. In 1864 he emigrated to Canada with his parents, was educated at Montreal High School, and studied medicine at Bishop's College, Lennoxville. For a time he was Professor of Medical Jurisprudence at Bishop University. In 1897 appeared his first volume of verse, *The Habitant*, written in the French-Canadian dialect of English. Others were *Phil-o-Rum's Canoe* (1901), *The Voyageur* (1905), and *The Great Fight* (1908). In 1902 he was made an LL.D. of Toronto.

Dryden, John (9 Aug. 1631—1 May 1700), poet, dramatist, and critic, was born at Aldwinkle Rectory, Northamptonshire. His father, from whom he inherited a small estate, was Erasmus, third son of Sir Erasmus Driden; his mother was Mary Pickering, also of good family; both families belonged to the Puritan side in politics and religion. He was educated at Westminster School and Trinity College, Cambridge, and thereafter, in 1657, came to London. While at college he had written some not very successful verse. His *Heroic Stanzas on the Death of Oliver Cromwell* (1658) was the first considerable poem. It was followed, in 1660, by *Astraea Redux*, in honour of the Restoration. The interval of 18 months had been crowded with events, and though much has been written against his apparent change of opinion, it is fair to remember that the whole cast of his mind led him to be a supporter of *de facto* authority. In 1663 he married Lady Elizabeth Howard, daughter of the Earl of Berkshire. The Restoration introduced a revival of the drama in its most debased form, and for many years Dryden was a prolific playwright, but though his vigorous powers enabled him to work effectively in this department, as in every other in which he engaged, it was not his natural line, and happily his fame does not rest upon his plays, which show the usual immorality of the age. His first effort, *The Wild Gallant* (1663), was a failure; his next, *The Rival Ladies* (1664), a tragi-comedy, established his reputation, and among his other dramas are *The Indian Queen* (1665), *Amboyna* (1673), *Tyrannic Love* (1669), *Almanzor and Almahide* (1670), ridiculed in Buckingham's *Rehearsal*, *Aurungzebe* (1675), and his greatest play, *All for Love* (1678), which deals with the same story as Shakespeare's *Antony and Cleopatra*. During the great plague of 1665 Dryden left London, and lived with his father-in-law at Charlton. On his return he published his first poem of real power, *Annus Mirabilis*, of which the subjects were the great fire and the Dutch War. In 1668 appeared his *Essay of Dramatick Poesie* in the form of a dialogue, fine alike as criticism and as prose. Two years later he became Poet Laureate and Historiographer Royal with a pension of £300 a year.

Dryden was now in prosperous circumstances, having received a portion with his wife, and besides the salaries of his appointments, and his profits from literature, holding a valuable share in the King's playhouse. In 1671 the Duke of Buckingham produced his *Rehearsal*, in ridicule of the overdone heroics of the prevailing drama, and satirizing Dryden as Mr Bayes. To this Dryden made no immediate reply, but bided his time. The next years were devoted to the drama. But by this time public affairs were assuming a critical aspect. A large section of the nation was becoming alarmed at the prospect of the succession of the Duke of York, and a restoration of popery, and Shaftesbury was supposed to be promoting the claims of the Duke of Monmouth. And now Dryden showed his full powers. The first part of *Absalom and Achitophel* appeared in 1681, in which Charles figures as 'David,' Shaftesbury as 'Achitophel,' Monmouth as 'Absalom,' Buckingham as 'Zimri,' in the short but crushing delineation of whom the attack of the *Rehearsal* was requited in the most ample measure. The effect of the poem was tremendous. Nevertheless the indictment against Shaftesbury for high treason was ignored by the Grand Jury at the Old Bailey, and in honour of the event a medal was struck, which gave a title to Dryden's next stroke. His *Medal* was issued in 1682. The success of these powerful satires raised a storm round Dryden. Replies were forthcoming in Elkanah Settle's *Absalom and Achitophel Transposed*, and Pordage's *Azaria and Hushai*. These compositions, especially Pordage's, were comparatively moderate. Far otherwise was Shadwell's *Medal of John Bayes*, one of the most brutal and indecent pieces in the language. Dryden's revenge—and an ample one—was the publication of *MacFlecknoe*, a satire in which all his opponents, but especially Shadwell, were held up to the loathing and ridicule of succeeding ages, and others had conferred upon them an immortality which, however unenviable, no efforts of their own could have secured for them. The following year, 1683, saw the publication of *Religio Laici* (The Religion of a Layman). In 1686 Dryden joined the Church of Rome, for which he has by some been blamed for time-serving of the basest kind. On the other hand his consistency and conscientiousness have by others been as strongly maintained. The change, which was announced by the publication in 1687 of *The Hind and the Panther, a Defence of the Roman Church*, at all events did not bring with it any worldly advantages. It was parodied by Charles Montague and Prior in the *City Mouse and Country Mouse*.

At the Revolution Dryden was deprived of all his pensions and appointments, including the Laureateship, in which he was succeeded by his old enemy Shadwell. His latter years were passed in comparative poverty, although the Earl of Dorset and other old friends contributed by their liberality to lighten his cares. In these circumstances he turned again to the drama, which, however, was no longer what it had been as a source of income. To this period belong *Don Sebastian* (1690), *Amphitryon* (1690), *King Arthur* (1691), *Eleanora* (1692), *Cleomenes* (1692), and his last play, *Love Triumphant* (1694). A new mine, however, was beginning to be opened up in the demand for translations which had arisen. This gave Dryden a new opportunity and he produced, in addition to translations from Juvenal and Persius, his famous rendering of Virgil (1697). About the same time appeared *The Ode for St Cecilia's Day*, and *Alexander's Feast*, and in 1700, the year of his death, the *Fables*, largely adaptations from Chaucer and Boccaccio. He was buried in Westminster Abbey beside Chaucer. In his own line, that of argument, satire, and declamation, Dryden is without a rival in our literature: he had little creative imagination and no pathos. His dramas, which in bulk are the greatest part of his work, add almost nothing to his fame; in them he was meeting a public demand, not following the native bent of his genius. In his satires, and in such poems as *Alexander's Feast*, he rises to the highest point of his powers in a verse swift and heart-stirring. In prose his style is clear, strong, and nervous. He seems to have been almost insensible to the beauty of Nature.

Duff, Sir Mountstuart Elphinstone Grant (21 Feb. 1829—12 Jan. 1906), diarist, born at Eden, Aberdeenshire, and educated at Edinburgh Academy and Oxford, was called to the Bar in 1854, and from 1857 to 1881 sat as M.P. for Elgin Burghs, then becoming a very successful governor of Madras. He published *Studies of European Politics* (1866), and a series of *Notes from a Diary* in 14 volumes (1897—1905). He was a Fellow of the Royal Society.

Dufferin, Helen Selina, Lady (1807—13 June 1867), song-writer, was a grand-daughter of Sheridan the dramatist, and oldest of the three beautiful Sheridan sisters. In 1813 she was taken by her parents to the Cape of Good Hope, but returned home with her mother on her father's death in 1817 and lived at Hampton Court Palace through the hospitality of the Regent. In 1825 she married Commander Blackwood, who succeeded as Baron Dufferin in 1839. After his death two years later she accompanied her son on his travels, and in 1862 she married George Hay, Earl of Gifford, on his death-bed. In 1863, after a trip up the Nile she wrote *Lispings from Low Latitudes*. Her songs, including the famous 'Lament of the Irish Emigrant' were published in 1894.

Duffy, Sir Charles Gavan (12 April 1816—9 Feb. 1903), journalist, born in Monaghan, son of a shopkeeper, was mainly self-educated. He became one of the founders of the *Nation* newspaper, and one of the leaders of the Young Ireland movement. Thereafter he went to Australia, where he became a leading politician, and rose to be Premier of Victoria. His later years were spent chiefly on the Continent. He did much to stimulate in Ireland a taste for the national history and literature, started a shilling series of books, *The Library of Ireland*, and made a collection, *The Ballad Poetry of Ireland*, which was a great success. He also published an autobiography, *My Life in Two Hemispheres* (1898).

Dugdale, Sir William (12 Sept. 1605—10 Feb. 1686), herald and antiquary, was born at Shustoke, near Coleshill, Warwickshire, and educated at Coventry School. From early youth he showed a strong bent towards heraldic and antiquarian studies, which led to his appointment, in 1638, as a Pursuivant-extraordinary, from which he rose to be Garter-King-of-Arms. In collaboration with Roger Dodsworth he brought out the first volume of *Monasticon Anglicanum* (1655—73), containing the charters of the ancient monasteries. In 1656 he published the *Antiquities of Warwickshire*, which maintains a high place among county histories, and in 1666 *Origines Judiciales*.

His great work, *The Baronage of England*, appeared in 1675—6. His *Life, Diary, and Correspondence* was printed in 1827.

du Maurier, Daphne (13 May 1907—   ), novelist, born in London, was a daughter of Sir Gerald du Maurier, the famous actor, and grand-daughter of George du Maurier (q.v.) Two of her most interesting books are *Gerald* (1934), a study of her father, and *The du Mauriers* (1937), which relates the story of three generations. Educated at home and in Paris, she disliked town life, her favourite pursuits being walking, gardening, and sailing. In 1932 she married Colonel F. A. M. Browning, D.S.O., who became Comptroller of Princess Elizabeth's Household in 1947. Her novels, which often have an element of melodrama, include *The Loving Spirit* (1931), *I'll Never Be Young Again* (1932), *The Progress of Julius* (1933), *Jamaica Inn* (1936), *Rebecca* (1938), *Frenchman's Creek* (1942), *Hungry Hill* (1943), *The King's General* (1946), *My Cousin Rachel* (1951), and *Mary Anne* (1954). *The Apple Tree* (1952) is a collection of short stories. In 1951 she published an edition of her grandfather's letters, and in 1962 she completed Quiller-Couch's unfinished novel, *Castle Dor*.

du Maurier, George Louis Palmella Busson (6 March 1834—6 Oct. 1896), artist and novelist, was born in Paris. His father was descended from an old French family and his mother was English, so George was bilingual; he had a fine singing voice. His early childhood is described in the novel *Peter Ibbetson* (1891), and his schooldays in *The Martian* (1897). For a time he worked at chemistry at London University, but after his father's death in 1856 he studied art in Paris. Later he used his experiences there in his novel *Trilby* (1894), which had a great success. In 1859 he lost the sight of one eye, and in the following year started drawing for *Punch*, specializing in society pictures which introduced beautiful women. From 1874 to 1894 he lived in Hampstead.

Dunbar, William (1465?—1530?), poet, born probably in East Lothian and educated at St Andrews University, was for a time a Franciscan Friar. He served James IV as both court poet and diplomatic envoy, and was granted by him a pension of £80. In 1503 he wrote his first great poem, *The Thistle and the Rose*, which celebrates the King's marriage with an English princess and the Anglo-Scottish treaty of peace; about 1508 he followed this with *The Golden Targe*, an allegory of Love, Beauty, and Reason. Both of these poems follow Chaucerian models, but Dunbar was soon to strike an individual note. *The Dance of the Seven Deadly Sins*, and *The Twa Merrit Women and the Wedo*, two fine satires, were followed by his splendid *Lament for the Makaris* (poets) bewailing the deaths of his predecessors. A peculiarly Scottish form of verse is represented by *The Flyting of Dunbar and Kennedy*—'flyting' means scolding. The date and circumstances of Dunbar's death are uncertain, some holding that he fell at Flodden, others that he was alive as late as 1530. Greatest of the so-called Scottish Chaucerians, he was a major poet of wide and varied range with a richness of imagery allied to masculine verve and rollicking humour. His verse forms

H*

greatest of Scottish poets, ranking him above Burns.   Unfortunately his antique language forms a difficulty for the modern reader.

Duncan, Ronald (6 Aug. 1914—   ), poet and playwright, was educated in Switzerland and at Cambridge.   From 1947 he farmed in Cornwall.   His plays include *This Way to the Tomb* (1945), *The Rape of Lucretia* (1946), *The Eagle Has Two Heads* (1946), *Stratton* (1948), and *The Typewriter* (1948).   Among his other publications are *The Dull Ass's Hoof* (1941), *Postcards to Prunella* (1942), *Journal of a Husbandman* (1944), *Home Made Home* (1947), *Jan's Journal* (1948), *The Mongrel and Other Poems* (1950), *The Blue Fox* (1951), *Jan at the Blue Fox* (1952), and *Where I Live* (1953).   He edited the *Songs and Satires* of the Earl of Rochester (1948) and Pope's *Letters* (1948).

Dunkerley, William Arthur (12 Nov. 1852—23 Jan. 1941), novelist and religious poet who wrote under the name John Oxenham, was born in Manchester, son of a wholesale provision merchant, and educated at Old Trafford School and Victoria University.   Between 1870 and 1881 he travelled in Europe and the United States in connection with his father's business, but after that, taking up a writing career, he joined with J. K. Jerome (q.v.) in launching *The Idler* in 1882.   Following a Fleet Street period he wrote some 40 novels, beginning with *God's Prisoner* (1898), and including *Bondman Free* (1903), *Hearts in Exile* (1904), *Pearl of Pearl Island* (1908), *The Quest of the Golden Rose* (1912), and *Flower of the Dust* (1916). In 1913 he published a book of verse, *Bees in Amber*, at his own expense, as publishers thought it a hopeless venture; it sold over a quarter of a million copies, and he followed it with *The King's Highway* (1916), and *The Vision Splendid* (1917), which were extremely popular during the First World War; his *Selected Poems* appeared in 1925.   In his later years he wrote a number of books on the life of Christ, including *The Cedar Box* (1924), *The Hidden Years* (1925), and *The Man Who Would Save the World* (1927).   Although he had Roman Catholic sympathies, he remained a Congregationalist all his life.   His biography was written by his daughter Erica in 1942.

Dunlap, William (19 Feb. 1766—28 Sept. 1839), playwright and historian, was born at Perth Amboy, New Jersey, son of an Irish shopkeeper.   An injury at play caused the loss of an eye, but although this interfered with his schooling he took up drawing, and going to London in 1784 studied art with Benjamin West.   While there he started writing plays, his first success being *The Father of an Only Child*.   In 1796 he became manager of a New York theatre and wrote other plays including *André* (1798) and *The Italian Father* (1799), both in blank verse.   His theatrical venture failed, and thenceforward he alternated between painting and the theatre.   His *History of the American Theatre* (1832), still of value, was followed by a *History of New York* (1840).

Dunlop, John Colin (1785?—Feb. 1842), historian, son of a Lord Provost of Glasgow, where and at Edinburgh he was educated, was called to the Bar in 1807, and became Sheriff of Renfrewshire.   He wrote a *History of Fiction* (1814), a *History of Roman Literature to the*

Augustan Age (1823—8), and *Memoirs of Spain during the Reigns of Philip IV and Charles II* (1834). He also made translations from the Latin Anthology.

Dunne, Finley Peter (10 July 1867—24 April 1936), humorist who wrote under the pseudonym Mr Dooley, was born in Chicago, where after an elementary school education he worked on the *Evening Post* and the *Times-Herald* from 1892 to 1897, then became editor of the *Journal*, and later edited *Collier's Weekly*. He is remembered as the author of a number of books in which Mr Dooley, ostensibly an Irish saloon-keeper, comments with shrewd philosophy on contemporary events, his Irish dialect giving him a sort of license to speak his mind freely on humbug and hypocrisy. The first volume in the collection, *Mr Dooley in Peace and War* (1898) was followed by *Mr Dooley in the Hearts of his Countrymen* (1899), *Mr Dooley's Philosophy* (1900), his *Opinions* (1901), his *Observations* (1902), his *Dissertations* (1906), the *New Dooley Book* (1911), and lastly *Mr Dooley on Making a Will and Other Necessary Evils* (1919).

Dunne, John William (1875—24 Aug. 1949), philosopher, son of General Sir J. H. Dunne, was educated at private schools. During the Boer War he was a trooper in the Yeomanry; later he was attached to a government balloon factory, and made a number of aeronautical experiments. Studying the philosophical problems of existence, he propounded the theory of serialism, which he worked out in a number of books, *An Experiment with Time* (1927), *The Serial Universe* (1934), *The New Immortality* (1938), and *Nothing Dies* (1940).

Duns Scotus, Johannes (1265?—1308?), philosopher nicknamed *doctor subtilis*, was born at Maxton in Roxburgh. He may have been at Oxford, is said to have been a regent or professor at Paris, and was a Franciscan. He was a man of extraordinary learning, among his many works on logic and theology being a philosophic grammar, and a work on metaphysics, *De Rerum Principio* (Of the Beginning of Things). His great opponent was Thomas Aquinas, and schoolmen of the day were divided into Scotists and Thomists, or realists and nominalists. In later days his subtleties were derided, and his name gave rise to the term 'dunce.'

Dunsany, Edward John Moreton Drax Plunkett, 18th Baron (24 July 1878—25 Oct. 1957), poet and playwright, was born in London. Educated at Eton and Sandhurst, he succeeded to the title on his father's death in 1899. During the Boer War he served with the Coldstream Guards, and in the First World War was a captain in the Inniskilling Fusiliers. In the Second World War he held the chair of Byron Professor of English Literature at Athens, and was there when the Nazis captured the city. By contrast with his work, which consists of delicate faery fantasies, he was an extremely athletic person, standing 6 feet 4 inches in height; he once estimated that 97 per cent of his time was spent in sport and soldiering, the rest in writing. His first book was a novel, *The Gods of Pegana* (1905); others of his novels are *Time and the Gods* (1906), *The King of Elfland's Daughter* (1924), *The Charwoman's Shadow*

(1926), and *The Wise Woman* (1933). *The Sword of Welleran* (1908) is a volume of short stories. In 1909, on Yeats's invitation, he wrote a play, *The Glittering Gate*, for the Abbey Theatre, and followed it with many others, including *The Gods of the Mountain* (1911), *A Night at an Inn* (1916), *The Laughter of the Gods* (1919), *The Tents of the Arabs* (1920), *If* (1921), *Alexander* (1925), *Lord Adrian* (1933), and *Plays for Earth and Air* (1937). He also published two volumes of verse, *Fifty Poems* (1930) and *Mirage Water* (1939), and a series of autobiographies, *Patches of Sunlight* (1938), *While the Sirens Slept* (1944), *The Sirens Wake* (1945), and *To Awaken Pegasus* (1949).

Durant, William James (5 Nov. 1885—   ), philosopher, was born at North Adams, Massachusetts, of a French Canadian family, and educated at St Peter's College, Jersey City. For a time he was a reporter on the New York *Evening Journal*, then obtained a Ph.D. of Columbia University, where he taught philosophy, and in 1935 was appointed Professor of Philosophy at the University of California. His book *The Story of Philosophy* (1926) made him famous. Others are *The Case for India* (1930), *The Tragedy of Russia* (1933), and his monumental work *The Story of Civilization*, which was published in successive parts—*Our Oriental Heritage* (1935), *The Life of Greece* (1939), *Caesar and Christ* (1944), *The Age of Faith* (1950), and *The Renaissance* (1953). His novel *Transition* (1927) is mainly autobiographical.

D'Urfey, Thomas (1653—26 Feb. 1723), poet and dramatist, was born at Exeter, of Huguenot descent. A well-known man-about-town, he was a companion of Charles II, and lived on to the reign of George I. He is best known in connection with a collection of songs entitled, *Pills to Purge Melancholy* (1719—20). Addison describes him as a 'diverting companion,' and 'a cheerful, honest, good-natured man.' His writings are nevertheless extremely gross. His plays include *The Siege of Memphis* (1676), *Madame Fickle* (1677), *The Virtuous Wife* (1680), and *The Campaigners* (1698).

Durrell, Lawrence George (27 Feb. 1912—   ), poet, was born in India of Irish descent and went to the College of St Joseph, Darjeeling, then was sent to England and attended St Edward's College, Canterbury. For a time he led a Bohemian life in London, at one time being a pianist in a night club. Before the Second World War he lived in Corfu, which forms the background to his novel, *Prospero's Cell* (1946), and during the war he was at the British Embassy in Cairo. Later he was Director of British Council Institutes in Greece and Argentina, his lectures being published as *A Key to Modern Poetry* (1952). Volumes of his verse are *Ten Poems* (1933), *Transition* (1934), *The Pied Piper of Lovers* (1935), *Private Country* (1943), *Cities, Plains, and People* (1946), *On Seeming to Presume* (1948), and *The Tree of Idleness* (1955). His novel *Panic Spring* (1937) was published under the name Charles Norden; under his own are *The Black Book* (1938), *Cefalu* (1947), *Reflections on a Marine Venus* (1953), *Justine* (1957), and *Bitter Lemons* (1957), which received the Duff Cooper Memorial Prize. In 1954 he was elected a Fellow of the Royal Society of Literature.

Dwight, Timothy (14 May 1752—11 Jan. 1817), scholar and poet, was born at Northampton, Massachusetts, son of a merchant. A precocious child, he could read the Bible at the age of 4, and at 13 entered Yale, where he studied fourteen hours a day, to the injury of his health and eyesight. From 1771 to 1777 he was a tutor at Yale, and from 1783 to 1795 Congregationalist minister at Greenfield Hill, Connecticut. His poem *America* (1772) was followed by *The Conquest of Canaan* (1785) the first American epic, and *Greenfield Hill* (1794), a poem in the eighteenth-century tradition. Various books of sermons followed. In 1795 he was appointed President of Yale, and wielded great influence, being nicknamed 'Pope Dwight'; from his administration Yale dates its modern era.

Dyce, Alexander (30 June 1798—15 May 1869), scholar, son of a general, was born in Edinburgh, and educated there and at Oxford. He took orders, and for a short time served in two country curacies. Then, leaving the Church and settling in London, he made his life-work editing English dramatists. His first work, *Specimens of British Poetesses*, appeared in 1825; and thereafter at various intervals editions of Collins's *Poems*, and the dramatic works of Peele, Middleton, Beaumont and Fletcher, Marlowe, Greene, Webster, and others. His great edition of Shakespeare's works in 9 volumes appeared in 1827. He also edited various works for the Camden Society, and published the *Table Talk of Samuel Rogers*.

Dyer, Sir Edward (born 1545? buried 11 May 1607), poet, born at Sharpham Park, Somerset, and educated at Oxford, was introduced to the Court by the Earl of Leicester, and sent on a mission to Denmark in 1589. He was in 1596 made Chancellor of the Order of the Garter, and knighted. In his own day he had a reputation for his elegies among such judges as Sidney and Puttenham. For a long time there was doubt as to what poems were to be attributed to him, but about a dozen pieces have now been apparently identified as his. The best known is that on contentment beginning, 'My mind to me a kingdom is.'

Dyer, John (13 Aug. 1699—1758), poet, was born at Llanfynydd in Caermarthenshire. In his early years he studied painting, but finding that he was not likely to attain a satisfactory measure of success, took orders, and became vicar of Calthorp, Leicestershire, in 1741. He has a definite, if modest, place in literature as the author of three poems, *Grongar Hill* (1727), *The Ruins of Rome* (1740), and *The Fleece* (1757). The first of these is the best, and the best known, and contains much true natural description of South Wales scenery. Wordsworth had a high opinion of Dyer as a poet, and addressed a sonnet to him.

E

Eadmer *or* **Edmer** (died 1124?), priest and chronicler, was a monk of Canterbury and a close friend of Archbishop Anselm. His *Historia Novorum in Anglia*, a Latin account of events in England from the Norman Conquest to his own day, is reliable and well written. He also wrote a number of ecclesiastical biographies, including lives of Anselm, St Dunstan, and St Oswald. In 1120 he was appointed Archbishop of St Andrews by Alexander I, King of Scotland, but resigned owing to a dispute about who should consecrate him.

Ealhwine, *see* **Alcuin.**

Earle, John (1601?—17 Nov. 1665), clergyman and essayist, was born at York and educated at Oxford, where he was a Fellow of Merton. He took orders, was tutor to Charles II, a member of the Assembly of Divines at Westminster in 1643, and Chaplain and Clerk of the Closet to Charles when in exile. On the Restoration he was made Dean of Westminster, in 1662 Bishop of Worcester, and the next year Bishop of Salisbury. He was learned and eloquent, witty and agreeable in society, and was opposed to the 'Conventicle' and 'Five Mile' Acts, and to all forms of persecution. He wrote *Hortus Mertonensis* (the Garden of Merton) in Latin, but his chief work was *Microcosmographie, or a Piece of the World discovered in Essays and Characters* (1628), the best and most interesting of all the 'character' books.

Eastaway, Edward, *see* **Thomas, Philip Edward.**

Eastlake, Elizabeth, Lady (17 Nov. 1809—2 Oct. 1893), critic and biographer, daughter of Dr Edward Rigby of Norwich, spent her earlier life on the Continent and in Edinburgh. In 1849 she married Sir Charles L. Eastlake, the famous painter, and President of the Royal Academy. Her first work was *A Residence on the Shores of the Baltic* (1841). From 1842 she was a frequent contributor to the *Quarterly Review,* in which she wrote a very bitter criticism of *Jane Eyre.* She also wrote various books on art, and lives of her husband, of Mrs Grote, and of Gibson the sculptor.

Echard, Laurence (1670?—16 Aug. 1730), historian, born at Barsham, Suffolk, and educated at Cambridge, took orders and became Archdeacon of Stow. He translated Terence, part of Plautus, D'Orleans's *History of the Revolutions in England,* and made numerous compilations on history, geography, and the classics. His chief work, however, was his *History of England* (1707—20), which covers the period from the Roman occupation to his own times.

Eddington, Sir Arthur Stanley, O.M. (28 Dec. 1882—22 Nov. 1944), astronomer, was born at Kendal, Westmorland, where his father was a headmaster, and educated at Manchester University and Cambridge, becoming Senior Wrangler and a Fellow of Trinity. From

1906 to 1913 he was chief assistant at the Royal Observatory, Greenwich, and then was appointed Professor of Astronomy at Cambridge. He received the medals of the Royal Society and the Royal Astronomical Society, was knighted in 1930, and in 1938 was awarded the Order of Merit. He was well-known outside scientific circles for his popular writings on astronomy. His works include *Space, Time, and Gravitation* (1920), *Stars and Atoms* (1927), *The Nature of the Physical World* (1928), *Science and the Unseen World* (1929), and *The Expanding Universe* (1933).

Edgar, John George (1834—22 April 1864), writer of books for boys, was born at Hutton, Berwickshire, son of a clergyman. Among his books are *Boyhood of Great Men* (1853), *Runnymede and Lincoln Fair* (1866), *Footprints of Famous Men* (1853), and *Cressy and Poictiers* (1865). He was the first editor of *Every Boy's Magazine*.

Edgeworth, Maria (1 Jan. 1767—22 May 1849), novelist, was born at Black Bouston, Oxfordshire, daughter of Richard Lovell Edgeworth, an Irish landowner and M.P. Her father, who was himself a writer on education and mechanics, bestowed much attention on her training, and she assisted him in his literary labours, especially in *Practical Education* (1798), and the *Essay on Irish Bulls* (1802); she also wrote stories to amuse her father's large family by his four wives, with the last of whom she enjoyed a close friendship. She soon discovered that her strength lay in fiction, and from 1800, when her first novel, *Castle Rackrent*, appeared, until 1834, when her last, *Helen*, was published, she continued to produce a series of novels and tales characterized by ingenuity of invention, humour, and acute delineation of character, notwithstanding a tendency to be didactic, and the presence of a 'purpose' in most of her writings. It was the success of Miss Edgeworth in delineating Irish character that suggested to Sir Walter Scott the idea of rendering a similar service to Scotland. Miss Edgeworth, who had great practical ability, was able to render much aid during the Irish famine. In addition to the novels above mentioned, she wrote *Belinda* (1801), *Leonora* (1806), *Tales of Fashionable Life* (two series, 1809, 1812), *The Absentee* (1809), *Ormond* (1817), and completed her father's *Memoirs* (1820). She also published a number of books for or about children, including *Moral Tales* (1801), *Popular Tales* (1804), *Frank* (1822), and *Harry and Lucy* (1825); she was one of the first to portray children as real human beings.

Edmer, *see* **Eadmer.**

Edwards, Jonathan (5 Oct. 1703—22 March 1758), theologian, was born at East Windsor, Connecticut, son of a clergyman, and entered Yale at the age of 12. After two years of theological study he became a minister in New York and then in Northampton, Massachusetts, where he remained till 1750. Thereafter he worked as a missionary among the Indians, and in 1757 was appointed President of Princeton, but died of smallpox almost immediately afterwards. His creed of Calvinism tempered by philosophy had a great influence on American theology of his time, his most important works being

Concerning the Religious Affections (1746), *On the Freedom of the Will* (1754), and *On Original Sin* (1758).

Edwards, Richard (1523?—31 Oct. 1566), poet and playwright, born in Somerset and educated at Oxford, was entered at Lincoln's Inn but apparently never practised law. He became Master of the Children of the Chapel Royal, and had a high reputation for his comedies and interludes. His *Palamon and Arcite* was acted before Elizabeth at Oxford in 1566, when the stage fell and three persons were killed and five hurt, the play nevertheless proceeding. *Damon and Pythias* (1577), a comedy, is his only extant play. He compiled one of the early anthologies, *The Paradise of Dainty Devices* (1576), which contains many of his own poems.

Egan, Pierce (1772—3 Aug. 1849), sporting journalist, was born in London. He satirized the Prince Regent in *The Lives of Florizel and Perdita* (1814), but is best remembered by *Boxiana: or, Sketches of Modern Pugilism* (1818—24), and *Life in London: or the Day and Night Scenes of Jerry Hawthorn and his elegant friend, Corinthian Tom* (1821), which gives a picture of the sports and amusements of London in the days of the Regency, and was illustrated by George Cruikshank.

Egerton, George, *see* **Bright, Mary Chavelita.**

Eggleston, Edward (10 Dec. 1837—2 Sept. 1902), minister and novelist, was born at Vevay, Indiana, son of a lawyer. Ill health prevented his attending any college, but he became a Methodist minister and Bible agent and in 1866 took up journalism. His first novel, *The Hoosier Schoolmaster* (1871), was followed by *The Circuit Rider* (1874), *Roxy* (1878), *The Hoosier Schoolboy* (1882), and *The Graysons* (1888). He also wrote some historical works.

Eliot, George, *see* **Evans, Mary Ann.**

Eliot, Thomas Stearns, O.M. (26 Sept. 1888—   ), poet and critic, was born at St Louis, Missouri, of a distinguished Boston family which included the founder of Washington University. He was educated at Smith Academy and Harvard, where from 1909 to 1910 he edited the *Harvard Advocate*, subsequently going on to the Sorbonne and in 1914 to Merton College, Oxford. For a time he was a master at Highgate School, and after that worked in Lloyd's Bank. In 1915 his first important poem, 'The Love-Song of J. Alfred Prufrock' appeared in *Poetry*, and in the same year he married Vivienne Haigh-Wood. In 1917 he published *Prufrock and Other Observations* and a study of Ezra Pound, and from 1917 to 1919 he was assistant editor of the *Egoist*, the periodical of the Imagist movement. When the United States entered the First World War he tried to enlist in the Navy, but was rejected. Other publications of his early period were *Poems* (1919), and *The Sacred Wood* (1922), a volume of critical essays.

In 1922 *The Waste Land* won the 2,000-dollar *Dial* award and brought Eliot fame. An allusive and frequently obscure poem, it symbolized the disillusionment and disgust of the post-war generation. While some critics saw in it the reflection of contemporary chaos, others labelled it unintelligible, and one called it 'the greatest hoax of the century.'   But its influence on modern literature was enormous, and it was translated into French, German, and Spanish. In the same year Eliot established his own magazine, the *Criterion*, which lasted for seventeen years.   In 1925 appeared a collection of his work, *Poems 1909—25*, and in 1932 *Selected Essays 1917—32*. In the latter year, having now become naturalized as a British subject, he paid his first visit to America for eighteen years, and held the post of Professor of Poetry at Harvard.   His later poems include *Ash Wednesday* (1930), *Four Quartets* (1943), and the diverting children's book, *Old Possum's Book of Practical Cats* (1939).

His first serious play, *Sweeney Agonistes* (1932), described as 'an Aristophanic melodrama,' was followed by *The Rock* (1934), and he reached a high level of poetic drama with *Murder in the Cathedral* (1935), and *Family Reunion* (1939); *The Cocktail Party* (1949) is a comedy.   In 1948 he was awarded the Nobel Prize for Literature, and in the same year received the Order of Merit.   His critical work includes essays on Dryden, Milton, Andrew Marvell, and Dante, and his anthology *A Choice of Kipling's Verse* (1941) contains a brilliant introduction.   *The Idea of a Christian Society* (1940) embodies his religious views.   In one of his books he claimed that he was 'an Anglo-Catholic in religion, a classicist in literature, and a royalist in politics.'

Elizabeth, *see* **Russell, Elizabeth, Countess.**

Elizabeth I (7 Sept. 1533—24 March 1603), Queen of England, was born at Greenwich, daughter of Henry VIII and Anne Boleyn. Roger Ascham (q.v.) was her tutor, and for her time she was well read in Latin and Greek as well as French and Italian.   She translated Boethius, Plutarch's *De Curiositate*, and Horace's *De Arte Poetica*.   Her letters to James VI, published in 1849, show a creditable command of English, and she wrote a number of short poems.

Elliot, Jean *or* **Jane** (1727—29 March 1805), poetess, was born at Minto House in Teviotdale, daughter of Sir Gilbert Elliot, Bart., who was Lord Justice Clerk of Scotland.   She is remembered as the writer of the beautiful 'Flowers of the Forest,' a poetic lament for Flodden, but is not known to have written any other verse.   The poem, composed as the result of a bet with her brother Gilbert, was published anonymously as an old ballad, and Burns was one of the first to declare that it must be a contemporary work.

Elliott, Ebenezer (17 March 1781—1 Dec. 1849), poet, born at Masborough, Yorkshire, and descended from Border raiders, worked in his father's iron-foundry, and in 1821 took up the same business on his own account with success.   His *Vernal Walk* (1801) was written at the age of 16, and followed by *Night* (1818), but he is best known by his poems on behalf of the poor and oppressed, and especially for his denunciations of the Corn Laws, which gained for him the title of the Corn Law Rhymer.   His principal poems are *The Village Patriarch* (1829), *Corn Law Rhymes* (1831), and *Splendid Village* (1850).

Ellis, George (1753—10 April 1815), scholar and satirist, son of a West Indian planter, gained some fame by his *Poetical Tales by Sir Gregory Gander* (1778). He also had a hand in the *Rolliad*, a series of Whig satires which appeared about 1785. Changing sides, he afterwards contributed to the *Anti-Jacobin*. He accompanied Sir J. Harris on his mission to the Netherlands, and there collected materials for his *History of the Dutch Revolution* (1789). He edited *Specimens of the Early English Poets* (1790), and *Specimens of the Early English Romances* (1805), both works of scholarship. He was a friend of Scott, who dedicated the fifth canto of *Marmion* to him.

Ellis, Henry Havelock (2 Feb. 1859—8 July 1939), psychologist, was born at Croydon and named after Sir Henry Havelock, the hero of the Indian Mutiny, to whom his mother was related. When he was 7 he sailed round the world with his father, a sea captain, and at 16 he made a sea voyage to Australia for his health and stayed there for four years. In 1879 he returned to England and studied medicine at St Thomas's Hospital. In 1891 he married Edith Lees, and he had also a lifelong attachment to Olive Schreiner the novelist (q.v.), to whom he wrote passionate letters till her death in 1920. Between 1897 and 1910 he published six volumes of *Studies in the Psychology of Sex*, and a seventh was added in 1928. Others of his books on the same subject are *Man and Woman* (1894), *The Erotic Rights of Women* (1918), and *Little Essays of Love and Virtue* (1922, 1931). He also wrote three volumes of essays on art, *Impressions and Comments* (1914, 1921, 1924), and edited the 'Mermaid' series of English dramatists. His autobiography *My Life* appeared posthumously.

Ellwood, Thomas (Oct. 1639—1 March 1713), poet, was born at Crowell, Oxfordshire. A Quaker, he was imprisoned for his beliefs. He was a friend of Milton, who showed him the manuscript of *Paradise Lost*, on which he made the famous comment, 'Thou hast said much of "Paradise Lost," but what hast thou to say of "Paradise Found?"' Some months later Milton showed him the second poem, *Paradise Regained*, and said that its composition was due to the remark. Ellwood himself wrote a sacred poem, *Davideis* (1712), and an interesting autobiography.

Elphinstone, Mountstuart (6 Oct. 1779—20 Nov. 1859), statesman and historian, fourth son of the 11th Lord Elphinstone, was educated at Edinburgh, and entered the Bengal Civil Service in 1795. He was Governor of Bombay (1819—27), and prepared a code of laws for that Presidency. In 1829 he was offered, but declined, the position of Governor-General of India. He wrote a *History of India* (1841) and *The Rise of the British Power in the East* published in 1887.

Elton, Oliver (3 June 1861—4 June 1945), scholar, son of a clergyman, educated at Marlborough and Oxford, was a lecturer in English at Manchester, and from 1900 to 1925 Professor of English at Liverpool. His works include *The Augustan Ages* (1899), *Michael Drayton* (1905), three *Surveys of English Literature* (1912, 1920, 1928), which together cover the period between 1730 and 1880,

The English Muse (1933), *Essays and Addresses* (1939), and a number of translations.   He was a Fellow of the British Academy.

Elwin, Whitwell (26 Feb. 1816—1 Jan. 1900), clergyman and critic, was born at Thurning, Norfolk, studied at Cambridge, and took orders; from 1849 till his death he was rector of Boston.   He was an important contributor to the *Quarterly Review*, of which he became editor in 1853.   He undertook to complete Croker's edition of Pope, and brought out 5 volumes, when he dropped it, leaving it to be finished by W. J. Courthope (q.v.).

Elyot, Sir Thomas (1490?—20 March 1546), diplomat, doctor, and writer, was born in Wiltshire, son of a judge.   He became Clerk of the King's Council and held many diplomatic appointments.   He wrote *The Book Named the Governor* (1531), a treatise on education, in which he advocated gentler treatment of schoolboys; *The Castle of Health* (1534), a medical work; and *A Defence of Good Women* (1545). He also in 1538 published the first Latin-English dictionary, and made various translations which did much to popularize the classics.

Emerson, Ralph Waldo (25 May 1803—27 April 1882), essayist, poet, philosopher, was born at Boston.   His father, a minister, died when the boy was 8, leaving his widow with six children to keep, but by taking in boarders she was able to give her sons a good education, four of them going to Harvard.   Emerson was not particularly distinguished there, and later had poor health; he was for a time a schoolmaster before studying for the ministry, to which he was admitted without having to pass the examination, on the ground that his eyes were weak.   In 1829 he became pastor of a Unitarian church, and in the same year married Ellen Louisa Tucker.   Two years later his wife died at the age of 19, and shortly afterwards Emerson suffered further bereavement in the deaths of his two brothers Edward and Charles.   In 1832 he resigned from his pastorate, ostensibly because of a disagreement about the celebration of the sacrament, but in reality because his religious views had changed, and he now felt that 'the day of formal religion was past.'   At this time he made his first visit to Europe; in England he met Landor, Coleridge, and Wordsworth, and commenced a lifelong friendship with Carlyle.

Returning to Boston in 1833, he began a course of lecturing, which for the rest of his life was the main source of his livelihood and took him all over America.   In 1853 he married Lydia Jackson and settled at Concord, which was his home till his death.   His first book, *Nature*, appeared in 1834, and in 1837 he delivered, as the Phi Beta Kappa address at Harvard, his famous essay on *The American Scholar*.   His influence as a philosopher was now extending rapidly. In 1836 the Transcendental Club was formed for the discussion of the new movement, and in 1840 was founded its periodical, the *Dial*, to which Emerson was a frequent contributor.   Meanwhile his lectures were published with the title *Essays* in two series (1836, 1841).   In 1847 he paid a second visit to England, delivering a course of lectures on *Representative Men* (1850) which classes itself with Carlyle's *Heroes and Hero-Worship*.   This trip also furnished him with materials for his book *English Traits* (1856), and in 1860 he published *The Conduct of Life*. Honours were now showered on him. In 1866 he was made an LL.D. of Harvard. In 1872 he made his third visit to Europe, and in 1874 he was nominated for the Lord Rectorship of Glasgow University; though defeated by Disraeli he regarded the honour as 'the fairest laurel that had ever fallen on him.' During his last years he suffered from loss of memory and passed into a serene senility.

Emerson's first volume of poems appeared in 1846, the second in 1867, his most famous pieces being 'The Problem,' 'The Snow-Storm,' 'The Rhodora,' the 'Concord Hymn,' 'Brahma,' and 'Days.' But even in his verse he is rather a thinker than a singer. He stands out in American literature as the greatest of the 'transcendentalist' group which included Thoreau and Hawthorne. In philosophy he was basically an idealist, seeking to combine Platonism with Christianity as a practical creed. But he cannot be said to have formulated any systematic doctrine, which indeed would have been the negation of his own belief that the source of religious authority should be within and not without, and that the soul of each man must be the supreme judge for himself in spiritual matters. He wrote down the intuitions and suggestions of the moment, indifferent as to whether these harmonized with his previous statements, and his mysticism is the mysticism of a glorified common sense. 'Hitch your wagon to a star' is one of the inspired precepts which mark him as the most stimulating and influential writer in American literature.

Erceldoune, Thomas of *or* **Thomas the Rhymer** *or* **Thomas Learmont** (1220?—1297?), seer and poet, lived at Erceldoune, now Earlston, in Berwickshire. A number of prophetic sayings were attributed to him, from which he got the name of True Thomas. A semilegendary figure like the English Merlin, he was supposed to have been carried off to Elfland by the fairies but allowed to revisit the earth for a time. He was the reputed author of a poem on the Tristram legend.

Erigena *or* **Scotus, John** (810?—870?), philosopher, was born in Ireland, and later resided at the court of Charles the Bald in France, where he had charge of the Palatine Academy. An early schoolman, he was one of the originators of mystical thought in the Middle Ages. His great work *De Divisione Naturae* (On the Division of Nature), in which he sought to reconcile reason with authority, was condemned by the Church. He also made a number of translations from the Alexandrian philosophers. According to one tradition he became Abbot of Malmesbury and was stabbed to death with their pens by his scholars.

Erskine, Ralph (15 March 1685—6 Nov. 1752), clergyman and poet, was born at Monilaws, Northumberland, son of a Covenanting minister, and educated at Edinburgh. He became minister of Dunfermline, and, with his brother Ebenezer, was involved in the controversies in the Church of Scotland, which led to the founding of the Secession Church in 1736. He has a place in literature as the writer of devotional works, especially his *Gospel Sonnets*, of which 25 editions had appeared by 1797, and *Scripture Songs* (1754).

Erskine, Thomas (1788—20 March 1870), theologian, was educated at Edinburgh High School and University. He was called to the Bar in 1810, but ceased to practise after succeeding, on his brother's death, to the estate of Linlathen. He devoted himself largely to the study of theology, and published various works, including *The Internal Evidence for the Truth of Revealed Religion* (1820), *Unconditional Freeness of the Gospel* (1828), and *The Spiritual Order* (1871). His *Letters* were edited by Dr W. Hanna (1877—8).

Ervine, St John Greer (28 Dec. 1883—   ), playwright and dramatic critic, was born in Belfast but moved to Dublin as a young man and was associated with the Abbey Theatre, becoming its manager in 1915. His best-known plays of this period are *Jane Clegg* (1911), and *John Ferguson* (1914). In the First World War he served with the Dublin Fusiliers and lost a leg. After the war he settled in London and wrote *Mary, Mary, Quite Contrary* (1923), and *The First Mrs Fraser* (1931) a highly successful comedy; others were *People of Our Class* (1934), *Robert's Wife* (1937), *Friends and Relations* (1940), and *Private Enterprise* (1947). Among his novels are *Changing Winds* (1917), *The Wayward Man* (1927), and *Sophia* (1941), and he also wrote biographies of General William Booth and Viscount Craigavon, as well as several books on theatre craft. Dramatic critic for various newspapers, from 1933 to 1936 he was Professor of Dramatic Literature for the Royal Society of Literature, of which he was made a Fellow, and he held honorary degrees of St Andrews and Belfast.

Etherege *or* **Etheredge, Sir George** (1635?—1691), Restoration wit and dramatist, was at Cambridge, travelled, read a little law, became a man-about-town, the companion of Sedley, Rochester, and their set, and held some diplomatic posts. He originated Restoration drama with three lively comedies, *Love in a Tub* (1664), *She would if she Could* (1668), and *The Man of Mode* (1676), all characterized by the grossness of the period. He was sent on a mission to Ratisbon, where he broke his neck when lighting his guests downstairs after a drinking bout. His *Letter-Book* was published in 1928.

Eusden, Laurence (baptized 6 Sept. 1688, died 27 Sept. 1730), Poet Laureate, a son of the rector of Spofforth, Yorkshire, was educated at St Peter's School, York, and Trinity College, Cambridge, of which he became a Fellow. In 1717 he wrote a flattering poem to celebrate the marriage of the Duke of Newcastle, and the Duke, who as Lord Chamberlain had the nomination of the Poet Laureate, appointed him to this post in succession to Nicholas Rowe (q.v.). The choice caused a good deal of ridicule, for Eusden was quite unworthy of the distinction. About 1725 he took orders, was chaplain to Lord Willoughby de Broke, and became rector of Coningsby in Lincolnshire. In Pope's *Dunciad* he is satirized as a drunken parson. He wrote a number of metrical panegyrics and some translations from Statius and Claudian which are better than his original work, and made some contributions to the *Spectator*.

Evans, Abel (Feb. 1679—18 Oct. 1737), clergyman and epigrammatist, was educated at Merchant Taylors' and Oxford, where he took orders in 1700 and obtained a D.D., becoming rector of Cheam in 1725. In 1710 he published *The Apparition*, a theological satire, and in 1713 a poetical epistle entitled *Vertumnus*. An intimate friend of Pope, he enjoyed a reputation for his epigrams, of which the best-known is the epitaph on Sir John Vanbrugh.

Evans, Sir Arthur John (8 July 1851—11 July 1941), archaeologist, was born at Nash Mills, Hertfordshire, son of Sir John Evans, also an archaeologist, and was educated at Harrow, Oxford, and Göttingen, afterwards travelling in the Balkans and studying folk culture. From 1884 to 1908 he was Keeper of the Ashmolean Museum, Oxford. Engaged in archaeological work in Crete from 1893 onwards, he discovered the early Minoan civilization, thus revolutionizing ideas of ancient Mediterranean history. After excavating the Minoan palace at Knossos he gave the site to the British School at Athens. In 1910 he was appointed Professor of Prehistoric Archaeology at Oxford. He held many distinctions and awards, being knighted in 1911. His works include *Scripta Minoa* (1909) and *The Palace of Minos* (1922—35).

Evans, Caradoc (31 Dec. 1878—11 Jan. 1945), novelist, was born at Pantycroy, Llandyssul, Wales, son of an estate agent, and educated at Rhydlewis board school, Cardiganshire, and the Working Men's College, London. Apprenticed to a draper in Carmarthen at 14, he was employed in this business for twelve years. Moving first to Cardiff, then London, he entered journalism, perfecting his English by study of the Bible, and became editor of *T. P.'s Weekly*. In 1933 he married the Countess Barcynska, an Englishwoman whose maiden name was Jervis and who wrote novels as Oliver Sandys. His books consist largely of vitriolic satires on his own land and people. His first collection of short stories, *My People: Stories of the Peasantry of West Wales* (1915) was suppressed in Wales; other collections are *Capel Sion* (1916), *My Neighbours: Stories of the London Welsh* (1919), and *Pilgrims in a Foreign Land* (1942). His best-known novels are *Nothing to Pay* (1930), *This Way to Heaven* (1933), *Wasps* (1934), and *Morgan Bible* (1943). When his play *Taffy* was produced in London in 1925 riots occurred. His life was written by his wife.

Evans, Mary Ann *or* **Marian** (22 Nov. 1819—22 Dec. 1880), novelist who wrote under the name George Eliot, was born at Arbury Farm, near Nuneaton, Warwickshire, daughter of an estate agent. Her education was completed at a school in Coventry, and after the death of her mother in 1836, and the marriage of her elder sister, she kept house for her father until his death in 1849. In 1841 they gave up their house in the country, and went to live in Coventry. Here she made the acquaintance of Charles Bray, a writer on phrenology, and his brother-in-law Charles Hennell, a rationalistic writer on the origin of Christianity, whose influence led her to renounce the narrow religious views in which she had been brought up. In 1846 she engaged in her first literary work, the completion of a translation begun by Mrs Hennell of Strauss's *Life of Jesus*. On her father's death she went abroad with the Brays, and, on her return in 1850, began to write for the *Westminster Review*, of which from 1851 to 1853 she was assistant-editor. There she was much thrown into the society of Herbert Spencer and George Henry Lewes (q.v.), with the latter of whom in 1854 she entered into an irregular union which lasted until his death. In the same year she translated Feuerbach's *Essence of Christianity*, the only one of her writings to which she attached her real name.

She was nearly 40 years of age when she discovered the true nature of her genius; for it was not until 1857 that 'The Sad Fortunes of the Rev. Amos Barton' appeared in *Blackwood's Magazine*, and showed that a new writer of singular power had arisen. It was followed by 'Mr Gilfil's Love Story,' and 'Janet's Repentance,' all three being reprinted as *Scenes from Clerical Life* (1857). *Adam Bede* was published in 1859, *The Mill on the Floss*, in its earlier chapters largely autobiographical, in 1860, *Silas Marner*, perhaps the most artistically constructed of her books, in 1861. In 1860 and 1861 she visited Florence with a view to preparing herself for her next work, *Romola*, a tale of the times of Savonarola, which appeared in 1863, in the *Cornhill Magazine*. *Felix Holt the Radical* followed in 1866. Miss Evans now for a time abandoned novel-writing and took to poetry, and between 1868 and 1871 produced *The Spanish Gipsy*, *Agatha*, *The Legend of Jubal*, and *Armgart*. These poems, though containing much fine work, did not add to her reputation, and in fact in writing them she had departed from her true vocation. Accordingly, she returned to fiction, and in *Middlemarch*, which appeared in parts in 1871—2, she was by many considered to have produced her greatest work. *Daniel Deronda*, which came out in 1874—6, was greatly inferior, and it was her last novel. In 1878 she published *The Impressions of Theophrastus Such*, a collection of miscellaneous essays. In the same year Lewes died, an event which plunged her into melancholy, which was, however, alleviated by the kindness of John Cross, who had been the intimate friend of both Lewes and herself, and whom she married in March 1880. The union was a short one, being terminated by her death in the same year. Cross subsequently wrote her biography.

George Eliot will probably always retain a high place among writers of fiction. Her great power lies in the minute painting of character, chiefly among the lower middle classes, shopkeepers, tradesmen, and country folk of the Midlands, into whose thoughts and feelings she had an insight almost like divination, and of whose modes of expression she was complete mistress. Her general view of life is pessimistic, relieved by a power of seizing the humorous elements in human stupidity and ill-doing. There is also, however, much seriousness in her treatment of the phases of life upon which she touches, and few writers have brought out with greater power the hardening and degrading effects of continuance in evil courses, or the inevitable and irretrievable consequences of a wrong act. Her descriptions of rural scenes have a singular charm.

Evelyn, John (31 Oct. 1620—27 Feb. 1706), diarist, was born at

Wotton, Surrey, where his grandfather had the first gunpowder mills in the country. In 1637 he went to Balliol College, Oxford, having already been admitted as a student at the Inner Temple. He travelled much on the Continent, seeing all that was best worth seeing in the way of galleries and collections, both public and private, of which he has given an interesting account in his *Diary*. He was all his life a staunch Royalist, and joined the King as a volunteer in 1642, but soon after repaired again to the Continent. From 1652 he was at home, settled at Sayes Court, near Deptford, where his gardens were famous. After the Restoration he was employed in various matters by the Government, but his lofty and pure character was constantly offended by the manners of the Court. In addition to his *Diary*, kept from 1624 to 1706, and full of interesting details of public and private events, he wrote upon such subjects as sculpture, in *Sculptura* (1662); plantations, in *Sylva* (1664); gardening in the unpublished *Elysium Britannicum*; architecture; prevention of smoke in London; engraving; and was one of the founders of the Royal Society, of which he was for a time secretary.

Ewing, Juliana Horatia (3 Aug. 1841—13 May 1885), writer of books for children, was born at Ecclesfield, Yorkshire, where her father was vicar; all her life she was delicate. Her first book, *Melchior's Dream*, was published in 1862. In 1865 her mother, Margaret Gatty (q.v.) started *Aunt Judy's Magazine*, in which many of Juliana's best stories appeared, the first being *Mrs Overtheway's Remembrances*. In 1867 she married Major Alexander Ewing and went with him to Fredericton, New Brunswick, but they returned two years later and she continued with her children's books, of which the favourites were *A Flat Iron for a Farthing* (1872), *Lob Lie-by-the-Fire* (1874), *Six to Sixteen* (1875), *Jan of the Windmill* (1876), *Jackanapes* (1883), and *The Story of a Short Life* (1885). Her stories are still popular, though they are rather religious and sentimental for modern tastes.

F

Faber, Frederick William (28 June 1814—26 Sept. 1863), clergyman and hymn-writer, was born at Calverley, Yorkshire, and educated at Harrow and Oxford, where he won the Newdigate Prize for Poetry and came under the influence of Newman, whom he followed into the Church of Rome. Created a D.D. by the Pope, he wrote various theological treatises, but is remembered best for his hymns, which include 'The Pilgrims of the Night,' and other favourites.

Fabyan, Robert (died 28 Feb. 1535), chronicler, was a clothier in London, of which he became an alderman and sheriff. He kept a diary of notable events, which he expanded into a chronicle, which he entitled, *The Concordance of Histories*. It covers the period from the arrival of Brutus in England to the death of Henry VII, and deals mainly with the affairs of London. It was not printed until 1515, when it appeared under the title of *The New Chronicles of England and France*.

Fair, A. A., *see* **Gardner, Erle Stanley.**

Fairfax, Edward (born 1580, buried 27 Jan. 1635), translator, son of Sir Thomas Fairfax, lived a studious and retired life at Fuystone, near Knaresborough. His translation of Tasso's *Jerusalem Delivered* (1600), on which his fame is founded, is one of the comparatively few translations which in themselves are literature, and was highly praised by Dryden and Waller. The first edition appeared in 1600, and was dedicated to Queen Elizabeth. Fairfax also wrote *A Discourse of Witchcraft* (1621).

Fairfield, Dame Cicily Isabel (25 Dec. 1892—   ), novelist and critic who wrote under the name Rebecca West, was born in Kerry, but on the death of her father the family moved to Edinburgh, where she was educated at George Watson's Ladies' College. She then studied at a London dramatic academy, was on the stage for a short time, and adopted the pseudonym Rebecca West from the heroine of Ibsen's *Rosmersholm*, one of the parts she had played. In 1917 she was on the staff of the *Clarion*, and contributed to many other periodicals. In 1930 she married Henry Maxwell Andrews, a banker, and they settled in Buckinghamshire. Her first book was a study of Henry James (1916), and in 1930 she wrote *D. H. Lawrence, an Elegy*. *Black Lamb and Grey Falcon* (1941) is the record of a trip she made through Jugoslavia in 1937. Her novels include *The Return of the Soldier* (1918), *The Judge* (1922), *Harriet Hume* (1929), *The Harsh Voice* (1936), *The Thinking Reed* (1936), and *The Fountain Overflows* (1957). She also wrote two books about the war trials, *The Meaning of Treason* (1949) and *A Train of Powder* (1955). In 1949 she was made a C.B.E., and in 1959 a D.B.E.

Fairless, Michael, *see* **Barber, Margaret.**

Falconer, William (11 Feb. 1732—Dec. 1769), poet, born in

Edinburgh, son of a barber, became a sailor, and was thus thoroughly competent to describe the management of the storm-tossed vessel, the career and fate of which are pictured in his poem, *The Shipwreck* (1762), a work of genuine, though unequal, talent. The efforts which Falconer made to improve the poem in the successive editions which followed the first were not entirely successful, but the work gained for him the patronage of the Duke of York, through whose influence he obtained the position of purser on various warships; he met his death on the frigate *Aurora*, which foundered near Capetown. Falconer also wrote *The Demagogue* (1764), a political satire, and compiled the *Universal Marine Dictionary* (1769).

Falkner, John Meade (8 May 1858—22 July 1932), novelist, was born at Manningford Bruce, Wiltshire, son of a clergyman, and educated at Marlborough and Hertford College, Oxford. He became secretary to the board of Armstrong Whitworth, the great armaments firm, and eventually rose to be chairman. His holidays were spent walking in Oxfordshire and Berkshire, and he compiled handbooks to these counties. Of his novels the most popular was *Moonfleet* (1898), an adventure story; others are *The Lost Stradivarius* (1895) and *The Nebuly Coat* (1903).

Falkner, William Harrison, *see* **Faulkner.**

Fanshawe, Catherine Maria (6 July 1765—17 April 1834), painter and poetess, was born at Shabden in Surrey, but spent most of her life in Richmond. Deformed and a semi-invalid, she was nevertheless a gifted water-colour artist. Her poems were printed for private circulation in 1865, but the only piece widely remembered is the enigma on the letter H beginning ' 'Twas whispered in heaven, 'twas muttered in hell,' at one time ascribed to Lord Byron.

Fanshawe, Sir Richard (baptized 12 June 1608, died 26 June 1666), diplomat, translator, and poet, born at Ware Park, Hertfordshire, and educated at Cambridge, travelled on the Continent, and when the Civil War broke out sided with the King. He acted as Latin Secretary to Charles II when in Holland. After the Restoration he held various appointments, and was Ambassador to Portugal and Spain successively. He translated parts of Virgil and Horace, *The Lusiad* of Camoens (1655), and Guarini's *Pastor Fido* (1658).

Faraday, Michael (22 Sept 1791—25 Aug. 1867), physicist, was born at Newington Butts, Surrey, son of a blacksmith, and apprenticed to a bookbinder. He early showed a taste for chemistry, and attended the lectures of Sir H. Davy (q.v.), by whom he was, in 1813, appointed his chemical assistant in the Royal Institution. He became one of the greatest of British discoverers and popularizers of science, his discoveries being chiefly in the department of electro-magnetism. He had an unusual power of making difficult subjects clearly understood. Among his writings are *History of the Progress of Electro-Magnetism* (1821), *Experimental Researches in Electricity* (1839—55), *The Chemical History of a Candle* (1861), and *The Various Forces in Nature*.

Farjeon, Herbert (5 March 1887—3 May 1945), critic and playwright, was born in London, son of a novelist, and educated at University College School. In 1907 he joined the Manchester staff of the *Daily Mail*, and was subsequently dramatic critic for a large number of papers in succession, including the *Sunday Pictorial*, *Sphere*, and *Graphic*. His plays include *Friends* (1917), *Picnic* (1927), *Many Happy Returns* (1928), *Why Not To-Night?* (1934), *Spread It Abroad* (1936), *Nine Sharp* (1938), *Big Top* (1942), and (in collaboration with his sister Eleanor) *The Two Bouquets* (1936) and *The Glass Slipper* (1944). They also worked jointly in writing *Kings and Queens* (1932), a child's rhyming history of England.

Farmer, Richard (28 Aug. 1735—8 Sept. 1797), scholar, born at Leicester, son of a wealthy maltster, was educated at Cambridge, where he ultimately became Master of Emanuel College. He wrote an *Essay on the Learning of Shakespeare* (1767), in which he maintained that Shakespeare's knowledge of the classics was through translations, the errors of which he reproduced. It is a production of great ability. Farmer was a clergyman, a D.D., and a prebendary of St Paul's.

Farnborough, Baron, *see* May, Sir Thomas E.

Farnol, John Jeffrey (10 Feb. 1878—9 Aug. 1952), novelist, was born at Aston, Warwickshire, and educated privately. He began to write at the age of 19, though his parents had other plans and sent him first as an apprentice in a brass foundry and then to the Westminster School of Art. Having married an American girl, he went to New York, worked there as a scene painter, and wrote *The Broad Highway* (1910), which after initial rejections, became so successful that he was able to return to England and make writing his career. Most of his books are historical romances of the 'cloak and dagger' school, among the best-known being *The Amateur Gentleman* (1913), *The Chronicles of the Imp* (1915), *Our Admirable Betty* (1918), *The Geste of Duke Jocelyn* (1919), *Peregrine's Progress* (1922), *Charmian*, *Lady Vibàrt* (1932), and *The Glad Summer* (1951).

Farquhar, George (1678—29 April 1707), dramatist, born at Londonderry, son of a clergyman, was a sizar at Trinity College, Dublin. Intended for the Church, he became an actor instead, but met with no success, and in 1698 moved to London, where he started writing comedies, the earliest, *Love and a Bottle* (1698), *The Constant Couple* (1699), and *Sir Harry Wildair* (1701), being of the licentious type common in the Restoration period. *The Inconstant*, and *The Twin Rivals* (1702) have more human feeling. In 1700 he obtained a commission in the militia and served in Holland for a short time, afterwards using his army experiences for his last and best plays,. *The Recruiting Officer* (1706) and *The Beaux' Stratagem* (1707), both of which are marked by a good-humoured realism very different from the artificiality and cynicism of Restoration Comedy, of which he is reckoned the last representative. Unlucky in all his ventures, Farquhar married in 1703 a penniless lady who secured him as husband by pretending to be an heiress, and died in poverty before he was 30.

Farrar, Frederic William (7 Aug. 1831—22 March 1903), clergyman and novelist, was born in Bombay, where his father was a missionary. Brought to England at an early age, he was educated at King William's College, Isle of Man, where he became head of the school, T. E. Brown (q.v.) being one of his classmates. From there he went on to London University and Cambridge, then became a master first at Marlborough in 1854 and subsequently at Harrow. In 1858 appeared his famous school story *Eric, or Little By Little*, which is partly based on his own schooldays. Published a year after the classic *Tom Brown's Schooldays*, it ran through 36 editions in Farrar's lifetime. *Julian Home* (1859) drew on his Cambridge experiences, and *St Winifred's, or The World of School* (1862) was only a little less popular than *Eric*. In 1869 Farrar was appointed chaplain to Queen Victoria, and in 1871 became headmaster of Marlborough, where he wrote his *Life of Christ* (1874), which was translated into all the principal European languages, his *Life of St Paul* (1879), and *Early Days of Christianity* (1882). In 1877 he had raised a storm of criticism by a noteworthy series of sermons on eternal punishment, but was nevertheless made Archdeacon of Westminster in 1883 and Dean of Canterbury in 1895.

Farrell, James Thomas (27 Feb. 1904—   ), novelist, born in Chicago, was educated at St Cyril High School and Chicago University. He tried various jobs, working in a shoe store, a petrol station, a cigar company, a funeral undertaker's, and as a reporter on a newspaper. In 1936 he was awarded a Guggenheim Fellowship, and in the following year won the 2,500 dollar Book-of-the-Month Club prize for *Studs Lonigan*, a trilogy made up of *Young Lonigan* (1932), *The Young Manhood of Studs Lonigan* (1934), and *Judgment Day* (1935), all novels of the Chicago slums. He aimed to portray American life frankly as he saw it, and some of his books are so unpleasantly realist that the term 'emetic' has been applied to them. One of his early novels was the subject of a censorship trial, but the charges were dismissed. Others of his works are *Gas House McGinty* (1933), *Father and Son* (1940), *Ellen Rogers* (1941), *My Days of Anger* (1943), *The Life Adventurous* (1947), *The Road Between* (1949), *This Man and This Woman* (1951), and *The Face of Time* (1953).

Faulkner *or* **Falkner, William Harrison** (25 Sept. 1897—   ), novelist, was born at New Albany and educated at the University of Mississippi, Oxford, of which his father was treasurer. In the First World War he joined the Canadian Air Force and was wounded in France. After working for a time as a house painter he drifted to New Orleans, where he became a friend of Sherwood Anderson (q.v.), and wrote *Soldier's Pay* (1926), and *Mosquitoes* (1927). In 1929 he published *The Sound and the Fury*, first of his novels to be written in the 'stream of consciousness' style, which describes thoughts and reactions instead of actual happenings; it and *As I Lay Dying* (1930) made his reputation, though *Sanctuary* (1931), a horror story, was the first of his books to become really popular. *Sartoris* (1929) was the first of a series of novels dealing with a single family who form the centre-piece of a saga of Southern decadence; the action takes place in Yoknapatawpha County, Mississippi, and the county town Jefferson can be identified with Oxford.   In 1939 Faulkner won first prize in the O. Henry Memorial Award, and in 1950 he was awarded the Nobel Prize for Literature. Among his later novels are *Light in August* (1932), *Absalom, Absalom!* (1936), *The Wild Palms* (1939), *The Hamlet* (1940), *Intruder in the Dust* (1948), and *Requiem for a Nun* (1952).   *Idyll in the Desert* (1931), *Dr Martino* (1934), and *Go Down, Moses* (1942) are collections of short stories.   Grotesque and often obscure, his work has been described as in the tradition of Poe.

Fausset, Hugh I'Anson (16 June 1895—   ), critic, was born at Killington, Westmorland, son of a clergyman and grandson of a famous Biblical scholar.   His mother died a few days after his birth and he was brought up with excessive strictness by his father.   Educated at Sedbergh and Cambridge, he worked as critic and reviewer, and published penetrating studies of *Keats* (1922), *Tennyson* (1923), *Donne* (1924), *Coleridge* (1926), *Tolstoi* (1928), *Wordsworth* (1933), and *Whitman* (1942).   He was also the author of two volumes of poems and *A Modern Prelude* (1933), which is autobiographical.

Fawcett, Henry (26 Aug. 1833—6 Nov. 1884), statesman and economist, was born at Salisbury, where his father, a draper, had been mayor, and educated at King's College School, London, and Cambridge.   In 1858 he was blinded by a shooting accident, in spite of which he continued to prosecute his studies, especially in economics, and in 1863 published his *Manual of Political Economy*, becoming in the same year Professor of Political Economy in Cambridge.   Two years later he was returned as M.P. for Brighton and in 1880 he was appointed Postmaster-General, in which office he approved himself a capable administrator.   His works include *The Economic Position of the British Labourer* (1871) and *Protection and Free Trade* (1878).

Fawkes, Francis (baptized 4 April 1721, died 26 Aug. 1777), clergyman and poet, was born at Warmsworth, near Doncaster, where his father was rector, and educated at Cambridge, after which he took orders.   He translated Anacreon, Sappho, and other classics, modernized parts of the poems of Gavin Douglas, and was the author of two poems, *Bramham Park* (1745), and *Partridge Shooting* (1767). He also wrote 'The Brown Jug,' a very popular song.

Felltham, Owen (1602?—1668), essayist, lived in Suffolk.   At the age of 18 he published the first version of his book *Resolves, Divine, Moral, and Political*, containing 146 short essays.   It had great popularity in its day.   Felltham was for a time in the household of the Earl of Thomond as chaplain or secretary, and published in 1652 *A Brief Character of the Low Countries*.

Fenn, George Manville (3 Jan. 1831—26 Aug. 1909), novelist, born in Pimlico, was educated at Battersea Training College for Teachers, and became a schoolmaster in Lincolnshire, then a private tutor, then a printer. In 1862 he started a verse magazine, *Modern Metre*, which ran for six months. His first published story was accepted by Dickens for the periodical *All the Year Round* in 1864, and in 1867 he was appointed editor of *Cassell's Magazine*. He wrote more than 170 books, the most successful being his stories for boys, of which the first was *Hollowdell Grange* (1867). Others are *In Honour's Cause* (1896), *Fix Bay'nets* (1899), *Nat the Naturalist* (1899), *Dick o' the Fens* (1905), and *Shoulder Arms!* (1905). His last book, written in 1907, was a memoir of his friend G. A. Henty (q.v.).

Fenton, Elijah (20 May 1682—August 1730), poet and translator, was born at Shelton, near Newcastle-under-Lyme, the eleventh child of an attorney. Educated at Cambridge, for a time he acted as secretary to the Earl of Orrery in Flanders, and was then Master of Sevenoaks Grammar School. In 1707 he published a book of poems. He is best known, however, as the assistant of Pope in his translation of the *Odyssey*, of which he Englished the first, fourth, nineteenth, and twentieth books, catching the manner of his master so completely that it is hardly possible to distinguish between them; while thus engaged he published in 1723 a successful tragedy *Mariamne*. His latest contributions to literature were a *Life of Milton*, and an edition of Waller's poems (1729).

Ferber, Edna (15 Aug. 1887—   ), novelist, was born at Kalamazoo, Michigan, daughter of a shopkeeper, but spent her girlhood at Appleton, Wisconsin, to which they removed. Her father became blind, so she had to start working and became a reporter. Her first novel, *Dawn O'Hara* (1911) was followed by *The Girls* (1921), and she became a best-seller with *So Big*, which won the Pulitzer Prize in 1925. *Show Boat* (1926), which was made a musical play, a film, and a radio play, was followed by *Cimarron* (1929), *Come and Get It* (1935), *Saratoga Trunk* (1941), *Great Son* (1945), and *Giant* (1952). She also wrote a series of short stories about business women, and collaborated with George S. Kaufman (q.v.) in a number of plays, including *Dinner at Eight* (1932), *Stage Door* (1938), and *The Land is Bright* (1941). *A Peculiar Treasure* (1939) is auto-biographical. Though she lived latterly in New York, her outlook was mid-Western.

Ferguson, Adam (20 June 1723—22 Feb. 1816), philosopher and historian, son of the parish minister of Logierait, Perthshire, studied at St Andrews and Edinburgh University, in the latter of which he was successively Professor of Mathematics and of Moral Philosophy (1764—85). As a young man he was chaplain to the 42nd Regiment, and was present at the Battle of Fontenoy. In 1757 he was made Keeper of the Advocates' Library. Ferguson's principal works are *Essays on the History of Civil Society* (1765), *Institutes of Moral Philosophy* (1769), *History of the Progress and Termination of the Roman Republic* (1782), and *Principles of Moral and Political Science* (1792). He spent his later years at St Andrews, where he died at the age of 92, and was buried in the old cathedral, his epitaph being written by Sir Walter Scott, who was his intimate friend.

Ferguson, Sir Samuel (10 March 1810—9 Aug. 1886), poet and

I

antiquary, born at Belfast, the son of parents of Scottish extraction, was educated at Trinity College, Dublin, from which he received in 1865 the honorary degree of LL.D. He practised with success as a barrister, became Q.C. in 1859, and Deputy Keeper of the Irish Records in 1867, an appointment in which he gave valuable service, for which he was knighted in 1878. He was a contributor to *Blackwood's Magazine*, in which appeared his best known poem, 'The Forging of the Anchor,' and was one of the chief promoters of the Gaelic revival in Irish literature. His collected poems appeared under the title of *Lays of the Western Gael* (1865). *Congal, an Epic Poem* was published in 1872, and his prose tales posthumously (1887), as *Hibernian Nights' Entertainments*. His principal antiquarian work was *Ogham Inscriptions in Ireland, Wales, and Scotland* (1887).

Fergusson, James (22 Jan. 1808—9 Jan. 1886), writer on architecture, born at Ayr, son of a doctor, was engaged in commercial pursuits in India, where he became interested in the architecture of the country, and published his first work, *Picturesque Illustrations of Ancient Architecture in Hindustan* (1840), which was followed by *An Historical Inquiry into the True Principles of Beauty in Art* (1849), and *A History of Architecture in all Countries from the Earliest Times to the Present Day* (1865—67). He also wrote *Fire and Serpent Worship* (1869), and a book on the use of earthworks in fortification.

Fergusson, Robert (5 Sept. 1750—16 Oct. 1774), poet, was born in Edinburgh, son of a clerk, and educated at Edinburgh and Dundee High Schools and St Andrews University. Poverty and ill health compelled him to give up his plans of being a minister, and he became a lawyer's clerk in Edinburgh. From 1771 to 1773 he contributed poems to Ruddiman's *Weekly Magazine*, but unhappily started drinking to excess; a fall was followed by illness which turned to insanity and he finally died in an asylum and is buried in Canongate churchyard. His poems, a volume of which appeared in 1773, had a great influence on Burns. Fergusson began by writing English verse, but found his true vein in Scots poetry. Realist and humorist, in 'The Daft Days,' 'Hallow-fair,' and 'Leith Races' he depicts with vividness and gusto the rough hearty life of his native city, so that he has been termed 'the laureate of Auld Reekie.' His odes 'To the Bee' and 'To the Gowdspink' (goldfinch) show the feeling for country scenes which was to be such a feature of Burns's poetry, while his 'Farmer's Ingle' foreshadows 'The Cotter's Saturday Night.'

Ferriar, John (21 Nov. 1761—4 Feb. 1815), doctor and critic, was born at Oxnam near Jedburgh, son of a minister, and studied medicine at Edinburgh. At Manchester, where he became doctor to the Infirmary, he campaigned for better sanitary laws. His best-known literary works are *Illustrations of Sterne* (1798), and a poem, *The Bibliomania* (1809).

Ferrier, James Frederick (16 June 1808—11 June 1864), metaphysician, was born in Edinburgh. His father, a writer to the signet, was a brother of Susan Ferrier (q.v.), and his mother was a sister of

John Wilson (q.v.), better known by his pseudonym of Christopher North. Educated at Edinburgh High School and University and Oxford, Ferrier was called to the Scottish Bar in 1832, but devoted himself to literature and philosophy. In 1842 he was appointed Professor of History in Edinburgh, and in 1845 translated to the Chair of Moral Philosophy and Political Economy at St Andrews. He published in 1854 *Institutes of Metaphysics*, and edited the collected works of his father-in-law, Professor Wilson.

Ferrier, Susan Edmonstoune (17 Sept 1782—5 Nov. 1854), novelist, was the youngest of ten children of James Ferrier, one of the principal clerks of the Court of Session. In this office he was the colleague of Sir Walter Scott, so Miss Ferrier was introduced to the best literary circles. She wrote three excellent novels, *Marriage* (1818), *The Inheritance* (1824), and *Destiny* (1831), all characterized by racy humour and acute character-painting. Her cheerful and tactful friendship helped to soothe the last days of Sir Walter Scott.

Field, Eugene (2 or 3 Sept. 1850—4 Nov. 1895), journalist and poet, was born at St Louis, Missouri, son of a lawyer, and educated at the University of Missouri. After his father's death he spent most of his patrimony in travel, visiting Britain, France, and Italy. In 1873 he married Julia Sutherland Comstock, who was only 16, but who proved a helpful wife and a devoted mother to their eight children. Taking up journalism, he worked as a columnist for the Chicago *Morning News* from 1883 till his death. His column, called 'Sharps and Flats' was a whimsical miscellany, but he is best remembered by such humorous poems as 'A Little Peach' and by his verses for children, especially 'Little Boy Blue' and 'Wynken, Blynken, and Nod.' He also composed some humorous renderings of the odes of Horace.

Field, Michael, *see* **Bradley, Katharine Harris,** *and* **Cooper, Edith Emma.**

Field, Nathan (baptized 17 Oct. 1587, buried 20 Feb. 1633), actor and dramatist, born in London, was one of the six comedians of the Children of the Queen's Revels, and acted in plays by Shakespeare, Ben Jonson, and Beaumont and Fletcher. He wrote *A Woman's a Weathercock* (1612), *Amends for Ladies* (1618), and (with Massinger) *The Fatal Dowry* (1632).

Fielding, Henry (22 April 1707—8 Oct. 1754), novelist and playwright, was born at Sharpham Park, near Glastonbury. His father was General Edmund Fielding, descended from the Earls of Denbigh and Desmond, and his mother was the daughter of Sir Henry Gould of Sharpham Park. His childhood was spent at East Stour, Dorset, and his education was received at first from a tutor, after which he was sent to Eton, where he was contemporary with Pitt and Fox. Following a love affair with a young heiress at Lyme Regis he was sent to Leyden to study law, where he remained until his father, who had entered into a second marriage, and who was an extravagant man, ceased to send his allowance. Thrown upon his own resources, he came to London and began to write light comedies and farces, of which during the next few years he threw off nearly a score, *Love*

in Several Masques (1728), being followed by *The Temple Beau*
(1730), and the better-known *Tragedy of Tragedies, or Tom Thumb,*
a burlesque of contemporary playwrights. About 1735 he married
Miss Charlotte Cradock, a beautiful and amiable girl to whom,
though he gave her sufficient cause for forbearance, he was devotedly
attached. She is the prototype of his heroines Sophia and Amelia.
She brought him £1,500, and the young couple retired to East Stour,
where he had a small house inherited from his mother. The little
fortune was, however, soon dissipated; and in a year he was back
in London, where he formed a company of comedians, and managed
a small theatre in the Haymarket. Here he produced successfully
Pasquin, a Dramatic Satire on the Times, and *The Historical Register
for 1736*, in which Walpole was satirized. This enterprise was
brought to an end by the passing of the Licensing Act, 1737, making
the *imprimatur* of the Lord Chamberlain necessary to the production
of any play. Fielding thereupon read law at the Middle Temple, was
called to the Bar in 1740, and went the Western Circuit.

The same year saw the publication of Richardson's *Pamela*, which
inspired Fielding with the idea of a parody, thus giving rise to his
first novel, *Joseph Andrews*. But as the characters, especially
Parson Adams, developed in his hands, the original idea was laid
aside, and the work assumed the form of a regular novel. It was
published in 1742, and though sharing largely in the same qualities as
its great successor, *Tom Jones*, its reception, though encouraging, was
not phenomenally cordial. Immediately after this a heavy blow fell
on Fielding in the death of his wife. The next few years were
occupied with writing his *Miscellanies* (1743), which contained, along
with some essays and poems, two important works, *A Journey from
this World to the Next*, and *The History of Jonathan Wild the Great*, a
grave satire; and he also conducted two papers in support of the
Government, *The True Patriot* and *The Jacobite Journal*, on consideration of which he was appointed Justice of the Peace for Middlesex and Westminster, and had a pension conferred upon him. In
1746 he set convention at defiance by marrying Mary Daniel, who
had been his first wife's maid, and the nurse of his children, and who
proved a faithful and affectionate companion. Fielding showed
himself an upright, diligent, and efficient magistrate, and his *Inquiry
into the Increase of Robbers* (1751), with suggested remedies, led to
beneficial results. By this time, however, the publication of his
great masterpiece, *The History of Tom Jones, a Foundling* (1749),
had given him a place among the immortals. It established in
English literature the novel form, which Fielding himself described
as 'a comic epic poem in prose.' It has been criticized for its
coarseness, but there is a universal agreement as to the permanent
interest of the types of character presented, the profound knowledge
of life and insight into human nature, the genial humour, the wide
humanity, the wisdom, and the noble and masculine English of the
book. Of it Gibbon made the famous remark, 'that exquisite
picture of human manners will survive the palace of the Escorial and
the Imperial Eagle of the House of Austria.' His only other novel,
Amelia, which has less vigour and is to some extent autobiographical,

was published in 1751. His health was now thoroughly broken, and in 1753, as a forlorn hope, he went in search of recovery to Lisbon, where he died, and was buried in the English cemetery. His last work, the delightful *Journal of a Voyage to Lisbon*, was published in 1755.

Fielding, Sarah (8 Nov. 1710—14 April 1768), novelist, born at East Stour, Dorset, was the sister of the above, who had a high opinion of her talents. She wrote several novels, including *The Adventures of David Simple in Search of a Faithful Friend* (1744), *The Governess* (1749), and *The Countess of Dellwyn* (1759). She also translated Xenophon's *Memorabilia* and *Apologia* (1762).

Filmer, Sir Robert (1590?—1653?), political writer, son of Sir Edward Filmer, of East Sutton, Kent, was educated at Cambridge. He was an enthusiastic Royalist, was knighted by Charles I and, in 1671, was imprisoned in Leeds Castle, Kent. He is notable as the defender, in its most extreme form, of the doctrine of the divine right of kings, which he expounded in a succession of works, of which the latest and best known, *Patriarcha*, appeared in 1679. His theory is founded on the idea that the government of a family by the father is the original and method of all government.

Finch, Anne, *see* **Winchilsea, Countess of.**

Finlay, George (21 Dec. 1799—26 June, 1875), historian, of Scottish descent, was born at Faversham, Kent, where his father, an officer in the army, was inspector of government powder mills. Intended for the law, he was educated at Glasgow, Göttingen, and Edinburgh, but becoming an enthusiast in the cause of Greece, he joined Byron in the war of independence, and thereafter bought a property near Athens, where he settled and busied himself with schemes for the improvement of the country, which had little success. His great history of Greece, produced in sections between 1843 and 1861, was reissued in 1877 as *A History of Greece from the Roman Conquest to the Present Time*.

Fisher, Herbert Albert Laurens, O.M. (21 March 1865—17 April 1940), historian, born in London, was educated at Winchester, Oxford, and Göttingen. In 1888 he became a Fellow of New College and lecturer on history. In 1912 he was appointed Vice-Chancellor of Sheffield University, and in 1916 was elected M.P. for Hallamshire. As President of the Board of Education he was mainly responsible for the Burnham Award grading teachers' salaries. In 1925 he became Warden of New College, from 1928 to 1932 was President of the British Academy, and in 1937 received the Order of Merit. During the Second World War he was run over in the black-out in London and died from his injuries. Among his works are *Studies in Napoleonic Statesmanship* (1903), *A History of England, 1485— 1547* (1906), *Bonapartism* (1908), *The Republican Tradition in Europe* (1911), and *Napoleon* (1920), but his best-known book was his excellent one-volume *History of Europe* (1936). His autobiography, *Pages from the Past*, appeared in 1939.

Fisher, John (1469—22 June 1535), prelate, born at Beverley, son of a mercer, was educated at Cambridge, took holy orders, and became in 1504 Bishop of Rochester. He wrote in Latin against the doctrines of the Reformation, but was a supporter of the New Learning, and induced Erasmus to lecture on Greek at Cambridge. Through his influence the Lady Margaret Professorships of Divinity were founded at Oxford and Cambridge by Margaret Countess of Richmond, and in 1502 he became the first holder of the Cambridge chair; in the following year he was appointed Chancellor of the University, and from 1505 to 1508 he was President of Queens' College; he was also instrumental in founding Christ's and St John's Colleges. For refusing to acknowledge the king as supreme head of the church, he was beheaded; he was beatified in 1886. He wrote a number of theological works.

Fiske, John (30 March 1842—4 July 1901), historian, was born at Hartford, Connecticut, son of a Quaker lawyer, his original name being Edmund Fisk Green. Very precocious, he was said to have read 200 volumes by the age of 8, and before he was 20 could read French, German, Spanish, Italian, Portuguese, Latin, Greek, Anglo-Saxon, and several other languages. Educated at Harvard, he had articles published before he graduated, and soon became a popular writer on historical subjects. His books include *Myths and Myth-Makers* (1872), *The Critical Period of American History, 1783—89* (1888), *The Beginnings of New England* (1889), *The War of Independence* (1889), *The American Revolution* (1891), *The Discovery of America* (1892), *Old Virginia and Her Neighbours* (1897), and *Dutch and Quaker Colonies* (1899).

FitzGerald, Edward (31 March 1809—14 June 1883), translator and letter-writer, was born near Woodbridge, Suffolk, son of John Purcell, who took his wife's surname on the death of her father in 1818. He was educated at Bury St Edmunds and Cambridge, where he was a contemporary of Thackeray. Thereafter he lived in retirement and study with his parents until 1838, when he took a neighbouring cottage. In 1856 he married a daughter of Bernard Barton, the poet, from whom, however, he soon separated. Afterwards he lived at various places in the East of England, continuing his studies, with yachting for his chief recreation. Meanwhile he had become an author, having written *Euphranor*, a dialogue on youth (1851), and *Polonius, a Collection of Wise Saws and Modern Instances* (1852). Becoming interested in Spanish literature, he published translations of six dramas of Calderon. Thereafter turning his attention to Persian, he produced (1859), anonymously, his famous translation of the *Rubaiyat of Omar Khayyám*. In it he aimed not so much at a mere literal reproduction of the sense of the original, as at reproducing its effect on the reader, and in this he was extraordinarily successful. His entertaining *Letters* were published in 1901.

Fitzgerald, Francis Scott Key (24 Sept. 1896—21 Dec. 1940), novelist, was born at St Paul, Minnesota, of Irish descent. He was educated at Newman School in New Jersey and Princeton, which he left in 1917 to serve in the First World War. After that he was for a short time in an advertising agency. His first book, *This Side of Paradise* (1920), established him as a leading literary figure; his next,

The Beautiful and Damned (1922) was a perfect reflection of the cynical and hard-boiled generation that followed the war. In 1920 he married Zelda Sayre, also a writer, and they lived in Long Island. His finest novel, *The Great Gatsby* (1925) shows up the false values of his own generation, while *Tender is the Night* (1934) he called his 'novel of deterioration.' An unfinished novel, *The Last Tycoon*, was published posthumously. Collections of his short stories include *Flappers and Philosophers* (1920), *Tales of the Jazz Age* (1922), *All the Sad Young Men* (1926), and *Taps at Reveille* (1935). His note-books and letters were published after his death with the title *The Crack-Up* (1945).

Fitzstephen, William (died 1190?), adherent and intimate of Archbishop Thomas Becket, witnessed his murder, and wrote his biography, with an interesting account of London in the twelfth century.

Flatman, Thomas (1637—8 Dec. 1688), miniature painter and minor poet, born in London, was educated at Winchester and Oxford. As a miniaturist his reputation stands high, and among his contemporaries he was also esteemed for his Pindaric odes, light verse, and devotional poems. His *Poems and Songs* (1674) went into four editions. In 1668 he was elected a Fellow of the Royal Society.

Flavel, John (1627—26 June 1691), Presbyterian minister, born at Bromsgrove, studied at Oxford, and was settled at Dartmouth, but ejected from his living when the Act of Uniformity was passed in 1662, continuing, however, to preach there secretly. He was a voluminous and popular author. Among his works are *Husbandry Spiritualized* (1669) and *Navigation Spiritualized* (1671), titles which suggest some of his characteristics as an expositor.

Flecker, James Elroy (5 Nov. 1884—3 Jan. 1915), poet and play-wright, born in London, was the son of a clergyman who became headmaster of Dean Close School, Cheltenham. He was baptized Herman but changed the name to James and was usually called Roy. Educated at Uppingham and Trinity College, Oxford, he was a schoolmaster in Hampstead for a few weeks, then in 1908 studied oriental languages at Caius College, Cambridge, and qualified for the Consular Service. In the same year he published his first book of verse, *The Bridge of Fire*, which was followed by *Thirty-Six Poems* (1910), and *Forty-Two Poems* (1911). In June of 1910 he was posted to Constantinople, and while on leave married a Greek girl, Helle Skiadaressi. From 1911 till March 1913 he was vice-consul at Beirut; then his health broke down from consumption and he went to Switzerland, where he died. Among his later volumes of poetry are *The Golden Journey to Samarkand* (1913), and *The Old Ships* (1915); *Collected Poems* (1916) contains practically all his published verse. The most famous of his works was the play *Hassan* (1922), and he also wrote another play, *Don Juan* (1925). Flecker's avowed object as a poet was 'to create beauty'; he claimed to be a follower of the French Parnassian school, but his inspiration was as much oriental as classical.

Flecknoe, Richard (died 1678?), poet and playwright, born in Oxford, is said to have been a Jesuit priest. In course of travels he visited Rome, Constantinople, Portugal, and Brazil; at Rome Andrew Marvell visited him and wrote a satirical account of him which gave Dryden the idea of *MacFlecknoe*, by which the unhappy poet is chiefly remembered. In that poem Dryden depicts him as 'throughout the realm of nonsense absolute,' and deciding that his only worthy successor is Shadwell (the real object of the satire). Flecknoe published a volume of poems entitled *Miscellanea* (1653), and his plays include *Love's Dominion* (1664), and *Damoiselles à la Mode* (1667). He also wrote *A Short Treatise of the English Stage* (1664), attacking the prevailing indecency.

Fleming, Margaret (15 Jan. 1803—19 Dec. 1811), child author, known as Pet Margery, born at Kirkcaldy, was a niece of Mrs Keith of Ravelston, a friend of Sir Walter Scott. Scott made a pet of the child, who was most precocious, reading history at the age of 6 and making poems and a diary which is full of quaint reflections. She died after an attack of measles.

Fleming, Oliver, *see* **MacDonald, Philip.**

Fleming, Peter (31 May 1907—   ), writer of travel books, was born in London, son of an M.P. At Eton he edited the school paper and at Oxford got a First in English in 1929. Taking up journalism, he wrote at first under the pseudonym 'Moth.' Subsequently he travelled in Mexico, Brazil, China, Japan, and other countries, often as a special correspondent of *The Times*. In the Second World War he served with the Grenadier Guards and was mentioned in dispatches. His books include *Brazilian Adventure* (1933), *One's Company* (1934), *News from Tartary* (1936), *The Flying Visit* (1940), *A Story to Tell* (1942), *The Sixth Column* (1951), and *A Forgotten Journey* (1952).

Fletcher, Andrew (1655—Sept. 1716), statesman and political writer, was the son of Sir Robert Fletcher of Saltoun, East Lothian, to which estate he succeeded at an early age. Educated under the care of Bishop Burnet, who was then minister of Saltoun, he became one of the most accomplished Scots of his time. Being firmly opposed to the arbitrary measures of the Duke of York, afterwards James II, he went to Holland, where he joined Monmouth, whom he accompanied on his ill-starred expedition. Happening to kill, in a quarrel, one of the Duke's followers, he fled to the Continent, travelled in Spain and Hungary, and fought against the Turks. After the Revolution he returned to Scotland, and took an active part in political affairs. He opposed the Union, fearing the loss of Scottish independence, and advocated federation rather than incorporation. He introduced various improvements in agriculture. His principal writings are *Discourse of Government* (1698), *Two Discourses concerning the Affairs of Scotland* (1698), and *Conversation concerning a right Regulation of Government for the Common Good of Mankind* (1703) in which occurs his well-known saying: 'Give me the making of the songs of a nation, and I care not who makes its laws.'

Fletcher, Giles (1588?—1623), clergyman and poet, younger brother of Phineas Fletcher (q.v.), was born in London and educated at Westminster School and Cambridge, where he became Reader in Greek.   About 1618 he was appointed rector of Alderton in Suffolk. His chief literary work, done while he was still an undergraduate, was *Christ's Victory and Triumph in Heaven and Earth over and after Death* (1610), which imitates Spenser and is full of allegorical passages.   He also wrote a prose tract, *The Reward of the Faithful* (1623).

Fletcher, John (Dec. 1579—Aug. 1625), dramatist, cousin of Giles and Phineas Fletcher (qq.v.), was born at Rye, Sussex, son of the vicar, who afterwards became Bishop of London.   John was educated at Benet College, Cambridge, but very little is known of his life. From about 1606 to 1616 he carried on his famous literary partnership with Francis Beaumont (q.v.), and they collaborated in some dozen plays, of which the best are *The Scornful Lady* (1610), *Philaster* (1611), *The Maid's Tragedy* (1611), *A King and No King* (1611), *Bonduca* (1614), and *Thierry and Theodoret* (1616), but were credited with many more.   Of the pair, Fletcher is generally reckoned the more fluent and creative, and he was the sole author of some 16 plays, of which the most important, with their approximate dates, are *The Faithful Shepherdess* (1609), *Valentinian* (1618), *Monsieur Thomas* (1619), *The Humorous Lieutenant* (1619), *The Chances* (1620), *The Pilgrim* (1621), and *The Wild Goose Chase* (1621).   He probably collaborated with Shakespeare in *Henry VIII* (1613), and *The Two Noble Kinsmen* (printed 1623).   Fletcher also collaborated with Massinger in several plays, and probably also with Rowley and Middleton in others.   He died of the plague.

Fletcher, John Gould (3 Jan. 1886—10 May 1950), poet, was born at Little Rock, Arkansas, son of a Confederate soldier, and educated at Phillips (Andover) Academy and Harvard, where he was not a success.   From 1908 to 1914 he lived in London and was one of the founders of the Imagist group of poets.   His first book of verse was *Fire and Wine* (1913), and among his best are *Irradiations: Sand and Spray* (1915), *Breakers and Granite* (1921), and *The Black Rock* (1928).   In 1933 he returned to the United States for good, and in 1939 he won the Pulitzer Prize for his *Selected Poems*, the best of twenty-five years' work.   His later volumes, *The Epic of Arkansas* (1936), and *The Burning Mountain* (1946) deal with American subjects.   *Life is My Song* (1937) is autobiographical.   Like Amy Lowell (q.v.) the other main founder of the Imagists, Fletcher made use of 'polyphonic prose,' and Conrad Aiken described his poetry as having magic of phrase and sound but nothing else.

Fletcher, Joseph Smith (7 Feb. 1863—31 Jan. 1935), novelist, was born in Halifax, son of a minister.   Going to London at the age of 18, he became a freelance journalist and then a writer, pouring out a stream of poetry, biography, and fiction, and producing over 100 books.   He wrote an authoritative history of Yorkshire (1901) and lives of Lord Roberts and Cardinal Newman, as well as some historical novels, but was best known for his detective stories, of which the best

I*

are *Middle Temple Murder* (1918), popularized by President Wilson's approval, *The Charing Cross Mystery* (1923), and *Murder in the Squire's Pew* (1932). His *Collected Verse* was published in 1931, but most of his work was too facile to survive.

Fletcher, Phineas (8 April 1582—1650), clergyman and poet, son of Giles Fletcher, ambassador and poet, and cousin of John Fletcher the dramatist (q.v.), was born at Cranbrook, Kent, and educated at Eton and King's College, Cambridge, of which he was a Fellow from 1600 to 1616. From 1621 till his death he was rector of Hilgay in Norfolk. In 1614 he wrote a pastoral play, *Sicelides*, and in 1628 *Britain's Ida or Venus and Anchises*, a pretty piece in the style of Shakespeare's *Venus and Adonis*. But his chief work was *The Purple Island or The Isle of Man* (1633), a poem in 10 books, giving an allegorical account of the human body, its virtues and vices; it imitates Spenser's *Faerie Queen* in many respects. Published in the same volume with it was a series of *Piscatory Eclogues*.

Flint, Frank Stewart (19 Dec. 1885—   ), poet and translator, was born in London, son of a commercial traveller. Straitened circumstances caused him to leave school before he was 14, and at 19 he entered the Civil Service as a typist. Studying at night school, he found he had a remarkable gift for languages, and eventually was able to read ten. His first book, *In the Net of the Stars* (1909), consists mainly of love lyrics, and he was one of the originators of the Imagist Movement, with its belief in 'unrhymed cadence.' Later volumes of his poems were *Cadences* (1915) and *Otherworld* (1920). He also published a great number of translations. Eventually he became a high official in the Ministry of Labour.

Florence of Worcester (died 7 July 1118), chronicler, was a monk. His work the *Chronicon ex Chronicis* is founded upon that of Marianus, an Irish chronicler, supplemented by additions taken from the *Anglo-Saxon Chronicle*, Bede's *Lives of the Saints*, and Asser's *Life of Alfred*. After his death it was brought down to 1295.

Florio, John (1553?—1625), translator, son of a Florentine preacher who was exiled for his protestantism, was born in London and about 1576 set up as a private tutor of languages at Oxford. In 1581 he was admitted a member of Magdalen College, and teacher of French and Italian. Patronized by various noblemen, he became in 1603 reader in Italian to Anne of Denmark, Queen of James I. He published *First Fruites* (1578), *Second Fruites* (1591), consisting of Italian and English dialogues, and his great Italian dictionary entitled *A World of Words*, in 1598. His chief contribution to pure literature is his famous translation of *The Essays of Montaigne*, in stately if somewhat stiff Elizabethan English. He married Rosa, sister of Samuel Daniel (q.v.).

Flower, Robin Ernest William (16 Oct. 1881—16 Jan. 1946), scholar and poet, was born at Meanwood, Yorkshire, of Anglo-Irish parentage, and educated at Leeds Grammar School and Oxford. In 1906 he joined the staff of the British Museum, and from 1929 to 1944 was Deputy Keeper of Manuscripts. He learned Irish, made a number of important translations from Old Irish, and was appointed Honorary Lecturer in Celtic at University College, London.   He also at different times held lecturing appointments with the British Academy, the Royal Society of Literature, and the Universities of Boston, Yale, and Chicago.   His volumes of verse include *Eire* (1910), *Hymenea* (1918), *Monkey Music* (1925), *The Pilgrim's Way* (1927), *Poems and Translations* (1931), and *The Western Island* (1944).

Fonblanque, Albany William (1793—13 Oct. 1872), journalist, was of Huguenot descent, the son of a Commissioner in Bankruptcy. He was bred to the law, but deserted it for journalism, in which he took a high place.   He wrote much for *The Times* and *Westminster Review*, and subsequently became editor and proprietor of the *Examiner*.   His best articles were republished as *England under Seven Administrations* (1837).   He also wrote *How we are Governed* (1858).   In 1847 he was appointed Statistical Secretary to the Board of Trade.

Foote, Samuel (baptized 27 Jan. 1720, died 21 Oct. 1777), actor and dramatist, was born in Truro, where his father had been mayor, and educated at Worcester College, Oxford.   Although entered at the Temple he was never called to the Bar, but lived as a wealthy young man about town, and having used up his fortune, turned actor. When he first appeared on the stage in 1744 he essayed tragic roles and was a failure.   In 1750 he inherited a second fortune from an uncle, but quickly ran through it in Paris.   In 1752 he returned to England and started writing farces, in which he acted, finding that as a comedian he was a great success; a capital mimic, he sometimes got into trouble by his clever caricaturing of living people.   In 1766 he lost a leg as the result of a practical joke which caused him to fall from a horse, and as compensation was given a life-patent of a theatre in Westminster.   Among his plays are *Taste* (1752), *The Englishman in Paris* (1753), *The Author* (1757), *The Minor* (1760), *The Liar* (1764), *The Lame Lover* (1770), *The Bankrupt* (1776), *The Devil Upon Two Sticks* (1778), and *A Trip to Calais* (1778).   By his contemporaries he was nicknamed the English Aristophanes.

Forbes, James David (20 April 1809—31 Dec. 1868), scientist, son of Sir William Forbes, Bart., of Pitsligo, was born and educated at Edinburgh.   He studied law, and was called to the Bar, but devoted himself to science, in which he gained a great reputation both as a discoverer and teacher.   He was Professor of Natural Philosophy at Edinburgh from 1833 to 1859, when he succeeded Sir D. Brewster as Principal of the United College at St Andrews.   He was one of the founders of the British Association in 1831.   His scientific investigations and discoveries embraced the subjects of heat, light, polarization, and especially glaciers.   In connection with the last of these he wrote *Travels through the Alps* (1843), *Norway and its Glaciers* (1853), *Tour of Mont Blanc and Monte Rosa* (1855), and *Papers on the Theory of Glaciers* (1859).

Forbes, Joan Rosita (1893—   ), travel writer, was born at Swinderley, Lincolnshire, daughter of Herbert J. Torr, M.P. She married, first, Colonel Ronald Forbes, whom she divorced, and later Colonel Arthur T. McGrath of the War Office. Frail-looking, beautiful, and very feminine, she was nevertheless a great traveller, visiting such out-of-the-way parts as Libya, Abyssinia, Syria, the Yemen, the Balkans, Central Asia, and South America, as well as more frequented places; she once claimed to have visited every country except Tibet and New Zealand. During the First World War she drove an ambulance for the French Red Cross. Among her books are *From Red Sea to Blue Nile* (1925), *Angora to Afghanistan* (1931), *The Secret of the Sahara* (1931), *Eight Republics in Search of a Future* (1933), *Kabul to Samarkand* (1937), *A Unicorn in the Bahamas* (1939), *The Prodigious Caribbean* (1940), and *Islands in the Sun* (1949). She also wrote a biography of Morgan the pirate (1948) and several novels.

Ford, Ford Madox (17 Dec. 1873—26 June 1939), novelist, was born at Merton, Surrey, son of Dr Francis Hueffer, a German, once musical critic of *The Times*; Ford's grandfather was Ford Madox Brown, the artist, and his aunt married William Rossetti. After publishing *Poems for Pictures* (1897) he collaborated with Joseph Conrad (q.v.) in two novels, *The Inheritors* (1901) and *Romance* (1903), and wrote independently *The Fifth Queen* (1906) and *The Half Moon* (1909). In 1908 he founded the *English Review*. In the following year he left his first wife, whom he had married in 1894, and having refused to pay her an allowance was imprisoned for ten days in Brixton. During the First World War he served in a Welsh regiment and was gassed. *The Good Soldier* (1915) was the first of his novels to attract the attention of the critics. After the war, having changed his name to Ford, he published a series of war novels, *Some Do Not* (1924), *No More Parades* (1925), *A Man Could Stand Up* (1926), and *The Last Post* (1928). In 1924 he edited the *Transatlantic review* in Paris. His autobiographical works include *Thus to Revisit* (1921), *It Was the Nightingale* (1933), and *Memories and Criticisms* (1938). His last years were spent in Michigan.

Ford, John (baptized 17 April 1586, died 1640?), dramatist, was born at Ilsington, Devon, and probably educated at Oxford. Entered at Middle Temple, he was never called to the Bar, and very little more is known of his life. In 1613 he wrote his first play, *An Ill Beginning Has a Good Ending*, which has been lost. Influenced by Burton's *Anatomy of Melancholy* he composed with great power what would now be termed problem plays dealing with the horrible and unnatural. Among them are *The Lover's Melancholy* (1629), *'Tis Pity She's a Whore* (1633), *The Broken Heart* (1633), and *The Ladies' Trial* (1639). *Perkin Warbeck* (1634) was one of the best chronicle plays since Shakespeare, and *The Fancies, Chaste and Noble* (1638) is a comedy. Lamb called Ford the last of the Elizabethans.

Ford, Paul Leicester (23 March 1865—8 May 1902), novelist and biographer, was born at Brooklyn, son of a lawyer. Dwarfed by a spinal injury, he was educated by tutors and read in his father's extensive library. Having a private income, he formed the Historical Printing Club, which printed rare American historical works. Later he edited the *Writings of Thomas Jefferson* in 10 volumes

(1892—4), and published *The True George Washington* (1896) and *The Many-Sided Franklin* (1899). His best-known novels are *The Honourable Peter Stirling* (1894) and *Janice Meredith* (1899), a historical romance, which was later dramatized. He was murdered by his brother, who had been disinherited in his favour.

Ford, Richard (1796—1 Sept. 1858), travel writer, son of an M.P., educated at Winchester and Oxford, was called to the Bar at Lincoln's Inn but never practised. He travelled for several years in Spain, becoming intimately acquainted with the country and people. He wrote a *Handbook for Travellers in Spain* (1845), which is much more than a mere guide-book, and *Gatherings from Spain* (1846). An accomplished artist and art critic, he was the first to make the great Spanish painter, Velasquez, generally known in England.

Fordun, John of (died 1384), chronicler, born at Fordun, is said to have been a chantry priest and Canon of Aberdeen. He began the *Scotichronicon*, for which he prepared himself, it is said, by travelling on foot through Britain and Ireland in search of materials. He brought the history down to 1153, leaving, however, material to the time of his own death, which was subsequently worked up by Walter Bower (q.v.). He is the chief authority for Scottish history before 1400.

Forester, Cecil Scott (27 Aug. 1899—   ), novelist, was born in Cairo, son of a government official, and educated at Alleyne's School and Dulwich College, afterwards studying medicine at Guy's. His first book, a crime novel entitled *Payment Deferred* (1926) was very successful and was dramatized. With his first wife he went inland voyaging in a dinghy through England, France, and Germany, the log being published as *The Voyage of the 'Annie Marble'* (1929), followed by *The 'Annie Marble' in Germany* (1930). In 1936—7 he was war correspondent for *The Times* in Spain. Others of his novels are *Brown on Resolution* (1929), *The Gun* (1933), and *The Ship* (1943). In *The Happy Return* (1937) he introduced one of the most popular heroes of modern fiction, Captain Hornblower, who appeared also in *Flying Colours* (1938) and *A Ship of the Line* (1939), which was awarded the Tait Black Memorial Prize. Later stories in the same series are *The Commodore* (1944), *Lord Hornblower* (1946), *Mr Midshipman Hornblower* (1950), and *Hornblower and the 'Atropos'* (1953).

Forster, Edward Morgan (1 Jan. 1879—   ), novelist, born in London, was educated at Tonbridge School and King's College, Cambridge, where he formed a friendship with G. Lowes Dickinson (q.v.), whose life he wrote in 1934. Living in Italy for a time, he wrote two novels with Italian backgrounds, *Where Angels Fear to Tread* (1905), and *A Room with a View* (1908). *The Longest Journey* (1907) tells of Cambridge life, and he also published *Howards End* (1910) before going on a visit to India. Later his brilliant novel *A Passage to India* won the Femina Vie Heureuse and Tait Black Memorial Prizes in 1925. During the First World War he was at Alexandria. In 1927 he delivered the Clark Lectures at Cambridge, his subject being *Aspects of the Novel*, and in 1942 he published a study of Virginia Woolf. *The Celestial Omnibus* (1923) and *The Eternal Moment* (1928) are collections of his short stories. *The Hill of Devi* (1953) is a record of his early Indian experiences. In 1953 he was made a Companion of Honour, and in 1961 the Royal Society of Literature made him a Companion of Literature.

Forster, John (2 April 1812—2 Feb. 1876), biographer, born at Newcastle, educated at the Grammar School there, and at University College, London, became a barrister of the Inner Temple, but soon relinquished law for literature. In 1834 he joined the staff of the *Examiner*, became its dramatic critic, and was editor from 1847 to 1855, having previously been editor of the *Foreign Quarterly Review* (1842—3), and the *Daily News* (1846). Charles Lamb and Leigh Hunt were among his friends. His historical writings were chiefly biographies, among which are *Statesmen of the Commonwealth of England* (1836—9), and lives of *Goldsmith* (1854), *Landor* (1869), and *Dickens* (1872—4). He also left the first volume of a life of Swift.

Fortescue, Sir John (1394?—1476?), writer on constitutional law, was descended from a Devonshire family and educated at Oxford. He was an eminent lawyer, and held the offices of Lord Chief Justice of the King's Bench under Henry VI. During the Wars of the Roses he was a staunch Lancastrian. He fought at Tewkesbury, and was captured, but pardoned on condition of writing in support of the Yorkish claims, which he did, considering that his own party appeared to be hopelessly ruined. His works include two treatises, *De Laudibus Legum Angliae* (in Praise of the Laws of England), published in 1537, and *On the Governance of the Kingdom of England*, not printed till 1714.

Foss, Sam Walter (19 June 1858—26 Feb. 1911), journalist and humorist, was born in Candia, New Hampshire, son of a farmer, of Huguenot origin; he worked on the farm as a boy and during his vacations from Brown University. Afterwards he became a journalist, and from 1898 till his death was librarian of the Somerville Public Library. His books of verse include *Back Country Poems* (1892), *Dreams in Homespun* (1897), *Songs of War and Peace* (1899), and *Songs of the Average Man* (1907).

Foster, John (17 Sept. 1770—24 Sept. 1843), essayist, was born near Halifax, son of a farmer, and educated at Bristol for the Baptist ministry. Though a man of powerful and original mind he did not prove popular as a preacher, and devoted himself mainly to literature, his chief contribution to which is his four *Essays, in a Series of Letters* (1805)—'On a Man's Writing Memoirs of Himself,' 'On Decision of Character,' 'On the Epithet "Romantic,"' and 'On Evangelical Religion,' all of which attracted much attention. In 1819 appeared his *Essay on the Evils of Popular Ignorance*, in which he advocated a national system of education.

Foster, Stephen Collins (4 July 1826—13 Jan. 1864), song-writer, was born at Pittsburgh, son of a merchant, and educated at Jefferson College. An early taste for music was at first discouraged, and he worked as a book-keeper in Cincinnati, but a collection of songs which included 'Uncle Ned' was so successful that he made song writing his life's work and wrote about 175, including such universal favourites as 'Old Folks at Home' (1851), 'Massa's in de Cold Ground' (1852), and 'My Old Kentucky Home' (1853). Although he captured the spirit of the negroes so effectively, Foster knew nothing of the South at first hand until he visited it in 1852. In 1860 he removed from Pittsburgh to New York, but in spite of his success his last years were spent in drink, poverty, and obscurity.

Fowler, Henry Watson (10 March 1858—26 Dec. 1933), lexicographer, was born at Tunbridge Wells, son of a clergyman, and educated at Rugby and Balliol College, Oxford. A first-rate swimmer and skater, he kept up these sports all his life. He worked as a schoolmaster first at Fettes, then at Sedbergh, lived for a time in Chelsea, and then joined his brother Francis George Fowler in Guernsey. They collaborated in producing *The King's English* (1906) and the *Concise Oxford Dictionary* (1911), an abridgment of the great *Oxford English Dictionary*; this smaller work has become accepted as the standard working dictionary for everyday use. After the death of his brother in 1918 Henry also compiled *A Dictionary of Modern English Usage* (1926), which they had planned together. These three books have probably done more for the modern English language than any other similar reference works. Among Henry's independent publications were *Some Comparative Values* (1928), *If Wishes Were Horses* (1929), and *Rhymes for Darby and Joan* (1931).

Fox, Charles James (24 Jan. 1749—13 Sept. 1806), statesman, born in London, son of Lord Holland, and educated at Eton and Oxford, was one of the greatest orators who have ever sat in the House of Commons. His only serious literary work was a fragment of a proposed *History of the Reign of James the Second* (1808). His *Speeches* were published in 1815.

Fox, George (July 1624—13 Jan. 1691), founder of the Society of Friends, born at Fenny Drayton, Liecestershire, son of a weaver, was apprenticed to a shoemaker, but gave up this work at 19, and adopted a wandering life. The protests which he made against the prevailing beliefs and manners, and which sometimes took the form of interrupting Divine service, involved him in frequent trouble. The clergy, the magistrates, and the mob alike treated him with harshness amounting to persecution. None of these things, however, moved him, and friends, many of them influential, extended favour towards him. From 1659 onwards he made various missionary journeys in Scotland, Ireland, America, and Holland. Later he was repeatedly imprisoned, again visited the Continent, and died in 1691. Fox's literary works are his *Journal*, *Epistles*, and *Doctrinal Pieces*. He was not a man of strong intellect, and the defence of Quakerism was undertaken by the far more competent hand of his follower, Barclay (q.v.). The *Journal*, however, is full of interest as a sincere transcript of the singular experiences, religious and others, of a spiritual enthusiast and mystic.

Fox, John (1862—8 July 1919), novelist, was born at Paris, Kentucky, and educated at Transylvania University and Harvard. He worked as a special correspondent in the Spanish-American and Russo-Japanese Wars, and in 1887 was in the mining business in Virginia. His novels, which quickly became best-sellers, were largely idealized pictures based on his mining experiences. They include *The Little Shepherd of Kingdom Come* (1903), *The Trail of the Lonesome Pine* (1908), which sold well over a million copies, *The Heart of the Hills* (1913), and *Erskine Dale, Pioneer* (1920). He died of pneumonia contracted during a fishing trip.

Foxe, John (1516—18 April 1587), martyrologist, was born at Boston, Lincolnshire, and educated at Oxford, where he became a Fellow of Magdalen College. While there he gave himself to the study of the theological questions then in debate, and ended by becoming a Protestant, in consequence of which he in 1545 left his college. He then became tutor in the family of Sir T. Lucy of Charlecote, and afterwards to the children of the recently executed Earl of Surrey. During the reign of Mary he retired to the Continent, and published at Strasburg, his *Commentarii* (the first draft of the *Acts and Monuments*). Removing to Basel he was employed as a reader for the press by the famous printer Oporinus, who published some of his writings. On the accession of Elizabeth, Foxe returned to England, was received with kindness by the Duke of Norfolk, one of his former pupils, and soon afterwards (1563) published the work on which his fame rests, the English version of the *Acts and Monuments*, better known as *The Book of Martyrs*. Received with great favour by the Protestants, it was, and has always been, charged by the Roman Catholics with gross and wilful perversion of facts, but as an example of vigorous prose it had considerable literary influence. Foxe, who had been ordained a priest in 1560, became Canon of Salisbury in 1563.

Francis, Sir Philip (22 Oct. 1740—23 Dec. 1818), politician, was born in Dublin, son of a clergyman, and educated at St Paul's School. He became a clerk in the office of the Secretary of State and in 1762 principal clerk to the War Office. In the political controversies of the times he wrote a number of letters to the papers under pseudonymns, and it is commonly supposed that he may have been the author of the famous *Letters of Junius* (*see* Junius). Later he was a member of the Court of Bengal and found himself in conflict with Warren Hastings, with whom he had a duel. In 1780 he returned to England, became a Whig M.P. and worked in a most vindictive manner for the impeachment of Hastings. He was made a Knight Commander of the Bath in 1806.

Frankau, Gilbert (21 April 1884—4 Nov. 1952), novelist, educated at Eton, went into his father's wholesale cigar business, of which he became managing director. After the publication of his first book, *One of Us* (1912) he went for a business trip round the world. In the First World War he served with the Royal Field Artillery, in the second in the Royal Air Force. *The Guns* (1916) is a book of war poems, and his *Poetical Works* were collected in 1923. He made his reputation as a novelist with *Peter Jackson, Cigar Merchant* (1919), and followed this up with *Seeds of Enchantment* (1921), *Gerald Cranston's Lady* (1924), *Martin Make Believe* (1930), *Wine, Women, and Waiters* (1932), *Everywoman* (1933), *Three Englishmen* (1935), *The Dangerous Years* (1937), *Winter of Discontent* (1941), *Michael's Wife* (1948), and *Oliver Trenton, K.C.* (1951). *Self-Portrait* (1939) is an autobiography. He was married three times.

Frankau, Pamela (3 Jan. 1908—   ), novelist, daughter of the above, was educated at Stapleton. Taking up journalism, she joined the staff of the *Women's Journal* in London, and her book *Marriage of Harlequins* (1927) was written in the train while on her way to and from work. Later she was a copy-writer in an advertising agency. Her novels, which showed an increasing seriousness as her craftsmanship developed, include *Three* (1929), *She and I* (1930), *Born at Sea* (1932), *Foolish Apprentices* (1933), *Tassel-Gentle* (1934), *The Devil We Know* (1939), *A Democrat Dies* (1940), *Shaken in the Wind* (1948), *The Willow Cabin* (1949), *The Winged Horse* (1953), *A Wreath for the Enemy* (1954), and *The Bridge* (1957). During the Second World War she was in the women's Auxiliary Territorial Service and rose to the rank of major. She married Marshall Dill, and from 1945 lived in the United States. In 1942 she became a Roman Catholic.

Franklin, Benjamin (17 Jan. 1706—17 April 1790), printer, author, statesman, was born in Boston, the fifteenth of a tallow-chandler's seventeen children, and went to Boston Grammar School. At the age of 10 he started work in his father's shop as a soap-boiler, and later was apprenticed to his half-brother James, a printer. His earliest writing, some essays imitating the *Spectator*, appeared in the *New England Courant*, which James founded in 1721. In 1723, having quarrelled with James, he removed to Philadelphia, and in the following year went to London, where he worked as a compositor for two years. Back in America, he established a printing house, bought the *Pennsylvania Gazette* in 1729, and began to make a name for himself as a journalist. From 1732 to 1764 he published *Poor Richard's Almanack*, an annual compilation of shrewd maxims largely borrowed from Bacon and la Rochefoucauld, which became extremely popular. He taught himself to read French, Spanish, Italian, and Latin, and also studied science. Using a kite he carried out a dangerous experiment to prove that lightning is the same as electricity.

Latterly he became a political force, being Clerk of the Pennsylvania Assembly from 1736 to 1751 and a member from then till 1764, and holding the post of Postmaster General for the Colonies. Sent on a political mission to England, from 1757 to 1762 he acted as colonial agent in London. Returning to America, he was a member of the Second Continental Congress, and was one of the committee that drew up the Declaration of Independence. In 1776 he was sent to Paris to enlist the help of the French, where he remained till 1785 and helped to draw up the treaty between America and France in 1778. His last years were spent in Philadelphia. Among his many writings *The Way to Wealth* (1757) contains a number of pithy sayings, but his most famous work is his *Autobiography*, published in full in 1868, which reveals him as one of the most versatile geniuses the world has known.

Frazer, Sir James George, O.M. (1 Jan. 1854—7 May 1941), anthropologist, was born in Glasgow, son of a minister. He was educated at Larchfield Academy, Helensburgh, Glasgow University, and Trinity College, Cambridge, of which he became a Fellow; he also studied law, and was called to the Bar in 1879. Knighted in 1914, a Fellow of the Royal Society from 1920, and awarded the Order of Merit in 1925, he held honorary doctorates of Oxford, Cambridge, St Andrews, Glasgow, Durham, Manchester, Paris, Strasbourg, and Athens. An accomplished classical scholar, he made translations of Pausanias, Ovid, and Sallust, but his great work was *The Golden Bough*, an exhaustive study in 12 volumes of totemism and taboo, which appeared between 1890 and 1915. Among his other books are *Totemism and Exogamy* (1910), *Folklore in the Old Testament* (1918), and *The Gorgon's Head* (1927). The Frazer Lectures in Anthropology, delivered alternately at Glasgow and Oxford, were established in his honour.

Frederic, Harold (19 Aug. 1856—19 Oct. 1898), novelist, was born at Utica, New York, son of a furniture decorator. At the age of 14 he became office-boy on the *Utica Observer*, in 1882 was editor of the Albany *Evening Journal*, and from 1884 was London correspondent for the *New York Times*. His earliest writings were novels of local colour, *Seth's Brother's Wife* (1887), *The Lawton Girl* (1890), and *The Return of the Mahoney* (1892); *In the Valley* (1890) is an historical novel of the American Revolution, and *Marsena* (1894) is a collection of stories of the Civil War. His greatest work was *The Damnation of Theron Ware* (1896), after which he wrote three mediocre novels of English life.

Freeman, Edward Augustus (2 Aug. 1823—16 May 1892), historian, was born at Harborne, Staffordshire. He lost both his parents in childhood, and was brought up by his paternal grandmother. He was educated at private schools, and as a private pupil of the Rev. R. Gutch, whose daughter he afterwards married. In 1841 he went to Trinity College, Oxford, of which he became a Fellow, afterwards settling at Somerleaze, near Wells, where he occupied himself in study, writing for periodicals, and with the duties of a magistrate. In 1884 he succeeded Stubbs as Professor of Modern History at Oxford. He had always been an enthusiastic traveller, and it was when on a tour of Spain that he died of smallpox. Freeman was a voluminous author, and a keen controversialist. Among his more important works were *A History of Federal Government* (1863), *The History of the Norman Conquest* (6 volumes, 1867—9), *The Growth of the English Constitution* (1872), *The Historical Geography of Europe* (1881—2), *The Reign of William Rufus* (1882), and an unfinished *History of Sicily*. Besides these he wrote innumerable articles in periodicals, many of which were separately published and contain much of his best work. He was laborious and honest, but the controversial cast of his mind sometimes coloured his work.

Freeman, John (29 Jan. 1880—23 Sept. 1929), poet, was born at Dalston, Middlesex, son of a commercial traveller. At the age of 12 he left school to become a clerk in an insurance company, of which by 1927 he was secretary and director. His earliest books of verse were *Twenty Poems* (1909), *Fifty Poems* (1911), and *Stone Trees* (1916), which made his reputation; his *Poems New and Old* gained the Hawthornden Prize in 1920. After several more books of verse his *Collected Poems* appeared in 1928 and *Last Poems* after his death. He also wrote studies of *George Moore* (1922) and *Herman Melville* (1926). His *Letters* were published in 1936.

Freeman, Richard Austin (1862—30 Sept. 1943), writer of detective stories, was born in London, and after studying medicine at the Middlesex Hospital Medical College was appointed house physician in 1886. In 1889 he took part in a medical expedition to West Africa, of which he wrote in his first book, *Travels and Life in Ashanti and Jamau* (1898); contracting blackwater fever he was invalided out. In 1904 he gave up medicine for writing, except for the period of the First World War, when he served with the Royal Army Medical Corps. In 1907 he published his first detective story, *The Red Thumb Mark*, and his detective, Dr Thorndyke, became one of the most famous of scientific investigators, even giving some ideas to the official force. Others of his books are *John Thorndyke's Cases* (1909), *The Eye of Osiris* (1911), *The Great Portrait Mystery* (1918), *Dr Thorndyke's Case Book* (1923), *The Puzzle Lock* (1925), *As a Thief in the Night* (1928), and *When Rogues Fall Out* (1932). In *The Singing Bone* (1912) he used the innovation of describing the crime first, before showing how Thorndyke unravelled it.

Freeman, Thomas (fl. 1614), epigrammatist, born in Gloucestershire and educated at Oxford, settled in London. In 1614 he published a collection of epigrams in two volumes entitled *Rub and a Great Cast*, and *Run and a Great Cast: The Second Bowl*. It contains epigrams on Shakespeare, Daniel, Chapman, and Donne.

Freneau, Philip Morin (2 Jan. 1752—19 Dec. 1832), poet, was born in New York, son of a wine importer, and educated at the College of New Jersey. When the American Revolution broke out he wrote several poems satirizing the British. Working as a planter's secretary in Santa Cruz he wrote his well-known ' Jamaica Funeral' and 'House of Night.' While at sea he was captured by the British and nearly died in confinement; from this experience he wrote his poem *The British Prison-Ship* (1781). In his later life he was alternately sea-captain and journalist, and as editor of the *Nationalist Gazette* had considerable political influence. The most noted of his shorter poems are 'The Indian Burying Ground' and 'The Wild Honeysuckle.' He died in a blizzard while living on a New Jersey farm.

Frere, John Hookham (21 May 1769—7 Jan. 1846), diplomat, translator, and author, eldest son of a distinguished antiquary, was born in London, was a friend of Canning at Eton, and at Cambridge became a Fellow of Caius. He became a clerk in the Foreign Office, and subsequently entering Parliament was appointed Under-

Secretary for Foreign Affairs. In 1800 he was Envoy to Portugal, and was Ambassador to Spain 1802—4, and again 1808—9. In 1818 he retired to Malta, where he died. He was a contributor to the *Anti-Jacobin*, to Ellis's *Specimens of the Early English Poets* (1801), and to Southey's *Chronicle of the Cid*. He also published some masterly translations from *Aristophanes*. All Frere's writings are characterized no less by scholarship than by wit.

Frost, Robert Lee (26 March 1874—   ), poet, was born in San Francisco. His father, a New Englander, died when Robert was 10 and his Scottish mother, a teacher, moved to Lawrence, Massachusetts. After attending various schools and a year at Dartmouth, Frost went to work in a Lawrence textile mill. At 20 he married Eleanor Miriam White, and from 1897 to 1899 was at Harvard, but never got a regular degree, though he was later to have sixteen honorary degrees. He was in turn teacher, cobbler, editor, and finally farmer for eleven years at Derry, New Hampshire. In 1912 he went to England and settled at Beaconsfield, where he met Rupert Brooke, Lascelles Abercrombie, Edward Thomas, and other poets. From this point his poetical career may be said to have begun. His first book of verse, *A Boy's Will* (1913) was followed by *North of Boston* (1914). In 1915 he returned to the United States, where he was now famous, and became Professor of Poetry at Harvard. He was four times awarded the Pulitzer Prize for Poetry —in 1924, 1931, 1937, and 1943—and also received the medal of the American Academy of Art and Letters in 1938 and of the Poetry Society of America in 1941. Though born in California, his voice was the voice of New England, and he has been described as the purest classical poet of America. His books include *Mountain Interval* (1916), *New Hampshire* (1923), *West-Running Brook* (1928), *A Further Range* (1936), *A Witness Tree* (1942), *A Masque of Reason* (1945), *Steeple Bush* (1947), *A Masque of Mercy* (1947), and *Complete Poems* (1949).

Froude, James Anthony (23 April 1818—20 Oct. 1894), historian, was born at Dartington, Devonshire, his father being archdeacon of Totnes. He was educated at Westminster School and Oxford, where he became a Fellow of Exeter and came under Newman's influence; but *The Nemesis of Faith*, which he published in 1849, showed a change to a sceptical outlook in religion, and he had to resign his fellowship. At this time he began contributing to the *Westminster Review* and to *Fraser's Magazine*, which he edited from 1860 to 1874; his articles were later collected and published as *Short Studies on Great Subjects*. His great 12-volume work, *The History of England from the Fall of Cardinal Wolsey to the Spanish Armada*, was published between 1856 and 1870; it has supreme dramatic and descriptive power, but is sometimes marred by its prejudiced tone and even actual inaccuracy. In 1869 Froude was elected Lord Rector of St Andrews, and a few years later he published *The English in Ireland in the Eighteenth Century*. In 1849 he had made the acquaintance of Carlyle and had since become one of his chief disciples. When Carlyle died in 1881 Froude was his literary executor, and in this capacity he published Carlyle's *Reminiscences* (1881), *Letters and Memorials of Jane Welsh Carlyle* (1883), and a 4-volume biography of Carlyle, which aroused indignant criticism by what were regarded as indiscreet revelations and false views. After visits to Australia and the West Indies he embodied the results of his observations in *Oceana* (1886), and *The English in the West Indies* (1888). In 1892 he was appointed Professor of Modern History at Oxford, and subsequently published *Life and Letters of Erasmus* (1894) and *Englishmen Seamen in the Sixteenth Century* (1895).

Fry, Christopher (18 Dec. 1907—), playwright, was born in Bristol, son of a lay preacher, and educated at Bedford Grammar School. After a few years of schoolmastering he turned to the stage and worked as actor, script writer, and producer. From 1934 to 1936 he was director for the Tunbridge Wells Repertory Players, and in 1939 and 1940 his pageant plays *Thursday's Child* and *The Tower* were performed. In 1940 he became director of the Oxford Playhouse, but was called up and served in the Second World War from 1940 to 1944. In 1946 his play *A Phoenix Too Frequent* appeared, to be followed by *The Lady's Not for Burning* (1949), *Venus Observed* (1950), *A Sleep of Prisoners* (1951), and *The Dark is Light Enough* (1954). *The Firstborn* (1946) shows his tragic power. Written in flexible verse, his plays form a landmark in the revival of poetic drama in England. *An Experiment of Critics* (1952) is an essay.

Fuller, Sarah Margaret (23 May 1810—19 July 1850), journalist and critic, was born at Cambridgeport near Boston, daughter of a lawyer who was a member of Massachusetts Senate. Very precocious, she started Latin at 6, and was reading Ovid, Molière, and Cervantes before she reached her teens. One of the Transcendental circle, she was celebrated as a talker, and from 1839 to 1844 established 'conversations' in Boston—cultural classes of some twenty-five ladies. From their discussions she wrote *Woman in the Nineteenth Century* (1845). Joint editor of the short-lived *Dial* of the Transcendentalists, she later joined the New York *Tribune*. In 1846 she visited Europe and saw Carlyle, Wordsworth, George Sand, and Mazzini, but just missed the Brownings, who were busy eloping. In Rome she married Angelo Ossoli, a penniless nobleman, who gave her the right to the title of Marchioness Ossoli. Setting sail for America with the manuscript of a history she had written of the Roman Revolution, she perished in a shipwreck. *Literature and Art* (1846) is a collection of her articles, but she was known better by her personality than by her writings.

Fuller, Thomas (June 1608—16 Aug. 1661), clergyman and antiquary, was born at Aldwinkle, Northamptonshire, where his father was rector. Possessed of exceptional intelligence and a wonderful memory, he became a good scholar, and went to Queen's College, Cambridge, at the age of 13. Taking orders in 1630, he had rapid preferment, including the lectureship at the Savoy, and a chaplaincy to Charles II. He was a voluminous author, his works dealing with theology, morals, history, and antiquities. Among the chief are *History of the Holy War*, i.e. the Crusades (1643), *The Holy State and the Profane State* (1642), *Good Thoughts in Bad Times* (1645), *A Pisgah Sight of Palestine* (1650), *Church History of Britain, History of Cambridge University* (1655), and *Worthies of England* (1662). The outstanding characteristic of Fuller's writings is shrewd observation conveyed in a style of quaint humour. Lamb says: 'His conceits are often-times deeply steeped in human feeling and passion.' But in addition there is much wisdom and a remarkable power of casting his observations into a compact, aphoristic form. The *Worthies*, though far from being a systematic work, is full of interesting biographical and antiquarian matter which, but for the pains of the author, would have been lost. Coleridge says of him: 'He was incomparably the most sensible, the least prejudiced great man in an age that boasted a galaxy of great men.' Fuller was a strong Royalist, and suffered the loss of his preferments during the Commonwealth. They were, however, given back to him at the Restoration.

Fullerton, Lady Georgiana (23 Sept. 1812—19 Jan. 1885), novelist, was born at Tixall Hall, Staffordshire. Part of her early life was spent in Paris, where her father, Lord Granville Leveson Gower, afterwards he 1st Earl Granville, was ambassador, and there she married Alexander George Fullerton; he became a Roman Catholic in 1843, and she in 1846. *Ellen Middleton* (1844), her first novel, was followed by *Grantley Manor* (1845), and *Too Strange Not to be True* (1852), her most popular work. After her son's death in 1854 she gave up writing and, joining the Order of St Francis, devoted herself to charitable works.

Furnivall, Frederick James (4 Feb. 1825—2 July 1910), scholar, born at Egham, Surrey, son of a doctor, was educated at London University and Cambridge. There he was a member of his college eight, and all his life he was a keen oarsman. He went on to study law at Lincoln's Inn and later devoted himself to the cause of the working classes, helping to found the Working Men's College in 1854. But his great work was the promoting of organized research in English literature. In 1847 he joined the Philological Society, of which he was secretary from 1853 till his death, and in 1861 he became the second editor of the great *Oxford English Dictionary*, before Sir James Murray (q.v.) took charge. Concentrating next on Middle English literature, he edited many works for the Early English Text Society, which he founded in 1864. In 1868 he founded the Chaucer Society, in 1873 the New Shakespeare Society, for which he did a great deal of work, in 1881 the Wyclif Society and the Browning Society, and in 1886 the short-lived Shelley Society. The failure of a bank left him in straitened circumstances during his last years, and in 1884 he was awarded a Civil List pension of £150. Among the many honours he received, he was a D.Litt. of Oxford, a Ph.D. of Berlin, and an original Fellow of the British Academy.

Furphy, Joseph (26 Sept. 1843—13 Sept. 1912), novelist who wrote under the name of Tom Collins, was born at Yering Station, now

Yarra Glen, Victoria, son of an Irish immigrant who was head gardener on the station. Educated by his mother, Joseph learned passages of Shakespeare and the Bible by heart, and never forgot them. About 1855 his father leased a farm at Kyneton, and it was worked by Joseph and his brother. After ups and downs in farming Joseph got a good post in his brother's foundry at Shepparton and worked there for twenty years. His reading and writing were done in the evenings. In 1897 he completed a picaresque novel, *Such is Life*, which came out in 1903 and became an Australian classic. In 1905 *Rigby's Romance*, originally part of the earlier work, was published as a serial, and in the same year Furphy moved to Western Australia. His *Poems* were published in 1916.

Fyleman, Rose (1877—1 Aug. 1957), poetess, was born in Nottingham, of Jewish descent, and educated at University College there. After working as a teacher for a few years she studied singing in Germany and Paris. Fond of travelling, she toured all over Europe and visited the United States and Canada. Having started writing at an early age, she sent some poetical pieces to *Punch*, and was soon accepted as an accomplished writer of light tuneful verse for children. Her books include *Fairies and Chimneys* (1918), *The Fairy Green* (1919), *The Fairy Flute* (1921), *The Rainbow Cat* (1922), *Fairies and Friends* (1925), *Gay Go Up* (1929), *Fifty New Nursery Rhymes* (1931), *Runabout Rhymes* (1941), and *Nursery Stories* (1949). In 1933 she wrote a children's opera.

G

Gaimar, Geoffrey (fl. 1140?), poet, translated the chronicle of Geoffrey of Monmouth into Anglo-Norman verse for the wife of his patron, Ralph Fitz-Gilbert and added a continuation dealing with the Saxon Kings. His work is entitled *L'Estoire des Engles*.

Gale, Norman Rowland (4 March 1862—7 Oct. 1942), poet, was born at Kew and latterly lived at Bexhill. A rural poet, he has been compared to Herrick, and his first book of verse was called appropriately *A Country Muse* (1892). This was followed by *Orchard Songs* (1894), and *A Book of Quatrains* (1909); his *Collected Poems* appeared in 1914, and later volumes were *The Candid Cuckoo* (1918), *Verse in Bloom* (1925), and *Love-in-a-Mist* (1939). He also published a number of books of verse about cricket, including *Cricket Songs* (1894), *Messrs Bat and Ball* (1930), and *Close of Play* (1936), as well as some volumes of essays.

Gale, Zona (26 Aug. 1874—27 Dec. 1938), novelist and poet, was born at Portage, Wisconsin, and educated at the University of Wisconsin, which later conferred a doctorate on her. Taking up journalism, she worked first on Milwaukee papers, then became a reporter on the *New York World*. Her first story, 'Success,' was published in 1904. Her novels include *Romance Island* (1906), *Heart's Kindred* (1915), *A Daughter of To-morrow* (1917), *Birth* (1918), *Miss Lulu Bett* (1920), which was dramatized and awarded the Pulitzer Prize, *Faint Perfume* (1923), *Preface to a Life* (1926), *Borgia* (1929), *Papa Le Fleur* (1933), and *Light Woman* (1937). *The Secret Way* (1921) is a book of poems, and *When I Was a Little Girl* (1913) is autobiographical. In 1928 she married William L. Breese.

Gallico, Paul William (26 July 1897—   ), journalist and novelist, was born in New York City, son of a music teacher. As a child he visited Europe with his parents. He was captain of rowing at Columbia University, and tried many other sports, including golf, baseball, football, swimming, and boxing. Joining the staff of the New York *Daily News* in 1922, he was its sports editor for 12 years, and wrote of his experiences in *Farewell to Sport* (1958); *Confessions of a Story Writer* (1946) is also autobiographical. His novels show great variety of type. *The Adventures of Hiram Holliday* (1939) and its sequel *The Secret Front* (1940) have been styled escape fiction; *The Snow Goose* (1941) is a love idyll; *Jennie* (1950) a most realistic story of a cat; and *Snowflake* (1952) is a fantasy. Others are *Foolish Immortals* (1953), *Love of Seven Dolls* (1954), *Ludmilla* (1955), *Thomasina* (1957), and *Flowers for Mrs Harris* (1958). *The Steadfast Man* (1958) is a life of St Patrick.

Galsworthy, John, O.M. (14 Aug. 1867—31 Jan. 1933), novelist and dramatist, was born at Kingston Hill, Surrey, son of a well-to-do solicitor. Educated at Harrow, where he was captain of football, and at Oxford, where he studied law, he was called to the Bar by

Lincoln's Inn, but instead of practising he went on a trip to the Far East, making the voyage in merchant ships, in one of which he met Joseph Conrad (q.v.), who became his lifelong friend. Galsworthy's first published book was a volume of *short stories, *Four Winds* (1897); this was followed by two novels, *Jocelyn* (1898), *Villa Rubein* (1900), and another collection of stories, *A Man of Devon* (1901). All of these appeared under the pseudonym John Sinjohn, and they attracted little attention. Meanwhile, however, the writer was learning his craft, taking for his model the Russian novelists, particularly Turgenev. In 1905 he married the wife of his cousin, A. J. Galsworthy, and in the following year was fairly launched with the appearance of his novel *The Man of Property* and the presentation of his first play, *The Silver Box*.

It was appropriate that Galsworthy should be practically middle-aged before he attained success, for his art was always to be one of fastidious restraint rather than strong feeling. *The Man of Property* was the first part of what was later entitled *The Forsyte Saga*, which was made up of *In Chancery* (1920) and *To Let* (1921), with two additional interludes, *The Indian Summer of a Forsyte* and *Awakening*. All deal with the same family, the Forsytes, and form a clever and intimate study of that upper middle class which held a dominant position in the England of Victorian times but has been practically destroyed by two world wars and the establishment of the Welfare State. Galsworthy did not spare to depict the faults as well as the virtues of his characters, who have been accepted, especially in other countries, as typical of the English moneyed class. A second trilogy, dealing with a later generation of the same family, comprised *The White Monkey* (1924), *The Silver Spoon* (1926), and *Swan Song* (1928), the whole being entitled *A Modern Comedy* (1929). Later still, *Maid in Waiting* (1931), with its sequels *Flowering Wilderness* (1932) and *Over the River* (1933) appeared in one volume as *End of the Chapter* (1934) after the author's death. Others of Galsworthy's novels are *The Island Pharisees* (1904), *The Country House* (1907), *Fraternity* (1909), *The Patrician* (1911), *The Dark Flower* (1913), *The Freelands* (1915), and *Saint's Progress* (1919).

Of his plays, the theme is almost always sympathy with one form or another of the 'under-dog,' bearing out Conrad's description of Galsworthy as 'a humanitarian moralist.' But there is always aloofness in his sympathy, and he never really understands the under-privileged classes that he champions. *The Silver Box* (1906) shows that there is one law for the rich and another for the poor; *Strife* (1909) reveals the hardships that attend industrial problems; *Justice* (1910) shows up the horrors of prison life and was instrumental in bringing about some reforms. Later plays were *The Skin Game* (1920), *Loyalties* (1922), *Windows* (1922), *Old English* (1924), and *Escape* (1926). All show a departure in technique from the epigrammatic brilliance that Wilde and Shaw had made fashionable; instead, they have a restrained and simple dialogue which is nevertheless effective because of the author's skilful artistry. Similarly the construction of the plays is straightforward, without any elaborate theatrical ingenuity.

Galsworthy at different times used most literary forms. *Tatter-demalion* (1920) is a collection of short stories, as is *On Forsyte 'Change* (1930); *Motley* (1910) and *The Inn of Tranquillity* (1911) are volumes of sketches; *Castles in Spain* (1927) is a book of essays. His *Collected Poems* appeared in 1934, and might have won more attention had they not been overshadowed by his other work. His distinctions were many. Having refused a knighthood, he was awarded the Order of Merit in 1929, and in 1932 was given the Nobel Prize for Literature. He held honorary degrees of Oxford, Cambridge, St Andrews and several other universities. After his death his ashes were scattered on the Sussex Downs, a fitting end to the most English of modern writers.

Galt, John (2 May 1779—11 April 1839), novelist, was born at Irvine, Ayrshire, son of a sea captain. When he was 10 the family removed to Greenock, where after leaving school he was a clerk in the Customs House and then with a business firm. In 1804 he went to London and had his epic poem *The Battle of Largs* published; later he suppressed it. After studying law at Lincoln's Inn he travelled abroad for two years, visiting Greece and meeting Lord Byron, whose life he wrote in 1830. After his return in 1811 he published *Voyages and Travels* and *Letters from the Levant*, as well as a life of Wolsey, but his first great success was with *The Ayrshire Legatees* (1820), which appeared in *Blackwood* and was followed by his best work, *Annals of the Parish* (1821). In 1822 he published *Sir Andrew Wylie*, *The Steamboat*, and *The Provost*, and in the following year *The Entail*, *The Spaewife*, and *Rothelan*. In 1825 he went to Canada as secretary of a land company, but though he was fairly successful, founding the town of Guelph in 1827, and having Galt named after him, he met with much opposition and resigned in 1828; *Lawrie Todd* (1830) is a novel based on his Canadian experiences. Back in London he had to contend with broken health and debts, to meet which he rapidly threw off works of various types, including his *Autobiography* (1834). In this same year he returned to Greenock, to die soon after. Galt's reputation rests on his novels of Scottish life, which show humour, pathos, and a rare command of Scots dialect.

Galton, Sir Francis (16 Feb. 1822—17 Jan. 1911), scientist, born in Birmingham, son of a banker, was a cousin of Charles Darwin (q.v.). Educated at King Edward's School, he studied medicine at King's College, London, and then read mathematics at Cambridge. Having explored Damaraland and other parts of unknown Africa, he wrote *Tropical South Africa* (1853) and *The Art of Travel* (1855). In 1856 he was elected a Fellow of the Royal Society, and from 1863 to 1867 he was secretary of the British Association for the Advancement of Science. He did some important work on meteorology, but it is with eugenics, a word he coined himself, that his name is particularly associated. Having made a special study of the laws of heredity, he wrote *Hereditary Causes* (1869), *Human Faculty* (1883), *Natural Inheritance* (1889), and *Noteworthy Families* (1906); by his will he founded a chair of eugenics at London University. He was also the originator of the use of fingerprints in criminal investigations. He was knighted in 1909.

Gardiner, Alfred George (2 June 1865—3 March 1946), journalist and essayist, was born at Chelmsford, Essex. After fifteen years in provincial journalism he became editor of the *Daily News* from 1902 to 1919 and wrote many articles and essays under the pseudonym Alpha of the Plough. Among his books are *Prophets, Priests, and Kings* (1908), *Pillars of Society* (1913), *The War Lords* (1915), *Certain People of Importance* (1926), and lives of Sir William Harcourt (1923), and George Cadbury (1923). Collections of his essays include *Pebbles on the Shore* (1915), *Leaves in the Wind* (1918), and *Many Furrows* (1924).

Gardiner, Samuel Rawson (4 March 1829—23 Feb. 1902), historian, born at Ropley, Hampshire, was educated at Winchester and Christ Church, Oxford, of which he became a Student. In 1855 he married a daughter of Edward Irving, founder of the Catholic Apostolic Church, which he joined. Himself a descendant of Cromwell and Ireton, he determined to write the history of the Puritan Revolution, which he did most ably in his *History of England from the Accession of James I to the Outbreak of the Civil War, 1603—1642*, in 10 volumes (1863—82), *History of the Great Civil War, 1642—1649*, in 4 volumes (1886), and *History of the Commonwealth and Protectorate, 1649—1660*, in 3 volumes (1894—1903). Others of his works are *The Thirty Years War* (1874), and *Cromwell's Place in History* (1896). He was elected a Fellow of All Souls in 1884 and of Merton in 1892. From 1871 to 1885 he was Professor of History at King's College, London, and from 1891 onwards he edited the *English Historical Review*. Indefatigable in research, accurate and unbiased, with a plain clear style, he has been called the most trustworthy of nineteenth-century historians.

Gardner, Erle Stanley (17 July 1889—   ), detective story writer, was born at Malden, Massachusetts, son of a miner, and at 17 went to the Klondike. Later he studied law with the district attorney, was admitted to the Californian Bar and practised for twenty-two years. In 1921 he started writing and three years later took to it seriously, keeping up a steady rapid output by means of dictaphones, after the manner of Edgar Wallace. The best of his detective stories revolve round the lawyer-sleuth Perry Mason, who figured first in *The Case of the Velvet Claws* (1932), others of his cases being *The Lucky Legs* (1933), *The Howling Dog* (1934), *The Caretaker's Cat* (1935), *The Stuttering Bishop* (1936), *The Lame Canary* (1937), *The Shoplifter's Shoe* (1938), *The Perjured Parrot* (1939), *The Baited Hook* (1940), *The Empty Tin* (1941), *The Drowning Duck* (1942), *The Drowsy Mosquito* (1943), *The Lonely Heiress* (1948), *The Musical Cow* (1950), and *The Runaway Corpse* (1954). There is another series bringing in District Attorney Douglas Selby, who appears in *The D.A. Calls It Murder* (1937), *The D.A. Holds a Candle* (1938), *The D.A. Draws a Circle* (1939), and *The D.A. Calls a Turn* (1954). A poll held by the American Institute of Public Opinion showed that in his own time Gardner was the most popular detective story writer in the United States, Conan Doyle being placed second. Gardner also wrote mystery novels under the pseudonym A. A. Fair.

Garland, Hamlin (16 Sept. 1860—4 March 1940), novelist and essayist, was born in a log cabin near West Salem, Wisconsin. In 1869 his father moved to Iowa, and Hamlin was educated at Cedar Valley Seminary, Osage. As a boy he worked on the farm with his father, but in 1884 he went to Boston, where he became first a teacher, then a writer. In 1887 he published *Main-Travelled Roads*, a collection of grimly realistic stories describing the ugliness of farm life in the West. *Prairie Folks*, another collection, followed in 1892, and in the same year his first novel, *A Spoil of Office*, appeared. Others of his novels are *Rose of Dutcher's Coolly* (1895), *The Captain of the Gray-Horse Troop* (1902), *Hesper* (1903), *The Long Trail* (1907), and *The Forester's Daughter* (1914). *A Son of the Middle Border* (1917) is partly autobiographical, and its sequel, *A Daughter of the Middle Border* (1921) was awarded the Pulitzer Prize. Garland also published a volume of critical essays, *Crumbling Idols* (1894), and a life of *Ulysses S. Grant* (1898). When he was in his seventies he wrote several books about literary figures he had known, *Roadside Meetings* (1930) being the most interesting. He was sometimes called the dean of American novelists.

Garnett, David (1892—   ), novelist, born in Brighton, was a grandson of Richard Garnett (q.v.); his father and mother were both writers, so he grew up in a literary atmosphere. Educated at the Royal College of Science, South Kensington, he studied botany for five years. During the First World War he was a conscientious objector, and in 1919 he started a bookshop in Soho. His first book, a biological fantasy entitled *Lady Into Fox*, was awarded the Hawthornden and the Tait Black Memorial Prizes in 1923. It was followed by the fanciful *A Man in the Zoo* (1924), *The Sailor's Return* (1925), *Go She Must!* (1927), *No Love* (1929), and *The Grasshoppers Come* (1931). After learning to fly, he described his experiences in *A Rabbit in the Air* (1932), and in 1938 he edited the letters of T. E. Lawrence. *A Terrible Day* (1932) is a volume of short stories, and *The Golden Echo* (1953) is an autobiography.

Garnett, Richard (27 Feb. 1835—13 April 1906), librarian, was the son of an assistant keeper of Printed Books in the British Museum. Born at Lichfield, and educated at a school in Bloomsbury, he entered the British Museum in 1851 as an assistant librarian. There he remained for nearly fifty years, and rose to be Keeper of Printed Books. He acquired a marvellous knowledge of books, and of everything connected with pure literature. He made numerous translations from the Greek, German, Italian, Spanish, and Portuguese, and wrote books of graceful verse, biographical works on Carlyle, Milton, Blake, and Emerson, *The Age of Dryden* (1895), a *History of Italian Literature* (1897), and contributed many articles to encyclopaedias, and to the *Dictionary of National Biography*. His best original work, *The Twilight of the Gods* (1888) is a series of satirical fables.

Garrick, David (19 Feb. 1717—20 Jan. 1779), actor and dramatist, born at Hereford, got most of his education at Lichfield, to which his father belonged. He was also one of the three pupils who attended Johnson's School at Edial. With his great preceptor, whom he accompanied to London, he always remained on friendly terms, becoming a member of the celebrated Club. He took to the stage, and became the greatest of English actors. He also wrote various plays and adaptations, and did not scruple to undertake 'improved' versions of some of Shakespeare's greatest plays, including *Cymbeline*, *The Taming of the Shrew*, and *The Winter's Tale*, performing the same service for Jonson and Wycherley, in the last case with much more excuse. Of his original plays, *The Lying Valet* (1741) and *Miss in her Teens* (1747), are perhaps the best. He was the last actor to be buried in Westminster Abbey, and Johnson paid a famous tribute at his death, saying that it 'eclipsed the gaiety of nations.'

Garrison, William Lloyd (10 Dec. 1805—24 March 1879), reformer, was born at Newburyport, Massachusetts, son of a sea captain. After a brief schooling, he entered journalism and became editor of the local *Free Press*, in which he printed the earliest poems of Whittier, with whom he formed a lifelong friendship. Later he moved to Boston, where he became one of the earliest champions of the abolition of slavery, editing the abolitionist paper, *The Liberator*, from 1831 to 1865. In 1833 he formed the American Anti-Slavery Society, of which he became president. His efforts earned him a short imprisonment for libel and at one time the State of Georgia offered a reward of 5,000 dollars for his arrest. His books include *Thoughts on African Colonization* (1832) and *Sonnets and Other Poems* (1843).

Garth, Sir Samuel (1661—18 Jan. 1719), doctor and poet, born at Bolam in the county of Durham, and educated at Cambridge, settled as a physician in London, where he soon acquired a large practice. He was a zealous Whig, the friend of Addison and, though of different political views, of Pope, and he ended his career as physician to George I, by whom he was knighted in 1714. He is remembered as the author of *The Dispensary* (1699), a mock-heroic poem which had great popularity in its day. He also edited a translation of Ovid's *Metamorphoses*, to which Addison, Pope, and others contributed.

Gascoigne, George (1525?—15 Nov. 1577), poet and dramatist, descended from Sir William Gascoigne, the famous Chief Justice to Henry IV, was educated at Cambridge, and entered Gray's Inn in 1555. While there he produced two plays, both translations, *The Supposes* (1566) from Ariosto, which is the earliest English prose comedy extant, and *Jocasta* (1566) from Euripides. Disinherited on account of his prodigality, he married, in order to rehabilitate his finances, a widow, the mother of Nicholas Breton (q.v.). He had, nevertheless, to go to Holland to escape from the importunities of his creditors. While there he saw service under the Prince of Orange, and was taken prisoner by the Spaniards. Released after a few months, he returned to England, and found that some of his poems had been surreptitiously published. He thereupon issued an authoritative edition under the title of *An Hundred Sundrie Floures bound up in one Posie* (1572). Other works are *Notes of Instruction Concerning the Making of Verse* (1575), which is the earliest English critical essay; *The Glasse of Government* (1575); and *The Steele Glasse* (1576), a satire. He also contributed to the entertainments in honour of Queen Elizabeth at Kenilworth and appears to have had a share of Court favour. Gascoigne was a man of originality, and a pioneer in several branches of literature.

Gaskell, Elizabeth Cleghorn (29 Sept 1810—12 Nov. 1865), novelist, was born at Chelsea, daughter of William Stevenson, a Unitarian minister, and for some time Keeper of the Treasury Records. She was brought up by her aunt at Knutsford, Cheshire, which is the original of Cranford. She married William Gaskell, a Unitarian minister, at Manchester, and in 1848 published anonymously her first book, *Mary Barton*, in which the life and feelings of the manufacturing working classes are depicted with much power and sympathy. Other novels are *Lizzie Leigh* (1855), *Mr Harrison's Confessions* (1865), *Ruth* (1853), *Cranford* (1853), *North and South* (1855), and *Sylvia's Lovers* (1863). Her last work was *Wives and Daughters* (1865), which appeared in the *Cornhill Magazine*, and was left unfinished. Mrs Gaskell had some of the characteristics of Miss Austen, and if her style and delineation of character are less minutely perfect, they are, on the other hand, imbued with a deeper vein of feeling. She was the friend of Charlotte Brontë (q.v.), to whom her sympathy brought much comfort and whose life she wrote. Of *Cranford* Lord Houghton wrote 'It is the finest piece of humoristic description that has been added to British literature since Charles Lamb.'

Gasquet, Francis Neil (5 Oct. 1846—5 April 1929), cardinal and historian, was born in London of French origin, and educated at Downside, where for a time he taught history and mathematics. From 1878 to 1885 he was prior of the monastery there, taking the religious name of Aidan. He then engaged in research for some years at the British Museum and produced *Henry VIII and the English Monasteries* (1889), which made his reputation as a historian. In 1907 he was president of the Benedictine commission which was entrusted with the task of revising the Vulgate, and for this work he had to reside in Rome. In 1914 he was created cardinal, and in 1919 became librarian of the Holy Roman Church. Others of his works are *Parish Life in Medieval England* (1906) and *Monastic Life in the Middle Ages* (1922).

Gatty, Margaret (3 June 1809—4 Oct. 1873), writer of children's books, was born at Burnham Rectory, Essex, daughter of A. J. Scott, D.D., a navy chaplain, who served under, and was the trusted friend of, Nelson. She married Alfred Gatty, D.D., Ecclesfield, Yorkshire, and became a highly popular writer of tales for young people. Among her books may be mentioned *Parables from Nature*, *Worlds not Realised*, *Proverbs Illustrated*, and *Aunt Judy's Tales* (1859). She also founded *Aunt Judy's Magazine* in 1865, and wrote a book on British seaweeds. Juliana Ewing (q.v.) was her daughter.

Gauden, John (1605—20 Sept. 1662), theologian, was born at Mayfield in Essex, and educated at Cambridge. His claim to remembrance rests on his being the reputed author of *Eikon Basilike* (the Royal Image), a book purporting to contain the meditations of Charles I during his imprisonment. Published immediately after the King's execution in 1649, it produced an extraordinary effect, so much so that Charles II is reported to have said that, had it been published a week earlier, it would have saved his father's life. There seems now to be little doubt that Gauden was the author. At all events he claimed to be recompensed for his services, and was made Bishop successively of Exeter and Worcester. The work passed through 47 editions within a year, and was answered by Milton in his *Eikonoklastes* (the Image-breaker).

Gawsworth, John, *see* **Armstrong, Terence I. F.**

Gay, John (baptized 16 Sept. 1685, died 4 Dec. 1732), dramatist and poet, was born near Barnstaple of a good but decayed family. His parents dying while he was a child he was apprenticed to a silk-mercer in London, but not liking the trade, was released by his master. In 1708 he published a poem, *Wine*, and in 1713 *Rural Sports*, which he dedicated to Pope, whose friendship he obtained. A little before this he had received an appointment as secretary in the household of the Duchess of Monmouth. In 1714 he made his first decided hit with *The Shepherd's Week*, a set of six pastorals designed to satirize Ambrose Philips, which, however, secured public approval on their own merits. These were followed by *Trivia* (1716), in which he was aided by Swift, an account in mock heroic verse of the dangers of the London streets. Gay had always been ambitious of public employment, and his aspirations were gratified by his receiving the appointment of secretary to an embassy to Hanover, which, how-ever, he appears to have resigned in a few months. His first attempts at drama were a satirical farce entitled *What d'ye Call It* (1715), and a comedy, *Three Hours after Marriage* (1717), neither of which, however, took the public fancy. In 1720 he published a collection of his poems, which brought him £1,000, but soon after lost all his means in the collapse of the South Sea Company. After producing another drama, *The Captive*, he published his *Fables* (1727), which added to his reputation, and soon after, in 1728, achieved the great success of his life in *The Beggar's Opera*, a Newgate pastoral, sug-gested by Swift, in which the graces and fantasticalities of the Italian opera were satirized. A sequel, *Polly* (1729), was suppressed by the Lord Chamberlain as reflecting upon the Court, but was published and had an enormous sale. The last few years of Gay's life were passed in the household of the Duke of Queensberry, who had always been his friend and patron. He died after three days' illness, and is buried in Westminster Abbey. Of his songs, the best-remembered is 'Black-eyed Susan.'

Geddes, Alexander (1737—26 Feb. 1802), theologian and poet, of Roman Catholic parentage, was born at Ruthven, Banffshire. Educated for the priesthood at the local seminary of Scalan, and at Paris, he became a priest in his native county. His translation of

K

the *Satires* of Horace made him known as a scholar, but his liberality of view led to his suspension. He then went to London, where he became known to Lord Petre, who enabled him to proceed with a new translation of the Bible for English Roman Catholics, which he carried on as far as Ruth, with some of the Psalms, and which was published in 3 volumes (1792—6). This was followed by *Critical Remarks on the Hebrew Scriptures*, in which he largely anticipated the German school of criticism. The result of this publication was his suspension from all ecclesiastical functions. Geddes was also a poet, and wrote *Linton: a Tweedside Pastoral* (1781).

Geoffrey of Monmouth (1100?—1154), churchman and chronicler, born in Monmouth, and educated at Oxford, was probably a Benedictine monk. He is said to have been Archdeacon of Llandaff, and in 1152 was appointed Bishop of St Asaph. His *Historia Regum Britanniae* (History of the Kings of Britain) claims to be based on 'a most ancient book in the British tongue,' but its main sources are the works of Bede and Nennius (qq.v.). The chief authority for the Arthurian legends, it was translated into Anglo-Norman by Gaimar and Wace (qq.v.) and into English by Layamon (q.v.).

George, Henry (2 Sept. 1839—29 Oct. 1897), economist, was born in Philadelphia, one of a publisher's ten children. At the age of 14 he left school to become an errand boy, and after a brief period as a sailor became a printer and journalist, but was constantly in money difficulties. After the publication in 1880 of his great work *Progress and Poverty* he became a public figure and lectured on economic questions at home and abroad. His theory was that poverty could be abolished by the use of a single tax that would absorb all the economic rent of land. In 1881 he wrote *The Irish Land Question*, and a few years later visited Britain twice. He offered himself as a candidate for Mayor of New York, but was unsuccessful. Among his other works are *Social Problems* (1884), *Protection and Free Trade* (1886), and *The Science of Political Economy* (1897).

Gerald, Alexander (22 Feb. 1728—22 Feb. 1795), theologian, was born at Chapel of Garioch, Aberdeenshire, where his father was minister. Educated at Marischal College, he became professor, first of Philosophy and afterwards of Divinity, and one of the ministers of the city. As a professor he introduced various reforms. In 1756 he gained the prize for an *Essay on Taste* which, together with an *Essay on Genius*, he subsequently published.

Gibbings, Robert (23 March 1889—19 Jan. 1958), artist and travel writer, was born in Cork, son of a protestant clergyman. When the First World War broke out he was an art student; he joined the Royal Munster Fusiliers and was badly wounded at Gallipoli. After the war he settled in London, was proprietor for a time of the Golden Cockerel Press, and then became a lecturer in typography at Reading University. He wrote a number of travel books, illustrated with his own wood engravings. After *A Tahitian Journal* (1932), *Coconut Island* (1936), and *Blue Angels and Whales* (1938) he scored a notable success with *Sweet Thames Run Softly* (1940) and the succeeding books *Coming Down the Wye* (1942) and *Lovely is the Lee*

(1944).   He went back to the South Seas for *Over the Reefs* (1948) and home again for *Sweet Cork of Thee* (1951), *Coming Down the Seine* (1953), and *Till I End My Song* (1957).

Gibbon, Edward (27 April 1737—16 Jan. 1794), greatest of English historians, was born at Putney of an ancient Kentish family.   His father was a country gentleman and M.P.   Edward was the only one of a family of seven who survived infancy, and was himself a delicate child with a precocious love of study.   After receiving his early education at home he was sent to Westminster School, and when 15 was entered at Magdalen College, Oxford, where, according to his own account, he spent fourteen months idly and unprofitably. Oxford was then at its lowest ebb, and earnest study or effort of any kind had little encouragement.   Gibbon, however, appears to have maintained his wide reading in some degree, and his study of Bossuet and other controversialists led to his becoming in 1753 a Roman Catholic.   To counteract this his father placed him under the charge of David Mallet (q.v.), the poet, deist, and editor of Bolingbroke's works, whose influence, not unnaturally, failed of the desired effect, and Gibbon was next sent to Lausanne, and placed under the care of a Protestant pastor, M. Pavilliard, who reconverted him to his original faith.   At Lausanne he remained for over four years, and devoted himself assiduously to study, especially of French literature and the Latin classics.   At this time also he became engaged to Mademoiselle Suzanne Curchod; but on the match being peremptorily opposed by his father it was broken off; Gibbon, in his own words, 'sighed as a lover, obeyed as a son.'   With the lady, who eventually became the wife of Necker, and the mother of Madame de Staël, he remained on terms of friendship.   In 1758 Gibbon returned to England, and in 1761 published *Essai sur l'Etude de la Litterature*, translated into English in 1764.   From 1759 to 1770 he held the rank of captain in the militia, an experience which he found of value when he came to write of military history.   About this time he made a tour on the Continent, visiting Paris, where he stayed for three months, and thence proceeding to Switzerland and Italy.   There it was that, musing amid the ruins of the Capitol at Rome on 15 October 1764, he formed the plan of writing the history of the decline and fall of the Roman Empire.

He returned to England in 1765, and in 1770 his father died, leaving him the embarrassed estate of Buriton, which had been his usual home when in England.   With a view to retrieving his affairs, he left his estate and lived in London where, in 1772, he seriously set himself to realize the great plan which, since its conception, had never been out of his thoughts.   The progress of the work was delayed by the fact that Gibbon had meanwhile (1774) entered the House of Commons, where, as member for Liskeard, he was a steady, though silent, supporter of Lord North in his American policy.   He subsequently sat for Lymington, and held office as a Commissioner of Trade and Plantations 1779—82.   The first volume of the *Decline and Fall of the Roman Empire* appeared in 1776, and was received with acclamation, and it was not until some time had elapsed that the author's treatment of the rise of Christianity excited the attention and alarm of the religious and ecclesiastical world. When, however, the far-reaching nature of his views was at length realized, a fierce and prolonged controversy arose, into which Gibbon himself did not enter except in one case where his fidelity as an historian was impugned. The second and third volumes appeared in 1781, and in 1783 Gibbon returned to Lausanne, where he lived tranquilly with an early friend, M. Deyverdun, devoting his mornings to the completion of his history, and his evenings to society. At length, on the night of 27 June 1787, in the summer-house of his garden, the last words were penned, and the great work of his life completed. Of the circumstances, and of his feelings at the moment, he has himself given an impressive account in his *Autobiography*, published in 1796. The last three volumes were issued in 1788, Gibbon having gone to London to see them through the press. This being done he returned to Lausanne where, within a year, his beloved friend Deyverdun died. His last years were clouded by ill-health, and by anxieties with regard to the French Revolution. In 1793, though travelling was a serious matter for him, he came to England to comfort his friend Lord Sheffield on the death of his wife, and died suddenly in London.

The place of Gibbon among historians is in the first rank, and if the vast scale of his work and the enormous mass of detail involved in it are considered along with the learning and research employed in accumulating the material, and the breadth of view, lucidity of arrangement, and sense of proportion which have fused them into a distinct and splendid picture, his claims to the first place cannot be disputed. His style, though not pure, being tinged with Gallicisms, is one of the most noble in our literature, rich, harmonious, and stately; and though sources of information not accessible to him have added to our knowledge, and have shown some of his conclusions to be mistaken, his historical accuracy has been comparatively little shaken, and his work is sure of permanence. The standard edition of the *Decline and Fall* is that by J. B. Bury (q.v.), published 1896—1900; his *Miscellaneous Works* were first edited in 1796, his *Letters* in 1896.

Gibbons, Stella Dorothea (5 Jan. 1902—   ), novelist, was born in north London, daughter of a doctor, and as a girl used to entertain her brothers by telling them stories. Educated at the North London Collegiate School for Girls, she then took the course in journalism at University College, and worked for ten years in Fleet Street. In 1933 she married Allan Bourne Webb, an actor, and in the same year her first novel, *Cold Comfort Farm*, a clever skit on the rural novel, won the Femina Vie Heureuse Prize. *Christmas at Cold Comfort Farm* followed in 1940 and *Conference at Cold Comfort Farm* in 1949. Others of her novels are *Bassett* (1934), *Enbury Heath* (1935), *Miss Linsey and Pa* (1936), *Nightingale Wood* (1938), *My American* (1939), *The Bachelor* (1944), *The Matchmaker* (1949), and *The Shadow of a Sorcerer* (1955). *Beside the Pearly Water* (1954) is a collection of short stories, and her *Collected Poems* appeared in 1950.

Gibbs, Sir Philip Hamilton (1 May 1877—   ), journalist, son of a civil servant, was privately educated, and became literary editor successively of the *Daily Mail*, *Daily Chronicle*, and *Tribune*. His novel *The Street of Adventure* (1909) describes the changes and chances of Fleet Street. As special correspondent of the *Daily Chronicle* he did brilliant work with the Allied forces in the First World War, and was made a Knight of the Order of the British Empire in 1920. A number of books, including *Realities of War* (1920) were based on his war experiences. A Roman Catholic, he performed the great journalistic feat of interviewing the Pope. He wrote many novels, of which the most outstanding are *The Middle of the Road* (1922) and *The Cross of Peace* (1933). Among the best of his other books are *Ten Years After* (1924), *The Day After Tomorrow* (1928), *European Journey* (1934), and *The New Elizabethans* (1953), a study of the modern English people. *The Pageant of the Years* (1947) and *Crowded Company* (1949) are autobiographical.

Gibson, Wilfrid Wilson (2 Oct. 1878—   ), poet, was born at Hexham, Northumberland. Educated privately, he started writing poetry in early youth, and never had any other occupation. His first published poem appeared in the *Spectator* in 1897, and his first book of verse, *Mountain Lovers*, in 1902. During the First World War he was rejected four times for bad eyesight, but finally got himself accepted for service in 1917 and served as a private. One of the leaders of the Georgian group of poets, he revolted against the Tennyson tradition and wrote of common life, raising ordinary matter to poetic level. A realist, he has been called the poet of 'the industrial poor,' but he also made use of his native Northumbrian country scenery. His earlier verse was gathered together in *Collected Poems 1905—25* (1926); later volumes are *Hazards* (1930), *Islands* (1932), *The Outpost* (1944), and *The Island Stag* (1947). He also wrote a number of plays, including *Daily Bread* (1910), *Womenkind* (1912), *Kestrel Edge* (1924), and *Within Four Walls* (1950).

Gifford, Richard (1725—1 March 1807), poet, was born at Bishop's Castle, Shropshire, son of a clergyman. Educated at Oxford, he took orders and became vicar of Duffield in Derbyshire. In 1753 he published anonymously the poem *Contemplation*, four lines of which have won immortality by being quoted in Dr Johnson's dictionary.

Gifford, William (April 1756—31 Dec. 1826), critic and poet, was born at Ashburton, Devon, son of a glazier, and after being for a short time at sea, was apprenticed to a cobbler. Having, however, shown signs of a superior ability, and a desire for learning, he was befriended and educated, ultimately at Oxford. Becoming known to Lord Grosvenor, he was patronized by him, and in course of time produced his first poem, *The Baviad* (1794), a satire directed against the Della Cruscans, a clique of trifling sentimental poets. This was followed by another satire, *The Maeviad* (1795), against some minor dramatists. His last effort in this line was his *Epistle to Peter Pindar* (1800), inspired by personal enmity, which evoked from its victim Dr Walcot the reply, *A Cut at a Cobbler*. These writings had established the reputation of Gifford as a keen, and even ferocious critic, and he was appointed in 1797 editor of the *Anti-Jacobin*, which Canning and his friends had just started, and of the *Quarterly Review* (1809—24). In it he bitterly attacked Keats, Hazlitt, and the so-called Cockney School of poetry, being probably the author of the notorious denunciation of *Endymion* in 1818. As a critic he had acuteness, but was hide-bound and prejudiced. He also brought out editions of Massinger, Ben Jonson, and Ford.

Gilbert, Sir William Schwenck (18 Nov. 1836—29 May 1911), dramatist, was born in London, son of a novelist; he got his middle name from his godmother. As a child, when in Italy with his parents he was stolen by brigands and ransomed for £25. He was educated at Great Ealing School and King's College, London, where he had Ainger and Besant (qq.v.) as fellow-students. In 1855 he was entered at the Inner Temple and in 1857 got a commission in the militia just too late for the Crimean War. From then on he worked as a clerk in the Privy Council Education Department, and in 1863 was called to the Bar, but found law far from lucrative, making only £75 in two years. Meanwhile he contributed as both writer and artist to *Fun* and sometimes to *Punch*, to which in 1866 he offered his famous 'Yarn of the *Nancy Bell*'; it was rejected as 'too cannibalistic,' but later became one of the most famous of his *Bab Ballads* (1869), which were named after the nickname he had as a child. In the next few years he wrote a number of short plays, but his chief fame rests on the comic operas in which he collaborated with Arthur Sullivan, the composer.

The first of these, *Trial by Jury* (1875) was followed in 1878 by *The Sorcerer*, and *H.M.S. 'Pinafore'*; the latter, which pokes fun at the navy, was a great success in America, where *The Pirates of Penzance* was next presented in 1879. *Patience*, a delightful burlesque of the aesthetic movement, followed in 1881, *Iolanthe* in 1882, *Princess Ida* in 1884, *The Mikado*, best-known of all the series, in 1885, *Ruddigore* in 1887, *The Yeomen of the Guard*, which has more seriousness than the others, in 1888, and *The Gondoliers* in 1889. At this point Gilbert and Sullivan, who were constantly quarrelling, definitely parted, and though they worked together again later, *Utopia Limited* (1893) and *The Grand Duke* (1896) did not approach the popularity of their earlier operas, which were still playing to full houses seventy years after. A wealthy man, Gilbert built and owned the Garrick Theatre, and his house at Harrow had a miniature observatory for his hobby of astronomy as well as an open-air swimming-pool; this last was the occasion of his death, which occurred from heart failure after he had rescued a lady visitor from drowning in it. He had been knighted in 1907.

Gildas (516?—570), historian, was a monk who is said to have gone to Brittany about 550 and founded a monastery. About 547 he wrote *De Excidio et Conquestu Britanniae* (On the Overthrow and Conquest of Britain), tracing the history of the country from the Roman invasion to his own time. Obscure, wordy, and unreliable, he is of some value as a primary authority for events of the fifth and early sixth centuries.

Gilder, Richard Watson (8 Feb. 1844—18 Nov. 1909), poet and journalist, was born at Bordentown, New Jersey, son of a Methodist minister who kept a girls' school at which Richard was the only boy pupil. In 1863 he entered the Philadelphia Artillery and fought in the Civil War. Turning to journalism he became assistant editor of *Scribner's Monthly*, and then editor of *The Century*, which had a great influence on the artistic and social life of New York. He wrote many books of verse, being at his best in lyrics and sonnets; they include *The New Day* (1876), *The Celestial Passion* (1887), *The Great Remembrance* (1893), *Five Books of Song* (1894), *In Palestine* (1898), and *Poems* (1908). His *Letters* were edited by his daughter in 1916.

Gildon, Charles (1665—12 Jan. 1724), critic, born at Gillingham, in Dorset, belonged to a Roman Catholic family, was educated for the priesthood at Douay, but became an unsuccessful playwright, a literary hack, and a critic of little acumen or discrimination. He attacked Pope as 'Sawny Dapper,' and was in return embalmed in *The Dunciad*. He also wrote a life of Defoe.

Gilfillan, George (30 Jan. 1813—13 Aug. 1878), poet and critic, born at Comrie, Perthshire, where his father was minister, studied at Glasgow University, and was ordained minister of a church in Dundee. He was a voluminous author. Among his writings are *Gallery of Literary Portraits*, and a collection of British poets in 48 volumes, with introductions and notes. He also wrote lives of Burns, Scott, and others, and *Night* (1867), a poem in 9 books. His style was somewhat turgid, and his criticism rather sympathetic than profound.

Gilfillan, Robert (7 July 1798—4 Dec. 1850), poet, was born at Dunfermline, son of a weaver. In 1811 the family removed to Leith and he was apprenticed to a cooper, then becoming successively grocer's shopman, clerk, and collector of police rates. He wrote a number of Scottish songs, including 'Oh, why left I my Hame,' and was favourably mentioned in the *Noctes Ambrosianae* of J. Wilson (q.v.).

Gillespie, George (21 Jan. 1613—16 Dec. 1648), theologian, was born at Kirkcaldy, and studied at St Andrews. He became one of the ministers of Edinburgh, and was a member of the Westminster Assembly, in which he took a prominent part. He was one of the most formidable controversialists of a highly controversial age. His best known work is *Aaron's Rod Blossoming* (1646), a defence of the ecclesiastical claims of the high Presbyterian party. He was Moderator of the General Assembly in 1648.

Gillies, John (18 Jan. 1747—15 Feb. 1836), historian, born at Brechin, Forfarshire, and educated at Glasgow University, wrote a *History of Greece* (1786) from a strongly anti-democratic standpoint, a *History of the World from Alexander to Augustus* (1807), and a *View of the Reign of Frederick II of Prussia*. He also made various translations from the Greek. In 1793 he was appointed Historiographer Royal for Scotland.

Giraldus de Barri, called **Cambrensis** (1146?—1220), travel writer, was born at Manorbier in Pembrokeshire of a Norman family which intermarried with the royal family of Wales. He was an eminent scholar and churchman, whose object of ambition was the Bishopric of St David's, to which he was twice elected by the chapter, but from which he was kept out by the opposition of the King. When travelling in Ireland with Prince John he wrote *Topographia Hibernica* (1185), a valuable descriptive account of the country, and in 1188 he wrote *Itinerarium Cambriae,* a similar work on Wales. He left several other works, including an autobiography, *De Rebus a se Gestis* (Concerning his own Doings).

Gissing, George (22 Nov. 1857—28 Dec. 1903), novelist, was born at Wakefield, son of a chemist and writer. At Owens College, Manchester, he was one of the most brilliant students, but wrecked his career by his unpractical idealism, being found to have stolen money to assist a prostitute with whom he had formed an attachment. Subsequently he worked as a clerk in Manchester, as tutor and gas-fitter in Boston, and nearly starved in Chicago. His experiences at this time are described in *New Grub Street* (1891), and the misfortune which seemed to dog all his actions is responsible for the tone of gloomy pessimism which runs through all his books. In 1878 he returned to England and published *Workers in the Dawn* (1880), which was followed by *The Unclassed* (1884) and *Isabel Clarendon* (1886). *Demos* (1886), his first real success, and *Thyrza* (1887) both take for their theme the degradation caused by poverty, but *A Life's Morning* (1888) is more light-hearted. Best of his books are the novels *The Nether World* (1889), *The Odd Women* (1893), and *In the Year of Jubilee* (1894), together with the unclassifiable *Private Papers of Henry Ryecroft* (1903). He also wrote effective *Critical Studies of Dickens* (1898). Twice married, he was unfortunate in both unions.

Gladstone, William Ewart (29 Dec. 1809—19 May 1898), statesman, was born in Liverpool, son of a merchant of Scottish ancestry, and was educated at Eton and Oxford, where he was prominent in the Union. In 1832 he entered Parliament as member for Newark, and rose rapidly, after holding various offices, to be four times Prime Minister (1868—74, 1880—5, 1885—6, and 1892—3). The Grand Old Man, as he was latterly called, possessed an extraordinary influence over his contemporaries through his powerful personality and the richness of his eloquence. In spite of his preoccupation with politics he found time to write a number of books, the first being *The State in its Relations with the Church* (1839). His *Studies on Homer and the Homeric Age* (1858), admired at the time, is now outdated. Others of his works are *Juventus Mundi* (1869), *The Impregnable Rock of Holy Scripture* (1890), *Odes of Horace Translated* (1894), and *Gleanings of Past Years* (1897). He died at Hawarden in Flintshire, his home for nearly sixty years, and is buried in Westminster Abbey.

Glanvill, Joseph (1636—4 Nov. 1680), theologian, born at Plymouth, and educated at Oxford, took orders, and held various benefices, including the Rectory of Bath Abbey and a prebend at Worcester. He came under the influence of the Cambridge Platonists, especially of Henry More (q.v.). His contendings were mainly with the English Nonconformists. His chief work is the *Vanity of Dogmatizing* (1661) which contains the story of the 'scholar gipsy,' in later days turned to such fine account by Matthew Arnold. Glanvill wrote a fine literary style, at its best recalling that of Sir Thomas Browne.

Glapthorne, Henry (28 July 1610—1644?), dramatist, had a high reputation among his contemporaries, though now almost forgotten. He wrote two comedies, three tragedies, and a book of poems, which were all reprinted in two volumes in 1874. His best play is *Argalus and Parthenia* (1639), based upon Sidney's *Arcadia*. Others were *The Hollander*, *Wit is a Constable*, and *The Ladies' Privilege* (all 1640).

Glascock, William Nugent (1787?—8 Oct. 1847), novelist, was a captain in the navy, and from this drew the inspiration of his vigorous and breezy sea-stories, which include *Sailors and Saints* (1829), *Tales of a Tar* (1836), and *Land Sharks and Sea Gulls* (1838). He also compiled *Naval Service, or Officers' Manual* (1836), which was translated and adopted by several other countries.

Glasgow, Ellen Anderson Gholson (22 April 1874—20 Nov. 1945), novelist, was born at Richmond, Virginia, where she remained throughout her life. A delicate child, she educated herself by reading in her father's library. Her first published work was some anonymous verse, her first novel *The Descendants* (1897). She began realistic writing with *The Voice of the People* (1900), which she followed up with *The Battleground* (1902), *The Deliverance* (1904), and *The Wheel of Life* (1911). *Virginia* (1913) and *Life and Gabriella* (1916) deal with the problems of a rigid family code; *Barren Ground* (1925) is political; while *The Romantic Comedians* (1926) and *They Stooped to Folly* (1929) are novels of manners. *In This Our Life*, which satirized the traditions of the South, was awarded the Pulitzer Prize for 1942. Her autobiography, *The Woman Within*, appeared posthumously in 1954. A distinguished literary figure, conventional and sophisticated, she received honorary degrees from four universities and was an honorary member of Phi Beta Kappa.

Gleig, George Robert (20 April 1796—9 July 1888), novelist and biographer, son of the Bishop of Brechin, was born at Stirling and educated at the grammar-school there and at Glasgow University and Balliol. He became an ensign in the army, and served in the Peninsula and America. Returning to Oxford in 1816, he took orders, and after serving various cures became in 1834, Chaplain of Chelsea Hospital, and in 1844 Chaplain-General of the Forces, which office he held until 1875. He was a frequent contributor to reviews and magazines, especially *Blackwood's*, in which his best-known novel, *The Subaltern*, appeared in 1826, and he was also the author of lives of Warren Hastings, Clive, and Wellington.

Glen, William (14 Nov. 1789—Dec. 1826), poet, born in Glasgow,

K*

was for some years in the West Indies. An unsuccessful business man, he died in poverty. His *Poems, chiefly Lyrical* (1815) include the well-known Jacobite ballad 'Wae's me for Prince Charlie.'

Glover, Richard (1712—25 Nov. 1785), poet and dramatist, was a London merchant, and M.P. for Weymouth. A scholarly man with a taste for literature, he wrote *Leonidas* (1737), a poem in 9 books, later enlarged to 12, and a ponderous epic, *The Athenaid* (1787). Though not without a degree of dignity, they want energy and interest, and are now forgotten. He also produced a few dramas, which had little success. His ballad, 'Admiral Hosier's Ghost,' had at one time a great vogue.

Glyn, Elinor (17 Oct. 1864—23 Sept. 1943), novelist, was born in Jersey, a daughter of Douglas Sutherland, a civil engineer. Her father died before she was a year old and she was taken to Canada by her mother, who, however, married again and returned in 1871 to Jersey, where Elinor read widely in her stepfather's house. A red-haired, exotic beauty, she married Clayton Glyn, M.P., in 1892. Her first book, *The Visits of Elizabeth* (1900), was highly successful, and was followed by *The Reflections of Ambrosine* (1902) and *The Vicissitudes of Evangeline* (1906), but she is chiefly remembered by *Three Weeks* (1907), a novel of passion which caused a sensation and is said to have sold five million copies. Later novels are *His Hour* (1910), *The Career of Katherine Bush* (1916), *Man and Maid* (1925), and *The Price of Things* (1930). From 1920 to 1927 she lived in Hollywood, writing for the films. *Romantic Adventure* (1936) is an autobiography.

Godfrey, Thomas (4 Dec. 1736—3 Aug. 1763), poet and playwright, was born in Philadelphia, son of a glazier. Apprenticed first to a watchmaker, he was a lieutenant in the army for a few months, then became a factor in North Carolina. His blank verse tragedy, *The Prince of Parthia*, published in 1765, is considered to be the first play written by an American and produced by professional actors. His poem *The Court of Fancy* appeared in the same year as his early death from a fever.

Godkin, Edwin Lawrence (2 Oct. 1831—21 May 1902), editor, was born at Moyne, County Wicklow, son of a clergyman, ultimately of English stock. Delicate and precocious as a child, he was educated at Silcoates School, Wakefield, and Queen's College, Belfast, then went to London and became a writer. His first book, *A History of Hungary*, appeared in 1853, and in the years that followed he was special correspondent for the *Daily News* in the Crimea. Offered the editorship of the Belfast *Northern Whig*, he went instead to America, where he studied law and was admitted to the Bar in 1858. In 1865 he was one of the founders of *The Nation*, which he edited from then till 1900. It became one of the greatest of American weeklies, as Godkin was well informed in both history and economics and was completely independent and fearless in expressing his views; he was several times summoned for libel, but the cases never went to court. In 1901 he returned to England, where he died.

Godley, Alfred Denis (22 Jan. 1856—27 June 1925), scholar and poet, was a son of the rector of Carrigallen, County Leitrim, and a cousin of the first Baron Kilbracken. Educated at Harrow and Balliol College, Oxford, he was for a time a master at Bradfield College, then from 1883 to 1912 was a Fellow and Tutor of Magdalen; from 1910 he was Public Orator to the University of Oxford. A very fine classical scholar, he made translations of Herodotus, Tacitus, and Horace, and is especially remembered for his volumes of elegant and witty verse, which include *Verses to Order* (1892), *Lyra Frivola* (1899), and *Fifty Poems*, published in 1927 after his death. He also wrote *Aspects of Modern Oxford* (1893) and *Oxford in the Eighteenth Century* (1908), as well as editing the works of Praed (1909) and Thomas Moore (1910).

Godwin, Mary (27 April 1759—10 Sept. 1797), feminist, was of Irish extraction. Her father, E. J. Wollstonecraft, was a spend-thrift of bad habits, and at 19 Mary left home to make her way in the world. Her next ten years were spent as companion to a lady, in teaching a school at Newington Green, and as governess in the family of Lord Kingsborough. In 1788 she took to translating, and became literary adviser to Johnson the publisher, through whom she became known to many of the literary people of the day, as well as to certain Radicals, including Godwin, Paine, Priestley, and Fuseli, the painter. In 1792 she went to Paris, where she met Captain Imlay, with whom she formed a connection, the fruit of which was her daughter Fanny. Captain Imlay having deserted her, she tried to commit suicide at Putney Bridge, but was rescued. Thereafter she resumed her literary labours, and lived with W. Godwin, who married her in 1797. She died at the birth of their daughter Mary, who became the second wife of Shelley. Her chief original writings are her *Answer to Burke's Reflections on the French Revolution* (1791), *Vindication of the Rights of Women* (1792), which courageously assailed conventions of the day, and *Original Stories for Children* (1791), illustrated by W. Blake.

Godwin, William (3 March 1756—7 April 1836), philosopher and novelist, was born at Wisbech in Cambridgeshire, and educated at a school in Norwich, to which city his father, a Presbyterian minister, had removed, and subsequently at a Presbyterian college at Hoxton, with a view to the ministry. From 1778 to 1783 he acted as minister of various congregations near London; but his theological views having undergone important changes, he resigned his pastorate, and devoted himself to a literary career. His first work, a series of historical sketches in the form of sermons, failed. He then found employment as one of the principal writers in the *New Annual Register*, and became otherwise prominent as an advocate of political and social reform. In 1793 his *Inquiry Concerning Political Justice*, which advocated the overthrow of authority and the abolition of marriage, was published and made him famous. A year later he published his masterpiece, *Caleb Williams*, a novel embodying his social theories, and in 1797 he married Mary Wollstonecraft (*see* Mary Godwin), whose life he afterwards wrote. In 1799 his second great novel, *St Leon*, a tale of the miraculous, appeared. His other

novels, *Fleetwood* (1804), *Mandeville* (1817), and *Cloudesley* (1830),
are much inferior. In addition to these works Godwin brought out
an elaborate *Life of Chaucer* in two volumes (1803), *An Essay on
Sepulchres* (1808), containing much fine thought finely expressed, *A
History of the Commonwealth of England* (1824—8), and his last work,
Lives of the Necromancers (1834). For some time he engaged in the
publishing business, in which, however, he ultimately proved
unsuccessful. In his later years he had the office of Yeoman Usher
of the Exchequer conferred upon him. Godwin entered in 1801
into a second marriage with a widow, Mrs Clairmont, by whom he
had a daughter. This lady had already a son and daughter, the
latter of whom had an irregular connection with Byron. Sceptic
and anarchist, Godwin was the theorist of the Romantic Revival,
and had a great influence on Wordsworth, Coleridge, and Shelley.

Gogarty, Oliver St John (17 Aug. 1878—22 Sept. 1957), surgeon,
poet, and writer of memoirs, was born in Dublin and educated
at Stonyhurst and Trinity College, Dublin, where he was a
fellow-student of Joyce (q.v.), who depicts him as Buck Mulligan in
Ulysses. An opponent in politics of the Sinn Feiners, Gogarty was
kidnapped during the troubles in 1921, and from 1922 to 1936 was a
senator of the Irish Free State. Famous for his wit, he was
acquainted with the chief writers of the Irish Renascence, including
Yeats, George Moore, and G. W. Russell. Among his volumes of
verse are *Poems and Plays* (1920), *An Offering of Swans* (1924),
Others to Adorn (1938), and *Elbow Room* (1939), but he was best
known for his racy books of memoirs, *As I Was Going Down Sackville
Street* (1937), *Tumbling in the Hay* (1939), and *It Isn't This Time of
Year At All!* (1954). A Roman Catholic, Gogarty lived in Renvyle,
Galway, and also spent some time in the United States. As a
young man he won cups at motor-cycle racing, while his later hobbies
were archery and aviation.

Golding, Arthur (1536—10 May 1606), translator, son of a gentleman of Essex, was educated at Jesus College, Cambridge, and
translated theological works by Calvin, Beza, and others, but is
chiefly remembered for his versions of Caesar's *Commentaries* (1565),
and specially of Ovid's *Metamorphoses* (1565—7), the latter in ballad
metre. He also translated Justin's *History*, and part of Seneca.
His half-sister married the Earl of Oxford.

Golding, Louis (19 Nov. 1895—9 Aug. 1958), novelist, was
born in Manchester (the 'Doomington' of his best-known novels),
and educated at Manchester Grammar School, of which he wrote in
his first book *Forward from Babylon* (1920); at Oxford he conducted
an undergraduate magazine. After serving in the First World War
he travelled extensively, and wrote of his experiences in *Sunward*
(1924), *Sicilian Noon* (1925), and *Those Ancient Lands* (1928). His
novels include *Seacoast of Bohemia* (1923), *Day of Atonement* (1925),
The Miracle Boy (1927), *Store of Ladies* (1927), *Magnolia Street*
(1931), *Five Silver Daughters* (1934), *The Camberwell Beauty* (1935),
Mr Emmanuel (1939), *The Glory of Elsie Silver* (1945), and *To the
Quayside* (1953). He also wrote a study of *James Joyce* (1933) and
several books of verse.

Goldring, Douglas (7 Jan. 1887—9 April 1960), novelist, was born at Greenwich, son of an architect, and educated at Felsted and Oxford. In 1908 he joined the staff of *Country Life*, from it went to the *English Review*, and in 1910 founded and edited *The Tramp*, which was famous for its verse contributors. His own volumes of verse include *A Country Boy* (1910) and *In the Town* (1916). From 1925 to 1927 he was Lecturer on English at the University College of Commerce, Gothenburg. His novels include *The Permanent Uncle* (1912), *The Fortune* (1917), *Nobody Knows* (1923), *The Cuckoo* (1926), *The Façade* (1927), *Margot's Progress* (1929), and *Facing the Odds* (1940). He also wrote lives of Ford Madox Ford (1948), and Sir Thomas Lawrence (1951), and many books of travel. *Life Interests* (1948) is a book of reminiscences.

Goldsmith, Oliver (10 Nov. 1728—4 April 1774), poet, dramatist, and essayist, son of an Irish clergyman, was born at Pallas in Longford. His early education was received at various schools at Elphin, Athlone, and Edgeworthstown. At the age of 8 he had a severe attack of smallpox which disfigured him for life. In 1744 he went as a sizar to Trinity College, Dublin, whence, having come into collision with one of the college tutors, he ran away in 1746. He was, however, induced to return, and graduated B.A. in 1749. The Church was chosen for him as a profession, against his inclination. He presented himself before the Bishop of Elphin for examination —perhaps as a type of deeper and more inward incongruencies— in scarlet breeches, and was rejected. He next figured as a tutor; but had no sooner accumulated £30 than he quitted his employment and forthwith dissipated his little savings. A long-suffering uncle named Contarine, who had already more than once interposed on his behalf, now provided means to send him to London to study law. He, however, got no farther than Dublin, where he was fleeced to his last guinea, and returned to the house of his mother, now a widow with a large family. After an interval spent in idleness, he studied medicine at Edinburgh University from 1752 to 1754, when he proceeded to Leyden. After a year there he started on a walking tour, which led him through France, Germany, Switzerland, and Italy. How he lived it is hard to say, for he left Leyden penniless. It is said that he earned a livelihood by disputing at universities and playing the flute on his travels. All this time, however, he was gaining the experiences and knowledge of foreign countries which he was afterwards to turn to such excellent account. At one of the Universities visited at this time, he is believed to have secured the medical degree, of which he subsequently made use. Louvain and Padua have both been named as the source of it.

He reached London almost literally penniless in 1756, and appears to have been occupied successively as an apothecary's journeyman, a doctor of the poor, and an usher in a school at Peckham. In 1757 he was writing for the *Monthly Review*. The next year he applied unsuccessfully for a medical appointment in India; and the year following, 1759, saw his first important literary venture, *An Enquiry into the State of Polite Learning in Europe*. It was published anonymously, but attracted some attention, and brought him other work. At the same time he became known to Bishop Percy, the collector of the *Reliques of Ancient Poetry*, and he had written *The Bee*, a collection of essays, and was employed upon various periodicals. In 1761 began his friendship with Johnson, which led to that of the other great men of that circle, and he became a member of the Literary Club. His *Chinese Letters*, afterwards republished as *The Citizen of the World*, appeared in *The Public Ledger* in 1762. *The Traveller*, the first of his longer poems, came out in 1764, and was followed in 1766 by his novel, *The Vicar of Wakefield*. In 1768 his drama, *The Good-natured Man*, had considerable success. The next few years saw him busily occupied with work for the publishers, including *The History of Rome* (1769), and lives of Parnell the poet, and Lord Bolingbroke (1770); in the same year *The Deserted Village* appeared; *The History of England* was published in 1771. In 1773 he produced with great success his other drama, *She Stoops to Conquer*. His last works were *The Retaliation, The History of Greece*, and *Animated Nature*, all published in 1774. In that year, worn out with overwork and anxiety, he caught a fever, of which he died.

With all his serious and very obvious faults—his reckless improvidence, his vanity, and, in his earlier years at any rate, his dissipated habits—Goldsmith is one of the most lovable characters in English literature, and one whose writings show most of himself—his humanity, his bright and spontaneous humour, and 'the kindest heart in the world.' His friends included some of the best and greatest men in England, among them Johnson, Burke, and Reynolds. They all, doubtless, laughed at and made a butt of him, but they all admired and loved him. At the news of his death Burke burst into tears, Reynolds laid down his brush and painted no more that day, and Johnson wrote the famous Latin epitaph 'Nullum tetigit quod non ornavit' (He touched nothing he did not adorn). The poor, the old, and the outcast crowded the stair leading to his lodgings, and wept for the benefactor who had never refused to share what he had (often little enough) with them. Much of his work—written at high pressure for the means of existence, or to satisfy the urgency of duns—has, apart from a certain charm of style which no work of his could be without, little permanent value; but *The Traveller*, and *The Deserted Village*, *She Stoops to Conquer*, and, above all, *The Vicar of Wakefield* are accepted English classics.

Gollancz, Sir Israel (13 July 1864—23 June 1930), scholar, was born in London and educated at the City of London School, University College, and Cambridge, where he became the first lecturer in English in 1896. In 1905 he was appointed to the Chair of English at King's College, London, and did important work in developing the English department there. Fellow and Secretary of the British Academy from its foundation in 1902, he was also a director of the Early English Text Society and president of the Philological Society. In 1891 he published an edition of *Pearl*, and in 1895 one of the Exeter Book. He was also general editor of the Temple Classics, the Temple Dramatists, and the original Temple edition of Shakespeare. He was knighted in 1919.

Goodall, Walter (1706?—28 July 1766), historian, son of a Banffshire farmer, was educated at King's College, Aberdeen, and became assistant librarian to the Advocates' Library in Edinburgh. In 1754 he published an *Examination of the Letters said to have been written by Mary Queen of Scots*, in which he combats the genuineness of the 'Casket Letters.' He also edited, among other works, Fordun's *Scotichronicon* (1759).

Goodwin, Thomas (5 Oct. 1600—23 Feb. 1680), clergyman, was born at Rollesby in Norfolk, and educated at Cambridge, where he was vicar of Trinity Church. Becoming an Independent, he was a pastor in London, and thereafter at Arnhem in Holland. Returning to England he was made chaplain to Cromwell's Council of State, and President of Magdalen College, Oxford. He was the author of various commentaries and controversial pamphlets, was a member of the Westminster Assembly, and assisted in drawing up the amended Confession, 1658. He attended Oliver Cromwell on his deathbed.

Googe, Barnabe (11 June 1540—Feb. 1594), poet and translator, son of the Recorder of Lincoln, studied at both Cambridge and Oxford. He was a kinsman of Sir William Cecil, who gave him employment in Ireland. He translated from the Latin of Manzolli *The Zodiac of Life*, a satire against the Papacy, and *The Popish Kingdome* by T. Kirchmayer, a similar work; also *The Foure Bookes of Husbandrie* of Conrad Heresbach. In 1563 he published a volume of original poems, *Eglogs*, *Epytaphes*, and *Sonnettes*. His eclogues are among the earliest examples of English pastorals.

Gordon, Adam Lindsay (19 Oct. 1833—24 June 1870), poet, was born at Fayal in the Azores, but spent his boyhood at Cheltenham, where his father was Professor of Oriental Languages, and went to the Military Academy at Woolwich, where he had his namesake 'Chinese' Gordon as a classmate. A keen sportsman and rather a scapegrace, after various episodes he went to Australia with a commission in the Mounted Police, but soon left that to become an independent horse-breaker. Horses were a passion with him all his life, as is shown by two of his best-known poems, 'How We Beat the Favourite,' which has been called the best racing poem ever written, and 'The Sick Stock-Rider.' Shortly after his marriage to a Glasgow girl, Maggie Park, he inherited a legacy of £7,000 from his mother's estate and entered politics, becoming in 1865 a member of the South Australian House of Assembly, but his irresponsibility prevented his success there. In 1868, having moved to Victoria, he scored his greatest triumph by winning the Melbourne Hunt Cup, but two years later, disappointed over his unsuccessful claim to a family estate in Scotland and oppressed by poverty and gloom, he shot himself at the age of 37. He had not long before received the proofs of his second volume of poems, *Bush Ballads and Galloping Rhymes*; his *Sea-Spray and Smokedrift* had been published three years earlier. His poetry, though uneven and never of the highest order, reflects the vigour and virility of the country of his adoption, and has caused him to be accepted, though an immigrant, as one of the greatest Australian poets.

Gordon, Charles William (13 Sept. 1860—31 Oct. 1937), clergyman and novelist who wrote under the name Ralph Connor, was born at Glengarry, Ontario, son of a Scottish Presbyterian minister. Educated at Toronto University, he studied divinity at Knox College, was ordained in 1890, and went as a missionary among the miners and lumbermen of the Canadian Rockies. From 1894 till his death he was minister of St Stephen's Church, Winnipeg. There he started writing novels based on his missionary work, among the earliest being *Black Rock* (1898), *The Sky Pilot* (1899), *The Man from Glengarry* (1901), and *The Doctor* (1906). His pseudonym was the result of a mistake; he meant to use 'Cannor,' from the letter-heading 'Brit. Can. Nor. West Mission,' but his editor changed it to Connor and added the Ralph. In the First World War Gordon was a chaplain with the Canadian Expeditionary Force. His later novels include *The Major* (1917), *The Sky Pilot in No Man's Land* (1919), *The Gaspards of Pine Croft* (1923), and *The Girl from Glengarry* (1933). He received honorary degrees from Glasgow and Kingston, and was made a Companion of the Order of St Michael and St George in 1935.

Gordon, Neil, *see* **MacDonell, Archibald.**

Gore, Catherine Grace Frances (1799—29 Jan. 1861), novelist, born at East Retford, Nottinghamshire, was a daughter of C. Moody, a wine merchant. She married a Captain Gore, with whom she resided mainly on the Continent, supporting her family by her voluminous writings. Between 1824 and 1862 she produced about 70 works, the most successful of which were novels of fashionable English life. Among these may be mentioned *Manners of the Day* (1830), *Cecil, or the Adventures of a Coxcomb* (1841), and *The Banker's Wife* (1843). She also wrote for the stage, and composed music for songs.

Gore, Charles (22 Jan. 1853—17 Jan. 1932), prelate, was born at Wimbledon and educated at Harrow and Oxford, where he became a Fellow of Trinity. Ordained priest in 1878, he was two years later appointed Vice-Principal of Cuddesdon Theological College, and from 1884 to 1893 was librarian of Pusey House, where he had a great influence on the religious life of Oxford University, being an Anglo-Catholic and a leader of the modernist group. In 1894 he became a canon of Westminster, and then was appointed Bishop successively of Worcester (1902), Birmingham (1905), and Oxford (1911), from which last see he resigned in 1919. Subsequently he lectured on theology in King's College, London. Chief among his works are *The Church and the Ministry* (1889); *Belief in God* (1921), *Belief in Christ* (1922), and *The Holy Spirit and the Church* (1924), a trilogy issued as a single volume with the title *The Reconstruction of Belief* (1926); *A New Commentary on Holy Scripture* (1928), *Jesus of Nazareth* (1929), and *The Philosophy of the Good Life* (1930).

Gore-Booth, Eva Selena (22 May 1870—30 June 1926), poetess, was the daughter of Sir Henry Gore-Booth, 5th Baronet of Lissadell, Sligo. A delicate child, she was educated privately. In 1894 she travelled in the West Indies and America with her father. Later she lived in Manchester, taking an active part in the Women's Suffrage movement, but had to move south because the climate affected her health, and spent her last years in Hampstead, saddened by the tragedy of the Irish Rebellion of 1916, in which her sister was implicated. Her poetry shows the influence of both Irish legend and West Irish scenery, the latter inspiring her best-known poem 'The Little Waves of Breffny,' and there is also a strong vein of mysticism. Her volumes of verse include *Poems* (1898), *Unseen Kings* (1904), *The One and the Many* (1904), *The Three Resurrections* (1905), *The Egyptian Pillars* (1907), *The Agate Lamp* (1912), *The Perilous Light* (1915), *The Death of Finovar* (1916), *Broken Glory* (1918), *The Shepherd of Eternity* (1925), and *The House of Three Windows* (1926). *The Inner Kingdom* (1926) is a collection of essays and addresses.

Gorell, Ronald Gorell Barnes, 3rd Baron (16 April 1885—), poet and novelist, son of the 1st Baron, was educated at Winchester, Harrow, and Oxford, after which he studied law and was called to the Bar of Inner Temple in 1909, but turned to writing and from 1910 to 1915 worked for *The Times*. During the First World War he served with the Rifle Brigade, rose to the rank of colonel and was awarded the Military Cross; and in 1919 he was made a Commander of the Order of the British Empire. From 1933 to 1939 he edited the *Cornhill Magazine*. He published many novels and volumes of verse, his books including *Babes in the African Wood* (1911), *Love Triumphant* (1913), *Days of Destiny* (1917), *Pilgrimage* (1920), *Many Mansions* (1926), *Unheard Melodies* (1934), *In the Potter's Field* (1936), *Last of the English* (1939), *Luck* (1948), *Earle's End* (1951), and *He Walked in Light* (1954).

Gosse, Sir Edmund William (21 Sept. 1849—16 May 1928), critic, was born in London, son of a zoologist who was a Plymouth Brother and religious bigot. His home was a gloomy place, as Gosse's grim memoir, *Father and Son* (1907) reveals. Educated privately, in 1867 he became an assistant librarian in the British Museum, in 1875 transferred to the Board of Trade, was Lecturer in English Literature at Trinity College, Cambridge, from 1884 to 1890, and was librarian of the House of Lords from 1904 to 1914. Throughout his life he formed friendships with eminent authors. He early developed an enthusiasm for Scandinavian languages, popularized Ibsen through his translations, and in 1901 received a Norwegian knighthood. He was also an authority on French literature, and for many years was regarded as one of the foremost literary critics in this country. Among the best of his critical works are *Seventeenth Century Studies* (1883), *Gossip in a Library* (1891), *Critical Kit-Kats* (1896), *French Profiles* (1905), *Portraits and Sketches* (1912), *Books on the Table* (1921), and *Leaves and Fruit* (1927). He also wrote a *History of Eighteenth Century Literature* (1889), and a *Short History of Modern English Literature* (1897), as well as biographies of *Gray* (1882), *Congreve* (1888), *Donne* (1899), *Sir Thomas Browne* (1905), *Ibsen* (1908), and *Swinburne* (1917). Knighted in 1925, he was also a Commander of the Legion of Honour.

Gosson, Stephen (1555—13 Feb. 1624), poet, actor, and satirist, born in Kent, and educated at Oxford, went to London, and wrote plays, which are now lost, and pastorals; but, moved by a sermon preached at Paul's Cross in 1577 during a plague, he deserted the theatre, and became one of its severest critics in his prose satire, *The School of Abuse* (1579), directed against 'poets, pipers, players, jesters, and such-like caterpillars of a Commonwealth.' Dedicated to Sir P. Sidney, it was not well received by him, and is believed to have evoked his *Apologie for Poetrie* (1595). Gosson took orders, and died rector of St Botolph's, London.

Gough, Richard (21 Oct. 1735—20 Feb. 1809), antiquary, was born in London, son of a brewer, and studied at Cambridge. For many years he made journeys over England in pursuit of his antiquarian studies. He published about 20 works, among which are *British Topography* (1768), *Sepulchral Monuments of Great Britain* (1786—99), an edition of Camden's *Britannia*, a translation of *The Arabian Nights* (1798), and various other treatises on archaeology, topography, and numismatics.

Gould, Gerald (1885—2 Nov. 1936), journalist and poet, was born at Scarborough and educated at University College, London, and Oxford, where he was a Fellow of Merton from 1909 to 1916. Taking up journalism, he was on the staff of the *Daily Herald* from 1915 to 1922 and on the *Saturday Review* from then till 1926, as well as writing literary criticism for other papers. His volumes of verse include *Lyrics* (1906), *Poems* (1911), *The Happy Tree* (1919), and *Collected Poems* (1929). He also published an *Essay on the Nature of the Lyric* (1909), *The English Novel of To-day* (1924), and *Democritus, or, The Future of Laughter* (1929), as well as two collections of essays, *The Return of the Cabbage* (1926), and *Refuge from Nightmare* (1933).

Gould, Nathaniel (21 Dec. 1857—25 July 1919), sporting novelist who wrote as Nat Gould, was born in Manchester, and went to school in Southport, afterwards entering his father's tea business. Taking up journalism, he joined the staff of the *Newark Advertiser* in 1878, and in 1884 went to Australia and became a racing journalist in Sydney. The publication of his first book, *The Double Event* (1891) coincided with the Melbourne Cup Meeting, the great racing event in Australia, and so it had a good reception. Returning to England in 1895 he settled in Middlesex and wrote an average of four novels a year, *The Pace That Kills* (1899) being one of the best-known of some 130 books, which sold in all about 24 million. Gould made no pretensions to be a serious novelist, but produced good exciting racing stories; a few of the titles are *Thrown Away* (1894), *The Miner's Cup* (1896), *A Gentleman Rider* (1898), *A Stable Mystery* (1900), *The Rajah's Racer* (1904), and *A Run of Luck* (1907). Two books descriptive of Australian life are *On and Off the Turf in Australia* (1895) and *Town and Bush* (1896). *The Magic of Sport* (1909) is autobiographical.

Gower, John (1330?—1408), poet, appears to have been a man of wealth and importance, connected with Kent, well known at Court, and in possession of more than one estate. He was the friend of Chaucer, who gives him the title of 'moral Gower,' which has clung to him ever since. His first principal work was *Speculum Meditantis* (the Mirror of One Meditating) written in French on the subject of married life. Lost for centuries, it was discovered at Cambridge in 1895. It was followed by *Vox Clamantis* (the Voice of One Crying) written in Latin, giving an account of the peasants' revolt of 1381, and attacking the misgovernment and social evils which had led to it. His third, and only English poem, was *Confessio Amantis* (Lover's Confession), a work of 30,000 rhyming octosyllabic verses, consisting of tales and meditations on love, written at the request of Richard II. It is the earliest large collection of tales in the English tongue. In his old age Gower became blind. He had, when about 70, retired to the Priory of St Mary Overies, the chapel of which is now the Church of St Saviour, better known as Southwark Cathedral, where he spent his last years, and where his tomb is still to be seen. Gower represented the serious and cultivated man of his time, in which he was reckoned the equal of Chaucer, but as a poet he is heavy and prolix.

Grafton, Richard (died 1572), printer and chronicler, published various editions of the Bible and Prayer-book; also the Proclamation of the Accession of Lady Jane Grey, for which he was cast into prison, where he compiled an *Abridgement of the Chronicles of England* (1563). To this he added in 1568 *A Chronicle at Large*. Neither holds a high place as an authority.

Graham, Ennis, *see* **Molesworth, Mary L.**

Graham, Harry Jocelyn Clive (23 Dec. 1874—30 Oct. 1936), humorous writer, was born in London and educated at Eton and Sandhurst. After serving with the Coldstream Guards in the South African War he wrote *Ballads of the Boer War* (1902). During the First World War he rejoined the army and served in France. He first won literary fame with his *Ruthless Rhymes for Heartless Homes* (1899), pieces of mock frightfulness which started a fashion in children's verse; *More Ruthless Rhymes* appeared in 1930. Further volumes of light verse are *Verse and Worse* (1905), *Deportmental Ditties* (1909), and *The Motley Muse* (1913), while his collections of prose articles include *The Perfect Gentleman* (1912), *The Complete Sportsman* (1914), *The World We Laugh In* (1924), and *Strained Relations* (1926). He also collaborated in a number of successful plays.

Graham, James, *see* **Montrose.**

Graham, Robert (1735?—1797?), song-writer, was born at Gartmore, Stirlingshire, his mother being a daughter of the Earl of Glencairn. Educated at Glasgow University, he went to Jamaica, where he held the office of Receiver-General. In 1785 he was elected Rector of Glasgow University, and from 1794 to 1796 was M.P. for Stirlingshire. In 1796 he assumed the name of Cunninghame-Graham. He wrote a number of lyrics, of which the best-known is that beginning 'If doughty deeds my lady please.'

Graham, Robert Bontine Cunninghame (24 May 1852—20 March 1936), travel writer and politician, was born in London, son of a

Scottish laird, and grandson of Robert Graham (q.v.). Brought up by a Spanish grandmother, he learned that language before he knew English. He was educated at Harrow, but before he was 17 he went to the Argentine and travelled in South America. In 1879 he married a Chilean poetess, Gabriela de la Balmondière. In 1884 his father died, and he inherited the family estates, which were burdened with debt. Selling Gartmore, he settled in his estate of Ardoch and entered politics. From 1886 to 1892 he was M.P. for North-West Lanarkshire, and along with Keir Hardie he organized the Scottish Labour party; in 1887 he was imprisoned for leading the mob in the Trafalgar Square riots. In 1897 he went exploring in Morocco, but much of his later life was spent in South America. A close friend of Hudson and Conrad (qq.v.), he was of the type of adventurous traveller to which Doughty and Burton belonged. His travel books include *Mogreb-el-Acksa* (1898), about Morocco, *El Rio de la Plata* (1914), and *Cartagena and the Banks of the Sinu* (1920). He wrote more than 30, but is still better known for his stories and sketches, collections of which include *Thirteen Stories* (1900), *Success* (1902), *Faith* (1909), *Hope* (1910), *Charity* (1912), and *Scottish Stories* (1914). He also wrote several biographies. In 1928 he was elected first president of the Scottish National Party.

Graham, Stephen (1884—   ), travel writer, was attracted to Russia by the literature of the country, and roamed widely over it, living with peasants and students. Among his books about it and its people are *Undiscovered Russia* (1912), *With the Russian Pilgrims to Jerusalem* (1913), *With Poor Emigrants to America* (1914), and *Through Russian Central Asia* (1916). *A Private in the Guards* (1919) tells of his experiences in the First World War, when he served with the Scots Guards. After it he resumed his vagabond life, visited the United States, tramped with Vachel Lindsay (q.v.) in the West, and wrote about it in *Tramping with a Poet in the Rockies* (1922). Later he travelled in Mexico and then went back to Russia and the Balkans, frequently writing of his journeys in *The Times*. Among his later books are *In Quest of El Dorado* (1924), *Russia in Division* (1925), *The Gentle Art of Tramping* (1927), *African Tragedy* (1937), *The Moving Tent* (1939), *Summing Up on Russia* (1951), and lives of *Peter the Great* (1929), *Stalin* (1931), and *Ivan the Terrible* (1932).

Grahame, James (22 April 1765—14 Sept. 1811), poet, son of a lawyer, was born in Glasgow and went to the university there. After spending some time in a law office in Edinburgh, he was called to the Scottish Bar. His health being delicate, and his circumstances easy, he early retired from practice, and taking orders in the Church of England in 1809, was appointed curate successively of Shipton, Gloucestershire, and Sedgefield, Durham. He wrote several pleasing poems, of which the best is *The Sabbath* (1804), full of quiet observation of country sights expressed in graceful verse.

Grahame, Kenneth (3 March 1859—6 July 1932), essayist, was born in Edinburgh, son of an advocate and great-grand-nephew of James Grahame (q.v.). His mother died when he was very young, and he was brought up by his grandmother in Berkshire and educated at St Edward's School, Oxford.   Joining the staff of the Bank of England, he rose to be secretary from 1898 to 1907.   His earliest writing was *Pagan Papers* (1893), a collection of essays.   Then in 1895 he published *The Golden Age*, followed three years later by *Dream Days*, both made up of charming and delightful studies of children, which appealed to all adults who looked back with longing to their childhood.   In 1908, to entertain his son Alastair, nicknamed Mouse, who died at the age of 20, he wrote *The Wind in the Willows*, an animal story which became one of the most popular of children's classics and was dramatized by A. A. Milne (q.v.) as *Toad of Toad Hall*.   He also edited the *Cambridge Book of Poetry for Young People* (1916).

Grahame, Simon *or* **Simion** (1570—1614), born probably in Edinburgh, son of a burgess, led a dissolute life as a traveller, soldier, and courtier on the Continent.   He appears to have been a good scholar, and wrote the *Passionate Sparke of a Relenting Minde*, and *Anatomy of Humours*, the latter of which is believed to have suggested to Burton his *Anatomy of Melacholy*.   He became an austere Franciscan, and was presented by James VI to the prebendary of Brodderstanes.

Grainger, James (1721—16 Dec. 1766), poet, was born probably at Duns in Berwickshire, son of an exciseman.   He studied medicine at Edinburgh, was an army surgeon, and later settled in practice in London, where he became the friend of Dr Johnson, Shenstone, and other men of letters.   His first poem, *Solitude*, appeared in 1755. He subsequently went to St Christopher in the West Indies, where he made a rich marriage, and published his chief poem, *The Sugar-Cane* (1764), which was ridiculed for its flatness and bathos.

Granger, James (1723—14 April 1776), biographer, born of poor parents at Shaston, Dorset, went to Oxford and, having taken orders, became vicar of Shiplake, Oxfordshire.   He published a *Biographical History of England from Egbert the Great to the Revolution* (1769), which had blank pages for the insertion of engraved portraits, of which he himself collected 14,000.   'Grangerizing' became a craze for a time, and the term is particularly applied to interleaving a book with illustrations cut from others.

Grant, Anne (21 Feb. 1755—7 Nov. 1838), poetess and essayist, was born in Glasgow, daughter of Duncan McVicar, a farmer who joined the army and became barrack-master of Fort Augustus in 1773. In 1779 Anne married James Grant, the garrison chaplain, who died in 1801.   In 1802 she published a volume of poems, and in the following year *Letters from the Mountains*, which met with great success.   In 1811 there appeared her *Essays on the Superstitions of the Highlands*, and thereafter she lived in Edinburgh, where she was the friend of Sir Walter Scott and other eminent men, through whose influence she was granted a pension of £100.

Grant, James (1 Aug. 1822—5 May 1887), novelist, born in Edinburgh, was related to Sir Walter Scott through his mother.   With his father, an army chaplain, he spent six years in Newfoundland, returning to his own country in 1839. After a few years as an ensign in the 62nd Foot, he devoted himself to writing, and produced some 50 novels in a brisk breezy style. Among the best are *Adventures of an Aide-de-Camp* (1848), *Bothwell* (1854), *Frank Hilton* (1855), *The Yellow Frigate* (1855), and *Harry Ogilvie* (1856). He also wrote biographies of *Kirkcaldy of Grange* (1849) and *Montrose* (1858). In 1875 he became a Roman Catholic.

Grant, James Augustus (11 April 1827—11 Feb. 1892), travel writer, was born at Nairn, where his father was minister, and educated at Aberdeen Grammar School and Mareschal College. Adopting an army career, he obtained a commission in the Bengal Infantry in 1846, served in the Mutiny, and was at the relief of Lucknow. In 1858 he returned to England and from 1860 to 1863 accompanied the explorer John H. Speke (q.v.) in his African expeditions to investigate the sources of the Nile, subsequently writing of their experiences in *A Walk Across Africa* (1864), and receiving the gold medal of the Royal Geographical Society. In 1866 he was made a Companion of the Bath, and of the Star of India in 1868.

Granville-Barker, Harley (25 Nov. 1877—31 Aug. 1946), actor, dramatist, and critic, born in London, was educated at private schools. At the age of 13 he entered a dramatic school in Margate, and in the following year made his first appearance on the London stage. His first play was *The Weather Hen* (1899), in which he collaborated with Herbert Thomas. In 1900 he was actor and producer for the Stage Society, and in the following year wrote *The Marrying of Ann Leete*. In 1905 he became manager of the Court Theatre, where he played lead in plays by Shaw and Ibsen. In 1907 he married Lillah McCarthy, the actress; the marriage was dissolved in 1918. He did much translating and adapting of foreign plays, and he himself wrote ironical 'intellectual' dramas, of which the best-known are *The Voysey Inheritance* (1905), *Waste* (1907), *The Madras House* (1910), and *The Secret Life* (1923). His *Prefaces to Shakespeare* (1923—37) are a valuable contribution to Shakespearian criticism from the actor's point of view. Others of his works are *The Study of Drama* (1934), *On Poetry in Drama* (1937), and *The Perennial Shakespeare* (1937).

Grattan, Thomas Colley (1792—4 July 1864), travel writer and novelist, born in Dublin, son of a solicitor, was educated for the law, but did not practise. He wrote a few novels, including *The Heiress of Bruges* (4 volumes, 1830); but his best work was *Highways and Byways*, a description of his Continental wanderings, of which he published three series (1823, 1825, 1827). He also wrote a history of the Netherlands, and an autobiography, *Beaten Paths* (1862). He was for some time British Consul at Boston, U.S.

Graves, Alfred Perceval (22 July 1846—27 Dec. 1931), poet, was born in Dublin; his father was later Bishop of Limerick and a Fellow of the Royal Society. Educated at Windermere College and Trinity College, Dublin, he became a clerk in the Home Office, then an inspector of schools first in Manchester, then at Taunton, and from

1895 in Southwark. His original books of verse include *Songs of Killarney* (1872), *Irish Songs and Ballads* (1879), and *Father O'Flynn and Other Lyrics* (1889). A leader of the Irish Renascence, he edited *The Book of Irish Poetry* (1915) and *A Treasury of Irish Prose and Verse* (1915). His last years were spent at Harlech in north Wales, where he wrote his autobiography *To Return to All That* (1930), a reply to his son Robert's *Good-bye to All That* (q.v.).

Graves, Robert Ranke (26 July 1895—   ), poet and novelist, son of the above, was born in London and educated at Charterhouse. During the First World War he served with the Royal Welch Fusiliers in the same regiment as Siegfried Sassoon (q.v.); in this period he published three books of verse, *Goliath and David, Over the Brazier*, and *Fairies and Fusiliers*. In 1918 he married Nancy Nicholson, and in the following year went to Oxford, where they kept a shop at Boars Hill. In 1926 he took his degree and became Professor of English at Cairo for a year. In 1929 he published *Goodbye to All That*, an account of the first phase of his life. Resident in Majorca for the next few years, he ran the Seizin Press in partnership with Laura Riding (q.v.), and after the Second World War he returned to live there. His later volumes of poems are mostly named by the years they cover; his *Collected Poems* (1938) drew on 19 earlier volumes, and was followed by *Poems, 1938—1945*. To the general reading public he is best known as the author of a series of historical novels—*I Claudius*, which was awarded the Hawthornden and Tait Black Prizes for 1934; its sequel, *Claudius the God* (1934); *Count Belisarius*, which obtained the Femina Vie Heureuse Prize for 1939; *The Golden Fleece* (1944); and *Homer's Daughter* (1955). Among his critical works are *On English Poetry* (1922), and a book of essays, *The Common Asphodel* (1949). In 1961 he succeeded Auden (q.v.) as Professor of Poetry at Oxford.

Gray, David (29 Jan. 1838—3 Dec. 1861), poet, was the son of a hand-loom weaver of Kirkintilloch, Dumbartonshire. He gave early promise at school, was destined for the service of the Church, and was for four years at Glasgow University, while he maintained himself by teaching. His first poems appeared in the *Glasgow Citizen*. In 1860, however, he went with his friend Robert Buchanan to London, where he soon fell into consumption. He was befriended by Monckton Milnes, afterwards Lord Houghton, but after vainly seeking health at Torquay, returned home to die. His chief poem, *The Luggie* (1862), named from river of his birthplace, contains much beautiful description; but his genius reached its highest expression in a series of 30 sonnets written in full view of an early death and blighted hopes, and bearing the title, *In the Shadows*.

Gray, Thomas (26 Dec. 1716—30 July 1771), poet, was born in London, the son of a scrivener, who, though described as 'a respectable citizen,' was of so cruel and violent a temper that his wife had to separate from him. To his mother and her sister, who carried on a business, Gray was indebted for his liberal education at Eton (where he became a friend of Horace Walpole), and Cambridge. After completing his University course he accompanied Walpole to France and Italy, where he spent over two years, when a difference arising Gray returned to England, and went back to Cambridge to take his degree in law without, however, any intention of practising. Though he never became a Fellow of any college, he remained there, first at Peterhouse, then at Pembroke, for the rest of his life, passing his time in the study of the classics, natural science, and antiquities, and in visits to his friends, of whom Walpole was again one. It was in 1747 that his first poem, the *Ode on a Distant Prospect of Eton College*, appeared. It was followed in 1751 by his great *Elegy in a Country Churchyard*, and in 1758 by his *Pindaric Odes*, including *The Progress of Poesy* and *The Bard*, which were, however, somewhat coldly received. On the death of Colley Cibber he was offered the laureateship, which he declined; but in 1768 he accepted the Professorship of Modern History in his University. Having been drawn to the study of Icelandic and Celtic poetry he produced *The Fatal Sisters* and *The Descent of Odin* (1761), in which are apparent the first streaks of the dawn of the Romantic Revival. In 1769 he made a tour among the English lakes, of which he wrote in his *Journal* (1775), the best of his prose works. Gray's poems occupy little space, but what he wrote he brought to the highest perfection of which he was capable, and though he followed eighteenth-century conventions, he had a depth of feeling and a sensitivity to natural beauty which links him with a later age. Probably no poem has had a wider acceptance among all classes of readers than his *Elegy in a Country Churchyard*. In addition to his fame as a poet, he enjoys that of one of the greatest of English letter-writers, and of an accomplished scholar. He died at Cambridge after a short illness, and is buried at Stoke Poges, the scene of his *Elegy*.

Grayson, David, *see* **Baker, Ray Stannard.**

Greeley, Horace (3 Feb. 1811—29 Nov. 1872), journalist, was born at Amherst, New Hampshire, son of a farmer. Leaving school at 14, he became a journalist and printer. In 1831 he went to New York, and three years later he founded the *New Yorker*, which was later merged with the *Tribune* and became one of New York's most influential papers. As its editor till shortly before his death, Greeley shaped political thought with his puritanical outlook, in particular championing the abolition of slavery. During the Civil War he was a leader of the Republican party, and in 1872 he was nominated for the presidency, but sustained a crushing defeat and died soon afterwards. His works include *The American Conflict* (1864—6), *Essays on Political Economy* (1870), and the autobiographical *Recollections of a Busy Life* (1868).

Green, Henry, *see* **Yorke.**

Green, John Richard (12 Dec. 1837—7 March 1883), historian, was the son of a tradesman in Oxford, where he was educated, first at Magdalen College School, and then at Jesus College. He took orders and was for a time a curate in the East End of London but had to abandon parish work because of ill health, and in 1869 was appointed librarian at Lambeth Palace. Finding that his lungs were affected, he concentrated his energies on the preparation of his *Short History of the English People*, which appeared in 1874, and at once gave him an assured place in the first rank of historical writers. In 1877 he married Alice Stopford, by whose talents and devotion he was greatly assisted in carrying out and completing such work as his broken health enabled him to undertake during his few remaining years. Abandoning a projected history of the Angevins, he confined himself to expanding his *Short History* into *A History of the English People* in 4 volumes (1878—80), and writing *The Making of England*, of which one volume only, coming down to 828, had appeared when he died at Mentone. After his death appeared *The Conquest of England*. The *Short History* may be said to have begun a new epoch in the writing of history, making the social, industrial, and moral progress of the people its main theme. To infinite care in the gathering and sifting of his material Green added a style of wonderful charm.

Green, Julian Hartridge (6 Sept. 1900—   ), novelist, born in Paris of American parents, was educated at a French *lycée* and the University of Virginia, where from 1920 to 1930 he was on the staff of the history department. His first novel, *Avarice House* (1926), won him immediate recognition; it was followed by *The Closed Garden* (1927), *The Dark Journey* (1929), which won the 10,000 dollar Harper Prize Novel Contest, *Christine* (1930), *The Strange River* (1931), *The Dreamer* (1934), and *Midnight* (1936). All these were originally written in French, and Green was in all essentials a Frenchman. *Personal Record* (1939) and *Memories of Happy Days* (1942) are autobiographical. In 1953 his play *Sud* was produced in Paris.

Green, Matthew (1696—1737), poet and Quaker, is known as the author of *The Spleen* (1737), a lively and original poem in octosyllabic verse on the subject of low spirits and the best means of prevention and cure. It has life-like descriptions, sprightliness, and lightness of touch, and was admired by Pope and Gray. The poem owes its name to the use of the term in the author's day to denote depression. Green, who held an appointment in the Customs, successfully upheld the right of Custom House cats to an official milk allowance.

Green, Thomas Hill (7 April 1836—26 March 1882), philosopher, born at Birkin, Yorkshire, where his father was rector, was educated at Rugby and Balliol College, Oxford, where in 1878 he became Whyte's Professor of Moral Philosophy and, by his character, ability, and enthusiasm on social questions, exercised a powerful influence. His chief works are an *Introduction to Hume* (1874), in which he criticized Hume's philosophy severely from the idealist standpoint, and *Prolegomena to Ethics*, published posthumously.

Greene, Albert Gorton (10 Feb. 1802—3 Jan. 1868), poet, was born at Providence, Rhode Island, son of an architect, and educated at Brown University. He studied law and was admitted to the Bar in 1823. From 1832 he was clerk of Providence City Council, and a magistrate from 1858 to 1867. He wrote a number of poems, but ironically is remembered by the humorous verses on 'Old Grimes' which he composed at the age of 16.

Greene, Henry Graham (2 Oct. 1904—   ), novelist,
was born at Berkhamsted, Hertfordshire, where his father was a
headmaster, and educated there and at Balliol College, Oxford, where
he edited the *Oxford Outlook*. From 1926 to 1930 he was a sub-
editor on *The Times*. In 1927 he married Vivienne Dayrell-Brown-
ing, and about the same time was converted to Roman Catholicism.
In 1935 he made a visit to Liberia, of which he wrote in *Journey
Without Maps* (1936); *The Lawless Roads*, published three years later,
tells of his experiences in Mexico. In 1940 he was literary editor of
the *Spectator*, and from 1941 to 1944 was on the staff of the Foreign
Office. His novels include *The Man Within* (1929), *The Name of
Action* (1930), *Stamboul Train* (1932), *It's a Battlefield* (1934), *A Gun
for Sale* (1936), *Brighton Rock* (1938), *The Power and the Glory* (1940),
which was awarded the Hawthornden Prize, *The Heart of the Matter*
(1948), *The End of the Affair* (1951), and *Loser Takes All* (1955). In
1953 his first play, *The Living Room*, was produced in London. A
cousin twice removed of Robert Louis Stevenson, Graham Greene
was acknowledged to be one of the most powerful novelists of his
time, his books being intensely concerned with psychology, especially
of the sinister type.

Greene, Robert (July 1558—3 Sept. 1592), dramatist and pamphleteer, born probably at Norwich, was educated at St John's College,
Cambridge, where he formed a friendship with Thomas Nashe (q.v.),
and was later made a member of Oxford University. A Bohemian
in his habits, he travelled in many European countries and then,
having deserted wife and child, settled in London, where he earned a
precarious living as a freelance writer, alternating between bouts of
dissipation and repentance. As a playwright he is included among
the 'University Wits' who laid the foundations of English drama.
Those of his plays which survive are, in probable order of composition,
Alphonsus King of Aragon, and *Orlando Furioso*, mouth-filling
tragedies in the style of Marlowe; *Friar Bacon and Friar Bungay*, a
comedy which introduces magic; and *The Scottish History of James
the Fourth*, which is not, as one might imagine, a chronicle play, but
a romantic comedy with Oberon, king of the fairies, as one of its
characters; he has also been credited with *George a Greene, the Pinner
of Wakefield* (1599). Greene also wrote a number of prose romances,
the nearest thing the Elizabethans had to the modern novel; they
include *Guydonius, the Card of Fancy* (1584); *Pandosto* (1588), which
gave Shakespeare the plot for *A Winter's Tale*; *Perimedes the Blacksmith* (1588); *Menaphon* (1589), later reprinted as *Greene's Arcadia*;
and *Philomela* (1592). Some of these contain beautiful lyrical
pieces, in which Greene excelled.

In his pamphlets Greene turned from Arcadia to Alsatia and from
idealism to sordid realism. They include *Euphues, his Censure of
Philautus* (1587), a continuation of Lyly's work, which provoked
Gabriel Harvey (q.v.) to sneer at him as 'Euphues' Ape.' Others are
Greene's Mourning Garment (1590), *Never Too Late* (1590), *Farewell
to Folly* (1591), *A Quip for an Upstart Courtier* (1592), and the
autobiographical *A Groatsworth of Wit Bought with a Million of
Repentance* (1592), which contains the famous attack on Shakespeare

as 'an upstart crow.' Interesting accounts of low London life and
the swindlers that infested the city are contained in *A Notable
Discovery of Cozenage* (1591), *The Defence of Cony-Catching* (1592),
and *A Disputation between a He Cony-Catcher and a She Cony-
Catcher* (1592); 'cony,' it may be explained, was Elizabethan slang
for a simpleton or 'mug.' Greene is said to have died from a surfeit
of pickled herrings and Rhenish wine.

Greenwood, Walter (17 Dec. 1903—   ), novelist and
playwright, was born at Salford, Lancashire, son of a hairdresser and
a waitress; at the age of 12 he left the council school to become a
pawnbroker's clerk, and subsequently worked as office boy, stable
boy, sign-writer, chauffeur, warehouseman, and salesman. In 1933
he published *Love on the Dole*, a novel based on his life experiences;
it was dramatized and as a social document was instrumental in
bringing about some economic reforms, as well as making its author
famous as a proletarian novelist. Others of his books, which have
usually a strong element of propaganda, are *The Time is Ripe* (1934),
His Worship the Mayor (1934), *Standing Room Only* (1936), *The
Secret Kingdom* (1938), *Only Mugs Work* (1938), *Something in My
Heart* (1944), and *What Everybody Wants* (1954). *My Son's My
Son* (1935), *Give Us This Day* (1936), *The Cure for Love* (1945), and
So Brief the Spring (1945) are plays.

Greg, William Rathbone (1809—15 Nov. 1881), essayist, born in
Manchester, and educated at Bristol and Edinburgh, was for some
years engaged in his father's business as a mill owner at Bury.
Becoming deeply interested in political and social questions, he
contributed to reviews and magazines many papers and essays on
these subjects, which were republished as *Essays on Political and
Social Science* (1854), *Literary and Social Judgments* (1869), and
Miscellaneous Essays (1884). Other works of his are *Enigmas of
Life* (1872), *Rocks Ahead* (1874), and *Mistaken Aims and Attainable
Ideals of Working Classes* (1876). In his writings he frequently
manifested a distrust of democracy and a pessimistic view of the
future of his country. He held successively the appointments of
Commissioner of Customs and Controller of H.M. Stationery Office.

Gregory, Isabella Augusta, Lady (5 March 1852—22 May 1932),
dramatist, born at Roxburghe, County Galway, was a daughter of
Dudley Persse, a rich landowner. In 1881 she married Sir William
Gregory, M.P., a former governor of Ceylon, who died in 1892.
Meeting Yeats in 1898 she became interested in the Irish Renascence
and was for many years a supporter of the Abbey Theatre, acting as
its manager; *Our Irish Theatre* (1913) tells of her early work there.
For it she wrote many short plays which blend poetry with a gentle
irony. Among her best are *Spreading the News* (1904), *Hyacinth
Halvey* (1906), *The Rising of the Moon* (1907), *The Workhouse Ward*
(1908), and *The Story Brought by Brigit* (1924). She also published
The Kiltartan History Book (1909) and *The Kiltartan Poetry Book*
(1919). Her home at Coole, with its lake and gardens, became a
centre for the writers of the Celtic Revival, and her translations of
Irish legendary tales, such as *Cuchulain of Muirthemhne* (1902) and
Gods and Fighting Men (1904), were used by its poets.

Grenfell, Julian (30 March 1888—26 May 1915), soldier and poet, a son of Lord Desborough, was educated at Eton, where he edited the school paper, and at Balliol College, Oxford. A keen sportsman, he had been master of the Eton beagles, and later went in for polo. Choosing an army career, he served in the Royal Dragoons, was awarded the D.S.O. in the First World War, and wrote ' Into Battle,' one of the great war poems. He was fatally wounded by a shell splinter on the Menin Road.

Grenfell, Sir Wilfred Thomason (28 Feb. 1865—9 Oct. 1940), surgeon and writer, was born at Parkgate, near Chester, where his father was a headmaster. Educated at Marlborough and Oxford, he took a medical degree and became house surgeon at the London Hospital. In 1892 he sailed for Newfoundland in a small ketch fitted up as a hospital, and treated some 900 patients. From these modest beginnings there grew up the International Grenfell Association, with six hospitals and four hospital ships. Working as missionary and doctor for forty years, Grenfell became widely known as Grenfell of Labrador, and was knighted in 1927. He wrote many books of a religious nature as well as tales of adventure, among the best being *Adrift on an Ice Pan* (1910), *A Labrador Doctor* (1919), *Labrador Days* (1921), and *The Romance of Labrador* (1934).

Greville, Charles Cavendish Fulke (2 April 1794—18 Jan. 1865), diarist, educated at Eton and Oxford, was a page to George III, secretary to Earl Bathurst, and afterwards held the sinecure office of Secretary of Jamaica. In 1821 he became Clerk to the Privy Council, an office which brought him into close contact with the leaders of both political parties, and gave him unusual opportunities of becoming acquainted with all that was passing behind the scenes. The information as to men and events thus acquired he fully utilized in his *Journals of the Reigns of George IV, William IV, and Queen Victoria*, which, edited by Henry Reeve, of the *Edinburgh Review*, were published in three series between 1874 and 1887, the whole being entitled *The Greville Memoirs*. It covers the period from 1820 to 1860, and constitutes an invaluable contribution to the history of the time.

Greville, Fulke, *see* **Brooke, 1st Baron.**

Grey of Fallodon, Edward, 1st Viscount (25 April 1862—7 Sept. 1933), statesman, was born in London, son of an army officer, and inherited his grandfather's title of baronet in 1882. He was educated at Winchester and Oxford, where he studied law and was a tennis blue. Years afterwards he became Chancellor of the University. From 1885 to 1916 he was Liberal M.P. for Berwick-upon-Tweed. From 1905 he was Foreign Secretary, and was thus in charge of foreign policy when Britain entered the First World War. When Lloyd George became Prime Minister in 1916 Grey retired to Fallodon, and in the same year was created a viscount. A keen student of nature, he wrote *Fly Fishing* (1899), *Fallodon Papers* (1926), and *The Charm of Birds* (1927); *Twenty-Five Years, 1892—1916* (1925) is a series of memoirs.

Grey, Zane (31 Jan. 1872—23 Oct. 1939), novelist, was born at Zanesville, Ohio, son of a backwoodsman, and educated at Pennsylvania University. From 1898 to 1904 he worked as a dentist. In the latter year he published at his own expense *Betty Zane*, an historical novel. Soon afterwards he started writing the Westerns which made him famous. *The Last of the Plainsmen* (1908) and *The Heritage of the Desert* (1910), were followed by *Riders of the Purple Sage* (1912), which sold over a million copies and made its author's fortune. Grey's popularity was immense, and though his novels are of a facile type they contain vivid and true pictures of the country which forms their setting. Later books are *Desert Gold* (1913), *The Lone Star Ranger* (1915), *The U.P. Trail* (1918), *The Mysterious Rider* (1921), *The Call of the Canyon* (1924), and *Western Union* (1939). *Tales of Fishing Virgin Seas* (1925) and *An American Angler in Australia* (1937) attest his keenness for the sport of deep-sea fishing.

Grierson, Sir Herbert John Clifford (16 Jan. 1866—19 Feb. 1960), scholar, was born at Lerwick in the Shetlands and educated at King's College, Aberdeen, and Christ Church, Oxford. He was appointed Professor of English at Aberdeen in 1894 and at Edinburgh in 1915. He was knighted on his retirement in 1936, and from that year till 1939 was Lord Rector of Edinburgh University. Among his more important works are *Metaphysical Poets* (1921), *The Background of English Literature* (1925), *Lyrical Poetry from Blake to Hardy* (1928), *The Seventeenth Century* (1929), *Milton amd Wordsworth* (1937), and *Essays and Addresses* (1940); he also edited Donne's poems.

Grieve, Christopher Murray (11 Aug. 1892—   ), poet and critic, who used the pseudonym Hugh MacDiarmid, was born at Langholm, Dumfriesshire, and educated at Edinburgh University. A supporter of Scottish nationalism, he was one of the founders of the Scottish Nationalist party and of the Scottish section of the P.E.N. Club. As a poet, he was one of the leaders of the Scottish literary renascence, employing the Lowland Scots tongue ('Lallans') in his verse. His volumes of poetry include *Sangschaw* (1925), *Penny Wheep* (1926), *A Drunk Man Looks at the Thistle* (1926), *To Circumjack Cencrastus* (1930), *First* and *Second Hymn to Lenin* (1932, 1935), and *Scots Unbound* (1932). Critical works are *Contemporary Scottish Studies* (1924), *Albyn, or Scotland and the Future* (1927), *At the Sign of the Thistle* (1934), and *Scottish Eccentrics* (1936). He also edited the *Golden Treasury of Scottish Poetry* (1941). *Lucky Poet* (1943) is an autobiography. In 1957 he was made an honorary D.Litt. of Edinburgh.

Griffin, Bartholomew (died 15 Dec. 1602), poet, is thought to have been born at Coventry, and to have been an attorney, but practically nothing is known of his life. In 1596 he published a collection of 62 sonnets under the title of *Fidessa*, of which some are excellent.

Griffin, Gerald (12 Dec. 1803—12 June 1840), dramatist, novelist, and poet, son of a brewer, was born and educated in Limerick. He went in 1823 to London, where most of his literary work was produced. In 1838 he returned to Ireland and, dividing his property among his brothers, devoted himself to a religious life by joining the Teaching Order of the Christian Brothers. Two years thereafter he died, worn out by self-inflicted austerities. His chief novel, *The Collegians* (1829), was adapted by Boucicault as *The Colleen Bawn*, and among his dramas is *Gisippus*. His novels depict southern Irish life.

Grigson, Geoffrey Edward Harvey (1905—   ), poet and critic, was born at Pelynt, Cornwall, son of a clergyman, and educated at St John's, Leatherhead, and Oxford. He became a journalist and joined the staff of the *Yorkshire Post*. During the Second World War he worked as a monitor for the British Broadcasting Company. His volumes of verse include *Several Observations* (1939), *Under the Cliff* (1943), and *The Isles of Scilly* (1946). He compiled a number of anthologies, including *New Verse* (1939) and *Poetry of the Present* (1949), and wrote studies of Wyndham Lewis (1951) and Gerard Manley Hopkins (1955). He also published several books on flowers and on painting. *The Crest on the Silver* (1950) is autobiographical.

Grimald, Grimsald, *or* **Grimvald, Nicholas** (1519—1562), poet, born in Huntingdonshire, was probably the son of Giovanni Grimaldi, an Italian clerk. Educated at Cambridge and Oxford, he became chaplain to Bishop Ridley. He contributed 40 poems to *Tottel's Miscellany* (1557), wrote two dramas in Latin, *Archi-propheta* and *Christus Redivivus*, and made translations from Virgil and Cicero.

Grimshaw, Beatrice Ethel (1871—June 1953), novelist, was born at Cloona, Antrim, and educated at Bedford College, London, and Queen's University, Belfast. She became a journalist first in Dublin, then worked in London, and at one time held the women's 24-hour cycling record. After travelling extensively in the South Seas she settled there in 1906 and wrote several travel books, including *From Fiji to the Cannibal Islands* (1907) and *The New New Guinea* (1910). Most of her 30-odd novels are about the Pacific islands, among the best-known being *Vaiti of the Islands* (1906), *When the Red Gods Call* (1911), *Kriss-Girl* (1917), *Nobody's Island* (1917), *Queen Vaiti* (1921), *The Sands of Oro* (1924), *My Lady Far Away* (1929), *The Star in the Dust* (1930), and *Rita Regina* (1939). She also published several books of short stories. In 1940 she retired to Australia.

Grimvald, Nicholas, *see* **Grimald.**

Groome, Francis Hindes (30 Aug. 1851—24 Jan. 1902), Romany scholar, born at Monk Soham in Suffolk, where his father was archdeacon, was educated at Oxford and Göttingen. He married a wife of gipsy extraction, and lived in Edinburgh, where he wrote for various encyclopaedias. He was a student of the gipsies and their language, and published *In Gipsy Tents* (1880), *Gipsy Folk Tales* (1899), and an edition of Borrow's *Lavengro* (1900). Other works were *A Short Border History* (1887), *Kriegspiel* (1896), a novel, and *Two Suffolk Friends* (1895), a study of his father and Edward FitzGerald (q.v.).

Grosart, Alexander Balloch (18 June 1827—16 March 1899), editor, was born at Stirling, son of a builder, and became a minister of the English Presbyterian Church. While still at Edinburgh University he published an edition of Robert Ferguson's poems (1851). But his chief service to literature was his reprints, with notes, of rare Elizabethan and Jacobean literature, including *Fuller's Worthies Library*, 39 volumes (1868—76), *Occasional Issues of Unique and Very Rare Books*, 38 volumes (1875—81), and *Huth Library*, 33 volumes (1886).

Grose, Francis (1731?—12 May 1791), antiquary and lexicographer, born at Greenford, Middlesex, of Swiss extraction, was Richmond Herald from 1755 to 1763. He published *Antiquities of England and Wales* (1773—87), and thereafter set out on an antiquarian tour through Scotland, the fruit of which was *Antiquities of Scotland* (1789—91); it was of him that Burns wrote 'A chiel's amang you takin' notes.' He afterwards undertook a similar expedition to Ireland, but died suddenly at Dublin. In addition to the works above mentioned he wrote *A Classical Dictionary of the Vulgar Tongue* (1785), *A Provincial Glossary* (1787), and a *Treatise on Ancient Armour and Weapons* (1786—9). He was an accomplished draughtsman, and illustrated his works.

Grosseteste, Robert (1175?—9 Oct. 1253), churchman and scholar, was born of poor parents at Stradbrook, Suffolk, and studied at Oxford and possibly Paris. In 1224 he became the first rector of the Franciscans in Oxford, and obtained many preferments; but after an illness he refused to be longer a pluralist, and resigned all but a prebend at Lincoln. Later he was a strenuous and courageous reformer, as is shown by his refusing in 1253 to induct a nephew of the Pope to a canonry at Lincoln, of which he had been Bishop since 1235. He was equally bold in resisting the demand of Henry III for a tenth of the Church revenues. He exercised a profound influence on English thought of the next two centuries through his voluminous works, which include a *Compendium Scientiae* or classification of contemporary knowledge, treatises on husbandry, scientific subjects, and moral philosophy, as well as sermons, commentaries, and an allegory, the *Chateau d'Amour*. Roger Bacon was a pupil of his, and testifies to his amazing variety of knowledge.

Grossmith, George (9 Dec. 1847—1 March 1912), comedian, was born in London, son of a journalist, and educated at North London Collegiate School. He was a journalist himself for a few years, then went on the stage in songs and sketches. From 1877 to 1889 he was a member of the D'Oyly Carte opera company playing Gilbert and Sullivan, and ' created ' the parts of Bunthorne, Jack Point, Ko-ko, Major Stanley, and others. His literary fame rests on one book, *The Diary of a Nobody* (1894), which he wrote in collaboration with his younger brother Walter, and which became a classic of humour.

Grote, George (17 Nov. 1794—18 June 1871), historian, was born near Beckenham in Kent, eldest of a banker's eleven children, and was educated at Charterhouse. In 1810 he entered his father's bank, of which he became head in 1830. In 1832 he was elected one of the members of Parliament for the City of London. In 1841, he retired from Parliament, and in 1843 from the bank, thenceforth devoting his whole time to literature, which, along with politics, had been his chief interest from his youth. In 1826 he contributed to the *Westminster Review* a severe criticism of Mitford's *History of Greece*, and in 1845 published the first two volumes of his own, the remaining six volumes appearing at intervals up to 1856. Grote belongs to the school of philosophical historians, and his *History*, which begins with the legends, ends with the fall of the country under the successors of Alexander the Great. A standard work, it has been repeatedly reissued, and has been translated into French and German. Grote also published in 1865, *Plato and other Companions of Socrates*, and left unfinished a work on Aristotle. In political life Grote was, as might be expected, a consistent and somewhat rigid Radical. He was one of the founders of the first London University, a Trustee of the British Museum, D.C.L. of Oxford, LL.D. of Cambridge, and a Foreign Associate of the Académie des Sciences. He was offered, but declined, a peerage in 1869, and is buried in Westminster Abbey.

Grub, George (4 April 1812—23 Sept 1893), church historian, was born in Aberdeen, and educated at King's College there. He studied law, and was admitted in 1836 to the Society of Advocates, Aberdeen, of which he was librarian from 1841 until his death. He was appointed Lecturer on Scots Law in Marischal College, and was Professor of Law in the University (1881—91). He has a place in literature as the author of an *Ecclesiastical History of Scotland* (1861), written from the standpoint of a Scottish Episcopalian, which, though dry, is concise, clear, fair-minded and trustworthy. Grub also edited (along with Joseph Robertson) Gordon's *Scots Affairs* for the Spalding Club, of which he was one of the founders.

Guedalla, Philip (12 March 1889—16 Dec. 1944), historian, was born in London and educated at Rugby and Balliol College, Oxford, where he was President of the Union and an actor in the Oxford University Dramatic Society. While still an undergraduate he published *Ignes Fatui*, a volume of parodies, and *Metri Gratia, Verse and Prose*. From 1913 to 1923 he was a barrister of the Inner Temple, then retired to devote himself to writing. As historian and biographer he displayed a coruscating style of his own. His books include *The Partition of Europe 1715—1815* (1914), *The Second Empire* (1922), *Palmerston* (1926), *Bonnet and Shawl* (1928), *The Duke*, a life of Wellington (1931), *The Hundred Days* (1934), *The Hundred Years* (1936), *Rag-Time and Tango* (1938), *Mr Churchill: A Portrait* (1941), and *The Liberators* (1942).

Guest, Lady Charlotte Elizabeth (19 May 1812—15 Jan. 1895), translator, a daughter of the Earl of Lindsey, was born at Uffington House, Lincolnshire. Mainly self-educated, she learned French, German, Italian, Latin, Greek, Hebrew, and Persian. In 1833 she married Sir John Guest, owner of a great iron-works in south Wales. She then learned Welsh, and made a translation of the *Mabinogion* (1838—49), a collection of old Welsh tales. In 1852 Guest died and three years later she married Charles Schreiber, a Fellow of Trinity College, Cambridge, who died in 1884. In later life she made a collection of rare china and published a book on *Fans and Fan Leaves* (1888—90). Her *Journals* were published in 1911.

Guiney, Louise Imogen (7 Jan. 1861—2 Nov. 1920), poetess and essayist, was born at Roxbury, a suburb of Boston. Her father, a native of Tipperary, was a lawyer and fought in the Civil War. After six years at the Convent of the Sacred Heart at Elmhurst, Rhode Island, Louise worked for a time as a journalist, then became postmistress at Auburndale, Massachusetts. Later she worked in the cataloguing department of the Boston Public Library, and in 1895 went to England and studied at the Bodleian; she is buried at Wolvercote, near Oxford. Her volumes *Songs at the Start* (1884) and *Goose Quill Papers* (1885) first won notice and secured her literary friends. The best of her criticism is contained in *A Little English Gallery* (1894), and *Happy Ending* (1909) collects all the verse she wished to preserve. Her *Letters* were published in 1926.

Guiterman, Arthur (20 Nov. 1871—11 Jan. 1943), poet, was born in Vienna of American parents who returned with him to New York in his infancy. Educated at the College of the City of New York, he was a keen sportsman and amateur actor, and was elected to Phi Beta Kappa. He became a reporter, then a freelance writer, and was one of the best American writers of light verse. His books include *The Laughing Muse* (1915), *The Mirthful Lyre* (1918), *Ballads of Old New York* (1920), *A Poet's Proverbs* (1924), *Song and Laughter* (1929), *Death and General Putnam* (1935), *Gaily the Troubadour* (1936), and *Brave Laughter* (1943).

Gunn, Neil Miller (8 Nov. 1891—), novelist, was born at Dunbeath, Caithness, where his father had a fishing fleet, but spent part of his boyhood in Galloway. Educated at a village school, he worked in the Civil Service from 1906 to 1937, first in London, then in Edinburgh, and from 1934 as an officer of Customs and Excise at Inverness. His first novel, *Grey Coast* (1926) at once brought him recognition, and was followed by *Morning Tide* (1931), *The Lost Glen* (1932), *Sun Circle* (1933), *Butcher's Broom* (1934), and *Highland River*, which was awarded the Tait Black Memorial Prize for 1937. Later novels are *Wild Geese Overhead* (1939), *Second Sight* (1940), *The Drinking Well* (1947), *The Well at the World's End* (1951), and *Bloodhunt* (1952). *Hidden Doors* (1929) is a collection of short stories, while *Off in a Boat* (1938) and *Highland Pack* (1950) are travel books. Gunn excelled in depicting the ordinary life of the Highlands and as an interpreter of the psychology of the Celt.

Gunther, John (30 Aug. 1901—), journalist, was born in Chicago and educated at the University of Chicago, where he was editor of the college paper; he also had articles published in the regular press while still an undergraduate. From 1924 to 1934 he worked in Europe for the *Chicago Daily News*, moving about from London to Berlin, Vienna, Moscow, Rome, Paris. His *Inside Europe* (1936), a popular and colourful account of European politics sold about half a million copies. In 1937 and 1938 he travelled about Asia and then wrote *Inside Asia* (1939). *Inside Latin America* followed in 1941, *Inside U.S.A.* in 1947, and *Inside Africa* in 1955. Others of his books are *Death Be Not Proud* (1949), and *Eisenhower* (1952).

L

Guthrie, Thomas (12 July 1803—24 Feb. 1873), minister and philanthropist, was born at Brechin, son of a banker. At the age of 12 he went to Edinburgh University, where he spent ten years—four in Arts, four in Divinity, and two in Medicine and Science. Licensed to preach in 1825, he became in 1837 minister of Old Grey Friars, Edinburgh. Possessed of a commanding presence and voice, and a remarkably effective and picturesque style of oratory, he became perhaps the most popular preacher of his day in Scotland, and was associated with many forms of philanthropy, especially temperance and ragged schools, of the latter of which he was the founder. He was one of the leaders of the Free Church, and raised over £100,000 for manses for its ministers. Among his writings are *The Gospel in Ezekiel* (1855), *Pleas for Ragged Schools* (1847—62), and *The City, its Sins and Sorrows* (1857).

Guthrie, Thomas Anstey (8 Aug. 1856—10 March 1934), humorous novelist who wrote under the name F. Anstey, the F being originally due to a printer's error, was born in London, the son of a tailor. Educated at Cambridge, where he contributed a serial to the *Cambridge Tatler*, an undergraduate periodical, he studied law and in 1881 was called to the Bar, but turned to writing after the success in the following year of his fantasy *Vice Versa*, the story of a man who exchanges bodies with his schoolboy son. From 1887 to 1930 he was on the staff of *Punch*, to which he contributed a column entitled 'Voces Populi.' He is best remembered for his fairy-tale extravaganzas *The Tinted Venus* (1885), *A Fallen Idol* (1886), and *The Brass Bottle* (1900); he also attempted some serious novels, but with little success. *A Long Retrospect* (1936) is autobiographical.

Gwynn, Stephen Lucius (13 Feb. 1864—11 June 1950), poet and critic, was born in Dublin, his father being a Biblical scholar. Educated at St Columba's College, Rathfarnham, and Brasenose College, Oxford, he was for ten years a teacher of Classics in various schools, then moved to London and became a freelance writer. In 1904 he returned to Ireland, and from 1906 to 1918 was M.P. for Galway City. During the First World War he served with the Connaught Rangers and received the Legion of Honour. He was made a D.Litt. of the National University of Ireland in 1940 and of Dublin University in 1945. Among his critical works are *The Masters of English Literature* (1904), and studies or lives of *Tennyson* (1899), *Thomas Moore* (1904), *Sir Walter Scott* (1930), *Horace Walpole* (1932), *Mary Kingsley* (1932), *Dean Swift* (1933), *Goldsmith* (1935), and *Robert Louis Stevenson* (1939). His *Collected Poems* appeared in 1923, and the autobiographical *Experiences of a Literary Man* in 1926.

H

Habberton, John (24 Feb. 1842—24 Feb. 1921), novelist, was born in Brooklyn, New York. After working as salesman and telegraph operator he learned printing, served with the Union Army during the Civil War, and then entered journalism. From 1876 to 1893 he was literary critic of the *New York Herald*, and later was on the staff of *Collier's Weekly*. Although he wrote well over a score of books, he is remembered almost entirely by his story *Helen's Babies* (1876), based on the escapades of his own boys. It was very popular, and had two sequels, *Other People's Children* (1877) and *Budge and Toddie, or, Helen's Babies at Play* (1908).

Habington, William (4 Nov. 1605—30 Nov. 1654), poet, born at Hindlip, Worcestershire, son of a Roman Catholic antiquary, was educated at St Omer's, but refused to become a Jesuit. He married Lucy Herbert, daughter of Lord Powis, and immortalized her in his poem *Castara* (1634), in which he sang the praises of chaste love. He also wrote a tragi-comedy, *The Queen of Arragon* (1640), and a *History of Edward IV*. His verse is graceful and tender.

Haggard, Sir Henry Rider (22 June 1856—14 May 1925), novelist, was born at Bradenham, Norfolk, son of a barrister, and educated at Ipswich Grammar School. In 1875 he went to South Africa as secretary to Sir Henry Bulwer, Governor of Natal. From 1877 to 1879 he was registrar of Transvaal High Court. In the following year he married Mariana Margitson, returned to England, and started studying law, being called to the Bar in 1884 by Lincoln's Inn, but in 1885 his novel *King Solomon's Mines* was such a great success that he decided to give up the law and retired to Norfolk, where he made novel-writing his life work and rural economy his hobby. Among his books about farming are *A Farmer's Year* (1899), *Rural England* (1902), and *The Poor and the Land* (1905); for this work he was made a Knight Commander of the British Empire in 1919. But his fame rests on his thrilling African romances, of which the best are *She* (1887), *Allan Quatermain* (1887), *Allan's Wife* (1890), *Nada the Lily* (1892), *Montezuma's Daughter* (1894), *Pearl Maiden* (1903), *Ayesha* (1905), and *She and Allan* (1921). *The Days of My Life* (1926) is autobiographical.

Hailes, Sir David Dalrymple, Lord (28 Oct. 1726—29 Nov. 1792), judge and historian, was born in Edinburgh and educated at Eton and Utrecht. Belonging to a family famous as lawyers, he was called to the Bar in 1748, and in 1766 became a judge of the Court of Session, with the title of Lord Hailes. An excellent judge, he also produced several works of permanent value on Scottish history and antiquities, including *Annals of Scotland* (1776) and *Canons of the Church of Scotland* (1769). He was a friend and correspondent of Dr Johnson.

Hake, Thomas Gordon (10 March 1809—11 Jan. 1895), doctor and poet, was born in Leeds, educated at Christ's Hospital, and studied medicine at Edinburgh and Glasgow, subsequently practising at Brighton. He formed a friendship with Dante Gabriel Rossetti (q.v.), whom he attended when he was suffering from the effects of drug-taking. Nearly all Hake's poetry was written after he was 50. His books of verse include *Madeline* (1871), *Parables and Tales* (1872), *Maiden Ecstasy* (1880), and *The New Day* (1890), a collection of sonnets. *Memories of Eighty Years* (1892) is autobiographical.

Hakluyt, Richard (1553?—23 Nov. 1616), geographer, who belonged to a good Herefordshire family, was born either at Eyton in that county or in London, and educated at Westminster School and Christ Church, Oxford. The lives and adventures of our great navigators and discoverers became the ruling passion of his life; and in order to increase his knowledge of these matters he studied various foreign languages and the art of navigation. He took orders, and was chaplain of the English Embassy in Paris, Rector of Witheringsett, Suffolk, 1590, Archdeacon of Westminster, 1602, and Rector of Gedney, Lincolnshire, 1612. After a first collection of voyages to America and the West Indies he compiled, while at Paris, his great work, *The Principal Navigations, Voyages, Traffics, and Discoveries of the English Nation*. It appeared first in 1589, and in its final form (3 folio volumes) in 1599. Besides it he published *A Discourse of Western Planting*, and he left a vast mass of manuscript afterwards used (in far inferior style) by S Purchas (q.v.). In all his work Hakluyt was actuated not only by the love of knowledge, but by a noble patriotism: he wished to see England the great sea-power of the world, and his work gave a great impetus to discovery and adventure. In addition to his original writings he translated various works, among them being *The Discoveries of the World*, from the Portuguese of Antonio Galvano.

Haldane, John Burdon Sanderson (5 Nov. 1892—), biologist, born at Oxford, son of Professor J. S. Haldane, the physiologist, and nephew of Viscount Haldane, statesman, was educated at Eton and New College, Oxford, of which he became a Fellow. During the First World War he served with the Black Watch. While Reader in Biochemistry at Cambridge from 1922 to 1932 he was dismissed in connection with a divorce case but reinstated. In 1932 he was elected a Fellow of the Royal Society and in the following year became Professor of Genetics in London University. His works include *Daedalus, or, Science and the Future* (1924), *Callinicus: A Defence of Chemical Warfare* (1925), *Science and Ethics* (1928), *Enzymes* (1930), *Fact and Faith* (1934), *Science and Everyday Life* (1939), *Science in Peace and War* (1940), *New Paths in Genetics* (1941), *Science Advances* (1947), and *The Biochemistry of Genetics* (1954).

Hale, Edward Everett (3 April 1822—10 June 1909), minister and novelist, was born in Boston, son of the owner and editor of the *Daily Advertiser* there, and went to Harvard at the age of 13. In 1846 he became minister in Worcester, Massachusetts, and ten years later moved to the South Congregational Church in Boston, where he remained for many years. In 1863 his famous short story 'A Man Without a Country' appeared in the *Atlantic Monthly*; this, with other stories, made up, *If, Yes, and Perhaps* (1868), his first book of fiction. His novels include *Ten Times One is Ten* (1871) and *In His Name* (1873), but he is also remembered for his autobiographical works, *A New England Boyhood* (1893) and *Memories of a Hundred Years* (1902).

Hale, Sir Matthew (1 Nov. 1609—25 Dec. 1676), jurist, born at Alderley, Gloucestershire, son of a barrister, was educated at Oxford and Lincoln's Inn. Steering a neutral course during the political changes of his time, he served under the Protectorate and after the Restoration rose to be Chief Justice of the King's Bench. He was the author of several works on science, divinity, and law. Among them are *The Primitive Origination of Mankind* and *Contemplations, Moral and Divine*, both published posthumously. His chief legal work was a *History of the Common Law of England* (1713).

Hale, Sarah Josepha (24 Oct. 1788—30 April 1879), was born at Newport, New Hampshire, her maiden name being Buell. In 1813 she married David Hale, who died in 1822, leaving her with five children to support. Taking up writing, she published *Northwood, a Tale of New England* (1827), and in 1828 was appointed editor of the Boston *Lady's Magazine*, later the *Lady's Book*; as editor of this for forty years she had great influence on women's causes in America, but her most famous work is 'Mary had a Little Lamb,' which appeared in her *Poems for Our Children* (1830).

Hales, John (19 April 1584—19 May 1656), theologian, born at Bath, and educated there and at Oxford, became one of the best Greek scholars of his day, and lectured on that language at Oxford, where he became a Fellow of Merton. In 1616 he accompanied the English ambassador to the Hague in the capacity of chaplain, and attended the Synod of Dort, where he was converted from Calvinism to Arminianism. A lover of quiet and learned leisure, he chose scholarly retirement in a Fellowship of Eton. A treatise on *Schism and Schismatics* gave offence to Laud, but Hales defended himself so well that Laud made him a Prebendary of Windsor. Refusing to acknowledge the Commonwealth, he was deprived of his living, fell into poverty, and had to sell his library. After his death his writings were published in 1659 as *The Golden Remains of the Ever-Memorable Mr John Hales of Eton College*.

Haliburton, Thomas Chandler (Dec. 1796—27 Aug. 1865), humorous writer, was born at Windsor, Nova Scotia, and educated at school and college there. He studied law and finally succeeded his father as a judge. He is famous for *The Clockmaker: or, Sayings and Doings of Samuel Slick of Slickerville* (1837), in which under the guise of a travelling Yankee clockmaker he pokes fun at political humbug; there were several sequels, including *The Attaché, or, Sam Slick in England* (1843), all using the same Yankee dialect, and Artemus Ward declared Haliburton to be the founder of the American school of humour. In 1856 he retired and went to England, married, and was elected to the House of Commons as member for Launceston.

Halifax, Charles Montagu, 1st Earl of (16 April 1661—19 May 1715), statesman and wit, born at Horton, Northamptonshire, was educated at Westminster School and Trinity College, Cambridge, where he formed a lifelong friendship with Isaac Newton. Entering Parliament he became Chancellor of the Exchequer in 1694, and First Lord of the Treasury 1697. Vain and arrogant, he soon lost popularity and power. His chief literary effort was his collaboration with Prior in *The Town and Country Mouse* (1687), a parody of and reply to Dryden's *Hind and Panther*. Halifax was the friend and patron of Addison, Steele, Congreve, and many other writers of his day. He became a peer in 1701.

Hall, Anna Maria (6 Jan. 1800—30 Jan. 1881), novelist, was born in Dublin, her maiden name being Fielding, but left Ireland at the age of 15. Nevertheless, that country gave her the motive of several of her most successful books, such as *Sketches of Irish Character* (1829), *Lights and Shadows of Irish Life* (1838), *Marian* (1839), and *The White Boy* (1845). Other works are *The Buccaneer* (1832), an historical novel, *Midsummer Eve* (1849), a fairy tale, and many sketches in the *Art Journal*, of which Samuel Carter Hall, whom she married in 1824, was editor. With him she also collaborated in a work entitled *Ireland, its Scenery and Character* (1840).

Hall, Basil (31 Dec. 1788—11 Sept. 1844), travel writer, son of Sir James Hall, Bart., of Dunglass, Haddingtonshire, entered the navy, and rose to be captain. He was one of the first to visit Corea, and wrote *Voyage of Discovery to Corea* (1818), also *Travels in North America in 1827—8*, a lively work which gave some offence in the United States, *Fragments of Voyages and Travels* (1831—40), and some tales and romances. He was latterly insane.

Hall, or Halle, Edward (1499?—1547), chronicler, born in London, was educated at Eton and Cambridge, and studied law at Gray's Inn. He was M.P. for Bridgnorth, and served on various commissions. He wrote a history of *The Union of the two Noble and Illustre Families of Lancastre and Yorke*, commonly called *Hall's Chronicle*. Published after the author's death by Richard Grafton, it gives a valuable account of the time of Henry VIII.

Hall, Josef Washington (27 Feb. 1894—   ), journalist who wrote under the name of Upton Close, was born at Kelso, Washington, and educated at George Washington University. From 1916 to 1919 he held a government post in Shantung, and from his experiences wrote *In the Land of the Laughing Buddha* (1925). His pseudonym was invented when he wrote of the Japanese invasion, and put on his message 'up close' to indicate that he was near the front. Later he was foreign affairs chief under Wu Pei-fu, the war lord. Others of his books are *The Revolt of Asia* (1927), *Eminent Asians* (1929), *The Challenge Behind the Face of Japan* (1934), and two novels, *Moonlady* (1927) and *Son of Mine* (1936).

Hall, Joseph (1 July 1574—8 Sept. 1656), bishop and satirist, born at Ashby-de-la-Zouche, and educated at Cambridge, took holy orders, and became in 1627 Bishop of Exeter, and in 1641 Bishop of Norwich. He had a chequered career. He accompanied James I to Scotland in 1617, and was a Deputy to the Synod of Dort. Accused of Puritanism, and at enmity with Laud, he fell on troublous days, and was, in 1641, imprisoned in the Tower. Returning to Norwich he found that his revenues had been sequestrated, and his private property seized. In 1647 he retired to a small farm near Norwich, where he passed the remainder of his life. His *Characters of Virtues and Vices* (1608), sketches of single qualities, is the first professed imitation of Theophrastus in England; he also claimed to be the first of English satirists, with his *Virgidemiarum Sex Libri* (Six Books of Stripes), written before he was in orders, and condemned by Archbishop Whitgift to be burned. Pope, however, thought them 'the best poetry and truest satire in the English language.' Hall's *Divine Right of Episcopacy* (1640), gave rise to much controversy, in which Archbishop Ussher, Milton, and the writers who called themselves ' Smectymnuus ' (q.v.) took part.

Hall, Marguerite Radclyffe (1886?—7 Oct. 1943), novelist, was born in Bournemouth and educated at King's College, London, and in Germany. Her earliest works were four volumes of verse, and several of her pieces were set to music by well-known composers. In 1924 she published two novels, *The Forge* and *The Unlit Lamp*, followed by *Adam's Breed* (1926) which was awarded the Femina Vie Heureuse and Tait Black Memorial Prizes. *The Well of Loneliness* (1928), a sympathetic study of Lesbianism, was banned as obscene in Britain but finally passed for publication in America. Others of her novels are *The Master of the House* (1932) and *The Sixth Beatitude* (1936). *Miss Ogilvie Finds Herself* (1934) is a volume of short stories. All her life she took a great interest in psychical research.

Hall, Robert (2 May 1764—21 Feb. 1831), Baptist minister, born at Arnsby, near Leicester, was educated at Bristol Baptist Academy, and at the University of Aberdeen, from which he received the degree of D.D. in 1817. He ministered to congregations at Bristol, Cambridge, Leicester, and again at Bristol, and became one of the greatest pulpit orators of his day. After his death a collection of 50 of his sermons was published (1843), and *Miscellaneous Works and Remains* (1846).

Hallam, Henry (9 July 1777—21 Jan. 1859), historian, was born at Windsor, where his father was canon, and educated at Eton and Oxford. He was called to the Bar at the Inner Temple, and appointed a Commissioner of Stamps. Among his earliest writings were papers in the *Edinburgh Review*; but in 1818 he leaped into a foremost place among historical writers by the publication of his *View of the State of Europe during the Middle Ages*. This was followed in 1827 by *The Constitutional History of England from the Accession of Henry VII to the Death of George II*, and his third great work, *Introduction to the Literature of Europe in the 15th, 16th, and 17th Centuries*, in 4 volumes, appeared in 1837—9. All these, which have gone through several editions, and have been translated into the principal languages of Europe,.are characterized by wide and profound learning, indefatigable research, and judicial impartiality. Hallam had two sons of great promise, both of whom predeceased him. Of these the elder, Arthur Henry, is the subject of Tennyson's *In Memoriam*.

Halle, Edward, *see* **Hall.**

Halleck, Fitz-Greene (8 July 1790—19 Nov. 1867), poet, born at Guilford, Connecticut, wrote, with Rodman Drake, a young poet who died at 25, *The Croaker Papers*, a series of satirical and humorous verses. *Fanny* (1819), a Byronesque satire, is entirely his own. In 1822 he visited Europe, and the influence of this is seen in his lines on Burns, and on Alnwick Castle.

Halliburton, Richard (9 Jan. 1900—23 or 24 March 1939), travel writer, was born at Brownsville, Tennessee, but the family moved to Memphis while he was still a child. He was educated at Princeton, and afterwards went to sea and sailed and tramped all over the world, having a particular passion for repeating the feats of famous heroes. For instance, *The Glorious Adventure* (1927) tells of his travels in Greece, where he followed the trail of Ulysses and emulated Leander by swimming the Hellespont. He visited Yucatan and Mexico, swam through the Panama Canal (paying on his tonnage, like a liner, for using the locks!) went to Devil's Island, Timbuctoo, Mount Everest, and other places whose names are a synonym for 'the back of beyond,' and told of them in *New Worlds to Conquer* (1929), *The Flying Carpet* (1932), and *Seven League Boots* (1935). Eventually he was drowned while sailing in the Pacific on a Chinese junk.

Halliwell-Phillips, James Orchard (21 June 1820—3 Jan. 1889), scholar, was born in Chelsea, son of a business man, his name originally being Halliwell. Educated at Cambridge, he was a Fellow of the Royal Society before he was 19. He wrote a *Life of Shakespeare* (1848), *New Boke about Shakespeare and Stratford upon Avon* (1850), *Folio Edition of Shakespeare* (1853—65), and various other works relative to him, as well as a *Dictionary of Old English Plays* (1860). He also edited works for the Camden and Percy Societies, and compiled a *Dictionary of Archaic and Provincial Words*. In 1872 he added his wife's name of Phillips to his own.

Hamerton, Philip Gilbert (10 Sept. 1834—4 Nov. 1894), artist and art critic, son of a solicitor, was born near Oldham. Originally intended for the Church, he decided for art and literature. For a time he lived on an island in Loch Awe with his wife, who was a Frenchwoman, then settled in France, and devoted himself to writing on art. Among his works are *Etching and Etchers* (1868), *Painting in France after the Decline of Classicism* (1869), *The Intellectual Life* (1873), *Human Intercourse* (1884), *The Graphic Arts* (1882), and *Landscape* (1885), some of which were magnificently illustrated. He also left an autobiography.

Hamilton, Alexander (11 Jan. 1757—12 July 1804), statesman, was born on Nevis, one of the Leeward Islands, son of a Scottish merchant. Educated at what is now Columbia University, he took a prominent part in the war of American Independence and became Washington's private secretary. Returning to New York after the

L*

war he studied law, was admitted to the Bar, and from 1782 to 1783 was a Member of Congress. In 1787 he was elected to the New York Legislature, and as one of the delegates to the Constitutional Convention played a leading part in obtaining the ratification of the federal constitution. In this and the following years Hamilton wrote a series of essays, afterwards collected with the title *The Federalist*, in which the working of the constitution was explained. From 1789 to 1795 he was Secretary of the Treasury, and placed the country's finances on a sound basis. Later he had a conflict on policy with President John Adams, and finally was killed in a duel with Aaron Burr, a political adversary.

Hamilton, Clive, *see* **Lewis, Clive Staples.**

Hamilton, Elizabeth (21 July 1758—23 July 1816), novelist, was born in Belfast, but her father was a Scot and she was brought up in Stirlingshire. In 1788 she moved to London, and was after producing various works, including *The Hindoo Rajah* (1796), and *Letters on Education* (1802), which was later continued by *Essays on the Elementary Principles of the Human Mind* (1812), she published her most notable book, *The Cottagers of Glenburnie* (1808), a kind of early 'kailyard' novel about life in a poor Scottish hamlet. She also wrote the well-known song 'My Ain Fireside.' Her *Memoirs* were published in 1815.

Hamilton, Mary Agnes (8 July 1884—), novelist, was born in Manchester, but brought up in Glasgow, where her father Robert Adamson was Professor of Logic. From Glasgow Girls' High School she went to Newnham College, Cambridge, and also studied in Germany. For a year she taught history in the University of Cardiff, then worked in London on the staff of the *Review of Reviews*. In 1905 she married C. J. Hamilton. After the First World War she turned to politics, and in 1929 was returned as Labour M.P. for Blackburn. In the same year she was a member of the British delegation to the League of Nations, and from 1933 to 1937 she was a governor of the B.B.C. Her novels include *Less Than the Dust* (1912), *Yes* (1914), *Dead Yesterdays* (1916), *Slings and Arrows* (1918), *Full Circle* (1920), *Special Providence* (1930), *Murder in the House of Commons* (1931), and *Life Sentence* (1935). She also wrote a number of books on Greek and Roman history, and studies of *Ramsay Macdonald* (1925), *Margaret Bondfield* (1926), *Carlyle* (1926), *John Stuart Mill* (1933), and *Sydney and Beatrice Webb* (1933). Her autobiography *Uphill All the Way* appeared in 1949, and in the same year she was awarded the C.B.E.

Hamilton, Thomas (1789—7 Dec. 1842), novelist, brother of Sir William Hamilton (q.v.), wrote a novel, *Cyril Thornton* (1827), which was received with great favour. Educated at Glasgow University, he became an officer in the army, and, on his retirement in 1818, settled in Edinburgh, and became a contributor to *Blackwood*. He was also the author of *Annals of the Peninsular Campaign* (1829), and *Men and Manners in America* (1833).

Hamilton, William (of Bangour) (1704—25 March 1754), poet, son of an advocate, was born at Bangour, the family seat in Linlithgowshire. Cultivated and brilliant, he was a favourite of society, and began his literary career by contributing verses to Allan Ramsay's *Tea Table Miscellany*. He joined in the Jacobite rising of 1745, and celebrated the Battle of Prestonpans in *Gladsmuir*. After Culloden he wandered in the Highlands, where he wrote his *Soliloquy*, and escaped to France. His friends, however, succeeded in obtaining his pardon, and he returned to his native country. In 1750, on the death of his brother, he succeeded to the family estate, but died at Lyons of consumption soon afterwards. The first to translate Homer into blank verse, he is best remembered for his fine ballad 'The Braes of Yarrow.'

Hamilton, William (of Gilbertfield) (1665?—24 May 1751), poet, was born at Ladyland, Ayrshire. Son of an army officer, he also had a military career, after which he retired and lived as a country gentleman at Gilbertfield near Glasgow. He contributed a number of pieces to Watson's *Choice Collection of Comic and Serious Scots Poems*, and addressed to his friend Allan Ramsay (q.v.) *Seven Familiar Epistles* in verse, which set a model for Burns's similar poetic letters. He also put Blind Harry's *Wallace* into English verse.

Hamilton, Sir William (8 March 1788—6 May 1856), metaphysician, born in Glasgow, in the University of which his father and grand-father successively filled the Chair of Anatomy and Botany, educated there and at Balliol College, Oxford, was called to the Scottish Bar, at which he attained little practice, but was appointed Solicitor of Teinds. In 1816 he established his claim to the baronetcy of Hamilton of Preston. In 1821 he was appointed Professor of History at Edinburgh, and in 1829 he gave proof of his remarkable powers as a philosopher in a famous article in the *Edinburgh Review*, a critique of Victor Cousin's doctrine of the Infinite. This paper carried his name over Europe, and won for him the homage of continental philosophers, including Cousin himself. After this Hamilton continued to contribute to the *Review*, many of his papers being translated into French, German, and Italian. In 1852 they were published as *Discussions in Philosophy and Literature, Education, and University Reform*. In 1836 Hamilton was elected Professor of Logic and Metaphysics at Edinburgh, which office he held with great reputation until his death, after which the lectures he had delivered were edited by H. L. Mansel and J. Veitch (1858—60). His *magnum opus* was his edition of the *Works of Dr Thomas Reid*, left unfinished, and completed by Mansel. Hamilton was the last, and certainly the most learned and accomplished, of the Scottish school of philosophy, which he considered it his mission to develop and correlate to the systems of other times and countries, bringing British thought into contact with that of Kant and Hegel. He also made various important contributions to the science of logic.

Hammerton, Sir John Alexander (27 Feb. 1871—12 May 1949), editor and critic, born at Alexandria, Dunbartonshire, became a journalist and after holding various Scottish and provincial posts was an editor of magazines and books of reference in London. Many of the works which he edited were issued in weekly or fort-nightly parts, among the most important being the *Universal*

Encyclopaedia, Universal History, Peoples of All Nations, and *Countries of the World.* In 1912 he was appointed managing editor of *El Diccionario Enciclopedico Hispano-Americano,* and later he wrote about his experience of Latin America in *The Argentine Through English Eyes* (1917). In each of the two world wars he edited a weekly magazine, *War Illustrated,* recording its progress. Among his own writings are *Stevensoniana* (1903), *George Meredith in Anecdote and Criticism* (1909), *Memories of Books and Places* (1928), and *Barrie: The Story of a Genius* (1929). He was knighted in 1932.

Hammett, Samuel Dashiell (27 May 1894—10 Jan. 1961), writer of detective stories, was born in Maryland and educated at Baltimore Polytechnic, which he left at the age of 13. He then worked as newsboy, freight clerk, messenger boy, stevedore, advertising manager, and finally for seven years was one of Pinkerton's detectives thus obtaining first-hand knowledge of the world of criminals. In the First World War he served with the Motor Ambulance. By his novels he founded the American 'hard-boiled' school of detective fiction. His first book, *Red Harvest* (1929), was of the more extreme blood-and-thunder type, full of gangsters and brutality, but his realism became less extreme as he went on. *The Dain Curse* (1929) was followed by *The Maltese Falcon* (1932), often reckoned his best. Others are *The Glass Key* (1931) and *The Thin Man* (1932), which was filmed. Hammett's books are far above the mere shocker type, and his characters, though repulsive, are vivid and genuine.

Hanley, James (1901—   ), novelist, was born in Dublin of a working-class family. Leaving school at 13, he followed the sea from 1914 to 1924, and then worked variously as butcher, railwayman, cook, clerk, postman, and journalist. His first book, *Drift,* was published in 1930, and his first real success, *Boy,* in the following year, which saw also *The Last Voyage* and *Ebb and Flood.* *The Furys* (1934), together with *Secret Journey* (1936), and *Our Time Is Gone* (1940) make up a trilogy of Dublin slum life and show Hanley's power of depicting horror and misery. Others of his novels are *The Maelstrom* (1935), *The Wall* (1936), *Hollow Sea* (1938), *The Ocean* (1941), *Sailor's Song* (1943), *Winter Song* (1950), and *The Closed Harbour* (1952). *Soldier's Wind* (1938), *Between the Tides* (1939), and *Don Quixote Drowned* (1953) are collections of essays, and *Broken Water* (1937) is autobiographical. Hanley once declared himself 'interested mostly in the insignificant.' He married a niece of the Earl of Ancaster, lived in a cottage in Wales, and his recreation was playing the piano.

Hanna, William (26 Nov. 1808—24 May 1882), theologian and biographer, son of the Professor of Divinity in the Presbyterian College, Belfast, was born there and became a distinguished minister of the Free Church of Scotland. He wrote *Memoirs of Dr Chalmers* (1849—53), whose son-in-law he was, and edited his works. He also edited the *Letters of Thomas Erskine of Linlathen* (1877—8), and wrote various theological works.

Hannay, James (17 Feb. 1827—9 Jan. 1873), novelist and journalist, was born at Dumfries, and after serving for some years in the navy took to literature, and became editor of the *Edinburgh Courant* from 1860 to 1864. He wrote two novels, *Singleton Fontenoy* (1850) and *Eustace Conyers* (1855); also *Lectures on Satire and Satirists* (1854) and *Studies on Thackeray* (1869). For the last five years of his life he was British Consul at Barcelona.

Hannay, James Owen (16 July 1865—1 Feb. 1950), clergyman and novelist who wrote under the name George A. Birmingham, was born in Belfast, where his father was a vicar, and educated at Haileybury and Trinity College, Dublin. Ordained in 1889, he was a curate in Wicklow, rector in Mayo, in 1901 a lecturer at Dublin University, from 1912 to 1921 a Canon of St Patrick's Cathedral, and from 1924 to 1934 rector of Mells. His first book was *The Spirit and Origin of Christian Monasticism*, published under his own name in 1903. *Spanish Gold* (1908) established him as a novelist of Irish life with a racy humour all his own. Among the best of his other novels are *Lalage's Lovers* (1911), *The Major's Niece* (1911), *The Inviolable Sanctuary* (1912), *Good Conduct* (1920), *Goodly Pearls* (1926), *Fidgets* (1927), *Fed Up* (1931), *Angel's Adventure* (1933), and *Good Intentions* (1945). His play *General John Regan* caused a riot when it was produced in Mayo in 1913. Yachting was his hobby.

Hardy, Thomas, O.M. (2 June 1840—11 Jan. 1928), novelist and poet, was born at Upper Bockhampton in Dorset, the Wessex of his books, son of a builder who had musical tastes; among his ancestors was Nelson's famous flag-captain. Delicate and precocious, he was educated at a private school in Dorchester, a few miles from his home, and studied French, Latin, and later German and Greek. From 1856 to 1861 he was apprentice to an ecclesiastical architect in Dorchester, whom he assisted in some of his restoration work. In the following year he moved to London, where for five years he studied Gothic architecture under Sir Arthur Blomfield, and meanwhile attended evening classes at King's College. In 1863 he was awarded a medal of the Institute of British Architects.

Appropriately, his first published work was a sketch entitled 'How I Built Myself a House,' which appeared in *Chambers's Journal* in 1865. In 1871, at his own expense, he published his first novel, a murder story entitled *Desperate Remedies*. Two rather slight books, *Under the Greenwood Tree* (1872) and *A Pair of Blue Eyes* (1873), were then followed by his first great novel, *Far From the Madding Crowd* (1874). *The Hand of Ethelberta* (1876) shows a falling-off, but with *The Return of the Native* (1878) he again showed his full powers, less prominent in *The Trumpet-Major* (1880) and *A Laodicean* (1881). *The Mayor of Casterbridge* (1886) marked a turning-point, for at this time he moved into Max Gate, the house at Dorchester built to his own plans, where he spent the rest of his life. *The Woodlanders*, another novel of powerful character-drawing, was followed by *Tess of the D'Urbervilles* (1891), which challenged Victorian conventions of respectability and was his most famous book, but aroused much hostile criticism. *Jude the Obscure* (1895) caused such disgust in many quarters that Hardy gave up writing novels, though an unsuccessful fantasy, *The Well-Beloved*, appeared in 1897.

His collections of short stories include *Wessex Tales* (1888), *A Group of Noble Dames* (1891), *Life's Little Ironies* (1894), and *A Changed Man* (1913). Like the novels, they display the bitter pessimism which led G. K. Chesterton to describe Hardy scornfully as 'a sort of village atheist brooding and blaspheming over the village idiot.' 'Atheist' is hardly correct, for Hardy invents a 'President of the Immortals' who is pictured as amusing himself by torturing men and women. He has been compared with the Aeschylus of *Prometheus Bound*, and admittedly he has something of the rugged strength of that Greek dramatist. But his conviction of the futility of everything is really a weakness; the true greatness of his novels lies in the genuine picture they give of the English countryside and its people; his best fiction, like his best poetry, is redolent of the soil.

The Dynasts, his epic drama, which began to appear in 1904 and was completed in 1908, contains three parts, 19 acts, and 130 scenes. Written in blank verse, it is commonly regarded as Hardy's greatest work. It pictures the Napoleonic Wars as viewed by supernatural spectators, 'certain impersonated abstractions or intelligencies, called spirits,' who form a sort of transcendental chorus. The whole is acclaimed by all critics as a noble conception. His only other noteworthy excursion into the world of drama was *The Tragedy of the Queen of Cornwall* (1923), a play on the old legend of Tristan and Iseult.

Reversing the usual sequence of an author's development, poetry was the final phase of Hardy's work. Indeed, he is sometimes spoken of as a man who began writing poetry on the verge of old age, but this is a misconception. He had written verse before his novels appeared, and some of this early work was included in *Wessex Poems* (1898). Other volumes are *Poems of the Past and Present* (1901), *Time's Laughing Stocks* (1910), *Satires of Circumstance* (1914), *Late Lyrics and Earlier* (1922), *Human Shows* (1925), and *Winter Words* (1928). In all he wrote about a thousand pieces. As a nature poet Hardy stands high, with a verse whose strength redeems its ruggedness. His poetry, like his prose, is permeated by his barren pessimism, but it is not impossible that it may outlast his novels. Perhaps it was not inappropriate that his ashes were buried in the Poet's Corner at Westminster Abbey.

Hardy's life was uneventful. He was twice married, to Emma Lavinia Gifford in 1874, and after her death to Florence Emily Dugdale in 1914. He received many distinctions. In 1910 he was awarded the Order of Merit, and in 1912 received the gold medal of the Royal Society of Literature. He held honorary degrees of Oxford, Cambridge, St Andrews, Aberdeen, and Bristol.

Hare, Augustus John Cuthbert (13 March 1834—22 Jan. 1903), biographer and writer of guide-books, born in Rome, was a nephew of Augustus William Hare (q.v.), by whose widow he was brought up; later he wrote of her in *Memorials of a Quiet Life* (1876). Educated at Harrow and Oxford, Hare wrote guides to *Berks, Bucks, and Oxfordshire* (1860), and *Durham* (1863). From 1863 to 1870 he lived in Italy, and continued the series with *Walks in Rome* (1871),

Wanderings in Spain (1873), *Walks in London* (1878), and many others. Biographies of his distinguished family connections include *The Story of Two Noble Lives* (1893), which tells of Lady Canning and Lady Waterford, and *The Gurneys of Earlham* (1895). *The Story of my Life* (1896—1900) is a tedious autobiography. In 1878 he was given the Order of St Olaf by the King of Sweden.

Hare, Augustus William (17 Nov. 1792—18 Feb. 1834), clergyman, was the son of Francis Hare-Naylor, who married a cousin of the famous Duchess of Devonshire, and was the author of a history of Germany. He was sent by the widow of Sir W. Jones, whose godson he was, to Winchester, and New College, Oxford, in the latter of which he was for some time a tutor. Having taken orders, he became incumbent of the rural parish of Alton Barnes. In addition to writing in conjunction with his brother Julius (q.v.), *Guesses at Truth* (1827), a work containing short essays on multifarious subjects, which attracted much attention, he left two volumes of sermons.

Hare, Julius Charles (13 Sept. 1795—23 Jan. 1855), clergyman and essayist, younger brother of the above, was born at Vicenza in north Italy. Educated at Charterhouse and Cambridge, he took orders and, in 1832, was appointed to the rich family living of Hurstmonceaux in Sussex, where he had John Sterling (q.v.) for curate, and Bunsen for a neighbour. He was also Archdeacon of Lewes and a Chaplain to the Queen. His first work was *Guesses at Truth* (1827), jointly with his brother, and he also collaborated with Thirlwall (q.v.) in a translation of Niebuhr's *History of Rome*, wrote *The Victory of Faith* (1840), and other theological books, and published with a life the *Essays and Tales* of John Sterling (1848). He was an eccentric man of strong antipathies, unmethodical, and unpunctual.

Harington, James, *see* **Harrington.**

Harington, Sir John (1561—20 Nov. 1612), translator, born at Kelston Park near Bath, and educated at Eton and Cambridge, became a courtier of Queen Elizabeth, whose godson he was. In 1599 he served in Ireland under Essex, by whom he was knighted on the field, a stretch of authority which was much resented by the Queen. While there he wrote *A Short View of the State of Ireland*, published in 1880. He was noted for his epigrams, of which some have wit, but others are only indelicate. His translation of the *Orlando Furioso* of Ariosto, in the metre of the original, is a somewhat free paraphrase. Banished from the Court for his Rabelaisian writings, he nevertheless was made tutor to Prince Henry by James VI and I. His most valuable work is one which was published in 1769 by a descendant, under the title of *Nugae Antiquae* (Old-time Trifles), a miscellaneous collection from his writings and papers, containing many things of interest, such as a minute account of the Queen's last illness, and letters and verses by her and other eminent persons.

Harker, Lizzie Allen (1863—14 April 1933), novelist, was born in Gloucester, her maiden name being Watson, and educated at Cheltenham Ladies' College. She married James Allen Harker, a professor at the Royal Agricultural College, Cirencester. Her first novel was published in 1902, but her first great success was *Miss Esperance and Mr Wycherley* (1908); it and its sequel, *Mr Wycherley's Wards* (1912) are both delightful stories in which children are the main characters. Others of her books are *A Romance of the Nursery* (1909), *The ffolliots of Redmarley* (1913), *Allegra* (1919), and *The Really Romantic Age* (1922). *Children of the Dear Cotswolds* (1920) and *The Vagaries of Tod and Peter* (1923) are collections of short stories. In collaboration with F. R. Prior she wrote two plays, *Her Proper Pride* (1917) and *Marigold* (1927), which ran for eighteen months in London.

Harland, Henry (1 March 1861—20 Dec. 1905), novelist, was born in New York, son of a lawyer, and educated at the College of that city and at Harvard, where he studied divinity. From 1883 to 1886 he worked as a clerk, and in 1884 he married Aline H. Merriam, a talented musician. Under the pseudonym Sidney Luska he published *As It Was Written* (1885), *Mrs Peixada* (1886), and *The Yoke of Thoral* (1887), melodramatic stories with little attempt at style. In 1889 he went to London and became a member of the 'aesthetic' group, writing in a carefully studied style which came to have great charm. To this period belong his novels *Mademoiselle Miss* (1893), *Grey Roses* (1895), *Comedies and Errors* (1898), and the extremely popular *The Cardinal's Snuff-Box* (1900). With Aubrey Beardsley he founded the famous *Yellow Book*, and edited it from 1894 to 1897. Later novels were *The Lady Paramount* (1902) and *My Friend Prospero* (1904). He died at San Remo of tuberculosis.

Harraden, Beatrice (24 Jan. 1864—5 May 1936), novelist, born at Hampstead, was educated at Dresden, Cheltenham, Queen's College, and Bedford College, London, where she took honours in classics and mathematics. Her first book was a story for children, *Things Will Take a Turn* (1891). After writing many short stories she scored a striking success with *Ships that Pass in the Night* (1893), a novel marked by fine characterization; after initial rejections it sold over a million copies. Others of her novels are *Hilda Strafford* (1897), *Out of the Wreck I Rise* (1912), *The Guiding Thread* (1916), *Thirteen All Told* (1921), *Youth Calling* (1924), *Rachel* (1926), and *Search Will Find It Out* (1928). For some years she took an active part in the women's suffrage movement.

Harrington *or* **Harington, James** (7 Jan. 1611—11 Sept. 1677), political theorist, was born at Upton, Northamptonshire, and educated at Oxford. After leaving the university he travelled on the Continent, visiting, among other places, The Hague and Venice, where he imbibed republican principles. He was for some time a groom of the bedchamber to Charles I. On the outbreak of the Civil War he sided with the Parliament, but disapproved of the execution of the King, for whom he appears, notwithstanding his political theories, to have cherished a personal attachment. Thereafter he withdrew from active life, and devoted himself to composing his political romance, *The Commonwealth of Oceana*, which he published in 1656, and in which Oceana represents England, Marpesia Scotland,

and Panopaea Ireland. In this work he propounds the theory that the natural element of power in states is property, of which land is the most important. He further endeavoured to propagate his views by establishing a debating society called the Rota, and by his conversations with his friends. After the Restoration he was confined in the Tower, and subsequently at Plymouth. He issued several defences of *Oceana*, and made translations from Virgil.

Harris, James (20 July 1709—22 Dec. 1780), grammarian, born at Salisbury and educated at Wadham College, Oxford, studied law at Lincoln's Inn. He was a wealthy country gentleman and M.P., who held office in the Admiralty and the Treasury. He was the author of a singular and learned work entitled *Hermes, or a Philosophical Inquiry concerning Universal Grammar* (1751). For the purpose which it had in view it is useless, but it contains much curious matter. His son was the eminent diplomatist, James Harris, 1st Earl of Malmesbury.

Harris, Frank (14 Feb. 1856—26 Aug. 1931), journalist and author, was born in Galway of Welsh parentage, but at the age of 15 went to the United States, where he worked as bootblack, labourer, hotel clerk, and cow-puncher. Later he studied law in Kansas and was admitted to the Bar. Returning to Europe, he attended a continental university, then entered journalism and became editor successively of the *Fortnightly Review*, the *Saturday Review*, and *Vanity Fair*, in connection with which he was imprisoned for libel. He was also founder and editor of *The Candid Friend*. During the First World War he returned to America. His books include *The Man Shakespeare* (1909), *The Women of Shakespeare* (1911), five series of *Contemporary Portraits* (1915—30), *Oscar Wilde, his Life and Confessions* (1920), *Bernard Shaw* (1931), and the autobiographical *My Life and Loves* (1923—7). He also wrote several plays, including *Mr and Mrs Daventry* (1900) and *Shakespeare and his Love* (1910), as well as a number of novels.

Harris, Joel Chandler (9 Dec. 1848—3 July 1908), writer of folk tales, was born near Eatonton, Georgia, son of an Irish labourer. Educated locally, he became printer's devil on the *Countryman*, a weekly, and after the chaos of the Civil War established himself as a humorous journalist. In 1876 he joined the staff of the *Atlanta Constitution*, on which he remained for twenty-four years, writing articles of all kinds. In it his Negro folk tales, put into the mouth of an old darkie, Uncle Remus, made their first appearance, and at once the adventures of Brer Rabbit, Brer Fox, and other animals became extremely popular. Among the main collections of these stories from Negro folklore are *Uncle Remus: His Songs and Sayings* (1880), *Nights with Uncle Remus* (1883), *Uncle Remus and his Friends* (1892), *The Tar Baby* (1904), and *Uncle Remus and Brer Rabbit* (1906); and in 1900 Harris founded *Uncle Remus's Magazine*. He also wrote a number of novels of life in the plantations. Shy and retiring, he was a close friend of James Whitcomb Riley (q.v.).

Harrison, Frederic (18 Oct. 1831—14 Jan. 1923), lawyer and philosopher, was born in London and educated at King's College and Oxford; he then studied law and was called to the Bar in 1858. Attracted by the Comtist doctrine of positivism, he accepted it as a religion and became one of the leaders of a positivist movement which lasted into the twentieth century. Among his works are lives of *Cromwell* (1888), *William the Silent* (1897), *Ruskin* (1902), and *Chatham* (1905); *Studies in Early Victorian Literature* (1895); *Theophano* (1904), a medieval romance, and *Nicephorus* (1906), a blank verse tragedy; and *Autobiographic Memoirs* (1911). He received honorary degrees from Oxford, Cambridge, and Aberdeen.

Harrison, Jane Ellen (9 Sept. 1850—5 April 1928), scholar, was born at Cottingham, Yorkshire, daughter of a timber merchant, and educated at Cheltenham under Miss Beale, and at Newnham. Settling in London, she studied archaeology at the British Museum under Sir Charles Newton, and formed friendships with the two great Greek scholars, Professor Gilbert Murray and Dr Verrall. In 1882 she published *Myths of the Odyssey in Art and Literature*, and in 1885 *Introductory Studies in Greek Art*. After three visits to Athens she produced *The Mythology and Monuments of Ancient Athens* (1890), a commentary on the first book of Pausanias's *Description of Greece*. Her two most important works are *Prolegomena to the Study of Greek Religion* (1903) and *Themis, a Study of the Social Origins of the Greek Religion* (1912). During the First World War she studied Russian and from 1917 onwards lectured on that language at Newnham; in her old age she also studied Persian. Her *Reminiscences of a Student's Life* appeared in 1925.

Harry, Blind, *see* **Henry the Minstrel.**

Hart, Liddell, *see* **Liddell Hart, B. H.**

Harte, Francis Brett (25 Aug. 1836—5 May 1902), novelist who wrote under the name Bret Harte, was born in Albany, son of a schoolmaster. He had a poem published when he was 11, left school at 13, and at 16 was supporting himself. He read widely, especially Dickens, whose influence appears in his work. In 1853 the family moved to California, where he held various jobs, including that of schoolmaster and apothecary, and in 1860 he became a compositor on the San Francisco *Golden Era*, for which he wrote stories, including the famous 'Mliss.' After that he held a post in the branch mint for six years. In 1867 he published *The Lost Galleon*, a book of verse, and *Condensed Novels*, containing clever parodies of contemporary writers. In the following year he became editor of the *Overland Monthly*, to which he contributed ' The Luck of Roaring Camp,' a story of effective Western local colour, depicting the world of the forty-niners, and in 1870 wrote his humorous poem, 'The Heathen Chinee.' His reputation as a writer was now at its height; he went East and obtained a contract with the *Atlantic Monthly*, but found that his work there had no longer the inspiration of his Californian days. In 1878 he went to Europe as United States consul at Crefeld, Prussia, and later at Glasgow, but with a change in the American administration he lost his post and spent his closing years as a hack writer. Collections of his stories include *Mrs Skaggs's Husbands* (1873) and *Tales of the Argonauts* (1875); *Gabriel Conroy* (1876) is·a novel, and *Ah Sin* (1877) a play in which he collaborated with Mark Twain.

Hartley, David (baptized 21 June 1705, died 28 Aug. 1757), philosopher, born at Luddenden, near Halifax, and educated at Cambridge, studied for the Church, but owing to theological difficulties turned to medicine as a profession, and practised with success at various places, including London and Bath. He also attained eminence as a writer on philosophy, and indeed may be said to have founded a school of thought based upon two theories, the doctrine of vibrations, and the association of ideas. These he developed in an elaborate treatise, *Observations on Man, his Frame, his Duty, and his Expectations* (1749). His philosophy had a great influence on Coleridge.

Hartley, Leslie Poles (30 Dec. 1895—   ), novelist, born at Peterborough, son of a solicitor, was educated at Harrow and Balliol. During the First World War he was a second lieutenant with the Norfolk Regiment. His first novel, *Simonetta Perkins* (1925) was followed by *The Shrimp and the Anemone* (1944), a story about children who reappear as grown-up characters in *The Sixth Heaven* (1946), and *Eustace and Hilda* (1947), which was awarded the Tait Black Memorial Prize. Later novels are *The Boat* (1950), *My Fellow Devils* (1951), *The Go-Between* (1953), which won the Heinemann Foundation Award, and *A Perfect Woman* (1955); he also published some volumes of short stories. In 1956 he was awarded the C.B.E.

Harvey, Gabriel (1545?—1630), poet and critic, was born at Saffron Walden in Essex, son of a prosperous rope-maker. Educated at Christ's College, Cambridge, he became a Fellow of Pembroke, where he formed a lifelong friendship with the poet Spenser. Pedantic and strongly attached to classical models, he tried to convert Spenser to the principle that English poetry should dispense with rhyme and be written in Latin metres; he himself claimed to be the originator of the English hexameter. His conceited and quarrelsome nature led him to attack Robert Greene in *Four Letters and Certain Sonnets* (1592), and to carry on an acrimonious and unedifying controversy with Nashe, to which he contributed *Pierce's Supererogation* (1593) and *The Trimming of Thomas Nashe* (1597), the latter having the best of the exchanges with his *Have With You to Saffron Walden* (1596). Harvey also took part in the Martin Marprelate controversy. His *Letter Book* was published in 1884.

Haskins, Minnie Louise (12 May 1875—3 Feb. 1957), lecturer and poetess, was educated at Clarendon College, Clifton, and the London School of Economics, where later she became a lecturer on social science, retiring in 1944. She is remembered especially for her poem *The Gate of the Year*, which was quoted by King George VI in one of his Christmas broadcasts. Other volumes of her verse are *The Desert* (1908) and *Smoking Flax* (1942).

Hawes, Stephen (1475?—1523), poet, of whom very little is known with certainty, is believed to have been born in Suffolk, and may have studied at Oxford or Cambridge. He first comes clearly into view as a Groom of the Chamber in 1502, in which year he dedicated to Henry VII his *Pastyme of Pleasure*, first printed in 1509 by Wynkyn de Worde. In the same year appeared the *Convercyon of Swerers* (1509), and *A Joyful Meditacyon of all England* (1509), on the coronation of Henry VIII. He also wrote the *Exemple of Vertu*, an allegory of the life of man. Hawes was a scholar, and was familiar with French and Italian poetry. He represents the transition period between Chaucer and Spenser.

Hawker, Robert Stephen (3 Dec. 1803—15 Aug. 1875), poet and antiquary, was born at Stoke Damerel, Devon, and educated at Cheltenham and Oxford, where he won the Newdigate Prize for Poetry. Taking orders, he became vicar of Morwenstow, a smuggling and wrecking community on the Cornish coast, where he exercised a reforming and beneficent, though extremely unconventional, influence until his death, shortly before which he was received into the Roman Catholic Church. He wrote some poems of great originality and charm, *Records of the Western Shore* (1832—6), *The Quest of the Sangraal* (1863), and *Cornish Ballads* (1869). Of his short pieces, the best known is 'And Shall Trelawny Die?' which, based as it is on an old rhyme, deceived both Scott and Macaulay into thinking it an ancient fragment. He also published a collection of papers, *Footprints of Former Men in Cornwall* (1870).

Hawkins, Sir Anthony Hope (9 Feb. 1863—8 July 1933), novelist who wrote under the name Anthony Hope, was born in London, son of a headmaster, and was a cousin of Kenneth Grahame (q.v.). At Marlborough he distinguished himself as a runner, and at Oxford he was President of the Union. Taking up law, he was called to the Bar by Middle Temple in 1887. In 1894 he achieved success with two books of very different types—*The Dolly Dialogues*, whose sprightly wit and humour is now old-fashioned, and *The Prisoner of Zenda*, first of the Ruritanian cloak-and-dagger romances of which he became a master; *Rupert of Hentzau*, a sequel to it, appeared in 1898. Others of his novels are *Tristram of Blent* (1901), *The Intrusions of Peggy* (1902), *Sophy of Kravonia* (1906), *The Great Miss Driver* (1908), and *Lucinda* (1920). He frequently visited the United States, and in 1903 married an American girl, Elizabeth S. Sheldon. Knighted in 1918, he lived at Tadworth, Surrey, where he played the part of squire. *Memories and Notes* (1927) is a volume of reminiscences.

Hawthorne, Nathaniel (4 July 1804—19 May 1864), novelist, was born at Salem, Massachusetts, son of a sea captain, who died in 1808, after which his widow led the life of a recluse. A slight lameness shut the boy off from sports, and led to a taste for reading, which fostered literary aspirations. His education was completed at Bowdoin College, where he had Longfellow for a fellow-student. After graduating, he obtained a post in the Custom-House, which, however, he did not find congenial, and soon gave up, turning to literature, his earliest efforts, besides a novel, *Fanshawe* (1828),which had no success, being short tales and sketches, which, after appearing in periodicals, were collected and published as *Twice-told Tales* (two series, 1837, 1842). In 1841 he joined for a few months the socialistic community established by the Transcendental Club at Brook Farm, but soon tired of it, and in the next year he married Sophia Peabody, and set up house in Concord in an old manse, formerly tenanted by Emerson, whence proceeded *Mosses from an Old Manse* (1846). In 1850 he published his finest work, *The Scarlet Letter*, one of the greatest of American novels, and in the following year the equally famous *House of the Seven Gables*. Other works of this period are a volume of stories, *The Snow-Image* (1851), *The Blithedale Romance* (1852), and his children's books, *A Wonder Book* and *Tanglewood Tales*. Such business as he had occupied himself with had been in connection with Custom-House appointments at different places; but in 1853 he received from his friend Franklin Pierce, on his election to the Presidency, the appointment of United States Consul at Liverpool, which he retained for four years, when, in consequence of a threatened failure of health, he went to Italy and began his story of *The Marble Faun*, published in England in 1860 under the title of *Transformation*. The last of his books published during his lifetime was *Our Old Home* (1863), notes on England and the English. He had returned to America in 1860, where, with failing health and powers, he passed his remaining four years. After his death there were published *The Ancestral Footstep*, *Septimius Felton*, *Dr Grimshawe's Secret*, and *The Dolliver Romance*, all more or less fragmentary. Most of Hawthorne's work is pervaded by a strong element of mysticism, and a tendency to dwell in the border-land between the seen and the unseen. His style is characterized by a distinctive grace and charm, rich, varied, suggestive, and imaginative.

Hay, Ian, *see* **Beith, John Hay.**

Hay, John Milton (8 Oct. 1838—1 July 1905), poet and statesman, was born at Salem, Indiana, and educated at Illinois University and Brown University. Having studied law, he was admitted to the Bar, and for four years was the secretary and confidant of Abraham Lincoln. During the Civil War he rose to be a colonel, later serving on U.S. legations in Paris, Vienna, and Madrid. In 1871 he published *Pike County Ballads*, which contains the well-known 'Jim Bludso' and 'Little Breeches,' and a book of travel, *Castilian Days*. In 1896, as ambassador to Britain, he brought about better relations between the two countries, and in 1898 he was appointed Secretary of State. He collaborated with J. G. Nicolay in *Abraham Lincoln: A History* (10 volumes 1890), and an edition of Lincoln's *Complete Works* (1894).

Hayley, William (29 Oct. 1745—12 Nov. 1820), poet and biographer, was born at Chichester, and educated at Eton and Cambridge. He was a friend of Cowper, and it was to his influence with Pitt that the granting of a pension to the poet was due. In addition to several volumes of third-rate poems, which include *The Triumph of Temper* (1781), he wrote lives of *Milton* (1794), and *Cowper* (1803), some books of essays, and an amusing volume of *Memoirs* (1823). On the death of Thomas Warton in 1790 he was offered, but declined, the Laureateship. Of him Southey said: 'Everything about that man is good except his poetry.'

Hayne, Paul Hamilton (1 Jan. 1830—6 July 1886), poet, born in Charleston, South Carolina, son of a naval officer, was educated at Charleston College, studied law, but turned to writing and held several editorial posts. He published *Poems* (1855), *Sonnets and Other Poems* (1857), and *Avolio, a Legend of the Island of Cos* (1860). From 1857 to 1860 he edited *Russell's Magazine*. A supporter of the Confederates, after the Civil War he retired to Georgia and tried to live by his poetry, which had a following not only in America but in England, where Tennyson and Swinburne admired his work. *Legends and Lyrics* appeared in 1872 and his *Collected Poems* in 1882.

Hayward, Abraham (22 Nov. 1801—3 Feb. 1884), essayist, born at Wilton, near Salisbury, was educated at Blundell's School, Tiverton, studied law at the Inner Temple, and was called to the Bar in 1832. He had a great reputation as a *raconteur* and sayer of good things, and was a copious contributor to periodicals, especially the *Quarterly Review*. Many of his articles were reprinted in *Biographical and Critical Essays* (3 series, 1858, 1873, 1874), and *Eminent Statesmen and Writers* (1880); he also wrote lives of George Selwyn and Lord Chesterfield, and books on whist and *The Art of Dining*. His *Select Correspondence* appeared posthumously.

Hayward, Sir John (1564?—27 June 1627), historian, born at Felixstowe and educated at Cambridge, was the author of various historical works, the earliest of which, *The First Part of the Life and Reign of King Henry IV*, was published in 1599, and gave such offence to Queen Elizabeth that the author was imprisoned. He, however, managed to ingratiate himself with James I by supporting his views of kingly prerogative, and was knighted in 1619. He also, at the request of Prince Henry, wrote a *History of the three Norman Kings of England* (1613). *The Life and Reign of Edward VI* was published posthumously in 1630.

Haywood, Eliza (1693—25 Feb. 1756), novelist, daughter of a London tradesman named Fowler, made an unhappy marriage with a man named Haywood, and took to the stage, upon which she appeared in Dublin about 1715. She afterwards settled in London, and produced numerous plays and novels, into which she introduced scandalous episodes regarding living persons whose identity was very thinly veiled, a practice which, along with her political satires, more than once involved her in trouble, and together with certain attacks upon Pope, made in concert with Curll the bookseller, procured for her a place in *The Dunciad*. She is repeatedly referred to by Steele, and has been doubtfully identified with his 'Sappho.' Some of her works, such as *The History of Jemmy and Jenny Jessamy* (1753) had great popularity. Others were *The Fair Captive* (1721), *Idalia* (1723), *Love in Excess* (1724), *Memoirs of a Certain Island adjacent to Utopia* (1725), and *Secret History of Present Intrigues at the Court of Caramania* (1727), the last two being published anonymously. She also conducted *The Female Spectator*, and other papers.

Hazlitt, William (10 April 1778—18 Sept 1830), critic and essayist, born at Maidstone in Kent, was the son of a Unitarian minister, who removed to Boston, U.S.A., in 1783 and four years later returned to settle at Wern in Shropshire. At his father's request William studied for the ministry at a Unitarian College in Hackney. His interests, however, were much more philosophical and political than theological. The turning point in his intellectual development was his meeting with Coleridge in 1798, described in one of his finest essays, 'My First Acquaintance with the Poets.' Soon after this he studied art with the view of becoming a painter, and devoted himself specially to portraiture, but though so good a judge as his friend, J. Northcote, R.A., believed he had the talent requisite for success, he could not satisfy himself, and gave up the idea, though always retaining his love of art. He then definitely turned to literature, and in 1805 published his first book, *Essay on the Principles of Human Action*, which was followed by various other philosophical and political essays. About 1812 he became parliamentary and dramatic reporter to the *Morning Chronicle*; in 1814 a contributor to the *Edinburgh Review*; and in 1817 he published a volume of literary sketches, *The Round Table*. In the last named year appeared his admirable *Characters of Shakespeare's Plays*, which was severely attacked in the *Quarterly Review* and *Blackwood's Magazine*, to which his democratic views made him obnoxious. He defended himself in a cutting *Letter to William Gifford*, the editor of the former. The best of Hazlitt's critical work—his three courses of Lectures, *On the English Poets*, *On the English Comic Writers*, and *On the Dramatic Literature of the Age of Queen Elizabeth*—appeared successively in 1818, 1819, and 1820. His next works were *Table Talk*, in which he attacked Shelley (1821—2), and *The Spirit of the Age* (1825), in which he criticized some of his contemporaries. He then commenced what he intended to be his chief literary undertaking, a life of *Napoleon Buonaparte*, in 4 volumes (1828—30). Though written with great literary ability it embodied unpopular views, and failed of success. His last work was a *Life of Titian*, in which he collaborated with Northcote.

Hazlitt is one of the most honest and acute of English critics, and has been described as the common sensible man raised to a high degree. His chief principle of criticism as avowed by himself was that 'a genuine criticism should reflect the colour, the light and shade, the soul and body of a work.' In his private life he was not happy. His first marriage, entered into in 1807, ended in a divorce in 1822, and he then formed a foolish infatuation for his landlady's daughter; this episode is described in his *Liber Amoris* (1823). A second marriage with a Mrs Bridgewater ended by the lady leaving him shortly after. The fact is that Hazlitt was possessed of a peculiar temper, which led to his quarrelling with most of his friends. But few writers have bequeathed to posterity work of such uniformly high quality.

Head, Sir Francis Bond (1 Jan. 1793—20 July 1875), administrator and travel writer, was born at Higham, Kent, of Portuguese descent. Educated at the Royal Military Academy, Woolwich, he entered the

Royal Engineers and served at Waterloo, retiring in 1825. Afterwards he went to South America as manager of a mining company, which failed, and then turned to literature, and made considerable reputation by a book of travels, *Rapid Journeys across the Pampas and among the Andes* (1827), which was followed by *Bubbles from the Brunners of Nassau* (1834). He was Governor of Upper Canada 1835—7, and in 1836 was made a baronet. Thereafter he contributed to the *Quarterly Review*, republishing his articles as *Stokers and Pokers—Highways and Byways*, and wrote a life of Bruce, the Abyssinian traveller.

Headlam, Walter George (15 Feb. 1866—20 June 1908), scholar, was a descendant of Richard Bentley (q.v.). Educated at Harrow and Cambridge, he remained there all his life, becoming a Fellow of King's and devoting himself entirely to scholarship. Noteworthy among his works are *Fifty Poems of Meleager* (1890), *The Mimes of Herodas* (1891), *A Book of Greek Verse* (1907), containing verse translations both from and into Greek which reveal true poetic feeling, and *Letters and Poems* (1910).

Hearn, Lafcadio (27 June 1850—26 Sept. 1904), writer on Japan, was born on the Ionian island of Santa Maura, son of a British surgeon-major and his Greek wife. He was educated at St Cuthbert's College, a Jesuit school in Yorkshire, where he lost an eye while playing games. After further schooling in France he went to America, worked as message-boy and pedlar in Cincinnati, then turned to journalism and gained a reputation as a writer with an individual style and a taste for the macabre. Among his earlier books are *Stray Leaves from Strange Literatures* (1884), *Some Chinese Ghosts* (1887), and *Two Years in the French West Indies* (1890), but he is best known by his writings on Japan, to which he went in 1890. He married a Japanese girl, Setsu Koizumi, took Japanese nationality, assuming the name of Koizumi Yakumo, and held the Chair of English Literature at Tokio University. Books in which he strove to explain Japan to Western readers are *Glimpses of Unfamiliar Japan* (1892), *Ghostly Japan* (1899), *A Japanese Miscellany* (1901), and *Japan: An Attempt at Interpretation* (1904).

Hearne, Thomas (July 1678—10 June 1735), antiquary, was born at White Waltham in Berkshire, where his father was parish clerk, and went to St Edmund Hall, Oxford. In 1712 he became sublibrarian of the Bodleian Library, but had to resign four years later because of his Jacobite views. An indefatigable student of antiquities, he wrote *Reliquiae Bodleianae* (1703) and *Curious Discourses upon English Antiquities* (1720), and also edited Leland's *Itinerary* (1712), and *Collectanea* (1815), Camden's *Annals* (1717), and Fordun's *Scotichronicon* (1722). His *Lives of Leland, Hearne, and Wood* was published in 1772 and his *Remarks and Collections* in 11 volumes (1885—1921). Hearne is the Wormius of Pope's *Dunciad*.

Heber, Reginald (21 April 1783—3 April 1826), bishop and hymnwriter, born at Malpas, Cheshire, where his father was rector, was educated at Oxford, where he gained the Newdigate prize for his poem, *Palestine*, and was elected in 1805 Fellow of All Souls. After travelling in Germany and Russia, he took orders in 1807, and became rector of the family living of Hodnet. In 1822, after two refusals, he accepted the Bishopric of Calcutta, an office in which he showed great zeal and capacity. He died of apoplexy in his bath at Trichinopoly. In addition to *Palestine* he wrote *Europe*, a poem having reference specially to the Peninsular War, and left various fragments, including an Oriental romance based on the story of Bluebeard. Heber's reputation now rests mainly on his hymns, of which several, e.g., 'From Greenland's Icy Mountains,' and 'Brightest and Best of the Sons of the Morning,' are sung wherever the English language is known. He also wrote a *Life of Jeremy Taylor* (1822).

Helps, Sir Arthur (10 July 1813—7 March 1875), essayist and historian, was born at Streatham, Surrey, and educated at Eton and Cambridge. After leaving the University he was private secretary to various public men, and in 1841, his circumstances rendering him independent of employment, he retired to Bishop's Waltham, and devoted himself for twenty years to study and writing. Appointed, in 1860, Clerk to the Privy Council, he became known to, and a favourite of, Queen Victoria, who entrusted him with the task of editing the *Speeches and Addresses of the Prince Consort* (1862), and her own book, *Leaves from the Journal of our Life in the Highlands* (1868). Of his own publications the first was *Thoughts in the Cloister and the Crowd* (1835), a series of aphorisms, and there followed among others, *Essays written in the Intervals of Business* (1841), *Friends in Council* (4 series, 1847—59), *Realmah* (1869), and *Conversations on War and General Culture* (1871). In history Helps wrote *The Conquerors of the New World* (1848—52), and *The Spanish Conquests in America* (4 volumes 1855—61). He also tried the drama, but without success. His essays are his most successful work, containing as they do the thoughts and opinions of a shrewd experienced, and highly cultivated man, written in what Ruskin called 'beautiful quiet English.' He was knighted in 1872.

Hemans, Felicia Dorothea (25 Sept. 1793—16 May 1835), poetess, was the daughter of George Browne, a Liverpool merchant who removed to North Wales, where she was brought up. A volume of her verse, *Early Blossoms*, was published before she was 15, and drew a letter from Shelley. Her first important work, *The Domestic Affections*, appeared in 1812, in which year she was married to Captain Hemans, an Irish officer. The union, however, was not a happy one, and her husband practically deserted her and her five sons in 1818. Her literary activity was continued during the whole of her short life, and her works include, *The Vespers of Palermo*, a drama, which was not successful, *The Forest Sanctuary* (1826), her best poem, *Records of Woman* (1828), *Songs of the Affections* (1830), *Hymns for Childhood* (1834), and *Thoughts during Sickness* (1834), her last effort. In 1829 she visited Scotland, where she was the guest of Scott, who held her in affectionate regard. She also enjoyed the friendship of Wordsworth. Always somewhat delicate, her health latterly entirely gave way, and she died of a decline. Her shorter pieces, such as 'Casabianca' and 'The Better Land' had great popularity, and she was reckoned the greatest poetess of her time.

Hemingway, Ernest Miller (21 July 1898—2 July 1961), novelist, was born at Oak Park, Illinois, son of a doctor who was also a keen sportsman and helped to give the novelist his passion for fishing and shooting. Educated at public schools and in France, he started work at 16. His father wished him to study medicine, but he became a reporter, then served with the Italians in the First World War, was severely wounded and gained the Croce de Guerra. *A Farewell to Arms* (1929), based on his experiences, is one of the best war books. In 1921 he settled in Paris, where he made the acquaintance of Ezra Pound and Gertrude Stein. In 1926 he published a successful novel, *The Sun Also Rises*, and also *The Torrents of Spring*, a burlesque of Sherwood Anderson (q.v.). Next year he returned to the United States and settled first in Florida and then in Cuba. His *Death in the Afternoon* (1932) and *The Green Hills of Africa* (1935) are essays in the psychology of cruelty and death as shown in bullfighting and big game hunting. In 1936 he went to Spain as a special correspondent in the Civil War and got the material for his famous novel *For Whom the Bell Tolls* (1940), the title of which is taken from Donne, and for his play *The Fifth Column* (1938). Collections of his short stories are *Men Without Women* (1927), *Winner Takes Nothing* (1933), and *The First Forty-Nine* (1938). A later novel was *Across the River and into the Trees* (1950), and in 1954 he was awarded the Nobel Prize for Literature for the narrative art shown in *The Old Man and the Sea* (1952), which had already won the Pulitzer Prize. He was married four times.

Henley, William Ernest (23 Aug. 1849—11 June 1903), poet and critic, son of a Gloucester bookseller, was related through his mother to Joseph Warton (q.v.). At the Crypt Grammar School he was a pupil of T. E. Brown (q.v.). From childhood he was a victim of tuberculosis, which caused the amputation of one foot, after which he spent many months between 1873 and 1875 in an Edinburgh infirmary having the other saved from the same fate. There he wrote *Hospital Verses*, which won him the friendship of R. L. Stevenson, who called to see him. After his recovery he took up journalism, and became successively editor of *London* (1877), the *Magazine of Art* (1882), the *Scots Observer*, which became the *National Observer* (1889), and the *New Review* (1894). His volumes of poetry include *A Book of Verses* (1888), *London Voluntaries* (1893), and *For England's Sake* (1900), among his best-known pieces being 'Invictus,' and 'England, my England.' *Views and Reviews* (1890) is a collection of critical articles, and he also compiled *Lyra Heroica* (1891), a book of verse for boys, and a *Slang Dictionary* (1904). In collaboration with Stevenson he wrote the plays *Deacon Brodie* (1890), *Admiral Guinea* (1892), and *Beau Austin* (1897).

Henry VIII (28 June 1491—28 Jan. 1547), King of England, born at Greenwich, came to the throne in 1509. Educated by various tutors, including John Skelton (q.v.), he was reckoned highly accomplished, and had a talent for lyric verse. His book *Assertio*

Septem Sacramentorum (A Defence of the Seven Sacraments), published in 1521 and opposing Luther's teaching, won for him from
Pope Leo X the title of Defender of the Faith, which has been claimed
by English sovereigns ever since, though he was the first to break
away from this faith.

Henry of Huntingdon (1084?—1155), historian, son of a churchman,
spent his early years at Lincoln, and in 1109 became Archdeacon of
Huntingdon.   At the request of the Bishop of Lincoln he undertook
to compile an English chronicle, and this, the *Historia Anglorum*
(History of the English), which covers the period from 55 B.C. to
A.D. 1154, is probably original from 1127 onwards.   He also wrote
some books of epigrams, and treatises on herbs, spices, and jewels.

Henry the Minstrel (died 1492), poet commonly styled Blind Harry
because he was blind from birth, probably belonged to Lothian, of
which he uses the dialect.   There are records of his receiving three
annual payments of eighteen shillings from James IV.   He collected
the popular traditions about the national hero, William Wallace, in a
poem of some 12,000 lines of heroic couplets.   It shows some knowledge of Latin and of Scottish topography, but its historical accuracy
is often in doubt.   The poem *Wallace* was extremely popular throughout Scotland both in its original form and in the English version
made by Hamilton of Gilbertfield (q.v.).

Henry, Matthew (18 Oct. 1662—22 June 1714), Bible commentator,
was born at Broad Oak in Flintshire, son of a minister.   He was
originally destined for the law, and studied at Gray's Inn, but
turned his mind to theology, and in 1687 became minister of a Nonconformist church at Chester.   He wrote many religious works, but
is chiefly remembered by his *Exposition of the Old and New Testa-
ments*, which he did not live to complete beyond the Acts.

Henry, O., *see* **Porter, William Sydney.**

Henry, Robert (18 Feb. 1718—24 Nov. 1790), historian, born at
St Ninians, near Stirling, son of a farmer, and educated at Stirling
Grammar School and Edinburgh University, entered the Church
of Scotland, becoming one of the ministers of Edinburgh.   He
wrote the *History of Great Britain on a New Plan* (1771—93), in six
volumes, covering the period from the Roman invasion to the reign of
Henry VIII.   The novelty consisted in dividing the subjects into
different heads, civil history, military, social, and so on, and following
out each of them separately.   The work was mainly a compilation,
having no critical qualities, and is now of little value.   Notwithstanding the persistent and ferocious attacks of Dr Gilbert Stewart
(q.v.), it had a great success, and brought the author over £3,000, and
a government pension of £100.

Henryson, Robert (1430?—1506?), poet, graduated Master of Arts,
but it is not known at what university; he was a schoolmaster
attached to Dunfermline Abbey, and also practised as a notary.   Of
all the so-called Scottish Chaucerians he most resembles their
master.   Versed in the learning and general culture of his day, he
had a fine sense of form and a wit and macabre humour typically

Scottish. Of his most important poems, *The Moral Fables of Esope the Phrygian* (1571) containing that gem 'The Uplandis Mous and the Burges Mous' (Country and Town Mouse) shows him a born master of the beast-fable; *The Testament of Cresseid* (1593) a sequel to Chaucer's *Troilus and Cressida*, was for long attributed to the English poet; and *Robene and Makyne* was the first pastoral to be written in this country. Others of his pieces are *Orpheus and Eurydice* and *The Garment of Gude Ladies*.

Henty, George Alfred (8 Dec. 1832—16 Nov. 1902), novelist, was born at Trumpington, near Cambridge. A delicate child, he was bullied at Westminster School until he took boxing lessons, which left him with a lifelong enthusiasm for that exercise. Sailing was his other hobby, and he died on a bunk in his schooner at Weymouth. While he was at Caius College, Cambridge, the Crimean War broke out, and he joined the Hospital Commissariat, acting at the same time as special correspondent for the *Morning Advertiser*; later he represented the *Standard* in the Franco-Prussian War. He is remembered best for his 80-odd historical novels for boys, which were deservedly popular. A few of the better-known titles are *With Clive in India* (1884), *By Pike and Dyke* (1890), *Redskin and Cowboy* (1892), *Through the Russian Snows* (1896), *With Moore at Corunna* (1898), and *With Buller in Natal* (1901). He also wrote a number of ordinary novels.

Heraud, John Abraham (5 July 1799—20 April 1887), poet, born in Holborn, son of a stationer of Huguenot descent, was originally intended for a business career but turned to literature and, having a knowledge of German, tried to popularize Schelling's philosophy. Fascinated by the remote and terrible, he wrote two macabre poems, *The Descent into Hell* (1830) and *The Judgment of the Flood* (1834). He also published some plays and books of travel. A friend of Wordsworth, Coleridge, Southey, and the Carlyles, he was in later years dramatic critic of the *Athenaeum*.

Herbert, Sir Alan Patrick (24 Sept. 1890—   ), poet and humorist, was born in London, son of a civil servant, and educated at Winchester and Oxford, where he studied law. During the First World War he served with the Naval Division in Gallipoli and France. In 1918 he was called to the Bar, but never practised. He lived beside the river at Hammersmith and was an enthusiastic yachtsman. In 1910 he started contributing to *Punch*, and in 1924 joined its staff. In 1935 he was elected as M.P. for Oxford University, and was instrumental in securing a modification of the divorce laws, of which he had written in *Holy Deadlock* (1934). His volumes of witty and humorous essays include *Light Articles Only* (1921), *Misleading Cases in Common Law* (three series, 1929, 1930, 1933), *Mild and Bitter* (1936), and *General Cargo* (1939). Collections of light verse are *Laughing Anne* (1926), *She-Shanties* (1927), *Plain Jane* (1927), *Swan Song* (1940), and *Less Nonsense* (1944). *The Water Gipsies* (1930) is a novel, *Pools Pilot* (1953) is an unorthodox guide to football pools, and *Independent Member* (1950) is an autobiography. He was knighted in 1945.

Herbert of Cherbury, Edward, 1st Baron (3 March 1583—20 Aug. 1648), philosopher and historian, was born at Eyton, Shropshire; his father was sheriff of Montgomeryshire, and George Herbert the poet (q.v.) was his brother. At the age of 16, while at Oxford, Edward married a kinswoman four years his senior. Thereafter he returned to the university and devoted himself to study, and to the practice of manly sports and accomplishments. At the coronation in 1603 James I made him a Knight of the Bath, and in 1608 he went to the Continent, where for some years he was engaged in military and diplomatic affairs, not without his share of troubles. In 1624 he was created an Irish, and a few years later, an English, peer, as Baron Herbert, of Cherbury. On the outbreak of the Civil War he sided, though somewhat half-heartedly, with the Royalists, but he surrendered to the Parliament in 1644, received a pension, held various offices, and died in 1648. It was in 1624 that he wrote his treatise, *De Veritate* (Concerning Truth), 'an empirical theory of knowledge.' It is the first purely metaphysical work written by an Englishman, and gave rise to much controversy. It was reprinted in 1645, when the author added two treatises, *De Causis Errorum* (Conerning the Causes of Errors), and *De Religione Laici* (Concerning the Religion of a Layman). His other chief philosophical work was *De Religione Gentilium* (1663), of which an English translation appeared in 1705, under the title of *The Ancient Religion of the Gentiles and Cause of their Errors considered*. It has been called 'the charter of the Deists.' Among his historical works are *Expeditio Buckinghamii Ducis* (1656), a vindication of the Rochelle expedition, a *Life of Henry VIII* (1649), extremely partial to the King, and his *Autobiography*, which gives a brilliant picture of his contemporaries, and of the manners and events of his time, together with a somewhat vainglorious account of himself and his doings. He was also the author of some poems of a metaphysical cast. On the whole he is one of the most shining and spirited figures of the time.

Herbert, George (3 April 1593—1 March 1633), clergyman and poet, brother of Lord Herbert of Cherbury (q.v.), was educated at Westminster School and Trinity College, Cambridge, where he took his degree in 1616, and was public orator 1619—27. He became the friend of Sir H. Wotton, Donne, and Bacon, the last of whom is said to have held him in such high esteem as to submit his writings to him before publication. He acquired the favour of James I, who conferred upon him a sinecure worth £120 a year, and having powerful friends, he attached himself for some time to the Court in the hope of preferment. The death of two of his patrons, however, led him to change his views, and coming under the influence of Nicholas Ferrar, the Quietist of Little Gidding, and of Laud, he took orders in 1626 and, after serving for a few years as prebendary of Layton Ecclesia, or Leighton Broomswold, he became in 1630 rector of Bemerton, Wiltshire, where he performed his duties with saintly devotion, and wrote his religious poems. His health, however, failed, and he died in his fortieth year. His chief works are *The Temple, or Sacred Poems and Private Ejaculations* (1634), and two prose volumes, *The Country Parson* (1652) and *Jacula Prudentium*, a collection of pithy proverbial sayings. Not published until the year after his death, *The Temple* had immediate acceptance, 20,000 copies, according to Izaak Walton, who was Herbert's biographer, having been sold in a few years. Among its admirers were Charles I, Cowper, and Coleridge. Herbert wrote some of the most exquisite sacred poetry in the language, although his style, influenced by Donne, is at times characterized by artificiality and conceits. He was an excellent classical scholar, and an accomplished musician.

Herbert, Mary, *see* **Pembroke, Countess of.**

Herbert, Sir Thomas (1606—1 March 1682), travel writer and historian, belonged to an old Yorkshire family, studied at Oxford and Cambridge, and went in connection with an embassy to Persia, afterwards writing *A Description of the Persian Monarchy* (1634). On the outbreak of the Civil War he was a Parliamentarian, but was afterwards taken into the household of the King, to whom he became much attached, was latterly his only attendant, and was with him on the scaffold. At the Restoration he was made a baronet, and in 1678 published *Threnodia Carolina*, an account of the last two years of the King's life.

Herd, David (baptized 23 Oct. 1732, died 25 June 1810), anthologist, born at Marykirk in Kincardineshire, son of a farmer, was clerk to an accountant in Edinburgh, and devoted his leisure to collecting old Scottish poems and songs, which he first published in 1769 as *Ancient Scottish Songs, Heroic Ballads, etc.* Other and enlarged editions appeared in 1776 and 1791. Sir W. Scott made use of his manuscripts in his *Minstrelsy of the Scottish Border*.

Herford, Oliver (Dec. 1863—5 July 1935), humorous writer, was born in Sheffield, son of a Unitarian clergyman who moved to the United States and was minister of churches in Boston and Chicago. Educated at Antioch College, Ohio, the Slade School of Art, and Julien's in Paris, young Herford settled in New York and worked for magazines as versifier and artist. Among some 50 books of fanciful nonsense he published *Pen and Inklings* (1893), *Artful Anticks* (1894), *Rubaiyat of a Persian Kitten* (1904), *A Little Book of Bores* (1906), *Cupid's Encyclopaedia* (1910), *The Jingle-Jungle Book* (1913), *This Giddy Globe* (1919), and *The Deb's Dictionary* (1931).

Hergesheimer, Joseph (15 Feb. 1880—25 April 1954), novelist, born in Philadelphia, of German and Scottish descent, attended the Pennsylvania Academy of Fine Arts, but turned from painting to writing. His earliest published novel was *The Lay Anthony* (1914), but his first of real importance was *The Three Black Pennys* (1917), which was followed by *Tubal Cain* (1918); both of these are studies in the triumph of personality. *Java Head* (1919) and *The Bright Shawl* (1922) have oriental settings; *Linda Condon* (1919) and *Cytherea* (1922) have been described as problem stories; and *Balisand* (1924), *The Limestone Tree* (1931), and *The Foolscap Rose* (1934) are historical novels. He also wrote many short stories, of which the best-known, 'Tol'able David,' appears in the collection entitled *The Happy End* (1919). *From an Old House* (1925) is autobiographical.

Herrick, Robert (baptized 24 Aug. 1591, buried 15 Oct. 1674), clergyman and poet, was born in London, son of a goldsmith, and for ten years was an apprentice at the same trade with his uncle, Sir William Herrick. Thereafter he went to Cambridge, took orders, and was in 1629 presented by Charles I to the living of Dean Prior, a remote parish in Devonshire, from which he was ejected in 1647, returning in 1662. In the interval he appears to have lived in Westminster, probably supported, more or less, by the gifts of wealthy Royalists. His *Noble Numbers or Pious Pieces* was published in 1647, his *Hesperides or Works both Human and Divine* in 1648, and the two together in one volume in the latter year. Over 60, however, of the lighter poems included in *Hesperides* had previously appeared anonymously in a collection entitled *Wit's Recreations*. Herrick's early life in London had been a free one, and his secular poems, in which he appears much more at ease than in his sacred, show him to have been a thorough Epicurean, though he claims that his life was not to be judged by his muse. As a lyric poet Herrick stands in the front rank for sweetness, grace, and true poetic fire, and some of his love songs, such as 'To Anthea,' and 'Gather Ye Rose-buds,' are unsurpassed in their kind; while in such exquisite little poems as 'To Blossoms,' 'To Daffodils,' and others he finds a classic expression for his love of nature and country life. He has been described as 'the most frankly pagan of English poets.'

Herrick, Robert (26 April 1868—24 Dec. 1938), novelist, son of a lawyer, was born at Cambridge, Massachusetts, and educated at Harvard. After extensive travels in the American continent, in 1893 he joined the staff of Chicago University, where he became Professor of English. Later he was secretary to the Governor of the Virgin Islands, and died there of overwork. The first of his novels, *The Man Who Wins* (1890), was followed by many others, among which may be mentioned *The Gospel of Freedom* (1898), *The Web of Life* (1900), *The Common Lot* (1904), *The Master of the Inn* (1908), *Together* (1908), *One Woman's Life* (1913), *Clark's Field* (1914), *Waste* (1924), *Chimes* (1926), and *Sometime* (1933). Writing of the sordid side of modern civilization, Herrick was one of the earliest of the American realist school.

Herschel, Sir John Frederick William (7 March 1792—11 May 1871), son of Sir William Herschel, the eminent astronomer and discoverer of the planet Uranus, was born at Slough, and educated at Cambridge, where he was Senior Wrangler and first Smith's prizeman. He became one of the greatest of English astronomers. Among his writings are treatises on Sound and Light, and his *Astronomy* (1831) was for long the leading manual on the subject. He also published *Familiar Lectures on Scientific Subjects* (1867), and made translations from Schiller, and from Homer. He was made a baronet in 1838.

Hervey, James (26 Feb. 1714—25 Dec. 1758), religious writer, born at Hardingstone, near Northampton, and educated at Oxford, became rector of Weston Favell, Northamptonshire. He was the author of *Meditations and Contemplations* (1745—7), containing his famous 'Meditations Among the Tombs,' *Theron and Aspasio* (1755), and other works, which had a great vogue in their day. They are characterized by over-wrought sentiment, and overloaded with florid ornament. Hervey was a devout and unselfish man, who by his labours broke down a delicate constitution.

Hervey of Ickworth, John Hervey, Baron (15 Oct. 1696—5 Aug. 1743), writer of memoirs, was a son of the 1st Earl of Bristol. Educated at Westminster and Cambridge, he entered Parliament in 1725 as member for Bury St Edmunds, and held various offices, including that of Lord Privy Seal. He was a favourite with Queen Caroline, and a dexterous and supple courtier. He wrote *Memoirs of the Reign of George II*, which gives a very unfavourable view of the manners and morals of the Court. It is written in a lively, though often spiteful style, and contains many clever and discriminating character sketches. A close friend of Lady Wortley Montagu (q.v.), he was satirized by Pope under the names of 'Sporus,' and 'Lord Fanny.'

Hewlett, Maurice Henry (22 Jan. 1861—15 June 1923), novelist and poet, was born at Weybridge, Surrey, son of a civil servant of Huguenot extraction. Educated at the International College, Isleworth, he studied law and was called to the Bar in 1891 but never practised. In 1897 he succeeded to the post held by his father in the Record Office. His first book, *The Forest Lovers*, appeared in 1898. *Richard Yea-and-Nay* (1900), and *The Queen's Quair* (1904) are historical novels; stories of modern times are the trilogy *Halfway House* (1908), *Open Country* (1909), and *Rest Harrow* (1910), together with *Bendish* (1913) and *Mainwaring* (1920). Of his dozen books of verse perhaps the best is *The Song of the Plow* (1916). *Wiltshire Essays* appeared in 1921. A lover of the country, he settled latterly at Broadchalke, near Salisbury.

Heylin, Peter (1600—8 May 1662), historian, born at Burford, Oxfordshire, and educated at Oxford, took orders in 1624, and was one of the clerical followers of Charles I who suffered for their fidelity, being deprived under the Commonwealth of his living of Alresford, and other preferments. After the Restoration he was made sub-Dean of Westminster, but the failure of his health prevented further advancement. He was a voluminous writer, and a keen and acrimonious controversialist against the Puritans. Among his works are a *History of the Reformation* (1661), and a life of Archbishop Laud (1668).

Heyward, Du Bose (31 Aug. 1885—16 June 1940), novelist, was born at Charleston, South Carolina, of an aristocratic but impoverished Southern family. At the age of 9 he was selling newspapers, at 14 a clerk, and at 19 suffered from polio for three years, after which he worked as an insurance salesman. His first publications were books of verse, *Carolina Chansons* (1922) and *Skylines and Horizons* (1924), and he was one of the founders of the Poetry Society of South Carolina. His first novel, *Porgy* (1925), scored a striking success; a dramatic version which he wrote in collaboration with his wife won the Pulitzer Prize in 1927, and was made into an opera by George Gershwin, with the title *Porgy and Bess* (1935). Other novels are *Angel* (1926), *Mamba's Daughters* (1929), *The Half Pint Flask* (1929), *Peter Ashley* (1932), *Lost Morning* (1936), and *Star Spangled Virgin* (1939). All these have the primitive Negroes for their subject. Heyward held honorary degrees from the universities of North and South Carolina and Charleston and was an honorary member of Phi Beta Kappa.

Heywood, John (1497?—1580?), dramatist and epigrammatist, is believed to have been born at North Mimms, Hertfordshire. He married Elizabeth Rastell, niece of Sir Thomas More, and through him gained the favour of Henry VIII, and was at the court of Edward VI and Mary, for whom, as a young Princess, he had a great regard. Being a Roman Catholic, he enjoyed her favour, but on the accession of Elizabeth, he left the country, and went to Malines, where he died. He was famous as a writer of interludes, a species of composition intermediate between the old moralities and the regular drama, and displayed considerable constructive skill, and a racy, if somewhat broad and even coarse, humour. Among his interludes are *The Four P's*, first printed in 1569, *The Play of the Wether* (1532), *The Play of Love* (1533), and *The Pardoner and the Frere*. An allegorical poem is *The Spider and the Flie* (1556), in which the Spider stands for the Protestants, and the Flie for the Roman Catholics. Heywood was likewise the author of some 600 epigrams, and made one of the earliest collections of proverbs.

Heywood, Thomas (1574?—1650), playwright and pamphleteer, born in Lincolnshire, is thought to have been educated at Cambridge before he became an actor-dramatist in London, where in 1598 we find him a member of the Lord Admiral's Company, and later one of the Queen's Players. A prolific and versatile writer, he claimed to have written or collaborated in over 200 plays; a master of spectacle, he succeeded Dekker (q.v.) as writer of the London municipal pageants. Among his earlier plays are *The Four Prentices of London*, *A Woman Killed with Kindness* (1603), *If You Know Not Me, You Know Nobody* (1605), and *The Rape of Lucrece* (1608). Between 1611 and 1613 he wrote a series of dramas named after the four ages, in which he dramatized classical myths. Later plays are *The Fair Maid of the West* (1631) and *The English Traveller* (1633). Weak in plot-making, but with the charm of simplicity and sincerity, Heywood excelled in domestic drama, and was described by Lamb as 'a kind of prose Shakespeare.' Among his many other works are translations of various writers including Sallust (1608); *An Apology for Actors* (1612); poems, including *The Hierarchy of the Blessed Angels* (1635); the miscellany *Dialogues and Dramas* (1637); and numerous pamphlets.

Hichens, Robert Smythe (14 Nov. 1864—20 July 1950), novelist, born at Speldhurst in Kent, was educated at Clifton and the Royal College of Music, London; he also studied music in Bristol and had a year at a London school of journalism. After a winter in Egypt he wrote *The Green Carnation* (1894), which was very popular and was followed ten years later by the even more successful *Garden of Allah*,

M

which sold about 800,000 copies and was dramatized. Among his many other books are *The Call of the Blood* (1906), *Bella Donna* (1909), *The Way of Ambition* (1913), *The Spirit of the Time* (1921), *The Paradine Case* (1933), and *That Which is Hidden* (1939).

Higden, Ranulf *or* **Ralph** (died 12 March 1364), chronicler, became a Benedictine monk at St Werburg's, Chester, in 1299, and travelled in many parts of England. He wrote the *Polychronicon*, a universal history coming down to 1342; the most complete work of the kind that had yet appeared, it was popular for nearly two centuries. Written in Latin, it was translated into English by John of Trevisa in 1387 and printed by Caxton in 1482. Higden also wrote on theology.

Hill, Aaron (10 Feb. 1685—8 Feb. 1750), poet and dramatist, son of a country gentleman of Wiltshire, was educated at Westminster School, and thereafter made a tour in the East. He was the author of 17 dramatic pieces, some original, such as *Athelwold* (1731), others, such as his versions of Voltaire's *Zaire* and *Merope*, being adaptations. He also wrote a quantity of poetry, which, notwithstanding some good passages, is as a general rule dull and pompous. Having written some satiric lines on Pope in his *Progress of Wit* (1730), he received in return a niche in the *Dunciad*, which led to a controversy, in which Hill showed some spirit. Afterwards a reconciliation took place. He was a friend and correspondent of Richardson, whose *Pamela* he highly praised. In addition to his literary pursuits Hill was a great projector of impracticable business projects.

Hilton, James (9 Sept. 1900—20 Dec. 1954), novelist, was born at Leigh in Lancashire, but taken as a child to London, where his father was a schoolmaster, and educated at Leys School and Christ's College, Cambridge. At 17 he had an article published in the *Manchester Guardian*, and his novel *Catherine Herself* appeared while he was still an undergraduate. His famous story *Goodbye, Mr Chips* (1934) was written in four days and ran first as a serial in the *British Weekly*; as a book it was a best seller, it was dramatized and filmed, and was later followed by *To You, Mr Chips* (1938). *Lost Horizon* (1933) won the Hawthornden Prize and added the word 'Shangri-la' to the English language. Others of his books are *Knight Without Armour* (1933), *We Are Not Alone* (1937), *Random Harvest* (1941), *Nothing So Strange* (1947), and *Time and Time Again* (1953). Latterly he lived in Hollywood, where he died of cancer.

Hinkson, Katharine, *see* **Tynan.**

Hinton, James (1822—16 Dec. 1875), surgeon and philosopher, born at Reading, son of a Baptist minister, became a successful aurist, but his attention being arrested by social questions, he gave more and more of his time to the consideration and exposition of these. Openminded and altruistic, he sought to reconcile science and religion by his system of 'actualism.' Among his writings may be mentioned *Man and his Dwelling-place* (1859), *The Mystery of Pain* (1866), *The Law of Human Life* (1874), *Chapters on the Art of Thinking* (1879), and *Philosophy and Religion* (1881).

Hoadly, Benjamin (14 Nov. 1676—17 April 1761), bishop and controversialist, born at Westerham in Kent, was the son of a schoolmaster. Educated at Cambridge, he took orders in 1701 and rose to be Bishop successively of Bangor, Hereford, Salisbury, and Winchester. He was a great supporter of the Revolution, and controvertor of the doctrines of divine right and passive obedience. His works were generally either the causes of controversy or elicited by it. One of his sermons, *On the Nature of the Kingdom or Church of Christ* (1717) was the originating cause of what was known as the Bangorian controversy, which raged for a long time with great bitterness.

Hobbes, John Oliver, *see* **Craigie, Pearl Mary Teresa.**

Hobbes, Thomas (5 April 1588—4 Dec. 1679), philosopher, was born at Malmesbury, Wiltshire, where his father was vicar, and educated at Oxford. Thereafter he travelled as tutor through France, Italy, and Germany, with William Lord Cavendish, afterwards 2nd Earl of Devonshire, and remained as his secretary after the completion of the tour. While engaged in this capacity he became acquainted with Bacon (whose amanuensis he is said to have been), Herbert of Cherbury, and Ben Jonson. In 1629 he published the first of his works, a translation of *Thucydides*. After the death of his patron, he assumed the position of tutor to his son, afterwards the 3rd Earl, with whom he went in 1634 for a second Grand Tour When in Italy he met Galileo, Gassendi, and other eminent men. Returning to England he remained in the Earl's service, and devoted himself to his studies in philosophy and politics. The commotions of the times, however, disturbed him; and his Royalist principles, expounded in his treatise, *De Corpore Politico* (Concerning the Body Politic), led to his again, in 1641, leaving England and going to Paris, where he remained until 1652. While there, he entered into controversy on mathematical subjects with Descartes, published some of his principal works, including *Leviathan*, and received, in 1647, the appointment of mathematical tutor to the Prince of Wales, afterwards Charles II, who was then in that city. The materialist views expressed in his works, however, brought him into such unpopularity that the Prince found it expedient to break the connection, and Hobbes returned to England. In 1653 he resumed his relations with the Devonshire family, living, however, in London in habits of intimacy with Selden, Cowley, and Dr Harvey. On the Restoration the King conferred upon him a pension of £100, but like most of the Royal benefactions of the day, it was but irregularly paid. His later years were spent in the family of his patron, chiefly at Chatsworth, where he continued his literary activity until his death, which occurred in his ninety-first year.

Hobbes was one of the most prominent Englishmen of his day, and has continued to influence philosophical thought more or less ever since, generally, however, by evoking opposition. His fundamental proposition is that all human action is ultimately based upon self-interest (more or less enlightened), and he allows no place to the moral or social sentiments. Similarly in his political writings man is viewed as a purely selfish being who must be held in restraint by the strong hand of authority. His chief philosophical works are *De Corpore Politico*, already mentioned, published in 1640; *Philosophical Rudiments concerning Government and Society*, originally in Latin, translated into English in 1650; *Leviathan, or the Matter, Form, and Power of a Commonwealth, Ecclesiastical and Civil* (1651); and *Letters upon Liberty and Necessity* (1654). Generally speaking, all his works led him into controversy, one of his principal opponents being Clarendon. The *Letters upon Liberty and Necessity*, which is one of the ablest of them, and indeed one of the ablest ever written on the subject, brought him into collision with Bramhall, Bishop of Londonderry, whom he completely overthrew. He was not, however, so successful in his mathematical controversies, one of the chief of which was on the quadrature of the circle. Here his antagonist was the famous mathematician Wallis, who was able easily to demonstrate his errors. In 1672, when 84, Hobbes wrote his autobiography in Latin verse, and in the same year translated four books of the *Odyssey*, which were so well received that he completed the remaining books, and also translated the whole of the *Iliad*. Though accurate as literal renderings of the sense, these works fail largely to convey the beauties of the original, notwithstanding which three editions were issued within ten years, and they long retained their popularity. His last work was *Behemoth*, a history of the Civil War, completed just before his death. As a stylist he ranks high, writing a clear and effective English prose and having, as Saintsbury puts it, a strange and as it were cross-grained magnificence about him.

Hobhouse, John Cam, *see* **Broughton.**

Hoby, Sir Thomas (1530—13 July 1566), translator, born at Leominster, and educated at Cambridge, translated Bucer's *Gratulation to the Church of England*, and Castiglione's *The Courtier*, the latter of which had great popularity. He died in Paris while ambassador to France.

Hoccleve, Thomas, *see* **Occleve.**

Hocking, Joseph (7 Nov. 1860—4 March 1937), minister and novelist, younger brother of Silas K. Hocking (q.v.), was born at St Stephen's, Cornwall, and educated at Manchester University. After working for a short time as a land surveyor, in 1884 he was ordained as a Methodist minister. In 1887 he travelled in the Near East, and on his return became pastor of Woodford Green, Essex, where he remained till 1910. He wrote some 50 novels, mainly of middle-class life, with a few historical romances. They include *Ishmael Pengelly* (1894), *All Men Are Liars* (1895), *O'er Moor and Fen* (1901), *The Woman of Babylon* (1906), *The Trampled Cross* (1907), *God and Mammon* (1912), and *Prodigal Daughters* (1922).

Hocking, Silas Kitto (24 March 1850—15 Sept. 1935), novelist, son of a mine-owner, was born at St Stephen's, Cornwall, and educated at the grammar-school there. He was ordained a Methodist minister in 1870, and held pastorates at Liverpool and Manchester before going in 1883 to Southport, where he was a popular preacher.

In 1895 he retired to devote himself to writing. His first story, *Alec Green* (1878), was followed by *Her Benny* (1879), a tale of the Liverpool, streets, which sold over a million copies. Most of Hocking's 50-odd novels have a religious tendency, among the better-known being *Caleb Carthew* (1884), *In Spite of Fate* (1897), *Gripped* (1902), and *Who Shall Judge* (1910). At one time he was said to be the most popular English novelist. *My Book of Memory* (1923) is autobiographical.

Hodgson, Ralph (9 Sept. 1871—   ), poet, born in Yorkshire, was for some years editor of *Fry's Magazine*. In 1907 he published a slim volume of poems, *The Last Blackbird*. In 1913, with Lovat Fraser, the artist, and Holbrook Jackson (q.v.), he founded The Sign of the Flying Fame for publishing broadsides and chapbooks, including some of his own poems, and in the following year he was the last recipient of the Polignac Prize, awarded by the Royal Society of Literature for 'The Bull' and 'The Song of Honour.' Both of these pieces were included in a later collection, *Poems* (1917), which also contains the favourites 'Eve,' and 'Time, You Old Gipsy Man.' *Silver Wedding* (1941) and *The Muse and the Mastiff* (1942) were privately printed. Hodgson's poems are clear and simple with an indefinable magic all their own. In 1924 he was appointed Lecturer on English Literature at Sendai University, Japan, and in 1954 he was awarded the Queen's Gold Medal for Poetry. Very fond of animals, he was an authority on bull-terriers, which he bred. In later years he lived at Minerva, Ohio.

Hoffman, Charles Fenno (7 Feb. 1806—7 June 1884), poet and novelist, was born in New York, son of a lawyer. At the age of 11 he lost his right leg in an accident. Educated at Columbia College, he studied law and in 1827 was admitted to the Bar. His best-known work is *Greyslaer* (1840), a murder story based on fact. He held various editorial posts and published some volumes of verse, including *The Vigil of Faith* (1842) and *Love's Calendar* (1847). From 1850 onwards he was insane.

Hogben, Lancelot Thomas (9 Dec. 1895—   ), writer on science, was born at Portsmouth, where his father was a naval chaplain, but was taken to London at the age of 11 and educated at Tottenham County School and Cambridge. He was successively on the staff of London, Edinburgh, and McGill Universities, then held the chair of zoology at Cape Town. In 1936 he was appointed Professor of Natural History at Aberdeen, and in the same year was elected a Fellow of the Royal Society. His best-known books are those popularizing scientific knowledge, *Mathematics for the Million* (1936), *Science for the Citizen* (1938), and *From Cave Painting to Comic Strip* (1949), but he also wrote more abstruse books on physiology and biology. He was in Norway at the time of the Nazi invasion, and wrote of his escape in *Author in Transit* (1940).

Hogg, James (baptized 9 Dec. 1770, died 21 Nov. 1835), poet, son of an Ettrick farmer and constantly styled 'The Ettrick Shepherd,' began life by herding cows until he was old enough to be trusted with a flock of sheep. His imagination was fed by his mother, who was possessed of an inexhaustible stock of ballads and folklore. He had little schooling, and had great difficulty in writing out his earlier poems, but was earnest in giving himself such culture as he could. Entering the service of a friend of Scott, he was introduced to the poet, and assisted him in collecting material for his *Border Minstrelsy*. In 1796 he had begun to write his songs, and when on a visit to Edinburgh in 1801 published them under the title of *Scottish Pastorals, Poems, and Songs*, following this volume in 1807 with *The Mountain Bard*. A treatise on the diseases of sheep brought him £300, on the strength of which he embarked upon a sheep-farming enterprise in Dumfriesshire which, like a previous smaller venture in Harris, proved a failure, and he returned to Ettrick bankrupt. Thenceforward he relied almost entirely on literature for support. With this aim he settled in Edinburgh in 1810, published *The Forest Minstrel*, and started the *Spy*, a critical journal, which ran for a year. In 1813 *The Queen's Wake* showed his full powers, and finally settled his right to an assured place among the poets of his country. He joined the staff of *Blackwood*, and became the friend of Wilson, Wordsworth, and Byron. Other poems followed, *The Pilgrims of the Sun* (1815), *Madoc of the Moor* (1816), and *Queen Hynde* (1826); and in prose *Winter Evening Tales* (1820), *Confessions of a Justified Sinner* (1824), and *The Domestic Manners and Private Life of Sir Walter Scott* (1834). In his later years his home was a cottage at Altrive on seventy acres of moorland presented to him by the Duchess of Buccleuch. As might be expected from his almost total want of regular education, Hogg was often greatly wanting in taste, but some of his lyrics, like 'The Skylark,' are perfect in their spontaneity and sweetness, and his 'Kilmeny' is one of the most exquisite fairy-tales in the language. He is a leading character, partly idealized, partly caricatured, in Wilson's *Noctes Ambrosianae*.

Hogg, Thomas Jefferson (24 May 1792—27 Aug. 1862), biographer, born at Norton, in Durham, was educated at Durham Grammar School and University College, Oxford, where he made the acquaintance of Shelley, whose lifelong friend and biographer he became. Associated with Shelley in the famous pamphlet on *The Necessity of Atheism*, he shared in the expulsion from the University which it entailed, and thereafter devoted himself to the law, being called to the Bar in 1817. In 1832 he contributed to Bulwer's *New Monthly Magazine* his *Reminiscences of Shelley*, which was much admired. Thereafter he was commissioned to write a biography of the poet, of which the first two volumes, published in 1858, gave such offence that the material with which he had been entrusted was withdrawn, and the work remained unfinished.

Holcroft, Thomas (10 Dec. 1745—23 March 1809), dramatist and novelist, son of a London shoemaker, became in turn a pedlar and a Newmarket stable-boy. A charitable person having given him some education he became a schoolmaster, but in 1770 went on the provincial stage. He then took to writing plays, and was the first to introduce melodrama into England. Among his plays, *The Road to Ruin* (1792) is the best; others are *Duplicity* (1781) and *A Tale* *of Mystery* (1802). Among his novels are *Alwyn* (1780) and *Hugh Trevor* (1794). His *Memoirs* were edited by Hazlitt in 1816.

Holinshed *or* **Hollingshead, Raphael** (died 1580?), chronicler, was born, according to one account, at Sutton Downes, Cheshire, educated at Cambridge, and became a priest. He came to London, and was in the employment of Reginald Wolf, a German printer, making translations and doing hack-work. His *Chronicles of Englande, Scotlande, and Irelande*, from which Shakespeare drew much of his history, was based to a considerable extent on the collections of Leland, and he had the assistance of W. Harrison, R. Stanyhurst, and others. The introductory description of England and the English was the work of Harrison, Stanyhurst did the part relating to Ireland, and Holinshed himself the history of England and Scotland, the latter being mainly translated from the works of Boece and Major (qq.v.). Published in 1577, it had a wide and lasting popularity. It is a work of real value—a magazine of useful and interesting information, with the authorities cited. Its tone is strongly Protestant, its style clear.

Holland, Josiah Gilbert (24 July 1819—12 Oct. 1881), poet and novelist, was born at Belchertown, Massachusetts, son of a mechanic. After a few years of a medical course he gave it up and became a schoolmaster. His earliest works are volumes of verse, *Bitter Sweet* (1858), *Katrina* (1867), and *The Marble Prophecy* (1872). In 1870 he helped to found *Scribner's Monthly*, and edited it until he died suddenly of heart disease just as it was about to be transformed into the *Century Magazine*. In his later years he produced didactic novels, of which the best-known are *Arthur Bonnicastle* (1873), *Sevenoaks* (1875), and *Nicholas Minturn* (1877).

Holland, Philemon (1552—9 Feb. 1637), translator, born at Chelmsford, Essex, son of a protestant clergyman, and educated at Cambridge, was master of the free school at Coventry, where he also practised medicine. His chief translations, made in good Elizabethan English, are of Livy (1600), Pliny's *Natural History* (1601), Plutarch's *Morals* (1603), Suetonius (1606), Xenophon's *Cyropaedia* (1632), and Camden's *Britannia* (1610). There are passages in his Plutarch which have hardly been excelled by any later prose translator of the classics. His later years were passed in poverty.

Holland, Sir Richard (fl. 1450), poet, may have been chaplain to the Earl of Moray. He wrote the alliterative poem *The Book of the Howlat* between 1442 and 1452 for Elizabeth, Moray's daughter, who married the 7th Earl of Douglas; from it the Douglases took their motto 'Tender and true.' He is mentioned by Dunbar (q.v.) in his *Lament for the Makaris.*

Hollingshead, Raphael, *see* **Holinshed.**

Hollis, Maurice Christopher (29 March 1902—   ), historian, a son of the Bishop of Taunton, was educated at Eton and Oxford, where he was President of the Union. From 1926 to 1935 he was a master at Stonyhurst, and from 1935 to 1939 did economic research work at Notre Dame University, Indiana. In the Second

World War he was a squadron-leader in the Royal Air Force. Later he took up journalism and was on the staff of the *Tablet*. In 1945 he was elected Conservative M.P. for Devizes. His books include *Glastonbury and England* (1927), *The Monstrous Regiment* (1929), *Foreigners Aren't Fools* (1936), *Foreigners Aren't Knaves* (1939), *The Rise and Fall of the Ex-Socialist Government* (1947), *Can Parliament Survive?* (1949), and studies of Dr Johnson (1928), St Ignatius (1931), Erasmus (1933), Dryden (1933), Sir Thomas More (1934), Lenin (1938), G. K. Chesterton (1950), and Evelyn Waugh (1954).

Holme, Constance (1881—17 June 1955), novelist, was born at Milnthorpe, Westmorland, on the shores of Morecambe Bay, the youngest of a J.P.'s fourteen children. In 1916 she married Frederick B. Punchard, and three years later her novel *The Splendid Faring* won the Femina Vie Heureuse Prize. Most of her books are true regional literature, being written round her native county; they include *The Lonely Plough* (1914), *The Old Road from Spain* (1916), *Beautiful End* (1918), *The Trumpet in the Dust* (1921), *The Things Which Belong* (1925), and *He-Who-Came* (1930).

Holmes, Oliver Wendell (29 Aug. 1809—7 Oct. 1894), doctor, poet, essayist, was born at Cambridge, Massachusetts, educated at Phillips Andover Academy and Harvard, and studied medicine there and in Paris. After practising in Boston he became Professor of Anatomy at Dartmouth and then from 1847 to 1882 at the Harvard Medical School. In 1840 he married Amelia Lee Jackson, daughter of a judge. One of the Boston circle of writers, he published eight volumes of poems, among which the best-remembered are 'Old Ironsides,' 'The Chambered Nautilus,' and 'The Wonderful One-Hoss Shay.' His *Lectures on English Poets of the Nineteenth Century* were published in 1853. He is famous above all for his 'Breakfast Table' series of table talks, *The Autocrat of the Breakfast Table* (1857) meeting with such success that he followed it with *The Professor at the Breakfast Table* (1860), *The Poet at the Breakfast Table* (1872), and *Over the Tea-Cups* (1891). He also wrote three novels, *Elsie Venner* (1861), *The Guardian Angel* (1867), and *A Mortal Antipathy* (1885). He received honorary degrees from Oxford, Cambridge, and Edinburgh.

Holtby, Winifred (23 June 1898—25 Sept. 1935), novelist, born at Rudstone, Yorkshire, was educated at Queen Margaret's School, Scarborough, and Somerville College, Oxford. In the First World War she was a member of the Women's Auxiliary Army Corps. In 1921 she moved to London, where she lived with Vera Brittain (q.v.) and worked for the weekly *Time and Tide*. She also travelled in Europe, lecturing for the League of Nations Union. She died prematurely of overwork, just after she had finished her novel *South Riding* (1935), which is generally reckoned her best. Others of her novels are *The Land of Green Ginger* (1927), *Poor Caroline* (1931), and *Mandoa! Mandoa!* (1933). She also wrote *Eutychus, or, The Future of the Pulpit* (1928), two books of short stories, *Truth Is Not Sober* (1934) and *Pavements of Anderby* (1937), and a study of *Virginia Woolf* (1932).

Home, Alexander, *see* Hume.

Home, Cecil, *see* Webster, Julia.

Home, Henry, *see* Kames.

Home, John (21 Sept. 1722—5 Sept. 1808), dramatist, born at Leith, where his father was town clerk, was educated there and at Edinburgh University, where Robertson the historian and Adam Ferguson were his friends. He became a minister, but before doing so he had fought on the Hanoverian side in the '45, and had, after the Battle of Falkirk, been a prisoner in Doune Castle, whence he escaped. His ministerial life at Athelstaneford, East Lothian, was brought to an end by the action of the Church Courts on his producing the play of *Douglas*. This drama, which had been rejected by Garrick, but brought out in Edinburgh in 1756, created an immense sensation, and made its appearance in London the following year. Home then became private secretary to the Earl of Bute, and thereafter tutor to the Prince of Wales, who on his accession as George III conferred upon him a pension of £300. Other plays were *The Siege of Aquileia* (1760), *The Fatal Discovery* (1769), *Alonzo* (1773), and *Alfred* (1778), which was a total failure. He also wrote a *History of the Rebellion of 1745* (1802). In 1778 he settled in Edinburgh, where he was one of the brilliant circle of literary men of which Robertson was the centre. He supported the claims of Macpherson to be the translator of Ossian.

Hone, William (3 June 1780—6 Nov. 1842), author, compiler, and bookseller, born at Bath, became a clerk in Gray's Inn but left the law in 1800 to set up as a bookseller in Lambeth Walk. He published many satirical writings, which had immense popularity, among which were *The Political House that Jack Built* (1819), *The Man in the Moon* (1820), *The Political Showman* (1821), and *The Apocryphal New Testament*. For one of his earliest satires, *The Political Litany*, published in 1817, he was prosecuted, but acquitted. Later he brought out *Ancient Mysteries* (1823), *Every Day Book* (1826—7), *Table Book* (1827—8), and *Year Book* (1828). These works, in which he had the assistance of other writers, are full of curious learning on miscellaneous subjects, such as ceremonies, dress, and customs. His last literary enterprise was an edition of *Strutt's Sports and Pastimes* (1830). His *Every Day Book* was praised by Scott and Southey.

Hood, Thomas (23 May 1799—3 May 1845), poet, born in London, son of a Scottish bookseller, started work in a counting house at 13, but being threatened with consumption he was sent to Dundee, where the family had connections, and where he remained for three years. His health being restored, he returned to London, and entered the employment of an uncle as an engraver. Here he acquired an acquaintance with drawing, which he afterwards turned to account in illustrating his comic writings. After working for a short time on his own account he became at the age of 22, sub-editor of the *London Magazine*, and made the acquaintance of many literary men, including De Quincey, Lamb, and Hazlitt. His first separate publication, *Odes and Addresses to Great People*, appeared in 1825, and had an immediate success. Thus encouraged he produced in.

M*

the next year *Whims and Oddities*, and in 1829, he commenced *The Comic Annual*, which he continued for nine years, and wrote in *The Gem* his striking poem, 'Eugene Aram.' Soon afterwards the failure of his publisher involved him in difficulties which, combined with his delicate health, made the remainder of his life a continual struggle. The years between 1834 and 1839 were the period of most acute difficulty, and for a part of this time he was obliged to live abroad. In 1840 friends came to his assistance, and he was able to return to England. His health was, however, quite broken down, but his industry never flagged. During the five years which remained to him he acted as editor first of the *New Monthly Magazine*, and then of *Hood's Monthly Magazine*. In his last year a Government pension of £100 was granted to his wife. Among his other writings may be mentioned *Tylney Hall* (1824), a novel which had little success, and *Up the Rhine* (1839), which satirized the English tourist. There are two distinct sides to his work. He is best remembered for his comic poems, full of ridiculous puns, like 'Ben Battle,' which make a joke of tragedy. But he can also be graceful and tender in poems of true pathos like 'The Song of the Shirt,' and 'The Bridge of Sighs.'

Hood, Thomas (14 Jan. 1835—20 Nov. 1874), poet, son of the above, was born at Wanstead, Essex, and educated at University College School, London, Louth Grammar School in Lincoln, and Pembroke College, Oxford. After a year in Cornwall, where he edited the *Liskeard Gazette*, he worked as a clerk in the War Office from 1860 to 1865, when he became editor of the comic paper *Fun*. Like his father he had a gift for humorous verse, and was a clever parodist. His first published poem, 'Farewell to the Swallows' appeared in a magazine in 1853, and his first book, *Pen and Pencil Pictures*, was published in 1857. *Rules of Rhyme* (1869) is a guide to versification. Of his half-dozen novels *Captain Master's Children* (1865) was the most successful. In 1867 he started *Tom Hood's Annual*, which was continued after his death, and in 1877 a collection of his verse, *Favourite Poems*, was edited by his sister.

Hook, Theodore Edward (22 Sept. 1788—24 Aug. 1841), novelist and dramatist, son of a music-hall composer, was born in London, and educated at Harrow. As a boy he wrote words for his father's comic dramas. In 1805 he produced a comic opera, *The Soldier's Return*, which was followed by *Catch Him who Can*. Both of them were highly successful, and were followed by many others. He was noted for his witty conversation and his practical jokes. In 1812 he received the appointment of Accountant-General of Mauritius, which he held for five years, when serious irregularities were discovered, and he was sent home in disgrace, prosecuted by Government for a claim of £12,000, and imprisoned. It subsequently appeared that the actual peculation had been the work of a subordinate, and that Hook himself was only chargeable with gross neglect of duty, but though he was released the claims against him were not withdrawn. He then became editor of *John Bull*, a journal of high Tory and aristocratic proclivities, which he conducted with great ability; he also edited the *New Monthly Magazine*, and wrote many novels, among which were *Sayings and Doings* (9 volumes 1824—8), *Gilbert Gurney* (1836), and

Jack Brag (1837). Though making a large income, he was always in difficulties, and, after a long struggle with broken health and spirits, he died at Fulham.

Hook, Walter Farquhar (13 March 1798—20 Oct. 1875), biographer, son of the Dean of Worcester, was educated at Winchester and Oxford. Entering the Church, he held various benefices, and became Vicar of Leeds (where, largely owing to his exertions, twenty new churches and many schools were built), and afterwards Dean of Chichester. Besides his labours as a churchman he was a voluminous author, his works including a *Church Dictionary* (1842), *Dictionary of Ecclesiastical Biography* (1845—52), and *Lives of the Archbishops of Canterbury* (1860—75), on which he was still engaged at his death, and which he had brought down to Juxon. His sermon *Hear the Church* (1838), in which he affirmed the Apostolical succession of the Anglican episcopate, attracted much attention.

Hooker, Richard (1554—2 Nov. 1600), theologian, was born at Heavitree near Exeter, of a family the original name of which was Vowell. His ability and gentleness as a schoolboy recommended him to the notice of Bishop Jewel, who sent him to Corpus Christi College, Oxford, where he graduated and became a Fellow in 1577. His proficency in Hebrew led to his appointment in 1579 as Deputy Professor. Two years later he took orders. In 1584 he received the living of Drayton-Beauchamp, in Buckinghamshire, and in the following year was appointed Master of the Temple. Here he had for a colleague as evening lecturer Walter Travers, a man of mark among the Puritans. Though both men were of the finest moral character, their views on ecclesiastical questions were widely different, and as neither was disposed to conceal his opinions, it came to be said that in the Temple 'the pulpit spake pure Canterbury in the morning and Geneva in the afternoon.' Things developed into an animated controversy, in which Hooker was considered to have triumphed, and Archbishop Whitgift suspended Travers. The position, however, had become intolerable for Hooker, who respected his opponent in spite of their differences, and he petitioned Whitgift that he might retire to the country and find time and quiet to complete his great work, the *Ecclesiastical Polity*, on which he was engaged. He was accordingly, in 1591, presented to the living of Boscombe near Amesbury, and made sub-dean and a minor prebendary of Salisbury. Here he finished *The Four Books of the Lawes of Ecclesiastical Polity*, published in 1594. The following year he was presented by Queen Elizabeth to the living of Bishopsbourne, Kent. Here the fifth book was published (1597), and here he died in 1600. The sixth and eighth books were not published until 1648, and the seventh only appeared in 1662. The *Ecclesiastical Polity*, a defence of the Church of England in Queen Elizabeth's reign, is one of the greatest achievements alike in English theology and English literature, a masterpiece of reasoning and eloquence, in a style stately and sonorous, though often laborious and involved. The sixth book has been considered of doubtful authority, and to have no claim to its place, and the seventh and eighth are believed to have been put together from rough notes.

Hooker's life was written by Izaak Walton, but the epithet 'judicious' attached to his name first appears in the inscription on his monument at Bishopsbourne.

Hope, Anthony, *see* **Hawkins, Sir Anthony H.**

Hope, Laurence, *see* **Nicolson, Adela F.**

Hope, Thomas (1770?—3 Feb. 1831), collector and novelist, son of a wealthy Amsterdam merchant of Scottish descent, spent much of his early life in travel, studying architecture, and collecting objects of art. Returning, he settled in London, and occupied himself in arranging his vast collections. In 1807 he published a work on *Household Furniture and Decoration*, which had a great effect in improving the public taste in such matters. This was followed by two magnificent works, *On the Costume of the Ancients* (1809) and *Designs of Modern Costumes* (1812). Up to this time his reputation had been somewhat that of a transcendent upholsterer, but in 1819 he astonished the literary world by his novel, *Anastasius; or, Memoirs of a Modern Greek*, a work full of imagination, descriptive power, and knowledge of the world. This book, which was published anonymously, was attributed to Byron, and only credited to the author on his avowing it in *Blackwood's Magazine*. Hope also wrote a treatise on the *Origin and Prospects of Man*, and *Essays on Architecture*. He was a munificent and discerning patron of rising artists.

Hopkins, Gerard Manley (28 July 1844—8 June 1889), priest and poet, was born at Stratford, Essex, now part of London, son of the consul for Hawaii. He was educated at Highgate School, where one of the masters was R. W. Dixon (q.v.), with whom he corresponded about prosody in later years, the letters being published in 1935. From there he went to Oxford, where he met Robert Bridges (q.v.). While still an undergraduate he was converted to Roman Catholicism, and after teaching for some time at a school in Birmingham he decided to become a Jesuit. Ordained in 1877, he worked in London, Oxford, Liverpool, and Glasgow, and later was a teacher at Stonyhurst. In 1884 he was appointed Professor of Classics at University College, Dublin, but his sensitive nature made the work arduous. Hopkins himself published no verse, but his first characteristic poem 'The Wreck of the Deutschland' was written in 1875 and his famous 'Windhover' not long afterwards. Thirty years after his death Dr Bridges edited these and other poems in a slim volume whose appearance in 1918 was very apposite, for Hopkins was so far in advance of his time that poetic fashion had only then caught up with his work. Both his oddity and his obscurity are essentially modern, as is his 'sprung rhythm,' reckoning by stresses instead of syllables; this, although not really an innovation, was used by him for new and elaborate effects. His *Notebooks* were published in 1937.

Hopkins, John (died October 1570), versifier, was educated at Oxford, took orders and became a schoolmaster and later rector of Great Waldingfield in Suffolk. He collaborated with Thomas Sternhold (q.v.) in a metrical version of the Psalms which was for two centuries the standard hymn-book of the Church of England.

Hopkinson, Francis (2 Oct. 1737—9 May 1791), statesman and satirist, born in Philadelphia, son of a lawyer, was the first graduate of what is now the University of Pennsylvania. He practised law, wrote poems, and was the first native of the United States to compose music. *A Pretty Story* (1774) is a political satire, and his ballad *The Battle of the Kegs* (1778) ridicules the British; he also wrote a number of political pamphlets. Elected to the second Continental Congress, he was one of the signers of the Declaration of Independence, and designed the American flag, familiarly called the Stars and Stripes. In 1789 he was appointed a judge of the United States Court.

Hopkinson, Joseph (12 Nov. 1770—15 Jan. 1842), son of the above, was educated at the University of Pennsylvania and became a successful lawyer. In 1814 he was elected a member of Congress and in 1828 was made a judge. He is remembered chiefly as the writer of 'Hail Columbia,' which he produced in 1798 to oblige a young actor who wanted a popular song.

Horler, Sydney (18 July 1888—27 Oct. 1954), novelist, born at Leytonstone, Essex, was educated at Redcliffe and Colston Schools, Bristol. He intended at first to be a schoolmaster, but instead turned to writing. During the First World War he was with the Intelligence Department, a useful training for his later stories of mystery and adventure. In 1918 he joined the staff of *John o' London's Weekly*. The first of his thrillers, *The Mystery of No. 1* (1925) was followed by well over a hundred others, of which the slogan was 'Horler for excitement.' Among them may be mentioned *False Face* (1926), *The Secret Service Man* (1928), *The Screaming Skull* (1930), *Horror's Head* (1931), *Tiger Standish* (1932), with its various sequels written round the same hero, *The Man from Scotland Yard* (1934), *Murder for Sale* (1945), and *Murder is So Simple* (1954). He also wrote an autobiography, *Excitement* (1933), and a diary, *Strictly Personal* (1934).

Horne, Richard Henry *or* **Hengist** (1 Jan. 1803—13 March 1884), poet and critic, born in London and educated at Sandhurst, became a midshipman in the Mexican navy and had a highly adventurous early life. His first printed work was a poem 'Hecatompylos,' which appeared in the *Athenaeum* in 1828. In 1837 he published two tragedies, *Cosmo de Medici* and *The Death of Marlowe*. From 1839 to 1846 he carried on a correspondence with Elizabeth Barrett, which was published in 1877, and it was his official report on the employment of young persons that inspired her famous 'Cry of the Children.' In 1843 he published *Orion*, an epic poem, at the price of a farthing, and in the following year the work by which he is best known, *The New Spirit of the Age*, in which he was assisted by the Brownings; the book is a sort of sequel to Hazlitt's *Spirit of the Age*, and like it, consists of critical studies of contemporary writers. In 1852 Horne went to Australia, where he held various official posts, returning in 1869.

Horne, Thomas Hartwell (20 Oct. 1780—27 Jan. 1862), Biblical scholar, son of a barrister's clerk, was born in Chancery Lane and died in Bloomsbury Square. Educated at Christ's Hospital, where he was contemporary with Coleridge, he took orders, became a prebend of St Paul's, and from 1824 to 1860 was an assistant librarian in the British Museum. His chief work, used extensively as a text-book, was *An Introduction to the Critical Study and Knowledge of the Holy Scriptures* (1818). He also wrote *An Introduction to the Study of Bibliography* (1814).

Hornung, Ernest William (7 June 1866—22 March 1921), novelist, was born at Middlesbrough, Yorkshire, and educated at Uppingham. From 1884 to 1886 he lived in Australia for his health and afterwards he wrote two novels with an Australian background, *A Bride from the Bush* (1890) and *The Boss of Taroomba* (1894). Returning to England, he married Constance Doyle, sister of Conan Doyle (q.v.) in 1893. In 1899 his well-known book *The Amateur Cracksman* appeared, with its hero Raffles the gentleman-burglar making a sort of foil to his brother-in-law's detective Sherlock Holmes. Three further collections of these adventures appeared, *Raffles* (1901), *A Thief in the Night* (1905), and *Mr Justice Raffles* (1909). During the First World War Hornung travelled in France with a mobile library for the use of the troops. *Notes of a Camp Follower on the Western Front* (1919) tells of his experiences, and *The Young Guard* is a book of war poems.

Houghton, Richard Monckton Milnes, 1st Baron (19 June 1809—11 Aug. 1885), poet, son of an M.P. nicknamed single-speech Milnes, was born in London, and went to Trinity College, Cambridge, where he was a member of the 'Apostles,' and intimate with Tennyson, Hallam, and Thackeray. He sat in the House of Commons for Pontefract from 1837 to 1863, when he was raised to the peerage. His interests were, however, mainly literary and philanthropic, and it was said of him that he 'knew everybody worth knowing at home and abroad.' A dilettante and patron of poets, he got Tennyson the laureateship, was one of the first to recognize the genius of Swinburne, and wrote a life of Keats. He also published many volumes of poetry among which were *Poetry for the People* (1840) and *Palm Leaves* (1848). Though he had not the depth of mind or intensity of feeling to make a great poet, his verse is the work of a man of high culture, graceful and refined.

Houghton, William Stanley (22 Feb. 1881—11 Dec. 1913), dramatist, was born at Ashton-upon-Mersey, Cheshire, son of a cotton merchant, and educated at Manchester Grammar School. He went into his father's business, but spent his leisure in amateur dramatic work. From 1900 onwards he began to write for the stage and also did dramatic criticism. His first play, *The Dear Departed* (1908), was followed by *Independent Means* (1909), *The Younger Generation* (1910), and *Hindle Wakes* (1912), which was a great success, bringing him fame and fortune; it may be explained that Hindle is a town and the wakes are the annual Lancashire holiday. Subsequently he left the cotton business and moved first to London and then to Paris, where he died at an early age of meningitis.

Housman, Alfred Edward (26 March 1859—1 May 1936), poet and scholar, was born at Fockbury, Worcestershire, within sight of the

Shropshire country which figures in his poems. His father was a lawyer. Educated at Bromsgrove School and St John's College, Oxford, the son had an undistinguished record, getting only a pass degree; it was partly this disappointment that made him reserved and gloomy and gave a strong vein of pessimism to his verse. In 1882 he became a clerk in the Patent Office, but ten years later he was appointed to the Chair of Latin at University College, London, and in 1911 to the corresponding post in Cambridge. As a scholar his great work was his edition of Manilius, which is a model of textual criticism and marks him as one of the greatest English Latinists. As a critic of other people's work he was merciless and vitriolic. But it is as a poet that he is best known to the general public. Three small volumes, *A Shropshire Lad* (1896), *Last Poems* (1922), and *More Poems* (1936), with the addition of a volume of *Manuscript Poems*, edited in 1955, contain his entire output. His lyrics have the clear simplicity of the poems of the Greek Anthology, and as a critic has said 'There were few strings to his lyre, but those strings were nearly all pure gold.' A small book of criticism, *The Name and Nature of Poetry* (1933) embodies his poetical theories.

Housman, Laurence (18 July 1865—20 Feb. 1959), dramatist and novelist, younger brother of the above, born at Bromsgrove, Worcestershire, attended the school there and studied painting at South Kensington. He worked first as an illustrator, then wrote fairy tales and poems, illustrated by himself. His first book of verse, *Green Arras*, appeared in 1895, but he first won notice with the anonymous *An Englishwoman's Love Letters* (1900), which caused a minor sensation. In 1905 he started as a dramatist, and struck out a new line with his *Little Plays of St Francis* (1922), composed of a large number of playlets, each dealing with one episode in the Saint's life. Another series, telling of Queen Victoria, was refused a licence because of its subject, but in 1937, on the centenary of the Queen's accession, a group of them with the title *Victoria Regina* was produced in London, while *Happy and Glorious* followed in 1945. *Palestine Plays* appeared in 1943, and *Cynthia*, a verse pastoral, in 1947. In addition to many other plays Housman published *Select Poems* (1909), *John of Jingalo* (1912), a novel satirizing contemporary politics, and an autobiography, *The Unexpected Years* (1936).

Howard, Bronson Crocker (7 Oct. 1842—4 Aug. 1908), playwright, born in Detroit, of which his father was mayor, was educated at Russell's Institute, New Haven, Connecticut. He moved to New York, where his farce *Saratoga* was produced in 1870. Altogether he wrote more than 20 plays, of which the best are *Lillian's Last Love* (1873), rewritten as *The Banker's Daughter*, *Young Mrs Winthrop* (1882), *One of Our Girls* (1885), *The Henrietta* (1887), and *Shenandoah* (1888), a play of the Civil War, his most successful. He discussed dramatic theory in *The Autobiography of a Play* (1886).

Howard, Edward (died 30 Dec. 1841), novelist, was a lieutenant in the navy, and on his discharge started writing sea stories. *Rattlin the Reefer* (1836), his most successful book, was sometimes attributed to Marryat (q.v.), who had been Howard's shipmate. Others of his novels are *The Old Commodore* (1837), *Outward Bound* (1838), and *Jack Ashore* (1840). He also wrote *Memoirs of Admiral Sir Sidney Smith* (1839), *Sir Henry Morgan the Buccaneer* (1842), and *The Centiad* (1841), a poem in four books.

Howard, Henry, *see* **Surrey, Earl of.**

Howard, Sir Robert (1626—3 Sept. 1698), dramatist, was a son of the 1st Earl of Berkshire; his sister married Dryden. On the outbreak of the Civil War he was of the King's party, and in 1644 was knighted on the field for bravery. After the Restoration he was in favour with the Court, and held many important posts. He wrote some plays, of which the best was *The Committee* (1692), and collaborated with Dryden in *The Indian Queen*. He was at odds with him, however, on the question of rhyme, the use of which he wrote against in very indifferent blank verse.

Howe, John (17 May 1630—2 April 1705), clergyman, born at Loughborough, of which his father was curate, studied at Cambridge, and became, in 1652, minister of Great Torrington, Devonshire, where he was famous for the unusual length of his sermons and prayers. In 1657 Oliver Cromwell made him his resident chaplain at Whitehall, a position which he retained under Richard Cromwell, so long as the latter held the office of Protector. On the Restoration Howe returned to Great Torrington, from which, however, he was ejected in 1662. Thereafter he wandered from place to place, preaching in secret until 1671, when he went to Ireland as chaplain to Lord Massareene, and in 1675 he became minister of a dissenting congregation in London. Howe was the author of many excellent works of practical divinity, among which are *The Living Temple* (1675), *Inquiry into the Doctrine of the Trinity* (1694), and *The Divine Presence.* The substance of his writings is better than their style, which is involved and extremely diffuse.

Howe, Julia Ward (27 May 1819—17 Oct. 1910), poetess, was born in New York, daughter of Samuel Ward, a banker. In 1843 she married Samuel Gridley Howe, an anti-slavery reformer twenty years her senior. Becoming one of the Boston literary circle she wrote several volumes of verse, including *Passion Flowers* (1854) and *Words for the Hour* (1857), as well as two travel books and a play. She is best known as the writer in 1862 of 'The Battle Hymn of the Republic,' which begins 'Mine eyes have seen the glory of the coming of the Lord.'

Howell, James (born 1594? buried 3 Nov. 1666), pamphleteer and letter-writer, son of a clergyman at Abernant, Caermarthenshire, was at Oxford and spent the greater part of his earlier life travelling in various Continental countries, including the Low Countries, France, Spain, and Italy, on various matters of business, during which he became versed in many languages, and amassed stores of information and observations on men and manners. He was a keen Royalist, and was on this account imprisoned in the Fleet, 1643—51. He wrote a large number of books, including *Dodona's Grove* (1640), a political allegory, *Instructions for Foreign Travel* (1642), *England's Tears for the Present Wars*, and the work on which his reputation rests, *Epistolae Ho-Elianae, or Familiar Letters* (1655), chiefly written in the Fleet to imaginary correspondents, but no doubt based upon notes of his own travels. It is one of the most interesting and entertaining books of his time.

Howells, William Dean (1 March 1837—11 May 1920), novelist and critic, leader of American letters for a quarter of a century, was born at Martin's Ferry, Ohio, son of a journalist of Welsh extraction, and at the age of 9 was a compositor in his father's office. He had no college training, though in later years he was to receive honorary degrees from Oxford and five other universities. Among his earliest writings were some poems in the *Atlantic Monthly*, through which he made the acquaintance of Lowell, Emerson, Holmes, and other writers. From 1857 to 1860 he worked as a reporter in Columbus, and during the Civil War was United States consul at Venice, afterwards publishing a series of sketches, *Venetian Life* (1866). Returning to America he joined the staff of the *Atlantic Monthly*, and in 1871 became its editor; for ten years he held this post, encouraging realism among the contributors, who included Henry James, Mark Twain, and Bret Harte (qq.v.). Later he carried on the same policy as a member of the staff of *Harper's*, for which he wrote regularly from 1886 to 1892. Apart from journalism his own output was formidable, including 35 novels, among which may be mentioned *Their Wedding Journey* (1872), *The Undiscovered Country* (1880), *A Modern Instance* (1882), *The Rise of Silas Lapham* (1885), *A Hazard of New Fortunes* (1890), and *A Traveller from Altruria* (1894). His critical works include *Criticism and Fiction* (1891) and *My Literary Passions* (1895), while *Literary Friends and Acquaintances* (1900), *My Mark Twain* (1910), and *Years of My Youth* (1916) are books of reminiscence.

Howie, John (14 Nov. 1735—5 Jan. 1793), biographer, was a Renfrewshire farmer, who claimed descent from an Albigensian refugee. He wrote lives of the martyrs of Scotland from Patrick Hamilton, the first, to James Renwick, the last, under the title of *Scots Worthies* (1774). The work of an unlettered man, it has considerable merit as regards both matter and style, and was long a classic among the Scottish peasantry as well as higher orders of the people.

Howitt, Mary (12 March 1799—30 Jan. 1888), authoress, was born at Coleford in Gloucestershire, daughter of Samuel Botham, a prosperous Quaker, and went to school at Croydon. In 1821 she married William Howitt (q.v.) and they commenced a career of joint authorship. After they settled in Esher in 1836 Mary wrote a series of tales for children, and in 1846 she translated Hans Andersen's fairy tales under the title of *Wonderful Stories for Children*. She also translated the Swedish novels of Frederica Bremer, wrote a *Popular History of the United States*, and for three years edited *The Drawing-Room Scrapbook*. In her later years she became a Roman Catholic.

Howitt, William (18 Dec. 1792—3 March 1879), author, was born at Heanor, Derbyshire, son of a Quaker farmer, educated at the Friends' School, Ackworth, and apprenticed to a builder. In 1821 he married Mary Botham (*see* Mary Howitt), with whom he collaborated in many works, including two volumes of poems, *The Forest Minstrel* (1822) and *The Book of the Seasons* (1831). They settled in Nottingham, where they kept a chemist's shop from 1823 to 1835, then moving to Esher in Surrey. Howitt's own publications include *A Popular History of Priestcraft* (1833), *Rural Life in England* (1837), *The Boy's Country Book* (1839), and *Visits to Remarkable Places* (two series, 1840, 1842). In 1852 he visited Australia and wrote *A History of Discovery in Australia* (1865).

Hubbard, Elbert (19 June 1856—7 May 1915), essayist, was born at Bloomington, Illinois, son of a doctor. From school he went in 1872 to journalism, later working as salesman and as advertising writer. At the age of 36 he left his business and studied at Harvard, then visited Europe, where he met William Morris (q.v.), by whom he was greatly influenced. In 1895 he returned to America, settled in Buffalo, kept a shop that dealt in pottery, and published a Bohemian magazine called *The Philistine*, which attained great popularity. His best-known work is *A Message to Garcia* (1899), which tells of an incident in the Spanish-American War and is said to have had a circulation of several millions. He went down in the *Lusitania* when she was torpedoed. His books of essays include *Time and Chance* (1899), *The Man of Sorrows* (1906), and *Little Journeys* (14 volumes, 1915), which tells of visits to the homes of great men.

Huchoun *or* **Huchown** *or* **Hucheon** (mid fourteenth century), poet, is an extremely shadowy figure. He is named in the *Chronicle* of Andrew of Wyntoun (q.v.) as author of *The Gret Geste of Arthur*, *The Auntyrs* (Adventures) *of Gawain*, and the *Pistill* (Epistle) *of Susane*, but only the last-named poem, which relates in alliterative verse the Apocryphal story of Susanna and the Elders, has been traced with any certainty. Huchoun means 'little Hugh' and he has been very doubtfully identified with the statesman Sir Hugh of Eglinton, brother-in-law of Robert II, Chamberlain of Cunningham and Justiciar of Lothian; this would square with Wyntoun's calling him 'Huchoun of the Awle Ryale' (Hall Royal).

Hudson, William Henry (4 Aug. 1841—18 Aug. 1922), writer on nature, was born at Quilmes near Buenos Aires, of parents who came from the United States. Brought up on the pampas, he told later of his early life in *Far Away and Long Ago* (1918). At the age of 15 his health was injured by rheumatic fever, so that he was unequal to farm work, and roamed about studying wild life, especially birds. In 1869 he moved to England, but did not adopt British nationality till 1900. While dogged by illness and poverty he married Emily Wingreave, and for a time they kept a boarding-house in Bayswater. In 1901 he was granted a Civil List pension, which he afterwards relinquished. Practically all his books are on nature subjects. In 1885 he published *The Purple Land*, a novel with a South American setting, and in 1904 another novel, *Green Mansions*, whose heroine Rima was portrayed in stone by Epstein. Others of his books are *Idle Days in Patagonia* (1893), *British Birds* (1895), *Birds in London* (1898), *Nature in Downland* (1900), *Hampshire Days* (1903), *A*

Shepherd's Life (1910), *A Traveller in Little Things* (1921), and *A Hind in Richmond Park* (1922). Of his clear vivid style Conrad declared 'He writes as the grass grows.'

Hueffer, Ford Madox, *see* **Ford.**

Hughes, John (29 Jan. 1677—17 Feb. 1720), essayist and dramatist, born at Marlborough, Wiltshire, was a clerk in the Ordnance Office, then secretary for the Commission of the Peace. He contributed to the *Spectator*, *Tatler*, and *Guardian*, edited Spenser, and wrote several dramas, of which the best is *The Siege of Damascus*. It was his last, he having died on the first night of its performance. Addison thought so well of his dramatic talent that he requested him to write the conclusion of *Cato*, which, however, he actually finished himself. Hughes also wrote a number of poems.

Hughes, Richard Arthur Warren (19 April 1900—   ), novelist, of Welsh descent, was born at Weybridge in Kent and educated at Charterhouse and Oriel College. While still at Oxford he published a one-act play, *The Sister's Tragedy*, which was admired by Bernard Shaw, and a volume of poems, *Gipsy Night* (1922); *Confessio Juvenis*, a second book of verse, appeared in 1926. After travelling in the United States, Canada, and the West Indies he turned to novel writing and published *A High Wind in Jamaica* (1929) and *In Hazard* (1938). *A Moment of Time* (1926) and *Don't Blame Me* (1940) are collections of short stories. During the Second World War he worked in the Admiralty and received the O.B.E.

Hughes, Thomas (20 Oct. 1822—22 March 1896), novelist and biographer, born at Uffington, son of a Berkshire squire, was educated at Rugby and Oxford, and called to the Bar in 1848. Much the most successful of his books was *Tom Brown's Schooldays* (1856), which had an immense popularity, and perhaps remains the best picture of English public-school life in the language. Its sequel, *Tom Brown at Oxford* (1861), was a comparative failure, but his *Scouring of the White Horse* (1859) deals in a charming way with his own countryside. He also wrote lives of Alfred the Great, Bishop Fraser, and D. Macmillan, the publisher. From 1865 to 1874 he was a Liberal M.P., and in 1882 he was appointed a County Court Judge.

Hull, Edith Maude (   ), novelist, in 1921 attained prominence with *The Sheikh*, a novel of 'incandescent passion,' which obtained great publicity from being filmed with Rudolph Valentino as the hero. A sequel, *Sons of the Sheikh*, appeared in 1925. Others of her books are *The Shadow of the East* (1921), *The Desert Healer* (1923), *The Lion Tamer* (1928), *Captive of the Sahara* (1931), and *Jungle Captive* (1939). *Camping in the Sahara* (1927), a travel book, shows that she had real knowledge of the romantic background to her stories.

Hume *or* **Home, Alexander** (1560—4 Dec. 1609), poet, son of the 5th Lord Polwarth, educated at St Andrews, and on the Continent, was originally destined for the law, but devoted himself to the service of the Church, and was minister of Logie in Stirlingshire from 1598 till his death. He published in 1599 *Hymns and Sacred Songs*, including the beautiful 'Day Estival,' descriptive of a summer day.

Hume, David (26 April 1711—25 Aug. 1776), philosopher and historian, second son of Joseph Hume, laird of Ninewells, Berwickshire, was born in Edinburgh and, educated at the university there, was intended for the law. For this, however, he had no aptitude, and commercial pursuits into which he was initiated in a counting-house in Bristol proving equally uncongenial, he was permitted to follow out his literary bent, and in 1734 went to France, where he passed three years at Rheims and La Flèche in study, living on a small allowance made him by his father. In 1739 he published anonymously his *Treatise of Human Nature*, which attracted little attention. Having returned to Scotland, he wrote at Ninewells his *Essays, Moral and Political* (1741—2). He became in 1745 governor to the Marquis of Annandale, a nobleman whose state was little removed from insanity. Two years later he accepted the more congenial appointment of Judge-Advocate-General to General St Clair on his expedition to Port L'Orient, and in 1748 accompanied him on a diplomatic mission to France, whence he passed on to Vienna and Turin. About the same time he produced his *Philosophical Essays concerning Human Understanding* (1748), republished in 1758 as *An Enquiry concerning Human Understanding*, and including the famous essay *Of Miracles*, which gave rise to so much controversy. These were followed in 1751 by his *Enquiry concerning the Principles of Morals*, which he considered his best work; and in 1752 by his *Political Discourses*, which alone of his works had an immediate success.

In the same year he was appointed Keeper of the Advocates' Library in Edinburgh. The access to books and original authorities which this position gave him appears to have suggested to his mind the idea of writing a history, and the first volume of his *History of England*, containing the reigns of James I and Charles I, was published in 1754. Its reception was not favourable, but the second volume, which appeared in 1757, dealing with the Commonwealth, and the reigns of Charles II and James II was better received, and had the effect of 'buoying up its unfortunate brother.' Thereafter the tide completely turned, and the remaining 4 volumes, 1759 and 1762, in which he turned back and finished the history from the invasion of Julius Caesar to the accession of Henry VII, attained a vast popularity, which extended to the whole work. During the progress of the history Hume published in 1757 *Four Dissertations: the Natural History of Religion; of the Passions; of Tragedy; of the Standard of Taste*. Two others on *Suicide* and on *The Immortality of the Soul* were cancelled, but published posthumously. In 1763 Hume accompanied Lord Hertford to Paris, and for a few months acted as *chargé d'affaires*. While there he was introduced to the brilliant literary society for which the French capital was then famous. Among other acquaintances which he made was that of Rousseau, whom he persuaded to accompany him on his return home, and for whom he procured a pension. The suspicious and fickle character of Rousseau, however, soon brought the friendship to an end. Soon after his return Hume received a pension, and in 1767—8, he was Under-secretary to General Conway, then Secretary of State. In 1769 he retired, and returned to Edinburgh with an income of £1,000 a year which, time and place considered, was an ample competence, and there he spent the remainder of his days, the recognized head of the intellectual and literary society of the city.

The mind of Hume was one of the most original and penetrating of his own or any age. The father of modern rationalism, he has rightly been styled a sceptic. His philosophy was largely a questioning of the views of previous metaphysicians, and he occupied towards mind, considered as a self-subsisting entity, a position analogous to that assumed by Berkeley towards matter similarly considered. He profoundly influenced European thought, and by indirectly calling into being the philosophy of Kant on the one hand, and that of the Scottish School on the other, created a new era of thought. As a historian he showed the same originality. He introduced a new and better method of writing history than had previously been practised. Until his time only chronicles and contemporary memoirs had, generally speaking, been produced; and though his great work cannot, from its frequent inaccuracies and the fact that it is not based upon original documents, claim the character of an authority, its clear, graceful, and spirited narrative style, and its reflection of the individuality of the writer, constitute it a classic, and it must always retain a place among the masterpieces of historical literature.

Hume, Ferguson Wright (8 July 1859—12 July 1932), novelist who wrote under the name Fergus Hume, was born in England, son of a New Zealander. When the family returned home to Dunedin, he was educated at the University of Otago, studied law, and then went to Australia and lived in Melbourne. After he had tried play-writing without success, he turned to detective fiction, and wrote *The Mystery of a Hansom Cab*, which sold about half a million copies, and though now forgotten ranks as the most successful detective story of all time. It was published in 1886, a year before Sherlock Holmes made his debut in *A Study in Scarlet*. Two years later Hume went to England and settled in Essex. Others of his mystery stories are *The Piccadilly Puzzle* (1889), *The Lone Inn* (1894), *The Lady from Nowhere* (1900), and *The Caravan Mystery* (1926), but though he wrote well over 100 books, he never came near repeating his first success.

Humphreys, Eliza Margaret (died 1 Jan. 1938), novelist who wrote under the pen-name Rita, was born on the estate of her father, John Gilbert Gollan, near Inverness. Taken to Australia as a child, she spent five years in Sydney, then at the age of 14 returned to England. She lived at first in London, then made her home in Cork for a time, and after her books became profitable she travelled extensively. W. Desmond Humphreys was her second husband. Of some sixty novels, *Souls* (1903) was the one that made her really famous. Others are *Countess Daphne* (1880), *Two Bad Blue Eyes* (1884), *A Society Scandal* (1890), *A Husband of No Importance* (1891), *Asenath of the Ford* (1892), *Peg the Rake* (1894), *A Jilt's Journal* (1901), *The House Called Hurrish* (1909), *The Ink-Slinger* (1915), *Diana of the*

Ephesians (1919), *The Road to Anywhere* (1923), *The Great 'Perhaps'* (1926), *The Prince Errant* (1928), and *The Naughty Grandfather* (1932). In the days of Victorian conventions, she was reckoned a daring novelist. She also wrote a number of plays, and a volume of reminiscences, *Recollections of a Literary Life* (1936).

Hunnis, William (died 6 June 1597), poet, was a gentleman of the Chapel Royal to Edward VI, imprisoned during the reign of Mary, but after the accession of Elizabeth was released, and in 1566 made Master of the Children of the Chapel Royal. He wrote metrical versions of the Psalms, and some volumes of verse, including *A Hiveful of Honey* (1578) and *A Handful of Honeysuckles* (1583).

Hunt, James Henry Leigh (19 Oct. 1784—28 Aug. 1859), essayist and poet, was born at Southgate, Middlesex, son of a clergyman, and educated at Christ's Hospital. A selection of his earliest poems was published by his father in 1801 under the title *Juvenilia*. In 1805 he joined his brother John in conducting a paper, the *News*, which the latter had started. Thereafter the brothers embarked upon the *Examiner*, a paper of pronounced Radical views. The appearance in this journal of an article on the Prince Regent in which he was described in words which have been condensed into 'a fat Adonis of fifty,' led in 1813 to Hunt being fined £500, and imprisoned for two years. With his customary genial philosophy, however, the prisoner made the best of things, turning his cell into a study, with book-cases and a piano, and his yard into a garden. He had the sympathy of many, and received his friends, including Byron, Moore, and Lamb. On his release he published his poem, *The Story of Rimini*. Two other volumes of poetry are *The Feast of the Poets* and *Foliage*, published in 1814 and 1818 respectively. In the latter year he started the *Indicator*, a paper something in the style of the *Spectator* or *Tatler*, and after this had run its course the *Companion*, conceived on similar lines, took its place in 1828. In 1822 Hunt went to Italy with Byron, and there established the *Liberal*, a paper which did not prove a success. Disillusioned with Byron, Hunt returned home, and published in 1828 *Lord Byron and his Contemporaries*, a work which gave great offence to Byron's friends, who accused the author of ingratitude. In 1834 Hunt started the *London Journal*, which he edited for two years. Among his later works are *Captain Sword and Captain Pen* (1835); *A Legend of Florence* (1840), a play; *The Palfrey* (1842), a poem; *Imagination and Fancy* (1844); *Wit and Humour* (1846); *A Jar of Honey from Mount Hybla* (1848); *The Old Court Suburb* (1855); *Sir Ralph Esher* (1834), a novel; and his autobiography (1850). Although his poems have considerable descriptive power and brightness, he had not the depth and intensity to make a poet, and his reputation rests rather upon his essays, which are full of a genial philosophy, and display a love of books, and of everything pleasant and beautiful. He did much to popularize the love of poetry and literature in general among his fellow-countrymen. He was the original of Skimpole in Dickens's *Bleak House*.

Hunt, Violet (1866—16 Jan. 1942), novelist, born in Durham, daughter of A. W. Hunt, a pre-Raphaelite painter, was at school with the daughters of Morris and Burne-Jones, and grew up in the Rossetti circle. At first she studied art, but later changed to writing, her earliest novel, *The Maiden's Progress*, appearing in 1894. Others are *Unkist, Unkind!* (1897), *Sooner or Later* (1904), *The Wife of Altamont* (1910), *The Doll* (1911), *The House of Many Mirrors* (1915), *The Last Ditch* (1918), and *The Tiger Skin* (1924), and she also wrote two series of *Tales of the Uneasy* (1910, 1925). *The Wife of Rossetti* (1932) is biographical, and *The Flurried Years* (1926), a book of memoirs, gives interesting accounts of the famous people she met.

Huntly, Francis E., *see* **Mayne, Ethel Colburn.**

Hurd, Richard (13 Jan. 1720—28 May 1808), prelate, born at Congreve, Staffordshire, son of a farmer, was educated at Cambridge, took orders, and rose to be Bishop successively of Lichfield and Worcester. He produced an edition of the *Ars Poetica* of Horace (1749), *Dissertations on Poetry* (1757), *Dialogues on Sincerity* (1759), *Letters on Chivalry and Romance* (1762), and *An Introduction to the Prophecies* (1772). He was in 1783 offered, but declined, the Primacy.

Hurst, Fannie (18 Oct. 1889—   ), novelist, was born at Hamilton, Ohio, but spent her early years in St Louis; her father owned a shoe factory. At Washington University she distinguished herself in athletics and amateur acting. Training for fiction by gaining experience of life as shop-girl and waitress, she became a fluent and versatile writer, beginning with a book of short stories, *Just Around the Corner* (1914). In 1915 she married Jaques S. Danielson, a pianist. Her own favourite among her novels was *Lummox* (1923), a story of a servant-girl; others are *Star Dust* (1921), *Five and Ten* (1929), *Back Street* (1930), *Imitations of Life* (1933), *Lonely Parade* (1942), *Hallelujah* (1944), *The Hands of Veronica* (1947), and *Anywoman* (1950). *Gaslight Sonatas* (1918), *Humoresque* (1919), *Procession* (1929), and *We Are Ten* (1937) are books of short stories. She has been called 'the sob-sister of American fiction.'

Hutcheson, Francis (8 Aug. 1694—1 Nov. 1746), philosopher, was born in Dublin, son of a minister, and educated for the Presbyterian ministry at Glasgow University. After keeping an academy at Dublin for some years he published in 1720 his *Enquiry into Beauty and Virtue*, which won for him a great reputation. In 1729 he became Professor of Moral Philosophy at Glasgow, where he exercised a great influence over his students, and also upon the Scottish system of philosophy. In his philosophical views he was to some extent a disciple of Shaftesbury. He introduced the term, 'moral sense,' which he defined as a power of perceiving moral attributes in action. His *System of Moral Philosophy* appeared posthumously.

Hutchins, William, *see* **Tyndale.**

Hutchinson, Arthur Stuart Menteth (2 June 1879—   ), novelist, was born in India, son of a general who wrote several military text-books. Bad eyesight prevented the son from following a military career and for three years he studied medicine at St Thomas's, London, then changed over to journalism and rose to be editor of the *Daily Graphic*. In this period he wrote three novels,

Once Aboard the Lugger (1908), *The Happy Warrior* (1912), and *The Clean Heart* (1914). During the First World War he succeeded in enlisting, and served with the Royal Engineers. After the war he scored a remarkable success with his novel *If Winter Comes* (1920), which he followed with *This Freedom* (1922), *One Increasing Purpose* (1925), *Big Business* (1932), *As Once We Were* (1938), *He Looked for a City* (1940), and *It Happened Like This* (1942). In the Second World War he was a member of the Home Guard at Eastbourne. *A Year that the Locust* . . . (1935) is an autobiography.

Hutchinson, Lucy (29 Jan. 1620—1676?), biographer, daughter of Sir Allan Apsley, Lieutenant of the Tower of London, married in 1638 Colonel Hutchinson, one of those who signed the death-warrant of Charles I. He died in prison after the Restoration, and she has a place in literature for her life of her husband, one of the most interesting biographies in the language, not only on account of its immediate subject, but of the light which it throws upon the characteristics and conditions of the life of Puritans of good family. Originally intended for her family only, it was printed by a descendant in 1806. She also made a translation of Lucretius.

Hutton, Richard Holt (2 June 1826—9 Sept. 1897), theologian, born at Leeds, had a distinguished career at University College, London, and became a Unitarian minister like his father, but later joined the Church of England. He was a frequent contributor to various magazines and reviews, and assisted Walter Bagehot in editing the *National Review*. In 1861 he became joint-proprietor and editor of the *Spectator*. Among his other writings may be mentioned *Essays, Theological and Literary* (1871), *Modern Guides of English Thought* (1887), and *Contemporary Thought and Thinkers* (1894), which were more or less reprints or expansions of his work in periodicals, and a memoir of Bagehot prefixed to an edition of his works.

Huxley, Aldous Leonard (26 July 1894—   ), novelist, was born at Godalming in Surrey; T. H. Huxley the biologist was his grandfather and his mother was a niece of Matthew Arnold. Educated at Eton and Balliol, he intended to become a doctor, but was prevented by an eye affection which made him almost blind for a time; the psychological effect of this period during which he was thrown on his own resources coloured his whole life's outlook. Later his eyes partly recovered and he finished the English course at Oxford, taking his degree in 1915. In 1919 he married Maria Nys, a Belgian refugee. He then joined the staff of the *Athenaeum* and did a lot of miscellaneous literary work. From 1923 to 1930 he was in Italy, writing novels and associating with D. H. Lawrence (q.v.); in 1934 he visited Central America, and in 1937 settled permanently in California. His main work falls into two sections. There are the clever and sceptical novels of the period between the two World Wars—*Crome Yellow* (1921), *Antic Hay* (1923), *Point Counter Point* (1928), *Brave New World* (1932), *Eyeless in Gaza* (1936), and *After Many a Summer Dies the Swan* (1939). And there is a succession of books of essays which show a detached and equable judgment—*On the Margin* (1923), *Along the Road* (1925), *Proper Studies* (1927),

Brief Candles (1930), *Vulgarity in Literature* (1930), *Music at Night* (1931), *Texts and Pretexts* (1932), *Ends and Means* (1937), and *Themes and Variations* (1950). Later works are *Time Must Have a Stop* (1944), *Ape and Essence* (1948), and *The Devils of Loudun* (1952). *The Perennial Philosophy* (1945) is a study of mysticism, in which latterly he became absorbed. He also published several books of poems.

Huxley, Sir Julian Sorrell (22 June 1887—   ), zoologist, elder brother of Aldous Huxley (q.v.), was educated at Eton and Oxford, where he won the Newdigate Prize for Poetry. In 1910 he was appointed Lecturer in Zoology at Oxford, and in 1916 Professor of Zoology at the Rice Institute, Houston, Texas. During the First World War he was on the Headquarters staff in Italy. In 1927 he became Professor of Zoology at King's College, London, and was also Professor of Physiology at the Royal Institute and Director of Regents Park Zoo. His chief recreation was bird-watching. From 1946 to 1948 he was Director-General of Unesco. His works include *Essays of a Biologist* (1923), *The Outlook in Biology* (1924), *Essays in Popular Science* (1926), *Religion without Revelation* (1927), *A Scientist Among the Soviets* (1932), *At the Zoo* (1936), *Beginnings of Life* (1938), *The Uniqueness of Man* (1941), *Evolution Up to Date* (1942), and *Evolution in Action* (1953). He was knighted in 1958.

Huxley, Thomas Henry (4 May 1825—29 June 1895), scientist and writer, son of a master in a public school, was born at Ealing. From childhood he was an insatiable reader. In his thirteenth year he became a medical apprentice, and in 1845 took his medical degree at Charing Cross Hospital. Thereafter he was for a few months surgeon on board the *Victory* at Haslar, and was then appointed surgeon on H.M.S. *Rattlesnake*, which was sent to make surveys at Torres Strait. While in this position he made numerous observations, which he communicated to the Linnaean Society. In 1851 he became a Fellow of the Royal Society, and in 1854 Professor of Natural History at the School of Mines. Henceforth his life was a very full one, divided between scientific investigation and public work. He was recognized as the foremost English biologist, and was elected President of the Royal Society in 1883. He served on the London School Board and on various Royal Commissions. His writings are in the main distinguished by a clearness, force, and charm which entitle them to a place in literature; and besides the addition which they made to the stock of human knowledge, they did much to diffuse a love and study of science. Huxley was a keen controversialist, contending for the strictly scientific view of all subjects as distinguished from the metaphysical or theological, and coined the word 'agnostic,' to express his own philosophical outlook. He was a strong supporter of the theory of evolution. His published works, including scientific communications, are very numerous. Among the more important are *Man's Place in Nature* (1863), *Elementary Lessons on Physiology* (1866), *Lay Sermons, Addresses, and Reviews* (1870), *Science and Morals* (1886), *Essays upon some Controverted Questions* (1892), *Evolution and Ethics* (1893), and *Collected Essays* (9 volumes,

1893—4). He was also an admirable letter-writer, as appears from the *Life and Letters*, edited by his son in 1900.

Hychins, William, *see* **Tyndale.**

Hyde, Douglas (17 Jan. 1860—12 July 1949), poet, historian, statesman, was born at Frenchpark, County Roscommon, son of a clergyman, and educated at Trinity College, Dublin, where he took a law degree, but never practised.   In 1891 he was interim Professor of Modern Languages in New Brunswick, then returned to Ireland and devoted himself to the restoration of its culture.   In 1893 he founded the Gaelic League, of which he was President till 1915.   He was President of the Irish National Literary Society and of the Irish Texts Society, and from 1909 to 1932 Professor of Modern Irish in the National University of Ireland.   He then retired to Ratra, County Roscommon, but after serving two terms in the Senate of the Free State, at the age of 78, in 1938, he was elected, though a Protestant, to be the first President of Eire, an office which he held till 1945.   Familiar with Gaelic from his earliest years, he wrote much in that language, using for his early works the pseudonym An Craoibhin Aoibhinn (delightful little branch).   He was one of the founders of the Abbey Theatre, and his play *The Workhouse Ward* was translated into English by Lady Gregory (q.v.).   Among his best-known works in English are *Beside the Fire* (1890), a collection of Irish folk tales, *Love Songs of Connaught* (1894), a *Literary History of Ireland* (1899), *Medieval Tales from the Irish* (1899), *The Bursting of the Bubble and Other Irish Plays* (1905), and *Legends of Saints and Sinners from the Irish* (1915).

Hyde, Edward, *see* **Clarendon, Earl of.**

Hyne, Charles John Cutcliffe Wright (11 May 1865—10 March 1944), novelist, was born at Bibury, Gloucestershire, son of a clergyman, and educated at Bradford Grammar School and Clare College, Cambridge.   At 15 he was 6 feet 3 inches in height, and later he became a keen boxer, oarsman, and yachtsman.   Before starting his writing career he travelled all over the world, then worked as a hack for a time and was even 'Aunt Ermyntrude,' giving advice to inquirers in a magazine.   His immortal character Captain Kettle first appeared in a serial in *Answers*, but the best known of his stories are those published in *Pearson's Magazine* and later collected as *The Adventures of Captain Kettle* (two series, 1898, 1899), *Captain Kettle, K.C.B.* (1903), *The Reverend Captain Kettle* (1925), and another half dozen books, winding up with *Captain Kettle, Ambassador* (1932). Others of his stories are *The Lost Continent* (1900), *McTodd* (1903), and *The Trials of Commander McTurk* (1904).   *My Joyful Life* is an autobiography.

I

Inchbald, Elizabeth (15 Oct. 1753—1 Aug. 1821), novelist, dramatist, actress, daughter of John Simpson, a farmer, was born at Sunningfield, near Bury St Edmunds. At the age of 18 she left home to seek her fortune in London, and became acquainted with Inchbald the actor, who married her in 1772. Seven years later her husband died, and for the next ten years she was on the stage, chiefly in Scotland and Ireland. She produced many plays, including *Mogul Tale* (1784), *I'll Tell you What* (1785), *Appearance is against Them* (1785), *Such Things Are* (1788), *The Married Man* (1789), *The Wedding Day* (1794), and two prose romances, *A Simple Story* (1791), one of the earliest examples of the novel of passion, and *Nature and Art* (1796). She also made a collection of plays, *The Modern Theatre* (1811), in 10 volumes. Her life was remarkable for its simplicity and frugality, and a large part of her earnings was applied in the maintenance of a delicate sister.

Inge, William Ralph (6 June 1860—26 Feb. 1954), Dean of St Paul's, was born at Crayke, Yorkshire, son of the Provost of Worcester College, Oxford, and was educated at Eton and King's College, Cambridge, where he had a brilliant career. In 1884 he was appointed an assistant master at Eton, and in 1889 a Fellow of Hertford College, Oxford. In 1905 he became vicar of All Saints Church, Kensington, in 1907 Lady Margaret Professor of Divinity and a Fellow of Jesus College, Cambridge, and finally in 1911 Dean of St Paul's, an office he held for twenty-three years. He became famous for the powerful pessimism of his outlook, and the newspapers nicknamed him 'the Gloomy Dean.' Besides writing widely on topical subjects he was an acknowledged authority on Plotinus and the Neo-Platonists. In 1930 he was made a K.C.V.O., and in 1934 he retired. His most popular books were the two series of *Outspoken Essays* (1919, 1922), and of *Lay Thoughts of a Dean* (1926, 1931), but he also wrote many philosophical works, including *Christian Mysticism* (1899), *Truth and Falsehood in Religion* (1906), *The Philosophy of Plotinus* (1918), and *Mysticism in Religion* (1947). Others of his books are *Society in Rome under the Caesars* (1886), *England* (1926), *Modernism in Literature* (1938), and *The End of an Age* (1948). *Vale* (1934) is an autobiography.

Ingelow, Jean (17 March, 1820—20 July 1897), poetess and novelist, was born at Boston, Lincolnshire, daughter of a banker, but spent the latter part of her life in London. She wrote three books of poems, of which perhaps the best known individual piece is 'The High Tide on the Coast of Lincolnshire,' one of the finest of modern ballads. She also wrote several novels, including *Off the Skelligs* (1872), *Fated to be Free* (1875), and *Sarah de Berenger* (1879), as well as some excellent stories for children, including *Mopsa the Fairy* (1869).

Innes, Cosmo (9 Sept 1798—31 July 1874), historian and antiquary, born on Deeside, was educated at Aberdeen, Glasgow, and Oxford Universities. He was called to the Scottish Bar in 1822, and was appointed Professor of Constitutional Law and History in the University of Edinburgh in 1846. He was the author of *Scotland in the Middle Ages* (1860), and *Sketches of Early Scottish History* (1861). He also edited many historical manuscripts for the Bannatyne and other antiquarian clubs.

Innes, Michael, *see* **Stewart, John Innes Mackintosh.**

Innes, Thomas (1662—28 Jan. 1744), historian, was descended from an old Roman Catholic family in Aberdeenshire. He studied in Paris at the Scots College, of which he became Vice-principal. He was the author of two learned works, *Critical Essay on the Ancient Inhabitants of the Northern Parts of Britain* (1729), and *Civil and Ecclesiastical History of Scotland 80 to 818*, published by the Spalding Club in 1853.

Ireland, William Henry (1777—17 April 1835), forger of Shakespeare manuscripts, was born in London, son of an engraver. He claimed to have discovered the manuscripts in the house of a gentleman of fortune. The forgeries included various deeds, a Protestant confession of faith by Shakespeare, letters to Ann Hathaway, Southampton, and others, a new version of *King Lear*, and a complete drama, *Vortigern and Rowena*. He completely deceived his father and various men of letters and experts, but was detected by Malone, and the representation of *Vortigern* on the stage in 1796 completed the exposure. Ireland then tried novel-writing, in which he failed. He published a confession in regard to the forgeries, and ended in poverty as a bookseller's hack.

Iron, Ralph, *see* **Schreiner, Olive.**

Irving, Edward (4 Aug. 1792—7 Dec. 1834), minister, was born at Annan, son of a tanner, and went to Edinburgh University when he was 13. While a schoolmaster at Kirkcaldy, he formed a friendship with Carlyle. Ordained to the ministry of the Church of Scotland he became, in 1819, assistant to Dr Chalmers in Glasgow, after which he went to the Scotch Church in Hatton Garden, London, where he had an almost unprecedented popularity, his admirers including De Quincey, Coleridge, Canning, Scott, and others. The effect of his spoken oratory is not preserved in his writings, and was no doubt in a considerable degree due to his striking appearance and fine voice. Soon after removing to a new church in Regent Square he began to develop his views relative to the near approach of the Second Advent; and his *Homilies on the Sacraments* (1828) involved him in a charge of heretical views on the person of Christ, which resulted in his ejection from his church, and ultimately in his deposition from the ministry. Thereafter his views as to the revival, as in the early Church, of the gifts of healing and of tongues, to which, however, he made no personal claim, underwent rapid development, and resulted in the founding of a new sect, the Catholic Apostolic Church, the adherents of which are commonly known as 'Irvingites.'

Irving, Washington (3 April 1783—28 Nov. 1859), essayist and historian, was born in New York, son of a merchant who had emigrated from Scotland. He was in his youth delicate, and his education was somewhat desultory, but his father had a fine library, of which he had the run, and he was an omnivorous reader. In 1799 he entered a law office, but a threat of consumption led to his going, in 1804, on a European tour in search of health. On his return in 1806 he was admitted to the Bar. He did not, however, practise law, but joined his brothers in business as a sleeping partner, while he devoted himself to literature. In 1807 he conducted *Salmagundi*, an amusing miscellany, and in 1809 appeared *A History of New York by Diedrich Knickerbocker*, a burlesque upon the old Dutch settlers, which has become a classic in America. He made in 1815 a second visit to Europe, from which he did not return for seventeen years. In England he was welcomed by Thomas Campbell, the poet, and introduced to Scott, whom he visited at Abbotsford in 1817. The following year the firm with which he was connected failed, and he had to look to literature for a livelihood. He produced *The Sketch-Book* (1819), which contains 'Rip Van Winkle,' and 'The Legend of Sleepy Hollow.' Through Scott's influence it was accepted by Murray, and had a great success on both sides of the Atlantic. In 1822 he went to Paris, where he began *Bracebridge Hall*, followed in 1824 by *Tales of a Traveller*. In 1826 Everett, the American minister at Madrid, invited him to come and assist him by making translations relative to Columbus, which opened up to him a new field hitherto little cultivated. The result was a series of fascinating historical and romantic works, beginning with *History of the Life and Voyages of Columbus* (1828), and including *The Conquest of Granada* (1829), *Voyages of the Companions of Columbus* (1831), *The Alhambra* (1832), *Legends of the Conquest of Spain* (1835), and *Mahomet and his Successors* (1849). Meanwhile he had returned to England in 1829, and to America in 1832. In 1842 he was appointed Minister to Spain, and in 1846 he finally returned to America. In the same year he published a *Life of Goldsmith*. *Wolfert's Roost* (1855), a collection of tales and essays, was followed by his crowning work, the *Life of Washington* (1855—9). Irving was never married: in his youth he had been engaged to a girl who died, and whose memory he faithfully cherished. His last years were spent at Sunnyside, an old Dutch house near his 'sleepy hollow.' Though not a writer of commanding power or originality, Irving, especially in his earlier works, imparted by his style and treatment a charm to every subject he touched, and was the first to give American literature a permanent standing abroad.

Isherwood, Christopher William Bradshaw (26 Aug. 1904—), novelist, was born at Disley, Cheshire, son of an army officer who was killed at Ypres in 1915; he was educated at Repton and Corpus Christi, Cambridge. In 1928 he published his first novel, *All the Conspirators*, followed in 1932 by *The Memorial*. In 1933 he went to Berlin, taught English there for four years, and after that travelled all over Europe. In collaboration with W. H. Auden (q.v.), who had been his schoolfellow, he wrote three plays, *The Dog*

Beneath the Skin (1935), *Ascent of F 6* (1937), and *On the Frontier* (1938), all with an expressionistic technique. In 1938 he and Auden made a trip to China, of which they wrote in *Journey to a War* (1939). In 1940 Isherwood went on to California and worked for Metro-Goldwyn-Mayer, and in 1946 he became an American citizen. His novels, which are strongly realistic, include *Mr Norris Changes Trains* (1935), *Goodbye to Berlin* (1939), *Prater Violet* (1945), and *The World in the Evening* (1954). *The Condor and the Cow* (1949) tells of a visit to South America, and *Lions and Shadows* (1938) is autobiographical.

J

Jacks, Lawrence Pearsall (9 Oct. 1860—17 Feb. 1955), philosopher and clergyman, was born at Nottingham and educated at London University. Entering the Ministry, he adopted Unitarian views and became assistant to Stopford Brooke (q.v.), whose daughter he married in 1889 and whose life he wrote in 1917. In 1902 he became the first editor of the *Hibbert Journal*, and in the following year he was appointed Professor of Philosophy at Manchester College, Oxford, the seat of Unitarianism. From 1915 until his retirement in 1931 he was Principal of the college and the best-known Unitarian of his time. Among his books are several telling of Smokeover, an imaginary industrial city; they include *Legends of Smokeover* (1922), *Heroes of Smokeover* (1926), and *The Last Legend of Smokeover* (1939). He also wrote *All Men Are Ghosts* (1913), *From Authority to Freedom* (1920), *Responsibility and Culture* (1925), *Constructive Citizenship* (1927), *Education Through Recreation* (1932), and *The Revolt Against Mechanism* (1934). *Confessions of an Octogenarian* (1942) and *Observations of a Nonagenarian* (1952) are autobiographical.

Jackson, Helen Hunt (15 Oct. 1830—12 Aug. 1885), novelist, was born Helen Maria Fiske at Amherst, Massachusetts, daughter of a professor of classics, and was at school with Emily Dickinson (q.v.). In 1852 she married Edward Bissell Hunt, and after his death in 1863 she turned to authorship. In 1875 she married William Sharpless Jackson. Her book *A Century of Dishonour* (1881) championed the cause of the Red Indians, and her novel *Ramona* (1884) had a similar theme. *Mercy Philbrick's Choice* (1876) is a novel based on the character of Emily Dickinson.

Jackson, Holbrook (31 Dec. 1874—15 June 1948), literary historian, was born in Liverpool. Almost entirely self-educated, he began earning his living at 15, and published his first articles at 16. His first book was a study of Edward FitzGerald (1899). In 1907 he became joint editor of the *New Age*, and as a freelance wrote on a great variety of subjects. He was the author of the first study of Bernard Shaw (1907), and followed this with a biography of *William Morris* (1908), and *Great English Novelists* (1908). In 1910 he became associated with T. P. O'Connor, and edited both *T.P.'s Magazine* and *T.P.'s Weekly*. In 1913 he published *The Eighteen Nineties*, the best study of that period. From 1917 to 1924 he owned and edited a literary journal, *To-Day*. Among his other works are *Occasions* (1922), *End Papers* (1923), *The Anatomy of Bibliomania* (1930), *The Printing of Books* (1938), *Bookman's Holiday* (1945), *The Reading of Books* (1946), and *Dreamers of Dreams* (1948).

Jacob, Naomi Ellington (1 July 1889—   ), novelist, was born at Ripon, Yorkshire, and educated at Middlesborough High School. At 15 she started work as a teacher. In the First World

War she was a supervisor in a munition factory, developed consumption, and had to spend three years in a sanatorium. After that she went on the stage with considerable success, and published her first novel, *Jacob Ussher* (1926). In 1930 she was ordered south for her health and went to Italy, where she lived at Sirmione on Lake Garda till 1939, after which she worked with E.N.S.A. Her novels include *The Loaded Stick* (1935), *Barren Metal* (1937), *Straws in Amber* (1938), *The Cap of Youth* (1941), *White Wool* (1944), *Passage Perilous* (1948), and *Morning Will Come* (1953). She also wrote a life of Marie Lloyd (1936) and a series of autobiographical books, *Me : A Chronicle About Other People* (1933), *Me—Again* (1937), *Me and the Mediterranean* (1945), *Me—Looking Back* (1950), and *Me—Likes and Dislikes* (1954).

Jacob, Violet (1863—9 Sept. 1946), poetess and novelist, was born at Montrose, her maiden name being Violet Mary Augusta Frederica Kennedy-Erskine. She married Major Arthur Otway Jacob, of the 20th Hussars, and spent some years in India. Her novels include *The Sheep-Stealers* (1902), *The Interloper* (1904), *The History of Aythan Waring* (1908), and *Flemington* (1911). Volumes of her poems, many of them in the Angus dialect, are *Songs of Angus* (two series, 1916, 1918), *Bonnie Joann* (1922), and *Northern Lights* (1927); her *Scottish Poems* were collected in 1944. *The Lairds of Dun* (1931) is a study in the landed history of her own district. In 1936 she was made an honorary LL.D. of Edinburgh.

Jacobs, William Wymark (8 Sept. 1863—1 Sept. 1943), short-story writer, was born at Wapping, where his father was overseer of a wharf. From 1883 to 1899 he worked in the Savings Bank department of the Post Office, and started writing his delightfully humorous stories of coasting vessels and their crews. Many of these tales were made up during walking tours he took with Will Owen, his illustrator, whose pictures seem inseparable from Jacobs's work. *Many Cargoes* (1896), the first collection in book form, was followed by *The Skipper's Wooing* (1897), *Sea Urchins* (1898), *A Master of Craft* (1900), *Light Freights* (1901), *The Lady of the Barge* (1902), *Odd Craft* (1903), *Short Cruises* (1907), *Ship's Company* (1911), *Night Watches* (1914), *Deep Waters* (1919), and *Sea Whispers* (1926). Among the humorous stories occur one or two highly effective tales of horror, of which 'The Monkey's Paw' is the most famous. He also wrote a number of plays.

James I, King of Scotland (July 1394—20 Feb. 1437), poet, the third son of Robert III, was born at Dunfermline. In 1406 he was sent for safety and education to France, but on the voyage was taken prisoner by an English ship, and conveyed to England, where for 18 years he remained confined in various places, but chiefly in the Tower of London. He was then ransomed and, after his marriage to Lady Jane or Joan Beaufort, daughter of the Earl of Somerset, and the heroine of *The Kingis Quair* (or King's Book), crowned at Scone in 1424. While in England he had been carefully educated, and on his return to his native country endeavoured to reduce its turbulent nobility to due subjection, and to introduce various reforms. His efforts, however, ended disastrously in his assassination in the monastery of the Black Friars, Perth. James was a man of great natural capacity both intellectual and practical—an ardent student and a poet of no mean order. In addition to *The Kingis Quair*, one of the finest love poems in existence, and *A Ballad of Good Counsel*, which are very generally attributed to him, he has been more doubtfully credited with *Peeblis to the Play* and *Christis Kirke on the Greene*.

James VI of Scotland and I of England (19 June 1566—27 March 1625), born in Edinburgh, son of Mary Queen of Scots and Lord Darnley, had a very complete education from various tutors, including the erudite George Buchanan (q.v.). His earliest publications were *Essays of a Prentice in the Divine Art of Poesy* (1584) and *Poetical Exercises at Vacant Hours* (1591), containing a number of poems in Scots. But as a writer he is best known for his *Daemonology* (1599), a learned treatise on witchcraft; the *Basilicon Doron* (1599), written to instruct his son Henry in the duties of kingship; and the entertaining *Counterblast Against Tobacco* (1604).

James, George Payne Rainsford (9 Aug. 1801—9 May 1860), novelist and historian, son of a London doctor, was for many years British Consul at various places in the United States and on the Continent. At an early age he began to write historical romances, and continued his production with such industry that his works reach to 100 volumes. This excessive rapidity was fatal to his permanent reputation, but his books had considerable immediate popularity. Among them are *Richelieu* (1829), *Philip Augustus* (1831), *The Huguenot* (1838), *The Robber* (1838), *Henry of Guise* (1839), *The Man at Arms* (1840), *The King's Highway* (1840), *Agincourt* (1844). In addition to his novels he wrote *Memoirs of Great Commanders*, a *Life of the Black Prince*, and other historical and biographical works. He held the honorary office of Historiographer Royal.

James, Henry, O.M. (15 April 1843—28 Feb. 1916), novelist, was born in New York, son of a theological writer and brother of William James (q.v.); his father was wealthy and he was able to follow his own inclinations. A long visit to Europe during his boyhood laid the foundation of the passion which he had all his life for European culture. After an unsystematic education which included the study of law at Harvard, in 1865 he began contributing reviews, sketches, and short stories to various periodicals. In 1871 his first novel, *Watch and Ward*, appeared serially, and in 1875 his first volume of short stories was published. In the same year he removed to Europe, and in 1876 settled in London, where he lived for more than twenty years.

It has been generally said that his work falls into three periods, which Philip Guedalla irreverently labelled James I, James II, and the Old Pretender. In the first he was occupied with the impact of American life on the older European civilization. To this period belong *Roderick Hudson* (1875), his first successful novel, which marks the end of his apprentice stage, and the still greater *Portrait of a Lady*

(1881); others include *The American* (1877), *Daisy Miller* (1879), *The Princess Casamassima* (1886), and *The Bostonians* (1886). His middle period, during which he developed purely English themes, begins with *The Tragic Muse* (1890) and continues with *The Spoils of Poynton* (1897), *What Maisie Knew* (1897), and *The Awkward Age* (1899). In his third period he returned to his original theme of the contrast between American and European character, and concentrated on depicting psychological interplay with the minimum of action, thus bringing the accusation that 'nothing ever happens' in his books. The last three novels published in his lifetime were *The Wings of a Dove* (1902), *The Ambassadors* (1903), and *The Golden Bowl* (1904). Two long novels, *The Ivory Tower* and *The Sense of the Past* were left unfinished at his death.

His collections of short stories include *Terminations* (1895), *The Two Magics* (1898), and *The Altar of the Dead* (1909). Between 1890 and 1894 he tried his hand as a dramatist, but without great success. He also wrote a number of critical works, including *French Poets and Novelists* (1878) and a book on Hawthorne (1879). *Portraits of Places* (1883), *A Little Tour in France* (1885), and *Essays in London and Elsewhere* (1893) are descriptive sketches of travel, and *The American Scene* (1906) relates his impressions on returning to America after twenty years' absence. He also published three volumes of reminiscences, *A Small Boy and Others* (1913), *Notes of a Son and Brother* (1914), and *The Middle Years* (1917), which is unfinished; his *Letters* were edited in 1920. He became naturalized as a British subject in 1915, received the Order of Merit at the New Year Honours of 1916, and shortly afterwards died at Chelsea. He was never married. For the collected edition of his works, begun in 1907, he wrote a series of critical prefaces which summarize his theories of the art of fiction. As a writer he is subtle and fastidious, portraying with delicate psychological nuances the complex characters of ultra-civilized people.

James, Montague Rhodes, O.M. (1 Aug. 1862—12 June 1936), antiquary and palaeographer, was born at Goodnestone, Kent, where his father was curate, and educated at Eton and Cambridge, where he became Director of the Fitzwilliam Museum from 1893 to 1908. In 1905 he was elected Provost of King's, his old college, from 1913 to 1915 was Vice-Chancellor of Cambridge, and in 1918 became Provost of Eton. His work as a palaeographer was enormous. Between 1895 and 1932 he catalogued the manuscripts of every Cambridge college, as well as those at Eton, Lambeth, Westminster Abbey, the John Rylands Library, and Aberdeen University Library. He also did most valuable work on the Apocrypha, as well as writing extensively on the art and literature of the Middle Ages. In more popular vein were his two collections of *Ghost Stories of an Antiquary* (1905, 1911). In 1903 he was elected a Fellow of the British Academy and in 1930 he received the Order of Merit; he also held honorary degrees from Oxford, Cambridge, St Andrews, and Dublin.

James, William (11 Jan. 1842—26 Aug. 1910), philosopher and psychologist, was born in New York, son of a theologian and brother of Henry James (q.v.). After a boyhood largely spent in travelling over Europe with the family he entered the Lawrence Scientific School in 1861 and attended Harvard medical school in 1866, taking his degree in 1868. In 1872 he was appointed Instructor in Physiology at Harvard, and lectured on the relations of physiology with psychology. In 1880 he was appointed Assistant Professor of Philosophy and created the first American laboratory of psychology, and in 1884 he joined in founding the American Society for Psychical Research. His important work *Principles of Psychology* appeared in 1890. His philosophy has been described as a union of empiricism and voluntarism. Others of his works are *The Will to Believe and Other Essays* (1897), *The Varieties of Religious Experience* (1902), and *Pragmatism* (1907). In 1908 he delivered the Hibbert Lectures at Oxford, published with the title *A Pluralistic Universe.*

Jameson, Anna Brownell (17 May 1794—17 March 1860), critic, was born in Dublin, daughter of D. Brownell Murphy, a miniature painter. In 1798 the family moved to England and in 1825 she married Robert Jameson, a barrister, who later became Attorney-General of Ontario. The union, however, did not turn out happily: a separation took place, and Mrs Jameson turned her attention to literature, and specially to subjects connected with art. Among many other works she produced *Loves of the Poets* (1829), *Celebrated Female Sovereigns* (1831), *Beauties of the Court of Charles II* (1833), *Hand Book to the Galleries of Art in London* (1842), *Early Italian Painters* (1845), and *Sacred and Legendary Art* (1848). She is best remembered by her book *Shakespeare's Heroines*, formerly entitled *Characteristics of Women* (1832).

Jameson, Margaret Storm (1897—   ), novelist, was born at Whitby, Yorkshire, and came of a family of shipbuilders. Educated at Leeds University and London, she was at different times publicity writer, dramatic critic, and editor. She married Professor Guy Patterson Chapman. Three of her finest novels, *The Lovely Ship* (1927), *The Voyage Home* (1930), and *A Richer Dust* (1931), form a trilogy telling of a shipbuilding family like her own. Others of her books are *The Three Kingdoms* (1926), *Farewell to Youth* (1928), *Cousin Honore* (1940) with its sequel *Cloudless May* (1943), *The Other Side* (1945), *The Black Laurel* (1948), *The Green Man* (1952), and *The Hidden River* (1955). Among her critical works are *Modern Drama in Europe* (1920), which she wrote as a university thesis, and an historical essay, *The Decline of Merrie England* (1930). She also wrote *Full Circle* (1928), a play in one act, and an autobiography, *No Time Like the Present* (1933).

Jamieson, John (3 March 1759—12 July 1838), minister and lexicographer, was born in Glasgow, son of a Secession minister. He went to Glasgow University at the age of nine, then studied theology in Edinburgh. Ordained in 1779, he became a pastor in Forfar. His first literary efforts were poems, which had little merit. Of his theological works *Sermons on the Heart* (1790) was the most popular, while his *Vindication of the Doctrine of Scripture* (1795), a counterblast to Dr Priestley's *History of Early Opinions*, earned him a D.D. of the

College of New Jersey. In 1797 he was transferred from Forfar to Edinburgh, where he had wider literary opportunities. In 1808 he published two volumes of his great *Etymological Dictionary of the Scottish Language*, which had grown out of a collection he made of non-English words used in his parish; two supplementary volumes were added in 1825. In spite of many defects, this work, which he kept revising till his death, remained the standard Scots dictionary for a century and a half. In recognition of its value he was made an Associate of the Royal Literary Society.

Jeans, Sir James Hopwood, O.M. (11 Sept. 1877—16 Sept. 1946), astronomer, was born at Southport, Lancashire, and educated at Merchant Taylors' and Trinity College, Cambridge, of which he became a Fellow in 1901. From 1905 to 1909 he was Professor of Applied Mathematics at Princeton in America, then returned to Cambridge as Stokes Lecturer. From 1935 till his death he was Professor of Astronomy at the Royal Institution. A follower of Einstein and Planck, he did much important scientific work, but is best known for his popular books on astronomy, which include *The Universe Around Us* (1929), *The Mysterious Universe* (1930), *New Backgrounds of Science* (1933), *Through Space and Time* (1934), and *Physics and Philosophy* (1942). A Fellow of the Royal Society, he was President of the Royal Astronomical Society from 1925 to 1927, and of the British Association for the Advancement of Science in 1934. He was knighted in 1928 and received the Order of Merit in 1939.

Jebb, Sir Richard Claverhouse, O.M. (27 Aug. 1841—9 Dec. 1905), classical scholar, got his second name from being born in Dundee while his parents were visiting his grandfather, the Dean of Brechin. Brought up in Dublin, he was educated at St Columba's College, Charterhouse, and Trinity College, Cambridge, where he had a brilliant career. In 1875 he became Professor of Greek at Glasgow, and from 1889 held the corresponding chair at Cambridge, for a time representing Cambridge University in Parliament. His books include *A Primer of Greek Literature* (1877), *Attic Orators* (1879), and *An Introduction to Homer* (1887), but his greatest work was his monumental edition of the plays of Sophocles, one volume being devoted to each play; it is reckoned the best English commentary on any classical author. He was one of the founders of the Society for the Promotion of Hellenic Studies and of the British School of Archaeology at Athens, was an original Fellow of the British Academy, and held many honorary degrees. He was knighted in 1900 and received the Order of Merit in 1905.

Jefferies, Richard (6 Nov. 1848—14 Aug. 1887), naturalist and novelist, son of a farmer, was born near Swindon, Wiltshire. He began his literary career on the staff of a local newspaper, and first attracted attention by a letter in *The Times* on the Wiltshire labourer. Thereafter he wrote for the *Pall Mall Gazette*, in which first appeared his *Gamekeeper at Home* (1878), and *Wild Life in a Southern County* (1879). Both these works are full of minute observation and vivid description of country life. They were followed by *The Amateur*

Poacher (1880), *Wood Magic* (1881), *Round about a Great Estate* (1881), *The Open Air* (1885), and others on similar subjects. Among his novels are *Bevis* (1882), in which he draws on his own childish memories, and *After London, or Wild England* (1885), a romance of the future, when London has ceased to exist. *The Story of My Heart* (1883) is an idealized picture of his inner life. Jeffries died after a painful illness, which lasted for six years. In his own line, that of depicting with an intense feeling for nature all the elements of country and wild life, he has had few equals.

Jeffers, John Robinson (10 Jan. 1887—   ), poet, born at Pittsburgh, Pennsylvania, son of a teacher of theology, studied medicine at the University of Southern California and forestry at the University of Washington; at college he was a champion athlete. Having built himself a house on the Californian coast near Carmel, he lived there in seclusion, drawing from the primitive country people inspiration for his sombre allegories. The tragic and horrible are presented in his work with a kind of moral despair. Of some 20 books of verse the best-known are *Tamar* (1924), *Roan Stallion* (1925), *Cawdor* (1928), *Thurso's Landing* (1932), *Give Your Heart to the Hawks* (1933), *Be Angry to the Sun* (1941), *The Double Axe* (1948), and *Hungerfield* (1954). His *Selected Poetry* was published in 1938, and in 1946 he made a free rendering of the *Medea* of Euripides.

Jefferson, Thomas (13 April 1743—4 July 1826), 3rd President of the United States, was born at Shadwell, Virginia, son of a landowner. Educated at William and Mary College, he studied law and was admitted to the Bar in 1767. In 1770 he was elected a member of the Virginia House of Burgesses, and in 1774 he published *A Summary View of the Rights of British America*. At the age of 33 he was chosen chairman of the committee appointed to draw up the Declaration of Independence in 1776, and the finished document was largely his work. From 1779 to 1781 he was Governor of Virginia, and in 1819 he founded the University of Virginia; his *Notes on the State of Virginia* was published in 1784. Secretary of State under Washington, he became Vice-President and finally from 1801 to 1809 President of the United States. His *Works* were published in 10 volumes (1893—99) and his *Autobiography* in 1914.

Jeffrey, Francis (23 Oct. 1773—26 Jan. 1850), critic and political writer, son of a legal official, born in Edinburgh, was educated at the High School there, and at Glasgow and Oxford, where, however, he remained for a few months only. Returning to Edinburgh he studied law, and was called to the Bar in 1794. Brought up as a Tory, he early imbibed Whig principles, and this, in the then political state of Scotland, long hindered his professional advancement. Gradually, however, his ability, acuteness, and eloquence carried him to the front of his profession. He was elected Dean of the Faculty of Advocates in 1829 and, on the accession to power of the Whigs in 1830, became Lord Advocate, and had a large share in passing the Reform Bill, in so far as it related to Scotland. In 1832 he was elected M.P. for Edinburgh, and in 1834 he was raised to the Bench as Lord Jeffrey. His literary fame rests on his work in connection with the *Edinburgh Review*, which he edited from its commencement in 1802 until 1829, and to which he was a constant contributor. The founding of this periodical by a group of young men of brilliant talents and liberal sympathies, among whom were Brougham, Sydney Smith, and F. Horner, constituted the opening of a new epoch in the literary and political progress of the country. Jeffrey's contributions ranged over literary criticism, biography, politics, and ethics and, especially in respect of the first, exercised a profound influence; he was, in fact, regarded as the greatest literary critic of his age, and in spite of his failure to appreciate the poetry of the Romantic Revival, he did much to raise the standard of public taste. A selection of his papers, made by himself, was published in 1844.

Jeffrey, William (26 Sept. 1896—11 Feb. 1946), poet and journalist, was born at Kirk of Shotts, Lanarkshire, where his father was a colliery manager, and educated at Wishaw High School and Glasgow University. During the First World War he served in France with the Royal Garrison Artillery and was gassed. Taking up journalism in 1920, he became a leader-writer and dramatic critic on the *Glasgow Herald*. His first volume of verse, *Prometheus Returns* (1921) was followed by over half a dozen others, including *The Wise Men Come To Town* (1923), *The Lamb of Lomond* (1926), *Mountain Songs* (1928), *Eagle of Coruisk* (1933), and *Sea Glimmer* (1947), which marked him as one of the leading poets of the modern Scottish renaissance. *Selected Poems* with a memoir appeared in 1951.

Jepson, Edgar Alfred (28 Nov. 1863—11 April 1938), novelist, born at Kenilworth, Warwickshire, was educated at Leamington College and Oxford, where he got his blue for cross-country running. In 1889 he was a schoolmaster at Newport, Monmouth, and from 1890 to 1893 at Harrison College, Barbados. Returning to London, he became editor of *Vanity Fair*, and wrote a large number of romances of adventure, including *Sibyl Falcon* (1895), *The Keepers of the People* (1898), *The Girl's Head* (1910), *The Gillingham Rubies* (1915), *The Loudwater Mystery* (1919), *The Tragedies of Mr Pip* (1926), and *The Moon Gods* (1930). He also published a number of delightful stories about children, including *The Lady Noggs, Peeress* (1906), and *Pollyooly* (1911), each of which had two sequels, and *The Determined Twins* (1913). *Memories of a Victorian* (1933) and *Memories of an Edwardian* (1937) are autobiographical.

Jerome, Jerome Klapka (2 May 1859—14 June 1927), novelist and playwright, son of a Nonconformist preacher, was born at Walsall, Staffordshire. He got his peculiar middle name from George Klapka, an exiled Hungarian who was a frequent guest at the house. Later they moved to Poplar, and young Jerome was educated at Marylebone Grammar School, afterwards becoming a railway clerk at Euston Station. He was at different times reporter and schoolmaster, and also tried the stage, about which he wrote in *On the Stage and Off* (1885). In 1889 he became popular as a writer with *Idle Thoughts of an Idle Fellow* and his most famous book, *Three Men in a Boat,* which sold a million (pirated) copies in America. It was followed by *Three Men on the Bummel* (1900), an account of a tour in Germany, and a novel, *Paul Kelver* (1902). In 1892 Jerome was joint editor of *The Idler*, and in 1893 started his own twopenny weekly *To-Day*, with Stevenson's *Ebb-Tide* as the serial, but a costly lawsuit brought it to an end. Of his plays the most famous is *The Passing of the Third Floor Back* (1908), the scene of which is a Bloomsbury boarding-house. In the First World War Jerome was an ambulance driver. His autobiography, *My Life and Times*, appeared in 1926.

Jerrold, Douglas (3 Aug. 1893—   ), historian and editor, great-grandson of Douglas William Jerrold (q.v.), was born at Scarborough and educated at Westminster and Oxford. During the First World War he served with the Royal Naval Division, of which he wrote an account later; he also wrote *The War on Land, 1914—1918* (1928). Entering the Civil Service, he was first with the Ministry of Food and then with the Treasury. From 1930 to 1936 he was editor of the *English Review*, and from 1945 of the *New English Review*. His books include *An Introduction to the History of England* (1949), *England, Past, Present, and Future* (1950), and *The Lie About the West* (1954), a reply to Professor Toynbee's theory of the existing world situation. He also wrote two novels, *The Truth About Quex* (1927) and *Storm Over Europe* (1930).

Jerrold, Douglas William (3 Jan. 1803—8 June 1857), dramatist and humorist, was born in London, son of an actor, and himself appeared as a child upon the stage. From his tenth to his twelfth year he was a midshipman in the Navy. He then became apprentice to a printer, devoting all his spare time to self-education. He early began to contribute to periodicals, and in his eighteenth year he was engaged by the Coburg Theatre as a writer of short dramatic pieces. In 1829 he made a great success by his drama *Black-eyed Susan*, which he followed up by a series of plays, including *Bubbles of the Day* (1841), *Retired from Business* (1851), and *The Heart of Gold* (1854). In 1840 he became editor of a publication, *Heads of the People*, to which Thackeray was a contributor, and in which some of the best of his own work appeared. He was one of the leading contributors to *Punch*, in which *Mrs Caudle's Curtain Lectures* came out, and from 1852 he edited *Lloyd's Weekly Newspaper*. Among his novels are *St Giles and St James*, and *The Story of a Feather*. He had a great reputation as a wit.

Jesse, Edward (14 Jan. 1780—28 March 1868), writer on natural history, was born at Hutton-Cranswick, near Halifax, where his father was vicar. He became secretary to Lord Dartmouth, lived for a time in Richmond Park, where he developed his love for nature, and in 1830 was appointed Deputy Surveyor of the Royal Parks. His works include *Gleanings in Natural History* in three series (1832, 1833, 1835), *An Angler's Rambles* (1836), and *Lectures on Natural History* (1861). He also edited Walton's *Compleat Angler* and White's *Selborne*.

Jesse, Friniwyd Tennyson (1889—6 Aug. 1958), novelist, was the daughter of a clergyman and a great-niece of Tennyson the poet. At

N*

15 she studied painting, but turned to journalism and worked as a
freelance correspondent in the First World War, of which she wrote in
The Sword of Deborah (1919). After the armistice she worked for the
National Relief Commission of which Herbert C. Hoover was the
head. In 1918 she married H. M. Harwood, doctor and playwright,
and with him wrote a number of plays, including *Billeted* (1920), *The
Pelican* (1926), and *How to Be Healthy Though Married* (1930).
During the Second World War they collaborated in a series of war-
time letters collected as *London Front* (1940) and *While London
Burns* (1942). Her novels include *The Milky Way* (1913), *Secret
Bread* (1917), *The White Riband* (1921), *Tom Fool* (1926), *Moonraker*
(1927), *A Pin to See the Peepshow* (1934), which shows her interest in
criminology, *Act of God* (1936), and *The Alabaster Cup* (1950). She
also published several collections of short stories and a book of poems,
The Happy Bride (1920).

Jesse, John Heneage (1815—7 July 1874), historical writer, son
of Edward Jesse (q.v.), was educated at Eton and became a clerk in
the Admiralty. He wrote a series of court memoirs, and *Celebrated
Etonians* (1875).

Jevons, William Stanley (1 Sept. 1835—13 Aug. 1882), logician and
economist, was born in Liverpool, son of an iron merchant, his mother
being the daughter of W. Roscoe (q.v.). He was educated at the
Mechanics Institute High School, Liverpool, and at University
College, London. After studying chemistry for some time he
received in 1853 the appointment of assayer to the mint at Sydney,
where he remained until 1859, when he resigned his appointment,
and came home to study mathematics and economics. While in
Australia he had been a contributor to the *Empire* newspaper, and
soon after his return home he published *Remarks on the Australian
Goldfields*, wrote in various scientific periodicals, and from time to
time published important papers on economic subjects. In 1863
he was appointed tutor, and in 1866, Professor of Logic, Political
Economy, and Mental and Moral Philosophy in Owen's College,
Manchester. In 1864 he published *Pure Logic* and *The Coal Question*;
other works were *Elementary Lessons in Logic* (1870), *Principles of
Science* (1874), and *Investigations in Currency and Finance* (1884).
He was drowned while bathing alone near Hastings.

Jewett, Sarah Orne (3 Sept. 1849—24 June 1909), novelist, daughter
of a doctor, was born and spent most of her life at South Berwick,
Maine. She had little formal education, but read widely in her
father's library. In 1869 she had a story published in the *Atlantic
Monthly*, and her place among writers was established by *Deephaven*
(1877), a collection of sketches. She followed this with over a dozen
novels and collections of short stories depicting the old provincial
life of her own countryside; they include *A Country Doctor* (1884),
A Marsh Island (1885), *The King of Folly Island* (1888), *Tales of
New England* (1890), *The Country of the Pointed Firs* (1895), generally
regarded as her best, and *The Tory Lover* (1901). Her *Letters* were
printed in 1911.

Jewsbury, Geraldine Endsor (1812—23 Sept. 1880), novelist, born at Measham, Derbyshire, was a friend of the Carlyles. She wrote several novels, of which *Zoe*, *The Half-Sisters*, and *Constance Herbert* may be mentioned. She also wrote stories for children, and was a contributor to various magazines.

Joad, Cyril Edwin Mitchinson (12 Aug. 1891—9 April 1953), philosopher, born at Southampton, was educated at Blundell's School, Tiverton, and Oxford. During the First World War he was a conscientious objector. For sixteen years he worked in the Civil Service, first at the Board of Trade and then at the Ministry of Labour. In 1930 he became head of the department of philosophy and psychology, Birkbeck College, London, which gave him a D.Lit. in 1936. From 1941 to 1947 he was a prominent member of the B.B.C. 'Brains Trust.' His best-known books are *Essays in Common Sense Philosophy* (1919), *Introduction to Modern Political Theory* (1924), *Thrasymachus: or, The Future of Morals* (1924), *Mind and Matter* (1925), *Diogenes: or, The Future of Leisure* (1928), *The Meaning of Life* (1929), *Great Philosophies of the World* (1931), *Guide to Modern Thought* (1933), *Guide to Philosophy* (1936), *Philosophy for Our Times* (1940), *The Future of Life* (1944), *Decadence: A Philosophical Enquiry* (1948), *Introduction to Contemporary Knowledge* (1951), *The Pleasure of Being Oneself* (1951), and *The Recovery of Belief* (1952). *The Book of Joad* (1937), is autobiographical.

John of Salisbury (1120?—25 Oct. 1180), prelate, was born at Old Sarum and studied at Paris under Abelard. He became secretary to Theobald, Archbishop of Canterbury, and retained the office under Becket. In 1176 he was made Bishop of Chartres. He wrote in eight books, *Polycraticus, seu De Nugis Curialium et Vestigiis Philosophorum* (Polycraticus, or, Concerning the Trifles of the Courtiers and the Footsteps of the Philosophers). In it he treats of pastimes, flatterers, tyrannicide, the duties of kings and knights, virtue and vice, glory, and the right of the Church to remove kings if in its opinion they failed in their duty. He also wrote lives of Anselm and Becket. He was one of the greatest scholars of the Middle Ages.

John of Trevisa (1326—1402), translator, was born at Crocadon, near Saltash, Cornwall. Educated at Oxford, he was a Fellow of Exeter from 1362 to 1369 and a Fellow of Queen's from then till 1379. He became vicar of Berkeley, Gloucestershire, chaplain to the 4th Lord Berkeley, and canon of Westbury. He was a diligent translator, his greatest work being the rendering into English of the Latin *Polychronicon* or universal history of Ralph Higden, to which he added an introductory 'Dialogue on Translations' and a short continuation; written in 1387, it is one of the earliest examples of English prose.

Johnson, Lionel Pigot (15 March 1867—4 Oct. 1902), poet and critic, was born at Broadstairs, Kent, son of an army officer, and educated at Winchester and Oxford. Settling in London, he lived a secluded life, surrounded by books like an Oxford don, and kept himself by writing critical articles and reviews. In 1891 he was converted to Roman Catholicism and became deeply interested in the Irish Renascence. In his two publications, *Poems* (1895) and *Ireland and Other Poems* (1897), he drew much of his inspiration from the beauty of Celtic legend, though his most famous poem is 'By the Statue of King Charles at Charing Cross.' His health became undermined by drink and he died as the result of a fall in Fleet Street, just after writing an elegy on Walter Pater, who was one of the chief influences on his work. His *Reviews and Critical Papers* were published in 1921.

Johnson, Pamela Hansford (29 May 1912—   ), novelist, was born in south London and educated at Clapham County Secondary School. Her mother and aunt were both actresses in Henry Irving's company. After working for four years in a bank she published her first novel, *This Bed Thy Centre* (1935) and made literature her career. Among her other novels are *The Trojan Brothers* (1944), *An Avenue of Stone* (1947), *The Philistines* (1949), *Catherine Carter* (1952), *An Impossible Marriage* (1954), *The Last Resort* (1956), and *The Humbler Creation* (1959). She also wrote studies of Thomas Wolfe (1947) and Ivy Compton-Burnett (1951), and a play, *Corinth House* (1948). She was married first in 1936 to Gordon Stewart, then in 1950 to the novelist Sir Charles P. Snow (q.v.).

Johnson, Richard (baptized 24 May 1573, died 1659?), miscellaneous writer, was born in London, of which he became a freeman. While still an apprentice he wrote *The Nine Worthies of London* (1592). But his chief work was *The Famous History of the Seven Champions of Christendom* (1596), one of the most popular prose romances of the time, the seven champions being St George of England, St David of Wales, St Andrew of Scotland, St Patrick of Ireland, St Denis of France, St James of Spain, and St Anthony of Italy; a second part was published in 1608 and a third in 1616. In 1607 there appeared three works by Johnson: *The Pleasant Walks of Moorfields*; *The Pleasant Conceits of Old Hobson, the Merry Londoner*; and *The Most Pleasant History of Tom a Lincoln*. Other publications of his were *Anglorum Lachrimae* (1603), a lament for Queen Elizabeth; *Look on me, London* (1613), a pamphlet on London abuses; *The Golden Garland of Princely Pleasures and Delicate Delights* (1620), a collection of verse; *The History of Tom Thumb* (1621); and *Dainty Conceits* (1630).

Johnson, Samuel (1649—May 1703), clergyman and pamphleteer, is sometimes called 'the Whig' to distinguish him from his great namesake. Of humble extraction, he was educated at St Paul's School and Cambridge, took orders, and became domestic chaplain to Lord William Russell. He attacked James II in *Julian the Apostate* (1682), and was imprisoned. He continued, however, his attacks on the Government by pamphlets, and did much to influence the public mind in favour of the Revolution. Dryden gave him a place in *Absalom and Achitophel* as 'Ben-Jochanan.' After the Revolution he received a pension, but considered himself insufficiently rewarded by a Deanery, which he declined.

Johnson, Samuel (18 Sept. 1709—13 Dec. 1784), lexicographer, critic, poet, son of a bookseller at Lichfield, received his early education at his native town, and went in 1728 to Pembroke College, Oxford, but had, owing to poverty, to leave without taking a degree. For a short time he was usher in a school at Market Bosworth, but found the position so irksome that he threw it up, and gained a meagre livelihood by working for a publisher in Birmingham. In 1735 he published anonymously a translation of Father Lobo's *Voyage to Abyssinia*, and in the same year married Elizabeth Porter, a widow twenty years his senior, who brought him £800, and to whom he was sincerely attached. He started an academy at Edial, near Lichfield, which, however, had no success, only three boys, one of whom was David Garrick (q.v.), attending it. Accordingly, this venture was given up, and Johnson in 1737 went to London accompanied by Garrick. He contributed to *The Gentleman's Magazine*, furnishing the parliamentary debates in very free and generally much improved form, under the title of 'Debates of the Senate of Lilliput.' In 1738 appeared *London*, a satire imitated from Juvenal which, published anonymously, attracted the notice of Pope. His next work was the life of his unfortunate friend Savage (q.v.) in 1744; and in 1747 he issued the prospectus of his great *Dictionary of the English Language*. Another satire, *The Vanity of Human Wishes*, appeared in 1749, and in the same year *Irene*, a tragedy, which was however a failure. His next venture was the starting of the *Rambler*, a paper somewhat on the lines of the *Spectator*; but, sententious and grave, it had none of the lightness and grace of its model, and likewise lacked its popularity. It was almost solely the work of Johnson himself, and was carried on twice a week for two years until the death of his wife 'dear Tetty' in 1752.

In 1755 his *Dictionary* appeared. The patronage of Lord Chesterfield (q.v.), which he had vainly sought, was then offered, but proudly rejected in a letter which has become a classic. The work made him famous, and Oxford conferred upon him the degree of M.A. He had become the friend of Reynolds and Goldsmith; Burke and others were soon added. The *Idler*, a somewhat less ponderous successor of the *Rambler*, appeared in 1758—60, and the didactic romance, *Rasselas, Prince of Abyssinia*, was written in a week's time in 1759 to meet the funeral expenses of his mother, who then died at the age of 90. At last the tide of his fortunes turned. A pension of £300 was conferred upon him in 1762, and the rest of his days were spent in honour, and such comfort as the melancholy to which he was subject permitted. In 1763 he made the acquaintance, so important for posterity, of James Boswell; and it was probably in the same year that he founded 'The Club,' later known as 'The Literary Club.' In 1764 he was introduced to Henry Thrale, a wealthy brewer, and for years spent much of his time, an honoured guest, in his family. The kindness and attentions of Mrs Thrale, described by Carlyle as 'a bright papilionaceous creature, whom the elephant loved to play with, and wave to and fro upon his trunk,' were a refreshment and solace to him. In 1765 his edition of Shakespeare came out, and his last great work was the *Lives of the Poets*, in 10 volumes (1779—81). He had in 1775 published his *Journey to the Western Isles of Scotland*, an account of a tour made in the company of Boswell. His last years were darkened by the loss of friends such as Goldsmith and Thrale, and by an estrangement from Mrs. Thrale, on her marriage with Piozzi, an Italian musician. Notwithstanding a lifelong and morbid fear of death, his last illness was borne with fortitude and calmness, soothed by the pious attentions of Reynolds and Burke. He was buried in Westminster Abbey, and a monument in St Paul's was erected by the Club. Statues of him were also erected in Lichfield and Uttoxeter. He had received from Oxford and Dublin the degree of LL.D.

Though of rough and domineering manners, Johnson had the tenderest of hearts, and his house was for years the home of several persons, such as Mrs Williams and Levett, the surgeon, who had no claim upon him but their helplessness and friendlessness. As Goldsmith aptly said, he 'had nothing of the bear but his skin.' His outstanding qualities were honesty and courage, and these characterize all his works. One of the greatest and most honourable figures in English letters, he well merited the title jokingly given him by Smollett, of 'the Great Cham of literature.' Boswell's marvellous *Life* has made Johnson's bodily appearance, dress, and manners more familiar to posterity than those of any other man—the large, unwieldy form, the face seamed with scrofula, the purblind eyes, the spasmodic movements, the sonorous voice, even the brown suit, metal buttons, black worsted stockings, and bushy wig, the conversation so full of matter, strength, sense, wit, and prejudice, superior in force and sparkle to the sounding, but often wearisome periods of his written style. Of his works the two most important are the *Dictionary*, which, though now superseded, made an epoch in the history of the language, and the *Lives of the Poets*, many of them deformed by prejudice and wholly inadequate criticism, others almost perfect in their kind, and the whole written in a style less pompous and more natural and lively than his earlier works.

In addition to Boswell's *Life* there is much information about Johnson in a *Life* by Sir John Hawkins (1787), and in Mrs Piozzi's *Anecdotes of the Late Samuel Johnson* (1786). His *Letters* were edited in three volumes by R. W. Chapman in 1953.

Johnston, Arthur (1587—1641), doctor and poet, born at Caskieben, Aberdeenshire, studied medicine at Padua. After living for about twenty years in France, he returned to England, became physician to Charles I, and from 1637 was Rector of King's College, Aberdeen. He attained a European reputation as a writer of Latin poetry. Among his works are *Musae Aulicae* (1637), and a complete translation of the Psalms, and he edited *Deliciae Poetarum Scotorum*, a collection of Latin poetry by Scottish authors.

Johnston, Sir Harry Hamilton (12 June 1858—31 Aug. 1927), explorer and administrator, was born in London and educated at Stockwell Grammar School, King's College, London, and the Royal Academy of Arts. In 1879 he spent eight months in Tunis and learned Arabic. In 1882 he made an expedition to the Congo, followed in 1884 by one to Mount Kilimanjaro. As vice-consul in the Cameroons in 1885 he planned with Rhodes an 'all-red' route from the Cape to Cairo. After his work as Commissioner for South Central Africa from 1891 to 1896 he was given the K.C.B. In 1899 he was special commissioner in Uganda, and in 1901 he gained notoriety by discovering the okapi in the Congo. In the same year he was awarded the K.C.M.G. His books describing the countries he had visited include *The Uganda Protectorate* (1902), *Liberia* (1906), and *The Negro in the New World* (1910). He also wrote five novels and an autobiography, *The Story of My Life* (1923).

Johnstone, Charles (1719?—1800?), novelist, was born at Carrigo-gunnel in Limerick, and educated at Dublin University. Prevented by deafness from practising at the Irish Bar, he went about 1782 to India, where he was proprietor of a newspaper. He wrote one successful book, *Chrysal, or the Adventures of a Guinea* (1760), a somewhat sombre satire, and some others now forgotten.

Jones, Ebenezer (20 Jan. 1820—14 Sept. 1860), poet, born in Islington of a Welsh father, became a clerk. He wrote a good deal of verse of very unequal merit, but at his best shows a true poetic vein. He was befriended by Browning and Rossetti. His chief work was *Studies of Sensation and Event* (1843). His most widely appreciated poems were 'Winter Hymn to the Snow,' 'To Death,' and 'When the World is Burning,' all written towards the end of his life. He made an unhappy marriage, which ended in a separation.

Jones, Ernest Charles (25 Jan. 1819—26 Jan. 1868), poet, novelist, and Chartist, son of the Duke of Cumberland's equerry, was born in Berlin. He adopted the views of the Chartists in an extreme form, and was imprisoned for two years for seditious speeches, and on his release conducted a Chartist newspaper. Afterwards, when the agitation had died down, he returned to his practice as a barrister, which he had deserted, and also wrote largely. He produced a number of novels, including *The Maid of Warsaw*, *Womans' Wrongs*, and *The Painter of Florence*, also some poems, *The Battle Day* (1855), *The Revolt of Hindostan* (1857), and *Corayda* (1859).

Jones, Henry Arthur (20 Sept. 1851—7 Jan. 1929), dramatist, was born at Grandborough, Buckinghamshire, the son of a farmer of Welsh descent, and educated at a village school. From 1864 to 1879 he was employed in the drapery business. He began to write plays in 1869 and had his first production in 1878, a comedy entitled *It's Only Round the Corner*. Four years later his position was established with *The Silver King*, which ran for 289 nights and was the most celebrated melodrama of the day. From then onwards he had some thirty years of unbroken success with his plays, among the best-known being *Hard Hit* (1887) and *The Dancing Girl* (1891), in both of which Herbert Tree acted. *The Liars* (1897) and *Mrs Dane's Defence* (1900), his most effective serious plays, were followed by *The Hypocrites* (1906) and *The Lie* (1914). Though he has been described as 'a shrewd observer rather than a deep philosopher' Jones shares with A. W. Pinero (q.v.) the distinction of bringing back reality to the English theatre after a flat period of nearly a century.

Jones, Sir William (28 Sept. 1746—27 April 1794), oriental scholar and jurist, was born in London, and educated at Harrow and University College, Oxford, of which in 1766 he became a Fellow. He lost his father, an eminent mathematician, at 3 years of age. He early showed extraordinary aptitude for acquiring languages, specially those of the East, and learned twenty-eight. Devoting himself to the study of law he became one of the most profound jurists of his time. He was appointed one of the Judges in the Supreme Court of Bengal, knighted in 1783, and started for India, whence he never returned. While there, in addition to his judicial duties, he pursued his studies in Oriental languages, from which he made various translations. He was a pioneer in the study of Sanskrit and founded the Bengal Asiatic Society. He left various unfinished works which, with his other writings, were collected and edited by Lord Teignmouth. His chief legal work was *The Institutes of Hindu Law* (1794).

Jonson, Ben *or* **Benjamin** (11 June 1572?—6 Aug. 1637), dramatist and poet, was descended from the Scottish Johnstones of Annandale. Born at Westminster, he was sent to Westminster School, for which, his father being dead, he seems to have been indebted to the kindness of W. Camden (q.v.), who was one of the masters. His mother, meanwhile, had married a bricklayer, and he was for a time put to that trade, but disliking it, he ran away and joined the army, fighting against the Spaniards in the Low Countries. Returning to England about 1592 he took to the stage, both as an actor and as a playwright. In the former capacity he was unsuccessful. In 1594 he married Anne Lewis, 'a shrew yet honest,' and in 1598, having killed a fellow-actor in a duel, he was tried for murder, but escaped by benefit of clergy. About the same time he joined the Roman Catholic Church, in which he remained for twelve years. It was in 1598 also that his first successful play, *Every Man in his Humour*, was produced, with Shakespeare as one of the players. It was followed by *Every Man out of his Humour* (1599), *Cynthia's Revels* (1600), and *The Poetaster* (1601), satirizing the citizens, the courtiers, and the poets respectively. The last called forth several replies, the most notable of which was the *Satiromastix* (Whip for the Satirist) of Dekker (q.v.), a severe, though not altogether unfriendly, retort, which Jonson took in good part, announcing his intention of leaving off satire and trying tragedy. His first work in this kind was *Sejanus* (1603), which was not very favourably received. It was followed by *Eastward Ho*, in which he collaborated with Marston and Chapman. Certain reflections on Scotland gave offence to James I, and the authors were imprisoned, but soon released.

From the begining of the new reign Jonson devoted himself largely to the writing of Court masques, in which he excelled all his contemporaries, and about the same time entered upon the production of the three great plays in which his full strength is shown. The first of these, *Volpone, or the Fox*, appeared in 1605, *Epicoene, or the Silent Woman* in 1609, and *The Alchemist* in 1610. His second and last tragedy, *Catiline*, was produced in 1611. Two years later he was in

France as companion to the son of Sir W. Ralegh, and on his return he held up hypocritical Puritanism to scorn in *Bartholomew Fair*, which was followed in 1616 by a comedy, *The Devil is an Ass*. In the same year he collected his writings—plays, poems, and epigrams—in a folio entitled his *Works*. He had now reached the height of his fame, and was in essentials if not in actual title the Poet Laureate, with a court pension. In 1618 he journeyed on foot to Scotland, where he was received with much honour, and paid his famous visit to Drummond (q.v.) at Hawthornden. He also visited Oxford, where he was made an honorary M.A. In 1623 he suffered a crushing misfortune, all his books and manuscripts being destroyed by fire, and after the production in 1625 of his last great play, *The Staple of News*, he had a paralytic stroke, from which he never entirely recovered. His next play, *The New Inn*, was driven from the stage for which in its rapid degeneracy he had become too learned and too moral. A quarrel with Inigo Jones, the architect, who furnished the machinery for the Court masques, lost him Court favour, and he was obliged, with failing powers, to turn again to the stage, for which his last plays, *The Magnetic Lady* and *The Tale of a Tub*, were written in 1632 and 1633. Town and Court favour, however, turned again, and his pension was increased. In 1637, after some years of gradually failing health, he died, and was buried in Westminster Abbey. An admirer caused a mason to cut on the slab over his grave the well-known inscription, 'O Rare Ben Jonson.' He left a fragment, *The Sad Shepherd*, his only pastoral. His works include a number of epigrams and translations, and two collections of poems, *The Forest* (1616), and *Underwoods* (1640). His chief prose work was a commonplace-book, *Timber; or Discoveries Made upon Men and Matter* (1640). His works were edited in 11 volumes by C. H. Herford and P. and E. Simpson (1925—52).

Jonson was the founder of the so-called 'comedy of humours,' in which each character is an exaggerated representative of a single type. His characters, like many of Dickens's, are portrayed only in the flat, not in the round. He was a striking contrast to Shakespeare, being learned, artificial, correct, and an observer of the classical 'unities.' But though they follow classical models, his comedies provide a wonderful portrait-gallery of Elizabethan types.

Jortin, John (23 Oct. 1698—5 Sept. 1770), historian, son of a Huguenot exile, was educated at Charterhouse and Cambridge, and having taken orders held various benefices, becoming in 1764 Archdeacon of London. He published *Remarks on Ecclesiastical History* (1751—4), a Life of Erasmus, and various miscellaneous pamphlets and tracts; seven volumes of sermons appeared after his death.

Jowett, Benjamin (15 April 1817—1 Oct. 1893), scholar, was born at Camberwell, and educated at St Paul's School and Balliol College, where he had a distinguished career, becoming Fellow in 1838, and Master in 1870. He held the Regius Professorship of Greek from 1855 till his death, though for the first ten years he was, owing to the opposition of his theological opponents in the University, deprived of a large part of the usual emoluments. His essay on *The*

Interpretation of Scripture in the famous *Essays and Reviews*, which appeared in 1860, brought him into strong collision with powerful sections of theological opinion, to which he had already given offence by his commentaries on the *Epistles to the Thessalonians, Galatians, and Romans* (1855). Latterly he exercised an extraordinary influence in the University of which from 1882 to 1886 he was Vice-Chancellor, and under his mastership Balliol became pre-eminent among the colleges. His chief works are translations, with learned introductions, of *The Dialogues* of Plato (1871), of Thucydides (1881), and of the *Politics* of Aristotle (1885). He held the degree of LL.D. from the University of Edinburgh (1884), and Cambridge (1890), and Doctor of Theology of Leyden (1875).

Joyce, James Augustine Aloysius (2 Feb. 1882—13 Jan. 1941), novelist and poet, was born in Dublin, where his father was collector of rates, and educated at the Jesuit Clongowes Wood College, Belvedere College, where he became captain of the school, and University College, Dublin. For some time he studied naturalist and symbolist literature in Paris. After his marriage to Nora Barnacle in 1904 he left Ireland and lived on the Continent, teaching languages at Trieste and in Switzerland for more than ten years. His first publication was a volume of lyrics, *Chamber Music* (1907), which had a successor twenty years later in *Pomes Penyeach*, but the realistic short stories in *Dubliners* (1914) were the first indication of his genius. *Portrait of the Artist as a Young Man* (1916) is a biographical novel, and in 1918 he published a play, *Exiles*. But his fame rests on his novel *Ulysses* (1922), which was published in Paris because of the censorship elsewhere. It was reset six times by the printers, because Joyce kept rewriting every proofsheet, but eventually he got the first printed copy on his fortieth birthday. One eminent critic called it the greatest novel of the twentieth century, while another described it as the foulest book ever printed. For long it was banned in America, until in 1933 a judge ruled that while 'in many places it is somewhat emetic, nowhere does it tend to be aphrodisiac.' The story deals with a single day in Dublin, and has some affinities with Sterne's *Tristram Shandy*.

For the next seventeen years, during which he became almost blind, Joyce worked at *Finnegans Wake*, which deals with a single night and is the story of a dream. A chapter was published in 1928 with the title *Anna Livia Plurabelle*, and another as *Haveth Childers Everywhere* in 1931; finally the complete book appeared in 1939. Both it and *Ulysses* are used by the author as vehicles for psychological exploration, with a mass of recondite allusions, newly coined words and other literary and grammatical eccentricities which·in extreme cases become almost if not quite unintelligible; they form a remarkable experiment in the technique of writing which has had few imitators. During the Second World War Joyce found asylum at Zurich, where he died worn out by privations and worry.

Judd, Sylvester (23 July 1813—26 Jan. 1853), novelist and clergyman, born at Westhampton, Massachusetts, studied for the ministry at Yale, and from 1840 till his death was Unitarian pastor of Augusta, Maine.   He published *Philo*, a religious poem, followed by *Margaret, a Tale of the Real and the Ideal* (1845), and *Richard Edney* (1850). He also produced some theological works.

Juliana *or* **Julian** of Norwich (1342?—1413), anchoress and mystic, was probably a Benedictine nun, living as a recluse in Norwich.   Her *XVI Revelations of Divine Love* embody the most fervent piety, and have been described as the most perfect expression in England of medieval mysticism.

Junius was the pseudonym used by a writer who has never been identified with certainty.   His famous *Letters* appeared between 1769 and 1771 in the *Public Advertiser*, the leading periodical of the day.   Distinguished by bitter and trenchant invective, they were directed against the government and its supporters, and the knowledge which they revealed of the most intimate scandals of the time made the mystery of their authorship doubly tantalizing.   Some fifty names were suggested at different times, the most likely claimant being Sir Philip Francis (q.v.).   It was the *Letters* of Junius that started the fashion for the anonymity of leading articles in modern newspapers.

K

Kames, Henry Home, Lord (1696—27 Dec. 1782), judge and philosopher, born at Kames, Berwickshire, was admitted an advocate in 1723, and raised to the Bench as Lord Kames in 1752. In 1748 he published a collection of Decisions of the Court of Session. It is, however, on his philosophical and historical writings that his literary fame rests. His writings include *Essays on the Principles of Morality and Natural Religion* (1751), *An Introduction to the Art of Thinking* (1761), *The Elements of Criticism* (1762), in which he sought for principles based on the elements of human nature, and *Sketches of the History of Man* (1774). He was also an eminent authority upon agriculture, on which he in 1777 published a work entitled *The Gentleman Farmer*.

Kaufman, George Simon (16 Nov. 1889—2 June 1961), playwright, was born at Pittsburgh and educated at the High School there. He studied law, but gave it up and worked first as a surveyor and then as a commercial traveller. In 1908 he started writing and was a columnist on the New York *Evening Mail* and then on the *Herald-Tribune*. Most of his plays were written in collaboration with someone else, an exception being *The Butter and Egg Man* (1925). With Marc Connelly he wrote *To the Ladies* (1922), *Merton of the Movies* (1922), and *Beggar on Horseback* (1925); with Alexander Woollcott he wrote *The Channel Road* (1929), and *The Dark Tower* (1933); with Ring Lardner *June Moon* (1929), a satire on writers of popular songs; with Moss Hart *You Can't Take It With You*, which won the Pulitzer Prize in 1937, and *The Man Who Came to Dinner* (1939); with Leueen MacGrath (whom he married in 1949), *The Small Hours* (1951); and with H. Teichmann, *The Solid Gold Cadillac* (1954).

Kavanagh, Julia (1824—28 Oct. 1877), novelist, was born at Thurles, County Tipperary, daughter of a writer, and spent much of her early life in France, where the scenes of most of her novels are laid. They include *Madeleine* (1848), *Daisy Burns* (1853), and *Adèle* (1858); she also wrote *Woman in France in the 18th Century* (1850).

Kaye, Sir John William (1814—24 July 1876), historian, son of a London solicitor, was educated at Eton and Addiscombe. After serving for some time in the Bengal Artillery, he succeeded J. S. Mill as secretary to the political and secret department in the East India Office. He wrote a valuable series of histories and biographies illustrative of the British occupation of India, including *The War in Afghanistan* (1851), and *The Sepoy War in India*, which he did not live to finish, and which was completed by G. B. Malleson as *The History of the Indian Mutiny* (6 volumes, 1890); also histories of the East India Company and of Christianity in India, and lives of Sir

John Malcolm and other Indian soldiers and statesmen. He was made K.C.S.I. in 1871.

Kaye-Smith, Sheila (4 Feb. 1887—15 Jan. 1956), novelist, was born at St Leonards-on-Sea, daughter of a surgeon. Educated privately, she started writing as a child, her first published novel being *The Tramping Methodist* (1908), which was followed by *Starbrace* (1909), *Sussex Gorse* (1916), *Tamarisk Town* (1919), *Green Apple Harvest* (1920), *Joanna Godden* (1921), and *The End of the House of Alard* (1923), which was a great success. In 1924 she married T. Penrose Fry, who became a rector, and in 1929 both were converted to Roman Catholicism and settled in Sussex, where they farmed their own land. Among her later novels were *Shepherds in Sackcloth* (1930), *Ember Lane* (1940), *Tambourine, Trumpet, and Drum* (1943), *The Lardners and the Laurelwoods* (1948), *Treasures of the Snow* (1949), *Mrs Gailey* (1951), and *The View from the Parsonage* (1954). *Joanna Godden Married* (1926) is a volume of short stories, and she also published three books of verse, *Willow's Forge* (1914), *Saints in Sussex* (1923), and *Songs Late and Early* (1931), as well as an autobiography, *Three Ways Home* (1937). *The Weald of Kent and Sussex* (1953) is a descriptive book about her own countryside. With G. B. Stern she wrote two books on Jane Austen (1943, 1949).

Keable, Robert (6 March 1887—23 Dec. 1927), novelist, born in Bedfordshire, son of a minister, was educated at Whitgift School and Cambridge. Ordained in 1911, he went to Africa as a missionary and became rector at Leribe in Basutoland. During the First World War he was chaplain with the South African forces, and wrote of his experiences in *Standing By* (1919). After the war he decided to resign from the Church, and in 1921 he published a novel, *Simon Called Peter*, telling of his disillusionment and loss of faith; it was very successful and made him rich and famous. A sequel, *Recompense* (1925), was not so popular. Going to the South Seas in search of health he wrote *Tahiti: Isle of Dreams* (1926) and *The Great Galilean* (1929). It has been said that though he gave up the Church he was always a preacher even in his novels.

Keary, Annie (3 March 1825—3 March 1879), novelist, born at Bilton in Yorkshire, where her father, an Irishman, was rector, began by writing fairy-tales, and then wrote some good novels, including *Oldbury* (1869), *Castle Daly* (1875), and *A Doubting Heart* (1879).

Keats, John (29 or 31 Oct. 1795—23 Feb. 1821), poet, was born in London, son of a livery stable keeper who had married his master's daughter. He was educated at Enfield, where he formed a friendship with Charles Cowden Clarke, son of the headmaster. In 1804 his father was killed in a riding accident, and in 1810 his mother died of consumption. Left an orphan at 15, Keats was apprenticed to a surgeon in Edmonton, and five years later moved to London, where in 1816 he was appointed a dresser at Guy's Hospital and later qualified as a surgeon. Throughout these years he had been reading widely, especially on classical themes, and in 1815 he wrote his famous sonnet, 'On First Looking Into Chapman's Homer.' His work at this time was influenced by Spenser, for whom he had a great admiration. His former teacher Clarke introduced him to Leigh Hunt, who lived at Hampstead, then a country village outside London, and there he made the acquaintance of other literary notabilities including Shelley and Hazlitt; later he met Wordsworth and Lamb at the house of Haydon, the painter.

In 1817 he published his first volume of *Poems*, which included some fine sonnets, and though the book had no success he abandoned surgery for literature. *Endymion*, a long poem in heroic couplets, based on a legend of the Greek moon goddess, appeared a year later, having been written during his stay in the Isle of Wight and other places; for after his boyhood he never had a home of his own, but moved from one lodging to another. The poem was so savagely attacked in the *Quarterly Review* and *Blackwood's Magazine* that a story grew up, fostered by Byron and others, blaming these critics for the author's early death. But Keats, in spite of his beauty of face and his small size—he was not much over five feet tall—was not the languishing aesthete that these accounts suggest; as a schoolboy he was very pugnacious, and he never lacked courage. The first stage of his fatal illness was in fact brought on by over-exertion on a walking tour, and aggravated by bereavement and an unhappy love affair. In the summer of 1818 he went with his friend Charles Armitage Brown on an over-ambitious 'hike' which took in the English Lakes and the western highlands of Scotland, including an ascent of Ben Nevis. Keats had to cut it short on doctor's orders and returned to London only in time to nurse his dying brother Tom. And after Tom's death in December he moved by invitation into Brown's house at Hampstead; there he had fallen in love with Fanny Brawne, daughter of a neighbour, who, though kind and considerate, was not capable of responding to the poet's sensitive and passionate nature.

In Brown's house, which is now preserved as the Keats Memorial House and contains many souvenirs of the poet, he produced in rapid succession during the next year some of the finest poems in the English language, including the four great odes 'To Psyche,' 'To a Nightingale,' 'On a Grecian Urn,' and 'To Autumn'; that medieval gem 'La Belle Dame Sans Merci,' often reckoned his most perfect poem; the longer 'Eve of St Agnes,' 'Eve of St Mark,' and 'Lamia'; and the splendid fragment of 'Hyperion.' All these were included in his third volume, *Lamia and Other Poems*, published in 1820. In the same year he developed symptoms which with his medical knowledge he recognized as indicating the onset of fatal consumption. In a last quest for health he sailed for Naples, along with his friend Severn the artist, who nursed him devotedly till the last. He was buried in the Protestant cemetery at Rome, with the epitaph which he wrote himself, 'Here lies one whose name was writ in water'; Shelley, who was to follow to the same resting-place little over a year later, gave him a more splendid memorial in his elegy 'Adonais.' His *Life, Letters, and Literary Remains* were edited by Lord Houghton in 1848, and the standard biography was published by Sir Sidney Colvin in 1920.

It is difficult to assess the greatness of a poet who died at 25, an age by which the most celebrated writers have seldom accomplished anything of note. More than any other, Keats fulfils Milton's dictum that poetry should be 'simple, sensuous, and passionate.' He has no message to convey, no theory to work out, but simply pursues beauty for its own sake wherever it is to be found. Hence it is that he is the most direct and objective of English poets, and by a curious paradox the nearest to the Greeks of the English Romantics, though he knew little or no Greek. His poetry, one may say, is the purest, most unalloyed, poetry in our language, making its appeal direct to the senses, not to the mind. Add to this the personal charm of his nature, the pathos of his unhappy life and tragic death, and it is little wonder that Keats is one of the best-loved figures in our literature.

Keble, John (25 April 1792—29 March 1866), clergyman and poet, was born at Fairford, Gloucestershire, and educated by his father, a vicar, before going to Corpus Christi College, Oxford, where his friends included Thomas Arnold and Sir John Taylor Coleridge, who eventually wrote his biography. Taking a double First, he was elected a Fellow of Oriel. His ideal life, however, was that of a country clergyman, and having taken orders in 1815, he became curate to his father. Meantime he had been writing *The Christian Year* (1827), a collection of sacred poems which attained immense popularity. Though at first anonymous, its authorship soon became known, with the result that Keble was in 1831 appointed to the Chair of Poetry at Oxford, which he held until 1841. In 1833 his famous sermon on national apostasy gave the first impulse to the Oxford movement of which, after the secession of Newman to the Church of Rome, he, along with Pusey, was regarded as the leader, and in connection with which he contributed several of the more important *Tracts of the Times* in which were inculcated 'deep submission to authority, implicit reverence for Catholic tradition, firm belief in the divine prerogatives of the priesthood, the real nature of the sacraments, and the danger of independent speculation.' His father having died, Keble became in 1836 Vicar of Hursley, near Winchester, where he remained until his death. In 1846 he published another book of poems, *Lyra Innocentium*. Other works were a Life of Wilson, Bishop of Sodor and Man, and an edition of the works of Hooker. After his death appeared *Letters of Spiritual Counsel*, and 12 volumes of *Parish Sermons*. In 1869 Keble College, Oxford, was founded in his memory. Keble was one of the most saintly and unselfish men who ever adorned the Church of England, and, though personally shy and retiring, exercised a vast spiritual influence upon his generation.

Keightley, Thomas (Oct. 1789—4 Nov. 1872), historian, educated at Trinity College, Dublin, settled in London in 1824. At the request of Dr Arnold of Rugby he wrote a series of text-books on English, Greek, and other histories. His *History of Greece* was translated into modern Greek. Among his other books are *Fairy Mythology* (1828), and *Mythology of Ancient Greece and Italy* (1831).

Keith, Robert (7 Feb. 1681—26 Jan. 1757), prelate and historian, born at Uras in Kincardineshire, belonged to the family of the Earls

Marischal, and was Bishop of Fife in the Scottish Episcopal Church. He was deeply versed in Scottish antiquities, and published in 1734 a *History of the Affairs of Church and State in Scotland* during the Reformation. He also compiled *A Catalogue of the Bishops of Scotland* (1755).

Kellett, Ernest Edward (1864—1950), critic and essayist, son of a clergyman, was educated at Kingswood and Oxford. Until 1924 he was senior English master at Leys School, and during this period he edited *The Book of Cambridge Verse* (1911). At the age of 59 he turned to writing and produced two books of essays, *Suggestions* (1924) and *Reconsiderations* (1928). In 1929 he published *The Northern Saga*, translations from the Icelandic, and *The Story of Myths*. Further critical works were *Fashion in Literature* (1931) and *Literary Quotation and Allusion* (1933). *A Pageant of History* appeared in 1936 and *Aspects of History* in 1938. *As I Remember* is a book of memoirs.

Kelly, Hugh (1739—3 Feb. 1777), dramatist, born at Killarney, son of a publican, worked in London as a staymaker, 1760, and after editing various journals, wrote *Memoirs of a Magdalen* (1767). His play, *False Delicacy* (1768), had an extraordinary success, and was translated into French, German, and Portuguese. After some subsequent failures he left off writing for the stage in 1774, and endeavoured to practise as a barrister, but without success. He also wrote political pamphlets, for which he received a pension from the Government.

Ken *or* Kenn, Thomas (July 1637—19th March 1711), prelate and religious writer, son of an attorney, was born at Little Berkhampstead, educated at Winchester and Oxford and taking holy orders received the living of Brightstone, Isle of Wight, where he composed his *Morning, Evening, and Midnight Hymns*, perhaps the most widely known of English hymns, including 'Awake, my soul,' and 'Glory to Thee, my God, this night.' These he was accustomed to sing daily to the lute. After holding other benefices he became Bishop of Bath and Wells, and a chaplain to Charles II. He was one of the 'Seven Bishops' sent to the Tower by James II. Refusing to take the oaths to William and Mary, he was deprived, and spent his later years in retirement, at Longleat with Lord Weymouth. Izaak Walton was his brother-in-law. Ken wrote a manual of prayers for Winchester College, and other devotional works.

Kendall, Henry Clarence (18 April 1841—1 Aug. 1882), poet, born near Ulladulla, New South Wales, was taken while a boy by his uncle, a whaling captain, for a two years cruise in the South Sea Islands. Returning to Sydney, he started work in a solicitor's office, then entered the State Survey Department. His *Poems and Songs* were published in 1862, and having won a prize for his poems 'Death in the Bush' and 'The Glen of Arrawatta,' he moved to Melbourne, where in 1869 he published *Leaves from Australian Forests*. Discouraged by poverty and lack of success he went back to Sydney and became a clerk in a timber business. His *Songs from the Mountains* appeared in 1880, and in 1881 he was appointed Inspector of

State Forests; but prosperity came too late, his constitution gave way and he died a year later. Kendall is regarded as the father of Australian native poetry; he had a wonderful power of reproducing that country's scenery and atmosphere in his verses, which were collected in a single volume in 1903.

Kennedy, John Pendleton (25 Oct. 1795—18 Aug. 1870), statesman and novelist, born in Baltimore, became a barrister and rose to be Secretary of the Navy. He wrote three novels, *Swallow Barn* (1832), *Horse Shoe Robinson* (1835), and *Rob of the Bowl* (1838), which give a vivid presentation of life in the Southern States.

Kennedy, Margaret (23 April 1896—), novelist, was born in London, daughter of a barrister, but spent much of her early life in Kent and Cornwall. She was educated at Cheltenham and Somerville College, Oxford, where she studied history, her first publication being *A Century of Revolution* (1922). Her first published novel was *The Ladies of Lyndon* (1923), and in the following year she became famous with *The Constant Nymph*, which was later dramatized and filmed. In 1925 she married David Davies, a barrister. Others of her novels are *Red Sky at Morning* (1927), *Return I Dare Not* (1931), *Together and Apart* (1936), *The Mechanized Muse* (1942), *The Feast* (1950), *Troy Chimneys* (1953), which won the Tait Black Memorial Prize, and *Act of God* (1955). *Escape Me Never!* (1934) is a three-act play, and she also wrote a life of Jane Austen (1950).

Kennedy, Walter (1460?—1508?), poet, son of the 1st Lord Kennedy, who had great estates in Carrick, and nephew of the Bishop of St Andrews, was educated at Glasgow University, and is perhaps best known as Dunbar's antagonist in the *Flyting of Dunbar and Kennedy*. Other poems are *Praise of Aige* (Age), *Ane Ballat in Praise of Our Lady*, and *The Passion of Christ*.

Ker, William Paton (30 Aug. 1855—17 July 1923), scholar, was born in Glasgow, son of a merchant, and educated at Glasgow Academy and University and Balliol College, Oxford. In 1879 he became a Fellow of All Souls, and he was appointed Professor of English at Cardiff in 1883 and at University College, London, in 1889. In 1920 he became Professor of Poetry at Oxford and in 1922 Director of Scandinavian Studies at London University. He died of heart failure while climbing in the Alps at the age of 67. He was one of the greatest authorities on medieval literature, his chief works being *Epic and Romance* (1897), *The Dark Ages* (1904), *The Art of Poetry* (1920), *Essays on Medieval Literature* (1923), and *English Literature: Medieval* (1924).

Key, Francis Scott (1 Aug. 1779—11 Jan. 1843), born in Maryland, was educated at St John's College, Annapolis, studied law, and became an attorney in Washington. His famous poem 'The Star-Spangled Banner' was composed while he was watching the British attack on Baltimore, 5th September, 1814; it was printed in the *Baltimore American* and soon had wide popularity; it was officially designated the American National Anthem by Act of Congress, 9th

March 1931. A small collection of Key's verses was published in 1857.

Keyes, Frances Parkinson (22 July 1885—   ), novelist, was born in the University of Virginia, where her father, John Henry Wheeler, was Professor of Greek. She got what she has termed 'her alleged education' at Boston, Geneva, and Berlin, in the course of constant and extensive travelling, which she continued all her life. In 1904 she married Henry Wilder Keyes, who was Governor of New Hampshire from 1917 to 1919 and an American Senator from 1919 to 1937. Her first novel, *The Old Grey Homestead*, was published in 1919; her first article written from Washington, in 1920, was the forerunner of her *Letters from a Senator's Wife* (1924) telling of the important people she met. Later novels were *The Career of David Noble* (1921), *Queen Anne's Lace* (1930), *Senator Marlowe's Daughter* (1933), *Honor Bright* (1936), *All That Glitters* (1941), *Came a Cavalier* (1948), *Dinner at Antoine's* (1949), *Joy Street* (1950), and *The Royal Box* (1954). *The Cost of a Best Seller* (1950) is autobiographical. In 1939 she became a Roman Catholic.

Keyes, Sidney Arthur Kilworth (27 May 1922—29 April 1943), poet, was born at Dartford, Kent, son of an army officer, and was educated at Dartford Grammar School, Tonbridge, and Queen's College, Oxford, where he edited the *Cherwell*. Obtaining a commission in the West Kent Regiment, he died in the Tunisian campaign of the Second World War after only a fortnight's active service. His first book of verse, *The Iron Laurel*, appeared in 1942, his second, *The Cruel Solstice*, in 1944, when he was posthumously awarded the Hawthornden Prize. His *Collected Poems* were published in 1945. One of the most original poets of the war, he belonged to what was termed the ' neo-romantic ' group, which represented a reaction from the realism of the thirties.

Keynes, John Maynard Keynes, 1st Baron (5 June 1883—21 April 1946), economist, was born at Cambridge, where his father was registrar of the university. He was educated at Eton and King's College, Cambridge, of which later he became Fellow and Bursar. He worked in the Treasury during the First World War, and represented it at the Peace Conference, but resigned because of a disagreement over his plan for reparations, and in 1919 published his famous work *The Economic Consequences of the Peace*. In 1925 he married Lydia Lopokova, the Russian dancer. During the Second World War he took part in lend-lease negotiations and later represented Britain at the Bretton Woods Conference. In 1940 he became a director of the Bank of England and in 1942 he was made a baron. His books include *A Tract on Monetary Reform* (1923), *A Short View of Russia* (1925), *The End of Laissez-Faire* (1926), *A Treatise on Money* (1930), *The General Theory of Employment, Interest, and Money* (1936), and *How to Pay for the War* (1940).

Kickham, Charles Joseph (1826—21 Aug. 1882), novelist and poet, was born at Mullinahone, Tipperary, son of a shopkeeper. His plans to become a doctor were frustrated by a shooting accident which impaired his sight and hearing. In 1860 he joined the Fenians, and in 1865 was appointed to the supreme executive of the projected Irish Republic, but the rising was a failure and he was imprisoned; while in prison he wrote his first novel, *Sally Kavanagh, or, The Untenanted Graves* (1869). Set free after four years, he stood unsuccessfully as a candidate for Tipperary, and after that devoted himself to writing. His verses and stories, written from the nationalist point of view, were collected in *Poems, Sketches, and Narratives Illustrative of Irish Life* (1870). Novels which he wrote later were *Knocknagow, or, The Homes of Tipperary* (1879), and *For the Old Land, a Tale of Twenty Years Ago* (1886).

Kid, Thomas, *see* **Kyd.**

Killigrew, Thomas (7 Feb. 1612—19 March 1683), dramatist, was born in London, son of Sir Robert Killigrew, a courtier. In 1633 he became page to Charles I, and in 1642 was imprisoned for taking up arms in the royalist cause. He accompanied Charles II in exile and in 1660 was made his 'Groom of the Bedchamber. In 1663 he built the original theatre in Drury Lane, and ten years later was appointed Master of the King's Revels. In 1664 he published nine plays, said to have been written in nine different cities. His best-known comedy is *The Parson's Wedding*, remarkable chiefly for its obscenity. He was buried in Westminster Abbey.

Kilmer, Alfred Joyce (6 Dec. 1886—30 July 1918), poet and journalist, was born at New Brunswick, New Jersey; his father was a chemist, his mother an authoress, and he married Aline Murray, the poetess. Educated at Rutgers College and Columbia University, he taught Latin for a year, worked on the *Standard Dictionary* from 1909 to 1912, and then held various editorial posts on the *Churchman*, the *Literary Digest*, and the *New York Times*. He enlisted as a private in the First World War and was killed in action, being awarded the Croix de Guerre posthumously. His first book of poems, *Summer of Love* (1911), was followed by *Trees and Other Poems* (1914), the famous title poem of which had appeared the previous year. *Main Street and Other Poems* was published in 1917, and in 1918 his *Works* were edited with a memoir.

King, Henry (baptized 16 Jan. 1592, died 30 Sept. 1669), poet and prelate, son of a Bishop of London, was educated at Westminster School and Oxford. He took holy orders, and rose in 1642 to be Bishop of Chichester. The following year he was deprived, but was reinstated at the Restoration. He wrote many elegies on Royal persons and on his private friends, who included Donne, Izaak Walton, and Ben Jonson. A selection from his *Poems and Psalms* was published in 1843.

King, Kennedy, *see* **Brown, George Douglas.**

Kinglake, Alexander William (5 Aug. 1809—2 Jan. 1891), historian, born near Taunton, was educated at Eton and Trinity College, Cambridge, where he was contemporary with Tennyson and Thackeray. He was called to the Bar in 1837, and acquired a considerable practice, which in 1856 he abandoned in order to devote himself to literature and public life. His first literary venture had been *Eothen*, a brilliant and original work of Eastern travel, published in 1844; but his *magnum opus* was his *Invasion of the Crimea*, an exhaustive history of the Crimean War in 8 volumes (1863—87), which is one of the most effective works of its class.

Kingsford, William (23 Dec. 1819—28 Sept. 1898), historian, born in London, enlisted in the Dragoon Guards, and went with them to Canada, where later he was engaged in surveying work. He has a place in literature for his *History of Canada* in 10 volumes (1887—98), a work of careful research, though not distinguished for purely literary merits.

Kingsley, Charles (12 June 1819—23 Jan. 1875), novelist and historian, son of a clergyman, was born at Holne Vicarage near Dartmoor, but passed most of his childhood at Barnack in the Fen country, and Clovelly in Devonshire. A precocious child, he wrote sermons and poems at the age of 4; educated at King's College, London, and Magdalene College, Cambridge, he was intended for the law but entered the Church, and became, in 1842, curate, and two years later rector of Eversley, Hampshire. In the latter year he published *The Saints' Tragedy*, a drama, of which the heroine is St Elizabeth of Hungary. Two novels followed, *Yeast* (1848) and *Alton Locke* (1850), in which he deals with social questions as affecting the agricultural labouring class and the town worker respectively. He had become deeply interested in such questions, and threw himself heart and soul, in conjunction with F. D. Maurice and others, into the schemes of social amelioration, which they supported under the name of Christian socialism, contributing many tracts and articles under the signature of 'Parson Lot.' In 1853 appeared *Hypatia*, in which the conflict of the early Christians with the Greek philosophy of Alexandria is depicted; it was followed in 1855 by *Westward Ho!* perhaps his most popular work; in 1857 by *Two Years Ago*, and in 1866 by *Hereward the Wake*. *At Last* (1870), gave his impression of a visit to the West Indies. His taste for natural history found expression in *Glaucus, or the Wonders of the Shore* (1855), and other works. *The Water Babies* (1863) is a story for children written to inspire love and reverence of nature. Kingsley was in 1860 appointed to the Professorship of Modern History at Cambridge, which he held until 1869. The literary fruit of this was *Roman and Teuton* (1864). In the same year he was involved in a controversy with J. H. Newman, which resulted in the publication by the latter of his *Apologia*. Kingsley, who had in 1869 been made a Canon of Chester, became Canon of Westminster in 1873. He was of a highly nervous temperament, over-exertion resulted in repeated failures of health, and he died two years later. His *Collected Poems* had been published in 1872, and his *Letters* were edited by his wife in 1877. Though hot-tempered and combative, he was a man of eminently noble character. His type of religion, cheerful and robust, was described as 'muscular Christianity.'

Kingsley, Henry (2 Jan. 1830—24 May 1876), novelist, brother of

Charles Kingsley (q.v.) was born at Barnack, Northamptonshire, and educated at King's College, London, and Oxford, which he left without graduating. He went off to the Australian gold-diggings, being afterwards in the mounted police; his novel Geoffrey Hamlyn (1859) is based on his experiences there. On his return in 1858 he devoted himself industriously to literature, and wrote a number of novels of much more than average merit, including *The Hillyars and the Burtons* (1865), *Ravenshoe* (1861), and *Austin Elliot* (1863). Of these *Ravenshoe* is generally regarded as the best. In 1869 he went to Edinburgh to edit the *Daily Review*, and later was war correspondent for his paper during the Franco-German War.

Kingsley, Mary Henrietta (13 Oct. 1862—3 June 1900), traveller, daughter of George Henry Kingsley (himself a traveller, and author of *South Sea Bubbles*), and niece of Charles Kingsley (q.v.), was born at Islington. Wishing to study primitive religion, she went to West Africa, where she made valuable observations and collections. Her *Travels in West Africa* (1897) is one of the most original and stimulating books of its class. Mary Kingsley had a singular power of viewing the religious rites of savage peoples from their point of view. She was about to undertake another journey, but died while nursing Boer prisoners at Simon's Town.

Kingston, William Henry Giles (28 Feb. 1814—2 Aug. 1880), writer of tales for boys, was born in London, but spent much of his youth in Oporto, where his father was a merchant. His first book, *The Circassian Chief*, appeared in 1844. His first book for boys, *Peter the Whaler* (1851), had such success that he retired from business and devoted himself entirely to the production of this kind of literature. In the next thirty years he wrote upwards of 130 tales, including *The Three Midshipmen* (1862), *The Three Lieutenants* (1874), *The Three Commanders* (1875), and *The Three Admirals* (1877). He also conducted various papers, including *The Colonist*, and *Colonial Magazine and East India Review*. For services in negotiating a commercial treaty with Portugal he received a Portuguese knighthood, and for his literary labours a Government pension.

Kipling, Joseph Rudyard (30 Jan. 1865—18 Jan. 1936), short-story writer and poet, was the son of John Lockwood Kipling, a Methodist minister who studied art at South Kensington, and Alice MacDonald, daughter of a Wesleyan minister and sister-in-law of Sir Edward Burne-Jones. John Kipling got a post in the School of Art at Bombay, and Rudyard was born there and named after Rudyard Lake in Staffordshire, where his parents had first met. In 1871 he was sent home and lived for some years at Southsea in the care of a most unpleasant woman of whom he tells in 'Baa, Baa, Black Sheep,' but spent his holidays at Fulham with Burne-Jones. In 1877 his mother came home and rescued him, and in the following year he went to the United Services College at Westward Ho!, Devon, his schooldays being later immortalized in the pages of *Stalky and Co* (1899), where Kipling figures as Beetle, because of his short sight. Although not distinguished at school, he was a voracious reader, with a great capacity of literary absorption.

In 1882 he returned to India and joined the staff of the *Civil and Military Gazette* of Lahore, where his father was now curator of the government museum, and also wrote for the *Pioneer*. His great powers of recollection and his facility in writing made him a brilliant journalist, and he soon began producing verse and short stories. Following the publication of *Departmental Ditties* (1886), in the years 1887—9 he published a total of over 70 short stories, contained in *Plain Tales from the Hills, Soldiers Three, The Story of the Gadsbys, In Black and White, Under the Deodars, The Phantom Rickshaw,* and *Wee Willie Winkie*. In 1889, having returned to England by way of Japan and the United States, he settled in Villiers Street at Charing Cross, which he made the scene of his novel, *The Light that Failed* (1891). Short stories of this period are contained in two of his best collections, *Life's Handicap* (1891) and *Many Inventions* (1893). After a visit to America, from which he returned by way of New Zealand and Australia, he married an American girl, Caroline Starr Balestier, in 1892 and settled with her among her own people at Brattleboro, Vermont. But he did not get on well with his neighbours, particularly his brother-in-law Beatty Balestier, and after four years he returned to England.

At Naulakha, his house in Vermont, he had written the two *Jungle Books* (1894, 1895), which contain some of the finest animal stories ever written, and also the distinctively American *Captains Courageous* (1897), a tale of the fishermen of the Newfoundland Banks. Meanwhile in poetry he had published *Barrack Room Ballads* (1892) and *The Seven Seas* (1896), both proclaiming the greatness of Britain's imperial tradition. In 1895 he was offered the post of Poet Laureate in succession to Tennyson, but declined the honour, as he thought he could do more in an unofficial capacity. This was borne out when the Boer War began and he wrote 'The Absent-Minded Beggar,' which raised a quarter of a million for a newspaper fund. In 1898 he published *The Day's Work*, which contains some of his finest stories, and in 1901 *Kim*, a romance of the Indian road, which brings in many reminiscences of his own early life in India. In 1902, shortly after the tragic death of his eldest child Josephine, he published the delightful *Just So Stories for Children*, which he illustrated himself. This was followed by two other children's books, *Puck of Pook's Hill* (1905), and *Rewards and Fairies* (1910), both dealing in a romantic way with English history, a theme which he followed up in *A School History of England* (1911), written in collaboration with C. R. L. Fletcher. From 1902 onwards he made his home at Burwash in Sussex, wintering each year at Cape Town or on the Continent. Works of his later years were *A Diversity of Creatures* (1917), *Debits and Credits* (1926), and *Limits and Renewals* (1932). After the First World War, in which his son was killed, he wrote an account of his regiment, *The Irish Guards in the Great War* (1923).

In 1907 he was awarded the Nobel Prize for Literature, and he received many other distinctions. He was three times offered the Order of Merit but declined it, just as he had declined the Laureateship. In 1922 he was elected Lord Rector of St Andrews, and in 1926 he was awarded the gold medal of the Royal Society of Literature; he also received honorary degrees from Oxford, Cambridge, Edinburgh, Durham, Paris, Strasburg, Athens, and McGill. An unfinished autobiography, *Something of Myself*, was published in 1937, a year after he had been buried in Westminster Abbey, dying, with tragic appropriateness, two days before the death of King George V marked the end of an epoch. Ten years earlier the Kipling Society had been formed, 'to do honour to, and to extend the influence of, the most patriotic, virile, and imaginative of writers, who upholds the ideals of the English-speaking world.' Kipling's reputation as a prose writer has never faltered. Of the short story he is an acknowledged master, probably the greatest in our literature. Around his poetry controversy has always raged, all the more fiercely because he gained among unpoetic readers an audience wider than anyone had commanded since Burns. Those who make a grand mystery of poetry have disparaged him as a mere versifier. But if he is often lacking in spiritual depth, his mastery of rhythm is unquestioned, and to this is added an exquisite craftsmanship in words. His flamboyant imperialism is more open to criticism; but if his patriotic fervour seems out of date, that is only to say that he was a product of his age, the unofficial laureate of the British Empire at its greatest.

Kirkland, Joseph (7 Jan. 1830—29 April 1894), novelist, was born in Geneva, New York, where his parents kept a school, but spent his boyhood in the backwoods of Michigan. After little formal education he worked as a clerk. Later he studied law, was admited to the Bar in 1880 and practised as an attorney. The best-known of his novels are *Zury: the Meanest Man in Spring County* (1885), which describes the life of early American settlers, *The McVeys* (1888), and *The Captain of Company K* (1891), a tale of the Civil War, in which Kirkland took part.

Kitto, John (4 Dec. 1804—25 Nov. 1854), biblical scholar, son of a Cornish stonemason, was born at Plymouth. At the age of 12 a fall led to his becoming totally deaf. From poverty and hardship he was rescued by friends, to whom his mental powers had become known. Educated at Islington Missionary College, he became a valuable contributor to Biblical scholarship. He travelled much in the East in the pursuit of his favourite studies. Among his works are *Scripture Lands*, *Daily Bible Illustrations*, and *The Lost Senses* (1845) in two volumes, one dealing with deafness, the other with blindness. He also published *The Pictorial Bible* (1838), *The Cyclopaedia of Bible Literature* (1845), and edited the *Journal of Sacred Literature* from 1848 to 1853. He received a pension of £100 from the Government. In 1844 the University of Giessen conferred upon him the degree of D.D.

Knickerbocker, Diedrich, *see* **Irving, Washington.**

Knight, Charles (1791—9 March 1873), author and publisher, was born at Windsor, where his father was a bookseller. After serving his apprenticeship with him he went to London, and co-operated effectively with Brougham and others in connection with The Society for the Diffusion of Useful Knowledge. He was publisher for the Society, and issued *The Penny Magazine* (1832—45), *Penny Cyclopaedia* (1833—44), and the *Pictorial History of England* (1837—44). He edited with success *The Pictorial Shakespeare* (1838—41), and was the author of a volume of essays, *Once upon a Time* (1853), an autobiography, *Passages from a Working Life* (1863), and a *History of the Thirty Years' Peace*, which was completed by Harriet Martineau.

Knight, Henry Gally (2 Dec. 1786—9 Feb. 1846), a country gentle-man of Yorkshire, educated at Eton and Cambridge, was the author of several Oriental tales in verse, *Ilderim, a Syrian Tale* (1816), *Phrosyne, a Grecian Tale*, and *Alashtar, an Arabian Tale* (1817). He was also an authority on architecture, and wrote various works on the subject, including *The Normans in Sicily* (1838) and *The Ecclesiastical Architecture of Italy* (1842—4).

Knight, Sarah Kemble (19 April 1666—25 Sept. 1727), diarist, was born in Boston, daughter of Thomas Kemble, a merchant. Benjamin Franklin is said to have attended a writing school which she opened. Later she moved to Connecticut, speculated in land, and kept a shop. Her *Diary*, printed in 1825, forms an interesting commentary on early American history.

Knoblock, Edward (7 April 1874—19 July 1945), playwright and novelist, was born in New York and educated at Harvard; coming to England, he was naturalized as a British subject in 1916. He wrote many successful plays, including *The Faun* (1911), *Kismet* (1911), *My Lady's Dress* (1914), *Tiger, Tiger* (1918), *The Lullaby* (1923), *The Mulberrry Bush* (1930), and *Rolling Stone* (1936). He also collaborated with Arnold Bennett in *Milestones* (1912) and *London Life* (1924), and with Beverley Nichols in *Evensong* (1932). His novels include *The Ant Heap* (1929), *The Man with Two Mirrors* (1931), *Love Lady* (1933), and *Inexperience* (1941). *Round the Room* (1939) is an autobiography.

Knolles, Richard (born 1550? buried 2 July 1610), historian, was born probably at Cold Ashby, Northamptonshire, and educated at Lincoln College, Oxford, of which he became a Fellow. In 1603 he published *A General History of the Turks*, which was praised by Dr Johnson and Byron. Knolles was master of a school at Sandwich.

Knowles, Herbert (1798—17 Feb. 1817), poet, was born at Gomersal, near Leeds, and educated at Richmond Grammar School. Wishing to go to Cambridge, he sent to Southey his poem 'Three Tabernacles,' suggested by Matthew xvii. 4, and better known as 'Stanzas Written in Richmond Churchyard.' The verses, which are remarkably mature work for a schoolboy of 18, were extravagantly praised, and secured for Knowles the patronage he sought, but he died of consumption just after his election to a Cambridge sizarship.

Knowles, James Sheridan (12 May 1784—30 Nov. 1862), dramatist, son of James Knowles, schoolmaster and lexicographer, was born at Cork. He was the author of a ballad, *The Welsh Harper*, which had great popularity, and gained for him the notice of Hazlitt and others.

o

For some years he studied medicine, but turned to literature, and produced several plays, including *Caius Gracchus* (1815), *Virginius* (1820), *The Hunchback* (1832), and *The Love Chase* (1837), in some of which he acted. He gave up the stage in 1843, and became a Baptist preacher.

Knox, Edmund George Valpy (27 July 1881—), humorist, a son of the Bishop of Manchester and brother of Ronald Knox (q.v.), in 1912 married a daughter of the Bishop of Lincoln. He was educated at Rugby and Oxford, and during the First World War he served with the Lincolnshire Regiment and was wounded at Passchendaele. His first book of light verse, *The Brazen Lyre* (1911), was followed by *A Little Loot* (1919) and *Parodies Regained* (1921). He then joined the staff of *Punch*, usually writing under the pseudonymn Evoe, the Latin cry in the festival of Bacchus, and in 1932 succeeded Sir Owen Seaman as editor. His collections of humorous articles and poems include *These Liberties* (1923), *Quaint Specimens* (1925), *Here's Misery!* (1931), and *Folly Calling* (1932); he also edited an anthology, *Humorous Verse* (1931).

Knox, John (1505—24 Nov. 1572), minister, was born in Haddington, son of a farmer, and educated at Glasgow University, where he studied law and divinity. He was converted to Protestantism by George Wishart, who was burned in 1546. After the murder of Cardinal Beaton Knox was captured by the French in 1548 and sent to the galleys at Rouen. Released after a year, he preached for some time in England, but at the accession of Mary I fled to Dieppe and then to Geneva, where he consorted with Calvin. In 1559 he returned to Scotland, where he became head of the Presbyterians and had a prolonged struggle with the Scottish Queen Mary over matters of religion and politics. Two of his books are outstandingly important. *The First Blast of the Trumpet Against the Monstrous Regiment of Women* (1558) was directed against the Roman Catholic rulers Mary Tudor, Mary of Lorraine, and Catherine de Medici ('regiment' meaning government), but also got him the enmity of Queen Elizabeth; and his *History of the Reformation in Scotland* (1586) is vivid and vigorous.

Knox, Ronald Arbuthnot (17 Feb. 1888—24 Aug. 1957), priest and author, son of the Bishop of Manchester and brother of E. V. Knox (q.v.), was educated at Eton and Oxford, where he had a brilliant academical career and was President of the Union. He became a Fellow of Trinity, took orders, and was chaplain of the college for five years. In 1917 he was converted to Roman Catholicism, in 1919 he was ordained priest, and in 1925 was appointed Catholic chaplain in Oxford. In 1936 he was Domestic Prelate to the Pope, and in 1939 he retired from his posts to make a new translation of the Vulgate. His version of the Old Testament appeared in 1944, that of the New Testament in 1950. He also published a New Testament commentary in 1954. Among his religious works are *The Belief of Catholics* (1927), *The Mystery of the Kingdom* (1928), *Heaven and Charing Cross* (1935), *God and the Atom* (1946), and *Retreat for Lay People* (1955). In lighter vein are

Memories of the Future (1923), *Essays in Satire* (1928), and *Let Dons Delight* (1939). He also wrote several ingenious detective stories, including *The Viaduct Murder* (1925), *The Footsteps at the Lock* (1928), and *The Body in the Silo* (1933). *Barchester Pilgrimage* (1935) is a parody of Trollope, in which the adventures of the characters in the Barsetshire novels are continued down to 1934.

Knox, Vicesimus (8 Dec. 1752—6 Sept 1821), essayist, born at Newington Green, Middlesex, was educated at Merchant Taylors' and Oxford, and succeeded his father as headmaster of Tonbridge School. He published *Essays Moral and Literary* (1778), and compiled the formerly well-known miscellany, *Elegant Extracts* (1783, 1789).

Knox, William (17 Aug. 1789—12 Nov. 1825), poet, son of a farmer in Roxburghshire, wrote several books of poetry, including *The Lonely Hearth* (1818) and *The Harp of Zion* (1825), which gained him the friendship of Scott. He fell into dissipated habits, was latterly a journalist in Edinburgh, and died at 36.

Krutch, Joseph Wood (25 Nov. 1893—   ), critic, was born at Nashville and educated at the University of Tennessee and Columbia. He planned to be an engineer, but found his vocation as a literary critic. In 1917 he joined the English Department at Columbia, where after a period as lecturer at Vassar he subsequently became professor. He became dramatic critic of the *Nation* and edited the plays of Congreve and of Eugene O'Neill. His works include *Edgar Allan Poe, a Study in Genius* (1926), *The Modern Temper* (1929), *Five Masters* (1930), *Experience and Art* (1932), *The American Drama Since 1918* (1939), *Samuel Johnson* (1944), *Henry David Thoreau* (1948), and *Modernism in American Drama* (1953). *The Desert Year* (1952) is a descriptive study of South-west U.S.A., and *The Measure of Man* (1954) is a discussion of modern problems.

Kunst, Hermann, *see* Smith, **Walter C.**

Kyd *or* **Kid, Thomas** (1557?—1595?), dramatist, was born in London, son of a scrivener, and was a schoolfellow of Edmund Spenser at Merchant Taylors', but little is known of his life. He became one of the Bohemian literary set of his day, was a close associate of Marlowe in his last years, and like him was charged with atheism; after being imprisoned for this he spent his last years in poverty. Though sneered at by Nashe, his Senecan play *The Spanish Tragedy*, which piles horror on horror, is well constructed and was immensely popular in its day, being translated into Dutch and German. His *Pompey the Great* (1594) is a translation from the French. He probably wrote *Solyman and Perseda* (1592), and may also have been the author of an old lost play on the subject of Hamlet which served as a basis for Shakespeare's great tragedy. His *Works* were edited in 1901 by F. S. Boas.

L

Lacy, John, *see* **Darley, George.**

Laidlaw, William (19 Nov. 1780—18 May 1845), poet, son of a sheep-farmer, was born at Blackhouse, Selkirk, where he formed a friendship with James Hogg (q.v.). After several unsuccessful farming ventures he became in 1817 a sort of steward on the Abbotsford estate, and through time came to be Walter Scott's trusted friend and secretary. The only work of his own by which Laidlaw is remembered is the pathetic ballad 'Lucy's Flittin'.'

Laing, David (20 April 1793—18 Oct. 1878), antiquary, born in Edinburgh and educated at its university, was the son of a bookseller, with whom he was in partnership until his appointment, in 1837, as librarian of the Signet Library. He edited many of the publications of the Bannatyne Club, of which he was secretary (1823—61). He was also Honorary Professor of Antiquities to the Royal Scottish Academy. Among the more important works which he edited were Robert Baillie's *Letters and Journals* (1841—2), John Knox's *Works* (1846—64), and the poems of Sir D. Lyndsay, Dunbar, and Henryson.

Laing, Malcolm (1762—6 Nov. 1818), historian, born in Orkney and educated at Edinburgh University, was an advocate but devoted his leisure to historical research. He completed Henry's *History of Great Britain*, and wrote a *History of Scotland from the Union of the Crowns to the Union of the Kingdoms* (1802). He was an assailant of the authenticity of the Ossianic poems, and wrote a dissertation on the participation of Mary Queen of Scots in the murder of Darnley. He did much to improve the agriculture of Orkney.

Lamb, Lady Caroline (13 Nov. 1785—26 Jan. 1828), novelist, daughter of the 3rd Earl of Bessborough, married the Hon. William Lamb, afterwards Lord Melbourne and Prime Minister. She wrote three novels, which, though of little merit, attracted much attention. The first of these, *Glenarvon* (1816), contained a caricature portrait of Lord Byron, with whom the authoress had become infatuated. It was followed by *Graham Hamilton* (1822), and *Ada Reis* (1823). In 1824 she accidentally encountered Byron's funeral procession, and the shock permanently affected her mind.

Lamb, Charles (10 Feb. 1775—27 Dec. 1834), essayist and poet, was born in London, his father being confidential clerk to Samuel Salt, one of the benchers of the Inner Temple. After being at a school in the neighbourhood, he went to Christ's Hospital, where he remained from 1782 to 1789, and where he formed a lifelong friendship with Coleridge. He was then for a year or two in the South Sea House, where his elder brother John was a clerk. Thence he was in 1792 transferred to the India House, where he remained until 1825, when he retired with a pension of two-thirds of his salary. Salt died in 1792, and the family, consisting of the father, mother, Charles, and his sister Mary, ten years his senior, lived together in somewhat straitened circumstances, John, comparatively well off, leaving them pretty much to their own resources. In 1796 the tragedy of Lamb's life occurred. His sister Mary, in a sudden fit of insanity, killed her mother with a table-knife, and was removed to an asylum. Thenceforward, giving up a marriage to which he was looking forward, he devoted himself to the care of his unfortunate sister, who was permitted after a time to return home, and became, except when separated from him by periods of aberration, his lifelong and affectionate companion—the 'Cousin Bridget' of his essays. His first literary appearance was a contribution of four sonnets to Coleridge's *Poems on Various Subjects* (1796). In 1798 he published, along with his friend Charles Lloyd, *Blank Verse*, the little volume including 'The Old Familiar Faces,' and others of his best known poems, and his romance, *Rosamund Gray*, followed in the same year. He then turned to the drama, and produced *John Woodvil* (1802), a tragedy, and *Mr H——* (1806), a farce, both failures, for although the first had some echo of the Elizabethan music, it had no dramatic force. Meantime the brother and sister were leading a life clouded by poverty and by the anxieties arising from the condition of the latter, and they moved about from one lodging to another. Lamb's literary ventures so far had not yielded much either in money or fame, but in 1807 he was asked by W. Godwin (q.v.) to assist him in his 'Juvenile Library,' and to this he, with the assistance of his sister, contributed the now famous *Tales from Shakespeare*, Charles doing the tragedies and Mary the comedies. In 1808 they wrote again for children, *The Adventures of Ulysses*, a version of the *Odyssey*, *Mrs Leicester's School*, and *Poetry for Children* (1809).

At this time also he was commissioned by Longman to edit selections from the Elizabethan dramatists. To the selections were added criticisms, which at once brought him the reputation of being one of the most subtle and penetrating critics who had ever touched the subject. Three years later his extraordinary power in this department was further exhibited in a series of papers on Hogarth and Shakespeare, which appeared in Hunt's *Reflector*. In 1818 his scattered contributions in prose and verse were collected as *The Works of Charles Lamb*, and the favour with which they were received led to his being asked to contribute to the *London Magazine* the essays on which his fame chiefly rests. The name 'Elia' under which they were written was that of a fellow-clerk in the India House. The first series was printed in 1823, the second, *The Last Essays of Elia*, in 1833. In 1823 the Lambs had left London and taken a cottage at Islington, and had practically adopted Emma Isola, a young orphan, whose presence brightened their lives until her marriage in 1833 to E. Moxon, the publisher. In 1825 Lamb retired, and lived at Enfield and Edmonton. But his health was impaired, and his sister's attacks of mental derangement were ever becoming more frequent and of longer duration. During one of his walks he fell, slightly hurting his face. The wound developed into erysipelas, from which he died. His sister survived until 1847.

The place of Lamb as an essayist and critic is the very highest.

His only rival in the former department is Addison, but in depth and tenderness of feeling, and richness of fancy Lamb is the superior. In the realms of criticism there can be no comparison between the two. Lamb is here at once profound and subtle, and his work led as much as any other influence to the revival of interest in and appreciation of our older poetry. His own writings, which are self-revealing in a quite unusual and always charming way, and the recollections of his friends, have made the personality of Lamb more familiar to us than any other in our literature, except that of Johnson. His weaknesses, his oddities, his charm, his humour, his stutter, are all as familiar to his readers as if they had known him, and the tragedy and noble self-sacrifice of his life add a feeling of reverence for a character we already love.

Landon, Letitia Elizabeth (14 Aug. 1802—15 Oct. 1838), poetess, daughter of an army agent, was born in Chelsea. She was a prolific and, in her day, remarkably popular writer, but she wrote too much for permanent fame. Many of her poems appeared in the *Literary Gazette*, and similar publications, but she published separately *The Fate of Adelaide* (1821), *The Improvisatrice* (1824), *The Troubadour* (1825), and *The Venetian Bracelet* (1829). She also wrote a few novels, of which *Ethel Churchill* (1837) was the best, and a tragedy *Castruccio Castracani* (1837). She married George Maclean, Governor of Cape Coast Castle, one of the West African Colonies, where, shortly after her arrival, she was found dead from the effects of an overdose of poison, which it was supposed she had taken as a relief from spasms to which she was subject. She was best known by her initials, L. E. L., under which she was accustomed to write.

Landor, Walter Savage (30 Jan. 1775—17 Sept. 1864), poet and writer of 'conversations,' son of a doctor, was born at Ipsley Court, Warwick, the property of his mother, and educated at Rugby and Oxford, where he earned the nickname of 'the mad Jacobin,' and whence he was rusticated. His whole long life thereafter was a series of quarrels, extravagances, and escapades of various kinds, the result of his violent prejudices, love of paradox, and ungovernable temper. His earliest publication was *Poems* (1795); *Gebir* (1798), an epic, had little success, but won for him the friendship of Southey. In 1808 he went to Spain to take part in the war against Napoleon, and saw some service. His first work to attract attention was his powerful tragedy of *Don Julian* (1811). About the same time he married Miss Julia Thuillier—mainly, as would appear, on account of her 'wonderful golden hair'—and purchased the estate of Llanthony Abbey, Monmouthshire, whence, after various quarrels with the local authorities, he went to France. After a residence of a year there he went in 1815 to Italy, where he lived until 1818 at Como, which, having insulted the authorities in a Latin poem, he had to leave. At Florence, which was his residence for some years, he commenced his famous *Imaginary Conversations*, of which the first two volumes appeared 1824, the third 1828, fourth and fifth 1829. Other works were *The Examination of W. Shakespeare touching Deer-stealing* (1834), *Pericles and Aspasia* (1836), *Pentameron* (1837),

Hellenics (1847), and *Poemata et Inscriptiones* (1847). He quarrelled finally with his wife in 1835, and returned to England, which, however, he had to leave in 1858 on account of an action for libel arising out of a book, *Dry Sticks Fagoted*. He went to Italy, where he remained, chiefly at Florence, until his death. Landor holds a high place among prose-writers by his restrained and finished style, which resembles Greek models. His shorter poems, such as ' Rose Aylmer,' have the same classic simplicity.

Lane, Edward William (17 Sept. 1801—6 Aug. 1876), Arabic scholar, son of a prebendary of Hereford, where he was born, began life as an engraver, but going to Egypt in search of health, devoted himself to the study of Oriental languages and manners, and adopted the dress and habits of the Egyptian men of learning. He published *Manners and Customs of the Modern Egyptians* (1836), which remains a standard authority, and a translation of *The Thousand and One Nights* (1838—40), better known as the *Arabian Nights*. What was intended to be the great work of his life, his *Arabic Lexicon*, was left unfinished at his death, but was completed by his nephew, Professor S. L. Poole. Lane was regarded as the chief European Orientalist of his day.

Lang, Andrew (31 March 1844—20 July 1912), scholar, folklorist, poet, was born in Selkirk, son of the county sheriff-clerk, and educated at Edinburgh Academy, St Andrews and Glasgow Universities, and Balliol College, Oxford, later becoming a Fellow of Merton. In 1875 he married and settled in London to make a living by writing; in this he had great versatility, and could write at any time and in any surroundings. He began with two books of verse, *Ballads and Lyrics of Old France* (1872) and *Ballades in Blue China* (1880), which inaugurated a revival of old French lyric metres; later collections of verse were *Rhymes à la Mode* (1884) and *Grass of Parnassus* (1888). His volumes of literary essays, *Letters to Dead Authors* and *Books and Bookmen* both appeared in 1886, when he had already started on the more ambitious anthropological field with *Custom and Myth* (1884), which was followed by *Myth, Ritual, and Religion* (1887) and *The Making of Religion* (1898). His ability as a classical scholar was shown in his translations of Theocritus (1880) and the *Homeric Hymns* (1899). He also collaborated with Leaf (q.v.) and Myers in a prose translation of the *Iliad* and wrote three books on Homeric problems—*Homer and the Epic* (1893), *Homer and his Age* (1906), and *The World of Homer* (1910). Of his purely historical works the best is *Prince Charles Edward* (1900); he also published a *History of Scotland* (1900—7). Younger readers know him best by his delightful series of *Fairy Books*, called by the names of different colours, and his *Book of Romance* (1902). He received doctorates of St Andrews and Oxford.

Langhorne, John (March 1735—1 April 1779), poet and translator, was born at Winton, Westmorland, son of a clergyman; having taken orders, he was for two years a curate in London, and from 1776 Rector of Blagdon, Somerset, and Prebendary of Wells. He is chiefly remembered as being the translator, jointly with his brother

William, of *Plutarch's Lives*, but in his day he had some reputation for 'pretty verses,' his *Poetical Works* being published in 1766. In his *Country Justice* (1774—7) he dimly foreshadows Crabbe, as in his descriptive poems he dimly foreshadows Wordsworth. He was twice married, and both of his wives died in giving birth to a first child.

Langland *or* **Langley, William** (1331?—1400?), poet, was born in the West Midlands, according to one account at Cleobury Mortimer in Shropshire, was educated at the school of the Benedictine monastery at Malvern, and became a clerk in minor orders. Moving to London, he lived in Cornhill with his wife and daughters, making a precarious livelihood as a scrivener or by singing requiems for the dead, and sometimes being reduced to begging. As he himself puts it, he lived both *in* and *on* London, and his experience of poverty and hardship comes out in the vivid sincerity of the pictures he draws in his work. The first version of his great poem *The Vision of William Concerning Piers the Plowman* was written about 1362; around 1377 a greatly expanded version was produced, a third about 1392, and he went on revising and adding to it till his death. Some scholars have maintained that the versions show the work of more than one hand, but this view is not now generally accepted.

The poem takes the form of an allegory, the author having a vision of 'a fair field full of folk (the world) in which Reason, Theology, Conscience, the Seven Deadly Sins, and other abstractions are depicted as living and moving.' In a second section a search is made for Do-well, Do-bet, and Do-best, with the help of Thought, Wit, and Study. Later additions are concerned with the corruption of the Church, for Langland, though a good Catholic, was an earnest reformer, and the poem is a powerful though confused satire. Apart from its literary value, it is of the first importance for the light it throws on the social history of the time. Almost exactly contemporary with Chaucer, Langland forms an interesting contrast to him, for he represents the close of the old English tradition of alliterative verse, which was superseded by the French rhyming measures that Chaucer popularized.

Langley, Noel Aubrey (25 Dec. 1911—   ), novelist and playwright, was born at Durban, and educated at Durban High School and the University of Natal. His novels include *Cage Me a Peacock* (1935), which deals in unusual fashion with some ancient Roman personalities, *There's a Porpoise Close Behind Us* (1936), *Land of Green Ginger* (1937), *The Cabbage Patch* (1947), *Nymph in Clover* (1948), *The Inconstant Moon* (1949), and *The Rift in the Lute* (1952). *Queer Cargo* (1934), *Little Lambs Eat Ivy* (1947), and *Married Alive* (1952) are plays, and he also wrote extensively for the films.

Lanier, Sidney (3 Feb. 1842—7 Sept. 1881), poet, was born at Macon, Georgia, son of a lawyer, and educated at Oglethorpe College. His career was interrupted by the Civil War, in which he served four years with the Confederates, was made a prisoner and ruined in health. After working for a time in his father's law office, in 1867 he published a war novel, *Tiger Lilies*, and soon afterwards abandoned law for writing. In 1874 *Corn*, his first long poem, a plea on behalf of Southern agriculture, brought him popular recognition. Among other pieces generally admired were 'The Song of Chatta-hoochee,' 'The Marshes of Glynn,' and 'The Master.' From 1879 to 1881 he was a lecturer in English Literature at Johns Hopkins University, but died of tuberculosis while still a young man. *The Science of English Verse* (1881) shows his critical ability, as do his lectures on *The English Novel* and *Shakespeare and his Forerunners*, which were published after his death.

Lardner, Dionysius (3 April 1793—29 April 1859), scientific writer, son of a solicitor, was born in Dublin and educated at Trinity College there. He was intended for the law, but having no taste for it, he devoted himself to literary and scientific pursuits, and became a contributor to the *Edinburgh Review*, and various Encyclopaedias. In 1827 he was appointed Professor of Natural Philosophy and Astronomy in the University of London, and in 1829 began his great work, *The Cabinet Cyclopaedia*, which, was finished in 133 volumes 20 years later. He lived in Paris from 1845 until his death.

Lardner, Ringold Wilmer (6 March 1885—25 Sept. 1933), journa-list and short-story writer who wrote under the name Ring Lardner, was born at Niles, Michigan, and studied engineering at Armour Institute, Chicago. He worked as a freight agent and book-keeper before he became a reporter. From 1910 he edited *Sporting News* at St Louis, and from 1913 to 1916 was a columnist on the Chicago *Tribune*. He became famous as a writer on sport, especially baseball, and for his short stories, written in the semi-literate argot of the baseball fan, and giving a satirical picture of different aspects of American life. He died of heart disease at the age of 48. His best-known books are *Bib Ballads* (1915), *You Know Me, Al* (1916), *Gullible's Travels* (1917), *Treat 'Em Rough* (1918), *The Big Town* (1921), *What of It?* (1925), *The Love Nest* (1926), and *Lose with a Smile* (1933). *June Moon* (1930) is a play in which he collaborated with G. S. Kaufman (q.v.), and *The Story of a Wonder Man* (1927) a fanciful autobiography.

Laski, Harold Joseph (30 June 1893—24 March 1950), political scientist, was born in Manchester and educated at Manchester Grammar School and Oxford. After being a lecturer in history at McGill University in Canada and at Harvard he returned to London and joined the staff of the London School of Economics, becoming in 1926 Professor of Political Science at London. Though a follower of Karl Marx and an extreme Socialist he was not a Communist. His books include *Political Thought in England from Locke to Bentham* (1920), *A Grammar of Politics* (1925), *Communism* (1927), *Liberty in the Modern State* (1930), *Studies in Law and Politics* (1932), *The State in Theory and Practice* (1935), *Parliamentary Government in England* (1938), and *Faith, Reason, Civilization* (1944).

Latimer, Hugh (1485?—16 Oct. 1555), bishop and martyr, born at Thurcaston in Leicestershire, son of a farmer, went to Cambridge in 1500, and became a Fellow of Clare Hall. Taking orders, he was at

o*

first a defender of the ancient faith, but convinced by the arguments of Bilney, embraced the reformed doctrines. His opposition to the Pope, and his support of the King's supremacy, brought him under the notice of Henry, and he was appointed chaplain to Anne Boleyn, and in 1535 Bishop of Worcester. For preaching in favour of the reformed doctrines he was twice imprisoned in the Tower, in 1539 and 1546, and on the former occasion resigned his bishopric, which he declined to resume on the accession of Edward VI. On the accession of Mary he was with Ridley, Bishop of London, thrown into prison, and a year later burned at Oxford. His words of encouragement to his fellow-martyr are well known, 'Be of good comfort, Master Ridley, and play the man; we shall this day light such a candle by God's grace in England as I trust shall never be put out.' He holds his place in English literature by virtue of his sermons—especially that on 'The Ploughers'—which, like himself, are outspoken, homely, and popular, with frequent touches of kindly humour.

Lauder, Sir Thomas Dick (1784—29 May 1848), novelist and journalist, born at Fountainhall, Haddington, son of a Scottish baronet, wrote two novels, *Lochandhu* (1825), and *The Wolf of Badenoch* (1827), but is best known for his *Account of the Great Floods in Morayshire in 1829*. He also wrote *Legendary Tales of the Highlands* (1841), and contributed to scientific journals and magazines.

Laver, James (14 March 1899—   ), poet, novelist, and art critic, born in Liverpool, was educated at Liverpool Institute and Oxford, where in 1921 he won the Newdigate Prize for a poem on Cervantes. His books of verse include *His Last Sebastian* (1922), *Microcosmos* (1929), and *Ladies' Mistakes* (1933). In 1922 he became Assistant Keeper of the Print Room at the Victoria and Albert Museum, and in 1927 Keeper. He wrote several books of art criticism and on the history of English costume, and became Art Director of the Working Men's College in Camden Town, a post previously held by Ruskin, Burne-Jones, and Rossetti. His later books include two novels, *Nymph Errant* (1932) and *Background for Venus* (1934), and a biography of Whistler (1930).

Lavin, Mary (11 June 1912—   ), novelist and short-story writer, born in Massachusetts, was educated in Ireland. Taking her degree at the National University of Ireland, she settled in Meath. In 1943 the Tait Black Memorial Prize was awarded to her book of short stories *Tales from Bective Bridge*. Later collections of stories were *The Long Ago* (1944), *The Becker Wives* (1946), and *A Single Lady* (1951); *The House in Clewe Street* (1945) and *Mary O'Grady* (1950), are novels. In 1947 she married William Walsh, a Dublin lawyer.

Law, William (1686—9 April 1761), clergyman, born at Kingscliffe, Northamptonshire, son of a grocer, went to Cambridge, and was elected a Fellow of Emmanuel College, but later dismissed for refusing to take the oath of allegiance to the house of Hanover. In 1728 he became tutor to the father of Gibbon the historian. His earliest works were controversial, but his fame rests on his moral treatises, *A Practical Treatise on Christian Perfection* (1726), and his best known book, *A Serious Call to a Devout and Holy Life* (1728), which has had a profound influence upon the religious life of England, largely owing to the impression which it produced upon such minds as those of Dr Johnson, the Wesleys, and others; it came second only to the Bible in spreading evangelicalism. In 1737 Law became a student of the works of Jacob Boehmen, the German mystic, and devoted himself largely to the exposition of his views.

Lawless, Anthony, *see* MacDonald, Philip.

Lawrence, David Herbert (11 Sept. 1885—2 March 1930), novelist and poet, was born at Eastwood, Nottinghamshire. His father was a coal-miner, his mother a school-teacher; *Sons and Lovers* (1913) gives a vivid picture of his early life in sordid surroundings. Educated at the High School and University College, Nottingham, he was for a time a teacher in an elementary school at Croydon. In 1911 he published a novel, *The White Peacock*, and decided to make a living by his pen. In the following year he had a liaison with Frieda, the German wife of Professor Ernest Weekley and a cousin of von Richthofen, the famous air ace; she eloped with him and they lived together in Italy, where they were married after her divorce in 1914. At this time he published *Love Poems and Others* (1913), a novel, *The Trespassers* (1912), and a volume of short stories, *The Prussian Officer* (1914). His novel *The Rainbow* (1915) was suppressed as obscene. In 1916 he published a book of travel, *Twilight in Italy*, and in the following year *Look! We Have Come Through*, a volume of poems.

During the First World War the Lawrences had lived in England, but they now went back to Italy, where in 1920 he wrote *The Lost Girl*, which won the Tait Memorial Prize, and *Women in Love*. *Sea and Sardinia* (1921) is another travel book. In 1922 they went to Australia, and he wrote *Kangaroo*, then on to New Mexico, where a friend presented him with a ranch. *The Plumed Serpent* (1926) belongs to this period. Back in England, he published *Lady Chatterley's Lover* (1928), which was banned in both Britain and the United States. Finally he died in Vence, near Nice, of tuberculosis. His *Collected Poems* were published in 1922 and his *Letters* in 1932. Apart from his excessive preoccupation with sex, Lawrence was a powerful and sensitive writer, and had a considerable influence on his contemporaries.

Lawrence, George Alfred (25 March 1827—23 Sept. 1876), novelist, was born at Braxted, Essex, son of a clergyman, and educated at Rugby and Oxford. He wrote several novels, of which one, *Guy Livingstone* (1857), had great popularity and may be said to have introduced the muscular blackguard-hero to English fiction. On the outbreak of the American Civil War he went to America with the intention of joining the Confederate Army, but was taken prisoner and only released on promising to return to England.

Lawrence, Thomas Edward (16 Aug. 1888—19 May 1935), soldier and writer, commonly called Lawrence of Arabia, was born at Tremadoc, Carnarvonshire, and educated at Oxford High School and Jesus College, where he formed a taste for archaeology, on which he worked from 1912 to 1914 in Egypt under Sir W. M. Flinders Petrie. In the First World War he was with British Intelligence and organized the Arab tribesmen in their revolt against the Turks, carrying on an effective guerrilla warfare and becoming an almost legendary figure. After the war he was given the C.B. and the D.S.O., and was offered, but refused, the Victoria Cross and a knighthood; he was also elected a Fellow of All Souls. His monumental account of the Arabian campaign, *Seven Pillars of Wisdom* (1926), which became a classic comparable with Doughty's *Arabia Deserta*, met with a curious mishap, for he lost the manuscript by leaving it in Reading railway station, and had to rewrite nearly the whole of it from memory. An abridgment, *The Revolt in the Desert*, was published in 1927, and in 1932 he published a prose rendering of Homer's *Odyssey*. Meanwhile, dissatisfied with British policy in the Near East, he sought obscurity by joining the Royal Air Force under the name of Shaw; a few weeks after he left it he was accidentally killed while riding his motor-cycle.

Layamon (fl. 1200), poetical historian, whose name is more correctly Laghamon, meaning 'Law man,' was, according to his own account, a priest of Arley Regis in Worcestershire. He wrote a long poem, *The Brut*, giving the story of England from the legendary Trojan Brutus to Cadwallader. It is based on the French rendering by Wace (q.v.) of the Latin *History* of Geoffrey of Monmouth (q.v.), with additions from Breton legend which are especially interesting because they contain the stories of Arthur, Lear, Cymbeline, and Locrine. The first important poem written in Middle English, it is a confusing mixture, written mainly in alliterative lines but occasionally using rhyme and assonance; it thus shows English verse in transition.

Layard, Sir Austin Henry (5 March 1817—5 July 1894), archaeologist, was born in Paris, son of a civil servant of Huguenot descent. After spending some years in the office of a London solicitor, he set out in search of employment in Ceylon, but passing through Western Asia, became interested in the work of excavating the remains of ancient cities. Two books—*Nineveh and its Remains* (1848—9), and *The Ruins of Nineveh and Babylon* (1853)—brought him fame, and on his return home he received many honours, including the freedom of the City of London, the degree of D.C.L. from Oxford, and the Lord Rectorship of Aberdeen University. He entered Parliament, where he sat as a Liberal. He held the offices of Under-Foreign Secretary (1861—6), and Chief Commissioner of Works (1868—9), and was Ambassador to Spain and afterwards Constantinople; on his retirement in 1878 he was made G.C.B. He left an autobiography published in 1903.

Lazarus, Emma (22 July 1849—19 Nov. 1887), poet and essayist, was born in New York City and educated privately. Very precocious, she wrote verses from an early age, her *Poems and Translations* (1867) being made up of pieces written between 14 and 16; the volume attracted the attention of Emerson, who corresponded with her all her life, and a second volume, *Admetus*, was dedicated to him. In 1876 she published *Spagnoletto*, a poetic drama, and in 1881 a translation of Heine's poems. In her last years she became the leading American champion of the Jews, and published *Songs of a Semite* (1882). Lines from her sonnet to the Statue of Liberty were inscribed on its pedestal in 1886, a year before her death.

Leacock, Stephen Butler (30 Sept. 1869—28 March 1944), political scientist and humorist, was born at Swanmoor, Hampshire. His parents emigrated to Canada in 1876, and he was educated at the University of Toronto. From 1891 to 1899 he was a teacher in Upper Canada College, then studied at Chicago, took his Ph.D. in 1903, and from then onwards worked at McGill University first as lecturer and then as head of the department of economics and political science; his text-book on the latter subject is still a standard work. He is, however, best known by his satirically humorous short stories and essays, which made him the most popular humorist in America since Mark Twain. His books in this vein include *Literary Lapses* (1910), *Nonsense Novels* (1911), *Sunshine Sketches of a Little Town* (1912), *Arcadian Adventures with the Idle Rich* (1914), *Moonbeams from the Larger Lunacy* (1915), *Further Foolishness* (1916), *Frenzied Fiction* (1917), *Winsome Winnie* (1920), and *The Garden of Folly* (1924). He also wrote studies of Mark Twain (1932) and Dickens (1933).

Leaf, Walter (28 Nov. 1852—8 March 1927), scholar and banker, was born at Upper Norwood, London, son of a business man. Educated at Harrow and Trinity College, Cambridge, where he was one of the brilliant 'Apostles' group of scholars, he went into his father's business and afterwards turned to banking, becoming a director of the London and Westminster Bank in 1891. As a scholar he is remembered chiefly for his annotated edition of Homer's *Iliad* (1888), still a standard work, and for the excellent prose translation which he made in collaboration with Andrew Lang (q.v.) and E. J. Myers. In 1912 he published *Troy, a Study in Homeric Geography*, and in 1915 *Homer and History*.

Lear, Edward (12 May 1812—30 Jan. 1888), artist and nonsense poet, was born in London of Danish descent, one of a stockbroker's fifteen children. From early years he suffered from asthma and epilepsy. Educated mainly by an elder sister, he applied himself to drawing, his first commission being to make pictures of the parrots in the zoological gardens. This led to his being asked to provide illustrations for a book on the Earl of Derby's private zoo, and while at Knowsley, Lord Derby's seat, he produced his first *Book of Nonsense* (1846) to amuse his host's children, with whom he was a great favourite. After an interval during which he visited Italy he was engaged to give drawing lessons to Queen Victoria. In later years he made many distinguished friends, including Tennyson and Lord Cromer, travelled extensively in the Mediterranean, and wrote a number of books about it, eventually dying at San Remo. His works include *Nonsense Songs* (1871), *More Nonsense* (1872), *Laughable Lyrics* (1877), and *Teapots and Quails* (1853); favourite pieces are 'The Owl and the Pussy Cat' and 'The Jumblies.' Second only to Carroll as a master of nonsense, Lear is remembered above all as the practical originator of the limerick, that favourite verse-form for popular rhymes. His *Letters* were published in 1907.

Learmont, Thomas, *see* Erceldoune, Thomas of.

Leavis, Frank Raymond (14 July 1895—   ), critic, born in Cambridge, was educated at Perse School and Emmanuel College. In 1932 he was a co-founder of the review *Scrutiny*, which he edited. In 1935 he was elected a Fellow of Downing College, and in the following year became Lecturer in English at Cambridge. Owing to the unconventional views put forward in them, his critical works have aroused a good deal of controversy. Among his more important writings are *Mass Civilization and Minority Culture* (1930), *New Bearings in English Poetry* (1932), *Tradition and Development in English Poetry* (1936), *The Great Tradition: George Eliot, James, and Conrad* (1948), *The Common Pursuit* (1952), and *D. H. Lawrence, Novelist* (1955).

Lecky, William Edward Hartpole, O.M. (26 March 1838—22 Oct. 1903), historian, the son of a landed gentleman of Carlow, was born near Dublin, and educated at Cheltenham and Trinity College, Dublin. Originally intended for the Church, he devoted himself to a literary career. His first work of importance was *Leaders of Public Opinion in Ireland* (1861), consisting of essays on Swift, Flood, Grattan, and O'Connell. The study of Buckle's *History of Civilization* to some extent determined the direction of his own writings, and resulted in the production of two important works, *History of the Rise and Influence of the Spirit of Rationalism in Europe* (1865), and *History of European Morals from Augustus to Charlemagne* (1869), both remarkable for learning, clearness, and impartiality. Both, however, gave rise to considerable controversy and criticism. His principal work is *The History of England in the Eighteenth Century* (1878—90). His view of the American war, and the controversies which led to it, is more favourable to the English position than that of some earlier historians. Other works are *Democracy and Liberty* (1896), and *The Map of Life* (1899), a volume of reflections. Though of warm Irish sympathies, Lecky was strongly opposed to Home Rule. He sat in Parliament for his University from 1895 until his death. He received many academical distinctions, and was a Corresponding Member of the Institute of France, and one of the original members of the Order of Merit.

Lee, Harriet (1757—1 Aug. 1851), novelist, was born in London, daughter of an actor. Her earliest novels were *The Errors of Innocence* (1786) and *Clara Lennox* (1797), but her chief work was *The Canterbury Tales* (1797—1805), twelve stories supposed to be told by travellers who have met together, in which she was assisted by her sister Sophia (q.v.). One of them, 'Kruitzner,' made such an impression on Byron when he read it as a boy that in 1821 he dramatized it under the title of *Werner, or, The Inheritance*. In 1798

William Godwin (q.v.) offered marriage to Harriet, who however refused him.   Celebrated for her lively conversation, she lived to be 94, retaining her faculties to the last.

Lee, Manfred (11 Jan. 1905—   ), writer of detective stories, collaborated with his cousin Frederic Dannay under the name Ellery Queen.   Born in Brooklyn and educated at New York University, he was for a time an advertising writer for a film company.   Like Dannay, he was headed for a successful business career when their joint prize-winning production *The Roman Hat Mystery* (1929) led them to make detective stories their life work.   For an account of their publications as Ellery Queen, *see* Dannay.

Lee, Nathaniel (born 1653?— buried 6 May 1692), dramatist, son of a clergyman at Hatfield, was educated at Westminster School and Cambridge.   After leaving the University he went to London, and joined the stage as both actor and author.   He was taken up by Rochester and others of the same dissolute set, led a loose life, and drank himself into Bedlam, where he spent four years.   After his recovery he lived mainly upon charity, and met his death from a fall under the effects of a carouse.   His tragedies, which, with much bombast and frequent untrained flights of imagination, have occasional fire and tenderness, are generally based on classical subjects.   The best-known is *The Rival Queens* (1677); others are *Nero* (1675) and *Mithridates* (1678).   He also wrote a few comedies, and collaborated with Dryden in an adaptation of *Oedipus*, and in *The Duke of Guise*.

Lee, Sir Sidney (5 Dec. 1859—3 March 1926), biographer, born in London, was christened Solomon Lazarus.   He was educated at the City of London School and Balliol College, Oxford; although his record was not brilliant, on Furnivall's recommendation he was appointed in 1883 to be sub-editor of the *Dictionary of National Biography* under Leslie Stephen (q.v.).   For it he himself wrote 870 articles, and in 1891 he was appointed editor.   His *Queen Victoria*, originally written as a dictionary article, was expanded into a book in 1902, and his *Life of Shakespeare* (1915), long a standard work, was his dictionary article doubled in length.   In 1911 he was given a knighthood.   The first volume of his *Life of King Edward VII* was published in 1925, but he did not live to complete the second.

Lee, Sophia (1750—13 March 1824), novelist and dramatist, was born in London, a sister of Harriet Lee (q.v.).   In 1780 she wrote an opera, *The Chapter of Accidents*, which proved so successful that she was able to start a girls' school in Bath on the proceeds.   In 1785 she published *The Recess*, one of the earliest historical romances, and later contributed to the *Canterbury Tales* of Harriet.   She produced two more plays, a tragedy, *Almeyda, Queen of Granada* (1796) and a comedy, *The Assignation* (1807).   After giving up her school in 1803 she published *The Life of a Lover* in six volumes of letters.

Lee, Vernon, *see* **Paget, Violet.**

Le Fanu, Joseph Sheridan (28 Aug. 1814—7 Feb. 1873), novelist, son of a Dean of the Episcopal Church of Ireland, and grand-nephew of Richard Brinsley Sheridan, was educated at Trinity College,

Dublin, and became a contributor and ultimately proprietor of the *Dublin University Magazine*, in which many of his novels made their first appearance. Called to the Bar in 1839, he did not practise, and was first brought into notice by two ballads, *Phaudrig Croohoore* and *Shamus O'Brien*, which had extraordinary popularity. His novels, which number twelve, include *The Cock and Anchor* (1845), *Torlough O'Brien* (1847), *The House by the Churchyard* (1863), *Uncle Silas*, perhaps the most popular (1864), *The Tenants of Malory* (1867), *In a Glass Darkly* (1872), and *Willing to Die* (1873). They are generally distinguished by able construction, ingenuity of plot, and power of the presentation of the uncanny and supernatural.

Le Gallienne, Richard (20 Jan. 1866—14 Sept. 1947), poet and essayist, was born in Liverpool, of French descent. Educated at Liverpool College, he was intended to be a chartered accountant, but found himself a misfit in an office. Some of his earliest verses were sent to O. W. Holmes, who encouraged him to be a writer. His first book, *My Lady's Sonnets*, appeared in 1887. In 1891 he was literary critic of the *Star*, then worked as a publisher's reader, and in 1898 moved to America. He finally settled on the Riviera at Mentone. As a writer he belongs to the school of the nineties, his prose being precious and mannered, his poetry delicate and artificial. Among his books of verse the most characteristic is *The Lonely Dancer* (1913), while his most famous piece is ' What of the Darkness? Is it very fair?' His best books are the reminiscent *Quest of the Golden Girl* (1896), *The Romantic Nineties* (1926), and *From a Paris Garret* (1936). He also wrote studies of Meredith (1890), Whitman (1898), and Kipling (1900). He was married three times, Eva Le Gallienne the actress being his daughter by his second wife.

Lehmann, John Frederick (2 June 1907—   ), poet and essayist, was born at Bourne End in Buckinghamshire; his father was a well-known journalist and oarsman, his mother an American. After Eton and Cambridge he spent some years in Vienna and then returned to England, where he went into the publishing business, and also edited the book-periodical *New Writing* and from 1954 the *London Magazine*. His books of verse include *A Garden Revisited* (1931), *The Noise of History* (1934), *Forty Poems* (1942), *The Sphere of Glass* (1944), and *The Age of the Dragon* (1951). *Evil Was Abroad* (1938) is a novel, *Down River* (1939) a travel book, and *The Open Night* (1952) a collection of essays. *The Whispering Gallery* (1951) is autobiographical

Lehmann, Rosamund Nina (1903—   ), novelist, born in London, a sister of John Lehmann (q.v.) was educated at Girton College, Cambridge, which was the scene of her first book, *Dusty Answer* (1927). Others of her novels are *A Note in Music* (1930), *Invitation to the Waltz* (1932) with its sequel *The Weather in the Streets* (1936), *The Ballad and the Source* (1944), and *The Echoing Grove* (1953). *The Gipsy's Baby* (1946) is a collection of short stories, and *No More Music* (1939) a play. A sensitive and brilliant writer, she excelled in depicting the thought-processes of adolescent girls. She was twice married, first to Leslie Runciman and then to Wogan Philipps, the artist.

Leigh, Henry Sambrooke (29 March 1837—16 June 1883), poet, was born in London, son of an artist. He wrote a considerable number of fluent but slight lyrics, volumes of which include *Carols of Cockayne* (1869), *A Town Garland* (1878), and *Strains from the Strand* (1882). He also translated and adapted many French comic operas for the English stage.

Leighton, Robert (1611—25 June 1684), prelate, son of a doctor, was educated at Edinburgh University, after which he resided for some time at Douay. Returning to Scotland he received Presbyterian ordination, and was admitted minister of Newbattle, near Edinburgh. In 1653 he was appointed Principal and Professor of Divinity in the University of Edinburgh, which offices he held until 1662 when, forsaking Presbyterianism, he was appointed Bishop of Dunblane, under the new Episcopal establishment. He repeatedly but unsuccessfully endeavoured to bring about an ecclesiastical union in Scotland on the basis of combining the best elements in each system. In 1669 he was appointed Archbishop of Glasgow, from which position he retired in 1674. His sermons and commentaries, all published posthumously, maintain a high place among English religious classics, alike for thought and style.

Leland, Charles Godfrey (15 Aug. 1824—20 March 1903), poet and folklorist, born in Philadelphia and educated at Princeton, Heidelberg, and Munich, studied law, but turned to literature. In 1863 he enlisted in the army and was present at the battle of Gettysburg. In 1855 he published his first work, *Meister Karl's Sketch-Book*, and in 1864 *Legends of Birds*, but his fame rests on his *Breitmann Ballads* (1871), written in a patois known as Pennsylvania Dutch. From 1869 to 1879 he lived in London. Others of his books are *Algonquin Legends* (1884), *Legends of Florence* (1895), and a *Dictionary of Slang* (1889). He also wrote on gipsy lore, of which he made a study.

Leland *or* **Leyland, John** (1506?—18 April 1552), antiquary, born in London, was educated at St Paul's School, Christ's College, Cambridge, All Soul's, Oxford, and Paris. He was a good linguist, and one of the first Englishmen to acquire Greek, and he was likewise acquainted with French, Italian, Spanish, Welsh, and Anglo-Saxon. He became chaplain and librarian to Henry VIII, from whom he received the Rectory of Poppeling, near Calais, and in 1533 the appointment of King's Antiquary. Soon afterwards he was permitted to do his work in France by deputy, and was commissioned to go over England in search of documents and antiquities; and on the strength of this made his famous tour, which lasted for about six years and is recorded in his *Itinerary* (1710). He was able to do something to stem the destruction of manuscripts on the dissolution of the monasteries, and made vast collections of documents and information regarding the monuments and general features of the country, which, however, he was unable fully to digest and set in order. They formed, nevertheless, an almost inexhaustible quarry in which succeeding workers in the same field, such as Stow, Camden, and Dugdale, wrought. In his last years he was insane, and hence none of his collections appeared in his lifetime. His *Collectanea* was published in 1715 by T. Hearne (q.v.).

Lemon, Mark (30 Nov. 1809—23 May 1870), humorous writer, born in London, was for a time manager of a brewery before taking up a literary career. He wrote many theatrical pieces, and a few novels of which the best is *Falkner Lyle* (1866), others being *Leyton Hall* and *Loved at Last*. He also wrote stories for children, lectured and gave public readings, and contributed to various periodicals. He is best known as one of the founders and, from 1843 until his death, the first editor of *Punch*. His *Jest Book* appeared in 1864.

Lennox, Charlotte (1720—4 Jan. 1804), novelist, was a daughter of Colonel Ramsay, said to have been lieutenant governor of New York, and spent her childhood in Albany, coming to England about 1735. After trying the stage without success, she took to writing and published her first book, *Poems on Several Occasions* in 1737. In 1747 she married Alexander Lennox, who had a post in the Customs. Her novel *Harriet Stuart* (1750) was admired by Dr Johnson, with whom she formed a friendship, but Mrs Thrale said that though her books were generally approved, nobody liked her. Her most famous work, *The Female Quixote* (1752), burlesques the old French romances. Other novels are *The History of Henrietta* (1758), *Sophia* (1762), and *Euphemia* (1790).

Leonard, Frederick (5 Feb. 1881—4 April 1954), dramatist who wrote under the name Frederick Lonsdale, was born in Jersey. Before becoming a playwright he was bell-boy on·a liner, seaman, and for five years a private in the South Lancashire Regiment. In 1908 he had three plays produced—*The Early Worm, The King of Cadonia,* and *The Best People*—and later wrote many witty comedies, including *Aren't We All?* (1923), *Spring Cleaning* (1925), *The Last of Mrs Cheyney* (1925), *On Approval* (1927), *Canaries Sometimes Sing* (1929), *The Street Singer* (1929), and *Once is Enough* (1938). He also collaborated in a number of musical comedies, of which *The Maid of the Mountains* (1916) was the most successful.

Leslie *or* **Lesley, John** (29 Sept. 1527—30 May 1596), prelate and historian, a son of the rector of Kingussie, studied at Aberdeen and Paris, at the former of which he became, in 1562, Professor of Canon Law. A Roman Catholic, he was a Privy Councillor (1563), and Bishop of Ross (1566), and was the confidential friend of Mary Queen of Scots, who made him her ambassador to Queen Elizabeth. He became Vicar-General of the diocese of Rouen in 1579, and died at the monastery of Guirtenburg near Brussels. While in England he wrote in Scots vernacular his *History of Scotland* from the death of James I (where Boece left off) to his own time. At Rouen he rewrote and expanded it in Latin from which it was retranslated into Scots by James Dalrymple in 1596.

Leslie, Sir John Randolph Shane (29 Sept. 1885—   ), novelist and biographer, was born in London, son of an Irish baronet by his American wife, and was educated at Eton, Paris, and Cambridge. In 1907 he visited Russia and became a friend of Tolstoi, and in the following year was converted to Roman Catholicism. After spending some time in America, in 1912 he married Marjorie Ide, daughter of the Governor-General of the Philippines. From

1916 to 1925 he was editor of the *Dublin Review*, and in 1921 he was appointed Privy Chamberlain of Sword and Cape to the Pope. His novels include *The Oppidan* (1922), *Doomsland* (1923), *Masquerades* (1924), and *The Cantab* (1926) with its sequel *The Anglo-Catholic* (1929). Among his biographies are *Manning, his Life and Labours* (1921), *George the Fourth* (1926), *The Skull of Swift, an Extempore Exhumation* (1928), and *Cardinal Gasquet, a Memoir* (1953). He also published several books of verse, and an autobiographical work, *The Film of Memory* (1938).

L'Estrange, Sir Roger (17 Dec. 1616—11 Dec. 1704), journalist and pamphleteer, born at Hunstanton, youngest son of a Norfolk baronet, was probably at Cambridge, and in 1638 took arms for the King. Six years later he was captured, imprisoned in Newgate, and condemned to death. He, however, escaped to Holland, where he was employed in the service of Charles II. On receiving a pardon from Cromwell he returned to England in 1653. In view of the Restoration he was active in writing on behalf of monarchy, and in 1663 published *Considerations and Proposals in order to the Regulation of the Press*, for which he was made Surveyor of Printing-Presses and Licenser of the Press, and received a grant of the sole privilege of printing public news. His first newspaper, *The Intelligencer*, appeared in the same year, and was followed by *The News* and the *City Mercury, or Advertisements concerning Trade*. Thereafter his life was spent in editing newspapers and writing political pamphlets in support of the Court and against the Whigs and Dissenters. In 1685 he became M.P. for Winchester, and in the same year he was knighted. His controversies repeatedly got him into trouble, and after the Revolution he lost his appointments, and was more than once imprisoned. In addition to his political writings he translated Aesop's *Fables*, Seneca's *Morals*, and Cicero's *Offices*.

Lever, Charles James (31 Aug. 1806—1 June 1872), novelist, born in Dublin, and educated at Trinity College there, studied medicine at Göttingen, and practised at various places in Ireland. In 1837 he contributed to the *Dublin University Magazine* his first novel, *Harry Lorrequer*, and the immediate and wide acceptance which it found decided him to devote himself to literature. He accordingly followed it with *Charles O'Malley* (1840), his most popular book. After this scarcely a year passed without an addition to the list of his light-hearted, breezy, rollicking stories, among which may be mentioned *Jack Hinton* (1842), *Tom Burke of Ours* (1844), *Arthur O'Leary* (1844), and *The Dodd Family Abroad* (1854). *The O'Donoghue* (1845) and *The Knight of Gwynne* (1847) are more in the nature of historical romances. In 1864 he contributed to *Blackwood's Magazine* a series of miscellaneous papers, *Cornelius O'Dowd on Men, Women, and Things in General*. Lever's life was largely spent abroad. He practised medicine in Brussels from 1840 to 1842, and in 1845 went to Italy, settled at Florence, and thereafter was British Consul successively at Spezzia and Trieste, at the latter of which he died. He continued to produce novels up to the end of his life. Among the later ones are *Sir Brooke Fosbrooke, The Bramleighs of Bishop's Folly*, and *Lord Kilgobbin*.

Lewes, George Henry (18 April 1817—28 Nov. 1878), miscellaneous writer, born in London, was educated at Dr Burney's school in Greenwich, and in Jersey and Brittany. His early life was varied; he tried law, commerce, and medicine successively, and was then for two years in Germany, on returning from which he tried the London stage, and eventually settled down to journalism, writing for the *Morning Chronicle*, for the *Penny Encyclopaedia*, and various periodicals. Thereafter he edited the *Leader* (1851—4), and the *Fortnightly Review*, which he founded. His chief works are the *Biographical History of Philosophy* (1845), *Comte's Philosophy of the Sciences* (1853), *The Physiology of Common Life* (1859), *Studies in Animal Life* (1862), and *Problems of Life and Mind* (1873—9). He was an exceptionally able dramatic critic, and in this department produced *Actors and the Art of Acting* (1875), and a book on the Spanish drama. By far his greatest work, however, is his *Life and Works of Goethe* (1855), which remains the standard English work on the subject, and which by the end of the century had, in its German translation, passed into 16 editions. He also wrote two novels, *Ranthorpe* (1847) and *Rose, Blanche, and Violet* (1848), neither of which attained any success. Lewes's life was in its latter section influenced by his irregular union with Mary Ann Evans ('George Eliot'), with whom he lived for twenty-four years in close intellectual sympathy.

Lewis, Cecil Day (27 April 1904—   ), poet, was born at Ballintogher, Ireland, son of a clergyman; on the mother's side he was related to Goldsmith. The family moved to England, and he was educated at Sherborne and Wadham College, Oxford, where he edited the anthology *Oxford Poetry* in 1927. After working as a schoolmaster at Oxford, Helensburgh, and Cheltenham, in 1935 he abandoned teaching for writing. With Auden and Spender (qq.v.), who had been his contemporaries at Oxford, he formed a poetic group partly inspired by T. S. Eliot (q.v.) and voicing the current feeling of social discontent. His more important books of verse are *Collected Poems 1929—33* (1935), *Overtures to Death* (1938), *Word Over All* (1943), and *An Italian Visit* (1953); he also translated Virgil's *Georgics* (1941) and *Aeneid* (1952) into verse. His critical works have a general appeal, some being used as school text-books. They include *A Hope for Poetry* (1934), *Poetry for You* (1945), *Enjoying Poetry* (1952), and *The Grand Manner* (1952). He wrote some novels, including *The Friendly Tree* (1936), *Starting Point* (1937), and *Child of Misfortune* (1939), but is much better known for the excellent detective stories which he published under the pseudonym Nicholas Blake. Among the best of these are *A Question of Proof* (1935), *Malice in Wonderland* (1940), and *The Case of the Abominable Snowman* (1941). During the Second World War he was employed at the Ministry of Information, and from 1951 to 1955 held the Chair of Poetry at Oxford. He was twice married, in 1928 to Constance M. King, daughter of his old headmaster, and after this marriage was dissolved in 1951 to Jill A. H. Balcon.

Lewis, Clive Staples (29 Nov. 1898—   ), moralist and novelist, was born in Belfast, son of a solicitor, and educated at

Malvern and University College, Oxford, getting a double First in Literae Humaniores and English. During the First World War he served with the Somerset Light Infantry. From 1925 to 1954 he was a Fellow of Magdalen, and then was appointed Professor of Medieval and Renaissance English at Cambridge. Important books of criticism are *The Allegory of Love* (1936) and his *English Literature in the Sixteenth Century* (1954), but he is better known for his religious and ethical works, which include *The Pilgrim's Regress* (1933), *The Problem of Pain* (1940), *The Screwtape Letters* (1942), *Christian Behaviour* (1943), *Beyond Personality* (1944), and *Mere Christianity* (1952). There is a strong religious tone also in his scientific fiction, which includes *Out of the Silent Planet* (1938), an account of an imaginary voyage to Mars, and *Perelandra* (1943), a similar romance about Venus. He also wrote a number of delightful children's books, including *The Lion, the Witch, and the Wardrobe* (1950), *Prince Caspian* (1951), *The Voyage of the Dawn Treader* (1952), and *The Silver Chair* (1953). *Surprised by Joy* (1955) is autobiographical. His long poem *Dymer* (1926) was published under the name Clive Hamilton.

Lewis, Dominic Bevan Wyndham (1894—   ), journalist and biographer, was born in Wales, son of a clergyman. He went to Oxford, but his course was interrupted by the First World War, in which he served as a private. After it he quickly made a name as a humorous columnist, being successively 'Beachcomber' of the *Daily Express* (1919—24), 'At the Sign of the Blue Moon' in the *Daily Mail* (1925—30), and from 1934 'Timothy Shy' of the *News Chronicle*. Several volumes of his inspired nonsense were collected and published, and he also edited an anthology, *The Nonsensibus* (1936), as well as editing, with Charles Lee, an entertaining collection of the worst English verse with the title *The Stuffed Owl* (1930). An excellent French scholar, Wyndham Lewis also made a number of translations, including *The Anatomy of Dandyism* of Barbey d'Aurevilly (1928), and wrote studies of Villon (1928), Louis XI (1930), the Emperor Charles V (1932), and Ronsard (1944). He was a Roman Catholic.

Lewis, Sir George Cornewall (21 April 1806—13 April 1863), statesman and scholar, son of a Radnorshire baronet, was educated at Eton and Oxford. He studied law, was called to the Bar in 1831, and entered Parliament in 1847, where his intellect and character soon gained him great influence. After serving on various important commissions and holding minor offices, he became Chancellor of the Exchequer (1855—8), Home Secretary (1859—61), and Secretary for War (1861—3). His official labours did not prevent his entering into profound and laborious studies, chiefly in regard to Roman history, and the state of knowledge among the ancients. In his *Inquiry into the Credibility of Ancient Roman History* (1855), he combated the methods and results of Niebuhr. Other works are *On the Use and Abuse of some Political Terms* (1832), *Authority in Matters of Opinion* (1849), *The Astronomy of the Ancients* (1862), and a *Dialogue on the best Form of Government* (1863).

Lewis, Harry Sinclair (7 Feb. 1885—10 Jan. 1951), novelist, son of a doctor, was born at Sauk Center, Minnesota, which appears as Gopher Prairie in his novel, *Main Street*. His college career at Yale, where he had William Rose Benét as a classmate, was interrupted by various part-time occupations. After working for some years as freelance journalist and editor, he published his first novel, *Our Mr Wrenn* in 1914, and followed it with *The Job* (1917) and *Free Air* (1919). With the appearance of *Main Street* (1920), which sold half a million copies, he became world famous. It was followed by *Babbitt* (1922), a brilliant satire on the American business man, and *Arrowsmith* (1923), which was awarded the Pulitzer Prize. Others of his novels are *Mantrap* (1926), *Elmer Gantry* (1927), *Dodsworth* (1929), *Ann Vickers* (1933), *It Can't Happen Here* (1935), a bitter study of the Fascist menace, *The Prodigal Parents* (1938), and his last, *World So Wide* (1951). He also wrote a number of plays. *The Man from Main Street* (1954) is a collection of his essays, and his *Letters* were published in 1952. In 1930 he became the first American writer to be awarded the Nobel Prize.

Lewis, Matthew Gregory (9 July 1775—14 May 1818), novelist, born in London, son of a deputy secretary in the War Office, was educated at Westminster and Oxford. Thereafter he went to Germany. From his childhood tales of witchcraft and the supernatural had a powerful fascination for him, and in Germany he had ample opportunities for pursuing his favourite study, with the result that at the age of 20 he became the author of *The Monk*, a tale in which the supernatural and the horrible predominate to an unprecedented extent, and from which he is known as 'Monk Lewis.' The same characteristic appears in all his works, which include *Tales of Terror* (1779), *Tales of Wonder* (1801), to which Sir W. Scott contributed, and *Romantic Tales* (1808). From 1796 to 1802 he was M.P. for Hindon. In 1817 he visited his West Indian estates to arrange for better treatment of the slaves, and died of yellow fever on the voyage home. His valuable *Journal of a West Indian Proprietor* was published in 1834.

Lewis, Percy Wyndham (1884—7 March 1957), artist, novelist, and essayist, born in Maine of English parents, was taken to England while still a child, and educated at Rugby, afterwards studying at the Slade School of Art. During the First World War he served with the Artillery. A leader of the Vorticist school of writing, he was co-founder with Ezra Pound (q.v.) of their organ, *Blast*, and afterwards edited some other short-lived periodicals. His first published book was *Tarr* (1918), a novel. Most of his works have been described as 'part novel, part essay, but all satire.' They include *Time and Western Man* (1927), *The Childermas* (1928), *The Apes of God* (1930), *The Hitler Cult* (1939), *America and Cosmic Man* (1948), and *The Writer and the Absolute* (1952). *One Way Song* (1933) is a volume of verse, *Rotting Hill* (1951) a book of short stories, while *Blasting and Bombardiering* (1937) and *Rude Assignment* (1950) are autobiographical. A distinguished artist, Wyndham Lewis has five works in the Tate Gallery.

Leyden, John (8 Sept. 1775—28 Aug. 1811), poet and orientalist, born at Denholm, Roxburgh, son of a shepherd, studied for the ministry at Edinburgh University, where he had a brilliant career, showing a special aptitude for languages and natural history. In 1800 he became a licentiate of the Church, but continued his scientific and linguistic studies, and also began to write. In 1799 he had published a sketch of the *Discoveries and Settlements of the Europeans in Northern and Western Africa*, and he contributed to Scott's *Minstrelsy of the Scottish Border*, and to 'Monk' Lewis's *Tales of Wonder*. In 1803 he published a poem, *Scenes of Infancy*, and in the same year, having qualified as a surgeon, sailed for India. He visited the Malay Peninsula, and some of the East Indian Islands, collecting vast stores of linguistic and ethnographical information, on which was founded his great *Dissertation on the Indo-Persian, Indo-Chinese, and Dekkan Languages* (1807). Soon after this Leyden was appointed a professor in the Bengal College, and a little later a judge in Calcutta. In 1811 he accompanied the Governor-General, Lord Minto, to Java. His health, however, had been undermined by his exertions, and immediately after landing he contracted a fever, of which he died in three days at the early age of 36. Two Oriental works translated by him, *Malay Annals* and *Commentaries of Baber*, were published respectively in 1821 and 1826. He knew more than thirty languages, and translated the Gospels into five.

Liddell Hart, Basil Henry (31 Oct. 1895—   ), military tactician and historian, was born in London and educated at St Paul's and Cambridge. During the First World War he served as a captain in the infantry, became recognized as a military expert, and in 1920 was given the task of writing the official post-war manual on military training; an exponent of the defence principle, he modernized both drill and tactics. He became military correspondent of the *Daily Telegraph* in 1925, and of *The Times* in 1935, and meanwhile lectured on military history at Cambridge. In addition to various works on tactics he wrote *A History of the World War* (1935), *The Defence of Britain* (1939), and studies of Scipio (1926), Sherman (1929), Foch (1931), and T. E. Lawrence (1934). *The Other Side of the Hill* (1948) is a study of the Second World War, and *The Defence of the West* (1950) discusses the threat from Russia; he also edited *The Rommel Papers* (1950). A very good lawn tennis player, he published *Lawn Tennis Masters Unveiled* in 1926.

Liddell, Henry George (6 Feb. 1811—18 Jan. 1898), scholar, born at Binchester in Durham, was educated at Charterhouse and Christ Church, Oxford, where he got a double First and in 1845 was appointed White's Professor of Moral Philosophy. From 1846 to 1855 he was headmaster of Westminster, and thereafter was Dean of Christ Church for thirty-six years, a record for this office. He is remembered best as the compiler, with Robert Scott, Master of Balliol, of the Greek lexicon which bears their names. He also wrote a *History of Rome* (1855). It was for Liddell's young daughter Alice that Dodgson wrote his *Alice in Wonderland*.

Liddon, Henry Parry (20 Aug. 1829—9 Sept. 1890), clergyman, son of a captain in the navy, was born at North Stoneham, Hampshire, and educated at King's College School, London, and Oxford. He took orders in 1853, was Vice-Principal of Cuddesdon Theological College from 1854 to 1859, Prebendary of Salisbury (1864), and Canon of St Paul's (1870). He was also Ireland Professor of Exegesis at Oxford from 1870 to 1882. In 1866 he delivered his Bampton Lectures on *The Divinity of Our Lord*, and came to be recognized as one of the ablest and most eloquent representatives of the High Church party. His sermons in St Paul's were among the leading features of the religious life of London.

Lightfoot, Joseph Barber (13 April 1828—21 Dec. 1889), theologian and scholar, born in Liverpool, and educated at King Edward's School, Birmingham, and Cambridge, took holy orders, and was successively Hulsean Professor of Divinity (1861), Chaplain to Queen Victoria (1862), member of the New Testament Company of Revisers (1870—1880), Margaret Professor of Divinity, Cambridge (1875), and Bishop of Durham (1879). He was probably the greatest scholar of his day in England, especially as a grammarian and textual critic. Among his works are commentaries on several of the minor Pauline epistles, a fragmentary work on the Apostolic Fathers, *Leaders in the Northern Church* (1890), and *The Apostolic Age* (1892).

Lillo, George (4 Feb. 1693—3 Sept. 1739), dramatist, of Dutch descent, was born in London, succeeded his father in business as a jeweller, and devoted his leisure to the composition of plays of the type termed domestic drama. He wrote in all seven of these, among which are *The London Merchant, or the History of George Barnewell* (1731), *The Christian Hero* (1735), and *Fatal Curiosity* (1736). He was a friend of Fielding, who said of him that 'he had the spirit of an old Roman joined to the innocence of a primitive Christian.'

Lincoln, Abraham (12 Feb. 1809—15 April 1865), President of the United States, was born in a log cabin in Kentucky, son of an illiterate backwoodsman. Till the age of 19 he was employed on farm work, then studied law and became an attorney, sitting in the Illinois legislature from 1834 to 1842. Strength of character made up for his imperfect education, and he rose to be a member of Congress from 1847 to 1849, and in 1861 to take office as President. It fell to him to steer the ship of state through the civil war that broke out a month later, and by his policy to preserve the American people as a united nation. One of the greatest of the world's champions of democracy, he takes his place in literary history through the simple but moving eloquence of his speeches, particularly the *Emancipation Proclamation* of 1862, which announced freedom for slaves; the *Gettysburg Address*, delivered in 1863 at the dedication of a national cemetery on the site of the Pennsylvania battle-field, and containing the memorable phrase 'government of the people, by the people, for the people'; and the *Inaugural Address* of 1865 at the opening of his second term of office, which was so tragically cut short by his assassination. There are several editions of his *Collected Works*, the latest being in 1953, and an *Autobiography* was edited in 1926.

Lindsay, Alfred William Norman (1879—   ), artist and novelist, was born at Creswick, Victoria, son of a doctor. At the age of 16 he joined the staff of a Melbourne paper as an illustrator, and later he became chief cartoonist of the famous *Sydney Bulletin* and the leading black-and-white artist of Australia. As a writer he was noted for his 'frank and funny' novels, one of which, *Red Heap* (1931), was banned in Australia; in many ways he recalled the days of the *Yellow Book*, and he has been compared with Beardsley. Others of his novels are *A Curate in Bohemia* (1913), *Saturdee* (1933), *Pam in the Parlour* (1934), *The Cautious Amorist* (1934), *Age of Consent* (1938), *The Cousin from Fiji* (1945), and *Dust or Polish* (1950). *Creative Effort* (1920) is a volume of essays. His hobby was making ship models.

Lindsay *or* **Lyndsay, Sir David** (1490—1555), poet and satirist, son of David Lindsay of the Mount in Fife, was born either there or at Garmylton near Haddington, and educated at St Andrews. Early in life he was at the Court of James IV, and on the King's death was appointed to attend on the infant James V, whose friend and counsellor he remained, though his advice was, unhappily for his country, not always given heed to. In 1522 he married Janet Douglas, the king's sempstress, and in 1529 he was knighted and made Lyon King at Arms. He was employed on various missions to the Emperor Charles V, and to Denmark, France, and England. He was always in sympathy with the people as against the nobles and the clergy, and was their poet. He favoured the Reformers, and was one of those who urged Knox to become a preacher. He did not, however, adhere to the reformed congregation, and died at least nominally in the Roman Church. Yet he lashed the vices of the clergy as they had never been lashed before, and only escaped their vengeance by the protection of the King, who also condoned the severities directed against himself. His latter days were spent at The Mount, where he died. His chief writings are *The Dreme* (1528), *The Complaynt to the King* (1529), *The Testament and Complaynt of our Soverane Lord's Papyngo* (Parrot) (1530), *Ane Pleasant Satyre of the Three Estaitis*, his greatest work, on which his reputation principally rests (1540), *A Dialogue betwixt Experience and a Courtier* (1552), *The Monarchy* (1554), and *The History of Squyer Meldrum*. Lindsay was a true poet, gifted with fancy, humour, and a powerful satiric touch and a love of truth and justice.

Lindsay, Jack (1900—   ), novelist and scholar, born in Melbourne, son of A. W. Norman Lindsay (q.v.) was educated at Brisbane Grammar School and University, taking a First in Classics; later he made many translations of Latin and Greek authors, including Theocritus, Catullus, Propertius, Petronius, and Ausonius. In 1926 he came to England and wrote a number of historical novels, including *Cressida's First Lover* (1932), *Rome for Sale* (1934), *Caesar Is Dead* (1935), *Last Days with Cleopatra* (1935), *Brief Light* (1939), and *Hannibal Takes a Hand* (1941). Stories of more modern times are *Rebels of the Goldfields* (1936), *Sue Verney* (1937), *Stormy Violence* (1947), *Fires in Smithfield* (1949), and *The Rising Tide* (1953). During the Second World War he worked at the War Office as a script-writer.

Lindsay, Nicholas Vachel (10 Nov. 1879—5 Dec. 1931), poet, born at Springfield, Illinois, was educated at Hiram College. Later he attended classes at Chicago Art Institute while working in a shop during the day, and then studied at New York Art School, but could not sell his drawings. He then turned to writing and went tramping through the West, making a livelihood by reciting his poems; this was more or less the career he followed all his life, reciting or lecturing, and preaching what he termed the gospel of beauty; the boredom of his monotonous round is reflected in the falling-off in his work after the initial volumes. After his marriage in 1925 he lived for a time in his wife's home at Spokane, Washington, then returned to Springfield, where in despair he committed suicide. As will be realized from 'The Congo' and 'General Booth Enters Heaven,' the title-poems of his first two volumes, his poems were written for chanting, and he has been called 'the jazz Blake.' Later books of his verse are *The Chinese Nightingale* (1917), *The Golden Whales of California* (1920), and *Every Soul Is a Circus* (1929). *A Handy Guide for Beggars* (1916) was based on his own experiences on the road.

Lindsay of Birker, Alexander Dunlop Lindsay, 1st Baron (14 May 1879—18 March 1952), scholar, was born in Glasgow, where his father was Principal of the United Free Church College, and was educated at Glasgow Academy and University and at University College, Oxford, where he was President of the Union. From 1906 to 1922 he was a Fellow and Tutor of Balliol, and from 1924 to 1949 Master; from 1922 to 1924 he was Professor of Moral Philosophy at Glasgow, and from 1935 to 1938 he was Vice-Chancellor of Oxford. During the First World War he did staff work in France with the rank of lieutenant colonel and was made a C.B.E. In 1945 he was created Lord Lindsay, and in 1949 was appointed Principal of the new University College of North Staffordshire. His works include *The Philosophy of Bergson* (1911), *The Philosophy of Kant* (1913), *The Nature of Religious Truth* (1927), *General Will and Common Mind* (1928), *The Essentials of Democracy* (1929), *Christianity and Economics* (1933), *Kant* (1934), *The Moral Teaching of Jesus* (1937), *The Two Moralities* (1940), and *The Modern Democratic State* (1943).

Lindsay, John Maurice (21 July 1918—   ), poet and critic, was born in Glasgow and educated at Glasgow Academy. He studied at the Scottish National Academy of Music, and was for a time music critic of a Scottish newspaper. In 1946 he edited *Modern Scottish Poetry: An Anthology of the Scottish Renaissance, 1920–1945*; he also edited *Poetry Scotland* from 1943 to 1949, and in 1950 the *Scots Review*. Volumes of his own verse are *No Crown for Laughter* (1943), *The Enemies of Love* (1946), *Hurlygush* (1948), *At the Wood's Edge* (1950), and *Ode for St Andrew's Night* (1950). His critical works include *The Scottish Renaissance* (1948), a study of *Robert Burns* (1954), and a *Burns Encyclopaedia* (1959). *The Lowlands of Scotland* (1953) and *Clyde Waters* (1958) are topographical books.

Lindsay, Robert (1500?—1565?), historian, born at Pitscottie, Fife, wrote a history entitled *The Chronicles of Scotland*, intended as a continuation of that of Boece. It deals with the period 1436—1515, and though often inaccurate in detail, is vivid and quaint.

Lingard, John (5 Feb. 1771—17 July 1851), historian, born at Claxby, Lincolnshire, son of a carpenter, was in 1782 sent to the English College at Douay, whence he escaped from the revolutionaries in 1793, and returning to England, went to Crookhall College, near Durham, and afterwards to Ushaw. Ordained a priest in 1795, he became Vice-President and Professor of Philosophy at the latter college. In 1806 he published *The Antiquities of the Anglo-Saxon Church*, and while a missioner at Hornby, Lancashire, began his *History of England to the Accession of William and Mary* (8 volumes, 1819—30). In the preparation of this work Lingard had access to material hitherto unpublished, and not available for Protestant historians, such as documents in the Vatican and other Roman Catholic sources, and was consequently able to throw new light on various parts of his subject. It gives an account of the Reformation period viewed from the side of the enlightened Roman Catholic priesthood.

Linklater, Eric (1899—), novelist, born at Dounby in the Orkney Islands, was educated at Aberdeen Grammar School and Aberdeen University, where he started to study medicine but finished up with an English degree. In the First World War he served with the Black Watch and was severely wounded at Passchendaele. For a time after the war he was assistant editor of *The Times of India* at Bombay. In 1927 he was an assistant in the English Department at Aberdeen, and from 1928 to 1930 travelled in the United States with a Commonwealth Fellowship; during this time he wrote *Poet's Pub*, his first novel. In 1933 he married Marjorie MacIntyre, and they made their home in Orkney, but he still made numerous trips abroad. A member of the Scottish Nationalist movement, Linklater was famous for his satirical and picaresque novels, of which the best are *Juan in America* (1931), *The Men of Ness* (1932), *The Crusader's Key* (1933), *Ripeness Is All* (1935), *Juan in China* (1937), *The Impregnable Women* (1938), *Judas* (1939), *Cornerstones* (1941), *Sealskin Trousers* (1949), and *The House of Gair* (1953). *A Year of Space* (1953) is a book of travel, and *The Man on My Back* (1941), an autobiography. From 1945 to 1948 he was Lord Rector of Aberdeen University.

Linton, Eliza (10 Feb. 1822—14 July 1898), novelist, was born at Keswick, daughter of James Lynn, a clergyman. She settled in London in 1845, and next year produced her first novel, *Azeth, the Egyptian; Amymone* (1848), and *Realities* (1851), followed. None of these had any great success, and she then joined the staff of the *Morning Chronicle*, and *All the Year Round*. In 1858 she married W. J. Linton, an eminent wood-engraver, who was also a poet of some note. In 1867 they separated in a friendly way, the husband going to America, and the wife devoting herself to novel-writing, in which she attained wide popularity. Her most successful works were *The True History of Joshua Davidson* (1872), *Patricia Kemball* (1874), and *Christopher Kirkland* (1885). She was a severe critic of the 'new woman.'

Lister, Thomas Henry (1800—5 June 1842), novelist, born near Lichfield and educated at Westminster and Cambridge, became the first Registrar-General for England and Wales. He wrote several novels, among which are *Granby* (1826), *Herbert Lacy* (1828), and *Arlington* (1832). He was also the author of a life of Clarendon.

Lithgow, William (1582—1645?), traveller, born at Lanark and educated at the grammar school there, claimed at the end of his various peregrinations to have tramped 36,000 miles in nineteen years. Previous to 1610 he had visited Shetland, Switzerland, and Bohemia. In that year he set out for Palestine and Egypt. His next journey (1614—16) was in Tunis and Fez; but his last (1619—1621), to Spain, ended unfortunately in his apprehension at Malaga and torture as a spy. He gave an account of his travels in *Rare Adventures and Paineful Peregrinations* (1632), and wrote *The Siege of Breda* (1637), *The Siege of Newcastle* (1645), and *Poems*.

Livingstone, David (19 March 1813—30 April 1873), missionary and explorer, born at Blantyre, Lanarkshire, spent the years between 10 and 24 as an operative in a cotton mill there. Qualifying as a medical missionary, and entering the service of the London Missionary Society, he sailed in 1841 to South Africa. He subsequently made exploration expeditions, in which he discovered Lake Ngami in 1849, and the River Zambesi in 1851. In 1856 he visited England, published his *Missionary Travels* (1857), and retired from the service of the London Missionary Society. He was Consul at Quilimane 1858—64, and in 1858 commanded an expedition for exploring Eastern and Central Africa, discovering Lakes Shirwa and Nyassa in 1859. Again visiting England he published his second book, *The Zambesi and its Tributaries* (1865). Returning to Africa he organized an expedition to the Nile basin, discovered Lake Bangweolo, and endured terrible sufferings and dangers, from which he was rescued just in time by H. M. Stanley (q.v.). His last journey was to discover the sources of the Nile, but it proved fatal, as he died at a village in Ilala. His remains were brought home and buried in Westminster Abbey. Livingstone ranks among the greatest explorers and philanthropists. The diary which he kept was published as *Last Journals of David Livingstone in Central Africa* (1874).

Livingstone, Sir Richard Winn (1880—   ), scholar and educationist, born in Liverpool, son of a clergyman, was educated at Winchester and New College, Oxford. For a short time he was an assistant master at Eton. From 1924 to 1933 he was Vice-Chancellor of Queen's University, Belfast, and thereafter till 1950 President of Corpus Christi College, Oxford, being also Vice-Chancellor of the University from 1944 to 1947. His works include *The Greek Genius and its Meaning to Us* (1912), *A Defence of Classical Education* (1916), *The Pageant of Greece* (1923), *The Mission of Greece* (1928), *Greek Ideals and Modern Life* (1935), *The Future in Education* (1941), *Education for a World Adrift* (1943), *Some Tasks for Education* (1947), and *Education and the Spirit of the Age* (1952). Knighted in 1931, he held many other distinctions, including honorary degrees of seven universities.

Llewellyn, Richard, *see* **Lloyd.**

Lloyd, Richard David Vivian Llewellyn (1907—   ),
novelist and playwright who wrote under the name Richard
Llewellyn, born at St David's, Pembrokeshire, was educated there
and in Cardiff.   At the age of 16 he was sent to Italy to learn hotel
management, and studied painting and sculpture in his spare time.
From 1926 to 1931 he served in the regular army, then took up film
work, beginning as an extra and rising to be production manager and
director.   This experience was useful when he was writing his plays
Poison Pen (1937) and *Noose* (1947).   His highly successful novel
How Green Was My Valley (1939), telling of a South Wales mining
family, was followed by *None But the Lonely Heart* (1943) and *A Few
Flowers for Shiner* (1950).   During the Second World War he was
Chief Transport Officer for E.N.S.A., and later served as a captain
in the Welsh Guards.

Lloyd, Robert (1733—15 Dec. 1764), poet, born in Westminster,
where his father was a schoolmaster, was educated there, having
Cowper, Charles Churchill, and Warren Hastings as his schoolmates,
and afterwards going on to Cambridge.   For a time he was a master
at Westminster, but gave this up and took to writing.   In 1760 he
published *The Actor*, and in 1762 a collection of other poems.   In the
following year he was arrested for debt and confined in the Fleet
Prison, where he died in spite of assistance given him by Churchill,
to whose sister he was engaged.   Lloyd's comic opera *The Capricious
Lovers* was staged only a fortnight before his death.

Locke, David Ross (20 Sept. 1833—15 Feb. 1888), journalist who
used the pseudonym Petroleum V. Nasby, was born at Vestal, near
Binghamton, New York.   Leaving school at the age of 10, he at
once began newspaper work.   During the Civil War he came into
prominence by writing illiterate letters signed Nasby, championing
slavery and the Democrats, and so bringing ridicule on them.   A
first volume of these, *The Nasby Papers* (1864) was followed by other
collections.   Locke's later books include *The Morals of Abou Ben
Adhem* (1875) and a political novel, *The Demagogue* (1891).

Locke, John (29 Aug. 1632—28 Oct. 1704), philosopher, son of an
attorney, was born at Wrington, near Bristol, and educated at Westminster School, where he was a schoolfellow of Dryden, and at
Oxford.   In 1660 he became lecturer on Greek, in 1662 on Rhetoric,
and in 1664 he went as secretary to an Embassy to Brandenburg.
While a student he had turned from the subtleties of Aristotle and
the schoolmen, had studied Descartes and Bacon, and becoming
attracted to experimental science, studied medicine, and practised a
little in Oxford.   At the same time his mind had been much exercised
by questions of morals and government, and in 1667 he wrote his
Essay on Toleration.   In the same year he became secretary to Lord
Ashley, afterwards 1st Earl of Shaftesbury, in whose house he went
to reside.   Here he made the acquaintance of Buckingham, Halifax,
and other leading men of the time, and was entrusted by Ashley with
the education of his son, and afterwards of his grandson, the famous
3rd Earl of Shaftesbury (q.v.).   In 1672 when Ashley became

Chancellor he bestowed upon Locke the office of Secretary of Presentations, and afterwards a post at the Board of Trade. In 1675 Locke took his medical degree, and in the same year went for the benefit of his health, which had always been delicate, to Montpelier, where there was then a celebrated medical school, and subsequently to Paris, where he became acquainted with most of the eminent Frenchmen of the day. Recalled by Shaftesbury in 1679 he returned to England but, his patron having in 1682 been obliged to take refuge in Holland from a prosecution for high treason, he followed him. After Shaftesbury's death Locke remained there until the Revolution, when he returned to England in the fleet which carried the Princess of Orange.

He was now in favour with Government, and was appointed a Commissioner of Appeals. In 1698 he was an adviser of the Government on the question of the coinage, and was made a member of the newly instituted Council on Trade, which position he resigned in 1700. During his last years he lived with Sir Francis and Lady Masham at Oates in Essex, where Lady Masham, who was a daughter of Ralph Cudworth (q.v.), and an old friend, assiduously tended his last years. The services of Locke to his country in civil and religious matters were various and great; but it is upon his philosophical writings, and chiefly on his *Essay on the Human Understanding* (1690) that his fame rests. It is divided into four books, of which the first treats of innate ideas (the existence of which he denies), the second traces the origin of ideas, the third deals with language, and the fourth lays down the limits of the understanding. Other works of his are *Treatises on Government* (1690), *Letters on Toleration* (1689—92), *Thoughts concerning Education* (1693), and *The Reasonableness of Christianity* (1695). If not a very profound or original philosopher Locke was a calm, sensible, and reasonable writer, and his books were very influential on the English thought of his day, as well as on the French philosophy of the next century. His style is plain and clear, but lacking in brightness and variety.

Locke, William John (20 March 1863—15 May 1930), novelist, was born at Demerara, British Guiana, son of a banker, and educated at Queen's Royal College, Trinidad, and Cambridge. From 1890 to 1897 he was a schoolmaster at Clifton and then at Glenalmond, but found the work uncongenial; thereafter for ten years he was secretary to the Royal Institute of British Architects. *At the Gate of Samaria* (1895) was his first novel, but it was not until the publication of *The Morals of Marcus Ordeyne* (1905) and *The Beloved Vagabond* (1906) that he achieved real success. Others of his romances are *Septimus* (1909), *Simon the Jester* (1910), *The Joyous Adventures of Aristide Pujol* (1912), *Stella Maris* (1913), *The Wonderful Year* (1916), *The Golden Adventures of Mr Paradyne* (1924), and *The Great Pandolfo* (1925). He also wrote a number of plays.

Locker, *later* **Locker-Lampson, Frederick** (29 May 1821—30 May 1895), poet, was born at Greenwich Hospital, where his father was civil commissioner. Educated at various London schools, he became in 1837 a clerk in Mincing Lane, then in Somerset House and finally in the Admiralty. In 1850 he married a daughter of the Earl of Elgin and soon afterwards left the government service. In 1857 he published his only volume of poetry, *London Lyrics*, which was extended and rearranged in ten subsequent editions; it contains light witty verses in the style of Praed. Ten years later he compiled *Lyra Elegantiarum*, an excellent anthology of *vers de société*. In 1872 his first wife died, and two years later he married Hannah J. Lampson, whose name he added to his own. *My Confidences* (1896) is a volume of reminiscences.

Lockhart, John Gibson (14 July 1794—25 Nov. 1854), biographer and novelist, was born at Cambusnethan, Lanarkshire, where his father was minister, and educated at Glasgow and Oxford. He studied law at Edinburgh, and was called to the Scottish Bar in 1816, but had little taste for the profession. Having, however, already translated Schlegel's *Lectures on the History of Literature*, he devoted himself more and more to a literary life. He joined John Wilson, and became one of the leading contributors to *Blackwood's Magazine*. After bringing out *Peter's Letters to his Kinsfolk* (1819), sketches of Edinburgh society, he produced four novels, *Valerius* (1821), *Adam Blair* (1822), *Reginald Dalton* (1824), and *Matthew Wald* (1824). His *Life of Burns* appeared in 1828. He was editor of the *Quarterly Review* from 1824 to 1853. In 1820 he had married Sophia, daughter of Sir Walter Scott, which led to his writing his famous *Life of Scott* (1838), undoubtedly one of the greatest biographies in the language. His later years were overshadowed with deep depression caused by the death of his wife and children. A reserved and cold manner led to his being regarded with dislike by many, but his intimate friends were warmly attached to him.

Lockhart, Sir Robert Hamilton Bruce (2 Sept. 1887—), journalist, was born at Anstruther, Fife, and educated at Fettes and the Universities of Paris and Berlin. In 1907 he went to Malaya to work on a rubber plantation. Later he entered the consular service and between 1911 and 1917 was British vice-consul and then consul in Moscow. When an attempt was made in 1918 to assassinate Lenin he was condemned to death on suspicion of being implicated, but was afterwards exchanged for Litvinoff, whom the British had arrested in reprisal. For ten years from 1919 onwards he was engaged in various financial enterprises, then worked on the staff of the *Evening Standard* till 1937. During the Second World War he was deputy under-secretary at the Foreign Office, and in 1943 he was made a Knight Commander of St Michael and St George. Most of his books tell of different aspects of his career. They include *Memoirs of a British Agent* (1932), *Retreat from Glory* (1934), *Return to Malaya* (1936), *My Scottish Youth* (1937), *Comes the Reckoning* (1947), and *My Europe* (1952).

Lodge, Sir Oliver Joseph (12 June 1851—22 Aug. 1940), scientist, was born at Penkhull, Staffordshire, and educated at Newport Grammar School, Shropshire, which he left to assist in his father's pottery business. Taking up the study of physics, he became a demonstrator at University College, London, where he took his

D.Sc. in 1877. From 1881 to 1901 he was Professor of Physics at Liverpool University, and after that Principal of Birmingham. As one of the world's leading physicists, he was awarded the Rumford and Albert Medals of the Royal Society, of which he was elected a Fellow in 1887, and in 1913 he was President of the British Association for the Advancement of Science. He was knighted in 1902. Some of his most important work was done on electro-magnetism and wireless telegraphy, and he published many scientific works, including *Life and Matter* (1905), *Man and the Universe* (1908), *Atoms and Rays* (1924), *Ether and Reality* (1925), and *Science and Human Progress* (1927). He became widely known for his interest in psychical research, especially after the death in the First World War of his son, of whom he wrote in *Raymond* (1916); *My Philosophy* followed in 1933. *Past Years* (1931) is an autobiography.

Lodge, Thomas (1558—Sept. 1625), dramatist and writer of romances, a son of the Lord Mayor of London, was educated at Merchant Taylors' and Trinity College, Oxford; he studied law at Lincoln's Inn but abandoned it for letters. In 1580 he published *A Defence of Plays* in answer to Gosson's *School of Abuse*, and in 1584 *An Alarum Against Usurers*; another of his moral pamphlets was *Wit's Misery and the World's Madness* (1596). About 1588 he wrote an historical play, *Wounds of the Civil War*, and a year or two later collaborated with Greene (q.v.) in *A Looking Glass for London*. But Lodge was heavy as a dramatist. His most important works were his romances, the Elizabethan counterpart of the modern novel. Two of these are *The History of Forbonius and Prisceria* (1584) and *Rosalynd, Euphues' Golden Legacy* (1590), which was written to pass the time during a voyage to the Canaries, and is remembered as providing the plot for Shakespeare's *As You Like It*. Lodge also excelled in lyrics, which are often used to diversify his romances. Separate poetical works are *Scilla's Metamorphosis* (1589), a poem on classical mythology; *Phillis* (1593), a series of love sonnets; and *A Fig for Momus* (1595), containing satires on the Horatian model. Later he published translations of Josephus (1602) and Seneca (1614). About 1595 he went to Avignon to study medicine, and on his return obtained an Oxford degree, but fell a victim to the plague, which he courageously stayed in London to combat.

Lofting, Hugh (14 Jan. 1886—26 Sept. 1947), writer of children's books, was born at Maidenhead, Berkshire, and educated at a Jesuit boarding school in Derbyshire; later he studied at the Massachusetts Institute of Technology and London Polytechnic, worked as a civil engineer in Canada, Africa, and the West Indies, and in 1912 settled in New York. During the First World War he served with the British forces in Flanders, and the idea of children's books came to him when he was trying to write interesting letters home from the front; he was impressed with the part animals were playing in the war, so Dr Dolittle, with his great interest in pets, came into being. There is a whole series of books telling of the doctor's adventures, from *The Story of Dr Dolittle* (1920) to *Dr Dolittle and the Green Canary* (1950). Others of Lofting's children's books are *The Story* *of Mrs Tubbs* (1923), and *Noisy Norah* (1929). In 1922 he was awarded the Newbery Medal, an American distinction given specially for children's books.

Logan, John (1748—25 Dec. 1788), minister and poet, son of a small farmer at Soutra, Midlothian, was educated at Musselburgh Grammar School and Edinburgh University, and became minister of South Leith in 1773. In 1770 he edited the poems of Michael Bruce (q.v.), who had been a fellow-student. Unfortunately, he appears to have claimed to be the author of some of Bruce's poems, and inserted them in a volume of his own, published eleven years later. The 'Ode to the Cuckoo,' which Burke once declared to be the most beautiful lyric in the language, became a particular subject of controversy. But the evidence appears conclusive that Bruce wrote it. Logan fell into dissipated habits, resigned his ministerial charge, and went to London, where he became a journalist.

London, John Griffith (12 Jan. 1876—22 Nov. 1916), novelist who wrote under the name Jack London, was born in San Francisco, the illegitimate son of an Irish vagabond and an American girl who afterwards married John London, a grocer. Brought up in poverty, he worked at all sorts of odd jobs, but read omnivorously. About the age of 19 he attended Oakland High School for a short time and then had a year at the University of California. But an ordered existence was impossible to him. The open sea and the open road were his passions, and at one time he was arrested as a vagrant. In 1897 he took part in the Klondike gold rush; he got no gold, but from his experiences he afterwards wrote *The Call of the Wild* (1903), which sold nearly a million and a half copies. In 1904 he was a special correspondent in the Russo-Japanese War, and in 1907 he set off with his wife for a world cruise; after visiting Honolulu they abandoned the voyage at Australia, and he wrote of it in *The Cruise of the Snark* (1911). In 1912 he sailed round the Horn. At this time he was reckoned the best paid and most popular writer in America, but drink and extravagance caused his work to deteriorate, and he finally committed suicide. He is best remembered for his primitive and sensational stories, such as *The God of his Fathers* (1901), *The Sea Wolf* (1904), *White Fang* (1905), *Before Adam* (1906), *Smoke Bellew* (1912), *John Barleycorn* (1913), *The Star Rover* (1914), and *Jerry of the Islands* (1917).

Long, George (4 Nov. 1800—10 Aug. 1879), scholar, born at Poulton, Lancashire, son of a merchant, was educated at Macclesfield Grammar School and Trinity College, Cambridge. He was Professor of Ancient Languages in the University of Virginia, Charlottesville, from 1824 to 1828, of Greek at University College, London, from 1828 to 1831, and of Latin there, from 1842 to 1846. He did much for the diffusion of education, was one of the founders and secretary of the Royal Geographical Society, and editor of the *Penny Cyclopaedia*. He translated Marcus Aurelius (1862), and *The Discourses of Epictetus* (1877), and wrote *Two Discourses on Roman Law* (1847), a subject on which he was the greatest English authority.

P

Long, Margaret Gabrielle (29 Oct. 1888—23 Dec. 1952), novelist who wrote under the names Marjorie Bowen, George R. Preedy, and Joseph Shearing, was born at Hayling Island, Hampshire, her maiden name being Campbell, and studied art at the Slade School and in Paris. She married her first husband, Zeffirino Emilio Costanzo, a Sicilian, in 1912; he died in 1916 and in the following year she married Arthur L. Long. Her first novel was published when she was 16, and altogether she wrote more than a hundred books in a fluent and easy style, with great fertility of invention, being especially successful with her Dutch and Italian tales. Her best-known novel is *The Viper of Milan* (1906); *The Golden Roof, The Triumphant Beast,* and *Trumpets at Rome* form a trilogy on Renaissance history; others of her works are *General Crack* (1928), *My Tattered Loving* (1937), *The Circle in the Water* (1939), *The Abode of Love* (1944), and *Within the Bubble* (1950). An autobiography, *The Debate Continues* (1939), was published under her maiden name.

Longfellow, Henry Wadsworth (27 Feb. 1807—24 March 1882), poet, was born at Portland, Maine, the son of a lawyer. From childhood he cared little for games, but was always devoted to reading. In 1822 he was sent to Bowdoin College, of which his father was a trustee, and after graduating was appointed to a new Chair of Modern Languages, which the college had decided to establish, and with the view of more completely qualifying him for his duties, he was sent to Europe for a three years' course of study. He accordingly went to France, Spain, and Italy. Returning in 1829 he commenced his professional duties, writing also in the *North American Review*. In 1831 he married Mary Potter, and in 1833 he published his first books, a translation from the Spanish, followed by the first part of *Outre-Mer: A Pilgrimage beyond the Sea* (1835), giving an account of his travels. At the end of the year Longfellow was invited to become Professor of Modern Languages at Harvard, an offer which he gladly accepted. He paid a second visit to Europe accompanied by his wife, who, however, died at Amsterdam. He returned to his duties in 1836, and in 1838 appeared *Voices of the Night*, containing the 'Psalm of Life' and 'Excelsior,' which had extraordinary popularity, and gave him a place in the affections of his countrymen which he held until his death. The same year saw the publication of *Hyperion*. His next work was *Ballads and other Poems* (1842), containing 'The Wreck of the Hesperus' and 'The Village Blacksmith.'

In 1843 he married his second wife, Frances Appleton, and in the same year appeared *The Spanish Student*, a drama. The *Belfry of Bruges* and *Evangeline* (1847), generally considered his masterpiece, followed. In 1849 he published *Kavanagh*, a novel which added nothing to his reputation, and in 1851 *Seaside and Fireside*, and *The Golden Legend*. Having now a sufficient and secure income from his writings, he resigned his professorship, and devoted himself entirely to literature. *Hiawatha* appeared in 1855, and *The Courtship of Miles Standish* in 1858. In 1861 his wife was accidentally burned to death, a tragedy which told heavily upon him. Later works were a translation of Dante's *Divina Commedia* (1865—7), *Tales of a Wayside*

Inn (1863), *The New England Tragedies* (1868), and *The Divine Tragedy*, the last two of which he combined with *The Golden Legend* into a trilogy, which he named *Christus* (1872). In 1868 he paid a last visit to England, where he was received with the highest honour. Among his last works were *Three Books of Song* (1872), *Aftermath* (1873), and *Ultima Thule* (1880—2). Longfellow lacked the intensity of feeling and power of imagination to make him a great poet; but though he never soars to the heights or sounds the deeps of feeling he touches the heart by appealing to universal and deep-seated affections.

Lonsdale, Frederick, *see* **Leonard.**

Loos, Anita (26 April 1893—), novelist, was born at Sisson, California, daughter of a theatrical producer, and appeared on the stage at the age of 5. Educated at San Diego High School, she wrote several scenarios, in one of which Mary Pickford played, and became a humorous columnist on the New York *Evening Telegram*. In 1919 she married John Emerson, and they wrote several films for Douglas Fairbanks, latterly having their own film unit. *Gentlemen Prefer Blondes* (1925), her first novel, a satirical account by a hard-boiled gold-digger of her adventures, was a tremendous success, and sold 400,000 copies. Its sequel *But Gentlemen Marry Brunettes* (1928) was not so popular. *A Mouse Is Born* (1951) is a novel about Hollywood.

Lovelace, Richard (1618—1658), poet, born at Woolwich, son of Sir William Lovelace, was educated at Charterhouse and Gloucester Hall, Oxford, where he was styled by Anthony Wood 'the most amiable and beautiful person that eye ever beheld.' He was an enthusiastic Royalist, and spent his whole fortune in support of that cause. For presenting 'the Kentish petition' in favour of the King, he was imprisoned in 1642, when he wrote his famous song, 'To Althea from Prison.' After his release he served in the French army, and was wounded at Dunkirk. Returning, he was again imprisoned, 1648, and produced his *Lucasta* (1649). He lives in literature by a few of his lyrics which, though often careless, are graceful and tender. He died in poverty.

Lover, Samuel (24 Feb. 1797—6 July, 1868), novelist, song-writer, and portrait painter, was born in Dublin, son of a stockbroker. He produced a number of Irish songs, of which several such as 'Molly Bawn' and 'The Low-backed Car,' attained great popularity. He also wrote some novels, of which *Rory O'More* (1837), which was in its first form a ballad, and *Handy Andy* (1842) are the best known, and short Irish sketches, which, with his songs, he combined into a popular entertainment called, *Irish Nights*. He joined with Dickens in founding *Bentley's Magazine*.

Lowell, Amy (9 Feb. 1874—12 May 1925), poetess and critic, was born in Brookline, Massachusetts, which was her home all her life. A collateral descendant of James Russell Lowell (q.v.) she belonged to one of the first American families, one of her brothers being President of Harvard. Educated privately, she made many trips abroad, and was at first interested chiefly in public life, but about 1902 started writing poetry. In 1913 she met Ezra Pound (q.v.) in England, became one of the Imagist group which he helped to found, and edited the collection *Some Imagist Poets*. Later she became an exponent of 'polyphonic prose,' a kind of rhythmic prose akin to free verse, her best-known piece being 'Patterns.' Among her volumes of verse are *A Dome of Many-Coloured Glass* (1912), *Sword Blades and Poppy Seeds* (1914), *Men, Women, and Ghosts* (1916), *Legends* (1921), and *East Wind* (1926). As time went on she became a legendary figure, celebrated for such eccentricities as smoking cigars and sleeping on sixteen pillows. But her biography *John Keats* (1925) was a work of careful scholarship, and her death from cerebral haemorrhage in the year of its publication was due mainly to the intensive labour it involved.

Lowell, James Russell (22 Feb. 1819—12 Aug. 1891), poet and critic, born at Cambridge, Massachusetts, son of a Unitarian minister, was educated at Harvard. At first he aimed at the law, but in 1840 he turned to a literary career, his early verse showing the influence of Keats. In 1844 he married Maria White, and first showed his real worth as a writer with the verse *Fable for Critics* (1848) and the racy dialect poems known as the *Biglow Papers* (two series, 1848, 1867). After his wife's death in 1853 he succeeded Longfellow as Professor of Modern Languages at Harvard. In 1857 he made a happy second marriage, and in the same year began his editorship of the *Atlantic Monthly* which set that periodical on the high road to success. From this time onwards he turned to prose and criticism rather than poetry and published the thoughtful essays *Among My Books* (two series 1870, 1876) and *My Study Windows* (1871). In 1877 he was appointed Minister to Spain, and from 1880 to 1885 was Minister to Britain. His preoccupation with public affairs was reflected in *Democracy and Other Essays* (1886), and *The Independent in Politics* (1888). In spite of the popularity of poetical pieces like 'The Courtin'' and the ironical 'Pious Editor's Creed,' Lowell's fame rests mainly on his literary criticism. He was the most cultured of American critics of the nineteenth century.

Lowell, Robert (1 March 1917—   ), poet, great-grandson of the above, was born in Boston and educated at Kenyon College, Louisiana State University, and Harvard. Brought up in the Puritan tradition of Boston and of his family, he nevertheless became a Roman Catholic, and further showed moral courage by standing out as a conscientious objector in the Second World War. In 1947 and 1948 he was Consultant in Poetry to the Library of Congress, and in the same years held a Guggenheim Fellowship. His volumes of verse include *Land of Unlikeness* (1944), *Lord Weary's Castle* (1946), and *The Mills of Kavanaughs* (1952). In 1947 he was awarded the Pulitzer Prize for Poetry. His sombre but powerful work has been said to mark him as one of the leading poets of his generation in America.

Lowes, John Livingston (20 Dec. 1867—15 Aug. 1945), scholar, was born at Decatur, Indiana, and educated at Washington and

Jefferson College, Leipzig and Berlin Universities, and Harvard. He was Professor of English successively at Hanover, Indiana (1895—1902), Swarthmore (1905—9), Washington (1909—18), and Harvard (1918—30), and was Francis Lee Higginson Professor from 1930 till he retired. His works include *Convention and Revolt in Poetry* (1919), *The Road to Xanadu* (1927), *Of Reading Books and Other Essays* (1930), *The Art of Geoffrey Chaucer* (1931), and *Essays in Appreciation* (1936). He also edited several of Shakespeare's plays. He held honorary degrees of several universities, including Oxford.

Lowndes, Marie Adelaide Belloc (1868—14 Nov. 1947), novelist, was a sister of Hilaire Belloc (q.v.), and like him had an intimate knowledge of both England and France. A Roman Catholic, she was educated at a convent school and began writing at the age of 16. In 1896 she married F. S. Lowndes, a member of the *Times* staff. Her first novel was *The Heart of Penelope* (1904), but she first became well known with the publication of *The Lodger* (1913), a murder story written round the legend of Jack the Ripper. Others of her novels are *The Uttermost Farthing* (1908), *When No Man Pursueth* (1910), *Love and Hatred* (1917), *The Lonely House* (1920), *The Terriford Mystery* (1924), *What Really Happened* (1926), *Thou Shalt Not Kill* (1927), *Letty Lynton* (1930), and *The House by the Sea* (1937). *Lizzie Borden, a Study in Conjecture*, appeared in 1939, and the autobiography *I Too Have Lived in Arcadia* in 1942.

Lowth, Robert (27 Nov. 1710—3 Nov. 1787), theologian and scholar, born at Winchester, son of a clergyman, was educated there and at Oxford. Taking holy orders, he became Bishop successively of St David's, Oxford, and London. In 1753 he published *De Sacra Poesi Hebraeorum* (On the Sacred Poetry of the Jews). He also wrote a *Life of William of Wykeham*, the founder of Winchester College, and made a new translation of Isaiah.

Lubbock, Sir John, *see* **Avebury.**

Lubbock, Percy (4 June 1879—   ), historian and biographer, born in London, was educated at Eton and King's College, Cambridge. From 1906 to 1908 he was librarian of Magdalene College, and had access to its famous Pepys collection, from which he published a study of the diarist in 1909. He also formed a friendship with the Master of the college, A. C. Benson, whose diary he edited in 1926. Among his other works are *The Craft of Fiction* (1921), an analysis of great novels; *Earlham* (1922), a book of recollections of his childhood in Norfolk; *Shades of Eton* (1929), containing reminiscences of his school; and a study of Edith Wharton (1947). In 1926 he married a daughter of the Earl of Desart, and in 1952 was made a C.B.E.

Lucas, Edward Verrall (12 June 1868—26 June 1938), essayist and editor, was born at Eltham in Kent of a Quaker family to which A. W. Verrall the classical scholar belonged. After various schools at Brighton he was apprenticed to a bookseller there, and from 1889 to 1892 was a reporter on the *Sussex Daily News*. He then had over a year at University College, London, writing meanwhile for the *Globe*. A very versatile writer, he compiled numerous anthologies, of which *The Open Road* (1899) was the most successful; wrote a dozen novels, among which *Over Bemerton's* (1908) is the best; published many travel books, including *Highways and Byways in Sussex* (1904) and *A Wanderer in London* (1906); contributed to *Punch* and was its assistant editor in its most successful days; and became head of a publishing house. But he is remembered above all as an authority on Charles Lamb, of whose works he published the definitive edition and whose life he wrote in 1905; and by his light conversational essays, of which there are some 30 volumes, including *Good Company* (1909), *Old Lamps for New* (1911), *Loiterer's Harvest* (1913), *Mixed Vintages* (1919), *Giving and Receiving* (1922), *Encounters and Diversions* (1924), and *Pleasure Trove* (1935). *Reading, Writing, and Remembering* (1932) is a volume of reminiscences.

Lucas, Frank Laurence (28 Dec. 1894—), scholar and poet, born at Hipperholme, Yorkshire, was educated at Rugby and Cambridge. During the First World War he served with the West Kent Regiment. In 1920 he was elected a Fellow of King's College and then became a Reader in English at Cambridge. His critical works include *Seneca and Elizabethan Tragedy* (1922), *Euripides and his Influence* (1923), *Authors Dead and Living* (1926), *Eight Victorian Poets* (1930), and *Studies French and English* (1934). He also published many translations from the Greek, including the popular selections *Greek Poetry for Everyman* (1951) and *Greek Drama for Everyman* (1954). His original works included books of verse, *Time and Memory* (1929), *Marionettes* (1930), and *Ariadne* (1932); plays, *The Bear Dances* (1932) and *Land's End* (1938); and several novels. In 1946 he was awarded the O.B.E. He was three times married, his first wife being Emily B. C. Jones, the novelist.

Luska, Sidney, *see* Harland, Henry.

Lyall, Edna, *see* Bayly, Ada Ellen.

Lydgate, John (1370?—1451?), poet, born at Lydgate in Suffolk, and educated at the Benedictine monastery of Bury St Edmunds, where he became a monk at the age of 16, and afterwards taught literature, is said to have studied at Oxford, Paris, and Padua. He appears to have been a bright, clear-minded, earnest man, with a love of the beautiful, and a faculty of pleasant, flowing verse. He wrote copiously and with tiresome prolixity whatever was required of him, moral tales, legends of the saints, and histories, and his total output is enormous, reaching 130,000 lines. His chief works are *Troy Book* (1412—20), written at the request of Henry V when Prince of Wales, *The Falls of Princes* (1430—38), and *The Story of Thebes*. Lydgate also wrote many miscellaneous poems. He was for a time Court poet, and was patronized by Humphrey, Duke of Gloucester; but the greater part of his life was spent in the monastery at Bury St Edmunds, whence he is often called the Monk of Bury. He was an avowed admirer of Chaucer, though he largely follows the French romanticists previous to him.

Lyell, Sir Charles (14 Nov. 1797—22 Feb. 1875), geologist, was born at Kinnordy, Forfarshire, son of a botanist, and brought up near the

New Forest. After going to school at various places in England, he was sent to Oxford, where under Buckland he imbibed a taste for science. He studied law, and was called to the Bar, but soon devoted himself to geology, and made various scientific tours on the Continent, the results of his investigations being published chiefly in the Transactions of the Geological Society, of which he was afterwards repeatedly President. His two chief works are *The Principles of Geology* (1830—33), and *The Elements of Geology* (1838). A later book was *Geological Evidence of the Antiquity of Man* (1863). He was Professor of Geology in King's College, London, from 1831 to 1833, President of the British Association in 1864, knighted in 1848, and created a baronet in 1864. He was buried in Westminster Abbey.

Lyly, John (born 1554? buried 30 Nov. 1606), dramatist and novelist, born in the Weald of Kent, was educated at Magdalen College, Oxford, of which he became a Fellow, and also studied at Cambridge. He wrote several dramas, most of which are on classical and mythological subjects, including *Campaspe* (1584), *Sapho and Phao* (1584), *Endymion* (1591), *Midas* (1592), and *The Woman in the Moon* (1597). His chief fame, however, rests on his two didactic romances, *Euphues, the Anatomy of Wit* (1579), and *Euphues and his England* (1580). These works exercised a powerful, though temporary, influence on the language, both written and spoken, commemorated in our words 'euphuism' and 'euphuistic.' The characteristics of the style have been set forth as 'pedantic and far-fetched allusion, elaborate indirectness, a cloying smoothness and drowsy monotony of diction, alliteration, punning, and such-like puerilities, which do not, however, exclude a good deal of wit, fancy, and prettiness.' Many contemporary authors, including Shakespeare, made game of it, while others, such as Greene, admired and practised it. Lyly also wrote light dramatic pieces for the children of the Chapel Royal, and contributed a pamphlet, *Pappe with an Hatchet* (1589) to the Marprelate controversy, in which he supported the Bishops. He sat in Parliament from 1589 to 1601.

Lynd, Robert (20 April 1879—6 Oct. 1949), essayist, born in Belfast, son of a clergyman, was educated at Queen's College. Moving to London, he entered journalism and became literary editor of the *News Chronicle*, and also for many years wrote weekly articles for the *New Statesman* over the signature Y.Y. In 1909 he married Sylvia Dryhurst, who was herself a poet and novelist. Lynd wrote a great number of essays on a vast variety of subjects, all in the Lamb tradition—intimate, inconsequential, with an artistry and charm all their own. Among collections of these are *The Art of Letters* (1920), *Books and Authors* (1922), *The Blue Lion* (1923), *The Orange Tree* (1926), *Both Sides of the Road* (1934), and *In Defence of Pink* (1939). He also wrote a number of books on Ireland, including *Irish and English* (1908), *Rambles in Ireland* (1912), and *Ireland, a Nation* (1919).

Lyndsay, Sir David, *see* Lindsay.

Lyte, Henry Francis (1 June 1793—20 Nov. 1847), hymn-writer, born at Ednam, near Kelso, of an ancient Somerset family, and educated at Trinity College, Dublin, took orders, and was incumbent of Lower Brixham, Devonshire. He published *Poems: Chiefly Religious* (1833). He is chiefly remembered for his hymns, one of which, 'Abide with Me,' is universally known and loved.

Lyttelton, George, 1st Baron Lyttelton (17 Jan. 1709—22 Aug. 1773), poet and statesman, son of Sir Thomas Lyttelton, of Hagley, Worcestershire, educated at Eton and Oxford, was the patron of many literary men, including Thomson and Mallet, and was himself a somewhat voluminous author. Among his works are *Letters from a Persian in England to his friend in Ispahan* (1735), a treatise *On the Conversion of St Paul* (1746), *Dialogues of the Dead* (1760), which had great popularity, and a *History of the Life of Henry the Second* (1767—1771), well-informed, careful, and impartial, but tedious. He is chiefly remembered by his *Monody* (1747) on the death of his wife. The stanza in *The Castle of Indolence* in which Thomson is playfully described (canto I, st. lxviii), is by Lyttelton, who is himself referred to in lxv. He took some part in public affairs, was Chancellor of the Exchequer in 1756, and was raised to the peerage in the same year.

Lytton, Edward George Earle Lytton Bulwer, 1st Baron (25 May 1803—18 Jan. 1873), novelist and statesman, was born in London, son of a general, and went to Cambridge, where in 1825 he won the Chancellor's Medal with a poem on *Sculpture*. In 1827 he made an unfortunate marriage with Rosina Wheeler, an Irish girl; they separated in 1836, but she persecuted him for the rest of his life, which was unhappy in spite of his material success. In 1831 he entered Parliament, and rose to be Colonial Secretary in 1858; in 1837 he was made a baronet, and in 1866 was raised to the peerage. In 1856 and 1858 he was elected Lord Rector of Glasgow University. Despite all this public activity he found time to produce a great number of novels, plays, and essays, and was for years the most popular author in England. Of his more important novels, *Pelham* (1828) belongs to the 'silver fork' school of fiction; *Eugene Aram* (1832) is based on the notorious murder; *The Last Days of Pompeii* (1834), *Rienzi* (1835), and *Harold, the Last of the Saxons* (1848) are historical novels; *The Caxtons* (1849) and *My Novel* (1853) are studies of contemporary life; and *The Coming Race* (1871) is an imaginary picture of the future. Among his plays *Richelieu* (1839) is outstanding; others are *The Lady of Lyons* (1838) and *Money* (1840). His poems included an epic, *King Arthur* (1849). Although he dazzled his contemporaries by his versatility and his uncanny ability to gauge the public taste, his reputation has not stood the test of time.

Lytton, Edward Robert Bulwer, 1st Earl of Lytton (8 Nov. 1831—24 Nov. 1891), poet and statesman, son of the above, was educated at Harrow and Bonn, and became private secretary to his uncle, Sir H. Bulwer, afterwards Lord Dalling and Bulwer (q.v.), at Washington and Florence. Subsequently he held various diplomatic appointments at other European capitals. In 1873 he succeeded his father in the title, and in 1876 became Viceroy of India. He was created an earl on his retirement in 1880, and was in 1887 appointed ambassador at Paris, where he died. He valued himself much more as a poet than as a man of affairs; but, though he had in a considerable degree some of the qualities of a poet, he never quite succeeded in commanding the recognition of either the public or the critics. His writings, usually appearing under the pseudonym of Owen Meredith, include *Clytemnestra* (1855), *The Wanderer* (1857), *Lucile* (1860), *Chronicles and Characters* (1868), *Orval, or the Fool of Time* (1869), *Fables in Song* (1874), and *King Poppy* (1892). As Viceroy of India he introduced important reforms, and his dispatches were remarkable for their fine literary form.

P*

M

Macaulay, Catherine (2 April 1731—22 June 1791), historian, born near Wye, Kent, was a daughter of John Sawbridge. Educated privately, in 1760 she married George Macaulay, a doctor, who died six years later, and in 1778 William Graham, who was then only 21. An advocate of republicanism, and a sympathizer with the French Revolution, she wrote a *History of England from the Accession of James I to the Elevation of the House of Hanover* (8 volumes, 1763—1783), which had great popularity in its day. She also published *A Reply to Burke's Thoughts on the Present Discontents* (1770), and *Letters on Education* (1790).

Macaulay, Dame Rose (1881—30 Oct. 1958), novelist, was born in Cambridge, where her father was a lecturer in English, but spent most of her childhood in Italy. She went to school and college at Oxford, and her first novel, *The Valley of Captives* (1911), was published while she was there. She first came into prominence with her satirical novel, *Potterism* (1920); this was followed by *Dangerous Ages* (1921), which was awarded the Femina-Vie Heureuse Prize, *Mystery at Geneva* (1922), *Told by an Idiot* (1923), *Orphan Island* (1924), *Crewe Train* (1926), *Keeping Up Appearances* (1928), *Staying with Relations* (1930), *They Were Defeated* (1932), *Going Abroad* (1934), *I Would Be Private* (1937), *And No Man's Wit* (1940), and *The World My Wilderness* (1950). *They Went to Portugal* (1948) and *The Fabled Shore* (1950) are travel books. She also published three books of verse, *The Two Blind Countries* (1914), *Three Days* (1919), and *Poems* (1927), as well as studies of *Milton* (1934) and *E. M. Forster* (1938). Clever and critical, she belonged to the Bloomsbury group of authors. In 1958 she was made a D.B.E.

Macaulay, Thomas Babington Macaulay, 1st Baron (25 Oct. 1800—28 Dec. 1859), historian, essayist, statesman, son of Zachary Macaulay, a West India merchant, and one of the leaders of the anti-slavery party, was born at Rothley Temple, Leicestershire, and educated at a private school and at Trinity College, Cambridge, of which he became a Fellow in 1824, and where he gained distinction as a classical scholar and debater, though he did not take a high degree, owing to his weakness in mathematics. About the time of his leaving the university his prospects were entirely changed by the failure of his father's firm. He accordingly read law, and in 1826 was called to the Bar, but literature had greater attractions for him. He had by this time made his first appearance in print, in *Knight's Quarterly Magazine*, and in 1825 he formed the connection with the *Edinburgh Review* which redounded so greatly to the fame of both. His first contribution was the famous essay on Milton, which, although he afterwards said of it that 'it contained scarcely a paragraph which his matured judgment approved,' took the reading public by storm, and at once gave him access to the first society in London, in which his extraordinary conversational powers enabled him to take a leading place.

He now began to turn his mind towards public life, and by favour of Lord Lansdowne sat in the House of Commons for his family borough of Calne. Entering the House in 1830 in the thick of the Reform struggle, Macaulay at once leaped into a foremost place as a debater, and after the passage of the Reform Bill sat as one of the two members for the new borough of Leeds, and held office as Secretary to the Board of Control. The acquaintance with Indian affairs which he thus gained led to his appointment as a member of the Supreme Council of India, whither he went in 1834. Here his chief work was the codification of the criminal law, which he carried out with great ability, and by which he wrote his name on the history of the Empire. In 1838 he returned to England, and next year he began *The History of England*, but for some time to come his energies were still divided between this task, the demands of the *Edinburgh Review*, and politics. He was elected for Edinburgh, for which he sat until 1847, when he was thrown out on the Maynooth question, and from 1839—41 was Secretary for War. In 1842 were published his stirring poems *The Lays of Ancient Rome*, to which were added in later editions 'Ivry' and 'The Armada'; and in the following year there appeared a collection of his contributions to the *Edinburgh Review*, with the title *Critical and Historical Essays*. In 1846 he joined the government of Lord John Russell as Paymaster-General, an office with light duties, his retirement from which, however, followed the loss of his seat in the next year.

He was now finally set free for his great work, which became thenceforth the leading interest of his life. The first and second volumes appeared in 1848, and were received with extraordinary applause. In 1852 he was offered, but declined, a seat in the coalition government of Lord Aberdeen, accepting, however, the seat in Parliament which Edinburgh, now repentant, gave him unsolicited. His health began about this time to decline, and he spoke in the House only once or twice. In 1855 the third and fourth volumes of the *History* came out, and meeting with a success both at home and in America unprecedented in the case of an historical work, were translated into various foreign languages. In 1857 Macaulay was raised to the peerage, and his last years were spent at Holly Lodge, Kensington; he was buried in Westminster Abbey.

Though never married, Macaulay was a man of the warmest family affections. Outside of his family he was a steady friend and a generous opponent, disinterested and honourable in his public life. Possessed of a phenomenal memory, knowledge of vast extent, and an unfailing flow of ready and effective speech, he shone alike as a parliamentary orator and a conversationalist. His mind was strongly cast in the mould of the orator and the pleader: and the vivid contrasts, antitheses, and even paradoxes which render his style so brilliant and stimulating do not always tend to secure a judicial view of the matter in hand. As a lucid and picturesque narrator of events he has few equals. But he tends to be superficial, and his Whig sympathies sometimes led him to misrepresentation of facts. He is probably most widely known by his *Essays*, which retain an extraordinary popularity.

MacCarthy, Denis Florence (26 May 1817—7 April 1882), poet, born in Dublin, and educated at Maynooth with a view to the priesthood, devoted himself, however, to literature, and contributed verses to *The Nation*. Among his other writings are *Ballads, Poems, and Lyrics* (1850), *The Bell Founder* (1857), and *Under-Glimpses* (1857). He also edited a collection of Irish lyrics, translated Calderon, and wrote *Shelley's Early Life* (1872).

MacCarthy, Sir Desmond (1877—17 June 1952), critic, born at Plymouth and educated at Eton and Cambridge, became a freelance journalist. During the First World War he served with the French Red Cross, and afterwards became literary editor of the *New Statesman*, for which he wrote weekly causeries under the name Affable Hawk. Later he was editor of *Life and Letters*. His books include *The Court Theatre* (1907), *Portraits* (1931), *Experience* (1935), *Drama* (1940), and studies of *Leslie Stephen* (1937) and *Shaw* (1950); in 1933 he edited the *Letters of the Earl of Oxford and Asquith*. He was knighted in 1951. Lord David Cecil (q.v.) was his son-in-law.

McCarthy, Justin (22 Nov. 1830—24 April 1912), historian and novelist, was born near Cork, son of the clerk to the city magistrates. At 17 he was a reporter on the *Cork Examiner*, in 1864 became editor of the *Morning Star* in London, and in 1871 a leader-writer on the *Daily News*. From 1879 to 1900 he was a member of Parliament; an advocate of Home Rule, he was chairman of the Irish Parliamentary party. He is best remembered by his historical ·vorks, *The Four Georges and William IV* (1884—1901), *The Reign of Queen Anne* (1902), and *A History of Our Own Times* (1905). Of his novels the most popular were *Dear Lady Disdain* (1875) and *Miss Misanthrope* (1878). He also published *Reminiscences* (1899) and *Irish Recollections* (1911).

McCarthy, Justin Huntly (1860—21 March 1936), novelist, son of the above, was educated at London University and from 1884 to 1892 was an M.P. In 1894 he married Cissie Loftus, the music-hall star; the marriage was dissolved in 1899. In 1901 he became famous through the dramatization of his novel *If I Were King*. Others of his novels are *Marjorie* (1903), *The Lady of Loyalty House* (1904), *The King Over the Water* (1911), *A Health Unto His Majesty* (1912), *Pretty Maids All in a Row* (1913), *In Spacious Times* (1916), and *The Golden Shoe* (1921). Among his plays are *The Candidate* (1884), *The White Carnation* (1892), and *The O'Flynn* (1910). He also wrote *A History of England Under Gladstone* (1884).

M'Cosh, James (1 April 1811—16 Nov. 1894), philosopher, born in Ayrshire, son of a farmer, and educated at Glasgow and Edinburgh Universities, was a minister first of the Church of Scotland, and afterwards of the Free Church. From 1851—68 he was Professor of Logic at Queen's College, Belfast, and thereafter went to America to be President of Princeton (then the College of New·Jersey), where he was also Professor of Philosophy. He wrote several works on philosophy, including *Method of the Divine Government* (1850), *Intuitions of the Mind Inductively Investigated* (1860), *Laws of Discursive Thought* (1870), *Scottish Philosophy* (1874), and *Psychology* (1886).

McCrae, John (30 Nov. 1872—28 Jan. 1918), doctor and poet, born at Guelph, Ontario, of Scottish parents, studied medicine at Toronto University, and in 1900 was appointed Fellow in Pathology at McGill. He was an artillery officer in the Boer War and a medical officer in the First World War. He wrote 'In Flanders Fields,' one of the great war poems, which appeared in *Punch* in 1915.

M'Crie, Thomas (Nov. 1772—5 Aug. 1835), biographer and ecclesiastical historian, born at Duns, Berwickshire, son of a linen-weaver, and educated at the University of Edinburgh, became a minister in Edinburgh and was from 1816 to 1818 Professor of Divinity. His *Life of Knox* (1813) ranks high among biographies for the ability and learning which it displays, and was the means of vindicating the great Reformer from a cloud of prejudice and misunderstanding in which he had been enveloped. It was followed by a *Life of Andrew Melville* (1819), Knox's successor as the leader of the Reformers in Scotland. M'Crie also published histories of the Reformation in Italy and Spain. He received the degree of D.D. in 1813.

McCutcheon, George Barr (26 July 1866—23 Oct. 1928), novelist, was born near Lafayette, Indiana, where later his father was sheriff. One of the Hoosier school of writers, he was a friend of George Ade and Booth Tarkington (qq.v.). Educated at Purdue University, he was for a time a reporter. His first and best novel *Graustark* (1901), a romance about an imaginary Balkan kingdom, made half a million dollars. Others in the same vein are *Castle Craneycrow* (1902), *Beverly of Graustark* (1904), and *The Prince of Graustark* (1914). *Brewster's Millions* (1903), a comic fantasy, was successfully dramatized. His own favourite among his books was *Mary Midthorne* (1911), a realistic story of Indiana.

MacDiarmid, Hugh, *see* **Grieve, C. M.**

MacDonagh, Thomas (1878—3 May 1916), poet, was born at Cloughjordan, County Tipperary. Both his parents were teachers, and he himself, after attending a monastery school, taught first in Kilkenny and then in St Enda's School, Dublin. Later he became Assistant Professor of English at the National University. A poet of the Irish literary renascence, he has been compared with Crashaw. His volumes of verse include *Through the Ivory Gate* (1902), *April and May* (1903), *The Golden Toy* (1906), *Songs of Myself* (1910), and *Lyrical Poems* (1913). He also published books on *Thomas Campion* (1913) and *Literature in Ireland* (1916). When the Irish Volunteers were organized in 1913 he was given command of a corps; and after the Easter Rising in 1916 was shot as a rebel by the English.

MacDonald, Betty (26 March 1908—8 Feb. 1958), humorous writer, was born at Boulder, Colorado, her maiden name being Anne Elizabeth Campbell Bond. Her father's work as a mining engineer took the family to Seattle, and she was educated at the Roosevelt High School and the University of Washington. In 1927 she married Robert E. Heskett, an insurance salesman, and they started a chicken ranch in the Olympic Mountains; she wrote a humorous account of this experiment in *The Egg and I* (1942), which sold over a million copies and brought her fame and fortune. Meanwhile she and Heskett had been divorced, and after working for a time in the United States Treasury Department she contracted tuberculosis and spent several months in a sanatorium, of which she wrote in *The Plague and I* (1948). *Anybody Can Do Anything* (1950) is an account of her job-hunting during the depression of the thirties, and *Onions in the Stew* (1955) tells of her life on an island in Puget Sound. She also wrote some children's books.

MacDonald, George (10 Dec. 1824—18 Sept. 1905), poet and novelist, son of a farmer, descended from one of the 120 MacDonalds who escaped the Massacre of Glencoe, was born at Huntly, Aberdeenshire, and educated at the University of Aberdeen, and at Highbury Theological College. He became Congregationalist minister at Arundel, but after a few years retired, on account partly of theological considerations, partly of a threatened breakdown of health. He then took to literature, and published his first book, *Within and Without* (1856), a dramatic poem. *Poems* followed in 1857, and *Phantastes, a Faerie Romance*, in 1858. He then turned to fiction, and produced numerous novels, of which *David Elginbrod* (1862), *Alec Forbes* (1865), *Robert Falconer* (1868), *The Marquis of Lossie* (1877), and *Sir Gibbie* (1879), are perhaps the best. He also wrote children's books of great charm and orginality, including *At the Back of the North Wind* (1871), *Ranald Bannerman's Boyhood* (1871), and *The Princess and the Goblin* (1872). As a novelist he had considerable narrative and dramatic power, humour, tenderness, a genial view of life and character, tinged with mysticism, and within his limits he was a true poet. His later years were spent mainly at Bordighera in Italy.

MacDonald, Philip (   ), writer of detective stories, grandson of the above, served with a cavalry regiment in Mesopotamia during the First World War, and from his experiences wrote the novel *Patrol* (1928). His first novel, *Gentleman Bill* (1922) was a boxing story, and he began the series of detective stories by which he is best known with *The Rasp* (1924). Others that followed are *The White Crow* (1928), *The Link* (1930), *The Noose* (1930), *Murder Gone Mad* (1931), *Escape* (1932), *Death on My Left* (1931), and *R.I.P.* (1933); in these Colonel Anthony Gethryn is the detective. MacDonald has also written under the pseudonyms Oliver Fleming, Anthony Lawless, and Martin Porlock, the last of these names appearing on *Mystery at Friar's Pardon* (1931) and *Mystery in Kensington Gore* (1932).

MacDonell, Archibald Gordon (3 Nov. 1895—16 Jan. 1941), novelist, born in Aberdeen and educated at Winchester, served in the First World War with the Royal Field Artillery, and from 1922 to

1927 was on the headquarters staff of the League of Nations Union. In 1933 he published a hilarious satire on English country life, *England, their England*; other satirical novels are *Lords and Masters* (1936) and *The Autobiography of a Cad* (1939). *A Visit to America* (1935) and *My Scotland* (1937) are descriptive. Macdonell was secretary of the Sherlock Holmes Society of London and wrote detective stories under the name Neil Gordon, two of them being *The New Gun Runners* (1928) and *The Shakespeare Murders* (1933). He was killed in an air raid.

McFee, William (15 June 1881—), writer of sea stories, was born appropriately on the *Erin's Isle*, a three-master owned by his father, a sea captain. Educated at Culford School, Bury St Edmunds, he became a marine engineer and in 1911 settled in the United States. During the First World War he served as a sub-lieutenant in the British Navy, and afterwards lived at Westport, Connecticut. His first book, *Letters from an Ocean Tramp*, appeared in 1908, but the novels, by which he is best known, are *Casuals of the Sea* (1916), *North of Suez* (1930), *No Castle in Spain* (1933), *The Beachcomber* (1935), *The Derelicts* (1938), and *The Watch Below* (1940). Collections of reminiscences include *Harbours of Memory* (two series, 1921, 1924), *Swallowing the Anchor* (1925), and *In the First Watch* (1946). His hobby was making ship models.

MacGill, Patrick (1890—), poet and novelist, was born in Donegal. After a few years at a county school he worked as farm servant, potato-digger, surfaceman, and navvy, from which he got the nickname of the Navvy Poet. In 1911 he joined the staff of the *Daily Express*, and when the First World War broke out he enlisted. Volumes of his verse are *Songs of a Navvy* (1911), *Songs of the Dead End* (1912), *Soldier Songs* (1917), and *Songs of Donegal* (1921). His novels include *The Rat-Pit* (1915), *The Amateur Army* (1915), *The Red Horizon* (1916), *The Brown Brethren* (1917), *Glenmornan* (1918), *Maureen* (1919), *Lanty Hanion* (1922), *Moleskin Joe* (1923), *Una Cassidy* (1928), *Tulliver's Mill* (1934), and *The House at the World's End* (1935). *Children of the Dead End* (1914) is largely autobiographical.

McGinley, Phyllis (21 March 1905—), poetess, was born at Ontario, Oregon, and educated at the universities of Utah and California. For a time she was a teacher at New Rochelle, New York, then entered journalism and became assistant editor of *Town and Country*. As a writer of humorous verse she has been compared to Ogden Nash (q.v.). Her publications include *On the Contrary* (1934), *One More Manhattan* (1937), *Pocketful of Wry* (1940), *Husbands Are Difficult* (1941), *Stones from a Glass House* (1946), and *The Love Letters of Phyllis McGinley* (1955), as well as a number of children's books, beginning with *The Horse Who Lived Upstairs*, (1944). A Roman Catholic, she married Charles Hayden in 1937. In 1955 she was elected to the American National Academy of Arts and Letters.

McGonagall, William (1830—), poetaster, was born

in Edinburgh, son of an Irish weaver whose search for work took him to Glasgow, where McGonagall had some eighteen months' schooling. Later the family moved to Dundee, where he learned the weaving trade. But his heart was in Shakespeare, whose works he read in penny editions, and he would recite extracts from the plays in public-houses, after taking up a collection. Later his own poems were used at these readings. He published his first book of verse in 1877, and in the following year tramped all the way to Balmoral, with some twopenny copies of the second edition, in the hope of showing them to Queen Victoria. About 1884 he visited London, and in 1887 made a voyage to New York in search of a new audience, but America was unresponsive, and he had to be indebted for his return fare to a Dundee patron. As a critic has observed, McGonagall is the only truly memorable bad poet, his work, in spite of bathos, irrelevance, and a disregard of rhythm, having a certain crude vigour and sincerity. A selection entitled *Poetic Gems* was published in 1890.

Machen, Arthur (1863—15 Dec. 1947), novelist and essayist, born at Caerleon-on-Usk, Wales, son of a clergyman, was dreamy and introspective as a child, solitary as an adult, and lived a life of poverty. For a time he was a clerk in a London publishing house, then tried teaching, and in 1902 became an actor with Benson's company. In 1912 at the age of nearly 50 he joined the staff of the London *Evening News*. It was in this paper that his war story of the angels of Mons appeared and was accepted by many as an account of actual fact; later it was included in *The Bowmen and Other Legends of the War* (1915). As a fiction writer he was a master of the super-natural, his novels including *The Great God Pan* (1894), *The Three Impostors* (1895), *The House of Souls* (1906), *The Hill of Dreams* (1907), *The Great Return* (1915), *The Terror* (1917), *The Shining Pyramid* (1923), and *The Green Round* (1933). Among his collections of essays are *The Anatomy of Tobacco* (1884), *Strange Roads* (1923), *Dog and . Duck* (1924), *Notes and Queries* (1926), and *Dreads and Drolls* (1926). He also made many translations, including one of *Casanova's Memoirs* in 12 volumes (1930). *Far-Off Things* (1922) and *Things Near and Fear* (1923) are autobiographical.

Mackail, Denis George (3 June 1892—   ), novelist and biographer, was born in Kensington, a son of J. W. Mackail (q.v.); his mother was a daughter of Burne-Jones the artist. Educated at St Paul's and Balliol College, Oxford, he was for many years interested in the stage and for a time was a stage designer; later he worked in the Print Room of the British Museum. He wrote a large number of light novels which were extremely popular and also many short stories for magazines. Among his best-known books are *Bill the Bachelor* (1922), *Summertime* (1924), *Greenery Street* (1925), *The Fortunes of Hugo* (1926), *Another Part of the Wood* (1929), *The Young Livingstones* (1930), *Ian and Felicity* (1932), *Having Fun* (1933), *London Lovers* (1938), *Life with Topsy* (1942), *Tales for a Godchild* (1944), *We're Here* (1947). and *By Auction* (1949). He also wrote *The Story of J. M. B.* (1941), which is the standard life of

Barrie, of whom he was an intimate friend. He was a Fellow of the Royal Society of Literature.

Mackail, John William, O.M. (26 Aug. 1859—11 Dec. 1945), scholar, born at Ascog in Bute, son of the minister there, was educated at Ayr Academy, Edinburgh University, and Balliol College, Oxford. In 1884 he joined the staff of the Ministry of Education, where he remained for forty-five years. From 1906 to 1911 he was Professor of Poetry at Oxford, and in 1924 was appointed Professor of Ancient Literature in the Royal Academy. In 1932 and 1933 he was President of the British Academy. His more important works are an edition of *Select Epigrams from the Greek Anthology* (1890), *Latin Literature* (1895), *The Springs of Helicon* (1909), *Lectures on Greek Poetry* (1910), *Lectures on Poetry* (1911), *Studies of English Poets* (1926), and *The Approach to Shakespeare* (1930). He also published translations of Virgil and of Homer's *Odyssey* and wrote the standard *Life of William Morris* (1899). He was awarded the Order of Merit in 1935.

Mackay, Charles (27 March 1814—24 Dec. 1889), poet and journalist, son of a naval officer, was born at Perth, and educated at the Royal Caledonian Asylum, London, and at Brussels, but much of his early life was spent in France. Settling in London in 1834, he engaged in journalism, and published *Songs and Poems* (1834), a *History of London* (1838), *Popular Delusions* (1841), and a romance, *Longbeard* (1841). He is best known by his songs, some of which, such as 'There's a Good Time Coming' and 'Cheer, Boys, Cheer,' had an astonishing popularity. In 1852 he became editor of the *Illustrated London News*, in the musical supplement to which other songs by him were set to old English music by Sir H. R. Bishop. Mackay acted as *Times* correspondent during the American Civil War, and in that capacity discovered and disclosed the Fenian conspiracy. He was made an LL.D. of Glasgow University in 1846.

Mackay, Mary (1 May 1855—21 April 1924), novelist who wrote under the name of Marie Corelli, was a daughter of Charles Mackay (q.v.) by Ellen Mills, who became his second wife. Educated by governesses, she showed a precocious talent for the piano, and planned a musical career, for which her pseudonym was originally chosen. Her first book, *A Romance of Two Worlds*, appeared in 1886, but her first real success was with *Barabbas* (1893), while *The Sorrows of Satan* (1895) made her the most popular novelist of her time in Britain. Others of her books are *Cameos* (1896), *The Mighty Atom* (1896), *Boy* (1900), *Temporal Power* (1902), *God's Good Man* (1904), *The Life Everlasting* (1911), *Innocent* (1914), *The Young Diana* (1917), and *The Love of Long Ago* (1920). Her *Poems* were published in 1925, after her death. During her later years she lived at Stratford-upon-Avon.

McKenna, Stephen (27 Feb. 1888—   ), novelist, was born in London and educated at Westminster School and Christ Church, Oxford. During the First World War he was in the Intelligence Section of the War Trade Department, and later took part in the Balfour Mission to America. Handicapped by delicate health, he travelled extensively in search of a climate that would suit him, but eventually settled in Lincoln's Inn. His first novel was *The Reluctant Lover* (1912), and his best known was *Sonia* (1917). Others are *Sonia Married* (1919), *An Affair of Honour* (1925), *The Secretary of State* (1927), *The Datchley Inheritance* (1929), *Namesakes* (1933), *The Undiscovered Country* (1934), *Sole Death* (1935), *Last Confession* (1937), *A Life for a Life* (1939), *Pearl Wedding* (1951), and *Life's Eventime* (1954). *While I Remember* (1921) is an autobiography, and he also wrote a memoir of his uncle, Reginald McKenna, the well-known statesman.

Mackenzie, Agnes Mure (1891—26 Feb. 1955), historian and novelist, was born at Stornoway in the Outer Hebrides, daughter of a doctor. From Stornoway High School she went to Aberdeen University, where she took honours in English, then becoming a lecturer first at Edinburgh University and afterwards at Birkbeck College, London. Her first book was a novel, *Without Conditions* (1922); later novels are *Keith of Kinellan* (1930), *Cypress in Moonlight* (1931), *Between Sun and Moon* (1932), and *Single Combat* (1934). *The Women in Shakespeare's Plays* (1924) and *A Historical Survey of Scottish Literature to 1714* (1933) show her literary knowledge. But her greatest work was her *History of Scotland to 1939* in six volumes (1934—41). She also wrote *The Arts and the Future of Scotland* (1942), *Scottish Principles of Statecraft and Government* (1942), and *A Scottish Pageant* (3 volumes, 1946—9). An LL.D of Aberdeen, she was made a C.B.E. in 1945. Her last years were spent in Edinburgh.

Mackenzie, Sir Compton (17 Jan. 1883—   ), novelist, was born at West Hartlepool, his name originally being Edward Montague Compton; both his parents were members of theatrical families, and his sister was Fay Compton, the well-known actress. Educated at St Paul's and Magdalen College, Oxford, where he was a member of the Oxford University Dramatic Society, he studied law at the Inner Temple but later turned to writing, his first work being a play, *The Gentleman in Grey* (1907). A successful first novel, *The Passionate Elopement* (1911), was followed by *Carnival* (1912) a story of theatre life, which sold nearly half a million copies. In the following year he published *Sinister Street*, a vivid picture of adolescent life at school and college, and in 1914 *Guy and Pauline*, a romance of the West Country. In the same year he became a Roman Catholic. During the First World War he served on the Dardanelles front, of which he wrote in *Gallipoli Memories* (1928), and was later employed on Secret Service work, which inspired *Extremes Meet* (1928). In 1919 he was awarded the O.B.E. He settled on the island of Barra in the Outer Hebrides, helped to found the Scottish Nationalist Party, and in 1931 was elected Lord Rector of Glasgow University. Among his later novels are *Poor Relations* (1919), *Rich Relations* (1920), *Extraordinary Women* (1928), *Our Street* (1931), *The Four Winds of Love* (1937), and *Whisky Galore* (1947) which was filmed with great success. *Greek Memories* (1932) and *Aegean Memories* (1940) are books of reminiscence. He was knighted in 1952.

Mackenzie, Sir George (1636—8 May 1691), lawyer and miscellaneous writer, a nephew of the Earl of Seaforth, was educated at St Andrews, Aberdeen, and Bourges, called to the Bar in 1659, and in 1677 became Lord Advocate. In this capacity he was the subservient minister of the persecuting policy of Charles II in Scotland, and the inhumanity and relentlessness of his persecution of the Covenanters gained for him the name of 'Bloody Mackenzie.' In private life, however, he was a cultivated and learned gentleman with literary tendencies, and is remembered as the author of various graceful essays, of which the best known is *A Moral Essay preferring Solitude to Public Employment* (1665). He also wrote legal, political, and antiquarian works of value, including *Institutions of the Law of Scotland* (1684), *Antiquity of the Royal Line of Scotland* (1686), and *Memoirs of the Affairs of Scotland from the Restoration of Charles II*, a valuable work which was not published until 1821. Mackenzie was the founder of the Advocates' Library in Edinburgh.

Mackenzie, Henry (26 Aug. 1745—14 Jan. 1831), novelist and essayist, was born in Edinburgh, son of a doctor, and educated at Edinburgh High School and University. He studied for the law, and became Controller of Taxes for Scotland. He published three novels, *The Man of Feeling* (1771), *The Man of the World* (1773), and *Julia de Roubigné* (1777), all written in a strain of rather high-wrought sentimentalism, in which the influence of Sterne is to be seen. He was also a leading contributor to *The Mirror* and *The Lounger*, two periodicals somewhat in the style of the *Spectator*. In his later days he was one of the leading members of the literary society of Edinburgh, and was sometimes called 'the Northern Addison.'

Mackintosh, Elizabeth (1897—13 Feb. 1952), novelist and playwright, who wrote under the names Gordon Daviot and Josephine Tey, was born in Inverness and educated at the Royal Academy there. After three years at Anstey Physical Training College in Birmingham, she held posts as physical instructress in various places. Her first book, *The Man in the Queue* (1929), introduces Inspector Grant, later to become familiar to readers of her excellent mystery stories, which were published under the name of her Suffolk great-great-grandmother, Josephine Tey. They include *A Shilling for Candles* (1936), *Miss Pym Disposes* (1947), *The Franchise Affair* (1949), *Brat Farrar* (1949), *To Love and be Wise* (1950), *The Daughter of Time* (1951), and *The Singing Sands* (1952). She was even more successful as a playwright, *Richard of Bordeaux* (1933), a two-act drama about Richard II, being very popular. Others which, like it, appeared under the name Gordon Daviot, were *Queen of Scots* (1934), *The Little Dry Thorn* (1946), and *The Stars Bow Down* (1949). In 1937 she published a biography of Claverhouse.

Mackintosh, Sir James (24 Oct. 1765—30 May 1832), philosopher, born at Aldourie, near Inverness, son of an army officer, studied medicine at Edinburgh. In 1787 he moved to London, and won distinction with his *Vindiciae Gallicae* (1791), championing the French Revolution. In 1795 he was called to the Bar, and from 1804 to 1811 he held important posts in India. On his return he was elected as M.P. for Nairn, and from 1818 to 1824 was Professor of Law at East India College, Haileybury. In 1831 he published *Dissertations on the Progress of Ethical Philosophy*, which embodied utilitarian views.

Macklin, Charles (1697?—11 July 1797), actor and dramatist, born at Westmeath in Ireland, son of William McLaughlin, was in 1713 a servant or 'skip' at Trinity College, Dublin. He became one of the most distinguished actors of his day, shining equally in tragedy and comedy. In 1735, having killed another actor in a quarrel at Drury Lane he was tried for murder but acquitted, and died a centenarian. He wrote, among other comedies, *Love à la Mode* (1759) and *The Man of the World* (1781), which were the only ones printed. He was the creator of Sir Pertinax Macsycophant, a famous burlesque character.

Maclaren, Ian, *see* **Watson, John.**

MacLeish, Archibald (7 May 1892—   ), poet, was born at Glencoe, Illinois, and educated at Yale and Harvard, where he studied law. His first book of verse, *The Tower of Ivory*, appeared while he was still at college. During the First World War he was a captain in the Field Artillery. In 1923 he gave up law practice and settled in France to make a living by poetry. Much of his work at this time shows the influence of Eliot and Ezra Pound. *Conquistador*, a long poem on Cortez, was awarded the Pulitzer Prize for 1932, and in 1939 he was appointed Librarian of Congress, and became an important force in American war propaganda. Among his other volumes of verse are *Happy Marriage* (1924), *Pot of Earth* (1925), *Streets in the Moon* (1928), *New Found Land* (1930), *Elpenor* (1933), *America Was Promises* (1939), *Colloquy for the States* (1943), and *Act Five* (1948); *Collected Poems 1917—1952* appeared in 1952. He also wrote a number of verse dramas, including *The Fall of the City* (1937), *Air Raid* (1938), and *The Trojan Horse* (1952). In 1949 he was appointed Professor of Rhetoric at Harvard.

M'Lennan, John Ferguson (14 Oct. 1827—16 June 1881), sociologist, born at Inverness, and educated at Aberdeen and Cambridge, was in 1857 called to the Scottish Bar, and was subsequently Parliamentary Draftsman for Scotland. His main contribution to literature is his original and learned book, *Primitive Marriage* (1865). Another work, *The Patriarchal Theory*, left unfinished, was completed by his brother. M'Lennan received the degree of LL.D. from Aberdeen in 1874.

Macleod, Fiona, *see* **Sharp, William.**

Macleod, Norman (3 June 1812—16 June 1872), minister and author, was born at Campbeltown, where his father was minister, studied at Glasgow and Edinburgh Universities, and was ordained in 1838. He became one of the most distinguished ministers, and most popular preachers of his Church, was made one of the Royal Chaplains in Scotland in 1857, and became a trusted friend of Queen Victoria. He was the first editor of *Good Words*, to which he contributed many articles and stories. His books include *The Earnest Student* (1854), *The Old Lieutenant* (1862), and *Wee Davie* (1864).

McMullan, Charles Walden Kirkpatrick (1889—   ),
playwright who wrote under the name C. K. Munro, was born at
Portrush, Antrim, son of a university professor, and educated at
Harrow and Cambridge. Entering the Civil Service, he rose to be
under-secretary at the Ministry of Labour. His first play, *The
Wanderers*, appeared in 1915, but his first real success was *At Mrs
Beam's* (1922), which he followed up considerably later with *Coronation Time at Mrs Beam's* (1937). Others of his plays are *The Rumour*
(1923), *Storm* (1924), *Progress* (1925), *The Mountain* (1926), *Bluestone
Quarry* (1931), *Veronica* (1933), and *Ding and Co.* (1934). His book
of essays *The True Woman* (1932) is subtitled 'a handbook for husbands.' In 1947 he was awarded the C.B.E.

MacNally, Leonard (1752—13 Feb. 1820), playwright, was born in
Dublin, son of a merchant, studied law, and in 1776 was called to the
Irish, in 1783 to the English, Bar. In 1792 he was counsel for Napper
Tandy in his action for false imprisonment. His house in Dublin
was a rendezvous for revolutionaries, whom he secretly betrayed to
the English Government, his treachery being discovered only after
his death. He wrote the well known song 'The Lass of Richmond
Hill' as a tribute to his first wife. His plays include *The Apotheosis
of Punch* (1779) and *Retaliation* (1782).

MacNeice, Louis (12 Sept. 1907—   ), poet, was born
in Belfast, son of the Protestant Bishop of Down, and educated at
Marlborough and Merton College, Oxford. From 1930 to 1936 he
was Lecturer in Classics at Birmingham, then became Lecturer in
Bedford College, London. At this time he went on a trip to Iceland
with W. H. Auden (q.v.), and collaborated with him in *Letters from
Iceland* (1937), which he followed with *I Crossed the Minch* (1938).
As a poet he belonged to the school of Auden and Spender, exhibiting
the same irony and satire. His books of verse include *Blind Fire-
works* (1929), *The Earth Compels* (1938), *Autumn Journal* (1939),
Plant and Phantom (1941), *Springboard* (1944), *The Dark Tower*
(1946), *Holes in the Sky* (1948), and *Ten Burnt Offerings* (1952). He
also translated the *Agamemnon* of Aeschylus and Goethe's *Faust*.
Modern Poetry (1938) is a book of criticism. In 1958 he was made a C.B.E.

McNeile, Herman Cyril (28 Sept. 1888—14 Aug. 1937), soldier and
novelist who wrote under the name Sapper, was born at Bodmin,
Cornwall, son of a captain in the navy. Educated at Cheltenham
College and the Royal Military Academy, Woolwich, he served in the
Royal Engineers from 1907 to 1919, winning the Military Cross and
finishing as a lieutenant-colonel. After publishing some war novels,
including *Men, Women, and Guns* (1916) and *No Man's Land* (1917),
he first became famous with his 'thriller' *Bulldog Drummond* (1920),
which is subtitled 'The Adventures of a Demobilized Officer Who
Found Peace Dull.' It had some half-dozen sequels, including *The
Black Gang* (1922), *The Third Round* (1924), *The Final Count* (1926),
and *Bulldog Drummond at Bay* (1935). These stories, with their
respectable though picaresque hero, were very popular with ex-army
men. Others of McNeile's novels are *Jim Maitland* (1923) and *The
Way Out* (1930).

Macneill, Hector (22 Oct. 1746—15 March 1818), poet, born near Roslin, Midlothian, son of an army captain, and educated at Stirling Grammar School, went to the West Indies, and was clerk on a naval flagship from 1780 to 1786. He wrote some political pamphlets, two novels, and several poems, including *The Harp* (1789), *The Carse of Forth*, and *Scotland's Skaith* (1795), the last against drunkenness, but is best known for his songs, such as 'My Boy Tammie' and 'Come Under My Plaidie.'

Macpherson, James (27 Oct. 1736—17 Feb. 1796), poet and translator, born at Ruthven, Invernesshire, son of a farmer, studied for the church at Aberdeen and Edinburgh, but gave that up and became a teacher. In 1758 he published *The Highlander*, a poem in six cantos, and in the following year met John Home (q.v.), who was greatly interested in Highland lore. With his help Macpherson published *Fragments of Ancient Poetry Translated from the Gaelic or Erse Language* (1760), which aroused widespread interest. Two years later, having searched the Highlands and Hebrides for further material, he published *Fingal*, an epic poem in six books, and next year *Temora*, in eight books; both poems purported to be translations from a third-century Gaelic poet called Ossian or Oisin. The sales of these were enormous, but their authenticity was soon called in question. Macpherson promised to produce the originals of his work, but did not do so, and many scholars, including Dr Johnson, considered him a forger. Controversy over the Ossianic poems raged for nearly two centuries. The truth appears to be that while Macpherson based his works on actual matter, he expanded and transformed it so much that the epics were practically his own work. The fact remains that these tales of Celtic romance took Europe by storm, had a great effect on the Romantic Movement then beginning, and were greatly admired by such diverse geniuses as Goethe and Napoleon. In 1764 Macpherson was appointed surveyor-general of the Floridas, in 1779 was agent to the Nabob of Arcot, and from 1780 to 1790 sat as M.P. for Camelford. He was buried at his own expense in Westminster Abbey.

Madden, Samuel (23 Dec. 1686—31 Dec. 1765), clergyman and poet, was born in Dublin, son of a doctor, and educated at Dublin University. In 1703 he succeeded to the family estates at Fermanagh and became a clergyman there. His tragedy *Themistocles, the Lover of his Country* (1729) was followed by a satire, *Memoirs of the Twentieth Century* (1733), and various pamphlets, but his chief claim to fame is that he was assisted by Dr Johnson in his long poem *Boulter's Monument* (1745).

Maginn, William (10 July 1793—21 Aug. 1842), journalist, born at Cork, son of a schoolmaster, entered Trinity College, Dublin, at a very early age. He became a contributor to *Blackwood's Magazine* and afterwards foreign correspondent to *The Representative*, a paper started by J. Murray, the publisher, and when its short career was run, one of the leading supporters of *Fraser's Magazine*. One of the most brilliant periodical writers of his time, he was also a clever parodist. In his later years he fell into intemperate habits, and died in poverty. A collection of his work, *Maginn's Miscellanies*, was published in 1857.

Mahon, Viscount, *see* **Stanhope, Earl.**

Mahony, Francis Sylvester (1804—18 May 1866), humorous writer who used the pseudonym Father Prout, was born in Cork, son of a wool manufacturer. Educated at the Jesuit College at Clongoweswood, Co. Kildare, at Amiens, and at Rome, he became a member of the Society, was Professor of Rhetoric at Clongoweswood, but was soon after expelled from the Order. He then came to London, and became a leading contributor to *Fraser's Magazine*. He was witty and learned in many languages. One form which his humour took was the professed discovery of the originals in Latin, Greek, or medieval French of popular modern poems and songs. Many of these *jeux d'esprit* were collected as *Réliques of Father Prout* (two series, 1836, 1876). He once described himself as 'an Irish potato seasoned with Attic salt.' Latterly he acted as foreign correspondent to various newspapers, and died in Paris reconciled to the Church.

Maine, Sir Henry James Sumner (15 Aug. 1822—3 Feb. 1888), jurist, born in India, was educated at Christ's Hospital and at Cambridge, where he became Regius Professor of Civil Law 1847—1854. In 1862 he went to India as legal member of the Government. On his return he was in 1870 appointed Professor of Comparative Jurisprudence at Oxford, which office he held until his election in 1878 as Master of Trinity Hall. He became Whewell Professor of International Law at Cambridge in 1887, and was the author of many valuable works on law and the history of political institutions, and profoundly influenced the study of jurisprudence. His most famous work is his *Ancient Law* (1861); others are *Village Communities* (1871), *Early History of Institutions* (1875), and *Dissertations on Early Law and Customs* (1883).

Mair, John, *see* **Major.**

Mais, Stuart Petre Brodie (4 July 1885—), journalist and critic, was born at Matlock, son of a clergyman, and educated at Denstone College and Oxford, where he got his Blue for running. From 1909 to 1920 he was games master successively at Rossall, Sherborne, and Tonbridge. Then for eighteen years he worked as a literary critic in Fleet Street, on the *Evening News*, *Daily Express*, and then *Daily Graphic*. His books of criticism include *From Shakespeare to O. Henry* (1917), *Books and Their Writers* (1919), *Some Modern Authors* (1923), *Books I Like* (two series, 1932, 1934), and *The Writing of English* (1935). A prolific and facile writer, he also published many novels and a great number of guide-books, such as *See England First* (1927), *It Isn't Far From London* (1930), *This Unknown Island* (1932), and a series beginning with *I Return to Scotland* (1947) and including *Switzerland* (1948), *Ireland* (1948), *Wales* (1949), and the *Riviera* (1950). *All the Days of My Life* (1937) and *Buffets and Rewards* (1952) are autobiographical.

Maitland, Sir Richard (1496—20 March 1586), lawyer and poet, was born in Haddingtonshire and educated at St Andrews and Paris.

Employed by James V on various diplomatic missions, he later became blind, but was nevertheless appointed a member of the Privy Council and was Keeper of the Great Seal from 1562 to 1567. He is chiefly remembered for his collection of ancient Scots poems, which passed into the hands of Pepys and are now in the library of Magdalene College, Cambridge. His services to literature were recognized by the formation at Glasgow in 1828 of the Maitland Club, which published his own poems two years later and subsequently edited many other ancient Scottish manuscripts, including his *History of the House of Seytoun*.

Major *or* **Mair, John** (1470?—1550), historian, born at North Berwick, and educated at Haddington Grammar School, Cambridge, and Paris, became a professor at Glasgow and was the teacher of John Knox and George Buchanan. In 1506 he was a Doctor of the Sorbonne, and in 1519 became Professor of Divinity at St Andrews. He wrote, in Latin, treatises on divinity and morals, and a *History of Greater Britain*, published at Paris in 1521, in which the separate histories of England and Scotland were brought together. In his writings, while upholding the doctrinal teaching of Rome, he was outspoken in condemning the corruptions of the clergy. He has been called 'the last of the schoolmen.'

Malcolm, Sir John (2 May 1769—30 May 1833), soldier, statesman, and historian, born at Burnfoot, Dumfriesshire, went to India in 1782, studied Persian, was employed in many important negotiations and held various distinguished posts, being Ambassador to Persia and Governor of Bombay 1826—30. He was the author of several authoritative works, including *A History of Persia* (1815), *Memoir of Central India* (1823), *Political History of India from 1784 to 1823* (1826), and *Life of Lord Clive* (1836).

Mallet, *originally* **Malloch, David** (1703?—21 April 1765), poet, born at Crieff, Perthshire, son of a farmer, was educated there and at Edinburgh University, where he became acquainted with James Thomson. In 1723 he went to London as tutor in the family of the Duke of Montrose. In the following year appeared his ballad of *William and Margaret*, by which he is chiefly remembered, and which made him known to Pope, Young, and others. In 1726 he changed his name to Mallet to make it more pronounceable by Southern tongues. His *Excursion*, an imitation of Thomson, was published in 1728. At the request of the Prince of Wales, whose secretary he had become, he wrote with Thomson a masque, *Alfred* (1740), in which 'Rule, Britannia' first appeared, but though he claimed the authorship, it is now generally attributed to Thomson. He also wrote a *Life of Bacon* (1740); and on Bolingbroke bequeathing to him his manuscripts and library, he published an edition of his works in 1754. On the accession of George III, Mallet became a zealous supporter of Lord Bute, and was rewarded with a sinecure. In addition to the works above named Mallet wrote some indifferent dramas, including *Eurydice* (1731), *Mustapha* (1739), and *Elvira* (1763). Dr Johnson said of him that he was 'the only Scotsman whom Scotsmen did not commend.'

Mallowan, Agatha, *see* **Christie.**

Malone, Edmond (4 Oct. 1741—25 April 1812), critic and editor, son of an Irish judge, born in Dublin, and educated at Trinity College there, studied for the law, but coming into a fortune, decided to follow a literary career. Acute, careful, and sensible, he was a useful contributor to the study of Shakespeare, of whose works he published a valuable edition in 1790. In the same year appeared his *Historical Account of the English Stage*. He also aided in the detection of the Rowley forgeries of Chatterton, and the much less respectable Shakespeare ones of Ireland. At his death he was engaged upon another edition of Shakespeare, which was brought out under the editorship of James Boswell (q.v.). Malone also wrote lives of Dryden and others, and was the friend of Johnson, Goldsmith, Reynolds, and Burke.

Malory, Sir Thomas (1400?—4 March 1470), translator, was born at Newbold Revell in Warwickshire, where his father was sheriff. He saw military service in France with the Earl of Warwick, and in 1445 sat in Parliament as knight of the shire. In 1451 he was arraigned on a long list of offences, including the attempted assassination of the Duke of Buckingham, and spent a great part of the rest of his life in prison, where he wrote his famous work the *Morte d'Arthur*. It is a fine prose rendering in 21 books of the Arthurian legends, made up from the French versions with additions of his own. Completed in 1469, it was printed by Caxton in 1485. Details of Malory's life previously lacking were supplied in a manuscript of his work discovered at Winchester in 1934. It was in Malory that Spenser, Tennyson, and other poets found the material for their Arthurian tales.

Malthus, Thomas Robert (17 Feb. 1766—23 Dec. 1834), economist, son of a landed proprietor, was born near Guildford, and educated at Jesus College, Cambridge, of which he became a Fellow. Taking orders he became incumbent of Albury, Surrey. He travelled much on the Continent, collecting information as to the means of livelihood and mode of life of various peoples. In 1798 the first edition of his famous *Essay on Population* appeared, and in 1803 a second greatly enlarged. Its leading proposition, supported by much learning, is that while population increases approximately in a geometrical ratio, the means of subsistence do so in an arithmetical ratio only, so that unless the former increase was controlled, food shortage was inevitable. The work gave rise to a great deal of controversy, much of it based on misunderstanding. Malthus was appointed Professor of Political Economy at Haileybury in 1815, and became a Fellow of the Royal Society in 1819.

Mandeville, Bernard de (1670?—21 Jan. 1733), satirist, a native of Dort in Holland, having studied medicine at Leyden, came over to England to practise his profession. In 1705 he published a short poem, *The Grumbling Hive*, which in 1714 reappeared with a prose commentary as *The Fable of the Bees, or Private Vices Public Benefits*, and in 1729 was made the subject of a persecution for its immoral tendency, its theme being the essential vileness of human nature.

It was also vigorously combated by, among others, Bishop Berkeley and William Law, author of *The Serious Call*. Another of Mandeville's works, *A Search into the Nature of Society* (1723), appended to the later versions of the *Fable*, also startled the public mind, which his last works, *Free Thoughts on Religion* and *An Enquiry into the Origin of Honour and the Usefulness of Christianity* did little to reassure.

Mandeville, Sir John (1300?—1372?), travel writer, was born, according to his own account, at St Albans, and began his travels in 1322. His book *The Voyage of Sir John Mandeville* was written at Liege, where he died. It sets out to be a guide for pilgrims to the Holy Land, but tells of many different countries, including Turkey, Tartary, Persia, and India. Immensely popular, it was accepted as genuine for centuries, but modern scholars have satisfied themselves that the work is a clever compilation, and that instead of making a tour of the known world the writer only made a tour of his library. Even the name Mandeville is suspect, for the original version appears to be in French, and one conjecture is that the book may have been written by Jean d'Outremeuse, a Frenchman.

Mangan, James Clarence (1 May 1803—20 June 1849), poet, born in Dublin, son of a small grocer, was brought up in poverty, and received most of his education from a priest who instructed him in several modern languages. He then became a lawyer's clerk, and was later an assistant in the library of Trinity College, Dublin. He contributed verses of very various merit to a number of Irish newspapers, and translations from the German to *The Dublin University Magazine*. By some critics his poetical powers were considered to be such as to have gained for him the first place among Irish poets; but addiction to drink and opium prevented him from rising to the heights his genius might have merited. He ultimately died of cholera. An edition of his *Poems* was published in 1859, and of his *Prose Writings* in 1904.

Manley, Mary de la Rivière (7 April 1663—11 July 1724), dramatist and satirist, born in Jersey, daughter of Sir Roger Manley, was decoyed into a bigamous connection with her cousin, John Manley. Her subsequent career was one of highly dubious morality, but considerable literary success. Her principal works are *The New Atalantis (sic)* (1709), a satire in which great liberties were taken with Whig notabilities, *Memoirs of Europe* (1710), and *Court Intrigues* (1711). She also wrote three plays, *The Royal Mischief, The Lost Lover*, and *Lucius*, and edited the *Examiner*. In her writings she makes great havoc with classical names and even with spelling. She was a vivacious and effective political writer.

Mannin, Ethel Edith (11 Oct. 1900—   ), novelist and travel writer, born in London of working-class parents, left school at fifteen and became a typist. In 1922 she published her first novel, *Martha*, which was followed by *Hunger of the Sea* (1924), *Sounding Brass* (1925), *Venetian Blinds* (1933), *The Pure Flame* (1936), *Darkness My Bride* (1939), *Red Rose* (1941), *The Blossoming Bough* (1943), *The Dark Forest* (1946), *Late Have I Loved Thee* (1948), *At Sundown* *the Tiger* (1951), and *Lover Under Another Name* (1953). The influence of A. S. Neill (q.v.) is shown in her educational studies *Commonsense and the Child* (1931), *Commonsense and the Adolescent* (1938), and *Commonsense and Morality* (1942). *All Experience* (1932), *Forever Wandering* (1934), *South to Samarkand* (1936), *Jungle Journey* (1950), and *Moroccan Mosaic* (1953) are travel books, and *Confessions and Impressions* (1929) and *Privileged Spectator* (1939) are autobiographical. She was married twice—to J. A. Porteous in 1920 and to Reginald Reynolds in 1938.

Manning, Anne (17 Feb. 1807—14 Sept. 1879), novelist, was born in London, daughter of an insurance broker. Her best known works are *Mistress Mary Powell*, which first appeared in *Sharpe's Magazine* in 1849, and *The Household of Sir Thomas More* (1851), a delightful picture of More's home life told in the form of a diary written by his daughter Margaret. Her writings have much literary charm, and show a delicate historical imagination.

Manning, Frederic (22 July 1882—22 Feb. 1935), novelist, was born in Sydney, where his father, Sir William Manning, was mayor. A delicate boy, he was educated privately except for six months at Sydney Grammar School. At the age of 15 he went to England, where his first volume of verse, *The Vigil of Brunhild*, was published in 1907. In that year he became a literary reviewer on the *Spectator*, and two years later he published *Scenes and Portraits*, which was followed by *Poems* (1910). During the First World War he served with the Shropshire Light Infantry, and his novel *Her Privates We* (1930) is based on his experiences at the front, the *double entendre* of the title being borrowed from Shakespeare's *Hamlet*.

Manning, Henry Edward (15 July 1808—14 Jan. 1892), cardinal, was born at Totteridge, Hertfordshire, and educated at Harrow and Oxford, where he became notable as an eloquent preacher, and as one of the ablest of the Tractarian party. He became rector of Woolavington-cum-Graffam in 1833, and Archdeacon of Chichester in 1840. In 1851 he entered the Church of Rome, in which he attached himself to the Ultramontane party. More even than Newman he was the leading spirit of the Roman Church in England. His writings consist of sermons, of which he published several volumes before his secession from the Church of England, and controversial works, including *Petri Privilegium* (1871), *The Vatican Decrees* (1875), in answer to Gladstone's *Vaticanism*, and *The Eternal Priesthood* (1883). He became Roman Catholic Archbishop of Westminster in 1865, and Cardinal in 1875.

Mannyng, Robert *or* **Robert of Brunne** (1264?—1340?), poet, was born, as his name indicates, at Brunne, now Bourne, in Lincolnshire. From 1302 to 1317 he was a canon of Sempringham. In 1303 he began writing *Handlyng Synne*, a verse treatise on the seven deadly sins, which run to over 12,000 lines. Adapted from the French *Manuel des Pechiez* attributed to the English writer William of Waddington, it includes many illustrative tales which give a valuable picture of the times. In 1338 Mannyng wrote in over 17,000 lines a verse *Chronicle of England* which drew extensively on another French work, by Peter of Langtoft.

Mansel, Henry Longueville (6 Oct. 1820—30 July 1871), metaphysician, was born at Cosgrave, Northamptonshire, where his father was rector, and educated at Merchant Taylors' School and Oxford. He took orders, was appointed Reader in Theology at Magdalen College in 1855, Bampton Lecturer in 1858, Professor of Ecclesiastical History in 1867, and Dean of St Paul's in 1869. Among his writings are *Prolegomena Logica* (1851), *The Limits of Demonstrative Science* (1853), *Limits of Religious Thought* (1858), *Metaphysics, or the Philosophy of Consciousness* (1860), and *Philosophy of the Conditioned* (1866). He was also joint editor of Sir W. Hamilton's *Lectures.*

Mansfield, Katherine, *see* **Beauchamp, Kathleen Mansfield.**

Map *or* **Mapes, Walter** (1137?—1209?), churchman and miscellanist, belonged to Hereford and studied in Paris. In favour at the Court of Henry II, he became a travelling justice and knew many leading men of the time. In 1179 he was sent on a mission to the Lateran Council at Rome, and after holding minor preferments he became canon successively of St Paul's, Lincoln, and Hereford, and in 1197 archdeacon of Oxford. His most important work is *De Nugis Curialium* (Of Courtiers' Trifles), a miscellany of tales, essays, and homilies, which throws much light on contemporary manners. He has also been credited, rather doubtfully, with a large collection of satirical poems in Latin, and with original Latin versions of the legends of Lancelot, the Holy Grail, and the death of Arthur.

Marjoram, J., *see* **Mottram, R. H.**

Markham, Edwin (23 April 1852—7 March 1940), poet, was born at Oregon City, son of a farmer, but was brought up on a ranch in California. Educated at San José Normal School and Christian College, Santa Rosa, he was for a time a school-teacher. In 1899 he wrote a poem, ' The Man with the Hoe,' inspired by Millet's famous picture of that name; it made his name a household word and he took to writing and lecturing. Hs second most famous poem is ' Lincoln,' published in 1901. His later work, of poorer quality, appears in *The Shoes of Happiness* (1915), *Gates of Paradise* (1920), *New Poems: Eighty Songs at Eighty* (1932), and *The Star of Araby* (1937). Shortly before his death he was awarded the 5,000 dollar prize of the Academy of American Poets.

Markham, Gervase *or* **Jervis** (1568—3 Feb. 1637), poet, translator, and writer on agriculture, was born at Cottam in Nottinghamshire and served as a soldier in the Low Countries and Ireland. Retiring into civil life about 1593 he displayed extraordinary industry as a translator, compiler, and original writer. Among his original writings are a poem on the last fight of Sir Richard Grenville's ship, the *Revenge* (1595), a continuation of Sidney's *Arcadia, The Discourse of Horsemanshippe* (1593), *Cavelarice, or, The English Horseman* (7 volumes, 1607), *Country Contentments* (1611), *A Way to Get Wealth* (1631), and various books on agriculture; also plays and poems, some of which are religious.

Marlowe, Christopher (baptized 26 Feb. 1564, died 1 June 1593), dramatist and poet, son of a shoemaker, was born at Canterbury, educated at the King's School there, and in 1581 went to Benet's (now Corpus Christi) College, Cambridge, where he graduated M.A. in 1587. Of his life after he left the University almost nothing is known. It has, however, been conjectured, partly on account of his familiarity with military matters, that he saw service, probably in the Low Countries. His first play, *Tamburlaine*, was acted in 1587 or 1588. The story is drawn from the Spanish Life of Timur by Pedro Mexia. Its resounding splendour, not seldom passing into bombast, won for it immediate popularity, and it shows a great advance on previous writers in the handling of blank verse. It was followed in 1604 by *Faustus*, a great advance upon *Tamburlaine* in a dramatic sense. The absence of 'material horror' in the treatment, so different in this respect from the original legend, has often been remarked upon. Marlowe's handling of the subject was greatly admired by Goethe, who, however, in his own version, makes the motive knowledge, while Marlowe's has power, and the medieval legend pleasure. In his next play, *The Jew of Malta*, Marlowe continues to show an advance in technical skill, but the work is unequal, and the Jew Barabas is to Shakespeare's Shylock as a monster to a man. In *Edward II*, Marlowe rises to his highest display of power. The rhodomontade of *Tamburlaine* and the piled-up horror of *The Jew* are replaced by a mature self-restraint, and in the whole workmanship he approaches more nearly to Shakespeare than any one else has ever done. Speaking of it Lamb says, 'The death scene of Marlowe's King moves pity and terror beyond any scene, ancient or modern, with which I am acquainted.' His next plays, *The Massacre of Paris* and *The Tragedy of Dido* (written with Nash, q.v.), both show a marked falling off; and it seems likely that in his last years, perhaps, breaking down under the effects of a wild life, he became careless of fame as of all else.

Greene, in his *Groat's Worth of Wit* reproaches Marlowe with his evil life and atheistic opinions, and a few days before his tragic death an information was laid against him for blasphemy. On the other hand, his friends, Shakespeare, Nash, Drayton, and Chapman, all make kindly reference to him. To escape the plague which was raging in London in 1593, he was living at Deptford, then a country village, and there he was killed by Ingram Frizer in a quarrel, so it was reported, over the payment for a meal at a tavern. The burial register of the parish bears the entry 'Christopher Marlowe slaine by ffrancis ffrezer; the ·1· of June.' Marlowe is the father of the modern English drama, and the introducer of the modern form of blank verse. In imagination, richness of expression, originality, and general poetic and dramatic power he surpasses all the Elizabethans except Shakespeare. In addition to his plays he wrote some short poems, of which the best known is 'Come live with me and be my love'; translations from Ovid's *Amores* and Lucan's *Pharsalia*; and a glowing paraphrase from Musaeus in his *Hero and Leander* (1598), a poem completed by Chapman.

Marmion, Shackerley (Jan 1603—Jan. 1639), dramatist, born at

Aynho, near Brackley, Northamptonshire, was educated at Oxford. After a youth of extravagance, he fought in the Low Countries. His writings consist of an epic, *Cupid and Psyche*, and three comedies in the manner of Ben Jonson, *Holland's Leaguer* (1632), *A Fair Companion* (1633), and *The Antiquary* (1634). His plays show some power of satire, and were popular, but he had little of the dramatist.

Marquand, John Phillips (10 Nov. 1893—16 July 1960), novelist, born at Wilmington, Delaware, was brought up at Rye, New York; his great-aunt was a famous blue-stocking. Educated at Harvard, he became a reporter on the Boston *Transcript*. During the First World War he served in the Artillery. His social satire *The Late George Apley* (1937) was awarded the Pulitzer Prize. Others of his novels are *The Unspeakable Gentleman* (1922), *Four of a Kind* (1923), *Black Cargo* (1925), *Ming Yellow* (1935), *Wickford Point* (1939), *H. M. Pulham, Esquire* (1941), *So Little Time* (1943), *Polly Fulton* (1946), and *Point of No Return* (1949). Detective stories in which the Japanese sleuth has a family resemblance to Biggers's Charlie Chan are *Thank You, Mr Moto* (1936), *Think Fast, Mr Moto* (1937), and *Last Laugh, Mr Moto* (1942).

Marquis, Donald Robert Perry (29 July 1878—29 Dec. 1937), journalist and poet, born at Walnut, Illinois, spent one year at Knox College and studied for a time at the Corcoran Art School. After he had tried working as teacher, clerk, reporter, and actor, Joel Chandler Harris (q.v.) made him assistant editor of *Uncle Remus's Magazine*. In 1912 he became a columnist, 'Sun Dial,' on the New York *Sun*, and later was 'Lantern' on the *Herald Tribune*. His last years were spent in illness and poverty. He is best remembered by the comic poems in *archy and mehitabel* (1927) and its sequels, supposed to be composed by archy, a cockroach, who types by butting the keys with his head, and uses no capitals because he cannot manipulate the shift key; mehitabel is a cat, and the antics and reflections of the pair provide an outlet for Marquis's views on life. He was less successful with his more serious works, which include *Poems and Portraits* (1922), the dramas *The Dark Hours* (1924) and *Out of the Sea* (1927), and some novels. *The Old Soak* (1921) is a kind of comic autobiography.

Marriott, John (1780—31 March 1825), clergyman and poet, born at Cotesbach, Leicestershire, where his father was rector, and educated at Rugby and Oxford, in 1808 became rector of Church Lawford in Warwickshire. Previous to this he lived at Dalkeith and was intimate with Sir Walter Scott, who addressed to him the second canto of *Marmion*. Later he contributed to Scott's *Minstrelsy of the Scottish Border*. His most famous poem was 'The Devonshire Lane.'

Marriott, Sir John Arthur Ransome (17 Aug. 1859—6 June 1945), historian, was educated at Repton and New College, Oxford. In 1884 he became a lecturer in history and a Fellow of Worcester College. His numerous works include *Makers of Modern Italy* (1889), *George Canning and his Times* (1903), *The Remaking of Modern Europe* (1909), *England Since Waterloo* (1913), *The European*

Commonwealth (1918), *England under the Tudors* (1922), *A History of Europe from 1815 to 1923* (1931), *The Evolution of Modern Europe* (1932), and *Modern England* (1934). From 1917 to 1922 he was M.P. for Oxford City, and from 1923 to 1929 for York.

Marryat, Frederick (10 July 1792—9 Aug. 1848), novelist and naval captain, son of an M.P. who was chairman of Lloyd's, was born in Westminster. In 1806 he entered the navy as a midshipman under Lord Cochrane, and saw much service in the Mediterranean, at Walcheren, and in the Burmese War of 1824. In 1819 he was elected a Fellow of the Royal Society for devising the mercantile code of signalling by flags, and in 1826 he was nominated C.B. The scenes and experiences through which he had passed were the preparation for and the foundation of his numerous novels, of which the first, *Frank Mildmay*, was published in 1829. It was followed by over 30 others, of which the best are *Peter Simple* (1834), *Jacob Faithful* (1834), *Mr Midshipman Easy* (1836), *Snarleyyow* (1837), *The Phantom Ship* (1839), and *Masterman Ready* (1841). He also wrote several books for boys. Marryat is the prince of sea story-tellers, with knowledge of the sea, vigorous definition of character, and hearty and honest, if somewhat broad, humour.

Marsh, Herbert (10 Dec. 1757—1 May 1839), theologian, born at Faversham in Kent, where his father was vicar, and educated at King's School, Canterbury, Cambridge, and Leipzig, was the first to introduce the German methods of Biblical criticism into England. Appointed Lady Margaret Professor of Divinity at Cambridge in 1807, he gave lectures on the subject, which excited great interest and controversy. In 1816 he was made Bishop of Llandaff, and was translated to Peterborough in 1819. His critical views and his opposition to the evangelical party in the Church, to the Bible Society, to hymns in Divine service, and to Catholic emancipation, involved him in controversy with high, low, and broad churchmen alike. He was the author of a *History of the Politics of Great Britain and France* (1799), *Comparative View of the Churches of England and Rome* (1814), and *Horae Pelasgicae* (1815).

Marsh, Ngaio Edith (23 April 1899—   ), writer of detective stories, was born at Christchurch, New Zealand, but claimed descent from the piratical de Mariscos, Lords of Lundy Island. Her first name (pronounced 'Ny-o') is Maori for 'light upon the water.' Educated at St Margaret's School, she studied for five years at Canterbury School of Art and then became a touring actress. From 1928 to 1932 she was a partner in a house-decorating business in London, where she wrote her first novel *A Man Lay Dead* (1934). After that she divided her time between London and Christchurch. Her other detective stories, which are among the best of their kind, include *Enter a Murderer* (1935), *Death in Ecstasy* (1937), *Vintage Murder* (1937), *Death in a White Tie* (1938), *Overture to Death* (1939), *Death at the Bar* (1940), *Surfeit of Lampreys* (1941), *Died in the Wool* (1945), *Final Curtain* (1947), *Opening Night* (1951), and *Spinsters in Jeopardy* (1954); Inspector Alleyn is her detective. In 1948 she was awarded the O.B.E.

Q

Marston, John (1576—25 June 1634), satirist, dramatist, and clergyman, born probably at Coventry, was educated at Oxford and studied law at the Middle Temple. He began writing in 1598 with an erotic poem, *The Metamorphosis of Pygmalion's Image*, which was burned by order of Archbishop Whitgift, and a satire, *The Scourge of Villainy*. He also took part in the satiric 'battle of the theatres,' *Histriomastix*, which he revised in 1599, satirizing Jonson, who held him up to ridicule in *The Poetaster*. But the feud was made up, and they both collaborated with Chapman in *Eastward Ho* (1605), a satire on Scottish adventurers, which gave such offence to King James that Marston and Chapman were imprisoned. Among Marston's own earliest plays are the satiric comedies *Jack Drum's Entertainment* (1600) and *What You Will* (1607); *The Dutch Courtesan* (1605) is a comedy of intrigue, and *Parasitaster* (1605) is in the style of Jonson. His tragedies *Antonio and Mellida* (1602) and its sequel *Antonio's Revenge* are full of rant and bombast, while *Sophonisba* (1605) appals by its horror. Sombre and caustic, Marston has been called 'a screech-owl among the singing birds.' In 1607 he abandoned writing, took holy orders, and was for fifteen years rector of Christchurch, Hampshire.

Marston, Philip Bourke (13 Aug. 1850—13 Feb. 1887), poet, was born in London, son of a doctor, and lost his sight when a child. His poems, *Song-tide* (1871), *All in All* (1875), *Wind Voices* (1883), and *Garden Secrets* (1887), bear, in their sadness, the impress of this affliction, and of a long series of bereavements. He was the friend of Rossetti and of Swinburne, the latter of whom wrote a sonnet to his memory.

Martin, Sir Theodore (16 Sept. 1816—18 Aug. 1909), poet, biographer, and translator, son of a solicitor, was born in Edinburgh and educated there at the High School and University. He practised as a solicitor in Edinburgh from 1840 to 1845, after which he went to London and became head of the firm of Martin and Leslie, parliamentary agents. His first contribution to literature was *The Bon Gaultier Ballads* (1845), written along with W. E. Aytoun (q.v.), full of wit and humour, which still retain their popularity. He also made numerous translations from Latin, German, and Danish authors. He is, however, perhaps best known for his *Life of the Prince Consort* (1874—80), the writing of which was committed to him by Queen Victoria and which he compiled with such ability and tact as to win for him her lifelong friendship. Later he wrote *Queen Victoria as I Knew Her* (1908). He married in 1851 Miss Helen Faucit the well-known actress, and authoress of studies on *Shakespeare's Female Characters*. He was nominated K.C.B. in 1880, and was Lord Rector of St Andrews in 1881.

Martin, Violet Florence (11 June 1865—21 Dec. 1915), novelist who wrote under the name Martin Ross in collaboration with her cousin Edith Somerville (q.v.), was born in County Galway at Ross House, from which she took her pseudonym. A daughter of the Deputy Lieutenant of Ireland, she was educated at Alexandra College, Dublin. From 1886 she lived with her cousin at Drishane, County

Cork, and in 1899 they started writing novels as a hobby, their first joint production being *An Irish Cousin*. Their best-known work is *Some Experiences of an Irish R.M.* (two series, 1899, 1908). For other works *see* under E. O. Somerville.

Martineau, Harriet (12 June 1802—27 June 1876), was born at Norwich, daughter of a cloth manufacturer of Huguenot descent. From her earliest years she was delicate and very deaf, and took to literary pursuits as an amusement. Afterwards, when her father had fallen into difficulties, they became her means of support. Her first publication was *Devotional Exercises for Young Persons* (1823). Becoming interested in political economy, she endeavoured to illustrate the subject by tales, of which two were *The Rioters* and *The Turn-out*. Later she published a more serious treatment of it in *Illustrations of Political Economy* (1832—4), *Poor Law and Paupers* (1833), and *Illustrations of Taxation* (1834). About this time she went to London, and was regarded as an authority on economic questions, being occasionally consulted by Cabinet Ministers. Among her books of travel are *Society in America* (1837), and *Eastern Life, Present and Past* (1848), which she considered her best book: in it she declared herself no longer a believer in revelation. She also wrote two novels, *Deerbrook* (1839), and *The Hour and the Man* (1840) and some books for children, of which the best is *Feats on the Fiord* (1844). Perhaps her most important work is her *History of England during the Thirty Years' Peace, 1816—46*, which appeared in 1849. She translated Comte's *Philosophy* (1853), and wrote an autobiography which was published the year after her death.

Martineau, James (21 April 1805—11 Jan. 1900), theologian, younger brother of the above, was born at Norwich, and had George Borrow (q.v.) as a schoolfellow at the Grammar School there. Possessed of considerable inventive and mathematical talents, he was originally intended for engineering, but studied for the Unitarian ministry, to which he was ordained in 1828. After serving as pastor in various places he became in 1840 Professor of Mental and Moral Philosophy in the Manchester New College (subsequently removed to London), and Principal in 1869. Among his writings, which were very influential, are *Rationale of Religious Inquiry* (1836), *Ideal Substitutes for God* (1879), *Study of Spinoza* (1882), *Types of Ethical Theory* (1885), *Study of Religion* (1888), *Seat of Authority in Religion* (1890), and religious poems and hymns.

Marvel, Ik, *see* Mitchell, D. G.

Marvell, Andrew (31 March 1621—18 Aug. 1678), poet and satirist, was born at Winestead in Holderness, Yorkshire, where his father was rector, educated at Hull Grammar School and Cambridge, and thereafter travelled for a time on the Continent. He sat in Parliament for Hull, proving himself an assiduous and incorruptible member, with strong republican leanings. In spite of this he was a favourite of Charles II, who took pleasure in his society, and offered him a place at Court, and a present of £1,000, which were both declined. In his own day he was best known as a powerful and fearless political writer, and for some time from 1657 was assistant to

Milton in the Latin or Foreign Secretaryship to the Council of State. After the Restoration he wrote against the Government, his chief work in this kind being his *Account of Growth of Popery and Arbitrary Government in England* (1677). He was also the author of *The Rehearsal Transpos'd* (1673) which condemns religious intolerance. His controversial style was lively and vigorous, but sometimes coarse and vituperative. His fame now rests on his poems which, though few, have many of the highest poetical qualities. Among the best known are the 'Song of the Emigrants in Bermuda,' the 'Horatian Ode upon Cromwell's Return from Ireland,' and 'Thoughts in a Garden.' Of the last Palgrave says that 'it may be regarded as a test of any reader's insight into the most poetical aspects of poetry.' The town of Hull voted Marvell a monument, which was, however, forbidden by the Court. His appearance is thus described, 'He was of middling stature, pretty strong-set, roundish-faced, cherry-cheeked, hazel-eyed, brown-haired.'

Masefield, John Edward, O.M. (1 June 1878—), Poet Laureate, was born at Ledbury, Herefordshire, son of a solicitor, and educated at King's School, Warwick, and the ship *Conway*, which trains boys for the merchant service. At the age of 15 he went to sea as an apprentice on a wind-jammer and made the voyage round Cape Horn. Turning ill in Chile, he abandoned the sea and lived in New York for three years, working successively in a bakery, a livery stable, a saloon, and a carpet factory. In 1897 he returned to London, and started writing for various periodicals. He became literary editor of the *Speaker*, and inaugurated the famous Miscellany column of the *Manchester Guardian*. His first book of poems, *Salt Water Ballads*, was published in 1902. *Ballads and Poems* followed in 1910, and in 1911 *The Everlasting Mercy*, a realist narrative poem which caused a sensation by its use of coarse everyday language. Other long poems of the same type are *The Widow in the Bye Street* (1912) and *Dauber* (1913). To this period belong also two plays, the grimly horrible *Tragedy of Nan* (1909) and *Pompey the Great* (1910). A small but excellent book on *Shakespeare* appeared in 1911, as also did *Jim Davis*, a boys' book in the tradition of *Treasure Island*.

During the First World War Masefield served with the Red Cross, and from it he drew on his experiences for *Gallipoli* (1916), *The Old Front Line* (1917), and *The Battle of the Somme* (1919). A new volume of verse, *Lollington Downs* (1917) was followed by his finest narrative poem, *Reynard the Fox* (1919). In 1923 appeared his *Collected Poems*, which sold over 200,000 copies. Next were two successful novels, *Sard Harker* (1924) and *Odtaa* (1926), which takes its peculiar title from the initials of the phrase 'one damned thing after another.' At this time he lived on Boars Hill, the 'poets corner' near Oxford, about a mile from Dr Bridges (q.v.), whom he succeeded as Poet Laureate in 1930. During the Second World War, when it was a centre of Air Force training, he removed to Cirencester. He had received a doctorate from Oxford in 1922, and in 1935 was awarded the Order of Merit; in 1961 the Royal Society of Literature made him a Companion of Literature. His autobiography *So Long to Learn* appeared in 1952, and its title may have a certain ironical aptness, since he has been criticized for his crudity, his faulty poetical technique, and lack of subtlety. But none can deny the tonic vigour of his verse, which looks back to two models—Chaucer, from whom he derived his power of telling a story in verse, and Kipling, who inspired his down-to-earth muscularity and feeling for the common man. In his prose writing he was most influenced by Conrad, the great sea writer.

Mason, Alfred Edward Woodley (7 May 1865—22 Nov. 1948), novelist, born at Dulwich and educated at Dulwich College and Oxford, became an actor with the Benson company. He began as an author with a series of mainly historical novels, including *A Romance of Wastdale* (1895), *The Courtship of Morrice Buckler* (1896), *The Philanderers* (1897), *Miranda of the Balcony* (1899), and *Clementina* (1901); *The Four Feathers* (1902) is a vivid story of Egypt, while *The Broken Road* (1907) tells of India, and *Running Water* (1907) describes the Brenva route on Mont Blanc. Later he published a number of detective stories in which Hanaud of the Sûreté, first fictional police detective since Lecoq, was much admired; they include *At the Villa Rose* (1910), *The House of the Arrow* (1924), *No Other Tiger* (1927), and *The Prisoner in the Opal* (1929). From 1906 to 1910 Mason was M.P. for Coventry, and during the First World War he served with Naval Intelligence.

Mason, Walt (4 May 1862—22 June 1939), humorist, was born at Columbus, Ontario, son of a wool dyer. In 1880 he came to the United States and arrived in Kansas with less than two dollars in his pockets. Writing in rhymed prose, a kind of slang doggerel, he has been called the Homer of the Middle West. His books include *Uncle Walt* (1910), *Walt Mason's Business Prose Poems* (1911), *Rippling Rhymes* (1913), *Horse Sense* (1915), *Terse Verse* (1917), and *Walt Mason, His Book* (1918).

Mason, William (12 Feb. 1724—7 April 1797), poet, son of a clergyman, was born at Hull, and educated at Cambridge. He took orders and rose to be a Canon of York. His first poem was *Musaeus* (1747), a monody on the death of Pope, and his other works include *Elfrida* (1752), and *Caractacus* (1759), dramas; a *Heroic Epistle* to Sir William Chambers, the architect, in which he satirized some modern fashions in gardening; *The English Garden* (1772—82), his largest work; and some odes. He was a close friend of Gray, whose life he wrote. His language was too magnificent for his powers of thought, but he has passages where the rich diction is effective.

Massey, Gerald (29 May 1828—29 Oct. 1907), poet, born near Tring, Hertfordshire, son of a canal boatman, started work in a silk mill at the age of 8, then became a straw-plaiter, then an errand boy. When he was 15 he came to London, where he was taken up by Maurice and Kingsley. In 1848 his first book, *Poems and Chansons*, was printed by a Tring bookseller, but he first attracted attention by *Babe Christabel* (1854). This was followed by *War Waits, Craigcrook Castle*, and *Havelock's March*. A selection from these was published in 1889, under the title of *My Lyrical Life*. Later he wrote and lectured on spiritualism, and produced prose works on the origin of myths and mysteries in *The Book of Beginnings* (1881), *The Natural Genesis* (1883), and *Ancient Egypt: the Light of the World* (1907). He also wrote a book on the sonnets of Shakespeare. Massey had a true lyrical vein, but though often musical, he was at times harsh and rugged.

Massinger, Philip (baptized 24 Nov. 1583, died 18 March 1640), dramatist, was born probably at Salisbury, and his father seems to have been in service with the Earl of Pembroke. Massinger was at Oxford, but left without a degree. A letter which he wrote to Henslowe in 1613 reveals him as living in London in poverty. At the start of his career as a dramatist he collaborated with Fletcher (q.v.) in over 30 plays, and after Fletcher's death in 1625 he was chief dramatist for the King's Men. Of his own tragedies the best are *The Duke of Milan* (1623) and *The Roman Actor* (1626). His comedies are more in the style of Jonson, the most effective being *The City Madam* (1632) and his greatest play of all, *A New Way to Pay Old Debts* (1633), which kept the stage till the nineteenth century. Other comedies are *The Parliament of Love* (1624), *The Picture* (1629), *Believe as you List* (1631), and *The Guardian* (1633). He also wrote several tragi-comedies in Fletcher's style, including *The Maid of Honour* (1628), *A Very Woman* (1634), and *The Bashful Lover* (1636). Massinger excelled in the construction and working out of a plot, and his blank verse is lucid and flexible.

Massingham, Harold John (25 March 1888—22 Aug. 1952), nature writer, was born in London, son of a journalist, and educated at Westminster and Oxford. Taking up journalism, in 1912 he became literary editor of the *Athenaeum*, and subsequently made a name as a nature writer. Among his earliest books are *Birds of the Countryside* (1921), *Sanctuaries for Birds* (1924), and *Birds of the Sea Shore* (1931). *In Praise of England* (1924), *World Without End* (1932), and *The Wisdom of the Fields* (1945) are general books; *English Downland* (1936), *Cotswold Country* (1937), and *Chiltern Country* (1940) tell of special districts; and *The Sweet of the Year* (1939), *The Fall of the Year* (1941), and *An Englishman's Year* (1948) with the changing seasons. *Remembrance* (1942) is an autobiography. He made his home at Long Crendon, near Aylesbury.

Masson, David (2 Dec. 1822—6 Oct. 1907), scholar and biographer, was born in Aberdeen, son of a stonecutter, and educated at Marischal College there and at Edinburgh, where he studied theology under Chalmers. He did not, however, enter the ministry, but began a literary career by editing a newspaper in Aberdeen. Going to London in 1847 he wrote extensively in reviews, magazines, and encyclopaedias. In 1852 he became Professor of English Literature in University College, London, in 1858 editor of *Macmillan's Magazine*, and in 1865 Professor of English Literature in Edinburgh. He was the author of many important works, including *Essays Biographical and Critical* (1856), *British Novelists* (1859), and *Recent British Philosophy* (1865). His *magnum opus* is his monumental *Life of John Milton* (6 volumes, 1859—80) the most complete biography of any Englishman, dealing as it does not only with the personal life of the poet, but with the history, political, social, and religious, of his time. Other books are *Drummond of Hawthornden* (1873), *De Quincey* (1878), *Edinburgh Sketches and Memories* (1892), and *Carlyle Personally and in his Writings*. He also edited the standard edition of De Quincey's works, and the Register of the Privy Council of Scotland, his introductions in connection with which are of great historical value. He was appointed Historiographer for Scotland in 1893. After his death his *Memories of London in the Forties* was published in 1908, and his *Memories of Two Cities* in 1911.

Masters, Edgar Lee (23 Aug. 1869—5 March 1950), poet, born at Garnett, Kansas, son of an attorney, was brought up in Petersburg and Lewistown, Illinois, which he made famous as the 'Spoon River Country.' Educated at Knox College, he studied law, was admitted to the Bar in 1891, and practised for a time in Chicago, then turning to literature. Influenced by reading a translation of epigrams from the *Greek Anthology*, he composed in imitation the *Spoon River Anthology* (1915), a collection of imaginary epitaphs from an Illinois cemetery, reflecting the spirit of the Middle West. Though he published nearly 50 volumes, he never repeated the success of this early venture, his later work being often dull and long-winded. His poetical works include *A Book of Verse* (1898), *Domesday Book* (1920), *The New Spoon River* (1924), and *The Fate of the Jury* (1929). He also wrote biographies of *Lincoln* (1931), *Vachel Lindsay* (1935), *Whitman* (1937), and *Mark Twain* (1938), some novels, and an autobiography, *Across Spoon River* (1937).

Mather, Cotton (12 Feb. 1663—13 Feb. 1728), theologian, was born in Boston, son of Increase Mather, a clergyman who became President of Harvard. The son created an all-time record by entering Harvard at the age of 12. In 1685 he became minister of the North Church in Boston, where he officiated all his life. Energetic, intolerant, and learned, a conservative in religion but a radical in science, he supported the burning of witches, but also approved of inoculation against smallpox, and was the first American to be elected a member of the Royal Society. Besides *Magnalia Christi Americana* (1702), an ecclesiastical history of New England, he wrote many theological works.

Mathias, Thomas James (1754?—Aug. 1835), satirist, son of a sub-treasurer of the Queen's household, was educated at Cambridge and became librarian at Buckingham Palace. He was an accomplished Italian scholar, and made various translations from the English into Italian, and vice versa. He also produced a fine edition of Gray, on which he lost heavily. His chief work, however, was *The Pursuits of Literature* (1794), an undiscriminating satire on his literary contemporaries, which went through sixteen editions.

Matthiessen, Francis Otto (19 Feb. 1902—1 April 1950), critic, born at Pasadena, California, was educated at Yale, and in 1923 went as a Rhodes Scholar to New College, Oxford, where he wrote a thesis on Goldsmith. After two years as an instructor at Yale, he went to Harvard and became Associate Professor of History and Literature from 1934 to 1942. His greatest work was *American Renaissance:*

Art and Expression in the Age of Emerson and Whitman (1941), a brilliant and sensitive study. Others of his books are *Sarah Orne Jewett* (1929), *The Achievement of T. S. Eliot* (1935), *Henry James: the Major Phase* (1944), *From the Heart of Europe* (1948), and *Theodore Dreiser* (1951). He committed suicide in Boston.

Maturin, Charles Robert (1782—30 Oct. 1824), novelist, born in Dublin of Huguenot ancestry, was educated at Trinity College there, and taking orders held various benefices. He was the author of a few dramas, one of which, *Bertram* (1816), had great success. He is, however, better known for his gruesome romances in the style of Mrs Radcliffe and 'Monk' Lewis. The first of these, *The Fatal Revenge*, appeared in 1807, and was followed by, among others, *The Milesian Chief* (1812), *Women* (1818), which was the most successful, and lastly by *Melmoth the Wanderer* (1820), in which he outdoes his models in the mysterious, the horrible, and indeed the revolting. His last work, *The Albigenses* (1824), is in a somewhat different style.

Maugham, William Somerset (25 Jan. 1874—), novelist, was born in Paris, where his father was solicitor to the British Embassy, and spoke French before he spoke English. An orphan before he was 10, he was brought up by a clergyman uncle in Whitstable, Kent, and went to school at King's School, Canterbury. After attending Heidelberg University he studied medicine in St Thomas's for six years, but never practised, except as a student in the London slums, from which he drew the materials for his sordid novel *Liza of Lambeth* (1897). He tells of these periods in *Of Human Bondage* (1915), often reckoned his finest novel. At first he was better known as a playwright than a novelist, though it was only after years of effort that he won success with *Lady Frederick* in 1907. During the First World War he served with the Intelligence Department, and so got the material for his spy story *Ashenden* (1928). In 1915 he married Lady Wellcome, daughter of Dr Barnardo; they were divorced in 1927. In 1930 he settled at Cap Ferrat, but lost nearly all his possessions in the German invasion of the Second World War. His best-known novels are *The Moon and Sixpence* (1919), *The Painted Veil* (1925), *Cakes and Ale* (1930), *The Razor's Edge* (1945), and *Catalina* (1948). Collections of short stories, of which he was an acknowledged master, are *Sadie Thompson* (1921) and *First Person Singular* (1931). From his fondness for life's bitter realities he has been called the English Maupassant. Most of his plays, however, are comedies of manners in the Wilde tradition. The best are *The Circle* (1921), *East of Suez* (1922), *Our Betters* (1923), *The Letter* (1925), *The Constant Wife* (1926), *The Sacred Flame* (1928), and *For Services Rendered* (1932). *Strictly Personal* (1941) is a book of reminiscences. In 1954 he was made a Companion of Honour, and in 1961 the Royal Society of Literature made him a Companion of Literature.

Maurice, Frederick Denison (29 Aug. 1805—1 April 1872), clergyman, son of a Unitarian minister, was born at Normanston, near Lowestoft, and studied at Cambridge. He went to London, and for a short time edited the *Athenaeum*. His theological views having changed, he joined the Church of England, went to Oxford, graduated and was ordained in 1834. He became Chaplain to Guy's Hospital, and held other clerical positions in London. In 1840 he was appointed Professor of English Literature and History at King's College, and subsequently Professor of Theology. He became a leader among the Christian Socialists, and for a short time edited their paper. In 1854 he was one of the founders of the Working Men's College, of which he became Principal, and in 1866 he was made Professor of Moral Philosophy at Cambridge. Among his writings are *The Religions of the World and their Relation to Christianity* (1838), *Theological Essays* (1853), *Social Morality* (1869), and *Moral and Metaphysical Philosophy* (1871—2).

Mavor, Osborne Henry (3 Jan. 1888—29 Jan. 1951), playwright who wrote under the name James Bridie, was born in Glasgow and educated at Glasgow Academy, High School, and University, where he edited the *University Magazine*. Qualifying as a doctor, he practised in Glasgow till 1938 and served with the R.A.M.C. in both World Wars. Known in Scotland by his early plays, *The Sunlight Sonata* (1928) and *What It Is To Be Young* (1929), he became widely celebrated through *Tobias and the Angel* (1930), which ran in London with great success. Others of his plays are *The Anatomist* (1930), *Jonah and the Whale* (1932), *A Sleeping Clergyman* (1933), *Susannah and the Elders* (1937), *Mr Bolfry* (1943), *The Forrigan Reel* (1944), *John Knox* (1947), *Dr Angelus* (1947) and *The Queen's Comedy* (1950). Full of humour and topsyturvy situations, but always with a substratum of sound philosophy, his work has been compared with Bernard Shaw's. A founder of the Glasgow Citizen's Theatre, he was made a C.B.E. in 1946. Reminiscences of his life are contained in *One Way of Living* (1939).

Max Müller, Friedrich (6 Dec. 1823—28 Oct. 1900), philologist, son of the German poet, Wilhelm Max Müller, was born at Dessau, and educated at Leipzig, Berlin, and Paris. In 1846 he was commissioned by the East India Company to edit the Sanskrit *Rigveda*. He settled at Oxford in 1848, and in 1850 was appointed deputy Taylorian Professor of Modern European languages, becoming Professor four years later, and Curator of the Bodleian Library in 1856. In 1858 he was elected a Fellow of All Souls, and ten years later first Professor of Comparative Philology. He edited *Sacred Books of the East,* a series of oriental religious classics, and wrote in English *Chips from a German Workshop* (1867—75). He did much to stimulate the study of comparative religion and philology, and he was made a Privy Councillor in 1896. His widow edited his *Life and Letters* (1902).

Maxwell, William Hamilton (1794—29 Dec. 1850), novelist, born at Newry, County Down, and educated at Trinity College, Dublin, entered the army, and saw service in the Peninsula, and at Waterloo. Afterwards he took orders, but was deprived of his living for non-residence. His novels, *O'Hara*, and *Stories from Waterloo*, both published in 1829, started the school of rollicking military fiction, which culminated in the novels of Lever. Maxwell also wrote a life of the Duke of Wellington, and a *History of the Irish Rebellion*.

Q*

May, Thomas (1595—13 Nov. 1650), poet, dramatist, and historian, born in Sussex, son of Sir Thomas May, of Mayfield, went to Cambridge, and thence to Gray's Inn, but discarded law for literature. In 1622 he produced his first comedy, *The Heir*, and also a translation of Virgil's *Georgics*. Six years later appeared his translation of *Lucan*, which gained him the favour of Charles I, at whose command he wrote two poems, *The Reigne of King Henry II*, and *The Victorious Reigne of King Edward III*, each in seven books. When the Civil War broke out May, to the disappointment of his friends, took the side of the Parliament, and was made Secretary to the Long Parliament, the historian of which he became, publishing in 1647, *The History of the Parliament of England, which began November the third, 1640*. May was also the author of several tragedies, including *Antigone* (1631).

May, Sir Thomas Erskine, 1st Baron Farnborough (8 Feb. 1815—17 May 1886), jurist and historian, was educated at Bedford Grammar School and called to the Bar by Middle Temple. After holding various minor offices he became in 1871 clerk to the House of Commons, retiring in 1886, when he was raised to the peerage. He had previously, in 1866, been made K.C.B. He was the author of *A Treatise on the Law, Privileges, Proceedings, and Usage of Parliament*, which, first published in 1844, reached in 1901 its 10th edition, and was translated into various languages. His *Constitutional History of England, 1760—1860* (1861—3) is practically a continuation of Hallam's great work. He also wrote *Democracy in Europe* (1877).

Mayne, Ethel Colburn (died 30 April 1941), novelist, daughter of an Irish magistrate, was educated at private schools, became a journalist, and made many translations. Her first published story appeared in the *Yellow Book* in 1895 under the pseudonym Francis E. Huntly. In 1898 she published, under her own name, a book of short stories, *The Clearer Vision*; other collections are *Things That No One Tells* (1910), *Nine of Hearts* (1923), and *Inner Circle* (1925). Her novels include *Jessie Vandeleur* (1902), *The Fourth Ship* (1908), and *One of Our Grandmothers* (1916). She was an authority on Byron, of whom she wrote a two-volume study in 1912, and she also wrote on *Browning's Heroines* (1913). *Enchanters of Men* (1909) is an account of famous courtesans.

Mayne, Jasper (baptized 23 Nov. 1604, died 6 Dec. 1672), clergyman and dramatist, born at Hatherleigh in Devonshire, and educated at Westminster and Oxford, took orders, and became Archdeacon of Chichester. He wrote two dramas, *The City Match* (1639) and *The Amorous War* (1648).

Mayne, John (26 March 1759—14 March 1836), poet, was born in Dumfries. In 1780 he published the *Siller Gun* in its original form in *Ruddiman's Magazine*. It is a humorous poem descriptive of an ancient custom in Dumfries of shooting for a trophy, and was admired by Scott. He was continually adding to it, until it grew to five cantos. He also wrote a poem on *Hallowe'en*, and a version of the ballad, *Helen of Kirkconnel*. He died in London, proprietor and editor of the *Star*.

Mayo, Katherine (1868—9 Oct. 1940), journalist, was born at Ridgeway, Pennsylvania, and educated at private schools. Her first book, *Justice to All* (1917), was a critical study of the American police system. During the First World War she went overseas to write about the Y.M.C.A., and did so in *That Damn Y* (1921). *Isles of Fear* (1925), was a criticism of American rule in the Philippines, and in 1927 appeared her most famous book, *Mother India*, exposing the iniquities of the child-bride system there; *Volume Two* (1931) consists of documentation of her statements in it. Others of her works are *The Face of Mother India* (1935) and *General Washington's Dilemma* (1938).

Mead, Margaret (16 Dec. 1901—   ), anthropologist, born in Philadelphia, daughter of a professor of economics of Quaker descent, was educated at De Pauw University, Bernard College, and Columbia. She took part in expeditions to Samoa and New Guinea, and in 1926 was appointed Assistant Curator of Ethnology at the American Museum of Natural History. Her publications, which are popular though authoritative, include *Coming of Age in Samoa* (1928), *Growing Up in New Guinea* (1930), and *Sex and Temperament in Three Primitive Societies* (1935), these three being collected as one volume with the title *From the South Seas* (1939). Later books are *Male and Female* (1949) and *Growth and Culture* (1951).

Mee, Arthur Henry (21 July 1875—27 May 1943), journalist, was born at Stapleford, Nottinghamshire, son of a railway fireman; both his parents were Baptists. On leaving the village school he became a reporter at the age of 16, and at 20 was editor of the *Nottingham Evening News*; later he went to Fleet Street and from 1903 to 1905 was literary editor of the *Daily Mail*. His prodigious memory was of great service in the reference works he compiled; they included a *Self-Educator* (1906), *History of the World* (1907), *The World's Great Books* (1909), *Harmsworth Natural History* (1911), *Popular Science* (1912), and *I See All* (1929), the first picture encyclopaedia. But his most famous work was his *Children's Encyclopaedia* (1908), which was translated into French, Spanish, Portuguese, Italian, Arabic, and Chinese, and was in a sense continued by his *Children's Newspaper*, begun in 1919 and still being issued forty years later. During his later years he wrote many children's books, and a series of county guides in 38 volumes, entitled *The King's England* (1936—43).

Melmoth, Sebastian, *see* **Wilde, Oscar.**

Melville, Herman (1 Aug. 1819—28 Sept. 1891), novelist and poet, was born in New York, son of a merchant of distinguished Scottish descent who died bankrupt in 1832, so that at the age of 15 Herman left Albany Academy and earned his living variously as clerk, farm hand, and teacher. In 1839 he began his long connection with the sea by shipping as cabin boy in the *Highlander* on a voyage to Liverpool; his experiences on this occasion were later the basis of his book *Redburn* (1849). His next voyage was from Fairhaven to the Pacific in 1841 on a whaler, the *Acushnet*, which gave him much of the material for his famous *Moby-Dick, or The Whale* (1851). He deserted the ship when it reached the Marquesas Islands, was captured by cannibals, with whom he lived for some weeks in friendship, and wrote about them eventually in *Typee: a Peep at Polynesian Life* (1846), his first publication. Escaping in an Australian whaler, the *Lucy Ann*, he was put ashore at Tahiti as one of a mutinous crew, and later made the Society Islands the subject of his second book, *Omoo, a Narrative of Adventure in the South Seas* (1847). Sailing from there to Honolulu, he came home as a seaman in the frigate *United States*, of which he wrote in *White-Jacket* (1850). In 1847 he married and settled in New York, and in addition to the above books published *Mardi* (1849), a satirical allegory which was not a success. In 1850 he bought a farm near Pittsfield, Massachusetts, and formed a friendship with Nathaniel Hawthorne (q.v.) who lived close by.

It was under Hawthorne's influence that he wrote *Moby-Dick*, which is not merely a vivid and stirring account of a whaling voyage but a cosmic allegory whose underlying theme is the enormity of evil, so that the book was declared by the author to have been 'broiled in hell-fire.' Misunderstood and only partly appreciated at first, it has come to be regarded as one of the great novels of American literature. Melville further developed the vein of symbolical fiction with *Pierre: or the Ambiguities* (1852), which was ignored by readers who preferred his exotic romances. *Piazza Tales* (1856) is a fine collection of short stories, but his only later prose works were *The Confidence Man* (1857), an unsuccessful satire, and a brilliant novelette, *Billy Budd*, written just before his death but not published till 1924, which was made into an opera by Benjamin Britten in 1950. During the last 35 years of his life Melville worked in the New York Customs House, and produced only some books of verse, *Battle Pieces* (1866), *Clarel* (1876), *John Marr and Other Sailors* (1888), and *Timoleon* (1891). For many years after his death his work was neglected, though in England especially he was always admired as a pioneer in the literature of the South Seas; but about the time of his birth centenary there was remarkable revival of interest in his books, and he is now reckoned one of the greatest of American authors, and an admirable prose stylist.

Melville, James (26 July 1556—13 Jan. 1614), diarist, born in Montrose, was a son of the laird of Baldovie, in Forfarshire, and nephew of the great reformer and scholar, Andrew Melville, by whom, when he was Principal of the University of Glasgow, James was chosen as a regent or professor. When, in 1580, Andrew became Principal of St Mary's College, St Andrews, James accompanied him, and acted as Professor of Hebrew and Oriental Languages. He wrote many poems, but his chief work was his *Diary*, an original authority for the period, written with much naïveté, and revealing à singularly attractive personality. Melville, who for his part in Church matters, had been banished to England, died at Berwick on his way back to Scotland.

Melville, Sir James (1535—13 Nov. 1617), historian, son of Sir John Melville, of Raith, in Fife, was a page to Mary Queen of Scots at the French Court, and afterwards one of her Privy Council.   He also acted as her envoy to Queen Elizabeth and the Elector Palatine. He was the author of an autobiography, *Memoirs of My Own Life*, which is one of the original authorities for the period.   The manuscript, which lay for long hidden in Edinburgh Castle, was discovered in 1660, and published in 1683.   A later edition was brought out in 1827 by the Bannatyne Club.   The work is written in a lively style.

Mencken, Henry Louis (12 Sept. 1880—29 Jan. 1956), critic, was born in Baltimore, son of a tobacco dealer of German descent, and was educated at Baltimore Polytechnic.   Turning to writing, he joined the staff of the Baltimore *Sun*, and soon showed himself a champion of heterodoxy by deliberately attacking conventional principles and morality.   In 1924 he founded the *American Mercury*, which he edited till 1933.   His first publication was a volume of poems, *Ventures into Verse* (1903), and he followed this with a critical work, *George Bernard Shaw: his Plays* (1905).   Later works are *A Little Book in C Major* (1916), *In Defence of Women* (1917), *A Book of Prefaces* (1917), *Damn—A Book of Calumny* (1917), *Prejudices* (six volumes 1919—27), and a study of *James Branch Cabell* (1927). His most important work of scholarship was *The American Language* (1919), which discusses the development of the English language in the United States and was several times revised; he also compiled *A New Dictionary of Quotations on Historical Principles* (1942). Humorous autobiographical volumes are *Happy Days* (1940), *Newspaper Days* (1941), and *Heathen Days* (1943).

Mercer, Cecil William (7 Aug. 1885—5 March 1960), novelist who wrote under the name Dornford Yates, was born in London, son of a solicitor, and educated at Harrow and Oxford, where he was president of the Oxford University Dramatic Society.   He was called to the Bar by Inner Temple, but forsook law for literature.   During the First World War he served in the London Yeomanry; in the second he was on the East Africa front and attained the rank of major.   His novels blend adventure with light-hearted farce, and have been said to combine the maximum of entertainment with the minimum of probability.   Among the earliest are *Berry and Co.* (1921), *Jonah and Co.* (1922), *And Five Were Fools* (1924), *The Stolen March* (1926), *Maiden Stakes* (1929), and *Storm Music* (1934); the 'Berry' series continues with *And Berry Came Too* (1936), *The House That Berry Built* (1945), and *The Berry Scene* (1947), while *As Berry and I Were Saying* (1952) consists of reminiscences in a fictional setting.

Meredith, George, O.M. (12 Feb. 1828—18 May 1909), novelist and poet, born at Portsmouth, son of a naval outfitter, who afterwards went to Cape Town, was educated at Portsmouth and Neuwied in Germany.   Owing to the neglect of a trustee, what means he had inherited were lost, and he was in his early days very poor.   Articled to a lawyer in London, he had no taste for law, which he soon exchanged for journalism, and at 21 he was writing poetry for magazines, his first printed work, a poem on the Battle of Chillianwallah, appearing in *Chambers's Journal*.   Two years later he published *Poems* (1851), containing the glorious 'Love in the Valley.' Meantime he had been editing a small provincial newspaper, and in 1866 was war correspondent in Italy for the *Morning Post*; and he also acted for many years as literary adviser to a publisher. By this time, however, he had produced several of his novels, and had become acquainted with Swinburne, the Pre-Raphaelites, and other eminent writers. *The Shaving of Shagpat* had appeared in 1856, *Farina* in 1857, *The Ordeal of Richard Feverel* in 1859, *Evan Harrington* in 1861, *Emilia in England* (subsequently renamed *Sandra Belloni*) in 1864, its sequel, *Vittoria*, in 1866, and *Rhoda Fleming* in 1865. In poetry he had produced *Modern Love and Poems of the English Roadside* (1862), generally regarded as his best poetical work.

These were followed by *The Adventures of Harry Richmond* (1871), *Beauchamp's Career* (1875), said to be the author's favourite, *The Egoist* (1879), which marks the beginning of a change in style characterized by an even greater fastidiousness in the choice of words, phrases, and condensation of thought than its predecessors, *The Tragic Comedians* (1880), and *Diana of the Crossways*, the first of the author's novels to attain anything approaching general popularity. The same period yielded in poetry, *Poems and Lyrics of the Joy of Earth* (1883), *Ballads and Poems of Tragic Life* (1887), and *A Reading of Earth* (1888). His later novels, *One of our Conquerors* (1891), *Lord Ormont and his Aminta* (1894), and *The Amazing Marriage* (1895), exhibit the tortuous and difficult style which denied general popularity to all of his works, and they did little to add to his reputation. In 1897 he published his lecture on *The Idea of Comedy and the Uses of the Comic Spirit*. In 1905 he received the Order of Merit. He was twice married, his first wife, who died in 1860, being a daughter of Thomas Love Peacock (q.v.). This union did not prove in all respects happy. His second wife was Marie Vulliamy, who died in 1885. In his earlier life he was vigorous and athletic, and a great walker; latterly he was disabled by paraplegia.

Though the writings of Meredith never were and probably never will be generally popular, his genius was, from the very first, recognized by the best judges. Few writers have striven to charge sentences and even words so heavily with meaning, or to attain so great a degree of condensation, with the result that links in the chain of thought are not seldom omitted and left for the careful reader to supply; hence Wilde's description of him as 'a prose Browning.' There is also a tendency to adopt unusual words and forms of expression where plainness and simplicity would have served as well, and these features taken together give reason for the charges of obscurity and affectation so often made. Moreover, the discussion of motive and feeling is often out of proportion to the narrative of events. But to compensate us for these defects he offers humour, often, indeed, whimsical, but keen and sparkling, close observation of and exquisite feeling for nature, a marvellous power of word-painting, the most delicate and penetrating analysis of character, and an invincible optimism which, while not blind to the darker aspects of life, triumphs over the depression which they might induce in a weaker nature.

Meredith, Owen, *see* **Lytton, 1st Earl of.**

Meres, Francis (1565—1647), clergyman and critic, was of a Lincolnshire family, studied at Cambridge and Oxford, and became rector of Wing in Rutland. He published in 1598 *Palladis Tamia: Wit's Treasury*, containing a comparison of English poets with Greek, Latin, and Italian. It has valuable references to Marlowe's death and Shakespeare's early plays.

Merivale, Charles (8 March 1808—27 Dec. 1893), historian, son of a writer, was born in London. Educated at Harrow, Haileybury, and Cambridge, he took orders, and among other preferments held those of chaplain to the Speaker of the House of Commons, and Dean of Ely. From his college days he was a keen student of Roman history, and between 1850 and 1864 he published his *History of the Romans under the Empire*, an able and scholarly work, though considered by some critics to be too favourable to the Emperors. An earlier work was *The Fall of the Roman Republic* (1853).

Merrick, Leonard (21 Feb. 1864—7 Aug. 1939), novelist, born in London, changed his original surname of Miller to Merrick by deed poll. Educated at Brighton College, he went to South Africa and worked as an overseer in the diamond fields. Returning to London at the age of 20, he spent two years on the stage, but he was always most at home in Paris, and many of his novels have a French atmosphere. They include *The Man Who Was Good* (1892), *This Stage of Fools* (1896), *One Man's View* (1897), *The Actor-Manager* (1898), *Conrad in Quest of his Youth* (1903), *The House of Lynch* (1907), *The Position of Peggy Harper* (1911), and *While Paris Laughed* (1918). *The Man Who Understood Women* (1908) and *The Little Dog Laughed* (1930) are volumes of short stories. Merrick's work was always more admired by other writers than by the general public, and a collected edition was published in his lifetime with introductions by Barrie, Wells, W. J. Locke, and others.

Merriman, H. Seton, *see* **Scott, Hugh Stowell.**

Meston, William (1688?—1745), scholar and poet, born at Midmar, Aberdeenshire, son of a blacksmith, was educated at Mareschal College, of which he became a regent. He took part in the rebellion of 1715, and had to go into hiding. His *Knight of the Kirk* (1723) is an imitation of *Hudibras*. It has little merit.

Mew, Charlotte Mary (15 Nov. 1869—24 March 1928), poetess, was born in Bloomsbury, daughter of an architect. Educated privately, she suffered all her life from illness and poverty, in spite of a small Civil List pension which was awarded to her in 1922, and finally died by her own hand. Beginning as a prose writer, she wrote some stories for the *Yellow Book*. Although she published only two books of verse, *The Farmer's Bride* (1915) and *The Rambling Sailor* (1929), Thomas Hardy thought her the best woman poet of her time. Reserved, secretive, over-restrained, she has been compared with Emily Dickinson.

Meynell, Alice Christiana Gertrude (22 Sept. 1847—27 Nov. 1922), poetess and essayist, born at Barnes, near London, spent most of her childhood in Italy. Her father, T. J. Thompson, was a friend of Dickens, and her sister, who became Lady Butler, was a famous painter of battle pictures. In 1872 Alice was converted to the Roman Catholic faith, and in 1875 she published her first volume of verse, *Preludes*. Two years later she married Wilfred Meynell (q.v.), whom she helped with his editorial work; theirs was a frugal but hospitable home, and they were on intimate terms with all the great writers of the time—Tennyson, Browning, Ruskin, Rossetti, George Eliot, Patmore, Meredith. They rescued and cared for Francis Thompson (q.v.), whose poems *Love in Dian's Lap* were a tribute to Mrs Meynell. A delicate and sensitive writer, she published several books of essays, including *The Rhythm of Life* (1893), *The Colour of Life* (1896), *London Impressions* (1898), *Ceres' Runaway* (1909), and *The Second Person Singular* (1921). But she is most famous for her poems, which are worthy to rank with those of Christina Rossetti (q.v.), and like hers have deeply religious undertones. Titles of the volumes are *Poems* (1893), *Other Poems* (1896), *Later Poems* (1902), *A Father of Women* (1917), and the posthumous *Last Poems* (1923). Her last work was an anthology for children, *The School of Poetry*.

Meynell, Viola (1886—27 Oct. 1956), novelist and poetess, daughter of the above, was born in Kensington and grew up in a household of brilliant literary activity. In 1922 she married John Dallyn, and they lived at Pulborough in Sussex. Her novels include *Modern Lovers* (1914), *Columbine* (1915), *Narcissus* (1916), *The Second Marriage* (1918), *Antonia* (1921), *A Girl Adoring* (1927), and *Follow Thy Fair Sun* (1935). Her poems were collected in *The Frozen Ocean* (1931), and she edited *The Poet's Walk, a Nature Anthology* (1936). In 1929 she published a memoir of her mother, and in 1942 she edited the *Letters of J. M. Barrie*.

Meynell, Wilfrid (17 Nov. 1852—20 Oct. 1948), journalist and poet, was born at Newcastle-on-Tyne, son of a colliery owner, and educated at Quaker schools in Croydon and York. At the age of 18 he became a Roman Catholic. Going to London, he took up journalism, and in 1881 became editor of the *Weekly Register*, a rival of the *Tablet*. His first book, *Journals and Journalism*, was published under the name of John Oldcastle. In 1877 he married Alice Thompson (*see* Alice Meynell), and they befriended the poet Francis Thompson (q.v.). Meynell's works include *The Man Disraeli* (1903), *Verses and Reverses* (1912), *Aunt Sarah and the War* (1914), *Rhymes With Reasons* (1918), and *Come and See* (1919). In 1934 he was awarded the C.B.E.

Mickle, William Julius (28 Sept. 1735—28 Oct. 1788), poet and translator, son of the minister of Langholm, Dumfriesshire, was educated at Edinburgh High School. He was for some time a brewer in Edinburgh, but failed. He then removed to Wheatley, near Oxford, where he was corrector for the Clarendon Press. After various literary failures and minor successes he produced his translation of the *Lusiad*, from the Portuguese of Camoens, which brought him both fame and money. In 1777 he visited Lisbon, where he was received with distinction. In 1784 he published the ballad of *Cumnor Hall*, which suggested to Scott the writing of *Kenilworth*.

Middleton, Conyers (27 Dec. 1683—28 July 1750), theologian, born in Yorkshire, where his father was a rector, went to Cambridge and was a brilliant and sceptical scholar. He was the author of *A Free Inquiry into the Miraculous Powers* (1749), which brought him into controversy with Waterland (q.v.) and others, and of a *Life of Cicero* (1741), largely plagiarized from William Bellenden, a Scottish writer of the seventeenth century.

Middleton, Richard Barham (28 Oct. 1882—1 Dec. 1911), poet, born at Staines, Middlesex, was descended, as his name indicates, from the author of the *Ingoldsby Legends*. Educated at St Paul's and Merchant Taylors', he became a clerk with an insurance firm in 1901, but after six years could endure it no longer and threw up the job to try to live by his pen. Despairing of success he poisoned himself with chloroform while in Brussels. As a writer Middleton belongs really to the nineties, and he had a great admiration for Dowson and Symons. In 1912, after his death, there appeared his *Poems and Songs* (two series), *The Ghost Ship*, a collection of stories, and *The Day Before Yesterday*, containing delightful child studies after the manner of Kenneth Grahame. His *Letters to Henry Savage* were published in 1929 and *The Pantomime Man*, a collection of prose pieces, in 1933.

Middleton, Thomas (April 1580—April 1627), dramatist, was born probably in London, and educated at Oxford, where he started writing poems while still an undergraduate. In 1604 he published two pamphlets about London, *The Black Book* and *Father Hubbard's Tales*. His early satirical comedies, also about London life, include *A Trick to Catch the Old One* (1606), *A Mad World, My Masters* (1608), and *A Chaste Maid in Cheapside* (1613). *The Roaring Girl* (1611) was written, like a number of others, in collaboration with Dekker, and *Anything for a Quiet Life*, of later date, has the same lively humour. From 1615 onwards Middleton turned to writing serious plays, which include *Women Beware Women* (1621), *The Changeling* (1622), and *The Spanish Gipsy* (1623), in which he collaborated with Rowley (q.v.). His last play, *A Game of Chess* (1624), ridiculed England's relations with Spain, and was withdrawn because the Spanish ambassador protested against it; Middleton was summoned before the Privy Council, but got off with a caution. He also wrote a number of masques, as well as pageants for the city ceremonies.

Mill, James (6 April 1773—23 June 1836), philosopher and historian, was born at Northwater Bridge, Forfarshire, son of a shoemaker, and showing signs of superior ability, was sent to the University of Edinburgh with a view to the ministry. He was licensed as a preacher in 1798, but gave up the idea of the Church, and going to London in 1802 engaged in literary work, edited the *St James's Chronicle* and wrote for the *Edinburgh Review*. In 1806 he began his *History of British India* (1817—18), in 1819 received the appointment of Assistant Examiner to the India Office, and in 1834 became head of the department. Mill was closely associated with Jeremy Bentham (q.v.), and became the chief exponent of his utilitarian philosophy. He was also one of the founders of the London University. His philosophical writings include *Elements of Political Economy* (1821), and *Analysis of the Human Mind* (1829).

Mill, John Stuart (20 May 1806—8 May 1873), philosopher, son of the above, born in London, was educated by his father with the view of making him the successor of Bentham and himself, as the exponent of utilitarianism. In all respects he proved an apt pupil, and by his fifteenth year had studied classical literature, logic, political economy, and mathematics. In that year he went to France, where he was under the charge of Sir Samuel Bentham, a brother of Jeremy, and after his return he became aquainted with Grote, the Austins, and other Benthamites. In 1823 he entered the India House as a clerk, and, like his father, rose to be examiner of Indian correspondence; on the dissolution of the Company he retired on a liberal pension. In 1825 he edited Bentham's *Rationale of Judicial Evidence*. During the following years he was a frequent contributor to Radical journals, and edited the *London Review*. His *System of Logic* appeared in 1843, and produced a profound impression; and in 1848 he published *Principles of Political Economy*. The years between 1858 and 1865 were very productive, his treatises on *Liberty*, *Utilitarianism*, and *Representative Government*, and his *Examination of Sir W. Hamilton's Philosophy* being published during this period. In 1865 he entered the House of Commons as one of the members for Westminster, where, though highly respected, he made no great mark. After this political interlude he returned to his literary pursuits, and wrote *The Subjection of Women* (1869), *The Irish Land Question* (1870), and an *Autobiography* (1873). Mill had married in 1851 Mrs Taylor, to whom he showed an extraordinary devotion, and whom he survived for 15 years. He died at Avignon. His *Autobiography* gives a singular, and in some respects painful account of the methods and views of his father in his education. Though remaining all his life an adherent of the utilitarian philosophy, Mill did not transmit it to his disciples altogether unmodified, but, finding it too narrow and rigid for his own intellectual and moral requirements, devoted himself to widening it, and infusing into it a certain element of idealism.

Millay, Edna St Vincent (22 Feb. 1892—19 Oct. 1950), poetess, was born at Rockland, Maine, and educated at Vassar College. She was a student there when her first poem, 'Renascence' was printed in 1912, and the same title was used for her first volume of verse in 1917. For some years she worked as a freelance in Greenwich Village, then in 1923 she married a Dutchman, Eugen Jan Boissevain. In the same year she was awarded the Pulitzer Prize for *The Harp-Weaver*, which showed her skill as a writer of sonnets. Others of her books of verse are *A Few Figs from Thistles* (1920), *Second April* (1921), *The Buck in the Snow* (1928), *Fatal Interview* (1931), *Wine from These Grapes* (1934), *Conversation at Midnight* (1937), *Huntsman*

What Quarry? (1939), and *Make Bright the Arrows* (1942). She also published three verse plays. An accomplished mistress of lyric, she was the most popular American poetess of her day.

Miller, Cincinnatus Hiner (10 March 1839—17 Feb. 1913), poet who wrote under the name Joaquin Miller, was born at Liberty, Indiana, son of a Quaker schoolmaster. His parents travelled the Oregon trail, but he ran away at 17, worked as cook in a Californian mining camp, and married an Indian woman. Later he returned to Oregon, studied law, and was admitted to the Bar in 1861, but instead of practising became a newspaper editor. After publishing two volumes of verse, *Specimens* (1868) and *Joaquin et al* (1869), he made a literary pilgrimage to England and wrote *Songs of the Sierras* (1871), which won favour there. After further travel he published *Songs of the Sun-lands* (1873), *Songs of Italy* (1878), and the narrative poem *Light* (1907). He also wrote several novels and three autobiographical books, *Life Amongst the Modocs* (1873), *Memorie and Rime* (1884), and *Overland in a Covered Wagon* (1930). Settling finally in Oakland, California, he was venerated as a relic of a past age.

Miller, Hugh (10 Oct. 1802—2 Dec. 1856), geologist, born at Cromarty, son of a sea captain of Scandinavian descent, had the ordinary parish school education, and early showed a remarkable love of reading and power of story-telling. At 17 he was apprenticed to a stonemason, and his work in quarries, together with rambles among the rocks of his native shore, led him to the study of geology. In 1829 he published a volume of poems, in 1834 became accountant in one of the local banks, and in the next year brought out his *Scenes and Legends in the North of Scotland*. In 1840 the popular party in the Church, with which he had been associated, started a newspaper, *The Witness*, and Miller was called to be editor, a position which he retained till the end of his life. Among his geological works are *The Old Red Sandstone* (1841), *Footprints of the Creator* (1850), *The Testimony of the Rocks* (1856), and *Sketch-book of Popular Geology*. Other books are: *My Schools and Schoolmasters* (1852), an autobiography of remarkable interest, *First Impressions of England and its People* (1847), and *The Cruise of the 'Betsy'* (1859). Of the geological books, perhaps that on the old red sandstone, a department in which Miller was a discoverer, is the best: but all his writings are distinguished by great literary excellence, and especially by a marvellous power of vivid description. The end of his life was most tragic. He had for long been overworking his brain, which at last gave way, and in a temporary loss of reason, he shot himself during the night.

Miller, Joaquin, *see* **Miller, Cincinnatus H.**

Miller, Thomas (31 Aug. 1807—24 Oct. 1874), poet and novelist, born at Gainsborough, son of a wharfinger, worked in early life as a basket-maker. He published *Songs of the Sea Nymphs* (1832). Going to London he was befriended by Lady Blessington (q.v.) and S. Rogers (q.v.), and for a time engaged in business as a bookseller, but was unsuccessful and devoted himself exclusively to literature, producing over 40 volumes, including the novels *Royston Gower*

(1838), *Gideon Giles the Roper* (1840), and *Godfrey Malvern* (1842—1843); and a volume of poems, *Rural Sketches* (1834). In his stories he successfully delineated rural characters and scenes.

Miller, William (Aug. 1810—20 Aug. 1872), poet, born in Glasgow, worked as a wood-turner. He made a reputation by his poems published in the Scots anthology *Whistle Binkie*, and is best remembered for 'Wee Willie Winkie' and other children's poems which earned him the title of laureate of the nursery. His *Scottish Nursery Songs* appeared in 1863.

Millin, Sarah Gertrude (1889—   ), novelist, was born near Kimberley, daughter of Isaiah Liebson, a diamond prospector. After a brilliant school record she had her first story printed when she was 19. She married Philip Millin, afterwards a judge of the Supreme Court of South Africa. Her novels include *The Dark River* (1920), *Middle Class* (1921), *The Jordans* (1923), *God's Stepchildren* (1924), *Mary Glenn* (1925), *An Artist in the Family* (1927), *The Coming of the Lord* (1928), *The Fiddler* (1929), *Three Men Die* (1934), *What Hath a Man* (1938), *Bucks Without Hair* (1941), *World Blackout* (1944), *King of the Bastards* (1950), and *The Burning Man* (1952). She also wrote a study, *The South Africans* (1926), lives of *Rhodes* (1933) and *Smuts* (1936), and a book of essays, *Men on a Voyage* (1930). Autobiographical works are *The Night is Long* (1941), and a series of *War Diaries* in six volumes (1944—8).

Milman, Henry Hart (10 Feb. 1791—24 Sept. 1868), historian and poet, son of a doctor, was born in London and educated at Eton and Oxford. Taking orders he became in 1835 Rector of St Margaret's, Westminster, and in 1849 Dean of St Paul's. He also held the professorship of Poetry at Oxford from 1821 to 1831. Among his poetical works may be mentioned *Samor* (1818), *The Fall of Jerusalem* (1820), *The Martyr of Antioch* (1822), *Anne Boleyn* (1826), and a play, *Fazio* (1815). It is, however, on his work as an historian that his literary fame chiefly rests, his chief works in this department being his *History of the Jews* (1830), *History of Christianity* (1840), and especially *The History of Latin Christianity* (six volumes 1854—6), which is one of the most important historical works of the century, characterized alike by literary distinction and by learning and research.

Milne, Alan Alexander (18 Jan. 1882—31 Jan. 1956), novelist and playwright, was born in London, son of a schoolmaster, and educated at Westminster and Cambridge, where he edited the *Granta*. In 1903 he became a freelance journalist in London, and from 1906 to 1914 was assistant editor of *Punch*. During the First World War he served with the Royal Warwickshires, and while at the front wrote his first play, *Wurzel-Flummery* (1917), which he followed up with *Mr Pim Passes By* (1919), *The Dover Road* (1923), *The Truth About Blayds* (1923), and other light comedies. In 1913 he had married Daphne de Sélincourt, and for their son, Christopher Robin, he wrote a series of books which have become children's classics; they include *When We Were Very Young* (1924), *Winnie the Pooh* (1926), *Now We Are Six* (1927), and *The House at Pooh Corner* (1928). *Toad of Toad*

Hall (1929) is a play based on Kenneth Grahame's *Wind in the Willows*. Milne's light humorous essays from his *Punch* days and later were collected in *The Day's Play* (1910), *The Holiday Round* (1912), and *The Sunny Side* (1922). *The Red House Mystery* (1921) is a detective story, *Peace With Honour* (1934) is a plea against war, and *It's Too Late Now* (1939) is an autobiography.

Milnes, Richard Monkton, *see* **Houghton, Baron.**

Milton, John (9th Dec. 1608—8 Nov. 1674), poet, was born in Bread Street, London. His father, a scrivener, was the son of a yeoman of Oxfordshire, who cast him off on his becoming a Protestant. From him the poet inherited his lofty integrity, and his love of, and proficiency in, music. Milton received his first education from a Scottish friend of his father's, Thomas Young, a Puritan of some note, one of the writers of *Smectymnuus* (q.v.). He was at St Paul's School, and in 1625 went to Christ's College, Cambridge, where for his beauty and his delicacy of mind he was nicknamed 'the lady.' His sister Anne had married Edward Phillips, and the death of her first child in infancy gave to him the subject of his earliest poem, 'On the Death of a Fair Infant' (1626). It was followed during his seven years at Cambridge by the poems, 'On the Morning of Christ's Nativity' (1629), 'On the Circumcision,' 'The Passion,' 'At a Solemn Music,' 'On May Morning,' and 'On Shakespeare,' all in 1630; and two sonnets, 'To the Nightingale' and 'On Arriving at the Age of Twenty-three,' in 1631. In 1632, having given up the idea of taking holy orders, for which his father had intended him, he lived for six years at Horton, near Windsor, devoted to further study. Here he wrote *L'Allegro* and *Il Penseroso* in 1632, *Arcades* in 1633, *Comus* in 1634, and *Lycidas* in 1637. The first celebrates the pleasures of a life of cheerful innocence, and the second of contemplative, though not gloomy, retirement, and the last is a lament for a lost friend, Edward King, who perished at sea. *Arcades* and *Comus* are masques set to music by Henry Lawes, having for their motives respectively family affection and maiden purity. Had he written nothing else these would have given him a place among the immortals. In 1638 he completed his education by a period of travel in France and Italy, where he visited Grotius at Paris, and Galileo at Florence. The news of impending troubles in Church and State brought him home the following year, and with his return may be said to close the first of three well-marked divisions into which his life falls. These may be called, first, the period of preparation and of the early poems; second, the period of controversy, and of the prose writings; and third, the period of retirement and of the later poems.

Soon after his return Milton settled in London, and employed himself in teaching his nephews, Edward and John Phillips, turning over in his mind at the same time various subjects as the possible theme for the great poem which, as the chief object of his life, he looked forward to writing. But he was soon to be called away to far other matters, and to be plunge into the controversies and practical business which were to absorb his energies for the next 20 years.

The works of this period fall into three classes—those directed against Episcopacy, including *Reformation of Church Discipline in England* (1641), and his answers to the writings of Bishop Hall (q.v.), and in defence of *Smectymnuus* (*see* under Calamy); those relating to divorce, including *The Doctrine and Discipline of Divorce* (1643), and *The Four Chief Places of Scripture which treat of Marriage* (1645); and those on political and miscellaneous questions, including the *Tractate on Education, Areopagitica, A Speech for the Liberty of Unlicensed Printing* (1644), his greatest prose work, *Eikonoklastes* (1649), an answer to the *Eikon Basilike* of Dr Gauden (q.v.), *The Tenure of Kings and Magistrates* (1649), in defence of the execution of Charles I, which led to the furious controversy with Salmasius and Milton's *Pro Populo Anglicano Defensio* (1650), the second *Defensio* (1654), which carried his name over Europe, and *The Ready and Easy Way to establish a Free Commonwealth*, written on the eve of the Restoration.

In 1643 Milton had married Mary Powell, the daughter of an Oxfordshire cavalier, a girl of 17, who soon found her new life as the companion of an austere poet, absorbed in severe study, too abrupt a change from the gay society to which she had been accustomed, and in a month returned to her father's house on a visit. When the time fixed for rejoining her husband arrived, she showed no disposition to do so, upon which he began to aim at a divorce, and to advocate in the works above mentioned 'unfitness and contrariety of mind' as a valid ground for it, views which incurred for him much notoriety and unpopularity. A reconciliation, however, followed in 1645, and three daughters were born of the marriage. In 1649 the reputation of Milton as a Latinist led to his appointment as Latin or Foreign Secretary to the Council of State, in the duties of which he was, after his sight began to fail, assisted by A. Marvell (q.v.) and others. In 1652 his wife died, and four years later he entered into a second marriage with Katharine Woodcock, who died in childbirth in the following year. To her memory he dedicated one of the most touching of his sonnets. At the Restoration he was, of course, deprived of his office, and had to go into hiding; but on the intercession of Marvell (q.v.), and perhaps Davenant (q.v.), his name was included in the amnesty. In 1663, being now totally blind and somewhat helpless, he asked his friend Dr Paget to recommend a wife for him. The lady chosen was Elizabeth Minshull, aged 25, who appears to have given him domestic happiness in his last years. She survived him for 53 years.

The Restoration closed his second, and introduced his third, and for his fame, most productive period. He was now free to devote his whole powers to the great work which he had so long contemplated. For some time he had been in doubt as to the subject, had considered the Arthurian legends, but had decided upon the Fall of Man. The result was *Paradise Lost*, which was begun in 1658, finished in 1664, and published in 1667. A remark of his friend, Thomas Ellwood (q.v.), suggested to him the writing of *Paradise Regained*, which, along with *Samson Agonistes*, was published in 1671. Two years before he had printed a *History of Britain*, written long before, which, however, is of little value. The work of Milton was now done. In addition to his blindness he suffered from gout, to which it was partly attributable, and, his strength gradually failing, he died 'of the gout struck in,' and was buried in the chancel of St Giles, Cripplegate.

In Milton the influences of the Renaissance and of Puritanism met. To the former he owed his wide culture and his profound love of everything noble and beautiful, to the latter his lofty and austere character, and both these elements meet in his writings. Leaving Shakespeare out of account, he holds an indisputable place at the head of English poets. For strength of imagination, delicate accuracy and suggestiveness of language, and harmony of versification, he is unrivalled, and almost unapproached. In his use of blank verse he has, for majesty, variety, and music, never been approached by any of his successors. He had no dramatic power and no humour. In everything he wrote, a proud and commanding genius manifests itself, and he is one of those writers who inspire reverence rather than affection. His personal appearance in early life has been thus described, 'He was a little under middle height, slender, but erect, vigorous, and agile, with light brown hair clustering about his fair and oval face, with dark grey eyes.' The standard life of Milton is by David Masson (q.v.).

Minot, Laurence (1300?—1352?), poet. Nothing is certainly known of him. He may have been a soldier. He celebrates in northern English and with a somewhat ferocious patriotism the victories of Edward III over the Scots and the French.

Minto, William (10 Oct. 1845—1 March 1893), critic and biographer, born at Alford, Aberdeenshire, and educated at Aberdeen and Oxford, went to London, and became editor of the *Examiner*, and also wrote for the *Daily News* and the *Pall Mall Gazette*. In 1880 he was appointed Professor of Logic and Literature at Aberdeen. He wrote a *Manual of English Prose Literature* (1873), *Characteristics of the English Poets* (1874), and a *Life of Defoe* (1879).

Mitchell, Donald Grant (12 April 1822—5 Dec. 1908), essayist who wrote under the name Ik Marvel (originally a misprint for J. K. Marvel), was born at Norwich, Connecticut, and educated at Yale, where he edited the college magazine. Between 1844 and 1846 he visited Europe, and his first book, *Fresh Gleanings* (1847) tells of his travels there. But he is best remembered for his pleasant fanciful sketches in *Reveries of a Bachelor* (1850) and *Dream Life* (1851). *My Farm of Edgewood* (1863), *Wet Days at Edgewood* (1865), and *Rural Studies* (1867) are reminiscences of his life as a gentleman farmer near New Haven.

Mitchell, John (3 Nov. 1815—20 March 1875), journalist, was born in Londonderry, son of a Presbyterian minister, and educated at Trinity College, Dublin. From 1840 he practised as a solicitor, but becoming acquainted with Thomas Davis (q.v.), he associated himself with the Young Ireland party, and was a leading contributor to the *Nation* newspaper. His political sympathies and acts were carried so far as to bring about in 1848 his trial for sedition, and his transportation for 14 years. He was sent to Bermuda, then the Cape of Good Hope, then Tasmania, from which in 1853 he escaped to America, where he resided chiefly at New York, edited various papers, and opposed the abolition of slavery. In 1874 he was elected M.P. for Tipperary, for which, however, he was declared incapable of sitting. On a new election he was again returned, but died before the resulting petition could be heard. He wrote a *Jail Journal* (1854), a work of great power, and a *History of Ireland* (1869).

Mitchell, Margaret Munnerlyn (1900—16 Aug. 1949), novelist, was born in Atlanta, Georgia, daughter of an attorney who was president of the Atlanta Historical Society. All the family were interested in American history, and she grew up in an atmosphere of stories about the Civil War. Educated at Washington Seminary and Smith College, Massachusetts, she worked for a time on the *Atlanta Journal*. In 1925 she married John R. Marsh, and between 1926 and 1936 she put on paper all the Civil War stories that she had heard in her childhood. The result was *Gone With the Wind* (1936), a mammoth novel of 1,000 pages, which won the Pulitzer Prize, sold eight million copies, and was translated into 18 languages. This, a record best-seller, was her only published work.

Mitchison, Naomi Margaret (1 Nov. 1897—), novelist, born in Edinburgh, was a sister of J. B. S. Haldane (q.v.) and married G. Richard Mitchison, a barrister, in 1916. Educated at Oxford, she first planned to be a scientist, but turned instead to writing novels and stories about ancient times. Books about Greece and Rome include *When the Bough Breaks* (1924), *Cloud Cuckoo Land* (1925), and *Black Sparta* (1928); *The Corn King and the Spring Queen* (1931) is an historical fantasy; and *The Swan's Road* (1954) tells of the Vikings. *Anna Comnena* (1928) is a biography, *Lobsters on the Agenda* (1952) a modern Scottish novel, and *The Laburnum Branch* (1926) a book of poems. In 1937 the Mitchisons settled at Carradale in Kintyre.

Mitford, Mary Russell (16 Dec. 1787—10 Jan. 1855), novelist, was born at Alresford, Hampshire. Her father, a doctor without prac-tice, selfish and extravagant, ran through three fortunes, his own, his wife's, and a lottery prize of £20,000 which Mary won at the age of 10. To her fell the task of supporting him, and after a volume of *Miscellaneous Poems* (1810) which attracted little notice, she pro-duced her powerful tragedy, *Julian* (1823). In 1819, what ultimately became the first volume of *Our Village* appeared in the *Lady's Maga-zine*. To this four additional volumes were added, the last in 1832. In these charming sketches of rural life Miss Mitford may be said to have created a new branch of literature. Her novel, *Belford Regis* (1835), is somewhat on the same lines. In addition to her dramas, *The Foscari* (1826), *Rienzi* (1828), and *Charles I* (1834), she wrote *Atherton and other Tales* (1852), and *Recollections of a Literary Life* (1854), and died in her cottage at Swallowfield, much beloved for her benevolent and simple character.

Mitford, Hon. Nancy Freeman (28 Nov. 1904—),

novelist, born in London, was a daughter of the 2nd Baron Redesdale, whose father was a cousin of Swinburne the poet. She was educated at home, and in 1933 married the Hon. Peter Rodd; the marriage was dissolved in 1958. Her early novels were *Highland Fling* (1931), *Christmas Pudding* (1932), *Wigs on the Green* (1935), and *Pigeon Pie* (1940). *The Pursuit of Love* (1945) was a notable success, and after it she made her home in Paris. Others of what have been termed her ironical comedies of manners are *Love in a Cold Climate* (1949) and *The Blessing* (1951). She also wrote two biographical studies, *Madame de Pompadour* (1954) and *Voltaire in Love* (1957). In 1956 she edited *Noblesse Oblige*, a book of satirical essays by various hands on English snobbery, defining what is regarded as ' U ' or upper-class and ' non-U ' or lower-class.

Mitford, William (10 Feb. 1744—10 Feb. 1827), historian, born in London, son of a barrister, was educated at Cheam School and Oxford. He studied law, but on succeeding to the family estates devoted himself to literature. His first publication was an *Essay on the Harmony of Language* (1774). His great work, *The History of Greece*, is said to have been undertaken at the suggestion of Gibbon, who was his fellow-officer in the South Hants Militia. This work, the successive volumes of which appeared at considerable intervals between 1784 and 1810, was long a standard one, but is marred by its anti-democratic bias. He sat in Parliament from 1785 to 1818.

Moffatt, James (4 July 1870—27 June 1944), minister and scholar, was born in Glasgow, son of an accountant, and educated at Glasgow Academy and University. Ordained in 1896 as a minister of the United Free Church of Scotland, he became a lecturer in London University in 1907, in 1911 was appointed Professor of Greek and New Testament Exegesis at Mansfield College, Oxford, in 1915 Professor of Church History at the United Free Church College, Glasgow, and from 1927 to 1939 occupied the corresponding Chair at the Union Theological Seminary, New York. He is principally remembered for his rendering of the Bible into modern English. His chief works were *The Historical New Testament, a New Translation* (1901), *Introduction to the Literature of the New Testament* (1911), *The Theology of the Gospels* (1912), *An Approach to the New Testament* (1921), *The Old Testament, a New Translation* (1924), and *A New Translation of the Bible* (1928).

Moir, David Macbeth (5 Jan. 1798—6 July 1851), poet and humorist, born at Musselburgh, practised medicine there and was a frequent contributor, under the signature of *Δ* (Delta) to *Blackwood's Magazine*, in which first appeared his *Mansie Wauch* (1828), a humorous Scottish tale. He also wrote *The Legend of Genevieve* (1824) and *Domestic Verses* (1843). His poetry was generally grave and tender, but occasionally humorous.

Molesworth, Mary Louisa (29 May 1839—20 July 1921), writer of children's books, was born in Rotterdam, of Scottish descent, her maiden name being Stewart, and was educated in Switzerland, but spent much of her girlhood in Manchester. In 1861 she married

Major R. Molesworth, a nephew of Viscount Molesworth. Beginning in 1869 with *Lover and Husband*, she wrote several 'grown-up' novels signed with the pseudonym Ennis Graham, which she discarded when she found her real province in children's books. Those she wrote divide into two distinct classes. There are the delightful fairy stories, of which the best-known are *The Cuckoo Clock* (1877), *The Tapestry Room* (1879), *Four Winds Farm* (1887), and her last book, *Fairies Afield* (1911). The second class consists of stories about real children, in which she excelled. Among these may be mentioned *Carrots—Just a Little Boy* (1876), *The Adventures of Herr Baby* (1881), *Two Little Waifs* (1883), *Us* (1885), *Silverthorns* (1887), *The Old Pincushion* (1889), *The Red Grange* (1891), and, what is considered by many her best book, *The Carved Lions* (1895). In all she wrote over a hundred books, and is by some reckoned our best writer for children.

Monboddo, James Burnett, Lord (1714—26 May 1799), judge, philosopher, and philologist, born at the family seat in Kincardineshire, was educated at the Universities of Aberdeen, Edinburgh, and Groningen, and called to the Scottish Bar in 1737. Thirty years later he became a judge with the title of Lord Monboddo. He was a man of great learning and acuteness, but eccentric and fond of paradox. He was the author of two large works, alike learned and whimsical, *An Essay on the Origin and Progress of Language* (six volumes 1773—92), and *Ancient Metaphysics* (six volumes 1779—1799). He maintained that men were originally monkeys, and gradually attained to reason, language, and civilization by the pressure of necessity. He was visited by Dr Johnson at Monboddo.

Monro, Harold (14 March 1879—16 March 1932), poet, son of a Scottish engineer, was born and spent his childhood in Brussels. Educated at Radley and Cambridge, he settled in London in 1911 and became known as the founder of the *Poetry Review* and later of the Poetry Bookshop in Bloomsbury. During the First World War he served in an anti-aircraft battery and in 1920 he married his second wife, Alida Klementaski. From 1919 to 1925 he edited *The Monthly Chapbook*, which he had founded. His volumes of verse include *Poems* (1906), *Judas* (1908), *Before Dawn* (1911), *Children of Love* (1914), *Trees* (1916), *Strange Meetings* (1917), *Real Property* (1922), *The Earth for Sale* (1928), and *Elm Angel* (1930). He also published a book of criticism, *Some Contemporary Poets* (1920), and an anthology, *Twentieth Century Poetry* (1929).

Monroe, Harriet (1860—26 Sept. 1936), poetess and critic, daughter of an attorney, was born in Chicago, and first attained notice with her *Columbian Ode* written for the Chicago Exposition of 1893. Educated at the Academy of the Visitation, Georgetown, she published several volumes of verse, including *Valeria* (1891), *The Dance of the Seasons* (1911), *You and I* (1914), and *The Difference* (1924). She was better known, however, as the founder and editor of *Poetry*, the first American periodical devoted exclusively to verse; it had a most stimulating influence on American literature and numbered many of the leading American poets among its contributors. She also collaborated in compiling *The New Poetry* (1932) an anthology of twentieth-century verse. *Poets and Their Art* (1932) is a book of essays, and *A Poet's Life* (1937) her autobiography.

Monsarrat, Nicholas John Turney (22 March 1910—), novelist, was born in Liverpool, son of a distinguished surgeon. He was educated at Winchester and Trinity College, Cambridge, where he took a law degree, but after two years in a law office turned to a writing career, his earliest novels being *Think of To-morrow* (1934), *At First Sight* (1935), and *The Whipping Boy* (1937). During the Second World War he served as a naval officer, and from his experiences wrote the non-fiction volumes *H.M. Corvette* (1942), *East Coast Corvette* (1943), and *Corvette Command* (1944). But his great success was his novel *The Cruel Sea* (1951), for which he received the Heinemann Prize for Literature. A later novel, *The Story of Esther Costello* (1953), is a work of sordid realism. From 1946 to 1956 Monsarrat was Director of the British Information Office first in Johannesburg, then in Ottawa. He was a Fellow of the Royal Society of Literature.

Monsell, John Samuel Bewley (2 March 1811—9 April 1875), hymn-writer, was born at St Columb's, Derry, where his father was archdeacon, and was educated at Trinity College, Dublin. Ordained in 1835, he had charges in Ireland and at Egham and Guildford, Surrey, where he died as the result of a fall from the roof of his church, which was being repaired. He is remembered by his hymns, of which he wrote over 70, including the well-known 'Fight the Good Fight.'

Montagu, Charles, *see* Halifax, Earl of.

Montagu, Elizabeth (2 Oct. 1720—25 Aug. 1800), hostess and critic, was born in York, daughter of Matthew Robinson, but spent her girlhood at Coveney, Cambridgeshire. She showed literary tastes at an early age, but was also very sociable, her nickname then being 'Fidget.' In 1742 she married Charles Montagu, a grandson of the Earl of Sandwich, and became a leader of society, her house in Mayfair being a centre for all the intellect and fashion of London; there she held *salons* frequented by Burke, Garrick, Reynolds, and Dr Johnson, who praised her conversation highly. One of the original 'blue-stockings,' she contributed three dialogues to Lyttelton's *Dialogues of the Dead*, but her most notable work was *An Essay on the Writings and Genius of Shakespeare* (1769), in which she answered Voltaire's hostile criticism. Her *Letters* were published in 1813.

Montagu, Lady Mary Wortley (baptized 26 May 1689, died 21 Aug. 1762), letter-writer, was the eldest daughter of Evelyn Pierrepont, who became the 1st Duke of Kingston. In her youth she combined the attractions of a reigning beauty and a wit. Her early studies were encouraged and assisted by Bishop Burnet, and she was the friend of Pope, Addison, and Swift. In 1712 she married against the wishes of her family, Edward Wortley-Montagu, a cousin of the celebrated Charles Montagu, Earl of Halifax (q.v.). Her husband having been appointed Ambassador at Constantinople in 1716, she accompanied him, and wrote the sparkling *Letters from the East*, published in 1763, which have given her a place high among the great letter-writers of the world. While in Turkey she became acquainted with the practice of inoculation against smallpox, which she did much to introduce into western countries. After her return to England she settled at Twickenham, and renewed her friendship with Pope, which, however, ended in a violent quarrel, arising out of her satirical *Town Eclogues* (1716). She was furiously attacked by both Pope and Swift, and was not slow to defend herself. In 1737, for reasons which have never been explained, she left her husband and country, and settled in Italy. On his death in 1761 she returned at the request of her daughter, the Countess of Bute, but died the following year.

Montague, Charles Edward (1 Jan. 1867—28 May 1928), journalist and novelist, was born at Twickenham, son of a former Roman Catholic priest, and was educated at the City of London School and Balliol College, Oxford, where he rowed in the college eight. In 1890 he joined the staff of the *Manchester Guardian*, and rose to be assistant editor to C. P. Scott (q.v.), whose daughter he married. His first novel, *A Hind Let Loose* (1910) is a skit on journalism. On the outbreak of the First World War he enlisted at the age of 47 as a private in the Royal Fusiliers. His later novels include *Disenchantment* (1922), *Rough Justice* (1926), and *Right Off the Map* (1927), while *Fiery Particles* (1923) and *Action* (1928) are volumes of short stories. Among his critical works are *Dramatic Values* (1911), *The Right Place* (1924), and *A Writer's Notes on his Trade* (1936).

Montgomerie, Alexander (1556?—1610?), poet, born probably at Beith in Ayrshire, was in the service of the Regent Morton and James VI, by whom he was pensioned. He is sometimes styled Captain, and was laureate of the Court. He appears to have fallen on evil days, was imprisoned on the Continent, and lost his pension. His chief work is *The Cherrie and the Slae* (1597), a somewhat poor allegory of Virtue and Vice, but with some vivid description in it, and with a comparatively modern air. He also wrote *The Flyting* (scolding) *betwixt Montgomerie and Polwart* (1621), and other pieces.

Montgomery, James (4 Nov. 1771—30 April 1854), poet, son of a pastor and missionary of the Moravian Brethren, was born at Irvine, Ayrshire, and educated at the Moravian School at Fulneck, near Leeds. After various changes of occupation and abode, he settled in Sheffield in 1792 as clerk to a newspaper. In 1796 he had become editor of the *Sheffield Iris*, and was twice imprisoned for political articles for which he was held responsible. In 1797 he published *Prison Amusements*; but his first book to attract notice was *The Wanderer of Switzerland* (1806). It was followed by *The West Indies* (1809), *The World before the Flood* (1812), *Greenland* (1819), and *The Pelican Island* (1828), all of which contain passages of considerable imaginative and descriptive power, but are lacking in strength and fire. He himself expected that his name would live, if at all, in his hymns, and in this his judgment has proved true. Some of these, such as 'For ever with the Lord,' are sung wherever the English language is spoken.

Montgomery, Lucy Maude (30 Nov. 1874—24 April 1942), novelist, was born at Clifton, Prince Edward Island, of Scottish descent, and brought up at Cavendish, near the sea, 11 miles from a town. As a girl she read omnivorously, and had a poem printed at the age of 15. Educated at Dalhousie University, Nova Scotia, she worked for three years as a teacher. In 1911 she married Ewan MacDonald, a Presbyterian minister, and they lived in Toronto. Her stories, however, have Prince Edward Island for a background. Her first novel, *Anne of Green Gables* (1908) was meant as a book for children, but delighted readers of all ages. Others are *Anne of Avonlea* (1909), *Kilmeny of the Orchard* (1910), *The Story Girl* (1911), *Chronicles of Avonlea* (1912), *Anne's House of Dreams* (1917), *Rainbow Valley* (1919), *Emily of New Moon* (1923), *Pat of Silver Bush* (1933), and *Anne of Ingleside* (1939). *The Watchman* (1917) is a book of poems. She was awarded the O.B.E.

Montgomery, Robert (1807—3 Dec. 1855), poetaster, born at Bath, illegitimate son of Robert Gomery, a comedian, was educated at Oxford and became a clergyman. He wrote some ambitious religious poems, including *The Omnipresence of the Deity* (1828) and *Satan* (1830) which were at first extravagantly praised and had a wide circulation. Macaulay devoted an essay to the demolition of the author's reputation, in which he completely succeeded.

Montrose, James Graham, 1st Marquis of (1612—21 May 1650), soldier and statesman, born at Old Montrose, was educated at St Andrews, after which he travelled in Europe. At first he supported the National Covenant which opposed the policy of Charles I, but in 1641 he was won over by the King and fought a brilliant but unsuccessful campaign on his side. After the King's execution he again fought for the royalist cause but was captured and hanged as a traitor. Montrose had the fashionable gentleman's talent for turning elegant verse, and wrote a number of lyrics, of which the best-known is 'My Dear and Only Love.'

Moody, William Vaughn (8 July 1869—17 Oct. 1910), dramatist and poet, was born at Spencer, Indiana, son of a steamboat captain. Educated at New Albany High School and Harvard, he became assistant in English there, and then assistant professor at the University of Chicago. His *Poems* (1901), which showed his gift for lyric verse, were followed by a textbook, *A First View of English Literature* (1905). Of his prose plays, *The Great Divide* (1905) was immensely popular, but *The Faith Healer* (1909) was less successful, though praised by the critics. Moody's greatest project was a trilogy of verse plays, *The Masque of Judgment* (1900), *The Fire-Bringer* (1901), and the unfinished *Death of Eve*. His *Letters* were edited in 1913.

Moore, Clement Clarke (15 July 1779—10 July 1863), scholar and poet, was born in New York, and educated at Columbia College, of which his father, Episcopal Bishop of New York, was president. He compiled a Hebrew lexicon and in 1821 became Professor of Biblical Learning in the General Theological Seminary, which he had helped to found. Later he was Professor of Oriental and Greek Literature.

He is chiefly remembered for his ballad ''Twas the Night Before Christmas,' which appeared anonymously in 1823, but was included in his collected *Poems* (1844).

Moore, Edward (22 March 1712—1 March 1757), fabulist and dramatist, son of a dissenting minister, was born at Abingdon, Berkshire. After being in business as a linen-draper, in which he was unsuccessful, he took to literature, and wrote a few plays; *The Gamester* (1753) had a great vogue, and was translated into various languages. He is best known by his *Fables for the Female Sex* (1744), which rank next to those of Gay (q.v.). He lived and died in poverty.

Moore, Francis (29 Jan. 1657—1715?), astrologer and almanac maker, was born at Bridgnorth, Shropshire, and moved to London, where he practised as a doctor. His *Vox Stellarum* (Voice of the Stars), an almanac containing forecasts based on astrology, first appeared in 1700, and is still published yearly as *Old Moore's Almanac*. It has a wide circulation and claims to have forecast the Second World War and the atomic bomb.

Moore, George Augustus (24 Feb. 1852—21 Jan. 1933), novelist and playwright, was born at Moore Hall, Mayo, son of an Irish landowner, and was educated at Oscott. In 1869 the family moved to South Kensington, and from 1872 to 1882 Moore studied painting in Paris. To this period belong his two books of verse, *Flowers of Passion* (1878) and *Pagan Poems* (1881). Returning to London, in 1883 he published his first novel *A Modern Lover*, followed by *A Mummer's Wife* (1885); both of these provoked criticism by diverging from Victorian traditions. His autobiographical *Confessions of a Young Man* (1888) told of his days in Paris. In 1894 appeared *Esther Waters*, greatest of his naturalistic novels. It was followed by the less successful *Evelyn Innes* (1898) and *Sister Teresa* (1901), after which Moore retired to Ireland, where he became High Sheriff of Mayo and turned Protestant. In 1906 he published *Memoirs of My Dead Life*, and in 1911 he moved back to London and wrote a long autobiography in three parts, *Ave* (1911), *Salve* (1912), and *Vale* (1914) called collectively *Hail and Farewell*. His last novels, which had both subtlety and power, were *The Brook Kerith* (1916), a novel of Christ's life, and *Heloïse and Abelard* (1921), a medieval romance. His plays, which belong to his later years, include *The Making of an Immortal* (1928) and the biblical *Passing of the Essenes* (1931). Moore's chief contributions to the development of English literature were the example of his polished style and the break that he made with the conventions of previous novelists.

Moore, George Edward, O.M. (4 Nov. 1873—24 Oct. 1958), philosopher, born in London, son of a doctor, was a brother of Thomas Sturge Moore (q.v.). From Dulwich College, where he was school captain for two years, he went to Trinity College, Cambridge, of which he became a Fellow. After some years spent first in Edinburgh and then at Richmond-on-Thames, in 1911 he became a lecturer on moral science at Cambridge, and in 1925 was appointed Professor of Philosophy. From 1921 to 1947 he was editor of *Mind*.

In 1939 he resigned his Chair and lectured at various American universities, and in 1951 was awarded the Order of Merit; he was also a Fellow of the British Academy. His published works, though few, have exerted a great influence on Western thought. They are *Principia Ethica* (1903), *Ethics* (1912), *Philosophical Studies* (1922), and *Some Main Problems of Philosophy* (1953).

Moore, John (1729—21 Jan. 1802), novelist and travel writer, son of an Episcopal minister, was born in Stirling. After studying medicine at Glasgow, he acted as a surgeon in the navy and the army, and ultimately settled in Glasgow as a doctor. In 1779 he published *A View of Society and Manners in France, Switzerland, and Germany*, which was well received. A similar work, relating to Italy, followed in 1781. The best of his novels is *Zeluco* (1789), which was admired by Byron. His last works were a *Journal during a Residence in France* (1792), and *Causes and Progress of the French Revolution* (1795), the latter of which was used by both Scott and Carlyle. Moore was one of the friends of Burns, and was the father of Sir John Moore, the hero of Corunna.

Moore, Marianne Craig (15 Nov. 1887—   ), poetess, was born at St Louis, Missouri, and educated at Bryn Mawr. After training at the Carlisle Commercial College, Pennsylvania, she taught shorthand for a time. From 1921 to 1925 she was assistant in New York Public Library. Previous to this she had contributed poems to the *Egoist*, the organ of the Imagist group, but they did not appear in book form until her friends had them published in London in 1921. A second collection of verse, *Observations* (1925) obtained the *Dial* Award, and later she won two more poetry prizes. Subsequent volumes are *The Pangolin* (1936), *What Are Years* (1941), and *Nevertheless* (1944); her *Collected Poems* appeared in 1951. Her work consists of free verse in disciplined but unconventional metrical patterns which are, however, distinct from the Imagist style. Witty and ironical, she has a vein of dry humour. *Predilections* (1955) is a book of essays.

Moore, Thomas (28 May 1779—25 Feb. 1852), poet, born in Dublin, son of a grocer, was educated at Trinity College, after which he went to London, and studied law at the Middle Temple. He took with him a translation of Anacreon, which appeared, dedicated to the Prince Regent, in 1800, and was well received. In the following year appeared his *Poems by Thomas Little*. In 1803 he received the appointment of Admiralty Registrar at Bermuda, and after visiting the island and travelling in America, he committed his official duties to a deputy and returned to England. The literary fruit of this journey was *Epistles, Odes, and other Poems* (1806). In 1807 Moore found his true poetic vocation in his *Irish Melodies*, the music being furnished by Sir John Stevenson, who adapted the national airs. The reception they met with was enthusiastic, and Moore became the national songwriter of Ireland. They continued to appear over a period of 25 years, and for each of the 130 songs he received 100 guineas. His charming singing of these airs, and his fascinating conversational and social powers made him sought after in the highest circles. In 1815 there appeared *National Airs* which, however, cannot be considered equal to the *Melodies*. He then turned to writing satirical and pungent verses on men and topics of the day, afterwards collected in *The Twopenny Post Bag*, in which the Prince Regent especially was mercilessly ridiculed, and about the same time appeared *Fables for the Holy Alliance*. In 1818 he produced the *Fudge Family in Paris*, written in that city, which then swarmed with 'groups of ridiculous English.' *Lalla Rookh*, a series of oriental tales in verse, with gorgeous descriptions of Eastern scenes and manners, had appeared in the previous year with great applause.

In 1818 the great misfortune of his life occurred through the dishonesty of his deputy in Bermuda, which involved him in a loss of £6,000, and necessitated his going abroad. He travelled in Italy with Lord John Russell, and visited Byron. Thereafter he settled for a year or two in Paris, where he wrote *The Loves of the Angels* (1823). On the death of Byron his memoirs came into the hands of Moore, who, in the exercise of a discretion committed to him, destroyed them. He afterwards wrote a *Life of Byron* (1830), which gave rise to much criticism and controversy, and he also edited his works. His last imaginative work was *The Epicurean* (1827). Thereafter he confined himself almost entirely to prose, and published lives of Sheridan (1827), and Lord Edward Fitzgerald (1831). Few poets have ever enjoyed greater popularity with the public, or the friendship of more men distinguished in all departments of life. He left behind him a mass of correspondence and autobiographical matter which he committed to his friend Lord John Russell for publication. They appeared in eight volumes (1852—6).

Moore, Thomas Sturge (4 March 1870—18 July 1944), poet and art critic, was born at Hastings, son of a doctor. Having left school at 14 because of ill health, he taught himself, studying art as much as literature, and wrote several books on modern artists. His chief poetical works are *The Vinedresser* (1899), *The Centaur's Booty* (1903), *Danaë* (1903), *The Gazelles* (1904), *Mariamne* (1911), *The Sea is Kind* (1914), *Medea* (1920), *Judas* (1923), and *Psyche in Hades* (1930). *Aphrodite against Artemis* (1901) and *Absalom* (1903) are plays. In 1920 he was granted a Civil List pension.

Mordaunt, Evelyn May (1877—25 June 1942), novelist and traveller who wrote under the name Elinor Mordaunt, was born at Cotgrove Place, Nottinghamshire, daughter of St John Legh Clowes. At the age of 20 she went to Mauritius, where she married a planter named Mordaunt; they were divorced later. While there she wrote a series of letters to preserve English memories, and in 1902 published them as *The Garden of Contentment*. In 1902 she sailed to Australia, where she married Robert Bowles. After another stay in England, she went off on travels which took her all over the world, and of which she wrote in *The Venture Book* (1926), *The Further Venture Book* (1927), *Purely for Pleasure* (1932), and *Traveller's Pack* (1933). She also published many novels, including *Lu of the Ranges* (1913), *The Rose of Youth* (1915), *Reputation* (1923), and *Cross Winds* (1932). *Sinabada* (1937) is an autobiography.

More, Hannah (2 Feb. 1745—7 Sept. 1833), dramatist and religious writer, was one of the five daughters of a schoolmaster at Stapleton, Gloucestershire. The family removed to Bristol, where Hannah began her literary efforts. Some early dramas, including *The Search after Happiness* (1762) and the *Inflexible Captive* (1774) bronght her before the public, and she went to London, where, through her friend Garrick, she was introduced to Johnson, Burke, and the rest of that circle, by whom she was highly esteemed. After publishing some poems, now forgotten, and a tragedy, *Percy* (1777), she resolved to devote herself to religious and reformative work, in which she was eminently successful. Books in this vein included *Hints towards forming the Character of a young Princess* (1805), written at the request of the Queen for the benefit of the Princess Charlotte; the novel *Coelebs in Search of a Wife* (1809); and a series of short tales, the *Cheap Repository*, among which was the popular tract *The Shepherd of Salisbury Plain*. This enterprise led to the formation of the Religious Tract Society. The success of Miss More's literary labours enabled her to pass her later years in ease, and her sisters having also retired on a competency made by conducting a boarding-school in Bristol, the whole family resided on a property called Barley Grove, which they had purchased, where they carried on with much success philanthropic and educational work among the people of the neighbouring district of Cheddar. *Letters of Hannah More* were published in 1925.

More, Henry (12 Oct. 1614—1 Sept. 1687), philosopher, born at Grantham and educated at Eton and Cambridge, took orders, but declined all preferment, including two deaneries and a bishopric, choosing rather a quiet life devoted to scholarship and philosophy. Becoming one of the Cambridge Platonists, he led a life of religious devotion, tinged with mysticism, and his writings had much popularity and influence in their day. Among them may be mentioned *Philosophical Poems* (1647), *The Mystery of Godliness* (1660), *The Mystery of Iniquity* (1664), and *Divine Dialogues* (1668).

More, Paul Elmer (12 Dec. 1864—9 March 1937), scholar and critic, was born at St Louis, Missouri, and educated at Washington University and Harvard. For a time he taught Sanskrit at Harvard and then Bryn Mawr, then was a literary critic on New York newspapers, and in 1914 retired to Princeton, where he gave lectures on philosophy. A leader of the New Humanist movement, in his *Shelburne Essays* (11 series, 1904—28) he criticized modern literature in the light of classical standards. Others of his works are *Hellenistic Philosophies* (1923), *The Christ of the New Testament* (1924), *The Demon of the Absolute* (1928), *The Catholic Faith* (1931), and *The Sceptical Approach to Religion* (1934). *Pages from an Oxford Diary* (1937) is autobiographical. He held honorary degrees of Columbia, Dartmouth, Princeton, and Glasgow.

More, Sir Thomas (7 Feb. 1478—6 July 1535), historian and humanist, son of a Justice of the King's Bench, was born in London. In his sixteenth year he was placed in the household of Morton, Archbishop of Canterbury. In 1497 he went to Oxford, where he

R

became the friend of Erasmus and others, and came in contact with the new learning. He studied law at New Inn and Lincoln's Inn, and for some time thought of entering the Church. He was, however, in 1504 sent up to Parliament, where his powerful speaking gained for him a high place. Meanwhile, he had brilliant success in the Law Courts, and was introduced by Wolsey to Henry VIII, with whom he soon rose into high favour. He became Chancellor of the Duchy of Lancaster, Speaker of the House of Commons in 1523, and was sent on missions to Charles V and Francis I. At length, on the fall of Wolsey, More was, much against his will, appointed Lord Chancellor, an office which he filled with great honour and success, though he was harsh in his dealings with persons accused of heresy. But differences with the King soon arose. More disapproved of Henry's ecclesiastical policy, as well as of his proceedings in regard to the Queen, and in 1532 he resigned his office. In 1534 he refused to take any oath that would impugn the Pope's authority, and for this he was imprisoned in the Tower, and finally beheaded. All Catholic Europe was shocked at the news of what was truly a judicial murder.

Among his works are a life of *Picus, Earl of Mirandula* (1510), and a *History of Richard III*, written about 1513. His great work, *Utopia*, was written in Latin in two books—the second in 1515, and the first in 1516. It had immediate popularity, and was translated into the principal European languages. It gives an account of an imaginary island and people, under cover of which it describes the social and political condition of England, with suggested remedies for abuses. More wrote many works of controversy, among which are *Dyaloge concerning Heresies*, and epigrams and dialogues in Latin. His *Correspondence* was edited in 1948. His pure and religious character, his sweet temper, his wit, his constancy and fortitude under misfortune combine to render him one of the most attractive and admirable figures in English history. He was canonized in 1935.

Morell, Thomas (born 18 March 1703, buried 19 Feb. 1784), scholar, born at Eton, was educated there and at Cambridge. Taking orders, he became curate of Kew, then rector of Buckland, Hertfordshire. In 1762 he compiled the *Thesaurus Graecae Poeseos*; he also published revised editions of other Greek and Latin dictionaries and of the *Gradus ad Parnassum*, and edited several Greek plays. In 1768 he was elected a Fellow of the Royal Society. The libretto which he supplied for Handel's *Joshua* contains the oft-quoted line 'See the conquering hero comes.'

Morgan, Charles Langbridge (22 Jan. 1894—6 Feb. 1958), novelist and playwright, was born in Kent, son of a railway engineer, and studied at the naval colleges of Osborne and Dartmouth. From 1911 to 1913 he served on the Atlantic and China stations, and in the First World War was made prisoner during the Naval Brigade's defence of Antwerp, but allowed on parole in Holland, where he spent four years. His knowledge of this country was used later in his novel *The Fountain* (1932), which won the Hawthornden Prize. After the war he studied at Oxford, where he was president of the

Oxford University Dramatic Society. In 1921 he became dramatic critic of *The Times* and in 1923 he married the novelist Hilda Vaughan. His novel *Portrait in a Mirror* (1929) won the Femina-Vie Heureuse Prize and gained him popularity in France, and *The Voyage* (1940) was awarded the Tait Black Prize. Others are *The Judge's Story* (1947) and *Breeze of Morning* (1951). His plays include *The Flashing Stream* (1938), *The River Line* (1952), and *The Burning Glass* (1954). He was a close friend of George Moore (q.v.) who made him his literary executor. Among other distinctions he was an Officer of the Legion of Honour and a Member of the French Academy.

Morgan, Sydney, Lady (1783?—13 April 1859), novelist, born in Dublin, daughter of Robert Owenson, an actor, married Sir Thomas Morgan, a surgeon, in 1812. She was the author of several vivacious Irish tales, including *The Wild Irish Girl* (1806), *O'Donnel* (1814), and *The O'Briens and the O'Flaherties* (1827); also two books on society in France and in Italy characterized by 'more vivacity and point than delicacy,' and a life of Salvator Rosa.

Morier, James Justinian (1780?—19 March 1849), diplomat, traveller, novelist, descended from a Huguenot family resident at Smyrna, where he was born, was educated at Harrow. Returning to the East he became in 1809 Secretary of Legation in Persia. He wrote accounts of travels in Persia, Armenia, and Asia Minor; also novels, in which he exhibits a marvellous familiarity with Oriental manners and modes of thought. The chief of these are *The Adventures of Hajji Baba* (1824), *Hajji Baba in England* (1828), *Zohrab the Hostage* (1832), *Ayesha* (1834), and *The Mirza* (1841). All these works are full of brilliant description, character-painting, and delicate satire.

Morison, James Augustus Cotter (20 April 1832—26 Feb. 1888), biographer, born in London, son of a quack doctor, spent his chilhood in Paris and was educated at Oxford. He wrote lives of *Gibbon* (1878), and *Macaulay* (1882); but his best work was his *Life of St Bernard* (1863). *The Service of Man* (1887) is written from a Positivist point of view.

Morley, Christopher Darlington (5 May 1890—28 March 1957), novelist and essayist, was born at Haverford, Pennsylvania, son of a professor of mathematics, graduated from Haverford College in 1910, and went to Oxford as a Rhodes Scholar. He worked as a columnist on the staff of various periodicals, and in 1937 edited a new edition of *Bartlett's Familiar Quotations*. The best-known of his novels are *Where the Blue Begins* (1922) and *Thunder on the Left* (1925); others are *Parnassus on Wheels* (1917), *The Haunted Bookshop* (1919), *Swiss Family Manhattan* (1932), *The Trojan Horse* (1937), *Kitty Foyle* (1939), and *The Man Who Made Friends with Himself* (1949). *Shandygaff* (1918) and *Mince Pie* (1919), books of essays, were followed by many others, including *Tales from a Rolltop Desk* (1921), *Inward Ho* (1923), *Off the Deep End* (1928), *Seacoast of Bohemia* (1929), *Hasta la Vista* (1935), *History of an Autumn* (1938), and *The Ironing Board* (1949). *The Rocking Horse* (1919), *Chimney-smoke* (1921), *Parson's Pleasure* (1923), and *The Middle Kingdom* (1944) are books of verse. He also wrote several one-act plays, and *John Mistletoe* (1931), an early autobiography.

Morley, Henry (15 Sept. 1822—14 May 1894), scholar and editor, was born in London and educated at King's College. He trained as a doctor, but was swindled by a dishonest partner, and turned to teaching and writing. From 1850 to 1865 he was on the staff of *Household Words* and then of *All the Year Round*; he also edited the *Examiner*, and wrote a number of biographies. In 1865 he was appointed Professor of English at University College, and in 1878 to the same post at Queen's College. Between 1887 and 1895 he produced *English Writers* in 11 volumes, a vast history of English literature which only got as far as Shakespeare. His *First Sketch of English Literature* (1873) went through over a dozen editions. His later years were spent in the valuable task of editing cheap reprints of the English classics, notably Morley's Universal Library (63 volumes) and Cassell's National Library (214 volumes). His *Early Papers and Some Memories* (1891) is autobiographical.

Morley of Blackburn, John Morley, 1st Viscount (24 Dec. 1838—23 Sept. 1923), statesman and biographer, was born at Blackburn, son of a surgeon. Educated at Cheltenham and Oxford, he was called to the Bar but never practised. Instead, he became a free-lance journalist in London, writing in particular for the *Saturday Review*, and becoming acquainted with many leading writers, including Meredith and John Stuart Mill. In 1867 he became editor of the *Fortnightly Review* and in 1880 of the *Pall Mall Gazette*. Essays written for the former were collected as *Critical Miscellanies* (1871—1877). He published noteworthy lives or studies of *Burke* (1867), *Voltaire* (1872), *Rousseau* (1873), *Diderot and the Encyclopaedists* (1879), *Cobden* (1881), *Walpole* (1889), *Cromwell* (1900), and *Gladstone* (1903). In 1883 he was elected Liberal M.P. for Newcastle, and became Gladstone's right-hand man. From 1892 to 1895 he was Secretary for Ireland, and from 1905 to 1910 Secretary for India. His *Recollections* were published in 1917.

Morris, George Pope (10 Oct. 1802—6 July 1864), journalist and poet, was born in Philadelphia, but moved to New York, where he worked in a printing office. From 1823 to 1842 he edited the *New York Mirror*, which became the mouthpiece of the Knickerbocker School, including among its contributors William Cullen Bryant and Fitz-Greene Halleck (qq.v.). His drama *Brier Cliff* (1826) had a long run but was never published. In 1830 he wrote a book of humorous sketches, *The Little Frenchman and his Water Lots*, but he is best remembered by his poems, especially 'Woodman, Spare That Tree,' which appeared in a collection *The Deserted Bride* (1838).

Morris, Sir Lewis (13 Jan. 1833—12 Nov. 1907), poet, born at Carmarthen, and educated at Sherborne and Oxford, was called to the Bar, and practised as a conveyancer until 1880, after which he devoted himself to the promotion of higher education in Wales; he helped to establish the University of Wales in 1893, and was knighted in 1895. In 1871 he published *Songs of Two Worlds*, which showed the influence of Tennyson, and was well received, though rather by the wider public than by more critical circles. It was followed in 1876—7 by *The Epic of Hades*, which had extraordinary popularity, and showed undeniable talent both in versification and narrative power, though it lacked the qualities of the higher kinds of poetry. It deals in a modern spirit with the Greek myths and legends. Others of his works are *A Vision of Saints, Gwen, The Ode of Life,* and *Gycia,* a tragedy.

Morris, William (24 March 1834—3 Oct. 1896), poet, artist, and socialist, was born at Walthamstow, and educated at Marlborough School and Exeter College, Oxford. After being articled as an architect he was for some years a painter, and then joined in founding the decorating firm, in which Rossetti, Burne-Jones, and other artists were partners. By this and other means he did much to influence the public taste in furnishing and decoration. He was one of the originators of the *Oxford and Cambridge Magazine,* to which he contributed poems, tales, and essays, and in 1858 he published *The Defence of Guenevere and other Poems. The Life and Death of Jason* followed in 1867, *The Earthly Paradise* in 1868—70, and *Love is Enough* in 1875. In the last mentioned year he made a translation in verse of Virgil's *Aeneid.* Travels in Iceland led to the writing of *Three Northern Love Stories,* and the epic of *Sigurd the Volsung* (1876). His translation of the *Odyssey* in verse appeared in 1887. A series of prose romances include *The House of the Wolfings* (1889), and *The Well at the World's End* (1896). A leader of the Socialist movement, he wrote *The Dream of John Ball* (1888) and the utopian *News from Nowhere* (1891) as Socialist propaganda. In 1800 Morris started the Kelmscott Press, for which he designed type and decorations. For his subjects as a writer he drew upon classic and Gothic models alike. A lifelong crusader against ugliness, he was inspired by the love of beauty for its own sake; his poetry is rich and musical, and he has a power of description which makes his pictures live and glow, but his narratives sometimes suffer from length and slowness of movement. The standard life of Morris is by J. W. Mackail (q.v.).

Morrison, Arthur (1 Nov. 1863—4 Dec. 1945), novelist, born in Kent, joined the staff of Henley's *National Observer,* in which his first book, *Tales of Mean Streets* (1894) first appeared. It was followed by *A Child of the Jago* (1896), a novel of the London slums, *London Town* (1899), *Cunning Murrell* (1900), and *The Hole in the Wall* (1902); *Divers Vanities* (1905) and *Green Ginger* (1909) are collections of short stories. He also wrote some good detective stories, *Martin Hewitt, Investigator* (1894) being followed by three other Martin Hewitt books, the last being *The Red Triangle* (1903). In 1911 he published a two-volume work on *The Painters of Japan,* and his collection of Chinese and Japanese paintings was eventually acquired by the British Museum.

Morton, Henry Vollam (26 July 1892—   ), travel writer, was born and educated in Birmingham, and started there as a journalist. During the First World War he served with the Warwickshire Yeomanry. He was on the staff of the *Daily Mail*, *Daily Express*, and *Daily Herald* successively, then gave up journalism to write topographical and travel books. The earliest of these were about London, and then *In Search of England* (1927) was so popular that a whole set of similar books followed, including *In Search of Scotland* (1929), *In Search of Ireland* (1930), and *In Search of South Africa* (1948). He also wrote several books on biblical scenes, including *In the Steps of the Master* (1934), *In the Steps of St Paul* (1936), *Through Lands of the Bible* (1938), and *Women of the Bible* (1940).

Morton, Thomas (1764?—28 March 1838), dramatist, born in Durham, came to London to study law, which he discarded in favour of playwriting. He wrote about 25 plays, of which *The Way to Get Married* (1796) and *Speed the Plough* (1798) were among the most popular. In the latter he introduced Mrs Grundy to the British public.

Moss, Thomas (1740?—6 Dec. 1808), poet and clergyman, educated at Cambridge, took orders and was for many years parson of Trentham, Staffordshire. In 1769 he published anonymously *Poems on Several Occasions*, which contains the well-known piece, 'A Beggar's Petition.' He also published some sermons and *The Imperfection of Human Enjoyments* (1783), a poem in blank verse.

Motherwell, William (13 Oct. 1797—1 Nov. 1835), poet, born in Glasgow and educated at Glasgow University, held the office of deputy sheriff-clerk at Paisley, at the same time contributing poetry to various periodicals. He had also antiquarian tastes, and a deep knowledge of the early history of Scottish ballad literature, which he turned to account in *Minstrelsy, Ancient and Modern* (1827), a collection of Scottish ballads with an historical introduction. In 1830 he became editor of the *Glasgow Courier*, and in 1832 he collected and published his *Poems, Narrative and Lyrical*. He also joined Hogg in editing the works of Burns.

Motley, John Lothrop (15 April 1814—29 May 1877), historian and diplomat, born in Boston, was educated at Harvard, where O. W. Holmes (q.v.), afterwards his biographer, was a fellow-student. After graduating he went to Europe, studied at Göttingen and Berlin, and visited Italy. On his return he studied law, and was admitted to the Bar in 1837. He did not, however, practise, and was in 1840 sent to St Petersburg as Secretary of Legation. Meanwhile, having published two novels, *Morton's Hope* and *Merry Mount*, which had little success, he turned to history, and attracted attention by some essays in various reviews. Having decided to write an historical work on Holland, he proceeded in 1851 to Europe to collect materials, and in 1856 published *The Rise of the Dutch Republic*. It was received with the highest approval by such critics as Froude and Prescott, and at once took its place as a standard work. It was followed in 1860 by the first two volumes of *The United Netherlands*.

The following year Motley was appointed Minister at Vienna, and in 1869 at London. His last work was a *Life of Barneveldt*, the Dutch statesman, published in 1874. Motley holds a high place among historical writers both on account of his research and accuracy, and his vivid and dramatic style, which shows the influence of Carlyle.

Mottram, Ralph Hale (30 Oct. 1883—   ), novelist, was born at Norwich, and educated at a school there and at Lausanne. He started work as clerk in a bank where his father was manager. In 1904 he formed a friendship with Galsworthy, who encouraged him to write, but it was not till after the First World War, during which he served in Flanders as an interpreter, that he won fame with his novel *Spanish Farm* (1924), which won the Hawthornden Prize and sold 100,000 copies; sequels to it were *Sixty-Four Ninety-Four* (1925) and *The Crime at Vanderlynden's* (1926), and the three books were published together in 1927 as *The Spanish Farm Trilogy*, which contains three additional pieces to join them together. Others of his novels are *The English Miss* (1928), *Europa's Beast* (1930), *Home for the Holidays* (1932), *Early Morning* (1935), *Flower Pot End* (1936), *Miss Lavington* (1939), *Bowler Hat* (1940), *The Gentleman of Leisure* (1947), *Come to the Bower* (1949), and *Over the Wall* (1955). He also published several volumes of short stories and (under the name J. Marjoram) two books of verse, *Repose* (1906) and *New Poems* (1909). *Autobiography with a Difference* appeared in 1939, and *The Broads*, telling of his own countryside, in 1952.

Moultrie, John (30 Dec. 1799—26 Dec. 1874), clergyman and poet, was born in London. At Eton his friends included W. M. Praed (q.v.), and at Cambridge he was intimate with Macaulay. He took orders and became rector of Rugby. As early as 1820 he had poems printed in the school magazine and elsewhere, among which 'My Brother's Grave' and 'Godiva' were much admired. Later volumes of verse included *The Black Fence* (1850) and *Altars, Hearths, and Graves* (1854).

Muir, Edwin (15 May 1887—3 Jan. 1959), novelist, poet, critic, was born at Deerness, Orkney Islands, son of a farmer, and educated at Kirkwall Burgh School. When he was 14 the family moved to Glasgow, where he worked as a clerk. Going to London, in 1919 he joined the staff of the *New Age*, and in the same year married Willa Anderson, the novelist. In 1921 they moved to Europe and lived in various countries while he wrote essays for *The Freeman*, then edited by Van Wyck Brooks; these were collected and published as *Latitudes* (1924). Later Muir settled at St Andrews in Scotland, where he and his wife made many translations from the German. His books of verse include *First Poems* (1925), *Chorus of the Newly Dead* (1926), *Variations on a Fine Theme* (1934), and *The Voyage* (1946); his *Collected Poems* appeared in 1952. His novels are *The Marionette* (1927), *The Three Brothers* (1931), and *Poor Tom* (1932). Books of criticism are *Transition* (1926), *The Structure of the Novel* (1928), *The Present Age* (1939), and *Essays on Literature and Society* (1949). He also wrote a life of *John Knox* (1929), and an autobiography, *The Story and the Fable* (1940).

Muir, John (21 April 1838—24 Dec. 1914), naturalist, was born at Dunbar in Scotland. In 1849 the family emigrated to the United States and he studied science at Wisconsin University. He lived for a while in the Yosemite, and was instrumental in having it made a national park. An admirer of Thoreau, he became a student of nature and had a passion for forests. In 1868 he removed to California; his journal of the trip, made mostly on foot, was published in 1916 as *A Thousand-Mile Walk to the Gulf*. Others of his books are *The Mountains of California* (1894), *Our National Parks* (1901), *Stickeen* (1909), a story of a dog, *My First Summer in the Sierra* (1911), *The Yosemite* (1912), and *The Story of My Boyhood and Youth* (1913). *Letters to a Friend* appeared after his death.

Mulford, Clarence Edward (3 Feb. 1883—10 May 1956), writer of Western stories, was born at Streator, Illinois, and educated there and at Utica, New York. He did newspaper work for a time, then was in the Civil Service. His first book, *Bar 20* (1907) was followed by some 30 others, all about cowboys and Western life, of which he made a careful study. Later books are *Hopalong Cassidy* (1910), *Bar 20 Days* (1911), *Buck Peters, Ranchman* (1912), *The Coming of Cassidy* (1913), *The Man from Bar 20* (1918), *The Bar 20 Three* (1921), *Hopalong Cassidy Returns* (1924), *The Bar 20 Rides Again* (1926), *Mesquite Jenkins* (1928), and *Hopalong Cassidy Serves a Writ* (1941). Mulford's lame, intrepid, two-gun hero Hopalong Cassidy became so famous that he appeared extensively on both films and television.

Müller, Friedrich Max, *see* **Max Müller.**

Mulock, Dinah Maria, *see* **Craik.**

Mumford, Lewis (19 Oct. 1895—   ), critic, was born at Flushing, Long Island, and made his home in New York. Educated at Stuyvesant High School and New York University, he served in the Navy during the First World War, visited London in 1920, and then worked as a freelance writer. His first book, *The Story of Utopias* (1922) was followed by *Sticks and Stones* (1924), *The Golden Day* (1926), *The Brown Decades* (1931), *Men Must Act* (1939), and *Faith for Living* (1940). Much of his work is an analysis of American culture and a plea for moral regeneration. *The Conduct of Life* (1952), which discusses man's nature and destiny, completes a series of which the earlier volumes are *Technics and Civilization* (1934), *The Culture of Cities* (1938), and *The Condition of Man* (1944). He also wrote a study of *Herman Melville* (1929), and lectured on education at several universities.

Munday, Anthony (born 1553, buried 10 Aug. 1633), playwright and ballad writer, was born in London, son of a draper. In 1576 he was apprenticed to a stationer, but gave that up and went to Rome as a sort of Protestant investigator in 1578. After writing several anti-Catholic pamphlets, in 1584 he was given a small appointment at Court. He translated a number of popular romances, including *Palladino of England* (1588) and *Amadis de Gaule* (1589—95). His plays include *John a Kent and John a Cumber* (1594), a highly popular romantic comedy, and a Robin Hood play, *The Downfall of Robert,*

Earl of Huntingdon (1601), which had as sequel *The Death of Robert, Earl of Huntingdon*, in which he collaborated with Henry Chettle (q.v.). He was famous for his pageants, being in 1605 appointed chief pageant writer for London, and composed a number of ballads. Stow the chronicler (q.v.) made Munday his literary executor.

Munro, C. K., *see* **McMullan, C. W. K.**

Munro, Hector Hugh (18 Dec. 1870—14 Nov. 1916), novelist who wrote under the name Saki, was born at Akyab, Burma, son of a police official of Scottish highland extraction, and was brought up by aunts at Pilton in Devon. Educated at Exmouth and Bedford Grammar School, he travelled with his father in France, Germany, and Switzerland, then was for a time in the police service in Burma but found the climate too unhealthy. Returning to England, he wrote for the *Westminster Gazette*, and from 1902 to 1908 was a foreign correspondent of the *Morning Post*. In the First World War he served as a private with the Royal Fusiliers and was killed at Beaumont-Hamel. His books of humorous short stories include *Reginald* (1904), *Reginald in Russia* (1910), *The Chronicles of Clovis* (1912), *Beasts and Super-Beasts* (1914), and *The Square Egg* (1924); *The Unbearable Bassington* (1912) and *When William Came* (1914) are novels. His pseudonym Saki is the name of the cup-bearer in *The Ruba'iyát* of Omar Khayyám.

Munro, Neil (2 June 1864—22 Dec. 1930), novelist, was born at Inveraray, Argyllshire, son of a farmer, and educated at the local school. For five years he worked in a law office, then went into journalism, and after working on various papers became editor of the *Glasgow Evening News* from 1918 to 1927. Latterly he lived at Craigendoran on the Firth of Clyde. His first book, *The Lost Pibroch* (1896), a collection of Celtic tales, was followed by a number of historical novels, including *John Splendid* (1898), *Gilian the Dreamer* (1899), *Doom Castle* (1901), and *Children of the Tempest* (1903). Of his humorous dialect stories, the Para Handy series, beginning with *The 'Vital Spark'* (1906) were the most popular; others are *Erchie* (1904), *The Daft Days* (1907), *Fancy Farm* (1910), *Ayrshire Idylls* (1912), and *Jaunty Jock* (1918). His books of verse include *Bagpipe Ballads* (1917), and *The Poetry of Neil Munro* (1931). *The Clyde: River and Firth* (1907) is descriptive. In 1908 he was made an honorary LL.D. of Glasgow.

Mure, William (9 July 1799—1 April 1860), scholar, born at Caldwell, Ayrshire, son of an army officer, and educated at Westminster, Edinburgh, and Bonn, sat in Parliament for Renfrewshire from 1846 to 1855. He was a sound classical scholar, and published *A Critical History of the Language and Literature of Ancient Greece* (five volumes, 1850—7). Mure was Lord Rector of Glasgow University 1847—8.

Murphy, Arthur (27 Dec. 1727—18 June 1805), actor and dramatist, born at Clomquin, Roscommon, and educated at St Omer, took up acting, then studied for the Bar, to which he was ultimately admitted after some demur on account of his connection with the

R*

stage. His plays were nearly all adaptations. They include *The Apprentice* (1756), *The Spouter*, and *The Upholsterer* (1758). He also wrote an essay on Dr Johnson, and a life of Garrick, and made a good translation of Tacitus.

Murray, Charles (28 Sept. 1864—12 April 1941), poet, was born at Alford in Aberdeenshire, but the more active part of his life was spent in South Africa, where he became manager of a mining company. In the Boer War he fought as a lieutenant in the Railway Pioneer Regiment. In 1901 he was appointed Deputy Inspector of Mines for the Transvaal, and in 1910 was Secretary for Public Works in the Union of South Africa, retiring in 1924 with a C.M.G. His books of verse include *Hamewith* (1900), *A Sough o' War* (1917), and *In the Country Places* (1920); his most famous poem is ' The Whistle,' written, like most of his verse, in the East Coast dialect, of which he was a master. A forerunner of the modern Scottish Renaissance, he spent his later years at Banchory in Aberdeenshire.

Murray, David Christie (13 April 1847—1 Aug. 1907), journalist, was born at West Bromwich, Staffordshire. Leaving school at 12, he was put to work in his father's printing office, then took up writing and joined the staff of the *Birmingham Morning News*. In 1865 he went to London without funds or prospects, and after a few months enlisted in the Irish Dragoon Guards, but was bought out by a great-aunt and went back to journalism. In 1871 he became parliamentary reporter for the *Daily News*, and in 1892 was editor of the short-lived *Morning*. His articles in the *Referee* were collected as *Guesses at Truth* (1908). He lived for a time in France, and in 1898 championed Dreyfus in the celebrated case. His most successful novels were *Joseph's Coat* (1881), *Val Strange* (1882), *By the Gate of the Sea* (1883), *Rainbow Gold* (1885), and *Aunt Rachel* (1886). *A Novelist's Notebook* (1887), *The Making of a Novelist* (1894), and *Recollections* (1908) are autobiographical.

Murray, David Leslie (5 Feb. 1888—), novelist, born in London, was educated at Harrow and Oxford. During the First World War he served with the Intelligence Department of the War Office. From 1920 to 1923 he was dramatic critic of the *Nation*, and from 1938 to 1944 editor of *The Times Literary Supplement*. His earliest book, a treatise on *Pragmatism* (1912) was followed by *Scenes and Silhouettes* (1926), and a study of *Disraeli* (1927). He then turned to novel-writing and published *The Bride Adorned* (1929), *Stardust* (1931), *The English Family Robinson* (1933), *Regency* (1936), *Commander of the Mists* (1938), *Tale of Three Cities* (1940), *Enter Three Witches* (1942), *Folly Bridge* (1945), *Leading Lady* (1947), *Royal Academy* (1950), and *Outrageous Fortune* (1952). He was a Fellow of the Royal Society of Literature.

Murray, George Gilbert Aimé, O.M. (2 Jan. 1866—20 May 1957), scholar and poet, was born in Sydney, New South Wales, where his father was President of the Legislative Council. Coming to England at the age of 11, he was educated at Merchant Taylors' and St John's College, Oxford, where he had a brilliant record and in 1888 was elected a Fellow of New College. In 1889 he married Lady Mary

Howard, daughter of the Earl of Carlisle. From that year till 1899 he was Professor of Greek at Glasgow University, and from 1908 to 1936 held the corresponding post at Oxford. Among his more important works are *A History of Ancient Greek Literature* (1897), *The Rise of the Greek Epic* (1907), *Four Stages of Greek Religion* (1912), *Euripides and his Age* (1913), *Religio Grammatici* (1918), *Aristophanes: a Survey* (1933), and *Aeschylus, the Creator of Tragedy* (1940). He made brilliant verse translations of plays of Aeschylus, Sophocles, Euripides, and Aristophanes, which from their poetic feeling deserve to rank almost as original work. A great public figure, he stood for Parliament several times and from 1923 to 1938 was chairman of the League of Nations Union. His works on public affairs include *Problems of Foreign Policy* (1921), and *Liberality and Civilization* (1938). A Fellow of the British Academy and of the Royal Society of Literature, he received honorary degrees from Oxford, Cambridge, Glasgow, and Birmingham, and was awarded the Order of Merit in 1941. He was buried in Westminster Abbey.

Murray, Sir James Augustus Henry (7 Feb. 1837—26 July 1915), lexicographer, was born at Denholm, near Hawick, and educated at Minto School. At the age of 17 he taught in a Hawick school where he became headmaster. Moving to London, he worked for eight years in a bank, then in 1870 became a master at Mill Hill and three years later took his B.A. degree at London University. A keen student of languages, he was appointed in 1879 editor of the *New English Dictionary on Historical Principles* which was being planned as a rival to *Webster's Dictionary*, but continued as a schoolmaster till 1885, when he removed to Oxford. Murray contracted with the Clarendon Press to complete the dictionary in 10 years, but it actually took nearly 50 from the time of his appointment, and he lived to edit only one half of it. The first section was published in 1884, the last in 1928, 13 years after Murray's death. A monumental piece of work, the *Oxford English Dictionary*, as it came to be called, marked a most important advance on all previous lexicography, and was taken as a model for succeeding works of the same type. Murray also edited a number of Scots texts. He was knighted in 1908 and received honorary degrees from nine universities.

Murray, Lindley (22 April 1745—16 Jan. 1826), grammarian, was born at Swatara, Pennsylvania, and practised as a lawyer. During the revolutionary war he amassed a fortune in commerce. From 1785 he lived in England, near York, and was for his last 16 years confined to the house. His *English Grammar* (1795) was long a standard work, and his main claim to a place in literature. His other writings were chiefly religious.

Murry, John Middleton (6 Aug. 1889—13 March 1957), critic, born at Peckham, London, son of a clerk at Somerset House, was educated at Christ's Hospital and Brasenose College, Oxford. Taking up journalism, he worked on the staff of the *Westminster Gazette* and later of the *Nation*. In 1913 he married Katherine Mansfield (q.v.), and his writing was much influenced by her and by their friend D. H. Lawrence (q.v.). In the First World War he worked in the Intelligence Department of the War Office, and became Chief Censor, receiving the O.B.E. in 1920. After the war he became editor of the *Athenaeum*, and in 1923 founded the *Adelphi*. Among his works of literary criticism are *Countries of the Mind* (two series 1922, 1931), *The Problem of Style* (1922), *Pencillings* (1923), *Discoveries* (1924), *Keats and Shakespeare* (1925), *Studies in Keats* (1930), *Son of Woman, the Story of D. H. Lawrence* (1931), *The Life of Katherine Mansfield* (1933), *William Blake* (1933), *The Mystery of Keats* (1949), and *Jonathan Swift* (1954). He also wrote a number of religious books, including *To the Unknown God* (1924), *The Life of Jesus* (1926), and *Christocracy* (1942). *Between Two Worlds* (1935) is an autobiography.

Myers, Frederic William Henry (6 Feb. 1843—17 Jan. 1901), poet and essayist, son of a clergyman, was born at Keswick, and educated at Cheltenham and Cambridge. He became an inspector of schools, and was the author of several volumes of poetry, including *St Paul* (1867). He also wrote *Essays Classical and Modern* (1883), and lives of Wordsworth and Shelley. Becoming interested in spiritualism he aided in founding the Society for Psychical Research, and was joint author of *Phantasms of the Living*. His last work was *Human Personality and its Survival of Bodily Death* (1903).

N

Nabbes, Thomas (fl. 1638), dramatist, matriculated at Oxford in 1621, but left without a degree. He lived in London, and wrote comedies, satirizing bourgeois society. He was most successful in writing masques, among which are *Spring Glory* and *Microcosmus*. He also wrote a continuation of Richard Knolles's *History of the Turks*.

Naidu, Sarojini (13 Feb. 1879—3 March 1949), poetess, born at Hyderabad, where her father was Principal of the Nizam's College, was educated at Madras University, King's College, London, and Girton. Her first book of poems, *The Golden Threshold* (1905), was followed by *The Bird of Time* (1914), and *The Broken Wing* (1917); from these collections of lyrics she gained the name of 'the Nightingale of India.' Later she forsook literature for politics and was the first Indian woman to preside over the National Congress. In 1908 she was awarded the Kaiser-i-Hind Medal, for work in connection with flood relief.

Nairne, Carolina, Baroness (16 Aug. 1766—26 Oct. 1845), songwriter, was born Carolina Oliphant at Gask in Perthshire (the 'auld house' of her poem). Though shy and delicate, she became an accomplished dancer and singer, and was known for her beauty as the Flower of Strathearn. In 1806 she married her second cousin, Major Nairne, who on reversal of attainder became 5th Lord Nairne. On his death, after residing in various places in England, Ireland, and on the Continent, she settled at the new house of Gask (the old one having been pulled down in 1801). Of her songs, 87 in number, many first appeared anonymously in *The Scottish Minstrel* (1821—1824); a collected edition with her name, under the title of *Lays from Strathearn*, was published after her death. Although the songs, some of which were founded on older compositions, had from the first an extraordinary popularity, the authoress maintained a strict anonymity during her life. For direct simplicity and poetic feeling Lady Nairne perhaps comes nearer than any other Scottish song-writer to Burns, and many of her lyrics are enshrined in the hearts of her fellow-countrymen. Among the best of them are 'The Land o' the Leal,' 'Charlie is my Darling,' 'Caller Herrin',' 'The Laird o' Cockpen,' 'The Auld House,' 'The Hundred Pipers,' and 'Will ye no come back Again?' The Jacobitism of some of these and many others was, of course, purely sentimental and poetical, like that of Scott.

Napier, Mark (24 July 1798—23 Nov. 1879), historian, son of a lawyer in Edinburgh, was called to the Bar, practised as an advocate, and was made Sheriff of Dumfries and Galloway. He published memoirs of the Napiers, of Montrose, and of Graham of Claverhouse, the last of which gave rise to much controversy. Napier wrote from a strongly Cavalier and Jacobite standpoint, and had remarkably little of the judicial spirit in his methods.

Napier, Sir William Francis Patrick (17 Dec. 1785—10 Feb. 1860), was one of the sons of the Hon. George Napier and Lady Sarah Lennox, daughter of the 2nd Duke of Richmond, and the object of a romantic attachment on the part of George III. One of his brothers was Sir Charles Napier, the conqueror of Scinde. Entering the army at 15, he served with great distinction in the Peninsula under Moore and Wellington. His experiences as a participator in the events of the war combined with the possession of remarkable acumen and a brilliant style to qualify him for the great work of his life as its historian. *The History of the War in the Peninsula* (1828—40) at once took rank as a classic, and superseded all existing works on the subject. It was translated into French, German, Spanish, Italian, and Persian. Napier also published *The Conquest of Scinde* (1844—1846), mainly a defence of his brother Charles, whose life he subsequently wrote. He became K.C.B. in 1848, and General in 1859.

Nasby, Petroleum V., *see* **Locke, David Ross.**

Nash, Frederic Ogden (19 Aug. 1902—   ), poet, born at Rye, New York State, was educated at St George's School, Rhode Island, and Harvard (1920—1). After a short period as a bond salesman he worked with a firm of publishers and in 1931 published two volumes of verse, *Hard Lines* and *Free Wheeling*, which at once attracted attention by their rich vein of humour, their freedom of scansion and their unconventionality of thought. Thereafter he became a prolific and very popular writer of humorous verse. In addition to his amusing or nonsensical poems he composed occasional serious pieces which showed great depth of feeling, and there is always an undercurrent of sage philosophy running through his work. After marrying Frances R. Leonard in 1931 he settled in Baltimore and had two daughters, Linell and Isabel, to whom a number of his poems are addressed. Among his best-known collections of verse are *The Face is Familiar* (1941), *Good Intentions* (1942), *Family Reunion* (1950), *Parents Keep Out* (1951), *The Private Dining Room* (1952), and *You Can't Get There From Here* (1957).

Nash *or* **Nashe, Thomas** (1567—1601), satirist, born at Lowestoft, son of a minister, graduated B.A. at Cambridge in 1586. A reckless life kept him in perpetual poverty, and a bitter and sarcastic tongue lost him friends and patrons. He cherished an undying hatred for the Puritans, and specially for Gabriel Hervey, with whom he maintained a lifelong controversy, and against whose attacks he defended Robert Greene (q.v.). Among his writings are *Anatomy of Absurdities* (1589), *Pierce Pennilesse, his Supplication to the Divell* (1592), and *Have with you to Saffron Walden* (1596), all against the Puritans. In his comedy *Summer's Last Will and Testament* (1600) occurs the well-known song, 'Spring, the sweet Spring, is the year's pleasant King.' *Christ's Tears over Jerusalem* (1593) may have indicated some movement towards repentance. Another work in a totally different style, *The Unfortunate Traveller, or the Life of Jack Wilton* (1594), a wild tale, may be regarded as the pioneer of the novel of adventure. It had, however, so little success that the author never returned to this kind of fiction. A comedy, *The Isle of Dogs* (now lost), adverted so pointedly to abuses in the state that it led to his imprisonment. His last work was *Lenten Stuffe* (1599), a burlesque panegyric on Yarmouth and its red herrings. Nash's verse is usually hard and monotonous, but he was a man of varied culture and great ability.

Nayler, James (born 1617? buried 21 Oct. 1660), Quaker theologian, son of a Yorkshire yeoman, after serving in the Parliamentary army, joined the Quakers in 1651, became one of Foxe's most trusted helpers, and exercised a powerful influence. By some of the more enthusiastic devotees of the sect he was honoured with such blasphemous titles as 'the Lamb of God,' which, however, he did not arrogate to himself, but asserted that they were ascribed to 'Christ in him.' He was found guilty of blasphemy, pilloried, whipped, and branded, and cast into prison, from which he was not released until after the death of Cromwell, when he made public confession and resumed preaching. He was the author of a number of short works both devotional and controversial which rank high for insight and depth of thought.

Neal, John (25 Aug. 1793—20 June 1876), novelist and poet, born at Portland, Maine, was self-educated, kept a dry goods store, and was afterwards a lawyer. He wrote several novels, which show considerable native power, but little art, and are now almost forgotten. Among those which show the influence of Byron and Godwin are *Keep Cool* (1818), *Logan* (1822), and *Seventy-six* (1823). His poems have the same features of vigour and want of finish. In 1823 he visited England, and became known to Jeremy Bentham. His autobiography, *Wandering Recollections of a Somewhat Busy Life* (1869), was written at the suggestion of Longfellow.

Neale, John Ernest (7 Dec. 1890—   ), historian, was born at Liverpool and educated at Liverpool University and University College, London, where he subsequently became an assistant in the Department of History. In 1925 he was appointed to the chair of Modern History at Manchester, and in 1927 he became Professor of English History at London University. His biography *Queen Elizabeth* (1934) was awarded the James Tait Black Memorial Prize. Later works of his were *The Elizabethan Political Scene* (1948), *The Elizabethan House of Commons* (1949), and *Elizabeth I and her Parliaments* (1953).

Neale, John Mason (24 Jan. 1818—6 Aug. 1866), clergyman and hymn-writer, was born in London, graduated B.A. from Trinity College, Cambridge, in 1840, and was for a time a tutor of Downing College. He held high church views and was one of the founders of the Cambridge Camden Society, which later became the Ecclesiological Society. From 1846 till his death he was warden of Sackville College, an almshouse at East Grinstead. He is chiefly remembered for his hymns, many of which were translated from Latin or Greek originals. One-eighth of the *Hymns Ancient and Modern* are his, including 'Jerusalem the Golden' and others equally famous.

Neaves, Charles, Lord (14 Oct. 1800—23 Dec. 1876), judge and author, born and educated in Edinburgh, was called to the Bar, and became a judge of the court of session. He was a frequent contributor to *Blackwood's Magazine*. His verses, witty and satirical, were collected as *Songs and Verses, Social and Scientific*. He wrote also on philology, and published a book on the Greek Anthology.

Neckham, Neckam, *or* **Necham, Alexander** (Sept. 1157—1217), scholar, born at St Albans, was foster-brother to Richard Cœur de Lion. He went to Paris in 1180, where he became a distinguished teacher. Returning to England in 1186 he became an Augustinian Canon, and in 1213 Abbot of Cirencester. He is one of our earliest men of learning, and wrote a scientific work in Latin verse, *De Naturis Rerum* (On the Nature of Things) in 10 books. Other works are *De Laudibus Divinae Sapientiae* (In Praise of the Divine Wisdom), *De Contemptu Mundi* (On Despising the World), and some grammatical treatises.

Neill, Alexander Sutherland (17 Oct. 1883—   ), educationist, born at Forfar and educated at Edinburgh University, was successively draper, teacher, and journalist before joining in founding the International School which was located in Germany, Austria, and then England. His unorthodox ideas on education and child psychology are set out in *A Dominie's Log* (1915), *A Dominie Dismissed* (1916), *A Dominie Abroad* (1922), *A Dominie's Five* (1924), *The Problem Teacher* (1939), *The Problem Family* (1948), and other books.

Nesbit, Edith (15 Aug. 1858—4 May 1924), novelist and writer of children's books, educated at a French convent, in Germany and at Brighton, spent her early youth in the country at Holstead Hall, Kent. She made her first appearance in print with a poem, 'The Dawn,' in the *Sunday Magazine* of 1876. After she married Hubert Bland in 1880 she continued writing articles, stories, and poems, but did not find her true vocation until *The Treasure Seekers*, a story for children, brought her financial success in 1899. *The Would-be Goods* (1901) and *Five Children—and It* (1902) were other favourites among her stories, which struck a new note by portraying young folk as real human beings. In 1915 she was granted a Civil List pension of £60 and in 1917, her first husband having died, she married Thomas Tucker, an engineer, and retired to New Romney.

Neville, Henry (1620—22 Sept. 1694), politician and novelist, was born at Billingbear, Berkshire, and went to Oxford, but left without a degree and then toured Europe. His political activities brought him into collision with Cromwell, who banished him from London in 1654. On Cromwell's death he became M.P. for Reading and published *Shuffling, Cutting, and Dealing in a Game of Picquet* (1659), a lampoon against the former Protector. He also translated Macchiavelli's works in 1675, but is chiefly remembered for his novel *The Isle of Pines*, published in 1668 and later translated into French, German, Italian, and Dutch.

Nevinson, Henry Woodd (1856—9 Nov. 1941), journalist, was born in Leicester and educated at Shrewsbury, Christ Church, Oxford, and Jena. After working as a teacher for a short time he turned to journalism and was a leader-writer for the *Daily Chronicle* from 1897 to 1903 and for the *Daily News* from 1908 to 1909. He was best known as a war correspondent, reporting the Greco-Turkish War of 1897, the Boer War of 1899—1902, and in 1904 exposing the Portuguese slave trade in Angola. During the First World War he represented the *Manchester Guardian* on various fronts from Flanders to the Dardanelles, and subsequently he reported the Washington conferences of 1921 and 1929. He received honorary degrees from Liverpool and Dublin. His best-known books are the autobiographical series *Changes and Chances* (1923), *More Changes, More Chances* (1925), and *Last Changes, Last Chances* (1928). He also wrote a book of verse entitled *Lines of Life* (1920), and a volume on Hardy the novelist, which was published after his death.

Newbolt, Sir Henry John (6 June 1862—14 April 1938), poet, was born at Bilston, Staffordshire, where his father was vicar, and educated at Clifton College and Corpus Christi, Oxford. Called to the Bar at Lincoln's Inn in 1887, he practised law for 12 years, and contributed extensively to the *Law Digest*. His first book, *Taken from the Enemy*, a story of the Napoleonic wars, appeared in 1892, and *Mordred*, a tragedy in blank verse, in 1895, but what made him famous was the poem 'Drake's Drum,' which was printed in *St James's Gazette* in 1896. *Admirals All*, a collection of verse including it, was followed by others of the same spirited type, *The Island Race* (1898), and *Songs of the Sea* (1904). In 1911 he was appointed Professor of Poetry in the Royal Society of Literature, and after the First World War he became official historian of its naval side. He was knighted in 1915, appointed a Companion of Honour in 1922, and received honorary degrees from Oxford, St Andrews, Glasgow, Bristol, Sheffield, and Toronto.

Newcastle, Margaret Cavendish, Duchess of (1624?—7 Jan. 1674), daughter of Sir Thomas Lucas, and a maid of honour to Queen Henrietta Maria, married in 1645 the 1st Duke of Newcastle (then Marquis), whom she regarded in adversity and prosperity with a singular and almost fantastic devotion, which was fully reciprocated. The noble pair collaborated (the Duchess contributing by far the larger share) in their literary ventures, which filled 12 volumes, and consisted chiefly of dramas (now almost unreadable), and philosophical disquisitions. One of her poems, *The Pastimes and Recreations of the Queen of Fairies in Fairyland*, has some good lines. Her life of her husband, in which she rates him above Julius Caesar, was said by Lamb to be 'a jewel for which no casket was good enough.'

Newell, Robert Henry (13 Dec. 1836—July 1901), poet and humorist, was born in New York, son of an inventor. In 1858 he became assistant editor of the New York *Sunday Mercury*. The outbreak of the Civil War was the occasion of the famous *Orpheus C. Kerr Papers*; the name was a garbled pun on 'office seeker,' a type then much in evidence, and the poems had the broad humour, gross misspelling and irreverence for all humbug, which the contemporary Artemus Ward and Mark Twain made popular. After various other journalistic appointments, Newell had to give up active employment in 1876. In 1870 he published *The Cloven Foot*, one of the many attempts to complete Dickens's unfinished *Edwin Drood*.

Newman, Francis William (27 June 1805—4 Oct. 1897), scholar and theological writer, brother of J. H. Newman (q.v.), was born in London and educated at Oxford, where he took a Double First in Classics and Mathematics. After spending three years in the East, he became successively classical tutor in Bristol College, Professor of Classical Literature in Manchester New College (1840), and Professor of Latin in University College, London, (1846—69). Both brought up under evangelical influences, the two brothers moved from that standpoint in diametrically opposite directions, Francis through eclecticism towards scepticism. His writings include a *History of the Hebrew Monarchy* (1847), *The Soul* (1849), and his most famous book, *Phases of Faith* (1850), a theological autobiography corresponding to his brother's *Apologia*; the publication of this led to much controversy, and to the appearance of Henry Rogers's *Eclipse of Faith*. He also published *Miscellanea* in four volumes, a dictionary of modern Arabic, and some mathematical treatises. He was a vegetarian, a total abstainer, and enemy of tobacco, vaccination, and vivisection.

Newman, John Henry (21 Feb. 1801—11 Aug. 1890), Cardinal, son of a London banker, and brother of the above, was educated at Ealing and Trinity College, Oxford, where he was the intimate friend of Pusey and Hurrell Froude. Taking orders he was successively curate of St Clement's 1824, and Vicar of St Mary's, Oxford, 1828. He was also Vice-principal of Alban Hall, where he assisted Whately, the Principal, in his *Logic*. In 1830 he definitely broke with the evangelicalism in which he had been brought up; and in 1832, accompanied by H. Froude, went to the South of Europe, and visited Rome. During this extended tour he wrote most of his short poems, including 'Lead Kindly Light,' which were published in 1834 as *Lyra Apostolica*. On his return he joined with Pusey, Keble, and others in initiating the Tractarian movement, and contributed some of the more important tracts, including the fateful No. XC, the publication of which brought about a crisis in the movement, which, after two years of hesitation and mental and spiritual conflict, led to the resignation by Newman of his benefice. In 1842 he retired to Littlemore, and after a period of prayer, fasting, and seclusion, was in 1845 received into the Roman Catholic Church. In the following year he went to Rome, where he was ordained priest and made D.D., and returning to England he established the oratory in Birmingham in 1847, and that in London in 1850. From 1854 to 1858 he was rector of Dublin Catholic University. A controversy with C. Kingsley, who had written that Newman 'did not consider truth a necessary virtue,' led to the publication of his *Apologia pro Vita Sua* (1864), one of the most remarkable books of religious autobiography ever written. Newman's later years were passed at the oratory at Birmingham. In 1879 he was summoned to Rome and created Cardinal of St George in Velabro. Besides the works above mentioned he wrote, among others, *The Arians of the Fourth Century*

(1833), *Romanism and Popular Protestantism* (1837), *Twelve Lectures* (1850), *Lectures on the Present Position of Catholics* (1851), *Idea of a University* (1852), and his poem, *The Dream of Gerontius* (1866). His collected works in 36 volumes were published 1868—81. Possessed of one of the most keen and subtle intellects of his age, Newman was also master of a style of marvellous beauty and power; to many minds, however, his subtlety not seldom appeared to pass into sophistry. His sermons place him in the first rank of English preachers.

Newton, Sir Isaac (25 Dec. 1642—20 March 1727), mathematician and scientist, was born at Woolsthorpe, Lincolnshire, the son of a small landed proprietor, and educated at the Grammar School of Grantham and at Trinity College, Cambridge. By propounding the binomial theorem, the differential calculus, and the integral calculus, he began in 1665 the wonderful series of discoveries in pure mathematics, optics, and physics, which place him in the first rank of the scientists of all time. He was elected Lucasian Professor of Mathematics at Cambridge in 1669, and in 1672 a Fellow of the Royal Society, over which body he presided for 25 years from 1703. In the same year his new theory of light was published in a paper before the society. His epoch-making discovery of the law of universal gravitation was not promulgated until 1687, though the first glimpse of it had come to him as early as 1665. The discovery of fluxions, which he claimed, was contested by Leibnitz, and led to a long and bitter controversy between the two savants. He twice sat in Parliament for his university, and was Master of the Mint from 1699, in which capacity he presented reports on the coinage. He was knighted in 1705. His writings fall into two classes, scientific and theological. In the first are included his famous treatises, *Light and Colours* (1672), *Optics* (1704), the *Principia* (1687), in Latin, its full title being *Philosophiae Naturalis Principia Mathematica*. In the second are his *Observations upon the Prophecies of Holy Writ* and *An Historical Account of Two Notable Corruptions of Scripture*. In character Newton was remarkable for simplicity, humility, and gentleness, with a great distaste for controversy, in which, nevertheless, he was repeatedly involved.

Newton, John (24 July 1725—21 Dec. 1807), clergyman and hymn-writer, son of a shipmaster, was born in London, and for many years led a varied and adventurous life at sea, part of the time on board a man-of-war and part as captain of a slaver. In 1748 he began to have strong religious convictions; he applied for orders in 1758, and was ordained curate of Olney in 1764. Here he became the intimate friend of Cowper, in conjunction with whom he produced the *Olney Hymns*. In 1779 he was translated to the Rectory of St Mary, Woolnoth, London, where he had great popularity and influence, and wrote many religious works, including *Cardiphonia, or the Utterance of the Heart* (1781). *An Authentic Narrative* of his early life appeared in 1764. He lives, however, in his hymns, among which are some of the best and most widely known in the language, such as 'Glorious things of Thee are Spoken,' 'How Sweet the Name of Jesus sounds,' and many others. In his latter years he was blind.

Nichol, John (8 Sept. 1833—1894), author, was the son of the Professor of Astronomy at Glasgow. He was educated at Glasgow University and Balliol College, Oxford, where he was president of the Old Mortality Club, to which belonged T. H. Green the philosopher, Bryce the historian, and the poet Swinburne. He was the first Professor of English Literature at Glasgow (1862—89). Among his writings are *Hannibal* (1873), a drama, *Death of Themistocles and other Poems* (1881), *Fragments of Criticism*, and *American Literature*; also lives of Bacon, Burns, Carlyle, and Byron.

Nichols, Anne (   ), actress and playwright, born in the United States, was famous for her play *Abie's Irish Rose*, which ran in New York from 1922 to 1927 for 2,327 performances, a record up to that time which has only twice been surpassed since. Others of her plays were *The Gilded Cage* (1920), *Love Dreams* (1921), and (in collaboration with Adelaide Matthews) *Just Married* (1921).

Nichols, John Beverley (9 Sept. 1898—   ), author and journalist, was born in Bristol, son of a solicitor, and educated at Marlborough and Oxford, where he edited the *Isis*, founded and edited the *Oxford Outlook*, was President of the Union, and published his first novel. Thereafter he combined writing with travel, and gained a reputation as a brilliant and unorthodox interviewer. To this period belong *Are They the Same at Home?* (1927), *The Star Spangled Manner* (1928), *Oxford-London-Hollywood* (1931), and his own autobiography, written when he was 25. Later he settled in Huntingdonshire, where he wrote *Down the Garden Path* (1932). His weekly column was a popular feature of the *Sunday Chronicle* for many years. He also wrote plays, including *The Stag* (1929), *Dr Mesmer* (1935), and *Shadow of the Vine* (1949); and some detective stories. *All I Could Never Be* (1949) is a continuation of his autobiography.

Nichols, Robert Malise Bowyer (16 Sept. 1893—17 Dec. 1944), poet, born at Shanklin, Isle of Wight, was educated at Winchester, and after one year at Oxford became a 2nd lieutenant in the Royal Field Artillery and served on the Western front. From 1921 to 1924 he was Profesor of English at the Imperial University, Tokio. After his marriage in 1922 he lived in Holywood for a time and worked on films with Douglas Fairbanks senior. Later he returned to England and settled at Winchelsea. His volumes of poems included *Invocations* (1915), *Ardours and Endurances* (1917), *Fisbo* (1934), and *Such was my Singing* (1942). He also wrote a play, *Guilty Souls* (1921).

Nicholson, Norman Cornthwaite (1914—   ), author, was born at Millom, Cumberland. His first book of verse, *Five Rivers*, appeared in 1944 and was succeeded by *Rock Face* (1948) and *The Pot Geranium* (1954). His play *The Old Man of the Mountains* (1945) tells the story of Elijah and the ravens in a lakeland setting, while *A Match for the Devil* (1953) is about the prophet Hosea.

The Fire of the Lord (1944) and *The Green Shore* (1947) are novels. He also wrote studies of H. G. Wells (1950), and Cowper (1951), and edited a selection of Wordsworth's poems with a critical introduction.

Nicoll, John Ramsay Allardyce (28 June 1894—   ), literary historian, educated at Stirling High School and Glasgow University, became lecturer and then Professor of English Language and Literature at King's College, London. After holding the Chair of Drama and Dramatic Criticism at Yale for a time he became Professor of English at Birmingham in 1945. A leading authority on the development of the drama, he wrote histories of *Restoration Drama* (1923), *Eighteenth Century Drama* (1925), *Late Eighteenth Century Drama* (1927), *Early Nineteenth Century Drama* (1930), and *Late Nineteenth Century Drama* (1939), as well as biographies of Blake (1922) and Dryden (1923). He also edited the annual *Shakespeare Survey* from its inception in 1948.

Nicoll, Sir William Robertson (10 Oct. 1851—4 May 1923), minister and journalist, was born at Lumsden in Aberdeenshire and educated at Aberdeen Grammar School and University, taking his M.A. in 1870. He then studied theology at the Free Church Divinity Hall, obtained his first charge at Dufftown in 1874, and moved in 1877 to Kelso, where he made a great reputation as a preacher. In 1885 ill health compelled him to resign and move south to London, where he became editor of the *Expositor*, a monthly theological magazine. From 1886 till his death he edited the *British Weekly*, and established it as one of the leading periodicals. In 1891 he founded the *Bookman*, a literary monthly, and in 1893 the *Woman at Home*, a women's magazine. Collections of his own contributions were published as *The Daybook of Claudius Clear* (his adopted pseudonym), and *A Bookman's Letters* (1913). From 1900 onwards he took a vigorous part in politics, supporting the Liberal cause. He was knighted in 1909 and made a Companion of Honour in 1921.

Nicolson, Adela Florence (4 April 1865—4 Oct. 1904), poetess, was born at Stoke Bishop, Gloucestershire, daughter of Arthur Cory, a colonel in the Indian army. She joined her parents in India and married Colonel Malcolm H. Nicolson of the Bengal Army, who was aide-de-camp to Queen Victoria from 1891 to 1894. In 1901 she published a volume of passionate poems with an Eastern setting, entitled *The Garden of Karma*, under the pseudonym Laurence Hope. Pieces from it, such as 'Pale hands I loved beside the Shalamar' became extremely popular as songs. General Nicolson died in Madras in 1904 and two months later his grief-stricken wife poisoned herself. Two more volumes of her verse were published after her death, *Stars of the Desert* and *Indian Love*.

Nicolson, Hon. Sir Harold George (21 Nov. 1886—   ), diplomat and author, was born at Teheran, where his father, afterwards Baron Carnock, was *chargé d'affaires*, and educated at Wellington College and Oxford. In 1909 he joined the Diplomatic Service and held posts at Madrid, Istanbul, Teheran, and Berlin. In 1929 he resigned, took up journalism, and joined the staff of the *Daily Express*. From 1935 to 1945 he sat as National Labour M.P. for

West Leicester, being part of the time Parliamentary Secretary to the Ministry of Information. In 1913 he married Victoria Sackville-West, the novelist. His works include a number of biographies—*Tennyson* (1923), *Byron, The Last Journey* (1924), *Swinburne* (1926), *Curzon: The Last Phase* (1934), *King George V* (1953)—and some political studies, such as *Peacemaking, 1919* (1933) and *Why Britain is at War* (1939). *The English Sense of Humour*, an essay, appeared in 1946. He was knighted in 1953.

Noel, Hon. Roden Berkeley Wriothesley (27 Aug. 1834—26 May 1894), poet, son of the 1st Earl of Gainsborough, was educated at Cambridge. He wrote *Behind the Veil* (1863), *Songs of the Heights and Deeps* (1885), and *Essays* on various poets, also a life of Byron. From 1867 to 1871 he was groom of the privy chamber to Queen Victoria.

Norden, Charles, *see* Durrell, Lawrence.

Norris, Frank (5 March 1870—25 Oct. 1902), novelist, was born in Chicago, son of a jeweller, and christened Benjamin Franklin Norris; later the family moved to San Francisco. In 1887 he studied art in London and Paris, then spent some time studying at the University of California and at Harvard. In 1895 he went to South Africa as a newspaper correspondent, and after that was a journalist in San Francisco and New York. In 1899 he published *McTeague*, a grim Zolaesque novel about the more sordid parts of San Francisco. He then planned a trilogy on the subject of wheat; *The Octopus* (1901) deals with its production, *The Pit* (1903) with the speculation that accompanies its marketing, and *The Wolf* was to have described the consumption of the bread in a famine-stricken village. But before he could complete this or another trilogy he had planned on Gettysburg, Norris succumbed to an attack of appendicitis at the age of 32. Others of his novels are *Moran of the Lady Letty* (1898), *Blix* (1899), *A Man's Woman* (1900), and *Vandover and the Brute* (1914). *A Deal in Wheat* (1903) and *The Third Circle* (1909) are collections of short stories, and *Responsibilities of the Novelist* (1903) is a book of essays.

Norris, John (1657—1711), philosopher and poet, was educated at Oxford, where he became a Fellow of All Souls. He took orders, and lived a quiet and placid life as a country parson and thinker. In philosophy he was a Platonist and mystic, and was an early opponent of Locke. His poetry, with occasional fine thoughts, is full of far-fetched metaphors and conceits, and is not seldom dull and prosaic. From 1692 he held G. Herbert's benefice of Bemerton. Among his works are *An Idea of Happiness* (1683), *Miscellanies* (1687), *Theory of the Ideal and Intelligible World* (1701—4), and a *Discourse concerning the Immortality of the Soul* (1708).

Norris, Kathleen (16 July 1880—), novelist, was born in San Francisco, daughter of James Alden Thompson, a banker. The unexpected death of both her parents made it necessary for her to start earning her living, and she worked as book-keeper, shop-girl, and teacher. Then she started to write for various San Francisco papers and took some courses at the University of California. In

1909 she married Charles Gilman Norris, brother of Frank Norris (q.v.), and they lived in New York. Her pleasantly sentimental novels include *Mother* (1911), *The Rich Mrs Burgoyne* (1912), *Poor Dear Margaret Kirby* (1912), *Certain People of Importance* (1922), *Barberry Bush* (1926), *Secret Marriage* (1936), *Lost Sunrise* (1939), *The Secret of the Marshbanks* (1940), *The Venables* (1941), *Love Calls the Tune* (1944), *Mink Coat* (1946), *High Holiday* (1949), *Shadow Marriage* (1952), and *Miss Harriet Townshend* (1955). *Noon* (1925) is an autobiography.

North, Christopher, *see* **Wilson, John.**

North, Sir Thomas (1535?—1601?), translator, 2nd son of the 1st Lord North, may have studied at Cambridge. He entered Lincoln's Inn in 1557, but gave more attention to literature than to law. He is best known by his translation of Plutarch's *Lives*, from the French of Amyot, in fine, forcible, idiomatic English, which was the repertory from which Shakespeare drew his knowledge of ancient history: in *Antony and Cleopatra* and *Coriolanus* North's language is often closely followed. Another translation was from an Italian version of an Arabic book of fables, and bore the title of *The Morale Philosophie of Doni*.

Norton, Caroline Elizabeth Sarah (1808—15 June 1877), authoress, was a grand-daughter of R. B. Sheridan (q.v.) and a sister of Lady Dufferin (q.v.). In 1827 she married the Hon. G. C. Norton, a union which turned out most unhappy, and ended in a separation. Her first book of poetry, *The Sorrows of Rosalie* (1829), was followed by *The Undying One* (1830), a romance founded upon the legend of the Wandering Jew. Among her novels were *Stuart of Dunleath* (1851), *Lost and Saved* (1863), and *Old Sir Douglas* (1867). The unhappiness of her married life led her to interest herself in the amelioration of. the laws regarding the social condition and the separate property of women and the wrongs of children, and her poems, *A Voice from the Factories* (1836), and *The Child of the Islands* (1845), had as an object the furtherance of her views on these subjects. Her efforts were largely successful in bringing about the needed legislation. In 1877 she married Sir W. Stirling-Maxwell, (q.v.).

Norton, Charles Eliot (16 Nov. 1827—21 Oct. 1908), Professor of the History of Art at Harvard (1875—1898), wrote *Church Building in the Middle Ages* (1876), translated Dante (1891), and edited the *Correspondence of Carlyle and Emerson* (1883), and *Carlyle's Letters and Reminiscences* (1887).

Norton, Thomas (1532—10 March 1583), playwright and poet, was born in London and educated at Cambridge. In 1555 he was entered at the Inner Temple, but devoted himself to literature as well as law and wrote a number of poems. In 1561 he collaborated with Thomas Sackville, Earl of Dorset (q.v.), in *Gorboduc, or Ferrex and Porrex*, usually reckoned the first English tragedy, Norton writing the first three acts and Dorset the other two. He was M.P. successively for Gatton, Berwick, and the City of London, of which he was appointed Remembrancer in 1571.

Novello, Ivor, *see* **Davies, David.**

Norway, Nevil Shute (17 Jan. 1899—12 Jan. 1960), engineer
and novelist who wrote as Nevil Shute, was the son of a post-office
official of Cornish ancestry and was educated at Shrewsbury and
Oxford. During the First World War he served in the Suffolk
Regiment and in the Second he became a lieutenant-commander
R.N.V.R. As an engineer he worked at Howden Airship Works
which made the R 100, and flew on her to Canada in 1924. When
the R 101 disaster put an end to airship construction he became
managing director of an aeroplane factory, and combined that with
writing novels under his two Christian names. His first novel,
Marazan (1926), was followed by *So Disdained* (1928), *Lonely Road*
(1932), and *What Happened to the Corbetts* (1939), which was a
realistic anticipation of the plight of a bombed-out family. Later
he went to Australia and settled at Langwarria, Victoria, and many
of his novels had an Australian setting. They include *Pastoral*
(1944), *No Highway* (1948), *A Town Like Alice* (1950), *The Far
Country* (1952), *In the Wet* (1953), and *The Breaking Wave* (1955).
Slide Rule (1954) is an autobiography.

Norwich, Viscount, *see* **Cooper, Alfred Duff.**

Noyes, Alfred (26 Sept. 1880—28 June 1958), poet, was born
in Wolverhampton, and educated at Exeter College, Oxford, where
he was notable as an oarsman. Encouraged by George Meredith,
he devoted himself to poetry and succeeded in making a livelihood by
it. His first volume, *The Loom of Years*, appeared in 1902, followed
by his popular sea epic *Drake* (1906—8). In 1913 he delivered the
Lowell Lectures in the United States, taking as his subject 'The Sea
in English Poetry,' and from 1914 to 1923 he was Professor of
Modern English Literature at Princeton. In 1918 he received the
C.B.E. Later he returned to England and settled in the Isle of
Wight, and in 1930 he was received into the Roman Catholic Church.
In his command of rhythm and melody Noyes belongs to the school
of Tennyson, the sea and fairyland being his special provinces. His
epics *The Flower of Old Japan* (1903) and *The Forest of Wild Thyme*
(1905) are the finest fairy poetry since the Elizabethans. His most
famous works are *Drake, Tales of the Mermaid Tavern* (1913), and
The Torchbearers (1922—30). A single volume of collected poems
was published in 1950. He also wrote several plays and a book of
critical essays, *Aspects of Modern Poetry* (1924). *Two Worlds for
Memory* (1953) is an autobiography.

O

O'Brien, Kate (3 Dec. 1897—   ), novelist, was born at Limerick and educated at Laurel Hill Convent there and at University College, Dublin. Moving to London, she worked for various newspapers and wrote a play, *Distinguished Villa* (1926), which she followed with *The Bridge* (1927). She then lived for some years in Spain. Her first novel, *Without my Cloak* (1931), was awarded both the Hawthornden Prize and the Tait Black Memorial Prize; its background, the Irish town of Mellick, appears in her other Irish stories, which are all characterized by witty and cultured dialogue. Later novels are *Mary Lavelle* (1936), *Pray for the Wanderer* (1938), *The Land of Spices* (1941), *The Last of Summer* (1943), *That Lady* (1946), and *The Flower of May* (1953). *Farewell Spain* (1937) is a travel book.

O'Casey, Sean (31 March 1884—   ), playwright, was born in Dublin of Protestant parents, and had only about three years schooling. As a boy he worked in a hardware shop for four shillings a week, and at 18 was a labourer. After initial failures, in 1923 he got his plays *The Shadow of a Gunman* and *Cathleen Listens In* produced at the Abbey Theatre. In the following year appeared his best-known play, *Juno and the Paycock*, which was awarded the Hawthornden Prize. After following it with *The Plough and the Stars* (1926), dealing with the Easter Rebellion, in which he himself took part, he came to England, and his play *The Silver Tassie* was produced in London in 1929. Later plays are *Within the Gates* (1934), *The Star Turns Red* (1940), *Purple Dust* (1940), *Red Roses for Me* (1942), *Oak Leaves and Lavender* (1946), *Cock-a-Doodle Dandy* (1949), and *The Bishop's Bonfire* (1955). Tragi-comedies of slum life, his plays are marked by racy dialogue and a shrewd wit. He wrote a lengthy autobiography, of which the six parts are *I Knock at the Door* (1939), *Pictures in the Hallway* (1942), *Drums Under the Window* (1945), *Inishfallen Fare Thee Well* (1949), *Rose and Crown* (1952), and *Sunset and Evening Star* (1954).

Occam *or* **Ockham, William of** (1290?—1349), philosopher, born at Ockham in Surrey and educated at Oxford and Paris, became a Franciscan. He was involved in the quarrel which this Order had with the Pope on the question of the vows of poverty, and was imprisoned at Avignon on a charge of heresy. Escaping, he spent the rest of his life in Munich. Known as 'the invincible doctor,' he was the last of the great schoolmen and one of the foremost medieval thinkers. With his condemnation of philosophic realism went his famous dictum known as Occam's razor, 'Entities are not to be unnecessarily multiplied.'

Occleve *or* **Hoccleve, Thomas** (1370?—1450?), poet, was born probably in London, and lived there in the Strand. At the age of 20 he became a clerk in the Privy Seal Office, and held this post for over 30 years. Pensioned off in 1424, he lived at the Priory of Southwick, Hampshire. His best-known work is *De Regimine Principum*, or *The Regiment of Princes* (1412), written for the Prince of Wales, who later became Henry V; it is an English rendering in rhyme royal of a Latin treatise by Aegisius on the duties of a ruler. It contains an interesting tribute to Chaucer, whose portrait appears in the original manuscript. Occleve also wrote a curious autobiographical poem, *La Male Regle* (1406), which tells of his moderately riotous life. Others of his works are two narrative poems based on tales from the *Gesta Romanorum*, *The Emperor Jereslaus's Wife*, and *Jonathas*; a dignified poem on death, *Ars Sciendi Mori*; and various shorter pieces.

Ockham, William of, *see* Occam.

Ockley, Simon (1678—9 Aug. 1720), scholar and clergyman, born at Exeter and educated at Cambridge, took orders and was vicar of Swavesey in Cambridgeshire. The greatest Orientalist of his day, he was in 1711 appointed Professor of Arabic in his university. His chief work is the *Conquest of Syria, Persia, and Egypt by the Saracens* (three volumes, 1708—57), which was largely used by Gibbon. The original documents upon which it is founded are now regarded as of doubtful authority.

O'Connor, Frank, *see* O'Donovan, Michael.

Odets, Clifford (18 July 1906—   ), playwright, was born in Philadelphia of Lithuanian Jewish parents, but brought up in the Bronx and educated at Morris High School, New York. At 15 he left and became an actor; later he was one of the founders of the Group Theatre. The first of his plays to be produced was *Waiting for Lefty* (1935), a one-act drama based on a New York cab strike. In the same year appeared *Awake and Sing*, a study of a Jewish family, which he had written in 1933. Others of his plays are *Till the Day I Die* (1935), *Golden Boy* (1937), *Rocket to the M on* (1938), *Clash by Night* (1941), *The Big Knife* (1949), *The Country Girl* (1951), *Winter Journey* (1952), and *The Flowering Peach* (1955). At one time he had three plays running on Broadway simultaneously. His work, which was influenced by that of O'Casey (q.v.), shows a command of realistic dialogue.

O'Donovan, Michael (1903—   ), novelist and playwright who wrote under the name Frank O'Connor, was born in Cork, where he was educated at the Christian Brothers School. He worked as a librarian, first in County Cork and then in Dublin, where he was for a time a director of the Abbey Theatre. His greatest success was with short stories, Yeats comparing him to Chekhov. Among his books are *The Saint and Mary Kate* (1932), *Bones of Contention* (1936), *Three Old Brothers* (1937), *Lords and Commons* (1938), *Dutch Interior* (1940), *Crab Apple Jelly* (1944), *The Common Chord* (1947), *Traveller's Samples* (1950), and *The Mirror in the Roadway* (1956). *In the Train* (1937), *Time's Rocket* (1939), and *The Statue's Daughter* (1940) are plays.

O'Faoláin, Seán (22 Feb. 1900—   ), novelist and
biographer, born in Dublin, was educated at the National University
of Ireland and Harvard. He took the Republican side in the civil
conflict of 1922, and was Director of Publicity for the Irish Republican Army. He then became a teacher and in 1929 was Lecturer in
English at Boston College. From 1930 till 1933 he held a similar
post at St Mary's Training College, Strawberry Hill, Middlesex. He
then returned to County Wicklow, and in 1932 his first book, a
collection of short stories entitled *Midsummer Night's Madness*,
appeared. His novels include *A Nest of Simple Folk* (1933), *Bird
Alone* (1936), *A Purse of Coppers* (1937), *Come Back to Erin* (1940),
and *Teresa* (1946). Of his biographies the best is *King of the Beggars:
a Life of Daniel O'Connell* (1938); he also wrote lives of *De Valera*
(1933) and *Constance Markievicz* (1934). He edited the works of
Thomas Moore (1929) and the autobiography of Wolfe Tone (1937).
She Had to Do Something (1938) is a play and *A Summer in Italy*
(1950) and *South to Sicily* (1952) are travel books.

O'Flaherty, Liam (1897—   ), novel-
ist, was born on the Aran Islands off the coast of Galway. Intended
for the priesthood, he went to Roman Catholic schools at Rockwell
and Blackrock and to the National University, Dublin. During
the First World War he enlisted in the Irish Guards and fought in
Belgium, but was invalided out in 1917. For the next few years he
roamed all over the world as deck-hand, porter, clerk, and labourer.
In the civil conflict of 1922 he fought for the Irish Republicans. His
first novel, *Thy Neighbour's Wife*, appeared two years later, and was
followed in 1926 by *The Informer*, which won the Tait Black Prize.
Later novels are *Mr Gilhooley* (1926), *The Assassin* (1928), *The House
of Gold* (1929), *The Puritan* (1931), *The Martyr* (1933), *Famine*
(1937), and *Insurrection* (1950). A master of the short story, in
which he is more poetical and less violent than in the novel, he
published many collections, including *Spring Sowing* (1926), *The
Tent* (1926), *The Fairy Goose* (1929), *The Mountain Tavern* (1929),
and *The Wild Swan* (1932). He also wrote a *Life of Tim Healy*
(1927) and *A Guide to Ireland* (1929). *Darkness* (1926) is a tragedy,
and *Two Years* (1930) and *Shame the Devil* (1934) are autobiographical.

Ogilvy, Gavin, *see* **Barrie, Sir James.**

O'Grady, Standish James (18 Sept. 1846—18 May 1928), historian,
was born at Castletown Berehaven, County Cork, son of a Protestant
clergyman, and was educated at Tipperary Grammar School and
Trinity College, Dublin, where he excelled in debating and sport. He
was called to the Irish Bar in 1872, but turned from law to writing,
and produced a *History of Ireland* in two volumes (1878—81) which
had a strong influence on the Celtic Revival, for it popularized Irish
legends, though its author did not know the Irish language. Others
of his works are *Early Bardic Literature of Ireland* (1879), *Finn and
his Companions* (1892), *The Bog of Stars* (1893), *The Coming of
Cuchulain* (1894), *The Chain of Gold* (1895), *The Flight of the Eagle*

(1897), *The Departure of Dermot* (1917), and *The Triumph and Passing of Cuchulain* (1919).

O'Hara, John Henry (31 Jan. 1905—   ), novelist, was born at Pottsville, Pennsylvania, son of a doctor. His father's death prevented him from going to Yale as planned, and after working on a great variety of jobs, as steward, goods checker, labourer, soda clerk, and secretary, he became a reporter, and moved about among various papers. His first novel, *Appointment in Samarra* (1934) was followed by *Butterfield 8* (1935), *Hope of Heaven* (1938), *A Rage to Live* (1949), and *The Farmer's Hotel* (1951). His best work is in his short stories, collections of which include *The Doctor's Son* (1935), *Files on Parade* (1939), *Pipe Night* (1945), and *Hellbox* (1947). Terse and hard-boiled rather in the manner of Hemingway, he has been called 'the voice of the hang-over generation.'

O'Keefe, John (24 June 1747—4 Feb. 1833), dramatist, born in Dublin, studied art but turned to the stage. He wrote a number of farces and dramatic pieces, many of which had great success. Among these are *Tony Lumpkin in Town* (1778), based on Goldsmith's *She Stoops to Conquer* (q.v.), *Love in a Camp* (1786), and *Wild Oats* (1791). Some of his songs, such as 'I am a Friar of Orders Grey' were very popular. He was blind from about 1797. His *Recollections* were published in 1826.

Oldham, John (9 Aug. 1653—9 Dec. 1683), poet, born at Shipton-Moyne in Gloucestershire, son of a minister, was at Oxford, and was the friend of most of the literary men of his time, by whom his early death from smallpox was deplored. He made clever adaptations of the classical satirists, wrote an ironical *Satire against Virtue* (1679), and four severe satires against the Jesuits. He is cynical to the verge of misanthropy, but independent and manly.

Oldmixon, John (1673—9 July 1742), historian, belonged to an old Somersetshire family, wrote some now forgotten dramas and poems which, along with an essay on criticism, in which he attacked Addison, Swift, and Pope, earned for him a place in *The Dunciad*. He was also the author of *The British Empire in America* (1708), *Secret History of Europe* (1712—15), and in his *Critical History* (1724—6) attacked Clarendon's *History of the Rebellion*. All these works are partisan in their tone. Oldmixon was one of the most prolific pamphleteers of his day.

Oldys, William (14 July 1696—15 April 1761), antiquary, born probably in London, the illegitimate son of a lawyer, wrote a *Dissertation on Pamphlets* (1731), a life of Sir W. Ralegh prefixed to an edition of his works (1736), and was joint editor with Dr Johnson of the *Harleian Miscellany*. He amassed many interesting facts in literary history, the fruits of diligent, though obscure, industry. The only poem of his that still lives is the beautiful little anacreontic beginning 'Busy, curious, thirsty Fly.' In 1755 he was appointed to the office of Norroy-King-at-Arms. He produced in 1737 *The British Librarian*, a valuable work left unfinished.

Oliphant, Laurence (1829—23 Dec. 1888), journalist and travel writer, born at Cape Town, where his father, Sir Anthony Oliphant, was Attorney-General, studied law and was called to the Bar. The first 38 years of his life were spent in desultory study, travel, and adventure, varied by occasional diplomatic employment. His travels included, besides Continental countries, the shores of the Black Sea, Circassia, America, China, and Japan. He was in the Crimean War, Indian Mutiny, Chinese War, the military operations of Garibaldi, and the Polish insurrection, and served as private secretary to Lord Elgin in Washington, Canada, and China, and as Secretary of Legation in Japan. In 1865 he was elected to Parliament for Stirling Burghs, and gave promise of political eminence, when in 1867 he came under the influence of Thomas L. Harris, an American mystic of questionable character, went with him to America, and joined the Brotherhood of the New Life. In 1870 he was correspondent for *The Times* in the Franco-German War. Ultimately he broke away from the influence of Harris and went to Palestine, where he founded a community of Jewish immigrants at Haifa. After revisiting America he returned to England, but immediately fell ill and died at Twickenham. Oliphant was a voluminous and versatile author, publishing books of travel, novels, and works on mysticism. The most important are *Journey to Khatmandu* (1852), *The Russian Shores of the Black Sea* (1853), *Minnesota and the Far West* (1855), *The Transcaucasian Campaign* (1856), *Patriots and Fillibusters* (adventures in Southern States) (1860), *Narrative of a Mission to China and Japan* (1857—9), *The Land of Gilead* (1880), *Piccadilly: a Fragment of a Contemporary Biography* (1870). *Altiora Peto* (1883) is a novel, *Scientific Religion* (1888) embodies his later mystical views, and *Episodes in a Life of Adventure* (1887) is autobiographical. His life was written by his cousin Margaret Oliphant (q.v.).

Oliphant, Margaret Oliphant (4 April 1828—25 June 1897), novelist and biographer, was born at Wallyford, near Musselburgh, daughter of Francis Wilson. In 1857 she married her cousin, Francis Wilson Oliphant, an artist. Her literary output began when she was little more than a girl, and was continued almost up to the end of her life. Her first novel, *Mrs Margaret Maitland*, appeared in 1849, and its humour, pathos, and insight into character gave the author an immediate position in literature. It was followed by an endless succession, of which the best were the series of *The Chronicles of Carlingford* (1861—5), including *Salem Chapel*, *The Perpetual Curate*, and *Miss Marjoribanks*, all of which, as well as much of her other work, appeared in *Blackwood's Magazine*, with which she had a lifelong connection. In addition to her novels of Scottish life, such as *The Minister's Wife* (1869), *Effie Ogilvie* (1886) and *Kirsteen* (1890), she wrote some tales of the unseen world, *A Beleaguered City* (1880), and *A Little Pilgrim in the Unseen* (1882). She did not, however, confine herself to fiction, but wrote many books of history and biography, including *Sketches of the Reign of George II* (1869), *The Makers of Florence* (1876), *Literary History of England 1790—1825* (1882), *Royal Edinburgh* (1890), and lives of *St Francis of Assisi*,

Edward Irving, Principal Tulloch, and her cousin *Laurence Oliphant* (q.v.). Her generosity in supporting and educating the family of a brother as well as her own two sons rendered necessary a rate of production which was fatal to the permanence of her work. She was negligent as to style, and often wrote on subjects to which her intellectual equipment and knowledge did not enable her to do proper justice. She had, however, considerable power of painting character, and a vein of humour, and showed untiring industry in amassing facts.

Oliver, George, *see* Onions, Oliver.

Oman, Carola Mary Anima (11 May 1897—), biographer and novelist, daughter of Sir Charles Oman (q.v.), was born at Oxford and educated at Wychwood School. During the First World War she was a nurse in France, and in 1922 she married Sir Gerald Lenanton. She is best known for her historical biographies, especially *Nelson* (1947), which won the *Sunday Times* Prize for English Literature, and *Sir John Moore* (1953), which was awarded the Tait Black Memorial Prize; others are *Prince Charles Edward* (1935) and *Henrietta Maria* (1936). She also wrote a number of historical novels, including *The Road Royal* (1924), *Princess Amelia* (1924), *Crouchback* (1929), *The Empress* (1932), *The Best of his Family* (1933), and *Over the Water* (1935). With these may be grouped her excellent children's books *Alfred, King of the English* (1939) and *Robin Hood* (1949). Among her novels of modern times are *The Holiday* (1928), *Fair Stood the Wind* (1930), *Nothing to Report* (1940), and *Somewhere in England* (1943). *The Menin Road* (1919) is a volume of poems.

Oman, Sir Charles William Chadwick (12 Jan. 1860—23 June 1946), historian, was born at Mozufferpore, India, son of a planter, and educated at Winchester and New College, Oxford. In 1883 he was elected a Fellow of All Souls, and in 1905 became Chichele Professor of Modern History at Oxford. He was a leading authority on military history, and his great work *The Art of War in the Middle Ages* appeared in 1898, to be followed later by *The Art of War in the Sixteenth Century* (1937). Others of his works are *Warwick the King-Maker* (1891), *A Short History of England* (1895), *A History of the Peninsular War* (1902—14), *Wellington's Army* (1912), and *Napoleonic Studies* (1929). *Things I Have Seen* (1933) and *Memories of Victorian Oxford* (1941) are books of reminiscences. M.P. for Oxford University from 1919 to 1935, he was knighted in 1920.

O'Neill, Eugene Gladstone (16 Oct. 1888—27 Nov. 1953), dramatist, was born in New York, son of a well-known actor; both his parents were Roman Catholics, and he was educated at Catholic boarding-schools and Princeton. After working variously in a mail-order firm, as a gold prospector in Honduras, and as a seaman, he took minor parts for a time in his father's company, then became a reporter. In 1914 he took a course in George Baker's '47 Workshop' at Harvard. His one-act play, *Bound East for Cardiff* (1916) was produced by the Provincetown Players; it and his next, *The Moon of the Caribbees* (1919) were drawn from his sea experiences. With his first full-length play, *Beyond the Horizon* (1919), he became accepted as America's leading playwright and was awarded the Pulitzer Prize, which later was also awarded for *Anna Christie* (1922) and *Strange Interlude* (1928). Others of his dramas are *The Emperor Jones* (1921), *The Hairy Ape* (1922), *All God's Chillun Got Wings* (1924), *The Great God Brown* (1925), *Desire Under the Elms* (1925), *Lazarus Laughed* (1926), and the trilogy *Mourning Becomes Electra* (1931). From 1934 to 1936 he worked on a series of dramas on a family's history, but this was not produced. Later plays are *The Iceman Cometh* (1946) and *A Moon for the Misbegotten* (1947). He left an autobiographical drama, *Long Day's Journey into Night*, which was produced after his death and won the Pulitzer Prize, making O'Neill's fourth award, a record for a playwright. Though many of his plays showed novel devices, the main theme of his serious work is the fundamental relation of man and fate. Among many other distinctions he was awarded the Nobel Prize in 1936. He was married three times, and his daughter Oona married Charles Chaplin the film comedian.

Onions, George Oliver (1873—9 April 1961), novelist, born at Bradford, changed his name in later life to George Oliver, but always wrote under his original one. He studied art in London and Paris, and worked for a time as illustrator and designer; in later years he designed his own book jackets. His first book was *The Compleat Bachelor* (1901), but his first real success was with the trilogy of novels *In Accordance with the Evidence* (1912), *The Debit Account* (1913), and *The Story of Louie* (1913). Others are *Good Boy Seldom* (1911), *Mushroom Town* (1914), *The New Moon* (1918), *A Case in Camera* (1920), *The Open Secret* (1930), *Cockcrow* (1940), *The Story of Ragged Robin* (1945), *Poor Man's Tapestry* (1946), which was awarded the Tait Black Memorial Prize, *Arras of Youth* (1949), and *Bells Rung Backwards* (1953). He also wrote highly effective ghost stories, collected in *Widdershins* (1911), *Ghosts in Daylight* (1924), and *The Painted Face* (1929). He married Berta Ruck, the novelist (q.v.).

Opie, Amelia (12 Nov. 1769—2 Dec. 1853), novelist, was born at Norwich, daughter of James Alderson, a doctor. In 1798 she married John Opie, the painter. Her first acknowledged work was *Father and Daughter* (1801), which had a favourable reception, and was followed by *Adeline Mowbray* (1804), *Temper* (1812), *Tales from Real Life* (1813), and others, all having the same aim of developing the virtuous affections, the same merit of natural and vivid painting of character and passions, and the same fault of a too great preponderance of the pathetic. They were soon superseded by the more powerful genius of Scott and Miss Edgeworth. In 1825 she became a Quaker. After this she wrote *Illustrations of Lying* (1825), and *Detraction Displayed* (1828). Her later years were largely devoted to philanthropic interests.

Oppenheim, Edward Phillips (1866—3 Feb. 1946), novelist, was born in London, son of a leather merchant, and educated at Wyggeston School, Leicester. He went into his father's business, but wrote in the evenings after hours. In 1890 he married an American, Elise

Hopkins, of Boston. *The Mysterious Mr Sabin* (1901) began his long series of romantic mysteries about secret international documents, shifty diplomats, and seductive adventuresses. Well over a hundred novels were compounded with this heady and popular mixture. Some of the more striking titles are *A Prince of Sinners* (1903), *Anna the Adventuress* (1904), *A Maker of History* (1906), *The Illustrious Prince* (1910), *Mr Grex of Monte Carlo* (1915), *The Great Impersonation* (1920), *The Mystery Road* (1924), *The Ostrakoff Jewels* (1932), and *Envoy Extraordinary* (1937). *The Pool of Memory* (1941) is an autobiography.

Orczy, Emmuska *or* **Emma Magdalena Rosalia Marie Josepha Barbara, Baroness** (23 Sept. 1865—12 Nov. 1947), novelist, was born at Tarnaörs, Hungary. Her father, Baron Felix Orczy, was a gifted composer of music, and as a child she met Wagner, Gounod, and Liszt. Although she knew no English till she was 15, all her books are in that language. Educated in Brussels and Paris, she studied art in London, where she met and married Montagu Barstow, and had some of her paintings hung in the Royal Academy. After writing many magazine stories she scored a striking success in 1905 with *The Scarlet Pimpernel*, a novel about an Englishman, Sir Percy Blakeney, who eludes and bamboozles the murderous emissaries of the French Revolution. It was dramatized successfully and had many sequels, from *The Elusive Pimpernel* (1908) to *The Scarlet Pimpernel Looks at the World* (1934). Other adventurous romances are *Beau Brocade* (1908) and *The Laughing Cavalier* (1914). She also published three volumes of good detective stories, *The Old Man in the Corner* (1909) with its sequel *Unravelled Knots* (1925), and *Lady Molly of Scotland Yard* (1910). *Links in the Chain of Life* (1947) is an autobiography.

Ordericus Vitalis (16 Feb. 1075—1142?), chronicler, was born at Shrewsbury, son of a French priest, and became a monk of the Abbey of St Evroul in Normandy. He wrote in Latin an *Ecclesiastical History of England and Normandy* which comes down to 1141 and gives a reliable though somewhat indistinct account of events in these countries.

O'Reilly, John Boyle (28 June 1844—10 Aug. 1890), journalist and poet, was born at Dowth Castle, near Drogheda, son of a schoolmaster, and at 11 was apprenticed as a newspaper compositor. Becoming a member of the Fenians, he had an adventurous life. In 1863 he enlisted in the 10th Hussars in order to spread sedition among them. He was detected and sentenced to death, but this was commuted to 20 years' penal servitude, and he was sent to Western Australia in 1868. In the following year he escaped to the United States on an American whaler, and went into journalism, becoming editor of the Boston *Pilot* in 1874. His volumes of verse include *Songs from the Southern Seas* (1874), *Songs, Legends, and Ballads* (1878), and *The Statues in the Block* (1881). His novel *Moondyne* (1870), a story of Australian convict life, went through 12 editions.

Orford, Earl of, *see* **Walpole, Horatio.**

O'Riordan, Conal Holmes O'Connell (29 April 1874—18 June 1948), novelist and playwright who used the pseudonym F. Norreys Connell in his earlier work, was born in Dublin, son of a barrister, and educated at Jesuit schools. He planned an army career, but had to give this up when injured by a fall from a horse; nevertheless during the First World War he was at the front as a Y.M.C.A. official. His first book was *In the Green Park* (1894), but his first real success was *The Fool and his Heart* (1896), which was followed by *The Nigger Knights* (1900), *Adam of Dublin* (1920) with its sequels *Adam and Caroline* (1921) and *Married Life* (1924), *Rowena Barnes* (1923), *Soldier Born* (1927), *Soldier of Waterloo* (1928), *Soldier's End* (1938), and *Judith Quinn* (1939). He succeeded J. M. Synge as director of the Abbey Theatre from 1909 to 1915, but his plays are not in the usual Abbey tradition. They include *Rope Enough* (1913), *His Majesty's Pleasure* (1925), and *The King's Wooing* (1929). From 1933 to 1934 he was Shute Lecturer on the Art of the Theatre at Liverpool University.

Orm *or* **Ormin** (thirteenth century), poet, lived probably in the eastern part of England. He was an Augustinian canon and wrote a poem named after him the *Ormulum*, which consists of a series of metrical homilies, based on the Gospel reading for each day, and runs to some 10,000 fifteen-syllable lines which have neither rhyme nor alliteration. As a poem the work is worthless, but it has a special interest from its use of a partly phonetic spelling of the author's devising, which provides valuable data for the philologist.

Orme, Robert (25 Dec. 1728—13 Jan. 1801), historian, born at Anjengo, in Travancore, son of an army doctor, was educated at Harrow and entered the service of the East India Company. Owing to failure of health he had to return home in 1760, and then wrote his *History of the Military Transactions of the British Nation in Indostan from 1745* (1763—78), a well-written and accurate work, showing great research. He also published *Historical Fragments of the Mogul Empire, the Morattoes, and English Concerns in Indostan from 1659* (1782). His collections relating to India are preserved at the India Office.

Ormin, *see* **Orm.**

Orrery, Roger Boyle, 1st Earl of (25 April 1621—16 Oct. 1679), statesman and author, son of the Earl of Cork, was born at Lismore and educated at Trinity College, Dublin. After having fought on the Royalist side he was, on the death of the King, induced by Cromwell to support him in his Irish wars and otherwise. After the death of the Protector he secured Ireland for Charles II, and at the Restoration was raised to the peerage. He wrote a romance in six volumes, entitled *Parthenissa* (1654), some plays, and a treatise on the *Art of War* (1677). He was one of the first to write tragedies in heroic couplets.

Orwell, *see* **Smith, Walter C.**

Orwell, George, *see* **Blair, Eric.**

Osborne, Dorothy (born 1627, buried 7 Feb. 1695), letter-writer, born at Chicksands, Bedfordshire, was a daughter of Sir Peter Osborne and niece of Francis Osborne, the writer. In 1648 she met Sir William Temple (q.v.) in France; they fell in love and carried on a courtship, mainly by correspondence, for seven years. Her love letters are celebrated as among the most exquisite of their kind, and have earned her a place in English literature by their tenderness of feeling and their prose style. After their marriage in 1655 she was a great help to her husband in his political schemes. A friend of Queen Mary II, she was buried in Westminster Abbey.

O'Shaughnessy, Arthur William Edgar (14 March 1844—30 Jan. 1881), poet, born in London and educated privately, became a junior assistant in the library of the British Museum, afterwards being transferred to the natural history department, where he became an authority on fishes and reptiles. He published various books of poetry, including *Epic of Women* (1870), *Lays of France* (1872), and *Music and Moonlight* (1874). Jointly with his wife he wrote *Toyland*, a book for children. He was associated with D. G. Rossetti and the other pre-Raphaelites. There is a certain remoteness in his poetry which will probably always prevent its being widely popular. He has a wonderful mastery of metre, and a haunting music all his own.

Ossian, *see* Macpherson, James.

O'Sullivan, Seumas, *see* Starkey, James Sullivan.

Otway, Caesar (1780—16 March 1842), travel writer, born in County Tipperary and educated at Trinity College, Dublin, took orders, and became one of Dublin's leading preachers. His writings, which display humour and sympathy with the poorer classes in Ireland, include *Sketches in Ireland* (1827), and *A Tour in Connaught* (1839). He was concerned in the establishment of various journals.

Otway, Thomas (born 3 March 1652, buried 16 April 1685), dramatist, was born at Trotton in Sussex, where his father was curate, and educated at Winchester and Oxford, which he left without graduating. His short life was marked by poverty and misery, and he appears to have died practically of starvation. Having failed as an actor, he took to writing for the stage, and produced various plays, among which *Alcibiades* (1675) and *Don Carlos, Prince of Spain* (1676), were successful, but an unreturned passion for one of his actresses drove him to enlist in the army in 1678, going to Holland and returning with health impaired. The plays by which he is best remembered are *The Orphan* (1680), and *Venice Preserved* (1682), both of which have been frequently revived. Otway made many adaptations from the French, and in his tragedy of *Caius Marius* incorporated large parts of Shakespeare's *Romeo and Juliet*. He has been called 'the most pathetic and tear-drawing of all our dramatists,' and he excelled in delineating the stronger passions. The grossness of his comedies has banished them from the stage.

Ouida, *see* Ramée, Louise de la.

Outram, George (25 March 1805—15 Sept. 1856), journalist and poet, was born at the Clyde Iron Works, Glasgow, of which his father was managing director. The family removed to Leith, and he was educated at the High School there and at Edinburgh University. In 1827 he was called to the Scottish Bar, but turned to journalism and became editor and part proprietor of the *Glasgow Herald*. He published *Lyrics, Legal and Miscellaneous* (1874), of which the most famous is 'The Annuity,' which extracts humour from the dry processes of law and insurance.

Overbury, Sir Thomas (baptized 18 June 1581, died 15 Sept. 1613), poet, born at Compton-Scorpion, Warwickshire, was educated at Oxford. He became the friend of Carr, afterwards Earl of Rochester and Somerset, and fell a victim to a Court intrigue connected with the proposed marriage of Rochester and Lady Essex, being poisoned in the Tower with the connivance of the latter. He wrote a poem on marriage, *A Wife now the Widow of Sir T. Overbury* (1614), and *Characters* (1614), short, witty descriptions of types of men, in the manner of the Greek Theophrastus; some by other hands are included with his.

Owen, John (1560?—1622?), epigrammatist, born at Plas Dhu, Carnarvonshire, was educated at Winchester and Oxford, and became headmaster of King Henry VIII's School at Warwick. His 11 books of Latin epigrams, which have both sense and wit in a high degree, gained him the name of 'the British Martial,' and were translated into English, French, German, and Spanish.

Owen, John (1616—24 Aug. 1683), theologian, was born at Stadhampton, Oxfordshire, where his father was vicar, and educated at Oxford, from which he was driven by Laud's statutes. Originally a Presbyterian, he passed over to Independency. In 1649 he accompanied Cromwell to Ireland, and in 1650 to Edinburgh. He was Dean of Christ Church, Oxford (1651—60), and Vice-Chancellor of the University in 1652. After the Restoration he was ejected from his deanery, but was allowed to preach to a congregation of Independents in London. His great learning and ability rendered him a formidable controversialist, specially against Arminianism and Romanism. His works fill 28 volumes; among the best known being *The Divine Original of the Scriptures* (1650), *Indwelling Sin* (1668), *Christologia* (1679), and a commentary on Hebrews.

Owen, Robert (14 May 1771—17 Nov. 1858), social reformer, was born at Newtown, Montgomeryshire, son of an ironmonger. After working as assistant first to a grocer in London and then to a haberdasher, he moved to Manchester and became manager of a cotton mill. In 1799 he married Anne Dale, daughter of the owner of New Lanark cotton mills, and next year began a pioneer experiment in social and educational reform by forming a model industrial community there, with good houses for his operatives and the first British infant school. New Lanark became a focus of interest for sociologists all over Europe, and was the forerunner of Port Sunlight, Bournville, and similar model villages. Owen also started a self-supporting community at Orbiston, Lanarkshire, but it was not an economic success. His *New View of Society* (1813—14) sets out his belief in the importance of environment in the formation of character.

He also wrote an interesting autobiography, which was published in 1857.

Owen, Wilfred (18 March 1893—4 Nov. 1918), poet, born at Oswestry, Shropshire, was educated at Birkenhead Institute and London University. Delicate and precocious, he was a great lover of poetry as a boy. From 1913 to 1915 he lived near Bordeaux as tutor to a French family. In the First World War he enlisted in the Artists' Rifles, but was invalided out in 1917 and sent to Craiglockhart War Hospital, where Siegfried Sassoon (q.v.) was his fellow-patient and encouraged him in his verse-writing. Sent back to France as a company commander, he won the Military Cross, but was killed a week before the Armistice in the crossing of the Sambre Canal. His *Poems* (1920) collected by Sassoon, are distinguished by extensive use of assonance in place of rhyme, a feature in which he looked forward to the later school of Auden and Spender.

Oxenham, John, *see* **Dunkerley, W. A.**

Oxford, Countess of, *see* **Asquith.**

Oxford, Edward De Vere, 17th Earl of (2 April 1550—24 June 1604), poet, educated at Cambridge, was a courtier of Queen Elizabeth, who lost his friends by his insolence and pride, and his fortune by his extravagance. He married a daughter of Lord Burghley, who had to support his family after his death. He had some reputation as a writer of short poems, many of which are in the *Paradise of Dainty Devices* and other Elizabethan miscellanies.

P

Paget, Violet (Oct. 1856—13 Feb. 1935), novelist and critic who wrote under the name Vernon Lee, was born at Boulogne of British parents. While they were travelling about in her early years she learned several languages and finally settled in Florence. In 1880 her *Studies of the Eighteenth Century in Italy* made her respected as a critic, and in the following year she visited England for the first time, meeting Whistler and other celebrities. The insight and erudition of her first book were repeated in *Euphorion* (1884), a study of Renaissance art, and in *Renaissance Fancies and Studies* (1895). *Gospels of Anarchy* (1908) and *Vital Lies* (1912) are philosophic and sociological works, and *The Beautiful* (1913) is a manual of aesthetics. She also wrote essays on the spirit of places, including *Genius Loci* (1898) and *The Enchanted Woods* (1904), and two novels. A dramatic trilogy, *Satan the Waster* (1920), embodied her belief in pacifism. In 1924 she was made an honorary D.Litt. of Durham.

Pain, Barry Eric Odell (28 Sept. 1864—5 May 1928), humorous writer, was born at Cambridge, son of a draper. He edited the school magazine at Sedbergh and the *Granta* at Cambridge; his contributions to the latter were later collected as *In a Canadian Canoe* (1891). After four years as an army coach he went to London, became a journalist, and succeeded Jerome K. Jerome (q.v.) as editor of *To-day*. During the First World War he served in the anti-aircraft section of the R.N.V.R. As a writer he excelled in humorous sketches of low life. His most successful book, *Eliza* (1900), which had four sequels, is supposed to be written by a suburban clerk; *Mrs Murphy* (1913) is the story of a charwoman, *Edwards* (1915) of a jobbing gardener. Others of his books are *Nothing Serious* (1901), *Wilhelmina in London* (1906), and *The Confessions of Alphonse* (1917). He also wrote some amusing parodies, including *Marge Askinfort* (1920), a burlesque of Margot Asquith's diaries, and *If Summer Don't* (1922), which 'guyed' A. S. M. Hutchinson's best-seller *If Winter Comes*.

Paine, Thomas (29 Jan. 1737—8 June 1809), political writer, son of a stay-maker and small farmer of Quaker principles at Thetford, Norfolk, became through his writings perhaps the most unpopular man in England. After trying various occupations, including those of schoolmaster and exciseman, and having separated from his wife, he went in 1774 to America where, in 1776, he published his famous pamphlet, *Common Sense*, in favour of American independence. He served in the American army, and also held some political posts, including that of secretary to a mission to France in 1781. Returning to England in 1787 he published his *Rights of Man* (1790—2) in reply to Burke's *Reflections on the French Revolution*. It had an enormous circulation, 1,500,000 copies having been sold in England alone; but he had to escape to France to avoid prosecution. Arrived in that country he was elected to the National Convention. He opposed the execution of Louis XVI, and was, in 1794, imprisoned by Robespierre, whose fall saved his life. He had then just completed the first part of his *Age of Reason*, of which the other two parts appeared respectively in 1795 and 1807. It is directed alike against Christianity and Atheism, and supports Deism. Becoming disgusted with the course of French politics, he returned to America in 1802, but found himself largely ostracized by society, and his opposition to the Federal party made him unpopular politically. He died at New York. Though apparently sincere in his views, and courageous in the expression of them, Paine was vain and prejudiced. The extraordinary lucidity and force of his style did much to gain currency for his writings.

Painter, William (1540?—1594), translator, born probably in London and educated at Cambridge, was successively schoolmaster at Sevenoaks, Kent, and Clerk of the Ordnance, in which position his intromissions appear to have been of more advantage to himself than to the public service. He was the author of *The Palace of Pleasure* (1566), largely consisting of translations from Boccaccio, Bandello, and other Italian writers, and also from the classics. It formed a quarry in which many dramatists, including Shakespeare, found the plots for their plays.

Paley, William (July 1743—25 May 1805), theologian, son of a minor canon of Peterborough, where he was born, went at 15 as a sizar to Christ's College, Cambridge, where he was Senior Wrangler, and became a Fellow and Tutor of his college. Taking orders in 1767 he held many benefices, and rose to be Archdeacon of Carlisle, and Sub-Dean of Lincoln. Paley, who holds one of the highest places among English theologians, was the author of four important works —*Principles of Moral and Political Philosophy* (1785), *Horae Paulinae* (1790), his most original, but least popular book, *View of the Evidences of Christianity* (1794), and *Natural Theology* (1802). These works had an immense popularity and influence in their day, and are characterized by singular clearness of expression and power of apt illustration. The system of morals inculcated by Paley is Utilitarian, modified by theological ideas. His view of the 'divine right of Kings' as on a level with 'the divine right of constables' was unpleasing to George III, notwithstanding which his ecclesiastical career was eminently successful.

Palgrave, Sir Francis (July 1788—6 July 1861), historian, was the son of Meyer Cohen, a Jewish stockbroker, but at his marriage in 1823, having previously become a Christian, assumed his mother-in-law's name of Palgrave. He studied law, and was called to the Bar in 1827. From 1838 until his death in 1861 he was Deputy Keeper of the Records, and in that capacity arranged a vast mass of hitherto inaccessible documents, and edited many of them for the Record Commission. His historical works include a *History of England in Anglo-Saxon Times* (1831), *Rise and Progress of the English Commonwealth* (1832), and *History of Normandy and England* (four volumes,

1851—64), published posthumously. He was knighted in 1832.

Palgrave, Francis Turner (28 Sept. 1824—24 Oct. 1897), poet and anthologist, son of the above, was born at Great Yarmouth but brought up mainly in Hampstead. Educated at Charterhouse and Balliol, where he was a friend of Matthew Arnold and Clough (qq.v.), he was elected a Fellow of Exeter. After a short time as assistant secretary to W. E. Gladstone, from 1850 to 1855 he was Vice-Principal of Kneller Hall, the teachers' training college. He then entered the Education Department, where he rose to be Assistant-Secretary. In 1854 he published *Idylls and Songs*, a small book of verse, and in 1858 *The Passionate Pilgrim*, a book of reflections. At this time he spent his holidays with Tennyson, of whom he was a close friend, and with his help Palgrave's great work *The Golden Treasury of Songs and Lyrics* took shape; it was published in 1861, quickly became a classic among anthologies, and has never been surpassed as a representative collection of English verse. A second series appeared in 1896, and Palgrave compiled a number of other anthologies, but none had anything approaching the success of the first. *Visions of England* (1881) and *Amenophis* (1892) were two more volumes of his original verse. In 1885 he was elected to the Oxford Chair of Poetry, which he occupied for 10 years; a volume of his lectures, *Landscape in Poetry*, was published in 1897.

Palmer, Herbert Edward (1880—17 May 1961), poet and critic, was born at Market Rasen, Lincolnshire, son of a Wesleyan minister, and educated at Woodhouse Grove School and Birmingham and Bonn Universities. From 1899 he was a master in various English, French, and German schools, but in 1921 gave up teaching for writing. His earlier verse was gathered together in *Collected Poems* (1932); later volumes are *Summit and Chasm* (1934), *The Vampire* (1936), *The Gallows-Cross* (1940), *A Sword in the Desert* (1946), *The Old Knight* (1949), and *The Ride from Hell* (1958). In 1932 he was awarded a Civil List pension for distinction as a poet. *The Judgment of François Villon* (1927) and *The Dragon of Tingalam* (1945) are plays. His prose works include *The Teaching of English* (1930), *Post-Victorian Poetry* (1938), and a volume of early reminiscence, *The Mistletoe Child* (1935).

Palmer, John Leslie (4 Sept. 1885—5 Aug. 1944), novelist and critic, was born in London and educated at King Edward's School, Birmingham, and Oxford. From 1910 to 1915 he was dramatic critic of the *Saturday Review*, then during the First World War worked in the War Trade Intelligence Department. In 1920 he joined the Permanent Secretariat of the League of Nations, where he met Hilary St George Saunders (q.v.), like himself a Balliol man, with whom he collaborated in writing thrillers under the names Francis Beeding and David Pilgrim. Palmer's own books include a number on the theatre, such as *The Comedy of Manners* (1913), *The Future of the Theatre* (1913), and *Studies in the Contemporary Theatre* (1927), as well as studies of *Bernard Shaw* (1915), *Rudyard Kipling* (1915), *Molière* (1930), and *Ben Jonson* (1934). His novels include

s*

Peter Paragon (1915), *The King's Men* (1916), *Jennifer* (1926), and *Timothy* (1931). He was awarded the O.B.E. in 1941. For the Beeding and Pilgrim books *see* H. St G. Saunders.

Paltock, Robert (1697—20 March 1767), romance writer, born in Westminster, was an attorney. His fame rests on a single work, *The Life and Adventures of Peter Wilkins, a Cornish Man* (1751), admired by Scott, Coleridge, and Lamb. It is somewhat on the same plan as *Robinson Crusoe*, the special feature being the *gawry*, or flying woman, whom the hero discovered on his island, and married. The description of Nosmnbdsgrutt, the country of the flying people, is a dull imitation of Swift, and much else in the book is tedious.

Panter-Downes, Mollie Patricia (25 Aug. 1906—   ), novelist, was born in London, daughter of a major in the Royal Irish Regiment who was killed at Mons in the First World War. She started writing at the age of 6, had verses printed in the *Poetry Review* when she was 12, and when she was 17 her first novel *A Shoreless Sea* was published. She was educated at Heathfield House, Horsham, where she founded a school magazine. In 1927 she married Clare Robinson. Among her other novels are *The Chase* (1925), *Storm Bird* (1929), *My Husband Simon* (1931), *Nothing in Common but Sex* (1932), and *One Fine Day* (1947). In the Second World War she wrote a weekly 'Letter from England' for the *New Yorker*.

Pardoe, Julia (1806—26 Nov. 1862), historian, novelist, and travel writer, was born at Beverley, Yorkshire, daughter of an army officer who fought at Waterloo. When she was 14 she published a volume of poems which went into a second edition. She became a voluminous and versatile writer, producing in addition to her lively and well-written novels many books of travel, and others dealing with historical subjects. She was a keen observer, and during her travels had obtained an accurate and deep knowledge of the peoples and manners of the East. Among her books are *The City of the Sultan* (1836), *Romance of the Harem* (1839), *Louis XIV and the Court of France* (1847), and *The Court and Reign of Francis I* (1849).

Paris, Matthew (1195?—1259), greatest of the medieval English chroniclers, became a monk of St Albans in 1217 and in 1236 succeeded Roger of Wendover as historiographer of the monastery; he continued his predecessor's work, *Flores Historiarum*, in *Chronica Majora* (Greater Chronicles), extending it from 1235 to 1259 and also expanding the earlier part and introducing accounts of events in foreign countries. Scholar and courtier, he enjoyed the favour of Henry III and was able to learn of happenings at first hand. His work excels that of other chroniclers in vividness, and he took great pains in verifying his facts.

Park, Mungo (10 Sept. 1771—Nov. 1806), explorer, born in a farm near Selkirk, studied medicine at Edinburgh. As a surgeon on an East Indiaman he visited Sumatra, and on his return attracted the attention of various scientific men by his botanical and zoological investigations. In 1795 he entered the service of the African

Association, and made a voyage of discovery on the Niger. His
adventures were published in *Travels in the Interior of Africa* (1799),
which had great success. He married and set up in practice in
Peebles; but in 1805 accepted an invitation by Government to undertake another journey in Africa. From this he never returned, having
been drowned in the Niger during a conflict with natives. His
narratives, written in a straightforward and pleasing style, are among
the classics of travel.

Parker, Dorothy (22 Aug. 1893—   ), satirist and
humorist, was born at West End, New Jersey, daughter of Henry
Rothschild, and educated at the Convent of the Blessed Sacrament,
New York. Becoming a journalist, she was on the staff successively
of *Vogue*, *Vanity Fair*, and the *New Yorker*, of which last she was
book-reviewer. Later she became a freelance. Though satirical
and ironical and celebrated for her 'wise-cracks' she could command
pathos, as in her story 'Big Blonds,' which won the O. Henry Prize
in 1929. Her books of verse include *Enough Rope* (1927), *Sunset
Gun* (1928), *Death and Taxes* (1931), and *Not so Deep as a Well*
(1936). *Laments for the Living* (1930) and *Here Lies* (1939) are
volumes of short stories. She married Edwin P. Parker in 1917;
they were divorced in 1928, and in 1933 she married Alan Campbell,
a film actor.

Parker, Sir Horatio Gilbert George, Bart. (23 Nov. 1862—6 Sept.
1932), was born at Camden East, Ontario, son of a captain in the
Canadian militia, and educated at Ottawa Normal School and
Trinity College, Toronto, where he became a lecturer in English in
1883. In 1885 his health broke down and he went for a voyage
round the world. At this time he was for four years assistant editor
of the Sydney *Morning Herald*. He now gave himself up to a literary
career, settling permanently in England in 1898, and from 1900 to
1918 sitting in Parliament as Conservative member for Gravesend.
In 1915 he was made a baronet for his services to war propaganda in
the United States. He has been called 'an imperialist of the old
romantic school,' and his most famous novel was *The Seats of the
Mighty* (1896), a story of the siege of Quebec. Others are *The
Trail of the Swords* (1894), *When Valmond Came to Pontiac* (1895),
The Battle of the Strong (1898), *The Right of Way* (1901), *A Ladder of
Swords* (1904), *You Never Know Your Luck* (1915), and *The Power
and the Glory* (1925). He also published several volumes of short
stories and an autobiographical work, *Tarboe* (1927).

Parker, Theodore (24 Aug. 1810—10 May 1860), clergyman and
reformer, born at Lexington, Massachusetts, and educated at Harvard, was an indefatigable student, and made himself master of many
languages. In 1837 he was settled at West Roxbury as a Unitarian
minister, but the development of his views in a rationalistic direction
gradually separated him from the more conservative portion of his
co-religionists. He travelled in Europe, and in 1845 settled in
Boston, where he lectured to large audiences, and exercised a wide
influence. He took a leading part in the anti-slavery crusade, and
was one of the secret committee abetting John Brown's raid at

Harper's Ferry. In 1859 his health, which had never been robust, gave way; he went to Italy in search of restoration, but died at Florence. Among the most outstanding of his writings are *A Discourse of Matters Pertaining to Religion* (1842) and *Sermons on Theism, Atheism, and the Popular Theology* (1853).

Parkman, Francis (16 Sept. 1823—8 Nov. 1893), historian, son of a Unitarian minister in Boston, Massachusetts, graduated at Harvard, qualified as a lawyer, but never practised, and though hampered by a state of health which forbade continuous application, and by partial blindness, devoted himself to the writing of the history of the conflict between France and England in North America. This he did in a succession of works—*The Conspiracy of Pontiac* (1851), *The Pioneers of France in the New World* (1865), *The Jesuits in North America* (1867), *La Salle and the Discovery of the Great West* (1869), *The Old Regime in Canada* (1874), *Count Frontenac and New France* (1877), *Montcalm and Wolfe* (1884), and *A Half Century of Conflict* (1892). Parkman spared no labour in collecting and sifting his material, much of which was gathered in the course of visits to the places which were the scenes of his narrative, and his books are the most valuable contributions in existence to the history of the struggle for Canada and the other French settlements in North America. He also wrote two novels, which had little success.

Parnell, Thomas (born 1679, buried 24 Oct. 1718), poet, born in Dublin and educated at Trinity College there, took orders in 1700, and was Vicar of Finglas and Archdeacon of Clogher. The death of his young wife in 1706 drove him into intemperate habits. He was a friend of Swift and Pope, a contributor to the *Spectator*, and aided Pope in his translation of the *Iliad*. He wrote various isolated poems showing a fine descriptive touch, of which the most important are 'The Hermit,' 'The Night Piece,' and the 'Hymn to Contentment.' Parnell was a scholar, and had considerable social gifts. His poems were collected and edited by Pope in 1721, and his life was written by Goldsmith.

Parr, Samuel (26 Jan. 1747—17 Jan. 1825), scholar, son of an apothecary, was born at Harrow and educated there and at Cambridge. He was successively an assistant-master at Harrow and headmaster of schools at Colchester and Norwich, and having taken orders, finally settled down at Hatton, Warwickshire, where he took private pupils. He was undoubtedly a great Latinist, but he has left no work to account for the immense reputation which he enjoyed during his life. His chief power appears to have been in conversation, in which he was bold, arrogant, and epigrammatic. He was nicknamed 'the Whig Johnson,' but fell very far short of his model. His writings, including correspondence, were published in eight volumes.

Parrish, Anne (12 Nov. 1888—6 Sept. 1957), novelist, was born at Colorado Springs and educated at private schools. Both her parents were artists, and she studied painting in Philadelphia, afterwards travelling a great deal. In 1915 she married her first husband, Charles A. Corliss, who died in 1936, and in 1938 her second,

Josiah Titzell, poet and novelist, with whom she settled in George-town, Connecticut. Best known of her novels is *The Perennial Bachelor*, which won the Harper Prize in 1925. Others are *A Pocketful of Poses* (1923), *Semi-Attached* (1924), *To-morrow Morning* (1926), *All Kneeling* (1928), *The Methodist Faun* (1929), *Loads of Love* (1932), *Sea Level* (1934), *Golden Wedding* (1936), *Mr Despondency's Daughter* (1938), *Pray for a To-morrow* (1941), *Poor Child* (1945), *A Clouded Star* (1948), and *And Have Not Love* (1954).

Partridge, Eric Honeywood (6 Feb. 1894—), lexico-grapher, was born at Gisborne, New Zealand, and educated at Queensland University. From 1910 to 1913 he was a schoolmaster, then during the First World War served as a private in the Australian infantry. From 1921 to 1923 he was a Queensland Travelling Fellow at Oxford, and from 1925 to 1927 a lecturer in English at Manchester and London Universities. His most important work was his great *Dictionary of Slang and Unconventional English* (1937), which was five times revised. A large work on similar lines is his *Dictionary of the Underworld* (1950). He also published a *Dictionary of Cliches* (1940); a *Dictionary of Abbreviations* (1942); *Usage and Abusage* (1947), a guide to good English; *Name into Word* (1949), a dictionary of proper names that have become common nouns; and *You Have a Point There* (1953), a guide to punctuation. After the Second World War, in which he served with the Royal Air Force, he collabor-ated in a *Dictionary of Forces Slang* (1948). In addition to these important reference works he published *British and American English Since 1900* (1951), and a large number of smaller books on language.

Passfield, Baron, *see* **Webb, Sidney.**

Pater, Walter Horatio (4 Aug. 1839—30 July 1894), critic, born in London, son of a doctor, was educated at King's School, Canterbury, and Queen's College, Oxford. He became a Fellow of Brasenose and spent most of his life there, travelling on the Continent or latterly living in London in the vacations. Through Ruskin's influence he became interested in art, and built up a reputation as an authority on aesthetics. He first made a name in 1873 with his *Studies in the History of the Renaissance*, and in 1878 he published his greatest work, *Marius the Epicurean*, a kind of historical novel of the time of Marcus Aurelius, which preached the pursuit of beauty. Among his books of criticism are *Imaginary Portraits* (1887), *Appreciations* (1889), and *Plato and Platonism* (1893); *Greek Studies* and *Miscellaneous Studies* appeared posthumously in 1895. In 1894 he was made an honorary LL.D. of Glasgow, and in the same year published his autobiographical study, *The Child in the House*. A master of polished and cultured prose, he taught the doctrine of 'art for art's sake,' and represents the most earnest side of the Aesthetic Move-ment.

Patmore, Coventry Kersey Dighton (23 July 1823—26 Nov. 1896), poet, son of P. G. Patmore, also an author, was born at Woodford, Essex, and became an assistant in the printed book department of the British Museum. He published *Tamerton Church Tower* (1853), and followed this with *The Betrothed* (1854), *The Espousals* (1856), *Faithful for Ever* (1860), and *The Victories of Love* (1862), four poems which, combined, form his masterpiece, *The Angel in the House*, a poetic celebration of married love. In 1864 he entered the Church of Rome. Thereafter he published *The Unknown Eros* (1877), *Amelia* (1878), and *Rod, Root, and Flower* (1895), odes and meditations chiefly on religious subjects, very different in both theme and treatment from the domesticity of his earlier work. His poems are full of graceful and suggestive thought, but occasionally suffer from length and discursiveness. He was successful in business matters, and in character was energetic, masterful, and combative. He numbered Tennyson and Ruskin among his friends, was associated with the Pre-Raphaelites, and was a contributor to their organ, the *Germ*. He was married three times.

Patrick, Saint (385?—17 March 461?), whose original Celtic name was Sucat, was the son of a Christian Roman named Calpurnius. Kilpatrick in Dunbartonshire claims to be his birthplace, but it is more probable that he was born in south Wales, from which at the age of 16 he was carried off to Antrim by Irish pirates. Escaping to France, he was educated there as a monk and was eventually entrusted by the Pope with the conversion of Ireland, to which he went in 433. He founded hundreds of churches and monasteries up and down the country, and within ten years he succeeded in Christianizing the whole island and fixed his see at Armagh. He left two important and well-authenticated works, his *Confession* and the *Epistle to Coroticus*, as well as an Irish hymn.

Pattison, Mark (10 Oct. 1813—30 July 1884), scholar and biographer, born at Hornby, Yorkshire, son of a clergyman, was educated privately and at Oxford, where in 1839 he became a Fellow of Lincoln College, and acquired a high reputation as a tutor and examiner. At first strongly influenced by Newman and the Tractarian movement, he ultimately abandoned the High Church party. In 1851, failing to be elected head of his college, he threw up his tutorship, and devoted himself to severe study, occasionally writing on educational subjects in various reviews. In 1861, however, he attained the object of his ambition, being elected Rector of Lincoln College. In 1875 he published a *Life of Isaac Casaubon*, and he left materials for a life of Scaliger, which he had intended to be his *magnum opus*. He also published a life of *Milton* and an edition of his sonnets. His introspective *Memoirs* appeared in 1885.

Paulding, James Kirke (22 Aug. 1778—6 April 1860), novelist and poet, born in Putnam County, New York, was chiefly self-educated. He became a friend of Washington Irving, and was part author with him of *Salmagundi*, a continuation of which by himself proved a failure. Among his other writings are *John Bull and Brother Jonathan* (1812), a satire, *The Dutchman's Fireside* (1831), a romance which attained popularity, a *Life of Washington* (1835), and some poems.

Pax, *see* Cholmondeley, Mary.

Payn, James (28 Feb. 1830—25 March 1898), novelist, born at Cheltenham, son of an official in the Thames Commission, was educated at Eton, Woolwich, and Cambridge. He was a regular contributor to *Household Words* and to *Chambers's Journal*, of which he was editor from 1859 to 1874, and in which several of his works first appeared; he also edited the *Cornhill Magazine* from 1883 to 1896. Among his novels—upwards of 60 in number—may be mentioned *Lost Sir Massingberd, The Best of Husbands, Walter's Word, By Proxy, A Woman's Vengeance, Carlyon's Year, Thicker than Water*, and *A Trying Patient*. He also wrote a book of poems and a volume of literary reminiscences.

Peabody, Josephine Preston (30 May 1874—4 Dec. 1922), poetess and dramatist, was born at Brooklyn, New York, and educated at the Girls' Latin School in Boston, and Radcliffe College. Her first book of verse, *The Wayfarers*, was published in 1898. From 1901 to 1903 she was an instructor in English at Wellesley College, and in 1906 she married Lionel S. Marks, a Harvard professor. A fervent admirer of Shakespeare, she won the Stratford-on-Avon Prize in 1910 with her play *The Piper*. From 1916 onwards she was an invalid. Her books of verse include *The Singing Leaves* (1903), *The Singing Man* (1911), and *Harvest Moon* (1916); her plays are *Marlowe* (1901), *The Wings* (1907), *The Wolf of Gubbio* (1913), and *Portrait of Mrs W.* (1922).

Peacock, Thomas Love (18 Oct. 1785—23 Jan. 1866), novelist, born at Weymouth, the only child of a glass merchant, was in boyhood at various schools, but from the age of 13 self-educated. Nevertheless, he became a really learned scholar. In 1819 he entered the service of the East India Company, and rose to be Chief Examiner from 1837 to 1856, coming between James Mill and John Stuart Mill. He was the author of several somewhat whimsical, but quite unique novels, full of paradox, prejudice, and curious learning, with witty dialogue and occasional poems interspersed. Among them are *Headlong Hall* (1816), *Nightmare Abbey* (1818), *Maid Marian* (1822), *Misfortunes of Elphin* (1829), *Crotchet Castle* (1831), and *Gryll Grange* (1860). He was the intimate friend of Shelley, memoirs of whom he contributed to *Fraser's Magazine*.

Pearson, Charles Henry (7 Sept. 1830—29 May 1894), historian, born at Islington, son of a clergyman, was educated at Rugby and King's College, London, where he became Professor of Modern History. Owing to a threatened failure of sight he went to Australia, where he remained for 20 years, and was for a time Minister of Education of Victoria. Returning to England in 1892 he wrote his *National Life and Character: a Forecast*, in which he gave utterance to very pessimistic views as to the future of the race. He also wrote a *History of England during the Early and Middle Ages* (1867).

Pearson, Hesketh (20 Feb. 1887—   ), biographer, born at Hawford, Worcestershire, was educated at Bedford Grammar School, then spent two years in a shipping office. In 1911 he went on the stage and became a successful actor, appearing in many London productions. During the First World War he enlisted as a private and ended as a captain, having served in Mesopotamia. After some further years as an actor he turned to writing, and had great success with his lively and vivid biographies, which include Sydney Smith in *The Smith of Smiths* (1934), *Gilbert and Sullivan* (1935), Anna Seward in *The Swan of Lichfield* (1936), *Tom Paine* (1937), John Nicholson in *The Hero of Delhi* (1939), *Bernard Shaw* (1942), *Conan Doyle* (1943), *Oscar Wilde* (1946), *Charles Dickens* (1949), Disraeli in *Dizzy* (1951), *The Man Whistler* (1952), and *Sir Walter Scott* (1955). He also published *Common Misquotations* (1937).

Pearson, John (28 Feb. 1613—16 July 1686), theologian, born at Great Snoring, Norfolk, where his father was rector, was educated at Eton and Cambridge, took orders, and after holding various preferments, including the archdeaconry of Surrey, and masterships of Jesus College, and Trinity College, Cambridge, was made, in 1673, Bishop of Chester. His *Exposition of the Creed* (1659) has always been regarded as one of the most finished productions of English theology, remarkable alike for logical argument and arrangement, and lucid style. He was also the author of other learned works, including a defence of the authenticity of the epistles of Ignatius. In his youth Pearson was a royalist, and acted in 1645 as a chaplain in the royal army.

Pecock, Reginald (1395?—1460?), theologian, born in Wales, took holy orders, and rose to be successively Bishop of St Asaph, 1444, and of Chichester, 1450. He was a strenuous controversialist, chiefly against the Lollards; but his free style of argument, and especially his denial of the infallibility of the Church, led him into trouble, and on being offered the choice of abjuration or death at the stake, he chose the former. He was nevertheless deprived of his bishopric, had his books burned, and spent his latter days in the Abbey of Thorney, Cambridgeshire. His chief work is *The Repressor of Overmuch Blaming of the Clergy* (1455), which, from its clear, pointed style, remains a monument of fifteenth-century English. *The Book of Faith* (1456) is another of his writings.

Peele, George (1558?—1597?), dramatist and poet, son of a London salter, was educated at Christ's Hospital and Oxford, where he had a reputation as a poet. Coming back to London about 1581 he led a dissipated life. He appears to have been a player as well as a playwright, and to have come into possession of some land through his wife. His works are numerous and consist of plays, pageants, and miscellaneous verse. His plays, which show great versatility are *The Arraignment of Paris* (1584), a pastoral masque; *Edward I* (1593), a chronicle play; *The Battle of Alcazar* (1594); *The Old Wife's Tale* (1595), a satirical drama; and *King David and Fair Bethsabe* (1599), a kind of miracle play. His poems include *Polyhymnia* (1590), and *The Honour of the Garter* (1593). One of the 'University Wits,' Peele wrote in melodious and flowing blank verse, with abundance of fancy and brilliant imagery, but his dramas are weak in construction, and he is often bombastic and extravagant.

Pemberton, Sir Max (19 June 1863—22 Feb. 1950), novelist, born in Birmingham, was educated at Merchant Taylors' and Cambridge. In 1892 he edited *Chums*, and from 1896 to 1906 *Cassell's Magazine*. He is best remembered for his exciting adventure stories, of which the most famous was *The Iron Pirate* (1893), with its sequel *Captain Black* (1911). Others are *The Sea Wolves* (1894), *The Impregnable City* (1895), *Kronstadt* (1898), *The Garden of Swords* (1899), *The House under the Sea* (1902), *My Sword for Lafayette* (1906), and *The Great White Army* (1915). In 1920 he founded the London School of Journalism, and in 1922 published a memoir of Lord Northcliffe, with whom he had been associated for many years. He was knighted in 1928, and in 1936 he wrote *Sixty Years Ago and After*, his own reminiscences.

Pembroke, Mary Herbert, Countess of (1555?—25 Sept. 1621), born at Ticknell in Worcestershire, was a sister of Sir Philip Sidney (q.v.). In 1577 she married Henry Herbert, Earl of Pembroke, and became patroness of a number of poets, including Samuel Daniel, Ben Jonson, and Nicholas Breton. Her own poems include ' The Lay of Clorinda,' once attributed to Spenser, and she collaborated with Sidney in a metrical version of the Psalms. She also revised his *Arcadia* and added to it, having first suggested its composition. She was the subject of a famous epitaph by William Browne (q.v.).

Penn, William (14 Oct. 1644—30 July 1718), founder of Pennsylvania, was born in London, son of Admiral Sir William Penn. At the age of 16 he went to Christ Church, Oxford, but was expelled from the university for adopting Quaker views, and was sent on a Continental tour by his irate father. Returning in 1667 he became an active Quaker, and was several times imprisoned for preaching in the street and publishing controversial tracts. While in prison he wrote the most famous of his books, *No Cross, No Crown* (1669), as well as a defence of his conduct, *Innocency with her Open Face* (1668). On his father's death in 1670 he succeeded to a fortune, and also to a claim against the Government for £16,000; this was settled in 1681, when Charles II granted him a large tract of land west of the Delaware, which was then named Pennsylvania in honour of the old admiral. Penn was appointed governor, and sailed there in the following year. Having founded and named the capital, Philadelphia, he drew up an enlightened constitution, organized the colony on broad and tolerant principles, and returned to England in 1684. On intimate terms with James VII and II, who was anxious to conciliate the Dissenters, Penn used his influence on behalf of the Quakers, but the revolution of 1688 brought him into disfavour and he had to live in retirement. From 1699 to 1701 he was again in America, dealing with conflicts that arose in Pennsylvania, and on his return to England was imprisoned for debt owing to an agent's defalcations, and died shortly after his release. A pioneer of liberal administration, Penn did much to further the cause of both religious toleration and democratic freedom.

Pennant, Thomas (14 June 1726—16 Dec. 1798), naturalist and traveller, born at Downing in Flintshire, and educated at Oxford, was one of the most distinguished naturalists of the eighteenth century, and published among other works on natural history, *British Zoology* (1768), and *History of Quadrupeds* (1781). In literature he is, however, best remembered by his *Tour in Scotland* (1771—5), which did much to make known the beauties of that country to England. He also travelled in Ireland and Wales, and on the Continent, and published accounts of his journeys. Dr Johnson said of him: 'he observes more things than anyone else does.'

Pepys, Samuel (23 Feb. 1633—26 May 1703), diarist, son of a London tailor, was educated at St Paul's School and at Cambridge. In 1669 he married Elizabeth le Marchant de St Michel, a girl of 15, and in 1676 entered the household of Edward Montagu, 1st Earl of Sandwich, who became his life-long patron. He held various Government posts, including that of Surveyor-General of the Victualling Office, in which he displayed great administrative ability and reforming zeal, and in 1672 he became Secretary of the Admiralty. After being imprisoned in the Tower on a charge in connection with the Popish plot, and deprived of his office, he was in 1686 again appointed Secretary of the Admiralty, from which, however, he was dismissed at the Revolution. Thereafter he lived in retirement chiefly at Clapham. Pepys was a man of many interests, combining the characters of the man of business, man of pleasure, and connoisseur, being skilled in music and a collector of books, manuscripts, and pictures. He was President of the Royal Society for two years. He wrote *Memoirs of the Royal Navy* (1690), but his great legacy to literature is his unique and inimitable *Diary*, begun 1 Jan. 1660, and coming down to 31 May 1669, when the failure of his sight prevented its further continuance. As an account by an eye-witness of the manners of the Court and of society it is invaluable, but it is still more interesting as, perhaps, the most singular example extant of unreserved self-revelation—all the foibles, peccadilloes, and more serious offences against decorum of the author being set forth with the most relentless naïveté and minuteness. It was written in a cipher or shorthand, which was translated into long-hand by John Smith in 1825, and edited by Lord Braybrooke, with considerable excisions. Later and fuller editions have followed. Pepys left his books, manuscripts, and collections to Magdalene College, Cambridge, where they are preserved in a separate library.

Percival, James Gates (15 Sept. 1795—2 May 1856), poet, born at Berlin, Connecticut, son of a doctor, was educated at Yale. With fatal versatility he tried one occupation after another, and was by turns doctor, teacher of chemistry, and journalist. He had also a considerable gift for languages and from 1827 to 1828 assisted Noah Webster (q.v.) in the compilation of his dictionary. Then he taught himself geology, and in 1835 made the first geological survey of Connecticut. With the same facility he wrote lyrics in the romantic style of Moore or Byron, his chief volumes of verse being *Poems* (1821), *Prometheus* (1822), and *The Dream of a Day* (1843). He was accounted the leading American poet of his time until he was eclipsed by Bryant (q.v.), but his work has not stood the verdict of posterity.

Percy, Thomas (13 April 1729—30 Sept. 1811), antiquary and poet, born at Bridgnorth, Shropshire, son of a grocer, was educated at Oxford, took holy orders, and became in 1778 Dean of Carlisle, and in 1782 Bishop of Dromore. He published various antiquarian works, chiefly with reference to the North of England; but is best remembered for his great service to literature in collecting and editing many ancient ballads, published in 1765 as *Reliques of Ancient Poetry*, which did much to bring back interest in the ancient native literature, and to usher in the revival of romanticism. Most of these pieces were taken from the Percy Folio, a seventeenth-century manuscript which he found by chance.

Pertwee, Roland (1885—   ), playwright and novelist, born at Brighton, studied at the Royal Academy School of Art and had pictures hung at the Academy Exhibition. Later he became an actor and then a writer. The first short story he wrote was accepted by the *Saturday Evening Post*, and during the First World War, while he was in France, he wrote many more. His plays, however, were his most serious work, the most successful being *Interference* (1927), in which he collaborated with H. Dearden. Others are *Seein' Reason* (1913), *Swank* (1914), *The Return of Imry* (1914), *Falling Upstairs* (1914), *Early Birds* (1916), *Ten Minutes Tension* (1917), *Hell's Loose* (1929), *Pursuit* (1930), *Pink String and Sealing Wax* (1943), and *School for Spinsters* (1947). He also wrote a number of novels, and an autobiography, *Master of None* (1940).

Petrie, Sir William Matthew Flinders (3 June 1853—28 July 1942), archaeologist, was a grandson of Captain Matthew Flinders the explorer. Educated privately, he attended no university, but nevertheless became the greatest Egyptologist of his time, and was Professor of Egyptology at University College, London, from 1892 to 1933. A Fellow of the Royal Society, he was knighted in 1923. His archaeological work began in England with his survey of Stonehenge in 1875, the results of which were published in 1880. He then applied similar methods to the pyramids and other remains of Egypt, and published a long series of works, beginning with *Pyramids and Temples of Gizeh* (1883), and including a *History of Egypt* (1903—5), *Revolutions in Civilization* (1911), *Eastern Exploration* (1918), and *Some Sources of Human History* (1919). *Seventy Years in Archaeology* (1931) is an autobiography.

Pettie, George (1548?—July 1589), translator, was born at Tetsworth, Oxfordshire, and educated at Christ Church, Oxford, then travelled on the Continent. In imitation of the popular *Palace of Pleasure* of William Painter (q.v.) he produced *A Petite Palace of Pettie his Pleasure* (1576), a collection of tales translated from Greek and Latin classics, which went through several editions. He also published a translation of Guazzo's *Civile Conversation* in 1681. He was the uncle of Anthony Wood (q.v.).

Phelps, William Lyon (2 Jan. 1865—21 Aug. 1943), scholar and critic, was born at New Haven, Connecticut, son of a minister, and educated at Yale and Harvard. In 1892 he joined the staff of Yale, and in 1901 became Lampson Professor of English Literature there. A gifted and popular teacher, he was the first to give a course of lectures on contemporary writers at an American university, and his influence on English studies in the United States may be compared with that of Quiller-Couch (q.v.) in England. Among his more important works are *The Beginnings of the English Romantic Movement* (1893), *Essays on Modern Novelists* (1910), *The Advance of the English Novel* (1916), *The Advance of English Poetry* (1918), and *The Twentieth Century Theatre* (1918). His great passions were Spenser, Browning, golf, and cats. In 1939 he published his *Autobiography with Letters*.

Philips, Ambrose (1675?—18 June 1749), poet, born in Shropshire and educated at Cambridge, wrote pastorals and dramas, was one of the Addison circle, and started a paper, the *Freethinker*, in imitation of the *Spectator*. He also made translations from Pindar and Anacreon, and a series of short complimentary verses, which gained for him the nickname of 'Namby Pamby.' His *Pastorals*, though poor enough, excited the jealousy of Pope, who pursued the unfortunate author with life-long enmity. Philips held various Government appointments in Ireland.

Philips, John (30 Dec. 1676—15 Feb. 1709), poet, born at Bampton, Oxfordshire, son of an archdeacon, and educated at Winchester and Oxford, is remembered by *The Splendid Shilling* (1705), a burlesque in Miltonic blank verse, and *Cyder* (1708), his chief work, an imitation of Virgil's *Georgics*, which has some fine descriptive passages. Philips was also employed by Harley to write verses on Blenheim as a counterblast to Addison's *Campaign*. He died at 33 of consumption.

Phillips, Samuel (28 Dec. 1814—14 Oct. 1854), novelist, son of a London shopkeeper of Jewish descent, studied for the Church at Göttingen and Cambridge, but his father dying, he was obliged to give up his intention and take to business, in which, however, he was unsuccessful, and fell into great straits. He then tried writing, and produced some novels, of which the best known was *Caleb Stukely*, which appeared in *Blackwood* in 1842. He was latterly a leader-writer for *The Times*.

Phillips, Stephen (28 July 1864—9 Dec. 1915), dramatist and poet, was born at Summertown, near Oxford, and educated at King's School, Peterborough, and Oundle. His mother was related to Wordsworth, and Laurence Binyon (q.v.) was his cousin. He studied for the Civil Service, but instead became an actor in the company of Frank Benson, another of his cousins, from 1885 to 1892, though with indifferent success. He came into literary prominence with the striking poem *Christ in Hades* (1897); and with his *Poems* (1898), which was awarded the thousand-guinea prize of the *Academy*, he established a reputation which lasted 10 years but has not been sustained since. He revived poetic drama with his *Paolo and Francesca* (1900), from which at one time he drew royalties of £150 a week. Later verse plays received with acclamation were *Herod* (1901), *Ulysses* (1902), and *Nero* (1906). But his range was very limited, and he now passed into a period of obscurity from which he emerged only to produce such inferior dramatic work as *The King* (1912), *Armageddon* (1915), and *Harold* (1927). His *New Poems* appeared in 1908 and *Panama* in 1915. From 1913 till his death he edited the *Poetry Review*.

Phillpotts, Eden (4 Nov. 1862—29 Dec. 1960), novelist and playwright, was born at Mount Aboo, India, where his father was a political agent. After attending a school in Plymouth he went to a dramatic school in London. From 1880 to 1890 he was a clerk in a fire insurance office, after which he earned a living by his pen, making his home first at Torquay, then at Exeter. Unsociable by nature, he directed all his energies to his writing, and published over 250 books. Best known of his novels are the Dartmoor series, which include *Children of the Mist* (1898), *Sons of the Morning* (1900), *The River* (1902), *The Secret Woman* (1905), *The Mother* (1908), *The Thief of Virtue* (1910), and *Widecombe Fair* (1913). Among his other novels are *The Good Red Earth* (1901), *The Jury* (1927), and *A Deed Without a Name* (1941). He also wrote some good mystery stories, including *The Grey Room* (1921), *The Red Redmaynes* (1922), *A Voice from the Dark* (1925), and *The Book of Avis* (1932—3), a trilogy, while *The Human Boy* (two series, 1899, 1908) is an excellent collection of school stories told from the boys' angle. Among his plays the most successful were *The Farmer's Wife* (1916), and *Yellow Sands* (1926), in which his daughter Adelaide collaborated. Phillpotts also published about a score of volumes of verse and a dozen books of essays. He has been said to have done for Devon what Hardy did for Dorset. *From the Angle of 88* (1951) is a book of reminiscences and reflections.

Picken, Andrew (1788—23 Nov. 1833), novelist, born in Paisley, was in business in the West Indies, then set up as a bookseller in Liverpool, but not being successful, went to London to try his fortunes in literature. His earlier writings, *Tales and Sketches of the West of Scotland* (1824) and *The Sectarian* (1829), gave offence by their satirical tone, but his next, *The Dominie's Legacy* (1830), had considerable success, and a book on *Travels and Researches of Eminent Missionaries* (1830) did something to rehabilitate him with those whom he had offended. His last work, *The Black Watch* (1833), had just appeared when he died of an apoplectic seizure. His best work is somewhat like that of Galt (q.v.).

Pickthall, Marmaduke William (7 April 1875—19 May 1936), Orientalist and novelist, son of the rector of Chillesford, Suffolk, was educated at Harrow and on the Continent. He lived among the peoples of the Near East, learned Arabic, acquired Eastern ways of thought, and turned Moslem. Sympathizing with the Turks, he published *With the Turk in Wartime* in 1914, but during the First World War he served with the British forces, and afterwards from 1920 to 1924 edited the *Bombay Chronicle*. His first and best-known novel was *Saïd the Fisherman* (1903); others are *Enid* (1904), *Brindle* (1905), *The Valley of the Kings* (1909), *Larkmeadow* (1912), *Veiled Women* (1913), *The House of War* (1916), *Knights of Araby* (1917), and *The Early Hours* (1921). *Oriental Encounters* (1918) is a travel book, and in 1930 he published an explanatory translation of the Koran.

Pierpont, John (6 April 1785—27 Aug. 1866), clergyman and poet, grandfather of John Pierpont Morgan, the multimillionaire, was born at Litchfield, Connecticut, son of a clothier. Educated at Yale, he studied law, but gave up his practice and went into the dry goods business in Baltimore. In 1816 he published *Airs of Palestine*, which put him in the front rank of the American poets of his day. In 1818 he entered the Harvard Divinity School, and became a Unitarian minister in Boston, but came into conflict with his congregation over his temperance and anti-slavery writings and resigned in 1845, eventually ending his years as a clerk in the United States Treasury Department.

Pike, Albert (29 Dec. 1809—2 April 1891), poet and lawyer, born in Boston, was in his early days a teacher, and afterwards a successful lawyer. His now little-remembered poems were chiefly written under the inspiration of Coleridge and Keats. His chief work, *Hymns to the Gods*, which appeared in *Blackwood's Magazine*, closely imitates the latter. During the Civil War he commanded Red Indian troops on the Confederate side.

Pilgrim, David, *see* Saunders, Hilary St G.

Pindar, Peter, *see* Wolcot, J.

Pinero, Sir Arthur Wing (24 May 1855—3 Nov. 1934), playwright, was born in London, son of a solicitor of Portuguese origin. Trained for the law, he gave this up to be an actor, and became a member of Henry Irving's company, but was never a success. After writing his first plays, *£200 a Year* (1877), *Daisy's Escape* (1879), and *The Money Spinner* (1880), he gave up acting. *The Squire* (1881) and *The Profligate* (1889) revealed his power of depicting character, and other plays of his early period are *The Magistrate* (1885), *Dandy Dick* (1887), and *The Amazons* (1893). With the first of his tragedies, *The Second Mrs Tanqueray* (1893), sometimes reckoned the beginning of modern British drama, he scored a sensational success; other serious plays which followed it were *The Notorious Mrs Ebbsmith* (1895), *The Gay Lord Quex* (1899), *Iris* (1901), *Letty* (1903), *His House in Order* (1906), and *Mid-Channel* (1909); *Trelawny of the Wells* (1898) was in part a tribute to the dramatist T. W. Robertson (q.v.). For 30 years London's most successful playwright, Pinero was knighted in 1909. He wrote over 50 plays, the best being realist dramas in the manner of Ibsen.

Pinkerton, John (17 Feb. 1758—10 March 1826), historian, born in Edinburgh and educated at Lanark Grammar School, was apprenticed to a lawyer, but took to literature, and moved to London in 1881. His first publication was *Select Scottish Ballads* (1783), some of which, however, were composed by himself. A valuable *Essay on Medals* (1784) introduced him to Gibbon and Horace Walpole. Among his other works are *Ancient Scottish Poems* (1786), *Dissertation on the Goths* (1787), *Medallic History of England* (1790), *History of Scotland* (1797), and his best work, *Treatise on Rocks* (1811). One of his many inveterate prejudices was against Celts of all tribes and times. He died in obscurity in Paris.

Pinkney, Edward Coote (10 Oct. 1802—11 April 1828), poet, was born in London, when his father was on a diplomatic mission from the United States. Educated at St Mary's College, Baltimore, he entered the American Navy and saw service against pirates in the West Indies. Resigning his commission in 1824 he set up in law practice, and in the same year he published *Rodolph*, a verse tale of lawless passion; a volume of *Poems* followed in 1825. His work was praised by Poe. In 1826 he was a professor at the University of Maryland, and later edited the *Marylander*, a periodical supporting John Quincy Adams.

Piozzi, Hester Lynch, *see* **Thrale, H. S.**

Pitter, Ruth (7 Nov. 1897—   ), poetess, was born at Ilford, Essex; both her parents were teachers. Educated at a school in Bow, she was in the War Office for two years, then worked with an arts and crafts firm on the east coast, and later set up her own business on the same lines in Chelsea. She started writing verse as soon as she could read, and was later encouraged by Hilaire Belloc. Belonging to no school or coterie, she found her inspiration mainly in the beauty of nature. In 1936 her volume *A Trophy of Arms* was awarded the Hawthornden Prize, and in 1953 *The Ermine* received the Heinemann Foundation Award. Others of her books of verse are *First and Second Poems* (1927), *Persephone in Hades* (1931), *A Mad Lady's Garland* (1934), *The Spirit Watches* (1938), *The Rude Potato* (1941), *The Bridge* (1945), *Pitter on Cats* (1947), and *Urania* (1951). In 1955 she was awarded the Queen's Gold Medal for Poetry.

Planché, James Robinson (27 Feb. 1796—30 May 1880), playwright and herald, was born in London, son of a watchmaker of Huguenot descent. In 1810 he was articled to a bookseller, but turned instead to the stage, and from 1818 onwards wrote a large number of plays and was manager at various theatres. In 1823 he designed the dresses for a revival of Shakespeare's *King John*, the first occasion that an historical play was produced with period costume. In 1829 he became known as a student of heraldry and antiquities, in 1854 the Duke of Norfolk appointed him Rouge Croix pursuivant at the Heralds' College, and in 1866 he was made Somerset Herald. His *History of British Costumes* (1834) was of great value to painters of historical scenes.

Plomer, William Charles Franklyn (10 Dec. 1903—   ), novelist, born at Pietersburg in Transvaal of English parents, was educated at Rugby. For health reasons he farmed in the Stormberg Mountains, then lived in Johannesburg, and after that was a trader in Zululand. He was associated with Roy Campbell (q.v.) in the production of the review *Voorslag*. Later he spent two years in Japan, and at the age of 25 was offered the Chair of English Literature at Tokio, but declined it and travelled in Europe instead, living for a time in Greece. His novels include *Turbott Wolfe* (1926), *Sado* (1931), *The Case is Altered* (1932), *The Invaders* (1934), *Ali the Lion* (1936), and *Museum Pieces* (1952); volumes of short stories are *I Speak of Africa* (1928), *Paper Houses* (1929), *The Child of Queen Victoria* (1933), and *Four Countries* (1949). He also published some books of poems and a biography of *Cecil Rhodes* (1933). *Double Lives* (1943) is an autobiography.

Plunkett, E. J. M. D. *see* **Dunsany, Baron.**

Poe, Edgar Allan (14 Jan. 1809—7 Oct. 1849), poet and short-story writer, was born in Boston, where his parents, who were both actors, were temporarily living. He was left an orphan in early childhood in destitute circumstances, but was adopted by John Allan, a merchant of Richmond, Virginia, from whom he took his middle name. By Allan and his wife Poe was treated with great indulgence, and in 1815 accompanied them to England, where they remained for five years, and where he received a good education which was continued on their return to America, at the University of Virginia. He distinguished himself as a student, but got deeply into debt through gambling, which led to his being removed. In 1829 he published a small volume of poems containing 'Al Aaraaf' and 'Tamerlane.' About the same time he proposed to enter the army, and was placed at the Military Academy at West Point. Here, however, he grossly neglected his duties, began those drinking habits which proved the ruin of his life, and was in 1831 dismissed. He then returned to the house of his benefactor, but his conduct was so objectionable as to lead to a rupture. In the same year Poe published an enlarged edition of his poems, and in 1833 was successful in a competition for a prize tale and a prize poem, the tale being the 'MS. found in a Bottle,' and the poem 'The Coliseum.' In the following year John Allan died without making any provision for Poe, and the latter, being now thrown on his own resources, took to literature as a profession, and became a contributor to various periodicals.

In 1836 he entered into a marriage with his cousin Virginia Clemm, a very young girl, who continued devotedly attached to him notwithstanding his many aberrations, until her death in 1847. *The Narrative of Arthur Gordon Pym of Nantucket* appeared in 1838, and from 1839 to 1840 Poe was editor of *The Gentleman's Magazine*, in which appeared a number of his best stories, In 1845 his famous poem, 'The Raven,' came out, in 1848 *Eureka, a Prose Poem*, a metaphysical work, and in the following year 'Annabel Lee' and 'The Bells.' The death of his wife gave a severe shock to his constitution, and a violent drinking bout on a visit to Baltimore led to his death in the hospital there. The literary output of Poe, though smallish in volume, limited in range, and very unequal in merit, bears the stamp of an original genius. In his poetry he sometimes aims at a musical effect to which the sense is sacrificed, but at times he has a charm and a magic melody all his own. His short stories, which were collected in *Tales of the Grotesque and Arabesque* (1840) and *Tales* (1845), are remarkable for their originality and ingenuity of construction, and in the best of them he rises to a high level of imagination, as in 'The Fall of the House of Usher,' while 'The Gold Bug' is one of the first examples of the cryptogram story; and in 'The Purloined Letter,' 'The Mystery of Marie Roget,' and 'The Murders in the Rue Morgue' he is the pioneer of the modern detective story.

Pollard, Albert Frederick (16 Dec. 1869—3 Aug. 1948), historian, born at Ryde, son of a J.P., was educated at Felsted and Jesus College, Oxford, where he had a brilliant career. In 1893 he was appointed assistant editor of the *Dictionary of National Biography*, to which he contributed about 500 articles, the equivalent of a whole volume of the work. From 1903 to 1931 he was Professor of Constitutional History at the University of London, and from 1908 to 1936 was a Fellow of All Souls, Oxford. In 1906 he founded the Historical Association, and from 1916 to 1922 he edited *History*. Among his more important works are *Henry VIII* (1902), *A Life of Thomas Cranmer* (1904), *Factors in Modern History* (1907), *A History of England* (1912), *The Reign of Henry VIII from Contemporary Sources* (1913—14), *The Life of Nelson* (1918), *A Short History of the Great War* (1920), *Factors in American History* (1925), and *Wolsey* (1929).

Pollard, Alfred William (14 Aug. 1859—8 March 1944), bibliographer, born in London, son of a doctor, was educated at King's College School and St John's College, Oxford. In 1883 he joined the staff of the British Museum as an assistant in the Department of Printed Books, and from 1919 to 1924 was Keeper. In 1915 he was Reader in Bibliography at Cambridge, and from 1919 to 1932 was Professor of English Bibliography in London. Among many other bibliographical works he collaborated in the *Short-Title Catalogue of English Books, 1475—1640*. In 1893 he published *A Chaucer Primer*, and in 1898 edited the Globe *Chaucer*. He made a most important contribution to the study of Shakespeare's text by his *Shakespeare Folios and Quartos* (1909) and *Shakespeare's Fight with the Pirates* (1917). In 1922 he was made a Companion of the Bath.

Pollok, Robert (19 Oct. 1798—18 Sept. 1827), poet, born at Eaglesham, Renfrewshire, son of a small farmer, was educated at Mearns School and Glasgow University. He qualified as a minister but ill health prevented his taking a permanent engagement. In 1824 he published anonymously *Tales of the Covenanters*, and in 1827, the year of his untimely death from consumption, appeared his poem, *The Course of Time*, which contains some fine passages, and occasionally faintly recalls Milton and Young. The poem went through many editions in Britain and America.

Pomfret, John (born 1667, buried 1 Dec. 1702), poet, son of the vicar of Luton, Bedfordshire, was educated at Bedford Grammar School and Cambridge, took orders, and became rector of Millbrook. His chief title to remembrance is a poem, *The Choice* (1701), which celebrates a country life free from care, and was very popular in its day.

Pope, Alexander (21 May 1688—30 May 1744), poet, was born in London, of Roman Catholic parentage. His father was a linen-merchant, who made a competence and retired to a small property at Binfield, near Windsor. Pope received a somewhat desultory education at various Roman Catholic schools, but after the age of 12, when he had a severe illness which left him a cripple, he was practi-

cally self-educated. Though never a profound or accurate scholar,
he had a good knowledge of Latin, and a working acquaintance with
Greek. By 1704 he had written a good deal of verse, which attracted
the attention of Wycherley (q.v.), who introduced him to town life
and to other men of letters. In 1709 his *Pastorals*, written, according
to his own account, at the age of 16, were published in Tonson's
Miscellany, and two years later *The Essay on Criticism* appeared,
and was praised by Addison. The *Rape of the Lock*, which came out
in 1714, placed his reputation on a sure foundation, and thereafter
his life was an uninterrupted and brilliant success. His industry was
untiring, and his literary output almost continuous until his death.
In 1713 *Windsor Forest* (which won him the friendship of Swift) and
The Temple of Fame appeared, and in 1715 the translation of the
Iliad was begun, and the work published at intervals between that
year and 1720. It had enormous popularity, and brought the poet
£5,000. It was followed by the *Odyssey* (1725—6), in which he had
the assistance of Broome and Fenton (qq.v.), who caught his style so
exactly as almost to defy identification. It also was very popular,
and increased his gains to about £8,000, which placed him in a
position of independence. While engaged upon these he removed to
Chiswick, where he lived from 1716 to 1718, and where he issued in
1717 a collected edition of his works, including the 'Elegy on the
Death of an Unfortunate Lady' and the 'Epistle of Eloisa to Abelard.'

In 1718, his father having died, he again removed with his mother
to his famous villa at Twickenham, the adornment of the grounds of
which became one of his chief interests. Here he received the visits
of his friends, who included the most distinguished men of letters,
wits, statesmen, and beauties, all ready to pay homage to the greatest
poet of the time. His next task was his edition of Shakespeare
(1725), a work for which he was not well qualified, though the
preface is a fine piece of prose. The *Miscellanies*, the joint work of
Pope and Swift, were published in 1727 and 1728, and drew down
upon the authors a storm of angry comment, which in turn led to the
production of *The Dunciad*, first published in 1728, and again with
new matter in 1729, an additional book—the fourth—being added
in 1742. In it he satirized with a wit, always keen and biting, often
savage and unfair, the small wits and poetasters, and some of a
quite different quality, who had dealt him real or supposed injuries.
Between 1731 and 1735 he produced his *Epistles*, the last of which,
addressed to Arbuthnot, is also known as the *Prologue to the Satires*,
and contains his ungrateful character of Addison under the name of
Atticus; and also, in 1733, the *Essay on Man*, written under the
influence of Bolingbroke. His last works were his *Imitations of
Horace*, published between 1733 and 1739, and the fourth book of
The Dunciad already mentioned. A naturally delicate constitution,
a deformed and undersized frame (he was only four feet six inches in
height), extreme sensitiveness, over-excitement, and over-work did
not promise a long life, and Pope died at the age of 56.

His position as a poet has been the subject of much contention
among critics, and on the whole is lower than that assigned him by
his contemporaries and immediate successors. Of the higher poetic

qualities, imagination, sympathy, insight, and pathos, he had no great share; but for the work which in his original writings, as distinguished from translations, he set himself to do, his equipment was supreme, and the medium which he used—the heroic couplet—he brought to the highest technical perfection of which it is capable. He wrote for his own age, and in temper and intellectual and spiritual outlook, such as it was, he exactly reflected and interpreted it. In the forging of condensed, pointed, and sparkling maxims of life and criticism he has no equal, and in painting a portrait has few rivals; while in the *Rape of the Lock* he has produced the best mock-heroic poem in existence. Almost no author except Shakespeare is so often quoted. His extreme vanity and sensitiveness to criticism made him often vindictive, unjust, and venomous. They led him also into frequent quarrels, and lost him many friends, including Lady Mary Wortley Montagu, and along with a weakness for finesse and stratagem, displayed especially in the circumstances attending the publication of his literary correspondence, make his character on the whole an unamiable one. On the other hand, he was often generous; he retained the friendship of such men as Swift and Arbuthnot, and he was a most dutiful and affectionate son.

Pope-Hennessy, Dame Una Constance (1876—16 Aug. 1949), biographer, was a daughter of Sir Arthur Birch, and in 1910 married Major-General Ladislaus Pope-Hennessy. Her biographical works include *Three English Women in America* (1929) and studies of *Edgar Allan Poe* (1934), *Charles Dickens* (1945), and *Charles Kingsley* (1948). *The Closed City* (1938) tells of a visit to Leningrad. In 1920 she was made a Dame Commander of the Order of the British Empire in recognition of her volunteer work during the First World War.

Porcupine, Peter, *see* **Cobbett, William.**

Pordage, Samuel (baptized 29 Dec. 1633, died 1691?), poet, son of a clergyman in Berkshire, was educated at Merchant Taylors', studied law at Lincoln's Inn, and made various translations, wrote some poems, two tragedies, *Herod and Marianne* (1673), and *The Siege of Babylon* (1678), and a romance, *Eliana*. He is best known by his *Azaria and Hushai* (1682), in reply to Dryden's *Absalom and Achitophel*, distinguished from the other replies by its moderation and freedom from scurrility.

Porlock, Martin, *see* **MacDonald, Philip.**

Porson, Richard (25 Dec. 1759—25 Sept. 1808), scholar, son of a weaver who was parish clerk of East Ruston, Norfolk, was distinguished from childhood by a marvellous tenacity of memory which attracted the attention of the curate of the parish, who educated him, after which he was sent by a neighbouring squire to Eton. Subsequently a fund was collected for the purpose of maintaining him at Cambridge, where he had a brilliant career, and became a Fellow of Trinity College. This position he lost by refusing to take orders. In 1792 he was appointed Professor of Greek in the University, but resided for the most part in London, where he was much courted by literary men, but unfortunately drank to excess. Porson was one of the very greatest of Greek scholars and critics;, but he has left little permanent work of his own. He edited Aeschylus and four plays of Euripides, the *Hecuba, Orestes, Phoenissae*, and *Medea*, and revolutionized the science of textual criticism. He is buried in the chapel of Trinity College.

Porter, Anna Maria (1780—21 Sept. 1832), novelist, sister of Jane Porter (q.v.), was born in Durham and educated in Edinburgh. At the age of 13 she began writing her *Artless Tales,* which were published two years later, in 1795, and followed by the novels *Walsh Colville* (1797) and *Octavia* (1798), after which she moved to London. Her chief work, *The Hungarian Brothers* (1807) is a tale of the French revolutionary war; others of her historical novels are *Don Sebastian* (1809) and *The Knight of St John* (1817). Her volume of verse *Ballad Romances* appeared in 1811.

Porter, Eleanor Hodgman (1868—23 May 1920), novelist, was born at Littleton, New Hampshire, daughter of Francis H. Hodgman. Because of poor health she left school to live an outdoor life, then studied at the New England Conservatory of Music. When she was 24 she married John L. Porter. Her earliest novels were *Cross Currents* (1907), with its sequel *The Turn of the Tide* (1908), and the cheerfully sentimental *Miss Billy* (1911), with its sequels *Miss Billy's Decision* (1912) and *Miss Billy Married* (1914). But meanwhile she scored a signal success with *Pollyanna* (1913), the story of a young girl who plays the 'glad game' of finding something to be glad about whatever happens. It sold over a million copies, and was followed by *Pollyanna Grows Up* (1915), which had the same effervescent optimism. Others of her novels are *Just David* (1916), *Dawn* (1919), and *Sister Sue* (1921). In 1924 her short stories were collected in *The Tangled Threads* and *Across the Years*.

Porter, Gene Stratton (17 Aug. 1868—6 Dec. 1924), novelist and nature writer, was born Geneva Grace Stratton, daughter of an Indiana farmer. In 1874 the family removed to Wabash, and in 1886 she married Charles D. Porter, a chemist, and they lived in a cabin on the edge of a primitive swamp called the Limberlost. Mrs Porter explored it with her camera and wrote nature articles, and made it the background of her novels *Freckles* (1904), which sold over two million copies, and *A Girl of the Limberlost* (1909). In 1911 she published *The Harvester*, based on her father's personality, and in 1913 *Laddie*, an idealized portrait of her brother Leander, who was drowned at 18. Later pleasantly sentimental novels were *Michael O'Halloran* (1915), and *A Daughter of the Land* (1918). Of her nature books *Homing with the Birds* (1919) has been compared with Fabre's work. She was killed in a motor accident in Los Angeles.

Porter, Jane (1776—24 May 1850), novelist, sister of Anna M. Porter (q.v.), was born in Durham and educated in Edinburgh; where Walter Scott was a frequent visitor at their house. As a girl she was fond of Spenser's poems and tales of chivalry. After moving to London she wrote *Thaddeus of Warsaw* (1803), an historical novel which went through a dozen editions, and followed this with *The Scottish Chiefs* (1810), the story of William Wallace's life, which has always been very popular with Scottish children and was translated into German and Russian.   Later works are *The Pastor's Fireside* (1815), a story of Stuart times, and *Tales Round a Winter's Hearth* (1824), which she wrote in collaboration with her sister.   She also tried writing plays, but with little success.

Porter, Katherine Anne (15 May 1894—   ), short-story writer, born at Indian Creek, Texas, and descended from the pioneer Daniel Boone, was educated at convent schools.   From her earliest years she made story-writing her life's work, but set her standard so high that she destroyed vast masses of manuscripts, and published nothing till she was 30.   She had no literary contacts and found it hard to make a living, but in 1931 she was awarded a Guggenheim Fellowship which enabled her to study abroad.   In 1933 she married Eugene Pressly, of the United States consular service, and after their divorce Albert R. Erskine, Professor of English at Louisiana University.   Her chief volumes of stories are *Flowering Judas* (1930), *Hacienda* (1934), *Noon Wine* (1937), *Pale Horse, Pale Rider* (1939), *The Leaning Tower* (1944), and *No Safe Harbour* (1949).   *The Days Before* (1952) is a collection of essays. Her work has been compared with Katherine Mansfield's.

Porter, William Sydney (11 Sept. 1862—5 June 1910), short-story writer who used the pseudonym O. Henry, was born at Greensboro, North Carolina, son of a doctor.   After leaving school he worked for five years in his father's dispensary, then went to Texas and was successively a ranch hand, a clerk, and a bank teller.   Some time later he was summonsed on a charge of having embezzled the bank funds, and though he seems to have been only technically guilty he cleared off to South America, where he associated with law breakers and refugees.   In 1897 he returned to Texas because of the illness of his wife, was arrested, and was sentenced to five years in the penitentiary, where he is thought to have taken the name of O. Henry from one of the prison guards.   Set at liberty in 1901, he roamed New York, living from hand to mouth and consuming an average of a quart of whisky a day.   He supported himself by his short stories, of which he wrote some 600, and eventually died in hospital of consumption.   His books of short stories include *Cabbages and Kings* (1905), *The Four Million* (1906), *Hearts of the West* (1907), *The Trimmed Lamp* (1907), *The Gentle Grafter* (1908), *Options* (1909), *Roads of Destiny* (1909), *Strictly Business* (1910), *Sixes and Sevens* (1911), and *Rolling Stones* (1913).   With their use of ironical coincidence and unexpected endings, avoidance of the sex motive, and skilful depicting of city types, they set a fashion in American literature.   In 1918 the American Society of Arts and Sciences founded the O. Henry Memorial Award for the best American short story of each year.

Post, Emily (1873—25 Sept. 1960), journalist, born in Baltimore, her maiden name being Price, became a columnist and wrote on social manners.   She is famous for her book *Etiquette in Society, in Business, in Politics, and at Home* (1922), which became a standard American work on behaviour, went through several editions, and has been called 'the blue book of social usage.' Others of her publications are *How to Behave Though a Debutante* (1928); *The Personality of a House* (1930), a book on house decoration; and *The Emily Post Cook Book* (1951).

Postgate, Raymond William (6 Nov. 1896—), historian and novelist, was born in Cambridge, where his father was Professor of Latin, and educated at Oxford. A conscientious objector in the First World War, he was imprisoned in 1916. He married a daughter of George Lansbury, the Labour leader, whose life he wrote in 1951, and like his sister, who married G. D. H. Cole (q.v.) he wrote both Socialist propaganda and detective stories. His political books include *Revolution from 1789 to 1906* (1920), a *History of the British Workers* (1926), and *Karl Marx* (1933). His detective stories are *Verdict of Twelve* (1940) and *Somebody at the Door* (1943).

Potter, Helen Beatrix (6 July 1866—22 Dec. 1943), writer of children's books, was born in Kensington, daughter of a wealthy barrister who never practised. She never went to school but was educated by governesses, who encouraged her taste for drawing and the study of natural history. Holidays in Scotland and the Lakes were a welcome relief from the formal London home where the adjacent block of museums was her chief relaxation. Devoted to animals, she kept as pets rabbits, mice, frogs, and a hedgehog. Letters to a convalescent child friend contained anecdotes about these, illustrated with her own drawings, which were collected in *Peter Rabbit* (1900), her first book. *Benjamin Bunny* (1904) was a sequel, and other animal tales were *Squirrel Nutkin* (1903) and *Mrs Tiggy-Winkle* (1905), the tale of a hedgehog. In 1906 she bought Hill Top Farm at Sawrey near Windermere, which became her other home. *Jemima Puddle-Duck* (1908) is about the farm itself; *The Pie and the Patty-Pan* (1905) is about the village; while *Ginger and Pickles* (1909) tells of the village shop. In 1913 at the age of 47 she married William Hellis, a solicitor from Appleby, and had 30 years of happy married life as a minor landowner. Her books have been translated into French, German, Spanish, and Welsh.

Potter, Stephen (1 Feb. 1900—), humorist, was educated at Westminster and Merton College, Oxford. He then became a lecturer in English at London and some other universities. In 1929 he published *The Young Man*, a novel which he himself confessed had no plot, no characters, and no action. In 1930 he wrote a study of D. H. Lawrence and in 1935 one of Coleridge. *The Muse in Chains* (1937) is a study in education. But he is chiefly known by his humorous books *The Theory and Practice of Gamesmanship or the Art of Winning Games Without Actually Cheating* (1947), *Some Notes on Lifemanship* (1950), and *One-Upmanship* (1952). His humour consists of a scientific and sympathetic analysis of different types of humbug, which he solemnly describes as a principle to be followed. A later book was *Sense of Humour* (1955).

Pound, Ezra Loomis (30 Oct. 1885—), poet and translator, distantly related to Longfellow on his mother's side, was born at Hailey, Idaho, and educated at Pennsylvania University and

Hamilton College. In 1907 he travelled in Europe, then settled in London, where he lived from 1908 to 1920, became friendly with T. S. Eliot, James Joyce, and Wyndham Lewis, and married Dorothy Shakespear. His most important volumes of verse at this time were *Personae* (1909), later enlarged, and *Ripostes* (1912), which may be reckoned the beginning of the Imagist Movement, of which he was one of the leaders. A great experimenter in verse, he also took part with the Vorticists, and from 1917 to 1919 was editor of the *Little Review*. *Quia Pauper Amavi* was published in 1919 and *Umbra* in 1920. From 1924 to 1945 he lived at Rapallo on the Italian Riviera, occupied with his great series of *Cantos*, over 70 of which were published in this period and had considerable influence on other writers. In 1928 he received the *Dial* Award for distinguished service to American letters, but his Fascist broadcasts during the Second World War brought him into ill repute. Taken to the United States in 1946, he was tried for treason, but acquitted as being of unsound mind and confined in a public mental hospital in Washington. Nevertheless in 1949 he was awarded the Bollingen Prize for his *Pisan Cantos*, which were written while he was in an American army prison camp in Italy. Pound also made many translations from French, Italian, and Chinese, and published several outspoken books of criticism, including *The Spirit of Romance* (1910), *Polite Essays* (1937), and *Literary Essays* (1954).

Powell, Anthony Dymoke (21 Dec. 1905—   ), novelist, was born in London, son of a lieutenant-colonel in the Welch Regiment. After a childhood spent in a variety of places to which his father was posted, including Finland, he was educated at Eton and Balliol College, Oxford, where he studied history. In 1934 he married Lady Violet Pakenham, daughter of the Earl of Longford. During the Second World War he held a commission in his father's old regiment for a year and a half, and was then transferred to the Intelligence Corps. His first novel, *Afternoon Men* (1931), was followed by *Venusberg* (1932), *From a View to a Death* (1933), *Agents and Patients* (1936), and *What's Become of Waring?* (1939). A linked series of novels, to have the general title ' The Music of Time,' included *A Question of Upbringing* (1951), *A Buyer's Market* (1952), *The Acceptance World* (1955), and *At Lady Molly's* (1957), which was awarded the Tait Black Memorial Prize. In 1948 he published a biography, *John Aubrey and his Friends*. He was made a C.B.E. in 1956, and also held some foreign decorations.

Powell, Frederick York (14 Jan. 1850—8 May 1904), historian, born in London, son of a doctor, was educated at Rugby and Oxford. Called to the Bar at Middle Temple in 1874, he was for a short time a lecturer on law and political economy. In 1894 he succeeded Froude as Professor of Modern History at Oxford, but published much less than his wide learning warranted, his chief works being *Early England to the Norman Conquest* (1876) and a *History of England from the Earliest Times to the Death of Henry VII* (1885). He also had a high reputation as a Scandinavian scholar, and collaborated in editing the *Corpus Poeticum Boreale* (1881), a collection of the whole' of ancient Northern poetry, with translation and commentary.

Powys, John Cowper (8 Oct. 1872—   ), poet, essayist, and novelist, was born at Shirley, Derbyshire, where his father was vicar; his mother was a collateral descendant of Donne and Cowper. Of the three brothers Powys, John is the best known.   Educated at Sherborne and Cambridge, he taught German at Brighton for a time, then became an Extension Lecturer for Oxford, Cambridge, and London; from 1928 to 1934 he lectured in the United States.   His first book of verse appeared in 1899 and was followed by *Wolfsbane Rhymes* (1916), *Mandragora* (1917), and *Samphire* (1922).   Of his novels the best are *Wolf Solent* (1929), *A Glastonbury Romance* (1932), and *Owen Glendower* (1940); others are *Rodmoor* (1916), *Ducdame* (1925), *Weymouth Sands* (1934), *Porius, a Romance of the Dark Ages* (1951), and *The Inmates* (1952).   Books of essays include *The Meaning of Culture* (1929), *In Defence of Sensuality* (1930), *A Philosophy of Solitude* (1933), *The Art of Happiness* (1935), *The Pleasures of Literature* (1938), and *The Art of Growing Old* (1944). He also wrote studies of *Dostoievsky* (1947) and *Rabelais* (1948). His *Autobiography* appeared in 1934.

Powys, Llewelyn (13 Aug. 1884—2 Dec. 1939), essayist and novelist, born at Dorchester, Dorset, and educated at Sherborne and Cambridge, was a brother of J. C. Powys and T. F. Powys (qq.v.). In 1909 he lectured in America, but fell ill of consumption, and for health reasons spent the years from 1914 to 1919 in Kenya as manager of a ranch.   From 1920 to 1925 he worked as a journalist in New York, then returned to Dorset with his American wife Alyse Gregory, and lived in a cottage on the south coast.   From time to time he travelled abroad, visited Palestine and the West Indies, and finally died in Switzerland of consumption.   His works include many stories and sketches from his years in Africa, including *Ebony and Ivory* (1922) and *Black Laughter* (1924).   Books of essays are *The Cradle of God* (1929), *Impassioned Clay* (1931), *Glory of Life* (1934), and *Dorset Essays* (1936); *Apples be Ripe* (1930) is a novel. *Confessions of Two Brothers* (1916) was written in conjunction with John Cowper Powys, to whom he was devoted; other biographical volumes are *Skin for Skin* (1925) and *The Verdict of Bridlegoose* (1926).

Powys, Theodore Francis (20 Dec. 1875—27 Nov. 1953), novelist, born in Shirley, Derbyshire, and educated at Dorchester Grammar School, was a brother of J. C. and Llewelyn Powys (qq.v.).   In 1905 he married and thenceforward lived a secluded and uneventful life at East Chaldon, Dorset.   His love of quiet appears in his *Soliloquies of a Hermit*, first published in America in 1916.   The most original of the three brothers, he wrote highly eccentric novels, of which *Mr Weston's Good Wine* (1927) is considered the best.   Others are *Black Bryony* (1923), *Mark Only* (1924), *Mr Tasker's Gods* (1925), *Unclay* (1931), *Captain Patch* (1935), and *Goat Green* (1937).   *The Left Leg* (1923), *The House with the Echo* (1929), *When Thou Wast Naked* (1931), and *Bottle's Path* (1946) are volumes of short stories.

Praed, Rosa Caroline (27 March 1851—10 April 1935), novelist who wrote as Mrs Campbell Praed, was born at Bromelton, Queensland, daughter of Thomas L. Murray-Prior, the Postmaster-General, and educated at Brisbane; in her youth she spent many hours in the ladies' gallery of the State Legislature. In 1872 she married Arthur Campbell Bulkley Praed, nephew of Praed the poet (q.v.). In 1876 she went to London and made her home in England. Her first novel, *An Australian Heroine* (1880) was followed by *Policy and Passion* (1881), *Nadine* (1882), *Moloch* (1883), *Zero* (1884), *The Romance of a Station* (1891), *December Roses* (1893), *The Other Mrs Jacobs* (1903), *Nyria* (1904), and *Opal Fire* (1910). She formed a friendship with Justin McCarthy (q.v.), and they collaborated in *The Ladies' Gallery* (1888) and *The Rival Princess* (1890). *My Australian Girlhood* (1902) tells of her early life.

Praed, Winthrop Mackworth (26 July 1802—15 July 1839), poet, born in London, son of a lawyer, was educated at Eton, where he edited a school magazine, and at Cambridge, where he twice won the Chancellor's Medal for English verse. In 1829 he was called to the Bar, and shortly afterwards became an M.P. He lost his seat with the passing of the Reform Act, but sat subsequently for Great Yarmouth and then Aylesbury, and in 1835 was Secretary to the Board of Control in Peel's Administration. A few years later he died of consumption. A collected edition of his poems was published after his death. Although Praed wrote a considerable amount of serious poetry, he is remembered chiefly as the supreme master of society verse—elegant trifles wittily depicting men and women as they appear in the fashionable world. Well-known examples of this are his 'Good-night to the Season' and 'Our Ball,' while 'The Vicar' shows his dexterity in what has been called metrical *genre*-painting.

Pratt, Edwin John (4 Feb. 1883—   ), poet, was born at Western Bay, Newfoundland, son of a Methodist minister. Educated at St John's High School and the University of Toronto, where he obtained a Ph.D., he was appointed to the English staff at Victoria College there in 1920, and became Professor of English, retiring in 1953. From 1936 to 1943 he edited the *Canadian Poetry Magazine*, and in 1941 he was awarded the Lorne Pierce Gold Medal of the Royal Society of Canada, of which he had been a Fellow since 1930. One of the greatest of modern Canadian poets, he was 40 before he became well known. Volumes of his poetry include *Newfoundland Verse* (1923), *The Witches' Brew* (1926), *Titans* (1926), *The Iron Door* (1927), *Verses of the Sea* (1930), *Many Moods* (1933), *The Loss of the Titanic* (1935), *The Fable of the Goats* (1937), *Dunkirk* (1941), *Still Life* (1943), *They Are Returning* (1945), *Behind the Log* (1947), and *Towards the Last Spike* (1952). Made a C.M.G. in 1946, he held honorary degrees of four universities.

Preedy, George R., *see* **Long, Margaret G.**

Prescott, William Hickling (4 May 1796—28 Jan. 1859), historian, born at Salem, Massachusetts, the son of an eminent lawyer, was educated at Harvard, where he met with an accident to one of his eyes which seriously affected his sight for the remainder of his life. He made an extended tour in Europe, and on his return to America

T

he married and abandoning the idea of a legal career, resolved to devote himself to literature. After 10 years of study, he published in 1837 his *History of Ferdinand and Isabella*, which at once gained for him a high place among historians. It was followed in 1843 by the *History of the Conquest of Mexico*, and in 1847 by the *Conquest of Peru*. His last work was the *History of Philip II*, of which the third volume appeared in 1858, and which was left unfinished. In that year he had an apoplectic shock, and another in 1859 was the cause of his death. In all his works he displayed great research, impartiality, and an admirable narrative power. The great disadvantage at which, owing to his very imperfect vision, he worked, makes the first of these qualities specially remarkable, for his authorities in a foreign tongue were read to him, while he had to write on a frame for the blind.

Preston, George F., *see* de Tabley.

Price, Richard (23 Feb. 1723—19 April 1791), writer on ethics' politics, and economics, was born at Tynton in Glamorgan, son of a minister, and educated at a school in London. He became a preacher at Newington Green and Hackney. In 1758 his *Review of the Principal Questions and Difficulties in Morals* a work of considerable metaphysical power, appeared; and it was followed in 1766 by a treatise on *The Importance of Christianity*. In 1769 his work on *Reversionary Payments* was published, and his Northampton Mortality Table was about the same time constructed. These, though long superseded, were in their day most valuable contributions to economical science. His most popular work, *Observations on Civil Liberty and the Justice and Policy of the War with America*, appeared in 1776, had an enormous sale, and led to his being invited to go to America and assist in establishing the financial system of the new Government. This he declined chiefly on the score of age.

Prichard, Katharine Susannah (1884—   ), novelist, was born in Fiji, daughter of a journalist, and taken to Australia as a child. She made her home in Western Australia, but travelled extensively, and lived in London for some years, working in Fleet Street. Her first novel, *The Pioneers* (1915) won the Hodder & Stoughton Prize of £1,000, and *Coonardoo* (1929) was awarded the Sydney Bulletin Prize of £500 for the best Australian novel. Others of her books are *Windlestraws* (1915), *Working Bullocks* (1926), *The Black Opal* (1921), which tells of Queensland, and a trilogy written round the Australian gold-fields—*The Roaring Nineties* (1946), *Golden Miles* (1948), and *Winged Seeds* (1950). In 1919 she married Hugo Vivian Hope Throssell, V.C., son of a West Australian premier; he died in 1933.

Prideaux, Humphrey (3 May 1648—1 Nov. 1724), clergyman and scholar, belonged to an ancient Cornish family, was born at Padstow, and was educated at Westminster School and Oxford, where he became Lecturer in Hebrew. He first attracted notice by his description of the Arundel Marbles (1676), which gained for him powerful patrons, and he rose to be Dean of Norwich. Among his other works are a *Life of Mahomet* (1697), and *The Old and New Testament connected in the History of the Jews and Neighbouring Nations* (1715—17), long an important work, of which many editions were brought out.

Priestley, John Boynton (13 Sept. 1894—   ), novelist, dramatist, and essayist, was born at Bradford, son of a schoolmaster. During the First World War he served with the Devonshire Regiment. After it he studied at Trinity Hall, Cambridge, and then went to London, where he worked as reviewer and critic. After publishing two novels, *Adam in Moonshine* (1927) and *Benighted* (1927) he scored a brilliant success with the long *Good Companions* (1929), which was awarded the Tait Black Memorial Prize and was very popular; *Angel Pavement* (1930) was also very successful. Others of his novels are *Wonder Hero* (1933), *They Walk in the City* (1936), *Let the People Sing* (1940), *Bright Day* (1946), *Jenny Villiers* (1947), *Festival at Farbridge* (1951), and *The Magicians* (1954). His hearty down-to-earth stories are in the tradition of Fielding. In 1932 he began as a dramatist with *Dangerous Corner*, and followed it with over a dozen plays, of which the chief are *Eden End* (1935), *Time and the Conways* (1937), *I Have Been Here Before* (1938), *Johnson Over Jordan* (1939), and the popular comedies *Laburnum Grove* (1933) and *When We Are Married* (1938), in which he himself played lead at short notice. His books of essays include *Brief Diversions* (1922), *Apes and Angels* (1928), *The Balconinny* (1929), *Postscripts* (1940), and *Delight* (1949). He also wrote lives of *George Meredith* (1926) and *Thomas Love Peacock* (1927), as well as *A Short History of the English Novel* (1927). *Midnight on the Desert* (1937) is autobiographical. He was married three times.

Priestley, Joseph (13 March 1733—6 Feb. 1804), clergyman and chemist, born at Fieldhead in Yorkshire, son of a draper, was brought up a Calvinist, but changed his views and at the age of 22 became a Unitarian minister at Needham Market, Suffolk. In 1761 he became a teacher of languages at Warrington Academy, and about the same time began to devote himself to science, alternating between that and preaching. In 1766 his *History of Electricity* won him election as a Fellow of the Royal Society. After officiating for five years as a minister in Leeds, in 1773 he travelled on the Continent as companion to Lord Shelburne, and made the acquaintance of various eminent scientists. In 1774 he made his famous discovery of oxygen. In 1780 he moved to Birmingham, but his championing of the French Revolution caused his house to be attacked and looted by the mob, and he had to escape to London. In 1794 he followed his three sons to America, where he was warmly welcomed and founded the first Unitarian church in Philadelphia. More distinguished in science than in theology, he has been called the father of modern chemistry.

Pringle, Thomas (5 Jan. 1789—5 Dec. 1834), poet, born at Blaiklaw, Teviotdale, son of a farmer, was lame from birth. Educated at Kelso Grammar School and Edinburgh University, he became known to Scott, by whose influence he obtained a grant of land in South

Africa, to which he, with his father and brothers, emigrated. He took to literary work in Cape Town, and conducted two papers, which were suppressed for their free criticisms of the Colonial Government. Thereupon he returned and settled in London, where he published *African Sketches* in 1834. He is remembered as a South African poet, for he was a pioneer in using that country's scenery and vocabulary in verse.

Prior, Matthew (21 July 1664—18 Sept. 1721), poet and diplomat, born near Wimborne Minster, Dorset, son of a joiner, was educated by an uncle, and sent to Westminster School. Befriended by the Earl of Dorset, he proceeded to Cambridge, and while there wrote, jointly with Charles Montague, *The Hind and the Panther Transversed to the Story of the Country and City Mouse* (1687), a burlesque of Dryden's *Hind and Panther*. After holding various diplomatic posts, in which he showed ability and discretion, he entered Parliament in 1700, and, deserting the Whigs, joined the Tories, by whom he was employed in various capacities, including that of Ambassador at Paris. On the death of Queen Anne he was recalled, and in 1715 imprisoned, but after two years released. In 1719 a folio edition of his works was brought out, by which he realized £4,000, and Lord Harley having presented him with an equal sum, he looked forward to the peace and comfort which were his chief ambition. He did not, however, long enjoy his prosperity, dying two years later. Among his longer poems are 'Henry and Emma,' a frigid modernization of the old ballad of 'The Nut-Brown Maid'; 'Alma, or the Progress of the Mind'; and his own favourite, 'Solomon on the Vanity of the World.' But these are now neglected for his shorter epigrammatic pieces, of which 'To a Child of Quality' is the best known. His chief characteristic is a certain elegance and easy grace, in which he is perhaps unrivalled. He was buried in the Poet's Corner of Westminster Abbey.

Procter, Adelaide Ann (30 Oct. 1825—2 Feb. 1864), poetess, born in London, was a daughter of Bryan Waller Procter (q.v.). Many of her poems were first published in *Household Words* and *All the Year Round*, and afterwards collected under the title of *Legends and Lyrics* (1858), of which many editions appeared. In 1851 she became a Roman Catholic. She took much interest in social questions affecting women, and wrote the well-known song 'The Lost Chord,' as well as many hymns.

Procter, Bryan Waller (21 Nov. 1787—5 Oct. 1874), poet who wrote under the name Barry Cornwall, an imperfect anagram of his Christian names, was born in Leeds. Educated at Harrow, he went to London and practised successfully as a solicitor. Thereafter he became a barrister, and was from 1832 to 1861 a Commissioner of Lunacy. By 1823 he had produced four volumes of poetry and a tragedy, *Mirandola* (1821). His works include *Dramatic Scenes* (1819), *A Sicilian Story* (1820), *Marcian Colonna* (1820), *The Flood of Thessaly* (1823), and *English Songs* (1832), which last will perhaps survive his other writings. Procter was the friend of most of his literary contemporaries, and was universally popular.

Prout, Father, *see* Mahony, F. S.

Prowse, William Jeffery (6 May 1836—17 April 1870), poet, born at Torquay, went to school in Greenwich, where he was fond of all sports, especially cricket. Drifting into journalism, he became a leader-writer on the *Daily Telegraph*, but his life was cut short by consumption. He was a brilliant writer of light verse and parody, one of his best-known pieces being 'The City of Prague.'

Prynne, William (1600—24 Oct. 1669), puritan pamphleteer, born at Swanswick in Somerset, was educated at Oxford and studied law at Lincoln's Inn, of which he became a bencher, but soon became immersed in the writing of controversial pamphlets. After the *Unloveliness of Lovelocks* and *Health's Sicknesse* (1627—30) appeared his best known work, *Histrio-Mastix: The Players Scourge or Actors Tragedie* (1633), a bitter attack on most of the popular amusements of the day. It was punished with inhuman severity. Prynne was brought before the Star Chamber, fined £5,000, pilloried, and had both his ears cut off. Undeterred by this he issued from his prison a fierce attack upon Laud and the hierarchy, for which he was again fined, pilloried, and branded on both cheeks with the letters S. L. (seditious libeller). Removed to Carnarvon Castle he remained there until liberated in 1641 by the Long Parliament. He soon after became a member of the House, and joined in the prosecution of Laud. He was among those expelled from the House of Commons by Cromwell, whom he had opposed in regard to the execution of the King with such asperity that he again suffered imprisonment, from which he was released in 1652. He supported the Restoration, and was by Charles II appointed Keeper of the Records in the Tower. Here he did good service by compiling the *Register of Parliamentary Writs* (1659-64) and *Records in the Tower of London* (1689).

Psalmanazar, George (1679?—3 May 1763), literary impostor. His real name is unknown, his pseudonym being taken from Shalmaneser, an Assyrian prince mentioned in the second Book of Kings He is believed to have been a native of France or Switzerland, but represented himself as a native of the island of Formosa, and palmed off a Formosan language of his own construction, to which he afterwards added a description of the island. For a time he was in the military service of the Duke of Mecklenburg, and formed a connection with William Innes, chaplain of a Scottish regiment, who collaborated with him in his frauds. Innes, however, was appointed chaplain to the forces in Portugal, and Psalmanazar was unable to maintain his impositions, and was exposed. After a serious illness in 1728 he turned over a new leaf and became a respectable and efficient literary hack; his works in his latter days included a *General History of Printing*, contributions to the *Universal History*, and an *Autobiography* containing an account of his impostures.

Puddicombe, Anne Adalisa (6 Oct. 1836—21 June 1908), novelist who wrote under the name Allen Raine, was born at Newcastle-Emlyn, Carmarthenshire, daughter of Benjamin Evans, a solicitor, and was educated at Cheltenham and Southfields. In 1872 she married Beynon Puddicombe, a bank employee, who became insane and died in 1906. After her first novel, *A Welsh Singer* (1897), a love story of peasant people, she turned out books very rapidly. Among the titles are *Torn Sails* (1898), *By Berwen Banks* (1899), *Garthowen* (1900), *A Welsh Witch* (1902), *On the Wings of the Wind* (1903), *Hearts of Wales* (1905), *Queen of the Rushes* (1906), *All in a Month* (1908), *Where Billows Roll* (1909), and *Under the Thatch* (1910).

Pulitzer, Joseph (10 April 1847—29 Oct. 1911), newspaper proprietor, born in Mako, Hungary, emigrated to the United States in 1864 and worked as a journalist in St Louis. Later he started his own paper there, and in 1883 he purchased the New York *World*. His name is perpetuated in the Pulitzer Prizes provided for in his will, to be awarded in journalism and literature. One each is awarded annually for the best novel, play, book of poems, biography, and history published by an American, the value being 500 or 1,000 dollars.

Purchas, Samuel (1575—1626), compiler of travels, born at Thaxted, Essex, and educated at Cambridge, took orders, and held various benefices, including the rectory of St Martin's, Ludgate Hill. The papers of R. Hakluyt (q.v.) came into his hands, and he made several compilations relating to man, his nature, doings, and surroundings. His three works are *Purchas his Pilgrimage, or Relations of the World and the Religions observed in all Ages and Places* (1612); *Purchas his Pilgrim, Microcosmus, or the History of Man* (1619); and *Hakluytus Posthumus, or Purchas his Pilgrimes, containing a History of the World in Sea Voyages and Land Travels* (1625). Although credulous, diffuse, and confused, these works have preserved many interesting and curious matters which would otherwise have been lost.

Pusey, Edward Bouverie (22 Aug. 1800—14 Sept. 1882), scholar and theologian, born at Pusey, Berkshire, and educated at Eton and Oxford, belonged to the family of Lord Folkestone, whose name was Bouverie, his father assuming that of Pusey on inheriting certain estates. After studying in Germany, he became in 1828 Regius Professor of Hebrew at Oxford. His first important work was an *Essay on the Causes of Rationalism in German Theology*, and the arrest of similar tendencies in England became one of the leading objects of his life. He was one of the chief leaders of the Tractarian movement, and contributed tracts on *Baptism* and on *Fasting*. In consequence of a sermon on the Eucharist, he was in 1843 suspended from the office of University Preacher which he then held. Later writings related to *Confession* and *The Doctrine of the Real Presence*, and in 1865 he issued an *Eirenicon* in support of union with the Church of Rome. He was prominent in all movements and controversies affecting the University. Pusey House, a theological centre in Oxford, was founded in his memory.

Putnam, George Palmer (7 Sept. 1887—4 Jan. 1950), writer and publisher, a grandson of the founder of Putnam's publishing house, was born at Rye, New York, and educated at Harvard and the University of California. He was four times married, his third wife being Amelia Earhart, the airwoman, with whom he collaborated in

Last Flight (1938). Others of his books are *In the Oregon Country* (1918), *Soaring Wings* (1939), *Duration* (1943), and *Wide Margins: A Publisher's Autobiography* (1942).

Puttenham, George (1530?—1590), critic, son of a country gentleman, travelled extensively on the Continent in his youth. He wrote a prose *Apologie* for Queen Elizabeth I's treatment of Mary Queen of Scots, and has also been credited with the authorship of the anonymous *Arte of English Poesie* (1589), the earliest detailed survey of English poetry, with sections on metre and poetic figures. Some authorities, however, attribute this to his elder brother Richard (1520—1601).

Pye, Henry James (20 Feb. 1745—11 Aug. 1813), Poet Laureate, was born at Faringdon, Berkshire, and educated at Magdalen College, Oxford. In 1784 he entered Parliament as member for Berkshire, and s pported Pitt, who had him appointed Poet Laureate in 1790. He duly produced official odes of impeccable loyalty and incredible dullness, which made him a byword in literary circles for flatness and frigidity. Among his works are *Naucratia, or Naval Dominion* (1798), *Adelaide, a Tragedy* (1800), *Alfred, an Epic* (1801), and a more valuable *Comment on the Commentators of Shakespeare* (1807). He also translated Aristotle's *Poetics*.

Q

Q, *see* Quiller-Couch, Sir Arthur T.

Quarles, Francis (8 May 1592—8 Sept. 1644), poet, born at his father's manorhouse of Stewards near Romford, was at Cambridge, and studied law at Lincoln's Inn. Thereafter he went to the Continent, and at Heidelberg acted as cup-bearer to Elizabeth of Bohemia, daughter of James I. He next appears as secretary to Archbishop Ussher in Ireland, and was in 1639 Chronologer of the City of London. On the outbreak of the Civil War he sided with the Royalists, and was plundered by the Parliamentarians of his books and rare manuscripts; this is said to have so grieved him as to bring about his death. His first book of poems was *A Feast for Worms* (1620); others were *Hadassa* (1621), *Sion's Elegies* (1625), and *Divine Emblems* (1635), by far his most popular book. His style was that fashionable in his day, affected, artificial, and full of 'conceits,' but he had both real poetical fire and genuine wit, mixed with much that was false in taste, and though quaint and crabbed, is seldom feeble or dull. He was twice married, and had by his first wife 18 children.

Queen, Ellery, *see* **Dannay, Frederic.**

Quennell, Marjorie (1884—   ), author and artist, born at Bromley Common, Kent, daughter of Allen Courtney, attended art schools at the Crystal Palace, Beckenham, and Westminster. In 1904 she married Charles Henry Bourne Quennell, an architect, and after his death in 1935 was curator of the Geffrye Museum, London, till 1941. In collaboration with her husband she published a noteworthy series of educational books, of which the first and most popular was *A History of Everyday Things in England* (four volumes 1918—34). It was followed by the 'Everyday Life' series, beginning with *Everyday Life in Prehistoric Times* (1921), and giving separate volumes to the *Old Stone Age* (1921), the *Bronze and Early Iron Ages* (1922), *Roman Britain* (1924), *Saxon and Norman Times* (1926), *Archaic Greece* (1931), and *Classical Greece* (1932); *The Good New Days* (1935) closed the series.

Quennell, Peter Courtney (9 March 1905—   ), poet, critic, and biographer, son of the above, was born in London and educated at Berkhamsted and Oxford. Freelancing in London, he wrote for various periodicals, then in 1930 was Professor of English in Tokio University, and wrote *A Superficial Journey through Tokio and Pekin* (1932). Back in London, he edited the *Cornhill Magazine* from 1944 to 1951. His first book of verse, *Masques and Poems* (1922), written while he was still at school, was followed by *Poems* (1926) and *Inscription on a Fountain Head* (1929). *The Phoenix-kind* (1931) is a novel, and *Sympathy* (1933) a volume of short stories. But he is best known for his biographies, *Byron: the Years of Fame* (1935) and *Byron in Italy* (1941), together with *Caroline of England*

(1939) and *John Ruskin, the Portrait of a Prophet* (1949). *Four Portraits* (1945) contains studies of Boswell, Gibbon, Sterne, and Wilkes, and *The Singular Preference* (1952) is a book of essays.

Quiller-Couch, Sir Arthur Thomas (21 Nov. 1863—12 May 1944), scholar and novelist, was born at Bodmin, Cornwall. Educated at Newton Abbot College, Clifton College, and Trinity College, Oxford, he lectured there in Classics in 1886 and 1887, then went to London and edited the *Speaker* till 1899. In 1910 he was knighted, and in 1912 succeeded A. W. Verrall in the King Edward VII Chair of English Literature which had been founded at Cambridge the previous year. He was known first for his novels, written under the pseudonym Q, among the best being *Dead Man's Rock* (1887), *Troy Town* (1888), *The Splendid Spur* (1889), *The Blue Pavilions* (1891), *The Delectable Duchy* (1893), *The Ship of Stars* (1899), *Fort Amity* (1904), and *Nicky Nan, Reservist* (1915); the unfinished *Castle Dor* was completed by Daphne du Maurier (q.v.) and published in 1962. His volumes of verse include *Verses and Parodies* (1893), *Poems and Ballads* (1896), and *The Vigil of Venus* (1912). A brilliant critic and an inspiring lecturer, he opened up new vistas in the study of English with his books *On the Art of Writing* (1916), *On the Art of Reading* (1920), *Studies in Literature* (three series, 1918, 1922, 1929), *Shakespeare's Workmanship* (1918), and *Charles Dickens and Other Victorians* (1925). His verse anthologies, which have become household works, include the *Oxford Book of English Verse* (1900), *Oxford Book of Victorian Verse* (1913), and *Oxford Book of Ballads* (1910), and he was joint editor of the New Cambridge edition of Shakespeare. He held honorary degrees of Aberdeen, Edinburgh, and Bristol, and in 1937 was elected mayor of Fowey. His chief recreations were yachting and rowing.

R

Radcliffe, Ann (9 July 1764—7 Feb. 1823), novelist, was born in London, daughter of William Ward, a tradesman. In her youth she met Mrs Piozzi and Mrs Montagu (qq.v.). In 1787 she married William Radcliffe, editor and proprietor of a weekly newspaper, the *English Chronicle*. In 1789 she published her first novel, *The Castles of Athlin and Dunbayne*, of which the scene is laid in Scotland. It, however, gave little promise of the future power of the author. In the following year appeared *The Sicilian Romance*, which attracted attention by its vivid descriptions and startling incidents. Next came *The Romance of the Forest* (1791), followed by *The Mysteries of Udolpho* (1794), best-known of her works, and *The Italian* (1797), a story of the Inquisition. *Gaston de Blondeville*, edited by Sergeant Talfourd, was brought out posthumously. Mrs Radcliffe has been called the Salvator Rosa of British novelists. She excels in the description of scenes of mystery and terror whether of natural scenery or incident: in the former displaying a high degree of imaginative power, and in the latter great ingenuity and fertility of invention. She had, however, little power of delineating character.

Raine, Allen, *see* **Puddicombe, Anne.**

Raine, Kathleen Jessie (14 June 1908—   ), poetess, was born in London. Her father and mother were both schoolteachers, and she spent her holidays with a grandmother who lived in Northumberland, on the Scottish border. After studying biology at Girton College, Cambridge, she married Charles Madge, who became a professor of sociology. Later the marriage was dissolved, and she retired to her beloved Border country, where she wrote her first volume of poems, *Stone and Flower* (1943). Afterwards she returned to London as a lecturer at Morley College. Further volumes of her work are *Living in Time* (1946), *The Pythoness* (1949), and *The Year One* (1952); her *Collected Poems* appeared in 1956. Most of her poems are short lyrics with a mystical atmosphere which has caused her to be compared with Blake, and she has also some kinship with the metaphysical poets.

Raine, William MacLeod (22 June 1871—25 July 1954), novelist, was born in London of Scottish parents and taken at the age of 10 to the United States, where he was educated at Sarcey College, Arkansas, and Oberlin College. He worked as a ranch hand, a schoolmaster, and then a reporter. Making his home in Denver, he started writing English romances and then Westerns, with which he was highly successful. Among his novels are *Wyoming* (1908), *Ridgway of Montana* (1909), *Bucky O'Connor* (1910), *A Texas Ranger* (1911), *The Yukon Trail* (1917), *Gunsight Pass* (1921), *Colorado*

(1928), *Square Shooter* (1935), *Hell and High Water* (1943), *Clattering Hoofs* (1946), and *Challenge to Danger* (1952). Other works are *Famous Sheriffs and Western Outlaws* (1929), *The Way of Life of a Frontier Peace Officer* (1941), and *Saddlebag Folk* (1942).

Ralegh *or* **Raleigh, Sir Walter** (1552?—29 Oct. 1618), explorer, statesman, historian, and poet, came of an old Devon family, and was born at Hayes Barton in that county. In 1568 he was sent to Oxford, where he greatly distinguished himself. In the next year he began his career of adventure by going to France as a volunteer in aid of the Huguenots, serving thereafter in the Low Countries. The year 1579 saw him engaged in his first voyage of adventure in conjunction with his half-brother, Sir Humphrey Gilbert. Their object was to discover and settle lands in North America; but the expedition failed, chiefly owing to opposition by the Spaniards. The next year he was fighting against the rebels in Ireland; and shortly thereafter attracted the notice of Queen Elizabeth, in whose favour he rapidly rose. In 1584 he fitted out a new colonizing expedition to North America, and succeeded in discovering and occupying Virginia, named after the Queen. On his return, he was knighted. In the dark and anxious days of the Armada, 1587—8, Ralegh was employed in organizing resistance, and rendered distinguished service in action. But his intrigue and private marriage with Elizabeth Throckmorton, one of the maids of honour, in 1593, lost him for a time the favour of the Queen. Driven from the Court he returned to the schemes of adventure which had so great a charm for him, and fired by the Spanish accounts of the fabulous wealth of Guiana, he and some of his friends fitted out an expedition which, however, though attended with various brilliant episodes, proved unsuccessful. Restored to the favour of the Queen, he was appointed an admiral in the expeditions to Cadiz, 1596, and in the following year was engaged in an attack on the Azores, in both of which he added greatly to his reputation.

The death of Elizabeth in 1603 was the turning point in Ralegh's fortunes. The new sovereign and his old enemies combined to compass his ruin. Accused of conspiring against the King he was, against all evidence, sentenced to death, and though this was not at the time carried out, he was imprisoned in the Tower and his estates confiscated. During this confinement he composed his *History of the World* (1614), which he brought down to 130 B.C. It is one of the finest specimens of Elizabethan prose, reflective in matter and dignified and grave in style. Released in 1615, he set out on his last voyage, again to Guiana, but this, like the former, proved a failure. He returned a broken and dying man, but met with no pity from his ungenerous King, who, urged, it is believed, by the King of Spain, had him beheaded on Tower Hill. Ralegh is one of the most striking and brilliant figures in an age crowded with great men. Of a noble presence, he was possessed of a commanding intellect and a versatility which enabled him to shine in every enterprise to which he set himself. In addition to his unfinished history he wrote *A Report of the Truth of the Fight about the Azores* (1591), which describes Sir Richard Grenville's famous encounter with the Spanish fleet, and

The Discoverie of the Empire of Guiana, besides various poems chiefly of a philosophic cast, of which perhaps the best known are 'The Pilgrimage,' and that beginning 'If all the world and love were young,' an answer to Marlowe's 'Passionate Shepherd.'

Raleigh, Sir Walter Alexander (5 Sept. 1861—13 May 1922), scholar, born in London, son of a Congregationalist minister, was educated at the City of London School, Edinburgh Academy, London University, and King's College, Cambridge, where he edited the *Cambridge Review* and was President of the Union. After two years as Professor of English at Aligarh in India, he held the Chair of English at Liverpool from 1890 to 1900, at Glasgow from 1900 to 1904, and was the first Professor of English Literature at Oxford, where his stimulating lectures had the same sort of inspiring influence as those of Quiller-Couch (q.v.) at Cambridge. In 1911 he was knighted, and after the First World War he was appointed official historian of the Royal Air Force, but lived to complete only the first volume, published in 1922. Contracting typhoid in Bagdad, where he had gone to get material for thé work, he died at his home in Ferry Hinksey. His books are comparatively few. They include *The English Novel* (1894), *Robert Louis Stevenson* (1895), *Style* (1897), *Milton* (1900), *Wordsworth* (1903), *Shakespeare* (1907), and *Six Essays on Johnson* (1910). After his death a collection of his lighter writings was made by his son with the title *Laughter from a Cloud* (1923), and his *Letters* were edited by his wife in 1926.

Ramal, Walter, *see* de la Mare.

Ramée, Louise de la (1 Jan. 1839—25 Jan. 1908), novelist who wrote under the name Ouida, her childish mispronunciation of Louise, was born at Bury St Edmunds, daughter of Louis Ramée, an instructor in French, and his English wife. In 1859 while living in London she met William Harrison Ainsworth (q.v.) who helped to launch her as a writer. Her first long novel, *Held in Bondage* (1863), was followed by *Strathmore* (1865), *Chandos* (1866), *Under Two Flags* (1867), *Tricotrin* (1869), *Puck* (1870), *Two Little Wooden Shoes* (1874), *Moths* (1880), and *In Maremma* (1882). *Bimbi* (1882) is a book of stories for children, and *Views and Opinions* (1895) and *Critical Studies* (1900) are collections of essays. From 1860 onwards she spent much of her time in Italy, where she maintained great style, but her popularity waned after 1890, and she lived in poverty for many years, being at last persuaded to accept a Civil List pension. Artificial and affected, she wrote of high life like a schoolgirl, and splendidly blasé guardsmen were the mainstay of her flamboyant novels, which had nevertheless qualities of vividness and vitality.

Ramsay, Allan (15 Oct. 1686—7 Jan. 1758), poet, was the son of a mine manager at Leadhills, Lanarkshire, who claimed kin with the Ramseys of Dalhousie. After leaving Crawford village school, in 1701 he came to Edinburgh as apprentice to a wig-maker, took to writing poetry, and joined the Easy Club, of which Pitcairn and Ruddiman, the grammarian, were members, and of which he was made 'laureate.' The club published his poems as they were thrown off, and their appearance soon began to be awaited with interest. In 1716 he published an additional canto to *Christ's Kirk on the Green*, a humorous poem sometimes attributed to James I, and in 1719 he became a bookseller, his shop being a meeting-place of the *literati* of the city. A collected edition of his poems appeared in 1720, among the subscribers to which were Pope, Steele, Arbuthnot, and Gay. It was followed by *Fables and Tales* (1722), and other poems. In 1724 he began the *Tea Table Miscellany*, a collection of new Scots songs set to old melodies, and the *Evergreen*, a collection of old Scots poems in editing which he took great liberties. *The Gentle Shepherd*, by far his best known and most meritorious work, appeared in 1725, and had an immediate popularity. It is a pastoral drama, and is rich in character, unaffected sentiment, and vivid description. After this success Ramsay, satisfied with his reputation, produced nothing more of importance. He was the first to introduce the circulating library into Scotland, and among his other enterprises was an unsuccessful attempt to establish a theatre in Edinburgh.

Ramsay, Edward Bannerman (31 Jan. 1793—27 Dec. 1872), a clergyman of the Scottish Episcopal Church, and Dean of Edinburgh in that communion from 1841, was born at Aberdeen and educated at Durham Grammar School and Cambridge. He has a place in literature by his *Reminiscences of Scottish Life and Character* (1858), which had gone through 22 editions at his death. It is a book full of the engaging personality of the author, and rich in entertaining anecdotes.

Randall, James Ryder (1 Jan. 1839—14 Jan. 1908), poet, was born in Baltimore, son of a merchant, and educated at Georgetown College. After trying various jobs he worked as a teacher in Louisiana. In 1861, at the beginning of the Civil War, he wrote 'Maryland, my Maryland,' which became the Marseillaise of the Confederates, being sung to the tune of 'Tannenbaum.' His *Poems* were collected and published in 1910.

Randolph, Thomas (15 June 1605—17 March 1635), poet and dramatist, born at Newnham-cum-Badby, Northamptonshire, son of a steward, and educated at Westminster School and Cambridge, was a friend of Ben Jonson, and led a wild life in London. He wrote six plays, including *The Jealous Lovers* (1632), *Amyntas*, and *The Muses' Looking-glass*, and a volume of *Poems* (1638). He was a scholar as well as a wit, and his plays are full of learning and condensed thought in a style somewhat cold and hard.

Ransom, John Crowe (30 April 1888—   ), poet and critic, born at Pulaski, Tennessee, was educated at Vanderbilt University and went to Oxford as a Rhodes Scholar. During the First World War he served in the Artillery. Joining the English staff at Vanderbilt, he was professor from 1924 to 1937, and later was Professor of Poetry at Kenyon College. He was one of a group of Nashville residents who founded *The Fugitive*, organ of the agrarian-distributists. His books of verse, which are marked by mordaunt humour, include *Poems about God* (1919), *Chills and Fever* (1924), *Grace after Meat* (1924), and *Two Gentlemen in Bonds* (1926).

Critical works are *God without Thunder* (1930), *The World's Body* (1938), *New Criticism* (1940), and *Studies in Modern Literature* (1951). In 1951 he received the Bollingen Prize for poetry.

Ransome, Arthur Michell (18 Jan. 1884—), critic and writer of children's books, was born in Leeds, where his father was Professor of History, and educated at Rugby. Entering a London publisher's office, he wrote some books of criticism, including studies of *Edgar Allan Poe* (1910) and *Oscar Wilde* (1912). Just before the First World War he went to Russia, where he learned the language, studied the folklore, and wrote *Six Weeks in Russia* (1919) and *The Crisis in Russia* (1921). In 1921 he went yachting in the Baltic, and later settled in Suffolk. His books for boys and girls are as carefully written as serious novels and are among the best of their kind. They include *Swallows and Amazons* (1931), *Peter Duck* (1933), *Winter Holiday* (1934), *Pigeon Post* (1936), *We Didn't Mean to Go to Sea* (1938), *Secret Water* (1939), *The Big Six* (1940), *The Picts and the Martyrs* (1943), and *Great Northern?* (1947). In 1953 he was made a Commander of the Order of the British Empire.

Rapin de Thoyras, Paul (25 March 1661—25 May, 1725), historian, born at Castres, Languedoc, belonged to a Protestant Savoyard family, and came to England on the revocation of the Edict of Nantes in 1686. He afterwards served with William III in Holland, and accompanied him to England in 1688. His *History of England*, written in French, was translated into English, and continued by various writers, and was the standard history until Hume's.

Raspe, Rudolf Eric (1737—1794), novelist, born in Hanover and educated at the universities of Göttingen and Leipzig, became a professor in Cassel, and keeper of the Landgrave of Hesse's antique gems and medals, in the purloining of some of which he was detected, and fled to England. Here he won for himself a certain place in English literature by the publication in 1785 of *Baron Munchausen's Narrative*, in which the hero narrates fantastic and impossible exploits. Only a small portion of the work in its present form is by Raspe, the rest having been added later by another hand. He appears to have maintained more or less during life his character of a rogue, and is the prototype of Dousterswivel in Scott's *Antiquary*.

Rattigan, Terence Mervyn (10 June 1911—), dramatist, was born in London and educated at Harrow and Oxford. During the Second World War he served as a gunner in the Royal Air Force. In 1936 he scored a success with his ingenious comedy *French without Tears*. Others of his plays are *After the Dance* (1939), *Follow my Leader* (1940), *Flare Path* (1942), *While the Sun Shines* (1943), *Love in Idleness* (1944), *The Winslow Boy* (1946), *The Browning Version* (1948), *Adventure Story* (1949), *The Deep Blue Sea* (1952), and *The Sleeping Prince* (1954). In 1958 he was made a C.B.E.

Rawlings, Marjorie Kinnan (8 Aug. 1896—14 Dec. 1953), novelist, born in Washington, D.C., daughter of an attorney, was educated at the University of Wisconsin and became a journalist. In 1919 she married Charles Rawlings; they were divorced in 1933 and in 1941 she married Norton S. Baskin. Her short story 'Gal Young Un' won the O. Henry Memorial Award in 1933. In the same year appeared her successful novel *South Moon Under*, while *The Yearling* (1938), a tale of a boy and his pet fawn, became a minor classic and was awarded the Pulitzer Prize. Others of her novels are *Golden Apples* (1935), *When the Whippoorwill* (1940), *Cross Creek* (1942), *Jacob's Ladder* (1950), and *The Sojourner* (1953). The backwoods of Florida, where she made her home, form the setting of many of her books. She was made an honorary LL.D. of Rollins College.

Rawlinson, George (23 Nov. 1812—6 Oct. 1902), clergyman and historian, a brother of Sir Henry Rawlinson (q.v.) was born at Chadlington, Oxfordshire, and educated at Swansea Grammar School and Trinity College, Oxford, where he was President of the Union. In 1840 he became a Fellow of Exeter, and in 1842 took orders, becoming a canon of Canterbury in 1872. From 1861 to 1889 he was Camden Professor of Ancient History at Oxford. He published a monumental edition of Herodotus (1858—60), to which his brother contributed articles. Later works embodying contemporary discoveries in the East were *The Five Great Monarchies of the Ancient Eastern World* (1862—7), *The History of Ancient Egypt* (1881), and a *History of Phoenicia* (1882).

Rawlinson, Sir Henry Creswicke, 1st Baronet (11 April 1810—5 March 1895), Assyriologist, brother of George Rawlinson (q.v.), was born at Chadlington, Oxfordshire. In 1827 he entered the service of the East India Company, of which he became a director in 1856. In 1859 he was British Minister in Persia, and from 1868 to 1895 a member of the Council of India. His most famous achievement was to discover and decipher the great inscription of King Darius cut on a cliff-face and set out in three languages—Persian, Babylonian, and Elamite. In 1846 he published the text with full notes as *The Persian Cuneiform Inscription at Behistun*. Others of his works are *Cuneiform Inscriptions of Western Asia* (1861), and *England and Russia in the East* (1875). He was successively President of the Royal Geographical Society and of the Royal Asiatic Society. In 1891 he was made a baronet.

Ray, John (29 Nov. 1627—17 Jan. 1705), naturalist, son of a blacksmith at Black Notley, Essex, was at Cambridge, where he became a Fellow of Trinity, and successively lecturer on Greek, Latin, and mathematics. His first publication was a Latin catalogue of plants growing near Cambridge, which appeared in 1660. Thereafter he made a tour of Great Britain, and published in 1670 his *Catalogue of the Plants of England and the adjacent Isles*. In 1663 he had travelled on the Continent for three years with his pupil-friend, F. Willughby, and in 1673 appeared *Observations* on his journeys, which extended over the Low Countries, Germany, Italy, and France, with a catalogue of plants not native to England. In the course of his botanical studies he also recorded proverbs and rare words. In 1670 he published his important *Collection of English Proverbs*, and in 1674 his *Collection of English Words not Generally*

Used. Among his later works are *Historia Plantarum Generalis* (1686—1704), and *Synopsis Methodica Animalium* (1693). He was for long popularly known by his treatise, *The Wisdom of God manifested in the works of the Creation* (1691), a precursor of Paley's *Natural Theology*. Ray is the father of English botany, and appears to have grasped the idea of the natural classification of plants, afterwards developed by Jussieu and other later naturalists. His greatest successors, including Cuvier, highly commended his methods and acquirements.

Read, Sir Herbert Edward (4 Dec. 1893—   ), poet and critic, was born at Kirbymoorside, Yorkshire, son of a farmer. His course at Leeds University was cut short by the First World War, in which he was a captain in the Yorkshire Regiment and won the D.S.O. and M.C. After two years in the Government Treasury Department, he became Assistant Keeper in the Victoria and Albert Museum from 1922 to 1931, and was then Professor of Fine Art in Edinburgh till 1933; thereafter till 1939 he edited the *Burlington Magazine*. A careful and conscientious craftsman of free verse, he published *Naked Warriors* (1919), *Eclogues* (1919), *Mutations of the Phoenix* (1923), *The End of a War* (1933), *Thirty-Five Poems* (1940), and *World Within a War* (1945). In criticism he belonged to the school of Coleridge, his works including *Reason and Romanticism* (1926), *English Prose Style* (1928), *The Sense of Glory* (1929), *Wordsworth* (1930), *Form in Modern Poetry* (1932), *In Defence of Shelley* (1935), *Essays in Literary Criticism* (1938), *The True Voice of Feeling* (1953), and a number of books on art. *The Innocent Eye* (1933) and *Annals of Innocence and Experience* (1940) are autobiographical. He was knighted in 1953.

Read, Opie Percival (22 Dec. 1852—2 Nov. 1939), humorous writer, born in Nashville, Tennessee, went to school in Gallatin and became a journalist in Kentucky. He wrote humorous novels which embodied a homely whimsical philosophy and were very popular for a time. · They include *A Kentucky Colonel* (1889), *A Tennessee Judge* (1893), *The Jucklins* (1895), *My Young Master* (1896), *On the Suwanee River* (1900), *An American in New York* (1905), and *The Mystery of Margaret* (1907). *I Remember* (1930) is an autobiography.

Read, Thomas Buchanan (12 March 1822—11 May 1872), poet, was born on a farm near Guthrieville, Pennsylvania. At school he showed a talent for drawing, and in 1841, after trying various different jobs, he set up a studio in Boston. Latterly he made Philadelphia his home, and became famous as one of America's leading poets. His volumes of verse include *The New Pastoral* (1855), *House by the Sea* (1855), *Sylvia* (1857), and *A Summer Story* (1865). Among his best-known pieces are 'Drifting' and 'Sheridan's Ride.'

Reade, Charles (8 June 1814—11 April 1884), novelist, son of a country gentleman of Oxfordshire, was educated at Magdalen College, Oxford, of which he became Vice-President, and was called to the Bar at Lincoln's Inn in 1843. He did not, however, practise, but began his literary career with some dramas, of which the most remarkable were *Masks and Faces*, *Gold*, and *Drink*. He afterwards rewrote the first of these as a novel, *Peg Woffington* (1852), which attained great popularity. *It is never too late to Mend* (1856) was followed by his historical novel, *The Cloister and the Hearth* (1861) generally regarded as his masterpiece, *Hard Cash* (1863), *Griffith Gaunt* (1867), *Foul Play* (1869), *Put Yourself in his Place* (1870), and *A Terrible Temptation* (1871). He was at his best a writer of unusual power and vividness. Nearly all are agreed as to the great excellence of *The Cloister and the Hearth*, Swinburne placing it 'among the very greatest masterpieces of narrative.' Many of his novels were written with a view to the reformation of some abuse; thus *Hard Cash* exposes certain private asylums.

Redfield, Martin, *see* **Brown, Alice.**

Reed, Henry Hope (11 July 1808—27 Sept. 1854), scholar, was born in Philadelphia, son of the State Attorney-General, and educated at the University of Pennsylvania, where he later became Professor of English. He died in a shipwreck. He was a sympathetic and delicate critic, and was among the first of American men of letters to appreciate the genius of Wordsworth, of whose works he brought out an edition in 1837. His lectures were published in several volumes after his death.

Reed, Herbert Langford (1889—March 1954), humorous writer, born at Clapham, was educated there and at Hove College. In 1910 he joined the staff of the *Daily Mail*. During the First World War he served in France, and during the second with the Royal Air Force. A collector and writer of limericks and nonsense verse, he published *The Complete Limerick Book* (1924), *The Anthology of Nonsense Verse* (1926), *Sausages and Sundials* (1927), *The Indiscreet Limerick Book* (1928), *The Child's Own Limerick Book* (1932), *Limericks for the Beach, Bathroom, and Boudoir* (1933), *The New Limerick Book* (1937), and *The Nondamsense Ballads* (1937). He also wrote a *Life of Lewis Carroll* (1932) and compiled *The Complete Rhyming Dictionary* (1936).

Reed, Talbot Baines (3 April 1852—28 Nov. 1893), writer of school stories, was born in Hackney, son of Sir Charles Reed, chairman of the London School Board. In 1868 he entered his father's firm of typefounders, and his *History of Old English Letter-Founders* (1877) is a standard work. In 1892 he helped to originate the Bibliographical Society, of which he became secretary. But he is best remembered for his excellent school stories, originally contributed to the *Boy's Own Paper*. Among the best are *The Adventures of a Three-Guinea Watch* (1880), *The Fifth Form at St Dominic's* (1881), *My Friend Smith* (1882), *The Willoughby Captains* (1883), *The Master of the Shell* (1887), and *The Cock-House at Fellsgarth* (1891).

Reeve, Clara (1729—3 Dec. 1807), novelist, was born at Ipswich, daughter of a clergyman. Educated by her father, she lived a quiet and retired life. In 1777 she published her best-known work, *The Champion of Virtue, a Gothic Story*, which was later renamed *The Old English Baron*; it was written in imitation or rivalry of Walpole's *Castle of Otranto*. Others of her novels are *The Two Mentors* (1783), and *The School for Widows* (1791). *The Progress of Romance* (1785) is an account of the fiction of her time.

Reeve, Henry (9 Sept. 1813—21 Oct. 1895), journalist, born in Norwich, son of a doctor, joined the staff of *The Times*, the foreign policy of which he influenced for many years. He was editor of the *Edinburgh Review* from 1855 till his death, and also edited the Greville Memoirs (1874—87). He held a leading place in society, and had an unusually wide acquaintance with men of letters all over the Continent.

Reid, Forrest (24 June 1875—4 Jan. 1947), novelist, was born in Belfast, the youngest of twelve children; his mother could trace her descent back to Henry VIII's queen, Katherine Parr. Reid was educated at the Royal Academical Institution, Belfast, and Christ's College, Cambridge. In his writing he was influenced by Henry James, to whom he dedicated his novel *The Garden God* (1905). Other novels are *The Bracknels* (1911), *Following Darkness* (1912, rewritten as *Peter Waring*, 1937), *The Gentle Lover* (1913), *At the Door of the Gate* (1915), *The Spring Song* (1916), *Pirates of the Spring* (1919), *Pender among the Residents* (1922), *Demophon* (1927), *Uncle Stephen* (1931), *The Retreat* (1936), and *Young Tom* (1944), the last three forming a trilogy on boyhood. He also wrote studies of Yeats (1915) and de la Mare (1929), and two autobiographies, *Apostate* (1926) and *Private Road* (1940). His favourite recreation was croquet.

Reid, Mayne (4 April 1818—22 Oct. 1883), born at Ballyroney, County Down, son of a minister, set off at the age of 20 for Mexico to push his fortunes, and went through many adventures, including service in the Mexican War. He also was for a short time settled in Philadelphia engaged in literary work. Returning to this country he began a long series of novels of adventure with *The Rifle Rangers* (1849). The others include *The Scalp Hunters* (1851), *Boy Hunters* (1852), *Young Voyageurs* (1853), *The White Chief* (1859), and *The Headless Horseman* (1866); they had great popularity, especially with boys.

Reid, Thomas (26 April 1710—7 Oct. 1796), philosopher, was the son of the minister of Strachan, Kincardineshire. At the age of 12 he was sent to Marischal College, Aberdeen, where he graduated, and thereafter resided for some time as librarian, devoting himself to study, especially of mathematics and the Newtonian philosophy. He was in 1737 ordained minister of New Machar, Aberdeen, and in 1748 he communicated to the Royal Society an *Essay on Quantity*. Four years later he became one of the Professors of Philosophy in King's College, Aberdeen, and in 1763 he was chosen to succeed Adam Smith as Professor of Moral Philosophy in Glasgow. In the following year he published his great work, *Inquiry into the Human Mind on the Principles of Common Sense*, directed against Hume's *Essay on Human Nature*. Up to the appearance of the latter work in 1739 Reid had been a follower of Berkeley, but the conclusions drawn therein from the idealistic philosophy led him to revise his theories, and to propound what is usually known as the 'common sense' philosophy, by which term is meant the beliefs common to rational beings as such. In 1785 he published his *Essay on the Intellectual Powers*, which was followed in 1788 by that *On the Active Powers*.

Reid, Sir Thomas Wemyss (29 March 1842—26 Feb. 1905), novelist, born at Newcastle-on-Tyne, son of a Congregationalist minister, became a journalist. From 1870 to 1887 he edited the *Leeds Mercury*, then moved to London, where from 1890 to 1899 he edited the *Speaker*. His novels include *The Land of the Bey* (1882), *Gladys Fane* (1883), and *Mauleverer's Millions* (1886), and he also wrote lives of *W. E. Forster* (1888), *Lord Houghton* (1891), *Lord Playfair* (1899), and *William Black* (1902). He was knighted in 1894.

Reynolds, Frederic (1 Nov. 1764—16 April 1841), dramatist, was born in London, son of an attorney, and educated at Westminster School. In 1782 he was entered at Middle Temple, but turned from law to playwriting. In 1785 appeared his first play, *Werter*, founded on Goethe's novel. Another tragedy, *Eloisa*, followed in 1786, and a highly successful comedy, *The Dramatist*, in 1789. Altogether he composed nearly a hundred plays, as well as a novel, *A Playwright's Adventures* (1831). His autobiographical *Life and Times of Frederic Reynolds* was published in 1826.

Reynolds, Sir Joshua (16 July 1723—23 Feb. 1792), painter and writer on art, was born at Plympton, Devonshire, son of a clergyman. After studying art in Italy, he settled in London, where he attained great fame as a portrait-painter. He is regarded as the greatest English representative of that art, and was first President of the Royal Academy. He was the intimate friend of Johnson, with whom he founded the famous Club, and of Burke, Goldsmith, and indeed most of the celebrated men of his time. He has also a place in literature for his *Fifteen Discourses* on painting, delivered to the Academy. He also contributed to the *Idler*, and translated Du Fresney's *Art of Painting*. He suffered from deafness, and in his latter years from failure of sight. He was knighted in 1769.

Rhodes, William Barnes (25 Dec. 1772—1 Nov. 1826), dramatist, started work in an attorney's office and then became a clerk in the Bank of England, where he rose to be chief teller. He wrote a popular burlesque *Bombastes Furioso* (1810) and also a number of epigrams.

Rhymer, Thomas the, *see* **Erceldoune, Thomas of.**

Rhys, Ernest (17 July 1859—25 May 1946), poet and editor, born in Islington, spent his childhood in his father's native town, Carmarthen. He was trained as a mining engineer, and his novel *Black Horse Pit* (1925) is based on his mining experiences. In 1885 he went to London and became a literary freelance. He became acquainted with Yeats, Dowson, and Lionel Johnson (qq.v.), and edited the Camelot Classics, but is best remembered as the editor of Everyman's Library, which reached its thousandth volume ten years after his death; many of the volumes in the series were edited by himself. His books of verse include *A London Rose* (1891), *Welsh Ballads* (1903), *Rhymes for Everyman* (1933), and *Song of the*

Sun (1937), while *English Lyric Poetry* (1913) is a book of criticism. He also wrote two delightful books of reminiscences, *Everyman Remembers* (1931) and *Wales England Wed* (1941).

Ricardo, David (19 April 1772—11 Sept. 1823), political economist, son of a Jewish stockbroker, himself followed the same business, in which he acquired a large fortune. On his marriage in 1793 he turned Christian. He was the founder of what is termed the classical school of political economy, his chief work being *The Principles of Political Economy and Taxation* (1817). After retiring from business he entered the House of Commons, where, owing to his remarkable power of lucid exposition, combined with his reputation as a highly successful man of business, he acquired great influence.

Ricaut, Sir Paul, *see* **Rycaut.**

Rice, Alice Caldwell Hegan (11 Jan. 1870—10 Feb. 1942), novelist, born at Shelbyville, Kentucky, was educated at private schools. Settling in Louisville, she wrote for local periodicals. Her first novel, *Mrs Wiggs of the Cabbage Patch* appeared in 1901 and was a great success. In the following year she married Cale Young Rice, the poet, with whom she collaborated in some books. Of her own novels *Lovey Mary* (1903) was the only one that approached her first in popularity. Others are *Sandy* (1905), *Mr Opp* (1909), *A Romance of Billy-Goat Hill* (1912), *Quin* (1921), and *Our Ernie* (1939). *Miss Mink's Soldier* (1918) is a book of short stories, and *The Inky Way* (1940) is an autobiography. She was made an honorary D.Litt. of Rollins College and of the University of Louisville.

Rice, Elmer (28 Sept. 1892—   ), playwright, was born Elmer Reizenstein in New York, but changed his name when he became a writer. Having studied law, he took his LL.B. in 1912, but turned playwright instead, his first piece, *On Trial*, being produced in 1913. For some years after that he wrote chiefly for amateur dramatic societies. In 1923 *The Adding Machine*, an expressionist play of office life, was produced with success. He then collaborated with Dorothy Parker in *Close Harmony* (1924) and with Philip Barry in *Cock Robin* (1929). His own *Street Scene* (1929), which depicts an ordinary day in the life of a tenement block, was awarded the Pulitzer Prize. Others of his plays are *Subway* (1929), *The Left Bank* (1931), *We, the People* (1933), *Judgment Day* (1934), *American Landscape* (1939), *Two on an Island* (1940), *Flight to the West* (1941), *Dream Girl* (1946), and *Grand Tour* (1952). He also wrote some novels, including *The Show Must Go On* (1949).

Rice, James (26 Sept. 1843—26 April 1882), novelist, born at Northampton and educated at Cambridge, studied law and was called to the Bar at Lincoln's Inn in 1871. In the following year he published the highly successful novel *Ready Money Mortiboy*, which he had written in collaboration with Walter Besant (q.v.). Other novels produced by the same partnership are *The Golden Butterfly* (1876), *The Monks of Thelema* (1877), *By Celia's Arbour* (1878), *The Chaplain of the Fleet* (1879), and *The Seamy Side* (1881). *A History of the British Turf* (1879) was written by Rice alone.

Rich, Barnabe (1540?—1617), writer of romances and pamphlets, born probably in Essex, saw military service in the Low Countries. He began to write in 1574, and took Lyly's *Euphues* as his model. Among his numerous romances are *The Strange and Wonderful Adventures of Simonides, a Gentleman Spaniard* (1581—4) and *Riche, his Farewell to the Military Profession* (1581), which furnished Shakespeare with the plot for *Twelfth Night*.

Richard de Bury, *see* **Bury.**

Richards, Ivor Armstrong (26 Feb. 1893—   ), critic, born at Sandbach, Cheshire, was educated at Clifton and Magdalene College, Cambridge, of which he became a Fellow, and from 1922 to 1929 was a lecturer in English. In the latter year he was a visiting professor of Tsing Hua University, Peking, and from 1944 onwards was a Professor of English at Harvard. A leading authority on semantics, the science of meaning, he collaborated with C. K. Ogden in *The Meaning of Meaning* (1923), and with him was the founder of Basic English, a simplified form of English which uses less than a thousand words; its value was set out in *Basic English and Its Uses* (1943). Richards's critical works, which have had a great influence on other writers, include *Principles of Literary Criticism* (1924), *Science and Poetry* (1925), *Practical Criticism* (1929), and *The Philosophy of Rhetoric* (1936). His chief recreation was mountaineering.

Richardson, Dorothy Miller (17 May 1873—17 June 1957), novelist, born at Abingdon, Berkshire, spent part of her early years in London. After leaving school she worked as a teacher, then as a clerk. She married Alan Odle, the artist, and latterly lived in Cornwall. *Pilgrimage* is the collective title she has given to her novels, which include *Pointed Roofs* (1915), *Backwater* (1916), *Honeycomb* (1917), *The Tunnel* (1919), *Interim* (1919), *Deadlock* (1921), *Revolving Lights* (1923), *The Trap* (1925), *Oberland* (1927), *Dawn's Left Hand* (1931), *Clear Horizon* (1935), and *Dimple Hill* (1938). Her work belongs to the so-called 'stream of consciousness' school, and she tries to reconstruct reality as a series of images or impressions in the mind of one person; in this she anticipated James Joyce and Virginia Woolf (qq.v.). She also wrote *The Quakers: Past and Present* (1914) and *John Austen and the Inseparables* (1930).

Richardson, Ethel Florence Lindesay (3 Jan. 1870—20 March 1946), novelist who wrote under the name Henry Handel Richardson, was born in Melbourne, daughter of an English doctor, and educated at the Presbyterian Ladies' College there. Having a talent for music, she studied the piano at Leipzig Conservatorium for three years. While there she married John G. Robertson, who became Professor of German at London University. In her early work she was influenced by Flaubert and the Russians. Her chief novels are *Maurice Guest* (1908), *The Getting of Wisdom* (1910), *The Fortunes of Richard Mahoney* (a trilogy made up of *Australia Felix* (1917), *The Way Home* (1925), and *Ultima Thule* (1929)), *Two Studies* (1931), and *The Young Cosima* (1939). *The End of a Childhood* (1934) is a volume of short stories, and *Myself When Young* (1948) an autobiography.

Richardson, Henry Handel, *see* **Richardson, Ethel.**

Richardson, Samuel (1689—4 July 1761), novelist, son of a joiner, was born somewhere in Derbyshire. As a boy he was a favourite of young women, and used to write their love letters for them. His father had intended him for the Church, but means failed, and at the age of 17 he went to London, and was apprenticed to a printer. Careful and diligent, he prospered in business and became printer of the Journals of the House of Commons. He was twice married, and each of his wives brought him six children, of whom, however, only four daughters were living at his death. Richardson, who was the originator of the modern novel, did not take seriously to literature until he was past 50 when, in 1740, *Pamela* appeared. It originated in a proposal by two printers that Richardson should write a collection of model letters for the use of persons unaccustomed to correspondence, but it soon developed in his hands into a novel in which the story is carried on in the form of a correspondence. Written about a maidservant, it struck a true note of sentiment, exploded the prevalent idea that dukes and princesses were the only suitable heroes and heroines, and won immediate and phenomenal popularity. In 1748 *Clarissa*, his masterpiece, was published, and in 1753 *Sir Charles Grandison*, in which the author embodies his ideal of a Christian gentleman. All his novels suffer from an elaboration of detail which often becomes tedious. As Dr Johnson said, 'If you were to read Richardson for the story your impatience would be so much fretted that you would hang yourself.' But in deep acquaintance with the motives of conduct, and especially of the workings of the female heart, they are almost unrivalled; their pathos also is genuine and deep. Richardson had an unusual faculty as the platonic friend and counsellor of women, and was the centre of an admiring circle who ministered to a vanity which became somewhat excessive. He has also the distinction of evoking the genius of Fielding, whose first novel, *Joseph Andrews*, was begun as a skit or parody upon *Pamela*. Richardson is described as 'a stout, rosy, vain, prosy little man.'

Richmond, Grace Louise (1866—   ), novelist, was born at Pawtucket, Rhode Island, daughter of Charles E. Smith, a clergyman, and educated at Syracuse High School. She married Nelson G. Richmond, a doctor, and they settled in Fredonia, New York State. When her family was grown up she started writing romantic fiction, her most successful books being a series written round the character of a doctor, *Red Pepper Burns* (1910), *Mrs Red Pepper* (1913), *Red Pepper's Patients* (1917), and *Red Pepper Returns* (1931). Others of her novels are *Around the Corner in Gay Street* (1908), *Strawberry Acres* (1911), *Red and Black* (1919), *Cherry Square* (1926), and *Bachelor's Bounty* (1931).

Ridge, William Pett (1860?—29 Sept. 1930), novelist, was born at Chartham, near Canterbury, and educated at Birkbeck Institution. After some years in the Civil Service, he became a journalist at the age of 30, and began writing novels of lower-class London. Among his books are *Mord Em'ly* (1898), *A Son of the State* (1899), *A Breaker* *of Laws* (1900), *'Erb* (1903), *Name of Garland* (1907), *Splendid Brother* (1909), *Nine to Six-Thirty* (1910), *Love at Paddington* (1912), *The Kennedy People* (1915), *The Amazing Years* (1917), *The Bustling Hours* (1919), *Rare Luck* (1924), and *Affectionate Regards* (1929); he also published several collections of short stories. *A Story Teller Forty Years in London* (1923) and *I Like to Remember* (1925) are books of reminiscence.

Riding, Laura (16 Jan. 1901—   ), poet and critic, was born in New York, daughter of an Austrian tailor of Socialist views, and was educated at Brooklyn Girls' High School and Cornell. While at college she married Louis Gottschalk, a history instructor; they were divorced in 1925. In 1924 her poems won a prize of 100 dollars awarded by the Fugitives, a group of Nashville poets. From 1925 to 1939 she lived in Europe, then returned to the United States and in 1941 married Schuyler Jackson, poet and farmer, with whom she collaborated in compiling a thesaurus-dictionary. Her critical works include *A Survey of Modernist Poetry* (1927), in which she collaborated with Robert Graves (q.v.), *Contemporaries and Snobs* (1928), and *Anarchism is not Enough* (1928). Her volumes of verse are *Poems: A Joking Word* (1930), *Poems: A Lying Word* (1933), *A Trojan Ending* (1937), and *Collected Poems* (1938).

Ridley, Maurice Roy (25 Jan. 1890—   ), scholar, was born at Orcheston St Mary, Wiltshire, where his father was rector, and was educated at Clifton and Balliol College, Oxford, where he had a brilliant record and won the Newdigate Prize for Poetry. From 1914 to 1920 he was a schoolmaster at Clifton and from then till 1945 a Fellow of Balliol. His most important work was the New Temple edition of Shakespeare (1934—6), which he followed with *Shakespeare's Plays, a Commentary* (1937). Others of his books are *Poetry and the Ordinary Reader* (1930), *Keats's Craftsmanship* (1933), studies of *Gertrude Bell* (1941) and *Abraham Lincoln* (1944), and a translation of *Sir Gawain and the Green Knight* (1944).

Riley, James Whitcomb (7 Oct. 1849—22 July 1916), poet, was born at Greenfield, Indiana, son of a lawyer. He left school at 16, took up painting, and became a house and sign painter. Later he started writing verses in the Hoosier dialect, as the vernacular of Indiana is called, and became an itinerant entertainer, giving readings and lectures enlivened by vivid Hoosier scenes and characters. His chief books of verse are *The Old Swimmin' Hole and 'Leven More Poems* (1883), which contains the famous 'When the Frost is on the Punkin,' *Afterwhiles* (1887), *Rhymes of Childhood* (1890), *Green Fields and Running Brooks* (1892), *Poems Here at Home* (1893), *Home Folks* (1900), and *Riley Songs o' Cheer* (1905). In Britain the best-known of his pieces is 'Little Orphant Annie.'

Rinehart, Mary Roberts (1876—22 Sept. 1958), novelist, was born in Pittsburgh, daughter of Thomas B. Roberts, a salesman. Trained as a nurse, she saw much of the tragic side of life. In 1896 she married Stanley M. Rinehart, a doctor. After the First World War they lived in Washington, and after her husband's death in 1932 Mrs Rinehart settled in New York. The earliest and greatest of America's group of women detective-story writers, though her plots are crude by later standards, she made a reputation with her first novel, *The Circular Staircase* (1908), which was successfully adapted for the stage as *The Bat*. Others of her novels are *The Man in Lower Ten* (1909), *The Amazing Adventures of Letitia Carberry* (1911), *The Amazing Interlude* (1917), and *The Red Lamp* (1925). She also published a series of humorous novels of which the heroine is an eccentric spinster, Tish; *Tish Plays the Game* appeared in 1926. Her plays include *Double Life* (1907) and *Cheer Up* (1913). *My Story* (1931) is an autobiography.

Rita, *see* **Humphreys, Eliza Margaret.**

Ritchie, Anne Isabella, Lady (9 June 1837—26 Feb. 1919), novelist, was born in London, a daughter of W. M. Thackeray, the novelist. Her father's close companion till his death in 1863, she knew everyone of literary note. In 1877 she married Richmond Thackeray Ritchie, her second cousin, who was later knighted. Her novels include *The Story of Elizabeth* (1863), *The Village on the Cliff* (1867), *Old Kensington* (1873), and *Mrs Dymond* (1885). Her highly interesting memoirs include *Records of Tennyson, Ruskin, and Browning* (1892), *Lord Tennyson and his Friends* (1893), and *Chapters from Some Memoirs* (1894). Her *Letters* were edited by her daughter in 1924.

Ritchie, Leitch (1800?—16 Jan. 1865), novelist, born in Greenock, was apprenticed in a firm trading with America, but it went bankrupt, and he moved to London and became a freelance writer. Commissioned to write a series of books of travel, he visited many places abroad in search of material. In his later years he was editor of *Chambers's Journal*. His novels include *Schinderhannes, the Robber of the Rhine* (1833), *The Magician* (1836), and *Wearyfoot Common* (1855). He also wrote *The Wye and its Associations* (1841) and *Windsor Castle and its Environs* (1848).

Ritson, Joseph (2 Oct. 1752—23 Sept. 1803), antiquary and critic, born at Stockton-on-Tees, settled in London as a conveyancer, at the same time devoting himself to the study of ancient English poetry. By his diligence as a collector and acuteness as a critic he rendered essential service to the preservation and appreciation of our ancient poetry. His chief works are *A Collection of English Songs* (1783), *Ancient Songs from Henry III to the Revolution* (1790), *A Collection of Scottish Songs* (1794), and *Ancient English Metrical Romances* (1802). Of a jealous and quarrelsome temper, Ritson was continually in controversy with his fellow-collectors and critics, including Johnson, Warton, and Percy. His acuteness enabled him to detect the forgeries of W. H. Ireland (q.v.). He died insane.

Robert of Brunne, *see* **Mannyng.**

Robert of Gloucester (*fl.* 1260—1300), chronicler, was probably a monk of Gloucester Abbey. He wrote in English verse a *Chronicle of England* from the earliest times down to the reign of Henry III. It has some spirited passages.

Roberts, Sir Charles George Douglas (10 Jan. 1860—26 Nov. 1943), nature writer, novelist, and poet, born at Douglas, New Brunswick, son of a minister, was a cousin of Bliss Carman (q.v.), whose place he took as leading Canadian poet. Educated at New Brunswick University, he became a headmaster, and then from 1885 to 1895 was Professor of English at King's College, Nova Scotia. From 1897 till 1907 he lived in New York, writing. On the outbreak of the First World War he enlisted in the Canadian army at the age of 54, and rose to be a major. In 1926 he was awarded the Lorne Pierce Medal of the Royal Society of Canada for his contribution to Canadian literature, and in 1935 he was knighted. His books of verse include *Songs of the Common Day* (1893), *New Poems* (1919), and *The Sweet o' the Year* (1925). He published much fiction, including *The Cruise of the Yacht 'Dido'* (1895), *The Forge in the Forest* (1896), *The Backwoodsmen* (1909), and *Lovers in Arcadie* (1924), but was most successful with his animal stories such as *The Kindred of the Wild* (1902), *The Feet of the Furtive* (1912), *They that Walk in the Wild* (1924), and *Eyes of the Wilderness* (1933). From 1934 to 1937 he edited the Canadian *Who's Who*. His recreations were camping and fishing.

Roberts, Kenneth Lewis (8 Dec. 1885—21 July 1957), novelist, was born at Kennebunk, Maine (the Arundel of his stories) and educated at Cornell. From 1900 to 1917 he was on the staff of the *Boston Post*, and also wrote for *Life* and *Puck.* From 1918 to 1919 he served with Army Intelligence, then was a correspondent for the *Saturday Evening Post*. He is noted for a series of novels of early American history, all embodying the most careful research. They include *Arundel* (1930), *Rabble in Arms* (1933), *Northwest Passage* (1937), *Oliver Wisewell* (1940), and *Lydia Bailey* (1946). *For Authors Only* (1935) is a book of essays, *Trending into Maine* (1938) is a eulogy of his native state, and *I Wanted to Write* (1949) is autobiographical.

Roberts, Morley (29 Dec. 1857—8 June 1942), novelist and travel writer, born in London, son of an income-tax inspector, was educated at Bedford School and Manchester University. From 1876 to 1879 he worked on Australian sheep and cattle stations, then after serving as a seaman on various ships was in different parts of North America from 1884 to 1886. Later he extended his travels to the South Seas, South Africa, and Central America. His books of travel include *The Western Avernus* (1887), *Land-Travel and Seafaring* (1891), *A Tramp's Notebook* (1904), *On the Earthquake Line* (1924), and *On the Old Trail* (1927). Among his novels are *The Mate of the Vancouver* (1892), *A Son of Empire* (1899), *The Way of a Man* (1902), and *The Private Life of Henry Maitland* (1912), which is based on the life of George Gissing (q.v.). Roberts also published many books of short stories, including *Red Earth* (1894), *The Keeper of the Waters* (1898), *The Blue Peter* (1905), and *Captain Spink* (1908). *Lyra Mutabilis* (1921) is a collection of verse.

Robertson, Frederick William (3 Feb. 1816—15 Aug. 1853), clergyman, son of an army officer, was born in London and educated at Edinburgh Academy and University, and Oxford. He took orders in 1840 and after holding various curacies became in 1847 incumbent of Trinity Chapel, Brighton, where his preaching, though it brought him under the suspicion both of the High and Evangelical parties in the Church, had an extraordinary influence. Always of delicate and highly strung constitution, his health gave way after his ministry in Brighton had extended to six years. His sermons, of which five series were published posthumously, had a very wide popularity.

Robertson, John Mackinnon (14 Nov. 1856—5 Jan. 1933), politician and critic, was born at Brodick, Arran, and educated at Stirling. He became a leader-writer on the Edinburgh *Evening News*, where he had William Archer (q.v.) as a colleague. In 1884 he went to London and joined the staff of the *National Observer*, working under Bradlaugh, after whose death he edited the paper from 1891 to 1893, then becoming a freelance. From 1906 to 1918 he was Liberal M.P. for Tyneside, and rose to be Parliamentary Secretary to the Board of Trade and a Privy Councillor. His *History of Free Thought in the Nineteenth Century* (1900) is a standard work, but he was better known as an acute Shakespearian critic. His works on that theme include *Montaigne and Shakespeare* (1897), *The Baconian Heresy* (1913), *Shakespeare and Chapman* (1917), *The Problem of Hamlet* (1919), *The Shakespeare Canon* (1922—3), and *The Problem of Shakespeare's Sonnets* (1926).

Robertson, Thomas William (9 Jan. 1829—3 Feb. 1871), dramatist, was born at Newark, son of an actor, and was brought up in an atmosphere of the stage. Coming to London in 1848 he worked as actor, prompter, and stage manager, and then started writing plays, the first to be produced being *A Night's Adventures* (1851). His first real success was *David Garrick* (1864), which was followed by *Society* (1865), and a comedy, *Ours* (1866), which confirmed his popularity. Others of his plays are *Caste* (1867), often reckoned his best, *Play* (1868), *School* (1869), *Home* (1869), and *M.P.* (1870). By his 'cup and saucer' comedies he broke away from the prevailing mode of stageyness, and set the fashion for a more natural type of play than had been in vogue earlier in the century.

Robertson, William (19 Sept. 1721—2 June 1793), historian, son of the parish minister of Borthwick, Midlothian, was educated at Dalkeith Grammar School and Edinburgh University, where John Home, author of *Douglas*, was one of his friends. In 1743 he became minister of Gladsmuir, near Prestonpans. In the '45 he showed his loyalty by offering himself to Sir J. Cope as a volunteer, a service which was, however, declined. He soon began to take a prominent part in the debates of the General Assembly, of which he rose to be the undisputed leader. In 1758 he became one of the city ministers of Edinburgh, and in the following year published his *History of Scotland*, which had an extraordinary success, and at once raised him to a foremost place among British historians. Preferment immediately followed: he was made Chaplain of Stirling Castle in 1759, King's Chaplain for Scotland in 1760, Principal of the University of Edinburgh in 1761, and Historiographer Royal for Scotland in 1763. In 1769 appeared his *History of the Reign of the Emperor*

Charles V, in 1777 *The History of America*, and in 1791 *Historical Disquisition on Ancient India*. In 1780 Robertson retired from the management of Church affairs, in which he had shown conspicuous ability, and gave himself to study. As a writer he possessed a finished style, clear, measured, and stately, which carried his well-arranged narrative as on a full and steady stream; he was also cool and sagacious but, like Hume, he was apt to take his facts at second hand, and the vast additional material which has been in course of accumulation since his day has reduced the value of his work.

Robinson, **Edwin Arlington** (22 Dec. 1869—6 April 1935), poet, was born at Head Tide, Maine, and educated at Harvard. After he had tried various jobs in New York, including that of subway inspector, his book of verse *Captain Craig* (1902) attracted the attention of President Theodore Roosevelt, who gave him a post in the Customs House, which he held from 1905 to 1910. His first volume *The Torrent and the Night Before* (1896) had been followed by *The Children of the Night* (1897) and *Town Down the River* (1910), which contains the well-known piece 'Miniver Cheevy,' but it was not until he was middle-aged that Robinson became famous with *The Man Against the Sky* (1916). In 1922 his *Collected Poems* won the Pulitzer Prize. Later poems, mainly psychological studies, include *Avon's Harvest* (1921), *The Man Who Died Twice* (1924) another Pulitzer Prize winner, *Dionysus in Doubt* (1925), *Cavender's House* (1929), *Matthias at the Door* (1931), *Amaranth* (1934), and *King Jasper* (1935). He also wrote several long narrative poems on Arthurian legends, *Merlin* (1917), *Lancelot* (1920), and *Tristram* (1927), which brought him his third Pulitzer Prize. A follower of convention and tradition, he was reckoned by many the leading American poet of his time. His *Selected Letters* were published in 1940.

Robinson, **Esmé Stuart Lennox** (4 Oct. 1886—14 Oct. 1958), dramatist, was born at Douglas, County Cork, son of a clergyman, and educated at Bandon Grammar School. His first play, *The Clancy Name*, was produced in 1908, and soon afterwards he moved to Dublin, where from 1910 to 1923 he was manager of the Abbey Theatre. Among many plays that he wrote for it are *The Cross-Roads* (1909), *The Dreamers* (1915), *The Lost Leader* (1918), *The White-Headed Boy* (1920), *Crabbed Youth and Age* (1922), *The White Blackbird* (1925), *The Big House* (1926), and *The Far-off Hills* (1928); he was at his best in comedies of Irish rural life. In 1947 he edited Lady Gregory's *Journals*, and in 1951 published *Ireland's Abbey Theatre 1899—1950*. He also compiled *The Golden Treasury of Irish Verse* (1925) and *The Little Anthology of Irish Verse* (1929), and wrote a study of W. B. Yeats (1939). *Curtain Up* (1942) is a volume of reminiscences. Six feet six inches tall, he was married to a daughter of Edward Dowden (q.v.), the Shakespearian scholar.

Robinson, **Henry Crabb** (13 March 1775—5 Feb. 1867), diarist, born at Bury St Edmunds, son of a tanner, was articled to an attorney in Colchester. Between 1800 and 1805 he studied at various places in Germany, and became acquainted with nearly all the great men of letters there, including Goethe, Schiller, Herder, and Wieland. Thereafter he became war correspondent to *The Times* in the Peninsula. On his return to London he studied for the Bar, to which he was called in 1813, and became leader of the Eastern Circuit. Fifteen years later he retired, and by virtue of his great conversational powers and other qualities, became a leader in society, going everywhere and knowing everybody worth knowing. He died unmarried, aged 91, and his *Diary, Reminiscences, and Correspondence*, which stands in the forefront of its class, was published in 1869.

Rochester, John Wilmot, 2nd Earl of (10 April 1647—26 July 1680), poet, son of the 1st Earl, was born at Ditchley in Oxfordshire, and educated at Oxford, where he became M.A. at 14. Later he saw some naval service in the Dutch War and showed conspicuous bravery. He became one of the most dissolute of the courtiers of Charles II, and wore himself out at 33 by his wild life. He was handsome and witty, and possessed a singular charm of manner. He wrote a number of light, graceful poems, and many which were extremely gross. Bishop Burnet, who attended him on his death-bed, believed him to have been sincerely repentant. In addition to his short pieces he wrote a *Satire against Mankind* (1675), and a tragedy, *Valentinian*, adapted from Beaumont and Fletcher.

Rodger, Alexander (16 July 1784—26 Sept. 1846), poet, was born at Mid-Calder, Midlothian, son of a farmer. Apprenticed to a silversmith in Edinburgh, he later moved to Glasgow, where he worked as a weaver, then was inspector of cloth in a print-works, a pawnbroker, and finally a journalist. At one time imprisoned for seditious writing, he had a gift for humorous and satirical verse which was sometimes more vigorous than refined. The best-known of his pieces is 'Robin Tamson's Smiddy.'

Rogers, Henry (18 Oct. 1806—20 Aug. 1877), theologian, born at St Albans, son of a surgeon, studied medicine for a time but turned to theology and in 1829 became a Congregationalist minister in Dorset. In 1832 he was appointed a lecturer at Highbury College, and soon after became Professor of English first at University College, London, and then at Birmingham, where he remained from 1839 to 1859. He contributed many theological articles to the *Edinburgh Review*, and was best known by his *Eclipse of Faith* (1852), which involved him in a controversy with Francis W. Newman (q.v.).

Rogers, Samuel (30 July, 1763—18 Dec. 1855), poet, born in London, son of a banker, received a careful private education, and entered the bank, of which, on his father's death, he became the principal partner. From his early youth he showed a marked taste for literature and the fine arts, and in his later years he was a well-known leader in society and a munificent patron of artists and men of letters, his breakfasts, at which he delighted to assemble celebrities in all departments, being famous. He was the author of the following poems: *The Pleasures of Memory* (1792), *Columbus* (1810), *Jacqueline* (1814), *Human Life* (1819), and *Italy* (1822). His writings, while full of allusion and finished description, rarely show passion or intensity of feeling; but are rather the reflections and memory-pictures of a man of high culture and refinement expressed in polished verse. His *Table Talk*, edited by A. Dyce (q.v.) in 1856, shows his powers as a conversationalist. On the death of Wordsworth he was offered, but declined, the laureateship.

Rogers, William Penn Adair (4 Nov. 1879—15 Aug. 1935), humorous writer, was born at Oologah, Oklahoma, of partly Red Indian stock, and educated at Kemper Military Academy, Missouri. During the Boer War he broke horses for the British in South Africa, and afterwards joined a Wild West show. Later he appeared in vaudeville, and from 1913 to 1919 was in the Ziegfield Follies. He wrote essays in which satiric humour was blended with a shrewd and homely philosophy, in the tradition of Artemus Ward and Mr Dooley, and his syndicated columns in the newspapers had a great following. At one time it was seriously suggested that he might run for the presidency. He was killed in an aeroplane accident in Alaska. His books include *The Cowboy Philosopher on Prohibition* (1919), *What We Laugh At* (1920), *Illiterate Digest* (1924), *Letters of a Self-made Diplomat to his President* (1927), *There's Not a Bathing Suit in Russia* (1927), and *Will Rogers's Political Follies* (1929). In 1949 a selection from his writings was published as his *Autobiography*.

Rohmer, Sax, *see* **Ward, Arthur.**

Rolfe, Frederick William Serafino Austin Lewis Mary (22 July 1860—26 Oct. 1913), novelist who called himself Baron Corvo, was born in London, son of a piano manufacturer. He became a Roman Catholic at the age of 26, and in 1887 entered Oscott College to study for the priesthood; in 1888 he was expelled from the Scots College at Rome after being there five months. After that he lived precariously, moving about the country from Christchurch to Aberdeen, then to Flintshire. His writing career started with *Stories Toto Told Me* (1898), which began publication in the *Yellow Book*; *In His Own Image* (1901) is another collection of stories, while *Hadrian VII* (1904) and *Don Tarquinio* (1905) are novels. His *Chronicles of the House of Borgia* appeared in 1901. He died in Venice, and was the subject of a brilliant biography by A. J. A. Symons, *The Quest for Corvo*.

Rolle, Richard (1300?—29 Sept. 1349), hermit, mystic, and poet, went to Oxford, but at 19 became a recluse, living in various parts of Yorkshire and finally settling at Hampole, near Doncaster. He wrote various religious treatises in Latin and English, turned the Psalms into English verse, and has been credited with a poem, *The Prick of Conscience* in seven books, in which is shown the attitude of protest which was rising against certain Papal pretensions and doctrines.

Rollock *or* **Rollok, Robert** (1555?—8 Feb. 1599), theologian and scholar, a son of the Laird of Powis, was educated at Stirling Grammar School and St Andrews University, where he was appointed one of the regents or professors. Afterwards he became the first Principal of the University of Edinburgh. He also held office as Professor of Theology, and was one of the ministers of the High Church.

He was one of the earliest of Protestant commentators. He wrote chiefly in Latin, but some of his sermons and commentaries are in vernacular Scots.

Rølvaag, Ole Edvart (22 April 1876—5 Nov. 1931), novelist, was born on the Norwegian island of Donne. Emigrating to the United States, he was educated at Augustana College, South Dakota, and St Olaf College, Minnesota, where in 1906 he joined the staff and rose to be head of the Norwegian department. In 1910 he became an American citizen, but his novels were all written in Norwegian. His greatest work, *Giants in the Earth* (1927), which takes its title from Genesis vi. 4, is a novel of pioneer life on the American prairies, and *Peder Victorious* (1929) is a sequel to it. Other novels are *Pure Gold* (1930) and *The Boat of Longing* (1933). In 1926 he was made a Knight of St Olaf.

Roosevelt, Franklin Delano (30 Jan. 1882—12 April 1945), 31st President of the United States, was a fifth cousin of Theodore Roosevelt (q.v.). Born at Hyde Park, New York State, he was educated at Harvard ánd Columbia Law School. In 1921 he contracted infantile paralysis, from which he only partially recovered. After holding office as Governor of New York, he was elected President in 1933 and remained till his death, being re-elected three times, an unequalled record. Guiding the country first through an unprecedented economic depression and then through the Second World War, he played a greater part in its fortunes than any President since Lincoln. His speeches and essays were collected in several volumes, including *Whither Bound?* (1926), *The Happy Warrior* (1928), *Government—Not Politics* (1932), *Looking Forward* (1933), and *On Our Way* (1934).

Roosevelt, Theodore (27 Oct. 1858—6 Jan. 1919), 25th President of the United States, born in New York City, was educated by tutors and at Harvard. Handicapped by ill-health, he made a gospel of fitness and wrote of this in *The Strenuous Life* (1900). He alternated political activity with the writing of history, his first work being *Naval History of the War of 1812* (1882). From 1896 to 1898 he was Assistant Secretary of the Navy, after which he organized an irregular troop, the Rough Riders, and led them in the Spanish-American War, becoming a popular hero; he wrote his own account of them in 1899. In 1898 he became Governor of New York, and in 1900 was elected Vice-President of the United States, succeeding to the Presidency when McKinley was assassinated in 1901. At 42 he was the youngest President in the country's history, and he held the post for two terms. Of his books *The Winning of the West* (1889—96) is counted among the most important. *African Game Trails* (1910) tells of his hunting trips, and *Through the Brazilian Wilderness* (1914) of an exploring expedition. He also wrote various political works and an *Autobiography* (1913).

Roper, William (1496—4 Jan. 1578), biographer, born at Canterbury, son of the sheriff of Kent, was educated at one of the universities and married Margaret, daughter of Sir Thomas More. He has a place in literature for his excellent and appreciative biography of his father-in-law.   He was a member of various Parliaments between 1529 and 1558.   Although he remained a Roman Catholic, he was permitted to retain his office of prothonotary of the Court of King's Bench after the accession of Elizabeth I.

Roscoe, William (8 March 1753—30 June 1831), historian, born in Liverpool, son of a market-gardener, for a time assisted his father, devoting all his spare time to mental improvement.   Subsequently he entered the office of an attorney, and later went into business on his own account.   In 1799 he joined a local bank as partner and manager, which proved an unfortunate step, as the bank was obliged, in 1816, to suspend payment.   In 1795 he rose into fame at a bound by his *Life of Lorenzo de' Medici*.   It was followed in 1805 by the *Life and Pontificate of Leo the Tenth*, which, though also a work of great ability, had not the same success, his treatment of the Reformation offending Protestants and Roman Catholics alike.   Both works were translated into various languages.   He also wrote some poems, including a piece for children, *The Butterfly's Ball and the Grasshopper's Feast* (1807), and several pamphlets on political questions, including the slave-trade, of which he was a determined opponent. He also took a leading part in the public life of Liverpool, which he represented in Parliament from 1806 to 1807.   He was an accomplished botanist.

Roscommon, Wentworth Dillon, 4th Earl of (born Oct. 1633, buried 21 Jan. 1685), poet, nephew of the famous Earl of Strafford, was born in Ireland.   Educated as a Protestant, he studied at Caen University and travelled on the Continent.   He enjoyed a considerable literary reputation in his own day on the strength of a poetical *Essay on Translated Verse* (1684), and translations from Horace's *Art of Poetry*.

Rose, William Stewart (1775—30 April 1843), poet and translator, was the son of a statesman.   Educated at Eton and Cambridge, he was M.P. for Christchurch from 1796 to 1800, then he was appointed Reading Clerk to the House of Lords.   He translated the romance of *Amadis de Gaul* (1803), and *Partenopex de Blois* (1807), and from 1823—31 was occupied with the principal work of his life, his translations from the Italian, including the *Orlando Furioso* of Ariosto, in which he was encouraged by Sir Walter Scott, whose friend he was.   He also produced a volume of poems, *The Crusade of St Louis* (1810).

Rosebery, Archibald Philip Primrose, 5th Earl of (7 May 1847—21 May 1929), statesman and biographer, was born in London, a grandson of the 4th Earl, and educated at Eton, where he was contemporary with A. J. Balfour (q.v.) and Lord Randolph Churchill. From there he went to Oxford, and in 1868 succeeded in the earldom. Possessed of a brilliant mind and great personal charm, he had a distinguished political career, becoming Foreign Secretary in the Gladstone Administrations of 1886 and 1892 and Prime Minister from 1894 to 1895.   His biographical writings include *William Pitt* (1891), *Sir Robert Peel* (1899), *Oliver Cromwell* (1899), *Napoleon, the Last Phase* (1900), *Lord Randolph Churchill* (1906), and *Chatham:*

U

his Early Life and Connections (1910), and show both vividness and accuracy. In 1881 he was elected Lord Rector of Edinburgh University, and 30 years later of St Andrews.

Rosman, Alice Grant (1887—   ), novelist, was born at Kapunda, South Australia, and educated at the Dominican Convent, Cabra, Adelaide.   As early as 1902 she had a story printed, and from 1908 to 1911 she wrote for an Adelaide paper as 'Rosna.' In 1911 she went to London and worked first on the staff of the *British Australian* and from 1920 to 1927 on the *Grand Magazine*. She first attained success as a novelist with her domestic romance *The Window* (1928), which sold 100,000 copies, and was followed by *Visitors to Hugo* (1929), another success.   Others of her novels are *The Young and Secret* (1930), *Jack the Scot* (1930), *The Sixth Journey* (1931), *Benefits Received* (1932), *Protecting Margot* (1933), *Somebody Must* (1934), *The Sleeping Child* (1935), *Mother of the Bride* (1936), *Unfamiliar Faces* (1938), *William's Room* (1939), and *Nine Lives* (1941).

Ross, Alexander (13 April 1699—20 May 1784), poet, was born in Aberdeenshire, son of a farmer, and educated at Mareschal College. He became a schoolmaster first at Aboyne, then at Laurencekirk, and finally from 1732 onwards at Lochlee, Angus, where he was also session clerk, precentor, and notary.   He wrote verse for amusement, and in 1768 published a volume *The Fortunate Shepherdess*, written in the Buchan dialect.   The best-known of his pieces is 'Woo'd, and Married, and A'.'

Ross, Barnaby, *see* **Dannay, Frederic.**

Ross, Martin, *see* **Martin, Violet.**

Rossetti, Christina Georgina (5 Dec. 1830—29 Dec. 1894), poetess, sister of Dante Gabriel Rossetti (q.v.), was born in London, where she lived all her life.   She began to write poetry in early girlhood, some of her earliest verse appearing in 1850 in the *Germ*, the magazine of the Pre-Raphaelites, of which her brother was one of the founders. Her subsequent publications were *Goblin Market and other Poems* (1862), *The Prince's Progress* (1866), *A Pageant and other Poems* (1881), and *Verses* (1893).   *New Poems* (1896) appeared after her death.   *Sing-Song* (1872) was a book of verses for children.   Her life was a very retired one, passed largely in attending on her mother, who lived until 1886, and in religious duties.   She twice rejected proposals of marriage.   Her poetry is characterized by imaginative power, exquisite expression, and simplicity and depth of thought. She rarely imitated any forerunner, and drew her inspiration from her own experiences of thought and feeling.   Many of her poems are definitely religious in form; more are deeply imbued with religious feeling and motive.   Critics have disputed whether she or Elizabeth Barrett Browning (q.v.) merits the title of greatest English poetess.

Rossetti, Dante Gabriel (12 May 1828—10 April 1882), poet and painter, born in London, was christened Gabriel Charles Dante. His father had been curator of antiquities in Naples Museum, but was compelled to fly because of his revolutionary activities, and became Professor of Italian in King's College, London. His mother was Frances Polidori, English on her mother's side, so that the poet was three-fourths Italian, and one-fourth English. He was educated at King's College School, began the systematic study of painting in 1842, and in 1848, with Holman Hunt, Millais, and others, founded the Pre-Raphaelite school of painting. In 1849 he exhibited the 'Girlhood of Mary Virgin,' and among his other pictures are 'Beata Beatrix,' 'Monna Vanna,' and 'Dante's Dream.' Simultaneously with art he worked hard at poetry; by 1847 he had written 'The Blessed Damozel,' which appeared in the *Germ*, the magazine of the Pre-Raphaelites, and in 1861 he brought out his first book, a volume of translations from the early Italian poets under the title of *Dante and his Circle*. The death of his wife in 1862, after a married life of less than two years, told heavily upon him, as did various attacks upon his poetry, including that of Robert Buchanan (q.v.) in ' The Fleshly School of Poetry ' (1871), to which he replied in ' The Stealthy School of Criticism.' His *Poems* which, in the vehemence of his grief, he had buried in the coffin of his wife, and which were afterwards exhumed, appeared in 1870; and his last literary effort, *Ballads and Sonnets*, containing the sonnets forming *The House of Life*, in 1881. In his later years he suffered acutely from neuralgia, which led to the habit of taking chloral. Rossetti was fastidious in composition; his poems are as remarkable for condensation, finish, and exact expression of the poet's thought as for their sumptuous colouring and rich concrete imagery. In later years he was subject to depression, and became somewhat embittered, and much of a recluse. His *Works* and *Letters* were edited after his death by his brother W. M. Rossetti (q.v.).

Rossetti, William Michael (25 Sept. 1829—5 Feb. 1919), critic and biographer, was born in London, a brother of Dante Gabriel and Christina Rossetti (qq.v.), and educated at King's College School. From 1845 to 1894 he worked in the Inland Revenue Department, where he rose to be senior assistant secretary. During his youth he took part in the Pre-Raphaelite Movement, and edited its periodical, the *Germ*. In 1865 he published a blank verse translation of Dante's *Inferno*, and about the same time wrote art criticisms for various periodicals, which were collected in *Fine Art, Chiefly Contemporary* (1867). In 1874 he married Lucy, daughter of Ford Madox Brown, the painter. Besides editing the works of his brother and sister, he brought out a series of English poets, and published the collected introductions as *Lives of Some Famous Poets* (1878). Others of his works are a *Life of Keats* (1887), *Memoir, with Family Letters, of Dante Gabriel Rossetti* (1895), *Some Reminiscences* (1906), and *Democratic Sonnets* (1907).

Rous, Francis (born 1579, buried 24 Jan. 1659), versifier and clergyman, was born at Dittisham, Devon, and educated at Oxford, where he wrote *Thule, or Virtue's History* (1598), a poem in imitation of Spenser. After further study at Leyden he was entered at Middle Temple, but turned from law to theology, and published several devotional works, including *The Art of Happiness* (1619). He was a member of both Short and Long Parliaments, and in 1643 was appointed Provost of Eton. His most notable work, however, was his version of *The Psalms of David in English Metre* (1643), which was adopted, after revision by a Scottish committee, by the General Assembly of the Church of Scotland in 1650, and became for the Scottish nation the form in which the Psalms were generally known. Though rough and often unduly literal, these versions have vigour and sincerity, and have retained their place in Scottish church worship along with modern hymns.

Row, John (baptized 6 Jan. 1569, died 26 June 1646), historian, born at Perth, son of an advocate, went to Edinburgh University and became minister of Carnock in Fife, and a leading opponent of Episcopacy. His *History of the Kirk of Scotland, 1558—1637*, left by him in manuscript, was printed in 1842 for the Wodrow Society. It is an original authority for the period.

Rowe, Nicholas (baptized 30 June, 1674, died 6 Dec. 1718), Poet Laureate, was born at Little Barford, Bedfordshire, son of a lawyer. Educated at Westminster School, he studied law at Middle Temple, but inheriting an income of £300 a year, he devoted himself to literature, and produced several dramas, including *The Ambitious Stepmother* (1700), *The Fair Penitent* (1703), and *Jane Shore* (1715). The last, which is his best, contains some scenes of true pathos. He also wrote some poems, and translated Lucan. Rowe, who was a man of very engaging manners, was the friend of Pope, Swift, and Addison, and received many lucrative appointments, including that of Under-Secretary of State. He has the distinction of being the first editor and biographer of Shakespeare (1709). He was appointed Poet Laureate in 1715, and was buried in Westminster Abbey, with an epitaph by Pope.

Rowley, Samuel (died 1624?), dramatist, was in 1598 associated with Philip Henslowe the theatrical manager, probably as a reviser of other writers' plays; in 1602 he made additions to Marlowe's *Faustus*. He himself wrote several plays on biblical subjects, but his only extant piece is *When You See Me You Know Me* (1605), a chronicle play of Henry VIII. *The Noble Soldier* (1634), a tragedy, has also been attributed to him, but doubtfully.

Rowley, William (1585?—1642?), actor and dramatist, did his best work in collaboration with Middleton (q.v.), with whom he wrote *A Fair Quarrel* (1617) and *The Changeling* (1621), while with Dekker and Ford he wrote *The Witch of Edmonton*, published in 1658. Plays published under his own name are *A New Wonder, a Woman Never Vexed* (1632), *All's Lost by Lust* (1633), *A Match at Midnight* (1633), and *A Shoemaker a Gentleman* (1638). *The Birth of Merlin* appeared in 1662 with the names 'William Shakespeare and William Rowley,' but the Shakespearian attribution was probably a publisher's publicity device.

Royce, Josiah (20 Nov. 1855—14 Sept. 1916), philosopher, was born at Grass Valley, California, of English parents, and educated at San Francisco schools and the University of California, after which he studied philosophy in Germany. In 1885 he joined the staff of

Harvard, where he became Alford Professor of Natural Religion, Moral Philosophy, and Civil Polity. A leading exponent of philosophic idealism, he embodied his theory of the Absolute in *The Religious Aspect of Philosophy* (1885). Others of his works are *The Spirit of Modern Philosophy* (1892), *The World and the Individual* (1900), *The Problem of Christianity* (1913), *Lectures on Modern Idealism* (1919), and *Fugitive Essays* (1920).

Royde-Smith, Naomi Gwladys ( ), novelist, was born at Llanwrst, Wales. The family moved to London, and she was educated at Clapham High School and Geneva. From 1912 to 1922 she was literary editor of the *Westminster Gazette*, and in 1926 she married Ernest Milton, a well-known actor. Her novels include *The Tortoiseshell Cat* (1925), *The Housemaid* (1926), *Summer Holiday* (1929), *The Delicate Situation* (1931), *The Bridge* (1932), *Pilgrim from Paddington* (1933), *All Star Cast* (1936), *Miss Bendix* (1938), *The Unfaithful Wife* (1941), *Mildensee* (1943), *Love in Mildensee* (1948), and *She Always Caught the Post* (1953). *A Balcony* (1926) and *Private Room* (1934) are plays.

Ruck, Berta (1878—), novelist, was born in Wales, daughter of an army officer, and educated at St Winifred's School, Bangor. She studied art at the Slade School and Colarossi's in Paris, but then turned to novel-writing, at which she was a popular success. *His Official Fiancée* (1914) her first book, was followed by over 50 others, some of the titles being *The Girls at his Billet* (1916), *The Girl Who Proposed* (1918), *Sweethearts Unmet* (1919), *Arrant Rover* (1921), *The Wrong Mr Right* (1922), *Kneel to the Prettiest* (1925), *Money for One* (1928), *To-day's Daughter* (1930), *Mock-Honeymoon* (1937), *Money Isn't Everything* (1939), *Spinster's Progress* (1942), *Love and Apron Strings* (1949), and *Fantastic Holiday* (1953). *A Story-teller Tells the Truth* (1935) is an autobiography. She married Oliver Onions (q.v.), the novelist.

Ruddiman, Thomas (Oct. 1674—19 Jan. 1757), grammarian, born at Boyndie in Banffshire, and educated at King's College, Aberdeen, became a schoolmaster at Laurencekirk. In 1709 he obtained a position in the Advocates' Library in Edinburgh, of which in 1730 he became Librarian. In 1714 he published his *Rudiments of the Latin Tongue*, which was for long the recognized Latin grammar in the schools of Scotland. He was made printer to the University in 1728. Ruddiman, who was one of the greatest of Scottish Latinists, produced an edition of the works of George Buchanan, and an edition of Livy once said to be 'immaculate.' He also reprinted, with notes, Gavin Douglas's version of the *Aeneid*.

Runyon, Alfred Damon (4 Oct. 1884—10 Dec. 1946), journalist and short-story writer, was born at Manhattan, Kansas, son of a printer, and brought up in Pueblo, Colorado. At the age of 14 he enlisted in the army and served in the Spanish-American War. He then became a newspaper reporter, was a war correspondent in Mexico in 1912 and through the First World War, and then a columnist. A favourite of the semi-literate American, he wrote always in the present tense, in a mixture of slang and wise-cracks, and depicted gangsters in their milder moments. The best-known of his books are *Guys and Dolls* (1932), *Blue Plate Special* (1934), *Money from Home* (1935), *My Wife Ethel* (1939), and *Take it Easy* (1939). *More Than Somewhat* (1937) and *Furthermore* (1938) are selections from these, published in Britain. *My Old Man* (1939) is a book of essays, and *Tents of Trouble* (1911) and *Rhymes of the Firing Line* (1912) are early volumes of verse.

Ruskin, John (8 Feb. 1819—20 Jan. 1900), writer on art, economics, and sociology, was born in London, the son of a Scottish wine merchant. Brought up under intellectually and morally bracing Puritan influences, until he went to Oxford in 1836 he was educated privately. In 1840 he had made the acquaintance of Turner, and this, together with a visit to Venice, constituted a turning point in his life. In 1843 appeared the first volume of *Modern Painters*, the object of which was to insist upon the superiority in landscape of the moderns, and especially of Turner, to all the ancient masters. The earnestness and originality of the author and the splendour of the style at once called attention to the work which, however, awakened a chorus of protest from the adherents of the ancients. A second volume appeared in 1846, the third and fourth in 1856, and the fifth in 1860. Meanwhile he had published *The Seven Lamps of Architecture* (1849), *The Stones of Venice* (1851—3), perhaps his greatest work, *Lectures on Architecture and Painting* (1854), *Elements of Drawing* (1856), and *Elements of Perspective* (1859).

During the 17 years between the first and the last volumes of *Modern Painters* his views alike on religion and art had become profoundly modified, and the necessity of a radical change in the moral and intellectual attitude of the age towards religion, art, and economics in their bearing upon life and social conditions had become his ruling idea. He now assumed the role of the prophet as Carlyle, by whose teaching he was profoundly influenced, had done, and the rest of his life was spent in the endeavour to turn the mind of the nation in the direction he desired. *The Political Economy of Art* (1857) showed the line in which his mind was moving; but it was in *Unto this Last*, published in the *Cornhill Magazine* in 1860, that he began fully to develop his views. It brought down upon him a storm of opposition and obloquy which continued for years, and which, while it acted injuriously upon his highly sensitive nervous system, had no effect in silencing him or modifying his views. There followed *Munera Pulveris* (1862), *Sesame and Lilies* (1865), *The Crown of Wild Olive* (1866), *Ethics of the Dust* (1866), *Time and Tide* (1867), and innumerable fugitive articles.

In 1869 Ruskin was appointed first Slade Professor of the Fine Arts at Oxford, and endowed a school of drawing in the University. His successive courses of lectures were published as *Aratra Pentelici* (Ploughs of Pentelicus) (1870), *The Eagle's Nest* (1872), *Ariadne Florentina* (1872), and *Love's Meinie* (1873). Contemporaneously with these he issued, with more or less regularity, as health permitted, *Fors Clavigera* (Chance the Clubbearer), a series of miscellaneous notes and essays, sold by the author himself direct to the purchasers, the first of a series of experiments, of which the Guild of St George, a tea room, and a roadmaking enterprise were other examples, in practical economics. After the death of his mother in 1871 he purchased a small property, Brantwood, in the Lake district, where he lived for the remainder of his life, and here he brought out his last work, *Praeterita*, an autobiography, 24 monthly parts of which appeared, bringing down the story to 1864. Ruskin was a man of noble character and generous impulses, but highly strung, irritable, and somewhat intolerant. He is one of our greatest stylists, copious, eloquent, picturesque, and highly coloured. His influence on his time was very great, at first in the department of art, in which he was for a time regarded as the supreme authority, later and increasingly in the realms of economics and morals, in which he was at first looked upon as an unpractical dreamer. He married in 1848, but the union proved unhappy, and was dissolved in 1855.

Russell, Bertrand Arthur William Russell, 3rd Earl, O.M. (18 May 1872—   ), scientist and philosopher, was born at Trelleck, Wales, grandson of the first Earl (q.v.), and succeeded to the title in 1931, but seldom used it. He was educated by tutors and at Trinity College, Cambridge, of which he became a Fellow in 1895. A genius at mathematics and philosophy, he wrote in collaboration with A. N. Whitehead *Principia Mathematica* (1910—13), which became a classic. A pacifist during the First World War, he spent four months in prison, during which he wrote *An Introduction to Mathematical Philosophy* (1919). Later he visited Russia, and for a year was Professor of Philosophy at Peking. From 1927 to 1932 he ran a progressive school for children in Sussex. One of the greatest thinkers of his time, he once described himself as a happy pessimist. Among his philosophical works are *The Problems of Philosophy* (1912), *Our Knowledge of the External World* (1914), *The Analysis of Mind* (1921), *The Analysis of Matter* (1927), *An Outline of Philosophy* (1927), *An Inquiry into Meaning and Truth* (1940), and *Human Knowledge: Its Scope and Limits* (1944). His books on science include *The ABC of Atoms* (1923), *Icarus: or The Future of Science* (1924), and *The ABC of Relativity* (1925). To sociology he contributed *Principles of Reconstruction* (1916), *Roads to Freedom* (1918), *Freedom and Organization* (1934), *New Hopes for a Changing World* (1951), *The Impact of Science on Society* (1952), and *Human Society in Ethics and Politics* (1955). In *The Amberley Papers* (1937) he edited his parents' diaries and letters. He received the Order of Merit in 1944, and in 1950 was awarded the Nobel Prize for Literature. He was married four times.

Russell, Elizabeth Mary Russell, Countess (1866—9 Feb. 1941), novelist who wrote under the name Elizabeth, was born in Sydney, daughter of H. Herron Beauchamp, and was a cousin of Katherine Mansfield (q.v.). She met her first husband, Count Henning August von Arnim, while travelling in Italy; they lived on his estate in East Prussia, and there she wrote *Elizabeth and her German Garden* (1898), a series of amusing sketches of her domestic life. It was followed by *The Solitary Summer* (1899), *The Adventures of Elizabeth in Rügen* (1904), *Princess Priscilla's Fortnight* (1906), and *The Caravanners*

(1909). The Count died in 1910, and she made a home for her five children in Switzerland. In 1916 she married John Francis Stanley Russell, 2nd Earl Russell, brother of Bertrand Russell (q.v.), but they separated after three years. She then wrote more novels, including *The Enchanted April* (1923), *Introduction to Sally* (1926), *The Jasmine Farm* (1934), and *Mr Skeffington* (1940). *All the Dogs of My Life* (1936) is an autobiography.

Russell, George William (10 April 1867—17 July 1935), poet and essayist who wrote under the initials Æ, was born at Lurgan, Armagh, of a Protestant family who moved to Dublin. There he attended Rathmines School and the School of Art, where he met W. B. Yeats (q.v.) ; he painted pictures all his life, but never exhibited or sold them. After working successively in a brewery, a warehouse, and a draper's shop, he became an active member of the Irish Literary Renascence and Home Rule movement and was one of the founders of the Abbey Theatre ; from 1910 onwards he edited the *Irish Statesman*. He died at Bournemouth of cancer. A theosophist from the year 1887, he wrote poems in which mysticism and a romantic love of nature were blent together. His signature Æ was originally the error of a printer who could not read the pseudonym ' Aeon.' His volumes of verse include *Homeward Songs by the Way* (1894), *The Earth Breath* (1897), *The Divine Vision* (1903), *The Nuts of Knowledge* (1903), *By Still Waters* (1906), *Gods of War* (1915), *Voices of the Stones* (1918), *Midsummer Eve* (1928), *Dark Weeping* (1929), *Enchantment* (1930), *Vale* (1931), and *The House of the Titans* (1931). *Deirdre* (1907) is a play. Books of essays are *Imaginations and Reveries* (1915), *The Interpreters* (1920), and *Song and Its Fountains* (1932).

Russell, George William Erskine (3 Feb. 1853—17 March 1919), politician and essayist, was born in London, a son of Lord Charles Russell, M.P., and educated at Harrow and Oxford. A member of Parliament from 1880 to 1885 and from 1892 to 1895, he rose to be Under-Secretary for India and then for the Home Department. His entertaining books of reminiscences include *Collections and Recollections* (two series, 1898, 1909), *A Londoner's Log-book 1901—1902* (1902), *Social Silhouettes* (1906), *A Pocketful of Sixpences* (1907), *Sketches and Snapshots* (1910), *Portraits of the Seventies* (1916), and *Politics and Personalities* (1917). He also edited Matthew Arnold's *Letters* (1895).

Russell, John Russell, 1st Earl (18 Aug. 1792—28 May 1878), statesman and historian, son of the 6th Duke of Bedford, was educated at Westminster School and the University of Edinburgh. He entered Parliament in 1813, and became one of the most eminent English statesmen of the nineteenth century. He uniformly acted with the Whig and afterwards with the Liberal party, advocated all measures of progress, especially the removal of tests, the extension of education, and Parliamentary reform. He was the leader of his party in the House of Commons from 1834 to 1855, represented the City of London from 1841 until raised to the peerage in 1861, and held the offices of Paymaster of the Forces, Home Secretary, Colonial

Secretary, Foreign Secretary, and Prime Minister, which last he held twice, from 1846 to 1852, and from 1865 to 1866. His contributions to literature were considerable, and include an *Essay on the English Constitution* (1821), *Memoirs of the Affairs of Europe from the Peace of Utrecht* (1824), *Correspondence of the 4th Duke of Bedford* (1842—6), *Life, Diary, and Letters of Thomas Moore* (1853—6), *Life and Times of Charles James Fox* (1859—67), *Essays on the Rise and Progress of the Christian Religion in the West of Europe* (1873), and *Recollections and Suggestions* (1875).

Russell, William (1741—25 Dec. 1793), historian, born at Windydoors, Selkirk, son of a farmer, was educated at Innerleithen and Edinburgh. Apprenticed to a bookseller in Edinburgh, he was patronized by Lord Elibank, and went to London, where he followed literature as a profession. He wrote poems and fables, a *History of America* (1779), and a *History of Modern Europe* in five volumes (1779—84).

Russell, William Clark (24 Feb. 1844—8 Nov. 1911), novelist, was born in New York, his father being a song composer, his mother a relative of the poet Wordsworth. Educated at private schools, he joined the merchant service as an apprentice on the ship *Duncan Dunbar*, and made several voyages to India and Australia which supplied him with material that was later worked into his books. In 1866 he left the sea to follow a literary career. His first novel *John Holdsworth, Chief Mate* (1875) was followed by *The Wreck of the 'Grosvenor'* (1877), which made his reputation as a graphic writer of sea stories, and he published more than 50 other novels, of which the best-known are *The Frozen Pirate* (1877), *A Sailor's Sweetheart* (1880), *An Ocean Tragedy* (1881), *The Death Ship* (1888), *List Ye Landmen* (1894), and *Overdue* (1903). He also wrote lives of *Dampier* (1889), *Nelson* (1890), and *Collingwood* (1891).

Russell, Sir William Howard (28 March 1820—10 Feb. 1907), journalist, born at Tallaght, County Dublin, and educated at Trinity College, was called to the Bar in 1850. Having joined the staff of *The Times*, he was sent as war correspondent to the Crimea, his letters from which caused a profound sensation, and led to an improved condition of things in regard to the army. In writing of Balaclava he used the phrase 'thin red line,' which has become a classic. He was also correspondent in India during the Mutiny, in America during the Civil War, and in the Franco-German War of 1870—1. Among his books are *The Adventures of Dr Brady* (1868), *Hesperothen* (1882), *A Visit to Chili* (1890), and *The Great War with Russia* (1895). He was knighted in 1895, and also received various foreign decorations.

Rutherford, Mark, *see* **White, William Hale.**

Rutherford, Samuel (1600?—29 March 1661), theologian, born at Nisbet, Roxburghshire, was educated at Edinburgh University, where he became in 1623 Regent of Humanity (Professor of Latin). In 1627 he was settled as minister of Anwoth in Galloway, whence he was banished to Aberdeen for nonconformity. On the re-establish-

u*

ment of Presbytery in 1638 he was made Professor of Divinity at St Andrews, and in 1651 Principal of St Mary's College there, and was one of the Scottish Commissioners to the Westminster Assembly. At the Restoration he was deprived of all his offices. Among his polemical works are *Due Right of Presbyteries* (1644) and *Lex Rex* (1644) which was, after the Restoration, burned by the common hangman, and led to the citation of the author for high treason, which his death prevented from taking effect. His chief fame, however, rested upon his devotional works, such as *Christ Dying and drawing Sinners to Himself* (1647).

Rycaut *or* **Ricaut, Sir Paul** (1628—16 Nov. 1700), historian, was born at Aylesford, Kent, son of a financier, and educated at Cambridge. After spending some 10 years in foreign travel, in 1661 he obtained a post on the embassy to Turkey, and later was consul at Smyrna. His most important work is *The Present State of the Ottoman Empire* (1668), and he also wrote *A History of the Turkish Empire from 1623 to 1677* (1679), which was a continuation of the *History of the Turks* by Knolles (q.v.). In 1685 he published a translation of Platina's Latin history of the Popes, and in the same year he was knighted.

Rymer, Thomas (1641—14 Dec. 1713), critic and archaeologist, born at Yafforth, Yorkshire, and educated at Cambridge, was called to the Bar at Lincoln's Inn. He gained notoriety through his *Tragedies of the Last Age Considered* (1678), in which he defended the classical against the Shakespearian manner, and for his *Short View of Tragedy* (1692), which condemned *Othello*. Appointed historiographer to William III, he made a valuable collection of English treaties, which were published in 20 volumes under the title *Foedera* (1704—35). He also wrote some poems, and a play entitled *Edgar, or the English Monarch*.

S

Sabatini, Rafael (29 April 1875—13 Feb. 1950), novelist, was born at Jesi, Italy, and educated at schools in Zoug, Switzerland, and Oporto. Greatly interested in history, he started to write historical romances in the Dumas tradition, his first book, *The Tavern Knight*, appearing in 1904. After his marriage in 1905 he settled in Herefordshire, and in the First World War he worked in the Intelligence Department. Among the best-known of his novels are *Scaramouche* (1921) and *Captain Blood* (1922), which had two sequels, *The Chronicles of Captain Blood* (1931) and *The Fortunes of Captain Blood* (1936). Others are *Love-at-Arms* (1907), *St Martin's Summer* (1909), *The Lion's Skin* (1911), *The Strolling Saint* (1913), *The Sea Hawk* (1915), *Fortune's Fool* (1923), *Bellarion* (1926), *The Lost King* (1937), *The Marquis of Carabas* (1940), and *The Gamester* (1949).

Sackville, Charles, *see* **Dorset, 6th Earl of.**

Sackville, Thomas, *see* **Dorset, 1st Earl of.**

Sackville-West, Hon. Edward Charles (13 Nov. 1901—), novelist, son of the 4th Baron Sackville and cousin of Victoria Sackville-West (q.v.), was educated at Eton and Oxford. An expert pianist, he was musical critic of the *Spectator* in 1924, and was on the staff of the *New Statesman* from 1926 to 1927. His novels include *Piano Quintet* (1925), *The Ruin* (1926), *The Apology of Arthur Rimbaud* (1928), *Simpson: A Life* (1931), and *The Sun in Capricorn* (1934); *A Flame in Sunlight* (1936) is a study of De Quincey, and *Inclinations* (1949) is a book of critical essays.

Sackville-West, Hon. Victoria Mary (9 March 1892—), poetess and novelist, daughter of the 3rd Baron Sackville, was born at Knole Castle, Kent, which her family received from Elizabeth I; she wrote of its history in *Knole and the Sackvilles* (1923). In 1913 she married Harold Nicolson (q.v.); *Passenger to Teheran* (1926) gives an account of the years they spent in Persia, where he was British Minister. In 1927 her poem *The Land* was awarded the Hawthornden Prize, and in 1946 *The Garden* received the Heinemann Prize. Other volumes of her verse are *Orchard and Vineyard* (1921), *King's Daughter* (1930), *Some Flowers* (1937), and *Solitude* (1938). Her novels include *Heritage* (1919), *Challenge* (1923), *Grey Wethers* (1923), *The Edwardians* (1930), *All Passion Spent* (1931), *Family History* (1932), *The Dark Island* (1934), *Pepita* (1937), *Grand Canyon* (1942), and *The Easter Party* (1953). She also wrote studies of Aphra Behn (1927), Andrew Marvell (1933), and Joan of Arc (1936); *The Eagle and the Dove* (1943) tells of two Carmelite saints. In 1948 she was made a Companion of Honour.

Sadleir, Michael Thomas Harvey (25 Dec. 1888—15 Dec. 1957), novelist and bibliographer, son of Sir Michael Sadler, the educationist, changed the spelling of his name so that they would not be confused together. He was educated at Rugby and Oxford. In the First World War he was in the Intelligence Department and afterwards worked in the League of Nations Secretariat. His best-known novel is *Fanny By Gaslight* (1940); others are *Privilege* (1921), *Desolate Splendour* (1923), *The Noblest Frailty* (1925), *Things Past* (1944), and *Forlorn Sunset* (1947). He also published studies of Sheridan (1912) and Trollope (1927), a memoir of his own father (1949), and a number of bibliographical works. In 1937 he was Reader in Bibliography at Cambridge, and in 1944 was President of the Bibliographical Society.

Saint-John, Henry, *see* **Bolingbroke, 1st Viscount.**

Saintsbury, George Edward Bateman (23 Oct. 1845—28 Jan. 1933), scholar, born at Southampton, was educated at King's College School, London, and Merton College, Oxford. After being successively a master at Manchester Grammar School and at Elizabeth College, Guernsey, and a headmaster in Elgin, he was from 1895 to 1915 Professor of English at Edinburgh University. Besides writing many text-books he contributed to various periodicals. His erudition was extremely wide, but he had a crabbed style which has been described as 'deplorably parenthetic.' His works include *A Short History of French Literature* (1882), *A History of Nineteenth Century Literature* (1896), *A Short History of English Literature* (1898), *A History of English Prosody* (1906—21), *A History of Elizabethan Literature* (1906), *A History of English Criticism* (1911), *A History of English Prose Rhythm* (1912), *The Peace of the Augustans* (1916), and studies of Dryden (1887), Matthew Arnold (1899), and Thackeray (1931). His miscellaneous essays were collected in *A Scrap Book*, (three series, 1922, 1923, 1924). A connoisseur of wines, he also wrote *Notes on a Cellar-Book* (1920).

Saki, *see* **Munro, Hector Hugh.**

Sala, George Augustus Henry (24 Nov. 1828—8 Dec. 1895), journalist and novelist, born in London of Italian ancestry, was at school in Paris with Dumas the Younger. He studied art, and became an illustrator of books and scene-painter, afterwards taking to literature. He contributed to many periodicals, including *Household Words* and the *Illustrated London News*, was the founder and first editor of *Temple Bar*, and was for many years on the staff of the *Daily Telegraph*. Among his novels were *The Buddington Peerage* (1860) and *Quite Alone* (1863). He also wrote books of travel and an autobiographical work, his *Life and Adventures* (1895).

Sale, George (1697?—13 Nov. 1736), Orientalist, son of a London merchant, was entered at Inner Temple in 1720 and became a solicitor. In 1734 he published a translation of the *Koran*. He also assisted in the *Universal History*, and was one of the correctors of the Arabic New Testament published in 1726.

Salisbury, John of, *see* **John of Salisbury.**

Sandburg, Carl (6 Jan. 1878—   ), poet, was born at Galesburg, Illinois, son of a Swedish blacksmith. Leaving school at

13, he worked successively as bricklayer, harvester, and kitchen hand in the Prairie States, then fought in Puerto Rico during the Spanish-American War. After that he worked his way through Lombard College, Galesburg, which later made him a D.Litt. While trying journalism in Milwaukee and Chicago he contributed Whitmanesque verse to *Poetry*, and in 1919 and 1920 was joint winner of the prize awarded by the Poetry Society of America. Moving about the country he earned his living by singing and reciting, and also collected folk-songs and ballads which he published in *The American Songbag* (1927). Volumes of his own verse, which combines robust vigour with impressionistic delicacy, include *In Reckless Ecstasy* (1904), *Chicago Poems* (1915), *Cornhuskers* (1918), *Smoke and Steel* (1920), *Slabs of the Sunburnt West* (1922), *Good Morning, America* (1928), and *The People, Yes* (1936); his *Complete Poems* were awarded the Pulitzer Prize in 1950. He also wrote a monumental *Life of Abraham Lincoln* which won the Pulitzer Prize in 1940, and an autobiographical work, *Always the Young Strangers* (1953).

Sanderson, Robert (1587—29 Jan. 1663), theologian, born at Rotherham in Yorkshire, was educated at Oxford. Ordained in 1611, he became Professor of Divinity in 1642, and in 1660 Bishop of Lincoln. His work on logic, *Logicae Artis Compendium* (1615), was long a standard treatise on the subject. His sermons also were admired; but he is perhaps best remembered by his *Nine Cases of Conscience Resolved* (1678), in consideration of which he has been placed at the head of English casuists.

Sands, Robert Charles (11 May 1799—16 Dec. 1832), poet, was born in New York, son of a wealthy merchant, and educated at Columbia University, where he studied law. In 1817 he published *The Bridal of Vaumond*, a narrative poem, and in 1820 another, *Yamoyden*, based on Indian legend. He also wrote short stories, of which the best-known is 'Boyuca,' and edited the *Life and Correspondence of John Paul Jones* (1830).

Sandys, George (2 March 1578—1644), traveller and translator, son of an Archbishop of York, was born at Bishopthorpe, Yorkshire, and educated at Oxford. In 1610 he travelled in Europe and the Near East, and later wrote of this in his popular *Relation of a Journey Begun An. Dom. 1610*. In 1621 he went to America and remained for ten years, becoming Treasurer of the Virginia Colony. While there he completed a translation of Ovid's *Metamorphoses* (1626), which marks an important stage in the development of the heroic couplet. His other works include poetic versions of the Psalms and the Song of Solomon, and a tragedy, *Christ's Passion*.

Santayana, George (16 Dec. 1863—26 Sept. 1952), philosopher, born in Madrid, was taken at an early age to America, where his mother had spent a great part of her life. He retained his Spanish nationality, but all his works were written in English. He was educated at Boston Latin School and Harvard, where he taught in the Philosophical Department from 1889 to 1912. From 1914 to 1918 he lived in England, later writing *Soliloquies in England* (1922). His earliest publications were *Sonnets and Other Verses* (1894) and

The Hermit of Carmel (1901) another book of poems. But his main works are philosophical, revealing in a rich poetic style a transition from orthodox Catholicism to a religion of beauty and nature. Greatest of these is *The Life of Reason* (1905—6), a general criticism of morals and arts. Others are *The Sense of Beauty* (1896), *Interpretations of Poetry and Religion* (1900), *Winds of Doctrine* (1913), *Dialogues in Limbo* (1926), *Platonism and the Spiritual Life* (1927), *The Realm of Spirit* (1940), *The Realm of Being* (1945), and *The Idea of Christ in the Gospels* (1946). *The Last Puritan* (1935) was a successful novel, while *The Background of My Life* (1944), *The Middle Span* (1945), and *My Host the World* (1953) are volumes of reminiscence.

Sapper, *see* **McNeile, Herman Cyril.**

Saroyan, William (31 Aug. 1908—   ), playwright and novelist, was born at Fresno, California, of Armenian parents. After leaving school he worked variously as telegraph boy, office boy, and farm labourer, then settled in San Francisco. He first gained notice with a volume of short stories, *The Daring Young Man on the Flying Trapeze* (1934). His earliest play, *My Heart's in the Highlands* (1939) was followed in the same year by *The Time of Your Life*, which was awarded the Pulitzer Prize. Others are *Love's Old Sweet Song* (1940), *The Beautiful People* (1941), *Get Away, Old Man* (1943), and *Jim Dandy* (1947). Novels and books of short stories are *The Human Comedy* (1942), *Dear Baby* (1944), *Adventures of Wesley Jackson* (1946), *Tracy's Tiger* (1951), and *The Laughing Matter* (1953). *The Bicycle Rider in Beverley Hills* (1952) is an autobiography.

Sassoon, Siegfried Lorraine (8 Sept. 1886—   ), poet and novelist, was born in Kent and educated at Marlborough and Cambridge. He enlisted at the outbreak of the First World War, served as a second lieutenant, and was awarded the Military Cross. His war experiences affected him deeply, and made him a pacifist. In 1919 he was literary editor of the *Daily Herald*. His volumes of poetry include *Twelve Sonnets* (1911), *Melodies* (1913), *Hyacinth* (1915), *The Old Huntsman* (1917), *Counter-Attack* (1918), *Satirical Poems* (1926), *Rhymed Ruminations* (1930), *Poems of Pinchbeck Lyre* (1931), and *Vigils* (1935). A trilogy of novels often taken as autobiographical are *Memoirs of a Fox-Hunting Man* (1928), which was awarded both the Hawthornden and the Tait Black Memorial Prizes, *Memoirs of an Infantry Officer* (1930), and *Sherston's Progress* (1936), together styled *The Complete Memoirs of George Sherston* (1937). His real autobiography is contained in *The Old Century and Seven More Years* (1938), *The Weald of Youth* (1942), and *Siegfried's Journey 1916—20* (1945). In 1946 he published a biography of Meredith. In 1951 he was made a C.B.E.

Saunders, Hilary Aidan St George (14 Jan. 1898—16 Dec. 1951), novelist, was born at Brighton, son of a clergyman, and educated at Downside and Oxford. During the First World War he was a second lieutenant in the Welch Guards and was awarded the Military Cross. From 1920 to 1937 he was on the Secretariat of the League of Nations, where he met John Leslie Palmer (q.v.), like himself a Balliol man, with whom he collaborated in writing thrillers. Under the pseudonym Francis Beeding they published *The Seven Sleepers* (1925), *The Hidden Kingdom* (1927), *The Six Proud Walkers* (1928), *The Five Flamboys* (1929), *The Four Armourers* (1930), *The Three Fishers* (1931), *Take It Crooked* (1932), *The Two Undertakers* (1933), *Mr Bobadil* (1934), *The One Sane Man* (1934), and other books; and as David Pilgrim they produced *So Great a Man* (1938), *No Common Glory* (1941), and *The Great Design* (1944). During the Second World War Saunders was attached to the Air Ministry as historian, and wrote *The Battle of Britain* (1941), a pamphlet which sold three million copies; he followed this with *Bomber Command* (1941), *Coastal Command* (1942), *Combined Operations* (1943), *The Green Beret* (1949), and *The Red Beret* (1950). From 1946 to 1950 he was librarian of the House of Commons, and in 1951 he was awarded the C.B.E.

Savage, Richard (1697?—1 Aug. 1743), poet, was probably of humble birth, but claimed to be the illegitimate son of the 4th Earl Rivers. He was the friend of Johnson in the early and miserable days of the latter in London; and in an account of his life Johnson has given his story as set forth by himself, which is, if true, a singular record of maternal cruelty. There are strong reasons, however, for doubting whether his account can be relied on. He led a wildly irregular life, killed a gentleman in a tavern brawl, for which he was sentenced to death, but pardoned; and by his waywardness alienated nearly all who wished to befriend him. For a time he had a pension of £50 from Queen Caroline on condition of his writing an ode yearly on her birthday, and on the death of Eusden in 1730 he tried to be appointed his successor as Poet Laureate, but Cibber was chosen. He wrote a comedy, *Love in a Veil* (1718), a tragedy, *Sir Thomas Overbury* (1723), and two poems, *The Bastard* (1728) and *The Wanderer* (1729). He died in prison at Bristol.

Savile, Sir Henry (30 Nov. 1549—19 Feb. 1622), scholar, born at Bradley, near Halifax, was educated at Oxford, where he lectured on mathematics. He was afterwards Warden of Merton College and in 1596 became Provost of Eton. In 1581 he made a translation from Tacitus entitled, *The Ende of Nero and Beginning of Galba*, and in the same year published *Rerum Anglicarum Scriptores post Bedam Praecipui*, a collection of some of the chronicles subsequent to Bede. He founded the Savilian Professorship of Astronomy and Geometry at Oxford, and was one of the most learned Elizabethans.

Saxby, Edward (died 1658), pamphleteer, was born in Suffolk, took service about 1643 in Cromwell's Horse, and rose to be a colonel. His extreme republican views, however, led him into the bitterest antagonism when Cromwell assumed the Protectorship. This received expression in his extraordinary pamphlet, *Killing no Murder*, in which the assassination of Cromwell is advocated and which displays in a remarkable degree perverted ingenuity of argument combined with considerable literary power. Saxby died demented in the Tower.

Sayce, Archibald Henry (25 Sept. 1845—4 Feb. 1933), philologist, was born at Shirehampton, near Bristol, where his father was curate, and was educated at Grosvenor College, Bath, and Queen's College, Oxford, of which he became a Fellow in 1869, taking orders in the following year. From 1876 to 1890 he was deputy to Max Müller, the Professor of Comparative Philology, and from 1891 to 1919 was Professor of Assyriology. Said to be the greatest linguist of his time, he carried out extensive archaeological work in the Near and Middle East, and was an authority on the Hittites. His works include *Principles of Comparative Philology* (1874), *An Introduction to the Science of Language* (1880), *Monuments of the Hittites* (1881), *The Hittites* (1889), *Ancient Empires of the East* (1884), *Babylonians and Assyrians* (1900), and *Archaeology of Cuneiform Inscriptions* (1907); in 1923 he published his *Reminiscences*. He received honorary degrees from Oxford, Aberdeen, Edinburgh, Dublin, and Oslo.

Sayers, Dorothy Leigh (13 June 1893—17 Dec. 1957), writer of detective stories, was born at Oxford, where her father was a head-master. Educated at Somerville College, she was one of the first women to get an Oxford degree. In 1926 she married Captain Atherton Fleming. Her first detective story, *Whose Body?* (1923) was followed by *Clouds of Witness* (1926), *Strong Poison* (1930), *Murder Must Advertise* (1933), in which she utilized her experience as a copy writer in an advertising agency, and *The Nine Tailors* (1934). *Gaudy Night* (1935) has an Oxford background, and *Busman's Honeymoon* (1937) carries on the romance of Lord Peter Wimsey, her erudite detective, modelled on one of the more popular dons of her day. In the introductions to her three collections of *Great Short Stories of Detection, Mystery, and Horror* (1928, 1931, 1934) she essays to classify the different types of thriller and to formulate rules for them. She also wrote a number of plays, including *The Zeal of Thy House* (1937), *The Devil to Pay* (1939), *The Man Born to be King* (1943), and *Just Vengeance* (1946), and published translations of Dante's *Inferno* (1949) and *Purgatorio* (1955).

Scarfe, Francis Harold (18 Sept. 1911—   ), poet and novelist, was born at South Shields, Durham, of a seafaring family. His father was lost at sea in 1916, and the son was educated at the Royal Merchant Seamen's Orphanage, Berkshire—which is described in his first novel, *Promises* (1950)—Durham University, Cambridge, and the Sorbonne. After a period as supervisor in French at Trinity College, Cambridge, he was appointed lecturer in French at Glasgow University. During the Second World War he was a lieutenant-colonel in the Army Educational Corps. Volumes of his verse are *Inscapes* (1940), *Poems and Ballads* (1942), and *Underworlds* (1950). Novels, of imaginative rather than realist type, are *Single Blessedness* (1951) and *The Unfinished Woman* (1954). Among his criticial works are *Auden and After* (1942), *Auden: a Study* (1949), and *The Art of Paul Valéry* (1954). He was a Fellow of the Royal Society of Literature.

Schreiner, Olive Emilie Albertina (24 March 1855—11 Dec. 1920), novelist, was born at Wittenbergen Mission, Basutoland, daughter of a Methodist missionary of German descent, and was mainly self-educated. At the age of 15 she became governess to a Boer family living on the edge of the Karroo desert. From 1881 to 1889 she lived in England, where her novel *The Story of an African Farm*, which she published in 1883 under the name Ralph Iron, won her fame and friends. In particular she formed a lifelong friendship with Havelock Ellis (q.v.). In 1894 she married Samuel Cronwright, who had been a member of the Cape Parliament. Among her later novels are *Trooper Peter Halket of Mashonaland* (1897), *From Man to Man* (1926), and *Undine* (1928); *Dreams* (1891), *Dream Life and Real Life* (1893), and *Stories, Dreams, and Allegories* (1920) are collections of short stories. Rationalist and feminist, she also wrote on political and social matters, her *Woman and Labour* (1911) being a classic. Her *Letters* were published in 1924.

Scott, Alexander (1530?—1584?), poet, lived in or near Edinburgh, and is said to have been a son of the Prebendary of the Chapel Royal. His work is preserved in the Bannatyne Manuscript. One of Scotland's greatest love poets, he was an accomplished master of lyric verse. Among his best pieces are ' A New Year Gift to Queen Mary,' ' The Rondel of Love,' and ' Jousting at the Drum.'

Scott, Duncan Campbell (2 Aug. 1862—10 Dec. 1947), poet, was born in Ottawa, son of a Methodist minister, and educated at Stanstead College, Quebec. Entering the Canadian Civil Service, he rose to be Deputy Superintendent General of the Department of Indian Affairs. His volumes of poetry include *The Magic House* (1893), *Labour and the Angel* (1898), *New World Lyrics and Ballads* (1905), *Via Borealis* (1906), *Lundy's Lane* (1916), *Beauty and Life* (1921), and *The Green Cloister* (1935). In 1899 he was elected a Fellow of the Royal Society of Canada, of which he became president, and in 1934 he was made a Companion of the Order of St Michael and St George. He held honorary doctorates of Toronto and Queen's University, Kingston.

Scott, Hugh Stowell (9 May 1862—19 Nov. 1903), novelist who wrote under the name Henry Seton Merriman, was born at Newcastle upon Tyne, son of a ship-owner, and educated at Loretto and Wiesbaden. For a time he worked as a clerk in an insurance office. His first book, *Young Mistley*, appeared in 1888, but his first real success came four years later with *The Slave of the Lamp* and *From One Generation to Another*. Developing a vein of historical fiction in the Dumas tradition, he wrote *With Edged Tools* (1894), *The Grey Lady* (1895), *The Sowers* (1896), *Flotsam* (1896), *In Kedar's Tents* (1897), *Roden's Corner* (1898), *Isle of Unrest* (1900), *The Velvet Glove* (1901), *Barlasch of the Guard* (1902), and *The Last Hope* (1904).

Scott, John (9 Jan. 1730—12 Dec. 1783), poet, was born at Bermondsey, son of a Quaker linen draper. He began writing verses for *The Gentleman's Magazine*, then visited London, was introduced to Johnson and became a friend of Beattie. In his later years he lived at the village in Hertfordshire which he celebrated in his descriptive poem *Amwell* (1776). Others of his works are *Four Moral Eclogues* (1778) and *Critical Essays* (1785).

Scott, Lady John, *see* **Spottiswood, Alicia Ann.**

Scott, Michael (1175?—1234?), translator, was probably born on the Scottish Border, and was educated at Oxford and Paris. One of the greatest scholars of his time, he studied Arabic, and translated part of Aristotle's works from that language into Latin. He became court astrologer to the Emperor Frederick II, and won a reputation as a magician, which is how Walter Scott writes of him in *The Lay of the Last Minstrel*. His supposed grave is shown in Melrose Abbey.

Scott, Michael (30 Oct. 1789—7 Nov. 1835), novelist, born in Glasgow and educated at the High School and University there, went to Jamaica in 1806 and set up business in Kingston. This led to his making frequent sea voyages, and thus yielded him experiences which he turned to account in two vivacious novels, *Tom Cringle's Log* and *The Cruise of the 'Midge,'* both of which first appeared in *Blackwood's Magazine*, and were published as books in 1836. The author, however, maintained a strict incognito during his life.

Scott, Sir Walter, Bart. (15 Aug. 1771—21 Sept. 1832), poet, novelist, critic, biographer, was born in Edinburgh, son of a lawyer. He was lame from childhood, owing to an illness. Educated at Edinburgh High School and University, where he had the reputation of being idle, he went on to study law, and in 1792 became an advocate. In 1799 he was appointed Sheriff-Depute of Selkirk, and in 1806 Clerk of Session in Edinburgh. Himself of Border descent, he took a great interest in the traditional songs and ballads of that region, and made a collection of them which he published with the title *Minstrelsy of the Scottish Border* (1802—3). The volume contained a number of essays and imitations, one of which outgrew its purpose and was published separately as *The Lay of the Last Minstrel* (1805), which proved very popular. Scott then followed it with the still more successful *Marmion* (1808) and *The Lady of the Lake* (1810), which by its descriptions of highland scenery did much to popularize that region to English visitors. About this time Scott became a partner in James Ballantyne's publishing business. Later works were *Rokeby* (1813), *The Bridal of Triermain* (1813), *The Lord of the Isles* (1815), and *Harold the Dauntless* (1817), his last long poem. During these years his celebrity as a poet was such that he was offered the Laureateship, but declined it in favour of Southey.

At the same time the success of Byron's exotic poetical romances gave Scott the feeling that his own homelier muse was being eclipsed, and he turned from poetry to prose, to become the first and in many ways the greatest writer of historical novels. Beginning with *Waverley* (1814), these appeared anonymously, for Scott at that time regarded novel writing as beneath the dignity of the eminent lawyer and country gentleman that he had become since the profits on his poems had enabled him to buy the estate of Abbotsford, near Melrose. Here he combined social activities with great literary industry, and published a long series of novels, all described as 'by the author of *Waverley*.' The secret of authorship was kept for ten years, during which Scott worked with almost incredible industry, turning out works to meet the heavy expenses of his estate. *Guy Mannering*

(1815), his second novel, was written in six weeks, and *The Bride of Lammermoor* (1819) in a fortnight. Of the whole series the most famous is *Ivanhoe* (1819), but others almost equally popular are *The Antiquary* (1816), *The Heart of Midlothian* (1818), *Kenilworth* (1821), *The Fortunes of Nigel* (1822), *Quentin Durward* (1823), and *The Talisman* (1825). Others are *Old Mortality* (1816), *Rob Roy* (1817), *The Legend of Montrose* (1819), *The Monastery* (1820), *The Abbot* (1820), *The Pirate* (1821), *Peveril of the Peak* (1823), *Redgauntlet* (1824), *St Ronan's Well* (1824), and *The Betrothed* (1825). In addition to this tremendous output of original work he had also published editions of Dryden and Swift, and a volume of *Lives of the Novelists* (1825).

Scott was now at the height of fame and fortune. In 1820 he had been made a baronet. He was Scotland's premier social host, and Abbotsford was 'like an inn' with its wealth of distinguished visitors. In 1822 he had organized the visit of George IV to Edinburgh. He entertained lavishly, and his expenses were in proportion. But in 1826 disaster overtook him. The publishing house of Ballantyne, with which he had become so closely involved, failed owing to mismanagement, with liabilities of over a quarter of a million pounds. How far Scott was responsible is a matter of controversy, but he felt himself under a moral obligation to satisfy the firm's creditors, and at the age of 55 set himself the heroic task of paying this enormous debt. 'This right hand shall work it off,' he declared, and prepared to drudge without intermission during the remainder of his life.

For a time he was able to keep up the pace, even though the death of his wife was a further blow. *Woodstock* came out in 1826, *Chronicles of the Canongate* in 1827, *The Fair Maid of Perth* in 1828, *Anne of Geierstein* in 1829, and in 1832 his last two novels, *Count Robert of Paris* and *Castle Dangerous*, in both of which it is apparent that his powers were failing. In 1827 he had published his *Life of Napoleon* and in 1830 *Tales of a Grandfather*, a history of Scotland to the close of the '45 rebellion. But the strain was too much. In 1830 he had an attack of apoplexy, and gave up his office of clerkship. A European tour made in search of health proved fruitless, and in June of 1832 he was brought back to Abbotsford in a state of extreme weakness. He died in the autumn and was buried in Dryburgh Abbey. In 1797 he had married Charlotte Carpenter, daughter of a French refugee, and they had four children. But with the death of his son the title became extinct, and Abbotsford eventually passed to his grandchild, the daughter of his son-in-law John Gibson Lockhart (q.v.), whose *Life of Scott* is one of the great biographies of English literature. His *Letters* were edited by H. J. C. Grierson (q.v.) in 1937. It is satisfactory to add that his creditors were finally paid off after his death by the sum realized from the sale of his copyrights.

In literary history Scott's work is of the first importance. He was one of the main forces in the Romantic Revival which affected English letters in the first part of the nineteenth century. His poetry reflects in its simplest form the love of nature which was one

of the main sides of the movement, while both it and his prose show
that interest in the storied past which was such a prominent feature
of the so-called Gothic Revival. He practically created the historical
novel, and in his own department of it has never been surpassed.
As a story-teller he has few equals, and his power of depicting
character is proved by the vividness of such minor figures as Dominie
Samson and Dandie Dinmont, Jeanie Deans and Meg Merrilees, for
whose portraits he could draw on his intimate knowledge of the folk
of his own beloved Border country. His influence on other authors
was far-reaching and extended all over Europe, where he was one of
the most popular of British writers. Alexandre Dumas and Victor
Hugo learned their trade from him. 'All is great,' said Goethe,
'in the Waverley Novels: material, effect, characters, execution.'
In his greatness and his wide humanity Scott takes a place beside
Homer and Shakespeare.

Scott, William Bell (12 Sept. 1811—22 Nov. 1890), poet and
painter, was born in Edinburgh, son of a painter, and educated at
Edinburgh High School. In 1837 he settled in London and worked
as a painter chiefly of historical subjects. He also published five
volumes of poetry, including *Hades* (1838) and *The Year of the World*
(1846), and wrote many fine sonnets. His works on painting include
Half-hour Lectures on Art (1861), *The Little Masters* (1879), and lives
of his own brother, the famous artist David Scott (1850) and of
Albrecht Dürer (1869). His *Autobiography* appeared in 1892.

Scotus, John, *see* **Erigena.**

Seaman, Sir Owen, Bart. (18 Sept. 1861—2 Feb. 1936), poet and
humorous writer, born in London, was captain of the school at
Shrewsbury and captain of the boats at Clare College, Cambridge.
For a time he worked as a schoolmaster at Rossall, then as Professor
of Literature at Durham College of Science. In 1897 he was called
to the Bar at Inner Temple and in the same year he joined the staff
of *Punch*, to which he had been contributing for some time. From
1906 to 1932 he was editor, succeeding Sir Francis Burnand (q.v.).
A brilliant writer of light verse and parody, he published many
volumes, including *Paulopostprandials* (1883), *Oedipus the Wreck*
(1888), *With Double Pipe* (1888), *Horace at Cambridge* (1894), *The
Battle of the Bays* (1896), *In Cap and Bells* (1899), *Borrowed Plumes*
(1902), *A Harvest of Chaff* (1904), *Salvage* (1908), *Made in England*
(1916), *From the Home Front* (1918), and *Interludes of an Editor*
(1929). Knighted in 1914, he was made a baronet in 1933; he held
honorary doctorates of Edinburgh and Durham.

Search, Edward, *see* **Tucker, Abraham.**

Sedgwick, Anne Douglas (28 March 1873—19 July 1935), novelist,
was born at Englewood, New Jersey, and educated by governesses.
At the age of 9 she was taken to London, and later she studied
painting in Paris. A follower of the Henry James tradition, she
commenced publication at 25 with *The Dull Miss Archinard*, but
made her reputation with *Tante* (1911). Others of her novels are
Franklin Winslow Kane (1910), *The Encounter* (1914), *The Third*

Window (1920), *The Little French Girl* (1924), *The Old Countess* (1927), *Dark Hester* (1929), and *Philippa* (1930). *The Nest* (1913) and *Autumn Crocuses* (1920) are books of short stories. An auto-biographical *Portrait in Letters* (1936) was edited by her husband, Basil de Selincourt, whom she married in 1908.

Sedley, Sir Charles (1639—20 Aug. 1701), poet and dramatist, born at Aylesford, son of a Kentish baronet, was at Oxford and, coming to the Court of Charles II, became one of the most popular and brilliant members of its dissipated circles. He was the author of two tragedies and three comedies, and of some poems and songs, of which the best known is 'Phyllis Is My Only Joy'; Dryden called him the Tibullus of his age. His only child was the witty and profligate Catherine Sedley, mistress of James II, who created her Countess of Dorchester. *Bellamira* (1687) and *The Mulberry Garden* (1668), founded respectively on Terence and Molière, are his best plays.

Seeger, Alan (22 June 1888—4 July 1916), soldier and poet, was born in New York and educated at Harvard, where he edited the *Harvard Monthly*. During the First World War he enlisted in the French Foreign Legion and was killed at Belloy-en-Santerre, after being awarded the Croix de Guerre and the Medaille Militaire. His *Collected Poems*, published in 1916 with an introduction by William Archer (q.v.) contain the famous war poem 'I Have a Rendezvous with Death.'

Seeley, Sir John Robert (10 Sept. 1834—13 Jan. 1895), historian and essayist, son of a publisher in London, was educated at the City of London School and Christ's College, Cambridge, where he was a contemporary of Calverley, Skeat, and Besant (qq.v.). In 1863 he became Professor of Latin at University College, London, and was Professor of Modern History at Cambridge from 1869 until his death. In 1865 appeared anonymously his *Ecce Homo*, a work which created intense excitement and keen controversy in the theological and religious world. Other works were *The Life and Times of Stein*, the Prussian statesman (1879), *Natural Religion* (1882), *The Expansion of England in the Eighteenth Century* (1883), *Life of Napoleon* (1885), and a work on Goethe. *The Growth of British Policy* (1895) was left finished but unrevised at his death. In recognition of his services to the empire in his political writings he was, in 1894, made K.C.M.G.

Selden, John (16 Dec. 1584—30 Nov. 1654), jurist and antiquary, son of a farmer, was born at Salvington, Sussex, studied at Oxford, and was called to the Bar at Middle Temple in 1612. One of the most learned men of his time, he published a great variety of works and also took an important part in public affairs. He sat in most of the Parliaments from 1621 to 1649, and was one of the members who were committed to the Tower. His works include a treatise on the *Duello or Single Combat* (1606); the still authoritative *Titles of Honour* (1614); *Analecton Anglo-Britannicon* (1615) a collection of Anglo-Saxon records; *De Deis Syris* (1617), an inquiry into polytheism, with special reference to heathen deities mentioned in the

Bible; *A History of Tithes* (1618), which was hotly criticized by the clergy; and *Mare Clausum* (1635) discussing the freedom of the seas. But he is best remembered for his delightful *Table Talk* (1689), collected during the last twenty years of his life by his secretary, Richard Milward. As Saintsbury has pointed out, this book shows the same difference, when compared with Selden's published work, as exists between the writings and the sayings of Dr Johnson; and like the latter, it is full of blunt practical wisdom.

Selincourt, Ernest de, *see* **de Selincourt.**

Sellar, William Young (22 Feb. 1825—Oct. 1890), scholar, born at Morvick, Sutherlandshire, his father being factor to the Duke of Sutherland, was educated at Glasgow University and Balliol College, Oxford. He became in 1859 Professor of Greek at St Andrews and, in 1863, of Latin at Edinburgh. He published a work on the *Roman Poets of the Republic* (1863), followed by *The Roman Poets of the Augustan Age* (1877), and *Horace and the Elegiac Poets* (1892).

Sempill, Francis (1616—12 March 1682), poet, son of Robert Sempill and grandson of Sir James Sempill (qq.v.), was born at Lochwinnoch, Renfrewshire, studied law, and became in 1677 sheriff-depute of Renfrew. Known as a poet and wit, he wrote *The Banishment of Poverty*, an autobiographical poem, and a number of lively ballads, including 'Maggie Lauder,' 'Hallow Fair,' and 'The Blythsome Bridal.' He is also credited with an early version of 'Auld Lang Syne.'

Sempill, Sir James (1566—Feb. 1626), satirist, a grandson of the 3rd Lord Sempill, lived at Lochwinnoch, Renfrewshire. He was educated by George Buchanan (q.v.) along with the future King James VI and I, was entrusted with a number of diplomatic missions, and was knighted in 1600. Among his controversial works is a satire on the Roman Catholic Church, *A Picktooth for the Pope, or the Packman's Paternoster* (1600).

Sempill, Robert (1530?—1595), poet, spent part of his life in Paris and was present at the Massacre of St Bartholomew. He held a position at the Scottish court, and was a supporter of Moray and the Reformation party. His *Regent's Tragedy* (1570) is a poem on the death of Moray, and *A Complaint upon Fortune* (1581) laments the fall of Morton.

Sempill, Robert (1595?—1665), poet, son of Sir James Sempill (q.v.) was educated at Glasgow University. He wrote *The Life and Death of Habbie Simpson, the Piper of Kilbarchan* (1640), a spirited example of the Scottish humorous elegy; its metre became traditional for Scottish elegiac verse and was a favourite with Burns, who used it in 'To a Mouse' and many other poems.

Senior, Nassau William (26 Sept. 1790—4 June 1864), economist and essayist, son of a clergyman, was born at Compton Beauchamp, Berkshire, educated at Eton and Oxford, studied law, and was called to the Bar in 1819. He twice held the Professorship of Political Economy at Oxford, from 1825 to 1830 and from 1847 to 1852, rendered important service as a member of the Poor Law Commission of 1833, and wrote its Report. Senior holds a high position among English economists, and made many contributions to the literature of the science, including *Outline of the Science of Political Economy* (1836). He was, moreover, a writer of considerable versatility, his works in general literature including *Essays on Fiction* (1864), *Historical and Philosophical Essays* (1865), and a series of *Conversations* with many eminent persons, chiefly political, such as De Tocqueville, Thiers, and Guizot, which combine fullness of information with discretion; he also published journals of his travels in Turkey, Greece, Egypt, and other countries.

Service, Robert William (16 Jan. 1874—11 Sept 1958), poet, was born at Preston but taken as a child to Glasgow, where he was educated at Hillhead High School and Glasgow University and afterwards worked in a bank. Emigrating to Canada at the age of 21, he worked at various occupations, including eight years with the Canadian Bank of Commerce in the Yukon. He then became a reporter, and in the First World War served as an ambulance driver and wrote *Rhymes of a Red Cross Man* (1916). After the war he made his home in France. Often styled the Canadian Kipling, he won great popularity with his vigorous frontier verses, which were collected in *Songs of a Sourdough* (1907), *Ballads of a Cheechako* (1909), *Rhymes of a Rolling Stone* (1912), *Ballads of a Bohemian* (1920), *Bar Room Ballads* (1940), *Songs of a Sun-Lover* (1949), *Rhymes of a Roughneck* (1950), and *Lyrics of a Lowbrow* (1951). His novels include *The Trail of '98* (1910), *The Pretender* (1914), *The Roughneck* (1923), and *The House of Fear* (1927). *Ploughman of the Moon* (1945) and *Harper of Heaven* (1948) are autobiographical.

Seton, Ernest Thompson (14 Aug. 1860—23 Oct. 1946), nature writer, was born at South Shields, Durham, his original name being Ernest Seton Thompson. Taken to Canada at the age of 6, he was brought up in the backwoods and educated at Toronto Collegiate Institute; later he studied art at the Royal Academy, London, and in Paris. A founder of the Boy Scouts of America, he wrote *Scouting for Boys* (1910), but is most famous for his books about animals, all of which were illustrated by himself. They include *Wild Animals I Have Known* (1898), *The Biography of a Grizzly* (1900), *Lives of the Hunted* (1901), *Two Little Savages* (1903), *Animal Heroes* (1905), *The Biography of a Silver Fox* (1909), *The Arctic Prairies* (1911), *Wild Animals at Home* (1913), *Wild Animals' Ways* (1916), *Woodland Tales* (1921), *Bannertail* (1922), and *The Biography of an Arctic Fox* (1937). *The Trail of an Artist-Naturalist* (1940) is an autobiography.

Settle, Elkanah (1 Feb. 1648—12 Feb. 1724), poet and dramatist, born at Dunstable and educated at Oxford, was the author of a number of turgid dramas, which in their day were held to rival those of Dryden, who pilloried Settle as Doeg in the second part of *Absalom and Achitophel*. Settle essayed a reply in *Absalom Senior*. He wrote against the Papists, but recanted, and made amends by a *Narrative of the Popish Plot*, in which he exposed the perjuries of Titus Oates. He was appointed City Poet, and died in the Charterhouse. His plays include *Cambyses* (1666), *Empress of Morocco* (1671), *Love and*

Revenge (1675), *The Female Prelate* (1680), *Distressed Innocence* (1691), and the *Ladies' Triumph* (1718).

Seward, Anna (12 Dec. 1747—25 March 1809), poetess known as 'the Swan of Lichfield,' was born at Eyam, Derbyshire, daughter of a clergyman. In 1754 the family removed to Lichfield, where she spent the rest of her life, living with her father and never marrying. Her earliest poems, 'An Elegy on the Death of Mr Garrick' and 'Ode to Ignorance,' appeared in the *Batheaston Miscellany*. In 1782 she published *Louisa, a Poetical Novel*, which went through five editions, and in 1799 a collection of sonnets. She was acquainted with Boswell, Mrs Piozzi, Dr Johnson (whom she disliked), and Walter Scott, who inserted one of her ballads among the imitations in his *Minstrelsy of the Scottish Border*. She bequeathed her literary remains to Scott, who edited her poetical works and wrote a verse inscription for her grave in Lichfield Cathedral. Her poetry is artificial and has been described as 'tinkling and tinsel'; her *Letters* were published in six volumes in 1813.

Sewell, Anna (30 March 1820—25 April 1878), authoress, was born at Yarmouth, daughter of Mary Sewell (q.v.). In 1835 the family went to Brighton, where her father got a post as bank manager. Lame from early childhood, Anna was an invalid nearly all her life. Her title to fame is her book *Black Beauty* (1877), the autobiography of a horse, which became a children's classic and has been described as the most successful animal story ever written.

Sewell, Mary (6 April 1797—10 June 1884), poetess, was born at Sutton, Suffolk, daughter of John Wright, a Quaker farmer. Educated mainly at home, she was a teacher for a time, and in 1819 married Isaac Sewell, who was successively shopkeeper, commercial traveller, and bank manager. She was 60 when she began writing verses for young people, always with a moral attached. Her *Homely Ballads* appeared in 1858, and her poem *Mother's Last Words* (1860) sold over a million copies, while *Our Father's Care* (1861) was only a little less popular. Others of her writings are *Children of Summerbrook* (1859), a tale in verse, and a prose story, *Patience Hart's Experience in Service* (1862).

Seymour, Beatrice Kean (died 31 Oct. 1955), novelist, was born in London, her maiden name being Stapleton. Brought up in a puritanical household where dancing and the theatre were forbidden, she went to a co-educational school and then took classes at King's College, London. Before her marriage to William Kean Seymour she worked as a typist. Among her best novels are *Intrusion* (1921) and *The Chronicles of Sally*, a trilogy made up of *Maids and Mistresses* (1932), *Interlude for Sally* (1934), and *Summer of Life* (1936). Others are *The Romantic Tradition* (1925), *Youth Rides Out* (1928), *False Spring* (1929), *Frost at Morning* (1935), *The Foot of Time* (1940), *Return Journey* (1942), *Joy as it Flies* (1944), *Tumbled House* (1946), *Family Group* (1947), *The Children Grow Up* (1949), and *The Wine is Poured* (1953). In 1937 she wrote a study of Jane Austen.

Shadwell, Thomas (1642?—19 Nov. 1692), Poet Laureate, born at

Weeting, Norfolk, son of a J.P., was educated at Cambridge. After studying law he travelled for a time, and on his return became a popular dramatist. Among his comedies, in which he displayed considerable humour and truth to nature, may be mentioned *The Sullen Lovers* (1668), *Royal Shepherdess* (1668), *The Humorists* (1671), and *The Miser* (1672). He attached himself to the Whigs, and when Dryden attacked them in *Absalom and Achitophel* and *The Medal*, had the temerity to assail him scurrilously in *The Medal of John Bayes* (1682). The castigation which this evoked in *Mac-Flecknoe* and in the second part of *Absalom and Achitophel*, in which Shadwell figures as 'Og,' has conferred upon him an unenviable immortality. He may have found some consolation in his succession to Dryden as Poet Laureate when, at the Revolution of 1688, the latter was deprived of the office.

Shaftesbury, Anthony Ashley Cooper, 3rd Earl of (26 Feb. 1671—4 Feb. 1713), philosopher, was born in London, grandson of the 1st Earl, the eminent statesman. After a private education under the supervision of Locke, and five years at Winchester College, he travelled much on the Continent. On succeeding to the earldom in 1699 he took a prominent part in the debates of the House of Lords, but devoted himself mainly to philosophical and literary pursuits. His collected writings were published in 1711 under the title of *Characteristics of Men, Manners, Opinions, and Times*. In his philosophy he maintains, as against Hobbes, the existence of a moral sense, a view subsequently developed by the Scottish school of philosophy. The style of Shaftesbury is stately and sonorous but laboured. He died at Naples, whither he had gone in search of health, at the early age of 42.

Shairp, John Campbell (30 July 1819—18 Sept. 1885), poet and critic, was born at Houston, West Lothian, son of an army officer, and educated at Edinburgh Academy, Glasgow University, and Oxford, where he won the Newdigate Prize for Poetry. In 1861 he was appointed Professor of Latin at St Andrews, in 1868 Principal of the United College there, and from 1877 to 1887 he was Professor of Poetry at Oxford. Among his writings are *Kilmahoe and other Poems* (1864), *Studies in Poetry and Philosophy* (1868), *Culture and Religion* (1870), *Burns* (1879), *Aspects of Poetry* (1881), and *Sketches in History and Poetry* (1887).

Shakespeare, William (baptized 26 April 1564, died 23 April 1616), dramatist and poet, was born at Stratford-upon-Avon. His father, John Shakespeare, a leading citizen of the town, was at one time its Mayor, or, as it was then termed, High Bailiff; he is variously described as butcher, glover, and dealer in wool. William's mother, Mary Arden, belonged to the landed gentry of Warwickshire. There is no definite information about his schooling, but he almost certainly went to Stratford Grammar School, where he would have a good education. In 1582, at the age of 18, he married Anne Hathaway, a farmer's daughter eight years older than himself; the little Hathaway farmhouse is still preserved in beautiful surroundings at Shottery on the outskirts of Stratford. Their first child, Susanna, was christened six months later, and twins, Hamnet and Judith, followed in 1585.

From then onwards there is a gap of about seven years in our knowledge of Shakespeare, until we hear of him as an actor-dramatist in London. Various traditions have been used to fill the gap. Aubrey, the seventeenth-century biographer, says that he was for a time a schoolmaster in the country, and Rowe, who edited the plays, recounts a story that he went poaching on the neighbouring estate of Charlecote, belonging to Sir Thomas Lucy, and went to London to avoid legal proceedings; it is suggested that he took revenge by ridiculing Lucy in the person of Justice Shallow in the *Merry Wives of Windsor*. His career as an actor is attested by the inclusion of his name in the list of those for two of Jonson's plays, but it is uncertain what parts he took in his own. According to one account he played the part of old Adam in *As You Like It*, and also the ghost in *Hamlet*; this is not incompatible with another tradition, that he was lame, though Aubrey informs us that he was 'a handsome well-shaped man.'

In 1592 Shakespeare was so well established as a playwright that Greene, one of the 'University Wits' who formed the leading lights of contemporary drama, made a spiteful attack on him in *A Groatsworth of Wit*, styling him 'an upstart crow beautified with our feathers.' This was countered a few months later by Henry Chettle, who writes in *Kind Heart's Dream* of Shakespeare's 'facetious (i.e. polished) grace in writing.' In the two following years Shakespeare published two poems, both dedicated to the Earl of Southampton in terms that imply a friendship between them, and in 1594 he is recorded as a member of the newly formed Lord Chamberlain's Company. In 1596, a year saddened by the death of his son Hamnet, his prosperity is attested by the granting to his father of a coat of arms, and in 1597 he purchased New Place, one of the finest houses in his native town. That Shakespeare was now at the top of his profession is shown by a tribute paid by Francis Meres in *Palladis Tamia* (1598), a literary survey, which ranks him highest of English playwrights.

In 1599 the Globe Theatre was built in Southwark, and Shakespeare was one of four members of the company who subscribed for a share in the venture. In 1603 King James took the company under his patronage as the King's Men, so that they became members of the royal household. Shakespeare now became so prosperous that he was able to purchase property in both Stratford and London; according to a later writer he spent at the rate of £1,000 a year, but this is certainly an exaggeration. In 1613 the Globe was burned during a performance of *Henry VIII*, the last play that contains work from his hand, and it is generally assumed that by this time he had retired to Stratford. In March 1616 he made his will, leaving New Place and most of his property to Susanna, now married to Dr John Hall. His other daughter, Judith, now the wife of a neighbour, Thomas Quiney, received a sum of money. He died in the following month and is buried in the parish church, where a monument, still extant, was erected over his grave. His widow died in 1623, and a few months later there was published the first collected edition of his plays, commonly termed the First Folio.

Shakespeare's career as a writer divides naturally into four periods, which correspond to four different phases of his work. As the dates of composition of the plays are partly conjectural, they are best considered in groups. In the first period, from his arrival in London to about 1594, he may be regarded as a writer learning the technique of his art and trying one experiment after another. To this time belong the poems *Venus and Adonis* (1593), which he himself styled 'the first heir of his invention' and the rather more mature *Rape of Lucrece* (1594). Some of his sonnets were at the same time in private circulation, but we have no means of dating them with certainty. The plays he produced at this time are all somewhat immature. First come the three parts of *Henry VI*, which are mere chronicle plays without any discernible plot; *Richard III* is little more than a sequence of double-dyed villainy, and *Titus Andronicus* is a farrago of horror. Somewhat less crude are the two slapstick farces, *The Comedy of Errors* and *The Taming of the Shrew*. But the best plays of this period are *The Two Gentlemen of Verona*, an early version of the 'girl disguised as boy' theme, and *Love's Labour's Lost*, a witty play which 'guys' the affectations of the age and is yet full of exquisite poetry.

In his second period, from 1594 to about 1600, Shakespeare attained full power as a dramatist and produced many of his most beautiful plays, though they lack the profundity that was to come later. There is intense poetical feeling in the first three plays, *Richard II*, *Romeo and Juliet*, and *A Midsummer Night's Dream*—an historical play, a tragedy, and a comedy. Consummate mastery of language is shown alike in King Richard's magnificent rhetoric, in the passionate love speeches of Juliet, and in the exquisite lyrics of the fairy play. A deeper study of character is developed in the historical plays of *1* and *2 Henry IV* and *Henry V*. Here too the comic scenes are Shakespeare's greatest achievement in masculine humour, Falstaff being acknowledged one of his greatest creations. *The Merry Wives of Windsor*, which depicts Falstaff as an unsuccessful wooer, is said to have been written at the special request of Queen Elizabeth.

To this second period belong also that famous group of comedies in which women play the leading part and men are little but foils to them—*The Merchant of Venice*, *Much Ado About Nothing*, *As You Like It*, and *Twelfth Night*. Three of these contain a story of a girl who disguises herself as a boy in order to be with the man she loves. This favourite device of Shakespeare gains special significance when we remember that in his day there were no actresses, and all the female parts were taken by boys. *The Merchant of Venice*, a model of clever stagecraft, is notable for the fine speeches it contains, while *Much Ado about Nothing* is famous for the 'skirmishes of wit' between Beatrice and Benedick, and for the comic constables Dogberry and Verges. Greatest of the four is *As You Like It*, in which Rosalind's happy sense of fun has a foil in the whimsical philosophy of the melancholy Jaques, but for sheer laughter-raising comedy the prize must go to *Twelfth Night*, with its hoaxing of the pompous Malvolio.

This takes us to the turn of the century, when Shakespeare was 36. Up to this time his plays reveal a spirit of youthful freshness and optimism. But with the approach of middle age he seems to have been overwhelmed by a feeling of disillusionment and in some degree to have lost his faith in human nature. There now follow the four great tragedies of *Hamlet*, *Macbeth*, *King Lear*, and *Othello*, all of which are marked by subtle character-drawing, skilful analysis of human motives, and philosophical reflections more profound than anything that appears in the earlier plays. Of these *Hamlet* is the greatest. Filled with Shakespeare's richest wisdom and philosophy, it has become so much a part of England's literary heritage that every other line is a well-known quotation. Next to it in popularity comes *Macbeth*, a murder play of which the horror is redeemed by passages of superb poetry. *King Lear* is basically a story of filial ingratitude, but contains scenes of such elemental passion that it seems like some titanic battle between the forces of good and evil. By contrast, *Othello* is a commonplace study of a husband's jealousy, but as a picture of ingenious human villainy it is masterly.

The other main group in this third period is that of the 'Roman plays' which borrow their plots from Plutarch's *Lives*. *Julius Caesar*, the first of these, shows consummate stagecraft and contains speeches which can hardly be equalled elsewhere in Shakespeare. *Antony and Cleopatra*, historically a sequel to it, depicts the passion of the Roman triumvir and the Egyptian queen. Last of the group is *Coriolanus*, the tragedy of an over-proud aristocrat. Linked with these are two plays on Greek subjects, *Troilus and Cressida*, whose theme is woman's faithlessness, and *Timon of Athens*, a depressing study of a misanthrope. Lastly there are two 'dark comedies,' *Measure for Measure* and *All's Well That Ends Well*, both of which have sordid plots and repulsive characters.

In his next and final period, the playwright had shaken off his black mood, had risen, as one critic puts it, from the depths to the heights, and produced a series of plays with an atmosphere of serene faith in the triumph of good over evil. Not comedies in the usual sense of the word, they have been styled 'romantic dramas,' and represent the sunset of Shakespeare's dramatic career. In each of these the heroine is a young girl who attains through trials and difficulties to happiness. Imogen of *Cymbeline* and Perdita of *The Winter's Tale* are among the most captivating of Shakespeare's creations, and the latter play, though confused in plot, is very effective on the stage. But the greatest of all is *The Tempest*, which the editors of the First Folio chose to commence the volume. The last complete play that Shakespeare wrote, it is in many ways his most perfect, depicting magic and young romance on an enchanted isle and even in its construction fulfilling the pedantic 'dramatic unities.'

Of Shakespeare's merits as playwright and poet it is difficult to write, for all superlatives seem inadequate. He is, of course, immeasurably the greatest of all English writers, and has been so recognized even in those periods that were antipathetic to the Elizabethan genius. Dr Johnson, always a severe critic, wrote 'The stream of time, which is continually washing the dissoluble fabricks of other poets, passes without injury by the adamant of Shakespeare.' Greatest of his gifts was the faculty of drawing character—an art so perfect that his creations often seem more real than the reader's own flesh-and-blood acquaintances. It was this power that led Coleridge to apply to him the epithet 'myriad-minded.' Nineteenth-century critics, indeed, praised him so indiscriminately that they provoked a reaction to 'this side idolatry.' During the twentieth century great advances were made in the study of Shakespeare's text, but the Cambridge edition of Clark and Wright is still used as a standard by most reference books. Editions which embody the latest research are the New Cambridge of Dover Wilson and Quiller-Couch (qq.v.), still unfinished in 1959, and the New Temple Edition (1935—6) of M. R. Ridley (q.v.). Practically all the known facts about Shakespeare and his life are collected in Sir Edmund Chambers's monumental *Shakespeare: A Study of Facts and Problems* (1930).

Shanks, Edward Richard Buxton (11 June 1892—4 May 1953), poet, novelist, and critic, born in London, was educated at Merchant Taylors' and Cambridge, where he edited the *Granta*. In the First World War he served with the South Lancashire Regiment. In 1919 he was the first winner of the Hawthornden Prize, with his poem *Queen of China*. From that year till 1922 he was assistant-editor on the *London Mercury*. In 1926 he was lecturer in poetry at Liverpool University, and from 1928 to 1935 he was a leader-writer on the *Evening Standard*. His volumes of verse include *Songs* (1915), *Poems* (1916), *The Island of Youth* (1921), *The Shadowgraph* (1925), and *Poems, 1912—32* (1933); *The Beggar's Ride* (1926) is a play. Among his novels are *The Old Indispensables* (1919), *The People of the Ruins* (1920), *The Richest Man* (1923), *Queer Street* (1932), *The Enchanted Village* (1923), and *Tom Tiddler's Ground* (1934). His critical works are *Essays in Literature* (two series, 1923, 1927), and studies of Bernard Shaw (1924), Edgar Allan Poe (1937), and Rudyard Kipling (1939).

Shapiro, Karl Jay (10 Nov. 1913—   ), poet, was born in Baltimore, of East European descent. Educated at the University of Virginia and Johns Hopkins, he was always deeply interested in poetry, and in 1935 he published his first volume. During the Second World War, while he was serving on the Pacific front, he wrote *Person, Place, and Thing* (1942) and *V-Letter* (1944), which won the Pulitzer Prize. In 1945 appeared his *Essay on Rime*, a blank-verse critique of modern poetry, and in the same year he received the Shelley Memorial Prize. In 1947 he was Consultant in Poetry to the Library of Congress, in 1948 he joined the staff of Johns Hopkins University, and in 1950 he became editor of *Poetry*. *Beyond Criticism*, a prose elaboration of his poetical theories, and *Poems 1940—53* both appeared in 1953.

Sharp, Luke, *see* **Barr, Robert.**

Sharp, Margery (1905—   ), novelist, was educated at Streatham High School and London University, where she took honours in French. Starting as a writer, she contributed to many periodicals, and became noted for her ingenious plots. Her novels include *Rhododendron Pie* (1930), *Fanfare for Tin Trumpets* (1932), *The Nymph and the Nobleman* (1932), *Sophy Cassmajor* (1934), *The Flowering Thorn* (1934), *Four Gardens* (1935), *The Nutmeg Tree* (1937), *Harlequin House* (1939), *The Stone of Chastity* (1940), *Three Companion Pieces* (1941), *Cluny Brown* (1944), *Britannia Mews* (1946), *The Gipsy in the Parlour* (1953), *The Tigress on the Hearth* (1955), *The Eye of Love* (1957), and *The Rescuers* (1959). In 1938 she married Major G. L. Castle, R.A.

Sharp, Robert Farquharson (31 Dec. 1864—3 Aug. 1945), critic and translator, was born in London and educated at Haileybury and Oxford. In 1888 he joined the staff of the British Museum, and rose to be Keeper of the Printed Books from 1924 to 1929. His publications include *A Dictionary of English Authors* (1897), *Masters of Music* (1898), *Architects of English Literature* (1900), *A Short History of the English Stage* (1909), and *A Short Biographical Dictionary of Foreign Literature* (1933). He also translated the plays of Ibsen and Björnson.

Sharp, William (12 Sept. 1855—14 Dec. 1905), novelist, was born in Paisley, son of a merchant, and educated at Glasgow Academy and University. After working for a time in a lawyer's office and in a bank, in 1881 he started trying to live by his pen, but had not much success at first. In 1882 he published a book of verse, *The Human Inheritance*, and in 1884 became art critic of the *Glasgow Herald*. In that year also he published *Earth's Voices* and edited the Canterbury Poets. In 1890, while on a visit to Rome, he started a series of romantic works which he published under the pseudonym Fiona Macleod; they were inspired by visions, and reflect the old Celtic paganism. They include *Pharais, a Romance of the Isles* (1893), *The Mountain Lovers* (1895), *The Washer of the Ford* (1896), *The Dominion* (1899), *The Divine Adventure* (1900), *Winged Destiny* (1904), and *The Immortal Hour* (1908). The secret of Fiona's identity was carefully preserved, Sharp even writing a biography of 'her' for *Who's Who*. He also published under his own name the novels *Wives in Exile* (1896) and *Silence Farm* (1899), and edited *Lyra Celtica* (1896), an anthology of Celtic poetry.

Shaw, George Bernard (26 July 1856—2 Nov. 1950), dramatist, was born in Dublin, son of a corn-factor who drank to excess; hence the son's teetotalism and puritanism. His mother, a gifted musician, left her husband, went to London, and worked as a music teacher. Shaw was educated at the Wesleyan School, and in 1871 became cashier in a Dublin land agency, but five years later threw up his job and joined his mother in London. After working for some months for the Edison Telephone Company he tried to make a living by writing, and produced four novels which were serialized in magazines, but they were not a success. The best is *Cashel Byron's Profession* (1886); others are *An Unsocial Socialist, Love Among the Artists*, and *The Irrational Knot*.

In 1885 he made use of the musical knowledge which he had learned from his mother to become music critic first of the *Star* and then of the *World*, writing under the pseudonym Corno di Bassetto; and in 1895 he became dramatic critic of the *Saturday Review*. From 1885 to 1898 he wrote assiduously as critic of art, music, literature, and drama, and made himself respected by his vitriolic pen. The work of these years is collected in his volumes *The Quintessence of Ibsenism* (1891), *The Sanity of Art* (1895), *The Perfect Wagnerite* (1848), and *Dramatic Opinions and Essays* (1907). Meanwhile he had become a Socialist in 1882, joined the Fabian Society in 1884, took part in innumerable debates, where his quick wit and skill in repartee were much in evidence, and wrote many pamphlets. In 1898 he had a breakdown from overwork, and in the same year married Charlotte Payne-Townshend, a Fabian like himself.

In spite of the fact that he was so active in the Socialist movement, his plays are not Socialistic, though they are often concerned with social reform; they are for the most part used as a pulpit for his satirical attacks on convention and humbug. In his first, *Widowers' Houses* (1892) he attacked slum landlords; *The Philanderer* (1893) is an Ibsenite play about the 'new woman'; and *Mrs Warren's Profession* is a study of prostitution. This last, however, was suppressed by order or the Lord Chamberlain, because of its subject. These three plays are grouped together as 'Plays Unpleasant.' A contrasted group, 'Plays Pleasant,' presenting satire in lighter vein, contains *Arms and the Man* (1894), debunking military heroism; *Candida* (1894), an unorthodox version of the 'eternal triangle'; and the farcical *You Never Can Tell* (1895). At the turn of the century came *The Devil's Disciple, Captain Brassbound's Conversion,* and *Pygmalion,* which caused a minor sensation by introducing in its dialogue the expletive 'bloody.' The long play *Man and Superman* (1903) brings in the idea of a Life Force which guides our destinies. Others of this period are *John Bull's Other Island* (1900), a comparison of the Irish and English characters, *The Doctor's Dilemma* (1906), which debunked doctors, and *Fanny's First Play* (1905), a satire on contemporary drama.

When the First World War started, Shaw published *Commonsense about the War* (1914), a drastic criticism of the Government's policy which brought him a torrent of abuse and caused him to be expelled from the Dramatists' Club. What may be termed his second main dramatic period had already started in 1912 with *Androcles and the Lion,* a play about religious persecution. *Heartbreak House* (1917) is a satire on English society, *Back to Methuselah* (1921) brings in once more the idea of the Life Force, and *Saint Joan* (1924), his greatest box-office success, is a sympathetic study of the Maid of Orleans. With it may be grouped his other historical plays, *Caesar and Cleopatra* (1900), *Great Catherine* (1913), and *In Good King Charles's Golden Days* (1939). *The Apple Cart* (1929) and *Geneva* (1938), which deal with international politics, were among the last well known to the general public, but his last play to be performed was *Buoyant Billions,* produced at Zurich in 1948. The long prefaces prefixed to many of his plays are practically tracts driving home the message that the plays are intended to convey; of a similar nature are *The Intelligent Woman's Guide to Socialism and Capitalism* (1928), which sets out his economic creed, and *Adventures of a Black Girl in Search of God* (1932).

In 1925 Shaw was awarded the Nobel Prize for Literature, and in 1934 the medal of the Irish Academy of Letters. When the Labour party first came into power he was offered a peerage and the Order of Merit, but declined both. In 1928 he visited Russia, and in 1931, at the age of 75, he made a world tour, visiting India, Africa, China, and America. Among his greatest friends were the Webbs, Sir Edward Elgar, and Lady Astor. He spent his last years at Ayot St Lawrence in Hertfordshire, for which he wrote a *Rhyming Picture Guide* illustrated with his own photographs (though none depicting his own six-foot person). *Sixteen Self Sketches* (1949) is autobiographical. His death at 94 followed his fracture of a leg while cutting a branch of a tree in his garden. An attempt was made after his death to convert his house into a public memorial, but popular support was lacking.

Shaw, Henry Wheeler (21 April 1818—14 Oct. 1885), humorous writer who used the pseudonym Josh Billings, was born at Lanesboro, Massachusetts. Famous for his practical jokes, he was expelled from Hamilton College for removing the clapper of the college bell. He then worked successively as farmer, steamboat owner, and later auctioneer in Poughkeepsie. He was 45 when he began to write, helped to a publisher by Artemus Ward (q.v.). His books include *Josh Billings, His Sayings* (1865), *Allminax* (1869—70), *Everybody's Friend* (1874), and *Josh Billings' Trump Kards* (1877). His humour depended largely on misspellings, bad grammar, malapropisms, and illogical reasoning.

Shearing, Joseph, *see* **Long, Margaret Gabrielle.**

Sheehan, Patrick Augustine (17 March 1852—5 Oct. 1913), priest and novelist, was born at Mallow, County Cork, and educated at St Colman's, Fermoy, and Maynooth College. Ordained in 1875, he began his pastoral work in England, first at Plymouth and then at Exeter. In 1877 he moved back to his birth-place, and in 1895 to Doneraile in the same county, where he was priest till his death, being made a canon of Cork Cathedral in 1905. He had already started writing for periodicals by 1881, and in 1895 he published his first novel, *Geoffrey Austin*, a story of student life, which had a sequel *The Triumph of Failure* (1899). In 1898 appeared his best-known work, *My New Curate*, a series of sketches of the life of a typical Irish priest. Of his other novels *The Blindness of Dr Gray* (1909) has a religious background, *Glenanaar* (1905) and *The Graves at Kilmorna* (1915) reflect aspects of Irish nationalism, while *Lisheen* (1907) and *Miriam Lucas* (1912) are concerned with social problems. He also published two volumes of essays, *Under the Cedars* and *Parerga*, and a devotional work, *Mariae Corona*.

Sheffield, John, *see* **Buckingham and Normanby, Duke of.**

Sheldon, Charles Monroe (26 Feb. 1857—24 Feb. 1946), clergyman

x

and author, born at Wellsville, New York State, was educated at Phillips Academy, Andover, Massachusetts, and Brown University. In 1886 he was ordained Congregational minister at Waterbury, Vermont, and afterwards was called to Topeka, Kansas. From 1920 to 1925 he was editor of the *Christian Herald*. He is remembered for his religious novel *In His Steps* (1896), which was one of America's greatest best-sellers of all time, and sold about six million copies, in spite of which the author made only a few hundred dollars by it. No such success was achieved by his other books, which include *His Brother's Keeper* (1895), *The Heart of the World* (1905), *Let's Talk It Over* (1929), and *He Is Here* (1931). *Charles M. Sheldon: his Life and Story* (1925) is an autobiography.

Sheldon, Edward Brewster (4 Feb. 1886—1 April 1946), dramatist, born in Chicago, was educated at Harvard, where he was the first President of the Dramatic Club. Settling in New York, he wrote plays, his first, *Salvation Nell* (1908), being followed by *The Nigger* (1909). *Romance* (1913) was one of the most famous hits in the days before the First World War. Others of his plays are *The Princess Zim-Zim* (1911) and *The High Road* (1912). In 1918 he contracted arthritis, which eventually made him a complete invalid, and later he became blind, but continued to work, carry on correspondence, and live a full life. Later plays, in which he collaborated with others, are *Bewitched* (1924), *Lulu Belle* (1926), *Jenny* (1929), and *Dishonored Lady* (1930).

Shelley, Mary Wollstonecraft (30 Aug. 1797—1 Feb. 1851), novelist, born in London, was the only child of William Godwin (q.v.) and Mary Wollstonecraft, his first wife. In 1814 she went to the Continent with P. B. Shelley (q.v.), and married him, on the death of his wife, two years later. When abroad she saw much of Byron, and it was at his villa on the Lake of Geneva that she conceived the idea of her famous novel *Frankenstein, or the Modern Prometheus* (1818), a ghastly but powerful work. None of her other novels, including *The Last Man* (1826) and *Lodore* (1835), had the same success. She contributed biographies of foreign artists and authors to Lardner's *Cabinet Cyclopaedia*, and edited her husband's poems after his death.

Shelley, Percy Bysshe (4 Aug. 1792—8 July 1822), poet and dramatist, was born at Field Place, near Horsham, Sussex, son of Timothy Shelley, a country squire. He went to school first at Sion House, Isleworth, and then at Eton. A beautiful, sensitive, imaginative boy, he was unsuited to the rough-and-tumble of public-school life, and was known to his schoolmates as 'mad Shelley.' While still at Eton he published two lurid romances of the Gothic school, *Zastrozzi* (1808) and *St Irvyne* (1810), as well as a little volume, *Original Poetry by Victor and Cazire* (1810), in which he collaborated with one of his sisters. He went on to University College, Oxford, where he continued his eccentric habits and filled his rooms with chemical apparatus. In 1811 his revolutionary trend found vent in the publication of a pamphlet, *The Necessity of Atheism*. The authorities were scandalized, and Shelley was expelled, along with his friend Thomas Jefferson Hogg, from a college which was later to erect an elaborate monument to his memory.

The two culprits took lodgings in London and, until his irate
father could be induced to make him an allowance, lived on borrow-
ings from his sisters' pocket money. Shelley, meanwhile, was thrown
together with one of their friends, Harriet Westbrook, daughter of a
retired coffee-house keeper. A romance in which she took the
initiative resulted in their elopement and marriage in Edinburgh.
Shelley was then only 19 and she was 16, and for a time they were in
great difficulties for money, till their fathers agreed to allow them
£400 a year. They moved about the country, staying at Keswick,
Lynmouth, and Tremadoc in Wales, and visiting Ireland, where
Shelley's missionary zeal led him to support the cause of Irish
nationalism, but he soon returned to London, where in 1813 Harriet
gave birth to a daughter Ianthe. At this time Shelley published
Queen Mab, a revolutionary poem, and met William Godwin (q.v.),
whose radical philosophy he embraced. He also met Godwin's
daughter Mary, who was far better able to respond to the depths in
his nature than the shallow Harriet. They fell in love and eloped
to the Continent in 1814. It is typical of Shelley's unpractical
affectionate nature that he invited his wife to join them. In 1815
his money difficulties were ended by the death of his grandfather, and
he was able to make adequate provision for her. He also published
at this time his first great poem, *Alastor, or the Spirit of Solitude*.

In 1816, a fateful year for Shelley, Mary gave birth to a son,
William, and in the summer they stayed at Geneva and met Byron,
between whom and Shelley there was always mutual respect and
admiration. At the end of the year Harriet was found drowned in
the Serpentine, and though Shelley was only partly responsible for her
suicide the courts denied him custody of his children by her. He was
now able to marry Mary, and they went to Italy, where he spent the
few remaining years of his life, during which he produced his greatest
poetry. In 1817 appeared the long poem *Laon and Cythna*, afterwards renamed *The Revolt of Islam*. In the following year he made
his translation of Plato's *Symposium*, and wrote *Julian and Maddalo*.
Two dramas, *The Cenci* and the splendid verse play *Prometheus
Unbound*, perhaps his finest work, were completed in 1819.

In 1820 the Shelleys moved to Pisa, where he wrote some of his
best-known lyrics, including the 'Ode to the West Wind,' 'The
Cloud,' and the 'Ode to a Skylark.' Next came *Epipsychidion*, a
product of his passing infatuation for the Countess Emilia Viviani,
and in 1821 he published *The Defence of Poetry* and was inspired by
Keats's death to compose *Adonais*, one of the most beautiful elegies
in English literature. *Hellas*, a play inspired by the Greek struggle
for freedom, appeared in the same year. In 1822 he moved house
again to a villa on the Gulf of Spezia, and in the summer he and his
friend Edward Williams purchased a small yacht which they named
the *Ariel*. Sailing back from Leghorn, where they had been welcom-
ing Leigh Hunt to Italy, their craft was caught in a squall and
foundered, and they were both drowned. The bodies, washed ashore
over a week later, were cremated in the presence of Leigh Hunt and
Byron, and Shelley's ashes were buried in the Protestant cemetery
at Rome near the grave of Keats, with, as epitaph, lines from Ariel's
song 'Full fathom five.'

In his own time Shelley was misunderstood and was denounced as bitterly as Byron, his direct antithesis, for the unpractical idealism of the one poet caused nearly as much tragedy as the unbridled sensuality of the other. Later critics viewed his life in better perspective, and the most commonly quoted word picture is Matthew Arnold's of 'a beautiful and ineffectual angel, beating in the void his luminous wings in vain.' Of his standing as a poet there has never been any real doubt. As a master of lyric in its purest form he is almost unsurpassed, and his ear for rhythm and musical cadence is unerring. The matter of many of his poems has an intangible spiritual quality which led Stopford Brooke to call him the Turner of poetry. He is not, like Keats, a lover of earthly things, but in his quest for beauty moves in a rarefied atmosphere all his own; as Francis Thompson wrote, 'He is gold-dusty with tumbling amidst the stars.' At its finest, his work is the distilled essence of poetry, purified of all grosser elements.

Shenstone, William (13 Nov. 1714—11 Feb. 1763), poet, was the son of Thomas Shenstone, owner of the Leasowes, a small estate at Halesowen, Worcestershire. In 1732 he went to Pembroke College, Oxford, where he was contemporary with Johnson. On his father's death he retired to the Leasowes, where he passed his time, and ran through his means in transforming it into a marvel of landscape gardening, visited by strangers from all parts of the kingdom. The works of Shenstone consist of poems and prose essays. Of the former, two, *The Schoolmistress* (1742), a humorous imitation of Spenser, with many quaint and tender touches, and the *Pastoral Ballad* (1755) in four parts, perhaps the best of its kind in the language, are outstanding. The essays also display good sense and a pointed and graceful style. The last years of Shenstone were clouded by financial embarrassments and perhaps also by disappointed affections. After his death his works were collected and published by Dodsley.

Sheridan, Richard Brinsley (30 Oct. 1751—7 July 1816), dramatist and politician, born in Dublin, the son of an actor, was educated at Harrow. In 1772 he eloped with Miss Linley, a famous singer, went with her to France, fought two duels, and married her in 1773. Sheridan has a reputation of the highest in two distinct walks, those of the dramatist and the Parliamentary orator. By his three great comedies, *The Rivals* (1775), *The School for Scandal* (1777), and *The Critic* (1779), he raised himself to the first place among the writers of the comedy of manners; and by his speeches, specially those in support of the impeachment of Warren Hastings, he has a position among the greatest of Parliamentary orators. Unfortunately he had little turn for business, and too great a love of pleasure and conviviality, which led to lifelong financial straits, completed by the destruction by fire of Drury Lane Theatre, of which he had become proprietor. Elected M.P. for Stafford in 1780, Sheridan supported the Whig party, and held the offices of Under-Secretary for Foreign Affairs, Secretary to the Treasury, and Treasurer of the Navy. He was also confidential adviser to George IV when Prince of Wales, but like everybody else who had to do with him suffered from the ingratitude of 'the first gentleman in Europe.' The accounts long prevalent of the poverty and misery of his last years have been shown to be greatly exaggerated, though he was in reduced circumstances. Like other Anglo-Irish dramatists he shines in the construction of amusing situations, and in a sparkling flow of witty dialogue which never flags. His only later play was *Pizarro* (1799), a patriotic melodrama. Lives of Sheridan were written by T. Moore (1825), and Mrs Oliphant (1883).

Sherlock, Thomas (1678—18 July 1761), prelate, son of William Sherlock (q.v.), was educated at Eton, where Robert Walpole and Henry Pelham were among his friends, and went on to Cambridge, where he became a Fellow and later Master of St Catharine's. Ordained in 1701, he became Master of the Temple in 1704, succeeding his father, and winning a great reputation as a preacher. In 1714 he was Vice-Chancellor of Oxford, then became Bishop successively of Bangor, Salisbury, and finally, in 1748, London. He wrote a number of pamphlets on religious controversies of the day, his most famous book being *A Trial of the Witnesses of the Resurrection of Jesus* (1729).

Sherlock, William (1641?—19 June 1707), clergyman and pamphleteer, born in Southwark and educated at Eton and Cambridge, took orders and became in 1684 Master of the Temple and in 1691 Dean of St Paul's. He was a voluminous writer, his most popular work being his *Discourse Concerning Death* (1689), while his principal controversial publication was a *Vindication of the Doctrine of the Trinity* (1690).

Sherman, Stuart Pratt (1 Oct. 1881—21 Aug. 1926), critic, was born at Anita, Iowa, son of a farmer, and educated at Troy Conference Academy and Williams College, Massachusetts, where he edited the college magazine. Later he wrote reviews for the *Nation*, and in 1911 was appointed Professor of English at the University of Illinois. In 1924 he became a book reviewer on the staff of the New York *Herald Tribune*, and two years later died of a heart attack while swimming. His first book was a study of Matthew Arnold, published in 1917. Others are *On Contemporary Literature* (1917), *Americans* (1922), *The Genius of America* (1924), *Points of View* (1924), *Men of Letters of the British Isles* (1924), *Critical Woodcuts* (1926), *The Main Stream* (1927), and *The Emotional Discovery of America* (1932). He also edited volumes I and II of the *Cambridge History of American Literature*.

Sherriff, Robert Cedric (6 June 1896—   ), playwright and novelist, was born at Kingston-upon-Thames, son of an insurance agent, and went into the same business after he left Kingston Grammar School. On the outbreak of the First World War he joined the East Surrey Regiment, was commissioned at 18, and was wounded at Ypres. Afterwards he worked at insurance for another 10 years, but in 1929 his play *Journey's End*, which had grown out of his letters home from the front, was produced and immediately made him famous, being staged in America and in five European countries. At the age of 35 he had a two-year course at Oxford, then went to Hollywood. His later plays, none of which approached his first success, were *Badger's Green* (1930), *Windfall* (1933), *Dark Evening*

(1949), *Home at Seven* (1950), and *The White Carnation* (1953). His
novels include *The Fortnight in September* (1931), *Greengates* (1936),
The Hopkins Manuscript (1939), *Chedworth* (1944), *Another Year*
(1946), and *King John's Treasure* (1954).

Sherrington, Sir Charles Scott, O.M. (27 Nov. 1861—4 March 1952),
physiologist, born in London and educated at Cambridge, became
Professor of Physiology first at Liverpool and in 1913 at Oxford.
From 1914 to 1917 he held the Fullerian Chair of the same subject
at the Royal Institution, and from 1936 to 1938 delivered the Gifford
Lectures at Edinburgh.   In 1922 he was made Knight Grand Cross
of the Order of the British Empire, in 1924 awarded the Order of
Merit, and in 1932 received the Nobel Prize.   From 1920 to 1925 he
was President of the Royal Society, and he held honorary degrees
of more than 20 universities.   A specialist on the brain and nervous
system, he wrote *The Integrative Action of the Nervous System* (1906),
Mammalian Physiology (1916), *Man on his Nature* (1941), and *Goethe
on Nature* (1946).

Sherwood, Mary Martha (6 May 1775—22 Sept. 1851), writer of
children's books, was born at Stanford, Worcestershire, daughter of
George Butt, clergyman and poet.   Her first book, *The Traditions*
(1794), was followed by *Margarita* and *Susan Gray*, both published
in 1802; the latter was written to instil religious principles in the
poor and was very popular.   In 1803 she married her cousin, Captain
H. Sherwood, and they lived in India from 1805 to 1816.   There she
wrote *The Infant's Progress* (1814) and *Little Henry and his Bearer*
(1815), and began *The History of the Fairchild Family* (three parts,
1818, 1842, 1847), which became a children's classic and is powerfully
written, though depressingly Calvinistic in tone.   Her autobiography
was edited by her daughter.

Sherwood, Robert Emmet (4 April 1896—14 Nov. 1955), playwright, was born at New Rochelle, New York State, son of a broker;
his mother was a well-known painter.   He was educated at Milton
Academy, Massachusetts, and Harvard, where he wrote his first
play, *Barnum Was Right*.   During the First World War he enlisted
in the Canadian Black Watch, making a striking figure with his six
feet seven inches, and was wounded at Amiens.   From 1924 to 1928
he was editor of *Life*.   His plays, which often develop serious ideas
through light situations, include *Road to Rome* (1927), *The Queen's
Husband* (1928), *This is New York* (1929), *Reunion in Vienna* (1931),
and *The Petrified Forest* (1935); *Idiot's Delight* (1936), *Abe Lincoln
in Illinois* (1938), and *There Shall be No Night* (1940) were all awarded
Pulitzer Prizes.   During the Second World War he was employed
at the War Information Office and came into contact with many of
the leading American figures; he used his experience in *Roosevelt
and Hopkins: An Intimate History* (1948).

Shirley, *see* **Skelton, Sir John.**

Shirley, Henry (died Nov. 1627), playwright, was born at Wiston
in Sussex; he was not related to the playwright James Shirley.
Practically nothing is known of him except the manner of his death.

He was stabbed by Sir Edward Bishop, M.P., when he demanded an annuity of £40 which was due to him; Bishop, who was said to have been drunk at the time, was afterwards pardoned. Only one of Shirley's plays has survived, *The Martyred Soldier* (1638), a mediocre work.

Shirley, James (born 18 Sept. 1596, buried 29 Oct. 1666), dramatist and poet, was born in London and educated at Merchant Taylors', Oxford, and Cambridge. He was ordained in the English Church, but was converted to Roman Catholicism and became a schoolmaster. From 1625 he lived in London, and after Massinger's death was chief playwright for the King's Men. He served as a Royalist in the Civil War, and died of shock and exposure in the Great Fire of London. He wrote about 40 plays, of which *The Maid's Revenge* (1626), *The Traitor* (1631), and *The Cardinal* (1641) are clever but artificial tragedies, while *The Young Admiral* (1633) and *The Royal Master* (1635) are tragi-comedies. His great achievement was in his comedies of manners, *The Witty Fair One* (1628), *Changes, or Love in a Maze* (1632), *Hyde Park* (1632), and *The Lady of Pleasure* (1635), which foreshadow the Restoration drama. His *Poems* were published in 1646, and his *Contention of Ajax and Ulysses* (1659), a dramatic entertainment, contains the famous dirge 'The glories of our blood and state.'

Shorter, Clement King (19 July 1857—19 Nov. 1926), journalist and critic, was born in London and educated at Birkbeck Institution. From 1877 to 1890 he worked in Somerset House. As a journalist he had an important influence on the English pictorial press. In 1890 he became editor of the *Illustrated London News*, in 1893 he founded and edited the *Sketch*, in 1900 he did the same for the *Sphere*, and in 1903 for the *Tatler*. A keen book collector, he had a fine library in his house at Great Missenden, Buckinghamshire. His critical works include *The Brontës and their Circle* (1896), *Immortal Memories* (1907), *The Brontës: Life and Letters* (1908), *George Borrow and his Circle* (1913), and two books on Napoleon. *C.K.S.* (1926) is an unfinished autobiography. In 1896 he married Dora Sigerson (q.v.), the Irish poetess.

Shorthouse, Joseph Henry (9 Sept. 1834—4 March 1903), novelist, born in Birmingham and educated at Tottenham College, began work in his father's chemical factory. Originally a Quaker, he joined the Church of England. His first, and by far his best book, *John Inglesant*, appeared in 1881, and at once made him famous. Though deficient in its structure as a story, it caught the High Church feeling of the day, and fascinated by the charm of its style and the 'dim religious light' by which it is suffused, as well as by the striking scenes occasionally depicted. His other novels, *The Little Schoolmaster Mark* (1883), *Sir Percival* (1886), *The Countess Eve* (1888), and *A Teacher of the Violin* (1888), though with some of the same characteristics, had no success comparable to his first. Shorthouse also wrote an essay, *The Platonism of Wordsworth* (1882).

Shute, Nevil, *see* **Norway.**

Shy, Timothy, *see* **Lewis, D. B. Wyndham.**

Sibbes *or* **Sibbs** *or* **Sibs, Richard** (1577—5 July 1635), clergyman, was born at Tostock, Suffolk, son of a wheelwright, and educated at Bury St Edmund's Grammar School and Cambridge. In 1608 he took orders and in 1626 was appointed Master of St Catharine's Hall, Cambridge, becoming a D.D. the following year. His devotional works include *The Saint's Cordials* (1629), *The Bruised Reed and Smoking Flax* (1630), and *The Church's Visitation* (1634). He also wrote some verse.

Sidgwick, Ethel (20 Dec. 1877—   ), novelist, was born at Rugby, where her father was a schoolmaster, and was a niece of Henry Sidgwick (q.v.). Educated at Oxford High School, she lived in that city all her life. Her novels include *Promise* (1910), *Le Gentleman* (1911), *Herself* (1912), *Succession* (1913), *A Lady of Leisure* (1914), *Duke Jones* (1914), *The Accolade* (1915), *Hatchways* (1916), *Jamesie* (1917), *Madam* (1921), *Restoration* (1923), *Laura* (1924), *When I Grow Rich* (1927), *The Bells of Shoreditch* (1928), and *Dorothy's Wedding* (1931). She also wrote a number of plays for children, and in 1938 a memoir of her aunt, Mrs Henry Sidgwick, Principal of Newnham.

Sidgwick, Henry (31 May 1838—28 Aug. 1900), philosopher, was born at Skipton, Yorkshire, where his father was a headmaster, and educated at Rugby and Trinity College, Cambridge, of which he became a Fellow. In 1876 he married a sister of A. J. Balfour (q.v.); his own sister was married to Archbishop Benson. From 1883 he was Professor of Moral Philosophy at Cambridge. The leading ethical philosopher of his day, he tried to combine intuitionism with utilitarianism, his most important work being *Methods of Ethics* (1874). Others are *The Principle of Political Economy* (1883), *Outlines of the History of Ethics* (1886), *The Elements of Politics* (1891), *Philosophy, Its Scope and Relations* (1902), *European Polity* (1904), and *Miscellaneous Essays* (1905).

Sidney *or* **Sydney, Algernon** (1622—7 Dec. 1683), political writer, son of the 2nd Earl of Leicester, and grand-nephew of Sir Philip Sidney, in his youth travelled on the Continent, served against the Irish Rebels, and on the outbreak of the Civil War, joined the side of the Parliament. He was one of the judges on the trial of Charles I, and though he did not attend, he thoroughly approved of the sentence. After the Restoration he lived on the Continent, but receiving a pardon, returned in 1677 to England. He, however, retained the republican principles which he had all his life advocated, fell under the suspicion of the Court, and was in 1683, on the discovery of the Rye House Plot, condemned to death on entirely insufficient evidence, and beheaded on Tower Hill. Sidney was deeply versed in political theory, and wrote *Discourses concerning Government*, published in 1698.

Sidney, Sir Philip (30 Nov. 1554—17 Oct. 1586), courtier, soldier, poet, and critic, son of Sir Henry Sidney, Lord-Deputy of Ireland and President of Wales, was born at the family seat of Penshurst, and educated at Shrewsbury School and Oxford. He was at the French Court on the fateful 24 August, 1572—the massacre of St Bartholomew—but left Paris soon thereafter and went to Germany and Italy. In 1576 he was with his father in Ireland, and the next year went on missions to the Elector Palatine and the Emperor Rudolf II. When his father's Irish policy was called in question, he wrote an able defence of it. He became the friend of Spenser, who dedicated to him his *Shepheard's Calendar*. In 1580 he lost the favour of the Queen by remonstrating against her proposed marriage with the Duke of Anjou. His own marriage with a daughter of Sir Francis Walsingham took place in 1583, a year after he had been knighted. In 1585 he was engaged in the war in the Low Countries, and met his death at Zutphen from a wound in the thigh. His death was commemorated by Spenser in his *Astrophel*.

Sidney has always been considered as the type of English chivalry; and his extraordinary contemporary reputation rested on his personal qualities of nobility and generosity. His writings consist of his famous pastoral romance *Arcadia*, his sonnets *Astrophel and Stella* (1591), and his *Apologie for Poetrie* (1595), afterwards called *Defence of Poesie*. The *Arcadia* was originally written for the amusement of his sister, afterwards Countess of Pembroke (q.v.), the ' Sidney's sister, Pembroke's mother,' of W. Browne's poem. Though its interest now is chiefly historical, it enjoyed an extraordinary popularity for a century after its appearance, and had a marked influence on the immediately succeeding literature. It was written in 1580—1 but not published until 1590, and is a medley of poetical prose, full of conceits, with occasional verse interspersed. His *Defence of Poesie*, written in reply to Gosson (q.v.) is in simple and vigorous English. Sidney also made a translation of the Psalms.

Sigerson, Dora (16 Aug. 1866—6 Jan. 1918), poetess, was born in Dublin, her father being a surgeon and a Gaelic scholar, her mother a writer. Like her greatest friends, Katherine Tynan and Louise Imogen Guiney (qq.v.) she was a Roman Catholic. In 1896 she married Clement Shorter (q.v.) and settled in London, but at the Easter Rebellion of 1916 she worked on behalf of the accused men, and carved a memorial sculpture group of the Irish patriots in Dublin cemetery. Her gift for narrative verse is shown in her publications *The Fairy Changeling* (1897), *Ballads and Poems* (1898), *The Father Confessor* (1900), *The Woman Who Went to Hell* (1902), *As the Sparks Fly Upward* (1904), *The Country House Party* (1905), *Through Wintry Terrors* (1907), *The Troubadours* (1910), *Madge Linsey* (1913), *Love of Ireland* (1916), *The Sad Years* (1918), *A Legend of Glandalough* (1919), and *Sixteen Dead Men and Other Ballads of Easter Week* (1919).

Sigourney, Lydia Howard Huntley (1 Sept. 1791—10 June 1865), poetess, born at Norwich, Connecticut, daughter of Ezekiel Huntley, a gardener, was a schoolmistress for a time. In 1819 she married Charles Sigourney, a hardware merchant. The popularity of her sentimental and melancholy verses caused her to be styled 'the American Hemans.' She published over 60 volumes, including *Pocahontas* (1841), *Poems, Religious and Elegiac* (1841), *Letters to Young Ladies* (1833), and the autobiographical *Letters of Life* (1866).

x*

Simms, William Gilmore (17 April 1806—11 June 1870), novelist, was born at Charleston, South Carolina, son of an Irishman. Apprenticed at first to a druggist, he turned to the study of law, then took to journalism and in New York formed a friendship with Bryant (q.v.). He wrote many frontier romances in the manner of Fenimore Cooper, including *Martin Faber* (1833), *Guy Rivers* (1834), *The Yemassee* (1835), and *Richard Hurdis* (1838). *The Partisan* (1835) and *Eutaw* (1856) are realistic novels of the War of Independence. He also published *A History of South Carolina* (1840) and *South Carolina and the Revolution* (1854). The Civil War left him ruined in health and purse.

Simpson, Helen de Guerry (1 Dec. 1897—14 Oct. 1940), novelist, was born in Sydney, daughter of a solicitor, and educated at Rose Bay Convent and Abbotsleigh, Waahroonga. During the First World War she served in England with the W.R.N.S., decoding messages for the Admiralty. Later she studied music at Oxford, but turned to writing, her book of verse *Philosophies in Little* (1921) being followed by a play, *A Man of the Time* (1923) and a novel, *Acquittal* (1925). In 1927 she married Denis John Browne, a nephew of T. A. Browne (q.v.), and in the following year published *Mumbudget*, a book of fairy stories. Her first great success was *Boomerang* (1932), which was awarded the Tait Black Memorial Prize. Later novels are *The Woman on the Beast* (1933), *Saraband for Dead Lovers* (1935), *Under Capricorn* (1937), and *Maid No More* (1940). She also wrote the historical biographies, *The Spanish Marriage* (1933) and *Henry VIII* (1934); *A Woman Among Wild Men* (1938) is an account of Mary Kingsley. She was killed in a London air raid.

Sims, George Robert (2 Sept. 1847—4 Sept. 1922), journalist and author, born in London, was educated at Hanwell College and Bonn. In 1874 he joined the staff of *Fun*, and from 1877 he contributed a column to the *Referee* under the pseudonym Dagonet; verses from this were collected as *Dagonet Ballads* (1882). In 1883 he published *How the Poor Live*, and subsequently he wrote many books about London and stories of London life, including *Living London* (1901), *Biographs of Babylon* (1902), *The Mysteries of Modern London* (1905), *London by Night* (1906), and *Behind the Veil* (1913). *Dorcas Dene, Detective* (1897) is a series of crime stories, and *Memoirs of a Mother-in-Law* (1913) a collection of humorous domestic sketches. He also wrote a number of plays, including *Lights o' London* (1881) and *Two Little Vagabonds* (1896). *My Life* (1916) contains personal reminiscences. In 1905 he was made a Knight of St Olaf, a Norwegian distinction.

Sinclair, May (1870—14 Nov. 1946), novelist, was born at Rock Ferry, Cheshire, and educated at the Ladies' College, Cheltenham. Her *Essays in Verse* were published in 1892, her first short story in 1895, and with the publication of *Audrey Craven* in the following year she was recognized as a leading novelist and a pioneer in the use of the 'stream-of-consciousness' technique; it was followed by *The Divine Fire* (1904) and *The Three Sisters* (1914). During the First World War she served with the Red Cross in Belgium. Later novels are *Mary Olivier* (1919), *Mr Waddington of Wyck* (1921), *Anne Severn and the Fieldings* (1922), *The History of Anthony Waring* (1927), *The Allinghams* (1927), and *Fame* (1929). *The Dark Night* (1924) is a novel in verse, and *Uncanny Stories* (1923), and *The Intercessor* (1931) are volumes of short stories. She also wrote a critical study, *The Three Brontës* (1912) and two books of philosophical essays, *A Defence of Idealism* (1917) and *The New Idealism* (1922).

Sinclair, Upton Beall (20 Sept. 1878—   ), novelist, was born in Baltimore, son of a liquor salesman whose excesses gave the writer a lifelong aversion to drinking. He worked his way through the College of the City of New York and Columbia by writing stories for cheap magazines. In 1900 he married and set out to make a living by his pen, but his first five novels brought in less than a thousand dollars. In 1906 *The Jungle*, a story of the Chicago stockyards, was a best-seller, but he was now a Socialist and lost most of the money when Helicon Hall, the communistic colony he had founded at Englewood, New Jersey, was burned down. His novels, though powerful, are rather like Socialistic tracts. *The Metropolis* (1908) attacks capitalism; *The Profits of Religion* (1918) criticizes organized religion; *Jimmie Higgins* (1919) is pacifist; *The Brass Check* (1919) denounces the Press; *The Goose Step* (1923) and *The Goslings* (1924) criticize the educational system; and *Oil* (1927) denounces business monopolies. Sinclair also wrote a fictional record of world history from 1913 onwards in the Lanny Budd series (so named after its hero), which comprises *World's End* (1940), *Between Two Worlds* (1941), *Dragon's Teeth* (1942), which won the Pulitzer Prize, *Wide is the Gate* (1943), *Presidential Agent* (1944), *Dragon Harvest* (1945), *A World to Win* (1946), *Presidential Mission* (1947), *O Shepherd, Speak* (1949), and *The Return of Lanny Budd* (1953). His books have been translated into nearly 50 languages.

Sinjohn, John, *see* **Galsworthy.**

Sitwell, Dame Edith (7 Sept. 1887—   ), poetess and critic, was born at Scarborough, daughter of Sir George Sitwell, Bart., and sister of Osbert and Sacheverell Sitwell (qq.v.); of striking appearance, she was nearly six feet tall, and habitually dressed in medieval fashions. In 1916, along with her brothers, she started the anthology *Wheels*, which represented a violent revolt against contemporary poetical fashions. Her volumes of verse are *The Mother* (1915), *Clowns' Houses* (1918), *The Wooden Pegasus* (1920), *Bucolic Comedies* (1923), *Rustic Elegies* (1927), *Gold Coast Customs* (1929), *Poems New and Old* (1940), *Green Song* (1944), *Façade* (1950), and *Gardeners and Astronomers* (1953). Her books of criticism include *Poetry and Criticism* (1925), *Alexander Pope* (1930), *The English Eccentrics* (1932), *Aspects of Modern Poetry* (1934), and *A Poet's Notebook* (1943). In 1933 she was awarded the medal of the Royal Society of London, and in 1954 was made a Dame Grand Cross of the Order of the British Empire; the same year she became a Roman Catholic. She held honorary doctorates of Oxford, Durham, and Leeds.

Sitwell, Sir Osbert, Bart. (6 Dec. 1892—   ), poet and novelist, brother of Edith and Sacheverell Sitwell (qq.v.), was born in London and educated at Eton. From 1912 to 1919 he served with the Grenadier Guards. During this period he contributed poems to the anthology *Wheels* edited by his sister. Volumes of his verse include *Argonaut and Juggernaut* (1919), *The Winstonburg Line* (1919), *Out of the Flame* (1923), *Winter the Huntsman* (1924), *England Reclaimed* (1927), and *Collected Satires and Poems* (1931). Novels are *Before the Bombardment* (1926), *The Man Who Lost Himself* (1929), and *Miracle on Sinai* (1933), while *Triple Fugue* (1924), *Open the Door* (1941), and *Death of a God* (1949) are collections of short stories. *Who Killed Cock Robin?* (1921) and *Dickens* (1932) are books of criticism, and *Sing High, Sing Low* (1944) is a collection of essays. He also wrote a series of family memoirs, *Left Hand, Right Hand!* (1944), *The Scarlet Tree* (1945), *Great Morning* (1947), *Laughter in the Next Room* (1948), and *Noble Essences* (1950). In 1956 he was made a C.B.E., and in 1958 a Companion of Honour.

Sitwell, Sacheverell (15 Nov. 1897—   ), critic and poet, born at Scarborough, brother of Edith and Osbert Sitwell (qq.v.), was educated at Eton and Oxford. During the First World War he served with the Grenadier Guards. A sensitive critic of art and music, he wrote *Southern Baroque Art* (1924), *German Baroque Art* (1927), *The Gothick North* (1929), *Spanish Baroque Art* (1931), and *Canons of Giant Art* (1933), as well as studies of Mozart (1932) and Liszt (1934). His volumes of poetry include *The People's Palace* (1918), *The Hundred and One Harlequins* (1922), and *The Cyder Feast* (1927). *Truffle Hunt* (1953) is a collection of essays, and *All Summer in a Day* (1926) is described as an autobiographical fantasia. From 1948 to 1949 he was Sheriff of Northamptonshire.

Skeat, Walter William (21 Nov. 1835—6 Oct. 1912), scholar, was born in London, son of an architect, and educated at King's College School, Highgate School, and Christ's College, Cambridge, where Walter Besant and Calverley (qq.v.) were among his friends. He took orders in 1860, was elected a Fellow of his college, and became curate first of East Dereham, Norfolk, and then of Godalming. Abandoning this owing to illness, in 1864 he became a mathematical lecturer at Cambridge, and then studied Old English to such purpose that in 1878 he was appointed Professor of Anglo-Saxon. His works include editions of *Piers Plowman* (1866—86), the *Anglo-Saxon Gospels* (1871—87), Aelfric's *Lives of the Saints* (1881—1900), and Chaucer's Works (1894—7), as well as many other volumes for the Early English Text Society. He also made an authoritative *Etymological Dictionary* (1879—82), and in 1873 founded the English Dialect Society.

Skelton, John (1460—21 June 1529), poet, born in Norfolk, was educated at Oxford and Cambridge, of both of which he was created Poet Laureate, and perhaps held the same office under the King. He was appointed tutor to Henry VIII, and notwithstanding his sharp tongue, enjoyed some favour at Court. In 1498 he took holy orders, and became Rector of Diss in his native county. Until then he seems to have produced some translations only, but about this time he appears to have struck upon the vein which he was to work with such vigour and popularity. He turned his attention to abuses in Church and State, which he lashed with caustic satire, conveyed in short doggerel rhyming lines peculiar to himself, in which jokes, slang, invective, and Latin quotations rush out pell-mell. His best works in this line are *Why come ye not to Court?* and *Colin Clout*, both directed against the clergy, and the former against Wolsey in particular. Piqued at his inconstancy, for Skelton had previously courted him, the Cardinal would have imprisoned him, had he not taken sanctuary in Westminster, where he remained until his death. Other works of his are *The Tunning* (brewing) *of Elynor Rummynge,* a coarsely humorous picture of low life, and the tender and fanciful *Death of Philip Sparrow*, the lament of a young lady over her pet bird killed by a cat. He also wrote an interlude, *Magnyfycence* (1533).

Skelton, Sir John (1831—19 July 1897), author who used the pseudonym Shirley, was born in Edinburgh and educated at the University there. Called to the Scottish Bar in 1854, he was Secretary and ultimately Chairman of the Local Government Board for Scotland. He wrote *Maitland of Lethington and the Scotland of Mary Stuart* (1887), *The Crookit Meg* (1880), *Essays of Shirley* (1882), and *The Table Talk of Shirley* (1895). He received the degree of LL.D. from Edinburgh in 1878, and was made K.C.B. in 1897.

Skene, Felicia Mary Francis (23 May 1821—6 Oct. 1899), novelist, sister of William Forbes Skene (q.v.) was born at Aix in Provence, brought up in Edinburgh, and as a child sat on Walter Scott's knee while he told her fairy stories. For a time she lived in Athens, later in Oxford. During the cholera epidemic of 1854 she organized a band of nurses, some of whom went to the Crimea during the war there, as a result of which she corresponded with Florence Nightingale. Her first book, *The Isles of Greece* (1843), a collection of poems, was followed by *The Divine Master* (1852), a devotional work, and a group of novels, *Hidden Depths*, *A Strange Inheritance*, and *The Lesters* (1886).

Skene, William Forbes (7 June 1809—29 Aug. 1892), historian, was born at Inverie, Knoydart. His father was a close friend of Sir Walter Scott. Educated at St Andrews and in Germany, he became a Writer to the Signet in Edinburgh, and Clerk of the Bills in the Court of Session. He wrote historical works of considerable authority, including *The Highlanders of Scotland* (1837), and his most important work, *Celtic Scotland* (1876—80), and edited *The Four Ancient Books of Wales* (1868), and other Celtic writings.

Skinner, Cornelia Otis (30 May 1901—   ), humorist, was born in Chicago, daughter of a famous actor-manager, and educated at Bryn Mawr and the Sorbonne. She studied acting in Paris and was successful on the stage, especially in monodramas. In 1928 she married Alden S. Blodget. She wrote a number of popular books of light essays, including *Tiny Garments* (1932), *Excuse It, Please!* (1936), *Dithers and Jitters* (1938), *Soap Behind the Ears* (1941), *Popcorn* (1943), *Nuts in May* (1950), and *Bottoms Up* (1955). *Our Hearts Were Young and Gay* (1944) and *Happy Family* (1950) are autobiographical. She was given honorary degrees by the universities of Pennsylvania and New York.

Skinner, John (30 Oct. 1721—16 June 1807), historian and song-writer, son of a schoolmaster at Birse, Aberdeenshire, was educated at Marischal College. Brought up as a Presbyterian, he became an Episcopalian and ministered to a congregation at Longside, near Peterhead, for 65 years. He wrote *The Ecclesiastical History of Scotland* (1788) from the Episcopalian point of view, and several songs, of which 'The Reel of Tullochgorum' is the best known, and he also rendered some of the Psalms into Latin. He kept up a rhyming correspondence with Burns.

Skipsey, Joseph (17 March 1832—3 Sept. 1903), collier and poet, was born at Tynemouth, son of a miner; he never went to school, but worked in the pits from the age of 7. In 1859 he published a volume, *Poems*, and in 1863 he was given an assistant librarian's post in Newcastle, but left that and worked in the mines again from 1864 to 1882, after which he and his wife were caretakers of a Newcastle school. His poems, based on his working life, were commended by Rossetti; volumes include *Collier Lad* (1864), *Carols from the Coal-fields* (1886), and *Songs and Lyrics* (1892). From 1889 to 1891 he was curator of Shakespeare's birth-place at Stratford.

Slingsby, Jonathan Freke, *see* **Waller, John Francis.**

Slingsby, Philip, *see* **Willis, Nathaniel.**

Smart, Christopher (11 April 1722—21 May 1771), poet, son of the steward to Lord Vane, was born at Shipbourne, Kent, and by the generosity of the Duchess of Cleveland sent to Cambridge, where he became a Fellow of Pembroke in 1745. Leaving the University he came to London and maintained himself by conducting and writing for periodicals. His *Poems on Several Occasions*, which contained 'The Hop Garden,' was issued in 1752, and *The Hilliad* in 1753 satirizing John Hill, a notoriety of the day who had attacked him. His mind ultimately gave way, and it was in confinement that he produced by far his most remarkable work, the *Song to David* (1763), a most original and powerful poem. Unfortunate to the last, he died in the King's Bench prison, to which he had been committed for debt. His *Rejoice in the Lamb* was published in 1939.

Smectymnuus was the pseudonym used by five Presbyterian ministers in a pamphlet which they published in 1641 against episcopacy. It was made up of their initials, their names being Stephen Marshal, Edmund Calamy, Thomas Young, Matthew Newcomen, and William Spurstow. The pamphlet was answered by Bishop Joseph Hall (q.v.) and defended by Milton.

Smedley, Francis Edward (4 Oct. 1818—1 May 1864), novelist generally known as Frank Smedley, was born at Great Marlow, Buckinghamshire, son of the High Sheriff of Westminster. A life-long cripple, he was educated by tutors. Of his books, which have a rich vein of comedy and show a love of sport, the best-known is *Frank Fairlegh, or Scenes from the Life of a Private Pupil* (1850). Others are *Lewis Arundel, or The Railroad of Life* (1852), and *Harry Coverdale's Courtship* (1855). He also collaborated with Edmund Yates in a book of nonsense verses, *Mirth and Metre* (1855); his own poems were published as *Gathered Leaves* in 1865.

Smiles, Samuel (23 Dec. 1812—16 April 1904), biographer and social reformer, born at Haddington and educated at the Grammar School there, studied medicine at Edinburgh, and settled in practice in his native town. Subsequently he turned to journalism, and edited a paper in Leeds. Afterwards he was secretary to various railways, and his first publication was *The Life of George Stephenson* (1857). *Self-Help*, his most popular work, followed in 1859; it had an immense circulation, and was translated into 17 languages. It was followed up by *Character* (1871), *Thrift* (1875), and *Duty* (1880). *The Lives of the Engineers* and *Industrial Biography* appeared in 1863, *The Huguenots, their Settlements, Churches, and Industries in England and Ireland* in 1867, and *The Huguenots in France* a little later. His *Autobiography* appeared in 1905. He received the degree of LL.D. from Edinburgh in 1878.

Smith, Adam (5 June 1723—17 July 1790), political economist, was born at Kirkcaldy, Fife, shortly after the death of his father, who was Controller of Customs there. The first and only adventure in his tranquil life was his being kidnapped by gipsies. After being at the Grammar School of Kirkcaldy, he went to the University of Glasgow, whence he proceeded to Oxford. In 1751 he was appointed to the Chair of Logic at Glasgow, which he next year exchanged for that of Moral Philosophy, and in 1759 he published his *Theory of the Moral Sentiments*. He received in 1762 the degree of LL.D. from his University, and two years later resigned his chair and became travelling tutor to the young Duke of Buccleuch, accompanying him to the Continent. He remained for nearly a year in Paris, and made the acquaintance of the brilliant circle of *savants* in that city. Returning to Kirkcaldy in 1766 he lived there with his mother for nearly 10 years in retirement and close study, the results of which were given to the world in 1776 in his epoch-making work, *An Inquiry into the Nature and Causes of the Wealth of Nations* (1776). This book may be said to have founded the science of political economy, and to have created a new department of literature; and very few works have, to the same extent, influenced the practical history of the world. In 1778 Smith was made a Commissioner of Customs, and settled in Edinburgh; and in 1787 he was elected Lord Rector of the University of Glasgow. In addition to the works above mentioned, he wrote various essays on philosophical subjects, and an account of the last days of David Hume. The style of his works was plain and lucid, and he had a remarkable faculty of apt illustration.

Smith, Albert Richard (24 May 1816—23 May 1860), humorist and novelist, was born at Chertsey, Surrey, son of a doctor, educated at Merchant Taylors', and studied medicine at Middlesex Hospital. One of the original contributors to *Punch*, he also wrote *The Adventures of Mr Ledbury* (1844), *The Adventures of Jack Holyday* (1844), and *The Scattergood Family* (1845). In addition he composed a number of public entertainments, including 'The Overland Mail,' 'The Ascent of Mont Blanc,' and 'China,' which he produced at the Egyptian Hall in London.

Smith, Alexander (31 Dec. 1830—5 Jan. 1867), poet and essayist, born at Kilmarnock, son of a pattern-designer, at first followed the same occupation in Glasgow, but having become known as a poet of promise was, in 1854, appointed Secretary of Edinburgh University. After contributing to the *Glasgow Citizen* he published *A Life Drama* (1853), which was widely admired. Thereafter appeared *War Sonnets* (in conjunction with S. Dobell (q.v.), *City Poems* (1857), and *Edwin of Deira* (1861). In prose he wrote a volume of essays entitled *Dreamthorp* (1863). *A Summer in Skye* (1865), and two novels, *Alfred Hagart's Household* and *Miss Dona M'Quarrie*. His poems were written in a rich and glowing style, but by some critics were held to show fancy rather than imagination. He belonged to what was called the 'spasmodic' school of poetry.

Smith, Charlotte (4 May 1749—28 Oct. 1806), poetess and novelist, was born in London, daughter of Nicholas Turner. In 1765 she married Benjamin Smith, a West India merchant of such improvident habits that they were reduced to poverty and in 1782 were imprisoned for debt. In these difficulties she managed to support herself and her family by her writings, which include *Elegiac Sonnets* (1784), and several novels, of which the best are *Emmeline* (1788) and *The Old Manor House* (1793).

Smith, Ernest Bramah (1868—23 June 1942), novelist who wrote under the name Ernest Bramah, spent part of his life in China, but lived latterly in Somerset. Farming was his earliest venture, but he could not make it pay, and his first book was *English Farming: Why I Turned It In* (1894). He is known mainly for his two creations, Kai Lung the Chinese philosopher, and Max Carrados the detective. Adapting Chinese conventions to the English language, he threw round his tales an atmosphere of profound oriental wisdom, which appears in *The Wallet of Kai Lung* (1900), *Kai Lung's Golden Hours* (1922), *Kai Lung Unrolls his Mat* (1928), *The Moon of Much Gladness* (1932), and *Kai Lung Beneath the Mulberry Tree* (1940). *Max Carrados* (1914) introduces a detective who has the unusual handicap of being blind, so that his discoveries seem preternaturally astute. He appears also in *The Eyes of Max Carrados* (1923) and *Max Carrados Mysteries* (1927).

Smith, Goldwin (13 Aug. 1823—7 June 1910), historian, was born at Reading, son of a doctor, and educated at Eton and Oxford, where he was a demy of Magdalen at the same time as Conington, who dedicated his great edition of Virgil to him. Entered at Lincoln's Inn, Smith was called to the Bar in 1850. From 1858 to 1866 he was Regius Professor of Modern History at Oxford, and was active in the cause of university reform. During the American Civil War he visited the United States, and in 1868 became Professor of English and Constitutional History at Cornell. In 1871 he settled in Toronto and edited various periodicals. His books include *Lectures on the Study of History* (1883), *Canada and the Canadian Question* (1893), and *Oxford and her Colleges* (1906).

Smith, Horace (1779—12 July 1849), poet and novelist, a brother of James Smith (q.v.), was baptized Horatio. Educated at a school at Chigwell, he began work as a clerk in a counting house, afterwards became a stockbroker, and retired in 1820. He wrote a poem praising the plays of Richard Cumberland (q.v.), who then introduced him to other writers, and he became the friend of Shelley, Keats, and Leigh Hunt. After publishing the novels *The Runaway* (1800), *Trevanion* (1802), and *Horatio* (1807), he collaborated in 1812 with his brother in a volume entitled *Rejected Addresses*, which contained parodies of contemporary poets, Horace doing those of Walter Scott and Moore. It was a phenomenal success, and next year they worked together again in *Horace in London*, which is, however, far inferior. Horace also wrote *Amarynthus* (1821), a pastoral drama, and a number of serious poems, but was always best in lighter efforts, such as his serio-comic 'Address to a Mummy.' *Brambletye House* (1826) is one of his later novels, and in 1831 he published *Festivals, Games, and Amusements, Ancient and Modern*.

Smith, James (10 Feb. 1775—Dec. 1839), humorous writer, brother of Horace Smith (q.v.), was born in London, son of a solicitor, and educated at a school at Chigwell. Entering his father's office, he succeeded him as solicitor to the Board of Ordnance. He collaborated with his brother in the highly successful *Rejected Addresses* (1812), and wrote the parodies of Wordsworth, Coleridge, and Crabbe. He also published occasional verse, and wrote the text for Charles Matthews's comic entertainments, but was most celebrated as a wit and diner-out.

Smith, John (baptized 9 Jan. 1580, died 21 June 1631), adventurer and historian, was born at Willoughby, Lincolnshire, and had a grammar-school education. He was apprenticed to a merchant, but gave that up to go soldiering on the Continent, where he had many adventures. In 1606 he sailed with other settlers to Jamestown in Virginia. Captured by Red Indians, he was condemned to death, but was saved, according to his own account, by the intervention of Pocahontas, the daughter of a chief. In 1608 he was elected President of the Council in Virginia, and in the following year returned to England. He wrote a number of books, of which the most important are *A True Relation of Such Occurrences and Accidents of Note as Hath Happened in Virginia Since the First Planting of the Colony* (1608), *A General History of Virginia, New England, and the Summer Isles* (1624), *The True Travels, Adventures, and Observations of Captain John Smith* (1630), and *Advertisements for the Unexperienced Planters of New England* (1631), which contains his autobiographical poem, 'The Sea-Mark.'

Smith, Lloyd Logan Pearsall (18 Oct. 1865—2 March 1946), essayist and bibliophile, was born at Millville, New Jersey, son of a Quaker glass manufacturer; his sister married Bertrand Russell (q.v.). Educated at Harvard and Oxford, Smith settled in England, where he counted Matthew Arnold and Whistler among his friends. He became well known by his collections of aphorisms and essays, *Trivia* (1902), *More Trivia* (1921), *Afterthoughts* (1931), and *Last Words* (1934), which were assembled in *All Trivia* (1934). An authority on English idioms, he published *The English Language* (1912) and *Words and Idioms* (1925). Among his critical works are *The Life and Letters of Sir Henry Wotton* (1907), *On Reading Shakespeare* (1933), and *Milton and his Modern Critics* (1940). *Songs and Sonnets* (1909) is a collection of his own verse, and *Unforgotten Years* (1939) is autobiographical; his philosophy appears in his famous remark, 'People say life is the thing, but I prefer reading.'

Smith, Naomi Royde, *see* Royde-Smith.

Smith, Samuel Francis (21 Oct. 1808—16 Nov. 1895), clergyman and poet, was born in Boston and educated at the Latin School there, and at Harvard. Afterwards he became a Baptist minister, having studied at Andover Theological Seminary. While there he was asked to provide verses for a song-book. One of the pieces was 'My Country, 'tis of Thee,' which he wrote in half an hour. With the title 'America' it was adopted as the national hymn of the United States in 1832. Smith's *Poems of Home and Country* were published in 1895, and he also wrote some travel sketches.

Smith, Sheila Kaye, *see* Kaye-Smith.

Smith, Sydney (3 June 1771—22 Feb. 1845), clergyman and author, was born at Woodford, Essex, the son of a gentleman of independent means, and educated at Winchester and Oxford. He took orders in 1794, becoming curate of Amesbury. He came to Edinburgh as tutor to a gentleman's son, was introduced to the circle of brilliant young Whigs there, and assisted in founding the *Edinburgh Review*. He then went to London, where he was for a time preacher at the Foundling Hospital, and lectured on moral philosophy at the Royal Institution. His brilliant wit and general ability made him a favourite in society, while by his power of clear and cogent argument he exercised a strong influence on the course of politics. His *Letters of Peter Plymley* (1807—8), did much to advance the cause of Catholic emancipation. He received various preferments, and became a canon of St Paul's. In politics he was a Whig, in his Church views an Erastian; and in the defence of his principles he was honest and courageous. Though not remarkable for religious devotion he was for 20 years a hard-working and useful country parson. By the death of a younger brother he in his later years came into a considerable fortune.

Smith, Sydney Goodsir (26 Oct. 1915—   ), poet and critic, was born at Wellington, New Zealand. Coming to Scotland, he became one of the chief figures of the modern Scottish Renaissance and a leader of the ' Lallans ' writers. Volumes of his verse are *Skail*

Wind (1941), *The Wanderer* (1943), *The Deevil's Waltz* (1946), *Under the Eildon Tree* (1948), *So Late into the Night* (1952), *Figs and Thistles* (1953), *Cokkils* (1954), and *Orpheus and Eurydice* (1955). *Carotid Cornucopius* (1947) is described as ' a Rabelaisian-cum-Joycean extravaganza,' *Colickie Meg* (1953) is a play, and his critical works include *A Short Introduction to Scottish Literature* (1951).

Smith, Walter Chalmers (5 Dec. 1824—20 Sept. 1908), poet, born in Aberdeen and educated at its Grammar School and at Marischal College, was ordained in 1850, and became a minister of the Free Church of Scotland at Orwell in Kinross, Glasgow, and Edinburgh successively. He attained considerable reputation as a poet. Among his works are *The Bishop's Walk* (1861), *Olrig Grange* (1872), *Hilda among the Broken Gods* (1878), *Raban* (1880), *Kildrostan* (1884), and *A Heretic* (1890). Some of these were written under the names of Orwell and Hermann Kunst. He received the degrees of D.D. and LL.D.

Smith, Sir William (20 May 1813—7 Oct. 1893), lexicographer, was born in London and educated at University College there. For a time he was a theological student, then studied law at Gray's Inn, but became a schoolmaster at University College School. He is noteworthy for the many excellent reference works he compiled, which include a *Dictionary of Greek and Roman Antiquities* (1842), a *Dictionary of Greek and Roman Biography* (1849), and a *Dictionary of Greek and Roman Geography* (1857). He also produced a *Bible Dictionary* (1860—5) and a *Classical and Biblical Atlas* (1874). From 1867 till his death he was editor of the *Quarterly Review*. Knighted in 1892, he held honorary degrees of Oxford, Glasgow, Dublin, and Leipzig.

Smith, William Robertson (8 Nov. 1846—31 March 1894), theologian and Orientalist, son of the Free Church minister of Keig, Aberdeenshire, was educated at the universities of Aberdeen, Edinburgh, Bonn, and Göttingen. In 1870 he was appointed Professor of Hebrew in the Free Church College at Aberdeen, a position which he had to resign on account of his advanced critical views. He became joint editor of the *Encyclopaedia Britannica*, and in 1883 Professor of Arabic at Cambridge. Smith was a man of brilliant and versatile talents. His works include *The Old Testament in the Jewish Church* (1881), and *The Religion of the Semites* (1889).

Smollett, Tobias George (baptized 19 March 1721, died 20 Sept. 1771), novelist, born at Dalquhurn, Dumbartonshire, was educated at Dumbarton Grammar School and Glasgow University, then served apprenticeship to a doctor-apothecary. In 1739 he proceeded to London with the object of having a tragedy, *The Regicide*, put on the stage; in this, however, he failed. In disappointment he took service as surgeon's mate on one of the vessels of the Carthagena expedition, 1741, an experience which he turned to account in his novels. On his return he settled in London, and endeavoured to acquire practice as a doctor, but was not very successful, and having discovered where his talent lay, he thenceforth devoted himself to literature. *Roderick Random* appeared in 1748, *Peregrine Pickle* in

1751, *Ferdinand, Count Fathom* in 1753, *Sir Lancelot Greaves* in 1766, and *Humphry Clinker*, generally considered his best novel, in 1770.

In 1766 he published his amusing but caustic *Travels in France and Italy*, which earned him the nickname from Sterne, of Smelfungus; and in 1769 his satire *The Adventures of an Atom*. Besides these works he translated Lesage's *Gil Blas* (1749), Cervantes's *Don Quixote* (1755), and the works of Voltaire (38 volumes, 1761—74), wrote a *History of England* in continuation of Hume's, an *Ode to Independence*, travels and satires, and contributed to various periodicals. He was repeatedly involved in acrimonious controversy, and on one occasion fined and imprisoned for a libel. This, with various private misfortunes, embittered his life, and he died disappointed and worn out near Leghorn. Had he lived four years longer he would have succeeded to his grandfather's estate of Bonhill. A master of the picaresque, Smollett displays great narrative power, and has a remarkable comic vein of a broad type, which enables him to present ludicrous scenes and circumstances with great effect. There is, however, a strong element of coarseness in his treatment of his subjects.

Snow, Sir Charles Percy (15 Oct. 1905—   ), scientist and novelist, was born in Leicester, son of a business man. Educated at Alderman Newton's School and University College, Leicester, he did research in physics at Cambridge, took a Ph.D. degree, and was a Fellow of Christ's from 1930 to 1950. From 1938 to 1940 he edited *Discovery*. During the Second World War he was a government science expert and was made a C.B.E., and in 1945 he was appointed a Civil Service Commissioner. His first novel, a detective story, *Death under Sail* (1932), was followed by *The Search* (1935). A sequence of novels dealing with the problems of the atomic age was *Strangers and Brothers* (1940), *The Light and the Dark* (1948), *Time of Hope* (1949), *The Masters* (1951), *The New Men* (1954), which was awarded the Tait Black Memorial Prize, *Homecomings* (1956), *The Conscience of the Rich* (1958), and *The Affair* (1959). *View over the Park* (1950) is a play. A Fellow of the Royal Society of Literature, Snow was knighted in 1957. In 1950 he married the novelist Pamela Hansford Johnson (q.v.).

Somerville, Edith Anna Oenone (2 May 1858—8 Oct. 1949), novelist, was born at Drishane, County Cork, daughter of an army officer. She studied art in Paris, Dusseldorf, and London, and later illustrated her own books. In 1903 she became the first woman Master of Foxhounds, a position she held till 1919, and in 1935 she published under her own name a hunting anthology, *Notes of the Horn*. All her other work appeared under the names of Somerville and Ross, the latter being her cousin Violet Martin (q.v.), with whom she collaborated from 1886 onwards. Among the best-known novels that they wrote together are *An Irish Cousin* (1889), *Naboth's Vineyard* (1891), *The Real Charlotte* (1895), *The Silver Fox* (1897), *Some Experiences of an Irish R.M.* (1899), and *Further Experiences of an Irish R.M.* (1908). They also collaborated in the travel books,

Through Connemara in a Governess Cart (1893), and *Some Irish Yesterdays* (1906).

Somerville, Mary (1780—29 Nov. 1872), writer on science, daughter of Admiral Sir William G. Fairfax, born at Jedburgh, was twice married, first to Captain Grieg, an officer in the Russian Navy, and second to her cousin Dr William Somerville, who was in full sympathy with her scientific tastes. They went to reside in London, and there her talents made her known in scientific circles. In 1823 she was requested by Lord Brougham to popularize the *Mechanique Celeste* of La Place. This she did with great success, publishing her work as *The Celestial Mechanism of the Heavens* (1830). She also published *The Connection of the Physical Sciences* (1834), and other works. She received a pension from the Government, and died aged 92 at Naples.

Somerville *or* **Somervile, William** (2 Sept. 1675—17 July 1742), poet, born at Colwich, Staffordshire, was educated at Winchester and Oxford and entered at the Middle Temple. Thereafter he spent his life as a country squire at the family seat of Edstone, near Henley-in-Arden, and was devoted to sport. His books include *The Chase* (1735), a poem in four books of blank verse, to which *Field Sports* (1742), a poem on hawking, is a kind of supplement, and *Hobbinol, or Rural Games* (1740), a burlesque.

Sotheby, William (9 Nov. 1757—30 Dec. 1833), translator, was born in London, son of an army officer, and educated at Harrow. He became an ensign in the 10th Dragoons, but in 1780 left the army and devoted himself to the study of the classics. In 1790 he published a volume of *Poems*, and in 1798 a translation of Wieland's *Oberon*, but he was best known for his verse renderings of Virgil's *Georgics* (1800), the *Iliad* (1831), and the *Odyssey* (1834), which were at one time greatly admired.

Soutar, William (28 April 1898—15 Oct. 1943), poet, was born at Perth, son of a carpenter, and educated at Edinburgh University. For the last 14 years of his life he was a bedridden invalid suffering from a form of paralysis. Writing both in English and in Scots with a delicate artistry and a rare humour, he was reckoned one of the most gifted poets of the Scottish revival. Among his books of verse are *Conflict* (1931), *Seeds in the Wind* (1933), *The Solitary Way* (1934), *A Handful of Earth* (1936), *Riddles in Scots* (1937), *In the Time of Tyrants* (1939), *But the Earth Abideth* (1943), and *The Expectant Silence* (1944). His *Collected Poems* appeared in 1948 and his *Diaries of a Dying Man* in 1954.

South, Robert (4 Sept. 1634—8 July 1716), clergyman, son of a London merchant, was born at Hackney, and educated at Westminster School and Oxford, where in 1660 he was appointed University Orator. He became domestic chaplain to the Lord Chancellor Clarendon, and in 1663 the degree of D.D. was conferred upon him. After accompanying an embassy to Poland he became Rector of Islip, and a chaplain to Charles II. He was opposed to the Romanizing measures of James II, but declined to associate himself in any way with the Revolution, to which nevertheless he submitted. He was an expert controversialist, but it is chiefly by his sermons, which are among the classics of English divinity, that he is remembered. He has the reputation of being the wittiest of English preachers.

Southerne, Thomas (1660—22 May 1746), dramatist, born near Dublin, and educated at Trinity College there, came to London and studied law at the Middle Temple. Afterwards he entered the army and saw service under the Duke of Berwick. His first great success, *The Fatal Marriage* (1694), was followed by the still more popular *Oroonoko* (1696), in which he appeals passionately against the slave-trade. Unlike most preceding dramatists he was a practical man, succeeded in his theatrical management, and retired on a fortune. Other plays are *The Loyal Brother* (1682), *The Disappointment* (1684), *The Wives' Excuse* (1692), and *The Spartan Dame* (1719).

Southey, Caroline Anne (7 Oct. 1786—20 July 1854), poetess, was born at Lymington, Hampshire, daughter of Captain Charles Bowles, who served with the East India Company. She sent a metrical tale, *Ellen Fitzarthur* (1820) to Southey for criticism, and this led to a friendship between them and to her becoming in 1839 Southey's second wife. His faculties were then failing and he died four years later. Of Caroline Southey's works the best-known is *Chapters on Churchyards* (1829), a series of stories. She also wrote several narrative poems, including *The Widow's Tale* (1822) and *The Birth-day* (1836).

Southey, Robert (12 Aug. 1774—21 March 1843), Poet Laureate, born in Bristol, son of an unsuccessful linen-draper, was sent to Westminster School, and in 1792 went to Balliol College, Oxford. His friendship with Coleridge began in 1794, and with him he joined in the utopian scheme of a 'pantisocracy.' In 1795 he married his first wife, Edith Fricker, and thus became the brother-in-law of Coleridge. Shortly afterwards he visited Spain, and in 1800 Portugal, and laid the foundations of his thorough knowledge of the history and literature of the Peninsula. Between these two periods of foreign travel he had attempted the study of law, which proved entirely uncongenial; and in 1803 he settled at Greta Hall, Keswick, to which neighbourhood the Coleridges had also come. Here he set himself to a course of indefatigable literary toil which only ended with his death. His long narrative poem *Thalaba* had appeared in 1801, and there followed *Madoc* (1805), *The Curse of Kehama* (1810), *Roderic, the Last of the Goths* (1814), and *A Vision of Judgment* (1821) which provoked Byron's brilliant satire of the same title; in prose a *History of Brazil*, lives of Nelson (1813), Wesley (1820), and Bunyan (1830), *The Book of the Church* (1824), *History of the Peninsular War* (1823—32), and *The Doctor* (1834—7), which contains the delightful fairy-tale of ' The Three Bears.' In addition to this vast amount of work he had been from 1808 a constant contributor to the *Quarterly Review*. In 1839 when he was failing both in body and mind· he married, as his second wife, Miss Caroline Ann Bowles, who had for 20 years been his intimate friend.

Though the name of Southey still bulks somewhat largely in the history of our literature, his longer poems, such as *Thalaba* and

Kehama, on which he himself based his hopes of lasting fame, are little regarded. To this result their length, remoteness from living interests, and the impression that their often splendid diction is rather eloquence than true poetry, have contributed. Some of his shorter poems such as 'The Battle of Blenheim' still live, but his fame now rests on his pure and unaffected prose and especially on his classic *Life of Nelson*. Like Wordsworth and Coleridge, Southey began life as a democratic visionary, and was strongly influenced by the French Revolution, but gradually cooled down into a pronounced Tory. He was himself greater and better than any of his works, his life being a noble record of devotion to duty and unselfish benevolence. He held the office of Poet Laureate from 1813, and had a pension from the Government. He was offered but declined a baronetcy.

Southhouse-Cheyney, Reginald Evelyn Peter (22 Feb. 1896—26 June 1951), crime novelist who wrote under the name Peter Cheyney, was born in London and educated at the Mercers School and London University. During the First World War he served with the Royal Warwickshire Regiment. He worked for a time as a law clerk, then became an actor, and after that a journalist; from 1933 to 1934 he was on the staff of the *Sunday Graphic*. His earliest publications were two books of verse, *Poems of Love and War* (1916) and *To Corona* (1917). His first successful crime novel, *This Man Is Dangerous*, appeared in 1936. Others are *Dames Don't Care* (1937), *Don't Get Me Wrong* (1938), *You Can't Keep the Change* (1940), *It Couldn't Matter Less* (1941), *Sorry You've Been Troubled* (1942), *You Can Always Duck* (1943), and *Dance Without Music* (1947).

Southwell, Robert (1561—21 Feb. 1595), Jesuit writer, born at Horsham St Faith's, Norfolk, of good Roman Catholic family, and educated at Douay, Paris, and Rome, became a Jesuit, and showed such learning and ability that he was appointed Prefect of the English College. In 1586 he came to England with Garnett, the superior of the English province, and became chaplain to the Countess of Arundel. His being in England for more than 40 days then rendered him liable to the penalty of death, and in 1592 he was apprehended and imprisoned in the Tower for three years, during which he was tortured 13 times. He was then put on trial and hanged at Tyburn. His verse includes *St Peter's Complaint* (1595) and 'The Burning Babe,' a short poem of great imaginative power; among his religious prose works are *Mary Magdalene's Funeral Tears* (1594), *The Triumphs Over Death* (1595), and *A Short Rule of Good Life* (1598).

Spade, Mark, *see* **Balchin, Nigel.**

Spedding, James (26 June 1808—9 March 1881), editor, son of a Cumberland squire, and educated at Bury St Edmunds and Trinity College, Cambridge, where he was one of the celebrated 'Apostles' group, was for some years in the Colonial Office. He devoted himself to the editing of Bacon's works, and the endeavour to clear his character against the aspersions of Macaulay and others. The former was done in conjunction with Ellis and Heath, his own being much the largest share in their great edition (seven volumes 1857—1859); and the latter, so far as possible, in *The Life and Letters* (seven volumes 1861—74), entirely his own. In 1878 he brought out an abridged *Life and Times of Francis Bacon*. He strongly combated the theory that Bacon was the author of Shakespeare's plays. His death was caused by his being run over by a cab.

Speed, John (1552?—28 July 1629), historian and cartographer, born at Farington, Cheshire, and brought up to his father's trade of a tailor, had a strong taste for history and antiquities, and wrote a *History of Great Britain* (1611), which was long the best in existence; in collecting material for it he had assistance from Cotton, Spelman, and other investigators. He also published useful maps of Great Britain and Ireland, and of various counties. His maps were collected and with descriptions published in 1611 as *Theatre of the Empire of Great Britain*.

Speke, John Hanning (4 May 1827—18 Sept. 1864), explorer, was born at Jordans in Somerset. Educated for the army, he served in the Sikh War and rose to be captain. In 1854 he accompanied Burton (q.v.) in the exploration of the Somali country, and in 1857 made another expedition with him in the course of which Speke discovered Lake Victoria Nyanza, which he assumed to be the source of the Nile; this was disputed, and on the morning that the subject was to be discussed before the British Association he accidentally killed himself while partridge shooting. Accounts of his journeys are given in his *Journal of the Discovery of the Source of the Nile* (1863) and *What Led to the Discovery of the Source of the Nile* (1864).

Spelman, Sir Henry (born 1564, buried 14 Oct. 1641), historian and antiquary, born at Congham, Norfolk, studied at Cambridge, and entered Lincoln's Inn. He wrote valuable works on legal and ecclesiastical antiquities, including a *History of Sacrilege* (1698), *Glossarium Archaeologicum* (1626), a glossary of obsolete law-terms, a *History of the English Councils* (1639), and *Tenures by Knight-service* (1641). His writings have furnished valuable material for subsequent historians. He sat in Parliament and on various commissions, and in recompense of his labours was voted a grant of £300.

Spence, James Lewis Thomas Chalmers (25 Nov. 1874—3 March 1955), poet and mythologist, was born at Broughty Ferry and educated there and at Edinburgh University. He studied dentistry, but turned to writing and in 1899 became a sub-editor on the *Scotsman*. From 1906 to 1909 he was on the staff of the *British Weekly*, and after that he wrote as a freelance. His dialect verse was one of the early influences in the modern Scottish Renascence, and he was also one of the founders of the Scottish National Party in 1929. His books of verse include *Le Roi d'Ys* (1910), *Songs, Satanic and Celestial* (1913), *The Plumes of Time* (1926), and *Collected Poems* (1953). He made a special study of the early civilizations of Mexico and Central America, and published *The Civilization of Ancient Mexico* (1911), *Myths of Mexico and Peru* (1913), and *The Gods of Mexico* (1923), a standard work. Others of his works on mythology and magic are *The Myths of Ancient Egypt* (1913), *An Introduction* *to Mythology* (1918), *An Encyclopaedia of Occultism* (1920), *The Problem of Atlantis* (1924), *The Magic Arts in Celtic Britain* (1945), *The History and Origins of Druidism* (1950), and *Second Sight* (1951).

Spence, Joseph (25 April 1699—20 Aug. 1768), anecdotist, born at Kingsclere, Hampshire, son of a clergyman, and educated at Eton, Winchester, and Oxford, took orders in 1724, held various preferments, including a prebend at Durham, and was Professor of Poetry at Oxford. He wrote an *Essay on Pope's Odyssey* (1726), which gained for him the friendship of the poet, of whose conversation he made notes, collecting likewise stories of him and of other celebrities which were published in 1820 with the title *Anecdotes*, and are of great value, inasmuch as they preserve much matter illustrative of the literary history of the eighteenth century which would otherwise have been lost.

Spencer, Herbert (27 April 1820—8 Dec. 1903), philosopher, was born at Derby, son of a schoolmaster, and at 13 was sent to the care of his uncle, a clergyman, near Bath. Declining a University career he became a school assistant, but shortly after accepted a situation as an engineer on the London and Birmingham railway, in which he remained until the great railway crisis of 1846 threw him out of employment. He now resolved to devote himself to journalism, and in 1848 was appointed sub-editor of the *Economist*. Thereafter he became more and more absorbed in the consideration of the problems of sociology and the development of the doctrine of evolution as applied thereto, gradually leading up to the completion of a system of philosophy which was the work of his life. His fundamental proposition is that society, like the individual, is an organism subject to evolution, and the scope of this idea is gradually expanded so as to embrace in its sweep the whole range of knowable things. Among the books which he published in exposition of his views may be mentioned *Social Statics* (1850), *Principles of Psychology* (1855), *First Principles* (1862), *Principles of Biology* (1867), *Data of Ethics* (1879), *Principles of Sociology* (1877), *Political Institutions* (1882), and *Man versus the State* (1884). His works have been translated into most European languages. The most characteristic qualities of Spencer as a thinker are his powers of generalization and analysis. He left an *Autobiography* (1904), in which he subjects his own personality to analysis with remarkable detachment of mind.

Spencer, William Robert (1769—24 Oct. 1834), poet, son of Lord Charles Spencer, was educated at Harrow and Oxford, and belonged to the Whig set of Fox and Sheridan. He wrote graceful *vers de societé*, made translations from Bürger, and is best remembered by his well-known ballad of *Gelert*. After a life of extravagance he died in poverty in Paris.

Spender, Stephen (28 Feb. 1909—   ), poet and critic, born in London, son of a journalist, was partly of German descent on his mother's side. He was educated at University College School and Oxford, where he became associated with Auden, Day Lewis, and MacNeice (qq.v.) in writing the so-called 'new' English poetry, with Communist trends; but in spite of this he was a strong individualist, and though he joined the Communist party later, he left it after a few weeks. About this period he travelled extensively on the Continent, often in company with Christopher Isherwood (q.v.). His volumes of verse include *Nine Entertainments* (1928), *Twenty Poems* (1930), *Poems* (1933), *The Still Centre* (1939), and *Ruins and Visions of Being* (1942). *The Destructive Element* (1934) and *The Creative Element* (1953) are critical works dealing with various modern writers. *Trials of a Judge* (1938) is a verse play; *The Burning Cactus* (1936) a volume of short stories; *The Backward Son* (1940) a novel; and *World Within World* (1951) an autobiography. During the Second World War he was a member of the Auxiliary Fire Service, and in 1941 he married the pianist Natasha Litvin.

Spenser, Edmund (1552?—16 Jan. 1599), poet, was born in East Smithfield, London, the son of John Spenser, described as gentleman and journeyman in the art of cloth-making, who had come to London from Lancashire. In 1561 the poet was sent to Merchant Taylors' School, then newly opened, and in 1569 he proceeded to Pembroke Hall, Cambridge, as a sizar, taking his degree in 1576. Among his friends there were Edward Kirke, who edited the *Shepheard's Calendar*, and Gabriel Harvey, the critic. While still at school he had contributed a number of sonnets to Van der Noot's miscellany, *Theatre for Worldlings* (1569). On leaving Cambridge Spenser went to the north, probably to visit his relations in Lancashire, and in 1578, through his friend Harvey, he became known to the Earl of Leicester and his brother-in-law, Philip Sidney. With Sidney, Dyer, and others he formed a literary circle styled the Areopagus. The next year, 1579, saw the publication of *The Shepheard's Calendar* in 12 eclogues. It was dedicated to Sidney, who had become his friend and patron, and was received with acclamation, all who had ears for poetry perceiving that a new and great singer had arisen.

The following year Spenser was appointed secretary to Lord Grey of Wilton, Deputy for Ireland, a strict Puritan, and accompanied him to Ireland. At the same time he appears to have begun the *Faerie Queene*. In 1581 he was appointed Registrar of Chancery, and received a grant of the Abbey and Castle of Enniscorthy, which was followed in 1586 by a grant of the Castle of Kilcolman in County Cork, a former possession of the Earls of Desmond, with 3,000 acres attached. Simultaneously, however, a heavy blow fell upon him in the death of Sidney at the Battle of Zutphen. The loss of this dear friend he commemorated in his lament of *Astrophel*. In 1590 he was visited by Sir Walter Ralegh, who persuaded him to come to England, and presented him to the Queen, from whom he received a pension of £50, which does not, however, appear to have been regularly paid, and on the whole his experiences of the Court did not yield him much satisfaction. In the same year his reputation as a poet was vastly augmented by the publication of the first three books of the *Faerie Queene*, dedicated to Elizabeth. The enthusiasm with which they were received led the publisher to bring out a collection of other writings of Spenser under the general title of *Complaints*, and including 'Mother-Hubbard's Tale' (a satire on the

Court and on the conflict then being waged between the old faith and the new), 'Teares of the Muses,' and 'The Ruins of Time.'

Having seen these ventures launched, Spenser returned to Kilcolman and wrote *Colin Clout's come Home Again*, one of the brightest and most vigorous of his poems, not, however, published until 1595. In the following year appeared his *Four Hymns* and the *Prothalamion* on the marriage of two daughters of the Earl of Worcester. He also published in prose his *View of the Present State of Ireland*, a work full of shrewd observation and practical statesmanship. In 1594 he was married to Elizabeth Boyle, whom he had courted in *Amoretti*, and his union with whom he now celebrated in the magnificent *Epithalamion*, by some regarded as his most perfect poem. In 1595 he returned to England, taking with him the second part of the *Faerie Queene*, published in 1596. In 1598 he was made Sheriff of Cork, and in the same year his fortunes suffered a final eclipse. The rebellion of Tyrone broke out, his castle was burned, and in the conflagration his youngest child, an infant, perished, he himself with his wife and remaining children escaping with difficulty. He returned to London, where he died, a broken man. He was buried in Westminster Abbey near Chaucer, and a monument was erected to his memory in 1620 by the Countess of Dorset.

The position of Spenser in English poetry is below Chaucer, Shakespeare, and Milton only. The first far excels him in narrative and constructive power and in humour, and the last in austere grandeur of conception; but for richness and beauty of imagination and exquisite sweetness of music he is unsurpassed except by Shakespeare. He has been called the poets' poet, a title which he well merits, not only by virtue of the homage which all the more imaginative poets have yielded him, but because of the almost unequalled influence he has exercised upon the whole subsequent course and expression of English poetry, which he enriched with the stanza which bears his name, and which none since him have used with more perfect mastery. His faults are prolixity, indirectness, and want of constructive power, and consequently the sustained sweetness and sumptuousness of his verse are apt to cloy. His great work, the *Faerie Queene*, is but a gorgeous fragment, six books out of a projected 12; but in its allegorical use of medieval romance and chivalry it embodies the noblest ideals of the Elizabethan age.

Spottiswood *or* **Spottiswoode, Alicia Ann** (1810—13 March 1900), poetess and composer, was born at Lauder in Berwickshire. In 1836 she married Lord John Scott, son of the Duke of Buccleugh, but after his death in 1860 she reverted to her maiden name and became known for her Scottish songs, 'Durrisdeer' and others. Among these is the famous 'Annie Laurie,' which was written in its original form by William Douglas of Fingland, Kirkcudbright, and published in 1824; she rewrote it and added a third stanza, besides composing the music for it.

Spottiswood, John (1565—26 Nov. 1639), prelate and historian, a son of the minister of Midcalder, was educated for the Church at Glasgow University. He gained the favour of James VI, and was his chief instrument in his endeavours to restore Episcopal church-government in Scotland. He became Archbishop successively of Glasgow and St Andrews, and in 1635 Lord Chancellor of Scotland. On the rising caused by the introduction of the service-book, he had to flee from Scotland, and was excommunicated by the General Assembly in 1638. He wrote a *History of the Church and State of Scotland* (1655) from the Episcopalian standpoint.

Sprague, Charles (26 Oct. 1791—22 Jan. 1875), banker and poet, was born in Boston. At the age of 13 he was apprenticed to a dry goods firm, but finally became a bank cashier and remained one for 40 years, writing only in his leisure. Among his poems 'Curiosity,' 'The Brothers,' and an ode on Shakespeare are reckoned the best. His *Writings* were collected in 1841.

Sprat, Thomas (1635—20 May 1713), prelate and author, born at Beaminster, Dorset, where his father was minister, and educated at Oxford, was a mathematician, and one of the group of scientific men among whom the Royal Society had its origin. His *History of the Royal Society* (1667) is his principal work, but he also wrote poems, and had a high reputation as a preacher. His literary style gives him a distinguished place among English writers. He held various high preferments, and died Bishop of Rochester and Dean of Westminster.

Spring, Howard (10 Feb. 1889—   ), novelist, was born in Cardiff, son of a jobbing gardener, and at the age of 11 left school to help to bring up his eight brothers and sisters. After working as messenger boy on a newspaper he became a reporter, joined the staff of the *Manchester Guardian*, where he remained till 1931, and later became literary critic of the *Evening Standard*. His first novel, *Shabby Tiger* (1934) had a sequel, *Rachel Rosing* (1935); his next, *O Absalom!* (1938), later called *My Son, My Son*, was a world best-seller, being translated into 11 languages. Others of his novels are *Fame is the Spur* (1940), *Hard Facts* (1944), *Dunkerleys* (1946), *There Is No Armour* (1948), *The Houses In Between* (1951), and *A Sunset Touch* (1953). *Book Parade* (1938) is a volume of criticism, and he also wrote some juvenile books, including *Darkie and Co.* (1932) and *Sampson's Circus* (1936). *Heaven Lies About Us* (1939), an autobiographical work telling of his poverty-stricken childhood, is continued in *In the Meantime* (1942) and *And Another Thing* (1946).

Spring-Rice, Sir Cecil Arthur (27 Feb. 1859—14 Feb. 1918), diplomat and poet, was a grandson of the 1st Baron Mounteagle. Born in London, and educated at Eton and Oxford, he became a clerk in the Foreign Office in 1882. After serving on various embassies he was appointed British Minister in Persia in 1906, and in the same year was made a Knight Commander of St Michael and St George. As British Minister in the United States from 1913 to 1918 he played a prominent part in Anglo-American relations during the First World War. His famous patriotic poem, 'I Vow to Thee, my Country,' was written on his last night in Washington, a few weeks before his death.

Spurgeon, Charles Haddon (19 June 1834—31 Jan. 1892), clergy-man, born at Kelvedon, Essex, left the Independents and joined the Baptist communion and became, at the age of 20, pastor of New Park Street Chapel, London, where he attained an unprecedented popularity. In 1859 the Metropolitan Tabernacle was erected for him. He possessed in an eminent degree two of the great requisites of effective oratory, a magnificent voice and a command of pure idiomatic Saxon English. His sermons, published weekly from 1855 to 1917, had an enormous circulation, and were regularly translated into several languages. In addition to his pastoral labours he super-intended an almshouse, a pastor's college, and an orphanage; and he was likewise a voluminous author, publishing, in addition to his sermons, over 100 volumes. His *Autobiography* appeared in 1898, and his *Letters* were edited by his son in 1923.

Squire, Sir John Collings (2 April 1884—20 Dec. 1958), poet and critic, born in Plymouth, was educated at Blundell's and St John's College, Cambridge. He became a freelance journalist, in 1913 was literary editor of the *New Statesman*, and from 1919 to 1934 editor of the *London Mercury*, in which he wrote under the name of Solomon Eagle. Among his other interests were architecture and archaeology. His books of verse include *Poems and Baudelaire Flowers* (1909), *The Three Hills* (1913), *The Survival of the Fittest* (1916), *The Lily of Malud* (1917), *The Birds* (1919), and *A Face in Candlelight* (1932). Among his critical works are *Books in General* (three series, 1918, 1920, 1921), *Life and Letters* (1920), *Essays at Large* (1922), and *Essays on Poetry* (1923). *The Grub Street Nights Entertainments* (1924) and *Outside Eden* (1933) are volumes of short stories. He also edited a number of anthologies, including *Selections from Modern Poets* (two series, 1921, 1924), *The Comic Muse* (1925), a collection of humorous verse, *Apes and Parrots* (1930), a volume of parodies, and *The Cambridge Book of Lesser Poets* (1927). In 1937 he published an autobiography, *The Honeysuckle and the Bee*. He was knighted in 1933.

Stables, William Gordon (21 May 1840—10 May 1910), novelist and writer of books for boys, was born at Aberchirder, Banffshire, and educated at Aberdeen Grammar School and University. He studied medicine and as a surgeon in the Navy from 1863 to 1871 voyaged extensively, but retired owing to ill health and settled at Twyford in Berkshire, where he started writing adventure stories for boys, based to some extent on his own experiences. Among the best-known are *Wild Adventures in Wild Places* (1881), *Wild Adventures Round the Pole* (1883), *The Hermit Hunter of the Wilds* (1889), *Westward with Columbus* (1894), *Kidnapped by Cannibals* (1899), and *In Regions of Perpetual Snow* (1904). He also wrote many historical novels. In 1886 he began living in a caravan, round which he wrote *The Cruise of the Land Yacht Wanderer* (1886).

Stacpoole, Henry de Vere (April 1863—12 April 1951), novelist, was born at Kingstown, Dublin, son of a clergyman, and educated at Malvern College. He studied medicine at London hospitals and practised for a time as a doctor; later he was made a Justice of the

Peace. He first won fame as a writer with *The Blue Lagoon* (1909), a romance of a South Sea island. Among his other novels are *The Pools of Silence* (1909), *The Ship of Coral* (1911), *The Street of the Flute Player* (1912), *The Pearl Fishers* (1915), *The Reef of Stars* (1916), *The Starlit Garden* (1918), *Men, Women, and Beasts* (1922), *The Gates of Morning* (1925), *Pacific Gold* (1931), and *Green Coral* (1935). He also published several books of verse, and translated the poems of François Villon (1913) and of Sappho (1920). *Men and Mice* (1942) and *More Men and Mice* (1945) are autobiographical.

Stanhope, Philip, *see* **Chesterfield.**

Stanhope, Philip Henry Stanhope, 5th Earl (30 Jan. 1805—24 Dec. 1875), historian, was born at Walmer, and educated at Oxford. He sat in the House of Commons for Wootton Bassett and Hertford, held some minor official appointments under Peel, and identified himself with many useful measures, specially in regard to literature and art. He founded the Stanhope Essay Prize at Oxford and helped to found The National Portrait Gallery. His writings include *The War of the Spanish Succession* (1832), *A History of England from the Peace of Utrecht to the Peace of Versailles* (1836—63), and *The Reign of Queen Anne* (1870), besides lives of the younger Pitt (1861) and of Lord Chesterfield (1845). As an author he is best known by his earlier title of Viscount Mahon.

Stanley, Arthur Penrhyn (13 Dec. 1815—18 July 1881), historian and theologian, son of the Bishop of Norwich, was born at Alderley, Cheshire, and educated at Rugby and Oxford, where he had a brilliant career. Taking orders in 1839 he became Canon of Canterbury in 1851, of Christ Church in 1858, and Dean of Westminster in 1864. He was also Professor of Ecclesiastical History at Oxford from 1856 to 1862. Throughout his life he supported all liberal movements in theology. He was a prolific author, his works including a *Life of Dr Arnold* (1844), whose favourite pupil he was, *Memorials of Canterbury* (1854), *Sinai and Palestine* (1855), *Lectures on the Eastern Church* (1861), *History of the Jewish Church* (1863), *Historical Memorials of Westminster Abbey* (1867), *Lectures on the History of the Church of Scotland* (1872), and various commentaries. His wife was Lady Augusta Bruce, daughter of the Earl of Elgin.

Stanley, Sir Henry Morton (29 June 1841—10 May 1904), explorer and journalist, was born at Denbigh in Wales, son of a grazier, his original name being John Rowlands. On the early death of his father he was brought up in St Asaph workhouse, from which he ran away after thrashing one of the masters. After trying his hand at various jobs he shipped in 1859 as cabin boy on an American ship, and landed penniless in New Orleans. Adopted here by Henry Stanley, a cotton broker, he took his benefactor's name and worked for a time in a store. In 1861 he served in the Civil War, and in subsequent years returned to the sea and made various voyages, of which he wrote later in *My Early Travels and Adventures in America and Asia* (1895). In 1865 he turned to journalism, and was so highly thought of as a special correspondent that in 1869 he was commissioned by the *New York Herald* to go and find Livingstone, who was missing in Africa. In November of 1871 he had his celebrated meeting with the great explorer at Ujiji, and a year later published *How I Found Livingstone*. In 1874, after Livingstone's death, Stanley himself crossed Africa from sea to sea, and wrote *Through the Dark Continent* (1878). In 1879 he explored the Congo, and in 1885 wrote *The Congo and the Founding of the Free State*, and was awarded the Order of Leopold by the King of the Belgians. After his last expedition of 1887, which laid the foundations of British East Africa, he wrote *In Darkest Africa* (1890). In 1895 he was elected Unionist M.P. for North Lambeth, and in 1899 was awarded the Grand Cross of the Bath. His *Autobiography* was edited by his wife in 1909.

Stanley, Thomas (1625—12 April 1678), poet, was born at Cumberlow, Hertfordshire, and educated at Cambridge. His mother was a cousin of the poet Lovelace, and he knew many of the writers of the day. Besides a volume of *Poems*, published in 1647, he made many translations, edited Aeschylus, and wrote a *History of Philosophy* (1655—62) which was long a standard work.

Stanyhurst, Richard (1547—1618), historian and translator, born in Dublin, son of the Speaker of the Irish House of Commons, was educated at Oxford, and studied law at Furnival's Inn and Lincoln's Inn. He wrote the history of Ireland in Holinshed's *Chronicles*, and made a stiff, clumsy, and prosaic translation of the first four books of Virgil's *Aeneid* into English hexameters. He also translated some of the Psalms.

Stapledon, William Olaf (10 May 1886—6 Sept. 1950), novelist, was born on the Wirral peninsula, near Liverpool, but spent much of his childhood in Egypt. Educated at Abbotsholme School and Oxford, he taught for a year at Manchester Grammar School, then worked in a shipping office, first in Liverpool, afterwards in Port Said. During the First World War he served with the Friends' Ambulance Unit and was awarded the Croix de Guerre. Later he took a Ph.D. at Liverpool University and was on the staff for some time. The success in 1931 of his *Last and First Men*, an imaginative story of the earth's future progress, led him to turn to writing as a livelihood. Other books of speculative fiction are *Last Men in London* (1932), *Waking World* (1934), *Old John* (1935), *Star Maker* (1937), and *Worlds of Wonder* (1949). He also wrote some philosophical works, including *A Modern Theory of Ethics* (1929), *Philosophy and Living* (1938), *Beyond the Isms* (1942), and *The Opening of the Eyes* (1951).

Stark, Freya Madeline (31 Jan. 1893—   ), travel writer, was born in Paris and educated at Bedford College and the London School of Oriental Studies. An accomplished linguist, she visited Syria in 1927 and after that explored the interior of Arabia and the less known parts of Persia. During the Second World War she did propaganda work among the Arabs for the British Government. She has been called the little Gertrude Bell, and was awarded the Burton Memorial Medal of the Royal Asiatic Society and the Mungo Park Medal of the Royal Scottish Geographical Society. Her most popular work was *The Valleys of the Assassins* (1934); other travel books are *The Southern Gates of Arabia* (1940), *Letters* *from Syria* (1942), *East Is West* (1945), *Traveller's Prelude* (1950), *Beyond Euphrates* (1951), and *Ionia: a Quest* (1955). *The Freya Stark Story* (1953) is autobiographical. In 1947 she married Stewart Henry Perowne, and they made their home at Asolo, in Italy.

Starkey, James Sullivan (1879—					), poet who wrote under the name Seumas O'Sullivan, was born in Dublin, son of a doctor, and educated at the Wesleyan College there. In 1923 he founded the *Dublin Magazine,* which he edited for the rest of his life. He was a foundation member of the Irish Academy of Letters, and was made an honorary Litt.D. of Trinity College, Dublin, in 1939. A mystical poet of the Celtic twilight school, he wrote *The Twilight People* (1905), *Verses Sacred and Profane* (1908), *The Earth-Lover* (1909), *Poems* (1912), *Requiem* (1917), *The Lamplighter* (1929), *Twenty-Five Lyrics* (1933), *Personal Talk* (1936), *Dublin Poems* (1946), and *Translations and Transcriptions* (1950). Collections of essays are *Impressions* (1912), *Mud and Purple* (1917), *Common Adventures* (1926), and *The Rose and Bottle* (1946).

Stead, Christina Ellen (17 July 1902—					), novelist, was born at Rockdale, New South Wales, daughter of a government official, and educated at Sydney University for the teaching profession, but turned instead to writing. In 1928 she went to London, and from 1930 to 1935 lived in Paris. After marrying the American novelist William Bleck, who wrote as William Blake, she settled in New York. Her books include *Salzburg Tales* (1934), *Seven Poor Men of Sydney* (1935), *The Beauties and the Furies* (1936), *House of All Nations* (1938), *The Man Who Loved Children* (1940), *Letty Fox, Her Luck* (1946), *A Little Tea, a Little Chat* (1948), and *The People with the Dogs* (1952).

Stedman, Edmund Clarence (8 Oct. 1833—18 Jan. 1908), poet and critic, was born at Hartford, Connecticut, son of a lumber merchant. In 1852 he was expelled from Yale for a youthful escapade and became a journalist. From 1869 to 1900 he was a stockbroker, writing only in his spare time. His best-known books of verse are *Poems Lyrical and Idyllic* (1860), *Alice of Monmouth* (1864), and *The Blameless Prince* (1869); he also compiled a number of anthologies. A leading literary critic of his day, he published *The Victorian Poets* (1875), *The Poets of America* (1885), and *The Nature and Elements of Poetry* (1882). He also wrote a *History of the New York Stock Exchange* (1905).

Steed, Henry Wickham (10 Oct. 1871—13 Jan. 1956), journalist, born at Long Melford, Suffolk, son of a solicitor, was educated at Sudbury Grammar School, the universities of Jena and Berlin, and the Sorbonne. In 1896 he joined the staff of *The Times,* rose to be foreign editor from 1914 to 1919, and was editor from then till 1922. From 1923 to 1930 he was owner and editor of the *Review of Reviews,* and from 1925 to 1938 he lectured at King's College, London, on Central European history. His works include *The Hapsburg Monarchy* (1913), *The Real Stanley Baldwin* (1930), *The Antecedents of Post-War Europe* (1932), *The Meaning of Hitlerism* (1934), *The Doom of the Hapsburgs* (1937), and *The Press* (1938). *Through Thirty Years* (1924) is an autobiography.

Steele, Sir Richard (baptized 12 March 1672, died 1 Sept. 1729), essayist and dramatist, son of a Dublin attorney, who died when his son was 5 years old, was, on the nomination of the Duke of Ormond, sent to the Charterhouse School, where his friendship with Addison began, and thence went to Oxford, but left without taking a degree, and enlisted in the Life Guards, for which he was disinherited by a rich relation. He, however, gained the favour of his colonel, Lord Cutts, himself a poet, and rose to the rank of captain. With the view of setting before himself a high ideal of conduct he at this time wrote a treatise on morals entitled *The Christian Hero* (1701). Abandoning this vein, he next produced three comedies, *The Funeral, or Grief à la Mode* (1702), *The Tender Husband* (1703), and *The Lying Lover* (1704). Two years later he was appointed Gentleman Waiter to Prince George of Denmark, and in 1707 he was made Gazeteer; and in the same year he married as his second wife Mary Scurlock, his 'dear Prue,' who seems, however, to have been something of a termagant. She had considerable means, but the incorrigible extravagance of Steele soon brought on embarrassment.

In 1709 he laid the foundations of his fame by starting the *Tatler*, the first of those periodicals which are so characteristic a literary feature of that age. In this he had the invaluable assistance of Addison, who contributed 42 papers out of a total of 271, and helped with others. The *Tatler* was followed in 1711 by the *Spectator*, in which Addison co-operated to a still greater extent. It was even a greater success, and ran to 555 numbers, exclusive of a brief revival by Addison in which Steele had no part, and in its turn was followed in 1713 by the *Guardian*. It is on his essays in these that the literary fame of Steele rests. With less refinement and delicacy of wit than Addison, he had perhaps more knowledge of life, and a wider sympathy, and like him he had a sincere desire for the reformation of morals and manners. In the keen political strife of the times he fought stoutly and honestly on the Whig side, one result of which was that he lost his office of Gazeteer, and was in 1714 expelled from the House of Commons to which he had just been elected. The next year gave a favourable turn to his fortunes. The accession of George I brought back the Whigs, and Steele was appointed to various offices, including a commissionership on forfeited estates in Scotland, which took him to Edinburgh, where he was welcomed by all the *literati*; and in 1715 he was knighted. But troubles now followed. His wife died; differences arose with Addison, who died before a reconciliation could be effected; and his remaining years were clouded by financial troubles and ill-health. His last work was a play, *The Conscious Lovers* (1722). He left London and lived in Hereford and at Carmarthen, where he died after a partial loss of his faculties from paralysis.

Steevens, George (10 May 1736—22 Jan. 1800), scholar, was born in London, son of a captain in the East India Company's service, and was educated at Eton and King's College, Cambridge. Having inherited a competence, he settled in Hampstead and devoted himself to the study of Shakespeare. In 1766 he published reprints of 20 Shakespeare quartos. He assisted Dr Johnson with his edition of the plays, and later brought out a new edition of his own, finally revised in 1793. Although cantankerous and constantly quarrelling with other literary men he was a member of The Club, the Society of Antiquaries, and the Royal Society. He detected a number of literary forgeries, including those of Chatterton and Ireland.

Steevens, George Warrington (10 Dec. 1869—15 Jan. 1900), journalist, born in London and educated at the City of London School and Oxford, where in 1893 he became a Fellow of Pembroke, took to journalism, in which he distinguished himself by his clearness of vision and vivid style. Connected successively with the *National Observer*, the *Pall Mall Gazette*, and the *Daily Mail*, he utilized the articles which appeared in these and other publications in various books, such as *The Land of the Dollar* (1897), *With Kitchener to Khartoum* (1898), *The Tragedy of Dreyfus* (1899), and *From Capetown to Ladysmith* (1900). His most striking work, however, was *Monologues of the Dead* (1895). He went as war correspondent to South Africa in 1900, and died of typhoid at Ladysmith.

Stein, Gertrude (3 Feb. 1874—27 July 1946), poet and critic, was born at Alleghenny, Pennsylvania, but spent her infancy in Vienna and Paris and her childhood in Oakland and San Francisco. She studied psychology under William James at Radcliffe College and medicine at Johns Hopkins. From 1903 she lived in Paris, where she was acquainted with Picasso and Matisse, and became a patron of the more advanced group of artists. Her first novel, *Three Lives*, appeared in 1908. A daring experimentalist in language, she wrote in a style so eccentric that critics were uncertain whether to take her seriously, but she had nevertheless considerable influence. Later novels were *Lucy Church Amiably* (1930) and *Things as They Are* (1950). In *Tender Buttons* (1914), a book of verse, she eschewed ordinary logic and grammar, and she published two books embodying her literary theories, *How to Write* (1931) and *Lectures in America* (1935). Books of reminiscence are *Autobiography of Alice B. Toklas* (Miss Toklas was her secretary, and the book is really about herself), and *Everybody's Autobiography* (1935). *Wars I Have Seen* (1945) told of her experiences in France, where she remained during the German occupation, and her last book, *Brewsie and Willie* (1946) is about the American infantryman.

Steinbeck, John Ernest (27 Feb. 1902—   ), novelist, born at Salinas, California, was of German descent. After studying science at Stanford University he worked successively as labourer, druggist, caretaker, fruit-picker, and surveyor. His first novel, *Cup of Gold* (1929), was about Morgan the pirate. *The Grapes of Wrath* (1939), his most popular book, tells of a migratory family seeking work in California; it was awarded the Pulitzer Prize, and has been compared in its influence with *Uncle Tom's Cabin*. Others of his novels are *To a God Unknown* (1933), *Tortilla Flat* (1935), *In Dubious Battle* (1936), *Of Mice and Men* (1937), *The Forgotten Village* (1941), *The Moon is Down* (1942), *Cannery Row* (1946), *The Wayward Bus* (1947), *The Pearl* (1947), *East of Eden* (1952), and *Sweet Thursday* (1954). *Pastures of Heaven* (1932), *Saint Katy the Virgin* (1936), *The*

Red Pony (1937), and *The Long Valley* (1938) are collections of short stories. *Russian Journey,* a travel book, describes a visit made in 1948. He was married three times.

Stephen, Sir James (3 Jan. 1789—14 Sept. 1859), statesman and historian, was born in Lambeth, son of a lawyer, educated at Cambridge, and called to the Bar at Lincoln's Inn in 1811. He became permanent counsel to the Colonial Office and Board of Trade in 1825, and from 1826 to 1847 was permanent Under-Secretary for the Colonies, in which capacity he exercised an immense influence on the colonial policy of the empire, and did much to bring about the abolition of the slave trade. Impaired health led to his resignation, when he was made K.C.B. and a Privy Councillor. He was afterwards Professor of Modern History at Cambridge from 1849 to 1859, and of the same subject at the East India College at Haileybury from 1855 to 1857. He wrote *Essays in Ecclesiastical Biography* (1849) and *Lectures on the History of France* (1852).

Stephen, James Kenneth (25 Feb. 1859—3 Feb. 1892), poet and parodist, son of Sir James Fitzjames Stephen, was educated at Eton, where he distinguished himself at games, and went on to King's College, Cambridge, of which he became a Fellow in 1885. After being called to the Bar he resided at Cambridge and took pupils. During this period he wrote two collections of light verse, *Quo, Musa, Tendis?* and *Lapsus Calami,* both published in 1891; his parodies are among the best of their kind.

Stephen, Sir Leslie (28 Nov. 1832—22 Feb. 1904), biographer, was born in Kensington and educated at Eton, King's College, London, and Trinity Hall, Cambridge, of which he became a Fellow. A good long-distance runner and a keen oarsman, he once walked from Cambridge to London in 12 hours. From 1865 to 1868 he was President of the Alpine Club, and among his early publications were *Peaks, Passes, and Glaciers* (1862) and *The Playground of Europe* (1871). In 1864 he settled in London and wrote for the *Saturday Review, Cornhill Magazine,* and other periodicals essays which were collected as *Hours in a Library* (three series, 1874, 1876, 1879). From 1871 to 1882 he was editor of the *Cornhill,* and knew many eminent writers. In 1882 he was given the task of editing the *Dictionary of National Biography,* which he carried out till 1891. His *English Literature and Society in the Eighteenth Century* was published on the day of his death. He married a daughter of Thackeray the novelist, and Virginia Woolf (q.v.) was his own daughter by his second wife. He was knighted in 1902.

Stephens, James (2 Feb. 1882—26 Dec. 1950), poet and story writer, was born in the slums of Dublin and brought up in poverty with practically no schooling. While working as a clerk he was discovered by George Russell (q.v.), who helped him to get his first book of poems, *Insurrections,* published in 1909. In 1911 he was co-founder of the *Irish Review,* in which appeared his first novel, *The Charwoman's Daughter.* In 1912 he won the Polignac Prize with *The Crock of Gold,* a prose fantasy, and in 1923 was awarded the Tailltean Gold Medal for *Deirdre,* a romance. His volumes of verse include *The Hill of Venus* (1912), *Songs from the Clay* (1915), *The Adventures of Seumas Beg* (1915), *The Rocky Road to Dublin* (1915), *Green Branches* (1916), *Reincarnation* (1918), and *Kings and the Moon* (1938). Collections of short stories are *Here Are Ladies* (1913) and *Etched in Moonlight* (1928). His tales are a strange blend of realism and fancy, full of mysticism and subtle wisdom. Under five feet in height and sometimes compared with a leprechaun, he appropriately made an anthology of *Irish Fairy Tales* (1920).

Stephens, Thomas (21 April 1821—4 Jan. 1875), historian and critic, born at Pont Nedd Fechan, Glamorganshire, son of a shoe-maker, was educated at Neath Grammar School and became a chemist. His works include *The Literature of the Kymry* (1849), *The History of Trial by Jury in Wales*, and an essay in which he demolished the claim of the Welsh under Madoc to the discovery of America. He also wrote on the life and works of the bard Aneurin. The critical methods which he adopted in his works often made him unpopular with the less discriminating enthusiasts for the glory of Wales, but he earned the respect of serious scholars.

Sterling, John (20 July 1806—18 Sept. 1844), author, son of a journalist, was born at Kames Castle, Bute, and educated at Glasgow University and Cambridge. At the latter he became acquainted with a group of brilliant men, including F. D. Maurice, Trench, and Monckton Milnes. He took orders and became curate to Julius Hare (q.v.); but intellectual difficulties and indifferent health led to his resignation within a year, and the rest of his life was passed in alternating between England and warmer climates. He wrote for *Blackwood's Magazine* and the *Westminster* and *Quarterly Reviews*, and published *The Election* (1841), a humorous poem, and *Strafford* (1843), a tragedy. His *Essays and Tales* were edited in 1848, but his memory, perpetuated in a remarkable memoir by Carlyle, lives rather by what he was than by anything he did.

Stern, Gladys Bronwyn (17 June 1890—   ), novelist, born in London, was educated at Notting Hill High School, after which she travelled in Germany and Switzerland and studied for two years at the London Academy of Dramatic Art. Her first novel, *Pantomime*, appeared in 1914 and was followed by *Grand Chain* (1917). In 1919 she married Geoffrey Lisle Holdsworth; later they were divorced. Her 'Matriarch' novels, in which the leading character is modelled on her great-aunt, who lived to be 90, include *Tents of Israel* (1924), *A Deputy Was King* (1926), *Mosaic* (1930), *Shining and Free* (1935), and *The Young Matriarch* (1942). Others of her books are *Dogs in an Omnibus* (1942), *Trumpet Voluntary* (1944), *Reasonable Shores* (1946), *No Son of Mine* (1948), *Benefits Forgot* (1949), *A Duck to Water* (1949), *The Donkey Shoe* (1952), and *A Name to Conjure With* (1953). She also wrote a study of Robert Louis Stevenson and collaborated with Sheila Kaye-Smith (q.v.) in two books on Jane Austen. *Monogram* (1936) and *Another Part of the Wood* (1941) are autobiographical. In 1947 she became a Roman Catholic, and described her conversion later in *All in Good Time* (1954).

Sterne, Laurence (24 Nov. 1713—18 March 1768), novelist, son of an officer in the army, and the great-grandson of an Archbishop of York, was born at Clonmel, County Tipperary, where his father's regiment happened to be stationed, and passed part of his boyhood in Ireland. At the age of 10 he was handed over to a relation who put him to school at Halifax, and thereafter sent him to Cambridge. He became a parson, a profession for which he was very indifferently fitted, and through family influence procured the living of Sutton, Yorkshire. In 1741 he married Elizabeth Lumley, daughter of a clergyman, whose influence obtained for him in addition an adjacent benefice, and he also became a prebendary of York. It was not until 1760 that the first two volumes of his famous novel, *Tristram Shandy*, appeared. Its peculiar and original style of humour, its whimsicality, and perhaps also its defiance of conventionality, and even its frequent lapses into indecorum, achieved for it an immediate and immense popularity. Sterne went up to London and became the lion of the day, and was presented by a nobleman with the perpetual curacy of Coxwold in Yorkshire. The third and fourth volumes appeared in 1761, the fifth and sixth in 1762, the seventh and eighth in 1765, and the last in 1767. Meanwhile he had published the *Sermons of Mr Yorick* (1760), and his remaining work, *The Sentimental Journey*, appeared in 1768. From the time of his finding himself a celebrity his parishioners saw but little of him, his time being passed either in the gaieties of London or in travelling on the Continent.

Latterly he was practically separated from his wife and only daughter, to the former of whom his behaviour had been anything but exemplary. His health, which had begun to give way soon after his literary career had commenced, finally broke down, and he died in London of consumption. His body was followed to the grave by one coach containing his publisher and another gentleman; and it was exhumed and appeared in a few days upon the table of the anatomical professor at Cambridge. He died in debt, but a subscription was raised for his wife and daughter, the latter of whom married a Frenchman, and is said to have perished under the guillotine. Contemptible as a man, Sterne possessed undoubted genius. He had wit, originality, and pathos, though the last not seldom runs into mawkishness, and an exquisitely delicate and glancing style. He has contributed some immortal characters to English fiction, including Uncle Toby and Corporal Trim. His great faults as a writer are affectation and a peculiarly deliberate kind of indecency, which his profession renders all the more offensive; and he was by no means scrupulous in adopting, without acknowledgment, the good things of previous writers.

Sternhold, Thomas (1500—23 Aug. 1549), versifier, is said to have been born at Southampton and educated at Oxford. He became one of the Grooms of the Robes to Henry VIII. Along with John Hopkins (q.v.) he was author of the metrical version of the Psalms which was formerly attached to the Prayer Book and was for two centuries the hymn book of the English Church. Compiled in 1562, it was gradually displaced by the later version of Tate and Brady.

It set the fashion for using ballad metre as the conventional verse form for psalms and hymns.

Stevenson, Burton Egbert (9 Nov. 1872—   ), compiler and novelist, was born at Chillicothe, Ohio, where he became librarian, a post he held all his life. He was educated at Princeton, paying his way by working as journalist and printer. In 1918 he was given the task of organizing the American Library in Paris. He compiled several large reference works, including *The Home Book of Quotations* (1934), *The Home Book of Shakespeare Quotations* (1937), *The Home Book of Proverbs, Maxims, and Familiar Phrases* (1948), and *The Home Book of Bible Quotations* (1949). He also wrote many detective stories, including *The Holladay Case* (1903), *The Marathon Mystery* (1904), and *The Mystery of a Boule Cabinet* (1912). He was a member of the National Institute of Arts and Letters.

Stevenson, Dorothy Emily (1892—   ), novelist, born in Edinburgh, was the daughter of an engineer of the Northern Lighthouse Board and a cousin of Robert Louis Stevenson; her mother was a cousin of Lord Roberts. In 1916 she married Major James R. Peploe, and eventually they settled at Moffat. Her best-known novels are *Mrs Tim of the Regiment* (1932), with its sequels *Golden Days* (1934), *Mrs Tim Carries On* (1941), *Mrs Tim Gets a Job* (1947), and *Mrs Tim Flies Home* (1952); and the Miss Buncle series, which includes *Miss Buncle's Book* (1934) and *Miss Buncle Married* (1936). Others are *Divorce from Reality* (1935), *A World in Spell* (1936), *Miss Bun the Baker's Daughter* (1938), *Green Money* (1939), *Spring Magic* (1941), *Kate Hardy* (1947), *Vittoria Cottage* (1949), *Winter and Rough Weather* (1951), and *Charlotte Fairlie* (1954). *It's Nice to Be Me* (1943) is a collection of verse for children.

Stevenson, Robert Louis (13 Nov. 1850—4 Dec. 1894), poet, novelist, and essayist, was born in Edinburgh, his original middle names being Lewis Balfour, and was educated at Edinburgh Academy and University. Both his father and his grandfather had been lighthouse builders, and it was at first intended that he also should be an engineer, but the lung weakness from which he suffered all his life made this inadvisable, and he studied law, being called to the Scottish Bar in 1875. His main interest, however, lay in literature, and by that time he had already written for various periodicals. In 1876 he made a trip through France by canoe and wrote of it in his first book, *An Inland Voyage* (1878); a later tour, made by land, was described in *Travels with a Donkey in the Cevennes* (1879). During these journeys he met and fell in love with Fanny Osbourne, an American woman ten years his senior who was estranged from her husband, and in 1879, when she secured a divorce, he sailed to America on an emigrant ship and married her in California. In the following year he returned to Scotland and began writing *Treasure Island*, which first appeared as a serial in *Young Folks*, and when published as a book in 1882 was recognized as one of the finest adventure stories for boys ever written.

Its success was a turning-point in Stevenson's career. Moving first to Switzerland, then to the Riviera in search of health, he wrote *The Black Arrow* (1888), another first-rate boy's story (though he himself deprecated its 'tushery'), and much of *A Child's Garden of Verses* (1885), which contains many delightful poems for children. Back in England, he lived at Bournemouth from 1884 to 1887, and wrote *Kidnapped*, in many ways his finest work; an exciting story, it has in Alan Breck an engaging hero, and has authentic Scottish atmosphere. In 1887 appeared a volume of poems, *Underwoods*, and in the same year he sailed again for America in search of a more congenial climate. This he eventually found at Apia in Samoa, where in his house 'Vailima' he lived from 1890 to 1894, venerated by the islanders, who gave him the native name Tusitala, or Teller of Tales. *The Master of Ballantrae*, one of his most powerful novels, appeared in 1889, and *Catriona*, a sequel to *Kidnapped* which contains the fine tale of Tod Lapraik, in 1893. He then began *St Ives* and *Weir of Hermiston*, both of which were left unfinished when he died suddenly of a brain haemorrhage at the age of 44. His letters written from Samoa were collected and published as *Vailima Letters* in 1895, and his *Collected Poems* in 1951. The standard life, by his cousin Sir Graham Balfour, appeared in 1901.

Stevenson was an accomplished stylist; he formed his technique carefully 'playing the sedulous ape,' as he himself relates, to various masters of English prose in turn. His most finished work appears in his books of essays, *Virginibus Puerisque* (1881), which takes its title 'To Maidens and Boys' from an ode of Horace, *Familiar Studies of Men and Books* (1882), and *Memories and Portraits* (1887). In his novels he ranged from the macabre study of *Dr Jekyll and Mr Hyde* (1886), and the spirited absurdities of the *New Arabian Nights* (1882), to the 'judicious levity' of those written in collaboration with Lloyd Osbourne, his stepson, *The Wrong Box* (1889) and *The Wrecker* (1892). His plays, *Deacon Brodie* (1880) and others written in collaboration with W. E. Henley (q.v.) were not a success. For all his many-sided genius, the volume of work which he left behind is not large, but it merits exceptional admiration because of the handicaps under which it was produced. Stevenson's whole life was a desperate struggle with ill health, and his determination to work strenuously even under the shadow of death makes him one of the most heroic figures in English literature.

Stewart, Alfred Walter (1880—1 July 1947), scientist who wrote detective stories under the name J. J. Connington, was born in Glasgow, son of a professor, was educated at Glasgow University and Marburg, and became Professor of Chemistry at Queen's University, Belfast. His *Recent Advances in Organic Chemistry* (1908) went through several editions. Among his detective stories are *Nordenholt's Millions* (1923), *Death at Swaythling Court* (1926), *The Dangerfield Talisman* (1926), *Murder in the Maze* (1927), *The Case with Nine Solutions* (1928), *The Eye in the Museum* (1929), *The Two Tickets Puzzle* (1930), *The Boat-House Riddle* (1931), *The Castleford Conundrum* (1932), *The Ha-Ha Case* (1934), *A Minor Operation* (1937), *For Murder Will Speak* (1938), *The Twenty-One Clues* (1941), and *Jack-in-the-Box* (1944). *Alias J. J. Connington* (1947) is an autobiography.

Stewart, Dugald (22 Nov. 1753—11 June 1828), philosopher, was born in Edinburgh, son of the Professor of Mathematics, and educated at Edinburgh High School and University. At the age of 19 he began to assist his father in his classes, receiving the appointment of regular assistant two years later. In 1785 he became Professor of Moral Philosophy, and rendered the chair illustrious by his learning and eloquence, his pupils including Lords Palmerston, Russell, and Lansdowne. Although he exercised great influence, Stewart was rather a brilliant expositor than an original thinker, and in the main followed Reid (q.v.). His works include *Philosophy of the Human Mind* (three volumes, 1792, 1813, 1827), *Outlines of Moral Philosophy* (1793), *Philosophical Essays* (1810), *Dissertation on the Progress of Metaphysical and Ethical Philosophy* (two parts, 1815, 1821), and *View of the Active and Moral Powers of Man* (1828). He also wrote memoirs of Robertson the historian, Adam Smith, and Thomas Reid. The Whig party, which he had always supported, on their accession to power, created for him the office of Gazette-writer for Scotland, in recognition of his services to philosophy. His later years were passed in retirement at Kinneil House on the Forth.

Stewart, John Innes Mackintosh (30 Sept. 1906—   ), scholar who wrote detective stories under the name Michael Innes, was born near Edinburgh and educated at Edinburgh Academy and Oxford, where he won the Matthew Arnold Memorial Prize. After five years as a lecturer at Leeds he was appointed in 1935 to the Chair of English at Adelaide University, and started writing stories to beguile the tedium of the long voyage to Australia. In 1945 he returned from there to become a lecturer at Queen's University, Belfast, and in 1949 was elected a Student (i.e. Fellow) of Christ Church, Oxford. His detective novels are high-brow and intellectual, sometimes over-erudite. His sleuth, Inspector Appleby, first appears in *Seven Suspects* (1936), which was followed by *Hamlet, Revenge!* (1937) and *Lament for a Maker* (1938), all highly successful. Later works are *The Spider Strikes* (1939), *A Comedy of Terrors* (1940), *The Secret Vanguard* (1941), *The Daffodil Affair* (1942), *What Happened at Hazlewood* (1946), *Operation Pax* (1951), *Private View* (1952), and *The Man from the Sea* (1955). Under his own name Stewart edited Florio's translation of Montaigne (1931) and wrote *Character and Motive in Shakespeare* (1949).

Stillingfleet, Edward (17 April 1635—27 March 1699), theologian, born at Cranbourne, Dorsetshire, and educated at Cambridge, took orders, and held many preferments, including a royal chaplaincy, the deanery of St Paul's (1678), and the bishopric of Worcester (1689). He was a frequent speaker in the House of Lords, and had considerable influence as a churchman. A keen controversialist, he wrote many treatises, including *The Irenicum* (1685), which advocated compromise with the Presbyterians, *The Unreasonableness of Separation* (1681), and *Origines Britannicae, or Antiquities of British Churches* (1685).

Stirling, James Hutchison (22 June 1820—19 March 1909), philosopher, born in Glasgow, and educated there and at Edinburgh, where he studied medicine, practised as a doctor until the death of his father in 1851, after which he devoted himself to philosophy. His *Secret of Hegel* (1865) gave a great impulse to the study and understanding of the Hegelian philosophy both at home and in America, and was also accepted as a work of authority in Germany and Italy. Other works, all characterized by keen philosophical insight and masterly power of exposition, are *Complete Text-book to Kant* (1881), *Philosophy and Theology* (1890), *What is Thought? or the Problem of Philosophy* (1900), and *The Categories* (1903). Literary studies include *Jerrold, Tennyson, and Macaulay* (1868), *Burns in Drama* (1878), and *Philosophy in the Poets* (1885).

Stirling, William Alexander, Earl of (1567—12 Sept. 1640), statesman and poet, born at Alva, Clackmannanshire, studied at Glasgow University and Leyden. A courtier, he followed James VI to England and received from him the grant of a vast tract of land in what is now Canada, but this was invalidated by the French conquests. In 1626 he became Secretary of State for Scotland, and in 1633 was made an Earl by Charles I. Two of his publications, *Aurora* (1604) and *Recreations with the Muses* (1637) consist of love lyrics and moral poems; he also wrote a long dreary epic on *Doomsday* (1614—37) and four 'Monarchic Tragedies,' *Darius* (1603), *Croesus* (1604), *The Alexandraean Tragedy* (1605), and *Julius Caesar* (1607), of which the theme is the downfall of ambition.

Stirling-Maxwell, Sir William, Bart. (8 March 1818—15 Jan. 1878), historian and writer on art, son of Archibald Stirling of Keir, was educated at Cambridge, and then travelled in Spain and the Levant. He sat in the House of Commons for Perthshire from 1852 to 1868 and from 1874 to 1880, served on various commissions and public bodies, and was Lord Rector successively of the University of St Andrews and Edinburgh, and Chancellor of that of Glasgow. His works include *Annals of the Artists of Spain* (1848), *The Cloister Life of the Emperor Charles V* (1852), and *Don John of Austria,* published posthumously in 1885. They were all distinguished by research and full information, and the last two are standard authorities. He married as his second wife Caroline Norton (q.v.).

Stockley, Cynthia (1877—15 Jan. 1936), novelist, was born at Bloemfontein, South Africa, and educated in England. In Rhodesia she married Philip George Watts Stockley, and after his death she married Captain H. E. Pelham Browne. In 1898 she came to England, worked for a time as a journalist in London and also was an actress in Benson's Shakespeare Company. Her works include *Virginia of the Rhodesians* (1904), *Poppy* (1910), *The Claw* (1911), *The Dream Ship* (1913), *Wild Honey* (1914), *Blue Aloes* (1918), *Pink Gods and Blue Demons* (1920), *Ponjola* (1923), *Perilous Women* (1927), *Three Farms* (1927), *Leopard in the Bush* (1928), *Tagati Magic* (1930), *Kraal Baby* (1933), and *Perilous Stuff* (1936).

Stockton, Frank Richard (5 April 1834—20 April 1902), novelist, was born in Philadelphia and worked as a wood engraver. After the success of *Ting-a-Ling* (1870), a volume of short stories for young

Y*

people, he turned from art to writing. Among a dozen volumes of short stories the most outstanding is 'The Lady or the Tiger' (1884), which left the reader with an impossible dilemma. He wrote a number of humorous novels full of absurdities, the best-known being *Rudder Grange* (1879), with its two sequels *The Rudder Grangers Abroad* (1891) and *Pomona's Travels* (1894); others are *The Casting Away of Mrs Lecks and Mrs Aleshine* (1886) and *The Adventures of Captain Horn* (1895).

Stoddard, Richard Henry (2 July 1825—12 May 1903), poet and critic, was born at Hingham, Massachusetts; his father, a sea captain, was drowned when the son was a baby. After a squalid upbringing in the course of which he moved to Boston and then to New York, he tried various jobs and at 18 became an iron moulder. After he became known through his poems in various periodicals Nathaniel Hawthorne got him an appointment in the Customs, which he held from 1853 to 1870. Later, from 1880 till his death, he was literary editor of the *Mail and Express*. His books include *Songs of Summer* (1857), *Poems* (1880), *The Lion's Cub* (1890), and *Recollections, Personal and Literary* (1903). He has been called the Nestor of American literature.

Stoker, Bram (1847—20 April 1912), novelist whose original name was Abraham, was born in Dublin, son of a government official. In his childhood he was an invalid, but in after years he became one of the leading athletes of Dublin University, as well as having a brilliant academic career there. For 10 years he worked in the Irish Civil Service, and in 1878 published *The Duties of Clerks of Petty Sessions in Ireland*. In the same year he became Henry Irving's acting manager at the Lyceum, and later he wrote *Personal Reminiscences of Henry Irving* (1906). After producing some unimportant novels, in 1897 he published *Dracula*, which has been styled the most blood-curdling horror story in English literature and sold over a million copies; a sequel, *Dracula's Guest*, appeared posthumously in 1914. Others of his books are *The Mystery of the Sea* (1902), *The Jewel of the Seven Stars* (1904), *The Lady of the Shroud* (1909), and *The Lair of the White Worm* (1911).

Stone, Louis (1871—23 Sept. 1935), novelist, was born in Leicester but taken by his parents to Australia in 1884. Educated at Sydney University, he became a master at Sydney Boys' High School. His first novel, *Jonah* (1911), a story of Sydney's underworld, was followed by *Betty Wayside* (1915). He married Abbie Allen, who shared his taste for music.

Storer, Thomas (1571—Nov. 1604), poet, born in London, and educated at Oxford, wrote a long poem, *The Life and Death of Thomas Wolsey, Cardinal* (1599).

Story, William Wetmore (12 Feb. 1819—7 Oct. 1895), poet and sculptor, was born at Salem, Massachusetts, son of Judge Joseph Story, whose *Life and Letters* he edited. After studying law at Harvard he settled in Italy, where he became a friend of the Brownings and was given honorary degrees by Rome and Bologna. His writings include *Roba di Roma* (1862), *The Tragedy of Nero* (1875), *The Castle of St Angelo* (1877), and *Excursions in Art and Letters* (1891).

Stout, Rex Todhunter (1 Dec. 1886—   ), novelist, was born of Quaker parents at Noblesville, Indiana, but was brought up in Kansas.   At 18 he joined the Navy, but left it after two years and planned to become a lawyer, eventually turning to writing instead. His first books were psychological novels, and he was 48 before the publication of *Fer-de-Lance*, his first crime story, in which the central figure is Nero Wolfe, the temperamental adipose detective with a passion for orchids.   Others of his books are *The League of Frightened Men* (1935), *Too Many Cooks* (1938), *Some Buried Caesar* (1939), *Over My Dead Body* (1940), *Black Orchids* (1942), *Not Quite Dead Enough* (1944), *Too Many Women* (1947), *Trouble in Triplicate* (1949), *Murder by the Book* (1951), *Prisoner's Base* (1952), *The Golden Spiders* (1953), and *The Black Mountain* (1954).

Stow, John (1525?—6 April 1605), historian and antiquary, born in London, son of a tailor, was brought up to the same trade.   He had, however, an irresistible taste for transcribing and collecting ancient documents, and pursuing antiquarian and historical researches, to which he ultimately entirely devoted himself.   This he was enabled to do partly through the generosity of Archbishop Parker.   He made large collections of old books and manuscripts, and wrote and edited several works of importance and authority, including *The Workes of Geoffrey Chaucer* (1561), *Summarie of Englyshe Chronicles* (1561), afterwards called *Annales of England*, and editions of the chronicles of Matthew Paris and Thomas Walsingham, and of Holinshed's *Chronicle*.   His principal work, however, is his *Survey of London* (1598), which gives a valuable description of the city in Shakespeare's time.   The only reward of his sacrifices and labours in the public interest was a patent from James I to collect 'among our loving subjects their voluntary contributions and kind gratuities.'

Stowe, Harriet Beecher (14 June 1811—1 July 1896), novelist, was born at Litchfield, Connecticut, daughter of Lyman Beecher, a Congregationalist minister who became President of Lane Theological Seminary, and was a sister of Henry Ward Beecher (q.v.); she was brought up under the strictest Puritan discipline.   In 1832 the family moved to Cincinnati, where she worked as a teacher.   In 1836 she married Calvin Ellis Stowe, Professor of Biblical Literature in her father's seminary.   In 1850 he became a professor at Bowdoin College in Maine, to which they removed.   Harriet Stowe's novel of slave life, *Uncle Tom's Cabin, or, Life Among the Lowly,* appeared as a serial in *The National Era* in 1851 and was published as a book in the following year.   It quickly became world famous, and had a powerful effect on promoting the cause of emancipation.   Of her later novels, *Dred* (1856) is another slavery story, while *The Minister's Wooing* (1859), *The Pearl of Orr's Island* (1862), and *Oldtown Folks* (1869) tell of life in the New England of her girlhood.   After the Civil War she lived in Florida, of which she wrote in *Palmetto Leaves* (1873).

Strachey, Giles Lytton (1 March 1880—21 Jan. 1932), critic and biographer, was born in London, son of General Sir Richard Strachey, and educated at Liverpool University and Cambridge, where he won the Chancellor's English Medal. Adopting a writing career, he worked for the *Spectator*, then edited by his cousin J. St Loe Strachey, wrote reviews and articles, and became the focus of the so-called Bloomsbury Group, which included E. M. Forster, Virginia Woolf, and Roger Fry. Breaking away from the tradition that biographies should chronicle only the subject's virtues, he created the new 'debunking' school. In particular he attacked the most famous Victorians, but attained his greatest success with his *Queen Victoria* (1921), in which his irony and cynicism was tempered with the affection he felt for the old queen; it was awarded the Tait Black Memorial Prize. Others of his works are *Landmarks in French Literature* (1912), *Eminent Victorians* (1918), *Books and Characters* (1922), *Pope* (1925), *Elizabeth and Essex* (1928), *Portraits in Miniature* (1931), and *Characters and Commentaries* (1933).

Straus, Ralph Sidney Albert (5 Sept. 1882—5 June 1950), novelist and critic, was born in Manchester and educated at Harrow and Cambridge. Of his novels the best-known is *The Orley Tradition* (1914); others are *The Man Apart* (1906), *The Dust Which is God* (1907), *The Scandalous Mrs Waldo* (1909), *5000 A.D.* (1911), *Carriages and Coaches* (1912), *Pengard Awake* (1920), *Volcano* (1922), *The Unseemly Adventure* (1924), *Married Alive* (1925), *Our Wiser Sons* (1926), and *Five Men Go to Prison* (1935). His critical and biographical works include *Robert Dodsley* (1910), *The Unspeakable Curll* (1927), *Dickens, a Portrait in Pencil* (1928), *Dickens, the Man and the Book* (1936), and *Sala, the Portrait of an Eminent Victorian* (1942).

Strickland, Agnes (19 Aug. 1796—13 July 1874), biographer, born in London, was educated by her father, and began her literary career with a poem, *Worcester Field*. She later published *Historical Tales of Illustrious British Children* (1833), *The Pilgrims of Walsingham* (1835), and *Tales and Stories from History* (1836). Her chief works, however, are *Lives of the Queens of England* (1840—8), and *Lives of the Queens of Scotland, and English Princesses Connected with the Royal Succession of Great Britain* (eight volumes, 1850—9), *Lives of the Bachelor Kings of England* (1861), and *Letters of Mary Queen of Scots* (1843); in some of her books she was assisted by her sister Elizabeth. Though laborious and conscientious she lacked the judicial faculty, and her style does not rise above mediocrity.

Strode, William (1602—11 March 1645), poet, was born at Plympton, Devonshire, and showing studious tendencies, was sent to Westminister School and Oxford. While at the University he began to manifest his poetic talents, and generally distinguished himself, being elected in 1629 Public Orator. He took orders and, on Richard Corbet (q.v.) becoming Bishop of Oxford became his chaplain. Later he was rector of East Bredenham, Norfolk, and of Badley, Northamptonshire, and Canon of Christ Church. On the outbreak of the Civil War he attached himself warmly to the cause of the King. he was a High Churchman, and had a reputation as 'a witty and

sententious preacher, an exquisite orator, and an eminent poet.'
As a poet he shines most in lyrics and elegies. With much of the
artificiality of his age he shows gracefulness, a feeling for the country,
and occasional gleams of tenderness. His play, *The Floating Island*,
a political allegory, was produced in 1633 and played before the Court
then on a visit to Oxford, where it was a subject of complaint that it
had more moralizing than amusement.

Strong, Leonard Alfred George (8 March 1896—16 Aug. 1958),
poet and novelist, was born near Plymouth, of Irish parents, and
often spent the summer with his grandparents in Dublin. Educated
at Brighton College and Oxford, where he worked as a schoolmaster
for 10 years, he moved to London in 1930. His volumes of verse
include *Dublin Days* (1921), *The Lowery Road* (1924), *At Glenan
Cross* (1928), *Northern Light* (1930), and *Call to the Swans* (1936).
Among his novels are *Dewer Rides* (1929), *The Jealous Ghost* (1930),
The Garden (1931), *Sea Wall* (1933), *Corporal Tune* (1934), *Mr
Sheridan's Umbrella* (1935), *Laughter in the West* (1937), *The Bay*
(1941), *The Director* (1944), and *Trevannion* (1948). Collections of
his short stories are *Doyle's Rock* (1925), *The English Captain* (1929),
Don Juan and the Wheelbarrow (1932), *Tuesday Afternoon* (1935),
The Travellers (1945), which was awarded the Tait Black Memorial
Prize, and *Darling Tom* (1952). He also wrote several detective
stories and a number of books for children. Critical works include
studies of Tom Moore (1937) and J. M. Synge (1941), and *The Sacred
River* (1949), a book about James Joyce.

Strype, John (1 Nov. 1643—11 Dec. 1737), ecclesiastical historian,
was born in London, son of a merchant from Brabant. Educated at
St Paul's School and Cambridge, he took orders and, among other
livings, held the rectory of Low Leyton, Essex, for upwards of 60
years. He made a large collection of original documents, chiefly
relating to the Tudor period, and was a voluminous author. Among
his works are *Memorials of Archbishop Cranmer* (1694), *Life of Sir
Thomas Smith, Secretary of State to Edward VI and Elizabeth* (1698),
Annals of the Reformation (1709—31), and *Ecclesiastical Memorials*
(1721); besides lives of Bishop Aylmer, and Archbishops Grindal,
Parker, and Whitgift. He was a painstaking and honest, but dull
and unmethodical, writer.

Stuart, Francis (29 April 1902—   ), novelist, was
born in Queensland of Irish parents. Coming to England, he was
educated at Rugby, then in 1920 went to live in Dublin and was
converted to Roman Catholicism. He fought in the Irish civil war,
was interned from 1922 to 1923, and then settled in Wicklow. His
volume of poems *We Have Kept the Faith* (1923) was awarded a prize
by the Royal Irish Academy. From 1939 to 1944 he was a lecturer
in English at the University of Berlin. His novels include *Women
and God* (1930), *Pigeon Irish* (1932), *The Coloured Dome* (1932), *Try
the Sky* (1933), *Glory* (1933), *In Search of Love* (1935), *White Hare*
(1936), *Julie* (1938), *The Great Squire* (1939), *The Silver Ship* (1940),
The Pillar of Cloud (1948), *Redemption* (1949), *The Flowering Cross*
(1950), *The Wild Wings* (1951), *The Chariot* (1953), and *Pilgrimage*
(1955). *Things We Live For* (1935) is autobiographical.

Stuart, Gilbert (1742—13 Aug. 1786), historian, born in Edinburgh, son of the Professor of Latin, was educated at Edinburgh High School and University. Among his publications were *An Historical Dissertation on the English Constitution* (1768), *Discourse on the Government and Laws of England* (1772), *A View of Society in Europe* (1778), and a *History of Scotland* (1782). He was a man of extremely jealous and implacable temper, and made venomous attacks on the historical works of Robertson and Henry. His own writings, though well-written, are inaccurate.

Stubbes *or* **Stubbs, Philip** (1555?—1610?), pamphleteer, studied at Oxford and Cambridge but took no degree. In 1583 he published *The Anatomy of Abuses*, a puritanical pamphlet denouncing the evils of the time; it contains a section on plays and is an important source of information for the Elizabethan theatre. Another of Stubbes's works is *A Crystal Glass for Christian Women* (1590).

Stubbs, William (21 June 1825—22 April 1901), historian, son of a solicitor, was born at Knaresborough, Yorkshire, and educated there and at the Grammar School of Ripon, and Oxford. In 1848 he became a Fellow of Trinity College, and in the same year took orders and was appointed to the collegiate living of Navestock in Essex, where he remained for 16 years, during which he began his historical researches, and published his earlier works. His first publication was *Hymnale Secundum Usum Sarum*. In 1858 appeared *Registrum Sacrum Anglicanum*, a calendar of English bishops from Augustine; and then followed editions of several Chronicles in the Rolls Series. The learning and critical insight displayed in these works commanded the attention and admiration of historical scholars both at home and on the Continent. In 1862 he was appointed librarian of Lambeth Palace, and in 1866 Professor of Modern History at Oxford. There he published in 1870 his *Select Charters*, and his chief work, *The Constitutional History of England* (three volumes, 1874—9), which at once became the standard authority on its subject. It covers the period down to 1485. In 1879 he was appointed a Canon of St Paul's and in 1884 Bishop of Chester, whence he was translated five years later to Oxford. As an active prelate he was necessarily largely withdrawn from his historical researches; but at Chester he edited two volumes of William of Malmesbury. Stubbs was greater as a historian than as a writer, but he brought to his work sound judgment, insight, accuracy, and impartiality. He was a member of the French and Prussian Academies.

Stukeley, William (7 Nov. 1687—27 Feb. 1765), antiquary, born at Holbeach, Lincolnshire, son of an attorney, was at Cambridge, studied medicine, and after practising as a doctor took orders in 1729 and held benefices at Stamford and in London. He made antiquarian tours through England, and was one of the founders of the Society of Antiquaries, to which he acted as secretary. He published *Itinerarium Curiosum* (1724) and *Stonehenge* (1740). He made a special study of Druidism, and was called 'the Arch-Druid.'

Suckling, Sir John (10 Feb. 1609—1642), poet and dramatist, son of a knight who had held office as Secretary of State and Comptroller of the Household to James I, was born at Twickenham, Middlesex, educated at Cambridge, and thereafter went to Gray's Inn. On the death of his father in 1627, he inherited large estates. After travelling in France and Italy, he is said to have served for a short time under Gustavus Adolphus. On his return he was knighted, and went to Court, where his wealth, generosity, and wit made him a general favourite. When Charles I was moving against the Scots Suckling fitted out a gorgeously appointed troop for his service which, however, were said to have fled at first sight of the Scots army at Duns, an exploit which is ridiculed in the ballad of *Sir John Suckling's Campaign*. He got into trouble in connection with a plot to rescue Strafford from the Tower, and fled to the Continent. He died in Paris, it is said by his own hand. He was a noted gambler, and has the distinction of being the inventor of the game of cribbage. He wrote four plays, *Aglaura* (1637), *Brennoralt* (1646), *The Goblins* (1646), and *The Sad One* (unfinished); his fame rests on his songs and ballads, such as 'The Wedding,' which are distinguished by a gay and sparkling wit and a singular grace of expression.

Surrey, Henry Howard, Earl of (1517?–21 Jan. 1547), poet, son of Thomas Howard, 3rd Duke of Norfolk, was educated by John Clerke, a learned and travelled scholar, and secretary to his father. He became attached to the Court, was cup-bearer to King Henry VIII, ewerer at the Coronation, and Earl Marshall at the trial of Anne Bullen. In 1542 he was made a Knight of the Garter a few weeks after the execution of his cousin, Queen Catherine Howard. He suffered imprisonment more than once for being implicated in quarrels and brawls, did a good deal of fighting in Scotland and France, and was the last victim of Henry's insensate jealousy, being beheaded on a frivolous charge of conspiring against the succession of Edward VI. The death of Henry saved Norfolk from the same fate. Surrey shares with Sir Thomas Wyatt (q.v.) the honour of being the true successor of Chaucer in English poetry, and of bringing the sonnet from Italy to England. He was also, in his translation of Virgil's *Aeneid*, the first to use blank verse. The poems of Surrey, though well known in courtly circles, were not published during his life; 40 of them appeared in *Tottel's Miscellany* in 1557. He also paraphrased part of Ecclesiastes and a few of the Psalms. The Geraldine of his sonnets was Elizabeth Fitzgerald, daughter of the Earl of Kildare, then a lonely child at Court, her father being imprisoned in the Tower.

Surtees, Robert Smith (1803—16 March 1864), novelist, was born at Durham and educated at the Grammar School there. He became a solicitor, and was later a Justice of the Peace and High Sheriff of the county. In 1831 he started the *New Sporting Magazine*, and while editing it invented the character John Jorrocks, a sporting Cockney grocer who blended engaging absurdity with good-humoured vulgarity. It was the success of *Jorrocks's Jaunts and Jollities* (1838) that inspired the start of the *Pickwick Papers*, and Jorrocks appeared again in *Handley Cross* (1843). Others of Surtees's novels are *Hillingdon Hall* (1845), *Hawbuck Grange* (1847), *Mr Sponge's Sporting Tour* (1853), *Ask Mamma* (1858), *Plain or Ringlets* (1860), and *Mr Facey Romford's Hounds* (1865).

Sutro, Alfred (7 Aug. 1863—11 Sept. 1933), playwright, born in London, was educated at the City of London School and in Brussels. Successful in business, after his marriage to Ethel Stella Isaacs, sister of the Marquis of Reading, he devoted himself to writing and translated most of the plays of Maeterlinck, who was his lifelong friend. Of his own plays *The Walls of Jericho* (1906) was the most successful. Others are *Women in Love* (1902), *The Foolish Virgins* (1904), *The Fascinating Mr Vanderveldt* (1907), *The Perplexed Husband* (1913), *The Marriage Will Not Take Place* (1918), *The Choice* (1919), *Uncle Anyhow* (1919), *The Laughing Lady* (1922), *The Great Well* (1923), *Far Above Rubies* (1924), *The Desperate Lovers* (1926), and *Living Together* (1929). *Celebrities and Simple Souls* (1933) is a volume of reminiscences.

Swan, Annie S. (1859—17 June 1943), novelist, was born in Edinburgh, daughter of a farmer, and brought up at Gorebridge, Midlothian. Educated at Edinburgh Ladies' College she started as novelist with *Ups and Downs* (1878), but her first success came in 1883 with *Aldersyde*, a Border story in the Oliphant tradition, which was followed by *Carlowrie* (1884), sometimes reckoned her best book, *A Divided House* (1885), and *Gates of Eden* (1888). Meanwhile she had married Dr James Burnett Smith, and they moved to London, where she contributed extensively to *The Woman at Home*, a magazine founded by W. Robertson Nicoll. Her later novels, which were very numerous, include *Maitland of Laurieston* (1891), *A Lost Ideal* (1894), *A Victory Won* (1895), *The Curse of Cowden* (1897), *The Ne'er-do-Weel* (1897), *Prairie Fires* (1913), *The Step-mother* (1915), *A Vexed Inheritance* (1924), *Ursula Vivian* (1927), *The Pendulum* (1928), and *Marching Feet* (1931); *Sir Roderick's Will* (1898) is a collection of short stories. During the First World War she worked at the Ministry of Food while her husband was attached to the Black Watch, and their house in Hertford was bombed by zeppelins. In 1930 she was awarded the C.B.E. Her autobiography, *My Life*, appeared in 1934, and her *Letters* were edited in 1945.

Swift, Jonathan (30 Nov. 1667—19 Oct. 1745), satirist, was born in Dublin of English parents. Dryden was his cousin, and he also claimed kinship with Herrick. He was a posthumous child, and was brought up in circumstances of extreme poverty. He was sent to school at Kilkenny, where Congreve (q.v.) was his schoolmate, and afterwards went to Trinity College, Dublin, where he gave no evidence of ability, but displayed a turbulent and unruly temper, and only obtained a degree by 'special grace.' After the Revolution he joined his mother, then resident at Leicester, by whose influence he was admitted to the household of Sir William Temple (q.v.) at Moor Park. Here he acted as secretary and having access to a well-stocked library, made good use of his opportunities, and became

a keen student. At Moor Park he wrote pindaric odes, one of which
is said to have provoked Dryden's remark, 'Cousin Swift, you will
never be a poet'; he also met Esther Johnson (Stella), an illegitimate
daughter of Sir William, who was afterwards to enter so largely into
his life. Dissatisfied, apparently, that Temple did not do more for
his advancement, he left his service in 1694 and returned to Ireland,
where he took orders, and obtained the small living of Kilroot, near
Belfast. While there he wrote his *Tale of a Tub*, a satire on 'corruptions in religion and learning,' and *The Battle of the Books*, describing
in mock-heroic style a contest between ancients and moderns; these
two satires were published together in 1704.

In 1698 he threw up his living at the request of Temple, who felt
the want of his society and assistance, and returned to Moor Park.
On the death of his patron in 1699 he undertook by request the
publication of his works, and thereafter returned to Ireland as chaplain to the Lord Deputy, the Earl of Berkeley, from whom he obtained
some small preferments, including the vicarage of Laracor, and a
prebend in St Patrick's Cathedral. At this time he made frequent
visits to London and became the friend of Addison, Steele, Congreve,
and other Whig writers, and wrote various pamphlets, chiefly on
ecclesiastical subjects. In 1710, disgusted with the Whigs' neglect
alike of himself and of the claims of his Church, he abandoned
them and attached himself to Harley and Bolingbroke. The next
few years were filled with political controversy. He attacked the
Whigs in papers in the *Examiner* in 1710, and in his celebrated
pamphlets, *The Conduct of the Allies* (1712), *The Barrier Treaty* (1713),
and *The Public Spirit of the Whigs* (1714). In 1713 he was made
Dean of St Patrick's, the last piece of patronage which he received.
The hostility of Queen Anne had proved an insurmountable obstacle
to his further advancement. On the destruction of his hopes Swift
retired to Ireland, where he remained for the rest of his life a thoroughly embittered man.

In 1713 he had begun his *Journal to Stella*, which sheds so strange
a light upon his character, and on his return to Ireland his marriage
to her is now generally believed to have taken place, though they
never lived together. Now also took place his final rupture with
Esther Vanhomrigh (Vanessa), who had been in love with him, with
whom he had maintained a lengthened correspondence, and to whom
he addressed his poem, *Cadenus and Vanessa* (1726). Though he
disliked the Irish and considered residence in Ireland as banishment,
he interested himself in Irish affairs, and attained extraordinary
popularity by his *Drapier's Letters*, directed against the introduction
of 'Wood's halfpence.' In 1726 he visited England and joined with
Pope and Arbuthnot in publishing *Miscellanies* (1727). In the same
year, 1726, he published *Gulliver's Travels*, his most widely and
permanently popular work; a bitter and misanthropical satire, it has
by a curious irony become, in expurgated form, one of the favourite
books of children. His last visit to England was paid in 1727 and
in the following year 'Stella,' the only being, probably, whom he
really loved, died. Though he had a circle of friends in Dublin, and
was, owing to his championing the people in their grievances, a

popular idol, the shadows were darkening around him. The fear of
insanity by which he had been all his life haunted, pressed more and
more upon him. He became increasingly morose and savage in his
misanthropy, and though he had a rally in which he produced some
of his most brilliant work—the *Rhapsody on Poetry, Verses on the
Death of Dr Swift,* and the *Modest Proposal* (a horrible but masterly
piece of irony)—he gradually sank into almost total loss of his
faculties. He was buried in St Patrick's Cathedral.

Swinburne, Algernon Charles (5 April 1837—10 April 1909), poet,
son of an admiral, was born in London but spent his childhood at
Bonchurch, on the Isle of Wight. He received his early education in
France, then was at Eton and at Balliol College, Oxford, where he
attracted the attention of Jowett, and gave himself to the study of
Latin, Greek, French, and Italian, with special reference to poetic
form. He left Oxford in 1860 without graduating, and in the next
year published two plays, *The Queen Mother* and *Rosamond,* which
made no impression on the public, though a few good judges recognized their promise. The same year he visited Italy, and there made
the acquaintance of Walter Savage Landor (q.v.). On his return he
lived for some time in Cheyne Row, Chelsea, with D. G. Rossetti
(q.v.), and G. Meredith (q.v.). The appearance in 1865 of *Atalanta
in Calydon* led to his immediate recognition as a poet of the first
order, and in the same year he published *Chastelard, a Tragedy,* the
first part of a trilogy relating to Mary Queen of Scots, the other two
being *Bothwell* (1874), and *Mary Stuart* (1881).

Poems and Ballads, published in 1866, created a profound sensation
alike among the critics and the general body of readers by its daring
departure from recognized standards of both politics and morality,
and gave rise to a prolonged and bitter controversy, Swinburne
defending himself against his assailants in *Notes on Poems and
Reviews.* His next works were the *Song of Italy* (1867) and *Songs
before Sunrise* (1871). Returning to the Greek models which he
had followed with such brilliant success in *Atalanta* he produced
Erechtheus (1876), the extraordinary metrical power of which won
general admiration. *Poems and Ballads,* second series, came out in
1878. It was followed by *Tristram of Lyonesse* (1882), *A Midsummer
Holiday* (1884), *Marino Faliero* (1885), *Locrine* (1887), *Poems and
Ballads,* third series (1889), *The Sisters* (1892), *Astrophel* (1894),
The Tale of Balen (1896), *Rosamund, Queen of the Lombards* (1899),
A Channel Passage (1904), and *The Duke of Gandia* (1908). Among
his prose works are two novels, *A Year's Letters* (1877) reissued in
1905 as *Love's Cross Currents,* and *Lesbia Brandon* (1952); *Under the
Microscope* (1872), an answer to R. Buchanan's *Fleshly School of
Poetry;* and critical studies of William Blake (1867), George Chapman
(1875), Shakespeare (1879), Victor Hugo (1886), and Ben Jonson
(1889).

Swinburne belongs to the class of 'poets' poets.' He never became
widely popular. As a master of metre he is hardly excelled by any
of our poets, but it has not seldom been questioned whether his marvellous sense of the beauty of words and their arrangement did not

exceed the depth and mass of his thought. The 'Hymn to Artemis' in *Atalanta* beginning 'When the hounds of Spring are on Winter's traces' is certainly one of the most splendid examples of metrical power in the language. As a prose writer he occupies a much lower place, and here the contrast between the thought and its expression becomes very marked, the latter often becoming turgid and even violent. In his earlier days in London Swinburne was closely associated with the Pre-Raphaelites, the Rossettis, Meredith, and Burne-Jones: he was thus subjected successively to the classical and romantic influence, and showed the traces of both in his work. He was never married, and for the last 30 years of his life lived with his friend, Theodore Watts-Dunton (q.v.), at 'The Pines,' near the foot of Putney Hill. For some time before his death he was almost totally deaf.

Swinnerton, Frank Arthur (12 Aug. 1884—), novelist and critic, was born in London, son of an engraver. Starting work at an early age he was for a time on the staff of the *Manchester Guardian*, and later was a publisher's reader. His most successful novels were *Nocturne* (1917), *September* (1919), *Young Felix* (1923), and *Harvest Comedy* (1937); others are *Coquette* (1921), *Sketch of a Sinner* (1929), *Elizabeth* (1934), *The Two Wives* (1939), *Thankless Child* (1942), *A Woman in Sunshine* (1944), *The Doctor's Wife Comes to Stay* (1949), *A Flower for Catharine* (1951), and *A Month in Gordon Square* (1953). *The Georgian Literary Scene* (1935) is a contemporary literary panorama, and he also wrote studies of George Gissing (1912) and R. L. Stevenson (1927). *Tokefield Papers* (1927) and *A London Bookman* (1928) are collections of essays, while *Swinnerton* (1937) is an autobiography.

Sydney, Algernon, *see* **Sidney.**

Sylvester, Joshua (1563—28 Sept 1618), poet and translator, born in Kent, son of a clothier, is chiefly remembered by his translation from the French of Du Bartas's *Divine Weeks and Works*, which is said to have influenced Milton and Shakespeare. In 1606 he was appointed Groom of the Chamber to Prince Henry. He seconded the *Counterblast against Tobacco* of James I with his *Tobacco Battered and the Pipes Shattered by a Volley of Holy Shot thundered from Mount Helicon* (1620), and also wrote *All not Gold that Glisters, Panthea: Divine Wishes and Meditations* (1630), and many religious, complimentary, and other occasional pieces. Sylvester, who was originally engaged in commerce, acted later as a sort of factor to the Earl of Essex.

Symonds, John Addington (5 Oct. 1840—19 April 1893), poet and critic, son of a doctor in Bristol, was educated at Harrow and Oxford. His delicate health obliged him to live abroad. He published *History of the Italian Renaissance* (seven volumes 1875—86), and translated the *Autobiography of Benvenuto Cellini* (1887). He also wrote some books of poetry, including *Many Moods* (1878) and *Animi Figura* (1882), and among his other publications were *Introduction to the Study of Dante* (1872), *Studies of the Greek Poets* (1873),

Shakespeare's Predecessors in the English Drama (1884), and lives of various poets, including Ben Jonson, Shelley, and Walt Whitman. He also made remarkable translations of the sonnets of Michelangelo and Campanella, and wrote upon philosophical subjects in various periodicals.

Symons, Alphonse James Albert (1900—25 Aug. 1941), biographer, was born in London. Owing to straitened family circumstances, he worked twelve hours a day for three years as a boy in a furrier's, a drudgery which he hated. Later he became a dandy and dilettante, founded the First Edition Club, and specialized in bibliography and biography. His best-known work is *The Quest for Corvo* (1934), a life of Frederick Rolfe (q.v.); other biographies are *Emin, Governor of Equatoria* (1928) and *H. M. Stanley* (1933). An authority on the eighteen-nineties, he published *An Anthology of Nineties Verse* (1930) and *The Nonesuch Century* (1936). Among his hobbies was the collection of Victorian musical boxes.

Symons, Arthur (28 Feb. 1865—22 Jan. 1945), poet and critic, was born in Wales of Cornish parents and educated privately. He started writing at a very early age, and having travelled in France and Italy was influenced in his work by the French Symbolist school. During the nineties he was on the staff successively of the *Athenaeum*, the *Saturday Review*, and the *Academy*, and contributed to the *Yellow Book*. His volumes of poetry, mainly in the decadent tradition of the time, include *Days and Nights* (1889), *Silhouettes* (1892), *London Nights* (1896), *Images of Good and Evil* (1899), *A Book of Twenty Songs* (1905), *The Fool of the World* (1906), *Knave of Hearts* (1913), and *Love's Cruelty* (1923). His more important critical works are *An Introduction to the Study of Browning* (1886), *Studies in Two Literatures* (1897), *The Symbolist Movement in Literature* (1899), *Studies in Prose and Verse* (1904), *The Romantic Movement in English Poetry* (1909), and *Studies in the Elizabethan Drama* (1919). He also wrote books on William Blake (1907), Thomas Hardy (1927), Oscar Wilde (1930), and Walter Pater (1932). *A Study in Pathology* (1930) is autobiographical.

Synge, John Millington (16 April 1871—24 March 1909), dramatist, was born near Dublin, son of a barrister. After studying at Trinity College he travelled in Germany, Italy, and France. In 1899, while studying in Paris, he met Yeats, who suggested that he should go back to Ireland and seek inspiration in the people of the Aran Islands. His book about them appeared in 1907, and his plays drew their characters from the same source. *In the Shadow of the Glen* (1903) was followed by *Riders to the Sea* (1904) and *The Well of the Saints* (1905); greatest of all is *The Playboy of the Western World* (1907), which nevertheless was hotly criticized when it was staged in Ireland. After it came *The Tinker's Wedding* (1909) and the unfinished *Deirdre of the Sorrows* (1910). The leading Irish dramatist of his time, Synge showed great power and range in his portrayal of Irish peasant life. A director of the Abbey Theatre from 1904, he was engaged to Maire O'Neill, its leading actress, but his death of cancer prevented their marriage.

T

Tabb, John Banister (22 May 1845—19 Nov. 1909), priest and poet, was born in Amelia County, Virginia. Having served on Confederate blockade-runners during the Civil War, he was captured and imprisoned. Afterwards he prepared for the Episcopalian ministry, but in 1872 was converted to Roman Catholicism and in 1884 was ordained priest, having studied at St Charles's College, near Baltimore, where he conducted classes in English all his active life. He first became known as a writer by his volume *Poems* (1894), which went through 17 editions; other publications were *Lyrics* (1897), *Later Lyrics* (1902), *The Rosary in Rhyme* (1904), and *Later Poems* (1910). His work has been compared with that of the seventeenth-century poets. *Child Verse* (1899) and *Quipps and Quiddits* (1907) show his taste for word-play and puckish humour. During his last years he was blind.

Tabley, de, 3rd Baron, *see* de Tabley.

Tagore, Sir Rabindranath (6 May 1861—7 Aug. 1941), poet and dramatist, was born in Calcutta, son of a wealthy Brahmin. Educated privately, he went to England in 1878 and studied at University College, London. He had by that time already published works in Bengali. In 1884 he married Mrinalinidebi, and they lived at Shilaida on the banks of the Ganges, where he came into close contact with native life and wrote many of his best-known works. In 1895 he published two collections of lyrics, *Chitra* (Beauty) and *Sonar Tari* (Golden Boat); better known are his two series of *Gitanjali* (Handful of Songs) published in 1912 and 1919; and in 1913 appeared *The Crescent Moon* and *The Gardener*. His early dramas *Chitrangada* and *Sacrifice* were followed by *The Post Office* (1912) and *The King of the Dark Chamber* (1914), while *Gora* (1908) and *Home and the World* (1916) are novels. In 1901 he had founded the Santiniketan (Home of Peace), a school for boys at Bolpur in Bengal, which became an international institute. His lectures delivered there were published in 1917 as *Personality* and *Nationalism*. In 1913 he was awarded the Nobel Prize and in 1915 he was knighted. Among his later works are *The Wreck* (1921), *Red Oleander* (1924), *Broken Ties* (1925), *Fireflies* (1928), and *The Religion of Man* (1931). *My Reminiscences* (1917) is autobiographical. Most of his works were written in Bengali and then translated by him into English, but he also wrote directly in English. A universal humanitarian, inspired by deep religious feeling and love of nature, he has been called the Bengal Shelley. In 1950 his poem 'Lord of the Heart of the People' was chosen as Indian's national anthem.

Talfourd, Sir Thomas Noon (26 May 1795—13 March 1854), judge and dramatist, son of a brewer at Reading, where he was born, and which he represented in Parliament from 1835 to 1841, was educated at Mill Hill School. He studied law, was called to the Bar in 1821, and became a judge in 1849. He died suddenly of apoplexy while charging the Grand Jury at Stafford. He wrote much for reviews, and in 1835 produced *Ion*, a tragedy, followed by *The Athenian Captive* (1838), and *The Massacre of Glencoe* (1840), all of which were acted with success. Talfourd was the friend and literary executor of Charles Lamb (q.v.), and published in two sections his *Memoirs and Letters*. In 1837 he introduced the Copyright Bill, which was passed with modifications in 1842.

Tannahill, Robert (3 June 1774—17 May 1810), poet, was born at Paisley, son of a weaver, and himself followed the same trade. Leaving school at the age of 13 he worked first at Lochwinnoch, then at Bolton in Lancashire, and finally returned to his native town, where in 1805 he helped in establishing the trades library for working men. He wrote many poems for Glasgow periodicals, and a volume which he published in 1807 had considerable popularity, but he became depressed through the problem of getting a revised edition produced, and drowned himself in Paisley canal at the age of 35. His poems, which have that 'singing' quality which seems to be the birthright of all minor Scots poets, include the well-known 'Bonnie Woods o' Craigielea,' 'Lass o' Arrenteenie,' and 'Braes o' Gleniffer.' 'Jessie the Flower o' Dumblane' was inspired by an unsuccessful love affair. After his death a statue was erected to him in the grounds of Paisley Abbey.

Tarkington, Newton Booth (29 July 1869—19 May 1946), novelist, was born at Indianapolis, Indiana, son of a lawyer, and educated at Purdue University and Princeton. He wanted first to be an artist, but later turned to writing. His first novel was *The Gentleman from Indiana* (1899), but he first became famous with the publication of *Monsieur Beaucaire* (1900), an historical romance. *The Magnificent Ambersons* (1918) and *Alice Adams* (1921) were both awarded Pulitzer Prizes; *Penrod* (1914), *Penrod and Sam* (1916), and *Seventeen* (1916) are delightful studies of adolescence; and others of his novels are *Cherry* (1903), *The Conquest of Canaan* (1905), *His Own People* (1907), *The Flirt* (1913), *Gentle Julia* (1922), *The Plutocrat* (1927), and *Clair Ambler* (1928).' Later were *The Heritage of Hatcher Ide* (1941), *Kate Fennigate* (1943), and *The Image of Josephine* (1945). He also wrote several plays, of which the most successful were *Clarence* (1921) and *Tweedles* (1923), in which he collaborated with Harry Leon Wilson. In 1902 he was elected to the Indiana House of Representatives, and wrote *In the Arena* (1905) from his experiences. *Looking Forward* (1926) is a book of essays, and *The World Does Move* (1928) is autobiographical. In 1942 he gained the Roosevelt Distinguished Service Medal, and in 1945 the Howells Medal of the American Academy of Arts and Letters. He held honorary degrees of Princeton, de Pauw, and Columbia.

Tate, John Orley Allen (19 Nov. 1899—), poet and novelist, born at Winchester, Kentucky, and educated at Vanderbilt University, worked for a time in his brother's coal business. In 1924 he married Caroline Gordon, also a writer. After holding a

Guggenheim Fellowship in 1928, he was on the English staff at the University of North Carolina and at Columbia. From 1939 to 1942 he was Fellow in Creative Writing at Princeton, and from 1944 to 1950 Fellow in American Letters of the Library of Congress, after which in 1951 he became Professor of English at the University of Minnesota. In 1936 he published *Reactionary Essays in Poetry and Ideas*, and in 1941 *Reason in Madness*, which marked him as one of the leading critics; later essays are *On the Limits of Poetry* (1948), *The Hovering Fly* (1949), and *The Forlorn Demon* (1952). His poetry, which shows the influence of Donne and T. S. Eliot, includes *The Winter Sea* (1945) and *Poems 1922—1947* (1948). He also published *Stonewall Jackson—The Good Soldier* (1928) and *Jefferson Davis—His Rise and Fall* (1929), and a novel, *The Fathers* (1938).

Tate, Nahum (1652—12 Aug. 1715), Poet Laureate, was born in Dublin, son of a clergyman named Faithful Teate, and was educated at Trinity College there. In 1672 he settled in London, and in 1677 published *Poems on Several Occasions*. In the self-imposed task of 'improving' Shakespeare he produced a version of *King Lear* in which Cordelia survives and marries Edgar; this monstrosity, which was defended by Dr Johnson, held the stage well into the nineteenth century. In 1682 Tate wrote, with Dryden's assistance, a second part to that poet's famous satire *Absalom and Achitophel*. In 1692 he was appointed Poet Laureate in succession to Shadwell, as a result of which Pope pilloried him later in *The Dunciad*; and in 1702 he was made historiographer royal. His chief original poem was *Panacea or a Poem on Tea* (1700), but he is remembered mainly for the metrical version of the Psalms in which he collaborated with Nicholas Brady (q.v.); published in 1696, it gradually superseded the earlier rendering of Sternhold and Hopkins (qq.v.).

Tatham, John (1612?—1664), poet and dramatist, wrote pageants for the Lord Mayor's show. His dramas include *Love Crowns the End* (1632), *The Distracted State* (1641), *The Scots Figgaries, or a Knot of Knaves* (1652), and *The Rump* (1660), a comedy on the Rump Parliament. He was a Cavalier, who hated the Puritans and the Scots, and invented a dialect which he believed to be their vernacular tongue.

Tautphoeus, Baroness von (23 Oct. 1807—12 Nov. 1893), novelist, was born at Seaview, Donegal, her maiden name being Jemima Montgomery, and in 1838 married Baron von Tautphoeus, Chamberlain at the Court of Bavaria. She wrote several novels dealing with German life of which the first, *The Initials* (1850), is perhaps the best. Others were *Cyrilla* (1853), *Quits* (1857), and *At Odds* (1863).

Taylor, Ann (30 Jan. 1782—20 Dec. 1866), poetess, was born in London, daughter of an engraver, and sister of Isaac and Jane Taylor (qq.v.). From 1786 the family lived in Suffolk, after which the father became a minister at Colchester. Ann and Jane collaborated in several books of poems for children, which had great popularity; they include *Original Poems for Infant Minds* (1804—1805), *Rhymes for the Nursery* (1806), and *Hymns for Infant Minds* (1810). Among Ann's more famous contributions are 'My Mother,'

'Meddlesome Matty,' and 'I Thank the Goodness and the Grace. In 1811 her father was transferred to a church at Ongar, and in 1813 she married Joseph Gilbert, a clergyman. Her last 40 years were spent in Nottingham, where she wrote *The Convalescent* (1839) and *Seven Blessings for Little Children* (1844).

Taylor, Bayard (11 Jan. 1825—19 Dec. 1878), poet, born in Kennett Square, Pennsylvania of Quaker descent, began to write verses at the age of 7. Apprenticed to a printer, he found the work uncongenial and, purchasing his indentures, went to Europe on a walking tour; thereafter he was a constant and enterprising traveller. After his return from Europe he edited a paper, joined the staff of the *New York Tribune*, and published several books of travel and poetry, among which are *Views Afoot* (1846), an account of his travels in Europe, and *El Dorado* (1850), which described the Californian goldfields. After some experience and some disappointments in the diplomatic sphere, he settled down to writing. His first novel, *Hannah Thurston* (1863), was very successful, and was followed by *John Godfrey's Fortunes* (1864), partly autobiographical, and *The Story of Kennett* (1866). His poetic works include *Poems of the Orient* (1854), *Poet's Journal* (1862), *Masque of the Gods* (1872), *Lars* (1873), and *Home Pastorals* (1875). *The Prophet* (1874) and *Prince Deukalion* (1878) are plays. In 1878 he was appointed to the German Embassy, and died in Berlin in the following year. His translation of Goethe's *Faust* (1870—1) is perhaps his best work. He was a man of untiring energy and great ability and versatility, but tried too many avenues to fame to advance very far in any of them.

Taylor, Sir Henry (18 Oct. 1800—27 March 1886), dramatist, was born at Bishop Middleham, Durham, son of a farmer. Educated at home, he became a midshipman in the navy, but made only one voyage. Later he became a clerk in the Colonial Office, and remained there for 48 years, during which he exercised considerable influence on the colonial policy of the Empire. In 1872 he was made a Knight Commander of St Michael and St George. He wrote four tragedies— *Isaac Comnenus* (1827), *Philip van Artevelde* (1834), *Edwin the Fair* (1842), and *St Clement's Eve* (1862); also a romantic comedy, *The Virgin Widow* (1850), which he renamed *A Sicilian Summer*. *The Eve of the Conquest and other Poems* (1847) is a volume of lyric verse. In prose he published *The Statesman* (1836), *Notes from Life* (1847), *Notes from Books* (1849), and an *Autobiography* (1885). Of all these *Philip van Artevelde*, the most successful, has great interest as a psychological study.

Taylor, Isaac (17 Aug. 1787—28 June 1865), philosopher, born at Lavenham, Suffolk, was a brother of Ann and Jane Taylor (qq.v.). He was trained as an engraver, the trade of his father and grandfather, and produced work which won the admiration of Rossetti. Later he turned to writing and produced *The Elements of Thought* (1823), and a translation of the *Characters* of Theophrastus (1824). In 1825 he settled near Ongar and married. Subsequently he published a *History of the Transmission of Ancient Books to Modern*

Times (1827) and started a series of semi-philosophical works which include *The Natural History of Enthusiasm* (1829), *Fanaticism* (1833), *The Restoration of Belief* (1855), and *The World of the Mind* (1857). *Personal Recollections* appeared in 1864. One of his recreations was making silhouettes.

Taylor, Jane (23 Sept. 1783—13 April 1824), poetess, was born in London, daughter of an engraver and sister of Isaac and Ann Taylor (qq.v.). A very vivacious child, she began planning books from the age of 8. In 1804 the two sisters collaborated in *Original Poems for Infant Minds*, which went through 50 editions and was translated into German, Dutch, and Russian. *Rhymes for the Nursery* followed in 1806, and in 1810 *Hymns for Infant Minds*, which went through 100 editions. Jane's best-remembered piece is 'Twinkle, Twinkle, Little Star.' The literary partnership ended when Ann was married in 1813. Jane went to Cornwall, where she wrote *Display, a Tale for Young People* (1815) and *Essays in Rhyme on Morals and Manners* (1816). Her last years were spent at Ongar, in Essex, where her father was then a preacher.

Taylor, Jeremy (baptized 15 Aug. 1613, died 13 Aug. 1667), bishop, was born at Cambridge, son of a barber. Educated at Perse School, he became a sizar at Gonville and Caius College. In 1636 he was elected a Fellow of All Souls College, Oxford, through the influence of Laud, who made him his chaplain. He also became a chaplain to the King, and soon attaining a great reputation as a preacher, was presented to the living of Uppingham. In 1639 he married his first wife, and in 1643 he was made Rector of Overstone. On the outbreak of the Civil War Taylor sided with the King, and was present at the battle fought in 1645 near Cardigan Castle, when he was taken prisoner. He was soon released, but the Royalist cause being practically lost, he decided to remain in Wales, and with two friends started a school at Newtonhall, Caermarthenshire, which had some success. Between 1647 and 1660 he laid the foundations of his splendid literary fame. The *Liberty of Prophesying* (that is, of preaching), one of the greatest pleas for toleration in the language, was published in 1647, *The Life of Christ* in 1649, *Holy Living* in 1650, and *Holy Dying* in 1651. These were followed by various series of sermons, and by *The Golden Grove* (1655), a manual of devotion which received its title from the name of the seat of his friend Lord Carbery. For some remarks against the existing authorities Taylor suffered a short imprisonment, and some controversial tracts on *Original Sin*, *Unum Necessarium* (The One Thing Needful), and *The Doctrine and Practice of Repentance* involved him in a controversy of some warmth in which he was attacked by both High Churchmen and Calvinists.

While in Wales Taylor had entered into a second marriage with a lady of some property which, however, was seriously encroached upon by the exactions of the Parliamentarians. In 1657 he ministered privately to an Episcopalian congregation in London, and in 1658 accompanied Lord Conway to Ireland, and served a cure at Lisburn. Two years later he published *Ductor Dubitantium, or the Rule of*

Conscience in all her General Measures, a learned and subtle piece of casuistry which he dedicated to Charles II. The Restoration brought recognition of Taylor's unswerving devotion to the Royalist cause; he was made Bishop of Down and Connor, and to this was added the administration of the see of Dromore. In his new position, though, as might have been expected, he showed zeal, diligence, and benevolence, he was not happy. He did not, probably could not, entirely practise his own views of absolute toleration, and found himself in conflict with the Presbyterians, some of whose ministers he had extruded from benefices which they had held, and he longed to escape to a more private and peaceful position. He died at Lisburn of a fever caught while ministering to a parishioner. Taylor is one of the great classical writers of England. Learned, original, and impassioned, he had an enthusiasm for religion and charity, and his writings glow with an almost unequalled wealth of illustration and imagery, subtle argument, and fullness of thought. With a character of stainless purity and benevolence, and gracious and gentle manners, he was universally beloved by all who came under the spell of his presence.

Taylor, John (24 Aug. 1580—Dec. 1653), poet and travel-writer usually known as 'the Water Poet,' was born in Gloucester, educated at the grammar school there, and apprenticed to a waterman. Pressed for the navy, he served at the siege of Cadiz, and when discharged with a lame leg resumed his occupation on the Thames, afterwards keeping inns first at Oxford, then in London. He had a talent for writing rollicking verses, enjoyed the acquaintance of Ben Jonson and other famous men, superintended the water pageant at the marriage of Princess Elizabeth in 1613, and composed the pageants at the Lord Mayor's shows. He made a journey on foot from London as far as to Braemar, of which he wrote an account, *The Pennyless Pilgrimage of John Taylor, the King's Majesty's Water Poet* (1618). He visited the Queen of Bohemia at Prague in 1620, and made other journeys, each of which was commemorated in a book. He was a well-known 'character,' and his doggerel pieces, crude but often diverting, have considerable historical and antiquarian interest.

Taylor, Philip Meadows (25 Sept. 1808—13 May 1876), novelist, was born in Liverpool, son of a merchant there. As a boy he went out to a mercantile situation in Calcutta, but in 1826 got a commission in the army of the Nizam of Hyderabad. From this he rose to a high civil position in the service of the Nizam, and entirely reorganized his government. After the Mutiny he was given charge of some districts of the Deccan, and in 1860 was made a Companion of the Star of India. He wrote several striking novels dealing with Indian life, including *Confessions of a Thug* (1839), *Tara* (1863), and *A Noble Queen* (1878). He left an autobiography, *The Story of my Life*, edited by his daughter.

Taylor, Rachel Annand (1876—15 Aug. 1960), poetess, was born in Aberdeen, daughter of John Wilson Annand, and educated at Aberdeen University, which in 1943 conferred on her the degree of

LL.D. In 1901 she married Alexander Cameron Taylor, and they lived in Dundee. Her first poems were contributed to the *British Weekly*. Her first published volume, *Poems* (1904), was followed by *Rose and Vine* (1908), *The House of Fiametta* (1909), a sonnet sequence, and its sequel *The End of Fiametta* (1923). Her poetry has been described by Gilbert Murray as 'instinct with a rich and dreamlike beauty of phrase.' Her prose works include *Leonardo the Florentine* (1927), *Renaissance France* (1930), and *Dunbar and his Period* (1931).

Taylor, Thomas (15 May 1758—1 Nov. 1835), translator, born in London, son of a staymaker, and educated at St Paul's School, devoted himself to the study of the classics and of mathematics. After being a bank clerk he was appointed assistant secretary to the Society for the Encouragement of Arts, in which capacity he made many influential friends, who furnished the means for publishing his various translations, which include works of Plato, Aristotle, Proclus, Porphyry, Apuleius, and others. His aim indeed was the translation of all the untranslated writings of the ancient Greek philosophers.

Taylor, Tom (19 Oct. 1817—12 July 1880), dramatist, born at Sunderland and educated at Glasgow and Cambridge, was Professor of English Literature in London University from 1845 to 1847. In 1846 he was called to the Bar, and from 1854 to 1871 he was secretary to the Local Government Board. He was the author of about 100 dramatic pieces, original and adapted, including *Still Waters run Deep* (1855), *The Overland Route* (1860), and *Joan of Arc* (1871). He was likewise a large contributor to *Punch*, of which he was editor from 1874 to 1880, and he edited the autobiographies of Haydon and Leslie, the painters, and completed the latter's *Life and Times of Sir Joshua Reynolds*.

Taylor, William (7 Nov. 1765—5 March 1836), translator, was born at Norwich, son of a cloth manufacturer. Sent to the Continent on business, he learned German, and became an enthusiastic student of German literature, which he was one of the first to introduce to his fellow-countrymen. His articles on the subject were collected and published as *Historic Survey of German Poetry* (1828—30). He translated Bürger's *Lenore*, Lessing's *Nathan*, and Goethe's *Iphigenia*. He also wrote *Tales of Yore* (1810) and *English Synonyms Described* (1813).

Teasdale, Sara (8 Aug. 1884—29 Jan. 1933), poetess, was born in St Louis, Missouri, and educated privately. A precocious child, she grew up neurotic and hypochondriac always unhappy, though she had many friends. After extensive travel in Europe and the Near East she settled in Chicago, where she met Vachel Lindsay (q.v.), who courted her for many years; after vacillating she married Ernest P. Filsinger, a business man, in 1914, but she was temperamentally unsuited to marriage and they were divorced in 1929. Her later years were spent in New York. Lindsay's suicide in 1931 was a great shock to her and little more than a year later she was found drowned in her bath. As a poetess she excelled in lyric verse, her earliest influence being Christina Rossetti, with whom she has been compared, and of whom she started to write a biography. Her volumes of poetry include *Sonnets to Duse* (1907), *Helen of Troy* (1911), *Rivers to the Sea* (1915), *Love Songs* (1917), which was awarded the Columbia University Prize, *Flame and Shadow* (1920), *Dark of the Moon* (1926), and *Strange Victory* (1933). *Stars To-night* (1930) consists of verses for children, and she also compiled some anthologies.

Temple, Sir William (1628—27 Jan. 1699), statesman and essayist, son of Sir John Temple, Master of the Rolls in Ireland, was born in London, and educated at Cambridge. He was for some time a member of the Irish Parliament. Later he was employed on various diplomatic missions, negotiated the Triple Alliance of England, Holland, and Sweden in 1668, and helped to arrange the marriage of the Prince of Orange and the Princess Mary. On his return he was much consulted by Charles II, but disapproving of the policy adopted, retired to his house at Sheen; this he afterwards left and purchased Moor Park, where Swift was for a time his secretary. He took no part in the Revolution, but acquiesced in the new *régime*, and was offered, but refused, the Secretaryship of State. His works consist for the most part of short essays collected in three series under the title of *Miscellanea* (1680, 1692, 1701), the second containing his famous 'Of Ancient and Modern Learning'; longer pieces are his *Essay upon the Present State of Ireland* (1668), and *Essay on the Original and Nature of Government* (1671). Temple is best known in literary history as being the recipient of the famous *Letters from Dorothy Osborne* (q.v.), who became his wife in 1655.

Tennant, Kylie (12 March 1912—   ), novelist, was born at Manly, New South Wales, and educated at Sydney University. In 1932 she married Lewis C. Rodd. Her first novel, *Tiburon* (1935), and *The Battlers* (1941) both won the Prior Memorial Prize, and the latter was also awarded the gold medal of the Australian Literary Society. Others of her novels are *Foveaux* (1939), *Ride On, Stranger* (1943), *Time Enough Later* (1943), *Lost Haven* (1946), and *The Joyful Condemned* (1953). In these she depicts with irony and gusto the life of the Australian poor, both urban and rural. She also wrote a number of plays, and *Australia, her Story* (1953).

Tennant, William (15 May 1784—14 Oct. 1848), poet and scholar, a cripple from his birth, was born at Anstruther (commonly called Anster) in Fife. As a youth he was clerk to his brother, a corn-merchant, but devoted his leisure to the study of languages, and the literature of various countries. In 1813 he became parish school-master of Lasswade, near Edinburgh, thereafter classical master at Dollar Academy, and in 1835 Professor of Oriental Languages at St Andrews. In 1812 he published *Anster Fair*, a mock-heroic poem, in *ottava rima*, full of fancy and humour, which at once brought him reputation. In later life he produced two tragedies, *Cardinal Beaton* (1823) and *John Baliol* (1825), and two poems, *The Thane of Fife* (1822), and *Papistry Stormed* (1827). He also issued a *Syriac and Chaldee Grammar*.

Tennyson, Alfred, 1st Baron (6 Aug. 1809—6 Oct. 1892), Poet Laureate, was the fourth son of George Tennyson, rector of

Somersby, Lincolnshire, where he was born. His father was himself a poet of some skill, and his two elder brothers, Frederick Tennyson and Charles Tennyson Turner (qq.v.) were poets of a high order. His early education was received from his father, after which he went to Louth Grammar School, whence in 1828 he proceeded to Trinity College, Cambridge. In the previous year had appeared a small volume, *Poems by Two Brothers*, chiefly the work of his brother Charles and himself, with a few contributions from Frederick, but it attracted little attention. At the University he was one of a group of highly gifted men, including Trench, Monckton Milnes, afterwards Lord Houghton, Lushington, his future brother-in-law, and above all, Arthur Hallam, whose friendship and early death were to be the inspiration of one of his greatest poems. In 1829 he won the Chancellor's medal with a poem on *Timbuctoo*, and in the following year he brought out his first independent work, *Poems chiefly Lyrical*. It was not in general very favourably received by the critics, though Wilson in *Blackwood's Magazine* admitted much promise and even performance. In America it had greater popularity. Part of 1832 was spent in travel with Hallam, and the same year saw the publication of *Poems*, which included 'The Lotus Eaters' and 'The Lady of Shalott.' In the next year Hallam died, and Tennyson began *In Memoriam* and wrote *The Two Voices*. He also became engaged to Emily Sellwood, his future wife, but owing to various cricumstances their marriage did not take place until 1850. The next few years were passed with his family at various places, and, so far as the public were concerned, he remained silent until 1842, when he published *Poems* in two volumes, containing 'Locksley Hall' and 'Ulysses,' and at last achieved full recognition as a great poet. From this time the life of Tennyson is a record of tranquil triumph in his art and of the conquest of fame. *The Princess* appearing in 1847 added materially to his reputation: in the lyrics with which it is interspersed, such as 'The Splendour Falls' and 'Tears, idle Tears' he rises to the full mastery of this branch of his art.

The year 1850 was the most eventful in his life, for in it took place his marriage, his succession to the Laureateship on the death of Wordsworth, and the publication of his great elegiac poem, *In Memoriam*. In 1852 appeared his noble *Ode on the Death of the Duke of Wellington*, and two years later *The Charge of the Light Brigade*. The publication of *Maud* in 1855 gave his rapidly growing popularity a perceptible set-back, but this was far more than made up for by the enthusiasm with which the first set of *The Idylls of the King* was received on its appearance four years later. *Enoch Arden*, with the *Northern Farmer*, came out in 1864; *The Holy Grail* and *Gareth and Lynette*, both belonging to the *Idyll* series, in 1869 and 1872 respectively. Three years later in 1875 Tennyson broke new ground by beginning a series of dramas with *Queen Mary*, followed by *Harold* (1876), *The Falcon* (1879), *The Cup* (1881), *The Promise of May* (1882), *Becket* (1884), and *Robin Hood* (1891), but these did not achieve permanent success. His later poems were *The Lover's Tale* (1879), *Tiresias* (1885), *Locksley Hall, Sixty Years after* (1886),

Demeter and other Poems (1889), including 'Crossing the Bar,' and
The Death of Œnone (1892). Tennyson, who cared little for general
society, though he had many intimate and devoted friends, lived at
Farringford, Isle of Wight, from 1853 to 1869, when he built a house
at Aldworth, near Haslemere, which was his home until his death.
In 1884 he was raised to the peerage. Until he had passed the three-
score years and ten he had, with occasional illnesses, enjoyed good
health on the whole. But in 1886 the younger of his two sons died,
a blow which told heavily upon him; thereafter frequent attacks of
illness followed, and he died in his eighty-fourth year, and received
a public funeral in Westminster Abbey.

The poetry of Tennyson is characterized by a wide outlook, by
intense sympathy with the deepest feelings and aspirations of
humanity, a profound realization of the problems of life and thought,
an exquisite sense of beauty, and a marvellous power of vivid and
minute description often achieved by a single felicitous phrase, and
heightened by the perfect matching of sense and sound. No poet
has excelled him in precision and delicacy of language and complete-
ness of expression. As a lyrist he ranks with the highest in English
poetry, and even of humour he possessed a share, as is shown in the
Northern Farmer and in other pieces. Patriotic, respectable, an
intimate friend of royalty, he was the ideal Poet Laureate. Above
all, he was the perfect mouthpiece of his age, both in its merits and
in its shortcomings; and for this reason his work was later to meet the
same disfavour as became attached to 'Victorianism.' But when
the volume, variety, and finish of his writings are considered, he must
be ranked among the greatest English poets.

Tennyson, Charles, *see* **Turner, Charles Tennyson.**

Tennyson, Frederick (5 June 1807—26 Feb. 1898), poet, born at
Louth in Lincolnshire, was the eldest brother of the above. Educated
at Eton and Cambridge, he passed most of his life in Italy and Jersey.
He contributed four pieces to the *Poems by Two Brothers*, and produced *Days and Hours* (1854), *The Isles of Greece* (1890), *Daphne*
(1891), and *Poems of the Day and Night* (1895). All his works show
passages of genuine poetic power.

Terhune, Albert Payson (21 Dec. 1872—18 Feb. 1942), writer of
animal stories, was born in his father's parsonage at Newark, New
Jersey, and after spending several years in Europe as a child was
educated at Columbia University. Later he travelled in Egypt and
Syria, lived with the Bedouin, and wrote *Syria from the Saddle* (1896).
Back in America, he became a journalist on the New York *Evening
World*, but from 1916 concentrated on writing about dogs, with which
his house was always filled. His first dog story, *Lad: a Dog* (1919)
had a sequel, *Further Adventures of Lad* (1922); other books are
Bruce (1920), *Buff, a Collie* (1921), *His Dog* (1922), *Wolf* (1924),
The Heart of a Dog (1925), *Bumps* (1927), *A Dog Named Chips* (1931),
The Way of a Dog (1934), and *A Book of Famous Dogs* (1937). *Now
That I'm Fifty* (1925) and *To the Best of My Memory* (1930) are
autobiographical.

Tey, Josephine, *see* **Mackintosh, Elizabeth.**

Thackeray, Anne, *see* Ritchie, Lady.

Thackeray, William Makepeace (18 July 1811—24 Dec. 1863), novelist, son of Richmond Thackeray, who held various important appointments in the service of the East India Company, and who belonged to an old and respectable Yorkshire family, was born at Calcutta, and soon after the death of his father which took place in 1816, sent home to England. After being at a school at Chiswick, he was sent to the Charterhouse School, where he remained from 1822 to 1826, and where he does not appear to have been very happy. Meanwhile in 1818 his mother had married Major H. W. C. Smythe, who is believed to be, in part at any rate, the original of Colonel Newcome. In 1829 he went to Trinity College, Cambridge, where he remained for a year only, and did not distinguish himself particularly as a student, but made many lifelong friends, including Spedding, Tennyson, FitzGerald, and Monckton Milnes, and contributed verses and caricatures to two undergraduate magazines, *The Snob* and *The Gownsman*. The following year, 1831, was spent chiefly in travelling on the Continent, especially Germany, where he visited Goethe. On his return he entered the Middle Temple, but having no liking for legal studies, he soon abandoned them, and turning his attention to journalism, became proprietor, wholly or in part, of two papers successively, both of which failed. These enterprises, together with some unfortunate investments and heavy losses at cards, stripped him of the comfortable fortune which he had inherited; and he now found himself dependent on his own exertions for a living. He thought at first of art as a profession, and studied for a time at Paris and Rome. In 1836, while acting as Paris correspondent for the second of his journals, he married Isabella, daughter of Colonel Shawe, an Irish officer, but the marriage was a tragic one, for his young wife became insane four years later, and remained in this condition for the rest of her life, dying in 1892.

In 1837 he returned to England and became a contributor to *Fraser's Magazine*, in which appeared *The Yellowplush Papers*, *The Great Hoggarty Diamond*, *Catherine*, and *Barry Lyndon*, the history of an Irish sharper, which contains some of his best work. Other works of this period were *The Paris Sketch-book* (1840) and *The Irish Sketch-book* (1843). His work in *Fraser*, while it was appreciated at its true worth by a select circle, had not brought him any very wide recognition: it was his contributions to *Punch*—the *Book of Snobs* and *Jeames's Diary*—which first caught the ear of the wider public. The turning point in his career, however, was the publication in monthly numbers of *Vanity Fair* (1847—8). This brilliant work gave him at once a place beside Fielding at the head of English novelists, and left him no living competitor except Dickens. *Pendennis*, largely autobiographical, followed in 1848, and fully maintained his reputation. In 1851 he broke new ground, and appeared, with great success, as a lecturer, taking for his subject *The English Humorists of the Eighteenth Century*, following this up in 1855 with *The Four Georges*, first delivered in America. Meanwhile *Henry Esmond*, perhaps his masterpiece, and probably the greatest novel of its kind, had appeared in 1852, and *The Newcomes* in 1853.

The Virginians, a sequel to *Esmond*, which, though containing
fine work, is generally considered to show a falling off as compared
with its two immediate predecessors, came out in 1857. In 1860 the
Cornhill Magazine was started with Thackeray for its editor, and to
it he contributed *Lovel the Widower* (1860), *The Adventures of Philip*
(1861—2), *The Roundabout Papers* (1860—3), a series of charming
essays, and *Denis Duval*, which was left a mere fragment by his
sudden death, but which gave promise of a return to his highest
level of performance.

In addition to the works mentioned, Thackeray for some years
produced Christmas books and burlesques, of which the best were
The Kickleburys on the Rhine (1850), and that delightful fairy tale,
The Rose and the Ring (1855). He also wrote graceful verses, some
of which, like 'Bouillabaisse' are in a strain of humour shot through
with pathos, while others are the purest rollicking fun. For some
years Thackeray suffered from spasms of the heart, and he died
suddenly in his fifty-third year. He was a man of the tenderest heart,
and had an intense enjoyment of domestic happiness; and the
interruption of this, caused by the permanent breakdown of his wife's
health, was a heavy calamity. This, along with his own latterly
broken health, and a sensitiveness which made him keenly alive to
criticism, doubtless fostered the tendency to what was often super-
ficially called his cynical view of life. He possessed an inimitable
irony and a power of sarcasm which could scorch like lightning, but
the latter was almost invariably directed against what is base and
hateful. To human weakness he was lenient and often tender, and
even where weakness passes into wickedness, he was just and com-
passionate. He saw human nature 'steadily and saw it whole,' and
painted it with a light but sure hand. He was master of a style of
great distinction and individuality, and ranks as one of the very
greatest of English novelists.

Thayer, Ernest Lawrence (14 Aug. 1863—21 Aug. 1940), journalist,
was born at Lawrence, Massachusetts, and educated at Harvard.
Taking up journalism, he worked for the Hearst newspapers, to
which he made a number of verse contributions, but is famous only
for his mock-heroic poem 'Casey at the Bat,' which first appeared in
the San Francisco *Examiner* in 1888, and describes the debacle of a
local baseball champion.

Theobald, Lewis (baptized 2 April 1688, died 18 Sept 1744), critic
and translator, born at Sittingbourne, became an attorney, like his
father, but turned to literature, translated from Plato, the Greek
dramatists, and Homer, and wrote also essays, biographies, and
poems. In 1715 he published *Shakespeare Restored*, in which he
severely criticized Pope's edition, and was in consequence rewarded
with the first place in *The Dunciad*, and the adoption of most of his
corrections in Pope's next edition. Theobald's own edition of
Shakespeare, published in 1734, contains many valuable emendations.

Thirkell, Angela Margaret (30 Jan. 1890—29 Jan. 1961), novelist,
born in London, was a daughter of J. W. Mackail and sister of Denis
Mackail (qq.v.). Educated at St Paul's Girls' School, she married

z

J. Campbell McInnes in 1911; they were divorced in 1917 and in the following year she married G. L. Thirkell of Tasmania, and they lived in Melbourne. She was 40 and had returned to England when she published her first book, *Three Houses*, containing memories of her childhood. Among her best-known novels are *August Folly* (1936), *Summer Half* (1937), *Pomfret Towers* (1938), *The Brandons* (1939), *Before Lunch* (1940), *Cheerfulness Breaks In* (1940), *Marling Hall* (1942), *Growing Up* (1943), *The Headmistress* (1945), *Miss Bunting* (1946), *Peace Breaks Out* (1947), *Love Among the Ruins* (1948), *County Chronicle* (1950), and *Happy Returns* (1952).

Thirlwall, Connop (11 Feb. 1797—27 July 1875), prelate and historian, was born in London, son of a clergyman. He read Latin and Greek at the age of 4, and when he was 11 his father published a volume of his compositions with the title *Primitiae*. Educated at Charterhouse and Cambridge, he studied law, was called to the Bar in 1825, and in the same year published a translation of Schleiermacher's *Critical Essay on the Gospel of St Luke*. After this, having changed his mind, he took orders in 1827, and the next year translated, with Julius Hare (q.v.), the first volume of Niebuhr's *History of Rome*, and published, also with him, *The Philological Museum* (1831—3). He was an advocate for the admission of Dissenters to degrees, and in consequence of his action in the matter had to resign his University tutorship. Thereupon Lord Brougham, then Lord Chancellor, presented him to the living of Kirkby Underdale. Between 1835 and 1847 he wrote his great *History of Greece*, which has a place among historical classics. In 1840 he was made Bishop of St David's, in which capacity he showed unusual energy in administering his see. He was buried in Westminster Abbey, in the same grave as George Grote (q.v.).

Thomas, Dylan Marlais (27 Oct. 1914—9 Nov. 1953), poet, born in Swansea, was educated at the grammar school there. A reporter for a time on the *South Wales Evening Post*, he had a number of poems printed in the *Sunday Referee*. His first book, *Eighteen Poems* (1934), containing some surrealist verse, was praised by Edith Sitwell. In 1936 he published *Twenty-Five Poems*, and in 1938 won a prize offered by the Chicago magazine *Poetry*. *The Map of Love*, a collection of stories and verse, appeared in 1939. Rejected for service in the Second World War, he worked for the British Broadcasting Corporation. In 1940 he published *Portrait of the Artist as a Young Dog*, a series of humorous autobiographical sketches. *Deaths and Entrances* (1946) and *In Country Sleep* (1951) are considered the finest volumes of his poetry, which has affinities with the works of Blake and Gerard Manley Hopkins; his *Collected Poems* appeared in 1952. Regarded by some as the outstanding poet of his generation, he died during a lecture tour of the United States. Posthumously published prose works are *Quite Early One Morning* (1954) and *Adventures in the Skin Trade* (1955). *Under Milk Wood* is a play.

Thomas, Philip Edward (3 March 1878—9 April 1917), poet and essayist, was born in London, son of a Civil Servant; both his parents were Welsh. He was educated at St Paul's and Lincoln College,

Oxford, where he studied history. His first book, *The Woodland Life*, appeared in 1897, and two years later, while still an under-graduate, he married Helen Noble. They lived in poverty in various parts of Kent while he tried to make a living by his books and by hack journalism. On the outbreak of the First World War, he enlisted as a private, but had received his commission as a 2nd lieutenant when he was killed at Arras. An intense love of the country is shown in his works, which include *Oxford* (1903), *Beautiful Wales* (1905), *The Heart of England* (1906), *The South Country* (1909), *The Isle of Wight* (1911), *The Icknield Way* (1913), *The Country* (1913), and *A Literary Pilgrim in England* (1917). He wrote no poetry till 1912, when he used the pseudonym Edward Eastaway; his *Collected Poems* (1920) in a style limpid and fastidious, were praised by Walter de la Mare. Thomas also published studies of Richard Jefferies (1909), Maeterlinck (1911), Swinburne (1912), Borrow (1912), Pater (1913), the Duke of Marlborough (1915), and Keats (1916). *The Happy-Go-Lucky Morgans* (1913) is a novel.

Thomas the Rhymer, *see* **Erceldoune, Thomas of.**

Thompson, Dorothy (9 July 1894—30 Jan. 1961), journalist, was born at Lancaster, New York State, daughter of a Methodist minister, and was educated at Syracuse University and Vienna. After working as an advertising copy writer she became a journalist and from 1920 to 1928 worked as a foreign correspondent, first in Vienna, then in Berlin. Later she was political commentator on the New York *Herald Tribune*, and wrote a syndicated column 'On the Record.' A provocative and sometimes maddening writer, she has been described as 'an intellectual Valkyrie.' Her books include *The New Russia* (1928), *I Saw Hitler!* (1937), *Refugees* (1938), *Political Guide* (1938), *Let the Record Speak* (1939), and *Listen, Hans* (1942). Her first two marriages, to Josef Bard, a Hungarian novelist, and to Sinclair Lewis (q.v.) ended in divorce; in 1943 she married Maxim Kopf. She held honorary degrees of six universities.

Thompson, Ernest Seton, *see* **Seton, Ernest Thompson.**

Thompson, Flora (5 Dec. 1877—21 May 1947), descriptive writer, was born at Juniper Hill, north Oxfordshire (the ' Lark Rise ' of her books), of working-class parents. After leaving the country school at 14 she became an assistant to the village postmistress. Later she kept up the connection by marrying a postmaster who was trans-ferred to Bournemouth, where she read extensively in the public library. Her first publication was a book of verse, *Bog Myrtle and Peat*. But she is remembered mainly for her three autobiographical volumes, *Lark Rise* (1939), *Over to Candleford* (1941), and *Candleford Green* (1945), which were reissued in one volume as *Lark Rise to Candleford* (1945). In these books she gives a delightful and truthful picture of English rural life in the latter half of last century. A further volume, *Still Glides the Stream*, appeared in 1948.

Thompson, Francis (16 Dec. 1859—13 Nov. 1907), poet, was born at Preston, Lancashire, son of a homoeopathist. He had two uncles who were writers, and was brought up a Roman Catholic. The family removed to Ashton-under-Lyne, near Manchester, where he lived till 1885. At Ushaw College he studied for the priesthood, but was found unfitted because of his neurotic temperament. He then was a medical student at Owens College for six years, but having failed three times in his final examinations he removed to London in 1885. There he lived in extreme poverty, selling matches or newspapers and becoming a laudanum addict. Having written some poems he sent them to the magazine *Merry England*, then edited by Wilfred Meynell (q.v.). After laying them aside for a time Meynell got in touch with the author in 1888 and was able to rescue him from the depths to which he had sunk. Thompson's health was restored at a monastery near Storrington in Sussex, where he wrote a number of poems, including his famous 'Hound of Heaven,' and for the rest of his life he made his home with the Meynells. His published volumes include *Poems* (1893), *Sister Songs* (1895), written for the little Meynell girls, and *New Poems* (1897). In prose he wrote *Health and Holiness* (1905), an *Essay on Shelley* (1909), and a *Life of St Ignatius Loyola* (1909). He died at 51 of tuberculosis. Among his diversions was watching cricket, on which he wrote various odd pieces of verse. One of the few modern Roman Catholic poets, for the splendour of his vision and the magnificence of his imagery he has been termed a greater Crashaw.

Thompson, Sylvia Elizabeth (4 Sept. 1902—), novelist, was born in Scotland but brought up at Lyndhurst, Hampshire, and educated at Cheltenham and Somerville College, Oxford. In 1926 she married an American artist, Theodore Dunham Peter Luling, and they lived in Venice till the Second World War. Her work reflects the spirit of youth between the World Wars, and her first novel, *Rough Crossing*, was published when she was 16. *The Hounds of Spring*, started when she was at Oxford, was a bestseller in 1925. Others of her novels are *A Lady in Green Gloves* (1924), *The Battle of the Horizons* (1928), *Chariot Wheels* (1929), *Winter· Comedy* (1931), *Summer's Night* (1932), *Helena* (1933), *Golden Arrow* (1935), *A Silver Rattle* (1935), *Recapture the Moon* (1937), *The Adventure of Christopher Columin* (1939), *The Gulls Fly Inland* (1941), *The People Opposite* (1948), and *The Candle's Glory* (1953).

Thoms, William John (16 Nov. 1803—15 Aug. 1885), antiquary, born in Westminster, son of a Treasury official, was for many years a clerk in the secretary's office of Chelsea Hospital. In 1845 he was appointed Clerk to the House of Lords, and subsequently became Deputy Librarian. He was the founder in 1849 of *Notes and Queries*, which for some years he also edited. Among his publications are: *Early Prose Romances* (1827—8), *Lays* and *Legends* (1834), *The Book of the Court* (1838), *Gammer Gurton's Famous Histories* (1846), *Gammer Gurton's Pleasant Stories* (1848), and the autobiographical *Gossip of an Old Bookworm* (1881).

Thomson, James (11 Sept. 1700—27 Aug. 1748), poet, son of the minister of Ednam, Roxburghshire, spent most of his youth, however, at Southdean, a neighbouring parish, to which his father was translated. He was educated at the parish school there, at Jedburgh, and at Edinburgh University, where he studied for the ministry. The style of one of his earliest sermons having been objected to by the Professor of Divinity as being too flowery and imaginative, he gave up his clerical views and went to London in 1725, taking with him a part of what ultimately became his poem of *Winter*. By the influence of his friend Mallet he became tutor to Lord Binning, son of the Earl of Haddington, and was introduced to Pope, Arbuthnot, Gay, and others. *Winter* was published in 1726, and was followed by *Summer* (1727), *Spring* (1728), and *Autumn* (1730), when the whole were brought together as *The Seasons*. Previous to 1730 he had produced one or two minor poems and the tragedy of *Sophonisba*, which, after promising some success, was killed by the unfortunate line, 'Oh! Sophonisba, Sophonisba, oh!' being parodied as 'Oh! Jemmy Thomson, Jemmy Thomson, oh!' In 1731 Thomson accompanied Charles Talbot, son of the Lord Chancellor, to the Continent as tutor, and on his return received the sinecure Secretaryship of Briefs which, however, he lost in 1737, through omitting to apply for its continuance to Talbot's successor. He then returned to the drama and produced *Agamemnon* in 1738, and *Edward and Eleanora* in 1739. The same year he received from the Prince of Wales a pension of £100, and was made Surveyor-General of the Leeward Islands which, after providing for a deputy to discharge the duties, left him £300 a year.

He was now in comfortable circumstances, and settled in a villa near Richmond, where he amused himself with gardening and seeing his friends. In conjunction with Mallet he wrote, in 1740, the masque of *Alfred*, in which appeared 'Rule, Britannia,' which Mallet afterwards claimed, or allowed to be claimed, for him, but which there is every reason to believe was contributed by Thomson. In 1745 appeared *Tancred and Sigismunda*, the most successful of his dramas, and in 1748 *Coriolanus*. In May of the latter year he published *The Castle of Indolence*, an allegorical poem in the Spenserian stanza, generally considered to be his finest work; it contains a stanza, describing himself as inmate of the castle, which was contributed by Lord Lyttelton. In August following he caught a chill which developed into a fever, and carried him off in his forty-eighth year. Though Thomson was undoubtedly a poet by nature, his art was developed by constant and fastidious polishing. To *The Seasons*, originally containing about 4,000 lines, he added about 1,400 in his various revisions. He was the first to give the description of nature the leading place, thus challenging the artificiality of the Augustans and leading the way to the Romantic Revival of the next century. His blank verse, though not equal to that of a few other English poets, is musical and wielded in a manner suitable to his subject. In all his poems he displays the genial temper and kindly sympathies by which he was characterized as a man. He was never married, and lived an easy, indolent life, beloved by his many friends.

Thomson, James (23 Nov. 1834—3 June 1882), poet, was born at Port-Glasgow, son of a ship's officer. With his mother dead and his father paralysed he was educated at the Royal Caledonian Asylum and the Military Asylum, Chelsea. In 1851 he became a teacher at Ballincolig, near Cork, where he met his lifelong friend Charles Bradlaugh; there also he fell in love with Matilda Weller, whose death in 1853 was a blow that shadowed his whole life. Subsequently he worked as an army teacher in Dublin, Aldershot, Jersey, and Portsmouth, but was discharged in 1862 for a breach of discipline. Living in London, first in Pimlico, then near the British Museum, he made a living as clerk and journalist, writing under the initials B. V., for Bysshe Vanolis, a combination of Shelley's middle name with an anagram on Novalis, the German poet. In 1874 he contributed to the *National Reformer* his best-known poem 'The City of Dreadful Night,' which made him famous as the poet of pessimism and despair; along with some other pieces it was published in 1880, and in 1881 a second volume of verse and a collection of essays appeared. A year later he died in University College Hospital, a victim of melancholia and drink.

Thomson, Sir John Arthur (8 July 1861—12 Feb. 1933), scientist, born at Pilmuir, East Lothian, son of a minister, was a contemporary of J. M. Barrie at Edinburgh University and afterwards studied at Jena and Berlin. He was Professor of Natural History at Aberdeen from 1899 till 1930, when he received a knighthood. His self-chosen task was to make science readable, and he published many popular works, of which the best-known are *Outline of Science* (1922), *The Bible of Nature* (1909), *Introduction to Science* (1911), *The Wonder of Life* (1914), *Secrets of Animal Life* (1919), *Science, Old and New* (1924), *Science and Religion* (1925), *Outlines of General Biology* (1931), and *Scientific Riddles* (1932).

Thoreau, Henry David (12 July 1817—6 May 1862), essayist, poet, and naturalist, was born at Concord, Massachusetts. His father, of French extraction, from Jersey, was a manufacturer of lead-pencils. He was educated at Concord Academy and at Harvard, where he became a good classical scholar. Subsequently he was a competent Orientalist, and was deeply versed in the history and manners of the Red Indians. No form of regular remunerative employment commending itself to him, he spent the decade after leaving college in the study of books and nature, for the latter of which he had exceptional qualifications in the acuteness of his senses and his powers of observation. Though not a misanthrope, he appears in general to have preferred solitary communion with nature to human society. 'The man I meet,' he said, 'is seldom so instructive as the silence which he breaks'; and he described himself as 'a mystic, a transcendentalist, and a natural philosopher.' He made such money as his extremely simple mode of life called for, by building boats or fences, doing agricultural or garden work, and surveying—anything almost of an outdoor character which did not involve lengthened engagement.

In 1837 he began his diaries, records of observation with which in 10 years he filled 30 volumes. In 1839 he made the excursion the record of which he in 1845 published as *A Week on the Concord and Merrimac Rivers*. Two years later, in 1841, he began a residence in the household of Emerson, which lasted for two years, when he assisted in conducting the *Dial*, and in 1845, after some teaching in New York, he retired to a hut near the solitary Walden Pond. There he lived alone for two years and wrote his most famous work, *Walden, or Life in the Woods* (1854), which embodies his doctrine of self-sufficiency and simplicity. Later works are *The Maine Woods* (1864), and *Cape Cod* (1865), accounts of excursions and observations, both published after his death. The deliberate aim of Thoreau was to live a life as nearly approaching nature as possible; and to this end he passed his time largely in solitude and in the open air. As he says, 'I went to the woods because I wished to live deliberately, to front only the essential facts of life, and see if I could not learn what it had to teach.' To his great powers of observation he added great powers of reflection, and two of the most characteristic features of his writings are immediateness and individuality in his descriptions of nature, and a remarkable power of giving permanent and clear form to the most subtle and evanescent mental impressions.

Thrale, Hester Lynch (27 Jan. 1741—2 May 1821), writer of memoirs, was born at Bodvel, Carnarvonshire, daughter of John Salusbury. In 1763 she was married, against her inclination, to Henry Thrale, a wealthy Southwark brewer. In 1765 Dr Johnson formed a close friendship with the Thrales, and for the next 16 years he was an inmate of their home at Streatham. Three years after Thrale's death in 1781 his widow married Gabriel Piozzi, an Italian Roman Catholic musician, though her daughters were opposed to the match; Johnson, much chagrined, never saw her again. The Piozzis lived happily in North Wales until he died in 1809, when the widow retired to Bath, where she died as a result of fracturing her leg. Vivacious, witty, and charming, Mrs Thrale wins immortality by her *Anecdotes of the late Samuel Johnson* (1786) and *Letters to and from the late Samuel Johnson* (1788). Her *Autobiography, Letters, and Literary Remains* appeared in 1861, and in 1942 there was published *Thraliana*, which contains her diaries and note-books from 1776 to 1809.

Thurber, James Grover (8 Dec. 1894— 2 Nov. 1961), humorist, was born at Columbus, Ohio, and educated at Ohio University. Rejected for service in the First World War because he was blind in one eye from a childhood accident, he worked as a code clerk. Later he became a journalist and artist and was on the Paris staff of the *Chicago Tribune* till 1926. He then returned to America and joined the staff of the *New Yorker*, of which he became the life and soul. In his first book, *Is Sex Necessary?* (1929) he collaborated with E. B. White. His other works, illustrated with his own drawings, include *The Owl in the Attic* (1931), *The Seal in the Bedroom* (1932), *The Middle-Aged Man on the Flying Trapeze* (1935), *Let Your Mind Alone* (1937), *The Last Flower* (1939), *Fables for our Times* (1940), *Men, Women, and Dogs* (1943), *The Great Quillow* (1944), *The Beast in Me and Other Animals* (1948), *The Thirteen Clocks* (1950), *The Thurber Album* (1952), and *The Thurber Country* (1953); *My Life and Hard Times* (1933) is autobiographical. His work has been described as a mixture of absurdity, inconsequence, and irony.

Latterly he lived in Connecticut, and was almost blind, seeing very imperfectly from his remaining eye.

Thurston, Ernest Charles Temple (23 Sept. 1879—19 March 1933), novelist, published a book of verse at the age of 16 and started to earn his living at 18. In 1901 he married Katherine Cecil Madden (*see* Katherine Thurston); she divorced him in 1910, and he was married on two other occasions. His first novel, *The Apple of Eden* (1904), was followed by *Sally Bishop* (1908), *The City of Beautiful Nonsense* (1909), *The Greatest Wish in the World* (1910), *The Garden of Resurrection* (1911), *Richard Furlong* (1913), *The Passionate Crime* (1915), *The Forest of Fire* (1919), *The World of Wonderful Reality* (1920), *Jane Carroll* (1927), and *A Hank of Hair* (1932). Of his plays *The Wandering Jew* (1920) is the best-known; others are *The Blue Peter* (1924) and *Charmeuse* (1930).

Thurston, Katherine Cecil (18 April 1875—5 Sept. 1911), novelist, was born in Cork, where her father, Paul Madden, had been Mayor. Educated privately, in 1901 she married Ernest Temple Thurston (q.v.), from whom she obtained a divorce in 1910. In 1904 she published her famous novel, *John Chilcote, M.P.*, a story of impersonation; it was very popular, and was dramatized. She treated the same theme in 1910 in *Max*, but did not repeat the success. Others of her novels are *The Circle* (1903), *The Gambler* (1906), *Mystics* (1907), and *The Fly on the Wheel* (1908).

Tickell, Thomas (1686—23 April 1740), poet, born at Bridekirk vicarage, Cumberland, and educated at Oxford, became the friend of Joseph Addison (q.v.) and accompanied him when he went to Ireland as secretary to the Lord Lieutenant. Tickell contributed to the *Spectator* and the *Guardian* and in 1712 published a poem *On the Prospect of Peace*. His translation of the first book of the *Iliad* came out at the same time as Pope's, and led to a quarrel between the latter and Addison, Pope imagining that the publication was a plot to interfere with the success of his work. On Addison becoming Secretary of State in 1717 he appointed Tickell Under-Secretary. Among the writings of Tickell are the ballad, *Colin and Lucy*, *Kensington Gardens*, a poem, and an elegy on the death of Addison, of which Macaulay says that it 'would do honour to the greatest name in our literature.' In 1725 he became secretary to the Lords Justices of Ireland, and retained the post until his death.

Ticknor, George (1 Aug. 1791—26 Jan. 1871), historian and biographer, son of a rich man, was born at Boston, and educated for the law, but abandoned this for literature. After being a professor at Harvard from 1819 to 1835 he went in the latter year to Europe, where he spent some years collecting materials for his greatest work, *The History of Spanish Literature* (1849). He also wrote lives of Lafayette and Prescott, the historian. His *Letters and Journals* were published in 1876, and are the most interesting of his writings.

Tighe, Mary (9 Oct. 1772—24 March 1810), poetess, was born in Ireland, daughter of William Blackford, a clergyman. In 1793 she married her cousin, Henry Tighe, but the union was unhappy, and she died of consumption. She wrote a good deal of verse; but her chief poem was a translation in Spenserian stanza of Apuleius's tale of *Cupid and Psyche*, which won the admiration of Moore and Keats.

Tillotson, John (baptized 10 Oct. 1630, died 22 Nov. 1694), prelate, was born at Halifax, son of a clothier, and educated at Cambridge, where his originally puritan views became somewhat modified. At the Savoy Conference in 1661 he was still a Presbyterian, but submitted to the Act of Uniformity, and became next year rector of Keddington, and in 1664 preacher at Lincoln's Inn, where he became very popular. In 1672 he was made Dean of Canterbury. He vainly endeavoured to secure the comprehension of the Nonconformists in the Church. After the Revolution he gained the favour of William III, who made him Clerk of the Closet, and Dean of St Paul's, and in 1691 he succeeded Sancroft as Archbishop of Canterbury. His sermons, which had extraordinary popularity, give him a place in literature, and he was one of those writers who, by greater simplicity and greater attention to clearness of construction, helped to introduce the modern style of composition.

Timrod, Henry (8 Dec. 1828—6 Oct. 1867), poet, was born at Charleston, South Carolina, son of a bookbinder, and educated at Franklin College, which later became the University of Georgia. He studied law, but gave that up and was for a time a schoolmaster and tutor. In 1860 he published a volume of verse, and some of his war poems, such as 'A Cry to Arms' and 'Carolina' were such an inspiration to the South that he was termed the 'Laureate of the Confederacy.' He enlisted in the Confederate forces in 1862 but was discharged because of tuberculosis. In 1864 he was part proprietor and editor of the *South Carolinian* in Columbia, but when Columbia was burned during the war he was reduced to beggary and died soon afterwards.

Tindale, William, *see* **Tyndale.**

Tobin, John (28 Jan. 1770—8 Dec. 1804), dramatist, was born in Salisbury, son of a merchant, and educated at Bristol Grammar School. Articled to a solicitor in Lincoln's Inn, he was more interested in playwriting, at which he tried his hand, at first with no success. After repeated rejections, he had almost given up hope when his blank verse play, *The Honey Moon*, was accepted for production. By this time he was in the last stages of consumption, and set off for the West Indies in quest of health, but died on the first day out; the vessel put back and he was buried at Cove near Cork. A few weeks later his play was produced amid great applause. The rejected pieces of his past years were now unearthed and printed, the best-known being *The Curfew* (1807) and *The School for Authors* (1808).

Toland, John (30 Nov. 1670—11 March 1722), deistical writer, born near Londonderry of Roman Catholic parentage, completed his education at Glasgow, Edinburgh, and Leyden Universities. Very early in life he had become a Protestant, and at Leyden he studied theology with the view of becoming a Nonconformist minister, but adopted rationalistic views. He then resided for some time at

z*

Oxford, and in 1696 published his first work, *Christianity not Myster-ious*, which was censured by Convocation and gave rise to much controversy. Next year he returned to Ireland, where, however, he was not more popular than in England, and where his book was burned by the common hangman. Returning to England he took to writing political pamphlets, including one, *Anglia Libera*, in support of the Brunswick succession, which gained him some favour at Hanover, and he was sent on some political business to the German Courts. He then served Harley in Holland and Germany practically as a political spy. His later years were passed in literary drudgery and poverty. Among his numerous writings may be mentioned *Account of Prussia and Hanover* (1705), *Origines Judaicae* (1709), *History of the Druids*, and a life of Milton.

Tomlinson, Henry Major (1873—5 Feb. 1958), novelist and travel writer, was born in the East End of London and grew up among the docks. At the age of 12 he became clerk to a shipping company, but disliked the work and started writing. In 1904 he joined the staff of the *Morning Leader*, and in 1912 he made a voyage up the Amazon, of which he wrote in *The Sea and the Jungle*. During the First World War he was a war correspondent, then was literary editor of the *Nation* from 1917 to 1923. He then travelled in the East Indies and wrote *Tidemarks* (1924). *Gallions Reach* (1927), a novel, was awarded the Femina-Vie Heureuse Prize; others of his novels are *All Our Yesterdays* (1930), *The Snows on Helicon* (1933), *All Hands!* (1937), and *Morning Light* (1946). But he is best known for his descriptive and travel books, *Old Junk* (1918), *London River* (1921), *Under the Red Ensign* (1926), *Between the Lines* (1928), *Out of Soundings* (1931), *The Wind Is Rising* (1941), *Turn of the Tide* (1945), and *Malay Waters* (1950). He also wrote studies of Thomas Hardy (1929) and Norman Douglas (1931); *A Mingled Yarn* (1953) is a collection of autobiographical essays.

Tooke, John Horne (25 June 1736—18 March 1812), philologist, son of a poulterer called Horne, added the name of Tooke in 1782 in anticipation of inheriting from his friend W. Tooke, of Purley. Educated at Westminster and Eton, he lost the sight of his right eye in a fight at school. Having studied at Cambridge, he took orders, but disliking the religious profession, travelled abroad. Returning he became prominent as a radical politician, and espoused the cause of Wilkes, with whom, however, he afterwards quarrelled. He also supported the revolted American colonists, and was fined and imprisoned for endeavouring to raise a subscription for them. An effort to be admitted to the Bar was unsuccessful; and in 1786 he published his *Diversions of Purley*, a pioneer philological work which stressed the importance of Gothic and Old English studies. Tooke twice endeavoured unsuccessfully to enter Parliament for West-minster, but ultimately sat for the rotten borough of Old Sarum, making, however, no mark in the House. He was the author of numerous effective political pamphlets.

Toplady, Augustus Montague (4 Nov. 1740—14 Aug. 1778), hymn-writer, son of an officer in the army, was born at Farnham, Surrey, and educated at Westminster and Trinity College, Dublin, after which he took orders and became incumbent of Broad Hembury. He was a strong Calvinist and entered into a bitter controversy with Wesley. His controversial works are forgotten; but he will always be remembered as the author of 'Rock of Ages,' one of the most widely known of English hymns.

Torrence, Frederic Ridgely (27 Nov. 1875—25 Dec. 1950), poet and playwright, born at Xenia, Ohio, was educated at Miami University and Princeton, where he helped to edit the college magazine. For six years he was a librarian in New York, then held various editorial posts, from 1920 to 1933 being poetry editor of the *New Republic*. After making a tour of Europe with his friend William Vaughn Moody (q.v.), he began writing verse plays and composed *El Dorado* (1903) and *Abelard and Heloise* (1907). These were followed by his plays for a Negro theatre, *Granny Maumee*, *The Rider of Dreams*, and *Simon the Cyrenian*, all produced in 1917. A pioneer in this type of production, he opened the way for others such as O'Neill's *Emperor Jones* and Connelly's *The Green Pastures*. Of his volumes of verse *Hesperides* appeared in 1925, *Poems*, which received the Shelley Memorial Prize, in 1941, and *Last Poems* in 1944.

Tourneur *or* **Turnour** *or* **Turner, Cyril** (1575?—28 Feb. 1626), poet and dramatist, somewhat resembles Marston (q.v.) in his work. Nothing is known of his early life. His poems include *The Transformed Metamorphosis* (1600), a satirical allegory; *A Funeral Poem* (1609) on Sir Frances Vere; and *A Grief on the Death of Prince Henry* (1613). Of the two plays attributed to him, *The Revenger's Tragedy* (1607) has sombre intensity and horror relieved by passages of poetic beauty; Lamb said of it that it made his ears tingle. *The Atheist's Tragedy* (1611) is not so effective, and the authenticity of both plays has been questioned. Tourneur served in the Netherlands and was Sir Edward Cecil's secretary in the unsuccessful Cadiz expedition of 1625; on its return he was put ashore in Ireland owing to illness and died at Kinsale.

Tovey, Sir Donald Francis (17 July 1875—10 July 1940), musical critic, was born at Eton, where his father was a master. He studied music, and took a classical degree at Balliol College, Oxford, of which he was later a Fellow. From 1914 till his death he was Professor of Music at Edinburgh, and he was knighted in 1935. His opera *The Bride of Dionysus* was produced in 1929, but he was best known as a musical critic. His works include *Essays in Musical Analysis* (six volumes, 1935—9), *The Main Stream of Music* (1938), and *A Musician Talks* (1941).

Toynbee, Arnold Joseph (14 April 1889—   ), historian, was born in London and educated at Winchester and Balliol College, Oxford, of which he was a Fellow from 1912 to 1915. In 1913 he married a daughter of Gilbert Murray (q.v.); they were divorced in 1946. During the First World War Toynbee was employed in the Foreign Office. From 1919 to 1924 he was Professor of Modern Greek and Byzantine History in London, then became Professor of International History there and Director of Studies at the Royal

Institute of International Affairs; he also edited the annual *Survey of International Affairs*. His monumental work, the 10-volume *Study of History*, published in sections between 1934 and 1954, forms a survey of the chief civilizations and seeks to construct a science of human progress. Others of his publications are *Nationality and the War* (1915), *Greek Civilization and Character* (1924), *Christianity and Civilization* (1940), *Civilization on Trial* (1948), *The Prospects of Western Civilization* (1949), and *The World and the War* (1953). He held honorary degrees of Oxford, Cambridge, Princeton, and Columbia, was a Fellow of the British Academy, and in 1956 was made a Companion of Honour.

Toynbee, Theodore Philip (25 June 1916—   ), novelist, was born at Oxford, son of Arnold Toynbee (q.v.), and educated at Rugby and Christ Church. At Oxford he published a novel, *The Savage Days* (1937), joined the Communist Party, and had the unique distinction of being a Communist President of the Union; but in 1939 he abandoned Communism and became a supporter of Labour. During the Second World War he served in the Guards, and later worked in the Intelligence Corps in London. In 1950 he joined the staff of the *Observer*. His novels include *School in Private* (1941), *The Barricades* (1944), *Tea with Mrs Goodman* (1947), and *The Garden to the Sea* (1953). *Friends Apart* (1954) is a memoir of two friends who were killed in the war.

Traherne, Thomas (1638?—27 Sept. 1674), mystical writer and poet, was born in Hereford, son of a shoemaker. Educated at Brasenose College, Oxford, he took orders and in 1657 was rector of Credenhill, near his birth-place; in 1667 he became chaplain to Sir Orlando Bridgeman, Lord Keeper of the Great Seal, in whose household at Teddington he passed the rest of his days. His *Roman Forgeries* (1673) and *Christian Ethics* (1675) have only historical interest, but *Centuries of Meditation*, first printed in 1908, consists of short reflections on religion in translucent prose of a wonderful musical quality which is sometimes more poetical than his verse, which has occasional technical faults. The discovery of his poems is a romance in itself. They were found in manuscript on a bookstall in 1896, and were at first thought to be the work of Vaughan. Bertram Dobell (q.v.) identified them as Traherne's, and published them in 1903. Pure and limpid, with brilliant natural imagery, they have affinities with Blake and Wordsworth, and rank with the best of the seventeenth-century lyrical poets.

Traill, Henry Duff (14 Aug. 1842—21 Feb. 1900), poet and critic, born in London, son of a magistrate, was educated at Merchant Taylors' and St John's College, Oxford. He studied law and was called to the Bar at Inner Temple in 1869. In 1871 he became an inspector in the Education Office. He then turned to writing, and was on the staff first of the *Pall Mall Gazette* and then of the *St James's Gazette*; from 1882 to 1897 he was a leader-writer on the *Daily Telegraph*. His humorous verses, which show a rare gift for parody, were collected as *Recaptured Rhymes* (1882) and *Saturday Songs* (1890). He published studies of Sterne (1882) and Coleridge

(1884), as well as of several statesmen, and wrote the standard life of Sir John Franklin (1896). *Number Twenty* (1892) and *The New Fiction* (1897) are volumes of essays, and *The New Lucian* (1884) is a series of dialogues of the dead.

Trapp, Joseph (baptized 18 Dec. 1679, died 22 Nov. 1747), poet and translator, was born at Cherrington, Gloucestershire, where his father was rector. Educated at New College School and Wadham College, Oxford, he took orders. In 1704 he published a tragedy, *Abramule, or Love and Empire*, and from 1708 to 1718 he was the first Professor of Poetry at Oxford; his lectures, delivered in Latin, were highly praised, though his name appears in the scurrilous pentameter of Oxford poets, 'Bubb, Stubb, Grubb, Crabb, Trapp, Young, Carey, Tickell, Evans.' In 1712 he was appointed chaplain to Lord Bolingbroke, and in 1728 was given the degree of Doctor of Divinity for writing tracts against the Roman Catholics. He wrote various poems on notable events of his time, but was known chiefly for his blank verse rendering of Virgil, published in 1735.

Treece, Henry (1912—), poet, novelist, critic, was born in the Midlands, of Welsh extraction, and educated at Wednesbury Grammar School and Birmingham University, where he was captain of boxing in 1932. During the Second World War he was a pilot officer in the R.A.F.V.R., and both before and after it worked as a schoolmaster. As a poet he was one of the leaders of the self-styled Apocalyptic movement, which represented a reaction against the realist and political poetry of the thirties and claimed kinship with the Book of Revelation. He was joint editor of their anthologies *The New Apocalypse* (1939), *The White Horseman* (1941), and *The Crown and the Sickle* (1945). Volumes of his verse include *Towards a Personal Armageddon* (1940), *Thirty-Eight Poems* (1940), *Invitation and Warning* (1942), *The Black Seasons* (1945), *The Haunted Garden* (1947), and *The Exiles* (1952). Turning then to fiction he wrote the novels *The Dark Island* (1952), *The Rebels* (1953), *Desperate Journey* (1954), *The Eagles Have Flown* (1954), *Hounds of the King* (1955), and *Vikings Dawn* (1955). Books of criticism are *How I See Apocalypse* (1946) and studies of Herbert Read (1944), Swinburne (1948), and Dylan Thomas (1949).

Trelawny, Edward John (13 Nov. 1792—13 Aug. 1881), adventurer and biographer, born in London, son of an army officer, in 1805 entered the navy, from which, however, he deserted, after which he wandered about in the East and on the Continent. In Switzerland he met Byron and Shelley, was living in close friendship with the latter when he was drowned, and was one of the witnesses at the cremation of his remains. He took part in the Greek war of independence, and married the sister of one of the insurgent chiefs. After various adventures in America he settled in London, where he was a distinguished figure in society, and enjoyed the reputation of a picturesque, but somewhat imaginative, conversationalist. He wrote *The Adventures of a Younger Son* (1831), an autobiographical work of striking distinction, and the intensely interesting *Records of Shelley*,

Byron, and the Author (1858). The last survivor of that brilliant group, he was buried by the side of Shelley.

Trench, Frederic Herbert (26 Nov. 1865—11 June 1923), poet and playwright, born at Avoncore, County Cork, was a great-nephew of Richard Chenevix Trench (q.v.). Educated at Haileybury, where he wrote *Haileybury Verses* (1882), and at Keble College, Oxford, in 1889 he was elected a Fellow of All Souls. After a period of travel in various parts of Europe he was Senior Examiner at the Board of Education from 1900 to 1909. During this time he published two volumes of verse, *Deirdre Wed* (1900) and *New Poems* (1907). From 1909 to 1911 he was artistic director of the Haymarket Theatre. His later publications include *Lyrics and Narrative Poems* (1911), an *Ode from Italy in Time of War* (1915), and *Poems, with Fables in Prose* (1918). *Napoleon* (1919) is a four-act play, and he was working on another, *Talleyrand*, when he died in Italy.

Trench, Richard Chenevix (5 Sept. 1807—28 March 1886), prelate and philologist, born in Dublin, son of a barrister, and educated at Harrow and Cambridge, took orders, and after serving various country parishes, became in 1847 Professor of Theology in King's College, London, in 1856 Dean of Westminster, and in 1864 Archbishop of Dublin. As Primate of the Irish Church at its disestablishment, he rendered valuable service in a time of trial. In theology his best known works are his *Hulsean Lectures* (1845), *Notes on the Parables* (1841), and *Notes on the Miracles* (1846). His philological writings, *The Study of Words* (1851) and *English Past and Present* (1855) are extremely interesting and suggestive, though now to some extent superseded. His *Sacred Latin Poetry* is a valuable collection of medieval Church hymns. He also wrote elegies and lyrics and some fine sonnets, besides two longer poems, *Justin Martyr* (1835), and *Sabbation* (1838).

Trevelyan, George Macaulay, O.M. (16 Feb. 1876—   ), historian, son of Sir George Otto Trevelyan (q.v.) and grand-nephew of Macaulay, was born at Stratford-upon-Avon and educated at Harrow and Trinity College, Cambridge, of which he became Master in 1940. In 1904 he married a daughter of Mrs Humphrey Ward. From 1927 to 1940 he was Professor of Modern History at Cambridge. During the First World War he was commandant of a British ambulance unit in Italy and was made a Chevalier of the Order of St Maurice and St Lazarus. In 1920 he was made a C.B.E. and in 1930 was awarded the Order of Merit; in 1961 the Royal Society of Literature made him a Companion of Literature. A Fellow of the British Academy, he held honorary degrees of Oxford, Cambridge, St Andrews, Edinburgh, London, Durham, Harvard, and Yale. In his writings he gave reality and colour to the dry bones of history and thus made it a living thing to a wide circle of readers. His best-known works are his *History of England* (1926) and *English Social History* (1942); others are *England Under the Stuarts* (1905), *Clio, a Muse* (1913), *British History in the Nineteenth Century* (1922), *England Under Queen Anne* (1930—4), *Trinity College* (1943), and *The Seven Years of William IV* (1952). He also wrote lives of John

Bright (1913), of his own father (1932), and of Lord Grey (1937), as well as several books on Garibaldi. *An Autobiography and Other Essays* appeared in 1949.

Trevelyan, Sir George Otto, 2nd Baronet, O.M. (20 July 1838—17 Aug. 1928), statesman and historian, was born at Rothley Temple, Leicestershire. At Harrow he was head of the school, and at Trinity College, Cambridge, he was noted for his light verse and satires. During his youth he was the favourite companion of his uncle, Lord Macaulay (q.v.). In 1862 he went to India as secretary to his father, Sir Charles Trevelyan, then a member of the Governor-General's Council. From 1868 to 1897 he was an M.P., being successively Secretary to the Admiralty (1881), Secretary for Ireland (1882), and Secretary for Scotland (1886 and 1892). His works include his edition of the *Life and Letters of Lord Macaulay* (1876), *The Early History of Charles James Fox* (1880), and his great six-volume *American Revolution* (1899—1914), which did much to vindicate the American point of view. In 1911 he was awarded the Order of Merit.

Trevelyan, Robert Calverley (28 June 1872—21 March 1951), poet and playwright, son of Sir George Trevelyan and brother of George Macaulay Trevelyan (qq.v.), was educated at Harrow and Trinity College, Cambridge. He made many translations from Greek authors and from the works of Leopardi. Volumes of his own verse include *Mallow and Asphodel* (1898), *Polyphemus* (1901), *The Bride of Dionysus* (1912), *The Foolishness of Solomon* (1915), *The Death of Man* (1919), *Poems and Fables* (1925), *The Deluge* (1926), *Rimeless Numbers* (1932), *Beelzebub* (1935), and *From the Shiffolds* (1947). Among his plays are *The Birth of Parsival* (1905), *Meleager* (1927), and *Cheiron* (1928). In prose he published *Thamyris, or the Future of Poetry* (1925) and a book of essays, *Windfalls* (1944).

Trevisa, John of, *see* **John of Trevisa.**

Trollope, Anthony (24 April 1815—6 Dec. 1882), novelist, was born in London and educated at Winchester and Harrow. His mother, Frances Trollope (q.v.), was a prolific writer, but his father, a barrister, ruined himself by speculation, and the family had to move to Belgium because of his debts. Anthony obtained a clerkship in the post office in 1834, and rose to be deputy postal surveyor at Banagher in Ireland, where he married Rose Heseltine and wrote his earliest stories, *The Macdermots of Ballycloran* (1847), *The Kellys and the O'Kellys* (1848), and *La Vendée* (1850). He first attained fame with the 'Barchester' series of novels, in which Church of England clergymen play a leading part. These 'Chronicles of Barset' comprise *The Warden* (1855), *Barchester Towers* (1857), *Doctor Thorne* (1858), *Framley Parsonage* (1861), *The Small House at Allington* (1864), and *The Last Chronicle of Barset* (1867). Other novels, which have a political rather than a clerical background, are *Phineas Finn* (1869), *Phineas Redux* (1876), and *The Eustace Diamonds* (1873). Essays and travel books added to the number of Trollope's writings, from which in all he is said to have made some £70,000. His *Autobiography* was published in 1883. The keynote of his work is contained in his definition of the novelist's task as 'the creation of human beings in whose existence one is forced to believe.' During the Second World War there was a considerable revival of interest in his books.

Trollope, Frances (10 March 1780—6 Oct. 1863), novelist and travel writer, was born at Stapleton near Bristol, daughter of William Milton, a clergyman. In 1809 she married Thomas Anthony Trollope who, after failing in this country as a barrister and as a farmer, went to Cincinnati, where he failed as a shopkeeper. After his death Mrs Trollope returned to England, where she brought herself into notice by publishing *Domestic Manners of the Americans* (1832), in which she gave a very unfavourable and grossly exaggerated account of the subject; a novel, *The Refugee in America*, followed similar lines. Next came *The Abbess* and *Belgium and Western Germany*, and other works of the same kind on *Paris and the Parisians* and *Vienna and the Austrians* followed. Thereafter she continued to pour forth novels and books on miscellaneous subjects, writing in all over 100 volumes. Though she possessed considerable powers of observation and a sharp and caustic wit, such an output was fatal to permanent literary success. She spent the last 20 years of her life at Florence. Her third son was Anthony Trollope, the well-known novelist (q.v.).

Trumbull, John (24 April 1750—11 May 1831), poet, was born at Westbury, Connecticut, son of a Congregationalist minister. Extremely precocious, he is said to have passed the entrance examination for Yale at the age of 7, but wisely did not matriculate till he was 13. In 1775 he removed to Boston, studied law, and ultimately became a judge. Most important of the group known as the Hartford Wits, he advocated departure from the prevailing neo-classical style of poetry, but nevertheless often followed it himself. *The Progress of Dulness*, a burlesque, and *The Correspondent*, a series of satirical essays, both appeared in 1773. Two years later he published his mock-epic *McFingal*, modelled on *Hudibras*; it satirized the stupidity of the British, and was very popular.

Tucker, Abraham (2 Sept. 1705—20 Nov. 1774), philosopher, born in London, and educated at Oxford, was a country gentleman, who devoted himself to the study of philosophy, and wrote under the name of Edward Search, *The Light of Nature Followed* (seven volumes 1768—78). It is rather a miscellany than a systematic treatise, but contains some original and acute thinking.

Tucker, George (20 Aug. 1775—10 April 1861), political economist, was born in Bermuda, son of the Mayor of Hamilton, and educated at the University of Virginia, where he became Professor of Moral Philosophy from 1825 to 1845. His early works include a novel, *The Valley of Shenandoah* (1824), and a satirical romance, *A Voyage to the Moon* (1827), but he is best known for his works on political economy, *Laws of Wages, Profits, and Rents Investigated* (1837), *The Theory of Money and Banks Investigated* (1839), *Progress of the United States in Population and Wealth in Fifty Years* (1843), and *Political*

Economy for the People (1859). He also published a life of Thomas Jefferson (1837), and a *History of the United States* (1856—7).

Tucker, Nathaniel Beverly (6 Sept. 1784—2 Aug. 1851), novelist and essayist, was born in Chesterfield County, Virginia, son of a judge, and was educated at the College of William and Mary, where ultimately he became Professor of Law.   In his novels he championed the rights of the South.   *George Balcombe* was highly praised by Poe, while *The Partisan Leader* prophesied the disunion that led to the Civil War, and was used as propaganda; both of these appeared in 1836, and *Gertrude* followed in 1845.   Of Tucker's treatises the most important are *A Discourse on the Importance of the Study of Political Science* (1840) and *The Principles of Pleading* (1846).

Tuckerman, Henry Theodore (20 April 1813—17 Dec. 1871), critic and essayist, was born in Boston, son of a merchant, and educated at the Latin School and Harvard.   He travelled in Italy and other parts of Europe, and wrote *The Italian Sketch Book* (1835), *Isabel, or Sicily, a Pilgrimage* (1839), and *A Month in England* (1853).   As a literary critic he followed Hazlitt in his *Thoughts on the Poets* (1846) and *Characteristics of Literature* (two series, 1849, 1851).   Other collections of essays are *The Optimist* (1850), *Leaves from the Diary of a Dreamer* (1853), *Essays Biographical and Critical* (1857), and *The Criterion* (1866).   He also wrote *America and her Commentators* (1864) and *The Book of the Artists* (1867).

Tulloch, John (1 June 1823—13 Feb. 1886), theologian and historian, born at Bridge of Earn, Perthshire, studied at St Andrews and Edinburgh.   After a period as minister in Dundee he became in 1854 Principal and Professor of Theology in St Mary's College, St Andrews.   He was a leader of the liberal party in the Church of Scotland, and wrote *Rational Theology and Christian Philosophy in England in the Seventeenth Century* (1872), a study of Pascal (1878), *Literary and Intellectual Revival of Scotland in the Eighteenth Century* (1883), and *Movements of Religious Thought in the Nineteenth Century* (1884—5).

Tupper, Martin Farquhar (17 July 1810—29 Nov. 1889), versifier, son of a doctor of Huguenot descent, was born in London, educated at Charterhouse and Oxford, and called to the Bar in 1835.   He, however, believed that literature was his vocation and wrote many works in prose and verse, only one of which, *Proverbial Philosophy* (1838), had much success.   But the vogue which it had was enormous, especially in America, where a million copies were sold.   It is a singular collection of commonplace observations set forth in a form which bears the appearance of verse, but has neither rhyme nor metre, though its rhythms, inspired by biblical passages, are said to have influenced Walt Whitman (q.v.).   Tupper's name has become a byword for the trite and platitudinous.   He also wrote *War Ballads* (1854), *Rifle Ballads* (1859), and *Protestant Ballads* (1874), various novels, and an autobiography, *My Life as an Author* (1886).

Turberville *or* **Turbervile, George** (1540?—1610), poet, belonging to an ancient Dorsetshire family, was born at Whitchurch, and educated at Winchester and Oxford.   He became secretary to

Thomas Randolph, Ambassador to Russia, and made translations from the Latin and Italian, and in 1567 published *Epitaphes, Epigrams, Songs, and Sonets*. He also wrote *The Booke of Faulconrie* and *The Noble Art of Venerie* (1575), and was one of the first to use blank verse.

Turner, Cyril, *see* **Tourneur.**

Turner, Charles Tennyson (4 July 1808—25 April 1879), poet, born at Somersby, Lincolnshire, was an elder brother of Alfred, Lord Tennyson (q.v.). Educated at Louth Grammar School and Cambridge, he took orders and became vicar of Grasby, Lincolnshire. He collaborated with Alfred in the little volume *Poems of Two Brothers*, published in 1827. In 1830 he changed his name to Turner on inheriting the property of a great-uncle. He wrote over 300 sonnets, published in several volumes and gathered together in *Collected Sonnets, Old and New* (1880).

Turner, Frederick Jackson (14 Nov. 1861—14 March 1932), historian, was born at Portage, Wisconsin, and educated at the University of Wisconsin and Johns Hopkins. In 1892 he became an assistant professor of history at Wisconsin, and from 1910 to 1924 occupied the Chair of History at Harvard. In 1893 he wrote a notable paper which became the chief essay in his book *The Frontier in American History* (1920) and had a profound effect on American historical thought. He was not a facile writer, and most of his work was in essay form. Among his books are *The Rise of the New West* (1906), *The Significance of Sections in American History* (1932), which was awarded the Pulitzer Prize, and *The United States, 1830—1850* (1935).

Turner, Sharon (24 Sept. 1768—13 Feb. 1847), historian, born in London, was a solicitor, and becoming interested in the study of Icelandic and Old English literature, published the results of his researches in his *History of the Anglo-Saxons* (1799—1805). Thereafter he continued the narrative in *History of England* (1814—29), carrying it on to the end of the reign of Elizabeth. These histories, especially the former, though somewhat marred by an attempt to emulate the grandiose style of Gibbon, were works of real research, and opened up, and to a considerable extent developed, a new field of inquiry. He also wrote a *Sacred History of the World* (1832), and a poem on Richard III.

Turner, Walter James Redfern (13 Oct. 1889—18 Nov. 1946), poet, novelist, music critic, was born in Melbourne, where his father was organist at St Paul's Protestant Cathedral, and educated at the Scotch College there. He attended the School of Mines for a time, but at the age of 17 came to London, and later studied at Munich and Vienna. During the First World War he served with the Royal Garrison Artillery. After it he became music critic of the *New Statesman* and dramatic critic of the *London Mercury*; from 1942 he was literary editor of the *Spectator*. Much of his verse is exotic, with rich and flowing language; volumes include *The Hunter* (1916), *The Dark Fire* (1918), *Paris and Helen* (1921), *Landscape of Cytherea*

(1923), *The Seven Days of the Sun* (1925), *New Poems* (1928), *Pursuit of Psyche* (1931), *Jack and Jill* (1934), *Songs and Incantations* (1936), and *Fables, Parables, and Plots* (1943). Among his novels are *The Man Who Ate the Popomack* (1922), *The Aesthetes* (1927), and *The Duchess of Popocatapetl* (1939). He also published many books on music.

Turnour, Cyril, *see* **Tourneur.**

Tusser, Thomas (1524?—3 May 1580), agricultural writer and poet, was born at Rivenhall in Essex. Having a good voice he was trained in music, and was a chorister in St Paul's and afterwards in Norwich Cathedral, and held the post of musician to Lord Paget. He tried farming at different places, but unsuccessfully; this did not, however, prevent his undertaking to instruct others, which he does with much shrewdness and point in his *Hundreth Goode Pointes of Husbandrie* (1557), expressed in rude but lively verse; thereafter he added *Hundreth Goode Pointes of Husserie* (Housewifery). The two joined, and with many additions, were repeatedly reprinted as *Five Hundredth Pointes of Goode Husbandrie united to as many of Goode Huswifery*. Many proverbs may be traced back to the writings of Tusser, who, in spite of all his shrewdness and talent, died in prison as a debtor.

Twain, Mark, *see* **Clemens, Samuel Langhorne.**

Tweedsmuir, Baron, *see* **Buchan, John.**

Tyler, Royall (18 July 1757—26 Aug. 1826), playwright and novelist, was born at Boston, his original name being William Clark Tyler. Educated at Harvard, he studied law, and was admitted to the Bar in 1780. In 1787 he wrote *The Contrast*, which is notable as the first comedy written by a native American and produced by a professional company, and the first play using local American dialect for comic purposes; it was highly successful, and he wrote other plays, which have not, however, been published. He also wrote *The Algerine Captive* (1797), a fine picaresque novel, and a number of poems, including *The Chestnut Tree*, written in 1824 but not printed till 1931, which gives an interesting picture of old village life in America.

Tynan, Katherine (23 Jan. 1861—2 April 1931), poetess and novelist, was born at Clondalkin, County Dublin, daughter of a farmer. A Roman Catholic, she was educated at Siena Convent, Drogheda. In 1883 she married Henry Albert Hinkson, a lawyer, and they made their home in London; later he was a resident magistrate in Mayo. Her first book of poems, *Louise de la Vallière*, was published in 1885. Others are *Ballads and Lyrics* (1890), *New Poems* (1911), and *Irish Poems* (1913); her *Collected Poems* appeared in 1930. The first of her pleasant and sentimental novels was *The Way of a Maid* (1895); altogether she wrote over a hundred, including *The Handsome Brandons* (1898), *A Midsummer Rose* (1913), *John-a-Dreams* (1916), *The Second Wife* (1920), *The Infatuation of Peter* (1926), and *The House in the Forest* (1928). She also published a series of autobiographical works, *Twenty-Five Years* (1913), *The Middle Years* (1917), *The Years of the Shadow* (1919), *The Wandering*

Years (1922), and *Memories* (1924). A well-known figure in the Celtic Revival, she knew most of the prominent Irish writers of her time. Alice Meynell (q.v.) was her close friend, and they are buried in London side by side.

Tyndale *or* **Tindale, William** (1484?—6 Aug. 1536), translator of the Bible, belonged to a northern family which, migrating to Gloucestershire during the Wars of the Roses, adopted the alternative name of Huchyns or Hychins, which Tyndale himself bore when at Oxford in 1510. After graduating there, he went to Cambridge, where the influence of Erasmus, who had been Professor of Theology, still operated. He took orders, and in 1522 was a tutor in the household of Sir John Walsh of Old Sodbury, and was preaching and disputing in the country round, for which he was called to account by the Chancellor of the diocese. At the same time he translated a treatise by Erasmus, the *Enchiridion Militis Christiani* (Manual of the Christian Soldier), and in controversy with a local disputant prophesied that he would cause that 'a boye that driveth the plough' should know the Scriptures better than his opponent. Having formed the purpose of translating the New Testament Tyndale went in 1523 to London, and lived in the house of a wealthy draper, Humphrey Monmouth, where he probably began his translation. Finding, however, that his work was likely to be interfered with, he proceeded in 1524 to Hamburg, whence he went to visit Luther at Wittenberg. He began printing his translation at Cologne the following year, but had to fly to Worms, where the work was completed, being published in 1525, with a revised edition in 1534.

The translation itself is entirely Tyndale's work, and is that of a thorough scholar, and shows likewise an ear for the harmony of words; a very great part of the much-praised Authorized Version is taken straight from it. The notes and introduction are partly his own, partly literal translations, and partly the gist of the work of Luther. From Germany the translation was introduced into England, and largely circulated until forcible means of prevention were brought to bear in 1528. In this year Tyndale removed to Marburg, where he published *The Parable of the Wicked Mammon,* a treatise on justification by faith, and *The Obedience of a Christian Man,* setting forth that Scripture is the ultimate authority in matters of faith, and the King in matters of civil government. Thereafter, having been at Hamburg and Antwerp, Tyndale returned to Marburg, and in 1530 published his translation of the *Pentateuch* and *The Practice of Prelates*, in which he attacked Wolsey and the proposed divorce proceedings of Henry VIII, the latter of whom endeavoured to have him apprehended. Subsequently he was involved in a controversy with Sir Thomas More. In 1533 he returned to Antwerp, Henry's hostility having somewhat cooled, and was occupied in revising his translations, when he was in 1535 betrayed into the hands of the Imperial officers and carried off to the Castle of Vilvorde, where the next year he was strangled and burned, his last words being, 'Lord, open the King of England's eyes.'

Tyndall, John (2 Aug. 1820—4 Dec. 1893), scientist, born at

Leighlin Bridge, County Carlow, was in early life employed in the ordnance survey and as a railway engineer. He was next teacher of mathematics and surveying at Queenswood College, Hampshire, after which he went to Marburg to study science, and while there became joint author of a memoir *On the Magneto-optic Properties of Crystals* (1850). In 1852 he was elected a Fellow of the Royal Society, and in 1853 was appointed Professor of Natural Philosophy in the Royal Institution, where in 1867 he succeeded Faraday as Superintendent. With Huxley (q.v.) he made investigations into the Alpine glaciers. Thereafter he did much original work on heat, sound, and light. In addition to his discoveries Tyndall was one of the greatest popularizers of science. His style, remarkable for lucidity and elegance, enabled him to expound such subjects with the minimum of technical terminology. Among his works are *The Glaciers of the Alps* (1860), *Mountaineering* (1861), and *Fragments of Science* (1871). He died from an overdose of chloral accidentally administered by his wife.

Tytler, Alexander Fraser (15 Oct. 1747—5 Jan. 1813), historian, son of William Tytler (q.v.), studied at Edinburgh, was called to the Bar in 1770 and raised to the Bench as Lord Woodhouselee in 1802. He was Professor of History in Edinburgh, and wrote *Elements of General History* (1801), *An Essay on the Principles of Translation* (1791), and various legal treatises.

Tytler, Patrick Fraser (1791—24 Dec. 1849), historian, son of the above, studied at Edinburgh, and was called to the Bar in 1813. Among his many writings are an *Essay on the History of the Moors in Spain*, *The Life of the Admirable Crichton* (1819), *History of Scotland, 1249—1603* (1828—43), *Lives of Scottish Worthies* (1831—3), and *England under the Reigns of Edward VI and Mary* (1839).

Tytler, William (12 Oct. 1711—12 Sept. 1792), historian, born in Edinburgh and educated at its High School and University, became a lawyer, and wrote *An Inquiry into the Evidence against Mary Queen of Scots* (1759), in which he combated the views of Robertson. He discovered the *King's Quhair* of James I, and published in 1783 *The Poetical Remains of James I, King of Scotland*, with a life.

U

Udall *or* **Uvedale, Nicholas** (born 1505, buried 23 Jan. 1556), dramatist, was born in Hampshire and educated at Winchester and Corpus Christi College, Oxford. He was one of the first Oxford tutors to support the Protestant movement. A friend of Leland the antiquary (q.v.) he was noted for the excellence of his Latin verses. About 1534 he became headmaster of Eton, where Thomas Tusser (q.v.) was one of his pupils. While there he published *Flowers for Latin Speaking*, a book of selections from Terence with translations, and for the college's St Andrew's Day celebrations he wrote the play *Ralph Roister Doister*, which is notable as the first native English comedy. In 1541 he was dismissed from his post for indecent offences, and until 1544 was vicar of Braintree in Essex. Later he enjoyed the favour of Edward VI and Mary I, and in 1554 became headmaster of Westminster School.

Underdown, Thomas (fl. 1566—1587), translator, was educated at Oxford. His translation of the *Aethiopica*, a novel of Helidorus, the third-century Greek writer, is a striking example of Elizabethan rhythmical prose; it opened up a new field of romance, and is thought to have influenced Sidney's *Arcadia*. In 1569 he also translated Ovid's *Ibis*.

Underhill, Evelyn (1875—15 June 1941), poetess and mystic, a daughter of Sir Arthur Underhill, was educated at King's College for Women, London, of which she became a Fellow. In 1907 she married Herbert Stuart Moore, a barrister like her father. In 1921 she was appointed Lecturer on the Philosophy of Religion at Manchester College, one of Oxford's theological colleges, and in 1939 she was made an honorary Doctor of Divinity of Aberdeen. Her works include *Mysticism* (1911), *The Mystic Way* (1913), *Practical Mysticism* (1914), *The Essentials of Mysticism* (1920), *The Life of the Spirit* (1922), *The Mystics of the Church* (1925), *Man and the Supernatural* (1927), *The House of the Soul* (1929), and *The Golden Sequence* (1932). *Immanence* (1912) and *Theophanies* (1916) are volumes of verse, and *The Grey World* (1904), *The Lost Word* (1907), and *The Column of Dust* (1909) are novels. In 1943 her *Letters* were published, and in 1946 her *Collected Papers*.

Underwood, Francis Henry (12 Jan. 1825—7 Aug. 1894), lawyer and novelist, was born at Enfield, Massachusetts, son of a farmer. After one year at Amherst he became a schoolmaster, but later studied law and was admitted to the Bar in 1847. Afterwards he became literary editor to a publishing house, and in 1857 helped to found the *Atlantic Monthly*. Of his novels the best is *Quabbin, the Story of a Small Town* (1893), which he wrote while in Scotland, where he was United States Consul first at Glasgow and then at Leith;

others are *Lord of Himself* (1874), *Man Proposes* (1885), and *Doctor Gray's Quest* (1895). He also wrote lives of Longfellow, Lowell, and Whittier.

Untermeyer, Louis (1 Oct. 1885—   ), poet and critic, born in New York and educated at the De Witt Clinton High School, at the age of 15 entered his father's jewellery business, in which he remained till 1923. He married successively Jean Starr and Virginia Moore, both poetesses, Esther Antin, a lawyer, and lastly Bryna Ivens. From 1928 he lived in the Adirondacks, and during the Second World War worked at the Office of War Information. Volumes of his own verse, which was influenced at first by that of Henley, include *First Love* (1911), *Challenge* (1914), *The New Adam* (1920), *Roast Leviathan* (1923), and *Burning Bush* (1928). A master parodist, he wrote many witty imitations of contemporary poets, gathered in *Collected Parodies* (1926). His critical works include *American Poetry Since 1900* (1923) and *Forms of Poetry* (1926), and he compiled some ten poetry anthologies, the most important being *Modern American Poetry* (1919) and *Modern British Poetry* (1920), both of which were later revised. From 1934 to 1937 he was poetry editor of the *American Mercury*. *From Another World* (1939) is autobiographical.

Urbanus, Sylvanus, *see* **Cave, Edward.**

Urquhart *or* **Urchard, Sir Thomas** (1611—1660), translator and miscellaneous writer, was a son of Sir Thomas Urquhart of Cromarty. Educated at King's College, Aberdeen, he then travelled in several European countries. Violently opposed to the Covenanters, he fought against them at Turriff in 1639, and had to take refuge in England, where he entered the service of Charles I, who knighted him in 1641. In the same year he published a book of *Epigrams*, and in 1645 followed this with *Trissotetras*, a work on trigonometry. For joining in a royalist rising in 1649 he was imprisoned in the Tower, where he wrote *The Jewel*, a panegyric on the Scots, and *Pantochronochanon*, a genealogy tracing his father's descent from Adam and his mother's from Eve in over 150 generations. In 1652 he produced *Ekskubalauron*, a denunciation of the Scottish Presbyterians, and in the following year *Logopandecteision*, a scheme for a universal language. His most important work, however, was his translation of the first three books of Rabelais in a euphuistic style; in this he was assisted by Peter Anthony Motteux, a Frenchman who had settled in England, and who continued the work. Urquhart combined great learning and originality with eccentricity which verged on insanity, and is said to have died from the effects of an uncontrollable fit of laughter when he received news of the Restoration.

Usk, Thomas (died 4 March 1388), allegorist, born in London, became secretary to John of Northampton, the Wyclifite Lord Mayor, and turned informer against his master to save himself. But after being appointed under-sheriff in 1387 by Richard II's mandate he was himself arraigned by the 'Merciless' Parliament and executed. During his imprisonment in Newgate he composed the

Testament of Love, an allegorical prose work long attributed to Chaucer.

Ussher, James (4 Jan. 1581—21 March 1656), prelate and scholar, born in Dublin, the son of a lawyer, and educated at Trinity College, took orders, and became Chancellor of St Patrick's, Dublin in 1605, and Professor of Divinity from 1607 to 1621. On the Irish clergy deciding to assert themselves as an independent church, Ussher had the main hand in drawing up the constitution. In 1621 he was made Bishop of Meath, and four years later Archbishop of Armagh. He constantly used his influence in favour of reform, and endeavoured to introduce such modifications of Episcopacy as would conciliate and comprehend the Presbyterians. The Rebellion in Ireland in 1641 drove him away, and he settled first at Oxford, but ultimately at the house of Lady Peterborough at Reigate, where he died. His works dealt chiefly with ecclesiastical antiquities and chronology, his best-known being *Annales,* a chronology of the world from the creation to the dispersion of the Jews in the reign of Vespasian, a work which gained him great reputation on the Continent as well as at home. The date of the creation was given as 4004 B.C., which was long universally received, but has, of course, been altogether disproved, alike by the discovery of ancient records, and by geology.

Uvedale, Nicholas, *see* Udall.

V

Vachell, Horace Annesley (30 Oct. 1861—10 Jan. 1955), novelist, born at Sydenham, Kent, was a great-grandson of the 1st Lord Lyttleton (q.v.). He went to Harrow, about which he wrote his famous school story *The Hill* (1905), and then to Sandhurst, obtaining a commission in the Rifle Brigade. In 1883 he resigned and emigrated to California, where he bought a ranch, married an American girl, Lydie Chawnay Philips, and settled down. In 1894 he produced his first novel, *The Romance of Judge Ketchum*, and followed it next year with *The Model of Christian Gay*. In the latter year Vachell's wife died, and in 1899 he returned to England and settled in Hampshire to make a living by his pen. His first really successful novel was *Brothers* (1904); among the best-known of many others are *John Verney* (1911), *Spragge's Canyon* (1914), *Quinney's* (1914), *The Triumph of Tim* (1916), *Fishpingle* (1917), *The Soul of Susan Yellam* (1918), *Quinney's Adventures* (1924) *Joe Quinney's Jodie* (1936), *Lord Samarkand* (1938), and *Quinney's for Quality* (1938). During the First World War he repeatedly tried to get into the army but was rejected as he was over 50. He wrote a number of plays as well as dramatizing some of his novels, and once had three plays running in London simultaneously. *Fellow Travellers* (1923) and *Distant Fields* (1937) are autobiographical, and his hundredth book, *Quests*, a collection of essays, was published shortly after his ninety-second birthday. Other late works are the anecdotal memoirs, *Methuselah's Diary* (1950) and *More From Methuselah* (1951). He was a Fellow of the Royal Society of Literature.

Vanbrugh *or* **Vanburgh, Sir John** (baptized 24 Jan. 1664, died 26 March 1726), dramatist and architect, born in London of Flemish descent, was in France from 1683 to 1685, studying architecture, for which he had early shown a taste. The next year he got a commission in the East Somerset Regiment, and in 1690 he was a prisoner on an unexplained charge, first at Vincennes and then in the Bastille. In 1696 he began his dramatic career with *The Relapse, or Virtue in Danger*, which had great success. *Aesop* followed in 1697, and *The Provoked Wife* in the same year. The latter was severely criticized by Jeremy Collier (q.v.) in his *Short View of the Immorality and Profaneness of the English Stage*, which produced a vindication by the author. In addition to these he wrote *The Confederacy* (1705) and started *The Provoked Husband*, which was finished by Cibber (q.v.) and brought out in 1728. His leading features as a dramatist are the naturalness of his dialogue and his lively humour. Like all his contemporaries he is frequently extremely gross. He obtained great fame as an architect as well as a dramatist. Among his most famous designs are Castle Howard, Blenheim Palace, and Seaton Delaval. He was knighted by George

I, was controller of the Royal works, and succeeded Wren as architect to Greenwich Hospital. He was a handsome and jovial person, and highly popular in society.

Van Dine, S. S., *see* **Wright, Willard H.**

Van Doren, Carl Clinton (10 Sept. 1885—18 July 1950), critic and biographer, was born at Hope, Illinois, son of a doctor, and educated at the University of Illinois, where he edited the college magazine, and at Columbia, where from 1911 to 1930 he was on the English staff. He was literary editor of the *Nation* from 1919 to 1922 and of the *Century Magazine* from then till 1925. From 1917 to 1921 he was general editor of the *Cambridge History of American Literature*. Said to be America's most popular biographer, he wrote lives of Thomas Love Peacock (1911), James Branch Cabell (1925) Dean Swift (1930), Sinclair Lewis (1933), and Benjamin Franklin (1938), this last being awarded the Pulitzer Prize. His critical works include *The American Novel* (1921) and *American and British Literature Since 1890* (1925), in which he collaborated with his brother Mark (q.v.). *The Ninth Wave* (1926) is a novel and *Three Worlds* (1936) an autobiography. His last important work was an edition of Benjamin Franklin's *Letters and Papers* (1947).

Van Doren, Mark Albert (13 June 1894—   ), poet and critic, younger brother of the above, was born at Hope, Illinois, and educated at the University of Illinois and Columbia, where he became Professor of English. During the First World War he served in the infantry. From 1924 to 1928 he was literary editor of the *Nation*, in succession to his brother, and in 1940 he was awarded the Pulitzer Prize for his *Collected Poems*. Separate volumes of his verse are *Spring Thunder* (1924) *7 P.M.* (1926), *Now the Sky* (1928), *Jonathan Gentry* (1931), *A Winter Diary* (1935), *The Last Look* (1937), *The Mayfield Deer* (1941), *The Seven Sleepers* (1944), *The Country Year* (1946), *New Poems* (1948), and *Spring Birth* (1953). He edited a number of anthologies, including *The Oxford Book of American Prose* and an *Anthology of World Poetry*. Among his critical works are studies of Thoreau (1916), Dryden (1920), Shakespeare (1939) and Hawthorne (1949), and he collaborated with his brother in *American and British Literature Since 1890* (1925). *The Transients* (1935) and *Windless Cabins* (1940) are novels.

Van Dyke, Henry (10 Nov. 1852—10 April 1933), essayist, poet, short-story writer, was born at Germantown, Pennsylvania, son of a Presbyterian minister. Educated at Brooklyn Polytechnic, Princeton, and Berlin, he studied theology. From 1879 to 1883 he was minister at Newport, Rhode Island, and from then till 1899 at a Presbyterian church in New York. In 1884 he published *The Reality of Religion*, but he is best known for his Christmas sermons *The Story of the Other Wise Man* (1896) and *The First Christmas Tree* (1897), which became celebrated and were translated into many European languages. In 1900 he was appointed Professor of English Literature at Princeton, and from 1913 to 1916 was American Minister to the Netherlands. In the First World War he was a naval chaplain and was awarded the Legion of Honour. His essays on outdoor life were collected in *Little Rivers* (1895) and *Fisherman's Luck* (1899), while books of short stories are *The Ruling Passion* (1901), *The Blue Flower* (1902), and *The Unknown Quantity* (1912). His *Collected Poems* appeared in 1911.

Vane, Henry Vane Sutton (1888—), a playwright like his father before him, began as an actor but joined up early in the First World War, and when discharged with shell shock returned to give theatrical performances behind the lines. After writing two plays of no special note he scored a striking success with *Outward Bound*, which he produced himself in 1923, all managers having rejected it; the plot is a fanciful one, depicting the voyage of a shipload of dead passengers who do not at first realize that they are dead, and the judgment that awaits them when they reach land. Later plays by the same author are *Time, Gentlemen, Please*, and *Marine Parade*, both produced in 1935.

Vanolis, Bysshe, *see* **Thomson, James.**

Vaughan, Henry (17 April 1622—23 April 1695), poet, born in the parish of Llansaintffraed, Brecknock, was a cousin of John Aubrey (q.v.). As a native of the land of the ancient Silures, he called himself 'Silurist.' He was at Jesus College, Oxford, and studied law in London, but finally settled as a physician at Brecon and Newton-by-Usk. In his youth he was a decided Royalist and, along with his twin brother Thomas, was imprisoned. His first book *Poems, with the Tenth Satire of Juvenal Englished*, appeared in 1646. *Olor Iscanus* (the Swan of Usk), a collection of poems and translations, was surreptitiously published in 1651. About this time he had a serious illness which led to deep spiritual impressions, and thereafter his writings were almost entirely religious. *Silex Scintillans* (1650), his best known work, consists of short poems full of deep religious feeling, fine fancy, and exquisite felicities of expression, mixed with a good deal that is quaint and artificial. It contains 'The Retreat,' a short exquisite poem which suggested to Wordsworth his *Ode on the Intimations of Immortality*, and 'Beyond the Veil,' one of the finest meditative poems in the language. *Flores Solitudinis* (Flowers of Solitude) and *The Mount of Olives* are devout meditations in prose. The two brothers were joint authors of *Thalia Rediviva: the Pastimes and Diversions of a Country Muse* (1678), a collection of translations and original poems.

Vaughan, Robert (14 Oct. 1795—15 June 1868), Congregationalist minister, born in the West of England, was Professor of History in London University from 1830 to 1843, and President of the Independent College, Manchester, from then till 1857. He founded and for a time edited the *British Quarterly*. He wrote, among various other works, *A History of England under the House of Stuart* (1840), *Revolutions in English History* (1859—63), and a life of Wycliffe (1853).

Vaux of Harrowden, Thomas Vaux, 2nd Baron (1510—Oct. 1556), poet, was educated at Cambridge and was created a Knight of the Bath at the coronation of Anne Bullen; he belonged to the cultured court circles of Henry VIII and Edward VI. His poems are mainly short lyrics with a tone of melancholy, two of them being printed anonymously in Tottel's *Miscellany*.

Veitch, John (24 Oct. 1829—3 Sept. 1894), philosopher and historian, son of an army sergeant, was born at Peebles and educated at its high school and at Edinburgh University. He became assistant to Sir William Hamilton (q.v.) in 1856, Professor of Logic at St Andrews in 1856, and from 1864 to 1894 occupied the corresponding Chair at Glasgow University. He was a voluminous and accomplished writer, his works including lives of Dugald Stewart (1857) and Sir William Hamilton (1869), *Tweed and other Poems* (1875), *History and Poetry of the Scottish Border* (1877), *Feeling for Nature in Scottish Poetry* (1887), *Merlin and other Poems* (1889), *Border Essays* (1896), and *Dualism and Monism* (1895).

Veblen, Thorstein Bunde (30 July 1857—3 Aug. 1929), economist, was born on a farm in Wisconsin, son of Norwegian immigrants. Brought up in Minnesota, he was educated at Carleton College, Johns Hopkins, Yale, and Cornell. He was on the staff successively of Chicago University, Stanford, Missouri, and the New School for Social Research in New York, and for a time edited the *Dial*; in every case he had to move because of scandals in his private life. His first book, *The Theory of the Leisure Class* (1899) at once won him recognition; others are *The Theory of Business Enterprise* (1904), *The Instinct of Workmanship* (1914), *The Vested Interests and the State of the Industrial Arts* (1919), *The Place of Science in Modern Civilization* (1919), *Absentee Ownership and Business Enterprise in Recent Times* (1923), and *Essays in Our Changing Order* (1934). He has been taxed with employing an abstruse and perplexing style, but his books had an important influence in introducing a more realistic attitude in economics.

Very, Jones (28 Aug. 1813—8 May 1880), poet, was born at Salem, Massachusetts, son of a ship's captain. After working as errand-boy and pupil-teacher he studied at Harvard, where he became a tutor. A mystic and visionary, he was sometimes thought insane, and actually spent some time in an asylum. He was a friend of the Transcendentalists, and Emerson helped him with the publication of his *Essays and Poems* (1839). Both this volume and his critical works have a mystical trend.

Victoria, Queen of Great Britain (24 May 1819—22 Jan. 1901), born in Kensington, a grand-daughter of George III, was educated by tutors, and came to the throne in 1837. In 1840 she married Prince Albert of Saxe-Coburg and Gotha, whose death in 1861 was a blow from which she never wholly recovered. Her long reign was a period of unprecedented prosperity in Britain. Never so happy as in her Scottish estate at Balmoral, she published in 1868 *Leaves from a Journal of our Life in the Highlands, 1848—61*, and in 1883 *More Leaves*. After her death her *Letters* were published in three series (1907, 1928, 1932).

Villiers, Alan John (23 Sept. 1903—   ), travel

writer, was born in Melbourne and educated at Essendon High School there. At the age of 15 he went to sea as a cadet in the barque *Rothesay Bay*, and thereafter sailed in square-rigged ships for five years. After a period as a journalist he returned to sea in the famous *Herzogin Cecilie*, of which he wrote in *Falmouth for Orders* (1929). After that he was part-owner of the four-master *Pamir*, in which he twice won the grain race from South Australia to England, with passages of 103 and 83 days. In 1934 he bought a full-rigged ship which he sailed 60,000 miles with a crew of cadets, afterwards telling of the voyage in *The Cruise of the 'Conrad'* (1937). During the Second World War he held the rank of lieutenant-commander R.N.V.R., had charge of a squadron of landing-craft during the Allied invasions, and was awarded the Distinguished Service Cross. His other books include *By Way of Cape Horn* (1930), *Last of the Windships* (1934), *Vanished Fleets* (1936), *The Coral Sea* (1949), *The Quest of the Schooner 'Argus'* (1952), for which he received the Portuguese Camoens Prize, and *The Way of a Ship* (1953). *The Set of the Sails* (1949) is autobiographical. In 1956 he was chosen to command the *Mayflower II*, a replica of the original ship of the Pilgrim Fathers, on a voyage to the United States to commemorate their crossing in 1620.

Villiers, George, *see* Buckingham, Duke of.

W

Wace, Robert (1100?—1174?), poet, was born in Jersey, grandson of the Duke of Normandy's chamberlain, and educated at Caen. He enjoyed the favour of Henry II, and in 1169 was given a prebend at Bayeux. He wrote metrical romances in Norman French, including *The Brut* (1155), named after Brutus the Trojan and telling the history of the Britons; based on Geoffrey of Monmouth's work, it embodied some of the Arthurian legends. At Henry's command he also wrote the *Roman de Rou*, an epic of Rolf, Duke of Normandy, and his successors; it is based on French originals. Wace had considerable influence on thirteenth-century vernacular literature.

Waddell, Helen Jane (31 May 1889—   ), scholar, was born in Tokyo, where her father was a Presbyterian minister, and learned to speak both Japanese and Chinese. Both her parents were Irish, and she was educated at Victoria College and Queen's University, Belfast. From 1920 to 1922 she was lecturer in Latin at Somerville College, Oxford, and after that was a Fellow of Lady Margaret Hall. A specialist in medieval Latin literature, she also made translations from the Chinese. In 1927 she was awarded the A. C. Benson Medal of the Royal Society of Literature, and in 1932 became a member of the Irish Academy of Letters. Her translations include *Lyrics from the Chinese* (1913), *Medieval Latin Lyrics* (1929), and *Beasts and Saints* (1934), the last being from Latin folk-tales. *The Wandering Scholars* (1927) is an account of the 'Vagantes' or Latin poets of the later Middle Ages. She also wrote books on the *Abbé Prevost* (1933), *The Desert Fathers* (1936), and *Poetry in the Dark Ages* (1948). *Peter Abelard* (1933) is a novel. She held honorary doctorates of Belfast, St Andrews, Durham, and Columbia.

Wade, Thomas (1805—19 Sept. 1875), poet, born at Woodbridge, Suffolk, published poems, dramas, sonnets, and a translation of Dante's *Inferno*. Among his writings are two volumes of poetry, *Tasso and the Sisters* (1825) and *Mundi et Cordis Carmina* (1835); *Duke Andrea* (1828), and *The Jew of Arragon* (1830), both tragedies, and the *Phrenologists* (1830), a farce.

Wakefield, Gilbert (22 Feb. 1756—9 Sept 1801), scholar and theologian, was born in Nottingham, where his father was a rector. Educated at Cambridge, he took orders, but becoming a Unitarian renounced them and acted as classical tutor in various Unitarian academies. He was a strong defender of the French Revolution, and was imprisoned for two years for writing a seditious pamphlet. He published editions of various classical writers, and among his theological writings are *Early Christian Writers on the Person of Christ* (1784), *An Examination of Paine's Age of Reason* (1794), and *Silva Critica* (1789—95), illustrations of the Scriptures.

Waley, Arthur David (19 Aug. 1889—   ), poet and translator, was born at Tunbridge Wells, his name being originally Arthur David Schloss. Educated at Rugby and King's College, Cambridge, of which he was made an honorary Fellow, he became one of the greatest authorities on Chinese literature. From 1912 to 1930 he was Assistant Keeper of the Department of Prints and Drawings at the British Museum, and he was also a lecturer at the School of Oriental Studies. During the Second World War he was at the Ministry of Information. One of the most important of his works is a translation of *The Tale of Genji*, a classic Japanese novel of about A.D. 1000, which he published in six volumes (1925—32). He also translated *The Pillow Book of Sei Shon Agon* (1928) and the *Analects* of Confucious (1938). He was best known, however, for his renderings of Chinese poems, which are so effective that they deserve to be regarded as poems in their own right; volumes of these appeared in 1918, 1919, 1927, and 1946. Works of a more general nature are *Japanese Poetry* (1919) and *Three Ways of Thought in Ancient China* (1939). A Fellow of the British Academy, he was made a Companion of Honour in 1956.

Wallace, Alfred Russel, O.M. (8 Jan. 1823—7 Nov. 1913), naturalist, was born at Usk, Monmouthshire, and educated at Hertford Grammar School. He learned surveying, and for a time succeeded his brother William in this work. While a schoolmaster in Leicester he met Bates the naturalist, and in 1848 they went on a joint expedition to the Amazon. After returning Wallace went alone to the Malay Archipelago, where he studied the fauna and flora and established the dividing line, now known as Wallace's Line, between the oriental and Australian sections of the islands. While in Borneo he wrote his essay in which he independently formulated the principle of the survival of the fittest, on which Darwin had been working. He sent it to Darwin, and they collaborated in a joint paper read in 1858 to the Linnaean Society. Wallace's reputation was now made, and he became the friend of many eminent men of science. His *Contributions to the Theory of Natural Selection* (1870) was followed by *The Geographical Distribution of Animals* (1876) and *Darwinism* (1889), which embodied his own theory of evolution. Others of his works are *Studies, Scientific and Social* (1900), *Man's Place in the Universe* (1903), and an autobiography, *My Life* (1905). In 1893 he was made a Fellow of the Royal Society and in 1910 was awarded the Order of Merit.

Wallace, Edgar (1 April 1875—10 Feb. 1932), journalist and novelist, born in Greenwich, the illegitimate son of an actor, was baptized Richard Horatio Edgar Wallace. Brought up by a Billingsgate fish-porter and his wife, he attended an elementary school at Peckham and left at 12 to become successively newsboy, errand boy, milk roundsman, and labourer. At 18 he enlisted in the Royal West Kent Regiment and served in South Africa. Discharged in 1899, he became a foreign correspondent of the *Daily Mail*, but was sacked for involving them in a libel suit. His first great success was *The Four Just Men* (1905), with its sequels *The Council of Justice* (1908) and *The Three Just Men* (1926). His early novels include a West

African series, *Sanders of the River* (1911), *Bones* (1915), and others, but it was by his thrillers and detective stories that he became really famous. Well meriting his nickname of 'fiction factory,' working with a dictaphone and a typist who held the record for speed-typing, he produced some 170 books. A few of the titles are *The Man Who Knew* (1919), *The Angel of Terror* (1922), *The Crimson Circle* (1922), *The Green Archer* (1923), *The Clue of the New Pin* (1923), *Room 13* (1924), and *The Mind of Mr J. G. Reeder* (1925); this last introduces a most realistic and human police detective. Wallace also wrote some excellent plays in which excitement and horror are skilfully relieved by touches of humour; among these are *The Squeaker* (1927), *The Ringer* (1929), *On the Spot* (1931), and *The Green Pack* (1933). *People* (1926) is an autobiography. He died in Hollywood of pneumonia, and left estate cumbered with £150,000 in debts, which his royalties paid off in two years. He was twice married.

Wallace, Lewis (10 April 1827—15 Feb. 1905), lawyer, diplomat, and novelist, was born at Brookville, Indiana; his father was later governor of the state. After studying law in his father's office, Lewis served in the Mexican War and with the Union Army in the Civil War, rising to be a major-general. From 1878 to 1881 he was Governor of New Mexico, and from 1881 to 1885 was American Minister to Turkey. His first novel was *The Fair God* (1873), a story of the Spanish conquest of Mexico, but his greatest success was *Ben Hur* (1880), an historical novel about the early days of Christianity; it sold some two million copies, and he followed it with *The Boyhood of Christ* (1888). He wrote another novel, *The Prince of India* (1893), a poem, *The Wooing of Malkatoon* (1898), and an *Autobiography* (1906) which was completed by his wife.

Wallas, Graham (31 May 1858—9 Aug. 1932), political scientist, was born in Sunderland, son of a clergyman, and educated at Shrewsbury and Corpus Christi College, Oxford. After being a master at Highgate, in 1895 he became a lecturer at the London School of Economics, where from 1914 to 1923 he was Professor of Political Science. From 1908 to 1928 he was a member of the Senate of London University. He was also one of the organizers of the Fabian Society, of which he was a member from 1886 to 1904. His most famous book was *The Great Society* (1914), a psychological analysis of social organization. Others are *Human Nature in Politics* (1908), *Our Social Heritage* (1921), *The Art of Thought* (1926), *Social Judgment* (1935), and *Men and Ideas* (1940). Describing himself as 'a working thinker' he advocated a closer connection between psychological and political studies. He held honorary degrees of Oxford and Manchester.

Waller, Edmund (3 March 1606—21 Oct. 1687), poet, born at Coleshill in what is now Buckinghamshire, and educated at Eton and Cambridge, belonged to an old and wealthy family, and in early childhood inherited the estate of Beaconsfield, worth £3,500 a year. He was related to John Hampden, and was distantly connected with Oliver Cromwell, his own family, however, being staunch Royalists. He studied law at Lincoln's Inn, and at the age of 16 became an

M.P., representing various constituencies for the greater part of his life. In 1631 he added to his fortune by marrying Anne Banks, a London heiress, who died in 1634, and he then paid assiduous but unsuccessful court to Lady Dorothea Sidney, to whom, under the name of Sacharissa, he addressed much of his best poetry. Though probably really a Royalist in his sympathies, Waller supported the popular cause in Parliament. In 1643, however, he was detected in a plot for seizing London for the King, was expelled from the House, fined £10,000 and banished. On this occasion he showed cowardice and treachery, humiliating himself in the most abject manner, and betraying all his associates. He went to the Continent, living chiefly in France and Switzerland, and showing hospitality to Royalist exiles. Returning by permission in 1652 he addressed some laudatory verses, among the best he wrote, to Cromwell, on whose death nevertheless he wrote a new poem entitled, *On the Death of the late Usurper, O.C.* At the Restoration the accommodating poet was ready with a congratulatory address to Charles II, who, pointing out its inferiority as a poem to that addressed to Cromwell, elicited the famous reply, 'Poets, Sire, succeed better in fiction than in truth.' The poem, however, whatever its demerits, succeeded in its prime object, and Waller became a favourite at Court, and sat in Parliament until his death. Much admired as a poet in the eighteenth century, he was regarded as a pioneer in the neo-classical style. His short poems, such as 'Go, lovely Rose,' often show fancy and grace of expression, but are frequently frigid and artificial. As a man, though agreeable and witty, he was time-serving, selfish, and cowardly. He married a second time and had five sons and eight daughters.

Waller, John Francis (1810—19 Jan. 1894), journalist and poet, born at Limerick, and educated at Trinity College, Dublin, became a contributor to and ultimately editor of the *Dublin University Magazine*, usually writing under the pseudonym of Jonathan Freke Slingsby. His poetical works include *Ravenscroft Hall* (1852), *The Dead Bridal* (1856), *Occasional Odes* (1864), and *Peter Brown* (1872).

Walpole, Horatio, *or* **Horace, 4th Earl of Orford** (24 Sept. 1717—2 March 1797), author and wit, son of Sir Robert Walpole, the great minister of George II, was born in London, and educated at Eton and Cambridge, after which he travelled on the Continent with Gray, the poet (q.v.). His father bestowed several lucrative appointments upon him, and he sat in Parliament for various places, but never took any prominent part in public business. By the death of his nephew, the 3rd Earl, he became in 1791 4th Earl of Orford. In 1747 he purchased the villa of Strawberry Hill, Twickenham, the conversion of which into a small Gothic Castle and the collection of the works of art and curios with which it was decorated became the main interest of his life. His position in society gave him access to the best information on all contemporary subjects of interest, and he was as successful in collecting gossip as curios. He also erected a private press, from which various important works, including Gray's *Bard*, as well as his own writings, were issued. Among the latter are

Letter from Xo Ho to his Friend Lien Chi at Pekin (1757), *The Castle of Otranto* (1765), forerunner of the romances of terror of Mrs Radcliffe and 'Monk' Lewis, and *The Mysterious Mother* (1768), a tragedy of considerable power. He also compiled *A Catalogue of Royal and Noble Authors* (1758), *Anecdotes of Painting* (1762), *Catalogue of Engravers* (1763), *Memoirs of the Last Ten Years of George II* (1822), and *Memoirs of the Reign of George III* (1845). But he is most famous for his *Letters*, edited in 19 volumes (1903—25), which are vivacious, interesting, and often brilliant. Walpole never married.

Walpole, Sir Hugh Seymour (13 March 1884—1 June 1941), novelist, was born at Auckland, New Zealand, son of a clergyman who became Bishop of Edinburgh. Sent to England, he was educated at King's School, Canterbury, and Cambridge. For a time he was a schoolmaster, then worked as a book reviewer. His first novel, *The Wooden Horse* (1909), was followed by *Maradick at Forty* (1910) and *Mr Perrin and Mr Traill* (1911) an effective study of a schoolmaster's life which is sometimes thought his best work. Other books of this period are *Fortitude* (1913) and *The Duchess of Wrexe* (1914). During the First World War he served with the Red Cross in Russia, received the Order of St George, and was made a C.B.E. Russia is the background of his novels *The Dark Forest* (1916) and *The Secret City* (1919), which told of the 1917 Revolution and was awarded the Tait Black Memorial Prize. In 1919 he began a trilogy of autobiographical stories of boyhood, *Jeremy* (1919), *Jeremy and Hamlet* (1923), and *Jeremy at Crale* (1927). *The Cathedral* (1922), which was dramatized in 1932, was the first of a series dealing with the Cornish town of Polchester; others were *The Old Ladies* (1924) and *Harmer John* (1926). *Portrait of a Man with Red Hair* (1925), a thriller, was followed by his most ambitious work, a family history styled the *Herries Chronicle*, covering a period of a century in the novels *Rogue Herries* (1930), *Judith Paris* (1931), *The Fortress* (1932), and *Vanessa* (1933). An able critic, he also wrote studies of Conrad (1916) and Trollope (1928). He was knighted in 1937. He was never married.

Walpole, Sir Spencer (6 Feb. 1839—7 July 1907), civil servant and historian, son of a barrister who became Home Secretary, belonged to the same family as Sir Robert Walpole. Educated at Eton, he became a clerk in the War Office, and was thereafter successively Inspector of Fisheries 1867, Lieutenant-Governor of the Isle of Man 1882, and Secretary to the Post Office, where he made a reputation as an efficient administrator, and was made K.C.B. in 1898. He published a *History of England from 1815* in 6 volumes (1876—86), bringing the story down to 1858, and followed it up with *The History of Twenty-five Years* (1904—8). He also wrote lives of Spencer Percival, the Prime Minister who was assassinated in the lobby of the House of Commons in 1812, and who was his maternal grandfather, and of Earl Russell. His latest book was *Studies in Biography* (1907).

Walsh, Maurice (2 May 1879—   ), novelist, was born at Ballydonohue, Kerry, son of a farmer, and educated at St Michael's

College, Listowell. In 1901 he entered the British Civil Service, and from 1922 to 1934 was in the Irish Free State Service. A lover of the Scottish highlands, he became acquainted with Neil M. Gunn (q.v.). His books are mainly adventure or detective stories or stories of Ireland. They include *The Key above the Door* (1923), *While Rivers Run* (1926), *The Small Dark Man* (1929), *Blackcock's Feather* (1932), *The Road to Nowhere* (1934), *Green Rushes* (1935), *And No Quarter* (1937), *The Hill is Mine* (1940), *Thomasheen James* (1941), *The Spanish Lady* (1943), *The Man in Brown* (1945), *Castle Gillian* (1948), *Trouble in the Glen* (1950), *Son of a Tinker* (1952), *The Honest Fisherman* (1954), and *Danger under the Moon* (1956).

Walsh, William (1663—18 March 1708), poet and critic, was born at Abberley, Worcestershire, and educated at Oxford. He became an M.P. and was Gentleman of the Horse in Queen Anne's household, but is chiefly remembered as a friend of Pope. His principal works were *Dialogue Concerning Women* (1691), which had a preface by Dryden, and *Poems* (1716). His life was written by Johnson.

Walsingham, Thomas (died 1422?), monk and chronicler, is thought to have been born in Norfolk and educated at the abbey of St Albans and Oxford. Afterwards at St Albans he was precentor and scriptorarius or head of the writing-room. From 1394 to 1409 he was prior of Wymondham, then returned to St Albans. He compiled a number of Latin Chronicles, including *Chronica Majora*, now lost, and *Chronicon Angliae*, an account of England from 1328 to 1388.

Walton, Izaak (9 Aug. 1593—15 Dec. 1683), angler and biographer, son of a farmer, was born in Stafford and after little schooling was apprenticed to an ironmonger. Subsequently he carried on business as a hosier in London, in which he made a modest competence, which enabled him to retire at 50, the rest of his long life of 90 years being spent in the simple country pleasures, especially angling, which he so charmingly describes. He was twice married, first to Rachel Floud, a descendant of Archbishop Cranmer, and second to Ann Ken, half-sister of the famous bishop. His first book was a *Life of Dr Donne* (1640), followed by lives of Sir Henry Wotton (1651), Richard Hooker (1662), George Herbert (1670), and Bishop Sanderson (1678). All of these, classics in their kind, short, but simple and striking, were collected into one volume. His masterpiece, however, was *The Compleat Angler*, the first edition of which was published in 1653. Subsequent editions were greatly enlarged; a second part was added by Charles Cotton (q.v.). With its dialogues between Piscator (angler), Venator (hunter), and Auceps (falconer), full of wisdom, kindly humour, and charity, its charming pictures of country scenes and pleasures, and its snatches of verse, it is one of the most delightful and care-dispelling books in the language. Walton's long and happy life ended in the house of his son-in-law, Dr Hawkins, Prebendary of Winchester, and his grave is in Winchester Cathedral.

Warburton, Bartholomew Elliott George (1810—4 Jan. 1852), historian usually known as Eliot Warburton, was born near Tulla-more, King's County, son of the Inspector-General of Police, and educated at Cambridge; in 1837 he was called to the Irish Bar. He led a roving life, travelled in the East, and wrote of his experiences in *The Crescent and the Cross* (1844). Others of his works are *Memoirs of Prince Rupert and the Cavaliers* (1849) and *Memoirs of Horace Walpole and his Contemporaries* (1851). In 1851 he planned to explore the isthmus of Darien, but perished in the burning of the *Amazon*, in which he sailed.

Warburton, William (24 Dec. 1698—7 June 1779), prelate and theologian, was born at Newark, where his father was an attorney, and educated at Oakham Grammar School, Rutland. Intended for the law, he was for a few years engaged in its practice, but abandoned it for the Church, and in 1728 was presented to the Rectory of Brand-Broughton, where he remained for many years. His first important work was *The Alliance between Church and State* (1736), which brought him into notice. But it was entirely eclipsed by his *Divine Legation of Moses*, of which the first part appeared in 1737, and the second in 1741. The work obtained for him the appointment of chaplain to Frederick, Prince of Wales. In 1739 Warburton gained the friendship of Pope by publishing a defence of *The Essay on Man*. Through Pope he became acquainted with most of the men of letters of the time, and he was made by the poet his literary executor, and had the legacy of half his library, and the profits of his posthumous works. On the strength of this he brought out an edition of Pope's works in 1751. In 1747 he had published an edition of Shakespeare with notes, which was somewhat severely criticized. He became Dean of Bristol in 1757 and Bishop of Gloucester in 1759.

Ward, Arthur Sarsfield (15 Feb. 1886—1 June 1959), novelist, who wrote under the name of Sax Rohmer, was born in Birmingham of Irish parents. He had a great interest in Egyptian things, but failed in his attempt to get a Civil Service appointment in the East. After working for a time as a journalist he became popular as a writer of exciting mystery stories. Many of his exotic thrillers are written round a sinister and inscrutable oriental villain, Fu Manchu. They include *Dr Fu Manchu* (1913), *The Yellow Claw* (1915), *The Sin Fan Mysteries* (1917), *The Quest of the Sacred Slipper* (1919), *The Golden Scorpion* (1920), *The Green Eyes of Bast* (1920), *Tales of Chinatown* (1922), *Yellow Shadows* (1925), *Moon of Madness* (1927), *Fu Manchu's Bride* (1932), *The Trail of Fu Manchu* (1934), and *The Drums of Fu Manchu* (1939). *Round in 50* (1922) and *The Eye of Siva* (1923) are plays.

Ward, Sir Adolphus William (2 Dec. 1837—19 June 1924), scholar, was born in London, but his father, a diplomat, was stationed in Germany from 1841 to 1870, so that young Ward went to school in Leipzig and formed a deep interest in things German. Later he went to King Edward VI School, Bury St Edmunds, and Peterhouse, Cambridge. He also studied law, and was called to the Bar in 1866, but never practised. After being a classical lecturer at Glasgow University he became Professor of History and English at Owens College, Manchester, in 1866. There he developed the history department and also helped in establishing the University of Manchester. In 1900 he left to become Master of Peterhouse. Meanwhile he produced many works of outstanding scholarship. His *History of English Dramatic Literature* (1875) is still a standard work. He wrote biographical studies of Chaucer (1879) and Dickens (1882) and published editions of many other authors. He took over the *Cambridge Modern History* from Acton and edited it from 1901 to 1912; from 1907 to 1916 he was one of the editors of the *Cambridge History of English Literature*, and from 1922 to 1923 of the *Cambridge History of British Foreign Policy*. One of the most important of his later works was *Germany 1815—1890* (1916—18). He was knighted in 1913, was President of the British Academy from 1911 to 1913 and of the Royal Historical Society from 1899 to 1901. He held honorary degrees of St Andrews, Glasgow, Manchester, and Leipzig.

Ward, Artemus, *see* Browne, Charles Farrar.

Ward, Mary Augusta Arnold (11 June 1851—24 March 1920), novelist better known as Mrs Humphry Ward, was born at Hobart; she was a grand-daughter of Dr Arnold of Rugby and a niece of Matthew Arnold. In 1865 her father returned to England and settled at Oxford, where she became familiar with a learned circle which included Dr Jowett, Pater, and T. H. Green. For a year she was secretary to Somerville College. In 1872 she married T. Humphry Ward, a Fellow of Brasenose College, and in 1881, when he joined the staff of *The Times*, they moved to London. Her first novel, *Miss Bretherton*, appeared in 1884, but she is best known for *Robert Elsmere* (1888), an attack on evangelical Christianity which caused a great sensation. Others of her novels were *David Grieve* (1892), *Marcella* (1894), *The Story of Bessie Costrell* (1895), *Helbeck of Bannisdale* (1898), *Eleanor* (1900), *Lady Rose's Daughter* (1903), *The Marriage of William Ashe* (1905), *Fenwick's Career* (1906), *The Testing of Dinah Mallory* (1908), and *The Case of Richard Meynell* (1911), a sequel to *Robert Elsmere*. All these were at first highly popular, but latterly they were condemned for their lack of feeling and humour. Mrs Ward did much good work among the poor of London, strongly opposed the suffragette movement, founding the Women's Anti-Suffrage League in 1908, and shortly before her death was appointed one of the first women magistrates in the country. Her autobiography, *A Writer's Recollections*, appeared in 1918.

Ward, Robert Plumer (19 March 1765—13 Aug. 1846), novelist, was born in London, son of a Gibraltar official. Educated at Westminster and Oxford, and called to the Bar in 1790, he held various political offices, and wrote some books on the law of nations; also three novels, *Tremaine, or the Man of Refinement* (1825), full of prolix discussions; *De Vere, or the Man of Independence* (1827), in which Canning is depicted under the character of Wentworth; and *De Clifford, or the Constant Man* (1841).

Ward, William George (21 March 1812—6 July 1882), theologian, was born in London, son of a financier, and educated at Winchester and Oxford. He came under the influence of J. H. Newman, whose famous Tract No. XC. he defended, and whom he followed into the

Church of Rome. In 1844 he published *The Ideal of a Christian Church* from the Romanist point of view, whence his soubriquet of 'Ideal Ward.' He was lecturer on moral philosophy at St Edward's College, Ware, and wrote various treatises on controversial theology.

Wardlaw, Elizabeth, Lady (April 1677—1727), authoress, daughter of Sir Charles Halket, Bart, of Pitfirrane, Fife, married Sir Henry Wardlaw, Bart, in 1696. In 1719 the ballad of *Hardyknute* was circulated by her as having been discovered in a vault in Dunfermline, but it is now believed to have been her own composition; it was included by Allan Ramsay in his anthology *Evergreen* (1724). Lady Wardlaw is said to have remodelled other ballads, including possibly *Sir Patrick Spens*.

Warner, Susan Bogert (11 July 1819—17 March 1885), novelist who wrote under the name Elizabeth Wetherell, was born in New York City. A devout Presbyterian, she was given to melancholy moods and was a great reader. To help the family finances, she wrote *The Wide, Wide World*, which was immensely popular when it appeared in 1850, and went through 13 editions in two years; its success is the more surprising since it has hardly any incidents, but chronicles with a wealth of emotional detail the moral and religious progress of an orphan. *Queechy* (1852) was almost as popular, and later novels of the same sentimental type were *The Old Helmet* (1863), *Daisy* (1868), *Diana* (1877), *My Desire* (1879), and *Nobody* (1882).

Warner, Sylvia Townsend (Dec. 1893—   ), novelist and poetess, was born at Harrow, Middlesex, daughter of a schoolmaster. Greatly interested in music, she was one of the editors of the 10-volume *Tudor Church Music*, and has been said to write like a composer. Her books of verse include *The Espalier* (1925), *Time Importuned* (1928), *Opus 7* (1931), and *Rainbow* (1932). Her poetry exhibits a graceful and inconsequent fancy which appears also in her novels *Lolly Willowes* (1926), *Mr Fortune's Maggot* (1927), *The True Heart* (1929), *Summer Will Show* (1936), *The Corner That Held Them* (1948), and *The Flint Anchor* (1954). *A Garland of Straw* (1943) and *Museum of Cheats* (1947) are volumes of short stories.

Warner, William (1558—9 March 1609), poet, born in London, studied at Oxford, and was an attorney in London. In 1585 he published a collection of seven tales in prose entitled *Pan his Syrinx*, and in 1595 a translation of the *Menaechmi* of Plautus. His chief work was a metrical history, *Albion's England*, published in 1586 in 13 books of fourteen-syllabled verse, and republished with three additional books in 1606. For about 20 years it was one of the most popular poems of its size—it contains about 10,000 lines—ever written, and he and Spenser were called the Homer and Virgil of their age. They must, however, have appealed to quite different classes. The plain-spoken, jolly humour, homely, lively, direct tales, vigorous patriotic feeling, and rough-and-tumble metre of Warner's muse, and its heterogeneous accumulation of material—history, tales, theology, antiquities—must have appealed to a lower and wider audience than Spenser's charmed verse.

A2*

Warren, John B. L., *see* de Tabley.

Warren, Robert Penn (24 April 1905—   ), poet,
novelist, critic, was born at Guthrie, Kentucky. Educated at
Vanderbilt University and Yale, he went to Oxford as a Rhodes
Scholar. He was appointed Professor of English at Louisiana State
University in 1934, and at the University of Minnesota in 1942, when
he also received the Shelley Memorial Prize for Poetry. Editor of
the *Southern Review* until it stopped issue, he was in 1950 Professor
of Play-writing at Yale Drama School. His earliest work was *John
Brown, the Making of a Martyr* (1929). His volumes of verse include
XXXVI Poems (1935), *Eleven Poems on the Same Theme* (1942),
and *Brother to Dragons* (1953). In 1946 his novel *All the King's
Men* was awarded the Pulitzer Prize; others are *Night Rider* (1938),
At Heaven's Gate (1943), and *World Enough and Time* (1950); *The
Circus in the Attic* (1948) is a volume of short stories.

Warren, Samuel (23 May 1807—29 July 1877), novelist, was born
near Wrexham, Denbighshire, son of a Wesleyan minister. After
studying medicine at Edinburgh he took up law, and became a
barrister, wrote several legal text-books, and in 1852 was made
Recorder of Hull. He sat in the House of Commons for Midhurst
1856—59, and was a Master in Lunacy 1859—77. He was the
author of *Passages from the Diary of a late Physician*, which appeared
(1832—7) first in *Blackwood's Magazine*, as did also *Ten Thousand a
Year* (1839). Both attracted considerable attention, and were often
reprinted and translated. His last novel, *Now and Then* (1847), had
little success.

Warton, Joseph (22 April 1722—23 Feb. 1800), poet and critic,
elder son of Thomas Warton, vicar of Basingstoke and Professor of
Poetry at Oxford, was born at Dunsfold, Surrey. At Basingstoke
Grammar School he had Gilbert White (q.v.) as a schoolfellow, and at
Winchester he had W. Collins, the poet. Going on to Oxford, he
took orders, held various benefices, and became headmaster of
Winchester College, and Prebendary of Winchester and of St Paul's.
He published miscellaneous verses, two volumes of *Odes* (1744 and
1746), in which he displayed what was then an unusual feeling for
nature, and revolted against the critical rules of Pope and his
followers. He was a good classical scholar, and made an approved
translation of the *Eclogues* and *Georgics* of Virgil. He and his brother
Thomas (q.v.) were friends of Johnson, and members of the Literary
Club. His last work of importance was an *Essay on the Writings and
Genius of Pope*, of which the first volume appeared in 1757, and the
second in 1782, and which gave an impulse to the romantic movement
in English literature. He also edited Pope's works, and had begun
an edition of Dryden when he died.

Warton, Thomas (9 Jan. 1728—20 May 1790), literary historian,
younger son of Thomas Warton and brother of the above, was born
at Basingstoke, educated at the Grammar School there, and went on
to Trinity College, Oxford, of which he became a Fellow, remaining
there all his life. At the age of 19 he published a poem of consider-

able promise, *The Pleasures of Melancholy*, and two years later attracted attention by *The Triumph of Isis* (1749), in praise of Oxford, and in answer to Mason's *Isis*. After various other poetical excursions he published *Observations on Spenser's Faerie Queene* (1754), which greatly increased his reputation, and in 1757 he was made Professor of Poetry at Oxford, which position he held for ten years. After bringing out one or two editions of classics and bio-graphies of college benefactors, he issued, from 1774—81, his great *History of English Poetry*, which comes down to the end of the Elizabethan age. The research and judgment, and the stores of learning, often curious and recondite, which went to its making render this work, though now in various respects superseded, a vast magazine of information; it did much to restore our older poetry to the place of which it had been unjustly deprived by the classical school, and had an important influence on the coming Romantic Revival. Warton was a clergyman, but if the tradition is to be believed that he had only two sermons, one written by his father and the other printed, and if the love of ease and of ale which he celebrates in some of his verses was other than poetical, he was more in his place as a critic than as a cleric. As a poet he hardly came up to his own standards. He was made Poet Laureate in 1785, and in the same year Camden Professor of History, and was one of the first to detect the Chatterton forgeries, a task in which his antiquarian lore stood him in good stead.

Waterland, Daniel (14 Feb. 1683—23 Dec. 1740), theologian, born at Walesby, Lincolnshire, where his father was rector, was educated at Magdalene College, Cambridge, of which he became Master in 1713. He was made Chancellor of York in 1722 and Archdeacon of Middlesex in 1730. He was an acute and able controversialist on behalf of the orthodox doctrine of the Trinity, on which he wrote several treatises. He was also the author of a *History of the Athanasian Creed* (1723).

Waterton, Charles (3 June 1782—25 May 1865), naturalist, was born at Walton Hall in Yorkshire, of an old Roman Catholic family, and was educated at Stonyhurst College. Sent out in 1804 to look after some family estates in Demerara, he wandered through the wildest parts of Guiana and Brazil, in search of plants and animals for his collections. His adventures were related in his highly spiced and entertaining *Wanderings in South America, the Northwest of the United States, and the Antilles* (1825), in which he details certain surprising episodes in connection with the capture of serpents, and specially of a cayman, on the back of which he rode. He also wrote three series of *Essays in Natural History* (1838, 1844, 1857).

Watson, John (3 Nov. 1850—6 May 1907), minister and novelist who wrote under the name Ian Maclaren, was born at Manningtree, Essex, son of a Scottish civil servant who moved to Perth shortly afterwards, John being educated at Stirling High School and Edin-burgh University. Having studied for the ministry, he became pastor at Logiealmond, Perthshire, the 'Drumtochty' of his stories. In 1877 he was called to a Glasgow church, and in 1880 to Liverpool, where he remained 25 years and won great popularity. He took a leading part in establishing the University of Liverpool and also Westminster College at Cambridge, of which he was appointed principal just before his death. His first published work was *Beside the Bonnie Brier Bush* (1894), a collection of sketches of Scottish life and character; it was so popular that it sold over three-quarters of a million copies. Later books were *The Days of Auld Langsyne* (1895), *Kate Carnegie and Those Ministers* (1897), *Afterwards and Other Stories* (1898), and *St Jude's* (1907), sketches of Glasgow life. In addition to these fictional works of the 'Kailyard School' he published a number of theological books, of which *The Mind of the Master* (1896) is the best known. He made two lecture tours in America and was given a D.D. of Yale.

Watson, Robert (1730?—1781), historian, son of an apothecary, was born in St Andrews, where and at Edinburgh and Glasgow, he was educated. He became a Professor of Logic, and afterwards Principal of St Salvador's College, at St Andrews, and wrote a *History of Philip II of Spain* (1777), and part of a continuation on Philip III, which were long standard works.

Watson, Thomas (1557?—1592), poet, born in London, was said to have been at Oxford, and studied law. He was a scholar, and made translations, one of which was a Latin version of the *Antigone* of Sophocles. In 1582 he published *Hecatompathia, or The Passionate Centurie of Love*, consisting of 100 eighteen-line poems, which he called sonnets. It was followed by *Amyntas* (1585) and *Teares of Fancie* (1593).

Watson, Sir William (2 Aug. 1858—11 Aug. 1935), poet, was born at Burley-in-Wharfedale, Yorkshire, son of a grocer, and educated at a school in Southport. His first volume of verse, *The Prince's Quest*, appeared in 1880, and ten years later he won fame with *Wordsworth's Grave and Other Poems*. In 1892 he wrote *Lachrymae Musarum*, the official elegy on Tennyson, which he followed with *Odes and Other Poems* (1894), *The Father of the Forest* (1895), and *The Purple East* (1896), in which he coined the name 'Abdul the Damned.' He was an obvious choice for the Laureateship, but lost favour owing to his anti-imperialist views, and it went to Alfred Austin (q.v.). Watson's 'Ode on the Day of the Coronation of King Edward VII' shows how well he would have filled that post. Among his last works was *The Muse in Exile* (1913). A conservative in his artistic values, and a follower of Tennyson, he excelled as an epigrammatist. He was given an honorary doctorate of Aberdeen in 1904, and in 1917 was knighted.

Watts, Alaric Alexander (16 March 1797—5 April 1864), poet, born in London, was at first an usher in a school in Fulham, then had an active career as a journalist. He founded the *United Service Gazette*, and edited various newspapers and an annual, the *Literary Souvenir*. His poems were collected as *Lyrics of the Heart* (1850). His numerous journalistic ventures finally resulted in bankruptcy.

Watts, Isaac (17 July 1674—25 Nov. 1748), hymn writer, was born at Southampton, son of a clothier who was at one time imprisoned for his religious beliefs. Educated at Southampton Grammar School and at a Nonconformist academy at Stoke Newington, he became minister of an Independent congregation in Mark Lane; but his health proving insufficient for his pastoral duties, he resigned, and gave himself chiefly to literary work, continuing to preach occasionally. For the last 36 years of his life he resided at Theobald's, the house of his friend, Sir Thomas Abney. Among his writings were various educational treatises, including those on *Logic* and *The Improvement of the Mind*, and some works on theological subjects. But his fame rests on his sacred poems and his hymns, which number over 500, and with much that is prosaic comprised 'There is a Land of Pure Delight,' 'O God our Help in Ages Past,' and 'When I survey the Wondrous Cross,' which has been called 'the most majestic hymn in English speech.' His *Horae Lyricae* (1706) was followed by *Hymns* (1707), *Divine and Moral Songs for Children* (1715), and *Metrical Psalms* (1719).

Watts-Dunton, Walter Theodore (12 Oct. 1832—6 June 1914), critic and novelist, was born at St Ives, Huntingdonshire, son of John King Watts, solicitor. In 1896 he added his mother's surname of Dunton to his own. Educated at a school in Cambridge, he became a solicitor and practised in London. He wrote literary criticism for the *Examiner* and the *Athenaeum*, became intimate with the Pre-Raphaelites, and had his interest in gipsy lore stimulated by meeting George Borrow in 1872. From 1879 onwards he became a sort of guardian to Swinburne, living with him in 'The Pines' at the foot of Putney Hill. Watts-Dunton's publications include *The Coming of Love* (1897), a collection of his poems, and the romantic novel *Aylwin* (1898), which had great popularity; *Old Familiar Faces* (1915) contains recollections of Borrow, Rossetti, Morris, and others. But he was greatest as a critic, as in *The Renascence of Wonder* (1903) and *Studies of Shakespeare* (1910).

Waugh, Alexander Raban (8 July 1898—), novelist, born in London, son of a publisher, was a brother of Evelyn Waugh (q.v.). He was educated at Sherborne, where he edited the school magazine, and at Sandhurst. His first novel, *The Loom of Youth* (1917), told of school life and caused his name to be removed from the school roll. In the First World War he held a commission in the Dorset Regiment and was taken prisoner; in the Second World War he served with it again in the Middle East, obtaining the rank of major. His novels include *The Lonely Unicorn* (1922), *Card Castle* (1924), *Kept* (1925), *Nor Many Waters* (1928), *So Lovers Dream* (1931), *Wheels within Wheels* (1933), *The Balliols* (1934), *Going Their Own Ways* (1938), *No Truce With Time* (1941), *Unclouded Summer* (1948), *When the Clock Strikes Twice* (1951), *Guy Renton* (1953), and *Island in the Sun* (1956). *The Coloured Countries* (1930) and *The Sunlit Caribbean* (1948) are travel books, and *Myself When Young* (1923) and *Thirteen Such Years* (1932) are autobiographical.

Waugh, Edwin (29 Jan. 1817—30 April 1890), poet, born at Rochdale, son of a shoemaker, has been called 'the Lancashire

Burns.' After very little schooling he worked as an errand boy and was then apprenticed to a printer. He read avidly and became assistant secretary to the Lancashire Public Schools Association. In 1859 he published *Poems and Lancashire Songs*, which make effective use of the local dialect. His prose works include *Besom Ben* (1865), which had several sequels, *Lancashire Sketches* (1869), *Lancashire Anecdotes* (1872), and *The Chimney Corner* (1879).

Waugh, Evelyn Arthur St John (28 Oct. 1903—   ), novelist, born in London, son of a publisher, was a younger brother of Alexander Waugh (q.v.). He was educated at Lancing, where he edited the school magazine, and at Hertford College, Oxford. After studying art in London he was a schoolmaster for a time. In 1927 he published a life of Dante Gabriel Rossetti, and in 1928 the first of his humorous satirical novels, *Decline and Fall*; others of the same type are *Vile Bodies* (1930), *Black Mischief* (1932), *A Handful of Dust* (1934), *Scoop* (1938), *Put Out More Flags* (1942), and *Brideshead Revisited* (1945). In 1928 he married Evelyn Gardner, daughter of Lord Burghclere; they were divorced in 1930 and in the same year he joined the Roman Catholic Church. In 1936 his life. of Edmund Campion was awarded the Hawthornden Prize, and in the following year he married Laura Herbert and settled in Gloucestershire. During the Second World War he was an officer first in the Marines and later in the Commandos. In 1950 he published a novel, *Helena*, about the mother of Constantine the Great; *Men at Arms* (1952) is the first novel of a trilogy on the war, and *Officers and Gentlemen* (1955) the second, while *Love Among the Ruins* (1953) is a satire on the welfare state. Waugh also wrote a number of travel books, including *Labels* (1930), *Ninety-Two Days* (1934), *Waugh in Abyssinia* (1936), and *The Holy Places* (1953).

Way, Arthur Sanders (13 Feb. 1847—25 Sept. 1930), translator, born at Dorking, Surrey, son of a clergyman, was educated at Kingswood School, Bath, and London University. From 1870 to 1876 he was classical master at Queen's College, Taunton, and after that vice-master of Kingswood School. In 1882 he went to Australia and for ten years was head of Wellesley College, Victoria. Then he returned and was for a time an examiner in Wales. He made a great number of verse translations of the classics, including Homer's *Odyssey* (1880) and *Iliad* (1886—9), Euripides (1894—8), Aeschylus (1906—8), Sophocles (1909—14), Theocritus (1913), Virgil's *Aeneid* (1916—24), Sappho (1920), Pindar (1921), and Aristophanes (1927).

Webb, Beatrice (22 Jan. 1858—30 April 1943), economist, was born at Standish, Gloucestershire, daughter of Richard Potter, a railway director. Educated privately, she was influenced by Herbert Spencer (q.v.), who was a friend of her father's, became interested in economics and socialism, and assisted Charles Booth in his investigation of poverty in London. In 1892 she married Sidney Webb (q.v.). From then onwards her life and career were bound up with his, and it was customary to speak, not of either individually, but of 'the Webbs.' They identified themselves with the British Labour movement, and worked and wrote tirelessly in support of it. Beatrice

Webb's own books include *The Co-operative Movement in Great Britain* (1891), *Men's and Women's Wages: Should They Be Equal?* (1919), and her autobiographical *My Apprenticeship* (1926), *Our Partnership* (1948), and *Diaries, 1912—1924* (1952). For joint works with her husband, see under Sidney Webb.

Webb, Mary Gladys (25 March 1881—8 Oct. 1927), novelist, was born at Leighton, Shropshire, daughter of George Edward Meredith, a schoolmaster, and educated at a school in Southport. In 1912 she married Henry Bertram Law Webb, a schoolmaster, and they lived first at Weston-super-Mare, then at Hampstead. Her life was a heroic struggle against illness and near-poverty, her literary success dating from the occasion when her work was praised by Stanley Baldwin, then Prime Minister. Her principal works consist of five novels, *The Golden Arrow* (1916), *Gone to Earth* (1917), *The House in Dormer Forest* (1920), *Precious Bane* (1924), which was awarded the Femina-Vie Heureuse Prize, and *The Armour Wherein he Trusted*, which was left unfinished at her death and published in 1929. *The Spring of Joy* (1917) is a book of essays. Her novels, written round her own county of Salop, are tragic and Hardyesque, permeated with a sense of grim fate; like Hardy too she excelled in descriptions of nature and country life.

Webb, Sidney, 1st Baron Passfield (13 July 1859—13 Oct. 1947), economist, was born in London and educated at Continental schools, the Birkbeck Institute, and the City of London College. From 1875 to 1891 he was in the Civil Service, then was elected to the London County Council, of which he was a Progressive member for 18 years. In 1892 he married Beatrice Potter (*see* Beatrice Webb). He helped to found the London School of Economics, in which he was Professor of Public Administration from 1912 to 1927, and in 1913 he started the *New Statesman*. From 1922 to 1929 he was Labour M.P. for Durham, and he became President of the Board of Trade in the first Labour Cabinet in 1924. The Webbs were the principal organizers of the Fabian Society, and were the guiding force behind the Labour movement, to which they dedicated their lives, producing together a vast number of authoritative studies on socialism. In 1929 Webb was created Baron Passfield, so that he could take his place in the second Labour Cabinet, in which he was Secretary for the Dominions and then for the Colonies. Both the Webbs were buried in Westminster Abbey. By himself Webb wrote *Socialism in England* (1890). Their joint works include *The History of Trade Unionism* (1894), *Industrial Democracy* (1897), *Problems of Modern Industry* (1898), *English Local Government* (15 volumes, 1906—22), *English Poor Law Policy* (1910), *The Prevention of Destitution* (1911), *The Decay of Capitalist Civilization* (1923), *English Poor Law History* (1927—30), *Soviet Communism* (1935), and *The Truth about Soviet Russia* (1942).

Webbe, William (born 1550) critic and translator, was educated at St John's College, Cambridge, where he knew Spenser and Gabriel Harvey. Later he was private tutor to certain distinguished families. He wrote a *Discourse of English Poetrie* (1586), in which he discusses metre and rhyme (the use of which he reprehends), and reviews English poetry up to his own day. He also translated the first two of the *Eclogues* of Virgil in singularly unmelodious hexameters.

Webster, Daniel (18 Jan. 1782—24 Oct. 1852), statesman and orator, was born at Salisbury, New Hampshire, of which his father was a founder, and educated at Philips Exeter Academy and Dartmouth College, where he made a name as a debater. Studying law, he built up a high reputation in his Boston practice, and in 1827 was elected a member of the United States Senate. He was twice appointed Secretary of State, in 1841 and again in 1850, and was famous as the greatest of American orators. His *Writings and Speeches* were collected in 18 volumes in 1903.

Webster, Jean (24 July 1876—11 June 1916), novelist, was born at Fredonia, New York State, daughter of a publisher. Her original name was Alice Jane Chandler Webster, and her mother was a sister of Mark Twain. Educated at Lady Jane Grey School, Binghamton, and Vassar, she first wrote stories for the Vassar *Miscellany*. Her delightful novel *Daddy-Long-Legs* (1912) was a great success both as a book, as a film starring Mary Pickford, and as a play. The sequel, *Dear Enemy* (1915), was not so successful. Others of her books were two school and college stories, *Patty and Priscilla* (1903) and *Just Patty* (1911), and some more general novels, *The Wheat Princess* (1905), *Jerry Junior* (1907), *The Four Pools Mystery* (1908), and *Much Ado About Peter* (1909). In 1915 she married Glenn Ford McKinney, and they lived in New York, but she was not yet 40 when she died soon after the birth of her daughter.

Webster, John (1580?—1625?), dramatist, was born probably in London. Little is known of his life, but he appears to have been the son of a tailor, and to have been a freeman of the Merchant Taylors' Company, and clerk of the parish of St Andrew's, Holborn. Four plays are known to be his, *The White Devil, or the Life and Death of Vittoria Corombona* (1612), *The Devil's Law Case* (1623), *The Duchess of Malfi* (1623), and *Appius and Virginia* (1654). He also collaborated with Dekker in *Westward Ho* and *Northward Ho*, and with Rowley in *A Cure for a Cuckold* and *Thracian Wonder*. He does not appear to have been much regarded in his own day, and it was only in the nineteenth century that his great tragic power began to be appreciated and expounded by such critics as Lamb and Hazlitt, and in later days Swinburne. Webster revels in the horrible, but the touch of genius saves his work from mere brutality, and evokes pity and sorrow where, without it, there would be only horror and disgust. His work is extremely unequal, and he had no power of construction, but his extraordinary insight into motives and feelings redeem all his failings and give him a place second only to Marlowe and Ben Jonson among the contemporaries of Shakespeare.

Webster, Julia Augusta (30 Jan. 1837—5 Sept. 1894), poetess and dramatist who wrote under the name Cecil Home, was born at Poole, Dorset, daughter of Vice-Admiral George Davies, and was educated at Cambridge, Paris, and Geneva. In 1863 she married Thomas Webster, a solicitor. As a poetess she excelled in the use of dramatic monologue, her volumes of verse including *Blanche Lisle* (1860), *Dramatic Studies* (1866), *Portraits* (1870), and *A Book of Rhyme* (1881). Among her plays are *Disguises* (1879) and *The Sentence* (1887). She also published translations of *Prometheus Bound* (1866) and *Medea* (1868), as well as a novel, *Lesley's Guardian* (1864).

Webster, Noah (16 Oct. 1758—28 May 1843), lexicographer, was born at West Hartford, Connecticut, son of a farmer, who mortgaged his farm to pay the son's expenses at Yale. Noah became a schoolmaster for a time, was admitted to the Bar, and also edited various newspapers, but his chief work was as an educational writer producing text-books that were distinctively American. His *Elementary Spelling Book* (1783) is said to have sold over 100 million copies. After long preparation he published in 1828 his monumental two-volume *American Dictionary of the English Language*, which became accepted as a standard authority in the United States, a position still held by subsequent editions. Webster had corresponded with Benjamin Franklin on spelling reform, and it was due to his ruling that spellings like 'center' and 'honor' became standard in America.

Weekley, Ernest (27 April 1865—7 May 1954), lexicographer, was born in London and educated at the universities of Cambridge, London, Paris, and Berne. From 1898 till 1938 he was Professor of French at University College, Nottingham. After that he lived in Richmond till his house was bombed in 1940, and then in Middlesex. His books popularized etymology and showed its fascination. They include *The Romance of Words* (1912), *The Romance of Names* (1914), *Surnames* (1916), *An Etymological Dictionary of Modern English* (1921), *Words Ancient and Modern* (two series, 1926, 1927), *Words and Names* (1932), and *Jack and Jill, a Study in our Christian Names* (1939).

Wells, Carolyn (died 26 March 1942), anthologist and detective story writer, was born at Rahway, New Jersey. Deaf from childhood as a result of scarlet fever, she studied under various teachers. Her first attempt at writing a book was made at the age of 6. Best known of her compilations is *The Nonsense Anthology* (1902); others are *A Parody Anthology* (1904), *A Satire Anthology* (1905), and *The Book of Humorous Verse* (1920). In 1918 she married Hadwin Houghton, a member of a well-known publishing family. She turned out some 75 detective stories at the rate of three a year, her chief sleuth being Fleming Stone, who gives his name to the *Fleming Stone Omnibus* (1931). In 1937 appeared her autobiography *The Rest of My Life*.

Wells, Charles Jeremiah (1800?—17 Feb. 1879), poet, born in London, went to school at Edmonton with Keats's brother Tom, and so had entry to London literary circles. He practised as a solicitor, and in 1822 published *Stories after Nature*, written in poetic prose, which attracted little notice, and a biblical drama, *Joseph and his Brethren* (1824), which had an almost similar fate until D. G. Rossetti called attention to it in 1863, giving it a high meed of praise. In 1874, stung by want of appreciation, he had burned his manuscripts of plays and poems; but on the new interest excited in his *Joseph* he added some new scenes. In his later years he lived in France.

Wells, Herbert George (21 Sept. 1866—13 Aug. 1946), novelist and sociologist, was born at Bromley in Kent. His father was a professional cricketer who kept a china shop, his mother had been a lady's-maid and was afterwards a housekeeper; the son thus belonged to the lower middle class. Educated at Midhurst Grammar School, he was apprenticed first to a draper and then to a chemist, but succeeded in winning a scholarship to the Royal College of Science, where he studied under Huxley and edited the college magazine. After that he became a kind of pupil-teacher at the University Correspondence College, Cambridge, obtained a B.Sc. degree in 1890, and so became a science instructor. In 1891 he married his cousin, Isabel Mary Wells, but the marriage was a failure; they separated in 1893 and were divorced two years later. Wells then married one of his pupils, Amy Catherine Robbins; they both held very advanced views and did not believe in marriage, but went through the ceremony as a concession to public opinion. She made him an ideal wife, and was the greatest help as housekeeper, secretary, and critic. After her death in 1927 he wrote about her in *The Book of Catherine Wells* (1928).

Wells began writing when his academic work was interrupted by a breakdown in health. He turned first to what is now termed science fiction, of which he was the most brilliant exponent we have had. His first real success was *The Time Machine* (1895), a fascinating story of a man who discovers how to move backwards and forwards in time. *The Invisible Man* (1897) is a circumstantial account of a man who is able to make himself invisible. *The War of the Worlds* (1898) shows the earth being invaded by Martians equipped with death-rays, and *The First Men in the Moon* (1901) tells of space travel. No writer, except perhaps Jules Verne, has ever succeeded in making his scientific romances so convincing and in many respects so accurate in the light of later scientific progress. Many of Wells's cleverest speculations are contained in his short stories collected in *The Country of the Blind* (1911). From scientific to sociological innovation was an easy transition, and even at this early date he was building the utopias which were the consuming passion of his life. *Anticipations* (1900), an early outline of hopes and ideals, was followed by *Mankind in the Making* (1903), *A Modern Utopia* (1905), and *New Worlds for Old* (1908). Always he was planning the ideal state in which the intellectually gifted should rule.

Meanwhile he was producing in his novels true and effective studies of lower middle-class life. *Kipps, the Story of a Simple Soul* (1905), in some ways his greatest book, has been called the first modern novel; in it he depicts with faithful but sympathetic realism the little, irrepressible, downtrodden man who forms the real rank and file of the nation. The same power of characterization is shown in such early novels as *Love and Mr Lewisham* (1900), *Ann Veronica* (1909), *Tono Bungay* (1909), *Mr Polly* (1910), *The Passionate Friends* (1913), and *Bealby* (1915), all of which have a wealth of human interest and are lightened by a happy sense of humour. In later novels such as *The New Machiavelli* (1911), *Mr Britling Sees It Through* (1916), *Joan and Peter* (1918), and *The World of William Clissold* (1926), the mission and the message have become more prominent, and the human interest is overlaid with propaganda. It was during this period that Wells joined the Fabian Society, but dropped out when he found that he could not adapt it to his own ideals.

In his final period he became a political and sociological writer pure and simple. The most popular of all his books was his *Outline of History* (1920), which traces the development of man from the dawn of creation to modern times. Trained historians regarded it as amateurish work, but it appealed to an enormous public, and is said to have sold over three million copies. Forming the first part of a trilogy, it was followed by *The Science of Life* (1929), in which Wells collaborated with Julian Huxley, and completed in *The Work, Wealth, and Happiness of Mankind* (1932), an outline of social science. In 1923 appeared *Men Like Gods*, one of the finest pictures of an ideal world, and in 1933 *The Shape of Things to Come*. But Wells's faith in man's ability to remake his destiny had been badly shaken by the events of the First World War, and was dealt a shattering blow by the Second. His final works, *The Fate of Homo Sapiens* (1939), *A Contemporary Memoir* (1942), and *Mind at the End of its Tether* (1945), reveal an increasing spirit of pessimism, and the atomic age, which he just lived to see, filled him with despair.

Wells's own account of his life is given in *Experiment in Autobiography* (1934). It has been said, somewhat flippantly, that he sold his birthright for a pot of message. Had he wished, he could have been the greatest novelist of his time. Instead, he followed those utopian ideals which revealed him as a reformer far in advance of his age. His appeal was universal in every sense, for in politics he was an internationalist. A visionary but always a practical visionary, the most widely read and influential British writer of his time, he viewed every problem in its universal aspect, yet ultimately from the standpoint of the plain unlettered man whose champion he was. Abroad as well as at home he was recognized as one of the greatest minds of the century, or as Anatole France styled him, 'the greatest intellectual force in the English-speaking world.'

Wendover, Roger de (died 6 May 1236), chronicler, born at Wendover, Buckinghamshire, was a monk of St Albans, became Prior of Belvoir, from which he was deposed for extravagance, but was recalled to St Albans, where he died. He wrote *Flores Historiarum* (Flowers of History), a history of the world in two books, the first from the creation to the incarnation, the second to the reign of Henry III, his own time. The latter is of value as a contemporary authority.

Wesley, Charles (18 Dec. 1707—29 March 1788), Methodist minister and hymn writer, was born at Epworth, Lincolnshire, eighteenth child of the rector, and educated at Westminster School and Oxford. He was all his life closely associated with his elder and greater brother John (q.v.), one of whose most loyal helpers he was, though not agreeing with him in all points. His chief fame is founded upon his hymns, of which he is said to have written the almost incredible number of 6,500, many of them among the finest in the language. They include 'Jesus, Lover of my Soul,' 'Love Divine all Loves excelling,' 'Come, oh Thou Traveller Unknown,' 'Hark the Herald Angels Sing,' and 'Come, let us join our Friends above.' His *Journal* was edited in 1849.

Wesley, John (17 June 1703—2 March 1791), clergyman, diarist, and founder of Methodism, was the second surviving son of Samuel Wesley, Rector of Epworth, Lincolnshire. The name was also written Westley and Wellesley, and the family appears to be the same as that to which the Duke of Wellington belonged. Wesley was educated at the Charterhouse and at Christ Church, Oxford, and was ordained deacon in 1725, and priest in 1728. After assisting his father for a short time as curate, he returned to Oxford, where he found that his brother Charles, along with G. Whitefield (q.v.) and others, had begun that association for religious improvement from which sprang the great religious movement known as Methodism. About the same time the two brothers came under the influence of William Law (q.v.), author of the *Serious Call*, and in 1735 John went on a mission to Georgia to preach to the Indians and colonists, and became closely associated with the Moravian Brethren. Difficulties of a personal character, however, led to his return in 1738 to London, where he continued to associate with the Moravians. It was at this time that, hearing Luther's preface to the Epistle to the Romans read at a meeting, he found his religious and ecclesiastical views revolutionized. Hitherto holding strong High Church views in some directions, he now assumed a position which ultimately led to his creating a separate ecclesiastical organization. As a result the pulpits of the Church were closed against him, and he began his marvellous career of itinerant and out-of-door preaching, which was continued to the close of his long life. He soon became a mighty power in the land; vast crowds waited on his ministrations, which were instrumental in producing a great revival of religious interest, and improved morality among the people. At the same time violent opposition was aroused, and Wesley was often in danger of his life from mobs. In the end, however, he lived down this state of things to a large extent, and in his old age was the object of extraordinary general veneration, while in his own communion he exercised a kind of pontifical sway.

During the 50 years of his apostolic journeyings he is said to have travelled 250,000 miles in Britain, Ireland, and the Continent; but notwithstanding this phenomenal activity he was able, by extreme economy of time, to write copiously, his works including educational treatises, translations from the classics, histories of Rome and England, a history of the Church, biblical commentaries, manifold controversial treatises and editions of religious classics. Most of them had a large circulation and they brought him in £30,000, all of which he expended on philanthropic and religious objects. The work, however, on which his literary fame chiefly rests is his *Journal*, extending from 1735 to 1790, and published in 1827, which is one of the most graphic and interesting records of its kind in existence. He also wrote many hymns, largely translations from the German, and had a considerable hand in giving final form to the almost innumerable hymns of his brother Charles. Wesley was a man of practical and organizing ability of the first order, of intense religious earnestness and sincerity, benevolent feelings, and agreeable manners. At the same time he was of an autocratic temper, and often showed severity and even intolerance in his controversies, which were largely against the extreme Calvinism of his old friend and fellow-labourer, Whitefield, and Toplady, the author of the hymn 'Rock of Ages,' himself a bitter polemic. In 1740 he had formally withdrawn from association with the Moravians. Wesley was married in 1751 to a widow, Mary Vazeille, with whom, however, he did not live happily, and who separated from him in 1776. His *Works* were published in 32 volumes (1771—4) and his *Letters* in eight volumes (1931).

West, Dame Rebecca, *see* **Fairfield, Dame Cicily.**

Westall, William Bury (7 Feb. 1834—9 Sept. 1903), novelist, born near Blackburn, Lancashire, son of a cotton spinner, was educated at Liverpool High School and then went into his father's business. In 1870 he turned to literature and lived abroad, becoming *Times* correspondent at Geneva and editor of the *Swiss Times*. His novel *Her Two Millions* (1897) tells of journalism in Geneva, while *The Old Factory* (1881) is a tale of Lancashire life. Others of his novels are *The Phantom City* (1886), *A Fair Crusader* (1888), *Strange Crimes* (1890), *Don or Devil* (1901), and *Her Ladyship's Secret* (1901).

Westmacott, Mary, *see* **Christie, Agatha.**

Wetherell, Elizabeth, *see* **Warner, Susan.**

Weyman, Stanley John (7 Aug. 1855—10 April 1928), novelist, was born at Ludlow, Shropshire, son of a solicitor. Educated at Shrewsbury and Oxford, he taught history at King's School, Chester, for a year. He then studied law, was called to the Bar at Inner Temple in 1881, and practised for eight years, but was too nervous to be a success. His first novel, *The House of the Wolf*, appeared in 1890, and he won great popularity with his romances of foreign adventure, *A Gentleman of France* (1893), *Under the Red Robe* (1894), *Count Hannibal* (1901), and *The Abbess of Vlaye* (1904). Stories with an English setting are *Shrewsbury* (1898), *Sophia* (1900), *Starvecrow Farm* (1905), *Chippinge* (1906), *The Great House* (1919), and *Ovington's Bank* (1922).

Wharton, Edith Newbold (24 Jan. 1862—11 Aug. 1937), novelist, was born in New York City, daughter of George Frederic Jones, and educated by governesses. In 1885 she married Edward Wharton; they travelled a great deal, and in 1906 removed to a flat in Paris. Wharton became insane, and they were divorced in 1912. Edith Wharton had begun writing with short stories in *Scribner's Magazine*, and she always excelled in this form of work, collections of which are *The Greater Inclination* (1899), *Crucial Instances* (1901), *The Hermit and the Wild Woman* (1908), *Tales of Men and Ghosts* (1910), *Xingu*

(1916), and *Here and Beyond* (1926). During the First World War she organized a French ambulance unit, and in 1924 she was made an officer of the Legion of Honour. Of her novels *Ethan Frome* (1911) is sometimes thought her greatest; *The Age of Innocence* (1920), a satire on society, was awarded the Pulitzer Prize, as also was *Old New York* (1924) in its dramatic form with the title *Old Maid*; other novels are *The Valley of Decision* (1902), *The House of Mirth* (1905), *The Reef* (1912), *The Custom of the Country* (1913), *Summer* (1917), *False Dawn* (1924), *The Children* (1928), *The Gods Arrive* (1932), and the unfinished *Buccaneers* (1938). *A Backward Glance* (1934) is a book of memoirs.

Wharton, Thomas Wharton, 1st Marquis of (Aug. 1648—12 April 1715), statesman, son of the 4th Baron Wharton, was born at Woburn, Bedfordshire. Brought up in an atmosphere of piety, he became the greatest rake in 'England. He entered the House of Commons in 1673, and was a supporter of the Exclusion Bill, and consequently obnoxious to James II. His only contribution to literature was the doggerel anti-Roman Catholic ballad, 'Lillibullero' (1688), which had so powerful a political effect that its author claimed to have sung a King out of three kingdoms. He was generally disliked and distrusted, but held for a short time, from 1708, the Lord Lieutenancy of Ireland, when he had Addison as his chief secretary.

Whateley, Richard (1 Feb. 1787—1 Oct. 1863), prelate, was born in London, son of a clergyman, and educated at a school in Bristol, and at Oxford, where he became a college tutor. Taking orders he became rector of Halesworth, Suffolk. In 1822 he delivered his Bampton lectures on *The Use and Abuse of Party Feeling in Religion*. Three years later he was made Principal of St Alban's Hall, in 1829 Professor of Political Economy, and in 1831 Archbishop of Dublin. He had no sympathy with the Oxford movement, was strongly anti-Calvinistic, and somewhat Latitudinarian, so that he was exposed to a good deal of theological odium from opposite quarters. He was a voluminous writer, and among his best known works are his treatises on *Logic* (1826), and *Rhetoric* (1828), his *Historic Doubts relative to Napoleon Buonaparte* (1819), intended as a *reductio ad absurdum* of Hume's contention that no evidence is sufficient to prove a miracle, *Essays on some Peculiarities of the Christian Religion* (1825), *Christian Evidences* (1837), and editions of Bacon's *Essays* and Paley's *Evidences*.

Whetstone, George (1544?—1587?) dramatist and poet, born in London, served as a soldier in the Low Countries, accompanied Sir Humphrey Gilbert's expedition to Newfoundland in 1578, and was at the Battle of Zutphen in 1586. He was a trenchant critic of the contemporary drama, contending for greater reality and rationality. His play, *Promos and Cassandra* (1578), translated from Cinthio's *Hecatommithi*, was used by Shakespeare in *Measure for Measure*.

Whewell, William (24 May 1794—6 March 1866), philosopher and scientist, was born at Lancaster, son of a joiner, and educated at Heversham Grammar School and Trinity College, Cambridge, where he had a brilliant career, winning the Chancellor's Medal with a poem on Boadicea, and being President of the Union. He became Professor of Mineralogy at Cambridge in 1828, of Moral Theology in 1838, was Master of Trinity from 1841 until his death, and he held the office of Vice-Chancellor of the University in 1843 and 1856. Whewell was remarkable as the possessor of an encyclopaedic fund of knowledge, perhaps unprecedented, and he was the author of a number of works of great importance on a variety of subjects. Among the chief of these may be mentioned his Bridgewater Treatise on *Astronomy and General Physics considered with Reference to Natural Theology* (1833), *History of the Inductive Sciences* (1837), *The Philosophy of the Inductive Sciences* (1840), *Elements of Morality* (1845), *History of Moral Philosophy in England* (1852), *Essay on the Plurality of Worlds* (1853), and *Platonic Dialogues for English Readers* (1859—1861). In addition to these he wrote innumerable articles, reviews, and scientific papers. It was as a co-ordinator of knowledge and the researches of others that Whewell excelled; he was little of an original observer or discoverer. He is described as a large, strong, erect man with a red face and a loud voice, and he was an overwhelming and somewhat arrogant talker.

Whibley, Charles (9 Dec. 1859—4 March 1930), journalist and author, born in Kent and educated at Cambridge, settled in London and began wriiting for the *Scots Observer*, later the *National Observer*. In 1892 he projected with W. E. Henley (q.v.) the series of reprints known as the Tudor Translations. Later he was on the staff of the *Pall Mall Gazette*, and wrote 'Musings Without Method' for *Blackwood's*. His own publications include *The Book of Scoundrels* (1897), *The Pageantry of Life* (1900), *Studies in Frankness* (1910), *Essays in Biography* (1913), *The Letters of an Englishman* (1915), and *Political Portraits* (1917). He has been described as an anachronism, belonging to the nineteenth century but publishing his works in the twentieth. He was twice married, first to Whistler's sister-in-law and then to Sir Walter Raleigh's daughter.

Whichcote, Benjamin (4 May 1609—May 1683), clergyman, born at Stoke in Shropshire, was educated at Cambridge, where he became Provost of King's College, of which office he was deprived at the Restoration. He was of liberal views, and is reckoned among the Cambridge Platonists, over whom he exercised great influence. His works consist of *Discourses* (1701) and *Moral and Religious Aphorisms* (1703). In 1668 he was presented to the living of St Lawrence Jewry, London, which he held until his death.

Whipple, Edwin Percy (8 March 1819—16 June 1886), critic, born at Gloucester, Massachusetts, and educated at Salem High School, worked for a time in a bank, but started writing for various periodicals and published his collected articles as *Essays and Reviews* (1848—9). He became a highly popular lecturer, his works including *Lectures on Subjects Connected with Literature and Life* (1850), *Character and Characteristic Men* (1866), and *Literature of the Age of Elizabeth* (1869). After his death there were published his *Recollec-*

tions of Eminent Men and *American Literature and Other Papers*. He was a close friend of Whittier (q.v.).

Whiston, William (9 Dec. 1667—22 Aug. 1752), clergyman and scientist, born at Norton, Leicestershire, of which his father was rector, was educated at Cambridge, where he succeeded Newton as Lucasian Professor of Mathematics, was a prominent advocate of the Newtonian system, and wrote a *New Theory of the Earth* (1696), opposing the views of Thomas Burnet (q.v.). He also wrote the theological works, *Primitive Christianity Revived* (1711) and the *Primitive New Testament* (1745). The Arian views promulgated in the former led to his expulsion from the University. His best-known work was his translation of *Josephus* (1737). He was a kindly and honest, but eccentric and impracticable man, and an insatiable controversialist.

White, Elwyn Brooks (11 July 1899—   ), journalist and essayist, was born at Mount Vernon, New York State, and educated at Cornell. During the First World War he served as a private. He became a reporter in Seattle, went to Alaska as a ship's steward, then worked in an advertising agency in New York. He joined the staff of the *New Yorker*, for which he wrote the 'Talk of the Town' column, and he also edited the section 'One Man's Meat' in *Harper's Magazine*. A brilliant humorist, he collaborated with Thurber (q.v.) in *Is Sex Necessary?* (1929). His own books include *Every Day is Saturday* (1934), *The Fox of Peapack* (1938), *Quo Vadimus* (1939), and *The Second Tree from the Corner* (1954). With his wife, whom he married in 1929, he edited *A Subtreasury of American Humour* (1941). His books for children, *Stuart Little* (1945) and *Charlotte's Web* (1952) became accepted classics.

White, Gilbert (18 July 1720—26 June 1793), naturalist, born at Selborne, Hampshire, son of a barrister, and educated along with the Wartons (q.v.) at their father's school at Basingstoke, went on to Oriel College, Oxford, took orders, and after holding various curacies settled again, in 1755, at Selborne. He became the friend and correspondent of Pennant the naturalist (q.v.), and other men of science, and published in the form of letters the work which has made him immortal, *The Natural History and Antiquities of Selborne* (1789), the only work of its kind which has been accepted as a classic of English literature. He was never married, but was in love with the well-known bluestocking Hester Mulso, afterwards Mrs Chapone, who rejected him. He had four brothers, all more or less addicted to the study of natural history.

White, Henry Kirke (21 March 1785—19 Oct. 1806), poet, was born at Nottingham, son of a butcher, and had only an elementary schooling when he was put to work at a stocking loom. Afterwards he worked in an attorney's office and began writing poetry, his *Clifton Grove* appearing in 1803. Southey took an interest in him and funds were raised to send him to Cambridge, where he entered St John's College as a sizar. He distinguished himself by his industry, but the work was too much for his health and he died in his college rooms. His *Remains* were edited, with a life, by Southey in 1807.

White, Joseph Blanco (11 July 1775—20 May 1841), poet, son of an Irish Roman Catholic resident at Seville, where he was born, went to work at the age of 8 in his father's mercantile house. At 14 he went to study at a Dominican college, and became a priest, but lost his religious faith and came to England, where he conducted a Spanish newspaper having for its main object the fanning of the flame of Spanish patriotism against the French invasion. He entered the Church of England, but latterly became a Unitarian. He wrote, among other works, *Internal Evidences against Catholicism* (1825), and *Second Travels of an Irish Gentleman in search of a Religion* (1833), in answer to T. Moore's work, *Travels, etc.* His most permanent contribution to literature, however, is his single sonnet on 'Night,' which Coleridge considered 'the finest and most grandly conceived' in our language.

White, Richard Grant (23 May 1821—8 April 1885), critic, was born in New York City, son of a merchant, and went to the university there. From 1861 to 1878 he was a clerk in the New York Customs, but employed his leisure in writing. Among his books are *Words and their Uses* (1870) and *Everyday English* (1880). An acute Shakespearian critic, he edited the Riverside edition of his works and also wrote *Studies in Shakespeare* (1886). *The Fate of Mansfield Humphreys* (1884) is a novel.

White, William Hale (22 Dec. 1831—14 March 1913), novelist who wrote under the name Mark Rutherford, was born in Bedford, son of a printer. Educated at Bedford Modern School, he studied for the ministry but was expelled from a theological college for his unorthodox views. In 1854 he entered the Civil Service, and was a clerk first in Somerset House and then in the Admiralty, retiring at the age of 60. His literary reputation depends mainly on his *Autobiography of Mark Rutherford* (1881) and its sequel *Mark Rutherford's Deliverance* (1885), which are a sort of personal confession. Other novels are *The Revolution in Tanner's Lane* (1887), *Miriam's Schooling* (1890), and *Catharine Furze* (1893). *Pages from a Journal* (three series, 1900, 1910, 1915), is a kind of miscellany. White also published some critical and philosophical works under his own name.

Whitehead, Charles (1804—5 July 1862), poet and novelist, was born in London, son of a wine merchant. He began as a clerk, but turned to literature, and is remembered for three works, all of which met with popular favour: *The Solitary* (1831), a poem, *The Autobiography of Jack Ketch* (1834), a novel, and *The Cavalier* (1836), a play in blank verse. He recommended Dickens for the writing of the letterpress for R. Seymour's drawings, which ultimately developed into *The Pickwick Papers*. In 1857 he went to Australia, where he died in poverty.

Whitehead, William (baptized 12 Feb. 1715, died 14 April 1785) Poet Laureate, born in Cambridge, son of a baker, and educated at Winchester School and Cambridge, became tutor in the family of the Earl of Jersey. In 1757 he succeeded Colley Cibber as Poet Laureate. He wrote plays of only moderate quality, including *The Roman Father* (1750), and *Creusa* (1754), tragedies, and *The School for* ·

Lovers (1762), a comedy. His poems include *The Enthusiast* and
Variety. His official productions as Laureate were severely attacked,
which drew from him in reply *A Charge to the Poets* (1762).

Whitman, Walt *or* **Walter** (31 May 1819—26 March 1892), poet,
was born at West Hills, Huntington, Long Island. His mother was
of Dutch descent, and the farm on which he was born had been in the
possession of his father's family since the early settlement. His first
education was received at Brooklyn, to which his father had removed
about 1823. At 13 he was in a printing office, at 17 he was teaching
and writing for the newspapers, and at 21 was editing one. The
next dozen years were passed in desultory work as a printer with
occasional literary excursions, but apparently mainly in 'loafing'
and observing his fellow-creatures. From 1846 to 1848 he was
editor of the Brooklyn *Daily Eagle*, but it was not till 1855 that his
first really characteristic work, *Leaves of Grass*, appeared; it discarded
rhyme and metre and used the rhapsodical rhythms of the Old
Testament. This first edition contained only 12 poems. Notwithstanding its startling departures from conventionality both in form
and substance it was well received by the leading literary reviews
and, with certain reserves to be expected, it was welcomed by
Emerson. It did not, however, achieve general acceptance, and was
criticized as being vulgar and irreverent. When a later edition was
called for, Emerson unsuccessfully endeavoured to persuade the
author to suppress the more objectionable parts, and in the year of
Whitman's death it reached its 12th edition. On the outbreak of
the Civil War Whitman volunteered as a nurse for the wounded, and
rendered much useful service. The results of his experiences and
observations were given in verse in *Drum Taps* (1865), and in prose
in *Specimen Days and Collect* (1882). From these scenes he was
removed by his appointment to a Government clerkship, from which,
however, he was soon dismissed on the ground of having written
books of an immoral tendency. This action of the authorities led to
a somewhat warm controversy, and after a short interval Whitman
received another Government appointment, which he held until
1873, when he had a paralytic seizure, which rendered his retirement
necessary. Other works besides those mentioned are *Democratic
Vistas* (1871) and *November Boughs* (1888). In his later years he
retired to Camden, New Jersey, where he died. Whitman is the
most unconventional of writers. Revolt against all convention was
in fact his self-proclaimed mission. In his verse he established a
new tradition of freedom of form and expression, while in his treatment of certain passions and appetites, and of unadulterated human
nature, he was at war with what he considered the conventions of an ·
effeminate society; but after all reservations, there is real poetic
insight and an intense and singularly fresh sense of nature in the best
of his writings.

Whitney, William Dwight (9 Feb. 1827—7 June 1894), philologist,
born at Northampton, Massachusetts, son of a banker, was educated
at Williams College and Yale, where he studied Sanskrit and in 1854
became professor of this subject. He edited a number of Sanskrit

texts and in 1879 published a *Sanskrit Grammar*. In his later years he was chief editor of the *Century Dictionary* (1889—91). He was a member of the American Philological Association from its foundation in 1869.

Whittier, John Greenleaf (17 Dec. 1807—7 Sept. 1892), poet, was born of Quaker parents at the village of Haverhill, Massachusetts. Brought up as a farmer's boy, he lived close to nature, and though he had little formal schooling he read avidly and drew inspiration from the poems of Burns. His own first poem to be printed appeared in 1826, and he became a journalist, holding various editorial positions. In 1833 he published an anti-slavery work, *Justice and Expediency*, and for thirty years he devoted himself to the abolitionist cause as writer and political worker, so that he became venerated in later years as the apostle of human freedom. After the Civil War he settled at Amesbury, Massachusetts, and led an uneventful life. His volumes of verse include *Songs of Labor* (1850), *The Chapel of the Hermits* (1853), *The Panorama* (1856), which contains the well-known 'Maud Muller' and 'Barefoot Boy,' *Home Ballads* (1860), *In War Time* (1864), containing the famous 'Barbara Frietchie,' *Snow-Bound* (1866), named from a poem that is sometimes accounted his best work, and *Among the Hills* (1869). Later volumes were *Miriam* (1871), *Hazel Blossoms* (1875), and *At Sundown* (1890). Greatest in his nature pieces, he was in his day the most popular American poet after Longfellow; his work has been compared with Cowper's.

Whymper, Edward (27 April 1840—16 Sept. 1911), engraver and mountaineer, was born in London. Succeeding his father in a wood-engraving business, he maintained a high standard of work, and his woodcuts were used in many books of travel. In 1860 he went to the Alps, primarily to make sketches, but became famous as a climber, and formed the ambition to conquer the Matterhorn. In 1865 he succeeded in this feat, but only at the cost of a terrible disaster, four of his party being killed in a fall. In 1871 he published an account of this and other ascents in *Scrambles among the Alps*. In 1888 he went to the Andes and climbed Chimborazo and Cotopaxi, telling of this later in *Travels among the Great Andes of the Equator* (1892). Others of his books are *Chamonix and Mont Blanc* (1896) and *Zermatt and the Matterhorn* (1897). He was awarded the medal of the Royal Geographical Society, and died among his loved mountains at Chamonix.

Whyte-Melville, George John (19 June 1821—5 Dec. 1878), writer of sporting novels, was born at Strathkinness in Fife, and educated at Eton. Commissioned first in the 93rd Highlanders and then in the Coldstream Guards, he saw service in the Crimea, retiring in 1859 as Major. Thereafter he devoted himself to field sports, on which he was an acknowledged authority, and to literature. He wrote a number of novels, mainly founded on sporting subjects, though a few were historical. They include *Kate Coventry* (1856), *The Queen's Maries* (1862), *The Gladiators* (1863), and *Satanella* (1873). He also wrote *Songs and Verses* (1869) and *The True Cross*

(1873), a religious poem. His *Riding Recollections* appeared in 1875.
He died from an accident in the hunting-field.

Wickham, Anna (1884—   ), poetess, was born at
Wimbledon of Australian parents, and was taken to Australia as a
child and educated at Sydney High School. At 21 she came back
to England, and studied singing in Paris. She married Patrick
Hepburn, the astronomer, who died in 1929. Her books of verse
include *The Contemplative Quarry* (1915), *The Man with a Hammer*
(1916), and *The Little Old House* (1921).

Wiclif, *see* **Wycliffe.**

Widdemer, Margaret (   ), poetess
and novelist, was born at Doylestown, Pennsylvania, daughter of a
minister. She trained as a librarian at Drexel Institute of Arts and
Sciences and studied at the University of Pennsylvania. In 1919
she married Robert Haven Schauffler. Her first published poem,
Factories (1915) won special notice from its humanitarian interest.
Others of her books of verse are *Old Road to Paradise* (1918), *Cross
Currents* (1921), *Ballads and Lyrics* (1925), and *Hill Garden* (1937).
In 1918 she shared with Carl Sandburg the prize of the Poetry
Society of America. Her novels include *The Rose Garden Husband*
(1915), which was a best-seller. *You're Only Young Once* (1918),
I've Married Marjorie (1920), *The Year of Delight* (1921), *Gallant
Lady* (1926), *Rhinestones* (1929), *Constancia Herself* (1945), *Red
Cloak Flying* (1950), *Lady of the Mohawks* (1951), and *The Golden
Wildcat* (1954).

Wiggin, Kate Douglas (28 Sept. 1856—24 Aug. 1923), novelist, was
born in Philadelphia, daughter of Robert Noah Smith, a lawyer, and
educated at Abbott Academy, Andover, Massachusetts. She studied
to be a teacher, and when the family moved to Southern California
she opened the first free kindergarten school on the Pacific Coast.
In 1881 she married Samuel Bradley Wiggin, who died in 1889, and
in 1895 she married George Christopher Riggs. Her first book was
The Story of Patsy (1883), followed by the more successful *Timothy's
Quest* (1890). Visits to England with her husband inspired the
Penelope books, *Penelope's Progress* (1898), her *English Experiences*
(1900), her *Irish Experiences* (1901), and her *Postscripts* (1915). In
1903 she published *Rebecca of Sunnybrook Farm*, a very popular
story which she followed up with *New Chronicles of Rebecca* (1907);
Rebecca has been called 'the nicest child in American literature.'
Other novels are *Rose of the River* (1905), *Susanna and Sue* (1909),
and *Mother Carey's Chickens* (1911). *My Garden of Memory* (1923)
is an autobiography.

Wilberforce, William (24 Aug. 1759—29 July 1833), philanthropist, born at Hull, of which his grandfather had been mayor,
was educated at Cambridge. He entered Parliament as member for
his native town, became the intimate friend of Pitt, and was the
leader of the crusade against the slave-trade and slavery. His chief
literary work was his *Practical View of Christianity* (1797), which had
remarkable popularity and influence. His *Appeal on Behalf of the*

Negro Slaves in the West Indies appeared in 1823. He was buried in Westminster Abbey.

Wilcox, Carlos (22 Oct. 1794—29 May 1827), poet, was born at Newport, New Hampshire, son of a farmer, and brought up in Vermont. Educated at Middlebury and Andover Theological Seminary, he was pastor successively at Hartford, Connecticut, and Danbury. He wrote *The Age of Benevolence*, a long poem in the style of Cowper with some good natural descriptions, but it was unfinished when he died of heart failure.

Wilcox, Ella Wheeler (5 Nov. 1850—30 Oct. 1919), poetess, was born at Johnstown Center, Wisconsin, daughter of Marius Hartwell Wheeler, a teacher of the violin, and was educated at the University of Wisconsin. Before she was 10 she had written a novel; soon she was writing two poems a day, and by the time she was 18 her earnings from her pen were substantial. Her earliest book of verse was a collection of temperance poems, *Drops of Water* (1872), which was followed by *Shells* (1873) and *Maurine* (1876), a narrative poem. Her first great success was with *Poems of Passion* (1883), which were criticized as immoral, though they seem very innocuous to a later age. In 1884 she married Robert Marius Wilcox, a silversmith, and they settled at Meriden, Connecticut. She travelled widely, and in 1913 was presented at Court in England. During the First World War she gave readings of her poems in army camps. She took her work most seriously, and published in all nearly 40 volumes. She was also interested in spiritualism and theosophy. *The Story of a Literary Career* (1905) and *The Worlds and I* (1918) are autobiographical.

Wilde, Oscar Fingal O'Flahertie Wills (16 Oct. 1854—30 Nov. 1900), born in Dublin, son of a surgeon, was educated at Trinity College, Dublin, and Magdalen College, Oxford, where he won the Newdigate Prize with a poem on Ravenna. While there he formulated his philosophy of 'Art for art's sake' and became the leader of the so-called aesthetic cult. A volume of his poems was published in 1881 and in 1882 he visited America. In 1884 he married Constance Lloyd, and in 1888 he published *The Happy Prince*, a book of children's fairy-tales with an occasional undercurrent of satire. The greater part of his literary work belongs to the next few years. In 1891 appeared *Lord Arthur Savile's Crime* and *The Picture of Dorian Gray*. Light comedies in the Anglo-Irish tradition of Sheridan were *Lady Windermere's Fan* (1892), *A Woman of No Importance* (1893), and *The Ideal Husband* (1895); *Salome* (1893), a fantastic play, was written in French but translated into English by Wilde's friend Lord Alfred Douglas. In 1895 appeared Wilde's last play *The Importance of Being Earnest*, and in the same year he was ill-advised enough to bring a libel action against Douglas's father, the Marquis of Queensberry, who had accused him of unnatural vice. Wilde lost his case, was arrested on a charge arising out of it, and sentenced to two years hard labour. This of course meant social and financial ruin. He came out of prison in 1897 and lived in France on the charity of his friends under the name Sebastian Melmoth. His last work was the somewhat rhetorical *Ballad of Reading Gaol* (1898). He died a Roman Catholic.

Wilder, Thornton Niven (17 April 1897—   ), novelist and dramatist, was born at Madison, Wisconsin, son of a newspaper editor who later became American consul-general at Hong-Kong. The boy was sent to school at Chefoo, and after that in Berkeley, California, going on from there to Yale and the American Academy at Rome.   In the First World War Wilder served in the artillery, and in the Second in the Air Corps.   His first novel, *The Cabala* (1925) was published while he was a teacher at Laurenceville School, New Jersey, but it was *The Bridge of San Luis Rey* (1927) that made him famous; it was a best-seller, received the Pulitzer Prize, was filmed, and started a fashion in fiction.   In 1928 he gave up teaching to concentrate on writing.   Later novels are *The Woman of Andros* (1930), *Heaven's My Destination* (1935), and *The Ides of March* (1948).   Of his plays, *Our Town* (1938) and *The Skin of Our Teeth* (1943), an allegorical comedy, were both awarded Pulitzer Prizes; others are *The Angel That Troubled the Waters* (1928) and *The Long Christmas Dinner* (1931).   Wilder's output is comparatively small, but of very high quality.

Wilkes, John (17 Oct. 1727—26 Dec. 1797), politician, born in London, son of a wealthy distiller, was educated at Leyden University.   Witty, resourceful, but unprincipled and profligate, he became from circumstances the representative and champion of important political principles, including that of free representation in Parliament.   His writings have nothing of the brilliance and point of his conversation, but his paper, *The North Briton*, and especially the famous issue in which he charged George III with uttering a falsehood in his speech from the throne, caused so much excitement, and led to such important results that they give him a place in literature.   He also wrote a highly offensive *Essay on Woman* (1764).   Wilkes was expelled from the House of Commons and outlawed, but such was the strength of the cause which he championed that, notwithstanding the worthlessness of his character, his right to sit in the House was ultimately admitted in 1774, and he continued to do so until 1790. He was also Lord Mayor of London.

Wilkie, William (5 Oct. 1721—10 Oct. 1772), poet, born at Dalmeny, Midlothian, son of a farmer, and educated at Edinburgh University, entered the Church, and became minister of Ratho, Midlothian, in 1756, and Professor of Natural Philosophy at St Andrews in 1759.   In 1757 he published the *Epigoniad*, an epic about the Epigoni, descendants of the seven legendary Greek champions who fought against Thebes, and so was nicknamed the Scottish Homer.   His *Moral Fables in Verse* appeared in 1768.

Wilkins, John (1614—19 Nov. 1672), prelate and scientist, born at Fawsley, Northamptonshire, son of a goldsmith, was educated at Oxford, took orders, held many preferments, and became Bishop of Chester.   He married a sister of Oliver Cromwell, and being of an easy temper and somewhat accommodating principles, he passed through troublous times and many changes with a minimum of hardship. He was one of the band of learned men whom Charles II incorporated as the Royal Society. Among his writings are *The Discovery of a World in the Moon* (1638), *Mathematical Magic* (1648), and *An Essay towards a Philosophical Language* (1668).

Wilkinson, Sir John Gardner (5 Oct. 1797—29 Oct. 1875), Egyptologist, was born in Chelsea, son of a Westmorland clergyman, and educated at Harrow and Oxford. In 1821 he went to Egypt, and remained there and in Nubia exploring, surveying, and studying the hieroglyphical inscriptions, on which he made himself one of the great authorities. He published two important works, of great literary as well as scholarly merit, *Materia Hieroglyphica* (1828), and *Manners and Customs of the Ancient Egyptians* (six volumes, 1837—41). He wrote various books of travel, and was knighted in 1839.

William of Malmesbury (1090?—1143?), historian, was a monk of the great monastery at Malmesbury. His name is said to have been Somerset, and he was Norman by one parent and English by the other. His history, written in Latin, falls into two parts, *Gesta Regum Anglorum* (Acts of the Kings of the English), in five books, bringing the narrative down from the arrival of the Saxons to 1120, and *Historia Novella* (Modern History), carrying it on to 1142. The work is characterized by a love of truth, much more critical faculty in sifting evidence than was then common, and considerable attention to literary form. It is dedicated to Robert, Earl of Gloucester, the champion of Queen Matilda. He also wrote *De Gestis Pontificum Anglorum* (On the Acts of the English Bishops), and a history of the Monastery of Glastonbury.

William of Newburgh, *or* **Newbury** (1136—1198?), historian, born at Bridlington, belonged to the monastery of Newburgh in Yorkshire. His own name is said to have been Little. His work, *Historia Rerum Anglicarum* (History of English Affairs), is written in good Latin, and has some of the same qualities as that of William of Malmesbury (q.v.). He rejects the legend of the Trojan descent of the early Britons, and animadverts severely on what he calls 'the impudent and impertinent lies' of Geoffrey of Monmouth (q.v.). His record is valuable for the reigns of Henry II and Richard I.

Williams, Sir Charles Hanbury (8 Dec. 1708—2 Nov. 1759), diplomat and satirist, was born at Pontypool, Monmouthshire, where his father, John Hanbury, owned an ironworks. The son assumed the name of Williams on inheriting a fortune from his father's friend of that name, entered Parliament as a supporter of Walpole, held many diplomatic posts, and was a brilliant wit with a great contemporary reputation for lively and biting satires and lampoons. His poems include *The Country Girl* (1742), *The Old Coachman* (1742), and *Tar Water* (1747). He finally became insane and committed suicide.

Williams, Emlyn (26 Nov. 1905—), playwright, was born at Penyffordd, Flintshire, son of an ironmonger, and spoke no English till he was 8. He was educated at Holywell, Dorset, and Christ Church, Oxford, where he was an active member of the University Dramatic Society and wrote a play, *Full Moon*. He soon became celebrated both as actor and as dramatist. His first real success was *A Murder Has Been Arranged* (1930), and he wrote several other effective horror dramas. His later plays include *Night Must Fall* (1935), *He Was Born Gay* (1937), *The Corn Is Green* (1938), *The Light of Heart* (1940), *Druid's Rest* (1944), *The Wind of Heaven* (1945), *Pepper and Sand* (1948), and *Accolade* (1951); *The Morning Star* (1942) tells of the bombing of London. He was also noted for his highly successful dramatic readings of Dickens and Dylan Thomas.

Williams, Tennessee (26 March 1912—   ), playwright, was born at Columbus, Mississippi, son of a commercial traveller, his original name being Thomas Lanier Williams. When he was 12 the family moved to St Louis. He was educated at the Universities of Missouri and Iowa, with an interval during which he worked as a clerk. In 1940 he received a Rockefeller Fellowship, and after working at various jobs he was employed by one of the film companies in Hollywood, where he wrote *The Glass Menagerie* (1945). This play, together with *A Streetcar Named Desire* (1947), which got its title from the trams of New Orleans, established him as one of America's leading dramatists. Later plays are *Summer and Smoke* (1948), *The Rose Tattoo* (1951), *Camino Real* (1953), and *Cat on a Hot Tin Roof* (1955). *27 Wagons Full of Cotton* (1946) is a collection of one-act plays, and *One Arm* (1948) and *Hard Candy* (1954) are volumes of short stories.

Williams, William Carlos (17 Sept. 1883—   ), poet and novelist, born at Rutherford, New Jersey, was educated at Geneva and the University of Pennsylvania, where he studied medicine. As a poet he began under Imagist influences, but afterwards set himself to develop a distinctive American technique which would be non-derivative. His volumes of verse include *Poems* (1909), *The Tempers* (1913), *Al Que Quiere?* (1917). *Kora in Hell* (1920), *Sour Grapes* (1921), *Spring and All* (1922), *Adam and Eve and the City* (1936), *Broken Span* (1941), *The Wedge* (1944), and his 'personal epic' *Paterson* (1946—51), which received the National Book Award. He wrote three novels which form a trilogy, *White Mule* (1937), *In the Money* (1940), and *The Build-Up* (1952); *The Knife of the Times* (1932), and *Make Light of It* (1950) are collections of short stories. He also wrote two books of critical essays, *The Great American Novel* (1923) and *In the American Grain* (1925), and an *Autobiography* (1951). He received honorary degrees of Pennsylvania, Buffalo, and Rutgers Universities.

Williams-Ellis, Amabel (1894—   ), novelist and critic, daughter of J. St Loe Strachey and cousin of Lytton Strachey (q.v.) was born at Newlands Corner, near Guildford. In 1915 she married Bertram Clough William-Ellis, an architect, and they lived in Wales. In 1922 she was literary editor of the *Spectator*, of which her father was editor. Her first book was a critical miscellany, *An Anatomy of Poetry* (1922). Her novels include *Noah's Ark* (1926), *The Wall of Glass* (1927), *Volcano* (1931), *To Tell the Truth* (1933), *The Big Firm* (1938), and *Learn to Love First* (1939). *Exquisite Tragedy* (1928) is a life of Ruskin, while *Women in War Factories*

(1943) and *The Art of Being a Woman* (1951) are sociological studies. She also wrote several books for children, including *Princesses and Trolls* (1950).

Williamson, Henry (1897—), novelist and nature writer, was born in Bedfordshire in a house which four generations of his family had occupied. As a boy he drew inspiration from the books of Richard Jefferies (q.v.). At the age of 17 he enlisted and served in France through the First World War; *The Wet Flanders Plain* (1929) tells some of his experiences. He worked in London as a struggling freelance, but was never happy in the town, and later settled in a cottage on Exmoor, afterwards moving to Norfolk. He first came into prominence through his tetralogy, *The Flax of Dreams*, made up of *The Beautiful Years* (1921), *Dandelion Days* (1922), *Dream of Fair Women* (1924), and *The Pathway* (1928). Other novels are *The Patriot's Progress* (1930) and *Star-born* (1933). But he is best known for his animal stories, such as *Tarka the Otter* (1927), which was awarded the Hawthornden Prize; others are *The Peregrine Saga* (1923), *The Old Stag* (1926), *Salar the Salmon* (1935), *The Phasian Bird* (1948), and *Tales of Moorland and Estuary* (1953). *Tales of a Devon Village* and *Life in a Devon Village* (1932) are partly autobiographical.

Willis, Browne (14 Sept. 1682—5 Feb. 1760), antiquary, born at Blandford St Mary and educated at Westminster and Oxford, studied law at the Inner Temple, and from 1705 to 1708 sat in the House of Commons. He visited all the cathedrals of England and Wales, and did extensive research in parish registers. His works include *Notitia Parliamentaria; or, an History of the Counties, Cities, and Boroughs in England and Wales* (1715—50) and *A Survey of the Cathedrals* (1727—30).

Willis, George Anthony Armstrong (2 Jan. 1897—), humorous writer who wrote under the name Anthony Armstrong, was born at Esquimault, British Columbia, but was educated in England at Uppingham and Cambridge. From 1915 to 1925 he served as a regular in the Royal Engineers, being awarded the Military Cross in 1916. After leaving the army he became a popular contributor to *Punch* over the initials A.A., and published some two dozen volumes of humorous articles, including *Warriors at Ease* (1926) and *Yesterdailies* (1931). He also wrote the light novels *Patrick, Undergraduate* (1926) and *No Dragon, No Damsel* (1929); the crime stories *The Trail of Fear* (1927) and *The Poison Trail* (1932); and the plays *Well Caught* (1929), *Full House* (1930), and *Ten Minute Alibi* (1932). During the Second World War he joined the R.A.F. Reserve, and in 1944 was awarded the O.B.E. Among his later books are *Nice Types* (1943) and *Whiskers Will Not Be Worn* (1945), in which he collaborated with William Hooper.

Willis, Nathaniel Parker (20 Jan. 1806—20 Jan. 1867), journalist and poet, born at Portland, Maine, and brought up in Boston, was educated at Yale and then worked as a journalist in Boston and New York. His *Fugitive Poetry* was published in 1829, and after visiting Europe and the Near East between 1832 and 1836 he wrote of his experiences in *Pencillings by the Way* (1835) and *Loiterings of Travel* (1840). While in England he published *Melanie and Other Poems* (1836) and (under the pseudonym Philip Slingsby) *Inklings of Adventure* (1836). Back in America he was a popular host at his country seat 'Idlewild' on the Hudson, and wrote various collections of verse and sketches and *Paul Fane* (1857), a novel.

Wills, James (1 Jan. 1790—Nov. 1868), poet and biographer, younger son of a Roscommon squire, was educated at Trinity College, Dublin, and studied law in the Middle Temple. Deprived, however, of the fortune destined for him and the means of pursuing a legal career by the extravagance of his elder brother, he took holy orders, and also wrote largely in *Blackwood's Magazine* and other periodicals. In 1831 he published *The Disembodied and other Poems*, and in 1835 *The Philosophy of Unbelief*, which attracted much attention. His largest work was lives of *Illustrious and Distinguished Irishmen* (1834—47), and his latest publication *The Idolatress* (1868). He helped to found the *Irish Quarterly Review*.

Wills, William Gorman (28 Jan. 1828—13 Dec. 1891), dramatist, son of the above, was born at Kilkenny and educated at Waterford Grammar School and Trinity College, Dublin, where he won the Vice-Chancellor's medal for poetry. Later he went to London and wrote for various periodicals. In 1857 he published a novel, *Old Times*. Of his plays, the best are *Medea in Corinth* (1872), *Charles I* (1872), and *Olivia* (1873), which is based on Goldsmith's *Vicar of Wakefield*; his last play was *A Royal Divorce* (1891). He also wrote *Melchior*, a poem in blank verse.

Wilson, Alexander (6 July 1766—23 Aug. 1813) ornithologist, born at Paisley, son of a weaver, was apprenticed to the same trade. In 1791 he published a volume of poems, his best piece of this period being 'Watty and Meg.' In 1794 he sailed to America, where he made his living as weaver and school-teacher, and published *The Foresters* (1805), a volume of nature poems. His interest in birds led to his being commissioned to compile a work on them, and the result was his unfinished *American Ornithology* (1808—14), a brilliant pioneer study. He died from a fever brought on by the labour and exposure entailed by his journeys in search of specimens.

Wilson, Sir Daniel (5 Jan. 1816—6 Aug. 1892), archaeologist, son of a wine merchant, was born in Edinburgh and educated at the high school and university there. From 1837 to 1842 he lived in London. In 1856 he became honorary secretary of the Scottish Society of Antiquaries, and in 1847 he published *Memorials of Edinburgh in Olden Time*, followed by *The Archaeology and Prehistoric Annals of Scotland* (1851). In 1853 he went to Toronto as Professor of History and English Literature, and from 1881 as President of the University greatly enhanced its standing through his administration. His later books include *Prehistoric Man* (1862), a study of the poet Chatterton (1869), *Caliban, the Missing Link* (1873), *Reminiscences of Old Edinburgh* (1878), *Anthropology* (1885), and *The Lost Atlantis* (1892). He was knighted in 1888.

Wilson, Edmund (8 May 1895—   ), critic and novelist, was born at Red Bank, New Jersey, son of a lawyer. Educated at Princeton, he became a reporter on the New York *Evening Sun*. During the First World War he served in the Intelligence Corps. In 1920 he became editor of *Vanity Fair*, in 1926 was on the staff of the *New Republic*, and from 1944 to 1948 was book reviewer for the *New Yorker*. He was one of the leading critics of his time, his greatest works being *Axel's Castle* (1931), a study of the Symbolist movement, and *To the Finland Station* (1940), a history of revolutionary traditions. Other books are *The American Jitters* (1932), *Travels in Two Democracies* (1936), *The Triple Thinkers* (1938), *The Wound and the Bow* (1941), *The Boys in the Back Room* (1941), and *Memoirs of Hecate County* (1946). He also wrote several plays, including *This Room and This Gin and These Sandwiches* (1937) and *Little Blue Light* (1951). *I Thought of Daisy* (1929) is a novel. He was married four times.

Wilson, Florence Roma Muir (1891—11 Jan. 1930), novelist who wrote under the name Romer Wilson, was born in Sheffield and educated at West Heath School, Richmond, and Girton College, Cambridge, where she studied law. During the First World War she worked at the Ministry of Agriculture. In 1923 she married Edward J. H. O'Brien, an American anthologist, and they settled in Switzerland. Her first novel, *Martin Schüler*, appeared in 1918, and in 1921 she won the Hawthornden Prize with *The Death of Society*. Others of her novels are *If All These Young Men* (1919), *The Grand Tour* (1923), *Dragon's Blood* (1926), *Latter Day Symphony* (1927), *Greenlow* (1927), *The Hill of Cloves* (1929), and *Tender Advice* (1935). *The Social Climbers* (1927) is a play, and *All Alone* (1928) is a life of Emily Brontë. She also edited three collections of fairy stories, *Green Magic* (1928), *Silver Magic* (1929), and *Red Magic* (1930).

Wilson, John (1627?—1696), playwright, was born in London, son of a Welshman, and educated at Exeter College, Oxford. After studying law at Lincoln's Inn he was called to the Bar in 1649, and about 1681 was appointed Recorder of Londonderry. He wrote several loyal works in support of James VII and II. His plays, which are in the Jonson tradition, comprise two lively comedies, *The Cheats* (1664) and *The Projectors* (1665); a tragedy, *Andronicus Commenius* (1664); and a tragi-comedy, *Belphegor, or the Marriage of the Devil* (1691). He also translated Erasmus's *Moriae Encomium, or The Praise of Folly* in 1668.

Wilson, John (18 May 1785—3 April 1854), journalist and essayist known better by his pseudonym of Christopher North, was born in Paisley, son of a wealthy manufacturer, and educated at Paisley Grammar School, Glasgow University, and Magdalen College, Oxford, where he won the Newdigate Prize for Poetry and distinguished himself as an athlete. Having succeeded to a fortune of £50,000 he purchased the small estate of Elleray in the Lake District, where he enjoyed the friendship of Wordsworth, Southey, Coleridge, and De Quincey. In 1812 he published *The Isle of Palms*, followed four years later by another poem, *The City of the Plague*, which gained for him a recognized place in literature. About this time he lost a large portion of his fortune, had to give up continuous residence at Elleray, came to Edinburgh, and was called to the Scottish Bar, but never practised. The starting of *Blackwood's Magazine* brought him his opportunity, and to the end of his life his connection with it gave him his main employment and chief fame. In 1820 he became Professor of Moral Philosophy in the University of Edinburgh, where, though not much of a philosopher in the technical sense, he exercised a highly stimulating influence upon his students by his eloquence and the general vigour of his intellect. The peculiar powers of Wilson, his wealth of ideas, felicity of expression, humour, and animal spirits, found their full development in the famous *Noctes Ambrosianae* (1822—35), a medley of criticism on literature, politics, philosophy, topics of the day and what not. *Lights and Shadows of Scottish Life* (1822) and *The Trials of Margaret Lyndsay* (1823) are contributions to fiction in which there is an occasional tendency to run pathos into rather mawkish sentimentality. In 1851 Wilson received a Government pension of £300. The following year a paralytic seizure led to his resignation of his professorial chair, and he died not long after. He was a man of magnificent physique, of shining rather than profound intellectual powers, and of generous character, though as a critic his strong feelings and prejudices occasionally made him unfair and even savage.

Wilson, John (11 Dec. 1804—1 Dec. 1875), missionary and orientalist, born at Lauder, Berwickshire, son of a farmer, and educated at Edinburgh for the ministry of the Church of Scotland, went in 1828 to India as a missionary, where, besides his immediate duties, he became a leader in all social reform, such as the abolition of the slave-trade and *suttee*, and a trusted adviser of successive Governors-General in regard to all questions affecting the natives. He was in addition a profound Oriental scholar, a Fellow of the Royal Society, and Vice-Chancellor of Bombay University. Among his works are *The Parsi Religion* (1812) and *The Lands of the Bible* (1847).

Wilson, Romer, *see* **Wilson, Florence, R. M.**

Wilson, Thomas (1525?—16 June 1581), scholar and statesman, born in Lincolnshire, was educated at Eton and King's College, Cambridge. He was intimate with Ascham (q.v.), and held various high positions under Queen Elizabeth I, becoming Secretary of State in 1579. He was the author of *The Rule of Reason containing the Arte of Logique* (1551), and *The Arte of Rhetorique* (1553), and made translations from Demosthenes. He endeavoured to maintain the purity of the language against the importation of foreign words.

Wilson, Thomas Woodrow (28 Dec. 1856—3 Feb. 1924), 27th President of the United States, was born at Staunton, Virginia, son of a Presbyterian minister. Educated at Davidson College, North Carolina, and Princeton, he studied law at the University of Virginia and in 1890 became Professor of Jurisprudence and Political Economy at Princeton, where from 1902 to 1910 he was president. Entering politics as a Democrat, he was elected Governor of New Jersey in 1910. In 1913 he became President of the United States; elected for a second term in 1917, he guided the country through the

First World War, and after it was instrumental in launching the League of Nations, from which, however, the United States withdrew. Wilson's writings, which belong to his academic period, include *Congressional Government* (1885), *The State: Elements of Historical and Practical Politics* (1889), *Division and Reunion, 1829—1889* (1893), *A History of the American People* (1902), and *Constitutional Government in the United States* (1908), as well as two books of essays, *An Old Master* (1893) and *Mere Literature* (1896).

Winchilsea, Anne Finch, Countess of (1660?—5 Aug. 1720), poetess, was born at Sidmonton, near Southampton, daughter of Sir William Kingsmill. She married Heneage Finch, who succeeded to the earldom of Winchilsea in 1712, and became a maid of honour to the Duchess of York. A friend of Pope and other writers, she wrote some Pindaric odes in the style of Cowley, but is more noteworthy as a pioneer in nature poetry, her 'Nocturnal Reverie' being commended by Wordsworth. Her volumes of verse include *The Spleen* (1701), *The Prodigy* (1706), and *Miscellany Poems* (1713); she also wrote *Aristomenes*, a tragedy.

Wingate, David (1828—1892), poet, born at Cowglen near Glasgow, son of a miner, was employed in the coal-pits near Hamilton from an early age. He published *Poems and Songs* (1862), which was favourably received, and followed by *Annie Weir* (1866). After this he studied at the Glasgow School of Mines, became a colliery manager, and devoted his increased leisure to study and further literary work. *Lily Neil* appeared in 1879, followed by *Poems and Songs* (1883), a different collection from the earlier volume of the same title, and *Selected Poems* (1890). He was twice married, his second wife being a descendant of Burns.

Winthrop, John (12 Jan. 1588—26 March 1649), administrator, was born at Edwardstone, Suffolk, and educated at Trinity College, Cambridge. He studied law at Gray's Inn and Inner Temple, and in 1630, having been appointed Governor of the newly formed Massachusetts Bay Company, he sailed to Salem with a party of Puritan immigrants. For the rest of his life he was governor, deputy governor, or magistrate, of the new colony. Establishing a two-chamber legislature, he framed a constitution which was a pattern for the other colonies. He wrote various papers on administration, and a journal, which was eventually published as *The History of New England from 1630 to 1649* (1875—6). He was married four times.

Winthrop, Theodore (28 Sept. 1828—10 June 1861), novelist, was born at New Haven, Connecticut. His father was a lawyer, his mother was related to six college presidents. Theodore was educated at Yale, from which he was rusticated for a time for breaking windows. He travelled in Europe, tried various occupations, including law, and then turned to literature. On the outbreak of the Civil War he enlisted in the 7th New York Regiment and was killed leading the advance at Great Bethel. His novels, all published after his death, had great popularity. They include *Cecil Dreeme* (1861), *John Brent* (1862), and *Edwin Brothertoft* (1862). More personal books are *The Canoe and the Saddle* (1863) and *Life in the Open Air* (1863).

Wise, Thomas James (7 Oct. 1859—13 May 1937), bibliographer and forger, was born at Gravesend, son of a tobacconist. He entered an oil business as a clerk, and eventually became a partner in it, retiring in 1912. He first began book-collecting at the age of 17, and gradually amassed the collection named the Ashley Library from his house in north London. Having learned the science of bibliography from Dr Furnivall (q.v.) he compiled bibliographies of Ruskin, Tennyson, Coleridge, Borrow, Wordsworth, the Brontës, Mrs Browning, Landor, Swinburne, and others. At the same time he made a business of faking first edition pamphlets which he sold to collectors. These were at last detected by discrepancies of paper and typography, and the swindle was exposed in 1934 when Carter and Pollard published *An Enquiry into the Nature of Certain Nineteenth Century Pamphlets*. Further revelations were made after Wise's death by W. Partington in his *Forging Ahead: the True Story of Thomas James Wise* (1939). Before his exposure Wise had received an honorary degree from Oxford.

Wither *or* **Withers, George** (11 June 1588—2 May 1667), poet and pamphleteer, born at Bentworth, near Alton, Hampshire, was at Oxford for two years, and then studied law at Lincoln's Inn. In 1613 he published a bold and pungent satire, *Abuses Stript and Whipt*, with the result that he was imprisoned for some months in the Marshalsea. While there he wrote *The Shepheard's Hunting*, a pastoral. *Wither's Motto* was written in 1618, and in 1622 he collected his poems as *Juvenilia*. The same year he published a long poem, *Faire Virtue, the Mistress of Philarete*, in which appears the famous lyric, 'Shall I wasting in despair.' Though generally acting with the Puritans he took arms with Charles I against the Scots in 1639; but on the outbreak of the Civil War he was on the popular side, and raised a troop of horse. He was taken prisoner by the Royalists, and is said to have owed his life to the intercession of a fellow-poet, Sir John Denham. After the establishment of the Commonwealth he was considerably enriched out of sequestrated estates and other spoils of the defeated party; but on the Restoration was obliged to surrender his gains, was impeached, and committed to the Tower. In his later years he wrote many religious poems and hymns, collected as *Hallelujah, or Britain's Second Remembrancer* (1641). Before his death his poems were already forgotten, and he was referred to by Pope in *The Dunciad* as 'the wretched Withers,' but interest in them was revived by Southey, Lamb, and others, who drew attention to his freshness, fancy, and delicacy of taste.

Wodehouse, Pelham Grenville (15 Oct. 1881—   ), novelist, was born at Guildford, Surrey, and educated at Dulwich College. He spent two years in a London bank, but found he was making more by freelancing, so gave it up. From 1906 to 1909 he was a columnist on the *Globe*. His earliest books were school stories, in one of which his popular character Psmith first appeared. In 1914 he married a widow, Ethel Rowley. Greatest humorous novelist of his time, he became well known after the First World

War with the publication of *Piccadilly Jim* (1918), one of his liveliest stories, but his greatest creation was Jeeves, the 'gentleman's personal gentleman' who is always equal to any crisis however desperate or involved, and behaves always with polished urbanity; he appeared in a number of books both before and after the *Jeeves Omnibus* (1931). A few of the more outstanding among Wodehouse's 60-odd novels are *The Coming of Bill* (1920), *Leave it to Psmith* (1923), *Ukridge* (1924), *Sam the Sudden* (1925), *The Small Bachelor* (1927), *Summer Lightning* (1929), *Hot Water* (1932), *Lord Emsworth and Others* (1937), *Uncle Fred in Springtime* (1939), *Full Moon* (1947), and *Pigs Have Wings* (1952). He also collaborated with Guy Bolton in over 20 musical comedies. Much of his life was spent in the United States, where latterly he lived in Long Island, and in 1955 he became an American citizen. He was given an honorary doctorate of Oxford. *Over Seventy* (1957) is a humorous autobiography, and *Performing Flea* (1953) is a collection of his letters.

Wodrow, Robert (1679—21 March 1734), historian, born in Glasgow, son of the Professor of Divinity, studied at Glasgow University, where he was librarian from 1697 to 1701. He became minister of Eastwood, near Glasgow, and remained there all his life. His principal work was *The History of the Sufferings of the Church of Scotland* (1721—2). He wrote when the memory of the persecutions was still fresh, and his work is naturally not free from partisan feeling and credulity. It is, however, thoroughly honest in intention, and is a work of genuine research, and of high value for the period with which it deals. Wodrow made large collections for other works which, however, were not published in his lifetime. *The Lives of the Scottish Reformers and Most Eminent Ministers* and *Analecta, or a History of Remarkable Providences*, were printed for the Maitland Club, and three volumes of his correspondence in 1841 for the Wodrow Society.

Wolcot, John (baptized 9 May 1738, died 14 Jan. 1819), satirist who wrote under the name Peter Pindar, was born at Dodbrooke, near Kingsbridge, Devon, son of a surgeon. He studied medicine and became an M.D. of Aberdeen. In 1767 he went as physician to Sir William Trelawny, Governor of Jamaica, whom he induced to present him to a church in the island then vacant, and was ordained in 1769. Sir William dying in 1772, Wolcot came home and, abandoning the Church, settled in medical practice at Truro, where he discovered the talents of Opie the painter, and assisted him. In 1780 he went to London, and commenced writing satires. The first objects of his attentions were the members of the Royal Academy, and these attempts being well received, he soon began to fly at higher game, the King and Queen being the most frequent marks for his satirical shafts. In 1786 appeared *The Lousiad, a Heroi-Comic Poem*, taking its name from a legend that on the King's dinner plate there had appeared a certain insect not usually found in such exalted quarters. Other objects of his attack were Boswell, the biographer of Johnson, of whom he wrote in *Bozzy and Piozzi*

(1786), and Bruce, the Abyssinian traveller. Wolcot had a remarkable vein of humour and wit, which, while intensely comic to persons not involved, stung its subjects to the quick. In other kinds of composition, as in some ballads which he wrote, an unexpected touch of gentleness and even tenderness appears. Among these are *The Beggar Man* and *Lord Gregory*.

Wolfe, Charles (14 Dec. 1791—21 Feb. 1823), clergyman and poet, was born in Dublin, where he completed his education at Trinity College, having previously been at Winchester. He took orders, and was rector of Donoughmore, but his health failed, and he died of consumption at 32. He is remembered for one short, but universally known and admired poem, 'The Burial of Sir John Moore,' which first appeared anonymously in the *Newry Telegraph* in 1817.

Wolfe, Humbert (5 Jan. 1885—5 Jan. 1940), poet and critic, was born in Milan of Jewish descent. His father, a wool merchant, moved to Bradford, and Humbert was educated at the grammarschool there and at Wadham College, Oxford. In 1908 he entered the Civil Service, where he showed great efficiency and rose to be Deputy Secretary of the Ministry of Labour. It was the strain of organization made necessary by the Second World War that brought about his death. His volumes of verse include *London Sonnets* (1919), *Shylock Reasons with Mr Chesterton* (1920), *Circular Saws* (1922), *Kensington Gardens* (1923), *Lampoons* (1925), *Requiem* (1927), *Snow* (1931), *Out of Great Tribulation* (1939), and *Kensington Gardens in War Time* (1940). Among his critical works are *Dialogues and Monologues* (1929), *Notes on English Verse Satire* (1929), and *Signpost to Poetry* (1931), as well as studies of Herrick (1928), Tennyson (1930), George Moore (1931), and Shelley (1933). *Now a Stranger* (1933) and *The Upward Anguish* (1938) are books of reminiscences. He was made a Commander of the Order of the British Empire in 1918 and a Companion of the Bath in 1925.

Wolfe, Thomas Clayton (3 Oct. 1900—15 Sept. 1938), novelist, was born at Asheville, North Carolina, son of a stonecutter. He was educated at the University of North Carolina, where he edited the college magazine, and later studied playwriting at the ' 47 Workshop' at Harvard. For a time he was instructor in English at New York University. His first book, *Look Homeward, Angel* (1929) had a great reception when eventually published after repeated rejections. After a visit to Europe he settled in Brooklyn, and produced *Of Time and the River* (1935) and *The Web and the Rock* (1939); *From Death to Morning* (1935) and *The Hills Beyond* (1941) are volumes of short stories. He died of pneumonia. His *Letters to his Mother* were published in 1943, and his collected *Letters* in 1956.

Wood, *or* à Wood, **Anthony** (17 Dec. 1632—29 Nov. 1695), antiquary, born at Oxford, was educated at New College School and Merton College. He inherited a competence and was inspired by the collections of Leland (q.v.) to visit and study the antiquities of his native county. This with history, heraldry, genealogies, and music occupied his whole time. By 1669 he had written his *History and Antiquities of the University of Oxford*, which was translated into

Latin not to his satisfaction by the University authorities, and he wrote a fresh English copy which was printed in 1786. His great work was *Athenae Oxonienses; an exact History of all the Writers and Bishops who have had their Education in the University of Oxford, to which are added the Fasti or Annals of the said University* (1691—2). For an alleged libel on the Earl of Clarendon in that work the author was expelled in 1694. He also wrote *The Ancient and Present State of the City of Oxford* (1773), and *Modius Salium, a Collection of Pieces of Humour* (1751), generally of an ill-natured cast. His *Autobiography* was published by Hearne (q.v.) in 1730.

Wood, Ellen (17 Jan. 1814—10 Feb. 1887), novelist better known as Mrs Henry Wood, was born in Worcester, daughter of Thomas Price, a glove manufacturer. Suffering from curvature of the spine while a girl, she was thrown much on her own resources, and read a great deal. In 1836 she married Henry Wood, head of a banking firm. They spent most of the next twenty years in southern France, but in 1850 settled at Norwood. Her first novel, *Danesbury House* (1860), won a prize offered by the Temperance League, but her great success was *East Lynne* (1861), which sold over half a million copies in this country, was dramatized repeatedly, and was translated into most European languages; other highly popular books were *Mrs Halliburton's Troubles* and *The Channings*, both published in 1862. In 1867 she became proprietor and editor of the *Argosy*, in which many of her later stories appeared. Among these are *Ashlydyat* (1863), *Roland Yorke* (1869), *Dene Hollow* (1871), *Within the Maze* (1872), *Edina* (1876), and *Pomeroy Abbey* (1878). Orthodox and conservative, she won popularity by her faithful depicting of middle-class life of the time.

Wood, John George (21 July 1827—3 March 1889), naturalist, born in London, son of a surgeon, was educated at home and at Oxford, where he worked for some time in the anatomical museum. He took orders, and was for a time chaplain to St Bartholomew's Hospital. He was a very prolific writer on natural history, though rather as a popularizer than as a scientific investigator, and was in this way very successful. Among his numerous works may be mentioned *Illustrated Natural History* (1853), *Common Objects of the Sea Shore* (1857), *Animal Traits and Characteristics* (1860), *Out of Doors* (1874), and *My Backyard Zoo* (1885). He also published books on sport and gymnastics, and an edition of White's *Selborne*.

Woodhouselee, Lord, *see* **Tytler, Alexander.**

Woods, Margaret Louise (1856—29 Nov. 1945), novelist and poetess, was born at Rugby, daughter of G. G. Bradley, Dean of Westminster. In 1879 she married H. G. Woods, who became President of Trinity College, Oxford. Her realistic novel *A Village Tragedy* (1887) was much admired, and she showed poetic gifts in her *Lyrics and Ballads* (1889). Others of her novels are *The Vagabonds* (1894), *Sons of the Sword* (1901), *The Invaders* (1907), *A Poet's Youth* (1924), and *The Spanish Lady* (1927). *Wild Justice* (1896) and *The Princess of Hanover* (1902) are poetic dramas, and her *Collected Poems and Plays* appeared in 1913.

B2*

Woodworth, Samuel (13 Jan. 1784—9 Dec. 1842), playwright and poet, was born at Sciutate, Massachusetts, son of a soldier. After desultory schooling he became a printer, settled in New York, and tried various journalistic ventures. His play *The Forest Rose* (1825) was a notable success, and he wrote a number of satirical poems, but is chiefly remembered as the writer of 'The Old Oaken Bucket.'

Woolf, Leonard Sidney (25 Nov. 1880—   ), historian, was born in London, son of a barrister, and educated at St Paul's and Cambridge. From 1904 to 1911 he was in the Ceylon Civil Service. In 1912 he married Virginia Stephen, better known as Virginia Woolf (q.v.). His earliest books were stories about Ceylon, *The Village and the Jungle* (1913), *The Wise Virgins* (1914), and *Stories of the East* (1916). In 1916 he joined the Fabian Society and published two reports on international government, and in the following year along with his wife he started the Hogarth Press. His works include *Co-operation and the Future of Industry* (1918), *Mandates and Empire* (1920), *Socialism and Co-operation* (1921), *Fear and Politics* (1925), *Hunting the Highbrow* (1926), *Imperialism and Civilization* (1928), *After the Deluge* (1931), and *Principia Politica* (1953).

Woolf, Virginia (25 Jan. 1882—28 March 1941), novelist, was born in London, daughter of Sir Leslie Stephen (q.v.) by his second wife, Julia Jackson. She was educated at home by reading in her father's library and conversing with his distinguished friends. In 1912 she married Leonard Woolf (q.v.) and in 1917 they started the Hogarth Press. Their home near the British Museum became the centre of the so-called 'Bloomsbury Group,' which included Lytton Strachey, E. M. Forster, Arthur Waley, Victoria Sackville-West, and J. M. Keynes. Her novels include *The Voyage Out* (1915), *Night and Day* (1919), *Jacob's Room* (1922), *Mrs Dalloway* (1925), *To the Lighthouse* (1927), *Orlando* (1928), and *The Waves* (1931). She evolved a technique of writing in which the words and actions of the characters were made subsidiary to the minute delineation of thought, but avoided the vagueness and obscurity often associated with the 'stream-of-consciousness school.' A thoughtful and penetrating critic, she published a collection of essays, *The Common Reader* (two series, 1925, 1932); *Flush* (1933), a biography of Elizabeth Barrett's dog; and a study of Roger Fry (1940). *A Room of One's Own* (1929) and *Three Guineas* (1938) were written in support of women's rights. She drowned herself during a mental breakdown brought on by the horrors of the Second World War. *A Writer's Diary* (1953) contains extracts from her journal.

Woollcott, Alexander Humphreys (19 Jan. 1887—23 Jan. 1943), journalist, was born at Phalanx, New Jersey, but spent his childhood in Kansas City. He went to school in Philadelphia, then studied at Hamilton College and Columbia. He was dramatic critic of the *New York Times* from 1914 to 1922, except for two years of the First World War when he served with a hospital unit in France, and from 1925 to 1928 he was on the staff of the *World*. He became famous both as a journalist and as a personality, and occasionally took parts on the stage, where he had made his debut at the age of 5. His books include *Mrs Fiske* (1917), *The Command is Forward* (1919), *Shouts and Murmurs* (1923), *Mr Dickens Goes to the Play* (1923), *Enchanted Aisles* (1924), *The Story of Irving Berlin* (1925), *Going to Pieces* (1928), *Two Gentlemen and a Lady* (1928), *While Rome Burns* (1934), and *Long, Long Ago* (1943). His *Letters* were edited by B. Kaufman and J. Hennesey in 1944.

Woolman, John (19 Oct. 1720—7 Oct. 1772), diarist and humanitarian, was born at Rancocas, New Jersey, and educated at a Quaker school. He began work as a farm labourer, then was a shopman, and finally a tailor. A deeply religious man, he became an itinerant Quaker preacher and an ardent opponent of slavery, against which he wrote in *Some Considerations on the Keeping of Negroes* (1753). In 1772 he went to England, where he died of smallpox. His *Journal* (1774) was much admired by Charles Lamb, and Whittier called it 'a classic of inner life.'

Woolner, Thomas (17 Dec. 1825—7 Oct. 1892), poet and sculptor, born at Hadleigh in Suffolk, went to school at Ipswich and studied drawing and modelling in London. At the age of 17 he exhibited some of his work. In 1847 he made the acquaintance of Rossetti, became one of the Pre-Raphaelite Brotherhood, and contributed to their magazine, *The Germ*; he was also a close friend of the Carlyles. Always struggling against poverty, he tried his luck in the Australian gold-fields in 1852, then came back to England and became known for his medallion portraits and busts. In 1874 he was made an R.A. His volumes of verse include *My Beautiful Lady* (1863), *Pygmalion* (1881), *Silenus* (1884), *Tiresias* (1886), and *Nelly Dale* (1886).

Woolsey, Sarah Chauncy (29 Jan. 1835—9 April 1905), who wrote children's stories under the name Susan Coolidge, was born in Cleveland, Ohio; her father's uncle, brother, and nephew were all presidents of Yale. Educated at private schools in Cleveland, she lived in New Haven, Connecticut, from 1855 to 1870, then travelled abroad for two years. She is best remembered for her books for girls, especially the series that began with *What Katy Did* (1872) and continued with *What Katy Did at School* (1873) and *What Katy Did Next* (1886). Others of her children's books are *Eyebright* (1879), *Cross Patch* (1881), *A Little Country Girl* (1885), *Clover* (1888), and *Just Sixteen* (1889). She was also a sound critic, and edited the letters of Frances Burney in 1880 and those of Jane Austen in 1892, as well as writing a short history of Philadelphia and three volumes of verse.

Wordsworth, Christopher (9 June 1774—2 Feb. 1846), scholar, youngest brother of William Wordsworth (q.v.), was born at Cockermouth, Cumberland, and educated at Hawkshead Grammar School and Trinity College, Cambridge. Taking orders, he was rector successively of Ashby in Norfolk, Woodchurch in Kent, and Bocking in Essex, then in 1817 became chaplain to the House of Commons. In 1820 he was appointed Master of Trinity College and also Vice-Chancellor of Cambridge, an office which he held again in 1826. He published *Ecclesiastical Biography* (1810) and *Who Wrote ' Eikon*

Basilike'? (1824), in which he argued that the author was Charles I.

Wordsworth, Christopher (30 Oct. 1807—21 March 1885), prelate, was born at Lambeth, youngest son of the above, and brought up at Bocking, Essex, and Sundridge, Kent. He was educated at Winchester and Trinity College, Cambridge, where he amassed a record list of prizes and honours and was made a Fellow of the college. In 1832 he travelled in Greece, and in 1836 was appointed headmaster of Harrow. In 1865 he became Archdeacon of Westminster and in 1869 Bishop of Lincoln. His greatest work was his monumental commentary on the Bible. He also wrote *Church History to A.D. 451* (1881—3) and *Athens and Attica* (1836), and edited Theocritus (1844).

Wordsworth, Dorothy (25 Dec. 1771—25 Jan. 1855), diarist, sister of William Wordsworth (q.v.), was his devoted companion for 50 years. She was a writer of beautiful prose, and her *Journals,* edited in 1941, reveal her sensitive love of nature and the debt which the poet owed to her, some of his poems being suggested by incidents she recorded. In 1829 she had a nervous breakdown, and for the rest of her life was an invalid. Among her works are *Recollections of a Tour in Scotland* (1804) and *Journal of a Tour on the Continent* (1820).

Wordsworth, Dame Elizabeth (22 June 1840—30 Nov. 1932), grand-niece of William Wordsworth (q.v.) was born at Harrow, where her father Christopher Wordsworth (q.v.) was headmaster. Educated at home, she had a strict and religious training. In 1878 she was appointed the first Principal of Lady Margaret Hall, the Oxford women's college which was opened in the following year. For 30 years she made the college her life work, building up the membership from 9 to 59. She also founded in 1886 another women's college, St Hugh's Hall, afterwards St Hugh's College. Her writings include *Glimpses of the Past* (1912), *Essays Old and New* (1919), *Poems and Plays* (1931), and a biography of her father. She received the honorary degrees of M.A. and D.C.L., and was made a Dame Commander of the Order of the British Empire.

Wordsworth, William (7 April 1770—23 April 1850), Poet Laureate, was born at Cockermouth in Cumberland, son of an attorney who was land agent to Lord Lonsdale. His mother died when he was 7 and his father when he was 13, but with the help of uncles he was given a good education at Hawkshead School and St John's College, Cambridge. His last summer vacation was spent in a walking tour in France, and after he had taken his degree in 1791 he paid a second visit to that country and was converted to Republicanism. He also fell in love with Annette Villon, daughter of a Blois surgeon, and she bore him a child, Caroline, whom he acknowledged at her christening. He wished to marry Annette, but their differing creeds, poverty, and the war were grave obstacles, and he returned home leaving her and escaping the fate of the Girondist party, with whom he was about to throw in his lot. His guardians wished him to take holy orders, but he was averse to any profession. Meanwhile the later excesses of the French Republicans had turned his early admiration to horror and for a time he embraced the rationalist philosophy of Godwin.

In 1793 appeared his first published works, *The Evening Walk* and *Descriptive Sketches of a Pedestrian Tour in the Alps*.

His meeting with Coleridge in 1795 confirmed him in his resolution to devote himself to poetry, and at the same time by a fortunate chance he was rendered independent by a legacy of £900 left him by his friend Raisley Calvert. With his sister Dorothy, who was to be his lifelong companion, he settled first at Racedown, Dorset, and then at Alfoxden in Somerset near Nether Stowey, where Coleridge was living. During this intimacy the two poets planned the *Lyrical Ballads*, that important landmark in English literature. To the volume Coleridge contributed 'The Ancient Mariner' and Wordsworth 'Tintern Abbey' and other pieces. The first edition appeared in 1798. With the profits from it Wordsworth went with his sister and Coleridge to Germany, where they stayed at Goslar and he began the *Prelude*, a poem descriptive of the development of his own mind. It was planned as the first part of a great philosophic poem to be called *The Recluse*, but the work was never finished. He also wrote at this time several shorter poems, including 'Ruth' and 'Lucy Gray.' In 1799 he and Dorothy settled at Grasmere in the Lake District, setting up house in Dove Cottage, and in 1800 the second edition of the *Lyrical Ballads* appeared, with Wordsworth's revolutionary *Preface* on the principles of poetry.

In the same year Lord Lonsdale died and the settlement of certain claims made by the Wordsworths supplied them with enough to live on in the simple manner which suited them. In 1802, having first visited Calais to meet Annette, Wordsworth married his cousin Mary Hutchinson, who, like his sister, gave him lifelong devotion and affection. In the following year he visited Scotland and began his friendship with Walter Scott, and in 1805 he completed the *Prelude*, which was not, however, published till after his death. Two years later he published a further collection of *Poems*, which contains some of his best work, including the 'Ode to Duty,' 'Ode on the Intimations of Immortality,' 'Yarrow Unvisited,' and 'The Solitary Reaper.' In 1813 the family removed to Rydal Mount, where he spent the rest of his life, and in the same year he was appointed Distributor of Stamps for Westmorland at a salary of £400. In 1814 he published *The Excursion*, the middle part of his projected philosophical poem, made another visit to Scotland, and wrote 'Yarrow Visited.' A period of classical influence at this time was responsible for the poem *Laodamia*. Later works were *The White Doe of Rylstone* (1815), *Peter Bell* and *The Waggoner* (both 1819), *The River Duddon* (1820), and *Memorials of a Tour on the Continent* and *Ecclesiastical Sonnets* (both 1822). An annuity left him by Sir George Beaumont enabled him at this time to indulge his passion for travel, and he visited France, Belgium, Switzerland, and Italy, as well as making another Scottish tour, followed by *Yarrow Revisited and Other Poems* (1835). In 1838 he received the degree of D.C.L. from Durham, and in 1839 the same from Oxford, and in 1843 he succeeded Southey as Poet Laureate. Unhappily, from 1829 onwards his sister's health had been impaired, and in 1847 he lost his daughter Dora, and never recovered from the blow. He is buried in

Grasmere churchyard. The *Letters of William and Dorothy Wordsworth* were published in six volumes (1935—9).

Wordsworth not only was one of the greatest of English poets, but had an exceptional importance in the development of English literature. The *Lyrical Ballads*, it may be said, ushered in the Romantic Revival and fundamentally changed the whole conception of poetic values in this country. There had, of course, been earlier revolts against the rigid rules of the Augustans, but Wordsworth's famous *Preface* was the first formulation of definite and determined opposition to those canons of taste that had held English poetry in fetters for a century and a half. The school of Dryden and Pope followed Latin models and used a stereotyped poetic diction derived from them; hence Wordsworth's contention that poetry should use the language of ordinary speech appeared to them the rankest heresy, and his principles were vehemently denounced. It is true that he himself does not always abide by them, but the general impression that his poetry gives is one of unadorned simplicity. Such lyrics as 'To the Cuckoo' and 'I Wandered Lonely as a Cloud' restored to English poetry a clarity and reality from which it had long been divorced. They also illustrate his second great gift to English literature, his philosophy of a return to nature. He re-awakened readers to the beauty of bird and tree and mountain. Nature to him was something to be worshipped, so that even the meanest flower could inspire 'thoughts that do often lie too deep for tears.' This feeling of a mystic union with nature is found throughout his poetry and above all in the 'Immortality Ode,' greatest of all Pindarics, which embodies the Neo-Platonist doctrine of a pre-existence of which earthly beauty serves to remind us. With his nature poetry he established a tradition which has lasted over a century and put all later poets in his debt.

Wotton, Sir Henry (1568—Dec. 1639), diplomat and poet, son of a Kentish gentleman, was born at Boughton Hall, near Maidstone, and educated at Winchester and Oxford. After spending seven years on the Continent, he entered the Middle Temple. In 1595 he became secretary to the Earl of Essex, who employed him abroad, and while at Venice he wrote *The State of Christendom or a Most Exact and Curious Discovery of many Secret Passages and Hidden Mysteries of the Times*, which was not, however, printed until 1657. Afterwards he held various diplomatic appointments, but Court favour latterly failed him and he was recalled from Venice and made Provost of Eton in 1624, to qualify for which he took deacon's orders. Among his other works were *Elements of Architecture* (1624). His writings in prose and verse were published in 1651 as *Reliquiae Wottonianae*. His poems include two which are familiar to all readers of Elizabethan verse, 'The Character of a Happy Life' and 'On his Mistress, the Queen of Bohemia.' He was the originator of many witty sayings.

Wraxall, Sir Nathaniel William, Bart (8 April 1751—7 Nov. 1831), historical writer, born in Bristol, was for a few years in the service of the East India Company, and thereafter employed on diplomatic missions, and sat for some years in the House of Commons. In addition to a book of travels and some historical works relating to the French and other foreign Courts, he wrote *Historical Memoirs of my own Time, 1772—84*, published in 1815. The work was severely criticized by both political parties, and in particular by Macaulay; but Wraxall made a reply which was considered to be on the whole successful. A continuation bringing the narrative down to 1790 was published in 1836. The *Memoirs* are valuable for the light they throw on the period, and especially for the portraits of public men which they give.

Wren, Percival Christopher (1885—23 Nov. 1941), novelist, was born in Devonshire and educated at Oxford, after which he roamed the world as tramp, schoolmaster, journalist, farm hand, explorer, hunter, and soldier. He was a trooper in a British cavalry regiment and served in the French Foreign Legion. For ten years he lived in India, and in the First World War was an officer in the Indian forces in East Africa. After being invalided home, he settled in London. Tall, distinguished, and monocled, he looked what he was, a retired officer. Of his romantic novels of adventure the most popular were those about the Foreign Legion, *Beau Geste* (1924), *Beau Sabreur* (1926), *Beau Ideal* (1928), and *The Good Gestes* (1929) in particular. Others are *Dew and Mildew* (1912), *Smoke and Sword* (1914), *The Wages of Virtue* (1916), *Stepsons of France* (1917), *The Mammon of Righteousness* (1930), *Valiant Dust* (1932), *Flawed Blades* (1932), *Port o' Missing Men* (1934), *Sinbad the Soldier* (1935), *Spanish Maine* (1935), *Fort in the Jungle* (1936), *Rough Shooting* (1938), and *The Uniform of Glory* (1941).

Wright, Harold Bell (4 May 1872—24 May 1944), novelist, was born on a farm at Rome, New York State, and educated at Hiram College, Ohio. He worked for a time as a house painter. Going to Missouri, he became an unqualified preacher there and in Kansas, and his first novel, *That Printer of Udell's*, was a study of church conditions. Having to go to the Ozark Mountains for his health, he wrote there *The Shepherd of the Hills* (1907), which was a great success, as was also *The Winning of Barbara Worth* (1911), which sold more than one and a half million copies. Among his other novels are *The Calling of Dan Matthews* (1909), *The Uncrowned King* (1910), *When a Man's a Man* (1916), *Helen of the Old House* (1921), *A Son of his Father* (1925), *God and the Groceryman* (1927), *Told Long Ago* (1929), *Ma Cinderella* (1932), *To My Sons* (1934), and *The Man Who Went Away* (1942). The chief criticism of his work comes from those who say he was a preacher, not a novelist.

Wright, Joseph (31 Oct. 1855—27 Feb. 1930), philologist, was born at Bradford, Yorkshire, son of a weaver. Starting work at the age of six, he was successively donkey-boy, mill hand, and wool sorter, but did not learn to read till he was 16. Later he studied French and German at evening classes, and in 1876 became a master at Springfield School, Bradford. From 1882 to 1885 he studied comparative philology at Heidelberg, and in 1888 was appointed deputy lecturer in Teutonic philology at Oxford. In the same year he published his primers of Old and Middle German, and of Gothic, and in 1901 he succeeded Max Müller (q.v.) as Professor of Comparative Philology. In 1891, on the recommendation of Skeat (q.v.), he had been chosen to compile the dialect dictionary projected by the English Dialect Society, and took over their collection of about a million reference slips, weighing a ton. Like many other lexicographers, he had inadequate financial backing; he spent all his own savings of about £2,000 in the undertaking, finally publishing the work at his own expense. The *English Dialect Dictionary* (1896—1905) is a standard reference work, and was compiled just in time to preserve many dialect words that were dying out. Wright also published elementary grammars of Old and Middle English. He was greatly assisted in his work by his wife, a former student of Lady Margaret Hall. He held honorary degrees of five universities, and was a Fellow of the British Academy.

Wright, Richard (4 Sept. 1908—   ), novelist, was born on a plantation near Natchez, Mississippi, son of a Negro who deserted his family. The boy was brought up partly by relations, partly in orphan asylums. At the age of 15 he went to Memphis and became a post office clerk; from there he moved to Chicago, then to New York. In 1938 he won a prize of 500 dollars with his novelette *Uncle Tom's Children*. Later he was awarded a Guggenheim Fellowship. In 1940 he was highly praised for *Native Son*, the story, partly founded on fact, of a young Negro murderer, and received the Spingarn Medal, highest award for work done in the Negro interest. *Twelve Million Black Voices* (1941) is a history of the persecution of the American Negro, and *Black Boy* (1945) is the story of his own youthful hardships. In 1946 he moved to Paris. Later books are *The Outsider* (1953) and *Black Power* (1954).

Wright, Thomas (23 April 1810—23 Dec. 1877), antiquary, born at Fenbury, Shropshire, son of a clothmaker, was educated at Ludlow Grammar School and Cambridge. His first work was a *History of Essex* (1831—6). In 1836 he went to London, and adopted literature as a profession, devoting himself specially to archaeology, history, and biography. He became a Fellow of the Society of Antiquaries, held office in the Camden, Percy, and Shakespeare Societies, and edited many works for them. In all he was the author of over 80 publications, of which some of the chief are *The Celt, the Roman, and the Saxon* (1852), *Biographia Britannica Literaria* (1842—6), *Queen Elizabeth and her Times* (1838), and *History of Domestic Manners and Sentiments in England during the Middle Ages* (1862). He was superintendent of the excavation of the Roman city at Wroxeter in 1859.

Wright, Willard Huntington (1888—11 April 1939), who wrote detective stories under the name S. S. Van Dine, was born at Charlottesville, Virginia. He was educated at St Vincent and Pomona Colleges, California, and at Harvard, afterwards studying in Munich and Paris. Between 1907 and 1914 he was literary critic for various Los Angeles papers. In 1916 he published a serious novel, *The Man of Promise*, but it had no success. He had two breakdowns in health, and during the second started a detective story, using an old family name, Van Dyne, with one vowel altered, and the initials for 'steam ship.' *The Benson Murder Case* (1926) was an immediate success, and was followed in the same year by *The 'Canary' Murder Case*, which broke all records and was filmed. Philo Vance, the languid dilettante who is the detective hero of these books, in many ways reflected the personality of Wright himself, and in his time he was undisputed leader of the 'highbrow' detective novelists in America, publishing a series entitled in a uniform formula the *Greene* (1928), *Bishop* (1929), *Scarab* (1930), *Kennel* (1932), *Dragon* (1933), *Casino* (1934), *Garden* (1935), and *Kidnap* (1936) Murder Cases. One more, *The Winter Murder Case*, appeared in the same year that he died of coronary thrombosis.

Wroth, Lady Mary (1586?—1640?), poetess, was a daughter of Robert Sidney, first Earl of Leicester, and brother of Sir Philip Sidney (q.v.). In 1604 she married Sir Robert Wroth, a landowner, who in 1613 became Sheriff of Essex. She became well known as a patroness of writers, and had poems addressed to her by Jonson, Chapman, and George Wither. In 1621 she published *The Countess of Montgomery's Urania*, an obvious imitation of the *Countess of Pembroke's Arcadia*; its title is a compliment to Lady Mary's neighbour, the wife of the Earl of Montgomery. It is a tedious prose romance, interspersed with over a hundred lyrics, some of which have merit.

Wyatt, Sir Thomas (born 1503, buried 11 Oct. 1542), diplomat and poet, born at Allington Castle, Kent, son of Sir Henry Wyatt, a servant of Henry VII, was educated at St John's College, Cambridge. Coming to Court, he was frequently employed by Henry VIII on diplomatic missions. He is said to have been an admirer of Anne Boleyn before her marriage, and on her disgrace was thrown into the Tower for a short time. In 1537 he was knighted, and two years later was against his will sent on a mission to the Emperor Charles V. On the death in 1540 of Thomas Cromwell, to whose party he belonged, Wyatt was accused of misdemeanours during his embassy and again imprisoned in the Tower, where he wrote a defence which resulted in his release. In 1542 he was sent to meet the Spanish Ambassador at Falmouth, and conduct him to London, but on the way caught a chill, of which he died. Wyatt shares with the Earl of Surrey (q.v.) the honour of being the first real successor of Chaucer, and also of introducing the sonnet into England. He may also be regarded as the reviver of the lyrical spirit in English poetry which, making its appearance in the thirteenth century, had fallen into abeyance. In the anthology known as *Tottel's Miscellany*, first published in 1557, 96 pieces by Wyatt appear along with 40 by Surrey, and others by different hands. Wyatt has less smoothness and sweetness than Surrey, but his form of the sonnet was much more difficult as well as more correct than that invented by the latter, and afterwards adopted by Shakespeare.

Wycherley, William (1640?—1 Jan. 1716), dramatist, was born at Clive, near Shrewsbury, where his father had an estate. He was at the Inner Temple in 1659, and at Queen's College, Oxford, in 1660. Part of his youth had been spent in France, where he became a

Roman Catholic, but at the Restoration he returned to Protestantism. He wrote four comedies, *Love in a Wood* (1672), *The Gentleman Dancing Master* (1673), *The Country Wife* (1675), and *The Plain Dealer* (1677), all produced in the reign of Charles II, and nothing of consequence afterwards, a volume of poems doing little to add to his reputation. About 1679 he married the widowed Countess of Drogheda, who died in 1681, and he entered into a second marriage eleven days before his death. In his later years he formed a friendship with Pope, then a boy of 16. Wycherley was one of the founders of the Comedy of Manners, the merit of his plays lying in smart and witty dialogue rather than in construction. *The Plain Dealer*, his best, is founded upon Molière's *Misanthrope*. His plays are notoriously coarse.

Wycliffe, *or* **Wyclif,** *or* **Wiclif, John** (1320?—1384), religious reformer and translator, born near Richmond, Yorkshire, studied at Balliol College, Oxford, of which he became in 1361 Master, and taking orders, became vicar of Fillingham, Lincolnshire, when he resigned his mastership, and in 1361 prebendary of Westbury. By this time he had written a treatise on logic, and had won some position as a man of learning. In 1372 he took the degree of Doctor of Theology, and became Canon of Lincoln, and in 1374 was sent to Bruges as one of a commission to treat with Papal delegates about certain ecclesiastical matters in dispute, and in the same year he became rector of Lutterworth, where he remained until his death. In 1376 he published his *De Dominio Divino* (On Divine Authority) arguing that all authority is founded on grace, hence wicked kings and priests should have no power. His views were taken up and exaggerated by the Lollards. His liberal and patriotic attitude on the questions in dispute between England and the Pope gained for him the favour of John of Gaunt and Lord Percy, who accompanied him when, in 1377, he was summoned before the ecclesiastical authorities at St Paul's. The Court was broken up by an inroad of the London mob, and no sentence was passed upon him. Another trial at Lambeth in the next year was equally inconclusive.

Wycliffe had now taken up a position definitely antagonistic to the Papal system. He organized his institution of poor preachers, and initiated his great enterprise of translating the Scriptures into English. His own share of the work was the Gospels, probably the whole of the New Testament and possibly part of the Old. The whole work was edited by John Purvey, an Oxford friend, who had joined him at Lutterworth, the task being completed by 1400. In 1380 Wycliffe openly rejected the doctrine of transubstantiation, and was forbidden to teach at Oxford, where he had obtained great influence. In 1382 a Court was convened by the Archbishop of Canterbury, which passed sentence of condemnation upon his views. It says much for the position which he had attained, and for the power of his supporters, that he was permitted to depart from Oxford and retire to Lutterworth, where, worn out by his labours and anxieties, he died of a paralytic seizure on the last day of 1384. His enemies, baffled in their designs against him while living, consoled themselves by disinterring his bones in 1428 and throwing them into the River Swift; of this Thomas Fuller (q.v.) has said: 'Thus this brook has conveyed his ashes into Avon, Avon into Severn, Severn into the Narrow Seas, they into the main ocean, and thus the ashes of Wicliffe are the emblem of his doctrine, which now is dispersed all the world over.'

Wylie, Elinor (7 Sept. 1885—16 Dec. 1928), novelist and poetess, was born at Somerville, New Jersey, daughter of Henry Martyn Hoyt, who was later Solicitor-General. She was educated in Washington. In 1904 she married Philip Hichborn, a wealthy Washingtonian, and in 1910 she eloped with Horace Wylie, a married man, and they lived in England. In 1915 they were married and returned to America, but in 1921 they were divorced and in 1923 she married William Rose Benét. They visited England, where she was injured by a fall, and on her return to America she died of a paralytic stroke. Very beautiful, but frail and high-strung, she was often compared with Shelley, for whose work she had a great admiration. Her poems, which combine fantasy with fine craftsmanship, include *Incidental Numbers* (1912), *Nets to Catch the Wind* (1921), *Black Armour* (1923), *Trivial Breath* (1928), and *Angels and Earthly Creatures* (1929). *The Orphan Angel* (1926) is a novel about Shelley; others are *Jennifer Lorn* (1923), *The Venetian Glass Nephew* (1925), and *Mr Hodge and Mr Hazard* (1928).

Wylie, Ida Alexa Ross (1885—4 Nov. 1959), novelist, was born in Melbourne, daughter of a Scottish barrister. She lost her mother at an early age and was left much to her own devices, travelling all over Europe by herself. She was educated at Brussels, Cheltenham, and Karlsruhe, stayed in Germany till 1911, and wrote about it in *My German Year* (1910) and *Eight Years in Germany* (1914). Of her 15 novels her own favourites were *Towards Morning* (1920), *The Silver Virgin* (1929), *To the Vanquished* (1934), *Furious Young Man* (1935), and *A Feather in Her Hat* (1937); later ones are *Where No Birds Sing* (1947) and *Candles for Therese* (1951). She was even more popular as a writer of short stories, collections of which are *Happy Endings* (1915), *Armchair Stories* (1916), *All Sorts* (1919), *Some Other Beauty* (1930), and *Storm in April* (1946). *My Life with George* (1940) is an autobiography.

Wylie, Philip Gordon (12 May 1902—   ), novelist, was born at Beverly, Massachusetts. His father was a Presbyterian minister, his mother and brother both writers. He was at Princeton for three years, then worked in factories, on farms, as press agent and advertising manager, and became editor of the *New Yorker*. He travelled in many parts of Europe, but finally made his home in Miami. His most controversial book was *A Generation of Vipers* (1942), which criticized the American civilization and popularized the word 'momism' meaning sentimentalization of motherhood. Other novels are *Gladiator* (1930), *Footprint of Cinderella* (1931), *The Savage Gentleman* (1932), *An April Afternoon* (1938), *The Other Horseman* (1941), *Night Unto Night* (1944), *Opus 21* (1949), and *To-morrow* (1953). He also wrote a series of books about fishing,

Fish and Tin Fish (1944), *Crunch and Des: Stories of Florida Fishing* (1948), and *Denizens of the Deep* (1953).

Wyntoun, Andrew of (1350?—1425?), chronicler, was a canon of St Andrews, who became Prior of St Serf's monastery in Loch Leven. His work, entitled *The Orygynale Cronykil*, begins with the creation of angels and men and comes down to 1406. It is poetic in form though rarely so in substance, and is of considerable historical value in its later parts and as regards the see of St Andrews.

X

X, pseudonym of **Eustace Budgell** (q.v.).

X, Flying Officer, pseudonym of **H. E. Bates** (q.v.).

Y

Yalden, Thomas (2 Jan. 1670—16 July 1736), poet, was born in Oxford, son of an exciseman, and educated at Magdalen College, where he became a friend of Addison and was made a Fellow. He took orders and held various livings. His *Ode for St Cecilia's Day* was published in 1693. An imitator of Cowley, he wrote Pindarics and some fables. His best poem is a 'Hymn to Darkness.'

Yates, Dornford, *see* Mercer, Cecil William.

Yates, Edmund Hodgson (3 July 1831—20 May 1894), journalist and novelist, was born in Edinburgh, where his father, an actor, was on tour. He was brought up in London and educated at Highgate and Dusseldorf. In 1847 he entered the service of the Post Office, and rose to be head of the Missing Letter Department. He wrote for various periodicals and became proprietor of the society paper *The World*; in 1874 he served a short term of imprisonment for a libel contained in it. His novels include *Running the Gauntlet* (1866), *Black Sheep* (1867), and *The Silent Witness* (1875). His *Recollections and Experiences* appeared in 1884.

Yeats, William Butler (13 June 1865—28 Jan. 1939), poet and dramatist, was born at Sandymount, near Dublin, son of an attorney who became an artist. The family, which was protestant, lived in Sligo, but the boy spent much of his childhood in London, and was educated at the Godolphin School in Hammersmith and then at the Erasmus Smith School in Dublin. From 1883 to 1886 he studied art, but preferred reading. In 1887 he went to London and became one of the group of 'decadent' writers associated with the *Yellow Book*. With Ernest Rhys he founded the Rhymers' Club, which included in its members Dowson and Lionel Johnson (qq.v.). He published several books full of the Celtic spirit. *The Wanderings of Oisin* (1889) contains poems on Irish legendary themes; *The Countess Kathleen* (1892) and *The Land of Heart's Desire* (1894) are verse plays; and *The Celtic Twilight* (1893) is a volume of essays. In 1895 he compiled an anthology, *A Book of Irish Verse*.

In 1896 he returned to Ireland and was caught up in the Celtic Renascence, of which he came to be the acknowledged leader. He became a Theosophist and a Rosicrucian and had an unsuccessful love affair with Maud Gonne, the actress, who inspired some of his finest lyrics. With Lady Gregory (q.v.) he founded in 1899 the Irish Literary Theatre, better known by its later name of the Abbey Theatre, of which he was a director till his death. Among the plays that he wrote for it were *Kathleen ni Houlihan* (1902), *The Pot of Broth* (1902), *The Hour Glass* (1903), *The King's Threshold* (1904), and *Deirdre* (1907). Besides writing himself, he influenced others, and started Synge on his dramatic career. His poetry had now shaken off the influence of the school of the nineties, and *The Wind*

Among the Reeds (1899), which shows kinship to the French symbolists, was followed by the maturer *In the Seven Woods* (1903) and *The Green Helmet* (1910). To this period belong several books of critical essays, including *Ideas of Good and Evil* (1903), *The Cutting of an Agate* (1912), and *Per Amica Silentia Lunae* (1918).

In 1917 he married Georgie Hyde Lees, a spiritualist medium, and they lived in a tower on the Irish coast. A new poetic vein was begun with *The Wild Swans at Coole* (1917). Along with *The Lake Isle of Innisfree* (1924), *The Tower* (1928), *The Winding Stair* (1929), and *Last Poems* (1939), it shows a more vigorous technique, so that Yeats is one of the few poets of whom it may be said that his later work is his best. In 1921 he wrote *Four Plays for Dancers*, which shows Japanese influence. From 1922 to 1928 he was a member of the Irish Senate, and in 1923 his literary pre-eminence was marked by the award of the Nobel Prize for Literature. In 1928 he published translations of two plays of Sophocles, *King Oedipus* and *Oedipus at Colonus*. As the greatest English-speaking poet of his age he was a natural choice for compiling *The Oxford Book of Modern Verse* (1936), but his selection, based on personal taste, caused some controversy. His *Autobiography* appeared in 1938, and he died at Roquebrune in France. Two collections of his letters were published, in 1940 and 1953.

Yeats-Brown, Francis Charles Claypon (15 Aug. 1886—19 Dec. 1944), soldier and author, was born in Genoa, where his father was British consul-general, and was educated at Harrow and Sandhurst. In 1906 he went to India as an officer in the Indian Cavalry. In the First World War he served first with the 5th Irish Lancers, and then in Mesopotamia with the Royal Flying Corps, and got the Distinguished Flying Cross; he was taken prisoner by the Turks but escaped. From 1926 to 1928 he was assistant editor of the *Spectator*. His best-known work is the autobiographical *Bengal Lancer* (1930), which was filmed. Other books are *Golden Horn* (1932), *Dogs of War* (1934), *Lancer at Large* (1936), *European Jungle* (1939), *Pageant of India* (1942), and *Martial India* (1945). A mystic, he also wrote *Yoga Explained* (1937).

Yendys, Sydney, *see* **Dobell.**

Yonge, Charlotte Mary (13 Aug. 1823—24 March 1901), novelist and writer of children's books, was born at Otterbourne, near Winchester, and was educated by her father, who had fought at Waterloo, but left the army when 27. Brought up very strictly, she was influenced by Keble, who lived close by. At the age of 7 she taught in the village Sunday-school, and continued this for 71 years. The first of her books was *Abbeychurch, or Self-Control and Self-Conceit* (1844), but it was not till 1853 that she became famous with the publication of *The Heir of Redclyffe*. To followers of the Oxford Movement this was not only a beautiful story but provided in its hero an ideal to follow; undergraduates and officers at the front in the Crimea read it with avidity. Later books, written for young people but enjoyed by readers of all ages, were *The Little Duke* (1854), *The Lances of Lynwood* (1855), *The Daisy Chain* (1856), *A Book of*

Golden Deeds (1864), *The Dove in the Eagle's Nest* (1866), and *Unknown to History* (1882). She wrote over a hundred books altogether, and from 1851 to 1889 was editor of *The Monthly Packet*, a children's magazine. Shy and retiring, she lived all her life in her own quiet village, and never married.

Yorke, Henry Vincent (1905—   ), novelist who wrote under the pseudonym Henry Green, was born near Tewkesbury and was a nephew of Lord Leconfield. While at Eton he wrote a novel, *Blindness*, which was published in 1926. After leaving Oxford he went into the family engineering business at Birmingham, of which he became managing director. His novel *Living* (1929) draws on his experience of factory workers. Others, which make up a list of unusual titles, are *Party Going* (1939), *Pack My Bag* (1940), *Caught* (1943), *Loving* (1945), *Back* (1946), *Concluding* (1948), *Nothing* (1950), and *Doting* (1952). He has been said to write with a kind of studied artlessness, as if viewing life for the first time. During the Second World War he was a full-time member of the National Fire Service.

Young, Andrew John (1885—   ), clergyman and poet, was born at Elgin and educated at the Royal High School, Edinburgh, and Edinburgh University. In 1920 he removed to Hove in Sussex, in 1941 became vicar of Stonegate and in 1948 a canon of Chichester Cathedral. Writer of many nature poems, he published *Songs of Night* (1910), *Boaz and Ruth* (1920), *The Bird Cage* (1926), *The New Shepherd* (1931), *Winter Harvest* (1933), *The White Blackbird* (1935), *The Green Man* (1947), and *Into Hades* (1952). He also wrote a verse play, *Nicodemus* (1937), and two books of botanical essays, *A Prospect of Flowers* (1945) and *A Retrospect of Flowers* (1950). In 1951 he was made an honorary LL.D. of Edinburgh, and in 1952 was awarded the Queen's Medal for Poetry.

Young, Arthur (11 Sept. 1741—20 April 1820), agriculturalist, was born in London, son of the rector of Bradfield, Suffolk, and went to school at Lavenham. In his early years he farmed, making many experiments, which though they did not bring him financial success, gave him knowledge and experience, afterwards turned to useful account. Various publications had made his name known, and in 1777 he became agent to Lord Kingsborough on his Irish estates. In 1780 he published his *Tour in Ireland*, and four years later started the *Annals of Agriculture*, 47 volumes of which appeared. His famous tours in France were made between 1787 and 1790, the results of his observations being published in *Travels in France* (1792). He was in 1793 appointed secretary to the newly founded Board of Agriculture, and published many additional works on the subject. His *Autobiography* was published in 1898. He is justly regarded as the father of modern agriculture. In his later years he was blind.

Young, Edward (baptized 3 July 1683, died 5 April 1765), poet, was born at Upham, Hampshire, where his father was rector. After being at Winchester College and Oxford, where in 1708 he was elected a law Fellow of All Souls, he accompanied the Duke of Wharton to Ireland. Young, who had always a keen eye towards preferment, and cultivated those who had the dispensing of it, began his poetical career in 1713 with *An Epistle to Lord Lansdowne*. Equally characteristic was the publication in the same year of two poems, *The Last Day* and *The Force of Religion*. The following year he produced an elegy *On the Death of Queen Anne*, which brought him into notice. Turning next to the drama he produced *Busiris* in 1719, and *The Revenge* in 1721. His next work was a collection of satires, *The Love of Fame, the Universal Passion* (1725—8). In 1727 he took orders, and was appointed one of the royal chaplains, and rector of Welwyn, Herts, in 1730. Next year he married Lady Elizabeth Lee, the widowed daughter of the Earl of Lichfield, to whom, as well as to her daughter by her former marriage, he was warmly attached. Both died, and sad and lonely the poet began his masterpiece, *The Complaint, or Night Thoughts* (1742—4), a mournful meditation in blank verse, which had immediate and great popularity. In 1753 he brought out his last drama, *The Brothers*, and in 1761 he received his last piece of preferment, that of Clerk to the Closet to the Princess Dowager of Wales. The poems of Young though in style artificial and sometimes forced, contain passages of passion and power which sometimes reach the sublime. But the feelings and sentiments which he expresses with so much force as a poet form an unpleasantly harsh contrast with the worldiness and self-seeking of his life.

Young, Emily Hilda (1880—8 Aug. 1949), novelist, was born in Northumberland. In 1902 she married J. A. H. Daniell, a solicitor, and they lived in Bristol; after he was killed in the First World War she moved to Wiltshire. Writing effectively of ordinary everyday persons, she has been called 'the apostle of quiet people.' Her novel *Miss Mole* gained the Tait Black Memorial Prize for 1930; others are *A Corn of Wheat* (1910), *Yonder* (1912), *Moor Fires* (1916), *William* (1925), *The Vicar's Daughter* (1928), *Jenny Wren* (1932), *The Curate's Wife* (1934), *Celia* (1938), *Caravan Island* (1940), *River Holiday* (1942), and *Chatterton Square* (1947).

Young, Francis Brett (1884—28 March 1954), novelist, was born at Halesowen, Worcestershire, son of a doctor. Educated at Epsom College, he studied medicine at Birmingham University and practised at Brixham from 1907 to 1914. In 1907 he married Jessie Hankinson, a singer. During the First World War he served with the Royal Army Medical Corps in East Africa, and wrote about this later in *Marching on Tanga* (1918). Invalided out, he settled with his wife in Capri, but returned to England in 1932. His first novel, *Deep Sea* (1914) was followed by *Pilgrim's Rest* (1922), *Cold Harbour* (1924) and several others, but his first great success was *Portrait of Clare* (1927), which was awarded the Tait Black Memorial Prize. Later novels are *My Brother Jonathan* (1928), *Black Roses* (1929), *Mr and Mrs Pennington* (1931), *The House under the Water* (1932), *White Ladies* (1935), *The Forest* (1936), *The City of Gold* (1939), and *The Man about the House* (1942). *Poems 1916—1918* appeared in 1919, and in 1944 *The Island*, a long poem about England. His last work was *In South Africa* (1952), a descriptive book, and he died at Cape Town.

Young, George Malcolm (29 April 1882—18 Nov. 1959), historian, was born at Greenhithe in Kent and educated at St Paul's and Balliol College, Oxford. In 1905 he was elected a Fellow of All Souls, and from 1906 to 1908 was a tutor at St John's. From 1908 to 1920 he was in the Civil Service, at first in the Board of Education, and in 1917 he was made a Companion of the Bath. His works include a *Life of Gibbon* (1932), *Origin of the West-Saxon Kingdom* (1934), *Victorian England* (1936), *Daylight and Champaign* (1937), *To-day and Yesterday* (1948), *Last Essays* (1950), and *Stanley Baldwin* (1952), which was awarded the Tait Black Memorial Prize. He held honorary doctorates of Cambridge and Durham.

Y. Y., *see* **Lynd, Robert.**

Z

Zangwill, Israel (14 Feb. 1864—1 Aug. 1926), novelist and playwright, born in London, son of a Russian refugee, was educated at the Jews' Free School and London University. For a year or two he was an elementary school teacher in Spitalfields, but having won a reputation by his writing he gave this up for literature. He published a series of masterly studies of Jewish history and Jewish life, of which the best known is *The Children of the Ghetto* (1892—3); it was followed by *Ghetto Tragedies* (1893), *The King of the Schnorrers* (1894), *Ghetto Comedies* (1907), and *Chosen Peoples* (1918); *Dreamers of the Ghetto* (1898) is a collection of essays on notable Jews of history. Others of his novels are *The Master* (1895), *They That Walk in Darkness* (1899), *The Mantle of Elijah* (1900), *The Grey Wig* (1903), and *Jinny the Carrier* (1919). *Merely Mary Ann* (1893), the story of a servant girl who inherits a fortune, was the most popular of his lighter works. He also wrote a number of plays, including *The Melting Pot* (1908), *Too Much Money* (1918), and *The Cockpit* (1922). Zangwill was the founder and first president of the International Jewish Territorial Organization.